THIRD EDITION

THE BEDFORD GUIDE FOR COLLEGE WRITERS

with Reader, Research Manual, and Handbook

X. J. KENNEDY, DOROTHY M. KENNEDY, and SYLVIA A. HOLLADAY

BEDFORD BOOKS of ST. MARTIN'S PRESS · BOSTON

For Bedford Books
Publisher: Charles H. Christensen
Associate Publisher/General Manager: Joan E. Feinberg
Managing Editor: Elizabeth M. Schaaf
Developmental Editors: Stephen A. Scipione, Ellen M. Kuhl, Katherine A. Retan
Production Editor: Tara L. Masih
Copyeditor: Barbara G. Flanagan
Text Design: Claire Seng-Niemoeller
Cover Design: Hannus Design Associates

Library of Congress Catalog Card Number: 92–52526

Manufactured in the United States of America

8 7 6 5 4 3

f e d

For information, write: St. Martin's Press, Inc.
175 Fifth Avenue, New York, NY 10010
Editorial Offices: Bedford Books *of* St. Martin's Press
29 Winchester Street, Boston, MA 02116

ISBN: 0–312–06549–3

Acknowledgments

Paula Gunn Allen. "Where I Come from Is like This." From *The Sacred Hoop* by Paula Gunn Allen. Copyright © 1986 by Paula Gunn Allen. Reprinted by permission of Beacon Press.

Sherwood Anderson. "Discovery of a Father." Reprinted by permission of Harold Ober Associates Incorporated. Copyright 1939 by The Reader's Digest Association, Inc. Copyright renewed 1966 by Eleanor Copenhaver Anderson.

Deborah C. Andrews. From "Words About Words." Excerpted with permission from *Chemical and Engineering Words*, March 13, 1989, 67(11), pp. 45–46. Copyright © 1989 American Chemical Society.

Russell Baker. "The Art of Eating Spaghetti." From *Growing Up* by Russell Baker, published by Congdon & Weed, Inc. Copyright © 1982 by Russell Baker. Reprinted by permission of Contemporary Books, Inc.

Mary Kay Blakely. "Psychic Income." Copyright 1981 by Mary Kay Blakely. Originally appeared in *The New York Times* and was included in Nancy Newhouse's *Hers: Through Women's Eyes*, Villard Books/Random House, 1985. Reprinted with permission.

Paul Bodanis. "What's in Your Toothpaste?" From *The Secret House* by Paul Bodanis. Copyright © 1986 by Paul Bodanis. Reprinted by permission of Simon & Schuster.

Daniel Boorstin. From *Hidden History*. Copyright © 1987 by HarperCollins Publishers.

Judy Brady. "I Want a Wife." From *Ms.*, December 1971. Reprinted by permission of the author.

Susan Brownmiller. "Pornography Hurts Women." From *Against Our Will* by Susan Brownmiller. Copyright © 1975 by Susan Brownmiller. Reprinted by permission of Simon & Schuster.

Acknowledgments and copyrights are continued at the back of the book, which constitutes an extension of the copyright page.

Preface:
To the Instructor

The third edition of *The Bedford Guide for College Writers* that you hold in your hand combines three books in one: a process-oriented rhetoric, a thematic reader, and a full research manual. If you prefer, a longer four-books-in-one version that includes a comprehensive handbook is also available.

Once again, the emphasis in *The Bedford Guide* is on students' writing, not just reading and talking about writing. Pressed immediately into the act of writing, students inductively learn by doing without being burdened by too much preliminary advice. This third edition not only incorporates the most recent findings of composition research but is an even more efficient, more practical, more useful tool for writing students. The book continues to be based on our belief that writing is the lively, usually surprising, often rewarding art of thinking while working with language. No one ever learned to swim or to play a musical instrument by reading a book or listening to an expert talk. Similarly, no one ever learned to write by reading or talking about writing. If a student is to learn to write well and confidently, practice is more valuable than theory and prescriptions. We hope the present structure of the book — reached after much trial and error — carries out our conviction with originality and common sense. The many discerning instructors whose students used the second edition and who made suggestions for the third edition helped us immeasurably as we made decisions on content and organization. Our goal has been to make this textbook valuable and easy to use for you and your students.

Let us highlight some of the significant elements of this new edition for you, book by book.

How the Rhetoric Is Built

Book One, *A Writer's Guide*, is a comprehensive process-oriented rhetoric which, as before, involves students immediately and repeatedly in the act of writing. It contains four parts.

In Parts One and Two, the chapters are structured alike. Part One, "A Writer's Resources," focuses on five major resources that writers draw on: recall (Chapter 1), observation (Chapter 2), reading (Chapter 3), conversation (Chapter 4), and imagination (Chapter 5). Part Two, "Thinking Critically," introduces students to five major critical strategies often used in writing: analyzing (Chapter 6), taking a stand (Chapter 7), proposing a solution (Chapter 8), evaluating (Chapter 9), and identifying causes and effects (Chapter 10). Each of these first ten chapters begins with "Learning from Other Writers" — two model essays, one by a professional and one by a student writer. Next, students are whisked into an assignment in "Learning by Writing." As they draw on the chapter's resource or deploy its critical strategy to write an essay, students are guided by assignment-specific suggestions for generating ideas, planning, drafting, developing, revising, and editing. "Learning by Writing" also features checklists for discovery, revision, and peer editing as well as tips for writing with a computer and for collaborative learning. After students learn by writing, an "Applying What You Learn" section links the resource or critical strategy with other courses across the curriculum and with real on-the-job situations. Each chapter ends with "Further Applications," a new section that connects the rhetorical information in the chapter to selections in Book Two, *A Writer's Reader*.

Part Three explores three special writing situations in which students are likely to find themselves: writing about literature, writing in class, and writing for business. Chapter 11, "Writing about Literature," guides students through writing a critique of a literary work, using professional and student samples of writing about both fiction and poetry. This new chapter also includes a section on specific strategies for writing about literature — synopsis, paraphrase, and comparison and contrast. Chapter 12, "Writing in Class," focuses on taking essay examinations, with particular emphasis on in-class competency exams. Chapter 13, "Writing for Business," has been restored and updated from the first edition of *The Bedford Guide for College Writers* and provides valuable information and models for students' personal and professional business writings.

Part Four, "A Writer's Strategies," presents in a handy sequence of chapters the basics of the writing process. It explains and exemplifies the various subprocesses, steps, and stages of writing and provides practical tips and exercises to help students improve both the process and the product of their writing. This part contains chapters on generating ideas (Chapter 14), planning (Chapter 15), drafting (Chapter 16), developing (Chapter 17), and revising and editing (Chapter 18). (And please note: for the first time we pay attention to proofreading as a skill separate from revising and editing.) Part Four also includes strategies for two special writing situations: working with other writers (Chapter 19) and writing with a computer (Chapter 20).

In this third edition, the rhetoric includes more readings (a total of twenty-nine, fourteen of which are new) and much more guidance on planning, drafting, developing, and revising essays than ever before.

How the Reader Is Built

Book Two, *A Writer's Reader*, is the only thematic reader in a book of this kind. Forty brief prose selections are arranged in six chapters, each focusing on a familiar theme: families, the sexes, American diversity, work, popular culture, and the environment. Introduced by a biographical headnote, each reading is followed by questions — on vocabulary, form, content, and connections to other selections — and suggested writing assignments. The reader mixes writings both new and familiar by writers who are culturally and professionally diverse. Here you can find perennial favorites such as E. B. White's "Once More to the Lake," Jessica Mitford's "Behind the Formaldehyde Curtain," and Judy Brady's "I Want a Wife" alongside contemporary essays by splendid writers such as Toni Morrison, Richard Rodriguez, Stephen Jay Gould, and Joyce Carol Oates. These selections supplement (and complement) the model readings of the rhetoric. We trust that *A Writer's Reader* will give students plenty to write about, on topics that they care about.

How the Research Manual Is Built

Book Three, *A Writer's Research Manual*, is the most comprehensive research guide in a combination textbook for composition courses. All the major information that students involved in research need to know about is here, in chapters expanded and updated since the last edition: writing from library research (Chapter 27), library resources (Chapter 28), writing from field research (Chapter 29), and documenting sources (Chapter 30). This edition features increased discussion of writing from sources and library resources (including technological sources such as databases and microforms) and a much expanded selection of both MLA and APA models (on tabbed pages for ease of reference). It is the only research section in a combination textbook to include annotated student papers in both MLA and APA formats and also an explanation of the number style used in documenting scientific papers. This book within a book can hold its own against discrete research guides.

How the Handbook Is Built

Book Four, *A Writer's Handbook*, is the most comprehensive handbook in a combination textbook. With its thorough coverage of all standard handbook topics, its tabs, and its highlighted rules, it looks and works like a conventional handbook. Its new editing checklists and its ESL guidelines exceed what conventional handbooks offer. The book includes sixty-one exercise sets for practice in and out of class (answers to the first five questions in each set are provided in the back of the book so that students can check their understanding). We believe that you will find that no other handbook at the back of a composition textbook is as useful as this one for student reference and practice.

Ancillaries

An instructor's manual, *Teaching with* The Bedford Guide for College Writers, is available in two volumes. The first volume, *Practical Suggestions*, written by Shirley Morahan of Northeast Missouri State University and revised for this edition by Linda LaPointe of St. Petersburg Junior College, offers resources and practical advice for busy composition instructors. It includes pop quizzes, syllabi, a guide to teaching the readings, and suggestions on helping students develop their critical thinking abilities. The second volume, *Background Readings*, is an anthology of articles on composition and rhetoric, covering theory, research, and pedagogy. Revised and updated by Shirley Morahan, *Background Readings* now includes new articles on using literature in the composition classroom and working with high-risk and ESL students. These readings are connected to *The Bedford Guide for College Writers* and to the classroom by introductions and exercises. Both volumes of the manual will be useful to inexperienced and experienced instructors alike. Finally, also available is *Writer's Prologue*, computer software designed by the award-winning Daedalus Group. A booklet links the software to the assignments in *The Bedford Guide for College Writers*.

Thanks and Appreciation

We continue to be grateful to the many people from whom we learned throughout the planning and writing of the first and second editions of *The Bedford Guide for College Writers*. We are especially grateful to Mike Rose, John J. Ruszkiewicz, Robert A. Schwegler, Jane Aaron, Patricia Bizzell, Robert DiYanni, Diana Hacker, Clayton Hudnall, Richard L. Larson, Sonia Maasik, Donald McQuade, Thomas P. Miller, Shirley Morahan, James C. Raymond, Robert Rudolph, Nancy Sommers, Josephine Koster Tarvers, Rise B. Axelrod, and Charles R. Cooper.

During the preparation of the third edition, our debts have increased. We are grateful to Joyce Burkhart, librarian in charge of the Michael M. Bennett Library of St. Petersburg Junior College, for reviewing, revising, and updating the chapter on library resources. We are appreciative to Lisa Hillenbrand, ESL instructor at St. Petersburg Junior College, for drafting the ESL guidelines and to Barbara Gaffney of the University of New Orleans, Mary Moya of Rutgers University–Newark, and Franklin Horowitz of Columbia University for reviewing and critiquing these guidelines. We thank Linda LaPointe of St. Petersburg Junior College for revising the first volume of the instructor's manual and Shirley Morahan of Northeast Missouri State University for revising and updating the second volume.

For reviewing the second edition and making suggestions to improve the third, we thank Chris Burnham of New Mexico State University, Rick Eden of the RAND Corporation, Barry Maid of the University of Arkansas, Dr. Elizabeth Metzger of the University of South Florida, and Michael Miller of Longview Community College. We also thank the graduate students who reviewed the instructor's manual: Liz Bryant and William Chernecky of the University of South Florida and Stephanie Zerkel of the University of Arkansas.

Instructors who responded to the publisher's questionnaire about our book are Phyllis R. Anderson, Longview Community College; Rosemary L. Arca, Foothill College; Mark Baker, Utah State University; Audrey J. Brubaker, Lancaster Bible College; Michael Scott Cain, Catonsville Community College; Rosemary Carey, Indiana University Northwest; M. Collings, Pepperdine University; Linda DiDesidero, Northwestern University; Sylvia Edwores, Longview Community College; Stacy Adrian Evans, Moorhead State University; Jacqueline Fuller, University of Southern Maine; Marti Gerdes, Lower Columbia College; Christine R. Gray, University of Maryland; Edween Ham, Utica College of Syracuse University; M. Kip Hartvigvsen, Ricks College; Kathryn Jansak, Kent State University; Barbara Jensen, Modesto Junior College; Elizabeth Dab Johnson, University of Maryland; Myrl Guy Jones, Radford University; Mary Luther, Muskegon Community College; Deborah L. Martin, Longview Community College, Blue Springs Campus; Pamela McLagan, Linn-Benton Community College; Mike Mullins, SUNY College of Technology at Canton; James R. Musgrave, Mesa College; Michael Olendzenski, Cape Cod Community College; Ruth Perkins, Chemeketa Community College; Susan Ross, Oklahoma City University; Victoria Sarkisian, Marist College; Martha Simonsen, William Rainey Harper College; Carolyn M. Squires, Utah State University; M. Thomas, San Diego City College; Martha A. Thomas, Grossmont College; Carmalletta M. Williams, Longview Community College. We thank you, one and all.

Working on the third edition, we realized anew that to write a textbook is to take part in a collaborative writing project different only in scope from those assigned to the students for whom we write. Many individuals have contributed significantly to our collaborative effort. Publisher Charles H. Christensen and Associate Publisher Joan E. Feinberg have provided unstinting encouragement and inspiration from the early beginnings of the book. Their creative suggestions and perceptive advice have guided us wisely, and their faith in our work has buoyed us through long hours at the computer screen. Editor Steve Scipione read and reread our manuscript, ferreting out the inconsistencies, spotting the problems, and coming up with sound solutions. His knowledgeable suggestions for improvements and refinements nudged us again and again toward a better book. Ellen Kuhl's patience and efficiency in the task of revising the research manual and the handbook helped us strengthen these two important books in this edition. We do not know how we could have prepared the thematic reader without Kathy Retan's conscientious assistance and acute editorial eye. Beth Castrodale oversaw the revision of the *Background Readings* with friendly efficiency. Tara Masih with her incisive attention to detail and her attention to deadlines kept all of us focused toward the completion of the project. She coordinated the production and layout of the book, expertly solving whatever problems arose. Once again, Barbara Flanagan did an excellent job of copyediting. Diane Carmody Wynne prepared the index. David Gibbs, a fine student and writer, cleared the copyright permissions. George Scribner and Donna Dennison brought unmatched creativity and flair to the promotion of the book; in particular, they oversaw the striking design of the cover. Others on the Bedford staff deserve thanks for their contributions, small and large; they include Managing Editor Elizabeth Schaaf, Terri Walton, Jennifer Henning, and Michele Biscoe. We also owe a debt of gratitude to Eugene Narrett, who drafted headnotes, and to Julia Sullivan, who was ever available on short notice for writing and rewriting.

Special thanks to all the students who have challenged us over the years to find better ways and to prepare better materials to help them learn. In particular we would like to thank those who granted us permission to use their essays in the first and second editions: Robert G. Schreiner, Sandy Messina, Rose Anne Federici, Michael R. Tein, Jennifer Bowe, Susan Fendel, Jeffrey Ting, Matthew A. Munich, and Katie Kennedy. And special thanks to Linnea Saukko, Jonathan Burns, and David Gibbs, whose works are significant new contributions in the third edition. We are appreciative to our mentors and colleagues in various universities and colleges across the country. We are grateful for each time you prompted us to reexamine our positions and defend our assertions, helping us to mature intellectually and academically. We thank our friends and families for their unstinting patience, understanding, and encouragement. All of you—student, colleague, friend, family member—have contributed to this book. In your honor, we hope the book will benefit other students and instructors.

Contents

A WRITER'S READER   423

A WRITER'S RESEARCH MANUAL   595

A WRITER'S HANDBOOK H–1

Introduction:
To the Student

You are already a writer with long experience. In earlier years, you wrote book reports and essays and term papers, answered exam questions, perhaps kept a journal. You have kept minutes for clubs and composed memos on the job. You've taken notes, written letters and postcards to family and friends, made shopping lists, maybe kept a diary, even tried your hand at writing stories and poetry. All this experience is about to pay off for you.

In college, you will combine what you already know about writing with the new techniques you will learn, and you will perform writing tasks more challenging than most you have faced before. Unlike parachute jumping, writing for a college course is something you go ahead and try without first learning all there is to it. In truth, nothing anyone can tell you about writing can help you so much as learning by doing. In this book we will suggest various writing situations and say, "Go to it." We will also recommend specific strategies that will make your writing go smoother.

To write a psychology or economics paper, you'll find that your mind has to stretch more than it did in writing a paper on flying squirrels or a letter of complaint. From now on, you will find yourself working in more complex disciplines, writing reports, gathering information from many sources, and above all thinking critically—not just reading books and stacking up facts, but analyzing what you learn, deciding what it means, weighing its value, taking a stand, proposing solutions to a problem. College instructors will expect you to question what they say and what you read, form your own judgments, and put them to use.

THE PROCESS OF WRITING

As you probably know, writing can seem at times an overwhelming drudgery worse than scrubbing kettles; at other moments, a sport full of thrills—like whizzing downhill on skis, not knowing what you'll meet around a bend.

Surprising and unpredictable though the writing process may be, you can understand what happens in it. Nearly all writers do similar things:

They generate ideas.
They plan, draft, and develop their papers.
They revise and edit.

These activities aren't lockstep stages: they don't always proceed in a straight line. You can skip around, taking up parts of the process in whatever order you like or work on several parts at a time. Gathering material, you may feel an urge to play with a sentence until it clicks. Writing a draft, you may decide to go back and look for more material. You may find yourself dashing off, crossing out, leaping ahead, backtracking, correcting, adjusting, questioning, trying a fresh approach, failing, trying still another approach, making a breakthrough, scrubbing, polishing—then in the end checking unfamiliar punctuation and looking up the spellings of any tricky words.

Briefly, let's run through a writer's basic activities.

Generating Ideas

Discovering what to write about   Finding a topic you honestly want to pursue, one about which you really have something to say, is half the task: find it, and words will flow. Although finding the topic is not always easy, often it lies near home. By observing the peacocks in her farmyard, Georgia writer Flannery O'Connor fired off an essay heard round the world. In college, of course, an instructor may give you a writing assignment that seems to hold no personal interest for you. In that case, you face the challenge of making it your own by finding a slant that does interest you. Take notes while you think, and jot down any likely possibilities.

Discovering material   You'll need information to back up your ideas—facts and figures, reports and opinions, examples and illustrations. How do you find this material to support your ideas and make them clear and convincing to your readers? Luckily, you have endless resources at your fingertips. You can *recall* your own knowledge and experience, you can go out and *observe,* you can *read,* you can *converse* with others, you can *imagine* "What if" possibilities. (These five great resources will be explored in Chapters 1–5.) All the while you look for material, you can be writing. You can be thinking on paper: making notes, summarizing what other writers have said, setting down your own rough ideas, making reminders for yourself:

When dealing with Gen. Franco, dictator of Spain, don't forget his friendship with Hitler.

OR

Remember to check the most recent laws on auto emissions for pollution control.

Planning, Drafting, and Developing Ideas

Having discovered a burning idea to write about (or at least a smoldering one) and material to back it up with (maybe not enough yet, but some), you sort out what matters most and decide on an order for your ideas. If right away you can see one main point you want to make in your paper, you're lucky. Try to state that point in writing; try various ways of expressing it. Next, you can arrange your ideas and material in what seems a clear and sensible order that will make your one point clear. To discover that order, you might group and label the ideas you have generated, or you might analyze the main idea. But if no one main point emerges quickly, never mind: you may find one while you draft—that is, while you write an early version of your paper. By the time you finish the paper, you should focus on a main point.

Usually your first version of a draft will be rough and preliminary. Writing takes time: a paper usually needs several drafts and perhaps a revision of your plan, especially if your subject is unfamiliar or complicated. You may decide to throw out your first attempt and start over because a stronger idea or a better arrangement hits you. Include explanations, definitions, illustrations, and evidence to make your ideas clear. If, as you draft, you discover you don't have enough specific evidence, work through your five resources again (recall, observe, read, converse, imagine). You can expect to keep discovering ideas, having insights, and drawing conclusions while you draft. By all means, welcome them, and work them in if they fit.

Revising and Editing

Rewriting occurs throughout the process of composing, not only after you have finished. When you complete a draft, you might think that your work is done, but very few writers can get their ideas across to others in a first draft. For most writers the time of revising is the time when work begins in earnest. In an apt comparison, Chinese-American writer Maxine Hong Kingston likens writing to gardening in Hawaii: a little time spent in planting, much more time spent in "cutting and pruning and hacking back." Novelist Ernest Hemingway, when asked what made him revise the ending of *Farewell to Arms* thirty-nine times, replied, "Getting the words right." Playwright Neil Simon puts it another way: "In baseball, you get only three swings and you're out. In rewriting, you get almost as many swings as you want and you know that, sooner or later, you'll hit the ball."

Revision—the word means "seeing again"—is more than a matter of just revising words: you sometimes revise what you know. Such changes may take place at any time while you're writing or at any moment when you stop writing to reread or to think. You can then shift your plans, decide to put in or leave out, move sentences or paragraphs around, connect ideas differently, or express them better. If you put aside your draft for a few hours or a day, you can reread it with fresh eyes and a clear mind.

When you revise, as humorist Leo Rosten has said, "you have to put yourself in the position of the negative reader, the resistant reader, the reader who doesn't surrender easily, the reader who is alien to you as a type, even the reader who doesn't like what you are writing." However, you should probably sit in the seat of the scornful only when your paper is well along. When your ideas first start to flow, you want to welcome them—lure them forth, not tear them apart—or they might go back into hiding. Get something on paper before you begin major tinkering. Don't be afraid to take risks: you'll probably be surprised and pleased at what happens.

Editing   Near the end of your labors, you'll *edit* what you have written: you'll correct any flaws that may stand in the way of your readers' enjoyment and understanding. Don't edit too early, though, because you may waste time on some part that you later revise out. In editing, you usually accomplish these repairs:

Get rid of unnecessary words.

Choose better words.

Check usage.

Correct grammar (make subjects agree with verbs, pronouns with what they stand for; make verb tense consistent).

Rearrange words into a stronger, clearer order.

Proofreading   A final activity, proofreading is giving your paper one last look, with a dictionary at your elbow, checking doubtful spellings, and fixing any typing mistakes. If you are using a word processor, take advantage of the computerized spell checker.

AUDIENCE AND PURPOSE

A big part of learning to write well is learning what questions to ask yourself. At any moment in the writing process, two questions are worth asking: Whom do I write for? and Why?

Writing for a reader   In fulfilling some relatively easy assignments—say, recalling an experience or reporting a conversation—you won't need to keep asking, Who's reading me? You'll know. In a college writing course like this one, you'll always have three or more readers: (1) yourself, (2) your instructor, and (3) your classmates.

Remember, as reading specialist Frank Smith says, "The writer is always the first reader." As your own first reader, you'll want to step back from a draft and reread it as though you weren't the writer but were someone else, detached and objective, and not too easy to please. You will also want to comb your writing for errors before you turn it in. That is merely to follow the Golden Rule of Writing: do unto your other readers as you trust other writers will do unto you.

If as you write a paper you believe it is going well, the chances are that your readers will think so too. But in tackling complex assignments, you'll write more effectively if you consider your audience. Say you wish to persuade your readers to take a certain action—to ban (or approve) a law regulating the hiring of women or the sale of pornography. At some point you might ask: What do my readers probably believe? Where are my statements likely to offend them? What objections are they likely to raise? What do they know already? What do they need to be told? You should know a great deal about your readers (what they know and don't know, what they believe, what they value) to aim your writing toward them. As you write, keep the uninformed reader, the reluctant reader, and the resistant reader in mind. Among your classmates you'll find all three types of readers, and in responding to your writing, your instructor will assume all three roles.

Writing for a reason   Usually a college writing assignment has a clear-cut purpose. Every assignment in this book asks you to write for a definite reason. In Chapter 1 you'll be asked to recall a memorable experience in order to explain how it changed you, and in Chapter 2, to observe a group of people or an event in order to share some telling insight about your subject. In Part Two, purposes will become especially important. You'll write papers to analyze (to understand something by breaking it into its components), to evaluate, to see causes or effects, to set forth an opinion, to propose a solution, to explain causes or effects. Aware that you write for a reason, you can concentrate on your task. From the start you can ask yourself, What do I want to do? And, in revising, Did I do what I meant to do? You'll find these are very practical questions. They'll help you cut the irrelevant that wanders into your writing, anything that hinders your paper from getting where you want it to go.

The reason you write and the readers you write for will always deserve consideration. Throughout this book, we'll remind you of these two points.

WHAT MATTERS MOST

In college writing, some qualities count more than mere neatness and correctness: mastering knowledge, discovering your own ideas, expressing them in your own words. The most important part of writing is getting something down on paper. Don't worry if your first draft isn't neat. Drafts are only sketches, made to be torn apart, reworked, filled in. Cross out words, draw arrows, move sentences and paragraphs. Scissor your draft to bits, then tape the pieces together in a stronger order. If your first draft looks like a bulldog has been chewing it, never mind—all a reader will see is your final version. If you're composing on the computer screen, you can move parts around easily, and don't hesitate to do so. Save several versions of your draft until you get it the way you want it. No writer is brilliant at all times. That's why writers have wastebaskets and computers have delete keys.

To keep thinking while you write, not merely beforehand, can yield surprising results. As your fingers type or move a pen, your brain keeps working. Often an idea will leap up and startle you. As the English writer E. M. Forster put it, "How do I know what I think until I see what I say?" Asked how she customarily wrote a poem, Anne Sexton said, "I will fool around on the typewriter. It might take me ten pages of nothing, of terrible writing, and then I'll get a line, and I'll think, 'That's what I mean.'" Though you don't need to include all the further thoughts that come to you, be willing to consider them.

USING THIS BOOK

In *The Bedford Guide for College Writers,* we too have a purpose. It is to help you write better, deeper-reaching, and more interesting, more satisfying papers than you have ever written before, and to do so by actually writing. Throughout the book we'll give you a lot of practice—in writing processes and strategies—to help you build your confidence.

How this book is built   Right away in *A Writer's Guide,* Part One encourages you to write, drawing on five basic resources for your ideas and material: recalling, observing, reading, conversing, and imagining. Part Two asks you to write papers that emphasize reading and thinking critically. You'll develop the critical skills of analyzing, taking a stand, proposing a solution, evaluating, and identifying causes and effects. Part Three leads you through special writing situations—writing about literature, writing in class, and writing for business. Part Four, "A Writer's Strategies," is packed with advice, tips, and exercises that you can unpack whenever you are hunting for ways to generate ideas, plan, draft, develop, revise, and edit your papers. You will also find strategies for working with other writers or for working with a computer. Browse through these chapters at your leisure, or refer to them in a pinch.

A Writer's Guide is only the first part of this package. In the pages that follow it you'll find three other parts.

A Writer's Reader contains a batch of brief essays on six evergreen themes: family, the sexes, ethnicity, work, popular culture, and the environment. The authors of the essays, experts from many fields, have faced the same decisions you must make as you write, so you can learn from studying their structures and techniques.

A Writer's Research Manual takes you through the challenging process of writing research papers, based on both reading and field investigation.

A Writer's Handbook is a practical guide to English rules and usage, covering matters such as grammar, spelling, punctuation, choice of words, and sentence structure—important matters to attend to when you revise and proofread.

Finally, to help you find your way quickly to all sections, terms, topics, and authors in the book, we include an index.

Taking it to the hoop   Like a hard game of basketball, writing a college paper is strenuous. Without getting in your way, we want to lend you all possible support and to provide guidance and direction for your efforts. So, no doubt, does your instructor, someone closer to you than any textbook writers. Still, like even the best coaches, instructors and textbook writers can improve your game only so far. Advice on how to write won't make you a better writer. You'll learn more and have more fun when you take a few sentences to the hoop and make points yourself.

As you know, other students can also help you—sometimes more than a textbook or an instructor. This book suggests opportunities for you to learn from your classmates and to help them learn from you. If your instructor asks you to exchange your work with other students, to give and receive reactions, you'll face a challenge: just how do you go about commenting on another student's writing? Throughout the book are useful hints for ways that you and other students can help one another discover ideas as you write and rewrite your papers. As you respond to your classmates' papers, you will learn to judge your own writing better.

A
WRITER'S
GUIDE

PART ONE

A WRITER'S RESOURCES

E very college writer wrestles with the question What should I write about? Sometimes one of your strong opinions will come to mind first; other times a memorable bunch of details. Then, after finding a topic, you'll ask yourself, What should I say? Why do I want to tell other people about this? What's my point? Fortunately, to answer those questions, you have five tremendous resources. With their aid, you'll never find yourself long at a loss for words.

None of these resources will be new to you. Already, you are adept at *recalling* what you know and at *observing* the world around you. You're accustomed to *reading* and *conversing* with people. And you've had experience with the richest resource of all: *imagining.* You already possess the major resources of a writer.

At the start of each chapter, we offer illustrations of good writing by two writers—a college student and a professional—who draw on the same resource. Then we suggest a writing assignment: a broad one that leaves you room to discover a specific topic you care about.

Immediately following the assignment you'll find suggestions to guide you in writing it. We pose questions that, if you like, you can ask yourself. Some of these questions will remind you of your audience and your purpose. Sometimes we report the experience of other students. We offer you rough guidance throughout the whole shifting, tentative, surprise-filled process of writing. But if, instead of reading our suggestions, you'd rather go ahead and write, please do. Our only aim in offering suggestions is to provide you with a trusty support system, for whenever you feel the need for it.

After you write your paper, you might care to read "Applying What You Learn." It will show you typical uses for the same kind of writing in your other college courses and in your career.

CHAPTER 1

Writing from Recall

Writing from recall is writing from memory, the richest resource a writer has, and the handiest. Novelist William Saroyan said that a writer observes—and then remembers having observed. This is clearly the case in an English course when you are asked to write of a personal experience, a favorite place, a memorable person. But even when an instructor hands you a subject that at first glance seems to have nothing to do with you, your memory is the first place to look. Suppose you have to write a psychology paper about how advertisers play on our fears. Begin with what you remember. What ads have sent chills down your back? (We recall a tire ad that showed the luckless buyer of an inferior product stuck with a blowout on a remote road on a stormy night, while the Frankenstein monster bore down on him.)

You may also need to observe, read more, talk with someone, and imagine. All by itself, memory may not give you enough to write about. But whenever you need to start writing, you will rarely go wrong if you start by jotting down something remembered. As you write, you'll remember more, so this is always a good way to get started.

LEARNING FROM OTHER WRITERS

In this chapter you will be invited to write a whole paper from recall. First, let's illustrate what we mean. Here are two samples of good writing—one by a professional writer, one by a college student. We begin with an excerpt from columnist Russell Baker's autobiography *Growing Up,* because autobiograph-ical writing so clearly demonstrates the uses of memory. Baker recalls what it was like to be sixteen in urban Baltimore, wondering what to do with his life.

THE ART OF EATING SPAGHETTI
Russell Baker

The only thing that truly interested me was writing, and I knew that sixteen-year-olds did not come out of high school and become writers. I thought of writing as something to be done only by the rich. It was so obviously not real work, not a job at which you could earn a living. Still, I had begun to think of myself as a writer. It was the only thing for which I seemed to have the smallest talent, and, silly though it sounded when I told people I'd like to be a writer, it gave me a way of thinking about myself which satisfied my need to have an identity.

The notion of becoming a writer had flickered off and on in my head since the Belleville days, but it wasn't until my third year in high school that the possibility took hold. Until then I'd been bored by everything as-sociated with English courses. I found English grammar dull and baffling. I hated the assignments to turn out "compositions," and went at them like heavy labor, turning out leaden, lackluster paragraphs that were agonies for teachers to read and for me to write. The classics thrust on me to read seemed as deadening as chloroform.

When our class was assigned to Mr. Fleagle for third-year English I anticipated another grim year in that dreariest of subjects. Mr. Fleagle was notorious among City students for dullness and inability to inspire. He was said to be stuffy, dull, and hopelessly out of date. To me he looked to be sixty or seventy and prim to a fault. He wore primly severe eyeglasses, his wavy hair was primly cut and primly combed. He wore prim vested suits with neckties blocked primly against the collar buttons of his primly starched white shirts. He had a primly pointed jaw, a primly straight nose, and a prim manner of speaking that was so correct, so gentlemanly, that he seemed a comic antique.

I anticipated a listless, unfruitful year with Mr. Fleagle and for a long time was not disappointed. We read *Macbeth.* Mr. Fleagle loved *Macbeth* and wanted us to love it too, but he lacked the gift of infecting others with his own passion. He tried to convey the murderous ferocity of Lady Macbeth one day by reading aloud the passage that concludes

. . . I have given suck, and know
How tender 'tis to love the babe that milks me.
I would, while it was smiling in my face,
Have plucked my nipple from his boneless gums. . . .

The idea of prim Mr. Fleagle plucking his nipple from boneless gums was too much for the class. We burst into gasps of irrepressible snickering. Mr. Fleagle stopped.

"There is nothing funny, boys, about giving suck to a babe. It is the— the very essence of motherhood, don't you see."

He constantly sprinkled his sentences with "don't you see." It wasn't a question but an exclamation of mild surprise at our ignorance. "Your pronoun needs an antecedent, don't you see," he would say, very primly. "The purpose of the Porter's scene, boys, is to provide comic relief from the horror, don't you see."

Late in the year we tackled the informal essay. "The essay, don't you see, is the. . . ." My mind went numb. Of all forms of writing, none seemed so boring as the essay. Naturally we would have to write informal essays. Mr. Fleagle distributed a homework sheet offering us a choice of topics. None was quite so simpleminded as "What I Did on My Summer Vacation," but most seemed to be almost as dull. I took the list home and dawdled until the night before the essay was due. Sprawled on the sofa, I finally faced up to the grim task, took the list out of my notebook, and scanned it. The topic on which my eye stopped was "The Art of Eating Spaghetti."

This title produced an extraordinary sequence of mental images. Surging up out of the depths of memory came a vivid recollection of a night in Belleville when all of us were seated around the supper table—Uncle Allen, my mother, Uncle Charlie, Doris, Uncle Hal—and Aunt Pat served spaghetti for supper. Spaghetti was an exotic treat in those days. Neither Doris nor I had ever eaten spaghetti, and none of the adults had enough experience to be good at it. All the good humor of Uncle Allen's house reawoke in my mind as I recalled the laughing arguments we had that night about the socially respectable method for moving spaghetti from plate to mouth.

Suddenly I wanted to write about that, about the warmth and good feeling of it, but I wanted to put it down simply for my own joy, not for Mr. Fleagle. It was a moment I wanted to recapture and hold for myself. I wanted to relive the pleasure of an evening at New Street. To write it as I wanted, however, would violate all the rules of formal composition I'd learned in school, and Mr. Fleagle would surely give it a failing grade. Never mind. I would write something else for Mr. Fleagle after I had written this thing for myself.

When I finished it the night was half gone and there was no time left to compose a proper, respectable essay for Mr. Fleagle. There was no choice next morning but to turn in my private reminiscence of Belleville. Two days passed before Mr. Fleagle returned the graded papers, and he returned everyone's but mine. I was bracing myself for a command to report to Mr. Fleagle immediately after school for discipline when I saw him lift my paper from his desk and rap for the class's attention.

"Now, boys," he said, "I want to read you an essay. This is titled 'The Art of Eating Spaghetti.' "

And he started to read. My words! He was reading *my words* out loud   12
to the entire class. What's more, the entire class was listening. Listening
attentively. Then somebody laughed, then the entire class was laughing,
and not in contempt and ridicule, but with openhearted enjoyment. Even
Mr. Fleagle stopped two or three times to repress a small prim smile.

I did my best to avoid showing pleasure, but what I was feeling was   13
pure ecstasy at this startling demonstration that my words had the power
to make people laugh. In the eleventh grade, at the eleventh hour as it
were, I had discovered a calling. It was the happiest moment of my entire
school career. When Mr. Fleagle finished he put the final seal on my happiness by saying, "Now that, boys, is an essay, don't you see. It's—don't
you see—it's of the very essence of the essay, don't you see. Congratulations, Mr. Baker."

For the first time, light shone on a possibility. It wasn't a very heartening   14
possibility, to be sure. Writing couldn't lead to a job after high school, and
it was hardly honest work, but Mr. Fleagle had opened a door for me. After
that I ranked Mr. Fleagle among the finest teachers in the school.

Questions to Start You Thinking

1. In your own words, state what Baker believes he learned in the eleventh grade
   about the art of writing. What incidents or statements help identify this lesson for
   readers of the essay? Tell what lesson, if any, you learned from the essay.

2. Why do you think Baker included this event in his autobiography?

3. What is the effect, in paragraph 3, of Baker's many repetitions of the words *prim*
   and *primly*? What other devices does Baker use to make vivid his characterization
   of Mr. Fleagle? Why do you think the author uses so much space to portray his
   teacher?

4. What does the quotation from *Macbeth* add to Baker's account? Had the quotation
   been omitted, what would have been lost?

5. How does Baker organize the essay? Why does he use this order?

6. Have you ever changed your mind about something you had to do, as Baker did
   about writing? Or about a person, as he did about Mr. Fleagle?

The next essay was written by a student, Robert Schreiner. He was asked
to recall a significant event from his childhood. As you read, notice the vivid
details that help bring the incident alive.

Student Essay

WHAT IS A HUNTER?
Robert G. Schreiner

What is a hunter? This is a simple question with a 1
relatively straightforward answer. A hunter is, according to
Webster's New Collegiate Dictionary, a person that hunts game
(game being various types of animals hunted or pursued for
various reasons). However, a question that is just as simple
but without such a straightforward answer is What characteristics make up a hunter? As a child, I had always considered
the most important aspect of the hunter's person to be his
ability to use a rifle, bow, or whatever weapon was appropriate to the type of hunting being done. Having many relatives
in rural areas of Virginia and Kansas, I had been exposed to
rifles a great deal. I had done extensive target shooting
and considered myself to be quite proficient in the use of
firearms. I had never been hunting, but I had always thought
that since I could fire a rifle accurately I would make a
good hunter.

One Christmas holiday, while we were visiting our grand- 2
parents in Kansas, my grandfather asked me if I wanted to go
jackrabbit hunting with him. I eagerly accepted, anxious to
show off my prowess with a rifle. A younger cousin of mine
also wanted to come, so we all went out into the garage,
loaded two .22 caliber rifles and a 20-gauge shotgun, hopped
into the pickup truck, and drove out of town. It had snowed
the night before and to either side of the narrow road swept
six-foot-deep powdery drifts. The wind twirled the fine
crystalline snow into whirling vortexes that bounced along
the icy road and sprayed snow into the open windows of the
pickup. As we drove, my grandfather gave us some pointers
about both spotting and shooting jackrabbits. He told us
that when it snows, jackrabbits like to dig out a hollow in
the top of a snowdrift, usually near a fencepost, and lie
there soaking up the sunshine. He told us that even though
jackrabbits are a grayish brown, this coloration is excellent

camouflage in the snow, for the curled-up rabbits resemble
rocks. He then pointed out a few rabbits in such positions
as we drove along, showing us how to distinguish them from
exposed rocks and dirt. He then explained that the only way
to be sure that we killed the rabbit was to shoot for the
head and, in particular, the eye, for this was on a direct
line with the rabbit's brain. Since we were using solid
point bullets, which deform into a ball upon impact, a hit
anywhere but the head would most likely only wound the
rabbit.

My grandfather then slowed down the pickup and told us   3
to look out for the rabbits hidden in the snowdrifts. We
eventually spotted one about thirty feet from the road in a
snow-filled gully. My cousin wished to shoot the first one,
so he hopped out of the truck, balanced the .22 on the hood,
and fired. A spray of snow erupted about a foot to the left
of the rabbit's hollow. My cousin fired again, and again,
and again, the shots pockmarking the slope of the drift. He
fired once more and the rabbit bounced out of its hollow,
its head rocking from side to side. He was hit. My cousin
eagerly gamboled into the snow to claim his quarry. He
brought it back holding it by the hind legs, proudly displaying it as would a warrior the severed head of his enemy. The
bullet had entered the rabbit's right shoulder and exited
through the neck. In both places a thin trickle of crimson
marred the gray sheen of the rabbit's pelt. It quivered
slightly and its rib cage pulsed with its labored breathing.
My cousin was about to toss it into the back of the pickup
when my grandfather pointed out that it would be cruel to
allow the rabbit to bleed slowly to death and instructed my
cousin to bang its head against the side of the pickup to
kill it. My cousin then proceeded to bang the rabbit's head
against the yellow metal. Thump, thump, thump, thump; after
a minute or so my cousin loudly proclaimed that it was dead
and hopped back into the truck.

The whole episode sickened me to some degree, and at   4
the time I did not know why. We continued to hunt throughout

the afternoon, and feigning boredom, I allowed my cousin and
grandfather to shoot all of the rabbits. Often, the shots
didn't kill the rabbits outright so they had to be killed
against the pickup. The thump, thump, thump of the rabbits'
skulls against the metal began to irritate me, and I was
strangely glad when we turned around and headed back toward
home. We were a few miles from the city limits when my
grandfather slowed the truck to a stop, then backed up a few
yards. My grandfather said he spotted two huge "jacks" sitting in the sun in a field just off the road. He pointed
them out and handed me the .22, saying that if I didn't shoot
something the whole afternoon would have been a wasted trip
for me. I hesitated, then reluctantly accepted the rifle.
I stepped out onto the road, my feet crunching on the ice.
The two rabbits were about seventy feet away, both sitting
upright in the sun. I cocked and leveled the rifle, my elbow
held almost horizontal in the military fashion I had learned
to employ. I brought the sights to bear upon the right eye
of the first rabbit, compensated for distance, and fired.
There was a harsh snap like the crack of a whip, and a small
jolt to my shoulder. The first rabbit was gone, presumably
knocked over the side of the snowdrift. The second rabbit
hadn't moved a muscle; it just sat there staring with that
black eye. I cocked the rifle once more and sighted a second
time, the bead of the rifle just barely above the glassy
black orb that regarded me so passively. I squeezed the
trigger. Again the crack, again the jolt, and again the
rabbit disappeared over the top of the drift. I handed the
rifle to my cousin and began making my way toward the rabbits. I sank into powdery snow up to my waist as I clambered
to the top of the drift and looked over.

     On the other side of the drift was a sight that I doubt   5
I will ever forget. There was a shallow, snow-covered ditch
on the leeward side of the drift and it was into this ditch
that the rabbits had fallen, at least what was left of the
rabbits. The entire ditch, in an area about ten feet wide,
was spattered with splashes of crimson blood, pink gobbets of

brain, and splintered fragments of bone. The twisted corpses
of the rabbits lay in the bottom of the ditch in small pools
of streaming blood. Of both the rabbits, only the bodies
remained, the heads being completely gone. Stumps of verte-
brae protruded obscenely from the mangled bodies, and one
rabbit's hind legs twitched spasmodically. I realized that
my cousin must have made a mistake and loaded the rifle with
hollowpoint explosive bullets instead of solid ones.

    I shouted back to the pickup, explaining the situation,   6
and asked if I should bring them back anyway. My grandfather
shouted back, "No, don't worry about it, just leave them
there. I'm gonna toss these jacks by the side of the road
anyway; jackrabbits aren't any good for eatin'."

    Looking at the dead, twitching bodies I thought only of   7
the incredible waste of life that the afternoon had been, and
I realized that there was much more to being a hunter than
knowing how to use a rifle. I turned and walked back to the
pickup, riding the rest of the way home in silence.

Questions to Start You Thinking

1. Where in the essay do you first begin to suspect the nature of the writer's feelings toward hunting? What in the essay or in your experience led you to this perception? Are other readers likely to have had a similar response? Why or why not?

2. What details in Schreiner's essay contribute to your understanding of his grandfather? From what the writer says about him, how would you characterize him? How would you characterize his cousin?

3. How did the writer's understanding of himself change as a result of his hunting lesson? Would the change in outlook presented in the essay be any less evident if the first paragraph were omitted? How else might the essay be strengthened or weakened by cutting out the opening paragraph?

4. Would Schreiner's essay be more or less effective if he explained in the last paragraph what he means by "much more to being a hunter"?

5. What are some of Schreiner's memorable images?

LEARNING BY WRITING

The Assignment: A Personal Experience

Write about a personal experience that took place at one moment in your life and that changed how you acted, thought, or felt from that moment on. Your purpose is not merely to tell an interesting story but to show your readers the importance that experience had for you. Your audience is your instructor and your classmates.

We suggest you pick an event that happened outside your head. An encounter with a person who for some reason greatly influenced you or with a challenge or obstacle or some activity will be far easier to look back on (and to make vivid for your reader) than a subjective, interior experience like a religious conversion or falling in love.

Some memorable student papers we have read have recalled experiences like those that follow—some heavy, some light:

> A man recalled guitar lessons with a teacher who at first seemed harsh but who turned out to be a true friend.

> A woman recalled her childhood fear that her mother, injured in a car crash, would no longer be able to take care of her. (The fear proved groundless.)

> A woman recalled how, as a small girl, she sneaked into a nun's room, out of curiosity stole some rosary beads, and discovered that crime does not pay.

> A man recalled meeting an American Indian who taught him a deeper understanding of the natural world.

> A man recalled how he conquered his fear of heights to rappel off a cliff.

To help you fulfill this assignment, let's consider: What does writing from personal experience call for?

Generating Ideas

You may find that the minute you are asked to write about a significant experience in your life, the very incident will flash to mind. If that is the case, start writing. Most writers, though, will need a little time to shake down their memories. If you are such a writer, the following suggestions may help.

Probably what will come to you first will be recent memories, but give long-ago memories time to surface, too. Novelist Willa Cather once said, "Most of the basic material a writer works with is acquired before the age of fifteen." As we might infer from her many stories of growing up on the plains of Nebraska, she was well aware of the value of searching early memories.

Be ready for any recollections that well up unexpectedly. Often, when you are busy doing something else—observing the scene around you, talking with someone, reading about someone else's experience—the activity can trigger a recollection from the past. When a promising one surfaces, write it down. It may be the start of your paper. Perhaps, like Russell Baker, you found success only when you ignored what you thought you were supposed to do in favor of what you really wanted to do. Perhaps, like Robert Schreiner, you learned from a painful experience. If nothing much surfaces, you might want to prod your memory with the following questions.

DISCOVERY CHECKLIST: SEARCHING YOUR MEMORY

- Did you ever break a rule or rebel against authority in some memorable way? Did you learn anything from your actions? If so, what?
- What were the causes and the results of the worst fight or argument you ever had?
- Did you ever succumb to peer pressure? Were the results of going along with the crowd good or bad? What did you learn from the experience?
- Did you ever regard a person in a certain way and then find you had to change your opinion of him or her?
- Did you ever have to choose between two equally attractive or equally dismal alternatives? What made the choice hard for you? What factors led you to decide as you did? Were you ultimately happy or unhappy with your choice? How might your life have been different if you had chosen the other alternative?
- Have you ever been appalled by witnessing an act of prejudice or cruelty or insensitivity? What did you do? Do you wish you had done something different?
- Did you ever make a serious error in judgment that led to disaster—or maybe to unexpected good fortune?
- Did you ever, as Robert Schreiner did, have a long-held belief or assumption challenged and toppled? Did you experience having one of your prejudices shattered?
- Was there ever a moment in your life when you decided to reform, to adopt a whole new outlook? In retrospect, would you characterize your attempt as successful, unsuccessful, laughable, painful, or what?
- Was there ever a moment in your life when you found, as Russell Baker did, that something you did just took off and seemed to do itself, and the result pleased you mightily, and perhaps pleased others, and you felt you had really learned something?
- Do you now have a strong belief or conviction that is different from what you were taught or once believed? Can you trace the change to one event or a series of events?

Try freewriting. You might still think, My life hasn't had any moments important enough to write about. Reassure yourself that what is important to you will probably be significant to others. If you still have difficulty recalling a meaningful experience, perhaps some other method of discovery might serve you. Spend ten or fifteen minutes freewriting—simply writing as fast as you can whatever comes into your head, regardless of whether it seems to have anything to do with the subject at hand. If you think you have nothing to say, write "I have nothing to say" over and over, until ideas come. They will come. Don't worry at all about spelling, punctuation, coherence, or anything else. Most of what you set down that way may have to be thrown out, but you may be surprised, when you read over what you have written, to find in it the germ of a good paper. (For more about freewriting, see p. 306 in Chapter 14.)

Try brainstorming. Alone or as part of a classroom exercise, brainstorming is another good way to jog your memory. When you brainstorm, you try to come up with as many ideas as you can, without any thought for their practical applications. Start with a suggestive word or phrase—*fight, painful lesson, peer pressure, good trip, friendship*—and list under that word or phrase as many ideas as occur to you through free association. Put them down at random, in the order in which they come to you, listing them quickly in words and phrases. Later you can see if anything on your list suggests a fruitful direction. (For more about brainstorming, see p. 303 in Chapter 14.)

Try reading. Browse in the autobiography of some famous person. (Helen Keller, Maya Angelou, and Alec Guinness are only a few authors of memorable autobiographies.) See Sherwood Anderson's "The Discovery of a Father" (p. 431) and what he learned from it. As you will find from your reading, not every decisive experience is earthshaking—Anderson learned a profound truth about himself by going swimming with his father.

Try a reporter's questions. Once you recall an experience you want to write about, ask yourself whether you feel the same about the event now as you did when it took place—or has the passage of time changed your view? Ask the reporter's questions, the "five *W*'s and an *H*" that journalists find useful in their work:

Who was there?
What happened?
When did it happen?
Where did the event take place?
Why?
How did the event or events happen?

Any one of these questions can lead to further questions—and, so, to further discovery. Take, for instance, Who was there? If there were people besides you involved in the incident, you might also ask: What did they look like? What information about them would a reader have to know to appreciate fully the point of your story? (Remember Mr. Fleagle in Baker's reminiscence.) What did the people do? What did they say? Can you remember, or approximate, what they said? If so, might their words supply a lively quotation for your paper? Or take the question What happened? Think about that, and you might also ask: What were your inmost thoughts as the event took place? At what moment did you become aware that the event was no ordinary, everyday experience? Or weren't you aware of that until later—perhaps only now that you are writing about it? (For more advice about putting these questions to work for you, see "Asking a Reporter's Questions" on p. 311.)

WRITING WITH A COMPUTER: RECALLING

If you write with a personal computer, you'll enjoy applying it to this assignment. You can set down your recollections rapidly, without pausing even to slam back a typewriter carriage. You might begin by making, as fast as you can, a simple on-screen list of the events you wish to record. This done, go back and flesh out the skeleton. Add any exact details that might make the experience real to your reader. Have you recalled a person? If so, add a sentence or two that will make him or her come alive ("a gray-haired gentleman who wore old white shirts with frayed collars, fond of consulting his gold pocket watch"). Did a certain locale shape your experience? (A shallow, snow-covered ditch is central to Schreiner's memoir "What Is a Hunter?" on p. 17.) What made that place so unforgettable? Keep recalling, dropping in memorable details. Before your eyes, your bare list will start becoming a meaty draft.

But if your list remains bare and you need more material, store your list and create a fresh document. Apply to your experience the five W's and an *H*. Ask yourself a reporter's questions and jot down your replies. With the power of word processing to lift the contents of one document to another, you can transfer to your draft all or any of the material you generate and work it in wherever it best fits. You can also try out different patterns of organization to see which works best. Move the thesis to the end, or try a flashback to start. If you don't like the changes, with word processing you can easily move the parts back or delete them.

Once you have a promising incident in mind, feel sure you can be honest in presenting it. If you find it too embarrassing to tell the whole truth, you might be better off choosing some other recollection.

Check your recollection. As we find out in a psychology course, the memory drops as well as retains. So it may be that you will want to check your recollections against those of anyone else who shared the experience. If possible, talk to a friend or family member. See that person, or phone him or her. Did you keep a diary at the time? If so, you might glance into it and refresh your memory. Was the experience public enough (such as a riot or a blizzard) to have been recorded in a newspaper or a news magazine? If so, perhaps you can read about it in a library. These are *possible* sources of material.

Planning, Drafting, and Developing

Now, how will you tell your story? If the one experience you want to write about is burning in your mind, it may be that you can start right in and write a draft without advance planning, writing and planning simultaneously, following the order of occurrence of events, shaping your story as you go along. Such a method might work for a personal memoir like the one this assignment calls for. But whether or not you plan and draft at the same time, you'll find it reassuring to have at your elbow any jottings you made as you searched your memory. If you need to plan, suggestions follow.

Establish a chronology. Retelling an experience is called narration, and the simplest way to organize the information is chronologically: relating events in the order in which they occurred. In doing so, you take the King's advice to the White Rabbit in *Alice's Adventures in Wonderland:* "Begin at the beginning, and go on till you come to the end: then stop." But sometimes because all experience flows together, you may not know just when to start or stop. If that occurs, stick to the essentials. Avoid giving a lot of background that is not related to the point you want to make. A good rule of thumb in relating an experience is to set down events chronologically—unless you see a good reason to set them down in some other way, such as beginning at an exciting moment in the middle and then using a flashback to tell your readers what else they need to know.

Show what happened. How can you best make your recollections come alive for your readers? Look again at Russell Baker's account of Mr. Fleagle teaching *Macbeth* and at the way Robert Schreiner depicts his cousin putting the wounded rabbits out of their misery. Both writers have done what good novelists and story writers do: they have not merely told us what happened, they have *shown* us, by creating scenes that we can see in our mind's eye. As you tell your story, include at least two or three such specific scenes of your own. Show your readers exactly what happened, where it occurred, what was said, who said it. What did the other people look like? How did they react? Were there any sounds that contributed to the scene? Smells or tastes or textures that you want to record?

Good fiction writers, and writers of true stories as well, know how to keep readers (or listeners) wondering, What happened next? They dole out essential information a little bit at a time so that readers have to keep reading or listening until the end to find out what they want to know. Both Baker and Schreiner save the meaning of their experiences for the end of their accounts. You can decide as you write whether you think that's the best place to discuss what your experience means to you. You might try it a couple of different ways.

Often, an account of a personal experience needs no introduction: it starts with something happening and then, through *flashback,* the writer fills in whatever background a reader needs to know. Richard Rodriguez, for instance, begins *Hunger of Memory,* a memoir of his bilingual childhood, with an arresting sentence:

> I remember, to start with, that day in Sacramento, in a California now nearly thirty years past—when I first entered a classroom, able to understand about fifty stray English words.

With such a limited vocabulary, we wonder, how will the child get along? The opening hooks our attention. In the rest of his essay, Rodriguez fills us in on his family history, on the gulf he came to perceive between the public language (English) and the language of his home (Spanish).

Revising and Editing

After you have written an early draft and have put it aside for a day or two (or, if time is tight, for a few hours), read it over as if seeing it for the first time.

When you revise, ask: What was so memorable about this experience? Do the details show what's memorable? Is it clear *why* the experience is memorable? Have you made it come alive, by recalling it in sufficient concrete detail? Can you *see* it? Be specific enough that your readers can see, smell, taste, hear, and feel what you experienced. Notice again Robert Schreiner's focus in his second paragraph on the world outside his own skin: his close recall of the snow, of the pointers his grandfather offered about the habits of jackrabbits and the way to shoot them. If you're recalling a fire, make your reader smell the smoke. As you revise, you may well recall more and more vivid details.

Remember your purpose. Keep in mind that you want to show how the experience was a crucial one in your life. So when you look back over your draft, make sure that this importance stands out. Ask again the question you probably asked yourself when you began: How did this experience alter your life? Have you got something in there about how life (or your view of it) has been different ever since? Pay a little extra attention to this major point. Be sure that the difference you point to is genuine and specific. Don't ramble on insincerely about "significances" that don't reflect the incident's real impact on you.

Here are some other questions for you to ask as you go over your paper.

REVISION CHECKLIST: WRITING FROM RECALL

- Have you fulfilled your purpose by demonstrating that this experience changed your life? How did you accomplish it?

- Why do you begin your narration as you do? Is there a place in the draft that would make a better beginning?

- What about the ending? Does it provide a sense of finality?

- Consider your audience. If you were in your readers' shoes, would you want to keep reading? Have you paid enough attention to what is most dramatic, instructive, or revealing? Can your readers experience (that is, see and feel) what you experienced?

- Why have you arranged the information as you have? If the events are not recorded in chronological order, is it easy to follow the organization you have chosen?

- Do you stick to the point? Is everything that is included relevant to your main idea or thesis? Does the draft contain extraneous thoughts, ideas, or events that ought to be struck out? (Draw a single line through any such wandering prose.)

- Do you portray any people? If so, have you told your readers enough about them to indicate their importance to you? Do you provide enough detail to make them seem real, not just shadowy figures?
- If there is dialogue, does it have the ring of real speech? Read it aloud. Record it on tape and listen to the way it sounds. Try it on a friend.

You may also find it helpful at this point to call on a classmate to read and criticize your draft. Your instructor may pair you with a classmate; if not, you may choose a friend or relative. Ask your peer editor to answer the following questions as carefully as possible.

PEER EDITING CHECKLIST: WRITING FROM RECALL

- What do you, the peer editor, see as you read the essay?
- Underline on the manuscript any sense images or descriptions that seem particularly effective.
- What details does the writer provide for you to see and convey?
- Tell the writer what you understand to be the importance of what he or she has recalled. What point do you think she or he wants to make?
- What emotions do the people (especially the main character) in the narration feel? Tell the writer also how you feel while reading the essay.
- Is the order of the occurrences and ideas easy to follow? List questions you still have about the event the writer has recalled.

In the light of the answers to the questions you have asked yourself and your peer editor, rewrite. Keep at it until you know you've related your experience and recorded its impact as well as you know how. This may take more than one new draft. It may take several. When you are satisfied, ask your peer editor to read it again and tell you if it is better than it was.

Then go over your paper one last time, proofreading for errors or problems you may have overlooked. Check spelling, punctuation, and word choice. Even the names of people and places you know well may need to be checked. Writing a paper about a remembered trip to New York, a high school student once consistently referred to "the Umpire State Building." Any encyclopedia could have put that writer straight.

When you have made all the changes you need to make, retype or recopy or print out your paper—and hand it in.

Other Assignments

1. Choose a person outside your immediate family who had a marked effect on your life, either good or bad, and jot down ten details about that person that might help a reader understand what he or she was like. In searching your memory for

FOR GROUP LEARNING

To gain dry-run practice in peer editing before trying your skills on a class-mate's paper, select from this book's table of contents any student-written paper and write a detailed response to it. Do this in the form of a short letter to the writer. Get together with others in your class who chose the same paper and compare comments. What did you notice in the paper? What did you miss that others noticed? If you have any doubts that it is worth your time to compare your responses with other people's, this activity will show you that several people can notice far more than one individual can.

details, consider the person's physical appearance, way of talking, and habits as well as any memorable incidents. When your list is finished, look back to "The Art of Eating Spaghetti" to identify the kinds of detail Baker used in his portrait of Mr. Fleagle, paying particular attention to the kinds of detail you might have included in your list but didn't. Then write a paper in which you portray that person and explore the nature of his or her impact on you. Include those details that help explain the effect the person had on you.

2. Write a paper in which you remember a place you were once fond of—your grandmother's kitchen, a tree house, a library, a locker room, a clubhouse, a vacation retreat, a place where your friends got together. Emphasize why this place was memorable. What made it different from every other place? Why was it important to you? Do you even now think back on it? What do you feel when you remember it? (No sentimental gush, now. But don't be afraid to set down honest feeling.)

3. Write a paper in which, from memory, you inform your readers about some traditional ceremony, ritual, or observation familiar to you. Such a tradition can pertain to a holiday, a rite of passage (confirmation, bar or bas mitzvah, gradu-ation, fraternity or sorority initiation), a sporting event, a special day on your college calendar. It might be a family custom. Explain the importance of the tradition to you, making use of whatever information you recall. How did the observation or custom originate? Who takes part? How has the tradition changed through the years? What does it add to the lives of those who observe it?

4. Narrate an experience in which you felt like an outsider, someone who didn't belong. Explore why you felt this way, and explain what you did as a result of this feeling.

APPLYING WHAT YOU LEARN: SOME USES OF WRITING FROM RECALL

Autobiographers and writers of informal essays rely extensively on recall. All of us depend on recall in much of our informal, everyday writing—when we pen a letter to friends or family members, when we write out directions for someone who doesn't know where we live, when we make a diary entry, when we fill out an accident report or an application form.

Students of creative writing often find themselves reaching into their memories for experiences to write about. Recall is also an important resource for the kind of paper in which you, the expert, are asked to explain how to do something—train a puppy, drive a car, build a coffee table, make a speech, catch a tarpon. But recall also plays a role in the writing you are asked to do for classes other than English. In most papers written for a college course, you are expected to investigate, to analyze, to explain, or to argue. Clearly it's not enough merely to recount a personal experience, but personal experience does have a place in academic writing as support for exposition and argument. Rebecca Shriver, a student who had spent a year living and working in St. Thomas, added life and verisimilitude to her research paper analyzing cultural differences between the Virgin Islands and the United States by including not only material gathered from books and periodicals but also this telling recollection:

> Among the first things an American in the Virgin Islands will notice are the driving and the drivers. St. Thomas retains the custom, a carryover from Danish rule, of driving on the left-hand side of the road. Drivers are extremely aggressive, vocal, and heedless of others. West Indians, especially the cab drivers, virtually own the road. They stop for minutes at a time at the bottom of steep hills to chat with friends or to pick up hordes of workers. The streets resound with honks and screams as drivers yell obscenities at each other. Hitchhikers, too, are aggressive. Often a West Indian jumps into the back of one's truck, or schoolchildren tap on one's window, soliciting a ride.
>
> The mind-set of left-hand driving surfaces in an unusual way: walking habits. Since St. Thomians are so used to driving on the left, they also walk on the left, and an American who is unused to this will bump into a lot of West Indians on the sidewalk.

The writer used this recollection to make an important point: that recognizing and understanding cultural differences provide the keys to understanding. In an article called "Sex and Size," paleontologist Stephen Jay Gould makes effective use of recollection to ease his readers into a seven-page essay on a challenging subject. (Linnaeus [1707–1778], a Swedish botanist, originated the system of classifying organisms in established categories.)

As an eight-year-old collector of shells at Rockaway Beach, I took a functional but non-Linnaean approach to taxonomy, dividing my booty into "regular," "unusual," and "extraordinary." My favorite was the common slipper limpet, although it resided in the realm of the regular by virtue of its ubiquity. I loved its range of shapes and colors, and the pocket underneath that served as a protective home for the animal. My appeal turned to fascination a few years later, when I both entered puberty and studied some Linnaean taxonomy at the same time. I learned its proper name, *Crepidula fornicata*—a sure spur to curiosity. Since Linnaeus himself had christened this particular species, I marveled at the unbridled libido of taxonomy's father.

When I learned about the habits of *C. fornicata*, I felt confident that I had found the key to its curious name. For the slipper limpet forms stacks, smaller piled atop larger, often reaching a dozen shells or more. The smaller animals on top are invariably male, the larger supporters underneath always female. And lest you suspect that the topmost males might be restricted to a life of obligate homosexuality by virtue of their separation from the first large female, fear not. The male's penis is longer by far than its entire body and can easily slip around a few males to reach the females. *Crepidula fornicata* indeed: a sexy congeries.

Then, to complete the disappointing story, I discovered that the name had nothing to do with sex. Linnaeus had described the species from single specimens in museum drawers; he knew nothing of their peculiar stacking behavior. *Fornix* means "arch" in Latin, and Linnaeus chose his name to recognize the shell's smoothly domed shape.

Disappointment finally yielded to renewed interest a few years later when I learned the details of *Crepidula*'s sexuality and found the story more intriguing than ever, even if the name had been a come-on. *Crepidula* is a natural sex changer, a sequential hermaphrodite in our jargon. Small juveniles mature first as males and later change to female as they grow larger. Intermediate animals in the middle of a *Crepidula* stack are usually in the process of changing from male to female.

Usually you have to research your subject in some depth before you can write an acceptable paper about it. You need to rely on resources other than memory. Yet even as you approach an academic writing assignment, a research paper, or an argument on a topic, you can *begin* by writing down your own relevant experiences. Whether or not you use them in your finished paper, they can help direct your research. Often you *will* use them, as Shriver and Gould did, in conjunction with more academic sources. A student who has worked in a day-care center can add vigor and authority to a sociology paper on day care in the United States today by including a few pertinent illustrations based on that experience. Or if you are the person writing the paper and you lack personal experience with day care, you can illustrate a point or two with lively anecdotes remembered from your reading or from interviewing someone with firsthand experience. In a paper for a course in corporate ethics, your next-door neighbor's gleeful account of a hostile takeover, divulged at the last block party you attended, might hammer home the point you're making more effectively than any statistic can. An economics paper about the recent growth of the fast-food industry could benefit immeasurably from an incident remembered from your harried days behind the counter at a McDonald's. If you grew up in the inner city, your recollections might lend enormous impact to a paper arguing for or against a particular city planning proposal.

Virtually every paper, no matter what it sets out to accomplish, stands to benefit from pat, vivid examples and illustrations. When you include such examples and illustrations in your writing, your memories can prove as valuable as hidden treasure.

Further Applications

Recall is probably the major resource for writers in all professions and from all walks of life. In *A Writer's Reader,* some of the writers recall and respond to events from childhood, others to events from adulthood. For example, in "Discovery of a Father" (p. 431), fiction writer Sherwood Anderson recalls events from his childhood that helped shape his ability to write novels and short stories. He recalls a series of episodes, culminating in one particular significant event through which he "discovered" his father. In "Japanese and American Workers" (p. 523), William Ouchi, a management consultant, draws on his experiences as an adult. He recalls visits to two Japanese factories to illustrate their "strong orientation to collective values, particularly a collective sense of responsibility"—a lesson for American business. These two writers, like Russell Baker (p. 14) and Robert G. Schreiner (p. 17), not only recall and report significant events in their lives, but they also reflect on the experiences and explain how they have changed their thoughts, feelings, and actions.

Some of the writers from various fields who use the resource of *recall* include novelist Paule Marshall, "From the Poets in the Kitchen" (p. 439), social historian Vivian Gornick, "Mama Went to Work" (p. 445), computer scientist Gary Katzenstein, "The Salaryman" (p. 528), editor Marcia Ann Gillespie, "A Different Take on the Ol' Bump and Grind" (p. 469), and television reporter Ti-Hua Chang, "Downtown Cousin" (p. 492). They look back over important events in their lives and interpret how the experiences have influenced them. For each essay, answer the following questions.

1. Does the author recall events from childhood or adulthood?
2. Is the perspective of the essay that of a child or an adult? How do you know? What does the author realize after reflecting on the events? Does the realization come soon after the experience or later, when he or she examines the events from a more mature perspective?
3. How does the realization change the individual?
4. How do you think recall is useful to the author in his or her field of work or study?

CHAPTER 2

Writing from Observation

Most writers, we said in Chapter 1, begin to write by recalling what they know. But sometimes when they sit down to write they look around the storehouse of the brain only to find empty shelves. In such a case, a writer has another resource: observation.

Not enough to write about? Open your eyes—and your other senses. Take in not only what you can see but also what you can hear, smell, touch, and taste. Then, when you write, report your experiences in concrete detail. Of course, you can't record everything your senses bring you. Keeping in mind your purpose in writing and your audience will help you to select those details important to the job at hand and to pay them the most attention. Writing an account of a football game for your college newspaper, trying to make it come alive for a reader who wasn't there, you might briefly mention the weather (overcast and cold) and the buttery smell of popcorn in the air. But, hewing to your purpose to tell which team won and why, you might stress other details: the condition of the playing field (deep mud), the most spectacular plays, and the players who scored.

Some writing consists almost entirely of observation: a news story by a reporter who has witnessed a fire, a clinical report by a doctor or nurse detailing a patient's condition, a scientist's account of a laboratory experiment. Travel writing, in which a traveler reports a visit to a distant place, consists largely of observation; so does descriptive writing that sets down a writer's observations of a person, place, or thing. (Such description occurs in both fiction and nonfiction.) In such kinds of writing, observation serves a definite purpose. In other kinds of writing, observation can provide supporting details to make ideas clear or convincing. Indeed, we can hardly think of a kind of writing that doesn't call for a writer to observe and report those observations.

LEARNING FROM OTHER WRITERS

Let's read two essays by writers who write from observation: a professional writer and a college student. Both essays arise from the authors' surroundings, but there the resemblance ends. The first is by freelance screenwriter Charlie Haas, who writes of crowd behavior with a perceptive eye. In this sprightly essay from *Esquire,* he takes a close look at Westwood Village, a neighborhood near the UCLA campus in Los Angeles from which national trends in clothes, food, music, and behavior emerge.

TINSEL TEENS
Charlie Haas

1 Some of us, years after graduating from college, still love college towns. We hit these little European pockets of America and feel right at home, happy to see an entire local economy running on strong coffee, imported cigarettes, and used books. The Vivaldi and chess in the bus-your-own coffeehouses, the day packs and bicycles aren't clichés to us, they're fraternal high signs. Some of us like these places so much that we graduate and never move away; others collect new college towns all our lives, always looking for these funky holdouts against a landscape that lights up, beeps, and buzzes.

2 Westwood Village is *nothing* like that. Westwood Village, which adjoins UCLA but looks like MTV, is a kids' chic business district so marvelously slick that you can enter it at twilight and glide all evening along the goofily curved and angled streets, feeling no friction and seeing, in a few blocks, the diet of hipness that will be fed to kids in slower regions for the next five years, after clearance from Westwood's spotless test boutiques.

3 If the currencies of past youth scenes were cultural ideas and political positions, the currency of Westwood is currency, and plenty of it: this is the Greenwich Village of moneyed leisure, the Left Bank of beautiful-brute hype. You can rummage in college towns for wisdom, but you go to West-wood for cleverness—clever clothes on clever bodies, droll food at arch tables. Westwood is your college town as remade by Hollywood. On week-end nights it is hardly a college town at all. On those nights Westwood is teen heaven.

4 Westwood doesn't attract teenagers with bitchin' surf, straight drag strips, hot dance floors, or anything so prosaically teen. If you ask a fifteen-

year-old girl in state-of-the-art *haute*-tramp exposed-midriff fashion and a two-hour eye-makeup job what she likes about Westwood and close your eyes as she answers, you can imagine that you're hearing an upper-middle-class, upper-middle-aged lady describe a favored destination in Europe: "Yes, well, there are a lot of nice *shops*, you know, the *gift* shops and so on, and there are, *ah*, some nice *restaurants*, and of course it's nice to, oh, go to a restaurant and then, say, a movie. . . ."

On a Saturday afternoon the kids start drifting in from all over the city 5 to kick things off with some serious clothes shopping. Boys who can name you every designer in their outfit, from Generra all-cotton jacket down, are heard to swear undying love for the shoes at Leather Bound. The Limited Express, with technopop on the PA, offers Day-Glo sweat-fleece cardigans and other punch-line looks; a few doors down, at the other Limited store, the emphasis is on foreign designs—Forenza, Kenzo. But what is key for the Westwood girl of the moment—even more key than Esprit—is Guess?, a line of sportswear heavy on soft-shaped whites, pastels, and denims. "They'll buy anything Guess?—the *label* sells," says a seventeen-year-old salesgirl at MGA. "They spend a lot of money, but then, *clothes* are a lot of money now." The biggest hit garment with the girls is a hugely oversize white jacket with overlapping seams, a jacket so shapeless and enveloping that its wearers look like sculptures waiting to be unveiled at adulthood.

In the meantime, there is Westwood, high school polite society. The 6 Village is easily walked across, but a pedicab service has sprung up, with all the "drivers" in black bow ties and some in formal dress. For those over twenty-one there are bars with alcohol, and they too are models of decorum: upstairs at T. J. Honeycutt's, clean-cut young people dance under a mirror ball to recorded pop you can talk over. At Baxter's downstairs bar, where the cocktail waitresses wear tiny sport shorts and satin team jackets, amiable chatter drowns out the rock videos on the multiple monitors, and a banner says WEDNESDAY NIGHT IS DYNASTY NIGHT—CHAMPAGNE 25¢, 9 P.M. There are video games in Westwood, but they are massed in one arcade, just as junk-jewelry vendors are confined to one courtyard, instead of lining several sleazy blocks as they do near UC Berkeley. If down these clean streets a man must go, he can do so for hours without being asked for spare change. There is a sprinkling of kids in the spirit-of-1976 punk look; an ambling few of them say that their idea of a hot time in Westwood, like anyone else's, is dinner and a movie—though, as hard-core anarchists, they make a point of copping meals and admissions from friends with jobs on the inside.

In the restaurants, fifteen-year-old diners place polite orders with six- 7 teen-year-old waitresses, but a full-course meal is not the only option: in Westwood, not even the junk food is junk. There are bulging falafels at Me & Me; Louisiana hot links at The Wurst; a clean, well-lit building housing an international arcade of GYRO SOUVLAKI TANDOORI CURRY KEBAB. There is Fatburger, "the last great hamburger stand," where the king chili-cheese-egg burger is so wetly unmanageable that watching someone eat one is an invasion of privacy. You can buy Bordeaux-chocolate-flavored popcorn in a gourmet popcorn store, order Heath Bar chips chopped into your raspberry custard ice cream with rum-soaked raisins poured on top at an ice cream place, eat New York-style pizza in a storefront decorated as a New York subway station. When a new method is discovered for achieving treats, the technology is rushed instantly to Westwood, the Silicon Valley of silly delight.

When a new movie is released, same deal: to go to a picture here is 8 to go to a *show*, to glide under the neon-crammed marquee of a heroic old theater, up to a cashier's cage where computers monitor ticket sales, past the studio's proudest die-cut star-photo stand-ups, across the lush undergrowth pictured on the old-fashioned lobby carpet, to projection and sound of a quality that has become rare.

But as sound-stage spectacles, movies in Westwood have to compete 9 with the stores. In the Nike sports-fashion store on Westwood Boulevard a giant fire-red 3-D plastic Nike swoosh logo hangs from the ceiling, its point sticking through the plate-glass window and out over the street, with faked burn damage in the masonry overhead. *Aahs!*, a store that sells the same Jetson-family T-shirts, naughty greeting cards, and candy-colored planning diaries as half a dozen other Westwood stores yet achieves distinction through sheer size, limits the number of customers, so kids line up on the sidewalk, patient victims of Saturday Night Browsing Fever. In one T-shirt store the salesgirl says that a shirt with a plain pink pig on it is her biggest seller ("I think because people consider themselves pigs"); at another, Lacoste-type knit shirts with pairs of screwing alligators are moving fast. At a third, the I FUCK ON THE FIRST DATE T-shirt is big, as are some devoted to Westwood's true compulsion: WHEN THE GOING GETS TOUGH, THE TOUGH GO SHOPPING, and I CAN'T BE OVERDRAWN, I STILL HAVE SOME CHECKS. But all of these, sweetly, are outsold by FEED THE WORLD and WAR IS STUPID.

By 10:00 P.M. the sidewalks are packed with kids from all over the city, 10 and the streets are filled with slow-cruising cars, kids striking up acquaintances in shouts, visiting one another in gridlocked Z's and Baja trucks. Even in Westwood, a fifteen-year-old's sophistication runs only so deep, and some of the kids are like farmers come to town: "Look at *that!* Look at *her!* Hey!" They are boisterous, but in a mild, vacationing way—Westwood is a place where people who live four freeway exits away become resort tourists in their own city. There are a lot of couples but also a lot of same-sex pairs and packs, and no urgent mating frenzy: a pack of boys sweeps up to a pack of girls on a corner, collects phone numbers, and breezes on. The kids are genuinely happy, which makes sense: sure, they live in the shadow of the nuclear bomb, but they also stand within walking distance of *two* all-night Fatburgers.

As it gets late a mass of kids crowd onto the wedge of sidewalk in front 11 of Glendale Federal Savings and Loan (it takes real style to look cool in front of posters about interest rates). A couple of LAPD° cops keep an eye

LAPD: Los Angeles Police Department.

on the crowd and hand out a few traffic tickets. "Westwood is orderly," one of them says, "because we keep it orderly. We have eight officers on foot patrol here on weekend nights, two during the week. Occasionally there will be trouble—a knife fight or something—because they're coming from all over now."

His fellow officer is letting a young woman talk him into signing a piece 12 of paper that says she got thirty-two people to sing "Row, Row, Row Your Boat." "It's for Lifespring," she says. "That's a self-awareness organization, but I'm not allowed to talk about it." Meanwhile six Asian teenage girls wearing Oreo-cookie costumes "as part of our Hell Week" for a sorority march through the crowd, followed by six Asian teenage boys who exchange graphic fantasies regarding the girls. Pledge a sorority, pledge a self-awareness scheme: one-stop shopping.

The cop's words aside, the Westwood kids look more inclined to diet 13 than riot. Adults who work in Westwood almost invariably describe weekend nights there as "a zoo." This is accurate, but perhaps in more ways than the speakers intend: Westwood is a place where kid wildness is neatly restrained, where the central pleasure is to check one another out like little loaned pandas. (Youth wants to know: Is your Guess? as good as mine?) The kids in front of Glendale Federal mill around just as they do at school recess, but this is gourmet recess, the all-city walking-around finals.

The conventional jive about L.A. is that the neighborhoods are insular, 14 that ethnic and racial groups don't mix, and that nobody walks. The Westwood kids, ignoring all that, have fashioned an integrated promenade that makes the adult visitors envious. Westwood is slick, but it is not a mall or an amusement park, not forged or run by a single intelligence. Instead, it's an actual urban neighborhood, with at least some randomness; if you've been growing up in Woodland Hills, this alone can seem a dizzying freedom. And Westwood actually invites kids, offers them a physical place to match their moment. Everyone is welcome—be a punk if you want, that's fine, punks add color, but be a *designer* punk, all right? Because this is not the Beach, not the Valley; tonight we are playing the Palace, the Carson show, of being a kid. A little élan; we are walking in *Westwood,* and what we do and wear here this Saturday night they will be doing and wearing six months from now in New York, two years from now in Cleveland, ten years from now at nostalgia-themed charity balls.

And on Sunday morning there is a ton of litter on the sidewalk in front 15 of Glendale Federal. All of it in the trash baskets.

Questions To Start You Thinking

1. How is this article appropriate for *Esquire* readers? If you aren't familiar with the magazine, visit the library or newsstand and look through an issue or two. Notice particularly not just articles but also advertisements.

2. Commented a UCLA student, "The guy who wrote this essay makes it seem as if only teenagers flock to Westwood Village. University students hang out there, too." Does anything in "Tinsel Teens" answer this criticism?

3. Is this essay primarily about a place or about the people who frequent that place? Give evidence to support your answer.

4. In one or two sentences, summarize the main impression the essay gives you of Westwood Village and the teenagers the author observes there. Do all of Haas's observations contribute to a single overall impression, or are you left with more than one?

5. To which of the five senses does "Tinsel Teens" especially appeal? Point to two or three vivid examples of sense imagery.

6. Haas wrote this essay in 1985. How do you imagine the scenes and the people in Westwood Village would be different today?

Sandy Messina, the student who wrote the following paper, submitted to both a course in freshman composition and another course—environmental biology. She looks closely at the desert and its inhabitants.

Student Essay

FOOTPRINTS: THE MARK OF OUR PASSING
Sandy Messina

No footprints. No tracks. No marks. The Navajo leave   1
no footprints because their shoes have no heels to dig into
the earth's womb. They have a philosophy--walk gently on
mother earth; she is pregnant with life. In the spring, when
the earth is ready to deliver, they wear no shoes at all.

As I walk across the desert, I look at my shoes etch the   2
sand dune. There they are following me: the telltale prints
left on the brown earth. Each footprint has a story to tell,
a story of change, a story of death. Many lives are marked
by our passing. Our steps can bring death to the life of a
flower, the life of a forest, the life of a friendship. Some
of our passages can bring death to the life of a nation.

I see my prints dug deeply into the spawning grounds of   3
the desert lavender, the evening primrose, the desert sun-
flower, and the little golden gilia. Life destroyed. Birth
aborted. There under each mark of my passing is death. The
fetuses--seeds of desert color, spring glory, trapped just

below the surface waiting parturition--crushed into lifeless-
ness. Man walks heavily on the earth.

He tramples across America, leaving giant footprints   4
everywhere he goes. He fills swamps, furrows hillsides,
forms roads, fells trees, fashions cities. Man leaves the
prints of his lifelong quest to subdue the earth, to conquer
the wilderness. He pushes and pulls and kneads the earth
into a loaf to satisfy his own appetites. He constantly tugs
at the earth, trying to regulate it. Yet, man was not told
to regulate, restrict, restrain the Garden of Eden but to
care for it and allow it to replenish itself.

I look at my own footprints in the sand and see nearby   5
other, gentler tracks. Here on the sandy hummock I see
prints, soft and slithery. The snake goes softly on the
earth. His willowy form causes no tyranny. He has no need
to prove his prowess: he graciously gives warning and strikes
only in self-defense. He doesn't mar the surface of the
earth by his entrance, for his home is found in the burrows
of the other animals.

The spidery prints of the roadrunner, as he escapes with   6
a lizard dangling from his beak, show that he goes mercifully
on the earth. He does not use his power of flight to feed
off wide distances but instead employs his feathers to insu-
late his body from high temperatures. He takes sustenance
from the earth but does not hoard or store it.

The wood rat scrambles over the hillock to burrow be-   7
neath the Joshua tree. His clawed plantigrade feet make
sensitive little marks. He is caring of the earth. He
doesn't destroy forage but browses for food and eats cactus,
food no other animal will eat. His home is a refuge of underground runways. It even provides protection for his enemy
the snake, as well as for himself, from the heat of the day.
He never feels the compulsion to be his own person or have
his own space but lives in harmony with many other animals,
under the Joshua tree.

The Joshua tree, that prickly paragon that invades the   8
desolation of desert, welcomes to its house all who would

dwell there. Many lives depend on this odd-looking creature, the Joshua tree. It is intimately associated with the moth, the lizard, the wood rat, the snake, the termite, the woodpecker, the boring weevil, the oriole. This spiky fellow is hospitable, tolerant, and kind on the earth. He provides a small world for other creatures: a world of pavilion, provision, protection from the harsh desert.

Unlike the Navajo's, my prints are still there in the   9
sand, but not the ruthless furrows I once perceived. My musings over nature have made my touch upon the earth lighter, softer, gentler.

Man too can walk gently on the earth. He must reflect   10
on his passing. Is the earth changed, bent and twisted, because he has traveled there, or has he considered nature as a symphony he can walk with, in euphony? He need not walk heavily on the earth, allowing the heat of adversity and the winds of circumstance to destroy him. He can walk gently on the earth, allowing life to grow undisturbed in seeming desert places until it springs forth.

Questions to Start You Thinking

1. Why doesn't the writer plunge right in and immediately start to report her observations? Of what use to her essay is her first paragraph?

2. In paragraph 2, how is the writer's way of walking across the earth seen as different from the Navajo way? Paragraph 3 isn't observation, but what does the writer accomplish in it? With paragraphs 4, 5, and 6, the writer returns to observing — for what purpose? What is the function of paragraphs 7, 8, and 9, 10?

3. How has the process of observing her own footprints changed the writer's behavior? How would she change the behavior of the rest of us?

4. What specialized words suggest that this essay was written for a readership familiar with biology (her instructor and other students)? Would any of the *jargon*, or technical terminology, interfere with Messina's communication of her ideas to a general reader?

LEARNING BY WRITING

The Assignment: Reporting on Group Behavior

Station yourself in a place where you can mingle with a group of people gathered for some reason or occasion. Observe the group's behavior and in a short paper report on it. Then offer some insight. What is your main impression of the group?

This assignment is meant to start you observing closely, so we suggest you don't write from long-ago memory. Go somewhere nearby, today or as soon as possible, and open your senses. Write for your classmates. Jot down what you can immediately see and sense. You may wish to take notes right there on the scene or minutes after you make your observations. After you have set forth your observations in detail, try to use them to form some general impression of the group or come to some realization about it. Expect to fill at least two typewritten or three handwritten pages.

Notice how the people in the group affect one another, how they respond. Which individuals stand out and seem to call for an especially close look? What details (of their dress, actions, speech, body language) make you want to remember them? Four student writers made these observations:

> One student recently observed a group of people nervously awaiting a road test for their driver's licenses. (She also observed them after their tests.)
>
> Another observed a bar mitzvah celebration that reunited a family for the first time in many years.
>
> Still another, who works nights in the emergency room of a hospital, observed the behavior of the community of people that abruptly forms on the arrival of an accident victim (including doctors, nurses, orderlies, the patient's friends or relatives, and the patient himself or herself).
>
> A fourth student observed a knot of people that formed on a street corner to inspect a luna moth perched on a telephone pole (including a man who viewed it with alarm, a wondering toddler, and an amateur entomologist).

Generating Ideas

Setting down observations might seem a cut-and-dried task, not a matter of discovering anything. But to reporter and essayist Joan Didion it is true discovery. "I write," she says, "entirely to find out what I'm thinking, what I'm looking at, what I see and what it means."

Do some brainstorming. First, you need to find a subject to observe. What groups of people come together for a reason? Get out your pencil and start brainstorming—listing rapidly and at random any ideas that come to mind (a technique often useful in getting started; for more advice about it, see p. 303). Here are a few questions to help you start your list.

DISCOVERY CHECKLIST: OBSERVING

- What people get together to take in some event or performance? (Spectators at a game, an audience at a play or concert. . . .)
- What people get together to participate in some activity? (Worshipers at a religious service, students in a discussion class. . . .)

- What people assemble to receive advice or instruction? (A team receiving a briefing from a coach, actors, musicians, dancers at a rehearsal. . . .)
- What people form crowds while they are obtaining something or receiving service? (Shoppers, students in a dining hall or student union, patients in a waiting room. . . .)
- What people get together for recreation? (People at a party, at a video arcade. . . .)
- What people gather at an unfortunate event? (To watch a fire, a street fight, the aftermath of a car crash. . . .)

Get out and look. After you make your list, go over it and put a check mark next to any possible subject that appeals to you. If no subject strikes you as compelling, go plunge into the world beyond your sleeping quarters and see what you will see. Your location might be a city street or a hillside in the country, a college building or a campus lawn, a furiously busy scene— a shopping mall, an airport terminal, a fast-food restaurant at lunch hour, or a student hangout—or one in which only two or three people are idling— sunbathers, dog walkers, anglers, or Frisbee throwers. It may be, as Haas says, a place where people "become resort tourists in their own city," similar to Westwood Village. You may soon find that you have picked a likely group to observe, or you may instead find that you're getting nowhere and want to move on to another location. Move around in a group, if possible. Stand off in a corner for a while, then mix in with the throng. Get different angles of view.

Record your observations. Sandy Messina's essay "Footprints" began as a journal entry. In her biology course, Sandy was asked to keep a *specialized* journal in which to record her thoughts and observations on environmental biology. When she looked back over her observations of a desert walk, a subject stood out—one wide enough for a paper that she could submit to her English course as well. As you can see from her final version, to keep such a journal or notebook, occasionally jotting down thoughts and observations, creates a trove of material ready and waiting for use in more formal writing. (For further thoughts on journal keeping, see p. 309.)

The notes you take on your subject—or tentative subject—can be taken in any old order or methodically. One experienced teacher of writing, Myra Cohn Livingston, urges her students to draw up an "observation sheet" to organize their note taking. To use it, fold a sheet of paper in half lengthwise. On the left make a column (which might be called Objective) and list exactly what you saw, in an impartial way, like a zoologist looking at a new species of moth. Then on the right make a column (called Subjective), and list your thoughts and feelings about what you observed. For instance, an observation sheet inspired by a trip to observe people at a beach might begin this way:

OBJECTIVE	SUBJECTIVE
Two kids toss a red beach ball while a spotted dog chases back and forth trying to intercept it.	Reminds me of when I was five and my beach ball rolled under a parked car. Got stuck crawling in to rescue it, cried, had to be calmed down, dragged free. Never much liked beach ball after that.
College couples on dates, smearing each other with suntan lotion.	Good way to get to know each other!
Middle-aged man eating a foot-long hot dog. Mustard drips on his paunch. "Hell! I just lost two percent!"	Guy looks like a business executive: three-piece-suit type, I bet. But today he's a slob. Who cares? The beach brings out the slob in everybody.

As your own list grows, it may spill over onto a fresh sheet. Write on one side of your paper only: later you can more easily organize your notes if you can spread them out and look at them all in one glance. Even in this sample beginning of an observation sheet, some sense is starting to take shape. At least, the second and third notes both suggest that the beach is where people come to let their hair down. That insight might turn out to be the main impression that the paper conveys. For this writing assignment, an observation sheet seems an especially useful device. The notes in column one will trigger more notes in column two. Observations, you will find, start thoughts and feelings flowing.

The quality of your finished paper will probably depend not on how much you rewrite but on the truthfulness and accuracy of your observations. If possible, while you write keep looking at your subject. Sandy Messina is a good, exact observer of nature: the details of the snake's "soft and slithery" print in the sand, the wood rat's "clawed plantigrade feet" (a technical word: *plantigrade* means walking with both sole and heel touching the ground).

Include images. Have you captured not just sights, but any sounds, touches, odors? A memorable *image,* or evocation of a sense experience, can do wonders for a paper. In his memoir *Northern Farm,* naturalist Henry Beston observes a remarkable sound: "the voice of ice," the midwinter sound of a whole frozen pond settling and expanding in its bed:

> Sometimes there was a sort of hollow oboe sound, and sometimes a groan with a delicate undertone of thunder. . . . Just as I turned to go, there came from below one curious and sinister crack which ran off into a sound like the whine of a giant whip of steel lashed through the moonlit air.

Apparently Beston's purpose in this passage is to report the nature of ice from his observations of it, and yet he uses accurate language that arrests us by the power of its suggestions.

When British journalist and fiction writer G. K. Chesterton wrote of ocean waves, he was tempted at first to speak of the "rushing swiftness of a wave" — a usual phrase. But instead, as he tells us in his essay "The Two Noises," he dusted off his glasses and observed a real wave toppling.

> The horrible thing about a wave is its hideous slowness. It lifts its load of water laboriously. . . . In front of me that night the waves were not like water: they were like falling city walls. The breaker rose first as if it did not wish to attack the earth; it wished only to attack the stars. For a time it stood up in the air as naturally as a tower; then it went a little wrong in its outline, like a tower that might some day fall.

Planning, Drafting, and Developing

Having been writing, however roughly, all the while you've been observing, you will now have some rough stuff to organize. Spread out your notes and look over all of them. If you have made an observation sheet, you can mark it up: you can circle whatever looks useful. Maybe you can plan best while rewriting your preliminary notes into a draft. Then you'll be throwing out details that don't matter, leaving those that do.

How do you map out a series of observations? One simple way would be to proceed *spatially*. You could map out your observations graphically or in a simple scratch outline. In observing a landscape, you might move from left to right, from top to bottom, from near to far, from center to periphery. One of these methods might be as good as any other. However, your choice may well depend on your purpose in writing.

You might see (or feel) a reason to *move from the most prominent feature to the less prominent.* If you are writing about a sketch artist at work, say, the most prominent and interesting feature to start with might be the artist's busy, confident hands. If you are describing a basketball game, you might start with the action under a basket.

Or you might *move from specific details to a general statement of an overall impression.* In describing Fisherman's Wharf in San Francisco, you might start with sellers of shrimp cups and souvenir fishnets, tour boats loading passengers, and the smell of frying fish and go on to say, "In all this commotion and commerce, a visitor senses the constant activity of the sea."

Or you could *move from common, everyday features to the unusual features you want to stress.* After starting with the smell of frying fish and the

How closely can you observe? Of these two copies of woodcuts by the sixteenth-century German artist known only by his signature, The Master I. B. with the Bird, one is the original, the other a forgery. Art critic William M. Ivins, Jr., remarked: "In this original the lines have

cries of gulls, you might go on: "Yet this ordinary scene attracts visitors from afar: the Japanese sightseer, perhaps a fan of American prison films, making a pilgrimage by tour boat to Alcatraz."

Consider your purpose. Perhaps your most important planning will take place as you answer the question What main insight or impression do I want to get across? To ask yourself this question may help you decide which impressions to include and which to omit.

intention and meaning. In the copy . . . the lines have lost their intention. They have all the characteristics of careless and unintelligent but laborious tracing." Which is which? The solution is on page 52.

Revising and Editing

Your rewriting, editing, and proofreading will all be easier if you have taken accurate notes on your observations. Clearly, that is what Charlie Haas did in Westwood Village.

But what if, when you look over your draft, you find that in observing you skimped and now you don't have enough notes? If you have any doubts

WRITING WITH A COMPUTER: OBSERVING

If you do find it necessary to make a second, follow-up trip to the scene, word processing will allow you to amplify your draft easily. You can simply open your draft file and insert further details wherever they will make your paper more vivid and lifelike.

Making your observations crackle with life, by the way, isn't just a matter of trying to intensify things with adverbs such as *very*. William Allen White, author and Kansas newspaper editor, hated such modifiers, which he believed are usually like fifth wheels. He once instructed his reporters to change every *very* they wrote to a *damn*, then cross out all the *damns*; they would then have stronger prose. Thanks to the miracle of word processing, you can—just for fun—readily William-Allen-White your own writing. Instruct your computer to conduct a global search-and-replace, changing every *very* to a *damn* throughout your paper. Print out the results and read it over. Then tell your computer to search out every *damn* and replace it with a space.

about your notes, go back to the scene and check them. Professional journalists often make such follow-ups.

Once you have made sure that you've accurately recorded your observations, you may find it useful to seek a classmate's reactions to your draft. If so, ask your peer editor to answer the following questions in writing.

PEER EDITING CHECKLIST: WRITING FROM OBSERVATION

- Give your overall reaction to the entire paper.
- Describe the main insight or impression you carry away from this piece of writing.
- How well has the writer used the evidence from his or her senses? Highlight with a marker details or description in the essay that you think use that evidence effectively.
- Which sense does the writer use particularly well in writing from observation? Does he or she neglect any sense that could be used?
- Are there any places in the writing where you think the writer could or should use more details? Put stars on the manuscript where you want more detail.
- Look at the way the writer has organized his or her observations. How well does the organization work? Do you recommend any changes?
- What three things do you like best about this piece of writing?
- On the manuscript, circle any spelling, punctuation, grammar, word choice, or sentence that made your reading of this essay more difficult than it should have been.

Not all writers rewrite in the same way. Some start tinkering early, perfecting little bits here and there. Even back in her original version of "Footprints," a few sheets of rough notes, Sandy Messina started making small improvements. In her first draft, she had written:

> Each of us must learn to walk gently on the earth. We must quit pushing and pulling and kneading it into a loaf to be our own bread.

Right away, she realized that by calling the earth "a loaf" she had already likened it to bread. So she crossed out "be our own bread" and substituted "suit our own appetites." She also crossed out verbs one at a time, as they occurred, until a strong verb came along.

> We ~~moved~~ ~~marched~~ trooped across America, leaving our giant footprints.

As a final test, to see what parts of your draft still need work when you rewrite, you might ask yourself these questions.

REVISION CHECKLIST: WRITING FROM OBSERVATION

- Have you gathered enough observations to make your subject understandable? Think of your audience: What can you assume your readers already know? What don't they need to be told?
- Do any of your observations need to be checked for accuracy?
- Have you observed with *all* your senses? (Smell isn't always useful, but it might be.)
- Have you accomplished your purpose: to convey clearly your overall impression of your subject and to share some telling insight about it?
- Why have you chosen the organizational pattern you have used? Is it the most effective pattern for your subject? Would another pattern be more effective?

Other Assignments

1. To develop your powers of observation, follow Sandy Messina's example. Go for a walk, recording your observations in two or three detailed paragraphs. Let your walk take you either through an unfamiliar scene or through a familiar scene perhaps worth a closer look than you normally give it (such as a supermarket, a city street, or an open field). Avoid a subject so familiar that it would be difficult for you to see it from a fresh perspective (such as a dormitory corridor or a parking lot). Sum up your impression of the place, including any opinion you form by your close observations.

2. Observe a place near your college or your home and the people who frequent this place (a mall, a strip, a club, a beach, a hangout). List the specific scenes, people, action, and events you see. What conclusions can you draw about the people? Describe the place, the people, and their actions so as to convey the spirit of the place.

3. Just for fun, here is a short, spontaneous writing exercise that might serve as a warmup for a long assignment. Lin Haire-Sargeant of Tufts University, whose students enjoyed the exercise, calls it "You Are the Detective." She asked her students to begin the assignment immediately after the class in which it was given and to turn it in the same afternoon.

> Go to a nearby public place—burger joint, library, copy center, art gallery—and select a person who catches your eye, who somehow intrigues you. Try to choose someone who looks as if she or he will stay put for a while. Settle yourself where you can observe your subject unobtrusively. Take notes, if you can do so without being observed yourself.
>
> Now, carefully and tactfully (we don't want any fistfights or lawsuits) notice everything you can about this person. The obvious place to start would be with physical characteristics, but focus on other things too. How does the person talk? Move? What does body language tell you?
>
> Write a paragraph describing the person. Pretend that the person is going to hold up a bank ten minutes from now, and the police will expect you to supply a full and accurate description of him or her.

4. Observe some bird, animal, or object and record your observations in a paragraph as long as necessary to make it vivid for your readers.

5. Charlie Haas writes from the perspective of a tourist, an outsider alert to details that reveal the distinctive character of places and people. If in the past year you, as an outsider, have visited some place, jot down from memory any details you noticed that you haven't been able to forget. Or spend a few minutes as a tourist right now. Go to a busy spot on or off campus and, in a few paragraphs, record your observations of anything you find amusing, surprising, puzzling, or intriguing.

Ask your instructor whether, for this assignment, you might write not a finished essay but a single draft. The idea would be to display your observations in the rough. If you and your instructor think it shows promise, it might be the basis for a later, more polished paper.

FOR GROUP LEARNING

Instead of soliciting written comments about your work, try reading aloud to your group the draft you have written for an assignment in this chapter. Prepare your reading beforehand and try to deliver it with some life and feeling. Ask others to stop you at any point when something isn't clear. Have pencil in hand to circle any such problem. After you've finished reading aloud, ask for reactions. If these are slow in coming, ask your listeners any of the questions in the peer editing checklist on page 46. Have your group's secretary record the most vital suggestions and reactions that your draft provokes. Be ready to serve as a listening critic for other writers in your group, to help them in return.

6. From among the photographs on pages 50–51, select one to observe. In a paragraph or two, capture in words its most memorable features. Does the photograph have any center that draws your attention? What main impression or insight does the picture convey to you? See if you can put a sense of the picture into the mind of a reader who hasn't seen it at all. What do you see that your classmates missed? What do they see that you missed?

APPLYING WHAT YOU LEARN: SOME USES OF WRITING FROM OBSERVATION

Many college courses designed to prepare students for a professional career involve field trips. In such courses, you are often expected to observe closely and later to write up your observations in a report. A sociology class (or maybe a class in prelaw) might visit a city police court on a Saturday morning to hear the judge trying the spouse abusers, drug pushers, streetwalkers, and peeping Toms hauled in on Friday night. A journalism class might visit the composing room of a large daily newspaper to see how a front page is made up. History students writing about local or recent events can add color by sharing their firsthand impressions of a nearby historic site. A class in early childhood education might visit a day-care center for intensive observation of one child, perhaps culminating in a written account of that child's behavior. After a visit to the coastal wetlands, biology students may be asked to describe or even draw the various forms of marine life they have observed. For a language development course, observers might be asked to report on the way in which a particular child communicates: Does the child's speech exhibit immaturity? How does the child cope when someone misunderstands him or her?

Practitioners in the helping professions often write case studies, sometimes for publication, sometimes not. Here, in *A Career in Speech Pathology* (1979), C. Van Riper illustrates the technique. He describes his initial observations of three severely deprived rural children in need of treatment.

> As I watched through the screen I saw the three children huddled in a corner like kittens in a cold barn, silent and not moving for almost five minutes. Then the oldest one separated from the tangle and tiptoed all around the edge of the room, listening and watching. Then he motioned the other two to come with him to the door which he found was locked. Then he spied a little blue truck which had been placed under the table (with a ball and other toys), made a dive for it, and suddenly the room was full of wild animals, fighting, snarling, making animal noises of every kind, barking, mewing, shrieking. I knocked on the door and they fled again to huddle in the corner, human again but silently frozen with terror. I sat down in a chair and played with the truck and talked to myself about what I was doing, occasionally giving them a slow smile. I held out a piece of candy but none of them would reach for it. It was an eerie first session.

Much writing in scientific and technical courses involves observation. In a report for a chemistry or biology course, you might be asked to report your

50

observations of a laboratory experiment ("When the hair was introduced into the condensing dish, bacteria collected in its follicles . . ."); in zoology, to observe and report on the behavior of animals. Here is a good illustration of scientific reporting from *Gorillas in the Mist,* written by Dian Fossey, a zoologist who for many years studied mountain gorillas in Rwanda, Africa. She records what a typical gorilla looks like at birth, based on her observations of scores of infant gorillas.

> The body skin color of a newly born gorilla is usually pinkish gray and may have pink concentrations of color on the ears, palms, or soles. The infant's body hair varies in color from medium brown to black and is sparsely distributed except on the dorsal surfaces of the body. The head hair is often jet black, short, and slick, and the face wizened, with a pronounced protrusion of the nasal region, giving a pig-snouted appearance. Like the nose, the ears are prominent, but the eyes are usually squinted or closed the first day following birth. The limbs are thin and spidery, and the digits typically remain tightly flexed when the baby's hands are not grasping the mother's abdominal hair. The extremities may exhibit a spastic type of involuntary thrusting movement, especially when searching for a nipple. Most of the time, however, a gorilla infant appears asleep.

In a college course in technical writing, and in many occupations, you are expected to write observations of objects, mechanisms, places of work, terrains, and other things. Richard J. Councill, chief geologist for the Seaboard System Railroad, turned in a report on two possible building sites in New Hanover County, North Carolina, for the use of a client of the railroad, a company deciding where to build a plant. Because the decision to build rested on whether adequate supplies of groundwater would be available, Councill wrote (in part):

> Both sites are characterized by rolling, sparsely wooded fossil sand dunes attaining a maximum elevation of 25–30 feet and lowlands ranging from near 0 feet to 10 feet. Depending upon elevation, the total thickness of the dunes is 45 to 60 feet. The surface and subsurface materials are essentially homogenous and consist of interbedded strata of fine to medium quartz sand, fine to coarse sand containing thin clayey sand and clay seams. Beneath these geologically young materials are intercalated beds of fine to very coarse quartz sand, glauconite, thin discontinuous broken shell beds, and clay-silt beds of the Pee Dee formation.

In this kind of writing, no doubt immensely valuable to decision making, the writer sets forth observations mingled with judgments and recommendations.

Solution to the Problem of the Two Woodcuts

If you identified the woodcut on page 45 as the original by the Master I. B. with the Bird, your powers of observation are excellent. If you were wrong, don't feel alone: in his scholarly book *The Woodcuts of the Master I. B. with the Bird* (Berlin, 1894), art historian F. Lippmann also mistook the forgery for the original.

Further Applications

Observation is a major resource for writers, one that often goes hand in hand with *recall*. Authors in *A Writer's Reader* use *observation* for a variety of purposes. Essayist E. B. White in "Once More to the Lake" (p. 425) reports his carefully juxtaposed observations of a lake in Maine as it was when he was a child and as it is when he returns as an adult. White feels there has been no passage of time: the place, the people, even the dragonfly seem to be the same. In "A Different Take on the Ol' Bump and Grind" (p. 469), editor Marcia Ann Gillespie observes quite a different scene—the Chippendales nightclub. She characterizes the women watching the male dancers and draws conclusions about contemporary society from her observations. Similar to White, Gillespie, and Charlie Haas (p. 33), novelist Paule Marshall in "From the Poets in the Kitchen" (p. 439) and reporter Trip Gabriel in "Call of the Wildmen" (p. 473) effectively use observation as a resource for analyzing group behavior. For these two essays, answer the following questions.

1. Specifically, what group does the author observe? Find some striking passages in which the author reports his or her observations. What makes these passages memorable to you?

2. For what purpose does the author draw on observation? How would the essay be weakened without the reported observations?

3. What conclusion does the author draw from reflecting on his or her observations?

CHAPTER 3

Writing from Reading

"A shut book," according to a saying, "is only a block of paper." So is an open book, until a reader interacts with it. Did you ever observe someone truly involved with a book? From time to time that reader may put down the book to ponder, to dream, or to doubt, may pick it up again, jot notes, underline, highlight, or star things, leaf backward for a second glance, sigh, mutter, fidget in discomfort, nod approvingly, perhaps laugh aloud, or disgustedly slam the book shut. Such a reader mixes in, interacts with the printed page, and reads with an individual style. Not all readers are so demonstrative. Some sit quietly, hardly moving a muscle, and yet they too may be interacting, deeply involved.

The act of reading is highly personal. Do all readers extract the same things from the same reading? Surely they don't. *The Divine Comedy,* said T. S. Eliot, has as many versions as that classic poem has readers. The point is not that a book can mean any old thing you want it to, but that each reader, like each visitor to a city, has different interests and so comes away with different responses and memories. Listening to a class discussion of an essay all have read, you may be surprised by the range of insights reported by different readers. If you missed some of those insights when you read alone, don't feel crestfallen. Just offer any insights that come to you. Other students may be equally surprised by what you see—something they missed entirely.

Like flints that strike against one another and cause sparks, readers and writers provoke one another. Often you go to books or journals to stimulate your own ideas. Sometimes you read in search of a topic to write about. Sometimes, when you already have a topic, you seek more information about it. Sometimes, when you have enough ideas, you turn to other writers to help you explain them or to back them up with examples and evidence. Sometimes you read because you have ideas you want to test. Reading can change your ideas. Reading may serve as the basis for your writing or as a stimulus or springboard for your own musings in writing.

LEARNING FROM OTHER WRITERS

Let's look at two examples of writing evidently inspired by reading. The first is by Lindsy Van Gelder, an editor at *Ms.* magazine whose reading of a fish and game manual provoked her to write a lively response.

THE GREAT PERSON-HOLE COVER DEBATE
Lindsy Van Gelder

A MODEST PROPOSAL FOR ANYONE WHO THINKS
THE WORD "HE" IS JUST PLAIN EASIER . . .

1 I wasn't looking for trouble. What I was looking for, actually, was a little tourist information to help me plan a camping trip to New England.

2 But there it was, on the first page of the 1979 edition of the State of Vermont *Digest of Fish and Game Laws and Regulations:* a special message of welcome from one Edward F. Kehoe, commissioner of the Vermont Fish and Game Department, to the reader and would-be camper, *i.e.,* me.

3 This person (*i.e.,* me) is called "the sportsman."

4 "We have no 'sportswomen, sportspersons, sportsboys, or sportsgirls,'" Commissioner Kehoe hastened to explain, obviously anticipating that some of us sportsfeminists might feel a bit overlooked. "But," he added, "we are pleased to report that we do have many great sportsmen who are women, as well as young people of both sexes."

5 It's just that the Fish and Game Department is trying to keep things "simple and forthright" and to respect "long-standing tradition." And anyway, we really ought to be flattered, "sportsman" being "a meaningful title being earned by a special kind of dedicated man, woman, or young person, as opposed to just any hunter, fisherman, or trapper."

6 I have heard this particular line of reasoning before. In fact, I've heard it so often that I've come to think of it as The Great Person-Hole Cover Debate, since gender-neutral manholes are invariably brought into the argument as evidence of the lengths to which humorless, Newspeak-spouting feminists will go to destroy their mother tongue.

7 Consternation about woman-handling the language comes from all sides. Sexual conservatives who see the feminist movement as a unisex plot and who long for the good olde days of *vive la différence*, when men

were men and women were women, nonetheless do not rally behind the notion that the term "mankind" excludes women.

But most of the people who choke on expressions like "spokesperson" 8 aren't right-wing misogynists, and this is what troubles me. Like the un-doubtedly well-meaning folks at the Vermont Fish and Game Department, they tend to reassure you right up front that they're only trying to keep things "simple" and to follow "tradition," and that some of their best men are women, anyway.

Usually they wind up warning you, with great sincerity, that you're jeop- 9 ardizing the worthy cause of women's rights by focusing on "trivial" side issues. I would like to know how anything that gets people so defensive and resistant can possibly be called "trivial," whatever else it might be.

The English language is alive and constantly changing. Progress—both 10 scientific and social—is reflected in our language, or should be.

Not too long ago, there was a product called "flesh-colored" Band-Aids. 11 The flesh in question was colored Caucasian. Once the civil rights move-ment pointed out the racism inherent in the name, it was dropped. I cannot imagine reading a thoughtful, well-intentioned company policy statement explaining that while the Band-Aids would continue to be called "flesh-colored" for old time's sake, black and brown people would now be consid-ered honorary whites and were perfectly welcome to use them.

Most sensitive people manage to describe our national religious tra- 12 ditions as "Judeo-Christian," even though it takes a few seconds longer to say than "Christian." So why is it such a hardship to say "he or she" instead of "he"?

I have a modest proposal for anyone who maintains that "he" is just 13 plain easier: since "he" has been the style for several centuries now—and since it really includes everybody anyway, right?—it seems only fair to give "she" a turn. Instead of having to ponder over the intricacies of, say, "Con-gressman" versus "Congressperson" versus "Representative," we can sim-plify things by calling them all "Congresswomen."

Other clarifications will follow: "a woman's home is her castle" . . . 14 "a giant step for all womankind" . . . "all women are created equal" . . . "Fisherwoman's Wharf." . . .

And don't be upset by the business letter that begins "Dear Madam," 15 fellas. It means you, too.

Questions to Start You Thinking

1. How did you respond to this essay? What did you star, question, highlight, under-line, or comment on as you read?

2. What problems does Van Gelder identify? What solution does she suggest? Is she serious? Does she convince you?

3. Is the order of information in Van Gelder's essay easy to follow? Why or why not?

4. How does Van Gelder develop her ideas? Is she specific enough to make her point clear?

5. Can you think of other examples to add to paragraphs 14 and 15?
6. This essay was written in 1980. Is the issue of sexist language the same now as then? Explain.

Rose Anne Federici had been assigned to read a medical book on eating disorders for her course in nursing education. As she read, looking for passages that encouraged "further thinking," one page stood out for her. Her reflections about it sent her thoughts beyond the book's immediate subject and crystallized into the following paper.

Student Essay

CONFLICTING MESSAGES: A LOOK AT A GENERATION TORN TWO WAYS
Rose Anne Federici

I belong to a generation constantly torn in two directions. This realization came to me unexpectedly as I was reading Eating Disorders: The Facts by Suzanne Abraham and Derek Llewellyn-Jones (Oxford: Oxford UP, 1984). These two medical writers ask why eating disorders are so prevalent among young women. Many people my age become victims of anorexia, or self-starvation, while others overeat to the point of obesity and become victims of bulimia, or abnormal craving for food.

Why does this happen? The writers offer several possible explanations. One is that women in our society today are bombarded by two conflicting messages--eat and don't eat. Growing confused, a person may go to either extreme, becoming a dieter who wastes away or a foodaholic. It is in the media, the writers point out, where we often find the two messages coming at us at once. In almost any women's magazine, right after an article on a sensational new diet guaranteed to help us lose weight comfortably with little effort or willpower, we get a recipe for a delectable chocolate cake or a creamy sauce. A television commercial shows us a diet drink or a low-calorie cereal followed by another commercial for a burger joint or pizzeria. One minute, we receive the

message that a woman's lifework is to be thin so as to be
healthy, happy, and loved by everyone. The next minute we
are told that eating not only satisfies the appetite but also
fulfills many inner wants. It is sensuous fun, which every
woman has a right to. Sometimes, Abraham and Llewellyn-Jones
add, the contradictions beamed forth from television are
reinforced by contradictory messages in the home.

> The social (and usually family) pressures are also
> contradictory: you must eat everything other people
> give you but you must not get fat.

> The provision of food is seen in our culture
> as a major sign of caring; and sharing food at a
> meal is seen as one of the prime social contacts.
> These cultural imperatives place a burden on a
> mother to provide abundant quantities of food, and
> on her loving daughter or son to eat that food. It
> is not surprising that in the face of the psycho-
> logical bombardment of two contradictory messages,
> most young women diet.

The writers suggest other possible explanations for eat-   3
ing disorders, but this one started me thinking. I believe
these writers are on to something important, and not only important for health care and preventive medicine. I suddenly
realized that in our society, people are constantly being
bombarded by contradictory messages, not only about eating
but about almost everything. For example, advertisers constantly make appeals that tug us in two different directions.
A television commercial tells us to get outdoors and explore
the wilds of America. However, while we are roughing it and
getting close to nature we are supposed to be living in a
camper with a TV set, a microwave oven, and the other comforts of home. The same discount store ad in the newspaper
that invites us to get plenty of exercise with a set of
weights also tells us to take life easy with an automatic
garage door opener.

Many of these conflicting messages are beamed at people   4
of college age. We are told to assert our individuality--but

to do so by wearing a name brand of makeup, or Jams, or Jordache jeans. How we can display our very own personalities when we are wearing what everyone else wears, we are not told. On television news and talk shows, glamorous unmarried mothers--Jessica Lange and Susan Sarandon, for example--are presented as stars worthy of our admiration. Recently, the same channels that feature such shows have been running public service messages aimed at unmarried women and girls: "Don't get pregnant."

Often our parents and teachers tell us one thing, and   5
television another. "Study hard and you will achieve success," I am told every time I go home. Meanwhile, on TV, I keep seeing people who are considered successes even though they have probably never opened a book. They simply buy a lottery ticket and they win a million dollars, or they record one hit song and become rich for life. Other conflicting messages bombard me every time I go home--"Study hard in college" and "Why don't you get out and meet people and enjoy yourself?"

In Mademoiselle magazine, an interview presents a woman   6
for us to admire. After starting her own business, she has scored a huge success and now has twenty employees. At the same time she has a husband and three children. She maintains a "gracious home" and gives dinner parties. There may be many miracle workers like that woman, but for me the two messages--be a successful executive, be a wonderful wife and mother--point in different directions. I wonder if there is not a built-in conflict in the whole idea of becoming a big success and still being a loving person, able to spend time with family and friends. Being both is not impossible, but for me it would be hard to achieve.

I realize that even on a national level, conflicting   7
messages are broadcast. We throw a big birthday party for the Statue of Liberty while doing our best to limit the number of immigrants allowed to enter the United States. We pride ourselves that we deinstitutionalize the mentally ill, but we do it by sending them out onto the streets while re-

fusing to give them the skills and the support to make it on
their own. We criticize the quality of our schools but pay
our public school teachers very little. We spend money for
Patriot missiles and at the same time call for world peace.
In the name of democracy, we send financial and military aid
to corrupt governments in other lands. No wonder that, although I do not suffer from anorexia or bulimia, I have an
increasing sense that I belong to a generation torn in different directions.

Questions to Start You Thinking

1. What idea of special interest does Rose Anne Federici find in the book *Eating Disorders*? What does she add to that idea?
2. Do you agree that all the messages Federici cites are necessarily contradictory? Can't one diet most of the time, yet on special occasions eat a sliver of chocolate cake?
3. What are the sources of the details Federici uses to develop her main point?
4. What other contradictory messages are you familiar with from magazine and television advertising, from films, from the news, or from family members and friends?

LEARNING BY WRITING

The Assignment: Reading for Insight

This assignment invites you to do some reading that will enlarge your area of knowledge and to use what you have read as a springboard for your writing. It asks you to look for passages that stimulate you to think, reflect on what you read, arrive at some original insight or observation that stems from what you have read, and then write a paper in which you use one source as the point of departure for your own ideas.

For at least five days, keep a reading journal in which you react each day to an essay, newspaper or magazine article, or chapter of a book—perhaps a textbook—that sends your thoughts in some new and interesting direction. Then look over your journal and select the most promising entry. Develop it into a paper in which you share with your readers what you have learned as well as your fresh insights and further ideas. Turn in your journal along with your paper.

Among the thoughtful papers we have seen in response to this assignment are these:

> A man who had recently read about the economic law of supply and demand set out to demonstrate that law by describing the behavior of both sellers and cus-
> tomers at a yard sale.

A woman, having read in her sociology textbook about the changes that city neighborhoods in the United States typically undergo in the course of fifty to a hundred years, thought about the changes that had taken place in a neighborhood she knew well and concluded that the textbook's generalizations in this case did not apply.

A man, after having read and thought about George Orwell's classic essay "Shooting an Elephant," agreed with the writer that whole governments can act unwisely, seemingly for no better reason than to save face. He used as his main example U.S. policy toward Vietnam in the 1960s and 1970s.

A man, inspired by Gradgrind, the tyrannical and shortsighted schoolmaster in Charles Dickens's novel *Hard Times,* humorously insisted he had encountered as much mindlessness in the elementary school he had attended as had Dickens's characters in Gradgrind's classroom.

A woman, appalled by newspaper accounts of the 1986 nuclear disaster at Chernobyl in the Soviet Union, weighed the risks inherent in nuclear power against possible benefits to humankind.

Generating Ideas

Check current periodicals. What will you read to find ideas for this assignment? There are numerous sources. Why not start in the library and browse through several current magazines, such as the *Atlantic, Harper's, New Republic, Commentary, Ms.,* and others likely to contain articles to spur you to thought. Never mind *People, Life,* and other periodicals written mainly to entertain. You want good, meaty articles, conducive to reflection; if they are a bit difficult to understand and need to be read twice, so much the better. Try not to start out with ideas you already have, looking only for confirmation. You'll do better if you stay open to fresh ideas that your readings may unexpectedly trigger.

Recall something you have already read. What have you read lately that has started you thinking and wondering? Classics like Sigmund Freud's *The Interpretation of Dreams,* Rachel Carson's *The Sea around Us,* or Henry David Thoreau's *Walden* bristle with challenging ideas. And why not draw on some reading you've been assigned for another course? It may be a chapter in a textbook, an essay in a reader used in your college English course, or a book assigned for outside reading.

We suggest you mix your choices for your journal. Try one of each: a classic, a current magazine article, a chapter from a textbook, the letters of some famous person, a thought-provoking short story, a book about art or music—whatever engages your interest. That way, your journal will contain a variety of possibilities from which you can choose the topic for your paper.

Skim and sample. As you begin your search for promising material, keep in mind that you're reading with a purpose. You can't afford the luxury of reading everything word by word; skim, skip, and sample ideas. When reading things for possible material, try reading just the first two paragraphs and the last two paragraphs. Those will probably alert you to the main points the writer makes. When you look into books to see if they're worth reading, skim through the first chapter and the last chapter. Then, if a book looks helpful, you can spend more time with it.

Once you zero in on a thought-provoking chapter, article, or essay, read slowly and carefully, giving yourself plenty of time to think between the lines. Try to discern the writer's opinions, even if they are unstated. Don't just soak up opinions and information. Criticize. Question. Wonder. Argue back. Dare to differ with the author whose work you're reading. Most printed pages aren't holy writ; you can doubt them. Opinions you don't agree with can be valuable if they set your own thoughts in motion.

Write while you read. Read with pencil in hand, and react in writing. Write brief notes to yourself (if you're using library materials), or mark up the text (if you own the book or magazine or have made a photocopy of it). Underline phrases and sentences that contain essentials. Star things you think are important. Make cross-references: "Contradicts what he said on p. 17." Jot thoughts in the margin. Besides helping you participate while you read, such notes are a wonderful help in reviewing what you have read.

On the next page, you can see how Rose Anne Federici reacted when she read Suzanne Abraham and Derek Llewellyn-Jones's *Eating Disorders: The Facts.* (By the way, she had a perfect right to mark up the copy: it was her textbook in her nursing education course.) We don't say you need to mark up every page you read. Evidently, Federici recognized that here was an especially valuable page, with an idea she would surely want to write about.

Keep a reading journal. As the assignment suggests, keep a journal of thoughts that arise in response to your reading. Each day, after reading and thinking about the day's selection, dash out a few sentences. What do you put into a journal entry? Well, first (and this is easy), put in the title, author, and source of any material you discuss. If as you read you come across passages you especially admire, copy them into the journal. Along with summaries and direct quotations, include your own reactions. See if you can arrive at any further insight.

This is what Rose Anne Federici did in preparing to write her essay. Shortly after she found herself interacting with this passage, Federici felt elated. In the last place she might have looked for it—a textbook for her nursing course—she had discovered a really interesting criticism of the

"Don't eat" and "Eat"—contradictory messages. I'm pretty sure we receive other c.m.s all the time.

What about the line on mental health? Yesterday in nursing class lecturer talked about how mental patients are "deinstitutionalized"—this saves cost and is supposed to be good for them. But they are turned loose on the streets without money or support. They get in trouble, commit crimes.

There's the line I get handed at home—"Study hard" vs. "Why don't you get out and meet people?"

Do advertisers sometimes contradict themselves? What about politicians? I want to find some more examples. How many conflicting messages are there in our society?

Eating disorders – the facts

THE SOCIAL EXPLANATION

In Western culture two contrasting messages about food and eating are offered by society, and particularly by the media. The first message is that a slim woman is successful, attractive, healthy, happy, fit, and popular. To become slim, with all that this implies, is deemed to be a major pursuit of many women. The second message is that eating is a pleasurable activity which meets many needs in addition to relieving hunger, and women have a right to have these needs met. In women's magazines these two contrasting messages tend to appear inextricably mixed. In nearly every issue the magazines publish 'exciting' new diets which 'guarantee weight loss with minimum discomfort or motivation', and these diets are often followed by recipes for, and superb photographs of, luscious cakes and foods with rich sauces. It is difficult to watch television without being confronted by an advertisement for a substitute diet-food alternating with a fast food advertisement, or its equivalent. The social (and usually family) pressures are also contradictory: you must eat everything other people give you but you must not get fat.

The provision of food is seen in our culture as a major sign of caring; and sharing food at a meal is seen as one of the prime social contacts. These cultural imperatives place a burden on a mother to provide abundant quantities of food, and on her loving daughter or son to eat that food. It is not surprising that in the face of the psychological bombardment of two contradictory messages, most young women diet. Some become 'foodaholics' and develop bulimia. Others become preoccupied with food and the avoidance of weight gain, developing bulimia or anorexia nervosa. Some decide that dieting is too disturbing to their way of life and return to eating more food than they require, becoming obese. These women may also find obesity protective against acceding to current social attitudes to sexuality, which they fear. Hidden in a fat body, they give the message that they are not attractive and do not want to form a sexual relationship.

[handwritten margin notes: "don't eat" & "eat"; YES!; Other contradictory messages we receive?]

28

society in which we live. This suggestion cast light not only on people who gorge or starve themselves, but on advertising, political pronouncements, and family life as well. Excited, Federici jotted her thoughts in her notebook, going beyond the ideas in the original. We give them on page 62 to illustrate a typical, spontaneous entry in a reading journal, like the one that our assignment calls for.

As you start writing your own reading journal, you might ask the questions in the discovery checklist.

DISCOVERY CHECKLIST: RECORDING YOUR READING

- How would you state what the writer takes for granted? If a writer begins, "The serious threat of acid rain was dismissed with a collective yawn in Washington again last week," then evidently he or she assumes that acid rain is a serious menace and that legislators too should take it seriously.
- Do the writer's assertions rest on evidence? What kind of evidence? Statistics? The results of surveys? Quotations from authorities? Historical facts? Photographs? Are you convinced?
- If you doubt the writer's statements, can you test them against anything you know or can find out?
- Do you agree with what the author has said? Does it clash with any ideas you hold dear? Does it question anything you take for granted? With what do you disagree? Why?
- From any facts the writer presents, what inferences can you draw? If the writer musters facts that lead to an inescapable conclusion, might any conflicting evidence be mustered? A portrait of an unfriendly country that showed all its citizens to be rapists, drunks, and drug addicts would leave much out; surely a different view would be possible.
- Has anything you read opened your eyes to new possibilities, new ways of looking at the world?
- Has the writer failed to tell you anything you wish you knew? If so, what?

If in your journal you write the answers to at least some of these questions, you'll have valuable thoughts on hand when you start drafting your paper.

Planning, Drafting, and Developing

Select an interesting entry. Faced now with your five journal entries, how do you decide which to expand into a paper? First, ask yourself which entry most interests you. Second, ask which of your reflections would most interest your possible readers—your classmates and your instructor. As you look over your journal entries, decide which most clearly seems to say something. Which arrives at a conclusion, however tentative? That's the one to develop.

If, before you begin writing, you feel the need for more ideas than there are in your journal entry, backtrack for a while. Look back over the passage you have selected and do more thinking. One of the strengths of Rose Anne Federici's paper is its convincing array of examples. After she wrote her journal entry, Federici decided it looked a little skimpy. She wished she might discover other contradictory messages. "I thought of the one about deinstitutionalizing the mentally ill but refusing to help them," she recalls, "and the one about 'get good grades but get out and see people'—I'd heard that one before. I knew there must be lots of other contradictory messages, but at first it was hard to think of any."

After a solitary, fruitless attempt at brainstorming, Federici had a conversation with three other students. She told them of her assignment, shared her preliminary thoughts, and asked, "What other contradictory messages have you heard lately?" They came up with ten further examples. Some of their ideas didn't fit Federici's specifications. It seemed easy enough to think of differing messages coming from two different sources—such as health warnings like "Don't smoke" and tobacco ads that urge the opposite. It was more difficult to come up with contradictory messages from the same source: for instance, the ad that calls on readers to "rough it in the wild" in a camper that boasts a microwave oven. As Federici began to draft, looking over the notes on her brainstorming session and on her conversation, new examples occurred to her.

WRITING WITH A COMPUTER: READING

Try sitting at your computer with a book in your lap, so that you can read and take notes at the same time. This way, you won't have to recopy any material you transcribe. You can write *around* it.

If you have long quotations that require extended proofreading, try this. Change your margin settings, and display your words in a narrow column with a justified right-hand margin. If a long passage looks like this, perhaps it will be more fun to proofread:

```
Benvenuto Cellini, the cele-
brated sculptor of the Ital-
ian   Renaissance,   designed
for Francis I a famous salt-
cellar  of  enamel  and  gold,
preserved  in  the  Vienna  Art
Museum.
```

In lines so short, any errors will stand out more readily. But lest you turn in a paper that looks like a newspaper, return your margins to their usual width after you finish proofreading.

A *portable* or *laptop* computer, by the way, is a great aid to reading and note taking in a library.

Borrow honestly. The first law of writing from reading is to acknowledge fully and honestly your debt to the writer from whom you derived anything, whether it be a quotation, information, or an idea. Not to do so is to lay yourself open to the charge of plagiarism (see p. 625). In general, identify any source of an idea or quotation right away, as soon as you mention it in your writing. You can do this informally, as Lindsy Van Gelder does in "The Great Person-Hole Cover Debate." It is enough in an informal paper, for example, to say, "Renowned feminist Betty Friedan states this idea convincingly in *The Feminine Mystique,*" and then quote Friedan.

You can use information from your sources in any of three ways.

Quoting. When an author expresses an idea in a way so incisive, so brilliant, or so memorable that you want to reproduce his or her words exactly, you can quote them word for word. Direct quotations add life and color and the sound of a speaking voice. If you do quote, be sure to quote exactly, including punctuation and capitalization. If you leave out part of a quotation, indicate the omissions with an ellipsis—three dots (. . .). If the ellipsis occurs at the beginning or end of a sentence *within* the quotation, it contains *four* dots. You don't need an ellipsis mark at the *beginning* or *end* of the quotation. Why leave anything out? Usually because, if left in, it would be too boring or cumbersome or distracting or needlessly long—perhaps because it adds some information that mattered to the author but doesn't matter to the point you are making. Also be careful that taking something out of context does not distort the meaning. For example, if a reviewer calls a movie "a perfect example of poor directing and inept acting," you should not say "perfect directing and acting."

Nutshelling. Also called *summarizing,* this is a useful way to deal with a whole paragraph or section of a work when what you're after is just the general drift. To save time and space and to focus on the idea, you don't want to quote word for word. Without doing violence to an idea, you put it in a nutshell: you express its main sense in a few words—*your own words*—and tell where you got the idea. Be sure you understand the passage before you attempt to condense it. You must take care not to distort the meaning. For example, Lindsy Van Gelder's account of what she read is in paragraphs 4 and 5 of her essay on p. 55.

Paraphrasing. This skill involves restating an author's ideas. When you put the author's thoughts into your own words, don't let the author's words keep slipping in. The style in paraphrasing, as in nutshelling, has to be yours. If some other writer says, "President Wilson called an emergency meeting of his cabinet to discuss the new crisis," and you say, "The president called on his cabinet to hold an emergency meeting to discuss the new crisis," that isn't far enough removed from the original. It looks like plagiarism. You could put quotation marks around the original sentence, although it seems unmemorable, not worth quoting word for word. Or, better, you could write: "Summoning his cabinet to an emergency session, Wilson laid forth the challenge before them." If you deal carefully with the material, you won't have to put quotation marks around anything in your paraphrase.

In Rose Anne Federici's "Conflicting Messages," you'll find all three methods in action: quotation, nutshell, and paraphrase. In her second paragraph in which she introduces the idea she discovered in the book she read, Federici sums it up in a nutshell:

```
One [explanation for eating disorders] is that women in
our society today are bombarded by two conflicting mes-
sages--eat and don't eat.  Growing confused, a person may
go to either extreme, becoming a dieter who wastes away
or a foodaholic.
```

Then, apparently feeling the need to explain more fully, she immediately goes on to paraphrase the writers' entire discussion of the two messages, with their illustrations from women's magazines and television advertising. Thus, without borrowing the writers' very language, she produces a new version true to their ideas. Better than quoting at great length, paraphrasing here serves her purposes. Freely, she arranges the writers' points in a different order, making the idea "contradictory messages" stand last in her own paragraph— and so giving it greater emphasis. She even invents specific examples where the original writers are vague: instead of their somewhat puzzling "a fast food advertisement, or its equivalent" (whatever its equivalent is!), she bravely and faithfully substitutes "commercial for a burger joint or pizzeria." Paraphrasing a British book, she thus retains its sense while making its examples recognizably American.

Her essay clearly gains, too, from an appropriate quotation. In her third paragraph, she quotes four sentences from her original—for what reason? "Because," she explains, "I wanted to keep the exact words about the mother and her loving daughter or son. Besides, I didn't know how to paraphrase 'cultural imperatives.' I could have said 'the dictates of society' or something, but that didn't sound as good. 'Cultural imperatives' was wonderful, and I wanted to leave it alone." (You can compare her nutshell and her paraphrase with the original text she read, reproduced on p. 57)

How do you condense another writer's thoughts? Before you paraphrase or nutshell, we suggest that you do the following.

1. Read the original passage over a couple of times. You can underline key parts or note them.
2. Without looking at it, try to state its gist—the main point it makes, the main sense you remember, and the major supporting points.
3. Then go back and reread the original one more time, making sure you got its gist faithfully. Revise your paraphrase as necessary.

Paraphrasing, incidentally, has another use: it is one way to understand a knotty passage that has baffled you. You can try to paraphrase it in writing, or perhaps just paraphrase it mentally. For more information on borrowing honestly from sources, see "Writing from Sources," p. 615.

Determine an order for your ideas. As you shape your draft, you must not only select the ideas to include but also begin to organize the information. You may start your draft with a quotation from your reading as Van Gelder does in "The Great Person-Hole Cover Debate" or with a personal account of the impact of your reading as Federici does. Perhaps you'll use a summary of your reading, a relevant anecdote, or a comment about the author to establish a basis for your reflections and insights. Then you'll decide on an arrangement of ideas in the body of your essay. Federici moves from a summary of what she has read on eating disorders to her own thoughts on contradictory messages in our society, drawing examples from her personal responses to ads, television, and family comments and from her observations of national events. If you are not sure how to organize your ideas, try several ways. To discover a satisfactory order, you might jot down your ideas and number them, or you might write a formal outline as a plan, or you might write several drafts, each organized differently. The strategy that works for you may not work for your classmates. The important thing is that you think and plan as you work. Finally you'll conclude your piece by referring to your main point, not by introducing a new idea. Look again at how Van Gelder and Federici allude to their main point in the conclusion of their essays.

Revising and Editing

Perhaps, as you look over your draft, you will feel the need to read further. Would your paper be stronger if it had more facts, statistics, or other evidence? Take the trouble to do additional reading if necessary. We don't ask you at this point to write a research paper. For this assignment, just have enough facts and information at your disposal to state your ideas with confidence and authority.

As you read and write at the same time, you may find your views changing. If you rearranged your ideas drastically since starting to write, cosmetic changes may not be enough—you may have to revise thoroughly. To see how much your ideas have changed since you first wrote your journal entry, you might try to state (to yourself or in writing) what insight you had then and what insight you have now.

In looking back over your paper, you might ask the following questions.

REVISION CHECKLIST: WRITING FROM READING

- Have you given emphasis to the significant and relevant points in the work you read?
- If you see any long stretches without a quotation, can you come up with a good, lively direct quotation to break the monotony? Look over your reading and see where it might be helpful (and interesting) to quote a writer's exact words.
- Would it ever help to state the other writer's ideas in a nutshell or to paraphrase?

- Did you make clear what you took from your source or sources?
- Is the order of your ideas easy to follow?
- Do you have enough details and examples to clarify and back up your assertions?
- Have you checked any summaries and quotations from your reading for accuracy?

Rose Anne Federici found that the hardest part of writing her paper was making the transition from the background material she felt her readers would need (paragraphs 1 and 2 of her finished essay) to the insights that reading the book had led her to. In her first draft she went on too long about the book she had read. Then she included in her transition almost all the suggestions that had arisen in the brainstorming session with her friends. As she set about revising, she realized that most of those ideas belonged later in the paper; and one or two, she finally had to admit, were too weak to be included at all. She coped with her problem by doing a lot of reorganizing and deleting.

~~Increasingly as I read, I realized what a valuable~~
~~book Eating Disorders was.~~ *The writers suggest* ~~It gave a whole lot of~~ other
So? reasons for eating disorders, ~~too--reasons that never~~
what? ~~would have occurred to me, like fear of sexuality, want-~~
~~ing to remain a child, and the need to rebel against~~
~~strict parents. All these were very interesting to me,~~
but ~~the~~ *this* one ~~I have quoted~~ started me thinking. I believe
these writers are on to something important, and not only *important*
for health care and preventive medicine. I ~~now know~~ *suddenly realized* that
in our society, people are constantly being bombarded ~~in~~
~~the media and elsewhere~~ by contradictory messages**,** ~~These~~
~~messages are~~ not only about eating but ~~also~~ about almost
everything. For example, advertisers constantly**,** *make* appeal**s**
~~to us in ways~~ that tug us in two different directions. A
television commercial tells us to *get outdoors* ~~rough it~~ and explore
the wilds of America. However, while we are roughing it
and getting close to nature we (supposed~~ly~~ are) ~~also resid-~~
~~ing~~ in a camper with a TV set, a microwave oven, and ~~all~~ *to be living*
the *other* comforts of home.~~^~~ The same discount ad in the news- *that invites* *plenty* *a set of*
paper **,** ~~inviting~~ us to get ~~lots~~ of exercise with **,** weights
also tells us to take life easy with an automatic garage
door opener.

Many of these conflicting messages are beamed at people of college age. We are told
~~Advertisers tell us~~ to assert our individuality--but
to do so by wearing a name brand of makeup, or Jams, or
Jordache jeans.   How (can we), *display our very own personalities*
~~"be ourselves"~~ when we are
wearing what everyone else wears, we are not told.   ~~They~~

?   ~~tell us to drive Porsches even though they ought to know~~
~~we can't afford them.~~ The media keeps showing us super-

I'm using
up all my
examples!   women with high-powered jobs and gorgeous, well-run homes
and beautiful, outstanding children.   Are we supposed to
study hard or be social successes?   ~~Are we supposed to~~   *What?*
Develop
later?   ~~support missile growth or stop paying taxes?~~   Mental patients are "deinstitutionalized," saving costs, but they
can't support themselves.   On television news and talk
                                     — Jessica Lange and Susan Sarandon, for example-
shows, glamorous unmarried mothers are presented as stars
worthy of our admiration.   Recently, the same channels
running public service announcements aimed at unmarried women and girls:
that feature such shows have been ~~advertising,~~ "Don't get
pregnant."

Really needed, a three-part organization for
these messages: those by advertisers, those
by government, and others

   Once you have a preliminary draft that you like, why not ask a friend or
classmate to read your paper and answer the following questions? In the light
of his or her suggestions, you can then make your final revisions.

PEER EDITING CHECKLIST: WRITING FROM READING

- ✔ What is your first reaction to the essay?
- ✔ Restate or quote the major insight that the writer shares from his or her reading.
- ✔ Look at the organization of the essay. Is it clear enough how parts of the essay connect to other parts? Do you recommend any changes in the ordering of parts? In the transitions or connections between parts?
- ✔ List any questions you have about what the writer wrote that you think he or she should answer when revising.
- ✔ Did you need any additional examples or explanations of ideas or illustrations anywhere in the paper? Put stars on the manuscript where the writer needs to develop the ideas more.
- ✔ How useful and how interesting to you are the quotations the writer uses? Does the writer introduce them smoothly enough?

- Is it difficult in any places to know when the writer is explaining his or her ideas and when he or she is nutshelling or paraphrasing from reading? Underline any parts of the essay where you're not sure whose ideas you are reading.
- Does the writer use any unfamiliar words that need quick definition?
- Circle on the manuscript any spelling, punctuation, grammar, or word choice that got in the way of your reading and understanding.
- Are there any revisions you think would be essential before the writer submits the paper to the instructor?

In writing from reading, your main concern will be to make sure you've produced a paper in which you convey to your readers some of the power and joy of thinking, not only with the prompting of another writer, but also by thinking on your own. However, you have other important responsibilities when you proofread your final draft. Be sure you indicated the sources of ideas and facts as well as of quotations and that you have borrowed honestly so as to avoid plagiarism. If you have used any direct quotations, check them against the original source. In copying a quotation into your paper, it's easy to omit something, perhaps something essential.

Other Assignments

1. Read several comments about a recent news event by columnists and commentators in magazines and newspapers. Find two writers who disagree in their analyses. Decide which view you favor, explain it in a few paragraphs, and tell why you favor it. In making your decision, you may find that you need to read still more, to learn as much about the event as possible.

2. Write a letter to the editor of your local newspaper in which you take exception to the recent conduct of some world leader or celebrity as reported in the paper or to some column the newspaper printed recently. By referring to what you have read, make the grounds of your complaint clear enough so that even someone who hasn't read the article you're criticizing will know what you're talking about.

3. To give yourself practice in skeptically analyzing what you read, study a story in a recent tabloid newspaper such as the *National Enquirer, Weekly World News,* or the *Star* that seems to you particularly hard to believe. Where was the story said to take place? What reliable witnesses were there? How could a skeptic verify the truth of the story? What inferences can you draw about the story, the reporter, and the newspaper that printed it?

4. Compare two history books in their accounts of a celebrated event—the Declaration of Independence, the bombing of Hiroshima, or any other event you wish to read more about. One of the books should be recent, the other at least thirty years old. Describe the differences in the two versions. How do you account for them?

5. Collect contradictory messages from television, songs, films, or advertisements, and use them as the basis of an essay.

FOR GROUP LEARNING

When your instructor assigns a paper in which you are to respond to some reading selection (or selections), first meet outside class with members of your writing group before you write. Let members of your group pool their reactions to their reading. Appoint a moderator to run a discussion. Each participant is free to take notes. To start the discussion, here are some questions that might be asked:

What problems did you have with this reading? What didn't you understand? (Be frank: no one always understands everything.) Were there any words or allusions you didn't get, that someone else might explain?

What do you take to be the author's purpose?

Is there any main point this author makes?

At any point, does the author cause you to disagree or doubt?

What, if anything, does the author do especially well?

What do you wish the author might have done instead?

What did you find out from this reading that you didn't know before?

The goal of this discussion is to give you a better understanding and appreciation of the reading than you alone might derive so that you might come up with more ideas for your own paper.

APPLYING WHAT YOU LEARN: SOME USES OF WRITING FROM READING

In college, writing from your reading is an activity you'll take part in almost daily. Many instructors, to encourage you to read and write continually, will ask you to keep a notebook of your reading and occasionally may ask you to turn it in for inspection. Writing about your reading, as you often do in taking tests and examinations, is intended to demonstrate your mastery of it. (For advice about writing essay examinations, see Chapter 12.)

For other college writing assignments, reading will be just one of your resources. An education course, to take an instance, might ask you to combine reading and observing: to watch a toddler for an hour a day over the course of a week, keep a detailed record of her appearance and her actions, compare those with what is average for a child of her age (information you would find by reading), and then draw some conclusions about her behavior. In the field of human development, students are constantly asked to make informed judgments on current issues (abortion, day care, and joint custody, to name a few) by learning to understand the differing views presented in the books and articles they are assigned to read. Further, they learn to be advocates for troubled children and their families not only by reading and researching legislative bills but also by writing letters against or in support of those bills.

At home or in high school you may have read general magazines like

Newsweek and *National Geographic,* which most literate readers can take pleasure in. But later in college, many of your courses will oblige you to read periodicals of a different kind: journals written and read by trained specialists. Many specialists, from physicists to physicians, write articles for others in their field, sharing what they know. Doctors and other health professionals report new diseases or new treatments; scientists and technicians advance new theories; literary critics make fresh ventures into literary criticism; historians address other historians, enlarging on and reinterpreting knowledge of the past. As part of your training in a special discipline, you may be introduced to the *Journal of Comparative Behavior, Nature, Educational Research, American Journal of Sociology, PMLA,* or *Foreign Affairs.* You will often be asked to report on an article, reading it critically, perhaps summarizing or paraphrasing its essentials, and finally adding a thoughtful comment. Doing so, you absorb the vocabulary and habits of thought of your chosen field of work and make them your own. You see how skilled writers prove and demonstrate, evaluate, explain, select useful details, assert, affirm, deny, try to convince.

Many a learned article begins with a short review of previous research, which the writer is about to dash to pieces. In some professional journals, though, summary or paraphrase of other writing may be an end in itself. Attorney Peter L. Knox, who in addition to practicing his profession writes articles about pension tax laws for professional journals such as *Taxation for Accountants* and the *Journal of Taxation,* says that writing for him is often a matter of reading difficult writing (like rulings of the tax court and the *Internal Revenue Manual*) and condensing it in plainer prose—"expressing in an organized, somewhat literary form a set of complex rules." You can see how such an article might greatly help other tax lawyers struggling to understand a long, crucially important entry about changing a pension plan, as in this example from *Final and Temporary IRS Regulations:*

> § 1.401(b)-1 Certain retroactive changes in plan [TD 7437, filed 9-23-76].
>
> (a) *General rule.* Under section 401(b) a stock bonus, pension, profit-sharing, annuity, or bond purchase plan which does not satisfy the requirements of section 401(a) on any day solely as a result of a disqualifying provision (as defined in paragraph (b) of this section) shall be considered to have satisfied such requirement on such date if, on or before the last day of the remedial amendment period (as determined under paragraphs (c), (d) and (e) of this section) with respect to such disqualifying provision, all provisions of the plan which are necessary to satisfy all requirements of sections 401(a), 403(a), or 405(a) are in effect and have been made effective for all purposes for the whole of such period.

The entry goes on like that for three and a half large pages of fine print divided into subsections, some with roman numerals. Bewildering as such material may be—probably no one reads IRS regulations for entertainment—thousands of a client's dollars may be riding on an attorney's ability to interpret that entry correctly. In an article explaining the passage to his fellow pension plan professionals, Knox helpfully begins, "Section 401(b) provides a way for retirement plans to be retroactively corrected" and goes on to tell how it is generally applied. Obviously, the law could not function without its interpreters, who translate its complex language into simpler directives that other people can follow. Besides, the interpreters foresee difficulties that can arise in real life when professionals try to apply the law. No mere exercise in translation, such specialized nutshelling and paraphrasing, it seems, calls for hard, even imaginative, thought.

We have been viewing books and articles as *immediately* useful sources of ideas and information. But sometimes there is a time lag: you read Melville's novel *Moby-Dick* or Thorstein Veblen's *The Theory of the Leisure Class* and, although your reading isn't immediately useful to the paper you have to write, something from it remains with you, perhaps nothing but a phrase, an example, a stray idea, a way of constructing a sentence. Perhaps months later, when you are writing another paper, it returns to the forefront of your mind. In truth, writing from reading is useful to you in ways we haven't begun to indicate. We hold this truth to be self-evident: that the better you read—the more alertly, critically, questioningly—the better you write.

Further Applications

Some writers use *reading* as a springboard for writing; others rely on it as a source of evidence for their writing. Either way, reading is a useful resource for writers. In *A Writer's Reader,* historian Joan Jacobs Brumberg uses reading for both purposes in her essay "The Origins of Anorexia Nervosa" (p. 451). Gleaned from her study of the history of the Victorian period, her essay draws on her knowledge of nineteenth-century society for evidence to support her stand. Scientist Stephen Jay Gould also depends on reading as a resource for his essay "The Terrifying Normalcy of AIDS" (p. 591). He uses what he read in Platt's paper as a springboard for his comments on AIDS and "the cardboard message of Epcot."

Just as Brumberg, Gould, Lindsy Van Gelder (p. 55), and student Rose Anne Federici (p. 57) use the resource of reading, other writers also draw on this important resource. The following writers use reading in different ways: feminist Susan Brownmiller, "Pornography Hurts Women" (p. 465), investigative reporter Jessica Mitford, "Behind the Formaldehyde Curtain" (p. 513), novelist Emily Prager, "Our Barbies, Ourselves" (p. 560), contributor to *Outside* magazine David Quammen, "A Republic of Cockroaches" (p. 582). Answer the following questions about each of these essays.

1. Is the information discovered in the reading a result of careful selection or an unexpected discovery?

2. How is the author's reading related to her or his occupation or area of study?

3. What does the author learn from reading? How does she or he use that information in this essay?

4. What original insight does the author arrive at as a result of reflecting on what she or he read?

CHAPTER 4

Writing from Conversation

Don't know what to write about? Go talk with someone. When you exchange facts, thoughts, and feelings with people, you both give and receive. Not only do you find out things from others that you didn't know, but by speaking your own thoughts and feelings you shape them and define them in words. Or listen closely to an hour's discussion between a class and an anthropology professor, and get material for a paper. Just as likely, you can get a paper's worth of information, thoughts, and feelings from a five-minute exchange with a mechanic who relines brakes. Both are experts. But even people who aren't usually considered experts may provide you with material.

As this chapter suggests, you can direct a conversation by asking questions to elicit what you want to find out. You do so in that special kind of conversation called the *interview*. Newspaper reporters, as you know, interview people all the time, and college writers can do so as well. An interview is a conversation with a purpose: usually to help you understand the other person or to find out what the other person knows.

LEARNING FROM OTHER WRITERS

Here are two fine essays whose writers met ordinary people face to face and reported their conversations. The first is by William Least Heat Moon — pen name of the part-Sioux writer William Trogdon. His conversation with Barbara Pierre is from his book *Blue Highways* (1982), written after he had traveled throughout the United States on small roads, visiting and talking with unsung people wherever he found them.

A VIEW OF PREJUDICE
William Least Heat Moon

Because of a broken sealed-beam headlight and Zatarain's Creole Mustard, an excellent native mustard, I met Barbara Pierre. I had just come out of Dugas' grocery with four jars of Zatarain's, and we almost collided on the sidewalk. She said, "You're not from St. Martinville, are you? You can't be."   1

"I'm from Missouri."   2

"What in the world are you doing here? Got a little Huck Finn in you?"   3

"Just followed the bayou. Now I'm looking for the Ford agency."   4

"Coincidences. I work there. I'll show you the way."   5

She was a secretary at the agency and took classes at the University of Southwestern Louisiana in Lafayette when she could. I asked about St. Martinville, but she had to start working before we could say much.   6

"Here's an idea," she said. "Come by at noon and we can have lunch at my place. I live in the project on the other side of the bayou."   7

I picked her up at twelve. She asked about the trip, especially about Selma and how things were as I saw them. "A white man griped about changes, and a black said there weren't enough changes to gripe about."   8

"That's us too. What we want is slow coming — if it's coming at all. Older blacks here are scared of whites and won't do much for change if it means risk. Others don't care as long as everything gets smothered over with politeness by whites. Young blacks see the hypocrisy — even when it's not there. But too many of them are juked on drugs, and that's where some of this town wants us."   9

"Don't any whites here try to help?"   10

"A few, but if a white starts helping too much, they get cut off or shut down by the others and end up paying almost the price we do. Sure, we got good whites — when they're not scared out of showing sympathy."   11

On Margaret Street, she pointed to her apartment in a small one-story brick building. Standard federal housing. As we went to the door, a shadowy face watched from behind a chintz curtain in another apartment.   12

"See that? Could be the start of bad news," she said.   13

"Maybe I should leave. I don't want to cause trouble for you."   14

"Too late. Besides, I live my own life here. I won't be pushed. But it'll come back in some little way. Smart remark, snub. One old white lady kicks me at the library. Swings her feet under the table because she doesn't want my kind in there. I could break her in two, she's so frail. She'll be kicking like a heifer if she gets wind of this."   15

Barbara Pierre's apartment was a tidy place but for books on the sofa.   16

Barbara Pierre in St. Martinville, Louisiana

"You can see I still use the library even with the nuisances. The kicking bitch hides books I return so I get overdue notices and have to go prove I turned the book in. I explain what's going on, but nothing changes. Simplest thing is trouble."

"That's what I heard in Selma."   17

"I'm not alone, but sometimes it seems like a conspiracy. Especially in   18
little towns. Gossip and bigotry—that's the blood and guts."

"Was that person who just looked out the window white?"   19

"Are you crazy? Nobody on this end of Margaret Street is white. That's   20
what I mean about us blacks not working together. Half this town is black,
and we've only got one elected black official. Excuse my language, but for
all the good he does this side of the bayou, he's one useless black mofo."

"Why don't you do something? I mean you personally."   21

"I do. And when I do, I get both sides coming down on me. Including   22
my own family. Everywhere I go, sooner or later, I'm in the courtroom.
Duplicity! That's my burning pot. I've torn up more than one court of law."

We sat down at her small table. A copy of *Catch-22* lay open.   23

"Something that happened a few years ago keeps coming back on me.   24
When I was living in Norristown, outside Philadelphia, I gained a lot of
weight and went to a doctor. She gave me some diet pills but never explained they were basically speed, and I developed a minor drug problem.
I went to the hospital and the nuns said if I didn't sign certain papers they
couldn't admit me. So I signed and they put me in a psychiatric ward. Took
two hellish weeks to prove I didn't belong there. God, it's easy to get somebody adjudicated crazy."

"Adjudicated?"   25

"You don't know the word, or you didn't think I knew it?"   26

"It's the right word. Go on."   27

"So now, because I tried to lose thirty pounds, people do a job on my   28
personality. But if I shut up long enough, things quiet down. Still, it's the
old pattern: any nigger you can't control is crazy."

As we ate our sandwiches and drank Barq's rootbeer, she asked whether   29
I had been through Natchitoches. I said I hadn't.

"They used to have a statue up there on the main street. Called the   30
'Good Darkie Statue.' It was an old black man, slouched shoulders, big
possum-eating smile. Tipping his hat. Few years ago, blacks made them
take it down. Whites couldn't understand. Couldn't see the duplicity in that
statue — duplicity on *both* sides. God almighty! I'll promise them one thing:
ain't gonna be no more gentle darkies croonin' down on the levee."

I smiled at her mammy imitation, but she shook her head. "In the sixties   31
I wanted that statue blown to bits. It's stored in Baton Rouge now at LSU,
but they put it in the wrong building. Ought to be in the capitol reminding
people. Preserve it so nobody forgets. Forgives, okay — but not forgets."

"Were things bad when you were a child?"   32

"Strange thing. I was born here in 'forty-one and grew up here, but I   33
don't remember prejudice. My childhood was warm and happy — especially
when I was reading. Maybe I was too young to see. I don't know. I go on
about the town, but I love it. I've put my time in the cities — New Orleans,
Philly. Your worst Southern cracker is better than a Northern liberal, when
it comes to duplicity anyway, because you know right off where the cracker
crumbles. With the Northerner, you don't know until it counts, and that's
when you get a job done on yourself."

"I'd rather see a person shut up about his prejudices."   34

"You haven't been deceived. Take my job. I was pleased to get it. 35
Thought it was a breakthrough for me and other blacks here. Been there
three weeks, and next Wednesday is my last day."

"What happened?" 36

"Duplicity's what happened. White man in the shop developed a bad 37
back, so they moved him inside. His seniority gets my job. I see the plot —
somebody in the company got pressured to get rid of me."

"Are you going to leave town?" 38

"I'm staying. That's my point. I'll take St. Martinville over what I've seen 39
of other places. I'm staying here to build a life for myself and my son. I'll
get married again. Put things together." She got up and went to the window.
"I don't know, maybe I'm too hard on the town. In an underhanded way,
things work here — mostly because old blacks know how to get along with
whites. So they're good darkies? They own their own homes. They don't live
in a rat-ass ghetto. There's contentment. Roots versus disorder." She
stopped abruptly and smiled. "Even German soldiers they put in the POW
camp here to work the cane fields wanted to stay on."

We cleared the table and went to the front room. A wall plaque: 40

> OH LORD, HELP ME THIS DAY
> TO KEEP MY BIG MOUTH SHUT.

On a bookshelf by the window was the two-volume microprint edition of the
Oxford English Dictionary, the one sold with a magnifying glass.

"I love it," she said. "Book-of-the-Month Club special. Seventeen-fifty. 41
Haven't finished paying for it though."

"Is it the only one in town?" 42

"Doubt it. We got brains here. After the aristocracy left Paris during the 43
French Revolution, a lot of them settled in St. Martinville, and we got known
as *Le Petit Paris*. Can you believe this little place was a cultural center only
second to New Orleans? Town started slipping when the railroad put the
bayou steamers out of business, but the church is proof of what we had."

"When you finish the college courses, what then?" 44

"I'd like to teach elementary school. If I can't teach, I want to be a 45
teacher's aide. But — here's a big 'but' — if I can make a living, I'll write
books for children. We need black women writing, and my courses are in
journalism and French. Whatever happens, I hope they don't waste my
intelligence."

She went to wash up. I pulled out one of her books: *El Señor Presidente* 46
by Guatemalan novelist Miguel Asturias. At page eighty-five she had underlined two sentences: "The chief thing is to gain time. We must be patient."

On the way back to the agency, she said, "I'll tell you something that 47
took me a long time to figure out — but I know how to end race problems."

"Is this a joke?" 48

"Might as well be. Find a way to make people get bored with hating 49
instead of helping. Simple." She laughed. "That's what it boils down to."

Questions to Start You Thinking

1. What feelings about her town and about the people in it does Barbara Pierre reveal as she talks? What reasons does she give for wanting to stay in St. Martinville?

2. Based on evidence from the essay, what proportion of his conversation with Pierre would you say the author has included? Why did he select the details he included? For what reasons do you think he omitted the rest?

3. What insights other than understanding of Pierre does the conversation provide?

4. Why doesn't the author add his personal reflections on and interpretations of the conversation?

5. Why doesn't the author state a main idea or thesis? What is his implied thesis?

6. Imagine that you have a chance to interview Barbara Pierre. Make a list of ten questions that you would ask her, questions that either extend topics covered in Least Heat Moon's essay or that cover areas on which you think Pierre's comments might be interesting.

The following essay by Michael Tein was written for a first-year composition course.

Student Essay

FLOWERS FOR CHAPEL STREET
Michael R. Tein

Few people on New Haven's Chapel Street ever notice   1
Louie Weisser. He presses his round back to the cement
storefront, his hands reach deep into his pockets rattling
his change, and he surveys his flowers. He sells them from
a pushcart the way he saw done on the Lower East Side of New
York City where he was born 72 years ago. He wears the same
clothes almost every day: a burgundy knit-collar shirt, a
stained tan V-neck, baggy herringbone trousers, and cloth
lace shoes. A blue nylon hunting cap with earflaps hugs his
head. It seems to be sewn right into his sparse scalp with
the threads of hair that remain. His cropped mustache has
browned under his nostrils from the smoke of thousands of
cigarettes. Louie draws a Lucky Strike from its box and
crimps the pack's edge so the remaining smokes stay huddled
together. The cellophane crinkles as he shoves them back

into his pocket. "I started smokin' these 'cause my father
smoked 'em. I used to steal them from him when I was a
kid."

Louie isn't much of a flower man. He drove a local bus   2
for 38 years ("a couple million miles, I would figure") before he started to help out his son's infant flower business.
His brother "got a B.S. and M.S. and all that" and was graduated from Yale, class of 1927. Lou thinks that he might have
prospered in business but has no regrets. Someone has to be
the working man.

Louie's years make him a remnant. He misses the five-   3
cent cup of coffee and the quarter pack of Luckys, but what
he remembers most is the prejudice. His brother's credentials could only get him a job driving his father's laundry
truck. "Are you Jewish?" job interviewers asked. "Well, we
don't hire Jews." Lou's former employer, the Connecticut
Transit bus company, spurned blacks from the payroll. "It
was strictly a white man's job. Now they got women, blacks,
they got everything now. They have quotas, they gotta.
It's a law now. It's not that they wanna do it, they're
forced to do it." He remembers going into a diner as a youth
and having the waitress refuse to serve his black friend.
"So we all walked out, in protest you know, to say 'the hell
with you.' We were kids, we almost started a riot there, you
know, my younger days." He laughs. "Ain't that stupid."

Louie cannot fathom stereotypes. "They say that all the   4
Jews have money," he remarks. "That's not true. You look
at the millionaires in this country and how many Jews do you
find? Kennedys aren't Jewish, the Rockefellers aren't Jewish. Why do they say the Jews have money? We never hurt,
robbed, or stole from anybody."

Lou balks at any distinction between races or religions. 5
He married a Protestant and his two sons were baptized at
Trinity Church a block away on the New Haven Green. "Just
live up to those ten commandments and you've got it made," he
says. "Everybody was Jewish before the advent of Christ.
Christians came from the word 'Christ' and Christ was Jewish.

I'm modernized," Lou proclaims. "I don't even go to <u>shul</u>
anymore."

A few times each day, Louie ventures into the Copper   6
Kitchen for a cup of coffee and a buttered Danish. He smokes
a cigarette, spins his ashtray back and forth, and tries to
work out the day's crossword, which he never finishes. He
files it in his back pocket. He eyes his cart through the
luncheonette entrance. Maybe a customer will come, maybe
not. "You may be wise, but I'm Weisser," he shrugs his
shoulders. "I got these old jokes." Lou chuckles to himself
as he waves his cigarette at the waitress to signal for a
refill.

Louie peddles all day until about six o'clock. The   7
construction work clouds the street with its refuse, jackhammers pound the pavement, and Yale students scurry by beneath the shadow of Vanderbilt and Bingham Halls. Lou is
oblivious to the tumult. His flowers are his Garden of Eden.
With each rose or swamp lily ("believe it or not, a swamp
lily") that he sells, his innocent, toothy, stubble-lined
smile reveals that this flower is his message of love and relief to a world which is far too complex, a world which has
swept him along, rudderless, in its current. His family
sailed from Russia to "the United States of America--the land
of opportunity." The terms are still interchangeable for
him. Lou was not the smart one. He drove a bus while his
brother studied chemistry. His sons are grown. One is a
teacher. The other is now his employer in the flower business. He worships both their achievements and failures, and
his eyes bulge out and shine when he speaks of them.

Lou's eyes are his most remarkable feature. The years   8
have pushed them back into the folds of skin, and a yellow
film coats the veiny whites. Each iris glows a deep purple.
Once, his eyes might have been a hazel or blue, but they have
filtered out so much darkness from his world that the residue
seems to persist. He sees only good.

"I made friends with these people." Louie points to the   9
stores behind him. "I don't hurt anybody or block anything."

Lou sets a high premium on friends. He needs them. An old
black man shuffles along behind Lou. A crumpled hat wraps
his head. He smiles at Lou through crooked and rotting teeth
as he pushes a grocery cart containing fifteen or so discarded cans. "That's my friend Richard. He looks about my
age. He used to work in a restaurant washing dishes, now
he's on social security." Richard does not beg. He returns
New Haven's cans for the five-cent deposit, and Lou respects
him for that. He pities the young bums who ask him for dimes
to buy cheap wine. After a while he stops giving. "I don't
think that I should support that."

    Lou is a terrible businessman. His heart beats with the   10
people and not with the buck. His son tells him to charge
two dollars per rose; "for you, one dollar," Louie says. But
with Louie, "for you" includes almost everyone, that is to
say, all of his friends.

    So Lou Weisser smiles and talks to Chapel Street, and   11
Chapel Street buys his flowers. The buses roll by, stores
open and close, but few are able to pass without a word to
Lou. "I'm really not the important part here," he says.
"I'm just the background."

Questions to Start You Thinking

1. What is the main point of this essay?
2. Which of Louie Weisser's physical characteristics does the writer choose to emphasize? Why?
3. Where in the essay does Tein rely directly on information from his conversation
   with Louie? How does he use this information?
4. Summarize what you think the old man's words reveal about his values and his
   outlook on life.
5. What it the author's attitude toward the old man? How do you know?
6. Besides conversing, which resources (recalling, reading, observing, imagining)
   does Tein rely on?
7. In its early drafts, "Flowers for Chapel Street" had one sentence added to its
   conclusion: "On the contrary, Lou, more like the director." Why do you think
   Tein removed it? Which ending do you prefer?
8. Why does Tein organize the information on Louie Weisser as he does? Is the
   order of ideas easy to follow? Could any of the parts be put in a different location
   (for example, paragraph 8 on Louie's eyes)?
9. Why did Tein choose his title? What other titles might he have used?

LEARNING BY WRITING

The Assignment: Interviewing

Write a paper about someone you know, a paper that depends primarily on a conversation with that person. Write about any acquaintance, friend, or relative whose traits, interests, activities, background, or outlook on life you think will interest your readers. Your purpose is to show as thoroughly as you can this person's character and personality as revealed through his or her conversation — in other words, to bring your subject alive for your readers.

Among student papers we have read that grew out of a similar assignment were the following.

A man wrote about a high school science teacher who had quit teaching for a higher-paying job in the computer industry only to return three years later to the classroom.

A man wrote about an acquaintance who had embraced the hippie lifestyle in the 1960s by "dropping out" of mainstream society.

A woman recorded the thoughts and feelings of a discouraged farmer she had known since childhood.

A man wrote what he learned about one woman's aspirations when he interviewed the most ardent feminist he knew.

A woman talked with an intern to help her decide whether she wanted to enter medical school.

A man learned about adjustment to life in a new country by talking to a neighbor from Vietnam.

If you would prefer not to write about a person but rather interview someone for information *about* something, see "Other Assignments."

Generating Ideas

It may be that the minute you read the assignment, an image of the perfect subject will flash into your mind. If that's the case, consider yourself lucky and go at once in search of that person to set up an appointment. If, on the other hand, you draw a blank at first, you'll need to spend a little time casting about for a likely person to interview. As you begin examining the possibilities, you may find it helpful to consider one or more of the following questions.

DISCOVERY CHECKLIST: INTERVIEWING

- Of the people you know, which ones do you most enjoy talking with?
- Are you acquainted with anyone whose life has been unusually eventful, stressful, or successful? If not, don't be discouraged. Even unspectacular

lives, as Tein and Least Heat Moon demonstrate, can make interesting reading.

- Do you know an expert who can help you solve a problem you have?
- Can you identify someone who is working in a job you would like to have?
- Do you know someone who has lived in a place where you would like to live?
- Do you know a younger person who has values and attitudes different from yours?
- Do you know an older person who can tell you what life was like thirty or even fifty years ago?
- Among the people you know, which have passionate convictions about society, politics, sex, childrearing, or any other topic on which you'd expect them to hold forth in lively words? A likely person may be someone actively engaged in a cause.
- Do you know anyone who has traits you particularly respect and admire — or deplore?
- Is there anyone whose background and life history you would like to know more about?
- Is there anyone in your area whose lifestyle is utterly different from your own and from that of most people you know?
- Is there anyone whose line of work you'd like to know more about? Someone's hobby — common or unusual?
- Is there an older relative who can tell you about your family?

Set up your interview. You might list the names of a few people you'd like to talk with and then find out whether your prospective source will grant you an interview. Make sure that the person can talk with you at some length — an hour, say. That should be enough time for you to conduct a thorough interview.

You'll want to make sure, too, that this person has no objections to appearing in your paper. If you sense any reluctance on the individual's part, probably your wisest course is to find another person.

There's an advantage to scheduling the interview on your subject's own ground: his or her home or workplace. As we've seen from both Tein's and Least Heat Moon's essays, an interviewer can learn a great deal from the objects with which a person surrounds himself or herself, and the interview becomes more realistic and the essay more vivid because of the details the writer can observe and include.

Don't be timid about asking for an interview. When you interview a subject, you acknowledge that person as someone with valuable things to say. Most people will be flattered by your interest in them and their lives.

Prepare questions. The interview will go better if you meet your subject at the appointed time and come prepared with some questions to ask. Give these careful thought. What kinds of questions will encourage your subject to open up? Questions about the person's background, everyday tasks, favorite leisure-time activities, hopes, and aspirations are likely to bring forth answers that you'll want to record. Sometimes a question that asks your subject to do a little imagining will elicit a revealing response. (If your house were on fire, what are the first objects you'd try to save from the flames? If you were stranded on a desert island, what books would you like to have with you?) You won't find out everything there is to know about the person you're interviewing. You'll have to focus on whatever aspect of that person's life you think will best reveal his or her personality. Good questions will enable you to lead the conversation where you want it to go and get it back on track when it strays too far afield. Such questions will also help you avoid awkward silences. Here are some of the questions Michael Tein had scribbled down before going to see Louie Weisser, a man with whom he seems to have had only a slight acquaintance:

> Where do you live?
> Does your family live in New Haven?
> When is business best?
> Where do you get your flowers?
> Who are your customers?
> Does the construction bother you?
> Does the noise bother you?
> Is this the best street corner?
> Any trouble with robbers?
> Competition?
> What got you involved in the flower business?

Probably Tein didn't have to use all those questions. One good question can get some people talking for hours. Some experts insist that four or five are enough to bring to any interview, but we believe it's better to err on the side of too many than too few. If, when you're actually talking with your subject, some of the questions you wrote strike you as downright silly, you can easily skip them. Some of Tein's questions would have elicited very brief answers. Others — like "What got you involved in the flower business?" — clearly inspired Louie to respond with enthusiasm.

Share with a classmate the questions you plan to use in your interview. Ask your classmate to respond to the following points about your questions.

PEER EDITING CHECKLIST: INTERVIEWING

- Are the questions appropriate for the person to be interviewed?
- Will the questions help the interviewer gather the information he or she is seeking?
- Are any of the questions not clear? Can you suggest rephrasing?

▱ What can you add to the list of questions?

▱ Do any of the questions seem redundant? Irrelevant?

Be open and observant. Be flexible: if the discussion is moving in a worthwhile direction, don't be a slave to your questions. Michael Tein was willing to let the conversation stray down interesting byways. Sometimes the key question, the one that takes the interview in its most rewarding direction, is the one the interviewer didn't write down in advance, one that simply grew out of something the subject said. Tein allowed Louie to answer some questions he hadn't even asked, and he really *listened* to what Louie was saying. William Least Heat Moon, in the account of his conversation with Barbara Pierre, demonstrates both the same flexibility and the same genuine interest in his subject. Of course, if the conversation heads toward a dead end, you can always bring it back by volunteering, "But to get back to what you were saying about. . . ."

During his interview, Least Heat Moon does something else that will later add vividness to his chapter about Barbara Pierre. In her apartment he uses his eyes as well as his ears. He observes what's in the room — books on the sofa, an open copy of *Catch-22* on the table, a wall plaque, an edition of the *Oxford English Dictionary,* a Guatemalan novel in which Pierre had underlined two sentences. He asks about the details that interest him, and he works Pierre's answers into his account. When you conduct an interview, you too can notice and ask about distinctive items in the subject's environment. It may encourage your subject to reveal unexpected facets of his or her personality. As you do so, keep in mind your purpose and the information you are seeking.

Sometimes a question won't interest your subject as much as you'd hoped it would. Sometimes the person you're interviewing may seem reluctant to answer a question, especially if you're unwittingly trespassing into private territory. Don't badger. If you have the confidence to wait silently for a bit, you might be rewarded. But if the silence persists, just go on to the next question.

Decide how to record the interview. Many interviewers advise against bringing a tape recorder to an interview on the grounds that sometimes it inhibits the person being interviewed and that it makes the interviewer lazy about really concentrating on what the subject is saying. Too often, the objections go, it tempts the interviewer simply to quote the rambling conversation as it appears on the tape without shaping it into good writing. If you do bring a tape recorder to your interview, be sure that the person you're talking with has no objections. Arm yourself with a pad of paper and a couple of pens or a few sharp pencils just in case the recorder malfunctions or the tape runs out before the interview ends. And don't let your mind wander. Martha Weinman Lear, a former editor with the *New York Times Magazine,* tape-records interviews but at the same time takes notes. "With the notes I hit all the high points, everything I know I want to use in the story. Then I can go back to expand on those points without having to listen to four hours of tapes, three-and-a-half hours of which might be garbage."[1]

Many interviewers approach their subjects without a tape recorder, with only paper and pen or pencil so that they can take notes unobtrusively as the interview proceeds. However, you won't be able to write down everything the person says as he or she is talking. It's more important to look your subject in the eye and keep the conversation lively than to scribble down everything he or she says. But be sure to record on the scene whatever you want to remember in exact detail: names and dates, numbers, addresses, whatever. If the person you're interviewing says anything that is so memorable that you want to record it exactly, take time to jot down the speaker's words just as he or she says them. Put quotation marks around them so that when you transcribe your notes later, you can quote them in your paper.

What about a telephone interview? It may sound like an easy way to work, but it is often less valuable than talking with the subject in person. You won't be able to duplicate by phone the lively interplay you can achieve in a successful face-to-face encounter. You'll be unable to observe the subject's possessions and environment, which so often reveal a person's personality, or see your subject's smiles, frowns, or other body language. Meet with your subject in person if at all possible.

As soon as the interview ends, rush to the nearest available desk or table and write down everything you remember but were unable to record during the conversation. Do this while the conversation is still fresh in your mind. The questions you took with you into the interview will guide your memory, as will any notes you took while your subject talked. Truman Capote, author of *In Cold Blood,* and other writers effectively use this technique for recall.

Planning, Drafting, and Developing

Now that you have gathered information on your subject, you are ready to start planning and writing your first draft. You probably have a good notion of what to include, what to emphasize, what to quote directly, what to sum up. But if your notes seem a confused jumble, you may need to approach your first draft more slowly. What are you to do with the bales of material you have amassed during the interview? Inevitably, much of what you collected will be "garbage," as Martha Weinman Lear calls it. Does that mean you should have collected less? No, it means that as you plan, you have to zero in on what is most valuable and throw out the rest. How do you do this?

Evaluate your material. Start by making a list of those details you're already pretty sure you want to include. To guide you as you sift and evaluate your material, you may find it useful to ask yourself a few questions.

What part of the conversation gave you the most insight into your subject's character and circumstances?

---

[1] Quoted in "The Art of Interviewing," text of a symposium, *The Author's Guild Bulletin* June–July 1982: 17.

Which of the direct quotations you wrote down reveal the most about your subject? Which are the most amusing, pithy, witty, surprising, or outrageous?

Which of the objects that you observed in the subject's environment provide you with valuable clues about your subject's interests?

What, if anything, did your subject's body language reveal? Did it give evidence of discomfort, pride, self-confidence, shyness, pomposity?

Did the tone of voice of the person you interviewed tell you anything about his or her state of mind?

Is there one theme, one emphasis that runs through the material you have written down? If so, what is it?

If you have a great deal of material and if, as often happens, your subject's conversation tended to ramble, you may want to emphasize just one or two things about him or her: a personality trait, the person's views on one particular topic, the influences that shaped the views he or she holds today. More than likely your notes will reveal some dominant impression around which to organize your portrait. If one is not immediately evident, study your material until you can generalize to state one. Grouping your details will help you discover a focus.

You may find yourself unable to read your hasty handwriting, or you may discover you need some crucial bit of information that somehow escaped you when you were taking notes. In such a case, telephone the person you interviewed to check out what you need to know. Have specific questions ready so that you do not need to take much of your subject's time.

Bring your subject alive. At the beginning of your paper, can you introduce the person you interviewed in a way that will frame him or her immediately in your reader's mind? A quotation, a bit of physical description, a portrait of your subject at home or at work can bring the person instantly to life.

From time to time you'll want to quote your subject directly. Be as accurate as possible, and don't put into quotation marks something your subject couldn't possibly have uttered. Sometimes you may care to quote a whole sentence or more, sometimes just a phrase. Tein smoothly works a brief direct quotation into paragraph 2 of "Flowers for Chapel Street":

```
His brother "got a B.S. and M.S. and all that" and
was graduated from Yale, class of 1927.
```

Only the words in quotation marks are actually Louie's, and they make clear the old man's rather casual attitude toward academic achievement. In the rest of the paragraph, Tein merely sums up much of what Lou has told him. Throughout his paper he moves gracefully back and forth between direct quotation and summing up.

In *Reporting,* a collection of interviews, noted reporter Lillian Ross suggests that when you quote directly the person you have interviewed, you

WRITING WITH A COMPUTER: CONVERSING

One problem with turning conversation into writing is that the results may not make easy reading. There are differences between what we say and what we write. When people talk, their facial expressions, voice inflections, and gestures can lend interest and emphasis to their words. But sometimes even the conversation of a lively speaker, transcribed word for word, will sound dull and long-winded.

Word processing can help you counter this problem. Type into the computer your subject's words as fully as you can recall. If you tape-recorded them, type them word for word. Then scroll through the results on the screen. What parts stand out? What remarks, just as they are, will be interesting and revealing and will help fulfill the purpose of your paper? Highlight these in bold or with underlining (which you can easily undo), or with another highlighting tool that your word processing program provides. Since you can delete with a couple of keystrokes, keeping the best material and cutting the rest will be easy. Or on the screen, you can readily replace any comment that seems tedious with a terse summary.

work hard to "find the quotations that get to the truth of what that person is. That does not mean that you make up quotations. Somewhere along the line, in the time you spend with your subject, you will find the quotations that are significant—that reveal the character of the person, that present as close an approximation of the truth as you can achieve." Keep writing until you believe you have come close to that truth.

Revising and Editing

Wait a few hours or a few days before you look again at the early draft you have written. As you pick it up to read it over, keep in mind that your purpose was to bring alive for your reader the person you interviewed. Your main task now is to make sure you have succeeded in doing that. This brief self-quiz may help you in reviewing your work.

REVISION CHECKLIST: WRITING FROM CONVERSATION

🖊 Have you merely skimmed over what the person said to you, or have you been careful to represent the conversation in enough detail to reveal a unique individual, worth paying attention to?

🖊 Are some statements you quoted of lesser importance, better suited to summarizing or indirect quotation ("He said that he had suffered enough") than to direct quotation ("He said, 'I have suffered enough' ")? Should some of what you merely summed up be given greater prominence by expanding it and adding specific quotations?

🖊 Have you included details that show what your subject most cares about?

- Have you put in a few of your own observations, inspired perhaps by objects you noticed in the place where the interview was conducted?
- Do the person's voice, bearing, and gestures come through in your writing?
- Read the direct quotations out loud. Do they sound likely to have come out of the mouth of the person you're portraying?
- Do the things he or she says reveal personality, character, mood? Are the individual's traits clear from the details you have selected?
- Are the details focused on a major trait or impression you want to emphasize? Are all the details relevant?
- Why have you organized the details as you have? Would a different organization be more effective?
- If any of your classmates are acquainted with your subject, do you think they would be able to recognize him or her from what you have written, even if the person's name were omitted from your account? Find out.
- Does any of the material you put into your paper strike you now as drivel? If so, be merciless about getting rid of it.
- Skim over your interview notes or listen again to selected parts of your tape recording for material whose significance may not have struck you while you were deciding what to include. Do any additional details, left out of your early draft, now seem worth putting in after all? If so, it's not too late to find a place for them and add them.
- Could your paper have a stronger beginning?
- What can you strike out?
- Is your ending satisfactory?

If you find it hard to criticize your own work, ask a classmate or a friend to read your draft and suggest how to make the portrait more vivid, clear, and honest.

PEER EDITING CHECKLIST: WRITING FROM CONVERSATION

- Give your overall reaction to the paper.
- What seems to make the person interviewed interesting to the writer? What do you understand to be the writer's major impression of or insight into the person? "Nutshell" this.
- Does the writer tell you anything about the person that seems unconnected to his or her major impression or insight?
- Do you have any questions about this person that you'd like answered in the paper but that aren't? Put stars where more details are needed.
- Do the words of the person interviewed "sound" real to you? Has the writer quoted anything that seems at odds with the general impression you now have of the person?

   ☞ Would you leave out any of the conversation the writer used? Underline any that you find not connected to the major impression or insight.

   ☞ Look at how the writer has arranged the materials. Would you suggest any changes in the organization?

   ☞ Does each part connect logically with other parts? Put a check mark anywhere that you think the writer needs to work more on transitions.

   ☞ Look particularly at the beginning of the essay. Did the writer make you want to get to know the person? If so, how? If not, what got in your way?

   ☞ Circle on the manuscript any problems with spelling, punctuation, grammar, or word choice that hindered you as you read.

Double-check your quotations. As you write your final draft, be sure that where you have omitted words from a direct quotation, you have substituted an ellipsis mark (. . .) — three dots that show where omissions have occurred — and that the sentence that contains the ellipsis makes sense and is coherent with the sentences before and after it. Suppose you want to quote Marta, who was interviewed by anthropologist Oscar Lewis for his landmark study of a poor Mexican family, *The Children of Sanchez* (New York: Random, 1961). Marta said, "I had been living in the Casa Grande, but there was an argument with Delila and I moved to my aunt Guadalupe's again, this time staying until just before Trini was born." Suppose that you want to quote just part of that sentence in your paper. You might do it like this: "I had been living in the Casa Grande, but there was an argument with Delila and I moved to my aunt Guadalupe's . . . staying until just before Trini was born." The sentence is faithful enough to the original so that it doesn't distort the speaker's words, but the three dots indicate that something has been omitted.

Occasionally you may have included a quotation within a quotation, as Lewis does a little later in his interview with Marta, who says, "When Guadalupe had gone begging Prudencia to let them stay in a corner of her room, she was told, 'My house is yours, but there is no room for your son.' " When you quote your subject quoting someone else, your subject's words appear in regular quotation marks, the other person's in *single* quotation marks. If your written interview, like William Least Heat Moon's, contains dialogue, be sure to start a new paragraph each time a different person speaks.

As you can see, quoting from conversation requires special attention to punctuation and formatting, and you should check your paper carefully for mechanical errors before you hand it in.

Other Assignments

1. Write a paper based on an interview with at least two members of your extended family about some incident that is part of your family lore. You may find yourself amused to notice that different people's accounts of the event don't always agree.

FOR GROUP LEARNING

Take part in a collective interview. Let your whole class or just your writing group interview someone who has some special knowledge or who represents a walk of life that you want to learn more about. Of course, this means finding a person likely to have something of interest to say who wouldn't mind meeting with your whole class or group. Public figures, like writers, who occasionally visit schools, are used to facing the questions of a whole class. Or perhaps someone on campus will be willing to be interviewed about a problem your group is interested in.

Before your subject arrives, let your class or your writing group take time to plan the discussion: What do you want to find out? What questions or lines of questioning do you wish to pursue? What topic will each student ask about? We suggest that when the interviewee is present, each questioner be allowed (as far as time permits) to ask all of his or her main questions before yielding the floor to the next questioner. This way each person can pursue a line of thought all the way. Later, students may write their individual papers based on the group interview, showing what they have learned not only from their own questions but from everybody's.

An alternative plan is to collaborate on the paper. The outcome of the interview may be one group-written paper. If so, the group might appoint two members to act as reporters or recording secretaries and take notes. If not, each of you should take notes. After the interview your writing group might meet to sift what you learned. The two reporters who took notes during the interview might show (or read aloud) their notes to the group to check the accuracy of both questions and answers. To parcel out the project fairly, these reporters shouldn't be asked to write the paper, too. Designate two or three others to write what the group has learned. One might write a draft and the others polish it, or several might write sections and then all of you put it together. A variation on this assignment is that the individuals in the group interview different people on the same subject and pool what all of you have learned into one paper.

If you can't reconcile them, combine them into one vivid account, noting that some details may be more trustworthy than others. Give credit to your sources. The paper that results might just be worth saving for young relatives.

2. Interview someone who is in a line of work you think you might like to enter yourself. Find out what this person recommends you do to prepare for the job that interests you. Then write a paper detailing your subject's advice.

3. Interview a mother or father about her or his reactions to a child's birth and how the child has changed the family's life.

4. After briefly questioning fifteen or twenty students on your campus to find out what careers they are preparing for, write a short essay summing up what you find out. What are their reasons for their choices? Are students at your college more intent on earning money than on other pursuits? How many of them are choosing lucrative careers because they have to pay back huge college loans? Are any of them unhappy with the direction they have chosen? Provide some

quotations to flesh out your survey. From the information you have gathered, would you call your classmates materialists? Idealists? Practical people?

5. Interview an older person in your family or neighborhood on what life was like when he or she was a child. Gather enough information to re-create the past world.

6. Interview someone on campus who has information on a current problem, and try to find a solution to the problem.

APPLYING WHAT YOU LEARN: SOME USES OF WRITING FROM CONVERSATION

Interviewing is a familiar tool of many writers in the world beyond college. Biographers who write about someone living often conduct extensive interviews with their subjects to guarantee accuracy. Usually they interview friends, relatives, and other associates to round out their picture of the person. Likewise, news reporters and commentators often rely on interviews with "informed sources" (generally public officials, some of whom don't want to be named). Another familiar kind of interview is that in which some author, actor, or political figure airs his or her views on a variety of subjects. Such interviews are written by people who have talked with their subjects, sometimes by telephone but usually face to face. James Dickey, the poet and novelist, has even published self-interviews to present his opinions.

Often in college writing you find yourself interviewing people not because you are interested in their personalities but because they can contribute valuable insights to what you are studying. Students of human development often interview people at various stages of the life cycle. They talk to men and women about the transition from student life to the working world, to mothers about the experience of giving birth, to older people about widowhood or retirement. One line of questioning, for instance, helps them find out how well these older men and women are carrying out the "life review" that therapists like Erik Erikson find so important to ending life with integrity. Sometimes, too, these students collect oral histories, either purely autobiographical ones or those that center on particular events from the past. In recent years historians themselves, acknowledging that "ordinary" people matter, both individually and collectively, have shown increasing interest in gathering and publishing oral histories and in mining those from the past. One such collection that throws vivid light on the civil rights movement is Howell Raines's *My Soul Is Rested* (New York: Putnam's, 1977). In the following excerpt the author records the words of Franklin McCain, who participated in the now famous sit-in at Woolworth's in Greensboro, N.C., on February 1, 1960.

> Once getting there . . . we did make purchases of school supplies and took the patience and time to get receipts for our purchases, and Joseph and myself went over to the counter and asked to be served coffee and doughnuts. As anticipated, the reply was, "I'm sorry, we don't serve you here." And of course we

said, "We just beg to disagree with you. We've in fact already been served; you've served us already and that's just not quite true. . . . We wonder why you'd invite us in to serve us at one counter and deny service at another. If this is a private club or private concern, then we believe you ought to sell membership cards and sell only to persons who have a membership card. If we don't have a card, then we'd know pretty well that we shouldn't come in or even attempt to come in." That didn't go over too well. . . . And the only thing that an individual in her case or position could do is, of course, call the manager. [Laughs]

A memorable quotation from an expert can lend great life and conviction to a factual paper or article. To write "The Superstars of Heart Research" for *Boston* magazine, reporter Philip Zaleski gathered information by talking with surgeons and scientists and, as in the following paragraph, with an official of a national health organization.

"If you ever want to alter people's lifestyles," says Barnie Duane of the American Heart Association, "let them watch a coronary bypass. It's the most horrendous thing I've ever seen. I watched my first one at Massachusetts General with a bunch of kids. Some of them fainted. We observed from a glass dome just four feet above the head of the surgeon, so we had a perfect view. Two teams of doctors worked simultaneously. One stood at the patient's feet, cutting a huge vein out of his leg. The other stood at his chest, ripping open the sternum with a saw — *zip!* Then they cracked open his ribs with giant clamps — *snap! snap! snap!* The surgeons lifted out a damaged artery and held it up to our view and squeezed. Cholesterol squirted out like toothpaste from a tube. It's guaranteed to change your life."

In professional scholarly research, dozens of interviews may be necessary. The five sociologists who wrote the much-acclaimed *Habits of the Heart: Individualism and Commitment in American Life* (Berkeley: U of California P, 1985) used as their sources not only books and periodicals but also extensive interviews with both ordinary citizens and professionals in various fields. Note how this example from a chapter written by Ann Swidler enlivens its discussion with pointed, informative quotations that read like spoken words:

Asked why she went into therapy, a woman summed up the themes that recur again and again in accounts by therapists and their clients: "I was not able to form close relationships to people, I didn't like myself, I didn't love myself, I didn't love other people." In the therapeutic ideology, such incapacities are in turn related to a failure fully to accept, fully to love, one's self.

As the therapist Margaret Oldham puts it, many of the professionally trained, upper-middle-class young adults who come to her, depressed and lonely, are seeking "that big relationship in the sky — the perfect person." They want "that one person who is going to stop making them feel alone." But this search for a perfect relationship cannot succeed because it comes from a self that is not full and self-sustaining. The desire for relatedness is really a reflection of incompleteness, of one's own dependent needs.

Before one can love others, one must learn to love one's self. A therapist can teach self love by offering unconditional acceptance. As a Rogersian therapist observes, "There's nobody once you leave your parents who can just say you are

O.K. with us no matter what you do." He continues, "I'm willing to be a motherer." ... Another, more behavioristic therapist concurs, saying he works by "giving them just lots of positive reinforcement in their selves; continually pointing out things that are good about them, feeding them with it over and over again." Thus the initial ingredient in the development of a healthy, autonomous self may be love from the ideal, understanding surrogate parent-lover-friend — the therapist. Unlike that of lovers, and friends, however, the purpose of the therapist's love is not to create a lasting relationship of mutual commitment, but to free people of their dependence so that ultimately they can love themselves.

Further Applications

Conversation is a resource used in nonfiction to make an essay realistic and interesting, similar to dialogue in fiction. In *A Writer's Reader,* several writers effectively draw on this resource. For example, in "The Men We Carry in Our Minds" (p. 461) Scott Russell Sanders, a professor of English at Indiana University, uses conversation to give his essay the ring of truth. In the introduction to his essay he uses direct conversation, but in other parts of his essay he uses indirect quotations, summarizing what he has learned from talking with other people. This technique is appropriate to his background as a literature professor. "Psychic Income" (p. 537) by Mary Kay Blakely, a professor of social research, is based on a discussion with a university administrator whose comments about "psychic income" stimulate the author to speculate — satirically — about inequalities in contemporary society.

Similar to Sanders, Blakely, William Least Heat Moon (p. 76), and student Michael R. Tein (p. 80), writers Paule Marshall in "From the Poets in the Kitchen" (p. 439), Ti-Hua Chang in "Downtown Cousin" (p. 492), and Trip Gabriel in "Call of the Wildmen" (p. 473) draw on conversation to bring their subjects alive. Answer the following questions about each of these essays.

1. Does the writer report conversation directly or indirectly?

2. Were the reported conversations the result of recall of informal discussions or of planned interviews? Which would be easier for a beginning writer? Why or why not?

3. What do the conversations show about the personality of the individual speaking? About the author/listener?

4. Why do you think this writer draws on conversation as a resource for writing?

CHAPTER 5

Writing from Imagination

"Imagination," said Albert Einstein, "is more important than knowledge." Coming from a theoretical physicist who widened our knowledge of the universe, the remark is striking. Although "imaginative writing" usually suggests stories, poems, or plays, storytellers, poets, and playwrights have no monopoly on imagination. Scientists and economists, historians and businesspeople need imagination just as much. The astronomer Copernicus *imagined* the earth revolving around the sun; he didn't see and report it. Economist John Maynard Keynes imagined the theory of aggregate demand before he set about proving it, and engineer and architect Buckminster Fuller conceived the geodesic dome before he could build one. Freud never saw the id; he imagined it. Anyone who comes up with a theory to explain a strange event or a hypothesis to account for a mysterious phenomenon uses imagination. Authors of college essays, blue book exams, and research papers will do well to call on the resource of imagination.

In one familiar sense of the word, imagining is nothing but daydreaming — imagining yourself wafted from a cold and rainy city street to a sunny beach in the tropics. Enlarging that definition a little, the *Shorter Oxford Dictionary* calls imagination "forming a mental concept of what is not actually present to the senses."

That definition is all right as far as it goes, but imagination is a far larger resource. According to mathematician Jacob Bronowski, "*To imagine* means to make images and to move them about inside one's head in new arrangements. When you and I recall the past, we imagine it in this direct and homely sense. . . . With the same symbolic vocabulary we spell out the future — not one but many futures, which we weigh one against another." He added that imagination and reason work together, beginning in childhood:

> When a child begins to play games with things that stand for other things, with chairs or chessmen, he enters the gateway to reason and imagination together. For the human reason discovers new relations between things not by deduction, but by that unpredictable blend of speculation and insight that scientists call induction, which — like other forms of imagination — cannot be formalized.

In the view of Samuel Taylor Coleridge, imagination is nothing less than a "magical power," one that can reveal in familiar objects "novelty and freshness." Sometimes it brings new things into existence by combining old things that already exist. Lewis Carroll, whose Alice books seem remote from actual life, drew the stuff of his fantastic adventures from his friendship with a real child and some of his fantastic characters from real persons in England. His portrait of the Mad Hatter, for instance, resembles Theophilus Carter, an eccentric Oxford furniture dealer. Instead of creating out of thin air, imaginative writers often build from materials they find at hand. "The imagination," said poet Wallace Stevens, "must not detach itself from reality."

Yet as many writers have testified, imagining is often playful: a fruitful kind of fooling around. Ursula Le Guin, writer of science fiction, calls imagination "the free play of the mind." In her essay "Why Are Americans Afraid of Dragons?" she explains:

> By "free" I mean that the action is done without an immediate object of profit — spontaneously. That does not mean, however, that there may not be a purpose behind the free play of the mind, a goal; and the goal may be a very serious object indeed. Children's imaginative play is clearly a practicing at the acts and emotions of adulthood; a child who did not play would not become mature. As for the free play of an adult mind, its result may be *War and Peace,* or the theory of relativity.

Though the result may not be Leo Tolstoy's classic novel or Einstein's theory, a college writer will find that such free play with language and ideas can be valuable and productive — and fun besides.

LEARNING FROM OTHER WRITERS

It appears that, to be a whole writer and a whole human being, each of us needs both a logical, analytical mind and what Shakespeare called "the mind's eye" — the faculty of imagining. In this chapter, we don't presume to tell you how to imagine. We only suggest how to use the imagination you already have. To begin, here are two examples of imaginative writing, the first by a professional writer and the second by a student of education. Both draw from their own knowledge, having to do little research. Anna Quindlen writes familiar essays based on her own experiences and reflections. In this essay from her collection, she fantasizes about mothers, those of other women and her own.

MOTHERS
Anna Quindlen

The two women are sitting at a corner table in the restaurant, their 1
shopping bags wedged between their chairs and the wall: Lord & Taylor,
Bloomingdale's, something from Ann Taylor for the younger one. She is
wearing a bright silk shirt, some good gold jewelry; her hair is on the long
side, her makeup faint. The older woman is wearing a suit, a string of
pearls, a diamond solitaire, and a narrow band. They lean across the table.
I imagine the conversation: Will the new blazer go with the old skirt? Is the
dress really right for an afternoon wedding? How is Daddy? How is his ulcer?
Won't he slow down just a little bit?

It seems that I see mothers and daughters everywhere, gliding through 2
what I think of as the adult rituals of parent and child. My mother died
when I was nineteen. For a long time, it was all you needed to know about
me, a kind of vest-pocket description of my emotional complexion: "Meet
you in the lobby in ten minutes—I have long brown hair, am on the short
side, have on a red coat, and my mother died when I was nineteen."

That's not true anymore. When I see a mother and a daughter having 3
lunch in a restaurant, shopping at Saks, talking together on the cross-
town bus, I no longer want to murder them. I just stare a little more
than is polite, hoping that I can combine my observations with a half-
remembered conversation, some anecdotes, a few old dresses, a photograph or two, and re-create, like an archaeologist of the soul, a relationship that will never exist. Of course, the question is whether it would have
ever existed at all. One day at lunch I told two of my closest friends that
what I minded most about not having a mother was the absence of that
grown-up woman-to-woman relationship that was impossible as a child or
adolescent, and that my friends were having with their mothers now. They
both looked at me as though my teeth had turned purple. I didn't need to
ask why; I've heard so many times about the futility of such relationships,
about women with business suits and briefcases reduced to whining children by their mothers' offhand comment about a man, or a dress, or a
homemade dinner.

I accept the fact that mothers and daughters probably always see each 4
other across a chasm of rivalries. But I forget all those things when one of
my friends is down with the flu and her mother arrives with an overnight
bag to manage her household and feed her soup.

So now, at the center of my heart there is a fantasy, and a mystery. 5
The fantasy is small, and silly: a shopping trip, perhaps a pair of shoes, a
walk, a talk, lunch in a good restaurant, which my mother assumes is the
kind of place I eat at all the time. I pick up the check. We take a cab to
the train. She reminds me of somebody's birthday. I invite her and my father
to dinner. The mystery is whether the fantasy has within it a nugget of fact.
Would I really have wanted her to take care of the wedding arrangements,
or come and stay for a week after the children were born? Would we have

talked on the telephone about this and that? Would she have saved my clippings in a scrapbook? Or would she have meddled in my affairs, volunteering opinions I didn't want to hear about things that were none of her business, criticizing my clothes and my children? Worse still, would we have been strangers with nothing to say to each other? Is all the good I remember about us simply wishful thinking? Is all the bad self-protection? Perhaps it is at best difficult, at worst impossible for children and parents to be adults together. But I would love to be able to know that.

Sometimes I feel like one of those people searching, searching for the   6 mother who gave them up for adoption. I have some small questions for her and I want the answers: How did she get her children to sleep through the night? What was her first labor like? Was there olive oil in her tomato sauce? Was she happy? If she had it to do over again, would she? When we pulled her wedding dress out of the box the other day to see if my sister might wear it, we were shocked to find how tiny it was. "My God," I said, "did you starve yourself to get into this thing?" But there was no one there. And if she had been there, perhaps I would not have asked in the first place. I suspect that we would have been friends, but I don't really know. I was simply a little too young at nineteen to understand the woman inside the mother.

I occasionally pass by one of those restaurant tables and I hear the   7 bickering about nothing: You did so, I did not, don't tell me what you did or didn't do, oh, leave me alone. And I think that my fantasies are better than any reality could be. Then again, maybe not.

Questions to Start You Thinking

1. What is the point of Quindlen's essay? How is the last phrase, "Then again, maybe not," related to that point?

2. Specifically what does Quindlen fantasize about? Why does she have these fantasies?

3. Might women fantasize similarly about their fathers? How about men about their fathers or mothers?

4. From this essay, what kind of person do you think Quindlen is?

5. Have you ever imagined what your life would be like if someone who died had not died? Or if someone who did not die, had?

6. Have you ever observed some people in a public place, perhaps on a bus or plane, and imagined who they are and why they are in that place at that time? Have you imagined the conversation they are having? What clues do you have to what they are saying? Try this kind of fantasizing the next time you go to the airport, the mall, or a restaurant, and share your imagined situation with your classmates. (This experience could also provide information for a paper.)

7. Have you ever drawn some conclusions about someone you have just met, only to discover later that you were wrong?

Student Jennifer Bowe faced this challenging assignment: "Imagine your ideal college. Conceive it to fit your own wishes and deepest desires. Then describe it in writing. Perhaps this college might bring together the strong points of several real colleges—faculty, curriculum, location, facilities, or other prominent features—in a new combination. Propose a philosophy for your college, one that might lead to original methods of instruction."

To generate ideas, Bowe first took part in a two-hour brainstorming session with three of her peers. She scribbled eight pages of ideas, pondered them, and then wrote. The following paper, though lighthearted, makes interesting criticisms of conventional methods of instruction.

Student Essay

IF I COULD FOUND A COLLEGE
Jennifer Bowe

Welcome to Sundial College. Jennifer Bowe, founder. 1
(That's me, that statue on horseback in front of the administration building.)

When you visit the campus of Sundial for the first time, 2
you notice something strange. The position of the sun never
changes, for Sundial College takes its name from its design,
which is as unique as its educational philosophy. The whole
campus rests on an enormous disk that rotates with the sun,
almost imperceptibly, so that the sun always shines down on
the college from the same direction. Rather than rising in
the east and setting in the west, the sun appears to rise
straight up and set straight down again. This odd design is
not merely an advertising gimmick to make the college sound
unique; it is quite practical. Classrooms are built to receive maximum sunlight at all times, thus saving in heating
costs more than enough to pay for running the giant motor
that turns the campus. Students reading on the lawn do not
need to keep moving their blankets to stay in the sun or the
shade. Greenhouses stay sunny all day long. Night Owl
Hall, the dorm for people who like to stay up late, has its
back to the sun, so that its late sleepers will receive no
unwanted morning light. Lark Hall, for early risers, lights
up with the dawn. Out of necessity, the Astronomy Department

is located just outside the central disk, so that its instruments are in harmony with the rest of the earth. At the hub
of the campus wheel is a great sundial--fixed, keeping faithful time.

Sundial College operates on the philosophy that college   3
should prepare one to think independently. It believes that
the best kind of learning takes place outside of class. For
this reason, there are no classes. I insisted on making this
experiment when I founded the college. In classes where
students talk a lot, too much time is spent on chatter. I
have heard some great lectures, but they have been frustrating. When you try to take notes on a lecture, you just get
all the names spelled wrong. I believe you can obtain
knowledge faster and more accurately by reading a book.

Sundial students take only one course at a time, so as   4
to concentrate on it without being distracted by other
courses. Each course lasts from two to six weeks, as long as
necessary. On the first day of a course, each student visits
the professor, who hands out a reading list and some writing
assignments. The college library is open day and night and
has bunk beds for people to take naps. Access to the professors is easy. Each student has a weekly appointment with
the professor (the one whose course he or she is now taking)
to ask questions and receive feedback on reading and writing
assignments.

In this college without classes, does the student lack   5
the stimulus of classroom-type discussion? On the contrary,
group discussions among students in a course take place
daily, outdoors in the sun, so that students can freely talk
together without being graded on what they say. At the end
of the course there is a test, not graded but marked pass or
fail. If a student fails, he or she goes to the instructor,
who finds out whether the student didn't do the work or
didn't understand it. Those who fail get a second chance.
If they fail again, they receive no credit for the course.
None of the courses prepares students for careers; the
courses only train their minds. I admit that careers are

naturally important to some students, and an active work-
study program finds paying jobs for those who want to take
off and work for a semester.

The students come from every walk of life and from every   6
country. The faculty, brilliant people in their twenties and
a few older scholars, come from all over the world. Enthusiasm for teaching, not famous publications, is the most important criterion in hiring them. More than half are women.
All have to be approved by a student council before they are
rehired. Besides these regular faculty, a group of "wanderng
scholars" spend their time roaming around campus engaging
students in intellectual bull sessions. Some are famous
scholars retired from other universities; some are just brilliant bums who can talk interestingly and stimulate students
to think.

Although the campus stays fixed in its place in the sun,   7
it is always in a whirl of exciting activity. Each student
sets time aside for strolling around the campus taking in
events. Foreign films, good Hollywood films, and documentaries of all kinds run day and night in a ten-screen theater. Lectures, plays, and concerts are held at all hours.
A computer room has every kind of educational software.
Rooms with VCR's contain thousands of videotapes. Everything
is designed to keep the student body thinking at all times.

The Sundial experience, of course, is not entirely an   8
intellectual one. There is a lively social life. When I
founded Sundial, I insisted on no fraternities, because frats
induce vomiting, especially at their beer parties. There
aren't any sororities either, to divide the student body into
castes. The students at Sundial are unified in spirit, and
campus parties and barbecues leave nobody out in the cold.
An essential center of society is the campus pub. Sundial's
has dark brown walls, booths with vinyl cushions, a dart
board, Sundialburgers (with a wedge of onion for the gnomon),
and several of the "wandering scholars" always hanging around
challenging students to argue with them. A friendly old
proprietor named Curly, who has been on the scene for thirty-

five years, gives out sympathy and five-dollar loans to
students short of cash.

Sports are laid-back and informal. The teams are really   9
just clubs, which anyone may join. I don't believe in sensational football and basketball teams with star players,
supported on money given by the alumni. Alumni always like
to support sports teams because they can't cheer for students
in class taking tests.

To finance such a college without alumni support is not   10
easy. Luckily, in founding Sundial I had several billion
dollars to endow it with. My continued generosity keeps the
tuition fees down to about half those at a community college.
Financial aid for those who need it is available and is the
highest in the country. No scholarships need to be repaid,
no part-time work is required, and substantial travel bonuses
are given to students who have to come a long way.

In fact, Sundial is such a pleasant place that it has   11
one serious problem: how to make everyone go home for the
summer. However, its problem has a built-in solution. Once
again, the design of its revolving campus proves the wisdom
and foresight of its founder. When the school year ends,
the dorms are locked, keeping everyone outside. Then the
huge disk of Sundial College accelerates, faster and
faster, reaching a dizzying speed, until every last student
takes off.

Questions to Start You Thinking

1. In what remarks does Jennifer Bowe seem to be kidding? Which does she apparently mean us to take seriously? Are any comments ironic?
2. What are Bowe's implied criticisms of traditional education?
3. What features of Sundial College appeal to you? Do any strike you as mistakes?
4. If you were designing your own ideal college, what would it be like? Compare your ideal college with the proposed colleges of your classmates.

LEARNING BY WRITING

The Assignment: "What If . . . ?"

Write an essay in answer to a question that begins "What if . . . ?"

You might imagine a past that unfolded differently: for instance, What if the airplane had never been invented? You might imagine a reversal of present-day fact: What if men had to bear children? Or you might imagine an event in the future: What if there were no more wars? or What if you were elected president of the United States?

Envision in specific detail a world in which the supposition is true. Your purpose is to make the supposition seem credible and convincing to your readers.

Unless your instructor encourages you to do so, don't write a story. To be sure, you could conceivably write this paper as science fiction. In answer to the question What if time travel were possible? you might begin: "As I walked into Me-opolis in 2500 A.D., the mayor rushed up to me. 'A terrible plague of headaches has struck our city!' he shouted. Luckily, I still had my bottle of Tylenol from the twentieth century. . . ." But instead, write imaginative *nonfiction*.

To help you start imagining, here are some topics that students generated for this assignment. Some may reveal interesting dimensions in your possible major field of study; some are less serious.

A DIFFERENT PAST

What if the Equal Rights Amendment had become law?

What if the South had won the Civil War?

What if continental drift had never taken place and the Americas, Africa, and Eurasia were still one connected landmass?

What if *Homo sapiens* had not straightened up but still walked on all fours? (One first thought: Basketball rims would be lower.)

What if Sigmund Freud had never lived?

What if John F. Kennedy or Martin Luther King, Jr., had not been assassinated?

A DIFFERENT PRESENT

What if no one needed to sleep?

What if knees bent the other way? (How would chairs, cars, and bicycles have to be redesigned?)

What if you could take a pill instead of eating?

What if the human eye could perceive only two dimensions?

What if it were possible to travel backward in time? If you could do so, to what earlier eras would you go? Why? (Alternative: What if you could meet any six prominent persons who ever lived? Whom would you choose? Why?)

A POSSIBLE FUTURE

What if a woman were elected the next president of the United States?

What if the United Nations were to create and control a powerful army?

What if a space station, capable of sustaining hundreds of people, were placed in orbit?

What if the salaries of all teachers in public schools and colleges were increased by fifty percent, effective immediately?

What if legislation were passed limiting couples to two children?

What if the ozone layer were depleted?

We know of several thought-provoking papers that resulted when students were asked to answer a question that began "What if . . . ?"

For a research paper in a course in European history, writing of the French Revolution, one student tried to imagine what it was like to be a citizen of Paris in 1789.

For a paper in economics, a man looked at government aid to disadvantaged people in the inner city, thinking and writing first as a liberal (his own conviction) and then — by an act of imagination — as a conservative.

In a research paper about space law, a student used both existing documents and his power to envision future conflicts and problems to propose answers to legal questions likely to be crucial in the future: Should discoverers of resources on the moon be allowed to keep them? Should probes be allowed for a scientific purpose (which might involve quarrying and removing material), or should international law protect the moon's existing surface? (And how should the law define a scientific purpose?)

A woman imagined a contemporary American child's day in a world in which television or computers had not been invented.

Generating Ideas

In making your own list of "What if" questions, you may find it helpful to brainstorm, either by yourself or (as Jennifer Bowe did) wth the aid of a group. Sometimes two or three imaginations are better than one. (For helpful tips on brainstorming, see p. 303.)

To help you generate "What if's," here are a few questions.

DISCOVERY CHECKLIST: IMAGINING POSSIBILITIES

- What event in history has always intrigued you?
- What common assumption — something we all take for granted — might be questioned or denied? (It might be a scientific opinion, such as the widely accepted knowledge that the ultraviolet rays of the sun are harmful to the skin.)
- What future event do you most look forward to?

⮫ What present-day problem or deplorable condition do you wish to see remedied?

⮫ What different paths in life might you have taken?

Jot down as many "What if" questions as you can think of, do some trial imagining, and then choose the topic that seems most promising. Say you pick as your topic "What if the average North American life span were to lengthen to more than a century?" You might begin by reflecting on some of the ways in which society would have to change. When ideas start to flow, start listing them. No doubt a lengthened life span would mean that a greater proportion of the populace would be old. Ask questions: How would that fact affect doctors and nurses, hospitals, and other medical facilities? How might city planners respond to the needs of so many more old people? What would the change mean for retail merchants? For television programming? For the social security system? For taxes?

Although there are no fixed rules to follow in imagining, all of us tend to imagine in familiar ways. Being acquainted with these ways may help you fulfill your assignment.

Shifting perspective   In imagining, a writer sometimes thinks and perceives from another person's point of view. In imagining her ideal college, Jennifer Bowe stops and realizes that many students, unlike herself, want a college to prepare them for a career, not just to help them learn. She then alters her concept of Sundial College to include a work-study program.

Envisioning   Imagining what might be, seeing in the mind's eye and in graphic detail, is the process of envisioning or imaging. A writer might imagine a utopia or ideal state, as did Thomas More in *Utopia* (1516), or an anti-utopia, as did George Orwell in his 1949 novel of a grim future, *Nineteen Eighty-Four*. By envisioning, you can conceive of other possible alternatives: to imagine, say, a different and better way of treating illness, of electing a president or a prime minister. The student who wrote about the French Revolution by imagining life in Paris in 1789 had to envision.

Sometimes in envisioning, you will find a meaningful order in what had seemed a chaotic jumble. Leonardo da Vinci, in his notebooks, tells how, when starting to conceive a painting, he would gaze at an old stained wall made of various stones until he began to see "landscapes adorned with mountains, rivers, rocks, trees, plains, . . . combats and figures in quick movement, and strange expressions of faces, and outlandish costumes, and an infinite number of things." Not everyone might see that much in a wall, but da Vinci's method is familiar to writers who have worked in an imaginative way—who also have looked into a confused and random array of stuff and envisioned in it a meaningful arrangement.

Synthesizing   Synthesizing (generating new ideas by combining previously separate ideas) is the opposite of analyzing (breaking down into component parts). In synthesizing, a writer brings together materials, perhaps old and familiar materials, and fuses them into something new. A writer makes fresh connections. Surely Picasso achieved a synthesis when, in making a metal sculpture of a baboon and needing a skull for the animal, he clapped on the baboon's neck a child's toy car. With its windshield like a pair of eyes and its mouthlike bumper, the car didn't just look like a baboon's skull: it *became* one. German chemist Friedrich August Kekulé rightly guessed the structure of the benzene molecule when, in reverie, he imagined a snake swallowing its own tail. In a flash he realized that the elusive molecule was a ring of carbon atoms, not a chain, as earlier chemists had believed. Surely to bring together the benzene molecule and a snake was a feat of imaginative synthesis.

Some things cannot be totally reduced to rule and line, and imagination is one of them. But we hope you will accept that imagining is a practical activity of which you are fully capable. The more words you put on paper, the more often you will find that you can discover surprising ideas, original examples, unexpected relationships. The more you write, the more you involve yourself with language, that fascinating stained glass window that invites you to find fresh shapes in it.

Planning, Drafting, and Developing

We trust we haven't given you the impression that all imagining takes place *before* you write. On the contrary, you'll probably find yourself generating more ideas—perhaps more imaginative and startling ideas—in the act of writing.

Though in writing a "What if" paper you are freely imagining, you'll still need to lay out your ideas in a clear and orderly fashion so that readers can take them in. Some writers prefer to outline (as we discuss on p. 331). However, you might find that in fulfilling this assignment all the outline you will need is a list of points not to forget. If in writing your "What if" paper you

---

WRITING WITH A COMPUTER: IMAGINING

Did you ever try "invisible writing"? This is a technique to make yourself less self-conscious while you write—as you'll especially need to be when you're imagining. Twist down the contrast control on your computer monitor so that you can't see any words appearing on your screen. Then write. Do you feel slightly at sea? Don't worry—keep writing. Then twist the contrast back up and behold what you have written. The advantage of this trick is that you won't be fussing over particular words (and spelling errors); you'll be able to devote your full attention to imagining.

enjoy yourself and words flow readily, by all means let the flow carry you along. In that happy event, you may be able to plan at the same time that you write your first draft.

To help your reader envision and share your imagined world just as vividly as you do, your "What if" needs an engaging (and convincing) opening. Anna Quindlen's "Mothers" has such a beginning. The author arrests our interest by describing in detail two women at lunch. This scene makes us feel as if we are there. With this basis in shared reality, we are then willing to share her fantasy as well. In relying on equally concrete specifics (such as her detail about the perpendicular sunrise), Jennifer Bowe makes her description of Sundial's campus ring almost true. Like Quindlen and Bowe, use specific details and concrete examples. You'll need to make your vision appear tangible, as if it really could exist.

The ending of Bowe's paper, too, works well. It pushes to an incredible extreme the notion of a campus built on a turntable. If we have been persuaded to accept the possibility of such a revolving campus, carried along by the writer's serious discussion of novel teaching methods, the ending takes us by surprise. Perhaps we laugh, feeling as though a rug has been yanked out from under us.

Often imaginative writing appeals to the mind's eye. For some accessible picture-filled writing, see the sports pages of a daily newspaper. Sports writer Bugs Baer once wrote of fireball pitcher Lefty Grove: "He could throw a lambchop past a wolf." Dan Shaughnessy in the *Boston Globe* described pitcher Roger Clemens: "Watching the Mariners try to hit Clemens was like watching a stack of waste paper dive into a shredder." Such language isn't mere decoration: it points to a truth and puts vivid pictures in the reader's "mind's eye." (For more about writing with *images*—language that evokes sense experiences, not always sight—look back over pp. 42–43.)

Imagination isn't a constant flame: sometimes it flickers and wavers. If in shaping your draft you get stuck and words don't flow, you may find it helpful to shift your perspective. Try imagining the past, present, or future *as if you were somebody else.* Perhaps you will then see fresh possibilities in your topic. Also helpful may be what all writers do now and then: take a walk, relax, do something else for a while. Then return to your draft and try to look at it with a *reader's* eyes.

Revising and Editing

As Jennifer Bowe reread her first draft, which she had typed, she thought of additional details: the scholarly bums who wander around provoking intellectual conversation, the Sundialburger with the onion casting a shadow. She added these details in pen, later incorporating them into her final version. Do you need more detail in places to make your vision clear and convincing? Then make yourself comfortable and do some more imagining.

In beginning to write her essay on Sundial College, Jennifer Bowe reported that her hardest problem was to introduce "the basically wacky idea" of a campus built on a turntable. "I didn't know how I'd ever get anybody to believe in that campus," she said, "so I tried to describe it in detail, keeping a straight face." She had to try several times before she achieved a result that pleased her. Here is an earlier draft of that troublesome paragraph.

When you   *for the first time, you*
~~Anyone who~~ visits the Sundial campus ∧notices something strange. ⸤Sundial College takes its name from its⸥
which is as
design∧ unique as its educational philosophy // ~~so~~ The posi-
for
tion of the sun never changes; At the hub of the campus

Good way to end the ¶!
wheel is a great sundial--fixed, keeping faithful time.
rests   *an enormous*   *rotates*
The whole campus ~~rotates~~ on ~~a big~~ disk that ~~moves~~ with
the sun, almost imperceptibly, so that the sun always
shines down on the college from the same direction. This

Reverse these two sentences.
odd design is not merely an advertising gimmick to make
the college sound unique; it is quite practical. Rather
than rising in the east and setting in the west, the sun
appears to rise straight up and set straight down again.

Classrooms are built to receive maximum sunlight at all times, thus saving in
~~The~~ heating costs ~~saved are~~ more than enough to pay for
running the giant motor that turns the campus. Students
reading on the lawn do not need to keep moving their
blankets to stay in the sun or the shade. Greenhouses
stay sunny   *Night Owl Hall, the dorm for people*
~~are in the sun~~ all day long. ~~and the dorm for anyone who~~
who like to stay up late,
~~likes to stay up late~~ has its back to the sun, so that
will   *no*
its late sleepers ~~don't~~ receive ∧unwanted morning light.
Lark Hall,   *with the*
~~There's also a hall~~ for early risers, ~~that~~ lights up∧ *dawn.*

Doesn't belong in this ¶
~~early.~~ Although the campus stays fixed in its place in
the sun, it is always in a whirl of exciting activity.

Jennifer Bowe could see that, to seem convincing to her readers, the paragraph needed reorganizing; and some details had to be more specific. Giving names to the dorms helped. The last sentence clearly introduced a whole new direction. Eventually it began paragraph 7. The sentence about the astronomy department was a later addition in the final essay, inspired by a peer reader's objection that Bowe's campus would play havoc with the study of astronomy.

Ask a classmate to let you know if he or she has any doubts about what you've written. Here is a list of questions for your peer reader to answer.

PEER EDITING CHECKLIST: WRITING FROM IMAGINATION

- What is your overall reaction to the paper?
- What do you like best about the writer's "What if" thinking?
- What did you find hardest to follow or imagine or accept? Is it difficult because of the ideas themselves or the way the writer presents them or both? List your problems with the "What if's" and explain why they are problems by asking the writer questions about them.
- Could what the writer imagines possibly exist? Where should he or she add any details, examples, description, or images to make it seem more possible? Put stars on the manuscript where the writer needs to make the ideas more plausible by being more specific.
- Look at the way the writer has arranged the materials. Would you make any changes in organization?
- Can you suggest any other effects of the writer's "What if" thinking?
- Circle on the manuscript any word choice that particularly obstructs your understanding of the essay.
- Put a check mark by any spelling, verb tense, grammar, or punctuation that needs attention.
- If you were handing in this paper for evaluation, what would you be certain to work further on?

A minor problem in envisioning may be to keep your verb tenses straight. As she imagined her ideal college, Jennifer Bowe found herself waffling between the future tense ("you *will notice* something strange") and the conditional ("the huge disk of Sundial College *would accelerate*"). Aware of this problem, she went through her draft and changed all tenses to the present. She had hit upon the simplest solution. In envisioning your imaginary world, why not hold it in the mind's eye as though it now exists?

The belief of poet William Butler Yeats that inspiration can come in rewriting as well as in writing may hold true when you write your "What if" paper. As you revise, you may find fresh and imaginative ideas occurring for the first time. If they occur, by all means let them in.

While you review your paper, you might consider the following points.

REVISION CHECKLIST: WRITING FROM IMAGINATION

- Is your vision consistent? Do all the parts of your vision get along with all the others? Or is some part discordant, needing to be cut out?
- Does your paper at any point need more information about the real world? If so, where might you find it: what can you read, whom can you talk with, what can you observe?
- Have you used any facts that need verifying, any words that need checking?

(Jennifer Bowe recalls: "I was glad about finding the right name for the upright hand in the middle of a sundial—the *gnomon*. I didn't know what to call it until I looked up *sundial* in my dictionary and found a picture of a typical sundial, with the names of its parts.")

✔ What difficulties did you run into in writing your "What if"? Did you overcome them? Are any still present that bother you? If so, what can you do about them? If you can't come up with solutions, ask your instructor or classmates to help you.

✔ Is your vision plausible? Could the world you imagine possibly exist? What physical details, vivid description, images, and illustrations can you add that will help make your vision seem real?

Other Assignments

1. Like Jennifer Bowe, author of "If I Could Found a College," imagine an ideal: a person, place, or thing that to your mind would be virtually perfect. Shape this ideal to your own desires. Then put it in writing. Perhaps this ideal might combine the best features of two or three real people, places, or things. Set forth your vision in writing as if you are trying to be useful to someone attempting to achieve something excellent for a practical reason: to improve himself or herself, to build a new town or city or college from the ground up.

   If, like Bowe, you envision your ideal college, you will have a decision to make early. Will you imagine a college as conceivably it could exist today (if you too had several billion dollars)? Or will you imagine a college of the future, which could be more nearly perfect (utilizing what science has not yet discovered)? If your ideal could exist only in the future, will you imagine the near future (say, 2000 A.D.) or a more remote future?

   In describing your ideal person, city, or college, you may be tempted to build up to a surprise ending. It might seem a great trick to reveal at the end (surprise, surprise!) that your ideal city is really good old Topeka, the best place on earth, or that your ideal mother is really your own real-life mother after all. But it probably won't be a convincing way to write your paper. Nothing that exists is ideal. Simply to describe what exists won't take any imagining.

2. Imagine two alternative versions of your own future, say, ten years down the road: the worst possible future you could have and the best possible. Describe each in detail. This assignment may help you in making long-term plans. (If you would prefer not to limit your vision to your own future, imagine the future of your hometown or city, your region, or your country, perhaps taking one current problem, such as violence or drug abuse, to a logical conclusion.)

3. Recall the way you envisioned something before you experienced it; then describe the reality you found instead. For instance: "My Dream of College and the Reality," "The London I Expected and the London I Found," "A Madonna Concert I Looked Forward To and What I Got." Your expectations, of course, might be good or bad; the reality might be a disappointment or a pleasant surprise. But if possible, pick some topic about which your ideas changed drastically. Write to show your fellow students how your mental picture changed. They might be interested because their mental pictures might coincide with yours (before or after your change).

4. Draw a connection between two things you hadn't ever thought of connecting before. Start with something that interests you — running, moviegoing, sports cars — and try relating it to something remote from it, running to writing or cars to clothes. See what both have in common and explain their similarity in two or three paragraphs: "The Pleasures of Running in Rain," "Moviegoing: Traveling Vicariously," "Sports Car Buffs as Grown-up Players with Toys," or whatever more appealing topic you can generate.

5. Try your hand at a short story, perhaps science fiction or historical fiction. Create an imaginary world different from the one we live in.

6. Imagine you are an endangered animal or bird.

7. Write your own "I Have a Dream" essay similar to Dr. Martin Luther King, Jr.'s speech quoted on page 116.

8. Here are a few short exercises designed to limber your imagination. Do them in your journal.

   a.   By penciling a big *X,* divide a sheet of paper into quarters. In each quarter draw a person, a bird, an animal, a fanciful monster, a machine, or anything else you wish. Diversify the drawings: don't draw birds in all four squares; mix up your subject matter. A wildly assorted mixture will work well for this. The drawings, which can be comic or serious or both, don't need to be of museum quality; they are only for your own use. When you are done, contemplate your four drawings. Then write a one-page story that brings all four subjects together.

   b.   Envision the place where you lived for the largest part of your life. Then visualize how it would have looked a hundred years ago or (if you like) how it will look a hundred years from now. Write a passage or paragraph rapidly, setting down any details you can see in your mind's eye.

   c.   Divide a sheet of paper into two columns. Write in the left column the names of a list of objects that (for no special reason) please you, intrigue you, or make you laugh. You might make this list from both memory and immediate observation — by just looking around. Then in the right column, for each object complete a sentence that makes a metaphor. For instance, one such list might begin:

   > An ant carrying something
   > My poodle
   > A sailboat
   > Althea's elbows

   Write rapidly, without trying to be brilliant. Compare each object with another object far removed from it, but in which you can find some similarity. The list might then give rise to metaphors such as these:

   > An ant carrying something is a piano mover.
   > My poodle is a barking marshmallow.
   > A sailboat is a bird with one wing.
   > Althea's elbows are a couple of unripe strawberries.

   Not all your metaphors will be worth keeping; not all will make sense to anyone else. You have to expect some kernels not to pop. But if you get any metaphors you like, why not share them with the class? (Metaphors like these, incidentally, are sometimes poems in their infancy. If any metaphor turns you on, by all means keep writing — whether in prose or in verse.)

d. Here is an exercise involving wordplay and other free play of the imagination. Choose a noun with interesting sounds or suggestions, a word or phrase you don't use daily: *luminosity, tyrannosaur, potato mashers, chromosome, platypus,* or perhaps a name such as *Amazon, Peter Ilyich Tchaikovsky.* Then rapidly write a series of statements, each beginning with that word or phrase. The statements need not follow logically or tell a story. Example:

> Peter Ilyich Tchaikovsky was always too shy to ask the prom queen for a date.
> Peter Ilyich Tchaikovsky attempted to fly by flapping his arms but usually fell on his face.
> Peter Ilyich Tchaikovsky couldn't cross the Delaware standing up in a row-boat like George Washington — the Delaware was always frozen and the rowboat leaked.

So far, without deliberate effort on the writer's part, connections are emerging: Peter Ilyich Tchaikovsky is becoming a distinctive and consistent character. That is how the imagination often operates. Our example may be absurd, but it exhibits a truth. "Language," says teacher and researcher Ann Berthoff, "enables us to make the meanings by whose means we discover further meanings."

APPLYING WHAT YOU LEARN: SOME USES OF WRITING FROM IMAGINATION

Imagination, we have suggested, is tremendously useful in much college writing, not only in a creative writing course. In scholarly writing, imagination is essential — as scholarly writers keep insisting. French philosopher of history Paul Veyne points out that a historian has to infer the motives of persons long dead. Understanding the past, Veyne argues, is often a matter of imaginatively "filling in" what cannot be completely documented. In the field of geography,

FOR GROUP LEARNING

Like Jennifer Bowe, who brainstormed with three friends before she wrote "If I Could Found a College," try a brainstorming session with your writing group to generate ideas for your own paper. When you do this as a group, appoint a recording secretary to set down ideas as fast as they can be transcribed. If possible, meet in an unused classroom or conference room with plenty of chalkboard space so that all present can see the ideas in the act of being recorded. Don't be surprised if this activity seems wild and chaotic; order can emerge from it. Limit your initial brainstorming session to ten or twelve minutes; then stop to discuss the results, circling on the chalkboard any items that draw strong reactions from the group. These may be the seeds that will grow a memorable paper. If nothing much comes out of this first session, brainstorm again. (For further advice on how to brainstorm, see p. 303.)

according to Robert W. Durrenberger in *Geographical Research and Writing,* a student who wishes to do research needs most of all to develop imagination. "Admittedly, an individual cannot be taught how to be creative," Durrenberger concedes. "But he can observe those who are creative and be on the lookout for new and original approaches to the solutions of problems."

To show you how you can usefully apply the ways of imagining to your writing in college and beyond, let's consider them one at a time: shifting perspective, envisioning, and synthesizing.

Shifting perspective The next time you are given an assignment in another course, try looking at the entire topic through someone else's eyes — someone unlike yourself. This way of imagining is often at work in specialized and professional writing. Philosophers and science writers challenge us, as Dr. Peter Saltzstein of Northeast Missouri State University puts it, to "step outside of received opinion or commonly held beliefs and examine those beliefs through the use of alternative perspectives." Thus John Locke, in his *Second Treatise of Government,* calls on his readers to imagine a world owned by all individuals in common, without private ownership. And science writer Garrett Hardin takes a skeptical look at some prevalent popular assumptions. In the following passage from *Naked Emperors: Essays of a Taboo-Stalker,* Hardin shifts perspectives. He imagines that an economist asks an ecologist, "Would you plant a redwood tree in your back yard?" When the ecologist says that he would, the economist charges him with being a fool — in economic terms.

> The economist is right, of course. The supporting economic analysis is easily carried out. A redwood tree can hardly be planted for less than a dollar. To mature [it] takes some two thousand years, by which time the tree will be about three hundred feet high. How much is the tree worth then? An economist will insist, of course, on evaluating the forest giant as lumber. Measured at a man's height above the ground, the diameter of the tree will be about ten feet, and the shape of the shaft from there upward is approximately conical. The volume of this cone is 94,248 board feet. At a "stumpage" price of 15¢ a board foot — the approximate price a lumberer must pay for a tree unfelled, unmilled, untransported — the tree would be worth some $14,000.
>
> That may sound like a large return on an investment of only one dollar, but we must not forget how long the investment took to mature: 2000 years. Using the exponential formula to calculate the rate of compound interest we find that the capital earned slightly less than one-half of 1 percent per year. Yes, a man would be an economic fool to put his money into a redwood seedling when so many profitable opportunities lie at hand.

Hardin, of course, is being unfair to economists, many of whom are undoubtedly capable of feeling awe before a giant redwood. But his momentary shift to the strict dollars-and-cents point of view enables him to conclude that, if we care for the future and for our descendants, we sometimes need to act without regard for economics.

Envisioning Some challenging assignments you'll meet in a college course will set forth a problem and ask you to envision a solution. The following question, from a final examination in an economics course, asks the student to imagine a better procedure:

> As we have seen, methods of stabilizing the dollar have depended on enlisting the cooperation of large banks and foreign governments, which has not always been forthcoming. Propose a better, alternative way for our own government to follow in protecting the value of its currency from severe fluctuations.

An effective answer to that question would be based on facts that the student has learned. What the exam question tries to provide is not just practice in recalling facts but also training in bringing them together and applying them.

Students in family science courses may be asked to envision ideal situations, play devil's advocate, even take a stand in opposition to their own when learning to debate issues informatively. In envisioning an ideal, as Jennifer Bowe does in her Sundial College paper, a writer sets up an imagined goal and perhaps also begins thinking about how to achieve it. In his epoch-making speech in Washington, D.C., on the 1963 centennial of Lincoln's Emancipation Proclamation, Martin Luther King, Jr., set forth his vision of an unsegregated future:

> I have a dream that one day on the red hills of Georgia the sons of former slaves and the sons of former slave owners will be able to sit down together at the table of brotherhood. . . . I have a dream that my four little children will one day live in a nation where they will not be judged by the color of their skin but by the content of their character.

Synthesizing   Combining unlike things and drawing unexpected conclusions may result in a lively and revealing paper. But in explaining almost anything, an imaginative writer can make metaphors and draw connections. Sylvan Barnet, in *A Short Guide to Writing about Art* (Boston: Little, 1989), questions whether a period of art can be entirely "Gothic" in spirit. To make a highly abstract idea clear, he introduces a brief *analogy,* a metaphor that likens the unfamiliar thing to something familiar:

> Is there really an all-embracing style in a given period? One can be skeptical, and a simple analogy may be useful. A family often consists of radically different personalities: improvident husband, patient wife, one son an idler and the other a go-getter, one daughter wise in her choice of a career and the other daughter unwise. And yet all may have come from the same culture.

To be sure, imagining has practical applications beyond the writing of college papers and scholarly articles. Asked why World War I took place, Franz Kafka, one of the most influential writers of our century, gave a memorable explanation: the war was caused by a "monstrous lack of imagination." Evidently if we are to survive, we would do well to imagine both World War III and its alternatives — not only the consequences of the problems we now face, but also the solutions.

Further Applications

Imagination can be the fount of powerful nonfiction. Various writers in *A Writer's Reader* effectively use this resource to convey their ideas and enhance their stands. Alice Walker, a novelist who has long been concerned about environmental problems, uses imagination to convey her concern about the future of our planet in "When a Tree Falls" (p. 567). She imagines an "intense" dialogue with the trees, concluding with their message: "The earth holds us responsible for our crimes against it, not as individuals, but as a species." In "Psychic Income" (p. 537), social researcher and critic Mary Kay Blakely shows how a serious professional can effectively use imagination to enhance her criticism of current social attitudes and economic practices. She complains to a university administrator about women being paid less than men at his institution, becomes upset by his response, and then imagines — satirically — how "psychic" money could change the world.

In addition to Walker, Blakely, Anna Quindlen (p. 99), and student Jennifer Bowe (p. 101), other writers who effectively use imagination as a resource in their nonfiction include essayist E. B. White, "Once More to the Lake" (p. 425), novelist Sherwood Anderson, "The Discovery of a Father" (p. 431), writer Judy Brady, "I Want a Wife" (p. 455), professor Noel Perrin, "A Part-Time Marriage" (p. 458), and novelist Toni Morrison, "A Slow Walk of Trees" (p. 496). Answer the following questions about each of these essays.

1. What "what-if" question does the author ask? What is the author's answer to the "what-if" question?

2. How does the writer use imagination as a resource? What does it add to this piece of nonfiction?

3. How does the imagined world differ from the real world as presented in the essay?

PART TWO

THINKING CRITICALLY

C *ritic,* from the Greek word *kritikos,* means "one who can judge and discern." If college leaves you better able to judge and discern—able to tell what is more important or less important, able to make distinctions and recognize differences, able to grasp involved concepts and get to the bottom of things, able to judge and choose wisely—then it will have given you your money's worth.

This part of the book will show you five typical college writing tasks in which you think critically and fulfill a purpose: analyzing, taking a stand, proposing a solution, evaluating, and identifying causes and effects. Not all of them will be news to you. You wrote evaluations back in grade school if you ever produced book reports that ended with statements like "I would recommend this book highly to anyone interested in polar bears." So, if you find anything old and familiar in the following five chapters, don't be surprised. However, a paper you write in college will go more deeply into the subject and will set forth your reasons for the recommendation. You will be writing for a more demanding audience who may not be as easily persuaded as a high school class or teacher.

CHAPTER 6

Analyzing

Many times in college you will be asked to understand some matter that seems complicated: an earthquake, the metabolism of a cell, the Federal Reserve Bank, the Protestant Reformation. Viewed as a whole, such a subject may look intimidating. But often you can simplify your task by *analyzing* your subject: by dividing it into its parts and then dealing with it one part at a time.

Analysis is already familiar to you. If you took high school chemistry, you probably analyzed water: you separated it into hydrogen and oxygen, its two elements. You've heard many a television commentator analyze the news. Did a riot break out in Bombay? Trying to help us understand what happened, the commentator tells us what made up the event: who the protesters were, whom they protested to, what they were protesting. Analyzing a news event may produce results less certain and clear-cut than analyzing a chemical compound, but the principle is similar: to take something apart and find out what makes it up, for the purpose of understanding it better. In a college writing assignment you might analyze anything from a contemporary subculture (What social groups make up the homeless population of Los Angeles?) to an ecosystem (What animals, plants, and minerals coexist in a rain forest?).

Not only can you analyze a subject, you can analyze an action as well. You can write a *process analysis,* a step-by-step explanation. You may choose one of two types of processes:

How something happens: how an unborn infant develops, how a glacier forms, how a music box works, how the music industry builds a song into a top-40 hit. This type is an *informative* process analysis, one that shows how something takes place by dividing it into its successive stages.

How to do something: how to ski, how to conduct yourself during a job interview, how to perform the Heimlich maneuver, how to build a hang glider, how to water ski. This is a *directive* process analysis, one that gives the reader step-by-step instructions on how to do something.

Whether you analyze a process, an idea, or some other subject, you'll be thinking in a basically similar way. You'll be dividing something into its components, the more readily to make sense of it.

LEARNING FROM OTHER WRITERS

Mathematician Paul Bodanis, in *The Secret House,* revels in what a microscope reveals. Analyzing items ordinarily found in an American household, Bodanis lets his readers in on surprising trade secrets. The essay that follows is taken from Bodanis's lively and eye-opening book.

WHAT'S IN YOUR TOOTHPASTE?
Paul Bodanis

Into the bathroom goes our male resident, and after the most pressing   1
need is satisfied it's time to brush the teeth. The tube of toothpaste is squeezed, its pinched metal seams are splayed, pressure waves are generated inside, and the paste begins to flow. But what's in this toothpaste, so carefully being extruded out?

Water mostly, 30 to 45 percent in most brands: ordinary, everyday   2
simple tap water. It's there because people like to have a big gob of toothpaste to spread on the brush, and water is the cheapest stuff there is when it comes to making big gobs. Dripping a bit from the tap onto your brush would cost virtually nothing; whipped in with the rest of the toothpaste the manufacturers can sell it at a neat and accountant-pleasing $2 per pound equivalent. Toothpaste manufacture is a very lucrative occupation.

Second to water in quantity is chalk: exactly the same material that   3
schoolteachers use to write on blackboards. It is collected from the crushed remains of long-dead ocean creatures. In the Cretaceous seas chalk particles served as part of the wickedly sharp outer skeleton that these creatures had to wrap around themselves to keep from getting chomped by all the slightly larger other ocean creatures they met. Their massed graves are our present chalk deposits.

The individual chalk particles—the size of the smallest mud particles   4
in your garden—have kept their toughness over the aeons, and now on the toothbrush they'll need it. The enamel outer coating of the tooth they'll have to face is the hardest substance in the body—tougher than skull, or bone, or nail. Only the chalk particles in toothpaste can successfully grind

into the teeth during brushing, ripping off the surface layers like an abrading wheel grinding down a boulder in a quarry.

The craters, slashes, and channels that the chalk tears into the teeth 5 will also remove a certain amount of build-up yellow in the carnage, and it is for that polishing function that it's there. A certain amount of unduly enlarged extra-abrasive chalk fragments tear such cavernous pits into the teeth that future decay bacteria will be able to bunker down there and thrive; the quality control people find it almost impossible to screen out these errant super-chalk pieces, and government regulations allow them to stay in.

In case even the gouging doesn't get all the yellow off, another substance is worked into the toothpaste cream. This is titanium dioxide. It 6 comes in tiny spheres, and it's the stuff bobbing around in white wall paint to make it come out white. Splashed around onto your teeth during the brushing it coats much of the yellow that remains. Being water soluble it leaks off in the next few hours and is swallowed, but at least for the quick glance up in the mirror after finishing it will make the user think his teeth are truly white. Some manufacturers add optical whitening dyes—the stuff more commonly found in washing machine bleach—to make extra sure that that glance in the mirror shows reassuring white.

These ingredients alone would not make a very attractive concoction. 7 They would stick in the tube like a sloppy white plastic lump, hard to squeeze out as well as revolting to the touch. Few consumers would savor rubbing in a mixture of water, ground-up blackboard chalk, and the whitener from latex paint first thing in the morning. To get around that finicky distaste the manufacturers have mixed in a host of other goodies.

To keep the glop from drying out, a mixture including glycerine glycol— 8 related to the most common car antifreeze ingredient—is whipped in with the chalk and water, and to give *that* concoction a bit of substance (all we really have so far is wet colored chalk) a large helping is added of gummy molecules from the seaweed *Chondrus Crispus*. This seaweed ooze spreads in among the chalk, paint, and antifreeze, then stretches itself in all directions to hold the whole mass together. A bit of paraffin oil (the fuel that flickers in camping lamps) is pumped in with it to help the moss ooze keep the whole substance smooth.

With the glycol, ooze, and paraffin we're almost there. Only two major 9 chemicals are left to make the refreshing, cleansing substance we know as toothpaste. The ingredients so far are fine for cleaning, but they wouldn't make much of the satisfying foam we have come to expect in the morning brushing.

To remedy that every toothpaste on the market has a big dollop of 10 detergent added too. You've seen the suds detergent will make in a washing machine. The same substance added here will duplicate that inside the mouth. It's not particularly necessary, but it sells.

The only problem is that by itself this ingredient tastes, well, too like 11 detergent. It's horribly bitter and harsh. The chalk put in toothpaste is pretty foul-tasting too for that matter. It's to get around that gustatory discomfort that the manufacturers put in the ingredient they tout perhaps the most of all. This is the flavoring, and it has to be strong. Double rectified peppermint oil is used — a flavorer so powerful that chemists know better than to sniff it in the raw state in the laboratory. Menthol crystals and saccharin or other sugar simulators are added to complete the camouflage operation.

Is that it? Chalk, water, paint, seaweed, antifreeze, paraffin oil, deter-   12
gent, and peppermint? Not quite. A mix like that would be irresistible to the hundreds of thousands of individual bacteria lying on the surface of even an immaculately cleaned bathroom sink. They would get in, float in the water bubbles, ingest the ooze and paraffin, maybe even spray out enzymes to break down the chalk. The result would be an uninviting mess. The way manufacturers avoid that final obstacle is by putting something in to kill the bacteria. Something good and strong is needed, something that will zap any accidentally intrudant bacteria into oblivion. And that some-thing is formaldehyde — the disinfectant used in anatomy labs.

So it's chalk, water, paint, seaweed, antifreeze, paraffin oil, detergent,   13
peppermint, formaldehyde, and fluoride (which can go some way towards preserving children's teeth) — that's the usual mixture raised to the mouth on the toothbrush for a fresh morning's clean. If it sounds too unfortunate, take heart. Studies show that thorough brushing with just plain water will often do as good a job.

Questions to Start You Thinking

1. What is the tone of Bodanis's essay? What does the essay gain from the author's use of this tone?
2. What is the author's main point?
3. Does your toothpaste tube list ingredients?
4. What is the author's apparent purpose? Is it more than just analyzing the ingre-dients in toothpaste? Does he address any particular audience?
5. Why does Bodanis discuss the elements of toothpaste in the order he does?

Linnea Saukko was a trained environmentalist working toward a degree in geology when she wrote this prizewinning essay for her first-year compo-sition class at Ohio State University in 1983.

Student Essay

HOW TO POISON THE EARTH
Linnea Saukko

Poisoning the earth can be difficult because the earth   1
is always trying to cleanse and renew itself. Keeping this

in mind, we should generate as much waste as possible from
substances such as uranium-238, which has a half-life (the
time it takes for half of the substance to decay) of one million years, or plutonium, which has a half-life of only 0.5
million years but is so toxic that if distributed evenly, ten
pounds of it could kill every person on the earth. Because
the United States generates about eighteen tons of plutonium
per year, it is about the best substance for long-term poisoning of the earth. It would help if we would build more
nuclear power plants because each one generates only 500
pounds of plutonium each year. Of course, we must include
persistent toxic chemicals such as polychlorinated biphenyl
(PCB) and dichlorodiphenyl trichloroethane (DDT) to make sure
we have enough toxins to poison the earth from the core to
the outer atmosphere. First, we must develop many different
ways of putting the waste from these nuclear and chemical
substances in, on, and around the earth.

     Putting these substances in the earth is a most impor-   2
tant step in the poisoning process. With deep-well injection
we can ensure that the earth is poisoned all the way to the
core. Deep-well injection involves drilling a hole that is
a few thousand feet deep and injecting toxic substances at
extremely high pressures so they will penetrate deep into
the earth. According to the Environmental Protection Agency
(EPA), there are about 360 such deep injection wells in the
United States. We cannot forget the groundwater aquifers
that are closer to the surface. These must also be contaminated. This is easily done by shallow-well injection, which
operates on the same principle as deep-well injection, only
closer to the surface. The groundwater that has been in-
jected with toxins will spread the contamination beneath
the earth. The EPA estimates that there are approximately
500,000 shallow injection wells in the United States.

     Burying the toxins in the earth is the next best method. 3
The toxins from landfills, dumps, and lagoons slowly seep
into the earth, guaranteeing that contamination will last a
long time. Because the EPA estimates there are only about

50,000 of these dumps in the United States, they should be located in areas where they will leak to the surrounding ground and surface water.

Applying pesticides and other poisons on the earth is another part of the poisoning process. This is good for coating the earth's surface so that the poisons will be absorbed by plants, will seep into the ground, and will run off into surface water.

4

Surface water is very important to contaminate because it will transport the poisons to places that cannot be contaminated directly. Lakes are good for long-term storage of pollutants while they release some of their contamination to rivers. The only trouble with rivers is that they act as a natural cleansing system for the earth. No matter how much poison is dumped into them, they will try to transport it away to reach the ocean eventually.

5

The ocean is very hard to contaminate because it has such a large volume and a natural buffering capacity that tends to neutralize some of the contamination. So in addition to the pollution from rivers, we must use the ocean as a dumping place for as many toxins as possible. The ocean currents will help transport the pollution to places that cannot otherwise be reached.

6

Now make sure that the air around the earth is very polluted. Combustion and evaporation are major mechanisms for doing this. We must continuously pollute because the wind will disperse the toxins while rain washes them from the air. But this is good because a few lakes are stripped of all living animals each year from acid rain. Because the lower atmosphere can cleanse itself fairly easily, we must explode nuclear test bombs that shoot radioactive particles high into the upper atmosphere where they will circle the earth for years. Gravity must pull some of the particles to earth, so we must continue exploding these bombs.

7

So it is that easy. Just be sure to generate as many poisonous substances as possible and be sure they are distributed in, on, and around the entire earth at a greater

8

rate than it can cleanse itself. By following these easy
steps we can guarantee the poisoning of the earth.

Questions to Start You Thinking

1. Where in the essay do you first realize that Saukko is not serious, that she is in fact being ironic (saying the opposite of what she means)?
2. Would her essay be as effective if it were straightforward instead of tongue-in-cheek? Of what, if anything, does she convince you?
3. The author organizes the ways of poisoning the earth into three parts: ways of putting poisons *in* the earth, *on* the earth, and *around* the earth. Why does she discuss poisons *in* the earth first?
4. Can you think of other ways we poison the environment?
5. Do some people treat their bodies in a similar manner? That is, do they poison their bodies? How might you write an ironic essay on how to poison your body?

LEARNING BY WRITING

The Assignment: Analyzing

Write an essay analyzing a subject *or* a process that you know well (or want to find out about). Make the process or subject clear to an audience of your classmates.

Here are instances of college writers who successfully responded to this type of assignment:

WRITERS WHO ANALYZED A SUBJECT

One student sliced the British Isles into geologic regions and assessed the mineral wealth in each.

A woman who plans a career as a consultant in time and motion study divided a typical day in the life of a college student into the segments that compose it (class time, study time, feeding time, grooming time, recreation time, social time, waste time) and suggested ways to make more efficient use of the student's time.

A student of psychology divided the human brain into its parts and described the function of each.

A speech student analyzed a piece of educational software for its assumptions about learning.

WRITERS WHO ANALYZED A PROCESS

A man who had trained to be a flight attendant explained the stages of training that an applicant goes through before receiving wings.

A woman who had worked in a clinic guided her readers through the steps by which a doctor examines a heart patient and conducts diagnostic tests.

A man wrote a step-by-step account of how a lobbyist seeks to influence a legislator.

A woman who had taken part in a summer seminar in wildlife management described, step by step, the process of banding birds to trace their patterns of migration.

A man told how to make grilled cheese sandwiches in a dorm room using an electric iron.

A woman analyzed the steps in breaking a wild horse.

Look over the preceding essay topics and discuss with your classmates the writer's purpose for each.

Generating Ideas

Your first task is to pick a topic you care about. The topics just listed may help start your own ideas flowing. Do some idle, relaxed thinking, with pencil and paper at hand. Or do some fast scribbling (see "Freewriting," p. 306). Try to come up with something complicated that you understand and would really like to analyze or something you would like to understand more clearly yourself (perhaps a mathematical procedure or a scientific process from one of the courses you are taking).

After you have decided on the type of analysis you intend to do — subject analysis or process analysis — and have chosen your topic (two decisions that are interwoven, by the way), follow the suggestions for subject analysis beginning on this page or for process analysis (p. 131) to complete your assignment.

Planning, Drafting, and Developing a Subject Analysis

Right away, decide on the principle you will follow in your analysis. Just as you can slice a carrot in many ways, you can find many ways to analyze a subject. You might divide your home state into geographic regions, or you might divide it on the basis of different patterns of speech heard in various areas. Before you begin, determine your reason for analyzing. What do you hope to demonstrate? If, for instance, you plan to write an analysis of New York City for the purpose of showing its ethnic composition, you might work through the city, dividing it into neighborhoods — Harlem, Spanish Harlem, Yorkville, Chinatown, Little Italy.

Ask yourself the following questions before you write.

DISCOVERY CHECKLIST: FOCUSING ON YOUR TASK

- Have you found a subject that interests you and that seems worthwhile to analyze?
- Is your basis — the principle you will follow in your analysis — clear to you, so that you can make it clear to your readers?

- In thinking about your essay, have you left out any obvious parts that a reader might expect to find? Some readers might object to an analysis dividing pop music into rap, rock, and jazz fusion on the grounds that it has a few holes.
- If you omitted some parts purposefully, what is your basis of selection?
- Exactly what will you be trying to achieve in your essay? Make sure before you begin that your analysis has a purpose: that it will demonstrate something or tell your readers something they didn't know before. Have a reason for analyzing.
- What is your principle of organization?

Many college assignments call for analysis, and a paper that analyzes a subject often turns out to be among the best essays that a college student writes. The secret is to care about what you say and to organize your essay so that it won't look (and read) like a lifeless stack of blocks. It is crucial to organize your material in some logical, easy-to-follow order. Some kind of outline—whether extremely detailed or rough—will save you time and avoid confusion.

The outline for a subject analysis might be a pielike circle with the slices labeled. If you make the size of the slices correspond to their relative importance, the sketch might give you some notion of how much time to spend

Pie outline of a radio station's broadcast day.

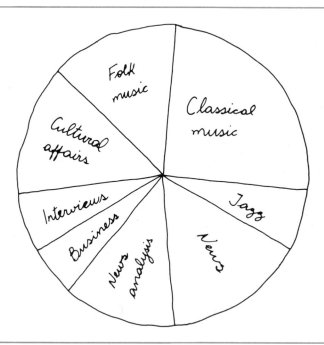

explaining each part. The pie outline for a paper analyzing the parts of a radio station's twenty-four-hour broadcast day might look like the illustration on page 129. Another way to plan your paper is to arrange your divisions from smallest to largest or from least important to most important — or any other order that makes sense to you.

Some writers like to start a subject analysis by telling their readers the divisions into which they are going to slice their subject ("A typical political party has these components..." or "The federal government has three branches"). Julius Caesar opens his *Commentaries on the Gallic War* with a famous division: "All Gaul is divided into three parts." That is one clear-cut way to go. Indicate the divisions and subdivisions in your writing so that your readers won't get lost. If you haven't already done so, invent a name or label for each part you mention to distinguish it from all the others. This device will help you keep your material clearly in mind and also help your readers keep the divisions straight. As you draft your essay, provide definitions of unfamiliar words, explain anything your readers may misunderstand, and clarify with examples.

Revising and Editing a Subject Analysis

As you revise, you'll find it useful to concentrate on making sure that your essay is meaty enough. If you find places that are thin, expand them with details and examples.

How can you make sure that your reader will be able to follow your thinking as you analyze? You can make your essay as readable as possible by using transitions, those valuable words and phrases that introduce and connect ideas. (See "Transitions," p. 354.)

If, on rereading your paper you find any sentence that now strikes you as awkward or murky, perhaps it needs a second try, or perhaps you can do without it altogether.

Once you have a legible draft, call on the services of a trustworthy peer editor. Ask him or her to answer the following questions.

PEER EDITING CHECKLIST: ANALYZING A SUBJECT

- Describe your first reaction to the paper.
- What seems to be the writer's purpose in this essay?
- Restate the writer's divisions by drawing a pie and labeling each slice. Are any of the slices disproportionate in size? Is it clear why the writer makes one slice larger or smaller?
- If the writer subdivided, has she or he clearly situated the subdivisions within the larger division? Tell the writer where he or she needs to be clearer.
- Circle on the manuscript any problems you find in spelling, grammar, word choice, or punctuation.

Once you have your peer editor's assessment in hand, go over your paper carefully, making every effort to incorporate his or her suggestions. Depending on how accurately or inaccurately your reader has seen your purpose, you'll want to accept more suggestions — or fewer. Then, as you prepare to write your final draft, ask *yourself* the following questions. Until you can answer them all to your complete satisfaction, you probably still have more work to do on your analysis.

REVISION CHECKLIST: ANALYZING A SUBJECT

- Does your introduction engage the reader?
- Have you explained each part completely enough that a reader will understand it?
- Have you shown how each part functions, how it relates to the whole?
- Have you made clear your basis for dividing — the principle on which you sliced?
- Do you give your audience a sense of having beheld the subject as a whole? Perhaps your concluding paragraph affords you a chance to bring all the separate parts back together and affirm what your dividing has explained.
- Is the purpose of your analysis clear?
- In your conclusion, do you show your readers that all this work has taught them something?

Planning, Drafting, and Developing a Process Analysis

What process will you analyze? It may be that at work, in the library, in a laboratory, or in a classroom, you have experienced, read about, or observed something done or something happening. If that is the case, you're an expert right now; you're well equipped to write. But if a workable idea doesn't spring to mind, drum up ideas by asking yourself a few questions.

DISCOVERY CHECKLIST: ANALYZING A PROCESS

- What processes are you already familiar with?
- Which ones might you observe?
- Which ones have you read about or would you like to read about?
- From among your friends (perhaps including your instructors), whose expertise can you tap?
- What processes can you imagine happening, say, in the future?
- What processes have you learned about in classes other than English? Has anyone in your family or among your friends ever asked you to explain one of them?
- Is there a process you've wondered about but have never had the time to investigate thoroughly? Can you do so now?

Brainstorm. For a start, do a little brainstorming. Jot down a list of titles that you think you could develop into essays worth reading. For an *informative* process analysis (explaining how something happens), possible topics might be "How a Hospital Emergency Room Responds to an Accident Case," "How a Large Telescope Functions," "How Glaciers Are Formed," "How an Artist Draws a Portrait," "What Would Have Happened if Halley's Comet Had Struck the Earth." (We'll get to the directive or "how to" kind of paper in a moment. For more suggestions on brainstorming, or rapidly listing ideas, see p. 303.)

What you include on such a list of topics will depend, of course, on what you know or can find out. At this point, though, you don't have to know every detail. It's always possible, at any stage, to fill in the gaps in your knowledge by reading, talking with experts, or, if possible, observing the process. What you need to do at first is just choose a couple of paths for your thoughts to follow and eventually narrow your choices to one.

If your expertise involves a skill that you can teach your readers, you can write a *directive,* or "how-to," process analysis. Do you know how to identify crystals with a microscope, navigate a sailboat, create graphs with a computer, teach someone how to drive, film a documentary, recognize the composer of a piece of chamber music, identify constellations? You'll find readers eager to learn those skills and many more. What process do you know most about? A list of possible topics might include "How to Renovate an Old House," "How to Choose Spreadsheet Software for a Small Business," "How to Record a Rock Group," "How to Train for Distance Running," "How to Silkscreen a Poster," "How to Recognize a Fourteenth-Century Italian Painting," "How to Repossess a Car."

Remember your readers. After you decide on a topic, keep asking questions about it. Is there background information your readers will need to understand the process? List any such information. Learn to anticipate questions readers will ask.

If you're writing a "how to" essay, do you know any trade secrets that will make what you're teaching easier for your readers to master? Jot them down.

What preliminary steps, if any, will the readers need to take to follow your directions? ("Sharpen a pair of shears. . . .") What materials are called for? List them: "a fifty-foot roll of sailcloth; a yardstick or measuring tape; one twelve-foot pine trunk at least twenty-four inches thick, trimmed of branches." Any ideas or information, however small, that you can put on paper now, as you discover and plan, you will be thankful for later.

If you have done enough thinking about your process analysis as you generated ideas, you'll have greatly lightened your next task: shaping, or mapping out the steps or stages in the process you are going to explain. You'll find a list of steps useful even if you're going to write just one paragraph.

Plot your paper. Let's say you are writing an *informative* process analysis. Into what stages will you divide the process? Make a list. In what order do these stages generally occur?

If you're writing a *directive* or "how to" analysis, what steps will your readers have to master to succeed in learning the skill? In what order do they need to perform those steps? Are any of the steps divided into subdivisions?

For either kind of process analysis, zero in on any parts that threaten to be complicated. Which stages or steps will take the most explaining? Underline or star these. This device will remind you, when you write your draft, to slow down and cover that stage or step with special care.

Arrange all the stages or steps in chronological order. This will be easy if you're writing a "how to" essay, perhaps harder if you're writing an informative paper about an event in which everything seems to happen at once, say, how a tornado strikes. If you cannot explain your subject step by step, try explaining it part by part — the tornado's action observed at its center, its action observed at its edge — until you have covered everything necessary to make the process understandable.

Review your list once more, making sure you've included every small stage or step necessary. Now your list of steps or stages can serve as an outline.

As you write your draft, concentrate on including every possible step in the process you're analyzing, even if it seems obvious. It's better at this point to put in too much detail than to put in too little. Later you can cross out what seems superfluous. Always keep in mind that what you're saying is probably news to your readers.

In drafting your paper, you may discover you have omitted a step. If so, put it in. Or you may realize two stages are really one. If so, collapse them. Include enough specific detail to make each part crystal clear to your readers, so that they will know exactly what occurs when and how. Help your readers follow the steps in your analysis by putting in *time markers*: words and phrases like *then, next, soon, after, while, first, a year, later, in two hours, by the following day, during the second week, as yet, at the same time, at present.* By making clear exactly when some action occurs relative to other actions, time markers serve as signposts to keep your readers from getting lost in a forest of details. You needn't overload your writing with time markers. Use

---

WRITING WITH A COMPUTER: ANALYZING A PROCESS

When you use *time markers*, you can set up your computer to help you determine whether your paper needs more of them.

Go through your draft and highlight any time markers in **boldface**, CAPITALS, or whatever form of highlighting your program allows. This will make them stand out. How frequently do you remember to use them? If you find no time markers at all, you could use some; if you find fewer than one or two in a hundred words, then you could probably use more. Word processing will let you drop these valuable transitions right into place. Remove all the highlighting, of course, before printing out your finished paper.

just enough so that the steps in the process will be clear. Not every sentence needs a time marker, and you'll want to avoid repeating the same ones too often ("After the seventh day . . . ," "After the eighth day . . ."). Vary them, use them with care, and they will keep your readers with you every step of the way through even the most complicated processes.

Revising and Editing a Process Analysis

Reread your draft in a picky, hard-to-please way. Put yourself in the place of a dim-bulb reader who can't follow any process without the writer leading him or her by the hand. This shift in perspective will help you notice any places where you (as a reader) need more help. Because your purpose is to provide your readers with information or a new skill that they will find truly valuable, now is a good time to see whether another person can understand your paper as well as you can. Enlist the services of a peer editor. Ask her or him to answer the following questions.

PEER EDITING CHECKLIST: ANALYZING A PROCESS

- Describe your first response to the essay.
- Do you think you understand this process well enough to explain it to someone else? If not, what questions do you have about the process?
- Even if the writer is analyzing a process that you didn't think you had any interest in, has she or he captured your interest? Underline any passages where the writer has failed to do so.
- Does the writer need to clarify any directions? Do you need any additional information? Put stars on the manuscript where you need more direction or help.
- Has the writer arranged the stages of the process in the clearest and most logical way that you can imagine? List any changes you would recommend.
- Do you have any trouble with the writer's word choice?
- Circle on the essay any problems with use of personal pronouns, tense, spelling, or punctuation that make this paper hard to read or follow.

Check your paper for inconsistencies of person. Process analysis tempts writers to switch from *I* to *one* to *you* without reason. If you used *I* at the start of your paper, make sure you've used it throughout.

Too heavy use of the passive voice ("It is known that . . .") is another pit that process analysis can fall into. Look for such constructions, and when you find any, change them to the active voice ("We all know that . . ."). An occasional passive is inevitable, but too many rob your writing of life. The exception to this advice occurs in scientific writing, where an objective tone is required and may be achieved with the use of the passive voice.

Look too for language that might give your reader difficulty. Circle any specialized or technical words. Do they need defining?

Here are a few more questions to ask yourself while you read as a hard-to-please reader.

REVISION CHECKLIST: ANALYZING A PROCESS

- Is the nature of the process clear: what will it lead to, what will it accomplish?
- Have you put your steps or stages in the most logical order possible?
- If your process includes a number of smaller steps or stages, have you left any out?
- Wherever you have circled a technical word or specialized language, can you put your idea in any simpler terms?
- Have you included enough time markers so that your readers can easily follow the steps in the process you have analyzed?
- If you're writing a directive paper, is there any moment in the process when things are likely to go wrong? Can you alert your reader to possible problems and give advice for solving them?
- Does your own interest in the knowledge you're sharing with your readers shine through? If not, what can you do to make that interest evident?

Other Assignments

1. In writing, analyze one of the following subjects by dividing it into its basic parts or elements.

    A college
    A newspaper
    A TV talk show
    A symphony orchestra
    A colony of insects, a flock of birds, a school of fish
    The human heart
    The United Nations organization
    A computer or other technological device
    A basketball, football, baseball, or hockey team
    A painting or statue
    A radio telescope
    A hospital or other institution
    An essay, short story, novel, or play
    Education
    Religion
    A family
    A marriage
    A scientific theory
    An era in history
    A child's first year
    A famous and influential idea

2. Write an informative process paper, explaining how any of the following takes place (or took place).

How a rumor starts
How a bird learns to fly
How a jury is selected
How the Grand Canyon was formed
How a cow dog does its job
How the ozone layer has been damaged by chemical agents
How someone becomes a Democrat or a Republican
How a closed-end equity mutual fund operates
How a psychiatrist diagnoses an illness
How acid rain is formed
How an expert detects an art forgery

3. Write a directive process analysis, explaining one of the following in a page or two.

How to get a job
How to do the breaststroke
How to buy a used car
How to make friends
How to save money
How to judge the effectiveness of an advertisement
How to choose an academic major
How to win an election
How to write a news story
How to overcome an addiction
How to harness solar energy to perform a useful task
How to administer the Heimlich maneuver
How to register a patent
How to take a market sampling
How to lodge a complaint with authorities *
How to prevent a certain sports injury
How to dissect a frog
How to teach a child the value of money

4. From any textbook you are currently using in another course, choose a chapter in which a process is analyzed. Psychology, geology, chemistry, physics, biology, botany, zoology, engineering, computer programming, business, nursing, and education courses are likely candidates to supply processes.

In a short paper of two or three paragraphs, including just the high points, explain the process. Your audience will be a fellow student who has not read the textbook or taken the course.

FOR GROUP LEARNING

We've all bought items we have to assemble ourselves: bicycles, stereos, can openers. Some come with instructions so confusing that even an engineer might be hard pressed to follow them. See if you can find such a set of instructions, whatever its quality. Read it aloud to your class or writing group. What makes it clear — or dense? Together, try to rewrite any puzzling instructions so that anyone may easily follow them.

This assignment is a matter of paraphrasing or "nutshelling" another writer's ideas and observations in your own words—a skill useful in many professional situations that involve writing from reading. (In a corporation, a senior executive might say, "Here, read all this stuff and write me a short report on what's in it.")

APPLYING WHAT YOU LEARN: SOME USES OF ANALYSIS

As you have no doubt seen already, many different college courses will give you an opportunity to analyze a subject. In explaining for a political science course how the power structure in Iran works, you might divide the government into its branches, explain each, and then factor in the influence of religion. In a nutrition class, you might submit an essay analyzing the components of a healthy diet. In a paper for a course on art history, you might single out each element of a Rembrandt painting: perhaps its human figures, their clothing, the background, the light.

You won't always write papers entirely devoted to analyzing. But you may often find analysis useful in writing *part* of an explanatory paper: a paragraph or a section. In the middle of his essay "Things Unflattened by Science," Lewis Thomas pauses to divide biology into three parts.

> We can imagine three worlds of biology, corresponding roughly to the three worlds of physics: the very small world now being explored by the molecular geneticists and virologists, not yet as strange a place as quantum mechanics but well on its way to strangeness; an everyday, middle-sized world where things are as they are; and a world of the very large, which is the whole affair, the lovely conjoined biosphere, the vast embryo, the closed ecosystem in which we live as working parts, the place for which Lovelock and Margulis invented the term "Gaia" because of its extraordinary capacity to regulate itself. This world seems to me an even stranger one than the world of very small things in biology: it looks like the biggest organism I've ever heard of, and at the same time the most delicate and fragile, exactly the delicate and fragile creature it appeared to be in those first photographs taken from the surface of the moon.

Analysis helps readers understand something complex: they can more readily take in the subject in a series of bites than in one gulp. For this reason, college textbooks do a lot of analyzing: an economics book divides a labor union into its component parts, an anatomy text divides the hand into the bones, muscles, and ligaments that make it up. In *Cultural Anthropology: A Perspective on the Human Condition* (1987), authors Emily A. Schultz and Robert H. Lavenda briefly but effectively demonstrate by analysis how a metaphor like "The Lord is my shepherd" makes a difficult concept ("The Lord") easy to understand.

> The first part of a metaphor, the **metaphorical subject**, indicates the domain of experience that needs to be clarified (e.g., "the Lord"). The second part of a metaphor, the **metaphorical predicate**, suggests a domain of experience which

is familiar (e.g., sheep-herding) and which may help us understand what "the Lord" is all about.

You will also find yourself from time to time being called upon to set forth an informative process analysis, tracing the steps by which something takes place: the formation of a star, a mountain, or a human embryo; the fall of Rome, the awarding of child custody in a divorce case, or the election of a president. Lab reports are good examples of such process analyses. For a marine biology course at his university, student Edward R. Parton did an experiment involving sea urchins, which he then described in a lab report. He began the "Materials and Methods" section of his report with this paragraph, which reveals how to tell a male sea urchin from a female. (Evidently this is not a problem for sea urchins, but it is one for biologists.)

> Because sea urchins (Strongylocentralus purpuratus)
> do not have any distinguishing characteristics that iden-
> tify their sex, several sea urchins were tested so that
> spermatozoa and eggs could be obtained. Five sea urchins
> were injected with 2.0 ml of 0.5 M potassium chloride
> (0.5 MKCl) by a hypodermic syringe into the soft, fleshy
> area on the oral side of each sea urchin. The injected
> sea urchins were set aside for 5 minutes with their oral
> sides facing up. The injected 0.5 MKCl made the gonad
> muscles of each sea urchin contract, thus releasing ga-
> metes to the external environment in a mucus-like fluid.
> If the fluid excreted was yellow, it signified the eggs
> of a female sea urchin. A male sea urchin excreted blue
> seminal fluid. But if the identification procedures
> didn't uncover both a male and female sea urchin from the
> sample of sea urchins, additional sea urchins were in-
> jected with 2.0 ml of 0.5 MKCl each, following the same
> identification procedures until at least one male and one
> female were obtained.

Here is an example from a professional writer of an informative process analysis — a passage from *The Perceptual World of the Child* by T. G. R. Bower. The author finds it necessary to stop partway through the chapter he calls "Some Complex Effects of Simple Growth" to explain in brief the workings of the human eye.

> Finally we come to the most complex sensory system, the eye and its as-
> sociated neural structures. The eye is an extremely intricate and complex organ.
> Light enters the eye through the cornea, passes through the anterior chamber
> and thence through the pupil to the lens. The lens is a soft transparent tissue

that can stretch out and get thinner or shorten and thicken, thus focusing the rays of light and enabling images of objects at different distances to be seen clearly. The lens focuses the light on the retina, which is the thin membrane covering the posterior surface of the eyeball. The nerve cells in the retina itself are sensitive to spots of light. Each nerve cell at the next level of analysis in the brain receives inputs from a number of these retinal nerve cells and responds best to lines or long edges in particular orientations. Numbers of these nerve cells feed into the next level, where nerve cells are sensitive to movement of lines in particular orientations in particular directions. There are other levels that seem sensitive to size, and still others that respond to specific differences in the signals from the two eyes.

Directive or "how to" writing is also demanded of college students. In an education class, you might be asked to describe how to write a lesson plan; in geometry class, how to introduce a new concept; in a psychology class, how to identify family types (open, closed, random, synchronous). In a course on communication disorders, you might be assigned papers on subjects as varied as how to approach a reluctant child in a therapy session, how to give a hearing test, and how to teach someone a new word.

Models of directive or "how to" writing are often found in textbooks such as *Surveying,* by Francis H. Moffitt and Harry Bouchard. The following passage instructs students in using a surveyor's telescope.

> When sighting through the telescope of a surveying instrument, whether it's a level, a transit, a theodolite, or an alidade, the observer must first focus the eyepiece system to *his individual eye*. This is most easily done by holding an opened field book about six inches in front of the objective lens and on a slant in order to obscure the view ahead of the telescope and to allow light to enter the objective lens. . . . The *eyepiece* is now twisted in or out until the cross hairs are sharp and distinct. Now, with the eyepiece system focused, the telescope is pointed at the object to be sighted, with the observer looking along the top of the telescope barrel (some telescopes are provided with peep sights with which to make this initial alignment). The rotational motion is then clamped. The object to be sighted should now be in the field of view. The tangent screw is then used to bring the line of sight directly on the point.

As you enter the world of work, you will probably find yourself called upon any number of times to analyze a process — in lab reports, technical writing of all sorts, business reports and memos, case studies, nursing records, treatment histories, and a host of other kinds of writing, depending on your career. You'll find it immensely useful to know how to explain a process from its beginning to its end.

Further Applications

Similar to Paul Bodanis (p. 122) and student Linnea Saukko (p. 124), writers often use *analyzing* in combination with other writing techniques to help them achieve their purposes. In the essay from *A Writer's Reader,* "From the Poets in the Kitchen" (p. 439), Paule Marshall first identifies the topics the Barbados women discuss, then analyzes the functions of their talking in order to explain its value to the women and its influence on Marshall as a writer. In "Family Codes" (p. 448), Margaret Mead draws on her expertise as an anthropologist to analyze cultural and family codes. In "A Republic of Cockroaches" (p. 582), environmentalist David Quammen uses process analysis to explain how cockroaches have survived for 250 million years.

A few other writers who use analysis are historian Joan Jacobs Brumberg, "The Origins of Anorexia Nervosa" (p. 451), journalist Susan Faludi, "Blame It on Feminism" (p. 482), computer scientist Gary Katzenstein, "The Salaryman" (p. 528), investigative reporter Jessica Mitford, "Behind the Formaldehyde Curtain" (p. 513), and novelist and playwright Joyce Carol Oates, "Rape and the Boxing Ring" (p. 562). Answer the following questions about each of these essays.

1. Does the author analyze subject or process? What is the principle of analysis?

2. What is the purpose of the analysis? How is the analysis related to the writer's occupation or field of interest?

3. What devices does the writer use to make the analysis clear and easy to follow?

CHAPTER 7

Taking a Stand

In college, both in class and outside of class, you'll hear controversial issues discussed: zero population growth, affirmative action, AIDS testing, gun control. In some fields of study, experts don't always agree, and issues go on and on being controversies for years. Ethical questions arise in the study of business, medical care, genetic engineering. That is why, in your college writing, you will soon find yourself taking up pen (or typewriter or word processor) in a cause. Taking a stand on an issue will help you understand the controversy and clarify what you believe.

Writing of this kind has a twofold purpose: to state an opinion and to win the reader's respect for it. The reader's own opinion might alter from reading what you say; then again, it might not. But at least, if you fulfill your purpose, your reader will see good reasons for your thinking the way you do.

In taking a stand, you do three things:

You state what you believe.

You enlist your reader's trust. You do so by demonstrating that you know what you're talking about.

You consider and respect what your reader probably thinks and feels. As writers, in the words of writing specialist Maxine Hairston, "we have to care more about communicating with [readers] than about showing them the error of their ways."

Charles R. Lawrence III is a professor of law at Stanford University. In the following article, adapted from a speech at a conference of the American Civil Liberties Union, he sets forth a controversial opinion on First Amendment rights.

ON RACIST SPEECH
Charles R. Lawrence III

I have spent the better part of my life as a dissenter. As a high school 1 student, I was threatened with suspension for my refusal to participate in a civil-defense drill, and I have been a conspicuous consumer of my First Amendment liberties ever since. There are very strong reasons for protecting even racist speech. Perhaps the most important of these is that such protection reinforces our society's commitment to tolerance as a value, and that by protecting bad speech from government regulation, we will be forced to combat it as a community.

But I also have a deeply felt apprehension about the resurgence of 2 racial violence and the corresponding rise in the incidence of verbal and symbolic assault and harassment to which blacks and other traditionally subjugated and excluded groups are subjected. I am troubled by the way the debate has been framed in response to the recent surge of racist incidents on college and university campuses and in response to some universities' attempts to regulate harassing speech. The problem has been framed as one in which the liberty of free speech is in conflict with the elimination of racism. I believe this has placed the bigot on the moral high ground and fanned the rising flames of racism.

Above all, I am troubled that we have not listened to the real victims, 3 that we have shown so little understanding of their injury, and that we have abandoned those whose race, gender, or sexual preference continues to make them second-class citizens. It seems to me a very sad irony that the first instinct of civil libertarians has been to challenge even the smallest, most narrowly framed efforts by universities to provide black and other minority students with the protection the Constitution guarantees them.

The landmark case of *Brown v. Board of Education* is not a case that 4 we normally think of as a case about speech. But *Brown* can be broadly read as articulating the principle of equal citizenship. *Brown* held that segregated schools were inherently unequal because of the *message* that segregation conveyed — that black children were an untouchable caste, unfit to go to school with white children. If we understand the necessity of eliminating the system of signs and symbols that signal the inferiority of blacks, then we should hesitate before proclaiming that all racist speech that stops short of physical violence must be defended.

University officials who have formulated policies to respond to incidents   5
of racial harassment have been characterized in the press as "thought
police," but such policies generally do nothing more than impose sanctions
against intentional face-to-face insults. When racist speech takes the form
of face-to-face insults, catcalls, or other assaultive speech aimed at an
individual or small group of persons, it falls directly within the "fighting
words" exception to First Amendment protection. The Supreme Court
has held that words which "by their very utterance inflict injury or tend to
incite an immediate breach of the peace" are not protected by the First
Amendment.

If the purpose of the First Amendment is to foster the greatest amount   6
of speech, racial insults disserve that purpose. Assaultive racist speech
functions as a preemptive strike. The invective is experienced as a blow,
not as a proffered idea, and once the blow is struck, it is unlikely that a
dialogue will follow. Racial insults are particularly undeserving of First
Amendment protection because the perpetrator's intention is not to discover truth or initiate dialogue but to injure the victim. In most situations,
members of minority groups realize that they are likely to lose if they
respond to epithets by fighting and are forced to remain silent and
submissive.

Courts have held that offensive speech may not be regulated in public   7
forums such as streets where the listener may avoid the speech by moving
on, but the regulation of otherwise protected speech has been permitted
when the speech invades the privacy of the unwilling listener's home or
when the unwilling listener cannot avoid the speech. Racist posters, fliers,
and graffiti in dormitories, bathrooms, and other common living spaces
would seem to clearly fall within the reasoning of these cases. Minority
students should not be required to remain in their rooms in order to avoid
racial assault. Minimally, they should find a safe haven in their dorms and
in all other common rooms that are a part of their daily routine.

I would also argue that the university's responsibility for ensuring that   8
these students receive an equal educational opportunity provides a compelling justification for regulations that ensure them safe passage in all
common areas. A minority student should not have to risk becoming the
target of racially assaulting speech every time he or she chooses to walk
across campus. Regulating villifying speech that cannot be anticipated or
avoided would not preclude announced speeches and rallies—situations
that would give minority-group members and their allies the chance to
organize counterdemonstrations or avoid the speech altogether.

The most commonly advanced argument against the regulation of racist   9
speech proceeds something like this: We recognize that minority groups
suffer pain and injury as the result of racist speech, but we must allow this
hate mongering for the benefit of society as a whole. Freedom of speech
is the lifeblood of our democratic system. It is especially important for
minorities because often it is their only vehicle for rallying support for the

redress of their grievances. It will be impossible to formulate a prohibition so precise that it will prevent the racist speech you want to suppress without catching in the same net all kinds of speech that it would be unconscionable for a democratic society to suppress.

Whenever we make such arguments, we are striking a balance on the   10 one hand between our concern for the continued free flow of ideas and the democratic process dependent on that flow, and, on the other, our desire to further the cause of equality. There can be no meaningful discussion of how we should reconcile our commitment to equality and our commitment to free speech until it is acknowledged that there is real harm inflicted by racist speech and that this harm is far from trivial.

To engage in a debate about the First Amendment and racist speech   11 without a full understanding of the nature and extent of that harm is to risk making the First Amendment an instrument of domination rather than a vehicle of liberation. We have not all known the experience of victimization by racist, misogynist, and homophobic speech, nor do we equally share the burden of the societal harm it inflicts. We are often quick to say that we have heard the cry of the victims when we have not.

The *Brown* case is again instructive because it speaks directly to the   12 psychic injury inflicted by racist speech by noting that the symbolic message of segregation affected "the hearts and minds" of negro children "in a way unlikely ever to be undone." Racial epithets and harassment often cause deep emotional scarring and feelings of anxiety and fear that pervade every aspect of a victim's life.

Brown also recognized that black children did not have an equal op-   13 portunity to learn and participate in the school community if they bore the additional burden of being subjected to the humiliation and psychic assault contained in the message of segregation. University students bear an analogous burden when they are forced to live and work in an environment where at any moment they may be subjected to denigrating verbal harassment and assault. The same injury was addressed by the Supreme Court when it held that sexual harassment that creates a hostile or abusive work environment violates the ban on sex discrimination in employment of Title VII of the Civil Rights Act of 1964.

Carefully drafted university regulations would bar the use of words as   14 assault weapons and leave unregulated even the most heinous of ideas when those ideas are presented at times and places and in manners that provide an opportunity for reasoned rebuttal or escape from immediate injury. The history of the development of the right to free speech has been one of carefully evaluating the importance of free expression and its effects on other important societal interests. We have drawn the line between protected and unprotected speech before without dire results. (Courts have, for example, exempted from the protection of the First Amendment obscene speech and speech that disseminates official secrets, that defames or libels another person, or that is used to form a conspiracy or monopoly.)

Blacks and other people of color are skeptical about the argument that   15 even the most injurious speech must remain unregulated because, in an unregulated marketplace of ideas, the best ones will rise to the top and gain acceptance. Our experience tells us quite the opposite. We have seen too many demagogues elected by appealing to America's racism. We have seen too many good liberal politicians shy away from the issues that might brand them as being too closely allied with us.

Whenever we decide that racist speech must be tolerated because of 16 the importance of maintaining societal tolerance for all unpopular speech, we are asking blacks and other subordinated groups to bear the burden for the good of all. We must be careful that the ease with which we strike the balance against the regulation of racist speech is in no way influenced by the fact that the cost will be borne by others. We must be certain that those who will pay that price are fairly represented in our deliberations and that they are heard.

At the core of the argument that we should resist all government reg- 17 ulation of speech is the ideal that the best cure for bad speech is good, that ideas that affirm equality and the worth of all individuals will ultimately prevail. This is an empty ideal unless those of us who would fight racism are vigilant and unequivocal in that fight. We must look for ways to offer assistance and support to students whose speech and political participation are chilled in a climate of racial harassment.

Civil-rights lawyers might consider suing on behalf of blacks whose right 18 to an equal education is denied by a university's failure to ensure a non-discriminatory educational climate or conditions of employment. We must embark upon the development of a First Amendment jurisprudence grounded in the reality of our history and our contemporary experience. We must think hard about how best to launch legal attacks against the most indefensible forms of hate speech. Good lawyers can create exceptions and narrow interpretations that limit the harm of hate speech without opening the floodgates of censorship.

Everyone concerned with these issues must find ways to engage actively 19 in actions that resist and counter the racist ideas that we would have the First Amendment protect. If we fail in this, the victims of hate speech must rightly assume that we are on the oppressors' side.

Questions to Start You Thinking

1. Where in the essay does Lawrence's position first become clear to you?
2. What kinds of evidence does the writer use to support his argument? Is the evidence convincing to you? How is it organized?
3. What impression of Lawrence do you get from reading his essay? Is his argument primarily emotional or logical?
4. Why does the writer begin his essay as he does? Would this argument be as credible if it were written by a doctor or a musician instead of by a lawyer?
5. How does Lawrence show his awareness of people with views different from his?

Susan Fendel, inspired by an anatomy and physiology lecture, wrote the following student essay on AIDS for her English composition class. As she pondered the disease and its consequences, she felt that she wanted to change the minds of her audience, her classmates. She wished to "get under everyone's skin," to take a stand against the emotional isolation AIDS victims so often suffer, against injustices they receive at the hands of a frightened public.

Student Essay

AIDS: THE RETURN OF THE SCARLET LETTER
Susan Fendel

The word AIDS has become a part of our present lingo, 1
abbreviating acquired immune deficiency syndrome into a more palatable term for the mysterious virus. In the media and in casual conversation, the topic of AIDS quickly approaches epidemic proportions, as does the disease itself. Currently, AIDS ranks as the new disease of our times. The many serious and frustrating problems of stopping this virus, the fear that accompanies the explosion of AIDS in our country, and the consequent isolation caused by the stigmas placed on those afflicted with the disease are just a few of the issues that arise with this controversial topic.

Acquired immune deficiency syndrome is a name that con- 2
veniently describes the virus--more correctly called human T-lymphotropic type III--which forces the body's immunity to become deficient, rendering the human body useless in protection against infection.

Kaposi's sarcoma, for example, which is a form of skin 3
cancer unknown to North America before the onset of AIDS, develops into a fatal disease in itself in the AIDS-affected immune system. The cancer spreads from the endothelium cells of blood vessels into the dermis (skin) and throughout the body, making what should be a treatable form of cancer into a deadly disease.

Researchers have been frustrated for years by the puzzle 4
of how to kill a virus without killing the human cell it attaches itself to--called the host cell. AIDS introduces a

new kink to this enigma because it is a virus that manifests
itself in the immune system (more specifically, the T cell),
disabling the body's ability to produce defenses (called an-
tibodies) against invading infection and disease.   Therefore,
as in the previous example, other diseases like cancer act as
predators, attacking organs already weakened. This results
in a multidiseased body, complicated by the ever-present AIDS
virus within the cells, which reduces the chances of recovery
from the secondary diseases.

As scientists struggle to solve this puzzle, the public   5
reaction to this virus splashes upon our sexually revolutionized society like a bucket of cold water.   "Sexual partners
need to be carefully chosen" is the new national message.
The conservatives nod their heads wisely, considering this
disease to be a punishment wrought by God--like the plague--
to admonish the promiscuous of our culture. This belief was
even more prevalent when just a few years ago AIDS afflicted
the homosexual and drug addict groups almost exclusively.
The general population approached the subject of AIDS with a
shrug and a negligent comment about getting and deserving.

But AIDS finally struck a common nerve. It has become a   6
frightening disease because of its expansion into the "innocent" groups category.   Presently, children, hemophiliacs,
and heterosexuals are falling victim. The percentage of the
heterosexual group infected with the disease is increasing
rapidly. Out of 30,000 people affected, 3.8 percent of those
fall into the heterosexual group and close to 7 percent in
the other "low-risk" groups combined. This figure is expected to double by 1990.

Because of this disease's new lack of discrimination,   7
what was once considered a health problem for a few minorities has become a hazard for almost everyone. The security
once felt about not contracting AIDS has ended and has been
replaced with increasing anxiety. Also disconcerting is that
scientists have no idea of how to overcome this disease,
which is, in fact, reported to be 100 percent fatal.

Ultimately, the emotional isolation in which AIDS vic-   8

tims are instantly placed is perhaps the most tragic element
of the AIDS phenomenon. This disease tortures not only the
body but also the ego, the psyche, and the lifestyle of those
it afflicts. The distancing by others, which creates this
isolation, is a cruel and unacceptable reaction. Our culture
has been educated in the ways this disease is transmitted.
It is general knowledge that AIDS cannot be contracted
through casual contact; yet the ostracism continues.

    In 1986, a child in Denver was not allowed to attend   9
his public school because he had contracted AIDS through a
"tainted" blood transfusion. The courts overruled the
school's decision, saying that he had a right to attend because he offered no danger to the other students. Parents
responded by pulling their own children from the school,
still terrified by the unknown factors of the disease. The
psychological damage to this young child, already dealing
with a painful disease, seems unnecessarily cruel.

    Stigmas often spring from fear within individuals. To   10
isolate that which threatens us, to turn away regardless of
the facts or truths we have learned, remains, though perhaps
not admirable, a part of human nature. Within us still lies
the instinctive resistance to jeopardizing our own safety
from the deadly disease as we continue to set apart those afflicted with AIDS from those who are not. This unwillingness
to (literally) extend a hand will hopefully dissipate along
with the extinction of the lingering suspicion of contagion.

    Society has always shunned what it fears, ostracizing   11
people at a time when they most need support. But in the
case of AIDS, families often react so negatively to the diagnosis that the person suffering is cast out, losing contact
with loved ones. With other diseases (even cancer has carried less of a stigma in the last few years), the family
support system is an important part in the patient's reconciliation with the disease and pending death. Sadly, the
AIDS victim stands alone, labeled because of some presumed
indiscretion.

    The prejudice toward the people in high-risk cate-   12

gories--the homosexuals and addicts--continues to make the public unyielding in its harsh discrimination against anyone afflicted with AIDS.

But attention is finally focusing on the size of the AIDS problem. Support groups have been organized in almost all of the major cities, and research efforts to isolate the AIDS virus have been given important funding. Slowly, the awareness of the facts of this disease is growing. Perhaps the stigma of having AIDS will eventually lose its strength. 13

Public opinion is starting to come to terms with the disease and treat it as a deadly health problem rather than with embarrassment and disregard. It will take time before AIDS is not thought of as another venereal disease that points a finger at the promiscuous of our nation. 14

AIDS is frightening. Yet all of the current information emphasizes that the risk of contracting AIDS does not increase by being kind. So there is no need to place upon these people that scarlet letter A, ostracizing people at a time when they need comfort and acceptance. We have come too far as a culture to turn away from scientific data and to rely solely on our moral judgments to make responsible decisions. 15

In our civilized society, the key to understanding is accepting diversity and adversity; being able to distinguish the difference between real and exaggerated threats; and realizing that judgment does not cleanse us from that which we judge but instead burdens us with attitudes and fear that are contagious. 16

Questions to Start You Thinking

1. What do Fendel's first four paragraphs contribute to her essay? Would the paper be as convincing if she had omitted them?

2. Where in her essay does Fendel's stand emerge most clearly? Why do you think Fendel placed it there? Would it have been as effective if placed earlier in the essay?

3. Is the stand that Fendel takes clear to you? Does her evidence convince you to respect her opinion? Can you think of anything that would strengthen her position?

4. Does the writer consider what her readers probably think and feel?

5. Is Fendel's argument primarily emotional or rational?

6. Make a list of public attitudes about which you might take a stand. Choose one of these, and list examples and illustrations in support of your stand. Then list points that oppose your beliefs. Develop your notes into an essay.

LEARNING BY WRITING

The Assignment: Taking a Stand

Find a controversy that arouses your interest. It might be an issue currently in the news or it might be a long-lasting one such as "In our public schools, does creationism, the fundamentalist explanation for the origin of species, deserve equal time with Darwin's theory of evolution?" or "Are intercollegiate sports on campus a good thing or a baleful one?" Your purpose in this paper isn't to try to *solve* a large social or moral problem, but just to make clear where you stand on a large or small issue of importance to you, and why. First state your view and then your reasons for holding it. Or do as Fendel does: present your evidence first and build up to your stand at the end of your paper. Your readers, you can assume, are people who may be familiar with the controversy but who have not yet taken sides.

Recently we have read good papers that take a stand, written by students at several colleges. Here are brief summaries of a few of them.

A woman who earns her own way through college countered the opinion that working full- or part-time during the school year provides a college student with valuable knowledge. Citing her own painful experience in having to drop out of college twice, she maintained that a student who can devote full time to her studies is far better off.

A woman attacked her history textbook's account of the burning of Joan of Arc on the grounds that the author had characterized Joan as "an ignorant farm girl subject to religious hysteria."

A married couple, with the encouragement of their sociology instructor, collaborated on a paper in favor of early marriage.

A woman wrote a letter to her congressional representative calling a bill that would remove a parcel of recreational land from the administration of the Bureau of Land Management "a misguided proposal" that would encourage new development by builders heedless of the environment.

A man, citing history and Christian doctrine, gave his reasons for preferring to keep prayer out of public school classrooms.

A man, decrying the "emotional publicity" that follows shooting incidents, took a stand against gun control. He challenged arguments and statistics put forth by advocates of stricter gun control laws and defended the right of citizens to carry weapons.

A woman in an education course disputed the claim of E. D. Hirsch, Jr., in his book *Cultural Literacy,* that we must give schoolchildren a grounding in facts common to our culture, including history, literature, mythology, science, geography, and sports. As a Hispanic, she maintained that to absorb the culture of the majority isn't necessarily to answer children's greatest need. Children, she affirmed, should first study their own cultural backgrounds and should master basic skills for gathering information.

Generating Ideas

Start with any controversial topic that interests you. To understand it better, you may need to find out more about it. Turn to some of your trusty resources. Recall. Observe, if you can. Converse. What do others think? Do some reading in a library. In gathering material, you will discover more exactly where you stand.

As she strove to discover ideas for her paper, Susan Fendel kept a free-flowing notebook in which she recorded thoughts as they came to her and as she read them or heard them. Her notes reveal interesting facets of her writing processes. Many of the ideas she wrote down never actually made it into her final draft. Still, when she began writing, she had more than enough material to choose from. Part of her notebook is reproduced on the following page.

State your claim. It will help you focus your view if you state it in a sentence: a thesis, or statement of your claim. *Make your claim narrow enough.* For a paper due a week from now, "The city's waterfront has become a stodgy, run-down disgrace" can probably be supported by your own observations. But the claim "The welfare program in this country has become a disgrace" would take much digging, perhaps the work of years. (For more advice on this important point, see "Stating and Using a Thesis," p. 322.)

Supply evidence. Your claim stated, you'll need evidence to support it. This matter is crucial, so let's take time right now to examine it.

What is evidence? Anything that demonstrates the truth of your claim: facts and figures, expert opinions, illustrations and examples, reported experience. At this point, we won't discuss those tremendous sources of evidence you can obtain by *deeply* exploring a library or by doing field research: actual legwork and firsthand reporting to find evidence that no one has published before. We discuss such sources in detail in *A Writer's Research Manual.* For now, let's see how you select what will be trustworthy in supporting your claim. Evidence comes in several varieties:

1. **Facts.** Facts are statements that can be verified by objective means, such as going and looking or reading a reliable account. Of course, we take many of our facts from the testimony of others. We believe that the Great Wall of China exists, though we have never beheld it with our own eyes.

A fact is usually stated in an impersonal way: "Algonquian Indians still live in Old Orchard Beach"; "If you pump all the air out of a five-gallon varnish can, it will collapse." Sometimes a small fact casts a piercing light. Claiming that strip-mining in his hometown had injured the environment, one student recalled taking a walk through local hills before a mining operation had moved

11/14/87
AIDS
1) Frightening = consequence of sexual revolution
2) Frustrating = fatal, incurable, affecting "innocent groups"
3) Isolating = Instant ostracization, both physical and emotional distancing. Hard to overcome stigma.

Intro should have these three topics introduced

11/15/89
Heard on News:

Heterosexual couple found out that they had AIDS. Made a suicide pact. He dies. She was discovered before she died, and recovered.

Man's autopsy revealed no sign of AIDS. The woman did not have AIDS either. She was arrested for attempted suicide (suicide is illegal) and for facilitating her lover's suicide.

Modern Romeo and Juliet ←

Usable in paper? Intro?

11/17/89
Rough draft completed, needs more detail, more expansion. Should I write it again or save it for first revision?

Language works well, must review for "tightening" aspects.

Hawthorne—The Scarlet Letter—is this too confusing a concept to begin and end paper with?

Some of Susan Fendel's preliminary notes

in and being almost deafened by a din of birdcalls. The paper ended with a quiet statement of fact: "Yesterday, on that same walk, I heard no birds at all."

2. **Statistics.** Another valuable kind of evidence, statistics are facts expressed in numbers, gathered in answer to a question. What are the odds that an American child is on welfare? According to statistics compiled by the U.S. Department of Health and Human Services and the Census Bureau in 1991, the chances are 1 in 8. (A student cited that statistic in an essay arguing

FOR GROUP LEARNING
Here is a situation in which your writing group is likely to prove particularly valuable. Allow a day or two for members of the group to decide, at least tentatively, the positions they wish to take in their individual papers. Then hold a meeting at which each member takes a few minutes to set forth his or her position and to support it. Other members of the group may be invited to argue or to suggest any useful supporting evidence that may occur to them. One tremendous advantage of this activity is that, before you write, you'll probably hear some of the objections your readers are likely to raise. You'll be kept busy during this discussion; ask your group's recording secretary to list all the objections you get so that you'll remember them when writing your paper. If you can't answer any of the counter-arguments, ask other members of the group to help you generate a reply. Of course, this group discussion might change your mind, make you aware that your ideas are half-baked, and cause you to alter your whole stand. If this happens, give thanks: it will be easier to revise your ideas now than to revise your paper later.

that politicians should put themselves in the shoes of single mothers before denouncing "welfare handouts.")

Most writers, without trying to be dishonest, interpret statistics to help their causes. The statement "Fifty percent of the populace have incomes above the poverty level" might be used to back the claim that the government of an African nation is doing a fine job. Putting the statement another way, "Fifty percent of the populace have incomes below the poverty level" might use the same statistic to show that the government's efforts to aid the disadvantaged are inadequate. A writer, of course, is free to interpret a statistic; and it is only human to present a case in a favorable light. But statistics should not be used to mislead. On the wrapper of a peanut candy bar, we read that one one-ounce serving contains only 150 calories and 70 milligrams of sodium. The claim is true, but the bar weighs 1.6 ounces. Eat the whole thing, as you are more likely to do than serving yourself exactly 62½ percent of it, and you'll ingest 240 calories and 112 milligrams of sodium — a heftier amount than the innocent statistic on the wrapper leads you to believe.

Such abuses make some readers automatically distrust statistics. Use figures fairly, and make sure they are accurate. If you doubt a statistic or a fact, why not check it out? Compare it with facts and statistics reported by several other sources. A report that differs from every other report may well be true, but distrust it unless it is backed by further evidence.

3. *The testimony of experts.* By *experts,* we mean people with knowledge of a particular field gained from study and experience. The test of an expert is whether his or her expertise stands up to the scrutiny of others knowledgeable in that field. An essay by basketball player Michael Jordan explaining how to play offense or by economist John Kenneth Galbraith setting

forth the causes of inflation carries authority, while a piece by Galbraith on how to play basketball would not be credible. But consider whether your expert has any bias that would affect his or her reliability. Statistics on cases of lung cancer attributed to smoking might be better taken from government sources than from a representative of the tobacco industry. If you have special knowledge for writing about a subject you choose, establish your credentials to your readers early in your essay.

4. *Memory and observation.* Obviously, firsthand experience and observation are persuasive. They add life to any paper. Perhaps in supporting the claim "It's foolish to exercise too strenuously" you might recall your own experience: "As a lifeguard for two summers, I watched hundreds of people exhaust themselves in jumping the waves and once had to rescue the victim of a heart attack." As readers, most of us tend to trust the writer who declares, "I was there. This is what I saw."

If you'd like any questions to stimulate your search for evidence, try these.

DISCOVERY CHECKLIST: TAPPING RESOURCES

- What do you already know about this topic? What has convinced *you* of the truth of your claim?

- What testimony can you provide from your own firsthand experience?

- What have you observed, or what might you observe, that would probably support your stand?

- What have you read about this topic? What else might you read? (For suggestions, consult the catalog of your library and the *Readers' Guide to Periodical Literature,* discussed on pp. 604 and 665–667.)

- What expert might you talk with?

- What illustrations and examples can you imagine to back up your claim? (Don't assert that these are facts, of course!)

- Try to imagine yourself as your reader—what further evidence might persuade you?

For this assignment, you'll assemble evidence in written form. Take notes, in a notebook or preferably on large, 4-by-6-inch or 5-by-7-inch index cards. (Cards have the advantage of being shufflable, easily arranged in an order for writing a draft.) Perhaps you'll have clippings or photocopies. Spread all this stuff out on a table and choose the evidence that best supports your claim. Let's see how you decide.

Testing evidence   When is evidence useful and trustworthy? When—

It is accurate. A writer assumes all responsibility for verifying facts and figures.

It is reliable. To decide whether you can trust it, you'll need to evaluate its source, as we have detailed. Whenever possible, do some reading. Compare information given in one source with information given in another.

It is up to date. Statistics from ten-year-old encyclopedias, such as population figures or scientific research, are probably out of date. Take facts from the latest sources.

It is to the point. It backs the exact claim you're making in your paper. This point may seem too obvious to deserve mention, but you'd be surprised how many writers get hung up on an interesting fact or opinion that has nothing to do with what they're trying to demonstrate. Sometimes a writer will leap from evidence to conclusion without reason, and the result is a *non sequitur* (Latin for "it does not follow"): "Benito Mussolini made the trains run on time. He was one of the world's leading statesmen." The evidence about trains doesn't support a judgment on Mussolini's statesmanship. (For more about errors in reasoning, see pp. 381–383.) If the evidence you find contradicts or belies your claim, you shouldn't make the claim.

It is representative. Any examples you select should be typical of all the things included in your claim. If you claim that, in general, students on your campus are well informed about their legal rights, don't talk just to prelaw majors; talk to an English major, an engineering major, a biology major, and others. Probably most writers, in the heat of persuading, can't help unconsciously stacking the evidence in their own favor, but the best writers don't deliberately suppress evidence to the contrary. The writer for an airline magazine who tried to sell package tours to India by declaring "India is an attractive land of sumptuous wealth and splendor" might give for evidence the Taj Mahal and a luxury hotel while ignoring the slums of Bombay and Calcutta. The result might be effective advertising but hardly a full and faithful view.

It is sufficient and strong enough to back the claim. How much evidence you use depends on the size of your claim. It will take less evidence to claim that a downtown park needs better maintenance than to claim that the Department of the Interior needs reorganizing. How much evidence you need may depend, too, on how much your readers already know. Who will be reading your paper? A group of readers, all from Washington, D.C., and vicinity, will not need much evidence to be persuaded that the city's modern Metro transit system is admirable in its efficiency, but more evidence may be needed to convince readers who don't know Washington.

As you try to comprehend another person's beliefs and feelings, you can try to imagine yourself in that person's place and anticipate questions a reader will ask. If you do, you will probably think of more ideas — points to make, objections to answer — than if you think only of presenting your own view.

It is not oversimplified. Some writers fall into the error of *oversimplification,* supplying a too-easy explanation for a phenomenon that may be vast and complicated: "Of course our economy is in trouble. People aren't buying American-made cars." Both statements may be true, but the second seems insufficient to account for the first: obviously there is much more to the economy than cars alone. More information is called for. Whenever in doubt that you've given enough evidence to convince your readers, you are probably well advised to come up with more.

Not that mere quantity is enough. One piece of vivid and significant evidence—such as the firsthand testimony of an expert, given in that person's memorable words—may be more persuasive than a foot-high stack of statistics. In evaluating your evidence, you can ask yourself a few questions.

DISCOVERY CHECKLIST: TESTING EVIDENCE

- Does your evidence lead to the stand you want to take? (If it all leads you to a different opinion, then you'll want to revise your claim as you stated it in your thesis.)
- If you are writing about some current situation, is your evidence—especially any statistical information—up to date?
- Are facts and figures accurate? If you doubt a piece of information, try to check it against published sources. See reports by others and facts given in reference works. Be sure to copy correctly.
- If an important point rests on your quoting an opinion or citing information you receive from an expert, do you know that the person is respected in his or her field?
- Is your evidence sufficient? Does it at least reflect the full range of your topic? If it leads to a general claim ("Nursing homes in this city are firetraps"), does the general statement rest on a large and convincing number of examples?
- What are the characteristics of your readers—their attitudes, interests, priorities, hopes, fears? Is your evidence appropriate and sufficient for them?
- If you were to read an argument based on this evidence, would you understand the reasons for the author's position? Imagine your paper all written and yourself in a reader's place.

Planning, Drafting, and Developing

Once you have looked over your written evidence and sifted for the useful part, you will probably find it falling into shape. If you have taken notes on cards, you can group them according to subject and organize them into the order you think you'll follow in writing your draft. One useful pattern you might follow is the classical form of argument: (1) introduce the subject to get the readers' interest; (2) state your main point or thesis; (3) provide evidence to support your position; (4) refute the opposition; (5) reaffirm your main point.

Check your claim. Double-check the claim you expressed in your thesis when you started this assignment. Now that you have gathered your evidence, does it express the point you want to make? Can you support it with the evidence you have found? If not, change it.

Build on your claim. Having stated your claim, keep writing. Summarize your reasons for holding this view. List the supporting evidence. You will find your writing growing into an argument. The result may even be a condensed version of the essay you plan to write.

You may decide to make an outline (for methods, see p. 331). Your claim — the statement of your view — will most likely come early in the paper. Then you might give your reasons for holding your view. An effective way to organize your reasons is from the least effective to the most effective, building up to your strongest point.

Define your terms. As you start to write your draft, make clear any questionable terms used in your claim. If your claim reads, "Humanists are dangerous," you had better give a short definition of what you mean by *humanists* and by *dangerous* early in the paper. Clearly defined terms will prevent misunderstandings and help determine the course of your argument.

Spell out your beliefs, and give attention to those opposing yours. Sometimes in taking a stand you find yourself spelling out your personal beliefs, values, and assumptions. This is a fine idea. State them and you lay them out in the open for your reader to consider; the reader who readily accepts them is probably already on your side. If you declare, "I am against eating red meat because it contains fats and chemicals known to be harmful," you assert a claim and give evidence for it. The reader who responds, "That's right — I'm a vegetarian myself," is clearly in your camp. But even the reader who responds at first, "Oh, I don't know — a hamburger never killed anyone!" may warm to your view if you trouble to consider his or her assumptions. These might include the beliefs that a steak or a burger is delicious; that vegetables aren't; that red meat supplies needed protein; and that the chemicals haven't been proved dangerous. You should show that you are aware of these assumptions and that you have considered them seriously. You might even agree with some of them, perhaps accepting the first one — that meat tastes good. Then you might set forth, in a reasonable way, your own view. By spelling out your assumptions and by imagining those of a dissenting reader, you will win — at the very least — a respectful hearing.

Keep an eye on your reader. When you sense that your reader is likely to disagree, frankly acknowledge this fact. Student Marty Reich does so in a paper in favor of limiting population growth in the city of Tucson, Arizona: "The reader may feel that I have grossly exaggerated the dangers of overpopulation, that the economy and biostructure of this desert city can easily support a few thousand more citizens. But let us consider the quantity of fresh water that each man, woman, and child consumes daily. . . ."

Credit your sources. As you write, make your sources of evidence clear. If an expert whom you quote has outstanding credentials, you may easily be able to insert a brief citation of those credentials: "Lewis Thomas, chancellor of the Memorial Sloan-Kettering Cancer Center," or "Michael Scammell, author of the award-winning biography *Solzhenitsyn.*" If you have talked to your

> **WRITING WITH A COMPUTER: TAKING A STAND**
> If in taking your stand you'll be disputing the view of some other writer, start by creating a document. Type into it those passages from the book, magazine article, newspaper column, or editorial that has provoked you to dissent. Your time will be well spent: transcribing the other writer's very words will get you looking at them closely and will probably help you answer them. Besides, you'll have exact quotations at your fingertips. Then on the same disk create a second document to use in writing your draft.
>
> When you want to cite the other writer's very words, just tell your computer to INSERT or MOVE or COPY (or whatever command your program uses to move text from one document and drop it into the one you're working on). Your computer thus enables you to add an exact quotation instantly in an appropriate place. As you include another writer's words, blend them in with your text and put them within quotation marks.

experts and are convinced of their authority, state why you believe that your experts can be trusted. "From conversation with Mr. Dworshak, who showed me six model wind tunnels he has built, I can testify to his extensive knowledge of aeronautics." In the opening sentence of "On Racist Speech" (p. 142), Lawrence establishes himself as a convincing spokesperson on the subject of free speech.

In supplying evidence, cite exact numbers whenever you can. To report that a condition holds true "in thirty-four cases out of fifty" is more convincing than to say "in many cases." At least it shows that you haven't taken a mere woolly-eyed gawp at a scene but have taken the trouble to count. If you do use the word *many*, be sure the evidence supports the idea of multiple cases, not just *some*.

Revising and Editing

Does taking a stand seem harder than some earlier assignments? Most students find that it is. If you feel the need for special help with this assignment, enlist a couple of other students to read your draft critically and tell you whether they accept your arguments. They can use the following questions.

> **PEER EDITING CHECKLIST: TAKING A STAND**
>
> - State what you understand the writer's claim to be.
> - How persuasive is the writer's evidence? Do you have any questions about that evidence?
> - Can you suggest some good evidence the writer has overlooked?

- Is there anything more that the writer needs to be aware of about his or her audience to improve the essay?
- Do you have any problems following or accepting the reasons for the writer's claim? Would you make any changes in any of the reasoning?
- Has the writer provided sufficient transitions to guide you through his or her argument?
- Circle on the manuscript any spelling, punctuation, grammar, or word choice that impeded you in reading and understanding the writer's views.

When you're writing a paper taking a stand, you may be tempted to fall in love with the evidence you have gone to such trouble to collect. One of the hardest things for a writer to do is to take out information, but you must if it is irrelevant, redundant, or weak. Some of it won't help your case; some may just seem boring and likely to persuade nobody. If so, pitch it. Sometimes you can have too much evidence, and if you throw some out, a stronger argument will remain. Sometimes you can become so attached to old evidence that, when new evidence or new thoughts come along, you won't want to discard what you have on hand. But in taking a stand, as in any other writing, second thoughts often surpass the thoughts that come at first. Be willing to revise not only your words but your view.

When you're taking a last look over your paper, proofread with care. Wherever you have given facts and figures as evidence, check for errors in names and numbers and typing. This advice may seem trivial, but there's a considerable difference between "10,000 people" and "100,000 people." To refer to Sigmund Frued or Alvin Einstein won't persuade a reader that you know what you're talking about.

As you revise, here are some points to consider.

REVISION CHECKLIST: TAKING A STAND

- Does your view convince you? Or do you think you need still more evidence?
- In your paper, have you tried to keep in mind your readers and what would appeal to them? Have you answered their major objections?
- Is your tone or manner of expression suitable for them? Is there anything that may alienate them?
- Might the points in your argument seem stronger if arranged in a different sequence?
- Have you unfairly omitted any evidence that would hurt your case?
- In rereading your paper, do you have any excellent, fresh thoughts? If so, make room for them.

Other Assignments

1. Write a letter to the editor of your local newspaper or of a national news magazine (*Time, Newsweek, U.S. News & World Report*) in which you agree or disagree with the publication's editorial stand on a current question or with the recent words or actions of some public figure. Be sure to make clear your reasons for holding your view.

2. Write a short paper in which you agree or disagree with one of the following suggestions — or some other you have lately read that interests you. You need not propose an alternative action; just give your opinion of the suggestion.

   > Creationism and evolution should be given equal importance in high school science courses.
   > Public television should be abolished.
   > To protect certain endangered species of ocean fish, fish rationing should be imposed on consumers.
   > The United States should colonize Mars.
   > Japan should relax its import regulations more.

3. Write a short paper in which you express your view on one of the following topics or another that comes to mind. Make clear your reasons for believing as you do.

   > Bilingual education
   > Nonsmokers' rights
   > Beauty contests
   > Date rape
   > The fitness movement
   > The minimum wage
   > Mandatory drug testing for athletes (or for job applicants)
   > Destruction of rain forests

4. Write a short paper in which you agree or disagree with the following quotation from Gilbert and Sullivan's musical comedy *Ruddigore.* Use examples and evidence to support your view.

   > If you wish in this world to advance
   > Your merits you're bound to enhance;
   >   You must stir it and stump it,
   >   And blow your own trumpet,
   > Or, trust me, you haven't a chance.

APPLYING WHAT YOU LEARN: SOME USES OF TAKING A STAND

As you may have found out by now, not only writing assignments but also college examination questions sometimes ask you to take a stand on a controversy:

> Criticize the statement "There's too much science and not enough caring in the modern practice of medicine."

> Respond to the view that "there's no need to be concerned about carbon dioxide heating up the earth's atmosphere because a warmer climate, by increasing farm production, would be preferable to the one we have now."

Your answers to such exam questions indicate clearly to your instructor how firm a grasp you have on the material.

In your daily life, too, you'll sometimes feel the need to advance a view in writing. You never know when you'll be called on to represent the tenants of your apartment building by writing a letter of protest to a landlord who wants to raise your rent or when you'll feel moved to write to a store manager complaining about the treatment you received from a salesperson. As an active citizen, you'll wish from time to time to write a letter to the editor of your local newspaper or of a national news magazine. You may want to write to those who represent you in Congress and in the presidency, making clear your view of some current issue you feel strongly about.

When you enter the working world, you'll be glad you can state your views clearly in writing. There is hardly a professional position you can hold—lawyer, teacher, nurse, business manager, journalist—in which you won't be invited from time to time to state and support your views about some important matter, often for the benefit of others in your profession. Here is a sample of such writing, in which Mary Anne Raywid, in the *Journal of Teacher Education* (Sept.–Oct. 1978) defends professors of education against the constant charge that they use jargon when ordinary English would do:

> This is not to deny that educators speak a language of their own. Indeed they do; and it is very much a part of their specialized knowledge. These words become a way first to select out certain qualities, events, and phenomena for attention; and they expedite communication via shorthand references to particular combinations of these. To cite a familiar example, when an educationist talks about a *meaningful learning experience,* s/he is not just spouting jargon, but distinguishing out of all the events and phenomena of a given time and place, a particular set. Moreover, a substantial list of things is being asserted about what is going on—e.g., the words *learning experience* suggest that it is, or it is meant to be, an episode from which learning results. The term *meaningful* is not superfluous but does a specific job: it adds that it is likely to be or was (depending on temporal perspective) a successful exercise in learning—which not all learning experiences proffered by teachers can claim. To qualify as *meaningful* in advance—in other words, well calculated to succeed—a number of conditions must be met, ordinarily including learner comprehension, interest, motivation, capacity, and likely retention.

Scientists who do original research face the task of persuading the scientific community that their findings are valid. Routinely, they write and publish accounts of their work in scientific journals for evaluation by their peers. In such articles they report new facts as well as state opinions. Some scientists and medical people, to be sure, write not only for their professional peers but for us general readers. Here, for instance, is Gerald Weissmann, in an essay called "Foucault and the Bag Lady," airing his views on the recent trend to deinstitutionalize the mentally ill:

> It has always seemed to me to constitute a fantastic notion that the social landscape of our large cities bears any direct relationship to that kind of stable, nurturing community which would support the fragile psyche of the mentally ill. Cast into an environment limited by the welfare hotel or park bench, lacking

adequate outpatient services, prey to climatic extremes and urban criminals, the deinstitutionalized patients wind up as conscripts in an army of the homeless. Indeed, only this winter was the city of New York forced to open temporary shelters in church basements, armories, and lodging houses for thousands of half-frozen street dwellers. A psychiatrist of my acquaintance has summarized the experience of a generation in treating the mentally deranged: "In the nineteen-fifties, the mad people were warehoused in heated public hospitals with occasional access to trained professionals. In the sixties and seventies, they were released into the community and permitted to wander the streets without access to psychiatric care. In the eighties, we have made progress, however. When the mentally ill become too cold to wander the streets, we can warehouse them in heated church basements without supervision."

Weissmann's statement is a good illustration of a specialist writing for the rest of us—and forcefully taking a stand.

Further Applications

Writers often have strong opinions that they wish to share with other people. In *A Writer's Reader,* columnist Ellen Goodman in "Was the Woman Really Less Qualified?" (p. 534) takes a strong *stand* on affirmative action. As evidence for her position, she reports the court case of Diane Joyce and Paul Johnson on which a Supreme Court opinion was based. In "Year of the Blue-Collar Guy" (p. 521), Steve Olson expresses his opinion about blue-collar workers. Drawing from his personal experience as a construction worker gives credibility to his positive position about manual laborers.

In addition to lawyer Charles Lawrence (p. 142) and student Susan Fendel (p. 146) in this chapter, other writers who take a stand include feminist Susan Brownmiller, "Pornography Hurts Women" (p. 465), ethnologist Paula Gunn Allen, "Where I Come from Is like This" (p. 500), professor of African-American studies Henry Louis Gates, Jr., "2 Live Crew, Decoded" (p. 558), and scientist Stephen Jay Gould, "The Terrifying Normalcy of AIDS" (p. 591). Answer the following questions about each of these essays.

1. What stand does the writer take? Is it a popular opinion, or does it break from commonly accepted beliefs?

2. How does the writer support his or her position? Is the evidence sufficient to gain your respect? How does the writer's occupation or expertise contribute to the credibility of the stand?

CHAPTER 8

Proposing a Solution

Sometimes when you learn of a problem such as acid rain, the homeless, or famine, you say to yourself, "Something should be done about that." This chapter will show you one way to do something constructive yourself: by the powerful and persuasive activity of writing.

Your purpose in such writing, as political leaders and advertisers well know, is to rouse your audience to action. Thomas Jefferson and his cohorts who wrote the Declaration of Independence proved as much, and even in your daily life at college you find chances to demonstrate this truth often. Does some policy of your college administrators irk you? Would you urge students to attend a rally for a cause or a charity? Write a letter to your college newspaper or to someone in authority, and try to stir your readers to action.

The uses of such writing go far beyond these immediate applications, as we will see. Accordingly, a college course (of any kind) will sometimes ask you to write a *proposal:* a recommendation that an action be taken. In the previous chapter, you took a stand and backed it up with evidence. Now go a step further. If, for instance, you have made the claim "Our national parks are in sorry condition," you might urge readers to write to their representatives in Congress or donate funds to save endangered species or visit a national park and pick up trash. Or instead you may want to suggest that the Department of the Interior be given a budget increase to hire more park rangers, purchase additional park land to accommodate the increasing horde of visitors to the national parks, and buy more clean-up equipment. The first paper would be a call to immediate action on the part of your readers; the second, an attempt to forge a consensus about what needs to be done.

In making a proposal you set forth a solution, and you urge action by using words like *should, ought,* and *must:* "This city ought to have a Bureau of Missing Persons"; "Small private aircraft should be banned from flying closer than one mile to a major commercial airport"; "Every consumer must refuse to buy South African apples." Then you lay out, clearly and concisely, all the reasons you can muster to persuade your readers that your proposal deserves to be implemented, taking care not to become preachy and thus alienate your readers by your tone.

LEARNING FROM OTHER WRITERS

In recent years, some people have complained that certain rock lyrics incite listeners to violence. Rock singers and composers and listeners have protested against any attempt at censorship. In an article from the *Boston Globe,* Caryl Rivers, novelist and professor of journalism at Boston University, sets forth her own view of the question, together with pointed suggestions for action.

WHAT SHOULD BE DONE ABOUT ROCK LYRICS?
Caryl Rivers

After a grisly series of murders in California, possibly inspired by the   1
lyrics of a rock song, we are hearing a familiar chorus: don't blame rock
and roll. Kids will be kids. They love to rebel, and the more shocking the
stuff, the better they like it.

There's some truth in this, of course. I loved to watch Elvis shake his   2
torso when I was a teenager, and it was even more fun when Ed Sullivan
wouldn't let the cameras show him below the waist. I snickered at the
forbidden "Rock with Me, Annie" lyrics by a black rhythm and blues group,
which were deliciously naughty. But I am sorry, rock fans, that is not the
same thing as hearing lyrics about how a man is going to force a woman
to perform oral sex on him at gunpoint in a little number called "Eat Me
Alive." It is not in the same league with a song about the delights of slipping
into a woman's room while she is sleeping and murdering her, the theme
of an AC/DC ballad that allegedly inspired the California slayer.

Make no mistake, it is not sex we are talking about here, but violence.   3
Violence against women. Most rock songs are not violent — they are funky,
sexy, rebellious, and sometimes witty. Please do not mistake me for a Mrs.
Grundy. If Prince wants to leap about wearing only a purple jock strap, fine.
Let Mick Jagger unzip his fly as he gyrates, if he wants to. But when either
one of them starts garroting, beating, or sodomizing a woman in their
number, that is another story.

I always find myself annoyed when "intellectual" men dismiss violence 4
against women with a yawn, as if it were beneath their dignity to notice. I
wonder if the reaction would be the same if the violence were directed
against someone other than women. How many people would yawn and
say, "Oh, kids will be kids" if a rock group did a nifty little number called
"Lynchin," in which stringing up and stomping on black people were set to
music? Who would chuckle and say, "Oh, just a little adolescent rebellion"
if a group of rockers went on MTV dressed as Nazis, desecrating syn-
agogues and beating up Jews to the beat of twanging guitars?

I'll tell you what would happen. Prestigious dailies would thunder on 5
editorial pages; senators would fall over each other to get denunciations
into the *Congressional Record.* The president would appoint a commission
to clean up the music business.

But violence against women is greeted by silence. It shouldn't be. 6

This does not mean censorship, or book (or record) burning. In a society 7
that protects free expression, we understand a lot of stuff will float up out
of the sewer. Usually, we recognize the ugly stuff that advocates violence
against any group as the garbage it is, and we consider its purveyors as
moral lepers. We hold our nose and tolerate it, but we speak out against
the values it proffers.

But images of violence against women are not staying on the fringes 8
of society. No longer are they found only in tattered, paper-covered books
or in movie houses where winos snooze and the scent of urine fills the air.
They are entering the mainstream at a rapid rate. This is happening at a
time when the media, more and more, set the agenda for the public debate.
It is a powerful legitimizing force—especially television. Many people regard what they see on TV as the truth; Walter Cronkite once topped a poll
as the most trusted man in America.

Now, with the advent of rock videos and all-music channels, rock music 9
has grabbed a big chunk of legitimacy. American teenagers have instant
access, in their living rooms, to the messages of rock, on the same vehicle
that brought them Sesame Street. Who can blame them if they believe that
the images they see are accurate reflections of adult reality, approved by
adults? After all, Big Bird used to give them lessons on the same little box.
Adults, by their silence, sanction the images. Do we really want our kids to
think that rape and violence are what sexuality is all about?

This is not a trivial issue. Violence against women is a major social 10
problem, one that's more than a cerebral issue to me. I teach at Boston
University, and one of my most promising young journalism students was
raped and murdered. Two others told me of being raped. Recently, one
female student was assaulted and beaten so badly she had $5,000 worth
of medical bills and permanent damage to her back and eyes.

It's nearly impossible, of course, to make a cause-and-effect link be- 11
tween lyrics and images and acts of violence. But images have a tremendous power to create an atmosphere in which violence against certain
people is sanctioned. Nazi propagandists knew that full well when they
portrayed Jews as ugly, greedy, and powerful.

The outcry over violence against women, particularly in a sexual con- 12
text, is being legitimized in two ways: by the increasing movement of these
images into the mainstream of the media in TV, films, magazines, albums,
videos, and by the silence about it.

Violence, of course, is rampant in the media. But it is usually set in 13
some kind of moral context. It's usually only the bad guys who commit
violent acts against the innocent. When the good guys get violent, it's
against those who deserve it. Dirty Harry blows away the scum, he doesn't
walk up to a toddler and say, "Make my day." The A Team does not shoot
up suburban shopping malls.

But in some rock songs, it's the "heroes" who commit the acts. The 14
people we are programmed to identify with are the ones being violent, with
women on the receiving end. In a society where rape and assaults on
women are endemic, this is no small problem, with millions of young boys
watching on their TV screens and listening on their Walkmans.

I think something needs to be done. I'd like to see people in the industry 15
respond to the problem. I'd love to see some women rock stars speak out
against violence against women. I would like to see disc jockeys refuse air
play to records and videos that contain such violence. At the very least, I
want to see the end of the silence. I want journalists and parents and critics
and performing artists to keep this issue alive in the public forum. I don't
want people who are concerned about this issue labeled as bluenoses and
bookburners and ignored.

And I wish it wasn't always just women who were speaking out. Men 16
have as large a stake in the quality of our civilization as women do in the
long run. Violence is a contagion that infects at random. Let's hear something, please, from the men.

Questions to Start You Thinking

1. What specific problem does Rivers identify? What solutions does she propose?
   Can you think of others?

2. Does Rivers persuade you that action is necessary? Do you think she takes rock
   lyrics too seriously?

3. What are the sources of her evidence? Can you recall from your own experience
   any other evidence that might support her argument?

4. Where in her essay does Rivers present, even sympathize with, views opposed to
   her own? By doing so, does she strengthen or weaken her case?

5. What unspoken values and assumptions do you discern in Rivers that make her
   argue as she does?

6. Where in her essay does Rivers use the resource of imagination? For what
   purpose?

After pondering an old problem — people who mix drinking and driving —
Jeffrey Ting came up with an original solution. For a freshman writing seminar
called Contemporary Social Problems, he wrote the following proposal.

Student Essay

THE DRINKING AGE:
HOW WE SHOULD DETERMINE IT
Jeffrey Ting

Recent history has shown that the big problem when the 1
driver mixes alcohol and gasoline comes from people between
the ages of sixteen and twenty. The reason for this problem
is not that young people are irresponsible. After the Vietnam War an old point was popularly raised: "Well, if a person
can be old enough to fight in a war why isn't he old enough
to drink?" So in the 1970s the drinking age was lowered in
most states to eighteen. This proved an experiment that
failed. Fatalities rose on the highways. That is why the
federal government in 1984 passed the law requiring states
to raise the drinking age to twenty-one or else lose federal
funding for their highways. Many states promptly reacted and
in early 1985 raised the drinking age to twenty-one.

Some individuals will be ready to drink at seventeen, 2
and others never will be if they live to be ninety. Instead
of penalizing all the twenty-one-year-olds who have been
spoiling for a beer ever since they were seventeen and who
would be perfectly well qualified to handle it, I would like
to propose a completely new solution to the problem. It is a
drinking license.

We have a driver's license now, which is given out to 3
persons who demonstrate their ability to drive, and this has
proven an effective system. Why then do we not license
drinking to those who can prove their competence? I do not
suggest that, to win one's drinking license, it should be
necessary to chug-a-lug a pitcher of beer and then walk a
straight line. It seems to me that the best way to determine
the ability to handle alcohol would be to relate this ability
to the ability to drive.

Let me imagine the plan like this. Let us say that the 4
driver's license, in a certain state, may be obtained at seventeen. Then should follow a period of eighteen months in
which the young driver proves that he can keep an unblemished

record--no drinking-related accidents. This caution would be necessary, for you may be sure that seventeen-year-olds who drive can find someone to buy beer for them. If at the end of that eighteen months the driver's record is clean, he can apply for a drinking license. A written test should be administered, like the one most states require for a driving license, to determine that the applicant has at least a basic knowledge of alcohol and its effects. Questions should be included such as "How many drinks does it take to get a person weighing 150 pounds over the point at which he can be declared legally inebriated?" "How long does it take, after that many drinks, to sober up?" "What is the best cure for a hangover?" (Answer: Honey.) And "How many people were killed last year in alcohol-related car accidents?" The applicant, if he can pass all this, receives a temporary drinking license good for six months of beer and wine, with hard liquor not yet permitted. If at the end of that six months he can both drink and drive and not have any accidents, he gets a permanent drinking license. I say "permanent," but this license can always be revoked. If the person is involved in a drinking-related accident he loses both driver's license and drinking license. No drinking license will be required for people over twenty-one.

    At least two objections, I realize, can be leveled 5 against this plan. It will require more paperwork and more bureaucracy. I don't see this as a serious problem. Indeed, compared to the work that the present unworkable system creates for our courts, what with the charging of people for violating the drinking laws and the crushing burden of trials resulting from accidents, I believe this extra work would be relatively small. The states could charge a small fee for a drinking license, which the teenager would pay willingly, thus making money for the state.

    A more serious objection is that this plan would tie 6 drinking licenses to drivers' licenses, and what about people who don't drive? Would they never be able to drink? That is a good objection, and I propose that, for those individuals without wheels, a different means be created for them to prove their ability to drink without causing any problems for society. They would be required to affirm that they are not going to obtain drivers' licenses. They would have to keep this pledge or else have to fall subject to the usual requirements for drivers. They would have an eighteen-month period following their seventeenth birthdays, during which they would be required to keep a clean police record. At the end of this eighteen months, if they had shown themselves to be good citizens, they could apply for and receive their drinking licenses. They would be required to take the same written test as anyone else.

While, like all official attempts to regulate unpredict- 7 able humans, the plan I suggest would not work perfectly, I expect that it would work much more efficiently in keeping drunken drivers off the roads than the present confusion of laws and drinking ages. It would view the growing individual as going through a series of gauntlets in taking his or her rightful place as a responsible member of adult society. Right now the law unfairly discriminates against those who are willing and able to assume responsibility early. My plan would trust those individuals who can show society that they are ready to be trusted.

Questions to Start You Thinking

1. What, to your mind, is Ting's most convincing point in favor of his proposal? Which is least convincing?
2. Are there other objections to Ting's plan that he fails to deal with?
3. Which of the writer's five resources — recalling, observing, reading, conversing, imagining — does Ting use in his essay? On which one does he rely most heavily?
4. What other possible solutions to this same problem can you imagine?
5. How does Ting organize his essay?

LEARNING BY WRITING

The Assignment: Arguing for an Action

In this essay, you're going to accomplish two things. First, you'll carefully describe a social, economic, political, civic, environmental, or administrative problem — a problem you care about, one that irritates you or angers you, one that you strongly wish to see resolved. The problem may be large or small, but it shouldn't be trivial. (No comic essays about the awful problem of catsup that squirts from Big Macs, please. For this assignment you'll want to probe deeper and engage your thinking with real concerns.) The problem may be one that affects the whole country, or it may be one that affects mainly people in your locality: your city, your campus, or your classroom. Show your readers that this problem really exists and that it matters to you and to them. Write for an audience who, once made aware of the problem, may be expected to help do something about it.

After setting forth the problem, go on to propose a way to solve it or at least alleviate it. What should be done? Supply evidence that your proposal is reasonable, that it can work, that a way to improve the existing state of affairs is within our grasp.

Some recent student papers that cogently argued for actions include the following.

> A man argued that SAT, ACT, and placement test scores should be abolished as criteria for college acceptance. He demonstrated that the tests favor aggressive students from affluent families, who can afford to take courses and buy software programs designed to improve their scores.

> A woman made a case for drafting all eighteen-year-olds for a year and putting them to work at such tasks as feeding the homeless, tutoring students who need special help, teaching the illiterate to read, planting trees and flowers, eliminating litter and graffiti, helping patients in nursing homes, and staffing day-care centers.

> A student of education, suggesting that students in sixth through ninth grades are ill served by the big, faceless middle schools and junior high schools they now attend, proposed a return to small, personal elementary schools that teach children from kindergarten through eighth grade.

> A man, stressing the humanizing influence of light, sunshine, and green space, argued for a moratorium on all construction of high-rise buildings.

> A woman, setting forth her belief in the importance of new frontiers, advocated more and better-funded research into space travel.

Generating Ideas

In selecting a topic, your five familiar resources may supply you with knowledge of a problem that needs to be cured. Here are a few questions to help ideas start flowing.

DISCOVERY CHECKLIST: DRAWING FROM RESOURCES

- Can you recall any problem you have encountered in your own experience that you think needs a solution? If your topic is a problem you are well acquainted with, your writing task will be easier by far. Ask yourself what problems you meet every day or occasionally or what problems concern people near you.
- Consider how to improve systems (or ways of doing things) that you believe

to be flawed. Can you think of a better way for your college to run its course registration? A better way for your state or community to control dangerous drugs?

- Have you observed a problem recently? What conditions in need of improvement have you seen on television or in your daily activities? What action is called for?
- Have you read of any such problem in a newspaper or news magazine?
- Have you heard of any problem in recent conversation or class discussion?
- By putting yourself in the position of another person, perhaps someone of a different economic or ethnic background, can you imagine a problem of importance to that person? (This last suggestion may require you to do some reading.)

Brainstorming — compiling a list of possible writing topics — is a good way to begin. (See p. 303 for more advice on this useful strategy.)

Scan the news. One of the most convenient sources of information about real and current problems is a daily newspaper or a news magazine such as *Time, Newsweek,* or *U.S. News & World Report.* In a single newspaper published on the morning we wrote these words, we found discussions of the problems of acid rain, teenage pregnancy, the high school dropout rate, famine in the Sudan, hunger in America, a spurt in the highway death toll because of drunken drivers, unemployment, cases of crack abuse, the difficulty of apprehending parents suspected of child abuse, traffic congestion, a surplus of wine produced by California vintners, terrorist bombings, swindlers who sell worthless insurance, the disposal of toxic waste, and a sharp increase in severe injuries in professional football (prompting debate over whether the rules of the game need to be changed).

Think about solutions. Once you've chosen a problem, try to come up with solutions. Some problems — such as that of reducing international tensions — present no easy solutions. Still, give some thought to any problem that you feel seriously concerned with. You can't be expected to solve, in one college writing assignment, a problem that may have thwarted teams of experts. But sometimes a solution to a problem will reveal itself to a novice thinker. And for some problems, like the problem of reducing armaments, even a small contribution to a partial solution will be worth offering. Brainstorming — alone or with classmates — can be a valuable strategy to find solutions. Here are a few questions to help you think about the problem critically.

DISCOVERY CHECKLIST: UNDERSTANDING A PROBLEM

- How urgent is the problem? Does something need to be done about it immediately?

> ↙ For how long has this problem been going on?
>
> ↙ What causes for this problem can you find? What have been its effects?
>
> ↙ In the past, have any problems like this been solved or eliminated?
>
> ↙ How does this problem affect the reader's health, well-being, conscience, or pocketbook?
>
> ↙ How many possible solutions can you imagine? Don't dismiss any possibilities yet, no matter how farfetched they may seem.

Consider your readers. Think of your audience — the readers you seek to persuade. If you are addressing your classmates, maybe they haven't thought about the problem before. If you can discover any way to bring it home to them, any evidence to show that it affects and concerns them, your paper is likely to be effective. Do some more brainstorming. Try *freewriting,* the useful strategy of writing steadily, thinking as you write (see p. 306 for more advice about freewriting). As you write preliminary notes, consider the following points.

DISCOVERY CHECKLIST: UNDERSTANDING YOUR AUDIENCE

↙ Who are your readers? How would you describe them?

↙ Why should your readers care? Why is this a problem that concerns them personally?

↙ In the past, have they expressed any interest in this problem that you can recall?

↙ Do they belong to any organization, religious group, minority, or other segment of society that might make them especially likely to agree or disagree? What assumptions and values do they hold that you should be aware of?

↙ What attitudes have you in common with them? Do you and your readers already agree on anything?

Gather evidence. To show that the problem really exists, you'll need evidence and examples. Again, draw on your five familiar resources. While you think, scribble notes to yourself. Keep your pencil moving. If you feel that further reading in the library will help you know what you're talking about, now is the time. NewsBank, the *Readers' Guide to Periodical Literature,* and the library catalog are sources of relevant reading — to locate newspaper and magazine articles and books, respectively. (For advice on using these aids, see Chapter 28.)

Planning, Drafting, and Developing

Start with your proposal. A basic way to approach your paper is to state your proposal in a sentence: "A law should be passed enabling couples to divorce without having to go to court"; "The United States should secede from the United Nations." From such a statement, the rest of the argument may start to unfold. Usually a paper of this kind falls naturally into a simple two-part shape.

1. A claim that a problem exists. This is a long introductory part, explaining the problem and supplying evidence to suggest that it is intolerable.
2. A claim that something ought to be done about it. This part is the proposal for solution.

You can make your proposal more persuasive by including some or all of the following elements.

The knowledge or experience you have or the thinking you have done that qualifies you to propose a solution to the problem. If you are proposing changes in Little League baseball, your experience as a player or a coach can help establish you as a credible authority.

The values, beliefs, or assumptions that have caused you to feel strongly about the need for action. (Sample statement: "I believe that persons of fifteen are old enough to chart their own destinies and that it is morally wrong for them to remain under their parents' control with no say in the matter.")

What will be required — an estimate of money, people, skills, material. This part might include a list of what is readily available now and what else will have to be obtained.

Exactly what must be done, step by step, to achieve your solution.

How long the solution is likely to take to implement.

What possible obstacles or difficulties may need to be overcome.

Why your solution to the problem is better than others that have been proposed or tried already.

What tests, controls, or quality checks might be used to make sure that your solution is proceeding as expected.

Any other evidence to show that what you suggest is practical, reasonable in cost, and likely to be effective.

Look again at Ting's essay (p. 167) to see how he incorporates most of the elements in the preceding list in his essay.

When you come to set forth your proposal, you will increase the likelihood of its acceptance if you make the first step simple and inviting. A claim that

WRITING WITH A COMPUTER: PROPOSING A SOLUTION

Your computer's wonderful ability to lift and move blocks of words has a special usefulness for this assignment. It gives you the power to play around, arranging the points of your argument in whatever sequence seems most effective. You might place first whatever you expect to be your readers' most powerful objection to your proposal and then answer it right away. Place the second strongest objection next, and so on. But who knows? Reverse that order, putting the strongest objection last. Try different sequences until you find the one that works best. Your most convincing point might come last—for an effective clincher.

national parks need better care might begin by suggesting that the reader head for such a park and personally size up the situation.

If as you go along you find you don't know enough about a certain point, don't hesitate to backtrack to the library, or to converse with others, or to give your memory another rummage, or to go out and observe, or to do some more imagining.

Imagine your readers' objections. Perhaps you can think of possible objections your readers might raise: reservations about the high cost, the complexity, or the workability of your plan, for instance. It is wonderfully persuasive to anticipate a specific objection that might occur to members of your audience and lay it to rest. Jonathan Swift, in "A Modest Proposal," is aware of this rhetorical strategy. After arguing that it will greatly help the poor of Ireland to sell their babies to rich landlords for meat (he's being ironic, savagely condemning the landlords' lack of feeling), Swift goes on:

> I can think of no one objection that will possibly be raised against this proposal, unless it should be urged that the number of people will be thereby much lessened in the kingdom. This I freely own, and it was indeed one principal design in offering it to the world.

Cite sources carefully. When you collect ideas and evidence from outside sources, whether books and periodicals or nonprint sources, you'll need to document your evidence, that is, tell where you got everything. Check with your instructor on the documentation method he or she wants you to use. Chapter 30 contains extensive information on documentation systems, but for a short paper like the one assigned in this chapter, it will probably be enough to introduce brief lines and phrases to identify sources:

```
According to Newsweek correspondent Josie Fair . . .

As 1980 census figures indicate . . .

In his biography FDR: The New Deal Years, Kenneth S.
Davis reports . . .

While working as a Senate page in the summer of 1986, I
observed . . .
```

Revising and Editing

Try your draft on other students. Are they convinced that the problem you are writing about is of vital concern to them? If not, why don't they care? Are they persuaded that your solution is likely and workable? You can ask them to consult the peer editing checklist as they comment on your draft.

PEER EDITING CHECKLIST: PROPOSING A SOLUTION

- What is your overall reaction to this proposal? Does it make you want to go out and do something about the problem?
- Restate what you understand to be the major points.

  Problem:
  Proposal:
  Explanation of proposal:
      Procedure:
      Duration:
      Advantages:
      Disadvantages:
  Response to other solutions:
  Recommendation:
- Has the writer carefully enough disposed of the other solutions?
- List any additional solutions you think the writer should refute.
- Describe what you think makes the writer trustworthy as a proposer.
- Describe the reader whom the paper seems to be addressing. Has the writer paid enough attention to the reader?
- Would you recommend any changes?
- Circle on the manuscript any spelling, punctuation, grammar, or word choice that impeded your reading and understanding.

In drafting his essay, Jeffrey Ting encountered problems near the end. He wanted to come to an effective conclusion but, looking over the draft, he realized that he had not done so. After showing his paper to a friend and then studying it carefully, he made the following changes.

End with this!

~~The law I suggest~~ *It* would view the growing individual as going through a series of gauntlets in taking his or her rightful place as a responsible member of adult society. ~~While~~ Right now the law *unfairly* discriminates against those who are willing and able to assume responsibility early. ~~My~~ plan~~, at least,~~ would trust those individuals who can show society that they are ready to be trusted.

~~What objections might be raised to the plan I have suggested?~~ At least two objections, I realize, can be leveled against this plan. ~~More~~ *It will require* More paperwork and more bureaucracy~~, will be required. This is not~~ *I don't see this as* a serious problem. Indeed, compared to the work that the present unworkable system creates for our courts, what with the charging of people for violating the drinking laws and the crushing burden of trials resulting from accidents, I believe this extra work would be relatively small. The states could charge a small fee for a drinking license, *which* the teenager would ~~make~~ *pay willingly, thus making* money for the state~~, by paying willingly.~~

A more serious ~~Another~~ objection is that this plan would tie drinking licenses to drivers' licenses, and what about people who don't drive? *Would they never be able to drink? That is* ~~Being~~ a good objection, *and* I propose that, for ~~these~~ *those* individuals without wheels, a different means be created for them to prove their ability to drink without causing *any* problems for society~~, in any way.~~ Some individuals will be ready to drink at seventeen, and others never will be if they live to be ninety. *Put in ¶ 2*

They would be required to affirm that they are not going to obtain drivers' licenses. They would have to keep this pledge or else have to fall subject to the usual requirements for drivers. They would have an eighteen-month period following their seventeenth birthdays, during which ~~time~~ they would be required to keep a clean ~~and unblemished~~ police record. At the end of this eighteen months, if they had shown themselves to be good citizens, they could apply for and receive their drinking licenses. They would be required to take the same written test as anyone else. ¶ While, like all official attempts to regulate humans, the plan I suggest ~~could never~~ *would not* work perfectly, I expect that it would work ~~really better~~ *much more efficiently* in keeping drunken drivers off the roads than the present confusion of laws and drinking ages. *(Insert ¶)*

With the corrections, the paper was more forcefully organized, ending with a focus on the positive aspects of his plan. In going over his draft, Ting was also able to eliminate unnecessary words and, in general, improve the style. What emerged was the effective conclusion he wanted.

Be reasonable. Exaggerated claims for your solution will not persuade. Don't be afraid to express your own reasonable doubts that your solution will root out the problem forever. If you have ended your draft with a sort of resounding trumpet call or a horrific vision of what will happen if your plea should go unheard, ask yourself whether you have gone too far and whether a reader might protest, "Aaah, this won't mean the end of the world."

A temptation in writing a paper that proposes a solution is to simplify the problem so that the solution will seem all the more likely to apply. In looking back over your draft, if you have proposed an easy, three-step way to end war, famine, or pestilence, perhaps you have fallen into oversimplification. (For help in recognizing this and other errors in reasoning, see "Looking for Logical Fallacies," p. 381.) You may need to rethink both the problem and the solution.

In looking back over your draft once more, review these points.

REVISION CHECKLIST: PROPOSING A SOLUTION

- Does your introduction invite the reader in?
- Have you made the problem clear?
- Have you made it of immediate concern to your readers, so that they will feel it is their business?
- Have you anticipated the doubts they may have?
- Have you made clear the steps that must be taken to solve the problem?
- Have you demonstrated the benefits of your solution to the problem?
- Have you considered other possible solutions to the problem before rejecting them in favor of your own?
- Have you come on as the well-meaning, reasonable writer that you are, one willing to admit, "I don't know everything"?
- Have you made a reasonable claim, not promised that your solution will do more than it can possibly do? Have you made believable predictions for the success of your plan, not wild ones?

Other Assignments

1. If in Chapter 7 you followed the assignment and took a stand, now write a few additional paragraphs extending that paper, going on to argue for action. You may find it helpful to brainstorm with classmates first.

2. Write an editorial in which you propose to your town or city officials an innovation you think would benefit the whole community. Here are a few suggestions to get your own thoughts working:

FOR GROUP LEARNING
Here is a one-on-one activity. Exchange with some other student the papers you both have written for an assignment in this chapter. Then, instead of writing the brief comments you might ordinarily write on another student's paper, write each other at least a few hundred words of reactions and suggestions. Exchange comments and then sit down together to discuss your experiences. What did you find out about proposing a solution? About writing? About peer editing?

>   Requiring an economics course of all high school students
>   A drug and alcohol education program in the schools
>   A network of bicycle paths
>   Conversion of a vacant lot into a park
>   After-school programs for children of working parents
>   Getting people involved in a neighborhood program for crime prevention
>   Tests of the local water supply
>   A law against the dumping of hazardous wastes
>   Lowering college tuition
>   Protecting an endangered species

3. Write a letter to your congressional representative or your senator in which you object to some government policy with which you disagree. End your letter with a proposal for righting the wrong that concerns you.

4. Choose from the following list a practice that seems to you to represent an inefficient, unethical, unfair, or morally wrong solution to a problem. In a few paragraphs, give reasons for your objections. Then propose a better solution. (You might prefer not to choose a topic from the list, but let the list prompt you to think of another, different wrong solution.)

>   Censorship
>   Corporal punishment for children
>   Laboratory experiments on animals
>   Strip-mining
>   Surrogate motherhood
>   State lotteries
>   Dumping wastes in the ocean

APPLYING WHAT YOU LEARN: SOME USES OF PROPOSALS

In college we often think of a proposal as a specific thing: a written plan submitted to someone in authority who must approve it before you go ahead with your solution. Students embarking on a research project may be required to submit a proposal to an adviser or a committee in which they set forth what they intend to investigate and how they will approach their topic. Students who object to a grade can file a grievance to try to get the grade changed. Like writers of persuasive essays, they state a claim and supply evidence in its support.

In business, too, proposals for action are often useful: for persuading a prospective customer to buy a product or service, to solve a personal or business problem, for recommending a change in procedure, for suggesting a new project, or for urging a purchase of new equipment. An office manager might use a proposal as a means to achieve harmony with co-workers: first discussing with the staff a certain problem—poor morale, a conflict between smokers and nonsmokers—and then writing a proposal to outline the solution on which the group has agreed. Copies of the proposal are given to the people who agreed on it so they can put it into action.

Throughout this chapter, we have looked at proposals as more general than plans in need of okaying. We have seen them as any arguments with which we try to influence readers to act on our ideas or, at the very least, to agree with them. Most of us have ideas for doing something more effectively than it has been done in the past, for improving a situation in which we discern some annoying fault, for abolishing a practice that strikes us as unfair or outmoded. We are often given opportunities, in college and beyond, to propose a solution to a problem. Sometimes we're given such an opportunity when we answer a question on an exam or when we are assigned to write a paper arguing for an action. "How can environmentalists change people's attitudes and therefore their actions toward the natural world?" "What suggestions can you make to alleviate the plight of women who want to work but cannot afford day care for their children?"

Thoughtful, imaginative answers to such questions can be the first crucial step toward solving some of the world's knottiest problems. By laying out possible solutions, writers can at the very least encourage fruitful debate. Every day in the world around us, we encounter proposals—on the editorial pages of newspapers and magazines, in books new and old. For example, in this paragraph from an editorial written for a 1979 textbook to urge more funding for research on alternative energy sources, nuclear physicist David Rittenhouse endorses the value and practicality of harnessing the wind:

> As another example of inadequate effort, no one is building a giant windmill. One prototype, built on a limited experimental basis during World War II, fed 1,000 kilowatts into the electricity grid in Vermont. That experiment came just at the dawn of the atomic age and was not followed up, probably because of early rosy hopes for infinite, cheap, and trouble-free nuclear power. Now that those early dreams have faded, it is high time to follow up on wind power development. The potential is enormous—almost limitless. Modern engineering stands ready, without awaiting further research and development, to build large numbers of giant windmills either in the sparsely settled parts of the Great Plains or offshore near the edge of the continental shelf, where they will bother almost no one. They can generate hydrogen to be stored and provide a steady source of power. The immediate need is for a few million dollars to build the first full-scale prototypes to convince decision makers that thousands of windmills would provide as much power as the nuclear plants that are being proposed.

Sometimes an entire article, essay, or other document is devoted to arguing for an action. In other cases, a writer's chief purpose may be to explain something or perhaps to express an opinion. Such an article can *end* with a proposal, a call to action. Lewis Thomas, a distinguished physician and writer, in a 1983 article for the *New York Times Magazine* laments the way science has been perceived as *the* key to understanding the universe and blames teaching from this perspective for the widespread dislike and ignorance of science. Then he proposes a drastic change in how science is taught.

> I suggest that the introductory courses in science, at all levels from grade school through college, be radically revised. Leave the fundamentals, the so-called basics, aside for a while, and concentrate the attention of all students on the things that are not known. You cannot possibly teach quantum mechanics without mathematics, to be sure, but you can describe the strangeness of the world opened up by quantum theory. Let it be known, early on, that there are deep mysteries and profound paradoxes revealed in distant outline by modern physics. Explain that these can be approached more closely and puzzled over, once the language of mathematics has been sufficiently mastered.
>
> At the outset, before any of the fundamentals, teach the still imponderable puzzles of cosmology. Describe as clearly as possible, for the youngest minds, that there are some things going on in the universe that lie still beyond comprehension, and make it plain how little is known.

Like many proposals that you will read during your college years and beyond, Thomas's is controversial. Whether Thomas persuades or fails to persuade his readers, he performs a useful service. By giving us a thoughtful proposal on this crucial issue, he challenges us to think, too.

In time, some calls to action that at first are controversial become generally accepted. This has certainly been true of Dr. Elisabeth Kübler-Ross's views about how dying patients and their loved ones ought to be treated. Before she wrote her landmark book *On Death and Dying* (1969), terminally ill patients in hospitals were seldom told when they were close to death, and little was done to help them die with dignity. Their families felt uncomfortable about the silences and deceptions imposed on the dying. After studying the problem, Kübler-Ross evolved a number of suggestions that would ease a patient's transition into death—easing pain for the caregivers as well as for the patient. Among them is this one.

> There is a time in a patient's life when the pain ceases to be, when the mind slips off into a dreamless state, when the need for food becomes minimal and the awareness of the environment all but disappears into darkness. This is the time when the relatives walk up and down the hospital hallways, tormented by the waiting, not knowing if they should leave to attend the living or stay to be around for the moment of death. This is the time when it is too late for words, and yet the time when the relatives cry the loudest for help—with or without words. It is too late for medical interventions (and too cruel, though well meant, when they do occur), but it is also too early for a final separation from the dying. It is the hardest time for the next of kin as he either wishes to take off, to get it over with; or he desperately clings to something that he is in the process of losing forever.

It is the time for the therapy of silence with the patient and availability for the relatives.

The doctor, nurse, social worker, or chaplain can be of great help during these final moments if they can understand the family's conflicts at this time and help select the one person who feels most comfortable staying with the dying patient. This person then becomes in effect the patient's therapist. Those who feel too uncomfortable can be assisted by alleviating their guilt and by the reassurance that someone will stay with the dying until his death has occurred. They can then return home knowing that the patient did not die alone, yet not feeling ashamed or guilty for having avoided this moment which for many people is so difficult to face.

At their best, like Kübler-Ross's pioneering recommendations for facing death and dying, proposals are often the advance guard that comes before useful action.

Further Applications

Whenever we encounter a problem, we search for solutions. When we find an answer which satisfies us, we *propose a solution* to share our excitement with other people. In *A Writer's Reader,* African-American columnist William Raspberry in "The Myth that Is Crippling Black America" (p. 510) proposes a solution to the problem of racism being considered the dominant influence in the lives of black Americans. Attorney Peter P. Swire in "Tropical Chic" (p. 575) proposes a way to save the rain forests. By his argument and evidence, he tries to rouse the jury of his readers to action. Similar to professor of journalism Caryl Rivers (p. 164) and student Jeffrey Ting (p. 167), these writers propose a solution to a problem they feel strongly about.

Other writers who make proposals for solving problems in contemporary society are poet and activist scholar Manning Marable, "Racism and Corporate America" (p. 532), mass communications expert Jack G. Shaheen, "The Media's Image of Arabs" (p. 550), journalist Kirkpatrick Sale, "The Environmental Crisis Is Not Our Fault" (p. 579). Answer the following questions about each of these essays.

1. What problem does the writer identify? What solution does she or he propose?
2. How is the writer qualified to write on this subject?
3. What evidence for the proposed solution does the writer present? Does the writer convince you to agree with her or him? Does the writer rouse you to want to do something about the problem?

CHAPTER 9

Evaluating

Evaluating means judging. You do it when you decide what candidate to vote for, when you pick which camera to buy from among several on the market, when you watch a game and size up a team's prowess. All of us find ourselves passing judgments continually as we move through a day's routine.

Often, in everyday situations, we make quick snap judgments. A friend asks, "How was that movie you saw last night?" and you reply, "Terrific — don't miss it," or maybe, "Pretty good, but it had too much blood and gore for me." Those off-the-cuff opinions are necessary and useful. But to *write* an evaluation calls on you to think more critically. As a writer, you first decide on *criteria*, or standards for judging, and then come up with evidence to back up your judgment.

A written evaluation zeroes in on a definite subject. You inspect the subject carefully and come to a considered opinion. The subject might be a film, a book, a piece of music, a sports team, a group of performers, a concert, a product, a scientific theory, a body of research — the possibilities are endless.

LEARNING FROM OTHER WRITERS

Here are two good evaluations, the first by a professional writer, the second by a student. Terence Rafferty, a film critic for *The New Yorker,* reviews a box office success, an outlaw movie with a twist. In addition to presenting his own evaluation, Rafferty attempts to account for this success.

OUTLAW PRINCESSES
Terence Rafferty

Ridley Scott's *Thelma & Louise* is a crazily overstuffed Hollywood en- 1
tertainment. Its heroines, played by Geena Davis (Thelma) and Susan
Sarandon (Louise), are a couple of Arkansas women who set out for a
weekend in the mountains and wind up speeding through the Southwest,
on the run from the law. Following the tradition of movie outlaws, they're
headed for the Mexican border; they cross a fair number of state lines, and
genre lines, on the way. The act that puts the women on this reckless course
is a murder. To get themselves in the mood for their carefree weekend,
Thelma and Louise stop off at a roadside honky-tonk, where Thelma, elated
at the prospect of a few days' freedom from her obnoxious husband, Darryl
(Christopher McDonald), allows herself to be picked up by a smooth-talking
cracker named Harlan (Timothy Carhart). After whooping it up on the dance
floor for a while, Thelma, feeling sick, heads for the parking lot, and Harlan
tries to rape her; Louise shoots him dead. They hop in Louise's convertible
and flee the scene, because Louise is sure that the police won't believe
the women's version of events; she thinks that Thelma's flirtatious behavior
in the roadhouse would cast doubt on the story of attempted rape. Louise
makes this radical decision, to go on the lam rather than face the skepti-
cism of the authorities, instantaneously and with unanswerable conviction.
For the audience, the moment requires a leap of faith that is far greater
than the one the cops would have to make in order to believe the women's
story. And it's only the first of a series of leaps that the script, by Callie
Khouri, forces us to make if we want to stay with these unlikely desperadoes
on their wild ride. The women have plenty of opportunities to turn back, but
the movie is designed to keep pushing them farther and farther out there —
past the point of no return, into the vanishing point of a vast Western
landscape, and, finally, over the edge of the world.

Essentially, *Thelma & Louise* is an outlaw fantasy, and a mighty shame- 2
less one. The feminist justification that Khouri's script provides for the
heroines' behavior doesn't make their actions any less preposterous: the
characters would probably be more believable if the movie provided fewer
explanations of their motives — if it allowed us to see their mad dash to the
border as purely irrational (in the manner of, say, a Patricia Highsmith
novel). The way the script is constructed, we sometimes feel, unfortunately,
that the feminist ideas are being used opportunistically, just to keep the
narrative moving — that every time Thelma and Louise have a chance to give
themselves up, a man does something horrible and strengthens their conviction that they're better off on the run. The funny thing about *Thelma &
Louise* is that you can recognize the crudeness of the script's devices and
still have an awfully good time. The dopey ideas do at least give the picture
some momentum: the heroines' flight is fueled (however implausibly) by
impulses that are more powerful than the usual road-movie anomie. The
movie has the hellbent energy of a drive-in exploitation picture, and it's

eventful — it isn't just figures drifting dazedly through alienating landscapes. Thelma and Louise are lively, voluble good old girls, and they're
not given to brooding; they keep each other's spirits up. The audience's,
too. Davis and Sarandon are so vivid and likable that they carry us past the
plot's most obvious contrivances; a little disbelief seems a small price to
pay for being allowed to remain in their company.

Davis has the flashier role. Thelma is totally oppressed by her loud-   3
mouthed, beer-swilling, gold-chain-wearing husband, an irredeemable
male-chauvinist goon. Despite her grim servitude to this pig, she manages
to be pretty cheerful, in a girlish, spacey way. She seems never to have
grown up; when she sneaks off, without telling Darryl, for her weekend with
Louise, she giggles wickedly, like a teenager who has put one over on her
parents. It's a wonderful role for Geena Davis: she gets to show off her
(proven) talent for dizzy comedy, and to go through lots of emotional
changes besides. In her best scenes, she does both at once. After a one-
night stand with a sexy young hitchhiker (Brad Pitt, who has the sullen
handsomeness — and the white cowboy hat — of the country singer Dwight
Yoakam), Thelma sashays into the motel coffee shop with a big goofy grin
on her face and tells Louise, "I finally understand what all the fuss is
about." Davis's silly rapture makes this a classic scene, a sweetly funny
image of sexual bliss. Throughout the movie, Davis's large, changeable
features and her lanky frame serve the character beautifully; she seems to
combine the malleability of a cartoon character — which isn't inappropriate
here — with a kind of long-limbed Western grace. She gets terrific vocal
effects, too: she produces a lovely comic music out of laughs and shouts
and drawls. Davis is spectacular, but Sarandon, whose character has a less
extreme emotional range, is every bit as good. Louise, a fortyish diner
waitress who's involved with a kindhearted but unreliable musician (Michael
Madsen), is steadier, world-wearier, and more practical than her young
friend. She has a been-there look about her, and she doesn't trust people
much; she's always scolding Thelma for striking up conversations with
strangers. (And her suspiciousness always turns out to be justified.) In many
scenes, Sarandon plays straight person to Davis, and does it with the skill
and good humor of an extremely confident actress. She trains a penetrat-
ing, no-nonsense stare on her companion's antics; her looks of affectionate
disbelief often mirror the audience's reactions. And when she breaks down
and laughs, giving in to the craziness around her, her abandon is infectious.
Sarandon holds our attention by not betraying her character's emotions too
readily. Her held-in quality makes an effective contrast to Davis's overflow-
ing exuberance, and it has its own power, too; in a sense, Sarandon's
mysterious straight-ahead intensity is what propels the story forward.

There's an exhilarating ease and intuitiveness in the way these ac-   4
tresses work together; we feel, and share, their pleasure in surprising each
other. *Thelma & Louise* is at its best in its most casual, most aimless-
seeming moments, in the dawdling intervals between "important" scenes,
while the women are just zipping down the highway and trying to figure out

what to do next. (Or why they did what they did last. They often seem as dumbfounded by the story as the audience is.) And Ridley Scott provides an abundance of moments like these: scenes in which the women tease each other or get on each other's nerves or sing along with the car radio, as their hair blows all over their faces. The camera lingers on Davis and Sarandon as if it couldn't get enough of them: Scott seems to want to show us what they look like in every kind of light and every kind of mood. The director's entranced gaze slows down the rhythm of the narrative; quite a lot happens in this movie, but it has a leisurely, expansive air. Scott—the director of *The Duellists, Alien,* and *Blade Runner*—is known for his striking, even overpowering, visual style: the compositions in his films are meticulous, shiny, and elaborately textured. They frequently look too good to be true, and Scott has sometimes been seen as just another member of a school of filmmakers who developed a slick, manipulative craft in the British advertising industry—directors like Alan Parker (*Midnight Express* and *Mississippi Burning*), Adrian Lyne (*Flashdance* and *Fatal Attraction*), and Ridley's brother Tony Scott (*Top Gun* and *Days of Thunder*). Ridley Scott isn't really that kind of filmmaker, though. He has never been a cynical manipulator of audience reactions. He's a romantic, and rather an innocent and credulous one, at that, investing everything he works on with the passion and enthusiasm of an imaginative child. His images have a true believer's intensity, and if they're not always persuasive it's perhaps because Scott isn't terribly selective about what he believes in.

His fabulist's sensibility does wonders for *Thelma & Louise.* He dances   5 attendance on the outlaw princesses who are his heroines, and treats every stage of their journey as an occasion for awe. Truck stops, mesas, motel pools, deserted country roads, messy kitchens, and the packed ladies' room of the honky-tonk all have a hyper-real gleam to them, a luminous expressiveness. When Thelma and Louise are on the road, the movie has the look of a mirage, a jeweled shimmer that keeps us half hypnotized. (The trance is broken periodically by the intrusion of banal plot mechanics: cutaways to the police investigation, under the direction of a sympathetic cop played by Harvey Keitel. These are the movie's clumsiest scenes; we can feel Scott's impatience to get back to the women.) Scott's love of the women and the landscape doesn't quite transform Khouri's gimmicky, rabble-rousing script into something profound, but it has the welcome effect of softening the hard edges of the story; it gives the whole movie a pleasantly dreamy quality. In the end, *Thelma & Louise* seems less a feminist parable than an airy, lyrical joke about a couple of women who go off in search of a little personal space and discover that they have to keep going and going and going to find a space that's big enough.

Questions to Start You Thinking

1. Summarize Rafferty's opinion of this movie. Does he provide enough evidence from the film and sufficient explanation to convince you to agree with him?

2. What criteria does Rafferty establish for his evaluation? How does he apply these criteria to the film?

3. For what audience is Rafferty writing?

4. How does Rafferty integrate narrative details from the plot into his review?

In a lively paper written for a composition class, Matthew Munich examines a familiar form of entertainment and gives his opinion of it.

Student Essay

I WANT MY MTV
Matthew A. Munich

The concept of the music video, a short film in which 1
video images interpret a song, is not a new one. The beginnings date as far back as the 1960s in the Beatles' full-length film A Hard Day's Night or later in the Rolling Stones' movie Gimme Shelter. With cable television and some of its subsidiary channels, however, the music video has received a tremendous amount of attention and popularity. MTV, a channel devoted solely to showing music videos twenty-four hours a day, has made the music video not only a new medium but also a new form of art. While it may not be fair to judge the popularity of the music video as a cultural step backward, neither can we consider it, in its display of violence and sexist attitudes, a cultural step forward. Music video can be thought of as a step timed to society, a form that meets a new criterion of entertainment.

Music video did for music what television did to radio; 2
in fact, MTV is a television station for videos. Before music video, listening was a more active process. The listener created a personal image of the song. With MTV, however, so compelling is the visual image that it imprints on the brain; the song cannot be divorced from the video. This phenomenon resembles television's "laugh tracks" in that not only is the television showing us a picture but it's telling us what we should think is funny. In this sense, music videos do not require the viewer's active attention or imagination.

Music video does provide a place where new and important   3
film techniques can be tried and developed.   The Cars' video,
which won best video of 1984, exemplifies this stage of technological advancement.   This video employed some of the most
recent discoveries in film computer graphics.   Music video
can help exploit new ways of using film as an artistic
expression.

While the methods used by music videos might be new and   4
innovative, the content seems stereotypical and trite.   The
figure of women in music videos is a large part of this stereotyped content.   The "Spellbound" video by the group Triumph
is a good example of the treatment of women.   The video shows
a man driving at night, and as he approaches a nebulous figure his car starts to break apart.   When he sees that the
figure is a woman with fluffed-out hair, wearing ripped white
fabric, the car falls completely apart.   He emerges from the
wreckage and follows her in a trance.   She stops to let him
reach her, kisses him, and turns him into a statue.   The
video ends with the band playing the song on stage with the
statue.   The video suggests that, while women may be beautiful, they possess evil powers that will be the downfall of
men.   Modern props notwithstanding, this woman is a version of the Medusa who has been turning men to stone for
centuries.

Regressing to an earlier stage than classical myth,   5
people in music video frequently dress in tribal garb.   We
see people in tattered clothing, nonhuman hair styles, jungle
skins, and face paint.   Although the medium is new, then,
these painted creatures portray the primitive thrust of music
video.   A typical example is the "Talk to Me" video by the
group Iam Siam, which shows a young girl taken by force to
some tribal ritual where she is encircled by natives wearing
face paint and loincloths.   Watching this happen is a bald
person painted blue and white from top to bottom.   He decides
to rescue this woman from the ceremony and, once he gets her
back to safety, he touches her, instantly transforming her to
a creature with the same paint job.   Although music video

advances technologies, it returns ideologically to a primitive state.

The concept of the music video invades our lives in   6
other ways than just on television. Movies that appear to be
nothing more than two-hour music videos are becoming popular.
The Talking Heads' movie Stop Making Sense is nothing more
than an extended music video. Clearly the toleration for
this new art form reflects popular taste; Flashdance and
Footloose are other immense successes that reflect the music
video mode. Who is the audience for the hard-imaged, fantastical, and sometimes amusing but always loud and rhythmic
sounds? What, if anything, does the form tell us about our
culture?

If music video is art, it is art you can do your home-   7
work to. It speaks of a culture that loves gimmicks and
quick fixes and noise. MTV has a mesmerizing effect, almost
hypnotizing us and offering a visual counterpart to a drugged
state. Like a dope peddler, the video station fosters addiction by promising total coverage: we can watch it all the
time; we never have to give it up. It reflects our culture's
fascination with and, more ominously, return to a more primitive state. There is no subtlety; every idea and theme is
spelled out, not once but many times. Natives beat drums,
beat their chests, and beat women. Women, conversely, are
the stereotypical downfall of men. Music video is quintes-
sentially modern because it's so thin: quickly replaced, dis-
passionate, disposable. In the nuclear age, MTV is us.

Questions to Start You Thinking

1. What is Munich's final judgment on MTV? Do you agree or disagree?
2. How convincing is the evidence the author marshals to support his evaluation?
3. What knowledge other than an acquaintance with music videos does Munich bring to his essay?
4. Analyze the organization of the essay.
5. What is the purpose of paragraph 6?

LEARNING BY WRITING

The Assignment: Writing an Evaluation

Pick a subject to evaluate, one with which you have some personal experience and which you feel reasonably competent to evaluate. This might be a play or a movie, a TV program, a piece of music or a concert, a work of graphic art, a product new on the market, a government agency (such as the Postal Service), or — what else? Then, in a thoughtful essay, evaluate your subject.

In writing your evaluation, you will have a twofold purpose: (1) to set forth your assessment of the quality of your subject and (2) to convince your readers that your judgment is reasonable — that is, based on your having considered evidence. Remember that analysis and comprehension precede evaluation.

Among the lively and instructive student-written evaluations we've seen recently are these:

> A music major, asked to evaluate the work of American composer Aaron Copland, found Copland a trivial and imitative composer "without a tenth of the talent or inventiveness that George Gershwin or Duke Ellington had in his little finger." To support his negative view, he critically analyzed Copland's *Appalachian Spring, Rodeo*, and other works.

> A man planning a career in business management evaluated a computer firm in whose main office he had worked one summer, using the criteria of efficiency, productivity, ability to appeal to new customers, and degree of employee satisfaction.

> A woman from Brazil, whose family included two scientists and who had herself visited the Amazon rain forest and had seen at first hand the effects of industrial development, critically evaluated the efforts of the U.S. government to protect the ozone layer, comparing them with efforts being made (or advocated) by environmentalists in her own country.

> A student of history, assigned the task of evaluating the long-term effects of the Volstead Act of 1919 (prohibiting the manufacture and distribution of alcoholic beverages), found in favor of the maligned Prohibition law, giving evidence in its support.

> For an English course, a man writing an evaluation of *Going after Cacciato*, Tim O'Brien's novel of American soldiers in Vietnam (1978), favorably compared it, point by point, with Ernest Hemingway's much-praised novel of World War I, *A Farewell to Arms*.

Generating Ideas

For a start, why not do a little *freewriting,* setting down ideas as fast as they come to mind? (This strategy is discussed in detail on p. 306.) Think of the features of your subject worth considering: in the case of a popular entertainer such as Madonna or Michael Jackson, perhaps on-stage manner, rapport with the audience, musicianship, selection of material, originality. How well does the performer score on these points?

You'll want to spend time finding evidence to back your judgment. You might observe (as you would do if you were evaluating a performance or the prowess of a sports team) or read in a library, checking out reviews by other critics, or converse, to see what others think.

Establish your criteria. In evaluating, you may find it helpful to set up *criteria,* standards to apply to your subject. In evaluating the desirability of Atlanta as a home for a young careerist, you might ask: Does it provide an ample choice of decent-paying entry-level positions in growth firms, suitable for a college graduate? The availability of such jobs would be one criterion for testing Atlanta. Evidently, any criterion you use to judge has to fit your subject, your audience, and your purpose. Ample entry-level jobs might not matter to the writer of an article in *Modern Maturity* evaluating Atlanta as a place to live, addressing an audience of retirees. Criteria more appropriate for that article might be the clemency of the weather and the quality and cost of medical care. To take another example of useful and specific criteria: in a review of a new automobile for *Car & Driver,* addressed to a readership of serious car buffs, a writer might evaluate the car by criteria such as styling

---

WRITING WITH A COMPUTER: EVALUATING

If in writing your evaluation you plan to compare and contrast your subject with another of its kind, your computer just might be your best friend. Surely it will be if it has split-screen capability and can display what you write in double columns. You can put this feature to excellent use when you draw up your rough outline. Split the screen into two columns and type a heading for each: Subject A, Subject B. In the left-hand column list each point to be compared. Add notes indicating whatever evidence you have for Subject A. Then in the right-hand column do the same for Subject B, so that your outline will look like the following (for a paper for a film history course, comparing and contrasting a classic German horror movie, *The Cabinet of Dr. Caligari,* with the classic Hollywood movie *Frankenstein*).

```
     CALIGARI                 FRANKENSTEIN

1. sets and lighting:
     dreamlike, impression-   realistic, but with
     istic (deliberately an-  heavy Gothic atmosphere
     gular and distorted;     (as in climax: a night-
     deep shadows throw fig-  time scene, torches
     ures into relief)        highlighting monster's
                              face)
```

And so on, point by point. By displaying each point and each bit of evidence side by side, you can outline your comparison with great efficiency. Once you have listed them, decide on a possible order for the points.

and design, handling, fuel efficiency, value, safety features, and quality of the ride.

Early on, you might try jotting down a list of your criteria. If you can think of any, they will greatly help you evaluate. For each point you plan to consider, note any evidence that springs to mind. If none springs, or not enough, you can readily see where you'll need more material.

Try comparing and contrasting. Although not all writers of evaluations compare or contrast, doing so may be useful for evaluating. (When you *compare,* you point to similarities; when you *contrast,* differences.) Often you can readily size up the worth of a thing by setting it next to another of its kind. Which city—Dallas or Atlanta—holds more advantages for a young single person looking for a job? (The purpose of such a paper might be to recommend settling in one city or the other.) How does an IBM personal computer stack up against a Macintosh for word processing? (Purpose: to decide which to buy.) Such questions invite you to set two subjects side by side so that one may throw the other into sharp relief. To be comparable, of course, your two subjects need to have plenty in common. The quality of a sports car might be judged by comparing it with a racing car, but not by comparing it with a Sherman tank.

If you want to try this method, ask yourself: What would be comparable to my subject? When a likely thing occurs, make a list of points you wish to compare. What similarities and differences leap to mind? If you get interested in any of these points and feel the urge to keep on writing, do. Your list might turn into a scratch outline you can use in drafting your paper.

Try defining your subject. Another technique for evaluating is to *define* your subject, to indicate its nature so clearly that your readers can easily tell it from others of its kind. In defining, you help your readers understand your subject: its structure, its habitat, its functions. Evaluating MTV, Matthew Munich does some *extended* defining: he discusses the nature of the popular video channel, its techniques, its content, its view of women, its effects on its audience. This kind of defining isn't the same as writing a *short definition,* such as you'd find in a dictionary. (For how to do that, see "Defining," p. 369.) Munich's purpose is to judge MTV. So you might ask, What is the nature of my subject? Or, put differently, What qualities make it unique, unlike others of its sort? Scribble down any qualities that occur to you. As you can see, this is a demanding question. But write out your answer and you may find that you have written most of your paper and that you have formed an opinion of your subject as you wrote.

To help you zero in on a promising subject and some likely material, you might ask yourself a few questions.

DISCOVERY CHECKLIST: EVALUATING

What evidence can you recall to back up your judgments? If not from memory, from what other resource might you draw evidence?

 What criteria, if any, do you plan to use in making your evaluation? Are they clear? Will they be reasonably easy to apply?

 Would comparing and contrasting help in evaluating your subject? If so, with what might you compare or contrast your subject?

 What specific qualities set your subject apart from all the rest of its general class?

 What is your purpose for writing?

Planning, Drafting, and Developing

Reflect a moment: What is your purpose in this evaluation? What main point do you wish to make? Keep this point in mind as you write, and you'll be more likely to arrive at it.

You might want to make that point at the beginning of your paper, then demonstrate it by looking at specific evidence, and finally hark back to it again in your closing lines. Organizing your paper differently, you might open by wondering, "How good a film is *Rain Man*?" or "Is Keynes's theory of inflation still valuable, or is it hopelessly out of date?" or "Are organically grown vegetables worth their higher price?" — raising some such question about your subject to which your paper will reply. You then consider the evidence, a piece at a time, and conclude with your overall judgment. You might try both patterns of organization and see which works better for your subject and purpose.

Consider your criteria. Some writers like to spell out criteria to apply to whatever they're evaluating. Many find that a list of criteria gives them confidence and provokes ideas. But we should admit that that isn't the only possible way to approach your draft. To be a good evaluator, you don't absolutely have to have foreordained criteria. You can, of course, just move into your subject and thoughtfully sniff around. T. S. Eliot said that, in criticizing literature, criteria, standards, and touchstones (great works to hold lesser works up to) don't help all that much. In a statement that sounds snobbish but isn't when you think about it, he declared that all a good critic needs is to be very intelligent.

Consider outlining. Most writers find that an outline — even a rough list — facilitates writing a draft. An outline will help you keep track of points to make. If you intend to compare and contrast your subject with something else, one way to arrange the points is *subject by subject*. You have your say about subject A and then do the same for subject B. In writing a short paper comparing Atlanta and Dallas, you would complete your remarks about Atlanta and then head west. This method is workable for a short essay of two or three paragraphs, but for a longer essay it has drawbacks. In an essay of, say, a thousand or two thousand words, your reader might find it hard to remember all your points about Atlanta, ten paragraphs ago, while reading about Dallas.

A better way to organize a longer comparison is *point by point.* You take up one point at a time and apply it first to one subject, then to the other:

1. Job opportunities
   a. Dallas
   b. Atlanta
2. Recreation possibilities
   a. Dallas
   b. Atlanta

And so on, for however many points you want to compare.

Keep your outline simple, and don't be ruled by it. If, while you write your draft, good thoughts come to you, by all means let them in. (If you need a quick refresher course in outlining, see "Outlining," p. 331.)

Revising and Editing

Be fair. Make your judgments reasonable, not extreme. Few things on earth are all good or all evil. You need not find Atlanta or Dallas a paradise in order to recommend it to a career-minded young settler. A reviewer can find fault with a film and conclude that nevertheless it is worth seeing, as Rafferty does (p. 183). There's nothing wrong, of course, with passing a fervent judgment ("This is the trashiest excuse for a play I have ever suffered through"), but consider your readers and their likely reactions. Read some reviews in your local newspaper or watch some movie critics on television to see how they balance their judgments.

However strongly you word your judgments, make sure that no one will fail to see what you think. Enlist the help of a peer editor, who can read your draft and consider these questions.

PEER EDITING CHECKLIST: EVALUATING

- When you finish reading the essay, can you tell exactly what the writer thinks of the subject?
- What is your overall reaction to this essay? Does the writer make you agree with his or her evaluation?
- Does the writer give you sufficient evidence for his or her judgment? Put stars wherever more evidence is needed.
- What audience does the writer seem to have in mind?
- Are there any places in the essay where the writer ignores his or her readers, when it might have helped to be aware of them? Point out such places.
- Look at the way the writer has arranged his or her points. Would you recommend any changes in how the essay is organized? Do you need more signposts?

> ✓ Circle any instances where you think grammar, spelling, punctuation, or usage may need a polish.
>
> ✓ What did you like best about the essay? Suggest any revisions that might make it more successful.

If you do any comparing and contrasting, look back over your draft with special care. Make sure that, all along, you keep discussing the same points about each subject. It might confuse your reader to compare, say, job opportunities in Dallas with sports facilities in Atlanta. Make sure you haven't fallen into a monotonous drone: A does this, B does that; A looks like this, B looks like that. Compare and contrast with feeling, and the result may be a lively paper. And it won't be mechanical in its symmetry, like two salt and pepper shakers.

In thinking critically about your draft, you might find this checklist handy.

REVISION CHECKLIST: EVALUATING

> ✓ Have you given your readers evidence to support each point you make? Is your overall opinion clear? Have you recalled, observed, read, or picked up from conversation any definite facts that your readers might go and verify? If your draft looks a little thin for lack of evidence, from which resource or resources might you draw more?
>
> ✓ Have you been fair to both your subject and your readers? If you are championing something, have you deliberately skipped over any of its damning disadvantages or glaring faults? If condemning your subject, have you omitted any of its admirable traits?
>
> ✓ Do any of your judgments need rewording, to tone them down or qualify them? Consider your readers. Is your conclusion likely to make them think that you are a wild-eyed nut?
>
> ✓ If you anticipate that readers will make any objections to your views, can you insert any answers to their objections?
>
> ✓ Is the judgment you pass on your subject unmistakably clear? Reread like a reader. Rewrite, if need be, to give your evaluation more emphasis.
>
> ✓ If you compared one thing with another, do you look consistently for the same points in both?

Other Assignments

1. If you disagree with Matthew Munich in his evaluation of MTV, write an essay setting forth your own evaluation. If you agree with Munich, you might instead read some reviews of films, recordings, television, and books in recent magazines (*Time, Newsweek, Rolling Stone, The New Yorker,* or others) until you find a

review you think quite wrong-headed. Write a reply to it, giving your own evaluation.

2. After reading Munich's essay, write your own judgment of MTV or *Night Tracks* or *Soul Train* or *The Arsenio Hall Show*.

3. Write an evaluation of a college course you have taken or are now taking. (So that you can be completely objective, we suggest you work on some course other than your writing course.) Analyze its strengths and weaknesses. Does the instructor present the material clearly, understandably, and interestingly? Can you confer with the instructor if you need to? Is there any class discussion or other feedback? Are the assignments pointed and purposeful? How is the textbook: helpful, readable, easy to use? Does this course give you your money's worth?

4. Analyze a story, poem, or play (as we discussed in Chapter 6), and you will be in a good position to evaluate it. Here are two poems on a similar theme. Read them critically, seeing what you find in them, and decide which seems to you the better poem. Then, in a brief essay, set forth your evaluation. Some criteria to apply might be the poet's choice of concrete, specific words that appeal to the senses instead of vague generalities and his awareness of his audience. (Does anything in either poem prompt you to object to it?)

PUTTING IN THE SEED

You come to fetch me from my work tonight
When supper's on the table, and we'll see
If I can leave off burying the white
Soft petals fallen from the apple tree
(Soft petals, yes, but not so barren quite,   5
Mingled with these, smooth bean and wrinkled pea),
And go along with you ere you lose sight
Of what you came for and become like me,
Slave to a springtime passion for the earth.
How Love burns through the Putting in the Seed   10
On through the watching for that early birth
When, just as the soil tarnishes with weed,
The sturdy seedling with arched body comes
Shouldering its way and shedding the earth crumbs.
            —Robert Frost (1874–1963)

BETWEEN OUR FOLDING LIPS

Between our folding lips
God slips
An embryon life, and goes;
And this becomes your rose.
We love, God makes: in our sweet mirth
God spies occasion for a birth.
Then is it His, or is it ours?
I know not—He is fond of flowers.
            —T. E. Brown (1830–1897)

5. Visit a new restaurant, a museum, or a tourist attraction, and write an evaluation of it for others who might be considering a visit to the place. Be sure to specify your criteria for evaluation.

6. Analyze and evaluate a magazine you do not often read.

7. Analyze and evaluate one of the essays in this textbook, using the criteria for effective writing you have learned in this course.

FOR GROUP LEARNING

Before you write a paper evaluating a subject, get together with your writing group or your customary peer editors. Discuss the subject you plan to evaluate and see whether the group can help you arrive at a sound judgment of it. They will need to see what it is you're evaluating or hear your detailed report about it. If you are evaluating a short literary work or an idea expressed in a reading, it might be an excellent idea to read that short work or excerpt aloud to the group so that they all may be familiar with it. Ask your listeners to supply reasons for their own evaluations. Maybe they'll suggest reasons that hadn't occurred to you.

APPLYING WHAT YOU LEARN: SOME USES OF EVALUATING

In your college writing you'll be called on over and over to evaluate. On an art appreciation exam, you might be asked to evaluate the relative merits of Norman Rockwell and Andrew Wyeth as realistic painters. Speech pathology students, after considering the long-standing controversy that rages in education for the deaf, might be called on to describe and then evaluate three currently disputed teaching methods: oral/aural, signing, and a combination of the two. Students of language and linguistics may be asked to decide which of two methods of articulation therapy is more valuable: Skinner's behaviorist theory or Chomsky's theory of innate language acquisition. Outside of class, students on some campuses are invited to write comments for a student-run survey to evaluate their college courses.

In life beyond campus, every executive or professional needs to evaluate. An editor accepts and rejects manuscripts. A personnel director selects people to hire. A lawyer sizes up the merits of a case and decides whether to take it. A retailer chooses the best product to sell. A speech pathologist evaluates the speech and language skills of prospective patients. You can think of endless other examples of evaluating, a kind of critical thinking we do every day of our lives.

Familiar kinds of *written* evaluation abound. Daily newspapers and magazines contain reviews of films, books, TV programs, records, and videos. Many sportswriters, columnists, and political commentators evaluate. The magazine *Consumer Reports* contains detailed evaluations of products and services, like this one from "Is There a DAT [digital audio tape] in Your Future?" (Jan. 1989).

> While prices will surely decline over time, we don't think DATs are going to make CDs obsolete anytime soon. First, while DAT players are much faster than conventional cassette decks at locating song tracks, they'll never be able to hop from track to track as quickly as a CD player.
>
> Second, digital audio tapes aren't as impervious to wear as compact discs.

The tape comes into physical contact with a rotating recording head similar to a VCR's, and that will eventually degrade sound quality on the tape.

Finally, recording quality might not be quite as close to perfect as DAT makers have implied—and record companies feared. When we tried out the *Sony DTC 1000 ES* DAT recorder last year, we found that it didn't match the low background noise performance of CD players. Unless that noise was a problem unique to our tested machine, DAT sound doesn't equal the quality of CD sound.

For all of those reasons—price, durability, convenience, quality of sound, and the reluctance of the recording industry—we think that DAT will coexist with, rather than supplant, the compact disc in the years ahead.

Like many general magazines, professional journals contain book reviews that not only give a brief rundown of a book's contents but also indicate whether the reviewer considers the book worth reading. In the March 13, 1989, issue of *Chemical & Engineering News,* Deborah C. Andrews reviews the second edition of a textbook by H. J. Tichy called *Effective Writing for Engineers, Managers, Scientists.* Included in the review is an evaluation:

> What this text does well is to use words to talk about words. Pages are heavy with text, and visuals are exceedingly rare. Tichy writes within the framework of English (and French) literature as well as the literature of science, often calling upon the masters for clever phrases and telling anecdotes, some of them somewhat arcane—like a reference to an address before the French Academy by the 18th century naturalist Count Georges-Louis Leclerc de Buffon. In a section on figures of speech, she includes mention of some, like metonymy and litotes, that would stymie many English majors.

For a final example, Howard Gardner, in *Artful Scribbles,* an inquiry into what children's drawings mean, makes a sharp contrast between the drawings of younger children and those of older children.

> When drawings made by eight- or nine-year-olds are juxtaposed to those produced by younger children, a striking contrast emerges. There is little doubt about which came from which group: works by the older children feature a kind of precision, a concern for detail, a command of geometrical form which are lacking in the attempts by younger artists. Schemas for familiar objects are readily recognized, and attempts at rendering less familiar objects can initially be decoded. And yet one hesitates to call the drawings by the older children "better"— indeed, most observers and sometimes even the youngsters themselves feel that something vital which is present at the age of six or seven has disappeared from the drawings by the older children. A certain freedom, flexibility, *joie de vivre* [zest for life], and a special fresh exploratory flavor which mark the childlike drawings of the six-year-old are gone; and instead of being replaced by adult mastery, this loss has merely been supplanted by a product that is at once more carefully wrought yet also more wooden and lifeless.

As you'll notice, Gardner, while giving the strong points of each age group of artists, apparently favors the work of the young, despite its faults.

Further Applications

We judge events and ideas, objects and procedures, people and places, movies and television programs — anything with which we come into contact. In *A Writer's Reader,* social critic Barbara Ehrenreich in "The Wretched of the Hearth" (p. 543) *evaluates* the success of the sitcom "Roseanne." She praises this television series for its realistic portrayal of a blue-collar American family, claiming that such realism without condescension and without stereotypes is rare. In "American SF and The Other" (p. 540), Ursula K. Le Guin, who has won awards for her science fiction novels, draws on her knowledge of the field to analyze and evaluate it, criticizing its outdated authoritarian qualities. Just as Terence Rafferty (p. 183) and student Matthew A. Munich (p. 186), these writers choose subjects they feel they can competently evaluate.

Some of the other writers in *A Writer's Reader* also evaluate subjects in their fields of expertise, including novelist Paule Marshall, "From the Poets in the Kitchen" (p. 439), professor of African-American studies Henry Louis Gates, Jr., "2 Live Crew, Decoded" (p. 558), and management consultant William Ouchi, "Japanese and American Workers" (p. 523). Answer the following questions about each of these essays.

1. Do you consider the writer qualified to evaluate the subject he or she chose? Why or why not?

2. Is the writer's assessment of the subject clear?

3. Does the writer convince you that his or her judgment is reasonable?

CHAPTER 10

Identifying Causes and Effects

When a house burns down, an insurance company assigns a claims adjuster to look into the disaster and answer the question Why? The answer—the *cause* of the fire, whether it be lightning, a forgotten cigar, or a match that the homeowner deliberately struck—is given in a written report. The adjuster also details the *effects* of the fire: what was destroyed or damaged, what repairs will be needed, how much they will cost.

In assigning you to write a paper tracing causes, no instructor will expect you to set forth a definitive explanation with absolute certainty. To ask why a huge phenomenon took place, such as continental drift or the Depression of the 1930s, is to propose long and serious toil. After decades, historians are still trying to account for that remarkable burst of intellectual energy called the Italian Renaissance. Taken seriously, the simple statement "Herbert Hoover became unpopular because the stock market crashed" would call for months of effort to demonstrate for sure that the president's unpopularity resulted from the crash and from no other cause. To seek causes, even if a writer has all the time in the world, is at best an uncertain pursuit. "Causality," says French philosopher of history Paul Veyne, "is always accompanied by mental reservation."

Still, in the process of seeking causes and effects, both you and your readers learn a good deal and understand the subject more clearly. To probe causes and to detail effects, you have to think about a subject critically, to gather information and ideas, and to marshal evidence. Effects, by the way, are usually easier to demonstrate than causes. The results of a fire are apparent to an onlooker the next day, although its cause may be obscure.

The following two essays explore causes and effects. The first is by Jonathan Kozol, who gained fame in the 1960s and 1970s as a teacher, author, and stern critic of American education, a reputation he has extended into the 1990s with the publication of *Savage Inequalities* (1991). With the publication of *Rachel and Her Children* (1988), he also gained a reputation as an advocate for the homeless. Kozol's "Distancing the Homeless," which appeared in the Winter 1988 issue of the *Yale Review*, was the basis for this essay.

ARE THE HOMELESS CRAZY?
Jonathan Kozol

It is commonly believed by many journalists and politicians that the homeless of America are, in large part, former patients of large mental hospitals who were deinstitutionalized in the 1970s—the consequence, it is sometimes said, of misguided liberal opinion that favored the treatment of such persons in community-based centers. It is argued that this policy, and the subsequent failure of society to build such centers or to provide them in sufficient number, is the primary cause of homelessness in the United States. 1

Those who work among the homeless do not find that explanation satisfactory. While conceding that a certain number of the homeless are or have been mentally unwell, they believe that, in the case of most unsheltered people, the primary reason is economic rather than clinical. The cause of homelessness, they say with disarming logic, is the lack of homes and of income with which to rent or acquire them. 2

They point to the loss of traditional jobs in industry (two million every year since 1980) and to the fact that half of those who are laid off end up in work that pays a poverty-level wage. They point out that since 1968 the number of children living in poverty has grown by three million, while welfare benefits to families with children have declined by 35 percent. 3

And they note, too, that these developments have occurred during a time in which the shortage of low-income housing has intensified as the gentrification of our major cities has accelerated. Half a million units of low-income housing are lost each year to condominium conversion as well as to arson, demolition, or abandonment. Between 1978 and 1980, median rents climbed 30 percent for people in the lowest income sector, driving many of these families into the streets. Since 1980, rents have risen at even faster rates. 4

Hard numbers, in this instance, would appear to be of greater help than psychiatric labels in telling us why so many people become homeless. Eight million American families now use half or more of their income to pay their rent or mortgage. At the same time, federal support for low-income housing 5 dropped from $30 billion (1980) to $7.5 billion (1988). Under Presidents Ford and Carter, 500,000 subsidized private housing units were constructed. By President Reagan's second term, the number had dropped to 25,000.

In our rush to explain the homeless as a psychiatric problem even the words of medical practitioners who care for homeless people have been curiously ignored. A study published by the Massachusetts Medical Society, for instance, has noted that, with the exceptions of alcohol and drug use, the most frequent illnesses among a sample of the homeless population were trauma (31 percent), upper-respiratory disorders (28 percent), limb disorders (19 percent), mental illness (16 percent), skin diseases (15 percent), hypertension (14 percent), and neurological illnesses (12 percent). Why, we may ask, of all these calamities, does mental illness command so much political and press attention? The answer may be that the label of mental illness places the destitute outside the sphere of ordinary life. It personalizes an anguish that is public in its genesis; it individualizes a misery that is both general in cause and general in application. 6

There is another reason to assign labels to the destitute and single out mental illness from among their many afflictions. All these other problems—tuberculosis, asthma, scabies, diarrhea, bleeding gums, impacted teeth, etc.—bear no stigma, and mental illness does. It conveys a stigma in the United States. It conveys a stigma in the Soviet Union as well. In both nations the label is used, whether as a matter of deliberate policy or not, to isolate and treat as special cases those who, by deed or word or by sheer presence, represent a threat to national complacence. The two situations are obviously not identical, but they are enough alike to give Americans reason for concern. 7

The notion that the homeless are largely psychotics who belong in institutions, rather than victims of displacement at the hands of enterprising realtors, spares us from the need to offer realistic solutions to the deep and widening extremes of wealth and poverty in the United States. It also enables us to tell ourselves that the despair of homeless people bears no intimate connection to the privileged existence we enjoy—when, for example, we rent or purchase one of those restored town houses that once provided shelter for people now huddled in the street. 8

What is to be made, then, of the supposition that the homeless are primarily the former residents of mental hospitals, persons who were carelessly released during the 1970s? Many of them are, to be sure. Among the older men and women in the streets and shelters, as many as one-third (some believe as many as one-half) may be chronically disturbed, and a number of these people were deinstitutionalized during the 1970s. But to operate on that assumption in a city such as New York—where nearly half the homeless are small children whose average age is six—makes no sense. Their parents, with an average age of twenty-seven, are not likely to have been hospitalized in the 1970s, either. 9

A frequently cited set of figures tells us that in 1955 the average daily 10 census of nonfederal psychiatric institutions was 677,000, and that by 1984 the number had dropped to 151,000. But these people didn't go directly from a hospital room to the street. The bulk of those who had been psychiatric patients and were released from hospitals during the 1960s and early 1970s had been living in low-income housing, many in skid-row hotels or boardinghouses. Such housing—commonly known as SRO (single-room occupancy) units—was drastically diminished by the gentrification of our cities that began in the early '70s. Almost 50 percent of SRO housing was replaced by luxury apartments or office buildings between 1970 and 1980, and the remaining units have been disappearing even more rapidly.

Even for those persons who are ill and were deinstitutionalized during the decades before 1980, the precipitating cause of homelessness in 1987 is not illness but loss of housing. SRO housing offered low-cost sanctuaries for the homeless, providing a degree of safety and mutual support for those who lived within them. They were a demeaning version of the community health centers that society had promised; they were the de facto "halfway houses" of the 1970s. For these people too—at most half of the homeless single persons in America—the cause of homelessness is lack of housing. 11

Even in those cases where mental instability is apparent, homelessness itself is often the precipitating factor. For example, many pregnant women without homes are denied prenatal care because they constantly travel from one shelter to another. Many are anemic. Many are denied essential dietary supplements by recent federal cuts. As a consequence, some of their children do not live to see their second year of life. Do these mothers sometimes show signs of stress? Do they appear disorganized, depressed, disordered? Frequently. They are immobilized by pain, traumatized by fear. So it is no surprise that when researchers enter the scene to ask them how they "feel," the resulting reports tell us that the homeless are emotionally unwell. The reports do not tell us that we have *made* these people ill. They do not tell us that illness is a natural response to intolerable conditions. Nor do they tell us of the strength and the resilience that so many of these people retain despite the miseries they must endure. 12

A writer in the *New York Times* describes a homeless woman standing on a traffic island in Manhattan. "She was evicted from her small room in the hotel just across the street," and she is determined to get revenge. Until she does, "nothing will move her from that spot. . . . Her argumentativeness and her angry fixation on revenge, along with the apparent absence of hallucinations, mark her as a paranoid." Most physicians, I imagine, would be more reserved in passing judgment with so little evidence, but this reporter makes his diagnosis without hesitation. "The paranoids of the street," he says, "are among the most difficult to help." 13

Perhaps so. But does it depend on who is offering the help? Is anyone offering to help this woman get back her home? Is it crazy to seek vengeance for being thrown into the street? The absence of anger, some psychiatrists believe, might indicate much greater illness. 14

"No one will be turned away," says the mayor of New York City, as 15 hundreds of young mothers with their infants are turned from the doors of shelters season after season. That may sound to some like a denial of reality. "Now you're hearing all kinds of horror stories," says the President of the United States as he denies that anyone is cold or hungry or unhoused. On another occasion he says that the unsheltered "are homeless, you might say, by choice." That sounds every bit as self-deceiving.

The woman standing on the traffic island screaming for revenge until   16
her room has been restored to her sounds relatively healthy by comparison. If three million homeless people did the same, and all at the same time, we might finally be forced to listen.

Questions to Start You Thinking

1. According to Kozol, what are the immediate causes of homelessness in America? What are the remote causes?

2. What reason does Kozol give for the widespread perception that the homeless are, by and large, mentally ill? To what extent does he agree with this perception?

3. Where in the essay does Kozol switch from searching out causes to detailing the effects of homelessness? Is he guilty of going around in circles? Explain.

4. Read one newspaper or magazine article that probes the causes of some contemporary problem: the shortage of reasonable day-care options, for instance, or the low academic scores of American students compared with those of students in other developed countries. Can you suggest additional causes that the article writer seems to have ignored?

"Why We Burned a Wilderness," a student-written paper, draws conclusions likely to surprise readers. A major in recreation management, Katie Kennedy had the opportunity to work for a season at a wildlife sanctuary near Naples, Florida. The experience changed one of her previous beliefs. You'll notice that she draws her material from all five basic resources: recalling, observing, reading, conversing, and imagining.

Student Essay

WHY WE BURNED A WILDERNESS
Katie Kennedy

Here I was, slogging through a Florida swamp with a   1
lighted drip torch in my hand, leaving behind me a trail of
fire. I was going against everything I believed about fires
in the outdoors. It had been ingrained in me to take the
utmost caution in using fire in the woods, lest a blaze rage

out of control. Yet now I was purposely setting fire to the surrounding grasses, vines, and scrubby trees with the intent of burning them to the ground.

I imagined the upcoming scene: clouds of insects rising, birds and animals--snakes, frogs, turtles, deer, armadillos, raccoons, opossums, rabbits, and maybe a bobcat--fleeing the blaze. I tried not to think about the animals I was killing or leaving homeless. Smokey the Bear would be appalled. 2

Six of us had set out to do the day's burning, four naturalists including myself, Greg the warden-biologist, and Ed the sanctuary manager. First we did a small practice burn along the side of the road, where Ed told us about the drip torches and how to use them. Drip torches are three-gallon tanks of gas mixed with diesel fuel, with a long spout and nozzle. When inverted and lit, they emit a thin stream of fire, as a watering can spouts water. "Today we're going to try to use the wind," Ed explained. "We'll try to keep it at our backs. Then it will spread the fire in the direction we're walking." 3

I lit my torch and pulled a bandana over my nose and mouth. We spread out and tried to head in the same direc- tion, burning as we went along. The vegetation was very thick, but I had to keep moving and rip through it, since the fire was close behind. The heat was intense and the smoke bothered my eyes. We couldn't see one another because of the dense vines and shrubs but had to keep yelling back and forth to make sure we were all still heading in the right direction and, most important, not trapping someone inside a ring of fire. Dry, crackling grass makes a lot of noise as it burns, so we had to yell loudly. Sometimes I'd find a mucky ditch in my way, or a thorny vine, but there wasn't time to ponder an alternate route. I just had to forge ahead, sinking up to my knees in cold, muddy water. I always found it nerve- racking to be followed so closely by the fire, although after my first ditch crossing I was somewhat comforted by the thought that my soaked jeans and boots probably wouldn't burn. 4

    I never got over my uneasiness about being so close to   5
the fire. I didn't like going on controlled burns. Yet, as
a seasonal naturalist at the National Audubon Society's Corkscrew Swamp Sanctuary in the Big Cypress Swamp region of
South Florida, I soon learned that burns had to be done periodically to ensure the health of the swamp. One of my duties was to go along with the full-time staff to see how the
burns were done. Another duty, one I hadn't expected, was to
read books. I learned a lot from one of them, Fire in South
Florida Ecosystems, by the staff of the Southeast Forest Experiment Station in Asheville, North Carolina (Washington:
U.S. Forest Service, 1980). It convinced me that trees and
plants of the swamp need fire to survive.

    The interrelationship of vegetation with fire has   6
evolved over thousands of years. In the past, when South
Florida was covered with an unbroken canopy of vegetation,
fires would start naturally by lightning. Sometimes, they
would rage from one side of the Florida peninsula to the
other and die only on reaching the coast. Or they might
blaze until extinguished by the rains of the next wet season.
Yet, in as little as two weeks, fresh green growth would begin to cover the ground again. When people started to discover the beauty of South Florida and began to chop it down
to get to it, cutting through the wilderness with roads and
housing developments, they brought their prejudices against
fire with them. When natural fires were not allowed to take
their course, the delicate balance was upset, causing havoc
in the ecological system.

    At Corkscrew Swamp Sanctuary, there are a diversity of   7
habitats, including pineland, marsh, wet prairie, bald cypress and pond cypress stands, and hardwood hammocks. What
makes each distinct are the species of trees and plants found
there, depending on how much water each area receives, its
elevation, and other factors. Therefore, there are different
animals associated with each habitat too. One goal of the
sanctuary management is to keep this diversity of habitats
available. Plant diversity ensures animal diversity, since

certain animals prefer one habitat over another for food and shelter. Each habitat is burned on its own schedule. The wet prairie, for example, is burned every one to three years, while the pinelands, a more established plant community, are burned every five to seven years. If fire were kept out of an area, the natural progression would be toward hardwoods such as oaks. Eventually, all the areas would end up looking much the same, with the same plant composition. Burning ensures that areas such as marsh and wet prairie will remain that way.

In a wilderness, fire has still other valuable effects. 8
Fire recycles nutrients. By reducing the vegetation to ash, the nutrients locked up in growing trees and plants are returned to the soil so that they may be used again. Without fire, some plants would not be able to reproduce. The seeds of certain plants must germinate through an ash layer. Other plants are stimulated to drop seeds only after feeling intense heat, ensuring that after a fire, new seeds are released to carry on the species.

Fire is a wonderful cleanser. It acts as a check on 9
various diseases: the heat and flames kill off harmful plant parasites and bacteria. Another reason for burning is to get rid of leaf litter. If all the fallen leaves and decaying vegetation were allowed to pile up, a natural fire would be a disaster for the sanctuary. Eliminating the extra fuel ensures that minimal damage will occur if an uncontrolled fire should accidentally start.

Through their long association with fire, South Flori- 10
da's plants have evolved many adaptations to its recurrences. Florida slash pines have a thick, spongy bark that contains much moisture. When a fire passes by, the bark may be singed, but the tree is protected. Saw palmettos have a long thick stem or "runner" that hugs the ground, so that a fire, unable to take hold from below, passes right over it. And I have to admit that nothing is wasted in a fire, not even the lives of the insects. Many birds come to a burned-over area to feed. Red-shouldered hawks love toasted grasshoppers.

I learned to unlearn my belief that fire and plants are   11
enemies. Soaked to mid-thigh, muscles sore, face and arms
scratched, covered with seeds and burrs, I would emerge from
a tangle of vines with a fire close on my heels. Taking the
bandana from over my mouth and nose, I would gulp fresh air.
I had to tell myself that I was giving the plants a hand. I
was just helping a natural process that, until interrupted by
humans, had been going on for centuries. The trees needed
me. I looked across the fire lane at an area that had been
burned a few weeks before, and already the ground was covered
with light green. I'll have to have a talk with Smokey the
Bear. He may have to change a few of his ideas if he ever
retires to Florida.

Questions to Start You Thinking

1. What evidence do you find of the writer's critically rethinking an earlier belief and then revising it?
2. By beginning and ending with the writer's personal experience, what does the writer of this essay gain? Can it be charged that the memories recalled in the first four paragraphs and the last paragraph don't serve the main purpose of the paper — to explain the "why" behind the burns?
3. At any point, do you get the sense that the writer is criticizing human beings? If so, what is her point? Do you agree or disagree? For what reasons?
4. What phenomenon have you observed lately whose causes or effects might be worth exploring?

LEARNING BY WRITING

The Assignment: Understanding a Change

Pick a definite change that has taken place during your lifetime, and seek out the causes and effects to help you and your readers understand that change better.

By "change" we mean a noticeable, lasting transformation produced by an event or series of events. The change might be one that has affected only you, such as a move to another location, a decision you made that changed the course of your life, or an alteration in a strong personal opinion or belief. It might be a change that has affected not only you but also other people in your neighborhood or city (a new zoning law), in a region (the growth of high technology in the Silicon Valley of California), or in society at large (the arrival of the personal computer or the fall of communism in Europe). It might be a new invention, a medical breakthrough, or a deep-down shift in the structure or attitudes of society. We do not mean a trend or a passing fad likely to burn out in a year, like bungee jumping or the grapefruit diet.

Don't think you must choose an earthshaking topic to write a good paper. On the contrary, you will do a better job on a subject you are personally familiar with.

Write for an audience of your classmates. If you write about a change in your own life, assume that your readers will care to know more about you. If you write about some change in a region or in society at large, assume that they will want to compare their own impressions of this change with yours.

Papers written in response to this assignment have included the following.

A woman's recollection of how a year-long stay in rural Mexico caused her to change her outlook and opinions after her return to the United States.

A woman's view of a shift she has noticed in her lifetime: a change in male attitudes toward women. Now, she finds, women are treated with less "fake politeness" and with more respect. Her paper explores causes for this change besides the women's movement. One leading cause is that a shift in the economy from industry to service and technology has created more jobs in which women can shine.

A man's contention that, in quality of architectural design, new buildings constructed in Minneapolis have greatly improved over those designed before World War II. He surveys the reasons for this improvement, citing the influence of architects and city planners.

A woman's observation that in the United States popular interest in space travel has declined. She cites evidence to support this claim, such as children no longer wanting to be astronauts and the press now rarely mentioning the fact that people have walked on the moon. She then asks why and finds causes for the decline, including decreased funding for the space program and the *Challenger* disaster.

Generating Ideas

What change that has taken place in your lifetime would be enjoyable or instructive to explore? This assignment leaves you the option of writing either from personal experience or from what you know or can find out.

Search your memory. A random search of your memory may help get you started. You might let your thoughts wander back to how things were a few years ago or when you were a child. Then ask yourself: In what respects are things different today?

These changes might be any of the following kinds (or any others that occur to you).

DISCOVERY CHECKLIST: RECALLING CHANGES

 A change in how you live (caused by a new job; by a fluctuation in income; by personal or family upheaval following death, divorce, accident, illness, or good fortune; by starting college)

- A change in where you live
- A change in the environment (such as air pollution, natural events such as a flood or a storm, the coming of new industry to a locality, or the failure of an old industry)
- A change caused by growing up or gaining in maturity
- A change caused by a personal tragedy or a natural disaster
- A change caused by a new invention (computers, microchips, pocket calculators, VCRs) or discovery (a wonder drug, a better design for reeds for woodwinds)
- A change in social opportunities (women now more readily accepted as corporate executives, judges, governors, candidates for high political office; blacks and Hispanics increasingly prominent in sports as coaches and managers or media commentators)
- A change in your neighborhood, city, or state (such as traffic, population, condominiums, or health care)

Soon, when a few thoughts percolate, reach for a pencil and brainstorm — jot down a list of likely topics that come to mind. (For more tips on brainstorming, see p. 303). Then choose the idea that you care most about, one that promises to be neither too large nor too small. A paper that confined itself to the causes of a family's move from New Jersey to Montana might be only one sentence long: "My father's company transferred him." But the subsequent effects of the move (on the writer and other family members) might require a whole paper. So the writer would probably choose to include both causes and effects. On the other hand, unless you are writing a very long term paper, the causes of a change in women's roles during the past twenty years are likely to prove too many and too profound even to begin to sketch in fewer than ten thousand words. Instead, can you narrow your topic? You might consider just one aspect of these changes, such as why a woman in your family went to work or why more married women today hold full-time jobs.

List causes and effects. Your choice tentatively made, write for ten or fifteen minutes, identifying likely causes and effects.

In looking for causes, look first for *immediate causes* — those evident and close at hand that clearly led to a situation or development. Then look for *remote causes:* underlying, more basic reasons for the situation, not always evident to an observing eye — perhaps causes that came earlier. The immediate cause of unemployment in a town might be the closing of a factory. But the more remote cause of unemployment might be competition from a foreign business, against which the local company couldn't survive. The immediate cause of an outbreak of sunburn cases might be a week of blazing sunshine. But the more remote cause of the problem might be the thinning of the ozone layer, causing a greater amount of harmful radiation to seep through the atmosphere.

Look back in time only as far as seems necessary. A paper on the causes of the sexual revolution that began with the fall of Adam would probably be going back too far. The writer might better confine the inquiry to what has been happening since 1970 or 1980.

Using a pencil to mark your list, check, star, or underline any causes that stand out. Another way to rate the items on your list is to ask: Is this an *essential* cause? Is it something without which the change couldn't have happened? (Then it deserves a big star.) Or, without it, might the change have taken place nevertheless, for some other reason? (It might still matter, but less importantly.)

If you haven't figured out enough causes to explain the change to your satisfaction, you need to do some more digging. Remember, you have five major resources.

DISCOVERY CHECKLIST: USING BASIC RESOURCES

- *Recall.* Do you remember having lived through this change? Can you remember life before it, and after? How were things different afterward?
- *Observation.* Can you go out right now and see the effects of this change?
- *Conversation.* Whom might you ask about it?
- *Reading.* Have any books or magazine articles on this change been published lately? (You might check a library catalog or a periodical index.)
- *Imagining.* Can you imagine possible causes or effects of this change and then test your imaginings against reality? For instance, if you are writing about why married women want jobs, try putting yourself in the place of such a woman when she stays home full-time. What is her situation? Then talk to such a woman, either a homemaker or an ex-homemaker now employed. See how well you have imagined.

If your topic calls on you to account for people's behavior, consider some suggestions from Kenneth Burke. A literary critic and philosopher, Burke has proposed a set of questions designed to discover the deep-down causes of a person's actions. For a writer, Burke's questions often generate insights, observations, and hunches worth pursuing. Take a look at "Seeking Motives" (p. 313).

Planning, Drafting, and Developing

Katie Kennedy's "Why We Burned a Wilderness" follows a clear plan. In her first four paragraphs, Kennedy recalls the burning of the swamp; in the rest of the paper she shows why the swamp was burned. The essay was written from this brief scratch outline, which simply lists the causes and effects:

1. Going on the burn – I expected bad effects

2. Why was burn done?
History of South Fla. — nature needs help
Fire releases nutrients
Some plants need fire to reproduce
Fire diversifies vegetation
It checks disease
It gets rid of leaf litter
It guards against more serious fire

3. Bad effects not so bad at all
Plants adapt
Nothing wasted

The paper makes its point: it shows the reason for which professional natu-ralists act—to give nature a hand. And it shows that cause and effect are closely related: naturalists act in order to achieve desired effects. In paragraph 2, the writer *imagines* the disastrous effects of the fire: homeless creatures fleeing, some dying. Paragraph 6 sets forth the valuable effects of natural fires.

You can begin planning your paper by assigning relative importance to the causal relationships: classify the causes as major or minor ones; classify the effects as major or minor. If, for example, you are writing about the reasons why more married women hold jobs now than they did ten years ago, you might make a list that includes (1) boredom, (2) more jobs now open to women, and (3) economic necessity. Then on reflection you might decide that economic necessity—the necessity that both husband and wife contribute to family expenses to make ends meet—is a major cause; boredom,

---

WRITING WITH A COMPUTER: SEEKING CAUSES AND EFFECTS

Whether you're looking for causes or effects, word processing can simplify your job. In setting forth causes, you can make a list of causes and, next to each item on the list, insert your evidence for it. In writing a paper determining effects, you can make a similar list and flesh it out with evi-dence. ("The lowering of the tariff on Japanese-made cars worked havoc in the automotive industry"—that statement of an effect calls for evidence: a few facts to back it up.)

Does your evidence seem substantial? You can tell from a glance at your screen exactly where you need to generate more material. Highlight any skimpy parts with **boldface** or underlining so you won't forget these needy places when you revise. With a couple of keystrokes or mouse clicks, you can highlight a whole long passage. Later, after you've revised and strengthened the passage, you can delete the highlighting.

a minor one. Plan to give the economic cause more space and place it last to emphasize it.

Once you have a tentative order for the causes and/or effects, draft the first part of your paper: describe the change you want to explain. Then make clear to your readers which one of the three tasks (to explain the causes of the change, to explain the effects, or to explain both) you intend to accomplish, but do so subtly. We don't mean you ought to say, in a flat and mechanical fashion, "Now I am going to explain the causes of this change." You can announce your task more casually, more naturally, as if you were talking to someone: "At first, I didn't realize that keeping six pet cheetahs in our back yard would bother the neighbors." Or, in a paper about a writer's father's sudden move to a Trappist monastery: "The real reason for Father's decision didn't become clear to me for a long while."

Using your list of causes and/or effects, you are now ready to draft the main part of your paper. In the first section of your paper — taking no more than two or three paragraphs — describe the change you have isolated. Then show how the change came about (the causes) or what followed as a result (the effects) or both. More than likely, the organization of your ideas will follow one of these patterns:

I. The change	I. The change	I. The change
II. Its causes	II. Its effects	II. Its causes
		III. Its effects

Revising and Editing

As you know by now, ascertaining causes and effects takes hard thought. You'll want to set aside an especially generous amount of time to look back over, ponder, and rewrite this paper. Katie Kennedy wrote several drafts of "Why We Burned a Wilderness." As she approached the paper's final version, one of the problems she faced was making a smooth transition from recalling her own experience to probing causes.

This belongs in the preceding ¶.

I always found it ~~It always seemed~~ nerve-racking to be followed so closely by the fire. ~~,~~ *although* ~~After~~ my first ditch crossing**/** I was somewhat comforted by the thought that my soaked jeans and boots probably wouldn't burn. ¶I never got over my   *Start ¶ here!* uneasiness about being so close to the fire. ~~Although~~ I didn't like *going on controlled burns. Yet,* ~~it,~~ as a seasonal naturalist at the National Audubon Society's Corkscrew Swamp Sanctuary in the Big Cypress Swamp region of South Florida, I soon *learned* ~~was taught~~ that burns had to be done periodically to ensure the health of the *swamp* ~~sanctuary~~. One of my duties was to go

along with the full-time staff to see how the burns were
done. ~~The heat was intense and the smoke bothered my~~ *Doesn't belong*
~~eyes.~~ Another duty, ~~and this~~ one I hadn't expected, was *here. But where?*
to read books. *one of them,* I learned a lot from Fire in South
Florida Ecosystems, by the staff of the Southeast Forest Experiment Station in Asheville, North Carolina
(Washington, D.C.: U.S. Forest Service, 1980). *It* ~~I was~~
convinced *me* that trees and plants of the swamp need fire to
survive. ¶The interrelationship of ~~trees~~ *vegetation* with fire has
evolved ~~been an evolving thing~~ over thousands of years. In the
past, when South Florida was covered with *an* unbroken *canopy of* vegetation, fires would ~~be started~~ *start* naturally by lightning.
Sometimes, ~~there would be fire~~ *they would rage* from one side of the Florida peninsula to the other *and die only on reaching the coast*. Or they might blaze until
extinguished by the rains of the next wet season.
Yet, in as little as two weeks, fresh green growth
would begin to cover the ground again.

End ¶ here!

Kennedy started her revision on this troublesome section by eliminating
a few lifeless passive constructions and unnecessary words. She also made
some details more vivid, allowing the fires to *rage* and substituting *an unbroken canopy of vegetation* for *unbroken vegetation*. As she worked, she moved
one sentence to a more appropriate spot earlier in the essay. Finally, she
realized that paragraph 5 ought to be a tightly organized transition paragraph
and that paragraph 6 ought to begin in a new place.

In revising a paper that traces causes, you might ask yourself the following
questions.

REVISION CHECKLIST: ASKING WHY

- Why are you going to all the work of demonstrating causes? What is your
  point? Have you shown your readers that your paper has a point to it?
- Have you given enough evidence to convince readers that the causes you
  find are the real ones?
- If not, where can you discover more evidence? Look to your five basic
  resources: recalling, observing, reading, conversing, and imagining.
- Have you claimed remote causes you can't begin to prove?
- Have you stated the causes with cocksure, swaggering certainty, when in
  all honesty you might admit that you're only guessing?

☞ Have you fallen into any logical fallacies (see p. 381), such as *oversimplification* — assuming that there was only one small cause for a large phenomenon? Example: "The revolution in sexual attitudes began because Marilyn Monroe posed in the nude for a calendar."

Another common mistake in logic is the *post hoc* fallacy, from the Latin *post hoc, ergo propter hoc,* meaning "after this, therefore because of this." In other words, don't assume that one thing caused another just because it preceded it. This is the error of a writer who declares, "Sandra Day O'Connor was appointed to the Supreme Court; in the following year, there was a noteworthy increase in the number of convicted rapists." (There is no clear causal connection here: the Supreme Court doesn't try rapists.)

In revising a paper setting forth effects, you might ask yourself the following questions.

REVISION CHECKLIST: DETERMINING EFFECTS

☞ What possible effects have you left out? Are any of them worth adding?

☞ Do you make clear that these effects have indeed occurred? Have you given sufficient evidence — perhaps reported observations or testimony, perhaps quoted opinions from authorities?

☞ Could any effect you mention have resulted not from the change you describe but from some other cause?

Remember, unless you are writing a paper that sets forth exact scientific findings (reporting, say, the effects of combining two chemicals), your instructor won't expect you to write a definitive explanation. You'll be expected only to do what lies within your capacity: to write an explanation that is thoughtful, searching, and reasonable.

Before you type a final draft, let a peer reader check over your paper and answer the questions on one of the following checklists. The first applies to a paper identifying causes, the second to a paper concerned with effects.

PEER EDITING CHECKLIST: IDENTIFYING CAUSES

☞ What point is the writer trying to make? Does the writer do more than merely list causes?

☞ Does the writer present causes that seem logical and possible?

☞ Did other causes occur to you that you think the writer should consider? If so, list them.

☞ Can you suggest a more appropriate order for the causes?

- Do you see any logical fallacies in the essay?
- Does the writer give you enough detail to be clear? Enough evidence to convince you? Put stars where more evidence is needed.
- Circle on the manuscript any areas where spelling, punctuation, grammar, or word choice got in the way of your understanding of the essay.
- If you were going to hand in this essay for a grade, is there anything you'd be sure to revise?

PEER EDITING CHECKLIST: DETERMINING EFFECTS

- What seems to you to be the purpose of the essay? Does setting forth effects let the writer accomplish his or her purpose?
- Has the writer overlooked some effects that should be added? List any that occurred to you as you read the paper.
- Is the order of the effects reasonable and easy to follow?
- Are you convinced by the logic used in the paper? Do all the effects the writer gives seem to be the result of the change he or she describes? Point out any effects that you found hard to accept as results of the change the writer describes.
- For the effects set forth as fact, has the writer given you enough evidence that they are fact? List any you don't believe really happened.
- Circle on the manuscript any areas where spelling, grammar, punctuation, or word choice got in the way of your reading or understanding of the essay.
- If you were going to hand in this paper for a grade, what would you be sure to revise?

FOR GROUP LEARNING

Together in class or in your writing group, tell aloud a two-minute story that you invent to explain the causes behind any surprising event that you find reported in this morning's news. Either realistic explanations or tall tales will be acceptable. You'll need to prepare your story carefully in advance. Invite the others to comment on it and, with their reactions in mind, set down your story on paper to turn in at the next class. In writing it down, embellish and improve on your story as much as you desire.

Before you write *any* paper setting forth causes or effects, you will find it particularly helpful to talk over with your fellow students what you plan to say. Ask for their comments. Invite them to add to your list of causes or effects if they can. In discerning causes and effects, always a complex task, you will generally find that several heads are far better than one.

Other Assignments

1. In a short paper, explain *either* the causes *or* the effects of a situation that exists today in our society. Draw on your reading, your conversation, your memory, your observations — on any useful resource.

   Some possible topics are the difficulty of getting admitted to law school, the shortage of male elementary school teachers, the willingness of businesses to hire college graduates with degrees in the liberal arts — or whatever interests and concerns you.

   Your readers for this paper won't be sociologists or other professionals who would expect a profound explanation, but students with interests similar to your own who might appreciate what you have to say.

2. Explore your own motives, and explain your reasons for taking some step or for doing something in a customary way. (All of us do some things without first reasoning. If you need help in pinning down reasons for your own behavior, some of Kenneth Burke's suggestions on pp. 314–316 may be useful.)

3. In an introductory philosophy course at Loyola College in Maryland, Frank J. Cunningham asks his students to write, instead of a traditional research paper, a short original essay exploring their own ideas and opinions. Try his assignment yourself. The assignment calls for students first to describe an idea and then to ask themselves why they hold it:

   > Over the years, in the process of growing up and growing civilized, all of us have developed certain opinions about the way things happen, about what works and what doesn't work, about how things are. We have also developed certain expectations toward our world based on these opinions.
   >
   > Under ordinary circumstances, we live with these opinions and expectations unquestioningly, and, on the whole, we manage quite well with our lives. But . . . in philosophy we look at things we don't normally look at, question things we normally take for granted, analyze what we accept from day to day.
   >
   > As preparation for this somewhat unusual (some would say perverse) activity, I would like you to think about your own opinions. Think about your views of the world, your expectations, your certainties, and decide on something of which you are absolutely certain. It may be a part of your normal life, a truth derived from your education, something that you have learned through your years of experience, something you were told, something you figured out on your own. Now write a short essay (no more than two pages) describing the one thing about which you are absolutely certain and why this thing commands such certainty.
   >
   > Remember that an essay such as this requires thought as preparation. You should not expect to sit down immediately at the typewriter and produce it. Remember too that there are at least two separate thinking tasks to be performed. First you must consider your stock of truths to find one in which you have utmost confidence. This will probably take some time and effort since we are willing to let a lot of truths pass without putting them to the test. Second, you must consider the reason for your certainty. In working out this part of the essay it might be useful to pretend that you are trying to convince a very reasonable but thoroughly doubting person of the truth of your position.

4. Glen Baxter, a humorous artist, specializes in the curious scene that cries out for an explanation. From the group of his drawings here, pick a drawing that interests you. In a paragraph, set forth the causes that might have led to the scene depicted

HELMUT CHECKED THE BOULDER AT TWELVE-
MINUTE INTERVALS THROUGHOUT THE NIGHT

"WE'LL HAVE NO ALLITERATION IN THIS
HERE BUNKHOUSE!" SNORTED MCCULLOCH

IT WAS MRS. CRABTREE AND SHE WAS
IN NO MOOD FOR PLEASANTRIES

in it. Then in a second paragraph, give at least one effect that might follow from it. Allow your imagination free rein.

APPLYING WHAT YOU LEARN: SOME USES OF SEEKING CAUSES AND EFFECTS

Examination questions often pose a problem in causality: "Trace the causes of the decline of foreign sales of American automobiles." Equally familiar is the exam question that calls for a survey of effects: "What economic effects of the repeal of Prohibition were immediately evident in the early 1930s?" Problems of that very same sort, you'll find, will frequently turn up as paper topics. In a child development course, you might be asked to research what makes some people become child abusers. In a speech pathology course you might be called on to investigate the causes and effects of head trauma, fetal alcohol syndrome, learning disabilities or dyslexia, Down's syndrome—all of which are relevant to impaired communication skills.

But in fulfilling any kind of college writing assignment, even one that doesn't ask you to look for causes or effects, you may wish to spend *part* of your paper exploring one or the other or both. In a paper that deals with any phenomenon—say, a sociology course assignment to write about an increase in teenage pregnancies among middle-class suburbanites—a paragraph or two that explores the causes of that phenomenon or its effects might add considerable depth to your paper.

At any moment in a book or article that deals with some current phenomenon, the writer may ask why—in only a paragraph or a few paragraphs. In *The Economics of Public Issues*, a college textbook, Douglass C. North and Roger Leroy Miller make the surprising claim that the ban of cigarette advertising on television has had effects injurious to your health:

The banning of advertising has had dramatic effects in other industries too. In 1976, Congress banned the advertising of cigarettes on television in response to the Surgeon General's finding that cigarette smoking could lead to lung cancer. It was argued that captive TV watchers should not be subjected to the advertising of a hazardous product. The results of such a ban were just the opposite of the desired effect. The lack of cigarette advertising on TV has caused two distinct phenomena, both of which have led to possible increased health problems. Prior to the banning of cigarette advertising on TV, the American Cancer Society and the antismoking lobbyists succeeded in forcing free antismoking ads on TV. Under the Fairness Doctrine promulgated by the Federal Communications Commission, networks are supposed to air *both* sides of the story (as if there were only two sides to every argument). Thus, if TV networks were accepting money for cigarette advertisements, it was argued they must also accept antismoking ads (and for free). Thus, prior to 1976, there were several antismoking ads a day on each network. After the ban on TV advertising of cigarettes, however, the networks were no longer obligated under the Fairness Doctrine to show antismoking ads for free. Thus, the number of antismoking ads dropped dramatically. Apparently such ads were having an effect, especially among teenagers and women, for the percentage of teenagers and women who smoke has been rising since the time cigarette TV ads were banned. Perhaps that is coincidence, but perhaps not.

The other phenomenon that may be leading to increased health hazards on the part of the American public results from the fact that TV advertising is a powerful, and perhaps the single most effective, means to introduce new cigarettes into the marketplace. Once people are set on smoking a particular brand of cigarette, it is hard to get them to change or to be aware of new brands; but TV advertising did just that—it made them aware of what was available. Professor Ben Klein has found that since the banning of advertising on TV, the introduction of new low tar, low nicotine cigarettes has dropped by 42 percent. Presumably, smokers benefit by switching to low tar, low nicotine cigarettes because they reduce the probability of lung disease in the future. Thus, the banning of such advertising has led consumers to stick with their old brands of cigarettes, which are likely to have higher levels of tar and nicotine and, hence, are more of a health hazard.

In less formal writing, too, the method is used continually. Stephen King, in *Danse Macabre*, his study of horror movies, asks why the average American, living a life without terror or violence, will pay four or five dollars to see a horror movie. In several paragraphs, King considers "simple and obvious" reasons: to show that we aren't afraid, to have fun, to feel comfortable in our own essential normality. Then he considers a deeper reason for the films' appeal:

The mythic horror movie, like the sick joke, has a dirty job to do. It deliberately appeals to all that is worst in us. It is morbidity unchained, our most base instincts let free, our nastiest fantasies realized — and it happens, fittingly enough, in the dark. For these reasons, good liberals often shy away from horror films. For myself, I like to see the most aggressive of them — *Dawn of the Dead*, for instance — as lifting a trapdoor in the civilized forebrain and throwing a basket of raw meat to the hungry alligators swimming around in that subterranean river beneath. Why bother? Because it keeps them from getting out, man. It keeps them down there and me up here. It was Lennon and McCartney who said that all you need is love, and I would agree with that. As long as you keep the gators fed.

To be sure, King's suggested explanation doesn't end the inquiry, but it offers a provocative answer to the question Why?

In his article "Causation of Terror," social historian Feliks Gross seeks to explain a difficult, complex, and vitally important matter: the reasons for political assassinations and terrorism in Europe and Russia in the nineteenth and twentieth centuries. Gross recalls cases of political parties who have used terrorist tactics to overthrow moderate and democratic governments; he remembers the victims of oppressive rule who have used terrorist tactics to fight back: the histories of the Armenians and Bulgarians under Turkish rule, the Serbs under Croatian Ustasha government, the Polish underground fighters who resisted Nazi occupation. Tentatively, offering a vast generalization, Gross finds that economic hardship does not usually cause its victims to respond with terrorist tactics and political assassinations. Instead, the causes of terrorism appear to lie in ethnic tensions and clashes of political ideology.

"It is of paramount significance," Gross concludes, "to understand the conditions that are conducive to political assassination." By controlling such conditions, perhaps we might even prevent terrorism. Applied to such an end, exploring causes and effects is no mere game, but a way of seeking peace and ensuring it.

Further Applications

As human beings we often try to understand why something occurs by *identifying causal relationships,* or searching for causes and analyzing effects. Writers do much the same thing. An author's identification of causes and effects is often interwoven with analysis, stand, problem, solution, and evaluation. In "Black Men and Public Space" in *A Writer's Reader,* Brent Staples, a newspaper editor with a Ph.D. in psychology, traces the effects that he as a black man has on the people he encounters in public places and, in turn, the effects their reactions have on him (p. 507). Writer Emily Prager has wondered about the creation of the Barbie doll and its popularity for many years, so in "Our Barbies, Ourselves" (p. 560) she speculates about the causes of Barbie's popularity and suggests some effects Barbie has on little girls and women. Jonathan Kozol (p. 200) and student Katie Kennedy (p. 203) deal primarily with causes, attempting to identify reasons.

Some of the other writers in *A Writer's Reader* who identify causal relationships include anthropology professor Michael Dorris, "The Train Cake" (p. 435), historian Joan Jacobs Brumberg, "The Origins of Anorexia Nervosa"

(p. 451), construction worker Steve Olson, "Year of the Blue-Collar Guy" (p. 521), and lawyer Peter P. Swire, "Tropical Chic" (p. 575). Answer the following questions about each of these essays.

1. Does the writer identify causes, or effects, or both?
2. Is the evidence sufficient to clarify the causal relationships and to provide credibility to the essay?
3. How is the chain of causes and effects relevant to the writer's occupation or field of interest?

PART THREE

SPECIAL WRITING SITUATIONS

In college English and humanities classes you'll write papers about literature. For examinations and on competency tests you'll write extemporaneously in a limited amount of time. On the job and for personal dealings you'll write formal letters and memos. Each of these situations calls for a special kind of writing. In the next three chapters you'll find suggestions for responding to each of these special situations.

When you are asked to write about literature, you may write a synopsis, a paraphrase, a personal response, a review, or—most common in college—a literary critique. To write an effective critique, you analyze, interpret, and evaluate one or more works of literature. To explain the meaning and discuss the significance of the literary selections, you may draw from the five resources for writing: recall, observation, other reading, conversation, imagination (see Part One). To enhance your interpretation of the meaning, you may compare and contrast a selection with another piece of literature or with experiences in life. Professors often ask you to do this type of writing because it reveals how well you understand the literature; how perceptively you use critical thinking skill (analyzing, taking a stand, proposing a solution, evaluating, and identifying causes and effects [see Part Two]); and how effectively you adapt the strategies for planning, drafting, developing, and revising (see Part Four). The following chapter (Chapter 11) provides guidance for writing various types of papers about literature.

Furthermore, as a student you often find yourself in testing situations in which you must demonstrate your knowledge of a subject as well as your proficiency in writing. More than likely, you will have a time limit for responding to exam questions and prompts. To do this type of writing well requires you to use special skills: reading carefully, planning globally, composing quickly, proofreading independently. Chapter 12 gives valuable tips on how not only to survive but also to thrive on in-class writings.

Finally, there are times when you'll want to respond in writing to a business situation. You may need to write a letter of application and a résumé for a job that will pay you more. You may want to write a letter to a manufacturer complaining of a faulty product. You may be asked to prepare a brief memo to update your supervisor at work about your progress on a project. Because time means money, business writing is concise and direct. Chapter 13 provides recommendations and samples for business writing, whether personal or corporate.

CHAPTER 11

Writing about Literature

In your college career you just might take one or more literature courses: literary study has long been recognized as an essential in most college curricula. Reading and understanding a literary masterpiece offers you rewards beyond those measurable in dollars and cents.

Literature, as countless readers know, gives pleasure and delight. Whether you are reading Dante or Danielle Steele, Stephen King or Stephen Crane, you can be swept up into an imaginative world where you can do and see things you can't in real life. You're held spellbound as you journey to distant lands and meet exotic folk. You think mighty thoughts and thrill to adventures until you emerge from the last page—maybe ready for another go.

Literature increases your understanding of life. Late nineteenth-century American writer and editor William Dean Howells said that it "widens the bounds of human sympathy"; contemporary novelist Ursula K. Le Guin, that it deepens "your understanding of your world, and your fellow men, and your own feelings, and your destiny." As you read, you meet characters similar to and different from yourself, and you encounter familiar as well as new ideas and ways of viewing life. By sharing the experiences of literary characters, you gain insight into your own problems and become more tolerant of others.

Time spent with Shakespeare's great play *Hamlet* or Kate Chopin's classic American novel *The Awakening,* with Shirley Jackson's short story "The Lottery" or D. H. Lawrence's poem "Snake" or any other piece of serious literature will help you develop critical thinking skills useful in the academic world as well as in the job market. As you develop these skills, you will truly become a *critic* in the sense of the Greek *kritikos,* one who can judge and discern. It's no wonder that personnel supervisors of large corporations often hire English majors as business managers.

More often than not, a writing assignment in a literature or humanities course will require you to read a literary work (short story, novel, play, or poem) closely, divide it into its elements, explain its meaning, and support your interpretation with evidence from the work. The analysis is not an end in itself; the purpose is to illuminate the meaning of the work, to help you and others understand it better. The more complex and challenging the literary selection, the more valuable analysis can be in determining meaning. You may also be asked to evaluate what you read and to compare and contrast individual selections with other pieces you have read.

There are various ways of writing about literature, each with its own purpose. We emphasize the *literary critique,* which requires that you analyze, interpret, and evaluate what you read. It demands that you exercise critical thinking skills. In this chapter we offer examples, strategies, and practices for writing about literature. We also provide an introduction to basic literary terms.

LEARNING FROM ANOTHER WRITER: ONE STUDENT'S EXPERIENCE

In a composition course, Jonathan Burns was given an assignment to write a critique of "The Lottery," a short story by the American writer Shirley Jackson. "The Lottery" caused a sensation when it was published in *The New Yorker* in 1948. In this piece, Shirley Jackson simultaneously conceals and reveals meaning. Students, teachers, and professional critics have offered varied interpretations of the work. Read it with care; try to figure out what it means. Then read on to see what Jonathan Burns makes of it.

THE LOTTERY
Shirley Jackson

The morning of June 27th was clear and sunny, with the fresh warmth   1
of a full-summer day; the flowers were blossoming profusely and the grass
was richly green. The people of the village began to gather in the square,
between the post office and the bank, around ten o'clock; in some towns
there were so many people that the lottery took two days and had to be
started on June 26th, but in this village, where there were only about three
hundred people, the whole lottery took less than two hours, so it could
begin at ten o'clock in the morning and still be through in time to allow the
villagers to get home for noon dinner.

The children assembled first, of course. School was recently over for   2
the summer, and the feeling of liberty sat uneasily on most of them; they

tended to gather together quietly for a while before they broke into boisterous play, and their talk was still of the classroom and the teacher, of
books and reprimands. Bobby Martin had already stuffed his pockets full
of stones, and the other boys soon followed his example, selecting the
smoothest and roundest stones; Bobby and Harry Jones and Dickie Delacroix—the villagers pronounced his name "Dellacroy"—eventually made a
great pile of stones in one corner of the square and guarded it against the
raids of the other boys. The girls stood aside, talking among themselves,
looking over their shoulders at the boys, and the very small children rolled
in the dust or clung to the hands of their older brothers or sisters.

Soon the men began to gather, surveying their own children, speaking 3
of planting and rain, tractors and taxes. They stood together, away from
the pile of stones in the corner, and their jokes were quiet and they smiled
rather than laughed. The women, wearing faded house dresses and sweaters, came shortly after their menfolk. They greeted one another and exchanged bits of gossip as they went to join their husbands. Soon the
women, standing by their husbands, began to call to their children, and
the children came reluctantly, having to be called four or five times. Bobby
Martin ducked under his mother's grasping hand and ran, laughing, back
to the pile of stones. His father spoke up sharply, and Bobby came quickly
and took his place between his father and his oldest brother.

The lottery was conducted—as were the square dances, the teenage 4
club, the Halloween program—by Mr. Summers, who had time and energy
to devote to civic activities. He was a round-faced, jovial man and he ran
the coal business, and people were sorry for him, because he had no children and his wife was a scold. When he arrived in the square, carrying the
black wooden box, there was a murmur of conversation among the villagers,
and he waved and called, "Little late today, folks." The postmaster, Mr.
Graves, followed him, carrying a three-legged stool, and the stool was put
in the center of the square and Mr. Summers set the black box down on it.
The villagers kept their distance, leaving a space between themselves and
the stool, and when Mr. Summers said, "Some of you fellows want to give
me a hand?" there was a hesitation before two men, Mr. Martin and his
oldest son, Baxter, came forward to hold the box steady on the stool while
Mr. Summers stirred up the papers inside it.

The original paraphernalia for the lottery had been lost long ago, and 5
the black box now resting on the stool had been put into use even before
Old Man Warner, the oldest man in town, was born. Mr. Summers spoke
frequently to the villagers about making a new box, but no one liked to
upset even as much tradition as was represented by the black box. There
was a story that the present box had been made with some pieces of the
box that had preceded it, the one that had been constructed when the first
people settled down to make a village here. Every year, after the lottery,
Mr. Summers began talking again about a new box, but every year the
subject was allowed to fade off without anything's being done. The black
box grew shabbier each year; by now it was no longer completely black but

splintered badly along one side to show the original wood color, and in some places faded or stained.

Mr. Martin and his oldest son, Baxter, held the black box securely on   6 the stool until Mr. Summers had stirred the papers thoroughly with his hand. Because so much of the ritual had been forgotten or discarded, Mr. Summers had been successful in having slips of paper substituted for the chips of wood that had been used for generations. Chips of wood, Mr. Summers had argued, had been all very well when the village was tiny, but now that the population was more than three hundred and likely to keep on growing, it was necessary to use something that would fit more easily into the black box. The night before the lottery, Mr. Summers and Mr. Graves made up the slips of paper and put them in the box, and it was then taken to the safe of Mr. Summers's coal company and locked up until Mr. Summers was ready to take it to the square next morning. The rest of the year, the box was put away, sometimes one place, sometimes another; it had spent one year in Mr. Graves's barn and another year underfoot in the post office, and sometimes it was set on a shelf in the Martin grocery and left there.

There was a great deal of fussing to be done before Mr. Summers   7 declared the lottery open. There were the lists to make up—of heads of families, heads of households in each family, members of each household in each family. There was the proper swearing-in of Mr. Summers by the postmaster, as the official of the lottery; at one time, some people remembered, there had been a recital of some sort, performed by the official of the lottery, a perfunctory, tuneless chant that had been rattled off duly each year; some people believed that the official of the lottery used to stand just so when he said or sang it, others believed that he was supposed to walk among the people, but years and years ago this part of the ritual had been allowed to lapse. There had been, also, a ritual salute, which the official of the lottery had had to use in addressing each person who came up to draw from the box, but this also had changed with time, until now it was felt necessary only for the official to speak to each person approaching. Mr. Summers was very good at all this; in his clean white shirt and blue jeans, with one hand resting carelessly on the black box, he seemed very proper and important as he talked interminably to Mr. Graves and the Martins.

Just as Mr. Summers finally left off talking and turned to the assembled   8 villagers, Mrs. Hutchinson came hurriedly along the path to the square, her sweater thrown over her shoulders, and slid into place in the back of the crowd. "Clean forgot what day it was," she said to Mrs. Delacroix, who stood next to her, and they both laughed softly. "Thought my old man was out back stacking wood," Mrs. Hutchinson went on, "and then I looked out the window and the kids was gone, and then I remembered it was the twenty-seventh and came a-running." She dried her hands on her apron, and Mrs. Delacroix said, "You're in time, though. They're still talking away up there."

Mrs. Hutchinson craned her neck to see through the crowd and found   9 her husband and children standing near the front. She tapped Mrs. Dela-croix on the arm as a farewell and began to make her way through the crowd. The people separated good-humoredly to let her through; two or three people said, in voices just loud enough to be heard across the crowd, "Here comes your Missus, Hutchinson," and "Bill, she made it after all." Mrs. Hutchinson reached her husband, and Mr. Summers, who had been waiting, said cheerfully, "Thought we were going to have to get on without you, Tessie." Mrs. Hutchinson said, grinning, "Wouldn't have me leave m'dishes in the sink, now, would you, Joe?" and soft laughter ran through the crowd as the people stirred back into position after Mrs. Hutchinson's arrival.

"Well, now," Mr. Summers said soberly, "guess we better get started, get this over with, so's we can go back to work. Anybody ain't here?"   10

"Dunbar," several people said. "Dunbar, Dunbar."   11

Mr. Summers consulted his list. "Clyde Dunbar," he said. "That's right. He's broke his leg, hasn't he? Who's drawing for him?"   12

"Me, I guess," a woman said, and Mr. Summers turned to look at her. "Wife draws for her husband," Mr. Summers said. "Don't you have a grown boy to do it for you, Janey?" Although Mr. Summers and everyone else in the village knew the answer perfectly well, it was the business of the official of the lottery to ask such questions formally. Mr. Summers waited with an expression of polite interest while Mrs. Dunbar answered.   13

"Horace's not but sixteen yet," Mrs. Dunbar said regretfully. "Guess I gotta fill in for the old man this year."   14

"Right," Mr. Summers said. He made a note on the list he was holding. Then he asked, "Watson boy drawing this year?"   15

A tall boy in the crowd raised his hand. "Here," he said. "I'm drawing for m'mother and me." He blinked his eyes nervously and ducked his head as several voices in the crowd said things like "Good fellow, Jack," and "Glad to see your mother's got a man to do it."   16

"Well," Mr. Summers said, "guess that's everyone. Old Man Warner make it?"   17

"Here," a voice said, and Mr. Summers nodded.   18

A sudden hush fell on the crowd as Mr. Summers cleared his throat and looked at the list. "All ready?" he called. "Now, I'll read the names—heads of families first—and the men come up and take a paper out of the box. Keep the paper folded in your hand without looking at it until everyone has had a turn. Everything clear?"   19

The people had done it so many times that they only half listened to the directions; most of them were quiet, wetting their lips, not looking around. Then Mr. Summers raised one hand high and said, "Adams." A man disengaged himself from the crowd and came forward. "Hi, Steve," Mr. Summers said, and Mr. Adams said, "Hi, Joe." They grinned at one another humorlessly and nervously. Then Mr. Adams reached into the black box and took out a folded paper. He held it firmly by one corner as he turned and   20 went hastily back to his place in the crowd, where he stood a little apart from his family, not looking down at his hand.

"Allen," Mr. Summers said. "Anderson. . . . Bentham." 21

"Seems like there's no time at all between lotteries anymore," Mrs. 22
Delacroix said to Mrs. Graves in the back row. "Seems like we got through with the last one only last week."

"Time sure goes fast," Mrs. Graves said. 23

"Clark. . . . Delacroix." 24

"There goes my old man," Mrs. Delacroix said. She held her breath 25
while her husband went forward.

"Dunbar," Mr. Summers said, and Mrs. Dunbar went steadily to the box 26
while one of the women said, "Go on, Janey," and another said, "There she goes."

"We're next," Mrs. Graves said. She watched while Mr. Graves came 27
around from the side of the box, greeted Mr. Summers gravely, and selected a slip of paper from the box. By now, all through the crowd there were men holding the small folded papers in their large hands, turning them over and over nervously. Mrs. Dunbar and her two sons stood together, Mrs. Dunbar holding the slip of paper.

"Harburt. . . . Hutchinson." 28

"Get up there, Bill," Mrs. Hutchinson said, and the people near her 29
laughed.

"Jones." 30

"They do say," Mr. Adams said to Old Man Warner, who stood next to 31
him, "that over in the north village they're talking of giving up the lottery."

Old Man Warner snorted. "Pack of crazy fools," he said. "Listening to 32
the young folks, nothing's good enough for *them*. Next thing you know, they'll be wanting to go back to living in caves, nobody work anymore, live *that* way for a while. Used to be a saying about 'Lottery in June, corn be heavy soon.' First thing you know, we'd all be eating stewed chickweed and acorns. There's *always* been a lottery," he added petulantly. "Bad enough to see young Joe Summers up there joking with everybody."

"Some places have already quit lotteries," Mrs. Adams said. 33

"Nothing but trouble in *that*," Old Man Warner said stoutly. "Pack of 34
young fools."

"Martin." And Bobby Martin watched his father go forward. "Over- 35
dyke. . . . Percy."

"I wish they'd hurry," Mrs. Dunbar said to her older son. "I wish they'd 36
hurry."

"They're almost through," her son said. 37

"You get ready to run tell Dad," Mrs. Dunbar said. 38

Mr. Summers called his own name and then stepped forward precisely 39
and selected a slip from the box. Then he called, "Warner."

"Seventy-seventh year I been in the lottery," Old Man Warner said as 40
he went through the crowd. "Seventy-seventh time."

"Watson." The tall boy came awkwardly through the crowd. Someone 41 said, "Don't be nervous, Jack," and Mr. Summers said, "Take your time, son."

"Zanini." 42

After that, there was a long pause, a breathless pause, until Mr. Summers, holding his slip of paper in the air, said, "All right, fellows." For a minute, no one moved, and then all the slips of paper were opened. Suddenly, all the women began to speak at once, saying, "Who is it?" "Who's got it?" "Is it the Dunbars?" "Is it the Watsons?" Then the voices began to say, "It's Hutchinson. It's Bill," "Bill Hutchinson's got it." 43

"Go tell your father," Mrs. Dunbar said to her older son. 44

People began to look around to see the Hutchinsons. Bill Hutchinson was standing quiet, staring down at the paper in his hand. Suddenly, Tessie Hutchinson shouted to Mr. Summers, "You didn't give him time enough to take any paper he wanted. I saw you. It wasn't fair!" 45

"Be a good sport, Tessie," Mrs. Delacroix called, and Mrs. Graves said, "All of us took the same chance." 46

"Shut up, Tessie," Bill Hutchinson said. 47

"Well, everyone," Mr. Summers said, "that was done pretty fast, and now we've got to be hurrying a little more to get done in time." He consulted his next list. "Bill," he said, "you draw for the Hutchinson family. You got any other households in the Hutchinsons?" 48

"There's Don and Eva," Mrs. Hutchinson yelled. "Make *them* take their chance!" 49

"Daughters draw with their husbands' families, Tessie," Mr. Summers said gently. "You know that as well as anyone else." 50

"It wasn't *fair*," Tessie said. 51

"I guess not, Joe," Bill Hutchinson said regretfully. "My daughter draws with her husband's family, that's only fair. And I've got no other family except the kids." 52

"Then, as far as drawing for families is concerned, it's you," Mr. Summers said in explanation, "and as far as drawing for households is concerned, that's you, too. Right?" 53

"Right," Bill Hutchinson said. 54

"How many kids, Bill?" Mr. Summers asked formally. 55

"Three," Bill Hutchinson said. "There's Bill, Jr., and Nancy, and little Dave. And Tessie and me." 56

"All right, then," Mr. Summers said. "Harry, you got their tickets back?" 57

Mr. Graves nodded and held up the slips of paper. "Put them in the box, then," Mr. Summers directed. "Take Bill's and put it in." 58

"I think we ought to start over," Mrs. Hutchinson said, as quietly as she could. "I tell you it wasn't *fair*. You didn't give him time enough to choose. *Every*body saw that." 59

Mr. Graves had selected the five slips and put them in the box, and he dropped all the papers but those onto the ground, where the breeze caught them and lifted them off. 60

"Listen, everybody," Mrs. Hutchinson was saying to the people around   61
her.

"Ready, Bill?" Mr. Summers asked, and Bill Hutchinson, with one quick   62
glance around at his wife and children, nodded.

"Remember," Mr. Summers said, "take the slips and keep them folded   63
until each person has taken one. Harry, you help little Dave." Mr. Graves
took the hand of the little boy, who came willingly with him up to the box.
"Take a paper out of the box, Davy," Mr. Summers said. Davy put his hand
into the box and laughed. "Take just *one* paper," Mr. Summers said. "Harry,
you hold it for him." Mr. Graves took the child's hand and removed the
folded paper from the tight fist and held it while little Dave stood next to
him and looked up at him wonderingly.

"Nancy next," Mr. Summers said. Nancy was twelve, and her school   64
friends breathed heavily as she went forward, switching her skirt, and took
a slip daintily from the box. "Bill, Jr.," Mr. Summers said, and Billy, his
face red and his feet overlarge, nearly knocked the box over as he got a
paper out. "Tessie," Mr. Summers said. She hesitated for a minute, looking
around defiantly, and then set her lips and went up to the box. She snatched
a paper out and held it behind her.

"Bill," Mr. Summers said, and Bill Hutchinson reached into the box and   65
felt around, bringing his hand out at last with the slip of paper in it.

The crowd was quiet. A girl whispered, "I hope it's not Nancy," and the   66
sound of the whisper reached the edges of the crowd.

"It's not the way it used to be," Old Man Warner said clearly. "People   67
ain't the way they used to be."

"All right," Mr. Summers said. "Open the papers. Harry, you open little   68
Dave's."

Mr. Graves opened the slip of paper and there was a general sigh   69
through the crowd as he held it up and everyone could see that it was
blank. Nancy and Bill, Jr., opened theirs at the same time, and both beamed
and laughed, turning around to the crowd and holding their slips of paper
above their heads.

"Tessie," Mr. Summers said. There was a pause, and then Mr. Summers   70
looked at Bill Hutchinson, and Bill unfolded his paper and showed it. It was
blank.

"It's Tessie," Mr. Summers said, and his voice was hushed. "Show us   71
her paper, Bill."

Bill Hutchinson went over to his wife and forced the slip of paper out   72
of her hand. It had a black spot on it, the black spot Mr. Summers had
made the night before with the heavy pencil in the coal-company office.
Bill Hutchinson held it up, and there was a stir in the crowd.

"All right, folks," Mr. Summers said. "Let's finish quickly."   73

Although the villagers had forgotten the ritual and lost the original black   74
box, they still remembered to use stones. The pile of stones the boys had
made earlier was ready; there were stones on the ground with the blowing
scraps of paper that had come out of the box. Mrs. Delacroix selected a

stone so large she had to pick it up with both hands and turned to Mrs.
Dunbar. "Come on," she said. "Hurry up."

Mrs. Dunbar had small stones in both hands, and she said, gasping   75
for breath, "I can't run at all. You'll have to go ahead and I'll catch up with
you."

The children had stones already, and someone gave little Davy Hutch-   76
inson a few pebbles.

Tessie Hutchinson was in the center of a cleared space by now, and   77
she held her hands out desperately as the villagers moved in on her. "It
isn't fair," she said. A stone hit her on the side of the head.

Old Man Warner was saying, "Come on, come on, everyone." Steve   78
Adams was in the front of the crowd of villagers, with Mrs. Graves beside
him.

"It isn't fair, it isn't right," Mrs. Hutchinson screamed, and then they   79
were upon her.

Questions to Start You Thinking

1. Where does this story take place? When?
2. Can you see and hear the people in the story? Do they seem real, or fantastic? Who is the most memorable character to you?
3. Are the events believable? Does the ending shock you? Is it believable?
4. How does this lottery differ from what we usually think of as a lottery? Why would people conduct a lottery such as this?
5. Is this a realistic story, or is Jackson using these events to represent something else?
6. What does this story mean to you?

As Jonathan Burns read "The Lottery," he was carried along quickly to
the startling ending. Right after the immediate impact of the story wore off,
Burns turned back and reread it, this time to savor some of the details he
had missed during his first reading. Then, knowing he had to write a literary
critique for his composition course, he wrote a summary or *synopsis* of "The
Lottery" to get a clear, concise fix on the literal events in the story. (We
reprint his synopsis on p. 254.)

But Burns knew that he could not write a good critique without reading
the story repeatedly and closely, marking key points in the text. Students who
read a complex work of literature only once, thinking that is enough, are
mistaken. Even if you are just trying to understand the literal level—what
happens in a story, or what a poet says—you'll need to read the work more
than once. If you are studying a literary selection to analyze, interpret, and
evaluate it, you'll find that several close readings are necessary.

For close reading, read the text at least three times, each time for a
different reason:

Read for the big picture. Read for an overall idea of what the work
contains.

Read for pleasure.

Read purposefully. Read with an eye for what you seek in the work: plot, characters, themes, form, or whatever. Read with pencil in hand. Make notes—in the margins if the copy is yours and on paper or index cards if it isn't. Is there an especially hard part? Try putting it into your own words. If you're analyzing a difficult piece, reading it aloud to yourself may help you make sense of it.

Later as you draft your literary critique, you will discover, just as Jonathan Burns did, that you have to reread specific sections over and over to check your interpretations and to be sure the evidence from the story supports your claims.

The Elements of Literature: Looking Closely at "The Lottery"

Every field—scuba diving, football, gourmet cooking, engineering, business— has its own vocabulary. If you are going to play football, you should know the difference between a blitz and a quarterback sneak. Before you start cooking, you'd better know the difference between basting and shirring. Literary criticism is no different. Before you can analyze and interpret a piece of literature or write a successful literary critique, you must be familiar with the *elements* of fiction, poetry, and drama and with the specialized terms critics and scholars use to talk about those elements.

Jonathan Burns knew he had to analyze the important elements in "The Lottery" to understand the story well enough to write about it. We list a few of the elements here—a handy glossary of terms that you can use to discuss any piece of literature:

Setting is the time and place where events occur. The season, the weather, the atmosphere, and people in the background may be part of the setting. Jonathan Burns recognized that Shirley Jackson describes the setting in the first sentence of "The Lottery": "The morning of June 27th was clear and sunny, with the fresh warmth of a full-summer day; the flowers were blossoming profusely and the grass was richly green" (226). That description is precise: Burns could almost feel the sun and smell the flowers. But he did not know the period of time—eighteenth century, nineteenth century, twentieth century? And he did not know where Jackson's village is located.

Characters are imagined people. The author lets you know what they are like through their actions, speech, thoughts, attitudes, and background. Sometimes a writer also tells you about physical characteristics or names or relationships—especially contrasts—with other people.

Burns reread the initial description of Mr. Summers: He "had time and energy to devote to civic activities. He was a round-faced, jovial man and he ran the coal business, and people were sorry for him, because he had no children and his wife was a scold" (227). These details introduce this official of the lottery. Later Burns learned more about him through what he says:

"Little late today, folks" (227); "Thought we were going to have to get on without you, Tessie" (229); "Well, now, . . . guess we better get started, get this over with, so's we can go back to work" (229). Burns decided that Mr. Summers is in charge of the situation and doesn't want any slip-ups. What does Mr. Warner's speech in "The Lottery" tell you about him?

And Burns learned about the characters through what they do, as when the Watson boy "blinked his eyes nervously and ducked his head" at the lottery (229) or when the villagers "only half listened to the directions; most of them were quiet, wetting their lips, not looking around" (229). What does Tessie do that gives you some insight into what she is like?

Plot is arrangement of events of the story—what happens to whom, where, when, and why. If the events follow each other logically and if they are in keeping with what we have been told about the characters, the plot is *plausible* or believable. Although the ending of "The Lottery" at first shocked Jonathan, when he looked back through the story, he found *foreshadowing,* hints that the author provides to help readers accept the "surprise" ending. Looking back he saw numerous clues that Tessie and the other villagers were nervous and hesitant about the lottery, not the usual reaction of people who expect someone to win a desirable prize of money, a car, or a vacation. See how many of these clues you can find.

The *protagonist,* or main character, is placed in a *dramatic situation*—in conflict with some other person or group of people, the *antagonist.* In "The Lottery," Burns identified Tessie Hutchinson as the protagonist, the villagers as the antagonist, and the dramatic situation as Tessie's joining the group waiting for the lottery. *Conflict* consists of two forces attempting to conquer each other or resisting being conquered. It is not merely any vaguely defined turmoil in a story. *External conflicts* are conflicts outside an individual— between two people, between a person and a group (Tessie Hutchinson versus the villagers), between two groups (those who support the lottery and those who want to do away with it), or even between a character and his or her environment. *Internal conflicts* are those within an individual, between two opposing forces or desires (such as reason versus emotion or fear versus hope in each villager as the slips of paper are drawn). The *central conflict* of a story is the primary internal conflict within the protagonist that propels and accounts for the action of the story. What is the central conflict within Tessie?

Events of the plot *complicate* the conflict (Tessie arrives late, Bill Hutchinson draws the slip with the black spot for his family, Tessie claims it wasn't fair) and lead to the *climax,* the moment at which the outcome is inevitable (Tessie draws the slip with the black dot). The outcome itself is the *resolution* or conclusion (the villagers stone Tessie Hutchinson). Some contemporary stories let events unfold without any apparent plot—action and change occur inside the characters.

Point of view is the angle from which a story is told. Who is the *narrator*—who tells the story? Through whose eyes are the events perceived? It might be the author, or it might be some character in the story. If a character, what part does he or she play, and what limits does the author place on that character's knowledge? Is the character aware of everything that is going on, or is he or she an outsider? Jonathan Burns tried to answer these questions to determine the point of view in "The Lottery." Three often used points of view are those of a *first-person narrator* (*I*), a *third-person narrator* (*he* or *she*) who is a major participant in the action (often the protagonist), and a *third-person narrator* who is an observer, not a participant in the action. The point of view may be *omniscient* (told through several characters' eyes), *limited omniscient* (told through one character's eyes), or *objective* (not getting into any character's mind). Burns realized that the point of view in "The Lottery" is that of a third-person narrator, an objective observer, seemingly looking on and reporting what is going on without knowing what any of the characters are thinking. Why do you think Shirley Jackson chose this point of view for "The Lottery"? How would the story be different if it were told from Tessie's point of view? From Mr. Summers's? From Old Man Warner's?

Theme is a main idea or insight a work contains. It is the author's observations about life, society, or human nature. Sometimes you can sum up a theme in a sentence: "honesty is the best policy," "human beings cannot live without illusion." In Aesop's fable of the fox and the grapes, the moral, which is stated at the end, is also the theme: "It is easy to scorn what cannot be attained." In the television program *Doogie Howser, M.D.*, Doogie types the theme into his computerized journal at the end of each episode.

In a complex work, however, a theme may be implied and difficult to discern. Any one piece of literature may have more than one theme, and a theme may be stated in various ways. In a critique of "The Lottery," the critics Cleanth Brooks and Robert Penn Warren assert, "We had best not try to restrict the meaning to some simple dogmatic statement. The author herself has been rather careful to allow a good deal of flexibility in our interpretation of the meaning, yet surely a general meaning does emerge."

To state a theme, find an important subject in the story and ask yourself, "What does the author say about this subject?" Details from the story itself should support your statement of theme, and your theme should account for all the details in the story. Be careful not to confuse a subject or topic of a story with a theme. Jonathan Burns listed some of the important subjects of "The Lottery": the unexpected, scapegoating, people's inhumanity to one another, outmoded rituals, victims of society, hostility, violence, death. What other subjects do you see in this story? How would you state what you see as the major theme? Burns focused on Tessie's claim that the lottery wasn't fair and the reaction of the Hutchinson children and the other villagers when the children did not draw the black dot, believing these to be significant occurrences leading to Jackson's meaning. From this interpretation, he stated the theme as "People are selfish, always looking out for number one."

Images are words or groups of words that refer to any sense experience:

Seeing. In his analysis of "The Lottery" Burns determined that Shirley Jackson uses many images of sight to help readers visualize what happens. The flowers bloom "profusely" and the grass is "richly green." Jackson describes the black box so precisely that Jonathan—and we—can

son describes the black box so precisely that Jonathan — and we — can see it clearly: It grows "shabbier each year" and is "no longer completely black but splintered badly along one side to show the original wood color, and in some places faded or stained" (227–28). When Mr. Graves drops all the slips of paper except the five for the Hutchinson family, "the breeze [catches] them and [lifts] them off" (231).

Hearing. Burns found several images of sound in Jackson's story. The children break into "boisterous play" (227). When Mr. Summers arrives in the square, a "murmur" spreads among the villagers; a "hush" falls upon the crowd when he speaks (227, 229). Nancy's friends breathe "heavily" as she goes forward to draw a slip of paper (232). Mrs. Dunbar is "gasping for breath" as the villagers move toward Tessie (233).

Smelling. Although Jackson doesn't include any smells in her story, Burns himself imagined the musty smell of Mr. Summers's coal company where the black box was locked away the night before the lottery and Mr. Graves's barn where the dusty black box had been stored for a year since the last lottery.

Tasting. What do you think the villagers tasted when they wet their lips?

Touching. The stones the children gather are smooth and round (227), and Tessie taps Mrs. Delacroix on the arm as she makes her way toward her husband (229).

Feeling. Do the characters feel heat or cold, fear or joy, pain or thirst? Jonathan saw that the villagers feel "the fresh warmth of a full-summer day" (226) and that "the feeling of liberty" sits "uneasily" on most of the children (paragraph 2). Then he realized that because of the point of view in "The Lottery," he wasn't told much more about what the villagers feel.

Figures of speech are defined by William Thrall and Addison Hibbard as "intentional departures from the normal order, construction, or meaning of words in order to gain strength and freshness of expression" (*A Handbook to Literature,* 1980). Some of the most common types of figurative language are the *simile,* a comparison using *like* or *as;* the *metaphor,* an implied comparison; and *personification,* the attribution of human qualities to inanimate or nonhuman creatures. Burns found several metaphors in "The Lottery." Bobby Martin, Harry Jones, and Dickie Delacroix *guard* their pile of stones "against the *raids* of the other boys" (paragraph 2). Tessie *cranes* her neck to find her family (paragraph 9). Old Man Warner says that the young people who want to give up the lottery will next "be wanting to go back to living in caves" (230).

A **symbol** is a tangible object or visible action or character that hints at meanings beyond itself. In "The Lottery," a story filled with symbols, Jonathan decided that the black box suggests outdated tradition, the mysteriously inexplicable, the past, resistance to change, evil, cruelty, and more. What does Old Man Warner suggest? In this story, as in others, if you can identify a central symbol and figure out what it suggests, you are well on your way to stating the theme.

Irony results from readers' sense of some discrepancy. A simple kind of irony, *sarcasm,* occurs when you say a thing but mean the opposite: "I just love scrubbing the floor" or "Of course, I don't want a Mercedes." In literature, an *ironic situation* sets up a wry contrast or incongruity. In "The Lottery," actions of evil cruelty and horror take place on a bright sunny June day in an ordinary village. *Ironic dialogue* occurs when a character says one thing but means something else. Mr. Summers says cheerfully to Tessie Hutchinson, "Thought we were going to have to get on without you" (229). When someone mentions that some people in the north village are talking of giving up the lottery, Old Man Warner snorts, "Next thing you know, they'll be wanting to go back to living in caves, nobody work anymore, live *that* way for a while. . . . First thing you know, we'd all be eating stewed chickweed and acorns" (230), implying that doing away with the lottery would cause them to return to a more primitive way of life. A story has an *ironic point of view* when we sense a difference between the author and the character through whose eyes the story is perceived or between the author and the narrator. Burns realized that Shirley Jackson does not condone the actions of the villagers, no matter what the reason. Find some other ironic events and comments in this story.

As you read literary criticism and discuss literature in your classes, you will discover other literary terms, but the basic ones listed here give you a foundation for analyzing literature.

After Jonathan Burns completed his analysis of the elements in "The Lottery," he was ready to begin his literary critique. He had thrashed around for a topic for his paper, some point on which he could focus his thoughts and comments. He immediately thought of the undertone of violence in the story but decided that the undertone was so subtle that it would be difficult to write about. Then he considered writing about the characters in the story. Mr. Summers and Old Man Warner were especially memorable. And then there was Tessie Hutchinson; he could hear her screams as the stones hit her. But he decided not to write about the characters because he could not think of much to say about them except that they were memorable, and he knew that that was too vague a statement. He considered the language and symbols, foreshadowing and ambiguity, and dismissed each in turn. All of a sudden he hit upon the surprise ending. How did Jackson manipulate all the details to generate such a shock?

To begin to focus his thinking, he brainstormed titles, some serious, others flippant: Death Comes as a Surprise; The Unsuspected Finish; Patience of the Devil; An Inquiry into the Implementation of Pure Reason; The Wrath of Grapes; Bob Dylan Was Right. He chose the straightforward title "The Hidden Truth."

After reviewing his notes from his analysis of the story, he realized that Jackson uses characterization, symbolism, and ambiguous description to prepare the reader for the ending. Writing about how the author shocks the reader at the end of the story would allow him to discuss several elements that interested him, and focusing on the techniques she used to build up to the ending would help him unify the aspects of his interpretation.

He listed details from the story under three headings — characters, symbols, and language. Then he drafted the following introduction:

> Unsuspecting, the reader follows Shirley Jackson's softly flowing tale of a rural community's timeless ritual, the lottery. Awareness of what is at stake--the savage murder of one random member--comes slow, only becoming clear toward the last fraction of the story. No sooner does the realization set in than the story is over. It is a shock ending.
>
> What created so great a shock as the reader experiences after reading "The Lottery"? Shirley Jackson takes great care in producing this effect, using elements such as language, symbolism, and characterization to lure the reader into not anticipating what is to come.

With his synopsis, his plan, his copy of the story, and this beginning of a draft, he wrote the following essay.

Student Essay

THE HIDDEN TRUTH:
AN ANALYSIS OF SHIRLEY JACKSON'S "THE LOTTERY"
Jonathan Burns

It is as if the first stone thrown strikes the reader as well as Mrs. Hutchinson. And even though there were signs of the stoning to come, somehow the reader is taken by surprise at Tessie's violent death. What factors contribute to the shock ending to "The Lottery"? Upon closer examination of the story, the reader finds that through all events leading up to the ending, Shirley Jackson has used unsuspicious characterizations, harmless symbolism, and ambiguous descriptions to achieve so sudden an impact. 1

By all appearances, the village is a normal place with normal people. Children arrive at the scene first, with school just over for the summer, talking of teachers and books, not of the fact that someone will die today (227). And as the adults show up, their actions are just as stereo- 2 typical: the men talk of farming and taxes, while the women gossip (227). No trace of hostility, no sense of dread in anyone: death seems very far away here.

The conversations between the villagers are no more ominous. As the lottery progresses, people laugh as wives command their husbands to go draw their slips of paper for the family (230). Mr. Summers is regarded as a competent and respected figure, despite the fact that his wife is "a scold" (227). Old Man Warner brags about how many lotteries he's seen and rambles on criticizing other towns that have given up the tradition (230). The characters' comments show the crowd to be more a closely knit community than a murderous mob.

Equally unthreatening are the symbols of "The Lottery." The stones collected by the boys (227) are unnoticed by the adults and thus seem a trivial detail. The reader thinks of the "great pile" (227) as a child's entertainment, like a stack of imaginary coins rather than an arsenal. Ironically, no stones are ever thrown during the children's play and no violence is seen in the pile of stones.

Similarly, Jackson describes the box and its history in great detail, but there seems nothing unusual about it. It is just another everyday object, stored away in the post office or on a shelf in the grocery (228). Every other day of the year, the box is in plain view but goes virtually unnoticed. The only indication that the box has lethal consequences is that it is painted black (227), yet this is an ambiguous detail, as a black box can also signify mystery or magic, mystical forces which are sometimes thought to exist in any lottery.

In her ambiguous descriptions, Jackson refers regularly to the village's lottery and emphasizes it as a central ritual for the people., The word lottery itself is ambiguous, as it typically implies a winning of some kind, like a raffle or sweepstakes. It is paralleled to square dances and to the teenage club, all under the direction of Mr. Summers (227), activities people look forward to. There is no implied difference between the occurrences of this day and the festivities of Halloween: according to Jackson, they are all merely "civic activities" (227). Equally ambiguous are the people's emotions: some are casual, such as Mrs. Hutchinson, who arrives late because she "clean forgot" what day it is (228), and some are anxious, such as Mrs. Dunbar, who repeats to her son, "I wish they'd hurry," without any sign of the cause of her anxiety (230). With these details the reader finds no threat or malice in the villagers, only vague expectation and congeniality.

Even when it becomes clear that the lottery is something 7 no one wants to win, Jackson presents only a vague sense of sadness and mild protest. The crowd is relieved that the youngest of the Hutchinsons, Davy, doesn't draw the fatal slip of paper (232). One girl whispers that she hopes it isn't Nancy (232), and when the Hutchinson children discover they aren't the winners, they beam with joy and proudly display their blank slips (232). It's like a theatrical scene, with growing suspense and excitement apparent only when the victim is close to being decided. And when Tessie is revealed to be the winner of the lottery (232), she merely holds her hands out "desperately" and repeats, "It isn't fair" (233).

With a blend of character, symbolism and description, 8 Shirley Jackson paints an overall portrait of a gentle-seeming rural community, apparently no different from any other. The tragic end is sudden only because there is no recognition of violence beforehand, despite the fact that Jackson has provided the reader with plenty of clues in the ample details about the lottery and the people. It is a haunting discovery that the story ends in death, even though such is the truth in the everyday life of all people.

Questions to Start You Thinking

1. How does this essay differ from a synopsis, a summary of the events of the plot? (For a synopsis of "The Lottery," see p. 254.)
2. Does Jonathan Burns focus on the technique of the short story or on theme?

3. What is his thesis?

4. Why does he explain characterization first, symbolism second, and description last? Would discussing these elements in a different order have made much difference in his essay?

5. Is his introduction effective? Compare and contrast it with the first introduction he drafted (p. 239). What did he change? Which version do you prefer?

6. Is his conclusion effective?

7. How does he tie his ideas together as he moves from paragraph to paragraph? Does he keep the focus on idea and technique instead of plot?

LEARNING BY WRITING

The Assignment: Writing a Critique of a Literary Work

A literary critic analyzes, interprets, and evaluates a work of literature. The critic sees and understands deeply not because he or she has some special inspiration or power, but because she or he has studied and analyzed the piece of writing very carefully. For this assignment you are to be a critic — analyzing, interpreting, and evaluating a literary selection for your classmates. You will deepen their understanding because you have devoted time and effort to digging out the meaning and testing it with evidence from the work itself. Even if they have studied the piece carefully, you will try to convince them that your interpretation is acceptable.

Write an essay interpreting one or more aspects of a literary work that intrigues you or that you think expresses a worthwhile meaning. Probably your instructor will want to approve your selection. After careful analysis of the literary work, you will become the expert critic, explaining the meaning you discern, supporting your interpretation with evidence from the literature itself as well as from your own experience, and evaluating the effectiveness of the elements and the significance of the theme. You may draw from any of your five resources — recall, observation, reading (the story as well as other sources), conversation, imagination. Probably you'll use several critical thinking skills — analyzing the parts of the work; taking a stand on your interpretation; comparing and contrasting characters in the story, or comparing and contrasting the work with other works you know; proposing a solution to a puzzling part of the work or to a problem posed by the author, perhaps as a theme; evaluating the quality of the work; and identifying causal relationships in the action of the work. Refer to Parts One and Two of this book to remind yourself about these resources and critical skills.

You cannot attempt to include everything about the work in your paper, so you should focus on one element (such as character, setting, or theme) or the interrelationship of two or three elements (such as Jonathan Burns's analysis of characterization, symbolism, and ambiguity in his interpretation of the surprise ending of "The Lottery"). The purpose of your essay is to help your classmates — who have read but not studied the selection as thoroughly as you have — to understand the meaning of the literature and to gain insight into their own lives just as you have through your careful study.

Your assignment is to analyze, to interpret, and to evaluate, not just to retell, the work. Although a summary, or *synopsis,* of it is a good beginning point for your ideas, it is not a satisfactory literary critique. Notice, for example, how Jonathan Burns uses details from the plot in the second and third paragraphs of his essay (pp. 239–40) but then moves beyond events of plot to an analysis of character, symbol, and description.

Here are instances of college writers who successfully responded to this type of assignment:

> A woman analyzed the plot of the short story "The Necklace" by Guy de Maupassant and concluded that the change in the protagonist Mathilde Loisel at the end of the story is unrealistic.

> A man demonstrated how the rhythm, rhymes, and images of Adrienne Rich's poem "Aunt Jennifer's Tigers" mesh to convey the poem's theme of tension between a woman's artistic urge and the constraints placed on her by society.

> A man explained how Carson McCullers in the short story "A Tree, a Rock, a Cloud" uses characterization to reveal the theme that severe emotional hurt caused by rejection in love can predispose an individual toward emotional detachment in subsequent relationships.

> A woman analyzed the reasons why the protagonist Charles Woodruff does what he does in the short story "Witness" by Ann Petry. She concluded that his motivation is sufficient and his actions, although tragic, are plausible.

> A woman majoring in psychology examined the relationship between Hamlet and Claudius in Shakespeare's *Hamlet* and concluded that it is in many ways representative of the relationship between stepsons and stepfathers.

> A woman explained how Walter Van Tilburg Clark uses symbols in "A Portable Phonograph" to reveal and intensify the theme of human beings' inhumanity to others because of selfishness.

> A man analyzed the foreshadowing in "Sonny's Blues" by James Baldwin and concluded that this story is tightly and effectively constructed.

> A man who was a musician analyzed the credibility of Sonny as a musician — his attitudes, actions, struggles, relationship with his instrument and with other musicians — and concluded that Sonny is a believable character.

Finding a Subject

Read several literary works until you find two or three you like. Perhaps one makes you nod your head in agreement as you read, or sends a chill up your spine when you finish, or leaves you puzzled at the end, or even makes you angry. Do you have a favorite author? A favorite short story among those you have read for this course? Any of these might make a suitable selection for your analysis. Then, slowly and carefully, reread the two or three that tweak your interest to decide which one you want to concentrate on. Choose the one that strikes you as especially significant — realistic or universal, moving or disturbing, believable or shocking. Choose the one that seems to have a meaning that you wish to share with your classmates.

Generating Ideas

Analyzing a literary work is the basis of interpreting meaning and evaluating literary quality. It also gives you ideas to write about and helps you understand the elements you will use in support of your interpretation. As you read the work you have selected, see it as divisible into its elements and analyze those elements as Jonathan Burns did the elements of "The Lottery." Then focus on *one* significant element. When you write your interpretation, restrict your discussion to that element and possibly its relationship to other literary elements.

As you begin to analyze a piece of literature, we provide checklists to guide you in studying different types of literature. Each analytical model is an aid to understanding; it is *not* an organizational outline for writing about literature.

DISCOVERY CHECKLIST: ANALYZING A SHORT STORY OR NOVEL

- What is your reaction to the story? Jot it down.
- Who is the *narrator*—not the author, but the one who tells the story? What is the *setting* (time and place)? What is the *atmosphere* or *mood*?
- What does the *plot* unfold? Write a synopsis, or summary, of the events in time order, including relationship between those events.
- What are the *characters* like? Describe their personalities and traits. Who is the *protagonist?* The *antagonist?* Do any characters change, and are the changes plausible or believable?
- How would you describe the story's *style*, or use of language? Is the style informal or conversational? Is it formal? Is there any dialect? Are there any foreign words?
- What are the *conflicts* (two forces in opposition) in the story? Determine the *external conflicts* (between a person and another person or between a person and an outside force such as nature or society) and the *internal conflicts* (inside a person). What is the *central conflict* (the major internal conflict within the main character)? Express the conflict using the word *versus*, such as "dreams versus reality" or "the individual versus society."
- What is the *climax* of the story—the peak of intensity of the central conflict, the point after which things will never be the same? Is there any *resolution* or falling action?
- What is the *point of view*—the angle of vision from which the story is told? It may be *omniscient* (getting into the minds of all the characters), *limited omniscient* (getting into the mind of only one or a few of the characters, often the protagonist), or *objective* (not getting into the minds of any character; simply reporting).

- Are there important *symbols?* What might they mean?
- What does the *title* of the story mean?
- Does the story have more than one *level of meaning?*
- What is the *theme* of the story, the universal idea implied by the author? State your interpretation of the theme. How is it relevant to your life?
- What other literary works or experiences from life does the story make you think of? Jot them down.

DISCOVERY CHECKLIST: ANALYZING A POEM

- What is your reaction to the poem? Jot it down.
- Who is the *speaker* — not the author, but the one who tells the story? What is the *setting* (time and place)? What is the *mood* (emotional atmosphere)?
- Can you put the poem into your own words — paraphrase it?
- What is striking about the language of the poem? Identify any unusual words or words used in an unusual sense. Look for *archaic* words (words no longer commonly used), *connotation* (suggestions of a word — *house* has a different connotation from *home*, although both may refer to the same place), *repetition* of words. Is the level of language colloquial or formal? What kind of figurative language is used: *imagery* (language that appeals to the senses), *metaphor* (implied comparison), *irony* (contrast between what is expected and what is)?
- Is the poem *lyric* (expresses emotion) or *narrative* (tells a story)?
- What is the structure of the poem? How is it divided? Are there *couplets* (two consecutive rhyming lines) or *quatrains* (units of four lines)? Notice especially the beginning and the end.
- Does the poem have *rhyme* (words that sound alike)? How does the rhyme contribute to the meaning?
- Does the poem have *rhythm* (regular meter or beat, patterns of accented and unaccented syllables)? How does the rhythm contribute to the meaning?
- What does the *title* of the poem mean?
- What is the *theme* of the poem? How does this underlying idea unify the poem? How is the theme relevant to your own life?
- What other literary works or experiences from life does the poem make you think of? Jot them down.

DISCOVERY CHECKLIST: ANALYZING A PLAY

- What is your reaction to the play? Jot it down.
- Because a play is written to be seen and heard, not read, how does this play differ from a short story or novel? Can you visualize the action? Can

you hear the words of the characters? If you were an actor, how would you interpret the stage directions and say the words? If you were the casting director, who would you cast in the major roles of the play?

- Is the play a *tragedy* (a serious drama that arouses pity and fear in the audience and usually ends unhappily with the death or downfall of the *tragic hero*) or a *comedy* (drama that aims primarily to amuse and that usually ends happily)?

- What is the *setting* (place and time) of the play? What is its *mood* (emotional atmosphere)?

- In brief, what happens? Summarize each act of the play.

- What are the characters like? Who is the *protagonist,* the main character? What *antagonist* opposes the main character? Are there *foil characters* (those who contrast to the main character and reveal his or her traits)? Which characters are in conflict with each other? Do any of the characters change?

- Which speeches seem especially significant?

- What is the plot? Identify the *exposition,* the background information needed to understand the story. Determine the main *external* and *internal* conflicts. What is the *central conflict*? What events *complicate* the central conflict? What is the *climax* of the play? Is there a *resolution* to the action? How are these elements of the *plot* spread throughout the acts of the play?

- What does the *title* mean?

- Can you identify any *dramatic irony,* words or acts of a character that carry meaning unperceived by the character but evident to the audience?

- What is the major *theme* of the play—a universal idea that underlies it? How is this theme related to your own life?

- What other literary works or experiences from life does the play make you think of? Jot them down.

Analysis precedes comprehension, so analysis of the elements of a literary work will provide insight into the author's attitudes and help you understand the meaning so that you can explain it to others.

As you write your critique, don't worry about impressing your readers with your brilliance. Though you need a critical vocabulary, use only terms that you understand. The writer who writes "The ironic symbolism in 'The Lottery' is portrayed as highly symbolic in theme" is about as clear as corned beef hash. Remember to assume that your readers, too, have read the work you're analyzing, but they have not studied it as carefully as you have. This assumption will help you determine how much evidence from the story you need to include and will save you a lot of wordy summarizing ("On the next page they bring out a black box, sit it on a three-legged stool, and put slips of paper in it"). We suggest that you regard your readers as friends in whose company you are discussing something already familiar to all of you. Your purpose is to explain the deeper meaning of the story to your friends, meaning that they may not be aware of after only a cursory reading.

DISCOVERY CHECKLIST: FINDING IDEAS

- Have you known people similar to those in the literary work? Are the characters believable? Is their motivation sufficient to cause them to act as they do? How do you know what they are like (through their actions, speech, habits, and so on)?
- Have similar things happened to you? Can you use some information from your experience to explain the meaning of the work?
- Are there any significant images that help illuminate the meaning? Any important symbols? Any irony? What about the setting and the atmosphere?
- Are the characters universal (representative of all human beings) or stereotypes?
- Is the theme you have isolated universal (applicable to all people everywhere at all times)?
- Have you selected a major element in the work to focus on? Have you avoided focusing on a minor element simply because it strikes your fancy?
- Do you know the main point you want to make about this work?
- Does the evidence in the work support the point you want to make?
- Are you using analysis to clarify meaning instead of as an end in itself?

Planning, Drafting, and Developing

After you have determined the element or the related elements of the work that you intend to focus on to interpret meaning, go through the work again to find all the passages that relate to your main point, marking them or taking notes as you find them. It's a good idea to put these relevant passages on note cards or in a computer file, just as you do when you are conducting library research. Remember to note the page references for the details you select, and if you use any quotations, quote them exactly.

Begin by trying to express the main point you want to convey in your critique. Suppose you start with a tentative thesis on the theme of "The Lottery." Note that the thesis statement identifies the literary work and the author.

```
In "The Lottery," Shirley Jackson reveals the theme.
```

But this statement is too vague, so you decide to rewrite it to be more precise:

```
In "The Lottery" by Shirley Jackson, the theme is
tradition.
```

This thesis is better, but still unsatisfactory. The statement of the theme of the story is not yet clear or precise: in her narrative, what does Jackson imply about tradition? You try several other ways of expressing your idea.

```
In "The Lottery" by Shirley Jackson, one of the major
themes is that outmoded traditions can be harmful.
```

You used the qualifier *one of* to indicate that this theme is not the only one in the story, but the rest of the thesis is vague. What does "outmoded" mean? How are the traditions harmful?

```
In "The Lottery" by Shirley Jackson, one of the major
themes is that traditions that have lost their meaning
can cause otherwise normal people to act abnormally by
rote.
```

This is a better thesis, one you might start writing from, but keep in mind that it may change as you develop the critique. You might decide to go beyond interpretation of Jackson's ideas to an evaluation of what she says. If so, you could write the following thesis:

```
In "The Lottery," Shirley Jackson reveals the tragic
theme that traditions that have lost their meaning can
cause otherwise normal people to act abnormally by rote.
```

In this thesis the word *tragic* reveals your evaluation of Jackson's observation of the human condition. Or you might say:

```
In "The Lottery," Shirley Jackson effectively uses sym-
bolism and irony to reveal the theme that traditions that
have lost their meaning can cause otherwise normal people
to act abnormally by rote.
```

When planning and organizing your essay, focus on ideas, not events. One way you might do so is to analyze your thesis. The thesis just presented could be divided into (1) use of symbolism to reveal theme and (2) use of irony to reveal theme. If you are writing about character change, say that of Mrs. Mallard in Kate Chopin's "The Story of an Hour" (p. 256), you might organize the information into her original character traits or attitudes, the events that cause the change, and her new traits or attitudes. In writing your critique, take care not to merely retell the story.

To start your critique, you might relate a personal experience that parallels that of the protagonist (for "The Story of an Hour," for instance, how you felt when someone close to you died) and tie your experience to that of the character in the work. Or you might focus on the universality of the character (pointing out that most people would feel as Tessie in "The Lottery" did and would probably shout "It isn't fair, it isn't right" if their name were drawn in the village lottery) or of the theme (discussing briefly how traditions seem to be losing their meaning in modern society). You might quote a striking line from the work ("And then they were upon her" or "Lottery in June, corn be heavy soon" or "we'd all be eating stewed chickweed and acorns" from "The Lottery"). More simply, you can start with a statement of what the work is about, or with your reaction to the work when you read it, or with a comment about a technique that writers use. You might begin with a "Have you ever?" question to draw the reader in to your interpretation. Be sure your beginning is tied to your main point.

As you write the body of your literary critique, include descriptions of setting and character, summaries of events, quotations of important comments of the characters, and other specific evidence from the story to support your interpretation. Cite the page numbers (for prose) or line numbers (for poetry) where details can be found in the work, placing the numbers in parentheses immediately after you mention the information from the work. Look again at how student writer Jonathan Burns (p. 239) used and documented information from "The Lottery." Integrate details from the story with your own comments and ideas.

Use transitions to keep the focus on ideas, not events. Use transition markers that refer to character traits and personality change, not those that refer to time. Say, "Although Mr. Summers was . . ." instead of "At the beginning of the story Mr. Summers was. . . ." Write "Tessie became . . ." instead of "After that Tessie was. . . ." State "The protagonist in 'The Lottery' realized . . ." or "The villagers in 'The Lottery' changed . . . ," not "On the next page . . ." or "In the following paragraph of the story . . ." or "At the end of the story she. . . ."

Provide a conclusion for your essay; don't just stop writing. Use the same techniques as you use for introductions — anecdote, personal experience, comment on technique, quotation — to provide a sense of finality and closing for the readers. Refer to or reaffirm your thesis. Often an effective conclusion ties in directly with the introduction. Notice how Jonathan Burns tied his conclusion (p. 241) to his introduction (p. 239).

In an essay for her writing class, Cindy MacDonald analyzed the change in the protagonist in a story by Meg Campbell. See how she starts and ends her essay.

INTRODUCTION

All many people think about is the good old days. They live in the past instead of living in the present. The character of Anne in the short story "Just Saying You Love Me Doesn't Make It So" by Meg Campbell is revealed as a young woman who lives in the past but changes to a person who is concerned with the present and the future.

CONCLUSION

When most people are forced to take an honest look at what they think of as the good old days, they sometimes realize that the good old days were not so good after all. If they start living in the present and making the future into what they want it to be, instead of dreaming of what might have been, they will find, as Anne did, that their lives are much happier.

In an analysis of the theme in "A Tree, a Rock, a Cloud" by Carson McCullers, student Diana Ward concludes her comments:

> Carson McCullers brings out the universal capacity to be deeply hurt by rejection in a close relationship and the necessity to overcome the adverse effects of this rejection. Without exception, inherent in love is its capacity to inflict the most intense kind of pain that a human being may experience. Unless a human being is able to control this pain, the pain will control the person.

Revising and Editing

Papers written in response to literature are often some of the most enjoyable and interesting essays you will write in college. Interpreting literature is a rewarding activity. You see yourself and your friends and family in the works you read, and the best writers provide you with insights into yourself and your relationships with others. As you read and analyze, solutions to problems you have struggled with may become clear, or you may just enjoy figuring out why a character does such crazy things or enjoy ferreting out the techniques an author uses to make you respond as you do. Once you understand the literary selection you are interpreting, you have the pleasure of sharing your insights with your readers and thus increasing their insights as well.

Here are some questions you can ask yourself as you shape your draft.

REVISION CHECKLIST: DEVELOPING A DRAFT

- Are your interpretations supported by evidence from the literary work?
- Are the passages and details from the work integrated smoothly into your comments and interpretations?
- Do the transitions focus on ideas and guide your readers easily from one section or sentence to the next?
- Is the essay unified, with everything related to your main point? Do you need to refine your thesis statement to fit what you have actually written?

- Do you use words you understand? Are any sentences not clear because of your use of literary terms?
- Are any of your sentences wordy or unnecessary?
- Have you tried to share your insights into the meaning of the work with your readers, or have you slipped into trying to impress them with your profound perceptions?

You may find that you need to recast problem areas; rephrase unclear passages, using words you understand; cut out deadwood; add or change transitions. Just keep your readers in mind.

To determine how well you have succeeded in communicating with your readers, ask one of your classmates to read your draft and answer the following questions about it.

PEER EDITING CHECKLIST: WRITING ABOUT LITERATURE

- What is your first reaction to the literary critique?
- Does the critique add to your understanding of the literary work? Add to your insights into life?
- Does the writer drift into any trite ideas or expressions?
- Does the introduction make you want to read the rest of the critique?
- Is the main point clear? Does the writer provide sufficient evidence from the work to back up that point? Put stars wherever additional evidence is needed. Is there anything in the critique that does not belong?
- Does the writer go beyond synopsis to analysis of elements, interpretation of meaning, and evaluation of literary merit?
- Is the critique organized by idea instead of events?
- Do the transitions guide you smoothly from one point to the next? Do the transitions focus on ideas, not on time or position in the story?
- Is the writer's use of literary terminology clear and appropriate?
- What would make the critique more effective?
- Circle on the manuscript any places where spelling, grammar, word choice, or punctuation looks problematic to you.

When you have your peer editor's responses to your draft, go over your critique again, noting his or her suggestions. Then before you write and proofread your final draft, answer the following questions about your own paper. Answer them honestly, and if your peer editor's responses or your own evaluation of your writing indicates that the piece needs more work, take the time to make the necessary changes.

REVISION CHECKLIST: TESTING THE EVIDENCE

- Have you clearly identified the literary work and the author near the beginning of the critique?

- Have you gone beyond synopsis? Have you organized your critique according to ideas, not events? Do your transitions focus on ideas, not on plot or time sequence?

- Is your main point clear?

- Have you focused on one element or a limited number of related elements in your analysis? Have you unified your ideas about those elements?

- Have you used literary terms properly?

- Have you found all the details in the work that support your interpretation? Is there any additional dialogue you can use? Any action? Any description? Are the details that you use really relevant to the points of analysis, or are they just interesting sidelights?

- Have you worked the details from the work smoothly into your text? Have you cited the correct page or line numbers for the details from the work?

- Have you sincerely tried to add to your classmates' understanding of this work?

- If you read your introduction, would you want to read the rest of the critique?

A Note on Documenting Sources

When you write a critique of a literary work, you should cite your source or sources.

If you are using only one primary source or piece of literature:

Put the page or line numbers in parentheses immediately after each paraphrase of an event, detail, or description from the work.

Put the page or line numbers in parentheses immediately after each direct quotation from the literary work.

Include a bibliographic entry at the end of your paper so that your readers can refer to the edition of the work you cite.

If you are using two or more primary sources or pieces of literature:

If the title of the literary work precedes your paraphrase or quotation from it, put only the page number in parentheses after the paraphrase or quotation.

If the title does not precede your paraphrase or quotation from the work and if the source of the information you cite could be confused, put the author's last name plus the page number in parentheses (Jackson 56). Use no punctuation between the name and the page number.

For further discussion of citing sources and for bibliographic forms, see Chapter 30.

Other Assignments

1. Use a poem, a play, or a novel instead of a short story to complete the assignment in this chapter.

2. Write an essay comparing and contrasting some element in two or three short stories or poems, similar to David Gibbs's essay on Emily Dickinson and D. H. Lawrence (p. 264).

3. Analyze and write a critical essay on the words of a song, a movie, or a television program. Because you won't have a written text in front of you, you probably will need to hear the work or view it more than once to pull out the specific evidence necessary to support your interpretation of it.

4. Read the following poem by Robert Frost. Then write an essay in which you use a paraphrase of this poem as a springboard for your thoughts on a fork in the road of your life — a decision that made a big difference for you.

    The Road Not Taken

    Two roads diverged in a yellow wood,
    And sorry I could not travel both
    And be one traveler, long I stood
    And looked down one as far as I could
    To where it bent in the undergrowth;

    Then took the other, as just as fair,
    And having perhaps the better claim,
    Because it was grassy and wanted wear;
    Though as for that the passing there
    Had worn them really about the same,

    And both that morning equally lay
    In leaves no step had trodden black.
    Oh, I kept the first for another day!
    Yet knowing how way leads on to way,
    I doubted if I should ever come back.

    I shall be telling this with a sigh
    Somewhere ages and ages hence:
    Two roads diverged in a wood, and I —
    I took the one less traveled by,
    And that has made all the difference.

5. Read the following poem by Edwin Arlington Robinson. Have you known and envied someone similar to Richard Cory, someone whom everyone else thought had it all? What happened to him or her? Did you discover that your impression of this individual was wrong? Write a personal response essay in which you compare and contrast the person you knew with Richard Cory. This assignment requires you to analyze the poem as well as draw on your own experience and knowledge.

    Richard Cory

    Whenever Richard Cory went down town,
    We people on the pavement looked at him:
    He was a gentleman from sole to crown,
    Clean favored, and imperially slim.

    And he was always quietly arrayed,
    And he was always human when he talked;

But still he fluttered pulses when he said,
"Good-morning," and he glittered when he walked.

And he was rich—yes, richer than a king—
And admirably schooled in every grace:
In fine, we thought that he was everything
To make us wish that we were in his place.

So on we worked, and waited for the light,
And went without the meat, and cursed the bread;
And Richard Cory, one calm summer night,
Went home and put a bullet through his head.

STRATEGIES FOR WRITING ABOUT LITERATURE: SYNOPSIS AND PARAPHRASE

Writing a Synopsis of a Story

Earlier in this chapter we mentioned that Jonathan Burns wrote a synopsis of "The Lottery" as part of his preparation for writing a literary critique of the story. A *synopsis* is a summary of the plot of a work of narrative literature—a short story, a novel, a play, or a narrative poem. It describes the first level of meaning, the literal layer. It condenses the story to only the major events and the most significant details but is more than an outline because it shows the relationship of each part to the whole and indicates how each part contributes to the meaning. You do not include your own interpretation in a synopsis but rather limit your comments to what the author has said. Writing a synopsis is valuable to you as a writer because it requires you to get the chronology straight, to pick out the significant events and details, and to see the relationship of the parts to each other and to the themes. In preparation for writing his literary critique of "The Lottery"—to make sure he had the sequence of events clear—Jonathan Burns wrote the following synopsis of the story.

A Synopsis of "The Lottery"

Jonathan Burns

Around ten o'clock on a sunny June 27, the villagers gathered in the square for a lottery, expecting to be home in time for lunch. The children came first, glad that school was out for the summer. The boys romped and gathered stones, the girls talked quietly in small groups, and the little ones hovered near their brothers and sisters. Then the men came, followed by the women. When parents called, the children came reluctantly.

Mr. Summers, who always conducted the town lottery,

arrived with the black wooden box and set it on the three-legged stool that Mr. Graves had brought out. The villagers remained at a distance from these men and didn't respond when Mr. Summers asked for help. Finally Mr. Martin and his son held the shabby black box as Mr. Summers mixed the papers in it. Although the townspeople had talked about replacing the box, they never had, but they had substituted paper slips for the original wooden chips. To prepare for the drawing, they listed the members of every household and swore in Mr. Summers. Although they had dropped many aspects of the original ritual, the official still greeted each person.

Tessie Hutchinson rushed into the square, telling her friend Mrs. Delacroix she had almost forgotten what day it was. Then she joined her husband and children.

When Mr. Summers asked if everyone was present, he was told that Clyde Dunbar was absent because of a broken leg but that his wife would draw for the family. Summers noted that the Watson boy was drawing for his mother and checked to see if Old Man Warner had made it.

The crowd got quiet. Mr. Summers reminded everybody of what they were to do and began to call the names in alphabetical order. People in the group joked nervously as the names were called. Mrs. Delacroix and Mrs. Graves commented on how fast time had passed since the last lottery, and Old Man Warner talked about how important the lottery was to the villagers. When Mr. Summers finished calling the roll, there was a pause before the heads of households opened their slips. Everybody wondered who had the special slip of paper, who had won the lottery. They discovered it was Bill Hutchinson. When Tessie complained that the drawing hadn't been done fairly, they told her to be a good sport.

Mr. Graves put five slips into the box, one for each member of Bill Hutchinson's family. Tessie kept charging that it wasn't fair. The children drew first, then Tessie, then Bill. The children opened their slips

first, smiled broadly, and held blank pieces of paper
over their heads.   Bill opened his and it was blank too.
Tessie wouldn't open hers; Bill had to do it for her.
Hers had a black spot on it.

Mr. Summers urged the villagers to finish quickly.
They picked up stones, even little Davy Hutchinson, and
started throwing them at Tessie, as she kept screaming,
"It isn't fair, it isn't right."   Then they stoned her.

Questions to Start You Thinking

1. Did Burns select the details necessary to let a reader know what happened in "The Lottery"? Why do you think he omitted certain details?

2. Are there any details, comments, or events that you would add to his synopsis? Why or why not?

3. Did Burns retell the story accurately and clearly? Did he get the events in correct time order? Did he show the relationships of the events to each other and to the whole? How?

4. Why isn't a synopsis as interesting as a short story?

5. Can you tell from this synopsis whether Burns understood Jackson's story beyond the narrative level?

6. Why didn't Burns include his own interpretation and responses to the story in this synopsis?

7. How does this synopsis differ from Burns's literary critique? (See p. 239.)

Exercise: Writing a Synopsis of a Story by Kate Chopin

Whenever you are having trouble understanding a story or if you have a lot of stories to read and are afraid you won't remember the specifics of each one, you will benefit from writing a synopsis to refer to later. Condensing five pages to 300 words forces you to isolate the most important details in the story and allows you to see clearly the sequence of events. This focus often leads you to a statement of theme. Kate Chopin is a nineteenth-century American writer. Her female characters search for their own identity and for freedom from domination and oppression. For practice, write a synopsis of 300–500 words of Chopin's short story "The Story of an Hour."

THE STORY OF AN HOUR
Kate Chopin

Knowing that Mrs. Mallard was afflicted with a heart trouble, great care   1
was taken to break to her as gently as possible the news of her husband's
death.

It was her sister Josephine who told her, in broken sentences, veiled 2
hints that revealed in half concealing. Her husband's friend Richards was
there, too, near her. It was he who had been in the newspaper office when
intelligence of the railroad disaster was received, with Brently Mallard's
name leading the list of "killed." He had only taken the time to assure
himself of its truth by a second telegram, and had hastened to forestall
any less careful, less tender friend in bearing the sad message.

She did not hear the story as many women have heard the same, with 3
a paralyzed inability to accept its significance. She wept at once, with
sudden, wild abandonment, in her sister's arms. When the storm of grief
had spent itself she went away to her room alone. She would have no one
follow her.

There stood, facing the open window, a comfortable, roomy armchair. 4
Into this she sank, pressed down by a physical exhaustion that haunted her
body and seemed to reach into her soul.

She could see in the open square before her house the tops of trees 5
that were all aquiver with the new spring life. The delicious breath of rain
was in the air. In the street below a peddler was crying his wares. The notes
of a distant song which someone was singing reached her faintly, and
countless sparrows were twittering in the eaves.

There were patches of blue sky showing here and there through the 6
clouds that had met and piled one above the other in the west facing her
window.

She sat with her head thrown back upon the cushion of the chair, quite 7
motionless, except when a sob came up into her throat and shook her, as
a child who has cried itself to sleep continues to sob in its dreams.

She was young, with a fair, calm face, whose lines bespoke repression 8
and even a certain strength. But now there was a dull stare in her eyes,
whose gaze was fixed away off yonder on one of those patches of blue sky.
It was not a glance of reflection, but rather indicated a suspension of
intelligent thought.

There was something coming to her and she was waiting for it, fearfully. 9
What was it? She did not know; it was too subtle and elusive to name. But
she felt it, creeping out of the sky, reaching toward her through the sounds,
the scents, the color that filled the air.

Now her bosom rose and fell tumultuously. She was beginning to rec- 10
ognize this thing that was approaching to possess her, and she was striving
to beat it back with her will — as powerless as her two white slender hands
would have been.

When she abandoned herself a little whispered word escaped her 11
slightly parted lips. She said it over and over under her breath: "Free, free,
free!" The vacant stare and the look of terror that had followed it went from
her eyes. They stayed keen and bright. Her pulses beat fast, and the cours-
ing blood warmed and relaxed every inch of her body.

She did not stop to ask if it were not a monstrous joy that held her. A 12
clear and exalted perception enabled her to dismiss the suggestion as
trivial.

She knew that she would weep again when she saw the kind, tender   13
hands folded in death; the face that had never looked save with love upon
her, fixed and gray and dead. But she saw beyond that bitter moment a
long procession of years to come that would belong to her absolutely. And
she opened and spread her arms out to them in welcome.

There would be no one to live for during those coming years; she would   14
live for herself. There would be no powerful will bending her in that blind
persistence with which men and women believe they have a right to impose
a private will upon a fellow creature. A kind intention or a cruel intention
made the act seem no less a crime as she looked upon it in that brief
moment of illumination.

And yet she had loved him—sometimes. Often she had not. What did   15
it matter! What could love, the unsolved mystery, count for in face of this
possession of self-assertion which she suddenly recognized as the strongest impulse of her being.

"Free! Body and soul free!" she kept whispering.   16

Josephine was kneeling before the closed door with her lips to the   17
keyhole, imploring for admission. "Louise, open the door! I beg; open the
door—you will make yourself ill. What are you doing, Louise? For heaven's
sake open the door."

"Go away. I am not making myself ill." No; she was drinking in a very   18
elixir of life through that open window.

Her fancy was running riot along those days ahead of her. Spring days,   19
and summer days, and all sorts of days that would be her own. She breathed
a quick prayer that life might be long. It was only yesterday she had thought
with a shudder that life might be long.

She arose at length and opened the door to her sister's importunities.   20
There was a feverish triumph in her eyes, and she carried herself unwittingly
like a goddess of Victory. She clasped her sister's waist, and together they
descended the stairs. Richards stood waiting for them at the bottom.

Someone was opening the front door with a latchkey. It was Brently   21
Mallard who entered, a little travel-stained, composedly carrying his grip-
sack and umbrella. He had been far from the scene of the accident, and
did not even know there had been one. He stood amazed at Josephine's
piercing cry; at Richards's quick motion to screen him from the view of his
wife.

But Richards was too late.   22

When the doctors came they said she had died of heart disease—of   23
joy that kills.

REVISION CHECKLIST: WRITING A SYNOPSIS OF A STORY

✔ Is your summary of the plot of the story true to the original? Are the details
   accurate? Are they in correct time order?

✔ Did you include only the major events and details of the story?

- ✓ Did you show the relationships of the parts without giving your personal opinions and interpretations?
- ✓ Did you use quotation marks to indicate any of the author's words you used?

Writing a Paraphrase of a Poem

In your literature courses you will often be asked to write synopses of short stories and novels but to paraphrase poems. Lika a synopsis, a *paraphrase* is a summary of the original piece of literature, showing understanding of meaning and relationships of the parts. Both assignments require you to dig out the literal level of the work.

In his composition course David Gibbs was asked to write a paraphrase of the poem "Snake" by D. H. Lawrence. His instructor wanted to know if he could comprehend the poem on his own. First David read the poem several times to be sure he understood it, marking important parts. He checked the definitions of words he was not sure of: *fissure* (line 7); *paltry, vulgar, mean* (line 65); *albatross* (line 67); *expiate* (line 74), *pettiness* (line 75). Then he divided the poem into sections and briefly summarized each in the margin of the text. Finally he drafted the paraphrase, connecting the parts of the paraphrase with transitions. Read the poem; then read David Gibbs's paraphrase of the poem.

SNAKE
D. H. Lawrence

A snake came to my water-trough
On a hot, hot day, and I in pyjamas for the heat,
To drink there.

In the deep, strange-scented shade of the great dark carob-tree
I came down the steps with my pitcher   5
And must wait, must stand and wait, for there he was at the trough
    before me.

He reached down from a fissure in the earth-wall in the gloom
And trailed his yellow-brown slackness soft-bellied down, over the edge
    of the stone trough
And rested his throat upon the stone bottom,
And where the water had dripped from the tap, in a small clearness,   10
He sipped with his straight mouth,
Softly drank through his straight gums, into his slack long body,
Silently.

Someone was before me at my water-trough,
And I, like a second comer, waiting.   15

He lifted his head from his drinking, as cattle do,
And looked at me vaguely, as drinking cattle do,
And flickered his two-forked tongue from his lips, and mused a moment,
And stooped and drank a little more,
Being earth-brown, earth-golden from the burning bowels of the earth   20
On the day of Sicilian July, with Etna smoking.

The voice of my education said to me
He must be killed,
For in Sicily the black, black snakes are innocent, the gold are
    venomous.

And voices in me said, If you were a man   25
You would take a stick and break him now, and finish him off.

But must I confess how I liked him,
How glad I was he had come like a guest in quiet, to drink at my
    water-trough
And depart peaceful, pacified, and thankless,
Into the burning bowels of this earth?   30

Was it cowardice, that I dared not kill him?
Was it perversity, that I longed to talk to him?
Was it humility, to feel so honoured?
I felt so honoured.

And yet those voices: 35
If you were not afraid, you would kill him!

And truly I was afraid, I was most afraid,
But even so, honoured still more
That he should seek my hospitality
From out the dark door of the secret earth.   40

He drank enough
And lifted his head, dreamily, as one who has drunken,
And flickered his tongue like a forked night on the air, so black;
Seeming to lick his lips,
And looked around like a god, unseeing, into the air,   45
And slowly turned his head,
And slowly, very slowly, as if thrice adream,
Proceeded to draw his slow length curving round
And climb again the broken bank of my wall-face.

And as he put his head into that dreadful hole,   50
And as he slowly drew up, snake-easing his shoulders, and entered
    farther,
A sort of horror, a sort of protest against his withdrawing into that horrid
    black hole,

Deliberately going into the blackness, and slowly drawing himself after,
Overcame me now his back was turned.

I looked round, I put down my pitcher,   55
I picked up a clumsy log
And threw it at the water-trough with a clatter.

I think it did not hit him,
But suddenly that part of him that was left behind convulsed in undigni-
    fied haste,
Writhed like lightning, and was gone   60
Into the black hole, the earth-lipped fissure in the wall-front,
At which, in the intense still noon, I stared with fascination.

And immediately I regretted it.
I thought how paltry, how vulgar, what a mean act!
I despised myself and the voices of my accursed human education.   65

And I thought of the albatross,
And I wished he would come back, my snake.

For he seemed to me again like a king,
Like a king in exile, uncrowned in the underworld,
Now due to be crowned again.   70

And so, I missed my chance with one of the lords
Of life.
And I have something to expiate;
A pettiness.

A PARAPHRASE OF "SNAKE"
David Gibbs

On a hot summer day in Sicily, when I went down to the   1
water pump to get some water, I saw a yellow-brown snake
draped over the trough quietly drinking. I waited and
watched him. He looked up at me and then drank some more.

I had been taught to kill poisonous gold snakes, so when   2
I hesitated, I felt like a coward. I realized I liked him
and was glad he was there. Yet I kept hearing the words of
my education: "If you were not afraid, you would kill him!"
I was afraid but also honored that he had sought my hospitality.

Slowly, regally, the snake began to climb the bank be-   3
hind the water trough. As he put his head in his dark hole

```
in the ground, I was suddenly horrified that he was going
into that blackness.  I threw a log at him, but I don't think
I hit him.  Fascinated, I watched as he rapidly drew himself
into the hole.
        Immediately I regretted my low act, despised myself for    4
striking out at the snake, and wished he would come back.
He seemed like a king of the underworld, and I was just a
petty human being who had allowed what other people said
about snakes to cause me to miss my chance of communing
with this fine creature.  And now I must make up for my
petty act.
```

Exercise: Writing a Paraphrase of a Poem by Emily Dickinson

When you study poetry, you can benefit from paraphrasing; that is, expressing the content of a poem in your own words. You may write your paraphrase in the margin of the poem or in your notebook. Writing a paraphrase forces you to divide the poem into logical sections, to figure out what the poet says in each section, and to discern the relationships of the parts.

To practice this way of writing about literature, write a paraphrase of "A narrow Fellow in the Grass" by Emily Dickinson. One of the most popular American poets, Dickinson lived as a recluse in nineteenth-century New England. She observed nature closely and wrote poems in which she used nature — sunflowers, grass, moss, rivers, birds, the sun — as a springboard for philosophical comment. In this poem she writes about a snake. Study her poem and then write a brief paraphrase of it.

A NARROW FELLOW IN THE GRASS
Emily Dickinson

A narrow Fellow in the Grass
Occasionally rides—
You may have met Him—did you not
His notice sudden is—

The Grass divides as with a Comb—   5
A spotted shaft is seen—
And then it closes at your feet
And opens further on—

He likes a Boggy Acre
A Floor too cool for Corn—   10
Yet when a Boy, and Barefoot—
I more than once at Noon

Have passed, I thought, a Whip lash
Unbraiding in the Sun
When stooping to secure it   15
It wrinkled, and was gone—

Several of Nature's People
I know, and they know me—
I feel for them a transport
Of cordiality—   20

But never met this Fellow
Attended, or alone
Without a tighter breathing
And Zero at the Bone—

DISCOVERY CHECKLIST: WRITING A PARAPHRASE OF A POEM

- How are the sections of the poem related? What are the relationships of the sections?
- Are there any words whose meanings you don't know? Are there any words that seem to be used in a special sense, a sense in which the usual meanings do not fit?
- Does the poet use any important images or pictures? Any metaphors? How do these contribute to the meaning?
- Do you leave your personal opinions out of your paraphrase?
- After you have completed the paraphrase, can you express the theme of the poem in one or two sentences?

OTHER WAYS OF WRITING ABOUT LITERATURE

A Comparison and Contrast Paper

One way to increase your understanding of the meaning of a piece of literature is to compare and contrast it with another work. As you identify similarities and differences, you deepen your knowledge of the technique and the meaning of both pieces. David Gibbs did just that in a comparison and contrast of two poems, "A narrow Fellow in the Grass" by Emily Dickinson and "Snake" by D. H. Lawrence.

Student Essay

SNAKES AND US: THE NATURE OF HUMAN AND BEAST IN TWO POEMS BY EMILY DICKINSON AND D. H. LAWRENCE
David Gibbs

Emily Dickinson's "A narrow Fellow in the Grass" and 1
D. H. Lawrence's "Snake" obviously deal with the same subject
matter. The two authors even use many of the same literary
devices in their depictions. Beyond these superficial similarities, however, lie deeper statements by both writers
about the relationship between nature and humanity.

Dickinson and Lawrence use some of the same stylistic 2
methods in their portrayal of the snake. In both poems, for
example, the snake is "humanized." Dickinson refers to the
animal as a "Fellow" (1) and even goes so far as to call all
animals "Nature's People" (17)--a personification that breaks
down the division between human and beast. Lawrence refers
to the snake throughout as "he," not "it," and recounts waiting patiently for the snake to finish drinking, as one would
wait in line behind another person.

Also common to both poems is temperature imagery, espe- 3
cially the contrast between hot and cold. Dickinson says
the snake lives in "a Floor too cool for Corn" (10). The
boy narrator, on the other hand, appears at noon--the hottest time of day. He sees the snake in the sun, where it
is most vulnerable. Hot versus cold is an even more important contrast in Lawrence's poem. His snake, like Dickinson's, is most open to attack in the "hot, hot day" (2),
"the day of Sicilian July, with Etna smoking" (22). His
refuge is to be found only in the inner regions of the cold,
dark hole. The water-trough represents relief for both man
and snake from the oppressive heat and thus becomes their
battleground.

But personification and temperature imagery are just de- 4
tails in the larger theme of both poems, that of the ambivalent mixture of fearful loathing and fascinated respect we
have for our fellow creatures.

Dickinson admires the symmetrical beauty of the snake   5
gliding through the grass, comparing its motion to that of
a comb through hair (5-8). But although she acknowledges a
"cordiality" (20) toward other creatures, she can't avoid
fearing the snake, a fear she describes as "a tighter breathing / And Zero at the Bone--" (23-24). Once more Dickinson
uses temperature imagery: the narrator is infected with the
very cold-bloodedness she loathes in the creature.

The relationship between Lawrence's man and snake is   6
even more complex. As in Dickinson's poem, the man both admires and fears the creature. The fear seems to stem from an
inner voice that tells him that his manhood (or perhaps his
very humanity) depends on killing the snake. This voice "of
my accursed education" (66) implies that only by destroying
the creature will the man prove that he is not afraid. The
voice taunts him into action in order to conquer his fear:
"If you were not afraid, you would kill him!" (37). But the
man realizes that far from making him less fearful and more
of a man, his act of violence has only brought out the part
of his nature we would normally consider "animalistic": "how
paltry, how vulgar, what a mean act!" (65). The man is
forced to question the so-called human values that have led
him to seek to destroy. As a result, he now sees the snake
as more of a human than himself. The initial shame he felt
over his fear of the snake has been replaced with the greater
shame of self-discovery: he is a violent creature. By the
end of the poem the man and the snake have traded places: the
man is a beast and the snake is a king.

Both Dickinson's and Lawrence's poems show that the re-   7
lationship between human and beast is far from simple or one-
dimensional. On the contrary, our feelings toward "Nature's
People" are always ambivalent, hovering between admiration
and repulsion. Going a step further, Lawrence's poem calls
into question any meaningful distinction between humanity and
the rest of nature, pointing out the human in the beast as
well as the beast in the human. It is perhaps this kinship
that we both admire and fear the most.

Questions to Start You Thinking

1. What elements of the poems does Gibbs compare and contrast? Can you identify others that he might have used?
2. How does he organize his essay?
3. Does he use sufficient evidence from the poems to support his interpretation?
4. Does he conclude that one or the other is a better poem?
5. Does his essay help you understand the two poems better?
6. Are there any similarities between these two poems and "The Lottery"? Can you think of other poems or stories that use similar literary devices or express similar themes? Any movies or television shows that have similar themes?
7. Have you had a similar experience with a reptile or an animal?

A Professional Critique

Literary critics write critiques of literature to introduce you to writers and to try to convince you to share their opinions of the literary selections. The critics explain how they arrived at their interpretation, and they cite evidence from the work to justify their evaluations. When you write about literature, you should do the same things.

Helen E. Nebeker is a professor of English at Arizona State University and a professional literary critic. In an article published in *American Literature* in 1974, she disagrees with other critics' interpretations of "The Lottery" and then sets forth her own, providing evidence from the story to back up her interpretation.

"THE LOTTERY": SYMBOLIC TOUR DE FORCE
Helen E. Nebeker

Numerous critics have carefully discussed Shirley Jackson's "The Lot- 1
tery" in terms of the scapegoat traditions of anthropology and literature, pointing out its obvious comment on the innate savagery of man lurking beneath his civilized trappings. Most acknowledge the power of the story, admitting that the psychological shock of the ritual murder in an atmosphere of modern, small-town normality cannot be easily forgotten. Nevertheless, beneath the praise of these critics frequently runs a current of uneasiness, a sense of having been defrauded in some way by the development of the story as a whole.

Virgil Scott, for example, writes that ". . . the story leaves one uneasy 2
because of the author's use of incidental symbolism. . . . the black box, the forgotten tuneless chant, the ritual salute—indeed the entire reconstruction of the mechanics of the lottery—fail to serve the story as they might have."[1] Robert Heilman discovers similar technical difficulties. While

---

[1] Virgil Scott, *Studies in the Short Story*, Instructor's Manual (New York, 1968) pp. 21–22.

approving the "deadpan narrative style" which screens us from the "horri-fying nightmare" to come, he nevertheless believes that the unexpected shock of the ending "crowds out" the impact of Jackson's thematic reve-lation. He suggests that the "symbolic intention" should be evidenced ear-lier in the story because, while "to set us immediately on the track of the symbolism" might reduce the shock, it might, on the other hand, "result in a more durable story."[2] Brooks and Warren praise the story for its "web of observations about human nature" and the "all-too-human tendency to seize upon a scapegoat," visiting upon it "cruelties that most of us seem to have dammed up within us." But then they indicate structural weakness by asserting that Jackson has "preferred to give no key to her parable but to leave its meaning to our inference," allowing "a good deal of flexibility in our interpretation,"[3] while yet insisting that "everything in the story has been devised to let us know how we are to 'take' the final events in the story."[4]

Perhaps the critical ambivalence illustrated above stems from failure 3 to perceive that "The Lottery" really fuses two stories and themes into one fictional vehicle. The overt, easily discovered story appears in the literal facts, wherein members of a small rural town meet to determine by lot who will be the victim of the yearly savagery. At this level one feels the horror, senses clearly the "dichotomy in all human nature,"[5] The "doubleness of the human spirit,"[6] and recoils in horror. This narrative level produces im-mediate emotional impact. Only after that initial shock do disturbing ques-tions and nuances begin to assert themselves.

It is at this secondary point that the reader begins to suspect that a 4 second story lies beneath the first and that Miss Jackson's "symbolic in-tentions" are not "incidental" but, indeed, paramount. Then one discovers that the author's careful structure and consistent symbolism work to present not only a symbolic summary of man's past but a prognosis for his future which is far more devastating than the mere reminder that man has savage potential. Ultimately one finds that the ritual of the lottery, beyond providing a channel to release repressed cruelties, actually serves to *gen-erate* a cruelty not rooted in man's inherent emotional needs at all. Man is not at the mercy of a murky, savage id; he is the victim of unexamined and unchanging traditions which he could easily change if he only realized their implications. Herein is horror.

The symbolic overtones which develop in this second, sub rosa story 5 became evident as early as the fourth word of the story when the date of June 27th alerts us to the season of the summer solstice with all its over-tones of ancient ritual. Carefully the scene is set—the date, the air of festivity, release, even license. The children newly freed from school play

---

[2] Robert B. Heilman, *Modern Short Stories; A Critical Anthology* (New York, 1959), pp. 384–85.
[3] Cleanth Brooks and Robert Warren. *Understanding Fiction,* 2nd ed. (New York, 1959), pp. 74–75.
[4] Ibid., p. 76.
[5] Scott, p. 21.
[6] Brooks and Warren, p. 76.

boisterously, rolling in the dust. But, ominously, Bobby Martin has already stuffed his pockets with stones and Harry Jones and Dickie Delacroix follow his example, eventually making a great pile of stones in the corner which they guard from the raids of other boys. By the end of just two paragraphs, Jackson has carefully indicated the season, time of ancient excess and sacrifice, and the stones, most ancient of sacrificial weapons. She has also hinted at larger meanings through name symbology. "Martin," Bobby's surname, derives from a Middle English word signifying ape or monkey. This, juxtaposed with "Harry Jones" (in all its commonness) and "Dickie Delacroix" (of-the-Cross) urges us to an awareness of the Hairy Ape within us all, veneered by a Christianity as perverted as "Delacroix," vulgarized to "Dellacroy" by the villagers. Horribly, at the end of the story, it will be Mrs. Delacroix, warm and friendly in her natural state, who will select a stone "so large she had to pick it up with both hands" and will encourage her friends to follow suit. Should this name symbology seem strained, superimposed, a little later we shall return to it and discover that every major name in the story has its special significance.

Returning to the chronology of the story, the reader sees the men   6
gather, talking of the planting and rain (the central issues of the ancient propitiatory rites), tractors and taxes (those modern additions to the concerns of man). The men are quieter, more aware, and the patriarchal order (the oldest social group of man) is quickly evidenced as the women join their husbands and call their children to them. When Bobby Martin tries to leave the group and runs laughing to the stones, he is sharply rebuked by his serious father, who knows that this is no game. Clearly this is more than the surface "idyllic" small-town life noted by Heilman;[7] the symbolic undercurrents prepare us to be drawn step by step toward the ultimate horror, where everything will fuse.

In the fourth paragraph, Mr. Summers, who ironically runs the "coal"   7
business, arrives with the postmaster, Mr. Graves, who carries the three-legged stool and the black box. Although critics have tended to see the box as the major symbol, careful reading discloses that, while the box is referred to three times in this paragraph, the stool is emphasized four times and in such strained repetition as to be particularly obvious. Further, in the next two paragraphs it will be stressed that the box rests upon, is supported by, the *three-legged stool.* It would thus seem that the stool is at least as important as the box: in my opinion, it is the symbol which holds the key to Jackson's conclusive theme. In the interest of structure and coherence, this point must be developed later in the article.

Returning to the symbol of the box, its prehistoric origin is revealed in   8
the mention of the "original wood color" showing along one side as well as in the belief that it has been constructed by the first people who settled down to make villages here (man in his original social group). The chips of wood, now discarded for slips of paper, suggest a preliterate origin. The

---

[7] Heilman, p. 384.

present box has been made from pieces of the original (as though it were salvaged somehow) and is now blackened, faded, and stained (with blood perhaps). In this box[8] symbol, Jackson certainly suggests the body of tradition—once oral but now written—which the dead hand of the past codified in religion, mores, government, and the rest of culture, and passed from generation to generation, letting it grow ever more cumbersome, meaningless, and indefensible.

Jackson does not, however, attack ritual in and of itself. She implies that, as any anthropologist knows, ritual in its origin is integral to man's concept of his universe, that it is rooted in his need to explain, even to control the forces around him. Thus, at one time the ritual, the chant, the dance were executed precisely, with deep symbolic meaning. Those chosen for sacrifice were not victims but saviors who would propitiate the gods, enticing them to bring rebirth, renewal, and thanking them with their blood. This idea explains the significance of Mrs. Delacroix's comment to Mrs. Graves that " 'there's no time at all between lotteries anymore' " and her reply that " 'Time sure goes fast.' " To the ancients, the ritual was a highly significant time marker: summer solstice and winter solstice, light versus dark, life versus death. These modern women only verify the meaninglessness of the present rite. Later, in a similar vein, when one of the girls whispers, " 'I hope it's not Nancy,' " Mr. Warner replies, " 'People ain't the way they used to be,' " implying that, anciently, honor and envy were accorded those chosen to die for the common welfare. Another neat symbolic touch tied to the meaningful ritualistic slaughter of the past is suggested by the character Clyde Dunbar. He lies at home, unable to participate in this year's lottery because of his broken leg. This reminds us that in every tradition of propitiation the purity and wholeness of the sacrifice was imperative. This "unblemished lamb" concept is epitomized in the sacrifice of Christ. In view of the interweaving of these ideas, it is difficult to see only "incidental symbolism" or to overlook the immediate and consistent "symbolic intention" of the narrative.

From the symbolic development of the box, the story moves swiftly to climax. Tessie Hutchinson hurries in, having almost forgotten the lottery in her round of normal, housewifely duties. She greets Mrs. Delacroix and moves good-humoredly into the crowd. Summers consults his list, discovers that Clyde Dunbar is missing and asks who will draw for him. When Janey Dunbar replies, " 'Me, I guess,' " Summers asks, " 'Don't you have a grown boy to do it for you, Janey?' *although Mr. Summers and everyone else in the village knew the answer perfectly well*" (italics added). In this seemingly innocent exchange the reader is jarred into a suspicion that the mentioned "grown boy" has been a previous victim and that his father cannot face the strain of being present, raising the question whether the breaking of his

[8] Etymologically, the closeness of our words "box" and "book" is indicated in the O.E. derivation from words meaning "evergreen tree or shrub" and "beech tree," probably from the habit of carving runic characters on the beech. The Latin words *codex* and *liber* have the same similarities.

leg has been accidental or deliberate. At any rate, this loss of a son will explain the unusual encouragement given Janey by the women as she goes to draw her slip of paper, her great anxiety as she awaits results with her remaining two sons—" 'I wish they'd hurry. . . . I wish they'd hurry' "—and her sending her older son with the news to her husband who, we may surmise, waits in agony for the outcome.

Significantly, the name Dunbar may in itself suggest that thin gray line   11 which separates those who have been personally marked by the horror of the lottery from those who have not. If this seems to be flagrant symbol hunting, we might remember that it is Mrs. Dunbar who, at the time of the stoning, holds back as Mrs. Delacroix urges her to action. Mrs. Dunbar, with only small stones in her hands, gasping for breath, says, " 'I can't run at all. You'll have to go ahead and I'll catch up.' " But we may believe that she will not. Marked by the loss of her son, she may still be a victim but she will not be a perpetrator. Herein lies the only humane hope raised in the story.

Next, because of the sequence of details, we are brought to consider   12 that Jack Watson is another villager touched personally by the lottery. Immediately after querying Mrs. Dunbar and making a note on his list, Mr. Summers asks, " 'Watson boy drawing this year?' " Note that the name Watson does not immediately succeed Dunbar; there seems to be a special quality about those whose names are checked previous to the actual lottery when the names will be called from A to Z. When Jack replies, " 'Here . . . I'm drawing for my mother and me,' " blinking nervously and ducking his head, the crowd responds with " 'Good fellow, Jack,' " and " 'Glad to see your mother's got a man to do it,' " encouraging him excessively as they do Mrs. Dunbar. Later, after the drawing, they will specifically ask, "Is it the Dunbars?' " " 'Is it the Watsons?' " Surely, at least the elder Watson—and maybe others in the family—has been a previous victim of the rite.

Now the symbolic names crowd upon us: "Old Man Warner," prototype   13 of the prophet of doom, voice of the past, foe of change, existing from everlasting to everlasting; Old Man Warner, seventy-seven (ancient magic number of indefiniteness) years old, the oldest of them all, juxtaposed with Jack Watson, the youngest patriarch, both part of the same unchanging horror. "Steve Adams"—Adam the father of the race and Stephen the first Christian martyr. "Baxter"[9] Martin, the eldest brother of Bobby, again suggesting primitive origins changed only superficially by even the best thought of the centuries. Tessie Hutchinson, more subtle in reference but "Hutchinson" reminiscent of early American Puritan heritage, while "Tessie," diminutive for "Theresa," derives from the Greek *theizein* meaning "to reap," or, if the nickname is for "Anastasia" it will translate literally "of the resurrection." What deliberate symbolic irony that Tessie should be the victim, not of hatred or malice or primitive fear, but of the primitive ritual itself.

---

[9] Richard Baxter was a seventeenth-century English Puritan minister and writer who postulated the doctrine of free grace.

Now, as Tessie stands at bay and the crowd is upon her, the symbols   14
coalesce into full revelation. "Tessie Hutchinson," end product of two thousand years of Christian thought and ritual, Catholic and Puritan merged,
faces her fellow citizens, all equally victims and persecutors. Mrs. "Of-the-
Cross" lifts her heavy stone in response to ritual long forgotten and perverted. "Old Man Warner" fans the coals (not fires) of emotions long sub-
limated, ritualistically revived once a year. "Mr. Adams," at once progenitor
and martyr in the Judeo-Christian myth of man, stands with "Mrs. Graves" —
the ultimate refuge or escape of all mankind — in the forefront of the crowd.

Now we understand the significance of the three-legged stool — as old   15
as the tripod of the Delphic oracle, as new as the Christian trinity. For that
which supports the present day box of meaningless and perverted superstition is the body of unexamined tradition of at least six thousand years
of man's history. Some of these traditions (one leg of the stool if you like)
are as old as the memory of man and are symbolized by the season, the
ritual, the original box, the wood chips, the names of Summers, Graves,
Martin, Warner (all cultures have their priesthoods!). These original, even
justifiable, traditions gave way to or were absorbed by later Hebraic per-
versions; and the narrative pursues its "scapegoat" theme in terms of the
stones, the wooden box,[10] blackened and stained, Warner the Prophet,
even the Judaic name of Tessie's son, David. Thus Hebraic tradition becomes a second leg or brace for the box.

Superimposed upon this remote body of tradition is one two thousand   16
years old in its own right. But it may be supposed the most perverted and
therefore least defensible of all as a tradition of supposedly enlightened
man who has freed himself from the barbarities and superstitions of the
past. This Christian tradition becomes the third support for the blood-
stained box and all it represents. Most of the symbols of the other periods
pertain here with the addition of Delacroix, Hutchinson, Baxter, and Steve.

With this last symbolic intention clearly revealed, one may understand   17
the deeper significance of Jackson's second, below-the-surface story. More
than developing a theme which "deals with 'scapegoating,' the human
tendency to punish 'innocent' and often accidentally chosen victims for our
sins"[11] or one which points out "the awful doubleness of the human spirit —
a doubleness that expresses itself in blended good neighborliness and
cruelty . . . ,"[12] Shirley Jackson has raised these lesser themes to one en-
compassing a comprehensive, compassionate, and fearful understanding
of man trapped in the web spun from his own need to explain and control
the incomprehensible universe around him, a need no longer answered by
the web of old traditions.

Man, she says, is a victim of his unexamined and hence unchanged   18
traditions which engender in him flames otherwise banked, subdued. Until
enough men are touched strongly enough by the horror of their ritualistic,

[10] The Ark of the Covenant itself is one of the earliest representations of the literal box.
[11] Scott, p. 20.
[12] Brooks and Warren, p. 76.

irrational actions to reject the long-perverted ritual to destroy the box completely—or to make, if necessary, a new one reflective of their own conditions and needs of life—man will never free himself from his primitive
nature and is ultimately doomed. Miss Jackson does not offer us much
hope—they only talk of giving up the lottery in the north village, the Dunbars
and Watsons do not actually resist, and even little Davy Hutchinson holds
a few pebbles in his hands.

Questions to Start You Thinking

1. What elements does Nebeker discuss—structure of plot, characterization, symbols, irony? How does she organize her discussion of these literary devices? How
   does she unify them, or tie them all together?
2. What does she see as the main theme of this story? Does she explain her interpretation clearly? Does she cite sufficient evidence from the short story?
3. Does Nebeker convince you that her interpretation of the story "The Lottery" is
   more valid than that of Virgil Scott, Robert Heilman, and Cleanth Brooks and
   Robert Penn Warren?

CHAPTER 12

Writing in Class

So far, we've been considering how you write when *you* control your writing circumstances. We've assumed that in writing anything from a brief account of a remembered experience to a hefty research paper, you can write lying down or standing up, write in the quiet of a library or in a clattering cafeteria. You can think, plan, draft, revise, and recopy. Although an instructor may have handed you a deadline to meet, it is usually a week or more away, and nobody is timing you with a stopwatch.

But as you know, often in college you do need to write on the spot. You face quizzes to finish in twenty minutes, final exams to complete in three or four hours, an impromptu essay to dash off in one class period, or a competency exam to take in an hour. Just how do you discover, shape, and put across your ideas in a limited time?

In this chapter we will discuss three types of in-class writings: the essay exam, the short-answer quiz, and the impromptu theme. These types of writing require thinking and composing processes different from those used for writing a paper over a period of several weeks. You have probably done all three before, but the tips in this chapter will help you write better under pressure. You will discover that you can use the same strategies for responding to an essay exam question and for writing a timed essay.

ESSAY EXAMINATIONS

First let's consider the techniques of writing an essay exam — in many courses the most important kind of in-class writing. Although lately multiple-choice tests, scored by computer, have been whittling down the number of essay exams that college students write, still the tradition of the essay exam endures. Instructors believe that such writing shows that you haven't just memorized a batch of material but that you understand it, can see connections in it, and can make your thoughts clear to someone else. To prepare for an essay exam and to write it are considered ways to lift knowledge out of textbook or notebook and bring it alive.

Preparing for the Exam

The days before an examination offer you a chance to review what you have learned and to fill in any blank spots that remain. Such reviewing enables you to think deeply about your course work, to see how its scattered parts all fit together. Sometimes the whole drift and purpose of a course may be invisible until you look back over it.

As you review your reading and any notes gleaned from lectures and class discussion, it's a good idea — if the exam will be closed book — to fix in memory any vitally important names, dates, and definitions. We said "vitally important" — you don't want to clutter your mind with a lot of spare parts selected at random. Also you might well be glad, on the day of the exam, to have a few apt quotations at your command. But preparation isn't merely a matter of decorating a vast glacier of ignorance with a few spring flowers of dates and quotations. When you review, look for the main ideas or themes in each textbook chapter. Then ask yourself: What do these main ideas have to do with each other? How might they be combined? What conclusions can I draw from all the facts? This kind of thinking is a practical form of imagining and critical thinking.

Some instructors favor open-book exams, in which you bring your books, and perhaps your notes as well, to class for reference. In an open-book exam, ability to memorize and recall is less important than ability to reason and to select what matters most. In such a writing situation, you have more opportunity than in a closed-book exam to generate ideas and to discover material on the spot.

When you study for either type of exam, you generate ideas, probably much more material than you'll be asked to use. The chief resource for most essay exams is your memory. What you remember may include observations, conversation, reading (usually important), and perhaps some imagination.

A good way to prepare in advance for any exam, whether the books are to be closed or open, is to imagine questions you might be asked, and then plan answers. We don't mean to suggest that you should try to psyche out your instructor. You're only slightly more likely to guess all the questions in advance than you are to clean out a slot machine in Las Vegas, but by thinking up your own questions, you review much material, imaginatively bring some of it together, and gain valuable experience in shaping answers. Sometimes, to help you get ready for an exam, the instructor will supply a few questions asked in former years. If you are given such examples, you can pattern new questions after them.

As you probably don't need to be told, trying to cram at the eleventh hour by going without sleep and food, consuming gallons of coffee or cola, and reducing yourself to a wreck with red-rimmed eyes is no way to prepare. You can learn more in little bites than in huge gulps. Psychologists testify that if you study something for fifteen minutes a day for eight days, you'll remember far more than if you study the same material in one unbroken sprint of two hours.

Learning from Another Writer

To start looking at techniques of answering *any* exam question, let's take one concrete example. A final exam in developmental psychology posed this question:

> What evidence indicates innate factors in perceptual organization? You might find it useful to recall any research that shows how infants perceive depth and forms.

In response, David Ian Cohn sat back in his chair for five minutes and thought over the reading he'd done for the course. What perception research had he heard about that used babies for subjects? He spent another five minutes jotting down ideas, crossed out a couple of weak ones, and drew lines connecting ideas that went together. (For an illustration of this handy technique, see "Linking," p. 328.) Then he took a deep breath and, without revising (except to cross out a few words of a sentence that seemed a false start), wrote this straightforward grade A answer:

> Research on infants is probably the best way to demonstrate that some factors in perceptual organization are innate. In the cliff box experiment, an infant will avoid what looks like a drop-off, even though its mother calls it and even though it can feel glass covering the drop-off area. The same infant will crawl to the other end of the box, which appears (and is) safe. Apparently infants do not have to be taught what a cliff looks like.
>
> Psychologists have also observed that infants are aware of size constancy. They recognize a difference in size between a 10-cm box at a distance of one meter and a 20-cm box at a distance of two meters. If this phenomenon is not innate, it is at least learned early,

for the subjects of the experiment were infants of sixteen to eighteen months.

When shown various patterns, infants tend to respond more noticeably to patterns that resemble the human face than to those that appear random. This seemingly innate recognition helps the infant identify people (such as its mother) from less important inanimate objects.

Infants also seem to have an innate ability to match sight with sound. When simultaneously shown two television screens, each depicting a different subject, while being played a tape that sometimes matched one screen and sometimes the other, infants looked at whichever screen matched what they heard—not always, but at least twice as often.

Questions to Start You Thinking

1. If you were the psychology instructor, how could you immediately see from this answer that Cohn had thoroughly dealt with the question and only with the question?

2. In what places is his answer concrete and specific, not vague and general?

3. Suppose Cohn had tacked on a concluding paragraph: "Thus I have conclusively proved that there are innate factors in perceptual organization, by citing much evidence showing that infants definitely can perceive depth and forms." Would that sentence have strengthened his answer?

4. Do you have any tried-and-true exam-answering techniques of your own that might have worked on that question or one like it? If so, share them with your class.

Generating Ideas

When, seated in the classroom, you begin your race with the clock, you may feel tempted to start scribbling away frantically. Resist the temptation. First read over all the questions carefully. Notice whether you are expected to make any choices, and decide which questions to answer. Choices are luxuries: they let you ignore questions you are less prepared to answer in favor of those you can tackle with more confidence. If you are offered a choice, just X out any questions you are *not* going to answer so you don't waste time answering them by mistake. And if you don't understand what a question calls for, ask your instructor right away.

Few people can dash off an excellent essay exam answer without first taking time to discover a few ideas and plan an answer. So take a deep breath, get comfortable, sit back, and spend a few moments in thought. Instructors prefer answers that are concrete and specific to answers that stay up in the clouds of generality. To come up with specific details may first take thought. David Cohn's answer to the psychology question cites evidence all the way through: particular experiments in which infants were subjects. A little time taken to generate concrete examples—as Cohn did—may be time wisely spent.

Some people have a rare talent for rapidly putting their thoughts in order. Many, however, will start writing an exam with a burst of speed, like race horses sprinting out of a paddock, only to find that, although they are moving fast, they don't know which way to run. Your pen will move more smoothly if you have a few thoughts in mind. These thoughts don't have to be definitive—only something to start you writing. You can keep thinking and shaping and adding your thoughts while you write.

Often a question will suggest a way to start your answer. Thought-provoking essay questions, to be sure, call for more than a regurgitation of your reading, but they often contain directive words that help define your task for you: *evaluate, compare, discuss, consider, explain, describe, isolate, summarize, trace the development of.* You can put yourself on the right track if you incorporate a form of such a directive word in your first sentence. For example:

QUESTION: Define romanticism, citing its major characteristics and giving examples of each.

ANSWER: Romanticism is defined as. . . .

OR

ANSWER: Romanticism is a complex concept, difficult to define. It. . . .

Planning: Recognizing Typical Exam Questions

Most examination questions fall into recognizable types, and if you can recognize them you will know how to organize them and begin to write. Here are specimens.

The cause and effect question   In general, these questions are easy to recognize: they usually mention *causes* and *effects.*

What were the immediate causes of the stock market crash of 1929?

Set forth the principal effects on the economy commonly noticed as a result of a low prime rate of interest.

The first question invites you to recall specific forces and events in history; the second question (from an economics course) invites an account of what usually takes place. For specific advice on writing to show cause or effect, see Chapter 10.

The compare and contrast question   One of the most popular types of examination questions, this calls on a writer to throw into sharp relief not one subject but two subjects. By pointing out similarities (comparing) and discussing differences (contrasting), you can explain both.

Compare and contrast *iconic memory* and *eidetic imagery.* (1) Define the two terms, indicating the ways in which they differ, and (2) state the way or ways in which they are related or alike.

After supplying a one-sentence definition of each term, a student proceeded first to contrast and then to compare, for full credit:

> <u>Iconic memory</u> is a picturelike impression that lasts for only a fraction of a second in short-term memory. <u>Eidetic imagery</u> is the ability to take a mental photograph, exact in detail, which later can be recalled and studied in detail, as though its subject were still present. But iconic memory soon disappears. Unlike an eidetic image, it does not last long enough to enter long-term memory. IM is common, EI is unusual: very few people have it. Both iconic memory and eidetic imagery are similar, however: both record visual images, and every sighted person of normal intelligence has both abilities to some degree.

A question of this kind doesn't always use the words *compare* and *contrast.* Consider this question from a midterm exam in basic astronomy:

> Signal at least three differences between Copernicus's and Kepler's models of the solar system. In what respects was Kepler's model an improvement on that of Copernicus?

What is that question but good old comparing and contrasting? The three differences all point to the superior accuracy of Kepler's model, so all a writer would need to do is list each difference and, in a few words, indicate Kepler's superiority.

> Distinguish between *agnosia* and *receptive aphasia.* In what ways are the two conditions similar?

Again, without using the words *comparison* and *contrast,* the question asks for both. When you distinguish, you contrast, or point out differences; when you tell how two things are similar, you compare.

> Briefly explain the duplex theory of memory. What are the main differences between short-term memory and long-term memory?

In this two-part question, the second part calls on the student to contrast (but not compare).

> Which bryophyta resemble vascular plants? In what ways? How do these bryophyta *differ* from the vascular plants?

Writers of comparison and contrast answers sometimes fall into a trap: in this case, they might get all wound up about bryophyta and fail to give vascular plants more than a few words. When you compare and contrast two things, pay attention to both, paralleling the points you make about each, giving both equal space.

The demonstration question   In this kind of question, you are given a statement and asked to back it up.

> Demonstrate the truth of Freud's contention that laughter may contain elements of aggression.

In other words, supply evidence to support Freud's claim. You might refer to crowd scenes you have experienced, perhaps quote and analyze a joke, perhaps analyze a scene in a TV show or film. Or use examples from your reading.

The discussion question   A discussion question may tempt an unwary writer to shoot the breeze.

> Name and discuss three events that precipitated Lyndon B. Johnson's withdrawal from the 1968 presidential race.

This question looks like an open invitation to ramble aimlessly about Johnson and Vietnam, but it isn't. Whenever a question says "discuss," you will be wise to plan your discussion. What it asks is "Why did President Johnson decide not to seek another term? List three causes and explain each a little."

> Discuss the economic uses of algae.

Here you might write a sentence or two on every use of pond scum you can think of ("Algae, when processed with yogurt cultures, become a main ingredient for a palatable low-calorie mayonnaise"). To deepen the discussion you might also tell how or why that use is important to the economy ("Last year, the sale of such mayonnaise increased by about thirty percent").

Sometimes a discussion question won't announce itself with the word *discuss,* but with *describe* or *explore*:

> Describe the national experience following passage of the Eighteenth Amendment to the Constitution. What did most Americans learn from it?

Provided you knew that the Eighteenth Amendment (Prohibition) banned the sale, manufacture, and transportation of alcoholic drinks and that it was finally repealed, you could discuss its effects — or perhaps the reasons for its repeal. (You might also assert that the amendment taught many Americans how to make whiskey out of rotten potatoes or how to fold a complete jazz band into a suitcase when the police raided a speakeasy, but probably that isn't what the instructor is after.)

The divide or classify question   Sometimes you are asked to slice a subject into parts, or sort things into kinds.

> Enumerate the ways in which each inhabitant of the United States uses, on the average, 1595 gallons of water a day. How and to what degree might each person cut down on this amount?

This two-part question invites you, for a start, to divide up water use into several parts: drinking, cooking, bathing, washing clothes, brushing teeth, washing cars, and so on. Then after you divide them, you might go on to give tips for water conservation and tell how effective they are ("By putting a water-filled, tight-capped plastic jug inside a toilet tank, each household would save 15 to 20% of the water required for a flush").

> What different genres of film did King Vidor direct? Name at least one outstanding example of each kind.

In this classification question, you sort things into categories — films into general kinds — possibly comedy, war, adventure, mystery, musical, western.

The definition question   You'll often be asked to write an extended definition on an essay exam.

> Explain the three dominant styles of parenting: *permissive, authoritarian-restrictive,* and *authoritative.*

This question calls for a trio of definitions. It might help to illustrate each definition with an example, whether recalled or imagined.

> Define the Stanislavsky method of acting, citing outstanding actors who have followed it.

Again, as part of your definition, you'd give examples.

The evaluation question   This is another favorite kind of question, much beloved by instructors because it calls on students to think critically. Here's a short example:

> Set forth and evaluate the most widely accepted theories to account for the disappearance of the dinosaurs.

Here's a longer example:

> Evaluate *two* of the following suggestions, giving reasons for your judgments:
> a. Cities should stop building highways to the suburbs and instead build public monorail systems.
> b. Houses and public buildings should be constructed to last no longer than twenty years.
> c. Freeways leading to the core of the city should have marked express lanes for buses and carpooling drivers and narrow lanes designed to punish with long delays individual commuters who drive their cars.

This last three-part question calls on you to argue for or against. Other argument questions might begin "Defend the idea of . . ." or "Show weaknesses in the concept of . . ." or otherwise call on you to take a stand.

The respond to the quotation question   "Test the validity of this statement," a question might begin, and then it might go on to supply a quotation for close reading. In another familiar form, such a question might begin:

> Discuss the following statement: High-minded opposition to slavery was only one cause, and not a very important one, of the animosity between North and South that in 1861 escalated into civil war.

The question asks you to test the writer's opinion against what you know. You would begin by carefully reading that statement a couple of times and then seeing whether you can pick a fight with it. It's a good idea to jot down any contrary evidence you can discover. If you end up agreeing with the statement, supply evidence to support it. (Sometimes the passage is the invention of the instructor, who hopes to provoke you to argument.)

Another illustration is the following question from an examination in women's literature:

> Was the following passage written by Gertrude Stein, Kate Chopin, or Tillie Olsen? On what evidence do you base your answer?
>
> > She waited for the material pictures which she thought would gather and blaze before her imagination. She waited in vain. She saw no pictures of solitude, of hope, of longing, or of despair. But the very passions themselves were aroused within her soul, swaying it, lashing it, as the waves daily beat upon her splendid body. She trembled, she was choking, and the tears blinded her.

The passage is taken from a story by an earlier writer than either Stein or Olsen: Kate Chopin (1851–1904). If you knew Chopin, who specializes in physical and emotional descriptions of impassioned women, you would know the answer to the examination question, and you might point to language (*swaying, lashing*) that marks it as her own.

The process analysis question   Often you can spot this kind of question by the word *trace*:

> Trace the stages through which a bill becomes a federal law.
>
> Trace the development of the medieval Italian city-state.

Both questions invite you to tell how something occurs or occurred. The other familiar type of process analysis, the "how-to" variety, is called for in this question:

> An employee has been consistently late for work, varying from fifteen minutes to a half hour daily. This employee has been on the job only five months but shows promise of learning skills that your firm needs badly. How would you deal with this situation?

For pointers on writing a process analysis, see Chapter 6. In brief, you divide the process into steps and detail each step.

The far-out question   Sometimes, to invite you to use your imagination, an instructor will throw in a question that at first glance might seem bizarre.

> Imagine yourself to be a trial lawyer in 1921, charged with defending Nicola Sacco and Bartolomeo Vanzetti, two anarchists accused of murder. Argue for their acquittal on whatever grounds you can justify.

On second glance, the question will be seen to reach deep. It calls on a prelaw student to show familiarity with a famous case (which ended with the execution of the defendants). In addition, it calls for knowledge of the law and of trial procedure. Such a question might be fun to answer; moreover, in being obliged to imagine a time, a place, and dramatic circumstances, the student might learn something. The following is another far-out question, this time from a philosophy course:

> What might an ancient Roman Stoic philosopher have thought of Jean-Paul Sartre's doctrine of anguish?

In response, you might try to remember what the Stoics had to say about enduring suffering, define Sartre's view and define theirs, compare their views with Sartre's, and imagine how they would agree (or, more probably, differ) with him.

Drafting: The Only Version

When the clock on the wall is ticking away, generating ideas and shaping an answer are seldom two distinct, leisurely processes: they often take place pretty much at the same time, and on scratch paper. Does your instructor hand you your own copy of the exam questions? If so, see if there's room in the margins to jot down ideas and roughly put them in order. If you can do your preliminary work right on the exam sheet, you'll have less confusion. Besides, you can annotate questions, underline points you think important, scribble short definitions. Write reminders that you will notice while you work: TWO PARTS TO THIS QUES.! or GET IN EXAMPLE OF ABORIGINES. To make sure that you include all necessary information without padding or repetition, you may care to jot down a brief, informal outline before setting pen to examination booklet. This was David Cohn's outline (p. 275):

Thesis: Research on infants is probably the best way to demonstrate that some factors in perceptual organization are innate.

cliff box – kid fears drop despite glass, mother, knows shallow side safe

size constancy – learned early if not intrinsic

shapes – infants respond more/better to face shape than nonformed

match sound w/sight – 2 TVs, look twice as much at right one

Budget your time   When you have two or more essay questions to answer, block out your time at least roughly. Sometimes your instructor will suggest how many minutes to devote to each question or will declare that one question counts twenty points, another ten, and so on. Obviously a twenty-point question deserves twice as much time and work as a ten-pointer. If the instructor doesn't specify, then after you have read the questions, decide for yourself how much time each question is worth. Make a little schedule so that you'll know that at 10:30 it's time to wrap up question 2 and move on. Allot extra minutes to a question that counts for the most points or looks complicated (such as one with several parts: a, b, c . . .) and fewer minutes to a simpler one. Otherwise, give every answer equal time. Then pace yourself as you write. A watch with an alarm you can set to buzz at the end of twenty or thirty minutes, alerting you that it's time to move on, might help—unless it would distract your classmates.

Begin with the easy questions   Many students find it helps their morale to start with the question they feel best able to answer. Unless your instructor specifies that you have to answer the questions in their given order, why not skip around? Just make sure you clearly number the questions and begin each answer in such a way that the instructor will immediately recognize which question you're answering. If the task is "Compare and contrast the depression of the 1930s with the recession of the 1970s," an answer might begin:

> Compared to the paralyzing depression that began in 1929, the recession of the 1970s seems a bad case of measles.

The instructor would recognize that question, all right, whether you answered it first or last. If you have a choice of questions, you can label your answer *a* or *b* or restate the question at the start of your essay so that your instructor will have no doubt which alternative you have chosen, as in the following example:

Question: Discuss *one* of the following quotations from the writings of Voltaire:
a.   "The truths of religion are never so well understood as by those who have lost the power of reasoning."
b.   "All roads lead to Rome."

ANSWER:

> When in September 1750, Voltaire wrote in a letter to Mme. de Fontaine, "All roads lead to Rome," his remark referred to more than the vast network of roads the ancient Romans had built—and built so well—throughout Europe. . . .

Try stating your thesis at the start   Some students find it useful to make their opening sentence a thesis statement—a sentence that makes clear right away the main point they're going to make. Then they proceed in the rest of the answer to back that statement up. This method often makes good sense. With a clear thesis statement to begin with, you will be unlikely to ramble into byways that carry you miles away from your main point. It also lets your instructor know right away that you know what you're talking about. (See "Stating and Using a Thesis," p. 322). That's how David Cohn opens his answer to the psychology question (p. 275). An easy way to get started off is to begin with the question itself. You might turn that question around, make it into a declarative statement, and *transform it into the start of an answer*:

> Can adequate reasons for leasing cars and office equipment, instead of purchasing them, be cited for a two-person partnership?

> I can cite at least four adequate reasons for a two-person partnership to lease cars and office equipment. For one thing, under present tax laws, the entire cost of a regular payment under a leasing agreement may be deducted. . . .

Stick to the point of the question   It's a temptation to want to throw into your answer everything you have learned in the course. But to do so defeats the purpose of the examination: not to parade your knowledge, but to put your knowledge to use. So when you answer an exam question cogently, you select *what matters* from what you know, at the same time shaping it.

Answer the whole question   Often a question will have two parts: it will ask you, say, to name the most common styles of contemporary architecture and then to evaluate one of them. Or it might say, "List three differences between the landscape paintings of Monet and those of Van Gogh" and then add, "Which of the two shows the greater influence of eighteenth-century neo-classicism?" When the dragon of a question has two heads, make sure you cut off both.

Stay specific   Pressed for time, some harried exam takers think, "I haven't got time to get specific here—I'll just sum up this idea in general." That's a mistake. Every time you throw in a large, general statement ("The Industrial Revolution was a beneficial thing for the peasant"), take time to include specific examples ("In Dusseldorf, as Taine tells us, the mortality rate from starvation among displaced Prussian farm workers now dropped to nearly zero, although once it had reached almost ten percent a year").

Leave room to revise   Incidentally, it's foresighted to write on only one side of the page in your examination booklet. Leave space between lines. Then later, should you wish to add words or sentences or even a whole paragraph, you can do so with ease. Give yourself room for second thoughts and last-minute inspirations. As you write and as you revise, you may well do further discovering.

Revising: Rereading and Proofing

If you have paced yourself, you'll have at least a few minutes left at the end of your examination period when, while some around you are still agonizingly trying to finish, you can relax a moment and look over your work with a critical eye.

Even if you should stop writing with an hour to spare, it probably won't be worth your time to recopy your whole exam. Use any time you have left not to improve your penmanship and the appearance of the paper but to test your ideas and how well they hang together.

Your foresight in skipping every other line will now pay off. You can add sentences wherever you think new ones are needed. Cross out any hopelessly garbled sentences and rewrite them in the blank lines. (David Cohn crossed out and rewrote part of his last sentence. Originally it read, "When simultaneously shown two television screens, each depicting a different subject, while being played *a tape that oscillated between which TV it was in time with....*" He rethought the last words, which we have italicized, found them confusing, crossed them out, and instead wrote on the line above: "a tape that sometimes matched one screen and sometimes the other.") If you recall an important point you forgot to put in, you can add a paragraph or two on a left-hand page that you left blank. So the grader will not miss it, draw an arrow indicating where it goes. If you find that you have gone off on a big digression or have thrown in knowledge merely to show it off, boldly X out that block of wordage. Your answer may look sloppier, but your instructor will think the better of it.

Naturally, errors occur oftener when you write under pressure than when you have time to edit and proofread carefully. Most instructors will take into consideration your haste and your human fallibility. On an exam, what you say and how forcefully you say it matter most. Still, to get the small details right will just make your answer look all the sharper. No instructor will object to careful corrections. You can easily add words with carets:

$$\text{Israeli } \overset{\text{foreign}}{\wedge} \text{policy}$$

Or you can neatly strike out a word by drawing a line through it. Some students like to use an erasable pen for in-class writing, but most instructors prefer cross-outs to the smeared letters of an erasable ink.

We don't expect you to memorize the following questions and carry them like crib notes into an examination. But when you receive your paper or blue book back and you look it over, you might learn more about writing essay exams if you ask them of yourself.

DISCOVERY CHECKLIST: EVALUATING YOUR PERFORMANCE

- Did you understand the question and what was expected?
- Did you answer the whole question, not just part of it?
- Did you stick to the point, not throw in information the question doesn't call for?
- Did you make your general statements clear by citing evidence or examples?

- Does your answer sprawl, or is it shaped?
- Does your answer, at any place, show a need for more knowledge and more ideas? Did you inflate your answer with hot air, or did you stay close to earth, giving plenty of facts, examples, and illustrations?
- Did you proofread for omissions and lack of clarity?
- On what question or questions do you feel you did a good job that satisfies you, no matter what grade you received?
- If you had to write this exam over again, how would you *now* go about the job?

Let's end with a few tips on two other common kinds of in-class writing.

SHORT-ANSWER EXAMINATIONS

Requiring answers much terser than an essay exam does, the *short-answer exam* may call on you to identify names or phrases from your reading, in a sentence or a few words.

> Identify the following: Clemenceau, Treaty of Versailles, Maginot line, Dreyfus affair.

You might answer such a question:

> *Georges Clemenceau*—This French premier, nicknamed The Tiger, headed a popular coalition cabinet during World War I and at the Paris Peace Conference demanded stronger penalties against Germany.

Writing a short identification is much like writing a short definition. Be sure to mention the general class to which a thing belongs:

> *Clemenceau*— French premier who....
> *Treaty of Versailles*—pact between Germany and the Allies that....
> *Maginot line*—fortifications which....

If you do so, you won't lose points for an answer like this, which fails to make clear the nature of the thing being identified:

> *Maginot line*—The Germans went around it.

TIMED WRITINGS

At some point in college you may need to prove your writing expertise on a competency exam (maybe at the end of a course or at the completion of a program). Most composition instructors, to give you experience in writing on demand, assign impromptu essays to be written in class. For such writings, your time is limited (usually forty-five minutes to an hour), the setting is controlled (usually you're sitting in a hard desk and you're not allowed to use a dictionary or a spell checker), and you can't choose your own subject. The purpose of timed writings is to test your writing skills, not to see how much information you can recall.

At first, this rapid-fire type of writing may cause you some anxiety—sweaty palms and a blank mind. It seems a lot different from the leisurely think-plan-draft-revise method of composing. It does require you to think and recall much faster, yet the way you write a timed essay doesn't differ greatly from the way you write anything else. Your usual methods of writing can serve you well, even though you have to use them in a hurry. With a few tips and a little practice, you can produce a top-notch piece that will please even the toughest readers.

Budget your time wisely   For any writing assignment, you must budget your time wisely. For an in-class essay, if you have forty-five minutes to write, a good rule of thumb is to spend ten minutes preparing, thirty minutes writing, and five minutes rereading and making last-minute changes. In the act of writing, you may find new ideas occurring to you and perhaps these exact proportions of time will change, or you may know from past experience that you need longer to plan or to proofread and check what you have written. Even so, a rough schedule like that will help you to allocate your time. Those last few minutes you leave yourself to read over your work and correct glaring errors may be the best-spent minutes of all. The worst mistake you can make is to spend so much time thinking and planning that you must rush through getting your ideas down on paper—the part you will be graded on.

Choose your topic wisely   For extemporaneous writing, you're given little choice of topic—usually one, two, or three. The trick is to make the topic your own. If you have a choice at all, choose the one you know the most about, not the one you think will impress your readers. They'll be most impressed by logical argument and solid evidence. If you have to write on a broad abstract subject (say, a world problem that affects many people), don't choose something you can't quickly recall much about (say, terrorism or the U.S. budget deficit or even saving the rain forests—unless you have recently done a lot of research in that area). You'll only end up being vague and general, while your readers will be expecting specifics to back up your claims. Instead, bring it down to something personal, something you have observed or experienced. Have you witnessed traffic jams, brownouts, and condos ruining beaches? Then write about increased population. If your doctor's and dentist's fees have gone up, if your insurance rates have increased, if you have put off a medical checkup, new glasses, or some dental work because it's so expensive, then write about the increasing costs of health care. If you have seen oil and garbage in lakes, junk piles out in the woods, warnings for people who have lung problems to stay indoors because of high ozone levels, write about pollution.

Think and plan before you begin writing   With limited time, your tendency will probably be to jump right in and start writing the essay. However, as with all effective writing, you need to think and plan before you start putting ideas into sentences and paragraphs. You should read the instructions and the topics or questions carefully, choose your topic thoughtfully, restrict it to something you know about, state a main idea for focus, and jot down the major divisions for development. While you're thinking, if a good hook for the introduction or conclusion occurs to you, make a note of it too. Just don't spend so much time on this part of the process that you can't finish the essay.

Don't try to be perfect   No one expects extemporaneous essays to be as polished as reports written over a period of a month. Realize that you may not be able to do everything you would like to do in so brief a time. Turn off your internal monitor. You can't polish every sentence or remember the exact word you want for every spot. Be satisfied with a less than perfect introduction. (We know one student who spent forty minutes crafting a smooth introduction — and then didn't have time to do anything else.) You may not have as many details as you would if you had more time, but do include some specifics. And you should never waste time recopying. A little messiness won't hurt, and you should devote your time to the more important parts of writing.

Save time to proofread   The last few minutes you leave yourself to read over your work and correct glaring errors may be the best-spent minutes of all. Cross out and make corrections neatly. Use asterisks (∗), arrows, and carets (^). (See more suggestions on how to make corrections in Chapter 18.) Especially check for the following:

Omitted letters (*-ed* or *-s*)

Added letters (develop*e*)

Inverted letters (rec*ie*ve)

Wrong punctuation (a comma instead of a period)

Omitted apostrophes (*dont* instead of *don't*)

Omitted words ("She going" instead of "she *is* going")

Wrong words (*except* instead of *accept*)

Misspelled words (mispelled)

You won't have time to do extensive revisions, but you can make time to proofread.

Types of Topics

Often you can expect the same type of questions or topics for in-class writings as for essay exams. If you are familiar with those recognizable types (discussed earlier in this chapter, pp. 277–82) and know how to organize them, you can do well. Just remember to look for the key words and do what they suggest.

What were the *causes* of World War I?

Compare and contrast the theories of capitalism and socialism.

How did the metaphysical poets of the seventeenth century *influence* the work of T. S. Eliot?

Define civil rights.

Another type of topic for timed writings is a general subject on which thousands of diverse students can write. This is the type of topic you can give your own personal twist. But again you should pay attention to key words.

A problem in education that is *difficult to solve.*

Ways to cope with stress.

Many well-known people in our world today influence other people and cause changes in our world. These people may be politicians, inventors, scientists, entertainers, educators, or others. Their influence may be considered positive or negative. Choose one person you believe has had a definite impact on some group of people in our world today. In an essay, *explain* the *influence* this person has had and whether it has been *positive or negative.*

A type of question you may be familiar with from the SATs is one in which you are given a short passage to read and then asked to respond to it. This type of question tests not only your writing ability but also your reading comprehension.

In one of William Wordsworth's most famous sonnets, he claimed, "The world is too much with us." *Explain* what he meant by that line, and *discuss* whether his assessment of the world still applies to our world today.

Thomas Jefferson stated, "If a nation expects to be ignorant and free, in a state of civilization, it expects what never was and never will be." *How* is his comment *relevant* to education today?

In "The Struggle against Surrender Never Ends," Maya Angelou stated, "Thomas Wolfe warned in the title of his great American novel that 'you can't go home again.' This book was splendid, but I never agreed with the title. One never can leave home. One carries the shadows and fears, the hopes and dreams of home eternally just under the skin." Do you agree with Wolfe or with Angelou? Write an essay *explaining* your position.

FOR GROUP LEARNING: BRAINSTORMING IDEAS

For practice in thinking and planning quickly, brainstorm with your class-mates how you might approach writing on the sample topics provided for essay exams and timed writings in this chapter. Include in your discussions possible thesis sentences, various patterns of organization, and specific evidence you might use. Don't expect everybody to come up with the same ideas.

CHAPTER 13

Writing for Business

In every business, people are continually writing: producing instructions, proposals, announcements, plans for sales campaigns, annual reports to stockholders, reports for the information of executives. Even where people work
elbow to elbow, you will sometimes hear: "I need a report on that. Write one
for me" or "That's a bright idea. Write me a memo about it, will you?"

Most of the world's business communication still takes place in writing.
The reasons are easy to understand. Although a telephone message may
conveniently be forgotten or ignored, a letter or a memorandum is a physical
thing that sits on a desk, calling for some action—if only to crumple it up
and pitch it into a wastebasket. Written documents can be kept on file, to be
checked for details later.

Personnel managers of large corporations, the people who do the hiring,
tend to be keenly interested in applicants who can write clearly, accurately,
and effectively. A survey conducted at Cornell University asked business executives to rate in importance the qualities they would like their employees
to possess. Skill in writing was ranked in fourth place, ahead of managerial
skill, ahead of skill in analysis. This fact is worth recalling if you ever wonder
what practical good you can do your career by taking a writing course.

In this chapter, we will show you three kinds of business writing likely to
prove useful to you.

BUSINESS LETTERS

In most college courses, you know your readers well—usually they are your instructor and other students—but the reader you address in a business letter may be unknown to you. If you write to a personnel manager seeking a job interview, chances are that you aren't personally acquainted with that mysterious person. Still, you can try to imagine him or her and supply information that this person needs to know: that you are capable of doing the job, how soon you will be available to go to work, and how you can be contacted. A good business letter is brief—if at all possible, limited to one page. It supplies whatever information the reader needs, no more. And the reader should be able to understand it in one reading. Why? In business, time is money.

Each of us, at least once in a while, has to write a letter for a business purpose: if not to apply for a job, then to apply for a scholarship or for acceptance at a graduate school; to request help, advice, or information; to order something by mail; to complain about a product or service; to answer a newspaper ad; or to express an opinion, as in a letter to the editor of a newspaper or to some elected official. Those are only a few common uses of a business letter in everyday life. Many college students enter the world of business on graduation, at which time they may find that writing business correspondence is a daily activity. But whether or not you plan a business career, knowing how to draft a good business letter is a skill that can serve you well in any job and in your personal business dealings.

Learning from Other Writers

An effective business letter is straightforward, forceful, but polite and considerate, concise, neat, and legible. Its purpose is to stimulate action: to get the reader to do what you need. Figure 13.1 contains a sample letter, its parts labeled and explained.

The *cc:* at the end of this letter indicates that the writer is sending a copy of her letter to an organization called the Fair Housing Committee. Another common reference at the end of a letter is *Enclosure* or *Enc.* (if the writer is enclosing some document in the envelope along with the letter). If the letter has been typed by someone other than the person who signs it, the initials of the signer, in capital letters, and the initials of the typist, in lowercase letters, appear at the left margin below the signature: *WF/br,* for example.

Notice the tone of Liggett's letter: the attitude she takes toward her landlord. Scrupulously, she avoids calling names, and she proposes a reasonable way for the landlord to satisfy herself that her tenants haven't done $500 worth of damage. The letter shows gumption, but it is diplomatic and considerate of the recipient's feelings.

The envelope for Jennifer Liggett's letter is shown in Figure 13.2.

When you don't know the name of the person who will read your letter, as when you write to someone at a large organization, it is acceptable to word

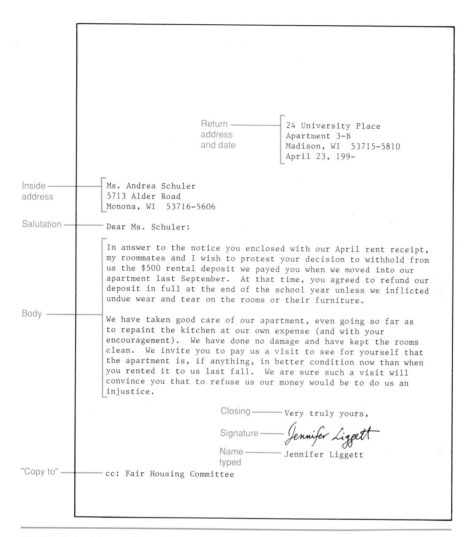

Return ——— 24 University Place
address   Apartment 3-B
and date   Madison, WI 53715-5810
               April 23, 199-

Inside ——— Ms. Andrea Schuler
address   5713 Alder Road
              Monona, WI 53716-5606

Salutation ——— Dear Ms. Schuler:

In answer to the notice you enclosed with our April rent receipt,
my roommates and I wish to protest your decision to withhold from
us the $500 rental deposit we payed you when we moved into our
apartment last September. At that time, you agreed to refund our
deposit in full at the end of the school year unless we inflicted
undue wear and tear on the rooms or their furniture.

Body ———
We have taken good care of our apartment, even going so far as
to repaint the kitchen at our own expense (and with your
encouragement). We have done no damage and have kept the rooms
clean. We invite you to pay us a visit to see for yourself that
the apartment is, if anything, in better condition now than when
you rented it to us last fall. We are sure such a visit will
convince you that to refuse us our money would be to do us an
injustice.

Closing ——— Very truly yours,

Signature ——— *Jennifer Liggett*

Name ——— Jennifer Liggett
typed

"Copy to" ——— cc: Fair Housing Committee

FIGURE 13.1 A letter of complaint

your salutation "Dear Editor" or "Dear Angell's Bakery" or to omit the "Dear" line. "Gentlemen" has become too sexist for contemporary use.

In a letter requesting information, try to be brief and to the point but clear, as in Figure 13.3.

If you ever find yourself on the opposite side of the desk, writing letters as a spokesperson for a company, you will face a special problem: do you write in the voice of an individual human being or try to write as an impersonal organization? Obviously you can't write to a complaining customer as though addressing a personal friend ("Keep your shirt on, old buddy . . .") or answer a request for information about a product line with an unwanted personal opinion ("Aren't these simulated oak cabinets cool-looking? I just love

Return address

Address double-spaced when less than four lines long

24 University Place
Apartment 3-B
Madison, WI 53715-5810

USA 29

Ms. Andrea Schuler

5713 Alder Road

Monona, WI 53716-5606

FIGURE 13.2   Envelope for a business letter

1981 Gerber Street
Chillicothe, OH 45601
April 2, 199-

Earthwatch Expeditions, Inc.
10 Juniper Road
Belmont, MA 02178

I read about your organization in the <u>Ohio Times</u> and would
like to spend my summer, or part of it, participating in
an Earthwatch expedition. Please send me your brochure
describing the programs available, including information
about dates and costs.

Thank you.

Sincerely yours,

William Schultz

FIGURE 13.3   A letter of inquiry

them!"). On the other hand, writing impersonally, you might sound stuffy ("It is the earnest wish of this agency..."). Hesitant to speak your own mind, you may render your thoughts obscure.

The solution to this dilemma is fourfold: (1) keep clearly in mind the reason for the letter and state it concisely in the first sentence; (2) size up the recipient of the letter and his or her needs; (3) use the *you* attitude: whenever possible, use *you* and *your*, not *we, I, our,* or *mine*; and (4) adopt a tone appropriate to the occasion: friendly but not backslapping; objective, but not cold or haughty. The letter writer who rejected a job applicant with the sentence "Sorry, but we have found someone better qualified than you are" was guilty of taking the wrong tone — cruelly frank — and it is no wonder that the recipient felt crushed and resentful. A better reply would have thanked the applicant for applying, explained that another applicant with more experience had also applied, and wished the recipient good fortune on another application. "Too often," notes a professor of business English, "inexperienced writers in the corporate world equate 'professional' with 'bureaucratic,' forgetting that every good writer — in or out of business — writes as one human being to another."

Formatting a Business Letter

In writing a business letter, observe these points.

Type your letter single-spaced, on good 8½-by-11 inch bond paper.

Type on only one side of the paper.

If you use a computer, use a letter-quality or laser printer.

Skip a line between the date and the inside address, the inside address and the salutation, the salutation and the body of the letter, and between paragraphs.

Skip two to four lines between the body and the closing, four lines between the closing and the typed signature.

Sign your name above the typed signature.

Letters look best if they are centered on the page, but there is more than one correct format for a business letter. It is not wrong, for instance, to indent your paragraphs, though you will usually find that letters written in large offices contain no such indentations. Some business letter writers line up all parts, including the addresses and salutation, date, closing, and signature along the left-hand margin. Others prefer the return address and date, the closing, and the signature closer to the right-hand margin. Let whatever pleases your eye govern your choices concerning such details, unless you're working for a company that prescribes a special form to follow. For your records, keep a carbon copy or photocopy of every business letter you write, even those you have saved on your computer disk.

When addressing a woman, unless you are aware that the recipient prefers *Miss* or *Mrs.*, use *Ms.* in your inside address and salutation.

LETTERS OF APPLICATION AND RÉSUMÉS

The most momentous business letter you write may be a letter applying for a job. Start by telling your prospective employer the position for which you are applying. Then state how you heard about the position. Don't be shy about briefly setting forth your qualifications and your reasons for wanting the job. You can enlarge on both in the résumé you send along with your letter. Indicate your willingness to appear for an interview.

It's a good idea to take pains with both letter and résumé. They will enable a busy personnel manager to decide quickly whether or not your application deserves any follow-up. Direct, persuasive, grammatically correct prose can help you stand out above the crowd. (See Figure 13.4.)

```
                                         Box 1277 Living/Learning
                                         University of Vermont
                                         Burlington, VT  05405-2293
                                         February 4, 199-

Educational Coordinator
Programs and Facilities Branch
Land Between the Lakes, TVA
Golden Pond, KY  42231

I wish to apply for one of the summer internships you offer to college
students.  I became keenly interested in your internship program after
reading the Land Between the Lakes brochure on file in the placement
office at the University of Vermont's School of Natural Resources.  The
practical experience of working in your campground during June, July,
and August would offer excellent preparation for my chosen career in
recreation management.  At the same time, I could serve your program
well by bringing to it skill and experience in working with teenagers
and young children.

As a high school student I was a full-time counselor for two summers in
my hometown's day camp, where I worked first with fifth graders and later
with seventh and eighth graders who took week-long canoe trips and
bicycle trips.  Last summer I volunteered as a nature guide at Hale
Reservation in Westwood, Massachusetts, and within a few weeks began
fulfilling additional duties and receiving additional pay for my efforts
there.

I am currently a sophomore at the University of Vermont, where I major
in recreational management.  During the third week in March, I will be
in Paducah, Kentucky, for a family visit and will be available for an
interview any time during that week.  My telephone number in Vermont is
(802) 650-3985.

                                 Very truly yours,

                                 Laura Baker

                                 Laura Baker

Enclosure
```

FIGURE 13.4   A letter to apply for a summer job

At the end of her letter, Baker alerts her reader to look for an enclosure, the accompanying résumé.

Surely every time you write a letter of application, you'll want to make the thing gleam like a jewel. Probably you'll draft it, ponder it, cut out unnecessary words, rephrase it, correct spelling, check grammar and punctuation, and rewrite it carefully. Here are some key questions to ask yourself when you revise.

REVISION CHECKLIST: WRITING A LETTER OF APPLICATION

- Does your letter make clear which job you're applying for? If you're responding to an ad, refer to it. If no job has been advertised, then describe briefly—but not too narrowly—what kind of job you seek: "I can meet people, take phone calls, and keep track of schedules—in short, handle most front-desk office assignments."

- Is your letter brief? Remember: one page only. A long-winded life history will quickly land in the wastebasket. Your purpose in writing is to make the recipient want to interview you. Accordingly your letter need do little more than introduce yourself in a sentence ("I expect to be graduated in June from Clark Community College with an A.S. degree in dental hygiene"), tell what sort of position you're seeking, when you will be available, and when and how you may be contacted for an interview. You need not repeat your qualifications in detail; they appear on your résumé. Keep your letter down to two or three short paragraphs.

- Do you leave yourself open to *other* possible jobs, in case the one you want is filled? Unless you are applying for a very specialized job that has been advertised, one in which you are highly trained, you might be wise not to make your aim too specific at this early stage: "I would be able to train new employees in methods of thread-waxing. . . ." Perhaps the recipient has more than one job available. You might be a likely prospect for some job quite different from what you have in mind.

- Do you respect yourself? Delete any statement that might seem hangdog: "Although I realize that I have not taken the necessary college courses to qualify me . . . ," "However young and inexperienced I may seem. . . ." Let the employer decide whether you lack the qualifications for the job. Why give him or her reasons to turn you down? Delete any statement such as "Any entry-level job you may have available, however temporary and low-paying . . ." or "I would be happy to work for you in any capacity. . . ." This last leaves the impression that the letter writer would thankfully lick boots. If you're worth hiring, you deserve a decent job.

- Do you sound like yourself? If you don't happen to feel brilliant, you don't need to try to radiate brilliance—all you are seeking is an invitation for an interview. And there's no need to force humor and charm. If jokes fall flat, they will only turn off the recipient's sympathy. Let the facts in your résumé do the charming for you.

- Do you leave the salary open to discussion? Better keep silent on this point. If you ask for too much, you will cut yourself out; if you ask for too little, you will seem to come cheap. If a prospective employer is interested in you, an offer is likely to follow.

✏ Is your letter businesslike: concise, crisp, clear, neat, free of distracting errors?

✏ The résumé you enclose with your letter of application lets a prospective employer see at a glance your qualifications for the job. Use it to set forth as full a picture of you as possible *in one page.* Figure 13.5 shows a résumé that, making clear the applicant's professional skills and experience, projects a positive impression. If the employer wants more information, you can provide it during the interview.

RÉSUMÉ

Valerie L. Brunn
21525 Saltair Avenue, #506
Los Angeles, CA 90025-4491
(213) 816-3688

Employment Objective	A position in advertising with special interest in new product marketing.
Education	University of California, Los Angeles B.A., Psychology/Business Administration Expected date of graduation: April 1993
	Courses in Business: Accounting, Principles of Economics, Practical Business Writing, Computer Programming, Statistics
	Courses in Human Behavior: Work Behaviors of Women and Men, Human Information Processing, Fundamentals of Learning, Psychology of Gender, Research Methods
Experience	The Best Service Company Los Angeles, CA
1/91 to present	Collector. Responsible for auto lease accounts. Prepare and approve affidavits for lawsuits. Confer with debtors and attorneys. Review correspondence and write replies. Created new form letter that increased debtor response and payments.
1/90-1/91	Mail Clerk. Responsible for postal distribution to accounts from more than two dozen banks. Supervised form letter input/output on word processor. Ran amortization and interest prime rate charts. Conducted investigations to locate debtors.
Summer 1988	K-Mart La Verne, CA Cashier. Developed public relations skills in a fast-paced environment. Reconciled receipts with sales.
Computer Skills	Experienced with IBM personal computer and WordPerfect word processor.
Interests	Aerobics, racquetball, jazz
References	Available on request.

FIGURE 13.5   A résumé

References are the names of people who know you well and who would respond favorably to your request for a letter of recommendation. Valerie Brunn apparently intends to supply the names of references only to a prospective employer seriously interested in her. There is nothing wrong, though, with listing names, addresses, and phone numbers in your résumé. The recipient may find such a list helpful. If your references are on file in your college placement office, mention this fact in your letter or résumé. Obtain permission from the people whose recommendations you seek before you submit their names. This is both common courtesy and wise policy. If you request a recommendation from someone who happens to be less than enthusiastic about you, he or she can refuse to write it or can spell out any reservations to you on the spot rather than in a letter to your prospective employer. Without having done yourself any harm, you will then be free to ask someone else instead.

Brunn strengthens her résumé by including relevant courses she has taken in college. You may also note relevant activities and honors in college (GPA, honor societies, service clubs).

MEMORANDA

The *memorandum,* or *memo* for short, is a form of communicaton used within a company to request or exchange information, to announce meetings or new

```
                          MEMORANDUM

          TO:   Sarah Uschold, Vice President for Sales
          FROM: James E. Kessler, Sales Representative J.E.K.
          DATE: May 28, 199-
          SUBJECT: Retailers' Reactions to Our Line of Corkscrews

              As you suggested in our conversation on May 2, I have conducted an
          informal survey among the hardware store owners in my territory about
          our current line of corkscrews.  Their sentiments are best summed up by
          Al Gaulke in Marshfield:  "You have to be a French waiter to get the
          cork out of a bottle of wine with one of these."  He presented me with
          this wing-type corkscrew (sample enclosed) as an example of the one he
          recommends to his customers because it works easily, anyone can use it,
          and it never drops bits of cork into the wine.  I tried it and, you
          know, Al is right!


          Enclosure
```

FIGURE 13.6   A sample memorandum

policies, or to confirm what has passed in conversation. Memoranda tend to be written in the first-person *I* or *we,* with headings if they are long, in simple, direct paragraphs if they are short. Be clear; be brief. Assume that your recipients will be busy people wanting a quick but accurate grasp of a single point.

The subject of a memo is always stated in very few words. Make this statement short and exact, and confine your memo to that subject and no other. In writing a memo, keep your probable reader in mind. Obviously, if you are writing a memo to Mr. Barker, the president and chairman of the board, you will keep it formal and respectful; if you address a memo to a fellow worker you know well, friendliness and even a touch of humor may be appropriate.

Sometimes memo sheets come preprinted in a standard form, with spaces to fill in the names of sender and recipient, the date, and the subject under discussion. Usually, instead of signing the memo, the writer simply initials it, in the space after his or her typewritten name. (See Figure 13.6.)

PART FOUR

A WRITER'S STRATEGIES

The following seven chapters constitute a manual offering special advice on strategies. The word *strategy* may remind you of warfare: in the original Greek sense of the word, it is a way to win a battle. Writing a college paper, you'll probably agree, is a battle of a kind. In this manual you'll find an array of small weapons to use — perhaps some heavy artillery.

Here are techniques you can learn, methods you can follow, good practices you can observe in writing more effectively. In earlier chapters, many of these strategies were briefly mentioned. In this section they will be fully discussed.

No strategy will appeal to every writer, and no writer uses every one for every writing task. Outlining is a strategy that has rescued many a writer from getting lost, but we know writers who never outline except in their heads.

This manual is meant to refer to when you need it. If you try out some of these strategies, we trust you'll be rewarded.

CHAPTER 14

Strategies for Generating Ideas

Learning to write is learning what questions to ask yourself. When you begin to write, no matter what the source of information—recalling, observing, reading, conversing, imagining—you need to start the ideas flowing. Sometimes that's easy: ideas appear quickly on the paper or screen. Often, however, the opposite occurs, and you sit staring at a blank. At these times you needn't throw up your hands in defeat or quit in frustration, because there are strategies you can use to generate ideas. This chapter presents five specific techniques for getting ideas started. Most of them involve your learning to ask yourself questions. You can use these strategies not only when you are thinking and planning but also at any point in the writing process when you find your flow of ideas drying up.

First are brainstorming and freewriting, useful for recalling information. Then comes advice on keeping a journal, a great way to ensure a constant supply of ideas. Finally are two sets of questions to ask yourself: a reporter's questions and questions for seeking motives. You may have used some of these strategies before, but all of them can help you prime the pump of ideas. If one doesn't work for a particular writing task, try one of the others.

BRAINSTORMING

A brainstorm is a sudden insight or inspiration, and brainstorming is free association for stimulating a chain of ideas. When you brainstorm, you start with a word or phrase to launch your thoughts in some direction. For a set length of time, say ten or fifteen minutes, putting the conscious, analytical part of your mind on hold, you scribble a list of ideas as rapidly as possible, writing down whatever comes to mind with no editing or going back. Then you look over the often surprising results.

For a college writing assignment, you might brainstorm to find a specific topic for a paper. If at any time in writing you need to generate some material such as an illustration or example, you can brainstorm. If you have already written a paper, you can brainstorm to come up with a title for it.

Brainstorming can be a group activity. In the business world, brainstorming sessions are common strategies to fill a specific need: a name for a product, a corporate emblem, a slogan for an advertising campaign. Members of a group sit facing one another. They designate one person as the recording secretary to take down on paper or a blackboard or flip chart whatever suggestions the others offer. If the suggestions fly too thick and fast, the secretary jots down the best one in the air at that moment. For several minutes, people call out ideas. Then they look over the secretary's list in hopes of finding useful results.

You can try group brainstorming like that with a few other students or your entire class. But you may find brainstorming also useful when, all by yourself, you need to shake an idea out of your unconscious. Here is how one student did just that. On the opening day of a writing course, Martha Calbick's instructor assigned a paper from recall: "Demonstrate that the invention of the computer has significantly changed our lives." Following the instructor's advice, Calbick went home and brainstormed. First, she wrote the key word *computer* at the top of a sheet of paper. Then she set her alarm clock to sound in fifteen minutes and began to scribble single words or phrases. The first thing she recalled was how her kid brother sits by the hour in front of a home computer playing Wizardry, a Dungeons and Dragons kind of game. The first recollection quickly led, by free association, to several more.

Wizardry
my kid bro. thinks computers are for kids
always trading games with other kids—
    software pirates
Mother says it's too bad kids don't play
    Wiffle Ball anymore
in 3rd grade they teach programming
hackers
some get rich
Ed's brother-in-law—wrote a program for
    accountants
become a programmer? big future?
guided missiles
computers in subway stations—print tickets
banks—shove in your plastic card

a man lucked out—deposited $100—computer
   credited him with $10,000
sort mail—zip codes
computers print out grades
my report card showed a D instead of a B—
   big fight to correct it
are we just numbers now?

When her alarm clock rang, Calbick dropped her pencil and took a coffee break. When she returned to her desk, she was pleased to find that a few of her random thoughts suggested directions that interested her. Much of the list she immediately discarded, going through it with a pencil and crossing out most entries. She didn't have any interest in Wizardry, and she didn't feel she knew enough to write about missiles. She circled the question "are we just numbers now?" It looked promising. Maybe some of the other ideas she had listed might express that very idea, such as the mindlessness of the computer that had credited the man with $10,000. As she looked over the list, she continued brainstorming, jotting down more thoughts, making notes on the list and adding to it. "Dealing with computers isn't dealing with people," she wrote next to the circled question. From her rough-and-ready list, an idea was beginning to emerge.

Calbick was later to write a paper focusing on the simple computer error in her high school office that had momentarily robbed her of a good grade. She recalled how time-consuming it had been to have that error corrected. She mentioned a few other cases of computer error, including that of the man who had struck it rich at the bank. Her conclusion was a wry complaint about computerized society: "A computer knows your name and number, but it doesn't know who you are."

You can see how brainstorming typically works and how it started one student going. It is valuable because it helps you personalize a topic and break it down into specifics. Whenever you try brainstorming, you might follow these bits of advice.

1. *Start with a key word or phrase*—one that will head your thoughts in the direction you wish to pursue.

2. *Set yourself a time limit.* Fifteen or twenty minutes is long enough—brainstorming can be strenuous.

3. *Write rapidly.* List any other words, any thoughts, phrases, fragments, or short sentences that surface in connection with your key word. Keep your entries brief.

4. *Don't stop.* While you're brainstorming, don't worry about misspelling, repetition, absurdity, or irrelevance. Write down whatever comes into your head, as fast as your pen will go. Now is not the time to analyze or to throw any suggestion away. Let your unconscious run free. Never mind if you come up with ideas that seem crazy or far out. Don't judge, don't arrange—just

produce. If your mind goes blank, keep your pencil moving, even if you are only repeating what you've just written.

When you finish, look over your list. Circle or check anything you want to think about further. If anything looks useless, or uninteresting, scratch it out.

You can now do some conscious organizing. Look over your edited list. Are any of the thoughts related? Can you group them? If so, maybe they will suggest a topic. If you succeed in finding a topic from your brainstorming session, you might then wish to try another technique—*freewriting*, the next strategy we discuss.

If you are writing and you need an example or some details, you can brainstorm at any time. In writing her paper on computers Martha Calbick couldn't think of a name for a typical computer store. She wrote down some real names she knew (Computer World, Computerland, OnLine Computers Plus), and those triggered a few imaginary ones. Within three minutes, she hit on one she liked: Byte City.

Whether you brainstorm at your writing desk or in a lounge with a group of friends, you will find this strategy calling up a rich array of thoughts from knowledge, memory, and imagination. Try it and see.

Exercise: Brainstorming

With the classmates in your peer group, choose one of the following subjects about which all of you have some knowledge. Then individually brainstorm for fifteen minutes.

travel	exercise	dreams
family	sports	animals
fear	dieting	automobiles
television	advertisements	education

Compare and contrast your brainstorming list with the lists of your classmates. Notice especially the differences—how each individual's list reflects his or her personal experiences. Although two or several writers may start with the same subject, each writer's treatment will be unique because of individual differences in experience and perspective.

FREEWRITING

Like brainstorming, freewriting is a way to fight writer's block by tapping your unconscious. To freewrite, you simply begin writing in the hope that good ideas will surface. You write without stopping for fifteen or twenty minutes, trying to keep words pouring forth in a steady flow. Freewriting differs from brainstorming in that you write a series of sentences, not a list. They don't have to be grammatical or coherent or stylish sentences; just let them leap to the paper and keep them flowing along. When you have just the beginning of an idea, freewriting can help open it up and show you what it contains. When you have an assignment that looks difficult, freewriting can get you under way.

Generally, freewriting is most productive if it has an aim. You have in mind — at least roughly — some topic, a purpose, or a question you want answered. Before you begin, you write a sentence or two summing up the idea you're starting out with. Martha Calbick, who found a topic by brainstorming (p. 304), headed the page on which she freewrote with the topic she had decided to pursue: "How life in the computer age seems impersonal." Then, exploring some of the rough ideas she had jotted down in her brainstorming session, she let words flow rapidly.

> Computers—so how do they make life impersonal? You push in your plastic card and try to get some cash. Just a glassy screen. That's different—not like looking at a human teller behind a window. When the computer tells you you have no money left in your account, that's terrible, frightening. Worse than when a person won't cash your check. At least the person looks you in the face, maybe even gives you a faint smile. Computers make mistakes, don't they? That story in the paper about a man—in Utica, was it?—who deposited a hundred dollars to his account and the computer misplaced a decimal point and said he had put in $10,000.

The result, as you can see, wasn't polished prose. It was full of false starts down distracting alleys and little asides to herself that she later crossed out. Still, in twenty minutes she produced a start that served (with much rewriting) as the basis for her finished essay.

If you want to try freewriting for yourself, here's what you do.

1. *Write a sentence or two at the top of your page or computer screen:* the idea you plan to develop by freewriting.

2. *For at least ten minutes, write steadily without stopping.* Start by expressing whatever comes to mind, even if it is only "I don't want to write a paper because I have nothing at all to say about any subject in the universe." If your mind goes blank, write, "My mind is blank, I have nothing to say, I don't know where to go next," and keep at it until some new thought floats into view. Write down whatever comes to mind.

3. *Don't censor yourself.* Don't stop to cross out false starts, misspellings, or grammatical errors. Never mind if your ideas have gaps between them. Later, when you look them over, some of the gaps may close. If you can't

think of the word that perfectly expresses your meaning, put in a substitute. (You might draw a squiggly line under it to remind yourself to search for a better word or phrase later.) Keep your pencil moving.

4. *Feel free to explore.* That sentence (or those sentences) you started with can serve as a rough guide, but it shouldn't be a straitjacket. If as you write you stray from your original idea, that change in direction may possibly be valuable. Sometimes, you may discover a more promising idea.

Some writers prepare for freewriting. They find it pays to spend a few prior minutes in thought. While you wait for the moment when your pencil starts racing, some of these questions may be worth asking yourself.

What interests you about this topic? What aspects of it do you most care about?

What does this topic have to do with you?

What do you recall about it from your own experience? What do you know about it that the next person doesn't?

What have you read about it?

What have you observed about it for yourself?

Have you ever talked with anyone about it? If you have, what did you find out?

How might you feel about this topic if you were someone else? (You might try thinking about it from the imagined point of view of a friend, a parent, an instructor, a person of the opposite sex, a person from another country.)

At the very least, your freewriting session may give you something to rewrite and make stronger. You can prod and poke at the parts that look most interesting to see if they will further unfold. In expanding and developing what you have produced by freewriting, here are a few questions you might ask.

What do you mean by that?
What interests you in that idea?
If that is true, what then?
What other examples or evidence does this statement call to mind?
What objections might your reader raise to this?
How might you answer them?

Additions based on your answers to such questions will be easy to insert if you have done your freewriting on a computer.

Exercise: Freewriting

Look over the list of one of the subjects you have brainstormed. Edit it: circle interesting notions, delete irrelevant or repetitious items, see which items you can group, and select one significant idea you can explore further. Put that idea at the top of a piece of paper or the top of your computer screen, and freewrite about it for fifteen minutes.

WRITING WITH A COMPUTER: FREEWRITING

Freewriting gives you an excellent opportunity to try "invisible writing" on a computer. After typing your topic across the top of the screen, turn down the contrast control on your monitor so that you can't see any letters. Then freewrite. Give your unconscious and your imagination free rein. Not being able to see the words and the punctuation, you can relax and concentrate on the ideas. If you feel somewhat uneasy, just keep typing and let the ideas flow through your fingers. After fifteen minutes of freewriting, turn the contrast back up, scroll to the beginning, and read what you have written.

KEEPING A JOURNAL

If you are already in the habit of keeping a journal, consider yourself lucky. If not, now is a good time to begin. Journal writing offers rich rewards to anyone who engages in it every day or several times a week. All you need is a notebook, a writing implement, and a few minutes for each entry; and you can write anywhere. There are students whose observations, jotted down during a bus ride, turned into remarkable journal entries and later into a series of essays. Not only is journal writing satisfying in itself, but a journal can also be a storehouse of material to write about.

What do you write? The main thing to remember is that <u>a journal is not a diary.</u> When you make a journal entry, the emphasis is less on recording what happened than on *reflecting* about what you do or see, hear or read, learn or believe. A journal is a record of your thoughts, for an audience of one: yourself.

In a journal you can plan your life, try out ideas, vent fears and frustrations. The following passage, from *The Journals of Sylvia Plath* (New York: Doubleday, 1982), was written in the early 1950s when the poet was a college freshman. Uncommonly sensitive and colorful, her journal exhibits the freedom and frankness of a writer who was writing for only her own eyes. In this entry she contrasts the happy fantasy world she inhabited as a child with the harsher realities of college life.

> After being conditioned as a child to the lovely never-never land of magic, of fairy queens and virginal maidens, of little princes and their rosebushes, of poignant bears and Eeyore-ish donkeys, of life personalized as the pagans loved it, of the magic wand, and the faultless illustrations — the beautiful dark-haired child (who was you) winging through the midnight sky on a star-path . . . of the Hobbit and the dwarves, gold-belted with blue and purple hoods, drinking ale and singing of dragons in the caverns of the valley — all this I knew, and felt, and believed. All this was my life when I was young. To go from this to the world of grown-up reality. . . . To feel the sex organs develop and call loud to the flesh; to become aware of school, exams (the very words as unlovely as the sound of chalk shrilling

on the blackboard), bread and butter, marriage, sex, compatibility, war, economics, death, and self. What a pathetic blighting of the beauty and reality of childhood. Not to be sentimental, as I sound, but why the hell are we conditioned into
the smooth strawberry-and-cream Mother Goose world, Alice-in-Wonderland fable, only to be broken on the wheel as we grow older and become aware of
ourselves as individuals with a dull responsibility in life? To learn snide and smutty
meanings of words you once loved, like "fairy." To go to college fraternity parties
where a boy buries his face in your neck or tries to rape you if he isn't satisfied
with burying his fingers in the flesh of your breast. To learn that there are a
million girls who are beautiful and that each day more leave behind the awkward
teenage stage, as you once did, and embark on the adventure of being loved. . . .
To be aware that you must compete somehow, and yet that wealth and beauty
are not in your realm.

Like Plath, to write a valuable journal you need only the honesty and the
willingness to set down what you *genuinely think and feel.* When you first
face that blank journal page, plunge boldly into your task by writing down
whatever observation or reaction comes to mind, in any order you like. No
one will criticize your spelling or punctuation, the way you organize or the
way you express yourself. A journal entry can be a list or an outline, a paragraph or a full-blown essay, a poem or a letter you don't intend to send.

To know what to put into your journal, you have only to *un*cover, *re*cover,
*dis*cover what is happening both inside and outside your head. Describe a
person or a place. As accurately as you can, set down a conversation you
have heard, complete with slang or dialect or colloquialisms. Record any
insights you have gained into your actions or those of others. Make comparisons. Respond to something you have read or to something mentioned in a
class. Do you agree with it? Disagree? Why? What was wrong with the last
movie or television show you watched? What was good about it? Have you
or has someone you know faced a moral dilemma? Was it resolved? If so,
how?

Perhaps you have some pet peeves. List them. What do you treasure?
Have you had an interesting dream or daydream? What would the world be
like if you were in charge? What are your religious convictions? What do you
think about the current political scene or about this nation's priorities? Have
you visited any foreign countries? Did you learn anything of worth from your
travels?

On days when your mind is sluggish, when you can come up with no
observations or insights to record, do a stint of freewriting or of brainstorming
in your journal, or just describe a scene, an object, or a person present before
you. Any of those activities may result in at least a few good thoughts to follow
up in future entries.

One further benefit rewards the faithful journal keeper. Well done, a journal is a mine studded with priceless nuggets: thoughts and observations,
reactions and revelations that are yours for the taking. When you have an
essay to write, chances are you will find that a well-stocked journal is a
treasure indeed. Rifle it freely—not only for writing topics, but for insights

and material. It can make your writing assignments far easier to fulfill. "This book is my savings bank," wrote Ralph Waldo Emerson in his journal. "I grow richer because I have somewhere to deposit my earnings; and fractions are worth more to me because corresponding fractions are waiting here that shall be made integers by their addition." Emerson refers to his personal writing process. In many of his lectures and essays, he would combine thoughts that had begun as disconnected entries. From the savings bank of his journal, the nineteenth-century Yankee philosopher made heavy withdrawals.

Your journal can also be used for the warm-up writing you do when you start collecting your thoughts in preparation for any assignment, whether short or long. In it you can group ideas, scribble outlines, sketch beginnings, capture stray thoughts, record relevant material from any one of the writer's five resources (recalling, observing, reading, conversing, imagining) that bear on your assignment.

A journal can be a catch-all or miscellany, like Emerson's, or it can be a focused, directed thing. Some instructors assign students to keep journals of their readings in a certain discipline. Faced with a long paper to write, and weeks or months to do it in, you might wish to assign *yourself* to keep a specialized journal. If, say, you were going to write a survey of current economic theories or an account of the bird life of your locality, you might keep a journal of economists whose work you read or the birds you are able to observe. Then, when the time comes to write your paper, you will have plenty of material to quarry.

Exercise: Keeping a Journal

Keep a journal for at least a week. Each day record your thoughts, feelings, and reactions. You may include some events, but go beyond what happens to how you respond to what happens. At the end of the week, bring your journal to class, select the entry you like best, and read it aloud to your classmates.

ASKING A REPORTER'S QUESTIONS

News reporters, assembling facts with which to write the story of a news event, ask themselves six simple questions, the five *W*'s —

> Who?
> What?
> Where?
> When?
> Why?

— and an *H:* How? In the *lead,* or opening (and most important) paragraph of a good news story, where the writer tries to condense the whole story into a sentence, you will find simple answers to all six questions:

The ascent of a giant homemade fire balloon (*what*)
startled residents of Costa Mesa (*where*)
last night (*when*)
as Ambrose Barker, 79, (*who*)
in an attempt to set a new altitude record, (*why*)
zigzagged across the sky at a speed of nearly 300 miles per hour. (*how*)

Such answers don't go deep. In a few words, they give only the bare bones of the story. If readers want to learn more, they keep reading. But answering the questions enables the writer to seize all the essentials of the story and give them to readers in brief.

Later in a news story, the reporter will relate in greater detail what happened. He or she can dig and probe and make the story more interesting. With a little thought on the reporter's part, the six basic questions can lead to further questions, generating more to write about than space will allow.

WHO is Ambrose Barker, anyway? (An amateur balloonist? A jack-of-all-trades? A retired professional aeronautical engineer?) Is he a major figure in balloonist circles? (Call a professional balloonist and ask, "Who is this Ambrose Barker? Ever hear of him?") What kind of person is he: a serious student of ballooning or a reckless nitwit? What do his neighbors and his family think of him? (Interview them.) What words spoken by Barker himself will show the kind of person he is? Is he proud of his flight? Humble? Disappointed? Determined to try again? What was his mental state at the moment he took off? (Elated and determined? Crazed? Inebriated?)

WHAT happened, exactly? Was Barker or anyone else hurt? What did his craft look like from close up? (How big was it? Any distinguishing features?) What did it look like to a spectator on the ground? (Did it resemble a shooting star? A glowing speck? Did it light up the whole sky?) Did Barker's flight terrify anybody? Did the police receive any phone calls? Did the nearest observatory? What has happened since the flight? (Will anyone sue Barker for endangering life and property? Will the police press charges against him? Has he received any threats, any offers to endorse products?)

WHERE did Barker take off from? (A ballfield? A parking lot? His back yard? What is his exact street address?) From where to where did he fly? Where did he land? Where did the onlookers live? In what neighborhoods? How far off was the most distant observer who sighted Barker's balloon? (Was it visible, say, from forty miles?)

WHEN, by the clock, did the flight take place? (What time did Barker take off? How long was he aloft? Exactly when did he touch down again?) Was the choice of evening for the flight deliberate? (Barker could have gone up in the daytime. Did he want to fly by night to be more noticeable?) Did he deliberately choose this particular time of year? When did Barker first conceive his plan to tour Costa Mesa in a fire balloon? (Just the other day? Or has he been planning his trip for thirty years?)

WHY did Barker want to set a record? What impelled him? What reasons did he give? (And might he have had any reasons other than the ones he gave?) Why did he wait till he was seventy-nine to take off? Was making such a flight a lifelong dream? Did he feel the need to soar above the crowd? Did he want his neighbors to stop laughing at him ("That thing will never get off the ground . . .")? Why did his balloon zigzag across the sky, not sail in a straight line? Why were spectators terrified (if they were)?

HOW did Barker make his odd craft airborne? What propelled it into the sky? (A bonfire? Jet fuel? Gunpowder?) Did he take off without aid, or did his wife or a friend assist? How did he construct the balloon: where did he get the parts? Did he make the whole thing with his own two hands or have help? How did he steer the craft? How did he land it? Was the landing smooth or did he come down in a heap? How was he greeted when he arrived?

Your topic in a college writing task may be less spectacular than a fire balloon's ascent: a team winning or losing a pennant, an experience of your own, an ancestor's arrival in America. It might be what happened at some moment in history (the firing on Fort Sumter at the start of the Civil War) or in social history (the rise of rock music). The six basic questions will help you discover how to write about all sorts of events and phenomena; and, given thought, your six basic questions can lead to many more.

Don't worry if some of the questions lead nowhere. Just try answering any that look promising: jot down any thoughts and information that come to you. At first, you can record these unselectively. You are just trying to gather a big bunch of ideas and material. Later, before you start to write, you'll want to weed out the bunch and keep only those buds that look as though they might just open wide.

Exercise: Asking a Reporter's Questions

Choose one of the following topics, or use one of your own.

an accident	a business opening
a sports event	an accomplishment on campus
a party or reception	an occurrence in your city
a concert	an important speech

Answer the six reporter's questions—the 5 *W*'s and an *H*—about the topic. Then write a *lead* for a news story in which you condense the whole story into one sentence. Briefly include the answers to all six questions in your lead.

SEEKING MOTIVES

In a surprisingly large part of your college writing, you try to explain human behavior. In a paper for history, you might show why Lyndon Baines Johnson decided not to seek a second full term as president. In a report for a psychology course, you might try to explain the behavior of people in an experimental situation. In a literature course, writing of Nathaniel Hawthorne's *The Scarlet Letter,* you might analyze the motives of Hester Prynne: why does she conceal the name of her illegitimate child's father? Because people, including characters in fiction, are so complex, this task is challenging. But here is a strategy useful in seeking out human motives.

If you want to understand any human act, according to philosopher-critic Kenneth Burke, you can analyze its components. To do so, you ask five questions. (To produce useful answers, your subject has to be an act performed for a reason, not a mere automatic reaction like a sneeze.)

> What was done?
> Who did it?
> What means did the person use to make it happen?
> Where and when did it happen and in what circumstances?
> What possible purpose or motive can you attribute to the person?

Answering those questions starts a writer generating ideas. Burke names the five components as follows.

1. The *act.*
2. The *actor:* the person who acted.
3. The *agency:* the means or instrument the actor used to make the act happen. (If the act is an insult, the agency might be words or a slap in the face; if it is murder, the agency might be a sawed-off shotgun.)
4. The *scene:* where the act took place, when, and in what circumstances.
5. The *purpose:* the motive for acting.

As you can see, Burke's *pentad,* or set of five categories, covers much the same ground as the news reporter's five *W*'s and an *H.* But Burke's method differs in that it can show how these components of a human act affect one another. This line of thought can take you deeper into the motives for human behavior than most reporters' investigations ever go.

How might the method be applied? Say you are writing a paper to explain your own reasons for taking some action. Burke's list of the components of an act may come in handy. Let's take, for example, the topic "Why I Enrolled in Prelaw Courses." You might analyze it like this:

1. The *act* is your decision.
2. The *actor* — that's you.
3. The *agency* is your enrolling in college and beginning a program of study.
4. The *scene* is your home last spring (where the circumstances might have included many earnest, knock-down, drag-out discussions with your family on the subject of what you should study in college).
5. The *purpose* is at least twofold: to make comfortable money and to enter a career you expect to find satisfying.

What happens when you start thinking about what each of these factors had to do with any other? What if you ask, say, "How did the *scene* of my decision influence the *actor* (me)?"

You may then recall that your father, who always wanted to be a racing car driver himself, tried to talk you out of your decision and urged you to hang around racetracks instead. In arguing with him you were forced to defend your notion of studying law. You came to see that, yes, by George, being a lawyer would be a great life for you. Maybe your brother was on the scene, too, and he said, "Why don't you go to law school? You always were a hardliner in arguments." Maybe that was a factor in your decision. You can pursue this line of thought. Then maybe you can try making another link: between scene and purpose. Ask, "How did my home motivate me?" Maybe then you realize that your brother gave you a real purpose: to show the world how well you can argue. Maybe you realize that your decision to go to law school was a way to prove to your father that you don't need to be a racing car driver — you can make good in a different career.

This example, to be sure, may not fit you personally. Perhaps you don't live with a father or a brother, and you can't stand the thought of studying law. But the point is that you can begin all sorts of fruitful lines of inquiry simply by asking questions that team up these components. Following Burke's method, you can pair them in ten ways:

actor to act	act to scene	scene to agency
actor to scene	act to agency	scene to purpose
actor to agency	act to purpose	agency to purpose
actor to purpose		

If you wish to understand this strategy, try writing one question for each pair; for example, for the second pair, "What does the actor have to do with the scene?" If you were writing about your move to study law, this question might be put: "Before I made my move, what connection existed, if any, between me and this college?" Try to answer that question and you may sense ideas beginning to percolate. "Why," you might say, "I came here because I know a good lawyer who graduated from the place." You'll get a head start on your writing assignment if, while trying to answer the questions, you take notes.

The questions will serve equally well for analyzing someone else's motives. If you were trying to explain, for a history course, why President Johnson chose not to run again, the five elements might perhaps be these.

Act: Announcing the decision to leave office without standing for reelection.

Actor: President Johnson.

Agency: A televised address to the nation.

Scene (including circumstances at the time): Washington, D.C., March 31, 1968. Protesters against the nation's involvement in Vietnam were gaining in numbers and influence. The press was increasing its criticism of the president's escalation of the war. Senator Eugene McCarthy, an antiwar candidate for president, had made a strong showing against Johnson in the New Hampshire primary election.

Purpose: Think of any *possible* purposes: to avoid a probable political defeat, to escape further personal attacks, to spare his family, to make it easier for his successor to pull the country out of the war, to ease bitter dissent among Americans.

If you started asking questions such as "What did the actor have to do with the agency?" you might come up with an answer like "Johnson apparently enjoyed facing the nation on television. Commanding the attention of a vast audience, he must have felt he was in control—even though his ability to control the situation in Vietnam was slipping."

Do you see the possibilities? The value of Burke's questions is that they can start you writing. Not all the questions will prove fruitful, and some may not even apply. But one or two might reveal valuable answers. Try them and see.

Exercise: Seeking Motives

Choose an action that puzzles you. It may be one of the following.

> Something you have done.
> An action of a family member or a friend.
> A decision of a historical or current political figure.
> Something in a movie or television program.
> An occurrence in a literary selection.

Then apply Burke's pentad to this action to try to determine the individual's motives. If Burke's five basic categories do not go far enough to help you understand the human act, team up the components (see p. 314) to perceive relationships that will help you delve more deeply into the motives for the act. When you believe you understand the individual's motivation, write a paragraph explaining the action, and share it with your classmates.

Now you have five specific strategies to generate ideas for writing. Seldom will you use all of them on one writing task, but if one approach doesn't help you think of sufficient information, try others. Think of these strategies as your arsenal of idea generators, techniques that you can call on at any point in the writing process.

CHAPTER 15

Strategies for Planning

Starting to write often seems a chaotic activity, but to reduce the chaos and create order when you shape a paper you can use the strategies in this chapter.

In general, especially when writing a paper that calls for critical thinking, you'll shape your draft around one central point (see "Stating and Using a Thesis" on p. 322). In nearly any kind of writing task, you can also organize your thoughts by various strategies (see "Grouping Your Ideas" and "Outlining" on pp. 328 and 331, respectively).

GETTING READY TO WRITE

For most writers, the hardest part of drafting comes first: the moment when they confront a blank sheet of paper. Fortunately, you can do much to get ready for it. Sometimes a simple trick or a playful change of your writing circumstances will ease you over that hard part and get you smoothly rolling along.

Experienced writers have many tested techniques to get moving. Many of the suggestions that follow may strike you as useless and far-out, even silly, but all have worked for some writers. Some work for us, and we hope a few will work for you. You may care to check or underline or highlight any suggestions that look useful. You're the only writer who can know which ideas might work for you.

Setting Up Circumstances

Get comfortable   We don't just mean turn on a bright light because it's good for your eyes. Why not create an environment? If you can write only with your shoes off or with a can of Orange Crush, by all means set yourself up that way. Some writers need a radio blaring heavy metal; others need quiet. Circumstances that put you in the mood for writing can encourage you.

Devote one special place to writing   Have one special location in which to write. Then when you go there, your mind and body will be ready to settle in and get to work. Not everyone has a room to devote to studying, so your place may be a desk in a corner of your bedroom, the dining room table, or a lap board on a den sofa. It should be a place with good lighting and plenty of space to spread out and leave projects you are working on. It should be a place where no one else will bother your materials and where everyone in the house will know you are working when you go there. Keep your pens, paper, typewriter or word processor, dictionary, and other reference materials there.

Establish a ritual   Many writers follow certain routines to get themselves in the mood for writing. You might try this technique — get a cup of coffee or a soda, turn on your light, turn the radio on (or off), sharpen your pencils or turn on the computer, check your paper supply, and straighten the things on your desk. Apprehensive writers also find that following a writing ritual relaxes them enough to think clearly and write effectively.

Relocate   Try writing in an unfamiliar place: a bowling alley, a bar, a bus station. Passers-by will wonder what you are doing there, scribbling away. Their curiosity might cause you to concentrate hard on your writing, just to show them that you aren't crazy but know what you're doing. We have heard of whole novels written in a cafeteria in midtown Manhattan.

Write in bed   This technique might help you relax and get more work done — provided you can keep your eyes open. At the helm of Britain during World War II, Winston Churchill usually did a morning's work in bed, reading dispatches and answering them, conducting an extensive correspondence with his generals. Marcel Proust, the French novelist, also liked to write while horizontal.

Write in the library   See if you can find a quiet corner where you can work surrounded by heads bowed in concentration. These good examples may start you concentrating too. Keep away from any corner of the library where a bull session is raging.

Reduce distractions   Most of us can't prevent interruptions when we are trying to concentrate, but we can reduce them. Answer all questions and take care of all needs of the people you live with before you start. If you are expecting your boyfriend to call, call him before you start. If you have small children, write when they are asleep or at school. If someone is ill, give him his medicine, get him comfortable, and turn on his television set before you go to your special place to write. Turn on the answering machine for the telephone. If you have an appointment you can't miss, set the alarm clock to remind you. Do all you can to let people around you know you are serious about writing and to allow yourself to give your full attention to the writing task.

Exhaust your excuses   Most writers are born experts at coming up with reasons not to write; and if you are one of those writers, you might find that it helps to run out of reasons. Is your room annoyingly jumbled? Straighten it. Drink that can of soda, sharpen those pencils, throw out that trash, and make that phone call home. Then, your mind swept clean, you can sit down and write. (If you still have good excuses not to write, jot down a list of them so you can take care of them later.)

Yield to inspiration   Classical Greek and Roman critics held that a goddess called a Muse would gently touch a poet and leave him inspired. Whether or not you believe in divine inspiration, sometimes ideas, images, metaphors, or vague but powerful urges to write will arrive like sudden miracles. Good writers stay alert for them. When they come, even if you are taking a shower or getting ready to go to a movie, you are wise to yield to impulse and set aside everything else and write. You will find, then, that words will flow with little exertion. Don't feel guilty if friends think you a hermit for declining that movie date. You may be a hermit, but at least you'll be a hermit with a finished paper. If going to that movie is irresistible, jot down enough notes beforehand to rekindle your ideas later when you can go back to writing.

Write at the time best for you   Some people think best early in the morning, others in the afternoon or late at night. If you don't know the time that is best for you, try writing in the small hours when the world is still. Before you are wholly awake, your stern self-critic might not be awake yet either. (When you edit and proofread, though, you want to be fully awake.) Poet Donald Hall likes to get up at dawn and start writing poems. He says that, his mind being closer to dream at that time, the results are often surprising and intriguing. Perhaps you might just find yourself staring at blank paper wishing for breakfast, but this time is worth at least one try. If you're a night person, take a nap in the afternoon and write from 10:00 P.M. until 2:00 or 3:00 A.M. Writing at dawn or midnight also has the advantage that most other people are asleep then, so you'll have fewer distractions.

Write on a schedule   Many writers find that it helps to have a certain predictable time of day to write. This method won't work for all, but it worked marvels for English novelist Anthony Trollope, a crack-of-dawn writer. Each day at 5:30 A.M., Trollope, before he dressed, would seat himself at his writing table, place his watch before him, spend half an hour rereading his work of the previous day, and then write 250 words every fifteen minutes until he had done his daily stint of 2500 words. His literary labors over at 8:30, he would then set off to his job at the General Post Office. "I have found," he noted dryly, "that the 250 words have been forthcoming as regularly as my watch went." (He wrote more than sixty books.) Trollope may have been a compulsive scheduler, but there is much to be said for forming the habit of writing daily. Over the desk of John Updike, a prolific writer of our own day, hangs the motto *Nulla dies sine linea* ("Never a day without a line"), a saying of the Roman writer Pliny. Even if you can't write every day, it may help to declare, first thing in the morning, "All right, today from 11 to 12 I'll sit down and write."

Defy a schedule   On the other hand, if you write on a schedule and your work isn't going well, break out of your usual time frame. If you are an afternoon writer, write at night.

Take regular short breaks   Even if you don't feel tired, take regular breaks every thirty minutes or every hour if you can work that long without losing your concentration. Get up, walk around the room, stretch, get a drink of water, or refill your coffee cup. Two or three minutes is enough to refresh your mind.

Change activities   When words won't come, do something quite different from writing for a while. Walk, run, throw a Frisbee, or work out at the gym. Exercise refreshes a tired brain with a shot of brand-new oxygen. Sometimes it helps to eat lunch, cook your favorite meal, take in a movie, check out an art exhibit, listen to music, take a nap, or go down to the supermarket and watch the cold cut slicer. Sometimes while you're not even thinking about the writing task before you, your unconscious mind will be working on it.

Switch instruments   Change the way your writing feels, looks, and sounds when it hits paper. Are you a typist? Try writing in longhand. If you are an inveterate pen user, type for a change. Try writing with a different kind of pencil or pen: a colored felt-tip, say, or an erasable pen. Try writing on note cards (which are easy to shuffle and rearrange) or on colored paper (yellow second-sheets, by the way, are cheaper than typing paper). Have you tried writing with a word processor? Many writers today compose much more easily on a computer. Perhaps you'll hit upon a new medium you'll enjoy much more.

Preparing Your Mind

Discuss your plans   Collar any nearby listener: roommate, student down the hall, spouse, parent, friend. Tell the other person why you want to write this particular paper, what you're going to put into it, how you're going to lay out your material. If the other person says, "That sounds good," you'll be encouraged; but even if the reaction is a yawn, at least you will have set your own thinking in motion.

Keep a notebook handy   Always have some paper in your pocket or purse or on the night table to write down those good ideas whenever they pop into your mind. We know an author who thought of a good introduction for her book while she was in the checkout lane of the supermarket. She whipped out her notebook and jotted down the main points before she got up to the cashier. Often you will have time to think while waiting in the doctor's office or during slow times on your job. Take advantage of those calm times, and write down your ideas so that you won't forget them.

Keep a daily journal   Use the journal to record your experiences as a writer. You don't want to make this a huge project. But you might be surprised how scribbling in a journal for fifteen minutes a day will nourish your writing. A small (5-by-7-inch) spiral-bound or looseleaf notebook is a nice, unintimidating size. Setting words down on a page becomes an everyday routine. In this, your writer's journal, you might note any writing problems you run into (and overcome), any ideas for things you'd like to write, any reactions to your writing you get from other people, any writing strategies that work well for you, anything about how to write that dawns on you. Journals can be kept for many purposes: a journal to record your reading and your reactions to it, a journal to track your progress in any course you take, a journal in which to save any stray thoughts you care to remember. (For more detailed suggestions about journals, see p. 309.) For a student paper that emerged from a journal kept for a biology class, see Sandy Messina's "Footprints: The Mark of Our Passing" (p. 37).

Doodle   At least you'll be pushing a pencil, even if you are only drawing rabbits, stick figures, or goofy faces. Who can tell? As you sit with pencil in hand, words might start to flow.

Shrink your immediate job   Break the writing task into several smaller parts and oblige yourself (for now) to do only the first one. It would look hard to hike cross-country, less hard if you knew you had to go only twenty miles by the first night. Similarly, writing a 750-word paper, you might get going faster if you vow to turn out, say, just the first three paragraphs.

Nutshell it   Write a very terse summary of the paper you want to write. Condense all your ideas into one small tight paragraph. Later you can go back and expand each sentence until the meaning is clear and all points are adequately supported. This technique works especially well if you compose on a computer screen.

Write a letter to your instructor   Tell your instructor just what you think of the assignment and what else you would rather be doing if you didn't have to write this paper. After getting that out of your system, keep writing. (When you turn in your finished paper, leave that letter out of it.)

State your purpose   In a sentence or a few lines, set forth what you want your paper to achieve. Are you trying to tell a story? If so, what is that story trying to do — prove a point or perhaps simply entertain? Are you trying to explain something? Win a reader over to your way of thinking? Sometimes doing this will define your job and bring blurred thoughts into focus. (For more about stating your purpose, see "Stating and Using a Thesis," below.)

Read for fun   Read whatever you feel like reading. The step from reading to writing is a short one. Even when you're just reading for kicks, you start to involve yourself with words. Who knows, you might by pure accident (which tends to happen to some writers) hit upon something useful for your paper.

Read purposefully   If you have a topic, or an area to search for one, set out to read what's being written about it. As you read, take notes. Naturally, the more you know about your topic, the more securely you will feel on top of it and ready to write.

Try the carrot-and-stick   This method may work when inspiration is on strike. Like a donkey encouraged to plod toward his destination by a juicy carrot suspended in front of his teeth, promise yourself a reward. Keep it simple: a trip to the refrigerator or the vending machine, a walk in the open air, a phone call to a friend, a fifteen-minute visit to a neighbor, a TV show — but only when you arrive at some moment in your labors at which you will truly feel you have earned your reward.

Seek a provocative title   Write down ten or twenty possible titles for your paper and then, looking over them, decide if any one sounds strikingly good to you. If so, you will probably be encouraged to write something rather than let such a promising title go to waste.

STATING AND USING A THESIS

Most pieces of effective writing make one main point. In "What Is a Hunter?" (p. 17), student Robert G. Schreiner maintains that there is more to being a hunter than knowing how to use a rifle. In "Conflicting Messages: A Look at a Generation Torn Two Ways" (p. 57), student writer Rose Anne Federici asserts the main idea that her generation is constantly pulled in two directions. After you have read such an essay, you can sum up the writer's main point in a sentence, even if the author has not stated it explicitly. We call this summary statement a *thesis sentence.*

Often the thesis — the writer's main point — will be plainly stated in the piece of writing itself. Federici states her thesis in the first sentence of her essay — "I belong to a generation constantly torn in two directions" — and repeats it in her conclusion — "I have an increasing sense that I belong to a generation torn in different directions." Such clear statements strategically placed as well as her title help readers see her main point unmistakably.

In some writing though, a thesis may be implied. In "Once More to the Lake," E. B. White (p. 425) clearly focuses on the realization of his own mortality. All the descriptive and narrative details from the past and the present, the references to time, and the allusions to his relationships with his father and his son culminate in the final sentence: "As he [son] buckled the swollen belt, suddenly my groin felt the chill of death." Although White does not state his main point in one concise sentence, after you have read his essay you know that he is keenly aware of the passing of family rituals from generation to generation, and you can state his thesis in your own words.

The purpose of most academic and business writing is to inform, to explain, or to convince, and to achieve these purposes the writer must make the main point crystal clear. A thesis sentence will help you clarify your main idea in your own mind, and it will also help guide you as you write by reminding you of the point you're driving at. It is an especially helpful strategy in writing an essay or explaining or arguing because it can help you stay on track and, incorporated into your essay, can help your reader readily see your point. Sometimes you may want to imply your thesis as White did in his essay, but implying your point makes understanding more difficult for your readers. For most of your writing, you will communicate more effectively with your readers if you do as Federici did in her essay: state your thesis so that the readers cannot miss it.

Discovering Your Thesis

On some writing tasks you will know what main point you intend to make before even setting a word on paper, but at other times you will struggle and make several attempts at expressing your main point—perhaps even write a whole draft—before you discover what you want to say and how to state it clearly and concisely. Don't be dismayed if your thesis does not come to you early in the writing process. Look back over the notes, the brainstorming, or the freewriting you did in preparation for this paper, and see if you can generalize from them. Write several tentative thesis sentences, changing words or word order or emphasis each time. Try some of the strategies for generating ideas or for getting started. Brainstorm titles (the title is usually a shortened form of the thesis). Freewrite the introductory paragraph or the conclusion to your paper. Or start in the middle of the essay and write the easiest part first. Nutshell: write a concise, one-paragraph summary of your paper. Write a complete draft. Talk it over with a friend, or tape-record your rambling thoughts about your topic. If one of these methods does not work for you on a particular writing task, try the others. When you get a thesis sentence that you feel comfortable with, try it out on your peer group or your instructor.

Exercise: Stating a Thesis

Practice generalizing from a group of details. State a thesis for each of the following groups of details. Then compare and contrast your thesis for each with that of your classmates in your peer group. What other information would you need to write a good paper on each of these topics?

1. Cigarettes are expensive.
   Cigarettes can cause fires.
   Cigarettes cause unpleasant odors.
   Cigarettes can cause health problems to the smoker.
   Secondhand smoke from cigarettes can cause health problems.

2. Clinger College has a highly qualified faculty.
   Clinger College has an excellent curriculum in my field.
   Clinger College has a beautiful campus.
   Clinger College is expensive.
   Clinger College has offered me a scholarship.

3. Crisis centers report that date rape is increasing.
   Most date rape is not reported to the police.
   Often the victim of date rape is not believed.
   Sometimes the victim of date rape is blamed.
   Sometimes the victim of date rape blames herself.
   The effects of date rape stay with a woman for years.

Often, during the interplay of a writer's mind, the English language, and a piece of paper or a computer screen, an insight will occur. Whenever such a discovery appears to you, you may wish — at that moment when in the midst of your work your thesis becomes clear to you — to set it down in a statement, even post it over your desk as a friendly reminder. Then it won't get away; and when you finish your draft, the thesis sentence will make it easier for you to evaluate what you have written. As you revise, you can reconsider your thesis statement and ask yourself, "Have I made that main point clear? Is everything I have written related to this point?"

If you decide to write on the topic "the decline of old-fashioned formal courtesy toward women," you indicate the area to be explored, but that topic doesn't tell you the *point* of your paper. If you say, "Old-fashioned formal courtesy toward women is a thing of the past," you are talking in circles and getting nowhere. What will you try to do in your paper, anyhow? Will you perhaps affirm something, or deny, or recommend? If you stick with that topic about old-fashioned formal courtesy declining—how women don't have coats or chairs held for them anymore—then your *thesis* might be "As the roles of men and women have changed in our society, old-fashioned formal courtesy toward women has declined." Then your paper would focus on how changing attitudes in society have caused many men to stop exercising the old-fashioned courtesies toward women. What other thesis sentences might you come up with for this topic? Discuss some other possibilities with your classmates.

If, to change topics, you plan to describe an old hotel, what possible point will you demonstrate? You might say to yourself, "I love the old Biltmore Hotel." But that statement gives you little direction for writing. What is it about the old hotel that you love? And what in the world do you mean by the word *love* anyway? You try again: "I love the quaintness of the old Biltmore Hotel." Now you intend to focus on the hotel's old-fashioned endearing quality. But then you wonder if *love* and *endearing* are repetitious, so you try again: "The Old Biltmore Hotel has a quaint beauty." This time you know you intend to describe the various aspects of old-fashioned beauty which have endeared the hotel to you. Although the way you state your thesis may change as you develop your ideas and as you discover new details, at least this thesis sentence gives you a place to start and a direction to move in.

If you are going to compare and contrast two things—for instance, two local newspapers in their coverage of a Senate election—ask yourself what is the point of that comparison and contrast. One possible thesis sentence you might come up with is "The *Herald*'s coverage of the Senate elections was more thorough than the *Courier*'s."

How to State a Thesis

Here are four suggestions for writing a workable thesis statement.

1. ***State the thesis sentence exactly.*** Use concise, detailed, and down-to-earth language. The statement "There are a lot of troubles with chemical wastes" is too huge and general. Are you going to deal with all chemical wastes, through all of history, all over the world? Are you going to list all the troubles they can cause? Make the statement more specific: "Careless dumping of leftover paint is to blame for a recent skin rash in Atlanta." Now you have a concise, restricted statement that you can use as the basis for a brief essay.

2. ***State just one central idea in the thesis sentence.*** If your paper is to focus on one point, to unify the writing your thesis should state only one main idea. This statement has one idea too many: "Careless dumping of leftover paint has caused a serious problem in Atlanta, and a new kind of biodegradable paint now looks promising." Either the first half or the second half of the statement would suffice and lead you to a unified essay.

3. ***State your thesis positively.*** You can usually find evidence to support a positive statement, but you can't prove a negative one. Write "The causes

of breast cancer remain a challenge for medical scientists" instead of "Medical scientists do not know what causes breast cancer." The former statement might lead to a paper about an exciting quest, the challenge that medical scientists face. But the latter statement seems to reflect a halfhearted attitude by the writer. Besides, to demonstrate that some medical scientists are still working on the problem would be relatively easy: you could show that after an hour of research in a library. To prove the negative statement, that not one medical scientist knows the answer, would be a very difficult task.

   4. *Limit your thesis sentence to a statement that is possible to demonstrate.* A thesis sentence should stake out enough territory for you to cover thoroughly within the assigned word length and the time available, and no more. To maintain throughout a 700-word paper the thesis "My favorite piece of music is Beethoven's Fifth Symphony" would be a difficult task unless you could go into voluminous detail, explaining how and why it is your favorite and contrasting it with *all* the other musical compositions you know. And how in the world could you sustain your readers' interest in such a listing for several pages? The statement "For centuries, popular music has been indicative of vital trends in Western society" wouldn't do for a 700-word paper either: that thesis would be enough to inform a whole encyclopedia of music in twelve volumes. "In the past two years, a rise in the number of preteenagers has resulted in a comeback for heavy metal on our local concert scene"— now that thesis idea sounds much more likely. You could cover it in a brief 500- to 700-word essay.

Let's try a few more examples of thesis sentences:

"Indian blankets are very beautiful." That statement is too vague and hard to demonstrate for a usual college writing assignment of 400 to 1000 words.

"American Indians have adapted to modern civilization." That sounds too large, too unrestricted, unless you plan to write a 5000-word paper in sociology.

"Members of the Apache tribe are skilled workers in high-rise construction." All right: you could probably find support for that thesis by spending a couple of hours doing research in a library.

Exercise: Examining Thesis Statements

Discuss each of the following thesis sentences with your peer group. Answer these questions for each:

   Is the thesis stated exactly?
   Does the thesis state just one idea?
   Is the thesis stated positively?
   Is the thesis sufficiently limited for 500 to 700 words?
   How might an essay based on this thesis be organized?

What information would I need to develop the essay?
Would the thesis lead to an interesting essay?
How might the thesis be improved?

1. Teenagers should not get married.
2. A person needs some old clothes.
3. Cutting classes is like a disease.
4. Going to college prepares an individual for the future, and it is increasingly expensive.
5. Students have developed a variety of techniques to conceal inadequate study from their instructors.
6. College is different from high school.
7. Older people often imitate teenagers.
8. There are many different types of students in college today.
9. Violence on television can be harmful to children.
10. Teachers have influenced my life.
11. Disney World is my favorite vacation spot.
12. Everyone in the office contributed to the Heart Fund.
13. I don't know how to change the oil in my car.
14. My hobbies are scuba diving, playing the guitar, and motocross racing.
15. Traveling is educational.

How to Use a Thesis

Often a good, clear, ample statement of a thesis will suggest an organization for your ideas. Say you plan to write a paper from the thesis "Despite the several disadvantages of living in a downtown business district, I wouldn't live anywhere else." That thesis sentence suggests how to organize your essay. You might start with several paragraphs discussing disadvantages of living in the business district, move on to a few paragraphs discussing the advantages, and then close with an affirmation of your fondness for downtown city life.

As you write, you don't have to cling to a thesis for dear life. If some facts or notions don't seem to fit, you may want to change your thesis while you write. Just putting your trial thesis into words can help you stake out the territory you need to know better. You might think that you want to write a paper on the thesis "Because wolves are a menace to people and farm animals, they ought to be exterminated." Suppose, though, that further investigation and conversation don't support that statement at all. Suppose, in fact, that what you learn contradicts it. Your thesis statement isn't chiseled in marble. You can change it to "The wolf, a relatively peaceful animal useful in nature's scheme of things, ought to be protected." The purpose of a thesis statement is to guide you on a quest, not to force you on a foolish and unheeding march to doom. You can restate it at any time: as you write, as you revise, as you revise again.

Not all writing tasks call for a thesis statement. In telling a story, writing a letter to a friend, or analyzing a process, you are not necessarily driving toward a single point. For most of your writing, however, you will find a thesis a useful strategy for helping you to plan, shape, draft, and revise.

GROUPING YOUR IDEAS

In any bale of scribblings you have made while exploring a topic, you will usually find a few ideas that seem to belong together. They make the same point ("Just what I need," you think, "*two* examples of how New Yorkers drive"). They might follow one another ("Here are facts on the frequency of New York traffic jams — from this, I can go to the point that New York drivers are frustrated").

As you look over your preliminary notes, you'll want to indicate to yourself any connections you find between your materials. You'll need to sort your notes into groups, arrange them in sequences. Here are six common ways to work.

1. ***Rainbow connections.*** Some writers list on a sheet of paper all the main points they're going to express. They don't recopy all their material — they just list each main point briefly, not worrying about order. Then, taking colored pencils, they circle with the same color any points that seem to go together. Others use various colors of highlight pens. When they write, they can follow the color code and deal with similar ideas at the same time.

2. ***Linking.*** Other writers, though they work in black and white, also start by making a list of major points. They draw lines that link similar ideas. Then they number each linked group, to remember in what sequence to deal with it. Figure 15.1 is an illustration of a linked list. This particular list was produced in a one-person brainstorming session. It is nothing but a brief jotting down of points the writer wants to make in an essay to be called "Manhattan Driving." The writer has drawn lines between points that seem to go together. He has numbered each linked group in the order he plans to follow when writing and has supplied each with a heading. When he writes his draft, each heading will probably inspire a topic sentence or a few lines to introduce each major division of his essay. One point failed to relate to any other: "Chauffeured luxury cars." In the finished paper, he would leave it out. This rough plan, if expanded three or four times, would make a workable outline for a short paper. It sifts out useless material; it arranges what remains.

3. ***Solitaire.*** Some writers, especially scholars, collect notes and ideas on roomy (5-by-8-inch) file cards. When they organize, they spread out the cards and arrange them in an order, as in a game of solitaire. When the order looks worth keeping, when each idea seems to lead to the next, they gather all the cards into a deck once more and wrap a rubber band around them. Then when they write, they deal themselves a card at a time and translate its

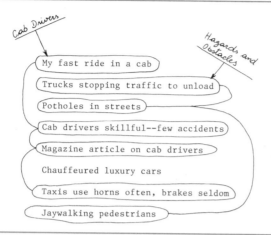

Cab Drivers

Hazards and Obstacles

(My fast ride in a cab)

(Trucks stopping traffic to unload)

(Potholes in streets)

(Cab drivers skillful--few accidents)

(Magazine article on cab drivers)

Chauffeured luxury cars

(Taxis use horns often, brakes seldom)

(Jaywalking pedestrians)

FIGURE 15.1   The linking method for grouping ideas

contents into readable writing. This technique is particularly helpful when you write about literature or when you write from research.

4. ***Scissors and tape.*** Other writers swear by scissors and tape. They lay out their rough notes before them. Then they group any notes that refer to the same point and that probably belong in the same vicinity. With scissors, they separate items that don't belong together. They shuffle the pieces around, trying for the most promising order. After throwing out any ideas that don't belong anywhere, they lock up the material into a structure. They join all the parts with tape. If they find places in the grand design where ideas and information are lacking, they make a note of what's missing and tape that note into place. Although this taped-together construction of cards or slips of paper may look sloppy, it can serve as a workable outline.

Some writers use this strategy not merely for planning, but for planning and drafting simultaneously. They tape together not just notes, but passages they have written separately. If you follow this method, you write whatever part you want to write first, then write the next most tempting part, and so on until you have enough rough stuff to arrange into a whole piece of writing. Try arranging the pieces on a wall or a blackboard to see how they fit together best. Then you'll need to add missing parts and to supply transitions (discussed on p. 354).

5. ***Clustering.*** Sometimes seeing a map of idea clusters with circles and lines showing connections will help you organize your thoughts. Clustering is useful for coming up with ideas, but it is just as valuable as a visual method of grouping those ideas. For clustering, take a piece of paper and in the middle of it write your topic in a word or a phrase. Then think of the major divisions into which this topic might be analyzed. For an essay called "Manhattan Drivers," the major divisions might be the *types* of Manhattan drivers: (1) taxi drivers, (2) bus drivers, (3) truck drivers, (4) drivers of private cars—New

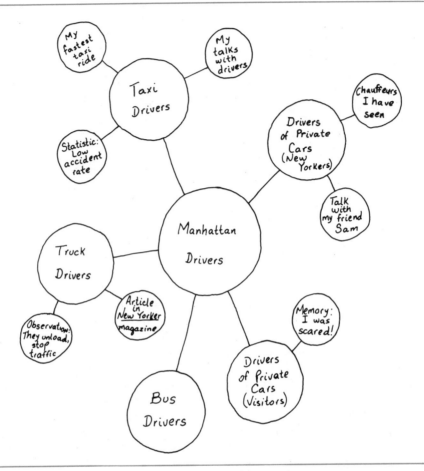

FIGURE 15.2 The clustering method for generating ideas

Yorkers, and (5) drivers of private cars—out-of-town visitors. Arrange these divisions around your topic on your page and circle them, too. Draw lines out from the major topic to the subdivisions. You now have the beginning of a rough plan for an essay.

Now, around each division, make another cluster of points you're going to include: examples, illustrations, facts, statistics, bits of evidence, opinions, whatever. On your page, make a brief notation ("My taxi ride," "Talk with New York friend," "Statistic on accidents") for each specific item, circle it, and connect it to the appropriate type of driver. When you write your paper, you can expand the details into one paragraph for each type of driver. Figure 15.2 presents a cluster for "Manhattan Drivers."

This technique lets you know where you have enough specific information to make your paper clear and interesting—and where you don't. If one of your subtopics has no small circles around it (such as "bus drivers" in Figure 15.2), you should think of some specific examples to expand it; if you can't, drop it. For a long paper (of, say, more than 1000 words), you would definitely need more material than you have in this example.

6. *The electronic game.* Many writers arrange their rough notes into groups right on a computer screen, moving items from place to place until they like the resulting plan. Some computer software is dedicated to outlining, making it possible for the writer to try out different schemes of organization before deciding on any one of them. (For detailed suggestions on writing with a computer, see Chapter 20, "Strategies for Writing with a Computer.")

Exercise: Clustering

Draw idea clusters or mind maps of three of the following topics. Share them with your peer group. Discuss which one of the three would probably help you write the best paper.

teachers	pets
cars	U.S. presidents
television programs	civil rights
my favorite restaurants	drug abuse
fast food	good health
leisure-time activities	technology

OUTLINING

Some writers start writing without any plan. "When I work," says novelist Norman Mailer, "I don't like to know where I'm going." Other writers plan extensively. Novelist John Barth says, "I don't see how anybody starts a novel without knowing how it's going to end. I usually make detailed outlines: how many chapters it will be and so forth." Yet whether they lay out thorough plans on paper or arrange ideas in their heads, good writers think and plan and organize what they write. In freshman composition you will not write novels like Mailer and Barth, but you too can benefit from using some strategies for organizing your essays.

In the previous section, "Grouping Your Ideas," we set forth ways to bring related thoughts together. Another, perhaps more familiar means to organize ideas is to outline. A written outline, whether brief or greatly detailed, serves as guide and friend. Even a detailed one shouldn't say *everything* you plan to write in your paper. You shouldn't use up all your thought and energy on your outline. If you forget where you are going or what you are trying to say, however, you can consult your written outline and get back on track. It's like a map that you make before setting out on a journey. It shows where to set out from, where to stop along the way, and where at last to arrive. While you drive along through your essay, occasionally consulting your map, you can easily revise your route.

How detailed an outline will you need? The answer depends in part on the kind of writer you are and in part on the kind of writing you are doing.

Some writers feel most comfortable when writing with a highly detailed outline: buoyed up as though by a pair of water wings. Others feel inhibited by such a thing, as though they were trying to swim in a straitjacket. Some writers like to lay out the job very carefully in advance; others prefer to lay it out more loosely and follow an outline more casually.

For most writing, most of the time, most college writers find it enough to use an informal outline — perhaps just a list of points to make. For timed writings and essay exams, that's all you have time to do; for short essays (two or three pages), that's probably all you'll need. If you are working with familiar material, a brief outline is enough. If you are dealing with complex, unfamiliar information, you'll probably need a full-blown outline to keep from getting lost. Do people tell you your writing isn't well organized and that they can't follow you? Then probably you need a more detailed plan. Do they tell you your writing sounds mechanical? Maybe your outline is constricting you.

Sometimes, when you have written the first draft of a paper that you suspect doesn't quite make sense, outlining can help you apply first aid. If you can't easily make an outline of what you have written, then probably your reader will have a hard time following your writing. Something is wrong with the paper's basic construction. Perhaps the main points don't follow clearly. Maybe the sequence of ideas needs rearranging. Maybe too many ideas are jammed into too few paragraphs. Maybe you don't have as many specific details and examples as you need. It is often easier to operate on your outline than on your ailing paper. Work on the outline until you get it into strong shape and then rewrite the paper to follow it.

Informal Outlines

For in-class writing and for brief essays, often a *short* or *informal outline,* also called a *scratch outline,* will serve your needs. It is just a brief list of points to make, in the order you plan to make them. The short outline is only for your eyes. When the writing job is done, you pitch the outline along with your unsatisfactory drafts into the trash basket.

The following is an informal outline for a 600-word paper contrasting city drivers with small-town drivers. Its thesis sentence is: "City drivers are quite different from small-town drivers." As for all good essays, you'll need plenty of facts, observations, and other specific evidence to back up that claim. One obvious way to proceed is to think of and list the specific areas of contrast (perhaps physical fitness, skill, and consideration). Then, for each quality, you would discuss first city drivers and then small-town drivers — how they do or don't exhibit the characteristic. You could put this plan in scratch form like this:

Introduction: Different driving habits

1. Physical fitness
   — City drivers: little time and space in which to exercise

— Small-town drivers: lifestyle conducive to physical ease
2. Skill at the wheel
— City drivers: small, crowded streets
— Small-town drivers: narrow streets
3. Consideration for others
— City drivers: tendency to vent their aggressions at the wheel
— Small-town drivers: laid-back attitude toward life reflected in driving habits

Conclusion: I'd rather drive in a small town.

A simple outline like that could easily fall into a five-paragraph essay. If you have a great deal to say about city drivers and small-town drivers, though, the essay might well run longer — perhaps to eight paragraphs: introduction, conclusion, and three pairs of paragraphs in between. You probably won't know until you write the paper exactly how many paragraphs you'll need.

An informal outline can be even briefer than the preceding one. If you were writing an in-class essay, an answer to an examination question, or a very short paper, your outline might be no more than an *outer plan* — three or four phrases jotted down in a list.

Physical fitness
Skill
Consideration for others

Often a clear thesis statement (see p. 322) will suggest a way to outline. If the thesis contains a plural word (such as *benefits* or *advantages* or *teenagers*), you can divide it. If one part of the thesis sentence is subordinate to the other (beginning with *because* or *since* or *if* or *although*), you can analyze according to the parts of the sentence. Let's say you are assigned, for an anthropology course, a paper on the people of Melanesia. You decide to focus on the following idea:

Thesis: Although the Melanesian pattern of family life may look strange to westerners, it fosters a degree of independence that rivals our own.

Laying out ideas in the same order as they follow in that thesis statement, you might make a short, simple outline like this:

l. Features that appear strange to westerners
— A woman supported by her brother, not her husband
— Trial marriages usual

> — Divorce from her children possible for any mother
> 2. Admirable results of system
>   — Wives not dependent on husbands for support
>   — Divorce between mates uncommon
>   — Greater freedom for parents and children

This informal outline might result in an essay that naturally falls into two parts: strange features, admirable results. In writing and thinking further, you might want to flesh out that outline with more material. The outline might expand accordingly.

Say you plan to write a "how-to" essay analyzing the process of buying a used car. Your thesis statement might read:

> Thesis: Despite traps that lie in wait for the unwary, you can get a good deal in a used car if you prepare yourself before you shop.

The key word in this sentence is *prepare,* and you ask yourself *how* the buyer should prepare himself or herself. What should he or she do before shopping for a used car? You think of several things, and you analyze the key word *prepare* into those parts:

> — Read car magazines and <u>Consumer Reports</u>
> — Check ads in the newspapers
> — Make phone calls to several dealers
> — Talk to friends who have bought used cars
> — Know what to look and listen for when you test drive
> — Consult a friend who's a mechanic

Follow this sequence of ideas in your paper. You can start your paper with some horror stories about people who get taken by car sharks and then proceed to list and discuss, point by point, your bits of advice. Of course, you can always change the sequence, add an idea or take one out, or revise your thesis sentence if you find it makes sense to do so as you go along. How might you end this paper? (Discuss possibilities with your classmates.)

Formal Outlines

A *formal outline* is the Mercedes-Benz of outlines: an elaborate job built with time and care. It is probably more than you need for brief writings. As a guide for long, complex papers, it can help you express your ideas in an orderly manner. It may be written in topic headings or sentence headings.

In college, a formal outline is usually used for ambitious projects. It is meant for a writer's own guidance, as well as for an instructor or a committee to ponder before (or after) the writer writes. Because long reports, research papers, and honors theses require so much work, some academic professors and departments ask a writer to submit a formal outline before going ahead and toiling for months, perhaps in vain. Some instructors in assigning an essay or a research paper ask for a special kind of formal outline — the *sentence outline* — to make the paper's organization easier to see and to discuss. For an example, see Lisa Chickos's sentence outline for her research paper on page 619. Writing such a detailed outline can pay off: by adding specifics and transitions, you can relatively easily turn the outline into a finished paper.

A formal outline offers the greatest amount of guidance that an outline can give. In a clear, logical way, it spells out where you are going to go and where you want your readers to follow. It shows how ideas relate one to another. It shows which ideas are equal (*coordinate*) and which are less important (*subordinate*). It ranks the points to be made according to their importance and inclusiveness: a point labeled with a roman numeral is a major point that takes in more territory, that is more general, than the points labeled with capital letters under it.

When you make a formal outline, you place your thesis sentence at the beginning. Then you divide it into your major points — those that most directly bear on your thesis — and express them in roman numerals: I, II, III. These points support and develop the main idea of your whole paper. Then you break down these points into divisions with capital letters, indenting them: A, B, C. You subdivide those into divisions with arabic numbers — 1, 2, 3 — indenting further, and then subdivide those into divisions with small letters — a, b, c — indenting yet again. Align like-numbered or -lettered headings under one another. As identations go farther in, ideas become more specific.

```
Thesis:
    I.
         A.
              1.
                   a.
                   b.
              2.
                   a.
                   b.
         B.
              1.
              2.
   II.
```

And the outline would continue until fully developed. If you have so much material that you have to subdivide still further, arabic numerals and small letters in parentheses are commonly used, but only hugely complicated writing projects need that much subdivision. Be sure to cast all headings in parallel grammatical form: phrases or sentences, but not both in the same outline.

Caution   Some readers and instructors grow wrathful if you write only one lonesome item as a subcategory, thinking that you can't divide anything into one part (and that's what an outline does — divide or analyze ideas). Let's say that in an outline on earthquakes you write:

```
D.  Probable results of an earthquake
    1.  Houses stripped of their paint
```

If you tell your reader — and yourself — that you are going to discuss the *probable results* of an earthquake, logically you need to include more than one result. If that one point is all you have to say, then why not just combine your categories:

```
D.  Houses stripped of paint during an earthquake
```

More likely, your use of only one subpoint indicates that you need to do more thinking, to discover more evidence. With a little more thought or reading, you might write:

```
D.  Probable results of an earthquake
    1.  Broken water mains
    2.  Collapsed bridges
    3.  Gaps in road surfaces
    4.  Cracks in foundations
    5.  Houses stripped of their paint
```

Not only have you now come up with more points, but you have also arranged them in an order of diminishing importance. This careful planning will save you some decisions when you write. ("Now, which of these results do I deal with first?")

A *formal topic outline* for a long paper about city and small-town drivers might be constructed like this. Notice that the writer decided to drop the subdivision "physical fitness" because it is not directly related to the subject of driving habits.

```
                 Drivers in Cities and Small Towns
Thesis: City drivers are quite different from small-town
drivers
   I.  Traits of drivers
       A.  City drivers
           1.  Fast-paced lifestyle
           2.  Aggressive
           3.  Impatient
           4.  Tense
           5.  Often frustrated
       B.  Small-town drivers
           1.  Slower-paced lifestyle
           2.  Laid back
           3.  Patient
           4.  Relaxed
           5.  Not easily upset
```

```
II.  Behavior as drivers
     A.  City drivers
         1.  Little consideration for other drivers
             a.  Horn blowing
             b.  Shouting
             c.  Not using proper signals
                 (1)  Turning across lanes
                 (2)  Stopping without warning
         2.  Disregard for pedestrians
         3.  Speeding
             a.  Running red lights
             b.  Having many accidents
     B.  Small-town drivers
         1.  Considerate of other drivers
             a.  Driving defensively
             b.  Less yelling
             c.  Signaling
                 (1)  For turning
                 (2)  For stopping
         2.  Regard for pedestrians
         3.  Driving within speed limits
             a.  Observing traffic lights
             b.  Fewer accidents
```

From this outline, you can see how a formal outline unfolds.

Sometimes you will need the top-of-the-line Mercedes—a *sentence outline*. If a topic outline is not thorough enough to help you know what you want to say or how to say it, or to indicate to you how ideas relate, you should consider changing the topic headings to sentence headings. In a sentence outline *every* heading is a complete sentence. The following is the outline on types of drivers with the headings changed from topic headings to sentence headings. Although you may not need to use a sentence outline for most of the brief papers you write in college, knowing how to construct such a complete outline will prove valuable to you for longer, complex papers.

```
            Drivers in Cities and Small Towns
Thesis: City drivers are quite different from small-town
drivers
    I.  The lifestyles and attitudes of city drivers and
        small-town drivers are different.
        A.  City drivers are always in a hurry.
            1.  They are impatient.
            2.  They are often frustrated and aggressive.
        B.  Small-town drivers live slower-paced lives.
            1.  They are relaxed.
            2.  They are seldom frustrated on the streets.
   II.  The behavior of city drivers and small-town drivers
        is different.
        A.  City drivers are aggressive.
```

     1. They show little consideration for other drivers.
       a. They blow their car horns often.
       b. They shout at other drivers frequently.
     2. They show no respect for pedestrians.
     3. They do not obey traffic laws.
       a. They do not use proper signals.
       b. They turn across lanes.
       c. They stop without warning.
       d. They speed.
     4. They have many accidents.
  B. Small-town drivers are laid back.
     1. They are considerate of other drivers.
       a. They drive carefully.
       b. They rarely yell or honk at other drivers.
     2. They show concern for pedestrians.
     3. They obey traffic laws.
       a. They use proper signals.
       b. They turn properly.
       c. They stop slowly.
       d. They speed less.
     4. They have fewer accidents.

A title goes at the top of a formal outline just as it goes at the beginning of an essay. For the contrast of city and small-town drivers, we used the title "Drivers in Cities and Small Towns," but with a little thought you could come up with something better to let your readers know what the essay is about as well as to get their attention. Your title should be clear and catchy, but not cute.

FOR GROUP LEARNING: OUTLINING

Discuss the topic outline on page 336 with your peer group or the entire class. Answer the following questions.

1. Would this outline guide a student writer in organizing an essay? Is the organization logical? Is it easy to follow? Try to think of other possible arrangements for the ideas.
2. Does this outline indicate sufficient details to develop a paper? About how many words would an essay developed from this outline be?
3. What would have to be added to this outline to make a satisfactory essay?
4. Do you think this outline would lead to an interesting essay? Why?
5. What possible pitfalls would the writer using this outline need to avoid?

Exercise: Outlining

1. Select one of your groups of ideas from the practices in Chapter 14, "Strategies for Generating Ideas." Using those ideas, construct a formal topic outline that might serve as a guide for an essay.
2. Now turn that topic outline into a formal sentence outline.
3. Discuss both outlines with your classmates and your instructor, bringing up any difficulties you encountered. If you get any better notions for organizing your ideas, change the outline.
4. Write an essay based on your outline.

CHAPTER 16

Strategies for Drafting

Learning to write well involves learning what questions to ask yourself. Some key questions are How can I get going on this draft? What shall I do if I get stuck? How can I flesh out the bones of my paper? How can I begin and end my paper effectively? How can I keep my reader with me? In this chapter we compile advice to get you going and keep you going on your draft, from the first paragraph to the last. We also show how your draft can achieve the coherence it needs to keep your reader cued.

STARTING YOUR DRAFT

Making a Start Enjoyable

Some writers find that if they can just make the art of writing start out playfully, like a game, they will find themselves at work before they know it.

Time yourself   Try being an Anthony Trollope: set your watch, alarm clock, or egg timer and vow to finish a page of draft before the buzzer sounds or your time expires. Don't stop for anything—if you find yourself writing drivel, which you can always cross out later, just push on. This is a way to prompt yourself to hurry, if your natural bent is to dawdle.

Slow to a crawl   If such speed quotas don't work for you—and some people might find them a source of sheer paralysis—time yourself to write with exaggerated laziness, completing, say, not a page every fifteen minutes, but a sentence. Maybe your speed will improve. At least you'll have a sentence.

Begin badly — on purpose For fun, begin by writing a deliberately crummy sentence, full of mistakes and misspellings and fuzzy mush-headedness. Then cross it out and write another, better sentence. This technique may help you clear the false starts out of the way quickly so that from then on your paper can only improve.

Begin on scrap paper There is something intimidating about a blank white sheet of paper that may have cost two or three cents. Some writers feel reluctant to mess up such a beautiful item. A bit of advice on that score comes from John Legget, novelist, biographer, and former director of the Writer's Workshop at the University of Iowa. To write preliminary notes, he uses the back of an old envelope or other scrap paper from his wastebasket. In this way, he told an interviewer, he is able to get started, feeling no guilt about "spoiling a nice piece of paper with my thoughts."

Tape-record yourself Talk a first draft of your paper into a tape recorder. Then play it back. Then write. Unless you are a skilled stenographer (and you have one of those tape recorders with a stop pedal that may be turned off and on easily while you type), you probably would find it hard to transcribe your spoken words, but this technique can sometimes set your mind in motion.

Imagine you're giving a speech On your feet, in front of an imaginary cheering crowd, spontaneously utter an opening paragraph. Then — quick! — write it down.

Write in a role Pretend you are someone else (your instructor? your best friend? a screen star? some writer whose work you know well?) and write in that person's voice. Or invent an imaginary character and write as that character would. William York Tindall, a literary scholar and critic, once confided that he had been unable to write his doctoral dissertation, couldn't get a handle on it, until one day he hit upon the notion of writing it as though he were Edward Gibbon, cool and cynical author of *The Decline and Fall of the Roman Empire*. Once he tried on Gibbon's voice, Tindall said, his own writing took off at a brisk clip.

Try the Great Chef method According to the legend, the great French chef Escoffier, by smelling a dish of food, could analyze it for its ingredients and then go into his kitchen and duplicate it. In similar fashion, analyze a paragraph by another writer — pick a paragraph you admire — and cook up a new paragraph of your own from its ingredients. Take care to avoid plagiarism (p. 625).

Write with excessive simple-mindedness   Do a whole paragraph or a whole paper the way a six-year-old talks: in plain, short, simple sentences. Karin Mack and Eric Skjei, in *Overcoming Writing Blocks,* call this technique "Dick-and-Janing," from those first-grade readers featuring Dick and Jane doing simple things in simple sentences. (For example, "See Dick run," or "Go, Jane, go.") Dick-and-Janing works like this. Suppose you're writing an essay on some complex topic, such as the influence of television on family life. You might begin: "Television is fun. It brings families together. They all watch *The Cosby Show.* Television is bad. Nobody talks. Nobody says how was your day. They watch the Huxtables' day . . ." and so on. Now, you wouldn't want to turn in a paper written like that; your readers would think you were still in third grade. But you have something down on paper that you can retool.

Address a sympathetic reader   Write as if you were writing to a close friend. You might even begin, "Dear Friend, How's the hometown treating you? I am writing a paper for an English class that I think you might like to read"—and so on. (You can cross out that beginning later.) If you have a picture of that friend, place it in front of you.

Begin writing the part you find most appetizing   Start in the middle or at the end. Novelist Bill Downey, in a book of advice on writing, *Right Brain . . . Write On!,* urges writers to tackle jobs for which they feel the most excitement. "This makes writing different from childhood," he observes, "when we were forced to eat our vegetables first and then get our dessert. Writers are allowed to have their dessert first." When you begin a writing task, try skipping the tough-looking steak for a while and start with the brownie. Set down the thoughts that come most readily to mind.

RESTARTING

When you have to write a long or demanding essay that you can't finish at one sitting, a special challenge often will arise. If a writing task drags on and on, sometimes you may return to it only to find yourself stalled. You tromp your starter and nothing happens. Your engine seems reluctant to turn over. In such a fix, don't call AAA for a jump-start—try the following suggestions for getting back on the road.

Reread what you have written   When you return to work, spend a few minutes rereading what you have already written. This method was a favorite of Ernest Hemingway, who, even when writing a novel, would begin a day's work by rereading his manuscript from page 1. Trollope urged this technique on any beginning writer: "By reading what he has last written, just before he recommences his task, the writer will catch the tone and spirit of what he is then saying, and will avoid the fault of seeming to be unlike himself." (Just don't let rereading become a way to evade the writing itself.)

Try snowplowing *Snowplowing* is the term invented by Jacqueline Jackson in her book about writing (and other things) *Turn Not Pale, Beloved Snail.* When you reach a point in a writing job that stops you cold — an obstinate passage or paragraph that won't come right — you imitate a snowplow and charge ahead through the difficulty:

> The plow gets to the bank and can't push it any farther. Then it goes back, revs up, comes barreling along the plowed snow, hits the bank and goes through — or at least a little farther.
>
> I reread the earlier paragraphs . . . and approach the impasse pretending it isn't there. I want to take it by surprise. Then when I'm suddenly upon it, I swerve. I don't reread it, for this would keep me in the same old rut. Instead I start writing madly, on the strength of the new thrust. This often gets me a few sentences farther, sometimes right through the bank.

Pause in midstream End a writing session by breaking off in mid-sentence or mid-paragraph. Just leave a sentence trailing off into space, though you may know perfectly well what its closing words should be. That way, when you return to your task, you can sit down and start writing again immediately.

Leave yourself hints for how to continue Maybe you're tired — it's been a long day, and you can't write any more. Quit, but if your head still holds any notions you have not yet expressed, jot them down. In a few words, tell yourself what you think might come next or write the first sentence of the next section. Then, when you come back to work, you will face not a blank wall but some rich and suggestive graffiti.

PARAGRAPHING

Even the most willing readers need occasionally to pause, to digest what you tell them. So prose is written not in large, indigestible lumps, but in *paragraphs* — small units, each beginning with an indent, each more or less self-contained, each contributing something new in support of the main point of an essay or article. Writers dwell on one idea at a time. They state it and develop it amply, illustrating it with an example or supporting it with a few facts. Then, finished with that point, they indent and start making a further point in a fresh paragraph.

A paragraph indentation signifies a pause, as if the writer were taking a breath, finished making one point and ready to begin another. Paragraphs can be as short as one sentence or as long as a page. Sometimes their length is governed by the audience for whom they are written, by the purpose of the writing, or by the medium in which they appear. News writers, for instance, tend to write in brief, one- or two-sentence paragraphs to make their stories easy to cut to fit a page. Newspaper readers, consuming facts like popcorn, find that the short paragraphing allows them to skim an article quickly. For long, meaty paragraphs in a newspaper, you have to read the editorials or the columns. Academic writers, on the other hand, assume some willingness on the part of their colleagues to read through long paragraphs in a specialized treatise.

Why pay attention to paragraphs? You have to keep your readers with you every step of the way. Paragraphing helps you develop each of your main points fully and clearly, providing signposts to guide your reader through what you say, using examples and abundant evidence, before going on. Paragraphing effectively means taking your readers by the hand and not only telling but *showing* them, with plenty of detailed evidence, exactly what you mean.

Using Topic Sentences

One tried-and-true way to draft an effective paragraph is to write down in advance one sentence that spells out what the paragraph's central point is to be. We call such a sentence a *topic sentence.* It supplies the foundation on which to build the rest of the paragraph. In expository writing, the topic sentence should be stated somewhere in the paragraph. Often when you read good clear prose, especially writing that explains or argues, you can pick out a paragraph's topic sentence.

Topic sentence as first sentence   Usually, as in this example from James David Barber's *The Presidential Character: Predicting Performance in the White House,* the topic sentence appears first in the paragraph, followed by sentences that clarify, illustrate, and support what it says. (In all the following examples, we have put the topic sentences in *italics.*)

> *The first baseline in defining Presidential types is activity-passivity.* How much energy does the man invest in his Presidency? Lyndon Johnson went at his day like a human cyclone, coming to rest long after the sun went down. Calvin Coolidge often slept eleven hours a night and still needed a nap in the middle of the day. In between, the Presidents array themselves on the high or low side of the activity line.

This paragraph moves from the general to the specific. The topic sentence clearly shows at the outset what the paragraph is to be about. The second sentence defines *activity-passivity.* The third and fourth sentences, by citing extremes at either end of the baseline, supply illustrations: active Johnson, passive Coolidge. The final sentence makes a generalization that reinforces the central point.

Topic sentence near the beginning of paragraph   Not every topic sentence stands at the beginning of its paragraph. Sometimes the first sentence of a new paragraph functions as a transition, linking what is to come with what has gone before, as in the following illustration from the essay "On Societies as Organisms" by science writer and physician Lewis Thomas. In such a paragraph the *second* sentence might be the topic sentence. The paragraph quoted here follows one about insects that ends, "and we violate science when we try to read human meanings in their arrangements."

> It is hard for a bystander not to do so. *Ants are so much like human beings as to be an embarrassment.* They farm fungi, raise aphids as livestock, launch armies into wars, use chemical sprays to alarm and confuse enemies, capture slaves. The families of weaver ants engage in child labor, holding their larvae like shuttles to spin out the thread that sews the leaves together for their fungus gardens. They exchange information ceaselessly. They do everything but watch television.

Topic sentence at end of paragraph   Occasionally a writer, especially one attempting to persuade the reader to agree, piles detail upon detail throughout a paragraph. Then, with a dramatic flourish, the writer *concludes* with the topic sentence. You can see this technique in the following paragraph, from student Heidi Kessler's paper in response to a writing assignment in sociology: to report on a contemporary social problem and voice an opinion on it.

> A fourteen-year-old writes to an advice columnist in my hometown newspaper that she has "done it" lots of times and sex is "no big deal." At the neighborhood clinic where my aunt works, a hardened sixteen-year-old requests her third abortion. A girl-child I know has two children of her own, but no husband. A college student in my dorm now finds herself sterile from a "social disease" picked up during casual sexual encounters. Multiply these examples by thousands. *It seems clear to me that women, who fought so hard for sexual freedom equal to that of men, have emerged from the battle not as joyous free spirits but as the sexual revolution's walking wounded.*

By the time you come to the end of the paragraph, you might be ready to accept the conclusion in the topic sentence. Reversing the most usual order of paragraph development (to make a general statement and back it up with particulars), this paragraph moves instead from the particular to the general: from the examples of individual girl-children and women to the larger statement about American women made in the topic sentence at the end.

Topic idea   It is also possible to find a perfectly unified, well-organized paragraph that has no topic sentence at all, like this one from "New York" by Gay Talese.

> Each afternoon in New York a rather seedy saxophone player, his cheeks blown out like a spinnaker, stands on the sidewalk playing *Danny Boy* in such a sad, sensitive way that he soon has half the neighborhood peeking out of windows tossing nickels, dimes and quarters at his feet. Some of the coins roll under parked cars, but most of them are caught in his outstretched hand. The saxophone player is a street musician named Joe Gabler; for the past thirty years he has serenaded every block in New York and has sometimes been tossed as much as $100 a day in coins. He is also hit with buckets of water, empty beer cans and eggs, and chased by wild dogs. He is believed to be the last of New York's ancient street musicians.

No one sentence neatly sums up the writer's idea. Like most effective paragraphs that lack a topic sentence, Talese's paragraph contains something just as good: a *topic idea*. The author doesn't allow his paragraph to wander aimlessly. He knows exactly what he wants to achieve: a description of how Joe Gabler, a famous New York street musician, plies his trade. Because Talese succeeds in keeping this main purpose firmly in mind, the main point—that Gabler meets both reward and abuse—is clear to the reader as well.

Question to answer   A paragraph is likely to have a strong topic idea, too, if you begin it with a question. You'll probably find it easy to organize the rest of the paragraph around the answer to that question. Here is a paragraph, by psychoanalyst Erik Erikson, organized by the question-and-answer method.

> Is the sense of identity conscious? At times, of course, it seems only too conscious. For between the double prongs of vital inner need and inexorable outer demand, the as yet experimenting individual may become the victim of a transitory extreme identity consciousness, which is the common core of the many forms of "self-consciousness" typical for youth. Where the processes of identity formation are prolonged (a factor which can bring creative gain), such preoccupation with the "self-image" also prevails. We are thus most aware of our identity when we are just about to gain it and when we (with that startle which motion pictures call a "double take") are somewhat surprised to make its acquaintance; or, again, when we are just about to enter a crisis and feel the encroachment of identity confusion.

Writing by the topic sentence method may not help every writer, but if you generally have trouble organizing an essay, you might try it. One foolproof way to plan is to make a sentence outline (see Lisa Chickos's outline on p. 619) and then write a paragraph enlarging on each section of the outline.

With practice, developing a paragraph around one main point can become almost second nature. A writer accustomed to this method can see exactly where more examples and illustrations are called for: if a paragraph looks skimpy and consists of little besides the topic sentence, then it probably needs more meat.

The more pointed and lively your topic sentence, the more interesting the paragraph. If your topic sentence leads off your paragraph, think of it as bait to hook your readers and tow them along with you. "There are many things wrong with television" may be a little dull and vague, but at least it's a start for a paragraph. Zero in on one specific fault, change the sentence to "Of all television's faults, the one I can't stand is its nightly melodramatization of the news" and go on to illustrate your point with two or three melodramatic newscasts that you remember. An arresting paragraph—and an arresting paper—will probably result from that topic sentence. For more specific suggestions on developing your ideas in paragraphs and essays, see Chapter 17, "Strategies for Developing."

Exercise: Topic Sentences

Discuss each of the following topic sentences with your peer group, answering
these questions:

> Is it clear?
> Is it limited?
> Is it eye-catching?
> Would it lead to an interesting paragraph?
> How might you develop the idea? Can you improve it?

1. College is an interesting place to be.
2. Television commercials stereotype people.
3. Teenagers face many problems growing up.
4. Getting money for college is difficult.
5. Living away from home for the first time is hard.
6. Being absent from class is like a disease.
7. Violence in movies can be harmful.
8. I have been influenced by teachers.
9. I like American-made cars.
10. Student parking at this college is a problem.
11. Housework is time-consuming.
12. It's good for a child to have a pet.
13. The flea market is a good place to buy jewelry.
14. Clothes for college have changed.
15. Friendship is important in life.
16. Pollution should be controlled.
17. Everybody should recycle wastes.
18. I taught my child the value of money.
19. *Casablanca* is my favorite movie.
20. With freedom comes responsibility.

Writing an Opening

Even writers with something to say occasionally find it hard to begin. Often
they are so intent on writing a brilliant opening paragraph that they freeze,
unable to write anything at all. Brilliant beginnings are fine if you can get
them, but they may be gifts of God. "Start with a bang," Richard Strauss
advised his fellow composers, and he opened his symphonic poem *Thus
Spake Zarathustra* with a sunrise: the whole orchestra delivers a tremendous
explosion of sound. But in most writing, brilliance and orchestral explosions
are neither expected nor required. In truth, when you sit down to draft an
essay, you can ease your way into the job by simply deciding to set words —
any words — on paper, without trying at all for an arresting or witty opening.
A time-honored approach to your opening paragraph is to write it *last,* after
you have written the body of your essay and know exactly in what direction
it is headed. Some writers like to write a first draft with a long, driveling

beginning and then in rewriting cut it down to the most dramatic, exciting, or interesting statement, discarding everything that has gone before. Others use the introduction as a summary guide for themselves and their readers. At whatever point in the writing process you set about fashioning an opening paragraph of your own, remember that your chief aim is to persuade your readers to lay aside their preoccupations and enter, with you as guide, the world set forth in your essay.

Begin with a story   Often a simple anecdote, by capturing your readers' interest, serves as a good beginning. Here is how writer Harry Crews opens his essay "The Car":

> The other day, there arrived in the mail a clipping sent by a friend of mine. It had been cut from a Long Beach, California, newspaper and dealt with a young man who had eluded police for fifty-five minutes while he raced over freeways and through city streets at speeds up to 130 miles per hour. During the entire time, he ripped his clothes off and threw them out the window bit by bit. It finally took twenty-five patrol cars and a helicopter to catch him. When they did, he said that God had given him the car, and that he had "found God."

Most of us, reading such an anecdote, want to read on. What will the author say next? What has the anecdote to do with the essay as a whole? Crews has aroused our curiosity.

Introduce your subject and comment on it   In some essays, the author introduces a subject and then turns momentarily away from it to bring in a vital bit of detail, as in this opening paragraph by contemporary American writer A. Alvarez from "Shiprock," an essay about climbing a mountain:

> I suppose the first sight of a mountain is always the best. Later, when you are waiting to start, you may grow to hate the brute, because you are afraid. And when, finally, you are climbing, you are never aware of the mountain as a mountain: it is merely so many little areas of rock to be worked out in terms of hand-holds, foot-holds and effort, like so many chess problems. But when you first see it in the distance, remote and beautiful and unknown, then there seems some reason for climbing.

That paragraph establishes the author as someone with firsthand knowledge. Alvarez proceeds smoothly from the opening paragraph about mountain climbing in general to the heart of his essay, with a sentence of transition at the start of his second paragraph: "I first saw Shiprock on a midsummer day."

Ask a question   A well-written essay can also begin with a question and answer, as writer James H. Austin begins "Four Kinds of Chance":

> What is chance? Dictionaries define it as something fortuitous that happens unpredictably without discernible human intention. Chance is unintentional and capricious, but we needn't conclude that chance is immune from human intervention. Indeed, chance plays several distinct roles when humans react creatively with one another and with their environment.

To ask a question like that and answer it with a clear definition is often an effective way to begin. The reader will expect the essay to supply an answer.

State an opinion   To challenge readers, a writer may begin with a controversial opinion, as writer Wade Thompson did:

> Unlike any other sport, football is played solely for the benefit of the spectator. If you take the spectator away from any other game, the game could still survive on its own. Thus tennis players love tennis, whether or not anyone is watching. Golfers are almost churlish in their dedication to their game. Ping-Pong players never look around. Basketball players can dribble and shoot for hours without hearing a single cheer. Even baseball might survive the deprivation, despite the lack of parks. Softball surely would. But if you took away the spectators, if you demolished the grandstands and boarded up the stadium, it is inconceivable to think that any football would be played in the eerie privacy of the field itself. No football team ever plays another team just for the fun of playing football. Army plays Navy, Michigan plays Purdue, P.S. 123 plays P.S. 124, only with the prospect of a loud crowd on hand.

After his first, startling remark, Thompson generalizes about games unlike football: "If you take the spectator away from any other game, the game could still survive on its own." Then the author backs up his generalization with examples of such games: tennis, golf, Ping-Pong, basketball, baseball, softball. Finally Thompson returns to his original point, thus emphasizing the direction his essay will take.

End with thesis sentence   An effective opening paragraph often ends, as does Thompson's, with a statement of the essay's main point. To end your opening paragraph this way, after first having captured your readers' attention, is to take your readers by the hand and lead them in exactly the direction your essay is to go. No one can ask more of any introduction. Such a statement can be brief, as in the second sentence of this powerful opening of an essay by educator George B. Leonard called "No School?":

HOW TO WRITE AN OPENING
If you find it difficult to write an opening paragraph, try these suggestions.

1. Don't worry *too* hard about capturing and transfixing your readers with your opening. It is enough to introduce an idea.
2. Open with an anecdote, a description, a comparison, a definition, a quotation, a question, or some vital background.
3. Set forth your thesis (as discussed on p. 322).
4. Hint in advance what you will say in paragraph two.

The most obvious barrier between our children and the kind of education that can free their enormous potential seems to be the educational system itself: a vast, suffocating web of people, practices and presumptions, kindly in intent, ponderous in response. Now, when true educational alternatives are at last becoming clear, we may overlook the simplest: no school.

Writing a Conclusion

The final paragraphs of an essay linger longest in the readers' minds. Here is a conclusion that certainly does so. In "Once More to the Lake," about returning with his young son to a vacation spot the author had known and loved as a child, essayist E. B. White conveys his confused feeling that he has gone back in time to his own childhood, that he and his son are one. Then, at the end of the essay, in an unforgettable image, he remembers how old he really is and realizes the inevitable passing of generations.

> When the others went swimming my son said he was going in, too. He pulled his dripping trunks from the line where they had hung all through the shower and wrung them out. Languidly, and with no thought of going in, I watched him, his hard little body, skinny and bare, saw him wince slightly as he pulled up around his vitals the small, soggy, icy garment. As he buckled the swollen belt, suddenly my groin felt the chill of death.

White's concluding paragraph is a classic example of an effective way to end. It begins with a sentence of transition that points back to what has gone before and at the same time looks ahead. After the transition, White leads us quickly to his final, chilling insight. Then he stops.

Yet even a quiet ending can be effective, as long as it signals clearly that the essay is finished. Sometimes the best way to conclude a story, for instance, is simply to stop when the story is over. This is what journalist Martin Gansberg does in his true account of the fatal beating of a young woman, Kitty Genovese, in full view of residents of a Queens, New York, apartment house, who, unwilling to become involved, did nothing to interfere. Here is the last paragraph of his account, "38 Who Saw Murder Didn't Call Police":

> It was 4:25 A.M. when the ambulance arrived to take the body of Miss Genovese. It drove off. "Then," a solemn police detective said, "the people came out."

For an essay that traces causes or effects, analyzes, evaluates, or argues, a deft concluding thought reinforces your main idea. Notice the definite click with which former heavyweight champion Gene Tunney closes the door on "The Long Count," an analysis of his two victorious fights with Jack Dempsey, whose boxing style differed markedly from Tunney's own.

> Jack Dempsey was a great fighter—possibly the greatest that ever entered a ring. Looking back objectively, one has to conclude that he was more valuable to the sport or "The Game" than any prizefighter of his time. Whether you consider it from his worth as a gladiator or from the point of view of the box office, he was tops. His name in his most glorious days was magic among his people, and today, twenty years after, the name Jack Dempsey is still magic. This tells a

volume in itself. As one who has always had pride in his profession as well as his professional theories, and possessing a fair share of Celtic romanticism, I wish that we could have met when we were both at our unquestionable best. We could have decided many questions, to me the most important of which is whether "a good boxer can always lick a good fighter."

   I still say yes.

It's easy to suggest what *not* to do at the end of an essay. Don't leave your readers suspended in midair, half expecting you to go on. Don't restate everything you've already said. Don't introduce a brand-new topic that leads away from the point of your essay. And don't feel you have to introduce your final paragraph with an obvious signal that the end is near. Words and phrases like "In conclusion," "As I have said," or "So, as we see," have their place, but do without them in the conclusion and your essay is likely to end more gracefully. In a long, complicated paper, a terse summation of your main points right before your concluding sentences may help your reader grasp your ideas; but a short paper usually requires either no summary at all or little more than a single sentence or two.

   "How *do* you write an ending, then?" you might well ask. An apt *quotation* can neatly round out an essay, as literary critic Malcolm Cowley demonstrates at the end of an essay in *The View from Eighty,* his discussion of the pitfalls and compensations of old age.

   "Eighty years old!" the great Catholic poet Paul Claudel wrote in his journal. "No eyes left, no ears, no teeth, no legs, no wind! And when all is said and done, how astonishingly well one does without them!"

In a sharp criticism of American schools, humorist Russell Baker uses another technique for ending his essay "School vs. Education": that of stating or *restating* his claim. Baker's main point is that schools do not educate, and he concludes:

   Afterward, the former student's destiny fulfilled, his life rich with Oriental carpets, rare porcelain and full bank accounts, he may one day find himself with the leisure and the inclination to open a book with a curious mind, and start to become educated.

It is also possible to introduce at the end of your essay not new topics that you haven't time to go into, but a few new *implications* concerning the topic you *have* covered. As you draw to a close and are restating your main point, ask yourself, "What now?" "What is the significance of what I have said?" Why not try to leave your reader with one or two provocative thoughts to ponder? Obstreperous 1920s debunker H. L. Mencken uses this technique in "The Libido for the Ugly," an essay about the ugliness of American cities and towns.

   Here is something that the psychologists have so far neglected: the love of ugliness for its own sake, the lust to make the world intolerable. Its habitat is the United States. Out of the melting pot emerges a race which hates beauty as it hates truth. The etiology of this madness deserves a great deal more study than it has got. There must be causes behind it; it arises and flourishes in obedience to biological laws, and not as a mere act of God. What, precisely, are the terms of those laws? And why do they run stronger in America than elsewhere? Let some honest *Privat Dozent*° in pathological sociology apply himself to the problem.

Exercise: Introductions and Conclusions

Introductions and conclusions frame an essay, contributing to the unity of the whole. The introduction sets up the subject and the main idea; the conclusion reaffirms the thesis and rounds off the ideas. Discuss the following introductions and conclusions with your peer group.

I. The following are two possible beginning paragraphs from a student essay on the importance of children learning how to swim.

A. Man inhabits a world made up of over 70 percent water. In addition to these great bodies of water, he has built millions of swimming pools for sports and leisure activities. At one time or another most people will be faced with either the danger of drowning or the challenge of aquatic recreation. For these reasons, it is essential that we learn to swim. Being a competitive swimmer and a swimming instructor, I fully realize the importance of knowing how to swim.

B. Four-year-old Carl, curious like most children, last spring ventured out onto his pool patio. He fell into the pool and, not knowing how to swim, helplessly sank to the bottom. Minutes later his uncle found the child and brought him to the surface. Since Carl had no pulse, his uncle immediately administered CPR on him until the paramedics arrived. Eventually he was revived. During his stay in the hospital, his mother signed him up for beginning swimming classes. Carl was a lucky one. Unlike thousands of other children and adults, he got a second chance.

1. Which introduction is more effective? Why?
2. What would the body of this essay be? What kinds of evidence would be included?
3. Write a suitable conclusion for this essay.

II. If you were to read the following introductions from professional essays, would you want to read the entire essay? Why?

A. During my ninth hour underground, as I scrambled up a slanting tunnel through the powdered gypsum, Rick Bridges turned to me and said, "You know, this whole area was just discovered Tuesday." (David Roberts, "Caving Comes into Its Golden Age: A New Mexico Marvel," *Smithsonian* Nov. 1988: 52)

B. From the batting average on the back of a George Brett baseball card to

Privat Dozent. A lecturer at a German university.

the interest rate fluctuations that determine whether the economy grows or stagnates, Americans are fascinated by statistics. (Stephen E. Nordlinger, "By the Numbers," *St. Petersburg Times* 6 Nov. 1988: 11)

C. "What does it look like under there?"

It was always this question back then, always the same pattern of hello and what's your name, what happened to your eye and what's under there. (Natalie Kusz, "Waiting for a Glass Eye," from *Road Song* [Farrar, Straus and Giroux]; reprinted in *Harper's,* Nov. 1990)

III. Evaluate the effectiveness of each of the following introductions from student essays.

A. On June 4, 1985, Los Angeles police arrested Jerald Curtis Johns. Police believe he may have raped as many as 100 women, ranging in age from 24 to 71, living in a ten block radius (*Time* 5 Sept. 1985). But of those 100 women, only 13 reported rape. This situation is commonplace: most rapes are not reported.

B. Is it possible for a young girl of twelve or so who has been sexually and mentally abused to recover her self-worth and have a productive and happy life? The movie *The Color Purple* attempts to answer that question.

IV. How effective are the following introductions and conclusions from student essays? Could they be improved? If so, how? If they are satisfactory, explain why. What would be an eye-catching yet informative title for each one's essay?

A. Recently a friend down from New York astonished me with stories of several people infected—some with AIDS—by stepping on needles washed up on the New Jersey beaches. This is just one incident of pollution, a devastating problem in our society today. Pollution is increasing in our world today because of greed, apathy, and Congress's inability to control this problem. . . .

Wouldn't it be nice to have a pollution-free world without medical wastes floating in the water and washing up on our beaches? Without garbage scattered on the streets? With every corporation abiding by the laws set by Congress? In the future we can have a pollution-free world, but it is going to take the cooperation of everyone, including Congress, to ensure our survival on this Planet Earth.

B. The divorce rate has risen 700 percent in this century and continues to rise. More than one out of every two couples who are married end up in divorce. Over one million children a year are affected by divorce in the family. From these statistics it is clear that one of the greatest problems concerning the family today is divorce and the adverse effects it has on our society. . . .

Divorce causes problems that change people for life. The number of divorces will continue to exceed the 700 percent figure unless married couples learn to communicate, to accept their mates unconditionally, and to sacrificially give of themselves.

Achieving Coherence

Effective writing is well organized. It proceeds in some sensible order, each sentence following naturally from the one before it. Yet even well-organized prose can be hard to read unless it contains *coherence*. To make your writing coherent, you can use various devices that tie together words in a sentence, sentences in a paragraph, paragraphs in an essay. When you write, you will probably use a combination of techniques to guide your readers through your ideas.

Transitions   You already use transitions every day, in both your writing and your speech. You can't help it. Instinctively you realize that certain words and phrases help your readers and listeners follow your line of thought. But some writers, in a rush to get through what they have to say, omit important links between thoughts. Mistakenly, they assume that because a connection is clear to them it will automatically be clear to their readers.

If your readers sometimes have trouble following you, you may find it useful to pay attention to transitions. Often just a word, phrase, or sentence of transition inserted in the right place will transform a seemingly disconnected passage into a coherent one.

Back in Chapter 6, we discussed time markers, those transitions especially useful for telling a story or analyzing a process because they make clear *when* one thing happens in relation to another. Time markers include words and phrases like *then, soon, the following day,* and *in a little while.* (For that discussion, see p. 133.) But not all transitions mark time. The English language contains many words and phrases that make clear other connections between or within sentences.

Consider choosing one of the following commonly used *transitional markers* to fit your purpose. They are grouped here by purpose or the kind of relation or connection they establish.

TO MARK TIME	then, soon, first, second, next, recently, the following day, in a little while, meanwhile, after, later, in the past
TO MARK PLACE OR DIRECTION	in the distance, close by, near, far away, above, below, to the right, on the other side, opposite, to the west, next door
TO SUMMARIZE OR RESTATE	in other words, to put it another way, in brief, in simpler terms, on the whole, in fact, in a word, to sum up, in short, in conclusion, to conclude, finally, therefore
TO RELATE CAUSE AND EFFECT OR RESULT	therefore, accordingly, hence, thus, for, so, consequently, as a result, because of
TO ADD OR AMPLIFY OR LIST	and, also, too, besides, as well, moreover, in addition, furthermore, in effect, second, in the second place, again, next
TO COMPARE	similarly, likewise, in like manner

TO CONCEDE	whereas, on the other hand, with that in mind, still, and yet, even so, in spite of, despite, at least
TO CONTRAST	on the other hand, but, or, however, unlike, nevertheless, on the contrary, conversely, in contrast, instead
TO INDICATE PURPOSE	to this end, for this purpose, with this objective
TO EXPRESS CONDITION	although, though
TO GIVE EXAMPLES OR SPECIFY	for example, for instance, in this case, in particular, to illustrate
TO QUALIFY	for the most part, by and large, with few exceptions, mainly, in most cases, some, sometimes
TO EMPHASIZE	it is true, truly, indeed, of course, to be sure, obviously, without doubt, evidently, clearly, understandably

Occasionally a whole sentence serves as a transition. Often, but not always, it is the first sentence of a new paragraph. When the transitional sentence appears in that position, it harks back to the contents of the previous paragraph while simultaneously hinting at the direction the new paragraph is to take. Here is a sample, excerpted from an essay by Marsha Traugot about adopting older and handicapped children, in which the transitional sentence (*in italics*) begins a new paragraph.

> ... Some exchanges hold monthly meetings where placement workers looking for a match can discuss waiting children or families, and they also sponsor parties where children, workers, and prospective parents meet informally.
> *And if a match still cannot be made?* Exchanges and other child welfare organizations now employ media blitzes as aggressive as those of commercial advertising. ...

By repeating the key word *match* in her transitional sentence and by inserting the word *still*, Traugot makes clear that in what follows she will build on what has gone before. At the same time, by making the transitional sentence a rhetorical question, Traugot promises that the new paragraph will introduce fresh material, in this case answering the question.

Transition paragraphs   Transitions may be even longer than sentences. When you write an essay, especially one that is long and complicated, you'll find that to move clearly from one idea to the next will sometimes require an entire paragraph of transition:

```
     So far, we have been dwelling on the physical and
psychological effects of driving nonstop for more than
two hundred miles.  Now let's reflect on causes.  Why do
people become addicted to their steering wheels?
```

Usually, such a paragraph will be shorter than other body paragraphs, but you'll want to allow it whatever space it may require. Often, as in the preceding example, it makes a comment on the structure of the essay, looking back and pointing forward. The writer is taking time out to explain what she is doing so that her readers may readily follow her.

Let a transition paragraph come to your aid, too, whenever you go off on one branch of argument and then return to your main trunk. Here's an example from a masterly writer, Lewis Thomas, in an essay, "Things Unflattened by Science." A medical doctor, Thomas has been complaining in his essay that biologists keep expecting medical researchers to come up with quick answers to intractable problems: cancer, schizophrenia, stress. He takes most of a paragraph to explain why he doesn't think medical science can solve the problem of stress: "Stress is simply the condition of being human." Now, to turn again to the main idea of his essay—what biological problems he would like to see solved—Thomas inserts a transition paragraph:

> But I digress. What I wish to get at is an imaginary situation in which I am allowed three or four questions to ask the world of biomedical science to settle for me by research, as soon as possible. Can I make a short list of top-priority puzzles, things I am more puzzled by than anything else? I can.

In a new paragraph, he continues: "First, I want to know what goes on in the mind of a honeybee." He wonders if a bee is just a sort of programmed robot or if it can think and imagine, even a little bit. Neatly and effectively, the transition paragraph has led to this speculation and to several further paragraphs that will come.

If you can do without transition paragraphs, do. Sometimes a question at the start of a paragraph will supply enough connection: "Why do people become addicted to their steering wheels?" That question neatly introduces a whole new idea. Use such a paragraph only when you sense that your readers might get lost if you don't patiently lead them by the hand. If the essay is short , one question or statement will be enough.

Repetitions   As we see in Traugot's passage about adoption, still another way to make clear the relationship between two sentences, two paragraphs, or two ideas is to *repeat* a key word or phrase. Such repetition, purposefully done, almost guarantees that the reader will understand how all the parts of even a complicated passage fit together. Note the transitional force of the word *anger* in the following paragraph (italics ours), from *Of Woman Born* by poet Adrienne Rich, in which the writer explores her relationship with her mother:

> And I know there must be deep reservoirs of *anger* in her; every mother has known overwhelming, unacceptable *anger* at her children. When I think of the conditions under which my mother became a mother, the impossible expectations, my father's distaste for pregnant women, his hatred of all that he could not control, my *anger* at her dissolves into grief and *anger for* her, and then dissolves back again into *anger* at her: the ancient, unpurged *anger* of the child.

The repetition of the one word *anger* in several contexts — a mother's anger toward her children and a child's anger, past and present, toward her mother — holds all the parts of this complex paragraph together, makes clear the unity and coherence of its ideas. Repetition of the word *mother* performs the same binding function.

Pronouns   Because they always refer back to nouns or other pronouns, pronouns serve as transitions by making the reader refer back as well. Note how certain pronouns (indicated by *italics*) hold together the following paragraph by columnist Ellen Goodman.

> I have two friends who moved in together many years ago. *He* looked upon this step as a trial marriage. *She* looked upon *it* as, well, moving in together. *He* was sure that in a matter of time, after *they* had built up trust and confidence, *she* would agree that marriage was the next logical step. *She,* on the other hand, was thrilled that here at last was a man *who* would never push *her* back to the altar.

Goodman's paragraph contains transitions other than pronouns, too: time markers like *many years ago, in a matter of time,* and *after they had built up trust; on the other hand,* which makes clear that what follows will represent a contrast from what has gone before; and repetition. All serve the main purpose of transitions: keeping readers on track.

CHAPTER 17

Strategies for Developing

In Part Two of this book, "Thinking Critically," you saw the usefulness of certain critical thinking strategies, valuable when you're writing a whole essay with a particular purpose: analyzing, taking a stand, proposing a solution, evaluating, and identifying causes and effects. You can use these strategies to help you develop not only essays but also paragraphs. To these strategies we now add other techniques for supporting and clarifying your ideas: giving examples, providing details, telling a story, classifying, defining, and comparing and contrasting. In a paragraph, or even in a brief essay, you may choose to use only one of these modes of developing your main idea, but in most essays you—like professional writers—will use a combination of developmental strategies.

GIVING EXAMPLES

An example—the word comes from the Latin *exemplum*, meaning "one thing chosen from among many"—is a typical instance that illustrates a whole type or kind. Here's an example, from *In Search of Excellence* by Thomas J. Peters and Robert H. Waterman, Jr., explaining why America's top corporations are so successful:

> Although he's not a company, our favorite illustration of closeness to the customer is car salesman Joe Girard. He sold more new cars and trucks, each year, for eleven years running, than any other human being. In fact, in a typical year, Joe sold more than twice as many units as whoever was in second place. In explaining

his secret of success, Joe said: "I sent out over thirteen thousand cards every month."

Why start with Joe? Because his magic is the magic of IBM and many of the rest of the excellent companies. It is simply service, overpowering service, especially after-sales service. Joe noted, "There's one thing that I do that a lot of salesmen don't, and that's believe the sale really begins *after* the sale—not before. . . . The customer ain't out the door, and my son has made up a thank-you note." Joe would intercede personally, a year later, with the service manager on behalf of his customer. Meanwhile he would keep the communications flowing.

Notice how Peters and Waterman focus on the specific, Joe Girard. They didn't write *corporation employees* or even *car salespeople,* but zeroed right in on one particular man to make the point come alive.

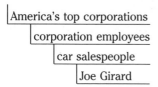

| America's top corporations |
| corporation employees |
| car salespeople |
| Joe Girard |

This ladder of abstraction moves from the general—America's top corporations—to a specific person—Joe Girard. Peters and Waterman's use of the specific example makes their point about the importance of closeness to the customer *concrete* to readers: he is someone readers can relate to.

Had a writer in love with generalities written that paragraph, he might have begun in the same way, with a generalization about "closeness to the customer." But then, instead of giving the example of Joe the car salesman and a sample of his speech, he might have gone on, still staying up in the clouds: "The need to consider the customer as an individual is very important to the operation of a successful business. The retailer is well advised to consider the purchaser as a person with whom he will have a continuing relationship," and so on, vaguely and boringly. Not only do examples make your ideas clear, but they also interest your readers. Writers who stay up in the clouds of generality may have bright ideas, but in the end readers may not care.

Giving examples as Peters and Waterman do, is one way to back up a general statement of the sort you make in a topic sentence. On page 344 James David Barber illustrates the main idea of his paragraph (that "activity-passivity" characterizes presidents) with examples of different presidential types: the drowsy Coolidge, the energetic Johnson. Barber too moves several levels down the ladder of abstraction to make his idea specific:

| presidents of the United States |
| presidential types |
| active presidents |
| Lyndon Johnson |
| passive presidents |
| Calvin Coolidge |

He brings the level of generality down to a specific, illustrative example of each type of president. If his purpose were to persuade rather than to explain, he would need more than one example. One example may illustrate satisfactorily, but it is not sufficient to convince thoughtful readers. To check the level of specification in one of your paragraphs or outlines, draw a ladder of abstraction for it. If you haven't gone down to the fourth or fifth level, you are probably too general and need to add examples. This strategy is also a way for you to restrict a broad subject to a topic manageable in a short essay.

Exercise: Giving Examples

To help you get in the habit of thinking specifically, fill in the ladder of abstraction for five of the following general subjects. Then share your ladders with your peer group and compare and contrast your specifics with theirs.

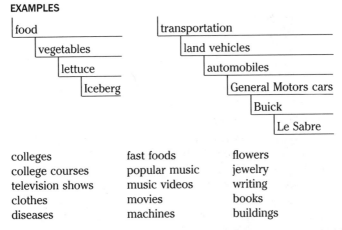

EXAMPLES

food	transportation
vegetables	land vehicles
lettuce	automobiles
Iceberg	General Motors cars
	Buick
	Le Sabre

colleges	fast foods	flowers
college courses	popular music	jewelry
television shows	music videos	writing
clothes	movies	books
diseases	machines	buildings

Giving examples to support a generalization is probably the most often used means of development. Examples for your writing abound: they are all around you. If you are writing a paper on bumper stickers, take a stroll through any parking lot, pen and notepad in hand. For a paper on sexism in advertising, watch television commercials or flip through a few magazines. After you have gathered a few examples on your topic, share them with your peer group, and they'll probably think of some to add to your list.

Science writer Heinz R. Pagels uses one sustained example to develop the topic sentence "Most people find evolution implausible":

> Most people find evolution implausible. Why is my spine erect, my thumb opposable? Can evolutionists *really* explain that? Once I attended a lecture given by the writer Isaac Bashevis Singer, and one of many biologists in the audience asked Singer about evolution—did he believe in it? Singer responded with the story of Paley's watch. He said there was an island upon which scientists were certain no human being had ever been. When people landed on the island they found a watch between two rocks—a complete mystery. The scientists when confronted with the evidence of the watch stuck to the view that the island was

uninhabited. Instead they explained that although improbable, a little bit of glass, metal, and leather had over thousands of years worked its way into the form of a watch. Singer's view differed from that of the scientists — as he summarized, "No watch without a Watchmaker." This story reflects the feeling many people share that random chemical interactions cannot explain the existence of life on earth. The reason it is hard for such people to grasp the evolutionary viewpoint — and for this our feelings do not help — is the difficulty in grasping the immense time a billion years actually is.

Using a variation of this strategy, writer Norman Cousins uses not one but four examples to make concrete the point of his long, complicated, and abstract topic sentence:

> The irony of the emphasis being placed on careers is that nothing is more valuable for anyone who has had a professional or vocational education than to be able to deal with abstractions or complexities, or to feel comfortable with subtleties of thought or language, or to think sequentially. The doctor who knows only disease is at a disadvantage alongside the doctor who knows at least as much about people as he does about pathological organisms. The lawyer who argues in court from a narrow legal base is no match for the lawyer who can connect legal precedents to historical experience and who employs wide-ranging intellectual resources. The business executive whose competence in general management is bolstered by an artistic ability to deal with people is of prime value to his company. For the technologist, the engineering of consent can be just as important as the engineering of moving parts. In all these respects, the liberal arts have much to offer. Just in terms of career preparation, therefore, a student is shortchanging himself by shortcutting the humanities.

DISCOVERY CHECKLIST: USING EXAMPLES TO DEVELOP IDEAS

Here's a revealing experiment you can easily make to test your skill at using examples. Glance back over the last essay you wrote for your composition course, and answer the following questions.

- ✓ How long are the paragraphs?
- ✓ Are they solid and stout? Or are they skimpy, undernourished?
- ✓ Is there hardly a paragraph longer than three sentences?
- ✓ If indeed you find your paragraphs tending toward frailty, ask yourself why.
- ✓ Do you use any examples?
- ✓ Do you use enough examples? Do you need to be more generous in giving examples?
- ✓ Are the examples you use relevant to the point you are making?
- ✓ Are the examples you use the best you can think of?
- ✓ Did you spend enough time trying to think of suitable examples?
- ✓ Are the examples really specific? Or do they just repeat generalities?
- ✓ From your paragraphs, can you draw a ladder of abstraction to at least the fourth level?

To find your own examples, do a little brainstorming or thinking. Review whatever you know. You can begin with your own experience, with whatever is near you. When you set out to draft a paragraph on a topic that you think you know nothing about — the psychology of gift giving, let's say — revolve it slowly in your mind. Maybe you will find yourself an expert on it. Did you ever know a person who gave large gifts people didn't want and felt uncomfortable accepting? Now why do you suppose he or she behaved that way? Was the gift giver looking for gratitude? A feeling of importance? Power over the recipient? How might you tell? If necessary, you might discover still more examples from conversation with others, from your reading, from digging in the library. By using examples, you make an idea more concrete and tangible. Examples aren't trivial doodads you add to a paragraph for decoration; they are what holds your readers' attention and shows them that your writing makes sense.

To give plenty of examples is one of the writer's chief tasks. We can't stress this truth enough. Most beginning writers don't give a reader enough examples. You'll want to cultivate the habit of example giving. Do something to remember its importance. Put a ring around this paragraph, or star it, or paint this motto over your writing desk: USE EXAMPLES! Or engrave it on your brain screen in letters of gold.

PROVIDING DETAILS

In truth, examples are only one kind of *evidence* — the factual basis for an argument or an explanation. Besides pointing to the example of President Coolidge, James David Barber gives a little evidence or specific detail to show that Coolidge was sleepy: the report that he would sleep eleven hours a night and then take a nap in midday besides. To back up your general statements, you would do well to supply such statements of fact, bits of historical record, your own observations. Mary Harris "Mother" Jones in old age published the story of her life as a labor organizer, *The Autobiography of Mother Jones*. In this view of a Pennsylvania coal miner's lot at the turn of the century, she makes a general statement and then with ample evidence lends conviction to her words.

> Mining at its best is wretched work, and the life and surroundings of the miner are hard and ugly. His work is down in the black depths of the earth. He works alone in a drift. There can be little friendly companionship as there is in the factory; as there is among men who build bridges and houses, working together in groups. The work is dirty. Coal dust grinds itself into the skin, never to be removed. The miner must stoop as he works in the drift. He becomes bent like a gnome.
>
> His work is utterly fatiguing. Muscles and bones ache. His lungs breathe coal dust and the strange, damp air of places that are never filled with sunlight. His house is a poor makeshift and there is little to encourage him to make it attractive. The company owns the ground it stands on, and the miner feels the precarious-

ness of his hold. Around his house is mud and slush. Great mounds of culm [the refuse left after coal is screened], black and sullen, surround him. His children are perpetually grimy from playing on the culm mounds. The wife struggles with dirt, with inadequate water supply, with small wages, with overcrowded shacks.

The miner's wife, who in the majority of cases worked from childhood in the nearby silk mills, is overburdened with child bearing. She ages young. She knows much illness. Many a time I have been in a home where the poor wife was sick in bed, the children crawling over her, quarreling and playing in the room, often the only warm room in the house.

Mother Jones, who was not a learned writer, wrote these memoirs in her mid-nineties. Her style may be heavy with short, simple sentences ("She ages young. She knows much illness"), but her writing is clear and powerful. She knows the strength of a well-chosen verb: "Coal dust *grinds* itself into the skin." Notice how she opens her description by making two general statements: (1) "Mining is wretched work" and (2) the miner's life and surroundings are "hard and ugly." Then she supports these generalizations with an overwhelming barrage of factual evidence from her own experience. The result is a moving, convincingly detailed portrait of the miner and his family.

Providing details—narrative, descriptive, factual, statistical—is one of the simplest yet most effective ways of developing ideas. All it takes on your part is close observation through the senses and recall for narration and description or a bit of research for facts and statistics.

Writer M. Scott Momaday describes the scene of the Kiowa celebration of the Gourd Dance on the Fourth of July at Carnegie, Oklahoma:

The celebration is on the north side. We turn down into a dark depression, a large hollow among trees. It is full of camps and cars and people. At first there are children. According to some centrifugal social force, children function on the periphery. They run about, making festival noises. Firecrackers are snapping all around. We park and I make ready; the girls help me with my regalia. I am already wearing white trousers and moccasins. Now I tie the black velvet sash around my waist, placing the beaded tassels at my right leg. The bandoleer of red beans, which was my grandfather's, goes over my left shoulder, the V at my right hip. I decide to carry the blanket over my arm until I join the dancers; no sense in wrapping up in this heat. There is deep, brick-red dust on the ground. The grass is pale and brittle here and there. We make our way through the camps, stepping carefully to avoid the pegs and guy lines that reach about the tents. Old people, imperturbable, are lying down on cots and benches in the shadows. Smoke hangs in the air. We smell hamburgers, popcorn, gunpowder. Later there will be fried bread, boiled meat, Indian corn.

His details are so vivid we as readers can share what he experienced—the sights, sounds, smells, even the heat. In this paragraph he arranges details spatially and chronologically. Notice his spatial transitions: "on the north side," "turn down," "on the periphery," "all around," "on the ground," "here and there," "through the camps," "in the shadows," "in the air." Look also at the time markers: "At first," "Now," "until," "Later." These transitions guide readers through the experience.

Quite different from Momaday's personalized details are George Alexander's objective details. At the beginning of his essay "Harnessing the Fires Below," he employs scientific data and factual description.

> The rain fell heavily on the Mayacmas Mountains, a range of low, softly rounded hills along the Pacific Coast, north of San Francisco. Much of the rainwater sluiced into creeks contributing to the Russian and Napa Rivers, but a large part also soaked into the ground. Over a period of many months, that water percolated slowly and steadily downward, through several hundred feet of sandy soil and sediments, then through a few thousand feet of shale, clay, sandstone and, here and there, through intrusive layers of volcanic rock. It passed through a network of cracks sometimes as wide as a knife blade and sometimes no wider than a very fine hair until, finally, it came down upon an impermeable layer of limestone, more than 5,000 feet below the surface. There, it flowed laterally out to the sides and, where the water contacted the perimeter of this stratum, it curled under the rim.
>
> The water had been getting warmer as it percolated downward, gaining approximately one degree Fahrenheit for every 100 feet of depth. But now, as it seeped around and under the caprock (as geologists call this umbrella-like layer), the water was effectively trapped in a natural pressure cooker. Above it was the caprock lid. Below it, under several thousand more feet of crystalline rock, was the firebox. The water temperature shot up to over 600 degrees Fahrenheit.
>
> The firebox is magma, or molten rock, created by naturally occurring radioactive elements deep in the earth's interior. Normally, this searingly hot matter—between 1,200 and 1,500 degrees Fahrenheit—is buried 20 miles or more beneath the earth's crust. But here and there, where the earth's crust has been fractured and thinned out, as it is in the boundaries between two huge drifting plates, the magma rises to within two or three miles of the surface and radiates enormous amounts of heat into the surrounding crustal material.
>
> Scientists call the energy derived from this heat "geothermal." It is the geothermal energy of a magma pool underlying a wide part of northern California that sends the temperature of the Mayacmas water soaring. Although the tremendous pressure exerted by several miles of rock and soil prevents the 600-degree water from flashing into steam, it has by now soaked up too much energy to remain buried down below.
>
> And so up it comes. Up through a different network of cracks, up through rock layers and sediment beds, the "superheated" water forces its way up until, finally, a thousand feet or so below the surface, the pressure of the overlying earth can no longer contain it in liquid form, and it flashes into steam. And now the steam bursts through the surface, a screeching, scalding vapor plume.

Based on his scientific knowledge, Alexander uses facts and figures to help readers understand the process by which geothermal energy is formed. He, like Momaday, includes spatial signposts and time markers to guide readers through the process. Find these transitions, and discuss with your classmates why Alexander uses each. Following this introduction packed with specific details, Alexander sets forth the advantages and disadvantages of geothermal energy as a natural source of power in future years.

Paula Gunn Allen uses a third type of detail—statistics. She heaps statistic upon statistic to convince the reader that ever since American Indians began making pacts with the U.S. government, their survival has been threatened. By the time we finish her paragraph, we share her alarm.

> Some researchers put our pre-contact population at more than 45 million, while others put it at around 20 million. The U.S. government long put it at 450,000 — a comforting if imaginary figure, though at one point it was put at around 270,000. If our current population is around one million; if, as some researchers estimate, around 25 percent of Indian women and 10 percent of Indian men in the United States have been sterilized without informed consent; if our average life expectancy is, as the best-informed research presently says, 55 years; if our infant mortality rate continues at well above national standards; if our average unemployment for all segments of our population — male, female, young, adult, and middle-aged is between 60 and 90 percent; if the U.S. government continues its policy of termination, relocation, removal, and assimilation along with the destruction of wilderness, reservation land, and its resources, and severe curtailment of hunting, fishing, timber harvesting and water-use rights — then existing tribes are facing the threat of extinction which for several hundred tribal groups has already become fact in the past five hundred years.

Exercise: Providing Details

To practice generating and using specific narrative and descriptive details, brainstorm with your peer group or alone on one of the following subjects. Then group them (see "Strategies for Planning," p. 328), and write a paragraph or a brief essay based on your specific details. Start off with a statement of main idea that says something about the subject you choose (not "My grandmother's house was in Topeka, Kansas" but "My grandmother's house was my childhood haven"). Be sure to include details of all five senses.

the things in my room	my old car
my grandmother's house	an unforgettable game
my childhood hideaway	an unusual person
my backyard	my favorite pet
my Shangri-la	a hospital room
the haunted house	a high school dance
my graduation	my first job interview

DISCOVERY CHECKLIST: PROVIDING DETAILS

- Do you have details of sights? sounds? tastes? touch? smells?
- Do you begin with a clear topic sentence that includes your subject plus your point of view toward the subject?
- Do all your details support your point of view?
- Have you arranged your details in an order that is easy to follow?
- Have you included transitional markers where they are needed to guide your readers through space and time?
- Have you included enough details to make your writing clear? to make it interesting?

CLASSIFYING

Another developmental strategy worth having in your personal artillery is classifying. To classify is to make sense of a complicated and potentially bewildering array of things—works of literature, mental illnesses, this year's movies—by sorting them into categories you can deal with one at a time. A literature book customarily arranges works of literature into three genres or classes: stories, poems, and plays. One paragraph in a discussion about movies might sort them by audience (children's movies, movies for teenagers, movies for mature audiences) or by subject matter (love-romance, mystery, science fiction, sports) and then go on to deal separately with each category. Your categories should be created according to the same principle of classification. In your discussion of movies, don't mix audience categories with subject matter categories (children's movies, mysteries, adult movies). In a textbook lesson on how babies develop, Kurt W. Fischer and Arlyne Lazerson (writing in *Human Development*) take a paragraph to describe a research project that classified individual babies into three types according to temperament:

> The researchers also found that certain of these temperamental qualities tended to occur together. These clusters of characteristics generally fell into three types—the easy baby, the difficult baby, and the baby who was slow to warm up. The *easy infant* has regular patterns of eating and sleeping, readily approaches new objects and people, adapts easily to changes in the environment, generally reacts with low or moderate intensity, and typically is in a cheerful mood. The *difficult infant* usually shows irregular patterns of eating and sleeping, withdraws from new objects or people, adapts slowly to changes, reacts with great intensity, and is frequently cranky. The *slow-to-warm-up infant* typically has a low activity level, tends to withdraw when presented with an unfamiliar object, reacts with a low level of intensity, and adapts slowly to changes in the environment. Fortunately for parents, most healthy infants—40 percent or more—have an easy temperament. Only about 10 percent have a difficult temperament, and about 15 percent are slow to warm up. The remaining 35 percent do not easily fit one of the three types but show some other pattern.

When you classify, you try to make order out of a jumble of stuff: you take many things and, to simplify your view of them, group them *by their similarities*. The simplest method is *binary* (or *two-part*) classification, in which the writer sorts things into two piles: things that possess a feature, things that don't possess that feature, as a chemist does in classifying solutions as either acids or bases. This method ignores fine gradations between two extremes, but sometimes it is clearly the right approach. You might classify people as scientists and nonscientists, literate and illiterate. In short, whenever you need to reduce complexity to an understandable order, don't be surprised to find yourself classifying.

Exercise: Classifying

To practice classifying, jot down at least three types for each of the following. Then compare the types you thought of with those the members of your peer group thought of. Did they classify according to the same principle you used? Did they think of any types you missed? You might use one of your classifications as the basis for a future paragraph or essay.

students	automobiles	worshipers
teachers	sports	writers
children	swimmers	drivers
customers	vacations	travelers
store clerks	families	politicians

DISCOVERY CHECKLIST: CLASSIFYING

🗸 Do you stick to one principle of classification? Do you use the most logical principle of classification for your purpose?

🗸 Are your classes clear? logical? interesting?

🗸 Can you think of specific examples of each class?

🗸 What is the best order for your classes? Why?

🗸 What generalization can you draw from your types that can serve as a statement of main idea—topic sentence or thesis sentence?

ANALYZING

Analyzing an Idea or Subject

You'll recall from Chapter 6 that analyzing means breaking a subject into its parts. You do so to understand your subject better. It's far easier to take in a subject, especially a complex subject, one piece at a time. In a common kind of analysis, *dividing,* a writer slices a subject into its components. This subject may be as concrete and definite as Manhattan (which a writer might divide into neighborhoods), or as abstract as, say, a person's knowledge of art (which the writer might divide into knowledge of sculpture, painting, drawing, and other forms). In the following paragraph from his college textbook *Wildlife Management,* Robert H. Giles, Jr., analyzes an especially large, abstract subject: the management of forest wildlife in America. To explain which professional environmentalists in America assume which duties and responsibilities, Giles divides forest wildlife management into six levels or areas of concern, arranged roughly from large to small. To a nonspecialist, this subject may seem head-stoppingly complicated. But see how neatly Giles divides it and explains it in a paragraph of less than 175 words.

> There are six scales of forest wildlife management: (1) national, (2) regional, (3) state or industrial, (4) county or parish, (5) intra-state region, management unit, or watershed, and (6) forest. Each is different. At the national and regional levels, management includes decisions on timber harvest quotas, grazing policy in forested lands, official stance on forest taxation bills, cutting policy relative to threatened and endangered species, management coordination of migratory spe-

cies, and research fund allocation. At the state or industrial level, decision types include land acquisition, sale, or trade; season setting; and permit systems and fees. At the county level, plans are made, seasons set, and special fees levied. At the intra-state level, decisions include what seasons to recommend, what stances to take on bills not affecting local conditions, the sequence in which to attempt land acquisition, and the placement of facilities. At the forest level, decisions may include some of those of the larger management unit but typically are those of maintenance schedules, planting stock, cutting rotations, personnel employment and supervision, road closures, equipment use, practices to be attempted or used, and boundaries to be marked.

Analyzing a Process

You can also analyze an action or a phenomenon: how a skyscraper is built, how a political revolution begins, how sunspots form on the sun's surface. Analyzing a process is one of the most useful kinds of writing: telling step by step how something is done or how to do something (see Chapter 6, "Analyzing"). This strategy will be familiar if you have ever followed directions in a cookbook, but it is also useful in writing about more complex processes. It can explain large, long-ago happenings that a writer couldn't possibly have witnessed, such as the formation of the Grand Canyon or the solar system. Here, for instance, is a paragraph of collaborative writing by a team of botanists, Peter H. Raven, Ray F. Evert, and Helena Curtis (from their college textbook, *Biology of Plants*).

> About 127 million years ago—when angiosperm pollen first appears in the fossil record—Africa and South America were directly linked with one another and with Antarctica, India, and Australia in a great southern supercontinent called Gondwanaland. Africa and South America began to separate at about this time, forming the southern Atlantic Ocean, but they did not move completely apart in the tropical regions until about 90 million years ago. India began to move northward at about the same time, colliding with Asia about 45 million years ago and thrusting up the Himalayas in the process. Australia began to separate from Antarctica about 55 million years ago, but their separation did not become complete until about 40 million years ago.

Notice the writers' use of transitional time markers—*about 127 million years ago, at about this time, until about 90 million years ago*. (Few of us will clearly imagine such vast extents of time, but at least the time markers make clear to us the sequence of events.) This paragraph illustrates the kind of process analysis that sets forth how something happens: an *informative* process analysis. Another familiar kind is the *directive* or "how-to" process analysis, which you often meet in the printed directions that come with merchandise in need of assembling. A directive process analysis instructs us in doing something— how to box, how to invest for retirement, how to clean a painting—or in making something—how to draw a map, blaze a trail, or put together a simple computer.

Exercise: Analyzing

Analyze one of the following topics. Take care not to confuse the parts of analysis with the types of classification. Use your analysis as the basis of a paragraph or short essay. When you write, remember that you must have a topic sentence in a paragraph or a thesis sentence in an essay to unify the writing. Then share your analysis with the analyses of your peer group. Can they follow your analysis or process easily? Do they spot anything you left out?

1. Analyze one of the following subjects into its parts.

the federal government	a family
a college	education
friendship	a football team
marriage	a computer

2. Analyze one of the following processes or procedures into its parts.

a hurricane	falling in love
registration for college classes	buying a used car
studying for a test	giving a speech
writing a research paper	cloud formation
influenza (or another disease)	osmosis

DISCOVERY CHECKLIST: ANALYZING

- ✔ Have you used one principle of analysis consistently?
- ✔ Have you analyzed your subject thoroughly?
- ✔ What is the purpose of your analysis? (It should be something more than just to analyze. Perhaps the purpose of an essay on the process of getting adjusted to living away from home would be to explain the difficulties. Someone else might write on the surprises, and another person might write on the ease of the process. Your experiences and your attitude will determine your purpose.)
- ✔ Is your explanation of the analysis suitable for an audience of nonexperts?
- ✔ Is the order of the parts of your analysis logical?
- ✔ Have you used appropriate transitions to connect the parts of the analysis?

DEFINING

Often in any paper that calls for critical thinking, you'll need to do some defining. *Define,* from the Latin, means "to set bounds to." You can define a thing, a word, or a concept.

If scientists and technical writers don't agree on the meaning of a word or an idea, they can't share knowledge. They often define their terms to be sure that they are communicating clearly. In his article "A Chemist's Definition of pH," Gessner G. Hawley makes his subject clear to readers who can follow him. Though he goes on to write an extended definition, he begins with a brief definition:

> pH is a value taken to represent the acidity or alkalinity of an aqueous solution; it is defined as the logarithm of the reciprocal of the hydrogen-ion concentration of a solution:

$$pH = \ln \frac{1}{[H^+]}$$

If you coin a word, you have to explain it or your readers won't know what you're talking about. Prolific word coiner and social prophet Alvin Toffler in *The Third Wave,* for instance, invents (among many others) the word *techno-sphere,* which he defines as follows:

> All societies — primitive, agricultural, or industrial — use energy; they make things; they distribute things. In all societies the energy system, the production system, and the distribution system are interrelated parts of something larger. This larger system is the *techno-sphere.*

In his later book *PowerShift,* Toffler picks up the word *screenie* from Jeffrey Moritz, president of National College Television, and adds his own boundaries to this coined term:

> Moritz uses the term *screenie* to describe this video-drenched generation, which has digested thousands of hours of television, imbibing its "video-logic." To that must be added, for many of them, more hours of interactive video games and, even more important, of work on their own personal computers. They not only follow a different logic, but are accustomed to make the screen do things, thus making them good prospects for the interactive services and products soon to hit the market. Above all, they are accustomed to choice.

Sometimes in writing you stop to define a standard word not often used (such as *exurbia* or *prescind* or *laconic*). You define it to save your readers a trip to the dictionary. Or you may define a word that is familiar but often misunderstood. What is equality? What is intelligence, socialism, preventive medicine, HMO, brand loyalty, minimum wage, a holding corporation? Whenever in your writing you need to indicate the nature of an idea, a thing, a movement, a phenomenon, an organization — then you'll find yourself defining. The more complex or ambiguous the subject, the longer the definition you need to clarify the term for your readers.

Exercise: Defining

Write an extended definition (a paragraph or so in length) of one of the following words. Begin with a one-sentence definition of the word. Then, to expand and clarify your ideas, use some of the strategies discussed in this chapter — examples, details, analysis, classification, comparison and contrast, causes, or effects. You may also use *negation* (explaining what something is by stating what it is not). Don't get most of your definition from a dictionary or textbook: personalize your definition. Remember, "Happiness is a warm puppy." Then share your definition with your peer group.

education	abuse	exercise	literacy
privacy	jazz	dieting	success
taboo	rock music	gossip	fear
prejudice	AIDS	ecology	gender

DISCOVERY CHECKLIST: DEFINING

- ✓ Have you tailored your definition to the needs of your audience?
- ✓ Do you start off with a brief statement of meaning to use as a springboard for your further explanation?
- ✓ Is your definition specific?
- ✓ Do you personalize your definition?
- ✓ What strategies for defining do you use? Could you use others to make the term clearer?

COMPARING AND CONTRASTING

Often, if your purpose is to explain or define or evaluate a subject, you can develop a paragraph effectively by setting a pair of subjects side by side and comparing and contrasting them. Working together, these twin strategies use one subject to clarify another. The dual method works well for a pair of things similar in nature: two cities, two films, the theories of two economists. It can show that a writer has clearly observed and thoroughly understood both. For this reason, college examiners will often ask you to compare and contrast (sample exam question: "Discuss the chief similarities and differences between nineteenth-century French and English colonial policies in West Africa").

Which city—Dallas or Atlanta—has more advantages and more drawbacks for a young single person thinking of settling down to a career? How does the IBM personal computer stack up against a Macintosh for word processing? As songwriters, how are Bruce Springsteen and Bob Dylan similar and dissimilar? Such questions invite answers that set two subjects side by side.

When you compare, you point out similarities; when you contrast, you discuss differences. In writing assignments that ask you to deal with two complicated subjects, usually you will need both to compare *and* contrast. Taking Springsteen and Dylan, you might find that each has traits the other has—or lacks. In writing about the two, you wouldn't absolutely have to conclude that one is great and the other inferior. You might look at their differences and similarities and then conclude that they're two distinct composer-performers, each with an individual style. Of course, such fence-straddling papers can seem to lack heart; if you had a passionate preference for either Dylan or Springsteen, you'd want to voice it. In a paper whose main purpose is to judge between two subjects (as when you'd recommend that a young single person move either to Dallas or to Atlanta), you would look especially for positive and negative features, weigh the attractions of each city and its faults, and then stick your neck out and make your choice.

In daily life, all of us frequently compare and contrast, as when we decide which menu selection to choose, which car (or other product) to buy, which magazine to read in a waiting room, which college course to sign up for. Though in making such everyday decisions we do not usually commit our reasoning to paper, comparing and contrasting (and weighing evidence for and against) are familiar habits of thought. Used in writing, this dual method is easy to follow. In a travel essay, "Venezuela for Visitors," written for the well-educated (and well-off) readers of *The New Yorker,* novelist John Updike sees Venezuelan society as polarized: it consists of rich people and Indians. In the following paragraph, Updike compares and contrasts the two classes.

> Missionaries, many of them United States citizens, move among the Indians. They claim that since Western civilization, with all its diseases and detritus, must come, it had best come through them. Nevertheless, Marxist anthropologists inveigh against them. Foreign experts, many of them United States citizens, move among the rich. They claim they are just helping out, and that anyway the oil industry was nationalized five years ago. Nevertheless, Marxist anthropologists are not mollified. The feet of the Indians are very broad in front, their toes spread wide for climbing avocado trees. The feet of the rich are very narrow in front, their toes compressed by pointed Italian shoes. The Indians seek relief from tension in the use of *ebene,* or *yopo,* a mind-altering drug distilled from the bark of the ebene tree and blown into the user's nose through a hollow cane by a colleague. The rich take cocaine through the nose, and frequent mind-altering discotheques, but more customarily imbibe cognac, *vino blanco,* and Scotch, in association with colleagues.

For most of this paragraph, you'll notice, Updike simply sets the two side by side: the feet of the poor, the feet of the rich; how the poor get high, how the rich do. But merely by doing so, he throws the two groups of people into sharp relief.

Writers use two basic methods of organization for comparison and contrast: the opposing pattern and the alternating pattern. A writer using the *opposing pattern* discusses all of the characteristics or subdivisions of the first subject in the first half of the paragraph or essay and then discusses all the characteristics of the other subject. A writer using the *alternating pattern* moves back and forth between the two subjects. This pattern places the specifics close together for immediate comparison and contrast. For example, a writer using the opposing pattern to compare and contrast two brothers Jim and Jack would discuss Jim's physical appearance, his personality traits, and his interests and would then discuss Jack's appearance, his personality, and his interests—discussing in both parts the same characteristics in the same order. A writer using the alternating pattern would discuss Jim's physical appearance, then Jack's physical appearance; Jim's personality, then Jack's; Jim's interests, then Jack's. Whichever pattern of order you choose, be sure to cover the same subpoints under each item and to do so in the same order in all parts.

In the paragraph about Venezuelan society, John Updike uses the alternating pattern to compare and contrast rich people and Indians. In the following paragraph (quoted earlier on p. 197), psychologist and educator Howard Gardner uses the opposing pattern to emphasize the differences between the drawings of older and younger children.

> When drawings made by eight- or nine-year-olds are juxtaposed to those produced by younger children, a striking contrast emerges. There is little doubt about which came from which group: works by the older children feature a kind of precision, a concern for detail, a command of geometrical form which are lacking in the attempts by younger artists. Schemas for familiar objects are readily recognized, and attempts at rendering less familiar objects can initially be decoded. And yet one hesitates to call the drawings by the older children "better"—indeed, most observers and sometimes even the youngsters themselves feel that something vital which is present at the age of six or seven has disappeared from the drawings by the older children. A certain freedom, flexibility, *joie de vivre* [zest for life], and a special fresh exploratory flavor which mark the childlike drawings of the six-year-old are gone; and instead of being replaced by adult mastery, this loss has merely been supplanted by a product that is at once more carefully wrought yet also more wooden and lifeless.

Gardner is not just setting things side by side; he is using the strategy to develop an evaluation of the children's drawings.

The alternating pattern can bring an array of differences and similarities into quick, sharp focus, but it can also slip into a Ping-Pong match of back-and-forth comparisons. See how Allen Lewis avoids the Ping-Pong trap by introducing slight variations to his comparison/contrast of American playwrights Tennessee Williams and Arthur Miller.

> Williams is absorbed with the instinctive and the behavioral, the cry for emotional freedom; Miller with the conceptual and the reasoned, the cry for social liberation. Williams makes of each individual a world unto himself. Miller goes beyond the individual to place blame on the forces that confine growth. Williams' characters are frustrated, sensitive, unfortunate people who preserve ideal images as bulwarks against the shipwreck of their lives. The characters in Miller's plays are often lonely, misguided, and self-seeking, but in the recognition of truth they find courage to sacrifice their own lives that others may profit. Both writers are gifted craftsmen able to create protagonists who are alive and self-propelled. Some of them, like Amanda and Willy Loman, have already been woven into the myths of a people. Williams' characters are lost in a struggle against the sadism of the insensitive; Miller's characters are lost by their refusal to adjust to social dishonesty. Neither author has discovered a redeeming faith; like O'Neill, they are in constant pursuit of freedom from unproductive anxieties. Williams is more descriptive, Miller more analytical. Williams is closer to the heart, and his com-

passion reaches out to the ill-adapted. His best characters are women. Miller is closer to the mind, his compassion being for all humanity. His best characters are men. *The Glass Menagerie* is a symbol of a broken world in which Laura is defeated by forces she does not understand. *The Crucible* is a symbol of the test of man's will, and Proctor succumbs after a conscious fight to purge stupidity and superstition. The opposing concepts of these two writers find expression in different images. The anarchy of the emotions becomes the lush, tropical sensuousness of Williams; the hope of order is reflected in the colder, northern austerity of Miller. Williams is closer to the subjective anguish of Strindberg; Miller to the social concern of Ibsen. Miller's few plays are carefully wrought. Williams is prolific and wasteful.

These brief examples may suggest that comparing and contrasting aren't just meaningless academic calisthenics. They are explaining devices that appeal to writers who have a passion for making things clear.

Exercise: Comparing and Contrasting

Write a paragraph or a short essay in which you compare and contrast the subjects in any of the following pairs, for the purpose of throwing light on both. In a short paper, you can hope to trace only a few similarities and differences. Use your own recall or observation, go to the library, or converse with a friendly expert if you need material.

> women and men as single parents
> baseball and football (or basketball)
> living in an apartment and living in a house
> two cities or towns you are familiar with
> two musicians
> two colleges
> two poems
> watching a sports event on television and in person
> two restaurants
> two college courses

DISCOVERY CHECKLIST: COMPARING AND CONTRASTING

- Have you chosen the *major* similarities and differences to write about?
- Have you used the same categories for each item? In discussing each feature, do you always look at the very same thing? (Don't compare and contrast, for example, Sarah's hair and height with Theresa's hair and weight. Don't compare and contrast American taste in clothes with British preferences in food. Compare and contrast like things.)
- Have you come to a conclusion about the two? To what extent do you prefer one over the other? What are your reasons for your preference? It's all right not to have a preference. You might not argue that Martina Navratilova is a superior tennis player to Chris Evert Lloyd, or vice versa. You might instead show how each throws the other into sharp relief.

- Is your reason for doing all the comparing and contrasting unmistakably clear? If not, your paper will seem an arbitrary exercise conducted in outer space. You should set out in a definite direction at the start of your paper and arrive somewhere at the end. Do you need to reexamine your goal: what is it you want to demonstrate, argue for, or find out?

- If you are making a judgment between your subjects, do you feel you have treated both fairly? Have you, for instance, left out any damning disadvantages or failures of the subject you're championing? Have you suppressed any of the losing subject's good points?

- Does your draft look thin for lack of evidence? If so, from which resources might you draw more?

- Have you dropped into a boringly mechanical, monotonous style ("On one hand, . . . now on the other hand")? Show your paper to a classmate and observe whether the friend begins to look glassy-eyed. If so, at what places can you break the monotony?

IDENTIFYING CAUSES AND EFFECTS

From the time we are children, we ask why. Why can't I go out and play? Why is the sky blue? Why do pickles taste sour? Why did my goldfish die? Our seeking causes and effects continues into adulthood. We try to understand our often puzzling world by searching for causes and identifying effects. So it's natural for one of the most used methods of development in writing to be causal relationships. Explaining causes and effects helps a writer to clarify a subject for readers. To use cause and effect successfully, you must think about the subject critically, gather evidence, draw judicious conclusions, and show relationships clearly. Chapter 10 gives you detailed information about how to write a complete essay identifying causes and/or effects, but let's look at a couple of brief examples of how this technique for development can be used in one paragraph of a longer essay.

Thomas McKeown, in a chapter called "The Diseases of Affluence" in his book *The Origins of Human Disease,* speculates on the *causes* of the attention that ill effects of smoking have received:

> There is probably no other hazard whose ill effects on health have been, or perhaps could be, charted as meticulously as those of tobacco. There are several reasons why it has received so much attention. First, it has been under investigation for almost exactly the period — the last four decades — in which the origins of non-communicable diseases have been seriously considered; until the end of the Second World War interest in the relation of behavior and environment to disease was almost confined to the infections. Second, the large increase in the frequency of smoking has occurred in the present century, when evidence from national statistics and other sources was much better than that available for diet and reproduction, in which some of the major changes occurred in the nineteenth

century. And third, the effects of smoking on health are so large and so obvious that they are accepted even by people who dismiss other features of behavior as scarcely worth attention.

Notice how McKeown clearly marks his *reasons*: "First," "Second," "And third."

Instead of focusing on causes *or* effects, often writers trace a *chain* of cause and effect relationships, as Charles C. Mann and Mark L. Plummer do in "The Butterfly Problem":

> More generally, the web of species around us helps generate soil, regulate freshwater supplies, dispose of waste, and maintain the quality of the atmosphere. Pillaging nature to the point where it cannot perform these functions is dangerously foolish. Simple self-protection is thus a second motive for preserving biodiversity. When DDT was sprayed in Borneo, the biologists Paul and Anne Ehrlich relate in their book *Extinction* (1981), it killed all the houseflies. The gecko lizards that preyed on the flies ate their pesticide-filled corpses and died. House cats consumed the dying lizards; they died too. Rats descended on the villages, bringing bubonic plague. Incredibly, the housefly in this case was part of an intricate system that controlled human disease. To make up for its absence, the government was forced to parachute cats into the area.

In Mann and Plummer's paragraph, trace the series of five results of the spraying of DDT in Borneo.

Exercise: Identifying Causes and Effects

1. Identify some of the *causes* of *five* of the following. Discuss possible causes with your classmates.

failing an exam	stress
an automobile accident	getting a job
poor health	losing a job
good health	losing weight
stage fright	going to college
losing or winning a game	getting a scholarship

2. Identify some of the *effects* of *five* of the following. Discuss possible effects with your classmates.

an insult	dieting
a compliment	speeding
poor attendance in class	drinking while driving
a child's running away from home	divorce
smoking cigarettes	increase in taxes

3. Identify some of the *causes and effects* of *one* of the following. You may need to do a little research in the library or in a textbook in order to identify the chain of causes and effects for the event. How might what you discovered be used as part of an essay? Discuss what you discover with your classmates.

the Civil War

the Vietnam War

Ronald Reagan's tenure as president

the discovery of atomic energy

a U.S. Supreme Court decision
  on abortion

the AIDS virus

recycling

smoking crack cocaine

the uses of solar energy

the hole in the ozone layer

racial tension

DISCOVERY CHECKLIST: USING CAUSES AND EFFECTS

- Have you used any causes and effects in developing your essay? Can you think of others that would strengthen your position?
- Is there a chain of causes and effects related to the subject?
- Are the causes you have identified actual causes? Can you find evidence to support them?
- Are the effects you have identified actual effects, or are they merely conjecture? If conjecture, would they be logical results? Can you find evidence to support them?
- Have you judiciously drawn conclusions concerning causes and effects? Have you avoided fallacies of thinking, such as hasty generalization and stereotyping? (See "Looking for Logical Fallacies," p. 381.)
- Do you need to add more transition words to make the relationships between causes and effects clear to readers?

CHAPTER 18

Strategies for Revising and Editing

Good writing is rewriting. When Ernest Hemingway was asked why he rewrote the last page of the novel *Farewell to Arms* thirty-nine times, he replied, "Getting the words right." His comment reflects the care serious writers take in revising their work.

The advice in this chapter is meant to help you revise what you write. It suggests strategies and lends you support in revising and editing a paper, whether you change all the major ideas or only polish the words and phrases. Sometimes a draft needs to be entirely rethought and recast into a new mold. We suggest how you can rethink and emphasize important ideas. This advice applies to rewriting whole essays. The section also gives hints for rewriting just *parts* of essays: sentences and paragraphs. In addition, we give you tips for proofreading and editing.

RE-VIEWING, RE-VISING, AND EDITING

Revision is much more than mere correction of grammar and spelling. *Revision* means "seeing again"—discovering again, conceiving again, shaping again. It is not something you do after you complete a paper. Rather, it is an integrated aspect of the total writing process; it may occur at all stages of the process.

How do you know when you need to rewrite? Rest assured that most writers do a lot of rewriting. Sometimes it's just tinkering with sentence structure or playing around with word choices. Other times it's more general— reordering ideas or finding additional information to develop an idea. You will be doing both types of revision—paying attention to the details of language use (sentences, words, punctuation) and also focusing on the rhetorical aspects of writing (purpose, voice, audience, unity, organization, development, coherence, clarity).

In previous chapters of this book, in the "Revising and Editing" sections, you found specific advice for such decision making. Here now are three *general* checklists of questions you might ask yourself as you reread and revise. You can use these questions for almost every writing task, but the questions will prove useful only if you allow time to give your work a thorough going-over. Allow your ideas to incubate. When you have a few hours to spare, these questions will guide you to make not just slight, cosmetic touch-ups, but major improvements.

REVISION CHECKLIST: REACHING YOUR GOAL

- Have you accomplished what you set out to do? If not, what still needs doing?
- Has your paper said everything that you believe needs to be said?
- Do you still believe everything you say? In writing the paper, have you changed your mind, rethought your assumptions, made a discovery? Do any of your interpretations or statements of opinion now need to be revised?
- Have you tried to take in too much territory, with the result that your coverage of your topic seems too thin? How might you—even now—reduce the scope of your paper? Could you cut material, perhaps write a new introduction making clear exactly what you propose to do?
- Do you know enough about your subject? Does more evidence seem called for? If so, try recalling, observing, reading, conversing, and imagining. Try some of the strategies for generating ideas (Chapter 14).
- If you have taken ideas and information from other writers, have you always given credit where it is due? Remember, you can refer to your sources in the body of the text ("Robert Sheridan claims . . .") or in parentheses.
- If you have written to persuade readers, can you sum up in a sentence the claim your paper sets forth? (For help, see "Stating and Using a Thesis," p. 322.)
- Have you emphasized what matters most? Have you kept the essential idea or ideas from being obscured by a lot of useless details and distracting secondary thoughts? (For help, see "Stressing What Counts," p. 383.)
- Have you avoided logical fallacies? (See p. 381.)

REVISION CHECKLIST: TESTING STRUCTURE

- Does the introduction set up the whole paper?
- Would any paragraphs make more sense or follow better if arranged in a different order? Try imagining how a paragraph might look and sound in a

new location. Scissor it out and stick it into a different place or move it on your word processor. Reread it and see whether it works well there.

⮑ Does your topic make itself clear early in the paper, or must the reader plow through much distracting material to come to it? Later in the draft, is there any passage that would make a better beginning?

⮑ Is your thesis clear? Is it given a position of emphasis? Are all the ideas relevant to the thesis?

⮑ Does everything follow clearly? Does one point lead to the next? If connections aren't clear, see "Achieving Coherence," page 354.

⮑ Does the conclusion follow from what has gone before? It doesn't seem arbitrarily tacked on, does it? (See "Writing a Conclusion," p. 350.)

⮑ Do you suspect that your paper is somewhat confused? If you suspect it, you are probably right. Suggestion: Make an informal outline of the paper as it now stands. Then look over the outline and try to spot places to make improvements—to change the order, to add specific details, to make the ideas cohere better. Revise the outline; then revise the paper. (For advice on outlining, see p. 331.)

REVISION CHECKLIST: CONSIDERING YOUR AUDIENCE

⮑ Who will read this paper? What are the readers like? Does the paper tell them what they will want to know? Or does it tell them only what they probably know already?

⮑ Does the beginning of the paper promise your readers anything that the paper never delivers?

⮑ Have you anticipated questions the readers might ask?

⮑ Are there any places where readers might go to sleep? If so, can such passages be shortened or deleted?

⮑ Do you take ample time and space to unfold each idea in enough detail to make it both clear and interesting? Would more detailed evidence help—perhaps an interesting brief story or a concrete example? (See "Giving Examples," p. 358.)

⮑ Can you cut any long-winded examples?

⮑ Are there places where readers might raise serious objections? How might you recognize these objections, maybe even answer them?

⮑ Have you used any specialized or technical language that your readers might not understand? Have you used any familiar words in a technical sense? If so, can you work in brief definitions?

⮑ What attitude toward your readers do you seem to take? Are you overly chummy, needlessly angry, cockily superior, apologetic? condescending? preachy? Do you still feel that way? How can you sound more congenial? Ask your peers for an opinion.

> ✓ From your conclusion, and from your paper as a whole, will your readers
> be convinced that you have told them something worth knowing?

After you have *re-viewed* and *re-vised* a draft, edit it. Go over what you have written, looking for specific pitfalls. Good writers learn to hunt down weaknesses in their prose and cut them out. You will soon learn what problems you need to be on the lookout for. Following are a few that most writers search for; they will be a good beginning for you.

LOOKING FOR LOGICAL FALLACIES

Logical fallacies are common mistakes in thinking — often, the making of statements that lead to wrong conclusions. Here are a few of the most familiar, to help you recognize them when you see or hear them and so guard against them when you write. If when you look back over your draft you discover any of these, cut them, think again, and come up with a different argument.

Non sequitur (From the Latin, "It does not follow.") This is the error of stating a claim that doesn't follow from your first premise (the statement you begin with): "Marge should marry Jergus. Why, in high school he got all A's." Come up with stronger reasons for Marge's decision — reasons that have to do with getting good grades *as a husband.*

Oversimplification This fallacy is evident when a writer offers neat and easy solutions for large, complicated problems: "If we want to do away with drug abuse, let's get tough — let's sentence every drug user to life imprisonment." (Even users of aspirin?)

Post hoc ergo propter hoc ("After this, therefore because of this.") This fallacy confuses cause and effect. We assume that when one event precedes another in time, the first is the cause of the second. "Because Jimmy Carter was obliged to leave the White House, the problem of inflation has been alleviated." Many superstitions result from post hoc reasoning: neither seeing a black cat nor strolling under a ladder cause misfortune. (In a way, this is another form of oversimplification: attributing huge effects to just one simple cause.)

Allness The *allness* fallacy means stating or implying that something is true of an entire class of things. There are exceptions to every rule, and your readers are likely to find them. Instead of saying "Students enjoy studying" (which implies that *all* students enjoy *all* types of studying *all* the time), qualify: "Some students enjoy studying math." Be wary of *allness* words: *all, everyone, no one, always, never.*

Proof by example (or too few examples) An example illustrates or helps to clarify, but it does not prove. This is another type of oversimplification: "Armenians are great chefs. My next door neighbor is Armenian and, boy, can he cook!" This type of overgeneralizing is the basis of much prejudice: "I once knew a Martian who was very messy, so I know Martians are bad housekeepers." Be sure you have sufficient evidence — enough examples, a large enough sampling — to draw a conclusion.

Begging the question Set out to prove a statement already taken for granted, and you beg the question. When you reason in a logical way, you state that because something is true, then another truth follows as a result. But when you beg the question, you repeat that what is true is true. If, for instance, you argue that rapists are a menace because they are dangerous, you don't prove a thing. Beggars of questions just repeat what they already believe, in different words. Sometimes this fallacy takes the form of *arguing in a circle,* demonstrating a premise by a claim and a claim by a premise: "He is a liar because he simply isn't telling the truth." Sometimes it takes the form of defining a word in terms of itself: "Happiness is the state of being happy."

Either/or reasoning This logical fallacy is a special brand of oversimplified thinking: assuming that there are only two sides to a question, that all statements are either true or false, that all questions demand either a yes or a no answer. "The nonbiologist," comments scientist Eric B. Lenneberg, "mistakenly thinks of genes as being directly responsible for one property or another; this leads him to the fallacy of dichotomizing everything as being dependent on either genes or environment." Other adherents to the either/or principle divide reality into either mind or body, sense or intellect, intelligence or stupidity, public or private, finite or infinite, humanity or nature, good or evil, competence or incompetence. An either/or reasoner assumes that a problem has only two possible solutions, only one of which is acceptable. "What are we going to do about acid rain? Either we shut down all the factories that cause it or we just forget about acid rain and learn to live with it. We've got no choice, right?" Realize that there are more than two choices or more than two causes. An individual isn't strong or weak but is a mixture of strengths and weaknesses.

Argument from dubious authority An unidentified authority can be used unfairly to shore up a quaking argument: "According to some of the most knowing scientists in America, smoking two packs a day is as harmless as eating a couple of oatmeal cookies. So let's all smoke." A reader should also doubt an authority whose expertise lies outside the subject being considered: "TV personality Pat Sajak says this insurance policy is the lowest-priced and most comprehensive available."

Argument ad hominem (From the Latin, "against the man.") This fallacy consists of attacking people's opinions by attacking their character. "Carruthers may argue that we need to save the whales, but Carruthers is the kind of person who always gets excited over nothing." A person's circumstances can also be turned against him: "Carruthers would have us spend millions to save whales, but I happen to know that he owns a yacht from which he selfishly enjoys watching whales."

Argument from ignorance This fallacy involves maintaining that, because a claim has not been disproved, it has to be accepted. "Despite years of effort, no one has conclusively proved that ghosts don't exist; therefore, we should expect to see them at any time." The converse is also an error: that because a conclusion has not been proved it should be rejected. "No one has ever shown that there is life on any other planet. Evidently the notion of other living things in the universe is unthinkable." This fallacy is widespread in politics: "Sure Candidate Smithers advocates this tax plan. It will put money in his pocket!" Judge the tax proposal on its merits, not on the character of its originator.

Argument by analogy The writer who makes this mistake uses a *metaphor* (a figure of speech that points to a similarity: "Her speech was a string of firecrackers") as though it were evidence to support a claim. In explanation, an analogy may be useful. It can set forth a complex idea in terms of something familiar and easy to imagine. For instance, shooting a spacecraft to a distant planet is like sinking a golf ball with uncanny accuracy into a hole a half mile away. But if used to convince, an analogy will be logically weak, though it may sound neat and clear. Dwelling only on similarities, a writer doesn't consider differences—since to admit them would only weaken the analogy. "People were born free as the birds. It's cruel to expect them to work." Hold on—human society and bird society have more differences than similarities. Because they are alike in one way doesn't mean they're alike in *every* way. In 1633, Scipio Chiaramonti, professor of philosophy at the University of Pisa, made this leaky analogy in arguing against Galileo's claim that the earth orbits the sun: "Animals, which move, have limbs and muscles. The earth has no limbs and muscles, hence it does not move."

STRESSING WHAT COUNTS

A boring writer writes as though every idea is no more important than any other. An effective writer cares what matters, decides what matters most, and shines a bright light on it.

You can't emphasize merely by underlining things, by putting them in quotation marks, or by throwing them into CAPITAL LETTERS. Such devices soon grow monotonous, and a writer who works them hard ends up stressing nothing at all, like a speaker whose every second word is a curse word. One Navy boatswain's mate, according to folklore, couldn't talk without emphasizing every noun with an obscene adjective. To talk that way cost him great effort. By the time he could get out an order to his crew to bail, the boat had swamped. Emphasis wasn't all that was lost.

An essential of good writing, then, is to emphasize things that count. How? This section offers suggestions.

Stating First or Last

One way to stress what counts is to put important things first or last. The most emphatic positions in an essay, or in a single sentence, are two: the beginning and the end. Let's consider each.

Stating first In an essay, you might state in your opening paragraph what matters most. Writing a paper for an economics course in which students had been assigned to explain the consequences of import quotas (such as a limit on the number of foreign cars allowed into a country), Donna Waite began by summing up her findings:

> Although an import quota has many effects, both for the nation imposing the quota and the nation whose industries must suffer from it, I believe that the most important effect is generally felt at home. A native industry gains a chance to thrive in a marketplace of lessened competition.

Her paper goes on to illustrate her general observation with evidence. Summing up the most important point right at the start is, by the way, a good strategy for answering a question in an essay examination. It immediately shows the instructor that you know the answer.

A paper that takes a stand or makes a proposal might open with a statement of what the writer believes.

> Our state's antiquated system of justices of the peace is inefficient.

> For urgent reasons, I recommend that the United States place a human observer in temporary orbit around the planet Mars.

The body of the paper would set forth the writer's reasons for holding the view, and probably the writer would hammer the claim or thesis again at the end.

That advice refers to whole essays. Now let's see how in a single sentence you can stress things at the start. Consider the following unemphatic sentence,

> When Congress debates the Hall-Hayes Act removing existing legal protections for endangered species, as now

```
seems likely to occur on May 12, it will be a consider-
able misfortune if this bill should pass, since the ex-
tinction of many rare birds and animals would certainly
be the result.
```

The coming debate, and its probable date, take up the start of the sentence. The writer might have made better use of this emphatic position.

```
The extinction of many rare birds and animals will
follow passage of the Hall-Hayes Act.
```

Now the writer stresses what he most fears: dire consequences. (In a further sentence, he might add the date of the coming debate in Congress and his opinion that passage of the legislation would be a misfortune.)

Consider these further examples (a sentence in rough draft and in a revision):

```
It may be argued that the best way to choose soft-
ware for a small business is to call in a professional
consultant, who is likely to be familiar with the many
systems available and can give helpful advice.
```

```
The best way to choose software for a small business
is to call in a professional consultant.
```

In the second version, the paper might go on: "Familiar with the many systems available, such an expert can give helpful advice." Notice that in the revision, the two most important ingredients of the idea are placed first and last, the emphatic positions in English sentences. *Best way* is placed up front, and *professional consultant,* standing last in the sentence, is also emphasized.

Stating last   In your reader's mind, an explosion of silence follows the final statement in your paper. To place an idea last can throw weight on it. One way to assemble your ideas in an emphatic order is to proceed from least important to most important.

This order is more dramatic: it builds up and up. Not all writing assignments call for drama, of course. In the papers on import quotas and justices of the peace, any attempt at a big dramatic buildup might look artificial and contrived. Still, this strategy is worth considering. Perhaps in an essay on city parks and how they lure shoppers to the city, the claim or thesis sentence — summing up the whole point of the essay — might stand at the very end: "For the inner city, to improve city parks will bring about a new era of prosperity." Giving all the evidence first and leading up to the thesis at the end is particularly effective in editorials and informal persuasive essays. Ask yourself: "Just where in my essay have I made my one main point, the point I most want to make?" Once you find it, see if you can place it last by cutting or shifting what comes after it.

This climactic order works not only in essays but also in sentences. A sentence that suspends its main point until the end is a *periodic* sentence. Waiting for someone to finish readying for a trip, you might say, "Now that you've packed your toothbrush and a change of clothing, let's roll!" By placing "let's roll" at the end of the sentence, you emphasize it. Notice how novelist Julian Green builds to his point of emphasis:

> Amid chaos of illusions into which we are cast headlong, there is one thing that stands out as true, and that is — love.

Repeating

In general, it's economical to say a thing once. But at times a repetition can be valuable. One such time is when a repetition serves as a transition: it recalls something said earlier. (We discuss such repetition on p. 356.)

Repetition can be valuable, too, when it lends emphasis. When Robert Frost ends his poem "Stopping by Woods on a Snowy Evening" by repeating a line, he does so deliberately:

> The woods are lovely, dark and deep,
> But I have promises to keep,
> And miles to go before I sleep,
> And miles to go before I sleep.

The effect of this repetition is to lay weight on the fact that, for the speaker, a long, weary journey remains.

This device — repeating the words that most matter — is more often heard in a speech than found in writing. Recall Lincoln's Gettysburg Address, with its promise that "government of the people, by the people, and for the people" will endure; and Martin Luther King's famous speech with the insistent refrain "I have a dream." This is a powerful device for emphasis. Break it out only when an occasion calls for it.

CUTTING AND WHITTLING

Like pea pickers who throw out dirt and pebbles, good writers remove needless words that clog their prose. They like to. One of the chief joys of revising is to watch 200 paunchy words shrink to a svelte 150. To see how saving words helps, let's first look at some wordiness. In what she imagined to be a gracious, Oriental style, a New York socialite once sent this dinner invitation to Hu Shi, the Chinese ambassador:

> O learned sage and distinguished representative of the numerous Chinese nation, pray deign to honor my humble abode with your noble presence at a pouring of libations, to be followed by a modest evening repast, on the forthcoming Friday, June Eighteenth, in this Year of the Pig, at the approximate hour of eight o'clock, Eastern Standard Time. Kindly be assured furthermore, O most illustrious sire,

that a favorable reply at your earliest convenience will be received most humbly and gratefully by the undersigned unworthy suppliant.

In reply, the witty diplomat sent this telegram:

CAN DO. HU SHI.

Hu Shi's reply disputes a common assumption: that the more words an idea takes, the more impressive it will seem. Most good contemporary writers know that the more succinctly they can state an idea, the clearer and more forceful it will be.

Since the sixteenth century, some English writers have favored prolixity and, like the woman who invited Hu Shi, have deliberately ornamented their prose. George Orwell, a more recent writer who favored concision, thought English writing in his day had set a new record for wind. Perhaps the verbosity he disliked has been due in part to progress in the technology of writing. Quill pens that had to be dipped have given way to pens with ball points or felt tips, to electric typewriters and word processors. These strides have made words easier to seize and perhaps have made them matter less. As a printer-reporter in Virginia City, Nevada, Mark Twain sometimes wrote while he set type, transferring letters of lead from a case to a composing stick in his hand. An editorial might weigh ten pounds. Twain said the experience taught him the weight of a word. He soon learned to use no word that didn't matter.

Some writers may begin by writing a long first draft, putting in every scrap of material, spelling out their every thought in detail. To them, it is easier to trim away the surplus than to add missing essentials. In their revising habits, such writers may be like sculptor Auguste Rodin, who when an admirer asked, "Oh, Monsieur Rodin, is sculpture difficult?" answered lightly, "Not at all! I merely behold the statue in the block of stone. Then I chip away everything else." Let us see how writers chip away.

CUT THE FANFARE

WORDY

```
As far as getting ready for winter is concerned, I put
antifreeze in my car.
```

REVISED

```
To get ready for winter, I put antifreeze in my car.
```

Some writers can't utter an idea without first sounding trumpets before it.

WORDY

```
The point should be made that . . .
I might hasten to add that . . .
Let me make it perfectly clear that . . .
In this paper I intend to . . .
In conclusion I would like to say that . . .
```

Why bother to announce that you're going to say something? Cut the fanfare. We aren't, by the way, attacking the usefulness of transitions that lead a reader along. You wouldn't chop a sentence like "Because, as we have seen, Chomsky's theory fails to account for the phenomenon of stuttering, let us consider the work of speech psychologist Wendell Johnson."

The phrases *on the subject of, in regard to, in terms of, as far as . . . is concerned,* and their ilk often lead to wind.

BE DIRECT

WORDY
```
He is more or less a pretty outstanding person in regard
to good looks.
```

REVISED
```
He is strikingly handsome.
In looks, he stands out.
```

Here's an especially grim example of corporate prose (before cutting and after):

WORDY
```
Regarding trainees' personal life in relation to domestic
status, it is not the intention of the management to ob-
ject to the marriage of any of its trainees at their own
individual discretions.
```

REVISED
```
Trainees may marry if they like.
```

Words can also tend to abound after *There is* or *There are.*

WORDY
```
There are many people who dislike flying.
```

This construction provides an easy way to open a sentence, but it takes words and shifts focus. You can cut it.

REVISED
```
Many people dislike flying.
```

Here's another instance:

WORDY
```
There is a lack of a sense of beauty in Wallace.
```

REVISED
```
Wallace lacks a sense of beauty.
Wallace is insensitive to beauty.
```

USE STRONG VERBS

Forms of the verb *to be* (*am, is, are, was, were*) can make a statement wordy when a noun or an adjective follows it.

WORDY

```
The Akron game was a disappointment to the fans.
```

Replace *was* by an active verb and revise the sentence:

REVISED

```
The Akron game disappointed the fans.
```

Not only do such changes save words, they enliven a sentence.

USE RELATIVE PRONOUNS WITH CAUTION

Often, when a clause begins with a relative pronoun (*who, which, that*), you can whittle it to a phrase:

WORDY

```
Venus, which is the second planet of the solar system, is
called the evening star.
```

REVISED

```
Venus, the second planet of the solar system, is called
the evening star.
```

WORDY

```
Bert, who is a prize-winning violist, played a work of
Brahms.
```

REVISED

```
Bert, a prize-winning violist, played a work of Brahms.
```

CUT OUT DEADWOOD

The more you revise, the more shortcuts you'll discover. The following sentences have words that can just be cut (indicated in *italics*). Try reading each sentence without them.

Howell spoke for the sophomores and Janet *also spoke* for the seniors.

Professor Lombardi is *one of the most* amazing *men.*

He is *somewhat of* a clown, but *sort of the* lovable *type.*

As a major in *the field of* economics, I plan to concentrate on *the area of* international banking.

The decision *as to* whether *or not* to go is up to you.

The vice-chairman *very much* regrets that he is *very* busy.

CUT DESCRIPTORS

Adjectives and adverbs are often dispensable. Consider the difference between these two versions.

WORDY

```
Johnson's extremely significant research led to highly
important major discoveries.
```

REVISED

```
Johnson's research led to major discoveries.
```

BE SHORT, NOT LONG

While sometimes a long word conveys a shade of meaning that its shorter synonym doesn't, in general it's a good idea to shun a long word or phrase when you can pick a short one. Instead of *the remainder,* try to write *the rest;* instead of *activate, start* or *begin;* instead of *expedite, rush;* instead of *adequate* or *sufficient, enough.* Wordiness, to be sure, doesn't always come from slinging overlarge words. Sometimes it comes from not knowing a right word — one that wraps an idea in a smaller package. The cumbersome expression *persons who are new to the sport of skiing* could be replaced by *novice skiers.* Consider these two remarks about a boxer:

WORDY

```
Andy has a left fist that has a lot of power in it.
```

REVISED

```
Andy has a potent left.
```

By the way, it pays to read. From reading, you absorb words like *potent* and *novice* and set them to work for you.

Here is a student essay that gained from cutting and whittling. John Martin, a business administration major, wrote this economics paper to fulfill the assignment "Set forth and briefly discuss a current problem in international trade. Venture an opinion or propose a solution." You can see the thoughtful cuts and condensations that Martin made with the help of his English instructor and his peer editor. Following the edited draft, you'll find the paper (p. 392) as he resubmitted it — in fewer words.

FIRST DRAFT

```
     Japan's Closed Doors:   Should the U.S. Retaliate?


                                                  is
     There is currently A serious problem⌃brewing in the
world of international trade; which may turn out to be a
cliché real tempest in a teapot, so to speak.  According to the
to cut latest National Trade Estimates report, several of the
```

U.S. trading partners deserve to be condemned for "unfair trade practices." The government has said it will use the report to single out countries to punish under the Super 301 provisions of the trade law.

The Super 301 section requires Carla Hills, the U.S. trade representative, to attack what she calls "priority unfair practices." She will be slashing at the same thing as impediments web of impediments that have denied American firms fast access to Japanese markets.

For long Japan has long been the prime candidate for a dose of Super 301. Over the past decade, industry groups have battered at the doors of Japanese markets, with some successes, but failed to make them swing wide. The U.S. trade deficit with Japan more than $50 billion last year, shows little sign of improving in 1990.

Some American businesspeople would take aim at Japan immediately. However, Clyde Prestowitz, a former Commerce Department official, doubts that it would be wise to name Japan for retaliation under Super 301: "It's hard to negotiate with guys you are calling cheats." No doubt many other observers share his view.

Evidently the administration has to

help

try to ~~pave the way for~~ U.S. exports ~~to~~ wedge their way

into ~~the~~ protected Japanese markets while keeping ~~it~~

~~firmly~~ in mind that the interests of both ~~the United~~

stronger

~~States and the Japanese~~ nations call for ∧a ~~strengthening~~

"ties" will
suffice.

~~of the~~ economic and military ties, ~~that bind both coun-~~

~~tries into a sphere of friendly relationship. It is my~~

~~personal conclusion that~~ **I**f the administration goes ahead,

~~with this,~~ it will ~~certainly~~ need to plan ~~ahead for the~~

~~future~~ carefully.

REVISED VERSION

    Japan's Closed Doors: Should the U.S. Retaliate?

    A serious problem is brewing in international trade.
According to the latest National Trade Estimates report,
several U.S. trading partners deserve to be condemned for
"unfair trade practices." The government has said it
will use the report to single out countries to punish under the Super 301 provisions of the trade law.

    The Super 301 section requires Carla Hills, the U.S.
trade representative, to attack what she calls "priority
unfair practices." She will be slashing at the web of
impediments that have denied American firms fast access
to Japanese markets.

    Japan has long been the prime candidate for a dose
of Super 301. Over the past decade, industry groups have
battered at the doors of Japanese markets, with some success, but failed to make them swing wide. The U.S. trade
deficit with Japan, more than $50 billion last year,
shows little sign of improving in 1990.

    Some American businesspeople would take aim at Japan
immediately. However, Clyde Prestowitz, a former Commerce Department official, doubts that it would be wise
to name Japan for retaliation under Super 301: "It's
hard to negotiate with guys you are calling cheats." No
doubt many other observers share his view.

    Evidently the administration has to try to help U.S.
exports wedge their way into protected Japanese markets

while keeping in mind that the interests of both nations
call for stronger economic and military ties. If the administration goes ahead, it will need to plan carefully.

Here is a final list of questions to use in slimming your writing.

REVISION CHECKLIST: CUTTING AND WHITTLING

- Are you direct and straightforward?
- Do you announce an idea before you utter it? If so, consider chopping out the announcement.
- Can you recast any sentence that begins *There is* or *There are*?
- What will happen if, wherever you use a form of the verb *to be* (*is, was, were*), you substitute an active verb?
- Have you used strong, precise nouns?
- Can you reduce to a phrase any clause beginning with *which is, who is,* or *that is*?
- Have you used too many adjectives and adverbs?
- Do you see any useless words that might go? Try omitting them.

PROOFREADING

Proofreading is the last step in writing. It helps you sell your ideas to your readers because they won't be constantly distracted by misplaced commas or misspelled words. In college, it can make the difference between a C and an A. On the job, it may help you get a promotion. Readers, teachers, and bosses like careful writers who take time to proofread.

Don't proofread too soon. In your early drafting, don't fret over the correct spelling of an unfamiliar word; the word may be revised or edited out in a later version. If the word stays in, you'll have time to check it later. Turn your internal monitor or editor off until you have the ideas right.

Most errors in writing occur unconsciously. Some result from faulty information in your memory. If you have never learned the difference between "its" and "it's," you'll probably misuse these words without realizing you're making a mistake. If you have never looked closely at the spelling of "environment," you may have never seen the second "n" and so you'll habitually spell it "enviroment." Such errors easily become habits and reinforce themselves every time you write them.

Split-second inattention or a break in concentration can also cause errors. Because the mind works faster than the pen or the pencil (or the typewriter or even the word processor), when you are distracted by someone's voice or a telephone ring, you may omit a letter or a whole word or you may put in the wrong punctuation.

The very way our eyes work leads to errors. When you read normally, you usually see only the shells of words — the first and last letters. You fix your eyes on the print only three or four times per line or less. (Think of how fast you can move down a column of names in the telephone book.) You take in the words between your fixation points with your peripheral vision, which gets less and less accurate the farther it is from the point of fixation. The average reader can "see" or take in only six letters accurately with one fixation and can retain only six items (whether letters, numbers, or words) in short-term memory. These physiological limitations mean that you have to fix your eyes on every word you have written, twice for longer words, to proofread accurately. Remember that to proofread you must look at the individual letters in each word and the punctuation marks between words and not slide over the individual symbols. Proofreading requires time and patience.

The skill of proofreading does not come naturally, but it is a skill you can develop, like touch typing or starting a car or playing the guitar. It is your responsibility as a writer to break old habits and develop this skill. It will pay off in the long run.

Tips for Proofreading

1. Turn off your internal monitor until you get the ideas right.

2. Realize that *all* writers make mistakes in their haste to get ideas on paper and must proofread to find and correct their errors.

3. Don't be egotistical about your writing: realize that you are human and you will make mistakes. Develop a healthy sense of doubt because mistakes are so easy to make. There is nothing bad about making mistakes, only about not taking time to find and correct them.

4. Budget enough time to proofread thoroughly.

5. Let a paper "get cold." Let it sit several days, or overnight, or at least a few hours before proofreading it.

6. Learn the grammar conventions you don't understand so you can spot and eliminate problems in your own writing. Practice until you easily recognize major errors, such as fragments and comma splices. Learn how to correct your own common problems. Ask for assistance in the writing center if your campus has one.

7. Read what you have written very slowly, looking at every word, every letter.

8. Read your paper aloud. Speaking forces you to slow down and see more, and sometimes you will hear a mistake you haven't seen.

9. Read what you have actually written, not what you think is there. Don't let your mind play tricks on you. Developing the objectivity to see what is really on the page or screen is one of the most difficult aspects of proofreading.

10. Use a dictionary or a spell checker whenever you can.

11. Double-check for your habitual errors (such as leaving off -s or -ed or putting in unnecessary commas). This is especially important for timed writings and tests on which you do not have access to a dictionary.

12. Read the essay backward. This will force you to look at each word because you won't get caught up in the flow of ideas.

13. Read the essay several times, focusing each time on a specific area of difficulty (once for spelling, once for punctuation, or even once for fragments if they cause recurrent problems for you).

14. Ask someone else to read your paper for you and tell you if it makes sense and is free of distracting errors. *Caution:* Don't let someone else do your work for you.

15. Take pride in your work.

REVISION CHECKLIST: PROOFREADING

- Have you omitted any words? any letters? any -s at the end of words? any -ed on verbs? any necessary marks of punctuation?
- Have you transposed any letters? Have you misplaced any punctuation marks?
- Have you added any unnecessary letters or punctuation?
- Have you checked your grammar? Look especially at verb tense, subject-verb agreement, pronoun agreement, pronoun case, and pronoun reference.
- Have you checked the spelling of the words you're unsure of? Of words you habitually miss?
- Have you in haste used the wrong word (*lay* instead of *lie*, *its* for *it's*, *advice* for *advise*, *their* for *they're*, *her's* for *hers*)?
- Have you slowed your mind down and focused your eyes on each word, each letter in each word, each punctuation mark?

Exercise: Proofreading and Editing

Proofread the following passage carefully. The organization of the paragraph is satisfactory, as is the sentence structure. You are to look for mistakes in spelling, grammar, punctuation, and capitalization and correct them. There are ten errors in the paragraph. After you have completed your editing of the passage, discuss with your classmates the changes you have made and your reasons for making those changes.

Robert Frost, one of the most popular American poets. He was born in San Francisco in 1874, and died in Boston in 1963. His family moved to new England when his father died in 1885. There he completed highschool and attended colledge but never graduate. Poverty and problems filled his life. He worked in a woolen mill, on a newspaper, and on varous odd jobs. Because of ill health he settled on a farm and began to teach school to support his wife and children. Throughout his life he dedicated himself to writing poetry, by 1915 he was in demand for public readings and speaking engagements. He was awarded the Pulitzer Prize for poetry four times — in 1924, 1931, 1937, and 1943. The popularity of his poetry rests in his use of common themes and images, expressed in everyday language. Everyone can relate to his universal poems, such as "Swinging on Birches" and "Stopping by Woods on a Snowy Evening." Students read his poetry in school from seventh grade through graduate school, so almost everyone recognize lines from his best-loved poems. America is proud of it's son, the homespun poet Robert Frost.

A NOTE ON MANUSCRIPT STYLE

Some instructors are sticklers in detailing how your paper ought to look; others maintain a benign indifference to such commonplaces. In writing for an instructor of either stripe, it is only considerate to turn in a paper easy to read and to comment on.

In case you have received no particular instructions for the form of your paper, here are some general, all-purpose specifications.

1. If you handwrite your paper, make sure your handwriting is legible. If you type, keep your typewriter keys clean.

2. Write or type on just one side of standard letter-size paper (8½-by-11 inches). Erasable typing paper, however helpful to a mistake-prone typist, may be irksome to an instructor who needs to write comments. The paper is easily smeared, and it won't take certain kinds of ink.

3. If you handwrite your paper, use 8½-by-11-inch paper with smooth edges (not torn from a spiral-bound notebook).

4. Use a black ribbon if you type, dark blue or black ink if you write. If you use a machine that lets you change type styles, don't do your paper entirely in italics or extra-fine characters. Pick an easy-to-read typeface.

5. For a paper without a separate title page, place your name, together with your instructor's name, the number and section of the course, and the date in the upper right corner of the first page, each item on a new line even with the right margin. Double-space and center your title. Don't underline the title; don't put it in quotation marks or type the title all in capital letters; and don't put a period after it. Capitalize the first and last words, the first word after a colon or semicolon, and all other words except prepositions, conjunctions, and articles. Double-space between the title and the first line of your text.

6. Number your pages consecutively, including the first page. For a paper of two or more pages, put your last name in the upper right corner of each sheet along with the page number. Do not type the word *page* or the letter *p* before the number and do not follow the number with a period or parenthesis.

7. Make sure you give your instructor plenty of room to write in, if need be. Leave ample margins — at least an inch — left and right, top and bottom.

If you type, double-space your manuscript; if you write, use wide-ruled paper or skip every other line.

8. Indent each new paragraph five spaces.

9. Leave two spaces after every period or other end stop, one after a comma, semicolon, or colon.

10. Try not to break words at the ends of lines. If you must break a word, divide it at the end of a syllable. If you're uncertain about where a syllable ends, check a dictionary.

11. Long quotations should be double-spaced like the rest of your paper but indented from the left margin—ten spaces if you're following Modern Language Association (MLA) guidelines, five if you're using American Psychological Association (APA) guidelines. Citations appear in parentheses two spaces after the final punctuation mark of the block quotation. (For more about citing sources, see Chapter 30.)

12. Label all illustrations, and make sure they are bound securely to the paper.

13. Covering a short essay—one of, say, five pages—in a hefty binder or giving it a title page with a blank sheet or two after it is unnecessary. Title pages are generally reserved for research papers and other bulky works.

14. Staples are the best bet; paper clips quit their posts. Put the staple in the top left corner. By the way, don't ever try to bind your pages together by folding the corners over and then ripping a notch in the fold. This method never works; the pages always come apart. Do not staple your pages all the way down the side; this practice makes turning the papers difficult.

15. For safety's sake and peace of mind, make a copy of your paper.

Additional Suggestions for Research Papers

For research papers the format is the same with the following additional specifications.

1. Type a title page, with the title of your paper centered about a third of the way down the page. Then go down two to four more spaces and type your name, then the instructor's name, the number and section of the course, and the date, each on a separate line. Repeat your title on the first page of your paper.

2. Do not number your title page; your outline, if you submit one with your paper, is numbered with small roman numerals (ii, iii, and so on).

3. Don't put a number on the first page of your text (page 1); all subsequent pages through your notes and works cited pages are numbered consecutively with arabic numerals in the upper right corner of the page.

4. Double-space your notes and your list of works cited. (For more instructions for making such a list, see Chapter 30.)

5. If you are asked to hand in your note cards along with your paper, be sure that they are in order and securely bound with a rubber band or placed in an envelope.

How to Make a Correction

Although you will want to make any large changes in your rough draft, not in your final copy, don't be afraid to make small corrections in pen when you give your paper a last once-over. No writer is error-free; neither is any typist. In making such corrections, you may find it handy to use certain symbols used by printers and proofreaders.

A transposition mark (∩) reverses the positions of two words or two letters:

```
The nearby star Tau Ceti closely resmebles our sun.
```

Close-up marks (⌒) bring together the parts of a word accidentally split when a typewriter stutters. A separation mark (⌐) inserts a space where one is needed:

```
The nearby star Tau Ceti closely re⌒sembles our⌐sun.
```

To delete a letter or a punctuation mark, draw a slanted line through it:

```
The nearby star Tau Ceti closely res/sembles our sun.
```

When you insert a word or letter, use a caret (∧) to indicate where the insertion belongs:

```
                                      s
The nearby star Tau Ceti closely re∧embles our sun.
```

The symbol ¶ before a word or a line means "start a new paragraph":

```
But lately, astronomers have slackened their efforts to
study dark nebulae. ¶ That other solar systems may support
life as we know it makes for still another fascinating
speculation.
```

You can always cross out a word neatly, with a single horizontal line, and write a better one over it (*never* type a correction right over a mistake).

```
                            closely
The nearby star Tau Ceti ~~somewhat~~ resembles our sun.
```

Finally, if a page has many errors on it, type or write it over again. (Repairing mistakes is, of course, child's play if you're writing with a word processor.)

CHAPTER 19

Strategies for Working with Other Writers:

Collaborative Learning

Some people imagine the writer all alone in an ivory tower, toiling in perfect solitude. But in the real world, writing is often a collaborative effort. In business firms, reports are sometimes written by teams and revised by committees before being submitted to top-level managers. People sit around a table throwing out ideas, which a secretary transcribes and someone else writes up. A crucial letter, an advertisement, or a company's annual report embodies the thinking and writing of many. Research scientists and social scientists often work in teams of two or more and collaborate on articles for professional journals. Even this book is the result of collaborative writing.

Student writers are often pleasantly surprised to find how genuinely helpful other students can be. When you are the writer, working with your classmates and friends gives you a very real sense of having a living, breathing, supportive audience. Asked to read an early draft, peers can respond to a paper, signal strengths in it, and offer constructive suggestions. In doing so, they explicitly guide you in revising. Students can give one another valuable help and support. That is why, in the body of this book, we include peer editing checklists and suggest activities for group learning.

In colleges today, more and more instructors are encouraging students to work together in small groups on their writing—to generate ideas, to provide constructive criticism of drafts, to respond to final papers, even to write collaborative essays. The writers not only benefit from the comments of peers on their writing, but also discover that giving reactions to other classmates helps them to write better.

If your instructor does not require collaborative writing or peer editing, you can arrange it on your own. Enlist one or more classmates or friends to read your work and comment on it. You can provide the same service in return. Before you show a draft to a friend, take a few minutes to write down two or three questions you'd like him or her to answer. If you are reading a classmate's work, ask the writer to give you a few specific questions.

If you don't know someone who is willing to respond to your writing for you, go to the writing center on campus. Here you can get help from special instructors and work with trained, experienced peer tutors. The lab staff will not do your work—planning, drafting, revising, proofreading—for you, but will help you fulfill your assigned task.

SERVING AS A READER

What does it take to be a helpful, supportive peer editor? Here are a few tips for you.

Look at the big picture. Your job isn't merely to notice misspelled words or misused semicolons (although it can't hurt to signal any that you see). Bend your mind to deeper matters: to what the writer is driving at, to the sequence of ideas, to the apparent truth or falsity of the observations, to the quantity and quality of the evidence, to the coherence or unity of the paper as a whole.

Be specific. Vague blame or praise won't help the writer. Don't say, "It's an interesting paper" or "I liked this essay a lot because I can relate to it." Such a response might make the writer feel glad, but statements like "That example in paragraph 9 clarified the whole point of the paper for me" will make the author feel glad for good reason.

Be tactful. Approach the work in a friendly way. Remember, you aren't out to pass godlike judgment on your peer's effort ("What confused garbage!"). Your purpose as a reader is to give honest, intelligent comments—to help make the other writer aware of what's written right, not only what's written wrong. When you find fault, you can do so by making impartial observations—statements nobody can deny. A judgmental way to criticize might be "This paper is confused. It keeps saying the same thing over and over again." But a more useful comment might be more specific: "Paragraph 5 makes the same point as paragraphs 2 and 3," suggesting that two of the three paragraphs might be eliminated.

Ask yourself questions. For help in looking for worthwhile, specific, tactful responses, skim the following checklist of readers' questions. Not all these points will apply to every paper.

FIRST QUESTIONS
What is your first reaction to this paper?

What is this writer trying to tell you? What does he or she most want you to learn?

What are this paper's greatest strengths?

Does it have any major weaknesses?

QUESTIONS ON MEANING

Do you understand everything? Is there any information missing from this draft that you still need to know?

Is what this paper tells you worth saying, or does it only belabor the obvious? Does it tell you anything you didn't know before?

Is the writer trying to cover too much territory? Too little?

Does any point need to be more fully explained or illustrated?

When you come to the end, do you find that the paper has promised you anything it hasn't delivered?

Could this paper use a down-to-the-ground revision? Would it be better on a different topic altogether—one the writer perhaps touches but doesn't deal with in this paper?

QUESTIONS ON ORGANIZATION

Has the writer begun in such a way that you're interested? Are you quickly drawn into the paper's main idea? Or can you find, at some point later in the paper, a better possible beginning?

Does the paper have one main idea, or does it struggle to handle more than one? Would the main idea stand out better if anything were removed?

Might the ideas in the paper be more effectively rearranged in a different order? Do any ideas belong together that now seem too far apart?

Does the writer keep to one point of view—one angle of seeing? (If he starts out writing as a college student, does he switch to when he was a boy without telling me? If he starts out as an enemy of smoking, does he end up as an advocate?)

Does the ending seem deliberate, as if the writer meant to conclude at this point? Or does the writer seem merely to have run out of gas? If so, what can the writer do to write a stronger conclusion?

QUESTIONS ON LANGUAGE AND WRITING STRATEGIES

Do you feel this paper addresses *you*? Or does the writer appear to have no idea who might be reading the paper?

At any point in the paper, do you find yourself disliking or objecting to a statement the writer makes, to a word or a phrase with which you're not in sympathy? Should this part be kept, whether or not you object, or should it be changed?

Does the draft contain anything that distracts you, that seems unnecessary, that might be struck?

Do you get bored at any point and want to tune out? What might the writer do to make you want to keep reading?

Can you follow the writer's ideas easily? Does the paper need transitions (words and phrases that connect), and, if it does, at what places?

Does the language of this paper stay up in the clouds of generality, referring always to *agricultural commodities* and *legality,* never to *pigs' feet* and *parking tickets*? If so, where and how might the writer come down to earth and get specific?

Do you understand all the words the writer uses, or are there any specialized words (such as scientific words or dialect) whose meaning needs to be made clearer?

LAST QUESTION

Now that you have lived with this paper for a while and looked at it closely, how well does it work for you?

Write comments. To show the writer just where you had a reaction, write notations in the margins of the paper. Then at the end write an overall comment, making major, general suggestions. Sum up the paper's strong and weak points — it can hardly be all good or all bad.

Here is a helpful comment by Maria Mendez on a draft of a paper by Jill Walker that ended up being titled "Euthanasia and the Law":

Jill—

The topic of this paper interested me a lot, because we had a case of euthanasia in our neighborhood. I didn't realize at first what your topic was—maybe the title "Life and Death" didn't say it to me. Your paper is full of good ideas and facts—like the Hemlock Society to help mercy-killing. I got lost when you start talking about advances in modern medicine (paragraph 6) but don't finish the idea. To go into modern medicine thoroughly would take a lot more room. Maybe euthanasia is enough to cover in five pages. Also, I don't know everything you're mentioning ("traditional attitudes toward life and death"). I could have used an explanation there—I'm from a different tradition. On the whole, your paper is solid and is going to make us agree with you.

Maria

LEARNING AS A WRITER

You, the writer whose work is in the spotlight, will probably find you can't just sit back and enjoy your fans' reactions. To extract all the usefulness from the process of peer reviewing, you'll need to play an active part in discussing your work.

Ask your reader questions. Probably your readers will give you more helpful specific reactions if you question them. Sometimes your instructor or your textbook will provide some questions for your readers. You as the writer, however, may already know that something is wrong with your early draft, so you should add your own questions. Direct the peer readers' attention to places in your paper where you especially want insights. Express any doubts you have. Point out parts you found difficult to write. Ask what they would

WRITING WITH A COMPUTER: SERVING AS A READER

If the writer wrote with a word processor, the two of you might sit down in front of the monitor screen together. You can scroll slowly through the document, commenting on the draft line by line. But if the writer doesn't want to stick around and watch you edit, you can put your comments and suggestions in brackets at whatever places in the draft they need to be made. Thanks to word processing, it will be easy for the writer, after reading all the comments, to search for every first bracket and delete each comment.

```
Harry S Truman had a folksy way of expressing him-
self, which makes us remember many of his sayings.
[Can you give an example?]  He was a folksy speaker
[Cut this repetition.] and developed his style in
the rough-and-tumble of Mississippi politics.  [You
mean Missouri.]
```

do about any weak spots. Get at the why's behind their responses. Ask pointed questions like these *in writing* for your editors to think about:

> When you read my conclusion, are you convinced that I'm arguing for the one right solution to this problem? Can you imagine any better solution?

> Paragraph four looks skimpy—only two short sentences. What could I do to make it longer?

> How clear is my purpose? Can you sum up what I'm trying to say? What steps can I take to make my point hit home to you?

Encourage your readers to be sympathetic but tough. Ask your peer editors not to be too easy on you. Let them know that you are willing to make deep structural changes in what you have written, not merely cosmetic repairs.

Be open to new ideas. You might get completely new ideas — for focus, for organization, for details — from the readers' reactions. They may also have some tips about where to find more, and more valuable, relevant material.

Take what's helpful. Occasionally students worry that asking another student, no wiser or brighter or more experienced than themselves, to criticize their work is a risk not worth taking. You have to accept such help judiciously. You want to be wary about following all the suggestions you receive. While some of them may help, others may lead down a dead-end street. At times when a reader finds fault with your work, you may want to make some change but not necessarily the very change your critic suggests. Sometimes it will strike a reader that something is wrong with a piece of writing, but he or she will not be sure just what it is and will not be able to come up with a surefire remedy. Not wanting to seem unhelpful, the reader will make a suggestion anyway.

Realize you're the boss. The important thing in taking advice and suggestions is to listen to your respondents but not be a slave to them. Trust yourself. Let your instincts operate. Make a list of the suggestions you receive. Do any of them cancel out others? Does any suggestion seem worth trying? If so, give it a try, but drop it if it doesn't work.

It takes self-trust to sift through criticism with profit. The final decision about whether or not to act on the advice you get from your fellow students is solely up to you. If you feel that one person's suggestions have not helped at all, you would be wise to get a second opinion, and maybe a third. When several of your readers disagree, only you can decide what direction to follow.

Learn to evaluate your own writing. As your writing skills continue to develop, you will find yourself relying less on your peers and more on your own ability to analyze and revise your early drafts. You can ask yourself the very same questions you use in evaluating other writers' papers. And when you learn to answer those questions searchingly, you'll become your own most valuable reader.

PEER EDITORS IN ACTION

The following brief histories point out how effectively classmates can help a revision. First, consider this early draft of an opening paragraph for the essay "Why Don't More People Donate Their Bodies to Science?" by Dana Falk, written in a tandem course in English and sociology.

> The question of why more organs and body parts are
> not donated "to science"--that is, for the use of organ
> transplants, medical research, and college education--is
> a puzzling one. As I have learned through my research,
> it is also a multidetermined one. There are a plethora
> of reasons that prevent there from being enough organs to
> go around, and in this paper I shall examine a number of
> the reasons I have uncovered, trying to evaluate the ef-
> fectiveness of efforts to alleviate the shortage and sug-
> gest possible alternate approaches myself. Primarily,
> though, we will simply look at the factors that prevent

```
health professionals from being able to supply body parts
each and every time a donor is needed.
```

Falk showed the paper to a classmate, Pamela Kong, who jumped at once on the opening sentence. "This could be rephrased as a question," she suggested, and she wrote "AWKWARD" next to the sentence that begins "There are a plethora of reasons that prevent there from being. . . ." "That sentence was pretty bad!" Falk later realized. Kong zeroed in on the stilted word *multidetermined* (apparently meaning "having several causes") and called for a clearer announcement of where the paper was going. After reading Kong's comments and doing some hard thinking, Falk recast the opening paragraph to read:

```
    The gap between the demand for human organs and
their current supply is ever-widening.  With the intro-
duction of cyclosporine, an immunosuppressant, the suc-
cess rate of transplants is way up, yet this bright spot
is clouded by the fact that many potential donors and
their families resist giving away their body parts, cre-
ating an acute shortage.  Why is it that people so fear
giving their bodies to science?  Let's examine the causes
of the shortage of transplantable organs and review some
possible solutions.
```

As you'll see if you compare the two passages, Falk's language becomes more concrete and definite with the use of two figures of speech. Now we have an "ever-widening gap" and a "bright spot" that is "clouded." The added detail about the newly successful drug lends the paper fresh authority—and no longer does the writer have to trumpet "my research." Pam Kong's suggestion to turn the question into an actual one (with a question mark) lends life to the sentence that now begins "Why is it that people so fear. . . ." The announced plan for the rest of the paper, now placed at the end of the paragraph, points toward everything that will follow. This hard job of rewriting (which continued throughout the whole paper) drew Falk's English instructor, Jeff Skoblow, to remark: "Your revising powers have grown formidable." No doubt some of the credit belonged to Pam Kong as well.

Now let's see how a peer editor helped a fellow student strengthen an entire paper. Kevin Deters wrote the following short essay for his English composition course. The assignment asked for a "reflective" essay in response to his own reading. Even in this early draft, you'll find, Deters's paper treats a challenging subject, and it comes to a thoughtful conclusion. But as the paper stands, what does it lack? For practice, try to critique the paper yourself before you look at the peer editor's comments.

FIRST DRAFT

Where Few Men Have Gone Before

Kevin Deters

Space: the final frontier. This is the subject addressed by the renowned writer Isaac Asimov in "Into Space: The Next Giant Step," a short piece published in the St. Louis Post-Dispatch. Asimov, the author of over four hundred science and science fiction books, writes about the space station that will be built in orbit around the earth in the near future. He examines the advantages and numerous possibilities of space travel that such a station would allow. This space station will give people the opportunity to be explorers, help conserve resources on earth, and unite the nations of the world as they forge the common goal of discovering knowledge of outer space.

"It is absolutely necessary that we build a base other than earth for our ventures into space. . . . The logical beginning is with a space station," Asimov says. The space station would serve as a stepping stone to future permanent bases on the moon and Mars. Adventurous settlers would pave the spaceways just as Daniel Boone and his followers blazed trails through the Kentucky wilderness. It is these space travelers "who will be the Phoenicians, the Vikings, the Polynesians of the future, making their way into the 21st century through a space-ocean far vaster than the water-ocean traversed by their predecessors."

These spacefarers will also find ways to help conserve valuable energy on earth. Asimov suggests that, using the space station as a base, lunar materials could be excavated from the moon to construct power stations to direct solar energy toward the earth. Thus, energy and money are saved, and this conservation could serve as a deterrent to the use of nuclear energy.

With this new surplus of energy, nuclear energy and all its applications such as power plants and missiles

would become unnecessary. A major threat to world safety
would be removed. The sun's never-ending supply of solar
energy could be harnessed to become the chief energy
source on earth, and dangerous forms of energy could be
done away with.

As a result, expensive heating bills and the like
would be unheard of. Energy costs would plummet as
earth's populace took advantage of the sun's plentiful
rays. The price decrease would snowball, affecting other
aspects of life, eventually resulting in a cheaper cost
of living.

The construction of such a space station could also
help unify the countries of the world. A massive project
like this enterprise would cost billions of dollars and
take a massive amount of time and hard work. Asimov suggests that if the United States and the Soviet Union were
to work together, costs and time could be considerably
lessened. Such joint U.S./U.S.S.R. missions are not unheard of. The Apollo-Soyuz venture, which linked together a spacecraft from each nation, was a success.

This joint effort could help promote global togetherness as well. If the world's nations could unite
to explore space, surely problems back home on earth
could be easily solved. Such quibbles as the nuclear
arms race and foreign trading disputes seem trivial and
inconsequential when compared to the grandeur of space
exploration.

And so, this space station will serve as a valuable
tool for humanity. Man must now reach for the heavens
above him, because if the earth's population keeps increasing, the planet will soon be too small to accommodate everyone. Space exploration is the only logical
answer. Space is indeed the final frontier that lies before us. We only have to take advantage of it.

Kevin Deters's classmate, Jennifer Balsavias, read his reflective essay and filled out a peer editing questionnaire. Here are the questions and her responses to them.

PEER EDITING CHECKLIST

1. First, sit on your hands and read the essay through. Then describe your first reaction.

This was a well-written report. The only time I really noticed any reflection on the reading was in the last paragraph.

2. What is "reflective" about this essay? What is the purpose of the essay and the major reflection?

The purpose of the essay was to show the importance of space to humans and their expansion into that final frontier. In the last paragraph, he lets us know his feelings on the information given. He doesn't reflect about the reading throughout the paper.

3. How skillfully has the writer used reading? Look at the way quotations or paraphrases are inserted. Is it clear when the writer is using reading and when the ideas are the writer's? Comment on any areas that were problematic to you.

He uses quotes and information from the reading very well. The writer is definitely using the reading and adds only a few thoughts of his own. Needs to reflect more !

4. Is the paper informed enough by reading? Where could the paper improve by more careful or detailed use of "secondary" (not personal) materials?

It's not very personal. His own feelings and reflections should be involved. There is enough about the reading. Maybe he shouldn't expand so much on the subject. Maybe stop after the first or second paragraph and REFLECT!

5. Who's the essay written to? Describe the audience.

I feel it is written to those interested in space and the new space programs. I found it interesting.

6. List any terms or phrases that are too technical or specialized or any words that need further definition.

None

7. If you were handing the essay in for a grade, what would you be sure to revise?

I'd put some of my own reflections in, not just facts.

8. Circle on the manuscript any problems with spelling, punctuation, grammar, or usage.

None that I saw!

In reading Jennifer Balsavias's evaluation, Deters was struck by her main criticism: "The only time I really noticed any reflection on the reading was in the last paragraph." "Needs to reflect *more*!" Deters's paper seemed more like a report on an article than an essay analyzing the article with some original thinking. It was difficult for the reader to tell Isaac Asimov's opinions from Deters's own. Perhaps Deters needed to express his views more clearly and not shun the first-person *I*. He reworked his draft, trying to set forth his own opinions, trying also to tighten and sharpen his prose. His revised essay begins on the following page.

REVISED VERSION

Where Few Have Gone Before

Kevin Deters

Space: the final frontier. The renowned writer Isaac Asimov addressed this subject in "Into Space: The Next Giant Step," a short piece published in the <u>St. Louis Post-Dispatch</u>. Asimov, the author of over four hundred science and science fiction books, writes about the space station that will be built in orbit around the earth in the near future. He examines the advantages and numerous possibilities of space travel that such a station would allow. From this article, I gathered that this space station will give people the opportunity to be explorers, help conserve resources on earth, and unite the nations of the world as they forge the common goal of discovering knowledge of outer space. I'm intrigued by each of these possibilities.

Asimov tells us, "It is absolutely necessary that we build a base other than earth for our ventures into space. . . . The logical beginning is with a space station." A space station would serve as a stepping stone to future permanent bases on the moon and Mars. I can imagine adventurous settlers who would pave the spaceways just as Daniel Boone and his followers blazed trails through the Kentucky wilderness. These space travelers Asimov describes as "the Phoenicians, the Vikings, the Polynesians of the future, making their way into the 21st century through a space-ocean far vaster than the water-ocean traversed by their predecessors."

The spacefarers will also find ways to help conserve valuable energy on earth. Asimov suggests that, with the space station as a base, lunar materials could be excavated from the moon to construct power stations that could direct solar energy toward the earth. Thus, along with our diminishing fossil fuels, energy could be conserved and money saved. I believe that this conservation could possibly serve as a deterrent to the use of nuclear

energy. With this new surplus of energy, nuclear energy
and all its applications such as power plants and missiles would become unnecessary. The sun's never-ending
supply of solar energy could be harnessed to become the
chief energy source on earth, and dangerous forms of energy could be done away with.

As a result, I suggest that undoubtedly expensive
heating bills and the like would be unheard of. Energy
costs would plummet as earth's populace would take advantage of the sun's plentiful rays. The price decrease
would snowball, affecting other aspects of life, eventually resulting in a cheaper cost of living.

The construction of the space station that Asimov
suggests could also help unify the countries of the
world. A project like this would cost billions of dollars and take a massive amount of time and hard work. No
one country could afford the project. Asimov suggests
that if the United States and the Soviet Union were to
work together, costs and time could be considerably lessened. I believe that without a doubt this joint effort
could help promote global togetherness as well. Joint
missions of the United States and other countries have
been conducted. For example, the Apollo-Soyuz venture
linked together spacecrafts from the two nations. If the
world's nations can unite to explore space, surely problems back home could be easily solved. Such quibbles
as the nuclear arms race and foreign trading disputes
seem trivial when compared to the grandeur of space
exploration.

Asimov suggests that the space station will serve as
a valuable tool for humanity. I concur, for I believe
the human race must now reach for the heavens. Space is
indeed the final frontier that lies before us. We can
all be Daniel Boones.

You'll notice that, as Jennifer Balsavias suggested, Deters seems to reflect
harder in his revised version. And by speaking out in his own voice, he makes

clear (as he didn't do in the earlier version) that many of his thoughts are his own, not Isaac Asimov's. Notice, too, Deters's smaller but effective alterations. At the end, he returns to his earlier, original comparison between pioneers in space and Daniel Boone. All his changes produce a more concise, readable, and absorbing paper, one that goes a little deeper—thanks in part to the services of an honest, helpful peer editor.

As your writing skills continue to develop, you may find yourself relying less on your peers and more on your own ability to analyze your early drafts. When you ask yourself what is right or wrong with your own paper, you can use the very same list of questions you used in evaluating other writers' papers. And when you learn to answer those questions searchingly, you'll become your own most valuable reader.

CHAPTER 20

Strategies for Writing with a Computer

"I love being a writer," declares novelist Peter De Vries. "What I can't stand is the paperwork."

If you have ever felt this way, you can appreciate the modern miracle of the word processor—a computer with the software necessary for writing. Some writers think word processing the greatest thing since Gutenberg invented movable type. Many find that, for the first time, writing becomes fun— like playing a video game, setting down ideas in bursts like gunfire, zapping out any that seem unnecessary.

Have you not yet tried word processing and do you want to know more about it? Then read on. On most college campuses you will find open-access labs where you can use a computer and a variety of programs as well as receive instruction in how to produce a professional-looking copy of your paper or report.

Are you, on the other hand, a practiced veteran who already writes with a computer? Then skip over to page 418 for some practical tips on making word processing work more effectively for you.

As you have probably noticed, earlier chapters of this book also contain suggestions for computer-assisted writing. And for particulars on how to format and print out a word-processed manuscript, see the end of this chapter.

WHAT WORD PROCESSING CAN DO

By enabling your work-in-progress to take shape on screen instead of on paper and by storing what you write, word processing does away with much of the mechanical work of rewriting. No more typing and retyping draft after draft. Word processing lets you do all the following:

revise easily
rearrange swiftly
insert short sentences or long sections into your paper
delete unwanted words, sentences, or passages
search for and replace a word or phrase
correct mistakes easily
format quickly
print many copies, all equally legible
store several hundred pages on a small disk

Supplemental programs can provide still greater assistance. Sometimes their features are built right into the word processing program; or you can get them as separate programs. Such programs can do the following:

feed you questions to prompt ideas
help you organize material
help you choose a better word
review grammar rules you may have forgotten
check your spelling
check your grammar
help you edit
help you proofread
detect clichés
count the number of words
automatically number the pages
put headings on each page
correctly format endnotes and bibliography entries
produce graphs
take notes in a database or on a notepad

All these features take the weight off the writer and free the mind for more essential considerations.

WHAT IT'S LIKE TO WRITE WITH A WORD PROCESSOR

"Everything you write comes out in a state of flux!" one writer complained, on first trying word processing. At first, for a writer accustomed to typing or pushing a pen, word processing may seem unnerving. You don't place marks directly on paper, where they stay put, to be corrected only by erasing, crossing out or whiting out, and rewriting or retyping. You arrange words in easily altered structures visible on a screen. These squiggles move and blink at your command. Most beginners need to have someone help them learn how to use word processing, but others just get an instruction manual and ferret out the directions for themselves, finding out what works by trial and error. Do whichever feels more comfortable for you, but don't fear the machine. Increasingly computer programs are "user friendly," meaning easy to learn and easy to use. You can learn to control this technology just as you program a VCR or operate an automobile.

Advantages

Ease of drafting   With word processing, you can throw down thoughts in whatever order they come to mind. Then you can move them around and arrange them as seems best. Of course, you can do this kind of thinking and revising with paper and scissors, too, but word processors encourage it and make it easy. They enable you to write an outline and flesh it out on the screen, working on it until it turns into a finished essay before your eyes. The process is a little like making a stew, adding an ingredient at a time, stirring and blending and cooking everything to a consistent thickness, all in the same pot. When you come across additional material, you can squeeze it right in where you want it, without recopying. If something doesn't taste right, you can lift it out. If you want to change a word throughout what you are writing, you tell the computer to search out that word and replace it each time it occurs. When you come to the end of a line, you don't have any typewriter carriage to return: the computer automatically begins a new line when it fills the old one to capacity. Unlike people who type on typewriters, writers who write with word processors may become more willing to draft quickly, less fearful of making mistakes. Some students also find that composing on a glowing screen helps concentrate their attention. Fascinated, as if playing a video game, they stay with the game until they win.

Ease of revising   The tremendous advantage of word processing is ease of revising; this is probably what enchants most writers. No more recopying a page because it is not legible or retyping a paragraph just because you wish to switch around the order of two sentences. You can make changes neatly, right on the screen, before the document is printed out. You can lift out words, sentences, and paragraphs and set them down somewhere else. You can readily add material or take it out. You can play around with the sequence of ideas, rearranging them into any order you like. You can feel the power of zapping bad writing with one stroke of the delete key.

Desktop publishing   Desktop publishing has made it possible to produce newsletters, brochures, and small magazines on personal computers — easily and inexpensively. With training, a single operator can produce good-looking pages resembling those of printed magazines in both quality and design. These may incorporate different styles and sizes of type, charts, graphs, and computer-generated art. If anyone in your class has the skill and access to the hardware and software necessary, desktop publishing might transform what you and your classmates write into a strikingly professional-looking magazine for campus circulation.

Disadvantages

Despite all the benefits, word processing has some drawbacks.

Loss of tactile experience   Some writers miss the touch of the manual keyboard or the feel of the pen and paper. According to author William Zinsser, others miss the satisfaction of being able to rip a page out of the typewriter and "crumble it in a fit of frustration or rage."

Size of display   Most screens display only about twenty-four lines at a time, some as few as sixteen. You won't be able to read all parts of what you write without "scrolling" your work backward or forward (but if you are working on paper, you go from page to page).

Size of equipment   Whereas you can carry a pen and paper with you anywhere, you can't easily carry a computer around with you in your pocket. Palm-sized computers are still too expensive for most people to use regularly.

Blabbing   Some writers become garrulous blabbers when they take to word processing. Finding to their surprise that they are enjoying writing, they run on and on. At one business firm, after word processors had been provided for the whole staff, the management found everyone happily writing not brief memoranda but endless dissertations. Will a word processor turn you into a blabber? We suspect that it will only make you a more extreme case of the kind of writer you are already. If you are the sort who likes to fuss, word processing makes fussing easier. If you love concision, it will spur you to zap out the fat, make your prose all the more terse. But if you tend to jaw on and on, it will make you more loquacious by the yard, leading you to grind out vapid passages of word processorese.

No substitute for the human mind   Some programs will check your spelling, word choice, clichés, or style for you. The spell checker works by matching what you type against words in a dictionary stored in the computer's memory. Unfortunately, none of those programs is a substitute for human proofreading. Even the wisest spell-check program won't point out certain errors: if you accidentally type *her* instead of *here,* the program won't see it as a mistake, for in its dictionary *her* is a perfectly good word. Grammar-check programs will check your grammar, show you what you did wrong, and suggest what to do about it. On the user's screen, IBM's word processing program Epistle will indicate a poorly structured sentence in red, alert the writer to the problem (or the broken grammatical rule) in blue, and suggest a correction in green. Such aids may help take the weight of editing and proofreading off the writer and free the mind for more essential things, but ultimately only you the writer can make the final decisions. Don't rely slavishly on computer checkers.

Possible loss of data A trouble with writing with a stream of electrons is that the stream may dry up, if, say, your roommate plugs in a hair dryer or someone in the next room starts using the microwave and blows a fuse while you have your word processor going. Poof! — there goes your term paper. Some people worry terribly about accidentally erasing what they have written, and they become afraid of writing with a computer. These fears are greatly exaggerated, unless you live in a place where the power is continually failing, like a Caribbean island, or where fuses continually blow, like an old apartment or college dormitory. In ten years of writing with word processors, we have lost only three pieces of copy — two of these because of human blunders, the other because of a momentary power failure. The answer to this problem, if it worries you, is to "save" your work frequently. Whenever you finish a few paragraphs, come to a blank moment or a pause or you want to knock off writing and think or vegetate for a short time, save what you've written: transfer it out of the computer's memory to the hard drive or to a disk. And make a backup copy of all your disks, updating them regularly. Making a backup takes only minutes and can save hours. But if a loss of data does occur to you, don't despair. Just know that it happens to everyone who uses computers sooner or later.

So literal-minded is a computer that it will follow instructions any sensible human being would know enough to ignore. Hit a wrong key in some programs, and you can move or delete a whole page. The computer merely does what you command it to. More devastating blunders are possible. You can lift a paragraph or a page, fully intending to set it down in another place. Then you can get so absorbed in working on some other paragraph that you forget what you intended to move. On some systems it is even possible, when you store something new, to erase by accident the piece you have previously lifted out. Because (unlike writing on paper) in some programs any words you move become invisible, you are usually wise, any time you move something, to deliver it promptly to its destination.

WRITING WITH WORD PROCESSING

Enthusiasts of word processing sometimes argue that to write with a computer is a more congenial way to think in language than to write with a typewriter or a pen. The latter, they charge, tends to direct the flow of words in a straight line, through the slow, laborious recopying of draft after draft. The latter process requires a writer to retype or recopy good passages left unchanged as well as those that need rewriting — a process that differs from that of the mind, which corrects only things that need correcting. The human mind seems to think in a nonlinear way. It stores up odd fragments of information at any old time, on any old subject; it leaps like a grasshopper from one idea to another idea far removed. Word processing seems tailor-made for the mind. It enables a writer to shape easily the amorphous blob of a first thought.

Writers who use word processors have widely different writing styles. Many prefer to write, revise, and edit entirely on screen, not even touching a piece of paper until they print out their finished product. Some like to set down alternative versions of a sentence or paragraph and look at them, decide which to keep, and destroy the rest. Others use some combination of word processing and more conventional technology. These writers still write a first draft in longhand and then enter their stuff into a word processor for revising or editing. Others write on screen, print out the draft, see what it looks like in black and white, then revise in pen or pencil, and finally go back to the word processor to make more alterations.

If you do all your work on screen, it may be wise to create a copy of the old document or print it out before beginning to edit it. Then if you ever want to go back to something you've revised out, you have a hard copy of it. If you like to revise a printout in pencil, you can triple-space or print it out with an unusually wide margin and give yourself plenty of revising room.

A Few Practical Tips

Reverse image. For a change if your word processing program lets you, reverse the image on your screen. The fresh look that all your words take on may render it a pleasure to write a draft.

Switch off. A temptation, when your work isn't going well, is to spend your time editing: tinkering with the surface of your work and trying to prettify it instead of coping with the large and demanding revisions that may be necessary. One way to get around this temptation is to switch off your screen or twist up the darkness control until the words you write become unreadable. Keep writing even though you can't see your words. When you want to reread and revise (and edit), then and only then take a look at them.

Print a hard (paper) copy. Because your screen will probably display only about twenty-four lines at a time, you may find it hard to hold in mind an entire piece of writing. In a long composition, large changes that involve several paragraphs may be harder to envision than if you have before you a stack of typed pages, which you can glance over in a flash. Of course, when you want to ponder several parts of your long document, you can scroll backward and forward, but then you have to hold in mind all that is not currently on the screen. The remedy if you find this a problem is to print out everything. Then you can ponder structural changes and other possible deep revisions much more easily and indicate with a pencil where you have work to do.

Avoid CRT fatigue. As people who work all day at computer terminals in offices know, watching a monitor can tire you out. Adjust the angle of your monitor and also its level of brightness for reading comfort. Take breaks now and then for stretching, exercise, and light refreshments. The quality of your prose just might improve.

Freewrite. Have trouble thinking up a title for your paper? Rapidly freewrite a long list of titles at the top of your essay. Then delete all but the best. Have trouble thinking of sufficient details? List details and nothing but details until you have a full screen. Then go back, select, delete, and group. You can use freewriting on the computer with ease.

Experiment. Do three different versions of a short paper or of a section of an essay (such as the introduction or the conclusion), starting a separate document for each. Then combine the best parts from all three versions.

Highlight. Does your draft seem ill organized? Go through it, highlighting in **bold** the main idea in each paragraph. You can then ponder whether any ideas are missing or need rearranging in a different order.

No computer will ever do all your thinking for you. The mind of a computer remains relatively simple compared with the human mind. If we regard computers with respect but not with slavish devotion, then with their aid we may be able to think-by-writing more swiftly and easily. More readily able to recall information, we may more readily deal with ideas of greater complexity. But the ideas have to be ours. A computer has no mind, no power to originate, no imagination at all—even though we call its spacious capacity a memory.

Formatting Your Manuscript with a Word Processor

Writing with a computer encourages neatness: you can make all your corrections before you print out your final copy—or as many as you can spot while your work is still on screen. Here are some points to remember in formatting a word-processed manuscript.

Breaking lines   Although when you write with a computer you don't need to keep watching for lines to end (there being no typewriter carriage to return), your computer may automatically break a few lines awkwardly. This tends to happen where you have an unusually long word or a phrase strung together with hyphens:

```
Speaking of his sociology classes, Professor Campbell

declared that he often met a

don't-give-a-damn-if-I-know-it-or-not attitude on the

part of some upperclassmen.   This attitude annoyed

him greatly.
```

Check through each page for similar awkward breaks before printing it out. Some word processing programs include a *hyphen-push* or *word-break* command that enables you to instruct the computer where to split a word.

```
Speaking of his sociology class, Professor Campbell

declared that he often met a don't-give-a-damn-if-I-know-

it-or-not attitude on the part of some upperclassmen.
```

Leaving margins   Allow the same generous margins you'd use if you typed or used pen. To get these margins you will have to make sure that your page breaks are accurate and instruct your printer carefully. Print out a sample page or two on scratch paper and, if the margins aren't right, give your computer fresh instructions.

Spacing   Before you break your document into pages, make sure it is set for double-space.

To justify or not to justify?   Many writers think it looks especially neat to use the power of a computer to *justify* their copy—that is, to make each line the same length, like lines in a printed book. Some feel, though, that shaggy right-hand margins look more like typewriting and are actually slightly more readable. Unless your instructor states any wishes on this score, we recommend not showing off the power of your computer but leaving the lines shaggy.

Choosing your printer   If you can, print out your paper on a laser printer or a letter-quality printer. Crisp black copy will enhance the readability of what you write. Some instructors dislike reading papers printed on a dot matrix printer, which produces each letter with a series of tiny dots. They claim that such manuscripts look like tapes from supermarket cash registers. Still, late-model dot matrix printers produce much sharper copy than the early models did. Even an old dot matrix printer may produce good dark copy if you use a fresh ribbon and instruct your computer to print each line boldface. If you have any doubts about the legibility of your copy, show your instructor a sample of your printer's work and make sure it will be acceptable.

Checking the ribbon   If you're using a letter-quality printer, a single-loop ribbon will produce the sharpest copy. If you're using a continuous-loop ribbon (one that keeps working until you change it), make sure it's fresh enough to produce a good black printout.

Choosing paper   Some printers print on continuous-form paper with a detachable perforated strip (*tractor feed*) at either edge. Cheaper grades of such paper (15-pound and 18-pound weight) may not take ink well. For a better-looking manuscript, use 20-pound continuous-form paper designated for word processing. For still handsomer results, use single sheets of bond paper, even if you have to feed them in by hand. But if you do use continuous-form paper, don't turn in a manuscript that looks like a strip of wallpaper. Take the pages apart. If only low-grade continuous-form paper is available, it might improve the looks of your manuscript to photocopy it and submit the photocopy instead.

Experimenting with typefaces   Some printers offer an array of several *fonts*, or typefaces, enabling you to use different styles of type for different purposes. You might use, say, one kind of type for quotations from books, another for quotations from conversation. To experiment not only might be fun but also might provide helpful guidance for your reader. But resist the temptation to produce a four-ring circus of various typography. In the end, the words you write are what matter, not the typeface you print them in.

A
WRITER'S
READER

CHAPTER 21

Families

E. B. (ELWYN BROOKS) WHITE was born in 1899 in Mount Vernon, New York. After serving in the army, he graduated from Cornell University and moved to Seattle to work as a reporter. His career led him back to the East Coast and he joined the staff of the recently established *New Yorker* magazine in 1927. For half a century his satires, poems, and essays helped define that magazine's distinctive style of elegant wit and social comment. He moved to Maine in 1933, and his widely read books for children, *Stuart Little* (1945), *Charlotte's Web* (1952), and *The Trumpet of the Swan* (1970), draw on his life in the country to celebrate life's blend of sadness, happiness, love, and loss. In the following essay, White reflects on the experience of returning with his son to a favorite scene from his own childhood.

ONCE MORE TO THE LAKE
E. B. White

AUGUST 1941

One summer, along about 1904, my father rented a camp on a lake in 1
Maine and took us all there for the month of August. We all got ringworm from some kittens and had to rub Pond's Extract on our arms and legs night and morning, and my father rolled over in a canoe with all his clothes on; but outside of that the vacation was a success and from then on none of us ever thought there was any place in the world like that lake in Maine. We returned summer after summer—always on August 1 for one month. I

have since become a salt-water man, but sometimes in summer there are days when the restlessness of the tides and the fearful cold of the sea water and the incessant wind that blows across the afternoon and into the evening make me wish for the placidity of a lake in the woods. A few weeks ago this feeling got so strong I bought myself a couple of bass hooks and a spinner and returned to the lake where we used to go, for a week's fishing and to revisit old haunts.

I took along my son, who had never had any fresh water up his nose   2
and who had seen lily pads only from train windows. On the journey over to the lake I began to wonder what it would be like. I wondered how time would have marred this unique, this holy spot—the coves and streams, the hills that the sun set behind, the camps and the paths behind the camps. I was sure that the tarred road would have found it out, and I wondered in what other ways it would be desolated. It is strange how much you can remember about places like that once you allow your mind to return into the grooves that lead back. You remember one thing, and that suddenly reminds you of another thing. I guess I remembered clearest of all the early mornings, when the lake was cool and motionless, remembered how the bedroom smelled of the lumber it was made of and of the wet woods whose scent entered through the screen. The partitions in the camp were thin and did not extend clear to the top of the rooms, and as I was always the first up I would dress softly so as not to wake the others, and sneak out into the sweet outdoors and start out in the canoe, keeping close along the shore in the long shadows of the pines. I remembered being very careful never to rub my paddle against the gunwale for fear of disturbing the stillness of the cathedral.

The lake had never been what you would call a wild lake. There were   3
cottages sprinkled around the shores, and it was in farming country although the shores of the lake were quite heavily wooded. Some of the cottages were owned by nearby farmers, and you would live at the shore and eat your meals at the farmhouse. That's what our family did. But although it wasn't wild, it was a fairly large and undisturbed lake and there were places in it that, to a child at least, seemed infinitely remote and primeval.

I was right about the tar: It led to within half a mile of the shore. But   4
when I got back there, with my boy, and we settled into a camp near a farmhouse and into the kind of summertime I had known, I could tell that it was going to be pretty much the same as it had been before—I knew it, lying in bed the first morning smelling the bedroom and hearing the boy sneak quietly out and go off along the shore in a boat. I began to sustain the illusion that he was I, and therefore, by simple transposition, that I was my father. This sensation persisted, kept cropping up all the time we were there. It was not an entirely new feeling, but in this setting it grew much stronger. I seemed to be living a dual existence. I would be in the middle of some simple act, I would be picking up a bait box or laying down a table fork, or I would be saying something and suddenly it would be not I but my

father who was saying the words or making the gesture. It gave me a creepy sensation.

We went fishing the first morning. I felt the same damp moss covering the worms in the bait can, and saw the dragonfly alight on the tip of my rod as it hovered a few inches from the surface of the water. It was the arrival of this fly that convinced me beyond any doubt that everything was as it always had been, that the years were a mirage, and that there had been no years. The small waves were the same, chucking the rowboat under the chin as we fished at anchor, and the boat was the same boat, the same color green and the ribs broken in the same places, and under the floor-boards the same fresh water leavings and debris—the dead hellgrammite, the wisps of moss, the rusty discarded fishhook, the dried blood from yesterday's catch. We stared silently at the tips of our rods, at the dragonflies that came and went. I lowered the tip of mine into the water, tentatively, pensively dislodging the fly, which darted two feet away, poised, darted two feet back, and came to rest again a little farther up the rod. There had been no years between the ducking of this dragonfly and the other one— the one that was part of memory. I looked at the boy, who was silently watching his fly, and it was my hands that held his rod, my eyes watching. I felt dizzy and didn't know which rod I was at the end of.

We caught two bass, hauling them in briskly as though they were mackerel, pulling them over the side of the boat in a businesslike manner without any landing net, and stunning them with a blow on the back of the head. When we got back for a swim before lunch, the lake was exactly where we had left it, the same number of inches from the dock, and there was only the merest suggestion of a breeze. This seemed an utterly enchanted sea, this lake you could leave to its own devices for a few hours and come back to, and find that it had not stirred, this constant and trustworthy body of water. In the shallows, the dark, watersoaked sticks and twigs, smooth and old, were undulating in clusters on the bottom against the clean ribbed sand, and the track of the mussel was plain. A school of minnows swam by, each minnow with its small individual shadow, doubling the attendance, so clear and sharp in the sunlight. Some of the other campers were in swimming, along the shore, one of them with a cake of soap, and the water felt thin and clear and unsubstantial. Over the years there had been this person with the cake of soap, this cultist, and here he was. There had been no years.

Up to the farmhouse to dinner through the teeming dusty field, the road under our sneakers was only a two-track road. The middle track was missing, the one with the marks of the hooves and the splotches of dried, flaky manure. There had always been three tracks to choose from in choosing which track to walk in; now the choice was narrowed down to two. For a moment I missed terribly the middle alternative. But the way led past the tennis court, and something about the way it lay there in the sun reassured me; the tape had loosened along the backline, the alleys were green with plantains and other weeds, and the net (installed in June and removed in

September) sagged in the dry noon, and the whole place steamed with midday heat and hunger and emptiness. There was a choice of pie for dessert, and one was blueberry and one was apple, and the waitresses were the same country girls, there having been no passage of time, only the illusion of it as in a dropped curtain — the waitresses were still fifteen; their hair had been washed, that was the only difference — they had been to the movies and seen the pretty girls with the clean hair.

Summertime, oh, summertime, pattern of life indelible with fade-proof lake, the wood unshatterable, the pasture with the sweetfern and the juniper forever and ever, summer without end; this was the background, and the life along the shore was the design, the cottages with their innocent and tranquil design, their tiny docks with the flagpole and the American flag floating against the white clouds in the blue sky, the little paths over the roots of the trees leading from camp to camp and the paths leading back to the outhouses and the can of lime for sprinkling, and at the souvenir counters at the store the miniature birchbark canoes and the postcards that showed things looking a little better than they looked. This was the American family at play, escaping the city heat, wondering whether the newcomers in the camp at the head of the cove were "common" or "nice," wondering whether it was true that the people who drove up for Sunday dinner at the farmhouse were turned away because there wasn't enough chicken. 8

It seemed to me, as I kept remembering all this, that those times and those summers had been infinitely precious and worth saving. There had been jollity and peace and goodness. The arriving (at the beginning of August) had been so big a business in itself, at the railway station the farm wagon drawn up, the first smell of the pine-laden air, the first glimpse of the smiling farmer, and the great importance of the trunks and your father's enormous authority in such matters, and the feel of the wagon under you for the long ten-mile haul, and at the top of the last long hill catching the first view of the lake after eleven months of not seeing this cherished body of water. The shouts and cries of the other campers when they saw you, and the trunks to be unpacked, to give up their rich burden. (Arriving was less exciting nowadays, when you sneaked up in your car and parked it under a tree near the camp and took out the bags and in five minutes it was all over, no fuss, no loud wonderful fuss about trunks.) 9

Peace and goodness and jollity. The only thing that was wrong now, really, was the sound of the place, an unfamiliar nervous sound of the outboard motors. This was the note that jarred, the one thing that would sometimes break the illusion and set the years moving. In those other summertimes all motors were inboard; and when they were at a little distance, the noise they made was a sedative, an ingredient of summer sleep. They were one-cylinder and two-cylinder engines, and some were make-and-break and some were jump-spark, but they all made a sleepy sound across the lake. The one-lungers throbbed and fluttered, and the twin-cylinder ones purred and purred, and that was a quiet sound, too. But now 10 the campers all had outboards. In the daytime, in the hot mornings, these motors made a petulant, irritable sound; at night in the still evening when the afterglow lit the water, they whined about one's ears like mosquitoes. My boy loved our rented outboard, and his great desire was to achieve single-handed mastery over it, and authority, and he soon learned the trick of choking it a little (but not too much), and the adjustment of the needle valve. Watching him I would remember the things you could do with the old one-cylinder engine with the heavy flywheel, how you could have it eating out of your hand if you got really close to it spiritually. Motorboats in those days didn't have clutches, and you would make a landing by shutting off the motor at the proper time and coasting in with a dead rudder. But there was a way of reversing them, if you learned the trick, by cutting the switch and putting it on again exactly on the final dying revolution of the flywheel, so that it would kick back against compression and begin reversing. Approaching a dock in a strong following breeze, it was difficult to slow up sufficiently by the ordinary coasting method, and if a boy felt he had complete mastery over his motor, he was tempted to keep it running beyond its time and then reverse it a few feet from the dock. It took a cool nerve, because if you threw the switch a twentieth of a second too soon you would catch the flywheel when it still had speed enough to go up past center, and the boat would leap ahead, charging bull-fashion at the dock.

We had a good week at the camp. The bass were biting well and the sun shone endlessly, day after day. We would be tired at night and lie down in the accumulated heat of the little bedrooms after the long hot day and the breeze would stir almost imperceptibly outside and the smell of the swamp drift in through the rusty screens. Sleep would come easily and in the morning the red squirrel would be on the roof, tapping out his gay routine. I kept remembering everything, lying in bed in the mornings—the small steamboat that had a long rounded stern like the lip of a Ubangi, and how quietly she ran on the moonlight sails, when the older boys played their mandolins and the girls sang and we ate doughnuts dipped in sugar, and how sweet the music was on the water in the shining night, and what it had felt like to think about girls then. After breakfast we would go up to the store and the things were in the same place—the minnows in a bottle, the plugs and spinners disarranged and pawed over by the youngsters from the boys' camp, the Fig Newtons and the Beeman's gum. Outside, the road was tarred and cars stood in front of the store. Inside, all was just as it had always been, except there was more Coca-Cola and not so much Moxie and root beer and birch beer and sarsaparilla. We would walk out with the bottle of pop apiece and sometimes the pop would backfire up our noses and hurt. We explored the streams, quietly, where the turtles slid off the sunny logs and dug their way into the soft bottom; and we lay on the town wharf and fed worms to the tame bass. Everywhere we went I had trouble making out which was I, the one walking at my side, the one walking in my pants. 11

One afternoon while we were at that lake a thunderstorm came up. It 12 was like the revival of an old melodrama that I had seen long ago with childish awe. The second-act climax of the drama of the electrical disturbance over a lake in America had not changed in any important respect. This was the big scene, still the big scene. The whole thing was so familiar, the first feeling of oppression and heat and a general air around camp of not wanting to go very far away. In midafternoon (it was all the same) a curious darkening of the sky, and a lull in everything that had made life tick; and then the way the boats suddenly swung the other way at their moorings with the coming of a breeze out of the new quarter, and the premonitory rumble. Then the kettle drum, then the snare, then the bass drum and cymbals, then crackling light against the dark, and the gods grinning and licking their chops in the hills. Afterward the calm, the rain steadily rustling in the calm lake, the return of light and hope and spirits, and the campers running out in joy and relief to go swimming in the rain, their bright cries perpetuating the deathless joke about how they were getting simply drenched, and the children screaming with delight at the new sensation of bathing in the rain, and the joke about getting drenched linking the generations in a strong indestructible chain. And the comedian who waded in carrying an umbrella.

When the others went swimming my son said he was going in, too. He   13
pulled his dripping trunks from the line where they had hung all through the shower and wrung them out. Languidly, and with no thought of going in, I watched him, his hard little body, skinny and bare, saw him wince slightly as he pulled up around his vitals the small, soggy, icy garment. As he buckled the swollen belt, suddenly my groin felt the chill of death.

Questions to Start You Thinking

1. How have the lake and the surrounding community, as White depicts them, changed since he was a boy?

2. How does White use recall and observation to compare and contrast past with present?

3. Define *primeval* (paragraph 3), *transposition* (paragraph 4), *hellgrammite* (paragraph 5), *undulating, cultist* (paragraph 6), and *petulant* (paragraph 10). What is White's purpose in using adult words rather than a child's words to look back on his childhood experience?

4. Both White and Michael Dorris in "The Train Cake" (p. 435) describe their efforts to please, and to draw closer to, their sons. Whose attempt seems more successful? Why?

Suggestions for Writing

1. Think of a place you were familiar with as a child and then visited again as an adult. Write an essay explaining how the place had changed and not changed.

2. Using observation and recall, describe a memorable place from your childhood. Draw on specific details to help your readers *see* the place as you recall it.

SHERWOOD ANDERSON (1876–1941) was born in Camden, Ohio. In his youth he worked as a stable groom and house painter, and as an adult he wrote advertising copy and manufactured a successful line of paint before setting out on a literary career. In his writing, exemplified by his most successful novel, *Winesburg, Ohio* (1919), he broke with established literary tradition by focusing on the psychology of his characters. His work influenced later writers, particularly Ernest Hemingway and William Faulkner. Anderson's psychological approach is evident in the following excerpt from his posthumous *Memoirs* (1942), in which he focuses on the process by which a son comes to acknowledge the ways in which he is truly his father's son.

DISCOVERY OF A FATHER
Sherwood Anderson

One of the strangest relationships in the world is that between father 1 and son. I know it now from having sons of my own.

A boy wants something very special from his father. You hear it said 2 that fathers want their sons to be what they feel they cannot themselves be, but I tell you it also works the other way. I know that as a small boy I wanted my father to be a certain thing he was not. I wanted him to be a proud, silent, dignified father. When I was with other boys and he passed along the street, I wanted to feel a glow of pride: "There he is. That is my father."

But he wasn't such a one. He couldn't be. It seemed to me then that 3 he was always showing off. Let's say someone in our town had got up a show. They were always doing it. The druggist would be in it, the shoestore clerk, the horse doctor, and a lot of women and girls. My father would manage to get the chief comedy part. It was, let's say, a Civil War play and he was a comic Irish soldier. He had to do the most absurd things. They thought he was funny, but I didn't.

I thought he was terrible. I didn't see how Mother could stand it. She 4 even laughed with the others. Maybe I would have laughed if it hadn't been my father.

Or there was a parade, the Fourth of July or Decoration Day. He'd be in 5 that, too, right at the front of it, as Grand Marshal or something, on a white horse hired from a livery stable.

He couldn't ride for shucks. He fell off the horse and everyone hooted 6 with laughter, but he didn't care. He even seemed to like it. I remember once when he had done something ridiculous, and right out on Main Street, too. I was with some other boys and they were laughing and shouting at him and he was shouting back and having as good a time as they were. I ran down an alley back of some stores and there in the Presbyterian Church sheds I had a good long cry.

Or I would be in bed at night and Father would come home a little lit   7
up and bring some men with him. He was a man who was never alone.
Before he went broke, running a harness shop, there were always a lot of
men loafing in the shop. He went broke, of course, because he gave too
much credit. He couldn't refuse it and I thought he was a fool. I had got to
hating him.

There'd be men I didn't think would want to be fooling around with him.   8
There might even be the superintendent of our schools and a quiet man
who ran the hardware store. Once, I remember, there was a white-haired
man who was a cashier of the bank. It was a wonder to me they'd want to
be seen with such a windbag. That's what I thought he was. I know now
what it was that attracted them. It was because life in our town, as in all
small towns, was at times pretty dull and he livened it up. He made them
laugh. He could tell stories. He'd even get them to singing.

If they didn't come to our house they'd go off, say at night, to where   9
there was a grassy place by a creek. They'd cook food there and drink beer
and sit about listening to his stories.

He was always telling stories about himself. He'd say this or that won-   10
derful thing happened to him. It might be something that made him look
like a fool. He didn't care.

If an Irishman came to our house, right away father would say he was   11
Irish. He'd tell what county in Ireland he was born in. He'd tell things that
happened there when he was a boy. He'd make it seem so real that, if I
hadn't known he was born in southern Ohio, I'd have believed him myself.

If it was a Scotchman, the same thing happened. He'd get a burr into   12
his speech. Or he was a German or a Swede. He'd be anything the other
man was. I think they all knew he was lying, but they seemed to like him
just the same. As a boy that was what I couldn't understand.

And there was Mother. How could she stand it? I wanted to ask but   13
never did. She was not the kind you asked such questions.

I'd be upstairs in my bed, in my room above the porch, and Father would   14
be telling some of his tales. A lot of Father's stories were about the Civil
War. To hear him tell it he'd been in about every battle. He'd known Grant,
Sherman, Sheridan, and I don't know how many others. He'd been particularly intimate with General Grant so that when Grant went East, to take
charge of all the armies, he took Father along.

"I was an orderly at headquarters and Sam Grant said to me, 'Irve,' he   15
said, 'I'm going to take you along with me.' "

It seems he and Grant used to slip off sometimes and have a quiet   16
drink together. That's what my father said. He'd tell about the day Lee
surrendered and how, when the great moment came, they couldn't find
Grant.

"You know," my father said, "about General Grant's book, his memoirs.   17
You've read of how he said he had a headache and how, when he got word
that Lee was ready to call it quits, he was suddenly and miraculously cured.

"Huh," said Father. "He was in the woods with me.   18

"I was in there with my back against a tree. I was pretty well cornered. 19
I had got hold of a bottle of pretty good stuff.

"They were looking for Grant. He had got off his horse and come into 20
the woods. He found me. He was covered with mud.

"I had the bottle in my hand. What'd I care? The war was over. I knew 21
we had them licked."

My father said that he was the one who told Grant about Lee. An orderly 22
riding by had told him, because the orderly knew how thick he was with
Grant. Grant was embarrassed.

"But, Irve, look at me. I'm all covered with mud," he said to Father. 23

And then, my father said, he and Grant decided to have a drink together. 24
They took a couple of shots and then, because he didn't want Grant to show
up potted before the immaculate Lee, he smashed the bottle against the
tree.

"Sam Grant's dead now and I wouldn't want it to get out on him," my 25
father said.

That's just one of the kind of things he'd tell. Of course, the men knew 26
he was lying, but they seemed to like it just the same.

When we got broke, down and out, do you think he ever brought any- 27
thing home? Not he. If there wasn't anything to eat in the house, he'd go
off visiting around at farm houses. They all wanted him. Sometimes he'd
stay away for weeks, Mother working to keep us fed, and then home he'd
come bringing, let's say, a ham. He'd got it from some farmer friend. He'd
slap it on the table in the kitchen. "You bet I'm going to see that my kids
have something to eat," he'd say, and Mother would just stand smiling at
him. She'd never say a word about all the weeks and months he'd been
away, not leaving us a cent for food. Once I heard her speaking to a woman
in our street. Maybe the woman had dared to sympathize with her. "Oh,"
she said, "it's all right. He isn't ever dull like most of the men in this street.
Life is never dull when my man is about."

But often I was filled with bitterness, and sometimes I wished he wasn't 28
my father. I'd even invent another man as my father. To protect my mother
I'd make up stories of a secret marriage that for some strange reason never
got known. As though some man, say the president of a railroad company
or maybe a congressman, had married my mother, thinking his wife was
dead and then it turned out she wasn't.

So they had to hush it up but I got born just the same. I wasn't really 29
the son of my father. Somewhere in the world there was a very dignified,
quite wonderful man who was really my father. I even made myself half
believe these fancies.

And then there came a certain night. Mother was away from home. 30
Maybe there was church that night. Father came in. He'd been off somewhere for two or three weeks. He found me alone in the house, reading by
the kitchen table.

It had been raining and he was very wet. He sat and looked at me for 31
a long time, not saying a word. I was startled, for there was on his face

the saddest look I had ever seen. He sat for a time, his clothes dripping. Then he got up.

"Come on with me," he said.   32

I got up and went with him out of the house. I was filled with wonder   33
but I wasn't afraid. We went along a dirt road that led down into a valley, about a mile out of town, where there was a pond. We walked in silence. The man who was always talking had stopped his talking.

I didn't know what was up and had the queer feeling that I was with a   34
stranger. I don't know whether my father intended it so. I don't think he did.

The pond was quite large. It was still raining hard and there were flashes   35
of lightning followed by thunder. We were on a grassy bank at he pond's edge when my father spoke, and in the darkness and rain his voice sounded strange.

"Take off your clothes," he said. Still filled with wonder, I began to   36
undress. There was a flash of lightning and I saw that he was already naked.

Naked, we went into the pond. Taking my hand, he pulled me in. It may   37
be that I was too frightened, too full of a feeling of strangeness, to speak. Before that night my father had never seemed to pay any attention to me.

"And what is he up to now?" I kept asking myself. I did not swim very   38
well, but he put my hand on his shoulder and struck out into the darkness.

He was a man with big shoulders, a powerful swimmer. In the darkness   39
I could feel the movements of his muscles. We swam to the far edge of the pond and then back to where we had left our clothes. The rain continued and the wind blew. Sometimes my father swam on his back, and when he did he took my hand in his large powerful one and moved it over so that it rested always on his shoulder. Sometimes there would be a flash of lightning, and I could see his face quite clearly.

It was as it was earlier, in the kitchen, a face filled with sadness. There   40
would be the momentary glimpse of his face, and then again the darkness, the wind and the rain. In me there was a feeling I had never known before.

It was a feeling of closeness. It was something strange. It was as   41
though there were only we two in the world. It was as though I had been jerked suddenly out of myself, out of my world of the schoolboy, out of a world in which I was ashamed of my father.

He had become blood of my blood; he the strong swimmer and I the   42
boy clinging to him in the darkness. We swam in silence, and in silence we dressed in our wet clothes and went home.

There was a lamp lighted in the kitchen, and when we came in, the   43
water dripping from us, there was my mother. She smiled at us. I remember that she called us "boys." "What have you boys been up to?" she asked, but my father did not answer. As he had begun the evening's experience with me in silence, so he ended it. He turned and looked at me. Then he went, I thought, with a new and strange dignity, out of the room.

I climbed the stairs to my room, undressed in darkness and got into   44
bed. I couldn't sleep and did not want to sleep. For the first time I knew that I was the son of my father. He was a storyteller as I was to be. It may

be that I even laughed a little softly there in the darkness. If I did, I laughed knowing that I would never again be wanting another father.

Questions to Start You Thinking

1. Although the subject of this essay is Anderson's relationship with his father, what does the piece imply about Anderson's feelings toward his mother?

2. What sorts of details does Anderson use in writing from recall? How well do they work to give you a sense of his relationship with his father?

3. Anderson's vocabulary is relatively simple, but some of his words and phrases were more easily understood in the early 1940s than they are today. Define *Decoration Day*, *livery stable* (paragraph 5), *lit up*, and *harness shop* (paragraph 7).

4. What kind of experience unites father and son in both Anderson's essay and E. B. White's "Once More to the Lake" (p. 425)?

Suggestions for Writing

1. Anderson begins the essay with a discussion of how ashamed his father made him. By the end of the essay, however, he seems to have resolved his feelings of shame and drawn closer to his father. Have you ever had a similar experience? Write an essay discussing a problem you have had with one or both of your parents and how you have resolved it. How was your experience different from Anderson's? How was it similar?

2. Think of an experience that helped shape your relationship with one or both of your parents, and explain it in a brief personal essay.

MICHAEL DORRIS, born in 1945 in Dayton, Washington, has been deeply influenced by his ethnic background as an American Indian and by his decision to become an adoptive single father. With degrees from Georgetown and Yale universities, Dorris has taught Native American Studies at Dartmouth College for the last fifteen years. His writings include *Native Americans: Five Hundred Years After* (1975), the popular novel *A Yellow Raft in Blue Water* (1987), and *The Crown of Columbus* (1991) coauthored with his wife, Louise Erdrich. His autobiographical work *The Broken Cord* (1989) focuses on his relationship with his son, Adam, who suffers the aftereffects of fetal alcohol syndrome. The following story, taken from *The Broken Cord*, reveals Dorris's sensitivity as an outsider and anthropologist, to the pressures that social groups exert on individuals.

THE TRAIN CAKE
Michael Dorris

. . . Adam was enrolled in what I assumed to be an enlightened day-care center, and I had thrown myself into the role of professional single parent. Still in my twenties, I was young enough to believe that all it took 1 to juggle family and career was organization and good intent. I was aggressively confident, well versed in the literature and jargon of child rearing, and prepared to quote statistics to prove that nurturing was a *human*, and not exclusively female, potential.

I was ready for the doubtful look or the arched eyebrow, I was ready to   2
exchange recipes and remedies while folding clothes in laundromats or waiting in line at Sears to have family portraits taken. I was not, however, expecting to vie with a population of high-achieving working parents — single or married — every bit as defensive as I about being employed outside the home.

The competition, I soon realized, would not be easy. The other moms   3
and dads had read and taken notes on every how-to-be-perfect manual on the market. Their progeny arrived in the morning dressed in color-coordinated outfits with matching watches and down-filled winter gear. Each boy and girl sported hairstyles that had to have taken an hour of dextrous adult early-morning labor to create. These kids all had famous idiosyncratic habits — aversions to synthetic cloth or allergies to dust — that required special instructions.

Birthdays were the one occasion for each child to be center stage. And   4
so lavish had the festivities apparently become the year before we arrived that the day-care center had made a rule limiting the gala spread to foods explicitly made *by* the actual parents *in* their actual homes. This seemed reasonable enough, but as fall turned into winter and I witnessed, at the end of occasional days, the excessive remains of one extravaganza after another, I began to suspect that some people were cheating. How else to explain the ice-cream cupcakes, the individual hot-dog-and-baked-bean quiches, the fluted papaya cups filled with *crème fraiche*?

Adam and I still lived in the small wooden house by Mascoma Lake —   5
the price was right for an instructor's salary. It was there that I retreated to think and plan as Adam's January birthday neared. Under no circumstances was I about to send him off with a concoction sneakily purchased at the bakery. I had something to prove.

I considered briefly the phyla of cream puffs and éclairs but rejected   6
them as too risky. I was not an experienced cook, and my oven, while dutifully heating, was not up to wild extremes or precise temperature calibrations. I contemplated the possibilities of puddings but rejected them as too unorthodox, too bizarre. From every unconventional excursion, I came back to cake.

"What would be the best cake you could imagine?" I asked Adam one   7
night as he played on the carpet with our Husky, Skahota. His reply was immediate and unsurprising, the declaration of his enduring passion.

"A choo choo train!" he announced, and went back to his game.   8

It was his birthday, so I didn't argue, didn't try to widen his horizon.   9
This once I took his fierce attachment seriously and called Nina, who knew more about baking than I. Culling through her recipe collection, she uncovered directions for specialized pans made from cardboard wrapped in

aluminum foil. Boxcars and caboose were a cinch, the coal car was a problem, and the locomotive was a challenge. But it was possible, it was Adam's enduring, maddening fantasy, and done right, it could be the most spectacular dessert ever to grace the two-foot-high day-care table. I gave the project a week of my life.

Mounted on a piece of plywood, each of the six cars was at base an   10
eight-by-four-inch-long rectangle of trimmed sponge cake, to which I attached paper wheels and connected toggles made of taffy. No food colors at the local grocery seemed bright or impressive enough, so I traveled one Sunday afternoon to a specialty outlet where, for two dollars each, I purchased small vials of blues and reds and yellows and greens so vivid, so ceramic in their luster, that a mere drop was sufficient to tint a bowl of white icing. But I was looking for more than a tint; I was after *bold*, so for good measure I mixed more and more edible dye into my palette until the hues that confronted me were dazzling. No caboose was ever so barn-red, no passenger car go grass-green, no plucky little locomotive, decorated with gumdrops, a hand mirror and a cheerful expression, so sky-blue. This was a little engine that *could*, and knew it. Black, for the coal car, was trickier, but I solved that dilemma with melted licorice that, when spread warm and allowed to harden, cemented the fragile sides into indestructible steel. I got behind in my lecture preparations, but finished the train at midnight the day before Adam's party. All around it I had constructed toy houses, cutout happy families (more than one shepherded by a lone adult male), grazing cartoon animals. Before going to bed, exhausted but smug, I asked Bea to come over and take photographs of Adam, Nina, and me standing before my creation. My son would have nothing to apologize for.

And it all came to pass just as I had imagined. When I carefully carried   11
the plywood base from the car, and negotiated the door of the center, the train cake was greeted with exclamations of delight and disbelief by the staff and children alike. Other parents, disrobing their sons and daughters from layers of mittens and boots and snowsuits, looked from the cake to me with expressions of betrayal and chagrin.

I had become the act to beat, the standard against which to measure.   12
With a spin of the mixer I had achieved the status of Ideal Parent, the adult for whom no task was too great, no child's dream too onerous to grant. Yes, I was employed full-time, but did I let that get in the way of my fatherly duties? The train cake told the story in capital letters.

The party, to which I returned to preside over later in the day, was   13
memorable. In the flickering light of six candles (one to grow on), the children's eyes were sugar-glazed. The volume of their voices was loud with greed, and once the clapping ceased, they made fast work of all my labors. Within twenty minutes my ordered platter had become a surrealistic swatch of colors, with only the indestructible coal car, chipped at but undismantled, remaining as solitary witness.

Adam, who had eaten almost none of the cake in his excitement, was   14

everyone's best friend, the hero of the day, and when we got into our blue
VW station wagon to go home, he leaned across the seat with a smile so
wide and happy it startled me.

"Thank you, Daddy," he said.   15

I looked at him, this little boy who really was, after all, what this was   16
for and about. In his dark eyes there was one message only, one idea: his
wish had come true. And I looked back in turn with a single realization of
my own: in him, my wish had come true, too.

"Happy Birthday," I said.   17

The story should have ended there, with the cake eaten and Adam   18
content and me reacquainted with the real meaning of things, but there
was one final chapter. About ten o'clock that night, I was at the kitchen
table trying hard to organize the next day's class notes when the phone
rang. It was the director of the day-care center, and her voice was frantic.

"What did you put in that thing?" she demanded.   19

"Why, nothing," I answered, worried that I had somehow violated some   20
interdiction about natural ingredients. "Just flour and sugar and a few
pieces of candy. What's wrong?"

"The parents have been calling me all night," she said. "They're hys-   21
terical. They're ready to take their children to the emergency room at the
hospital."

"Why?" Now I was scared.   22

"It's when they put the kids to bed," she said. "When they took them   23
to the potty. They noticed before they flushed! The water in the toilet bowl
was green! Or bright blue! Electric yellow! *Orange!*"

I closed my eyes and saw again the jaunty cars, lined up and ready to   24
roll. The train cake had made more of an impression than I had planned.

Days later, when every expensive hue had passed safely but remarkably   25
through the digestive system of each child, the day-care center's governing
council inaugurated an amendment to the party rule: henceforth, all birthday fixings must be normal. The like of the train cake would never be seen
again.

Questions to Start You Thinking

1. Why is Dorris so intent on making the perfect cake for Adam's birthday? What
   might the cake represent for father and son?

2. What details does Dorris give about the day-care center, Adam's classmates, and
   their parents? From Dorris's observations, what conclusions can you draw about
   these people and about Dorris's attitude toward them?

3. Define *progeny*, *dextrous*, *idiosyncratic* (paragraph 3), *phyla*, *calibrations* (paragraph 6).

4. Both Dorris's "The Train Cake" and Sherwood Anderson's "Discovery of a Father"
   (p. 431) focus on events that bring father and son together. How are these events
   alike? How are they different?

Suggestions for Writing

1. As described in this piece, Dorris's relationship with his son is powerfully influenced by the preconceptions of those around him. Write an essay explaining how, in your opinion, social pressures and expectations affect parents' relationships with their children.

2. Think of an unusual gift you have given someone. Write an essay explaining why you gave this gift and how it affected both you and the person to whom you gave it.

PAULE MARSHALL was born in Brooklyn in 1929 and has lectured on African American literature at such universities as Oxford, Columbia, and Cornell for more than thirty years. She is currently a professor of English and creative writing at Virginia Commonwealth University. Her first novel, *Brown Girl, Brownstones* (1959), explores the experience of a dual ethnic heritage—that of the United States, where Marshall grew up, and that of Barbados, from which her parents emigrated. In the following excerpt from *Reena and Other Stories* (1983), Marshall attributes the beginnings of her education as a writer to the conversations that filled her mother's kitchen.

FROM THE POETS IN THE KITCHEN
Paule Marshall

Some years ago, when I was teaching a graduate seminar in fiction at 1 Columbia University, a well-known male novelist visited my class to speak on his development as a writer. In discussing his formative years, he didn't realize it but he seriously endangered his life by remarking that women writers are luckier than those of his sex because they usually spend so much time as children around their mothers and their mothers' friends in the kitchen.

What did he say that for? The women students immediately forgot about 2 being in awe of him and began readying their attack for the question and answer period later on. Even I bristled. There again was that awful image of women locked away from the world in the kitchen with only each other to talk to, and their daughters locked in with them.

But my guest wasn't really being sexist or trying to be provocative or 3 even spoiling for a fight. What he meant—when he got around to explaining himself more fully—was that, given the way children are (or were) raised in our society, with little girls kept closer to home and their mothers, the woman writer stands a better chance of being exposed, while growing up, to the kind of talk that goes on among women, more often than not in the kitchen; and that this experience gives her an edge over her male counterpart by instilling in her an appreciation for ordinary speech.

It was clear that my guest lecturer attached great importance to this, 4 which is understandable. Common speech and the plain, workaday words that make it up are, after all, the stock in trade of some of the best fiction writers. They are the principal means by which characters in a novel or story reveal themselves and give voice sometimes to profound feelings and complex ideas about themselves and the world. Perhaps the proper measure of a writer's talent is skill in rendering everyday speech—when it is appropriate to the story—as well as the ability to tap, to exploit, the beauty, poetry and wisdom it often contains.

"If you say what's on your mind in the language that comes to you from 5 your parents and your street and friends you'll probably say something beautiful." Grace Paley tells this, she says, to her students at the beginning of every writing course.

It's all a matter of exposure and a training of the ear for the would-be 6 writer in those early years of apprenticeship. And, according to my guest lecturer, this training, the best of it, often takes place in as unglamorous a setting as the kitchen.

He didn't know it, but he was essentially describing my experience as 7 a little girl. I grew up among poets. Now they didn't look like poets—whatever that breed is supposed to look like. Nothing about them suggested that poetry was their calling. They were just a group of ordinary housewives and mothers, my mother included, who dressed in a way (shapeless housedresses, dowdy felt hats and long, dark, solemn coats) that made it impossible for me to imagine they had ever been young.

Nor did they do what poets were supposed to do—spend their days in 8 an attic room writing verses. They never put pen to paper except to write occasionally to their relatives in Barbados. "I take my pen in hand hoping these few lines will find you in health as they leave me fair for the time being," was the way their letters invariably began. Rather, their day was spent "scrubbing floor," as they described the work they did.

Several mornings a week these unknown bards would put an apron and 9 a pair of old house shoes in a shopping bag and take the train or streetcar from our section of Brooklyn out to Flatbush. There, those who didn't have steady jobs would wait on certain designated corners for the white housewives in the neighborhood to come along and bargain with them over pay for a day's work cleaning their houses. This was the ritual even in the winter.

Later, armed with the few dollars they had earned, which in their vo- 10 cabulary became "a few raw-mouth pennies," they made their way back to our neighborhood, where they would sometimes stop off to have a cup of tea or cocoa together before going home to cook dinner for their husbands and children.

The basement kitchen of the brownstone house where my family lived 11 was the usual gathering place. Once inside the warm safety of its walls the women threw off the drab coats and hats, seated themselves at the large center table, drank their cups of tea or cocoa, and talked. While my sister and I sat at a smaller table over in a corner doing our homework, they talked—endlessly, passionately, poetically, and with impressive range. No subject was beyond them. True, they would indulge in the usual gossip: whose husband was running with whom, whose daughter looked slightly "in the way" (pregnant) under her bridal gown as she walked down the aisle. That sort of thing. But they also tackled the great issues of the time. They were always, for example, discussing the state of the economy. It was the mid and late 30's then, and the aftershock of the Depression, with its soup lines and suicides on Wall Street, was still being felt.

Some people, they declared, didn't know how to deal with adversity.   12
They didn't know that you had to "tie up your belly" (hold in the pain, that is) when things got rough and go on with life. They took their image from the bellyband that is tied around the stomach of a newborn baby to keep the navel pressed in.

They talked politics. Roosevelt was their hero. He had come along and   13
rescued the country with relief and jobs, and in gratitude they christened their sons Franklin and Delano and hoped they would live up to the names.

If F.D.R. was their hero, Marcus Garvey was their God. The name of the   14
fiery, Jamaican-born black nationalist of the 20's was constantly invoked around the table. For he had been their leader when they first came to the United States from the West Indies shortly after World War I. They had contributed to his organization, the United Negro Improvement Association (UNIA), out of their meager salaries, bought shares in his ill-fated Black Star Shipping Line, and at the height of the movement they had marched as members of his "nurses' brigade" in their white uniforms up Seventh Avenue in Harlem during the great Garvey Day parades. Garvey: He lived on through the power of their memories.

And their talk was of war and rumors of wars. They raged against World   15
War II when it broke out in Europe, blaming it on the politicians. "It's these politicians. They're the ones always starting up all this lot of war. But what they care? It's the poor people got to suffer and mothers with their sons." If it was *their* sons, they swore they would keep them out of the Army by giving them soap to eat each day to make their hearts sound defective. Hitler? He was for them "the devil incarnate."

Then there was home. They reminisced often and at length about home.   16
The old country. Barbados—or Bimshire, as they affectionately called it. The little Caribbean island in the sun they loved but had to leave. "Poor— poor but sweet" was the way they remembered it.

And naturally they discussed their adopted home. America came in for   17
both good and bad marks. They lashed out at it for the racism they en- countered. They took to task some of the people they worked for, especially those who gave them only a hard-boiled egg and a few spoonfuls of cottage cheese for lunch. "As if anybody can scrub floor on an egg and some cheese that don't have no taste to it!"

Yet although they caught H in "this man country," as they called Amer-   18 ica, it was nonetheless a place where "you could at least see your way to make a dollar." That much they acknowledged. They might even one day accumulate enough dollars, with both them and their husbands working, to buy the brownstone houses which, like my family, they were only leasing at that period. This was their consuming ambition: to "buy house" and to see the children through.

There was no way for me to understand it at the time, but the talk that 19 filled the kitchen those afternoons was highly functional. It served as therapy, the cheapest kind available to my mother and her friends. Not only did it help them recover from the long wait on the corner that morning and the bargaining over their labor, it restored them to a sense of themselves and reaffirmed their self-worth. Through language they were able to overcome the humiliations of the work-day.

But more than therapy, that freewheeling, wide-ranging, exuberant talk 20 functioned as an outlet for the tremendous creative energy they possessed. They were women in whom the need for self-expression was strong, and since language was the only vehicle readily available to them they made of it an art form that — in keeping with the African tradition in which art and life are one — was an integral part of their lives.

And their talk was a refuge. They never really ceased being baffled and 21 overwhelmed by America — its vastness, complexity and power. Its strange customs and laws. At a level beyond words they remained fearful and in awe. Their uneasiness and fear were even reflected in their attitude toward the children they had given birth to in this country. They referred to those like myself, the little Brooklyn-born Bajans (Barbadians), as "these New York children" and complained that they couldn't discipline us properly because of the laws here. "You can't beat these children as you would like, you know, because the authorities in this place will dash you in jail for them. After all, these is New York children." Not only were we different, American, we had, as they saw it, escaped their ultimate authority.

Confronted therefore by a world they could not encompass, which even 22 limited their rights as parents, and at the same time finding themselves permanently separated from the world they had known, they took refuge in language. "Language is the only homeland," Czeslaw Milosz, the emigré Polish writer and Nobel Laureate, has said. This is what it became for the women at the kitchen table.

It served another purpose also, I suspect. My mother and her friends 23 were after all the female counterpart of Ralph Ellison's invisible man. Indeed, you might say they suffered a triple invisibility, being black, female, and foreigners. They really didn't count in American society except as a source of cheap labor. But given the kind of women they were, they couldn't tolerate the fact of their invisibility, their powerlessness. And they fought back, using the only weapon at their command: the spoken word.

Those late afternoon conversations on a wide range of topics were a 24 way for them to feel they exercised some measure of control over their lives and the events that shaped them. "Soully-gal, talk yuh talk!" they were always exhorting each other. "In this man world you got to take yuh mouth and make a gun!" They were in control, if only verbally and if only for the two hours or so that they remained in our house.

For me, sitting over in the corner, being seen but not heard, which was 25 the rule for children in those days, it wasn't only what the women talked about—the content—but the way they put things—their style. The insight, irony, wit and humor they brought to their stories and discussions and their poet's inventiveness and daring with language—which of course I could only sense but not define back then.

They had taken the standard English taught them in the primary schools 26 of Barbados and transformed it into an idiom, an instrument that more adequately described them—changing around the syntax and imposing their own rhythm and accent so that the sentences were more pleasing to their ears. They added the few African sounds and words that had survived, such as the derisive suck-teeth sound and the word "yam," meaning to eat. And to make it more vivid, more in keeping with their expressive quality, they brought to bear a raft of metaphors, parables, Biblical quotations, sayings and the like:

"The sea ain' got no back door," they would say, meaning that it wasn't 27 like a house where if there was a fire you could run out the back. Meaning that it was not to be trifled with. And meaning perhaps in a larger sense that man should treat all of nature with caution and respect.

"I has read hell by heart and called every generation blessed!" They 28 sometimes went in for hyperbole.

A woman expecting a baby was never said to be pregnant. They never 29 used that word. Rather, she was "in the way" or, better yet, "tumbling big." "Guess who I butt up on in the market the other day tumbling big again!"

And a woman with a reputation of being too free with her sexual favors 30 was known in their book as a "thoroughfare"—the sense of men like a steady stream of cars moving up and down the road of her life. Or she might be dubbed "a free-bee," which was my favorite of the two. I liked the image it conjured up of a woman scandalous perhaps but independent, who flitted from one flower to another in a garden of male beauties, sampling their nectar, taking her pleasure at will, the roles reversed.

And nothing, no matter how beautiful, was ever described as simply 31 beautiful. It was always "beautiful-ugly": the beautiful-ugly dress, the beautiful-ugly house, the beautiful-ugly car. Why the word "ugly," I used to wonder, when the thing they were referring to was beautiful, and they knew it. Why the antonym, the contradiction, the linking of opposites? It used to puzzle me greatly as a child.

There is the theory in linguistics which states that the idiom of a people, 32 the way they use language, reflects not only the most fundamental views they hold of themselves and the world but their very conception of reality. Perhaps in using the term "beautiful-ugly" to describe nearly everything, my mother and her friends were expressing what they believed to be a fundamental dualism in life: the idea that a thing is at the same time its opposite, and that these opposites, these contradictions make up the whole. But theirs was not a Manichaean brand of dualism that sees matter, flesh, the body, as inherently evil, because they constantly addressed each other as "soully-gal" — soul: spirit; gal: the body, flesh, the visible self. And it was clear from their tone that they gave one as much weight and importance as the other. They had never heard of the mind/body split.

As for God, they summed up His essential attitude in a phrase. "God," 33 they would say, "don' love ugly and He ain' stuck on pretty."

Using everyday speech, the simple commonplace words — but always 34 with imagination and skill — they gave voice to the most complex ideas. Flannery O'Connor would have approved of how they made ordinary language work, as she put it, "double-time," stretching, shading, deepening its meaning. Like Joseph Conrad they were always trying to infuse new life in the "old old words worn thin . . . by . . . careless usage." And the goals of their oral art were the same as his: "to make you hear, to make you feel . . . to make you see." This was their guiding aesthetic.

Questions to Start You Thinking

1. What does Marshall mean when she says that her mother and her friends were "poets"? How do they talk about the world around them?

2. How does Marshall use analysis to help her recall? How does she analyze her observations?

3. What is the contrast between Marshall's vocabulary and her mother's? Why does Marshall use words like *bards* (paragraph 9), *meager* (paragraph 14), and *exhorting* (paragraph 24)?

4. In Marshall's essay and Sherwood Anderson's "Discovery of a Father" (p. 431), how do the writers' attitudes toward their parents differ? Think about why they differ.

Suggestions for Writing

1. When Marshall describes her mother and her friends as in a state of "triple invisibility, being black, female, and foreigners" (paragraph 23), she is talking about social conditions of the 1930s and 1940s. How are things the same today? How have they changed? Write an essay comparing the challenges faced by Marshall's mother with the challenges an immigrant woman might face today.

2. Write an essay explaining how a favorite expression or a piece of advice from an older family member has influenced you.

VIVIAN GORNICK was born in 1935 and lives in New York City, where for three decades she has taught writing at numerous colleges and written for many publications, including *The Village Voice*. Her gift for personal and social history is the basis for much of her writing. The following selection is from *Fierce Attachments* (1987), a work for which the title emphasizes the complex and persistent power of family ties.

MAMA WENT TO WORK
Vivian Gornick

Mama went to work five weeks after my father died. He had left us two 1
thousand dollars. To work or not to work was not a debatable question. But
it's hard to imagine what would have happened if economic necessity had
not forced her out of the house. As it was, it seemed to me that she lay on
a couch in a half-darkened room for twenty-five years with her hand across
her forehead murmuring, "I can't." Even though she could, and did.

She pulled on her girdle and her old gray suit, stepped into her black 2
suede chunky heels, applied powder and lipstick to her face, and took the
subway downtown to an employment agency where she got a job clerking
in an office for twenty-eight dollars a week. After that, she rose each morning, got dressed and drank coffee, made out a grocery list for me, left it
together with money on the kitchen table, walked four blocks to the subway
station, bought the *Times*, read it on the train, got off at Forty-second
Street, entered her office building, sat down at her desk, put in a day's
work, made the trip home at five o'clock, came in the apartment door,
slumped onto the kitchen bench for supper, then onto the couch where she
instantly sank into a depression she welcomed like a warm bath. It was as
though she had worked all day to earn the despair waiting faithfully for her
at the end of her unwilling journey into daily life.

Weekends, of course, the depression was unremitting. A black and 3
wordless pall hung over the apartment all of Saturday and all of Sunday.
Mama neither cooked, cleaned, nor shopped. She took no part in idle chatter: the exchange of banalities that fills a room with human presence,
declares an interest in being alive. She would not laugh, respond, or participate in any of the compulsive kitchen talk that went on among the rest
of us: me, my aunt Sarah, Nettie, my brother. She spoke minimally, and
when she did speak her voice was uniformly tight and miserable, always
pulling her listener back to a proper recollection of her "condition." If she
answered the phone her voice dropped a full octave when she said hello;
she could not trust that the caller would otherwise gauge properly the abiding nature of her pain. For five years she did not go to a movie, a concert,
a public meeting. She worked, and she suffered.

Widowhood provided Mama with a higher form of being. In refusing to 4
recover from my father's death she had discovered that her life was en-
dowed with a seriousness her years in the kitchen had denied her. She
remained devoted to this seriousness for thirty years. She never tired of it,
never grew bored or restless in its company, found new ways to keep alive
the interest it deserved and had so undeniably earned.

Mourning Papa became her profession, her identity, her persona. Years 5
later, when I was thinking about the piece of politics inside of which we
had all lived (Marxism and the Communist party), and I realized that people
who worked as plumbers, bakers, or sewing-machine operators had thought
of themselves as thinkers, poets, and scholars because they were members

of the Communist party, I saw that Mama had assumed her widowhood in much the same way. It elevated her in her own eyes, made of her a spiritually significant person, lent richness to her gloom and rhetoric to her speech. Papa's death became a religion that provided ceremony and doctrine. A woman-who-has-lost-the-love-of-her-life was now her orthodoxy: she paid it Talmudic attention.

Papa had never been so real to me in life as he was in death. Always 6 a somewhat shadowy figure, benign and smiling, standing there behind Mama's dramatics about married love, he became and remained what felt like the necessary instrument of her permanent devastation. It was almost as though she had lived with Papa in order that she might arrive at this moment. Her distress was so all-consuming it seemed ordained. For me, surely, it ordered the world anew.

The air I breathed was soaked in her desperation, made thick and heady 7 by it, exciting and dangerous. Her pain became my element, the country in which I lived, the rule beneath which I bowed. It commanded me, made me respond against my will. I longed endlessly to get away from her, but I could not leave the room when she was in it. I dreaded her return from work, but I was never not there when she came home. In her presence anxiety swelled my lungs (I suffered constrictions of the chest and sometimes felt an iron ring clamped across my skull), but I locked myself in the bathroom and wept buckets on her behalf. On Friday I prepared myself for two solid days of weeping and sighing and the mysterious reproof that depression leaks into the air like the steady escape of gas when the pilot light is extinguished. I woke up guilty and went to bed guilty, and on weekends the guilt accumulated into low-grade infection.

She made me sleep with her for a year, and for twenty years afterward 8 I could not bear a woman's hand on me. Afraid to sleep alone, she slung an arm across my stomach, pulled me toward her, fingered my flesh nervously, inattentively. I shrank from her touch: she never noticed. I yearned toward the wall, couldn't get close enough, was always being pulled back. My body became a column of aching stiffness. I must have been excited. Certainly I was repelled.

For two years she dragged me to the cemetery every second or third 9 Sunday morning. The cemetery was in Queens. This meant taking three buses and traveling an hour and fifteen minutes each way. When we climbed onto the third bus she'd begin to cry. Helplessly, I would embrace her. Her cries would grow louder. Inflamed with discomfort, my arm would stiffen around her shoulder and I would stare at the black rubber floor. The bus would arrive at the last stop just as she reached the verge of convulsion.

"We have to get off, Ma," I'd plead in a whisper. 10

She would shake herself reluctantly (she hated to lose momentum once 11 she'd started on a real wail) and slowly climb down off the bus. As we went through the gates of the cemetery, however, she'd rally to her own cause. She would clutch my arm and pull me across miles of tombstones (neither of us ever seemed to remember the exact location of the grave), stumbling like a drunk, lurching about and shrieking: "Where's Papa? Help me find Papa! They've lost Papa. Beloved! I'm coming. Wait, only wait, I'm coming!" Then we would find the grave and she would fling herself across it, arrived at last in a storm of climactic release. On the way home she was a rag doll. And I? Numb and dumb, only grateful to have survived the terror of the earlier hours.

One night when I was fifteen I dreamed that the entire apartment was 12 empty, stripped of furniture and brilliantly whitewashed, the rooms gleaming with sun and the whiteness of the walls. A long rope extended the length of the apartment, winding at waist-level through all the rooms. I followed the rope from my room to the front door. There in the open doorway stood my dead father, gray-faced, surrounded by mist and darkness, the rope tied around the middle of his body. I laid my hands on the rope and began to pull, but try as I might I could not lift him across the threshold. Suddenly my mother appeared. She laid her hands over mine and began to pull also. I tried to shake her off, enraged at her interference, but she would not desist, and I did so want to pull him in I said to myself, "All right, I'll even let her have him, if we can just get him inside."

For years I thought the dream needed no interpretation, but now I think 13 I longed to get my father across the threshold not out of guilt and sexual competition but so that I could get free of Mama. My skin crawled with her. She was everywhere, all over me, inside and out. Her influence clung, membrane-like, to my nostrils, my eyelids, my open mouth. I drew her into me with every breath I took. I drowsed in her etherizing atmosphere, could not escape the rich and claustrophobic character of her presence, her being, her suffocating suffering femaleness.

I didn't know the half of it. 14

One afternoon, in the year of the dream, I was sitting with Nettie. She 15 was making lace, and I was drinking tea. She began to dream out loud. "I think you'll meet a really nice boy this year," she said. "Someone older than yourself. Almost out of college. Ready to get a good job. He'll fall in love with you, and soon you'll be married."

"That's ridiculous," I said sharply. 16

Nettie let her hands, with the lace still in them, fall to her lap. "You 17 sound just like your mother," she said softly.

Questions to Start You Thinking

1. Describe the personality of Gornick's mother. Are the author's memories of her positive or negative?

2. Discuss how Gornick uses images of physical illness to characterize her family's mental state. How do these help establish the essay's tone?

3. What do the words *doctrine*, *orthodoxy*, *Talmudic* (paragraph 5), and *ordained* (paragraph 6) have in common? What does the word *persona* (paragraph 5) mean?

4. How is Gornick's realization that she is like her mother (paragraphs 14–18) similar to Anderson's discovery that he is like his father in "Discovery of a Father" (p. 431)? How are the realizations different?

Suggestions for Writing

1. Write a personal essay explaining how you were affected by the depression of someone close to you. What were your feelings toward that person? How did his or her depression change your feelings? How did you try to help the person?

2. In a brief essay, explain how the death of someone close to you affected you or someone you know.

MARGARET MEAD (1901–1978) was among the most influential and admired Americans of this century. Born in Philadelphia, she earned degrees in anthropology at Barnard College and Columbia University and went on to work for fifty years at the American Museum of Natural History in New York City, where she served as Curator of Ethnology. She taught at Columbia from 1940 to 1978, twice refusing the offer of a full professorship so that she could continue her work at the museum. Mead's ground-breaking fieldwork in the South Pacific established new methods for studying family life and individual development. In scores of articles, books, and lectures, she spoke clearly and persuasively both to scholars and to a popular audience. In the following excerpt from *Male and Female* (1949), Mead argues that in American society, unlike more "primitive" cultures, each family has its own unique code of behavior.

FAMILY CODES
Margaret Mead

In the United States the striking characteristic is that each set of parents is different from each other set, that no two have exactly the same memories, that no two families could be placed side by side and it could be said: "Yes, these four parents ate the same food, played the same games, heard the same lullabies, were scared by the same bogeys, taught that the same words were taboo, given the same picture of what they would be as men and women, made ready to hand on unimpaired the tradition they received, whole, unravelled, unfaded, from their parents."

Every home is different from every other home, every marriage, even within the same class, in the same clique, contains contrasts between the partners as superficially striking as the difference between one New Guinea tribe and another. "In our family we never locked the bathroom door." "In our family you never entered another person's room without knocking." "Mother always asked to see our letters, even after we were grown." "The smallest scrap of paper on which one had written something was returned unread." "We were never allowed to mention our legs." "Father said that 'sweat' was a good deal honester word than 'perspiration,' but to be careful not to say it when we went to Aunt Alice's." "Mother said my hands would get rough if I climbed trees." "Mother said girls ought to stretch their legs and get some exercise while they were young." Side by side, next-door neighbors, children of first cousins, sometimes children of sisters or brothers, the ways of each household diverge, one family bringing up the children to prudery, privacy, and strongly marked sex roles, another to an open give-and-take that makes the girls seem tomboys. Then again comes marriage between the children with the different upbringings, and again the clash, the lack of timing, the lack of movement in step, of the new set of parents. Every home is different from every other home; no two parents, even though they were fed their cereal from silver porringers of the same design, were fed it in quite the same way. The gestures of the feeding hands, whether of mother, grandmother, Irish cook, English nurse, Negro mammy, country-bred hired girl, are no longer the assured, the highly patterned gestures of the member of a homogeneous society. The recently come foreigner's hand is unsure as it handles unfamiliar things and tries to thrust a spoon into the mouth of a child who acts and speaks strangely; the old American's hand bears marks of such uncertainties of former generations, and may tremble or clench anew over some recent contact with some newly arrived and little-understood stranger.

But just because every home is different from every other home, be- 3
cause no husband and wife can move effortlessly in step to the same remembered cradle-songs, so also is every home alike. The anthropologist who has studied a New Guinea tribe can often predict down to the smallest detail what will go on in each family if there is a quarrel, what will be said when there is a reconciliation, who will make it, with what words and what gestures. No anthropologist can ever hope to do the same thing for the United States. What the quarrel will be, who will make up and how, will differ in every home; what the highest moment between parents and child will be will differ. But the form, the kind of quarrel, the kind of reconciliation, the kind of love, the kind of misunderstandings, will be alike in their very difference. In one home the husband will indicate his importunate desire by bringing flowers, in another by kicking the cat playfully as he enters, in a third by making a fuss over the baby, in a fourth by getting very busy over the radio, while the wife may indicate her acceptance or rejection of his erotic expectation by putting on more lipstick or by rubbing off the lipstick she has on, by getting very busy tidying up the room, or by sinking in a soft dream into the other overstuffed chair, playing idly with her baby's curly hair. There is no pattern, no simple word or gesture that has been repeated by all husbands in the presence of all the small children who are to be future husbands, and all the small girls who are to be wives, so that when they grow up they will be letter-perfect in a ballet of approach or retreat.

In America the language of each home is different, there is a code in 4 each family that no one else knows. And that is the essential likeness, the essential regularity, among all these apparent differences. For in each American marriage there is a special code, developed from the individual pasts of the two partners, put together out of the accidents of honeymoon and parents-in-law, finally beaten into a language that each understands imperfectly. For here is another regularity. When a code, a language, is shared by everyone in the village, spoken by the gracious and the grim, by the flexible-tongued and the stubborn, by the musical voice and the halting and stammering voice, the language becomes beautifully precise, each sound sharply and perfectly differentiated from each other sound. The new-born baby, first babbling happily through his whole possible range of lovely and unlovely noise listens, and narrows his range. Where he once babbled a hundred nuances of sound, he limits himself to a bare half-dozen, and practices against the perfection, the sureness, of his elders. Later, he too, however stumbling his tongue or poor his ear, will speak the language of his people so that all can understand him. The perfected model made by the lips and tongues of many different sorts of people speaking the same words holds the speech of each newcomer clear and sharp enough for communication. And as with speech, so with gesture, so with the timing of initiative, of response, of command and obedience. The toddler falls in step with the multitude around him and cannot fail to learn his part.

But in a culture like modern America, the child does not see any such   5
harmonious, repetitive behavior. All men do not cross their legs with the same assured masculinity, or squat on wooden stools to protect themselves from a rear-guard attack. All women do not walk with little mincing steps, or sit and lie with thighs drawn close together, even in sleep. The behavior of each American is itself a composite, an imperfectly realized version, of the behavior of others who in turn had, not a single model — expressed in many voices and many ways, but still a single model — but a hundred models, each different, each an individually developed style, lacking the authenticity, the precision, of a group style. The hand held out in greeting, to still a tear, or to help up a strange child that has stumbled, is not sure that it will be taken, or if taken, taken in the sense in which it is offered. Where patterns of courtship are clear, a girl knows the outcome if she smiles, or laughs, casts down her eyes, or merely walks softly by a group of harvesting youths cradling a red ear of corn in her arms. But in America, the same smile may evoke a casual answering grin, embarrassed averted eyes, an unwelcome advance, or may even mean being followed home along a deserted street, not because each boy who answers feels differently about the girl, but because each understands differently the cue that she gives.

Questions to Start You Thinking

1. According to Mead, how are social and family codes interwoven?
2. How do the examples Mead cites from New Guinea contrast with the images she presents of American society?

3. Mead uses several terms that have specific meanings to anthropologists. Define *taboo* (paragraph 1), *clique, homogeneous* (paragraph 2), and *code* (paragraph 4). What do words like these add to her essay?

4. What kinds of social and family codes are presented in Michael Dorris's "The Train Cake" (p. 435), in Vivian Gornick's "Mama Went to Work" (p. 445), and in E. B. White's "Once More to the Lake" (p. 425)?

Suggestions for Writing

1. According to Mead, what traits characterize American culture? Write an essay supporting or challenging Mead's characterization of American society.

2. Write an essay explaining what qualities you feel should be central to family life. What types of behavior lead to successful family relationships? Support your ideas with examples from your own experience and observations.

JOAN JACOBS BRUMBERG was born in Mount Vernon, New York, in 1944. After graduating from the University of Rochester, she earned an M.A. at Boston College and a Ph.D. in history at Cornell University, where she now is director of women's studies. The following essay is excerpted from her award-winning study *Fasting Girls: The Emergence of Anorexia Nervosa as a Modern Disease* (1988), which traces the long social history of a disorder that has received serious attention only in the last decade.

THE ORIGINS OF ANOREXIA NERVOSA
Joan Jacobs Brumberg

Contrary to the popular assumption that anorexia nervosa is a peculiarly 1 modern disorder, the malady first emerged in the Victorian era — long before the pervasive cultural imperative for a thin female body. The first clinical descriptions of the disorder appeared in England and France almost simultaneously in 1873. They were written by two well-known physicians: Sir William Withey Gull and Charles Lasègue. Lasègue, more than any other nineteenth-century doctor, captured the rhythm of repeated offerings and refusals that signaled the breakdown of reciprocity between parents and their anorexic daughter. By returning to its origins, we can see anorexia nervosa for what it is: a dysfunction in the bourgeois family system.

Family meals assumed enormous importance in the bourgeois milieu, 2 in the United States as well as in England and France. Middle-class parents prided themselves on providing ample food for their children. The abundance of food and the care in its preparation became expressions of social status. The ambience of the meal symbolized the values of the family. A popular domestic manual advised, "Simple, healthy food, exquisitely pre-pared, and served upon shining dishes and brilliant silverware . . . a gentle blessing, and cheerful conversation, embrace the sweetest communions and the happiest moments of life." Among the middle class it seems that eating correctly was emerging as a new morality, one that set its members apart from the working class.

At the same time, food was used to express love in the nineteenth- 3 century bourgeois household. Offering attractive and abundant meals was the particular responsibility and pleasure of middle-class wives and moth-ers. In America the feeding of middle-class children, from infancy on, had become a maternal concern no longer deemed appropriate to delegate to wet nurses, domestics, or governesses. Family meals were expected to be a time of instructive and engaging conversation. Participation was expected on both a verbal and gustatory level. In this context, refusing to eat was an unabashedly antisocial act. Anorexic behavior was antithetical to the ideal of bourgeois eating. One advice book, *Common Sense for Maid, Wife, and Mother*, stated: "Heated discussion and quarrels, fretfulness and sul-len taciturnity while eating, are as unwholesome as they are unchristian."

Why would a daughter affront her parents by refusing to eat? Lasègue's 4 1873 description of anorexia nervosa, along with other nineteenth-century medical reports, suggests that pressure to marry may have precipitated the illness.

Ambitious parents surely understood that by marrying well, at an ap- 5 propriate moment, a daughter, even though she did not carry the family name, could help advance a family's social status — particularly in a bur-geoning middle-class society. As a result, the issue of marriage loomed large in the life of a dutiful middle-class daughter. Although marriage did not generally occur until the girl's early twenties, it was an event for which she was continually prepared, and a desirable outcome for all depended on the ability of the parents and the child to work together — that is, to state clearly what each wanted or to read each other's heart and mind. In the context of marital expectations, a daughter's refusal to eat was a provocative rejection of both the family's social aspirations and their good-will toward her. All of the parents' plans for her future (and their own) could be stymied by her peculiar and unpleasant alimentary nihilism.

Beyond the specific anxieties generated by marital pressure, the Vic- 6 torian family milieu in America and in Western Europe harbored a mélange of other tensions and problems that provided the emotional preconditions for the emergence of anorexia nervosa. As love replaced authority as the cement of family relations, it began to generate its own set of emotional disorders.

Possessiveness, for example, became an acute problem in Victorian 7 family life. Where love between parents and children was the prevailing ethic, there was always the risk of excess. When love became suffocating or manipulative, individuation and separation from the family could become extremely painful, if not impossible. In the context of increased intimacy, adolescent privacy was especially problematic: for parents and their sexually maturing daughters, what constituted an appropriate degree of privacy? Middle-class girls, for example, almost always had their own rooms or shared them with sisters, but they had greater difficulty establishing autonomous psychic space. The well-known penchant of adolescent girls for novel-reading was an expression of their need for imaginative freedom. Some parents, recognizing that their daughters needed channels for expressing emotions, encouraged diary-keeping. But some of the same parents who gave lovely marbled journals as gifts also monitored their content. Since emotional freedom was not an acknowledged prerogative of the Victorian adolescent girl, it seems likely that she would have expressed unhappiness in nonverbal forms of behavior. One such behavior was refusal of food.

When an adolescent daughter became sullen and chronically refused 8
to eat, her parents felt threatened and confused. The daughter was perceived as willfully manipulating her appetite the way a younger child might. Because parents did not want to encourage this behavior, they often refused at first to indulge the favorite tastes or caprices of their daughter. As emaciation became visible and the girl looked ill, many violated the contemporary canon of prudent childrearing and put aside their moral objections to pampering the appetite. Eventually they would beg their daughter to eat whatever she liked—and eat she must, "as a sovereign proof of affection" for them. From the parents' perspective, a return to eating was a confirmation of filial love.

The significance of food refusal as an emotional tactic within the family 9
depended on food's being plentiful, pleasing, and connected to love. Where food was eaten simply to assuage hunger, where it had only minimal aesthetic and symbolic messages, or where the girl had to provide her own nourishment, refusal of food was not particularly noteworthy or defiant. In contrast, the anorexic girl was surrounded by a provident, if not indulgent, family that was bound to be distressed by her rejection of its largess.

Anorexia nervosa was an intense form of discourse that honored the 10
emotional guidelines that governed the middle-class Victorian family. Refusing to eat was not as confrontational as yelling, having a tantrum, or throwing things; refusing to eat expressed emotional hostility without being flamboyant. And refusing to eat had the advantage of being ambiguous. If a girl repeatedly claimed lack of appetite she might indeed be ill and therefore entitled to special treatment and favors.

In her own way, the anorexic was respectful of what historian Peter Gay 11
called "the great bourgeois compromise between the need for reserve and the capacity for emotion." The rejection of food, while an emotionally charged behavior, was also discreet, quiet, and ladylike. The unhappy adolescent who was in all other ways a dutiful daughter chose food refusal from within the symptom repertoire available to her. Precisely because she was not a lunatic, she selected a behavior that she knew would have some efficacy within her own family.

Questions to Start You Thinking

1. Does Brumberg believe that the root of anorexic behavior lies in the individual or in society? Explain.

2. How does Brumberg use cause and effect in her analysis of Victorian social pressures and anorexia?

3. Define *anorexia nervosa, cultural imperative, dysfunction, bourgeois* (paragraph 1), *milieu* (paragraph 2), *gustatory* (paragraph 3), and *alimentary* (paragraph 5). How does Brumberg's use of this technical language support her authority as an expert?

4. In this selection, Brumberg outlines some of Victorian society's expectations of women. Compare and contrast these expectations with those described by Emily Prager in "Our Barbies, Ourselves" (p. 560).

Suggestions for Writing

1. In this essay, Brumberg analyzes some social pressures that produced anorexia nervosa in Victorian times. Write a brief essay analyzing some aspects of today's society that might drive people to anorexic behavior.

2. Compare and contrast the stereotypes of women in Victorian society, as Brumberg describes them here, with female stereotypes you see today.

CHAPTER 22

Men and Women

JUDY BRADY was born in 1937 in San Francisco, where she now makes her home after attending college in Iowa and studying class relationships in Cuba. She has recently edited the book *1 in 3: Women with Cancer Confront an Epidemic* (1991). In the following piece, which has been reprinted frequently since its appearance in *Ms.* magazine in December 1971, Brady considers the role of the American housewife. While she has said that she is "not a 'writer,' " this essay shows Brady to be a satirist adept at taking a stand and provoking attention.

I WANT A WIFE
Judy Brady

I belong to that classification of people known as wives. I am A Wife. 1
And, not altogether incidentally, I am a mother.

Not too long ago a male friend of mine appeared on the scene fresh 2
from a recent divorce. He had one child, who is, of course, with his ex-
wife. He is looking for another wife. As I thought about him while I was
ironing one evening, it suddenly occurred to me that I, too, would like to
have a wife. Why do I want a wife?

I would like to go back to school so that I can become economically 3
independent, support myself, and, if need be, support those dependent
upon me. I want a wife who will work and send me to school. And while I

am going to school I want a wife to take care of my children. I want a wife to keep track of the children's doctor and dentist appointments. And to keep track of mine, too. I want a wife to make sure my children eat properly and are kept clean. I want a wife who will wash the children's clothes and keep them mended. I want a wife who is a good nurturant attendant to my children, who arranges for their schooling, makes sure that they have an adequate social life with their peers, takes them to the park, the zoo, etc. I want a wife who takes care of the children when they are sick, a wife who arranges to be around when the children need special care, because, of course, I cannot miss classes at school. My wife must arrange to lose time at work and not lose the job. It may mean a small cut in my wife's income from time to time, but I guess I can tolerate that. Needless to say, my wife will arrange and pay for the care of the children while my wife is working.

I want a wife who will take care of *my* physical needs. I want a wife   4
who will keep my house clean. A wife who will pick up after my children, a wife who will pick up after me. I want a wife who will keep my clothes clean, ironed, mended, replaced when need be, and who will see to it that my personal things are kept in their proper place so that I can find what I need the minute I need it. I want a wife who cooks the meals, a wife who is a *good* cook. I want a wife who will plan the menus, do the necessary grocery shopping, prepare the meals, serve them pleasantly, and then do the cleaning up while I do my studying. I want a wife who will care for me when I am sick and sympathize with my pain and loss of time from school. I want a wife to go along when our family takes a vacation so that someone can continue to care for me and my children when I need a rest and change of scene.

I want a wife who will not bother me with rambling complaints about a   5
wife's duties. But I want a wife who will listen to me when I feel the need to explain a rather difficult point I have come across in my course of studies. And I want a wife who will type my papers for me when I have written them.

I want a wife who will take care of the details of my social life. When   6
my wife and I are invited out by my friends, I want a wife who will take care of the babysitting arrangements. When I meet people at school that I like and want to entertain, I want a wife who will have the house clean, will prepare a special meal, serve it to me and my friends, and not interrupt when I talk about things that interest me and my friends. I want a wife who will have arranged that the children are fed and ready for bed before my guests arrive so that the children do not bother us. I want a wife who takes care of the needs of my guests so that they feel comfortable, who makes sure that they have an ashtray, that they are passed the hors d'oeuvres, that they are offered a second helping of the food, that their wine glasses are replenished when necessary, that their coffee is served to them as they like it. And I want a wife who knows that sometimes I need a night out by myself.

I want a wife who is sensitive to my sexual needs, a wife who makes   7
love passionately and eagerly when I feel like it, a wife who makes sure

that I am satisfied. And, of course, I want a wife who will not demand sexual attention when I am not in the mood for it. I want a wife who assumes the complete responsibility for birth control, because I do not want more children. I want a wife who will remain sexually faithful to me so that I do not have to clutter up my intellectual life with jealousies. And I want a wife who understands that *my* sexual needs may entail more than strict adherence to monogamy. I must, after all, be able to relate to people as fully as possible.

If, by chance, I find another person more suitable as a wife than the wife I already have, I want the liberty to replace my present wife with another one. Naturally, I will expect a fresh, new life; my wife will take the children and be solely responsible for them so that I am left free. 8

When I am through with school and have a job, I want my wife to quit working and remain at home so that my wife can more fully and completely take care of a wife's duties. 9

My God, who *wouldn't* want a wife? 10

Questions to Start You Thinking

1. How does Brady define the role of the traditional wife? Does she feel that a wife should perform all of the duties she outlines? How can you tell?

2. How does Brady use observation to support her stand? What other resources does she use?

3. Why does Brady use such simple language in this essay? What is implied by her use of such phrases as *of course* (paragraph 2), *Needless to say* (paragraph 3), and *Naturally* (paragraph 8)?

4. Compare Brady's description of the role of the wife with Susan Faludi's description ("Blame it on Feminism," p. 482) of the status of women as currently perceived in American society. How are Brady's and Faludi's perceptions of women's rights and responsibilities similar? How do they differ?

Suggestions for Writing

1. How has the role of a wife changed in the twenty-plus years since this essay was written? Write a brief essay comparing and contrasting the wife of the 1990s with the kind of wife Judy Brady says she wants.

2. In a short personal essay, explain what you want or expect in a wife, husband, or life partner. How do your hopes and expectations differ from the social norm? Why might that be? Did your parents' marriage shape your ideals of relationships? If so, in what way(s)?

NOEL PERRIN was born in 1927 in New York City. He earned degrees at Williams College, Duke University, and Cambridge University and since 1959 has taught English at Dartmouth College. For all his academic credentials, much of his fame as a writer comes from three volumes of essays on part-time farming. In the following essay, first published in the *New York Times Magazine* on September 9, 1984, Perrin satirizes the postdivorce behavior of many middle-class couples and proposes a somewhat unorthodox solution to the problems that plague modern marriages.

A PART-TIME MARRIAGE
Noel Perrin

When my wife told me she wanted a divorce, I responded like any 1
normal college professor. I hurried to the college library. I wanted to get hold of some books on divorce and find out what was happening to me.

Over the next week (my wife meanwhile having left), I read or skimmed 2
about twenty. Nineteen of them were no help at all. They offered advice on financial settlements. They told me my wife and I should have been in counseling. A bit late for *that* advice.

What I sought was insight. I especially wanted to understand what was 3
wrong with me that my wife had left, and not even for someone else, but just to be rid of *me*. College professors think they can learn that sort of thing from books.

As it turned out, I could. Or at least I got a start. The twentieth book 4
was a collection of essays by various sociologists, and one of the pieces took my breath away. It was like reading my own horoscope.

The two authors had studied a large group of divorced people much 5
like my wife and me. That is, they focused on middle-class Americans of the straight-arrow persuasion. Serious types, believers in marriage for life. Likely to be parents—and, on the whole, good parents. Likely to have pillar-of-the-community potential. But, nevertheless, all divorced.

Naturally there were many different reasons why all these people had 6
divorced, and many different ways they behaved after divorce. But there was a dominant pattern, and I instantly recognized myself in it. Recognized my wife, too. Reading the essay told me not only what was wrong with me, but also with her. It was the same flaw in both of us. It even gave me a hint as to what my postdivorce behavior was likely to be, and how I might find happiness in the future.

This is the story the essay told me. Or, rather, this is the story the essay 7
hinted at, and that I have since pieced together with much observation, a number of embarrassingly personal questions put to divorced friends, and to some extent from my own life.

Somewhere in some suburb or town or small city, a middle-class couple 8
separate. They are probably between thirty and forty years old. They own a house and have children. The conscious or official reason for their separation is quite different from what it would have been in their parents' generation. Then, it would have been a man leaving his wife for another,

and usually younger, woman. Now it's a woman leaving her husband in order to find herself.

When they separate, the wife normally stays in the house they occupied 9 as a married couple. Neither wants to uproot the children. The husband moves to an apartment, which is nearly always going to be closer to his place of employment than the house was. The ex-wife will almost certainly never see that apartment. The husband, however, sees his former house all the time. Not only is he coming by to pick up the children for visits; if he and his ex-wife are on reasonably good terms, he is apt to visit them right there, while she makes use of the time to do errands or to see a friend.

Back when these two were married, they had an informal labor division. 10 She did inside work, he did outside. Naturally there were exceptions: She gardened, and he did his share of the dishes, maybe even baked bread. But mostly he mowed the lawn and fixed the lawn mower; she put up any new curtains, often enough ones she had made herself.

One Saturday, six months or a year after they separated, he comes to 11 see the kids. He plans also to mow the lawn. Before she leaves, she says, "That damn overhead garage door you got is off the track again. Do you think you'd have time to fix it?" Apartment life makes him restless. He jumps at the chance.

She, just as honorable and straight-arrow as he, has no idea of asking 12 for this as a favor. She invites him to stay for an early dinner. She may put it indirectly—"Michael and Sally want their daddy to have supper with them"—but he is clear that the invitation also proceeds from her.

Provided neither of them has met a really attractive other person yet, 13 they now move into a routine. He comes regularly to do the outside chores, and always stays for dinner. If the children are young enough, he may read to them before bedtime. She may wash his shirts.

One such evening, they both happen to be stirred not only by physical 14 desire but by loneliness. "Oh, you might as well come upstairs," she says with a certain self-contempt. He needs no second invitation; they are upstairs in a flash. It is a delightful end to the evening. More delightful than anything they remember from their marriage, or at least from the later part of it.

That, too, now becomes part of the pattern. He never stays the full 15 night, because, good parents that they are, they don't want the children to get any false hopes up—as they would, seeing their father at breakfast.

Such a relation may go on for several years, may even be interrupted 16 by a romance on one side or the other and then resume. It may even grow to the point where she's mending as well as washing his shirts, and he is advising her on her tax returns and fixing her car.

What they have achieved postdivorce is what their marriage should have 17 been like in the first place. Part-time. Seven days a week of marriage was too much. One afternoon and two evenings is just right.

Although our society is even now witnessing de facto part-time arrange- 18 ments, such as the couple who work in different cities and meet only on weekends, we have no theory of part-time marriage, at least no theory that has reached the general public. The romantic notion still dominates that if you love someone, you obviously want to be with them all the time.

To me it's clear we need such a theory. There are certainly people who   19 thrive on seven-day-a-week marriages. They have a high level of intimacy and they may be better, warmer people than the rest of us. But there are millions and millions of us with medium or low levels of intimacy. We find full-time family membership a strain. If we could enter marriage with more realistic expectations of what closeness means for us, I suspect the divorce rate might permanently turn downward. It's too bad there isn't a sort of glucose tolerance test for intimacy.

As for me personally, I still do want to get married again. About four   20 days a week.

Questions to Start You Thinking

1. How did Perrin's divorce affect him? What is his tone in this essay?

2. How does Perrin use cause and effect to support the solution he proposes?

3. Define *straight-arrow, pillar-of-the-community* (paragraph 5), *dominant* (paragraph 6), *self-contempt* (paragraph 14), *de facto* (paragraph 18), and *glucose tolerance test* (paragraph 19). Would you say that Perrin's vocabulary is typical of the "normal" college professor? Give some specific examples to support your answer.

4. Compare Perrin's view of marriage with Judy Brady's in "I Want a Wife" (p. 455). How do both writers react against traditional attitudes?

Suggestions for Writing

1. Take a stand on the solution Perrin proposes. In a short essay, agree or disagree with the idea of part-time marriage. Is it a constructive response to problems of marital incompatibility? Why or why not?

2. Write an essay on the causes and effects of divorce. In your experience, what are the main reasons for divorce? How has it affected you or those around you?

SCOTT RUSSELL SANDERS was born in 1945 in Memphis, Tennessee. Having received degrees at Brown University and Cambridge University, he has taught English at Indiana University since 1971. His numerous publications include *D. H. Lawrence: The Major Novels* (1974), *Fetching the Dead* (1984), a collection of stories, and *Paradise of Bombs* (1991), a collection of essays. Sanders has described his writing as "driven by a deep regard for particular places and voices . . . a regard compounded of grief, curiosity, and love." In the following essay, which first appeared in *Milkweed Chronicle* (1984), Sanders explains how the experience of growing up in a working-class community made it difficult for him to understand the grievances of women from more privileged backgrounds.

THE MEN WE CARRY IN OUR MINDS
Scott Russell Sanders

"This must be a hard time for women," I say to my friend Anneke. "They 1 have so many paths to choose from, and so many voices calling them."

"I think it's a lot harder for men," she replies. 2

"How do you figure that?" 3

"The women I know feel excited, innocent, like crusaders in a just 4 cause. The men I know are eaten up with guilt."

We are sitting at the kitchen table drinking sassafras tea, our hands 5 wrapped around the mugs because this April morning is cool and drizzly. "Like a Dutch morning," Anneke told me earlier. She is Dutch herself, a writer and midwife and peacemaker, with the round face and sad eyes of a woman in a Vermeer painting who might be waiting for the rain to stop, for a door to open. She leans over to sniff a sprig of lilac, pale lavender, that rises from a vase of cobalt blue.

"Women feel such pressure to be everything, do everything," I say. 6 "Career, kids, art, politics. Have their babies and get back to the office a week later. It's as if they're trying to overcome a million years' worth of evolution in one lifetime."

"But we help one another. We don't try to lumber on alone, like so many 7 wounded grizzly bears, the way men do." Anneke sips her tea. I gave her the mug with owls on it, for wisdom. "And we have this deep-down sense that we're in the *right*—we've been held back, passed over, used—while men feel they're in the wrong. Men are the ones who've been discredited, who have to search their souls."

I search my soul. I discover guilty feelings aplenty—toward the poor, 8 the Vietnamese, Native Americans, the whales, an endless list of debts— a guilt in each case that is as bright and unambiguous as a neon sign. But toward women I feel something more confused, a snarl of shame, envy, wary tenderness, and amazement. This muddle troubles me. To hide my unease I say, "You're right, it's tough being a man these days."

"Don't laugh." Anneke frowns at me, mournful-eyed, through the sas- 9 safras steam. "I wouldn't be a man for anything. It's much easier being the victim. All the victim has to do is break free. The persecutor has to live with his past."

How deep is that past? I find myself wondering after Anneke has left. 10 How much of an inheritance do I have to throw off? Is it just the beliefs I breathed in as a child? Do I have to scour memory back through father and grandfather? Through St. Paul? Beyond Stonehenge and into the twilit caves? I'm convinced the past we must contend with is deeper even than speech. When I think back on my childhood, on how I learned to see men and women, I have a sense of ancient, dizzying depths. The back roads of Tennessee and Ohio where I grew up were probably closer, in their sexual patterns, to the campsites of Stone Age hunters than to the genderless cities of the future into which we are rushing.

The first men, besides my father, I remember seeing were black con- 11
victs and white guards, in the cottonfield across the road from our farm on
the outskirts of Memphis. I must have been three or four. The prisoners
wore dingy gray-and-black zebra suits, heavy as canvas, sodden with sweat.
Hatless, stooped, they chopped weeds in the fierce heat, row after row,
breathing the acrid dust of boll-weevil poison. The overseers wore dazzling
white shirts and broad shadowy hats. The oiled barrels of their shotguns
flashed in the sunlight. Their faces in memory are utterly blank. Of course
those men, white and black, have become for me an emblem of racial
hatred. But they have also come to stand for the twin poles of my early
vision of manhood—the brute toiling animal and the boss.

When I was a boy, the men I knew labored with their bodies. They were 12
marginal farmers, just scraping by, or welders, steelworkers, carpenters;
they swept floors, dug ditches, mined coal, or drove trucks, their forearms
ropy with muscle; they trained horses, stoked furnaces, built tires, stood
on assembly lines wrestling parts onto cars and refrigerators. They got up
before light, worked all day long whatever the weather, and when they came
home at night they looked as though somebody had been whipping them.
In the evenings and on weekends they worked on their own places, tilling
gardens that were lumpy with clay, fixing broken-down cars, hammering on
houses that were always too drafty, too leaky, too small.

The bodies of the men I knew were twisted and maimed in ways visible 13
and invisible. The nails of their hands were black and split, the hands
tattooed with scars. Some had lost fingers. Heavy lifting had given many
of them finicky backs and guts weak from hernias. Racing against conveyor
belts had given them ulcers. Their ankles and knees ached from years of
standing on concrete. Anyone who had worked for long around machines
was hard of hearing. They squinted, and the skin of their faces was creased
like the leather of old work gloves. There were times, studying them, when
I dreaded growing up. Most of them coughed, from dust or cigarettes, and
most of them drank cheap wine or whiskey, so their eyes looked bloodshot
and bruised. The fathers of my friends always seemed older than the
mothers. Men wore out sooner. Only women lived into old age.

As a boy I also knew another sort of men, who did not sweat and break 14
down like mules. They were soldiers, and so far as I could tell they scarcely
worked at all. During my early school years we lived on a military base, an
arsenal in Ohio, and every day I saw GIs in the guardshacks, on the stoops
of barracks, at the wheels of olive drab Chevrolets. The chief fact of their
lives was boredom. Long after I left the arsenal I came to recognize the
sour smell the soldiers gave off as that of souls in limbo. They were all
waiting—for wars, for transfers, for leaves, for promotions, for the end of
their hitch—like so many braves waiting for the hunt to begin. Unlike the
warriors of older tribes, however, they would have no say about when the
battle would start or how it would be waged. Their waiting was broken only
when they practiced for war. They fired guns at targets, drove tanks across
the churned-up fields of the military reservation, set off bombs in the wrecks

of old fighter planes. I knew this was all play. But I also felt certain that when the hour for killing arrived, they would kill. When the real shooting started, many of them would die. This was what soldiers were *for*, just as a hammer was for driving nails.

Warriors and toilers: those seemed, in my boyhood vision, to be the   15 chief destinies for men. They weren't the only destinies, as I learned from having a few male teachers, from reading books, and from watching television. But the men on television — the politicians, the astronauts, the generals, the savvy lawyers, the philosophical doctors, the bosses who gave orders to both soldiers and laborers — seemed as remote and unreal to me as the figures in tapestries. I could no more imagine growing up to become one of these cool, potent creatures than I could imagine becoming a prince.

A nearer and more hopeful example was that of my father, who had   16 escaped from a red-dirt farm to a tire factory, and from the assembly line to the front office. Eventually he dressed in a white shirt and tie. He carried himself as if he had been born to work with his mind. But his body, remembering the earlier years of slogging work, began to give out on him in his fifties, and it quit on him entirely before he turned sixty-five. Even such a partial escape from man's fate as he had accomplished did not seem possible for most of the boys I knew. They joined the army, stood in line for jobs in the smoky plants, helped build highways. They were bound to work as their fathers had worked, killing themselves or preparing to kill others.

A scholarship enabled me not only to attend college, a rare enough   17 feat in my circle, but even to study in a university meant for the children of the rich. Here I met for the first time young men who had assumed from birth that they would lead lives of comfort and power. And for the first time I met women who told me that men were guilty of having kept all the joys and privileges of the earth for themselves. I was baffled. What privileges? What joys? I thought about the maimed dismal lives of most of the men back home. What had they stolen from their wives and daughters? The right to go five days a week, twelve months a year, for thirty or forty years to a steel mill or a coal mine? The right to drop bombs and die in war? The right to feel every leak in the roof, every gap in the fence, every cough in the engine, as a wound they must mend? The right to feel, when the lay-off comes or the plant shuts down, not only afraid but ashamed?

I was slow to understand the deep grievances of women. This was   18 because, as a boy, I had envied them. Before college, the only people I had ever known who were interested in art or music or literature, the only ones who read books, the only ones who ever seemed to enjoy a sense of ease and grace were the mothers and daughters. Like the menfolk, they fretted about money, they scrimped and made-do. But, when the pay stopped coming in, they were not the ones who had failed. Nor did they have to go to war, and that seemed to me a blessed fact. By comparison with the narrow, ironclad days of fathers, there was an expansiveness, I thought, in the days of mothers. They went to see neighbors, to shop in town, to run errands at school, at the library, at church. No doubt, had I looked harder at their lives, I would have envied them less. It was not my fate to become a woman, so it was easier for me to see the graces. Few of them held jobs outside the home, and those who did filled thankless roles as clerks and waitresses. I didn't see, then, what a prison a house could be, since houses seemed to me brighter, handsomer places than any factory. I did not realize—because such things were never spoken of—how often women suffered from men's bullying. I did learn about the wretchedness of abandoned wives, single mothers, widows; but I also learned about the wretchedness of lone men. Even then I could see how exhausting it was for a mother to cater all day to the needs of young children. But if I had been asked, as a boy, to choose between tending a baby and tending a machine, I think I would have chosen the baby. (Having now tended both, I know I would choose the baby.)

So I was baffled when the women at college accused me and my sex 19 of having cornered the world's pleasures. I think something like my bafflement has been felt by other boys (and by girls as well) who grew up in dirt-poor farm country, in mining country, in black ghettos, in Hispanic barrios, in the shadows of factories, in third world nations—any place where the fate of men is as grim and bleak as the fate of women. Toilers and warriors. I realize now how ancient these identities are, how deep the tug they exert on men, the undertow of a thousand generations. The miseries I saw, as a boy, in the lives of nearly all men I continue to see in the lives of many— the body-breaking toil, the tedium, the call to be tough, the humiliating powerlessness, the battle for a living and for territory.

When the women I met at college thought about the joys and privileges 20 of men, they did not carry in their minds the sort of men I had known in my childhood. They thought of their fathers, who were bankers, physicians, architects, stockbrokers, the big wheels of the big cities. These fathers rode the train to work or drove cars that cost more than any of my childhood houses. They were attended from morning to night by female helpers, wives and nurses and secretaries. They were never laid off, never short of cash at month's end, never lined up for welfare. These fathers made decisions that mattered. They ran the world.

The daughters of such men wanted to share in this power, this glory. 21 So did I. They yearned for a say over their future, for jobs worthy of their abilities, for the right to live at peace, unmolested, whole. Yes, I thought, yes yes. The difference between me and these daughters was that they saw me, because of my sex, as destined from birth to become like their fathers, and therefore as an enemy to their desires. But I knew better. I wasn't an enemy, in fact or in feeling. I was an ally. If I had known, then, how to tell them so, would they have believed me? Would they now?

Questions to Start You Thinking

1. Why does Sanders call himself an "ally" (paragraph 21) of the women he met in college? Do you agree that he was their ally? Explain.

2. Sanders uses recall as a resource in this piece. How does he use the experiences he recalls to support the stand he takes?

3. Sanders writes that when he was a boy "warriors and toilers" seemed to him to be the chief destinies for men (paragraph 15). What qualities do you associate with "warriors" and "toilers"? Are the connotations of these terms primarily positive or negative?

4. How do the images of men that Sanders acquired in his childhood differ from the images of women that Paula Gunn Allen ("Where I Come from Is like This," p. 500) acquired in hers?

Suggestions for Writing

1. Write a short essay explaining whether men's or women's roles are more difficult in today's society. Use examples from your own experience.

2. Using recall as a resource, describe a man whose qualities you "carry in your mind." Who was this man? How did he help shape your views of what masculinity is and should be?

SUSAN BROWNMILLER was born in 1935 in Brooklyn, New York. After attending Cornell University, she worked as a writer, editor, and reporter for *Newsweek, The Village Voice,* NBC, and ABC. Cofounder of New York Radical Feminists, Brownmiller has written extensively on women's issues. Her book *Femininity* (1984) examines the ideal qualities often ascribed to women. The following essay, which first appeared in her book *Against Our Will: Men, Women, and Rape* (1975), raises issues about gender and censorship that continue to be debated among feminists and civil libertarians.

PORNOGRAPHY HURTS WOMEN
Susan Brownmiller

Pornography has been so thickly glossed over with the patina of chic   1 these days in the name of verbal freedom and sophistication that important distinctions between freedom of political expression (a democratic necessity), honest sex education for children (a societal good) and ugly smut (the deliberate devaluation of the role of women through obscene, distorted depictions) have been hopelessly confused. Part of the problem is that those who traditionally have been the most vigorous opponents of porn are often those same people who shudder at the explicit mention of any sexual subject. Under their watchful vigilante eyes, frank and free dissemination of educational materials relating to abortion, contraception, the act of birth, and female biology in general is also dangerous, subversive and dirty.

(I am not unmindful that a frank and free discussion of rape, "the unspeakable crime," might well give these righteous vigilantes further cause to shudder.) Because the battle lines were falsely drawn a long time ago, before there was a vocal women's movement, the anti-pornography forces appear to be, for the most part, religious, Southern, conservative, and right-wing, while the pro-porn forces are identified as Eastern, atheistic, and liberal.

But a woman's perspective demands a totally new alignment, or at least 2 a fresh appraisal. The majority report of the President's Commission on Obscenity and Pornography (1970), a report that argued strongly for the removal of all legal restrictions on pornography, soft and hard, made plain that 90 percent of all pornographic material is geared to the male heterosexual market (the other 10 percent is geared to the male homosexual taste), that buyers of porn are "predominantly white, middle-class, middle-aged married males," and that the graphic depictions, the meat and potatoes of porn, are of the naked female body and of the multiplicity of acts done to that body.

Discussing the content of stag films, "a familiar and firmly established 3 part of the American scene," the commission report dutifully, if foggily, explained, "Because pornography historically has been thought to be primarily a masculine interest, the emphasis in stag films seems to represent the preferences of the middle-class American male. Thus male homosexuality and bestiality are relatively rare, while lesbianism is rather common."

The commissioners in this instance had merely verified what purveyors 4 of porn have always known: hard-core pornography is not a celebration of sexual freedom; it is a cynical exploitation of female sexual activity through the device of making all such activity, and consequently all females, "dirty." Heterosexual male consumers of pornography are frankly turned on by watching lesbians in action (although never in the final scenes, but always as a curtain raiser); they are turned off with the sudden swiftness of a water faucet by watching naked men act upon each other. One study quoted in the commission report came to the unastounding conclusion that "seeing a stag film in the presence of male peers bolsters masculine esteem." Indeed. The men in groups who watch the films, it is important to note, are *not* naked.

When male response to pornography is compared to female response, 5 a pronounced difference in attitude emerges. According to the commission, "Males report being more highly aroused by depictions of nude females, and show more interest in depictions of nude females than [do] females." Quoting the figures of Alfred Kinsey, the commission noted that a majority of males (77 percent) were "aroused" by visual depictions of explicit sex while a majority of females (68 percent) were not aroused. Further, "females more often than males reported 'disgust' and 'offense.' "

From whence comes this female disgust and offense? Are females sex- 6 ually backward or more conservative by nature? The gut distaste that a majority of women feel when we look at pornography, a distaste that, incredibly, it is no longer fashionable to admit, comes, I think, from the gut knowledge that we and our bodies are being stripped, exposed, and contorted for the purpose of ridicule to bolster that "masculine esteem" which gets its kick and sense of power from viewing females as anonymous, panting playthings, adult toys, dehumanized objects to be used, abused, broken, and discarded.

This, of course, is also the philosophy of rape. It is no accident (for   7 what else could be its purpose?) that females in the pornographic genre are depicted in two cleanly dilineated roles: as virgins who are caught and "banged," or as nymphomaniacs who are never sated. The most popular and prevalent pornographic fantasy combines the two: an innocent, untutored female is raped and "subjected to unnatural practices" that turn her into a raving, slobbering nymphomaniac, a dependent sexual slave who can never get enough of the big, male cock.

There can be no "equality" in porn, no female equivalent, no turning of   8 the tables in the name of bawdy fun. Pornography, like rape, is a male invention, designed to dehumanize women, to reduce the female to an object of sexual access, not to free sensuality from moralistic or parental inhibition. The staple of porn will always be the naked female body, breasts and genitals exposed, because as man devised it, her naked body is the female's "shame," her private parts the private property of man, while his are the ancient, holy, universal, patriarchal instrument of his power, his rule by force over *her.*

Pornography is the undiluted essence of anti-female propaganda. Yet   9 the very same liberals who were so quick to understand the method and purpose behind the mighty propaganda machine of Hitler's Third Reich, the consciously spewed-out anti-Semitic caricatures and obscenities that gave an ideological base to the Holocaust and the Final Solution, the very same liberals who, enlightened by blacks, searched their own conscience and came to understand that their tolerance of "nigger" jokes and portrayals of shuffling, rolling-eyed servants in movies perpetuated the degrading myths of black inferiority and gave an ideological base to the continuation of black oppression — these very same liberals now fervidly maintain that the hatred and contempt for women that find expression in four-letter words used as expletives and in what are quaintly called "adult" or "erotic" books and movies are a valid extension of freedom of speech that must be preserved as a Constitutional right.

To defend the right of a lone, crazed American Nazi to grind out propa-   10 ganda calling for the extermination of all Jews, as the ACLU has done in the name of free speech, is, after all, a self-righteous and not particularly courageous stand, for American Jewry is not currently threatened by storm troopers, concentration camps, and imminent extermination, but I wonder if the ACLU's position might change if, come tomorrow morning, the bookstores and movie theaters lining Forty-second Street in New York City were devoted not to the humiliation of women by rape and torture, as they currently are, but to a systematized, commercially successful propaganda machine depicting the sadistic pleasures of gassing Jews or lynching blacks?

Is this analogy extreme? Not if you are a woman who is conscious of   11
the ever-present threat of rape and the proliferation of a cultural ideology that makes it sound like "liberated" fun. The majority report of the President's Commission on Obscenity and Pornography tried to pooh-pooh the opinion of law enforcement agencies around the country that claimed their own concrete experience with offenders who were caught with the stuff led them to conclude that pornographic material is a causative factor in crimes of sexual violence. The commission maintained that it was not possible at this time to scientifically prove or disprove such a connection.

But does one need scientific methodology in order to conclude that the   12
anti-female propaganda that permeates our nation's cultural output promotes a climate in which acts of sexual hostility directed against women are not only tolerated but ideologically encouraged? A similar debate has raged for many years over whether or not the extensive glorification of violence (the gangster as hero; the loving treatment accorded bloody shoot-'em-ups in movies, books and on TV) has a causal effect, a direct relationship to the rising rate of crime, particularly among youth. Interestingly enough, in this area—nonsexual and not specifically related to abuses against women—public opinion seems to be swinging to the position that explicit violence in the entertainment media does have a deleterious effect; it makes violence commonplace, numbingly routine, and no longer morally shocking.

More to the point, those who call for a curtailment of scenes of violence   13
in movies and on television in the name of sensitivity, good taste, and what's best for our children are not accused of being pro-censorship or against freedom of speech. Similarly, minority group organizations, black, Hispanic, Japanese, Italian, Jewish, or American Indian, that campaign against ethnic slurs and demeaning portrayals in movies, on television shows, and in commercials are perceived as waging a just political fight, for if a minority group claims to be offended by a specific portrayal, be it Little Black Sambo or the Frito Bandido, and relates it to a history of ridicule and oppression, few liberals would dare to trot out a Constitutional argument in theoretical opposition, not if they wish to maintain their liberal credentials. Yet when it comes to the treatment of women, the liberal consciousness remains fiercely obdurate, refusing to be budged, for the sin of appearing square or prissy in the age of the so-called sexual revolution has become the worst offense of all.

Questions to Start You Thinking

1. Why does Brownmiller feel that pornography is "anti-female propaganda" that hurts women (paragraph 9)? Do you agree with her?

2. What evidence does Brownmiller use to support her stand? How does she use cause and effect?

3. Look up *pornography* in several dictionaries. How do their definitions differ? Why might this be? What does *pornography* mean to you?

4. How might Brownmiller respond to Henry Louis Gates's "2 Live Crew, Decoded" (p. 558)? Use specific examples from Brownmiller's essay to support your response.

Suggestions for Writing

1. "There can be no 'equality' in porn," writes Brownmiller, "no female equivalent, no turning of the tables in the name of bawdy fun" (paragraph 8). Do you agree or disagree? Write a brief essay in which you take a stand on this position.

2. Propose a solution to the problem of pornography. Draw on your own knowledge and cite examples from the media. Would change best be effected by government or by individual action?

MARCIA ANN GILLESPIE was born in 1944 in Rockville, New York, and graduated from Lake Forest College. She has been an editor at *Essence* magazine and is currently a contributing editor for *Ms.* magazine. In the following piece, which appeared in *Ms.* in 1987, Gillespie recalls an evening she spent with a group of women at a nightclub featuring male strip shows and compares and contrasts the ways in which men and women express erotic energy.

A DIFFERENT TAKE ON THE OL' BUMP AND GRIND
Marcia Ann Gillespie

Once upon a time only nasty girls, women my grandmother called floozies, gave men a top-to-bottom once-over checking chests, muscles, behinds, and crotches. Nice girls, ladies, and good women were supposed to keep their eyes, like their skirts, down at all costs. The last thing the ol' patriarchy ever wanted was sexually assertive women knowing, much less talking, about orgasms, discussing our right to sexual pleasure, assessing men's sexual potential or performances, acknowledging that we found men's bodies exciting or simply interesting to look at. But in clubs all around this country women are looking, laughing, and carrying on while men come on like Gypsy Rose Lee: who would have thunk it? 1

Recently a friend's mother turned seventy and she knew just where she wanted to celebrate that milestone: Chippendales! Now for those of you who don't know, Chippendales provides a revue where male dancers shake, shimmy, bump, grind, and strip down to their bikini briefs for an almost 2 exclusively female audience who wave dollar bills in the air for their favorites in exchange for slightly sweaty hugs and kisses. In some cities one can even order up a male stripper—who will make house, restaurant, or even office calls—to shake it down for private parties. All you need do is dial a number and have your credit card handy. Ain't modern life grand!

When asked to join this particular birthday party, in between bursts of 3 laughter, I said yes indeed. My girlfriend was clearly in need of moral support. I think she was a bit shocked that her mother had turned down dinner at The Plaza for Chippendales. (Makes you wonder who the really liberated women are, us or our mothers?) I also will admit to being downright curious about the show. Was it going to be slightly sleazy, or really raunchy? Who went? Who performed? Did the women come on in macha— "hey, baby, shake that thang"—style?

The nightclub scene: dark walls, flashing strobes, speakers blasting 4 heavy-bassed hot disco, utilitarian banquettes and benches lining a dance floor. Music videos and pinups of good-looking, well-muscled young men in stock seductive poses, on screens positioned around the room. A bevy of young men moved through the crowd, serving drinks, hugging new arrivals, smiling and joking with the customers. Like cocktail waitresses, whose uniforms are designed to expose beaucoup cleavage and much thigh, these waiters are obviously picked for their bodies. Shirtless, wearing tight black pants, collars and bow ties, there's not an inch of excess fat, not an undeveloped pectoral, nary a hairy chest in sight!

The nightclub was filled with women. Women of all ages and sizes, 5 races and ethnicities, married and single, careerists and workers, students and retirees, suburbanites and city dwellers, they'd come by twos, and in groups large and small. Some appeared to be regulars, who used the club as a girls'-night-out hangout, or came a-cruisin'. And then there were the first-timers: more than a few appeared hesitant, with "what in the world am I doing here" looks on their faces; others were obviously revved up and ready to kick it out!

"Ladies, welcome to Chippendales!" The show began with a Las Vegas— 6 style opener, a big dance routine that seemed to include every man in the place. Then the emcee, a Michael J. Fox type, led off with a reverse strip. Starting out in briefs he put it all on, and then proceeded to work the crowd for the rest of the show: a series of vignettes loosely based on a "fantasy weekend." The accommodating Room Service Waiter, the Souvenir Man in a cage, the Macho Motorcyclist, the James Deanish Rebel who makes a cause out of oiling his body, and the Friendly Chauffeur—all performed with a fun, shake-it-all-out sense of delivery. The guys seemed sweet and clearly wished to please their patrons, enjoyed seeing the women have fun, and obviously loved the attention.

The performances are billed as interpretations of women's fantasies. 7 Very safe middle-of-the-road fantasies (like those hairless chests), nothing that would shock, rock, or threaten. (Steve Merritt, the show's choreographer and director, later told me that he'd discussed the concepts with women friends and in fact used many of their fantasies in the show.) Though none of them came close to my Secret Garden, it's clear that many of the women found them to be right on the money or maybe they just got a thrill out of the idea itself. Whatever the reasons, as each guy came out the women carried on, laughing, acting out a bit, hugging, being hugged and kissed. Kissed with much gusto but rather chastely (quite sanely given the age), on the cheek.

In truth as good-looking and as sexy as the men may be, I wasn't moved.   8 Some man shaking his family jewels and flexing his muscles isn't my sexual dish. Besides, other than Robert DeNiro, white men rarely, as in almost never, make up the stuff of my erotic dreams. I'm told that in the Los Angeles and Atlantic City clubs, Chippendales has black performers, providing equal opportunity erotica. Yet, I hardly think I'd be more turned on if the stars covered a complete racial spectrum. Fantasies aside, how many variations of the same old bump and grind can there be?

And yet, though none of it made my toes curl, I clapped and laughed   9 and had a ball. I knew it was gonna be a good time from the moment I walked into that room, heard the music, looked around at the sea of women and felt all their energy. No matter how good, bad, or simply boring the show might be, the truly vital dynamic was female.

And the women do get down. One woman's enthusiasm seemed to spur   10 another's, until it was impossible to tell whether the cheers and clapping and screams were for the performers, or simply us women saluting ourselves and each other. As the show progressed, that often repressed, slightly raunchy girl in even the most sedate of us started coming out. Across the room in the front row sat an older black woman, clearly a church-going lady, stolid of body, solemn of mien, who reminded me of my maternal grandmother. From the moment I first spied her, I kept wondering what in the world she was doing there, and how she was going to react to the show. Fascinated, I kept my eyes on her most of the evening. At first she seemed detached from it all, but then ever so slowly her head began to nod, while her feet tapped out the beat. And then—with absolutely no change of expression or position—a dollar bill appeared like magic in her hand, over the head of one of the younger women she was with, who, I presumed, was her daughter. And suddenly to the younger woman's total surprise there was this very big, very blond, very undressed male dancer swooping down to give her a hug. Mama cracked up, and laughed even harder when the same dancer kissed her as well.

One woman had a lot more contact in mind, which she demonstrated   11 by leaping onto a performer and wrapping her legs firmly around his waist. She looked like she'd died and gone to heaven when he danced her around the room. My friend's mom, head bouncing to the music, got into the act as well. One minute she was sitting with us, and the next she was over by the dance floor with her dollar waving in the air, being swept up in a bare bear hug by another giant-looking dancer. She returned to the group grinning from ear to ear.

By the time the show was over everyone seemed to be in a really good, 12
up place. And that's when the real party began as women singly, and by
twos and threes moved out on the dance floor boogying back. I felt the pull
and responded up on my feet out on the floor, dancing with my friend's
mother, energized and feeling a very special high. High off being with so
many other women, and the feeling of safety and celebration. Where else
could women go out and kick back like that, maybe in a gay women's bar,
I don't know. But here straight women were able to be publicly free in ways
we still too rarely are, without a thought of how we looked or who was
looking at us, without giving a damn about men and about being hit on,
when in fact that was the furthest thing from mind.

I kept contrasting the evening and the place to those clubs where 13
women strip for primarily male audiences. I recalled a joint I'd been years
before, once again out of sheer curiosity, with a man friend of mine. The
women who performed seemed deadpan and wary, while the men's eyes
seemed to bore into them, and more than once along with the tucked-in
bills came intrusive probing fingers or superior smirks and demeaning remarks. No one seemed to be having a really good time, not the customers,
not the dancers, not the waitresses serving the drinks. I could not, cannot
imagine those men jumping up as we women did at the end of the show
dancing together. Or those women who performed sharing good-time hugs
and kisses with the tippers. Too bad, because it will be a better day for all
of us when men—as well as women—can raise the roof off erotic energy.

Questions to Start You Thinking

1. Was Gillespie's overall impression of Chippendales positive or negative? Does she
   seem to have had fun?

2. How does Gillespie use comparison and contrast in her evaluation of male and
   female dance shows?

3. What kind of language does Gillespie use to talk about sexuality? How explicit is
   she? Define *floozies* (paragraph 1), *macha* (paragraph 3), *pectoral* (paragraph 4),
   vignettes (paragraph 6), and *dynamic* (paragraph 9).

4. In "Pornography Hurts Women" (p. 465), Susan Brownmiller says, "There can be
   no 'equality' in porn, no female equivalent, no turning of the tables in the name
   of bawdy fun." Would Gillespie agree or disagree?

Suggestions for Writing

1. Gillespie concludes that "it will be a better day for all of us when men—as well
   as women—can raise the roof off erotic energy" (paragraph 13). Do you agree
   or disagree? Write a short essay taking a stand on this question.

2. In a brief essay, compare and contrast the images of male and female sexuality
   presented by the media. Are men made into sex objects by the media? How?

TRIP GABRIEL was born in 1955, received his B.A. from Middlebury College, and now lives in New York City. A freelance writer, he is a contributing editor for *Rolling Stone* and a correspondent for *Outside* magazine. The following article, which appeared in the *New York Times Magazine* in October 1990, reports on one facet of the quickly growing men's awareness and rights movement. As a professional reporter for an establishment publication, Gabriel writes as both a participant and a somewhat distant and skeptical viewer.

CALL OF THE WILDMEN
Trip Gabriel

It was spring in the Emerald Hill country of North Texas, a region of rolling fields clotted with purple asters, mustard and black-eyed Susans. Signs that hung beside the white-rail fences of prosperous-looking ranches boasted of the breeds of cattle raised there, Brangus and Herefords and Santa Gertrudis. One sign, as vast as a billboard, said, "Polled Herefords: the Big Bold Breed." At a freshly plowed field, I turned off the blacktop onto a muddy ranch road, following directions to something called the Wildman Gathering, a weekend of outdoor living that, the brochure promised, would put me in touch with my "deep masculinity." 1

Around the nation, increasing numbers of men have been gathering at similar retreats to discover an earthier, more self-assured version of themselves. The workshops are part of a loosely organized but rapidly growing phenomenon known as the men's movement. Adherents claim that there is a gruff, elemental "wildman" lying deep inside every regular guy. This wildman, who can be freed by such activities as drumming and dancing around bonfires, has long been suppressed by industrialization, the corporate culture and 20 years of feminism. 2

Certainly, I was in the right place to shuck off civilization. I was 50 miles south of Fort Worth, in the heart of Texas, home of that masculine icon, the cowboy. Arriving at the Bosque Creek Ranch, a scrub-covered spread with a modest cabin and corral, I parked my car alongside many others. A man checked me off a registration list that included more than 130 names. He turned out to be Marvin Allen, the weekend's organizer and director of the Austin Men's Center. When Allen helped start the center in 1988, he noted, Austin had more than a dozen resource centers for women, but not one for men. Today the men's center offers a support group for new and expectant fathers, a Men's Codependency and Emotional Release Therapy Group, men's poetry evenings and the Wildman Gathering, which takes place here three times a year and is so popular it is booked up months in advance with participants from many states. 3

The growing men's movement has spawned magazines like Wingspan   4
and Man!, and workshops along the lines of Allen's, some lasting a day
and others as long as a week, have been held in Boston, Seattle, Minneapolis, Mendocino, Calif., and the mountains of New Mexico. By one estimate, the gatherings have attracted 50,000 men. Situated at the
intersection of the personal growth movement and the new age, the phenomenon for years was known almost exclusively to adherents of holistic
healing or crystal collecting. But recently it has come up from underground
and is attracting mainstream attention. Interest was stirred this year by a
90-minute Bill Moyers television program on the poet Robert Bly, the grand-
daddy, so to speak, of the men's movement.

Marvin Allen created the Wildman Gathering so males could come to-   5
gether in semiwilderness, apart from women, to get in tune with their bodies and their feelings. Or, as he had told me on the phone, "We work on
joy and exuberance and fierceness." Now he said I could set up my tent
wherever I chose. Beside some brushy trees, I pounded in the tent stakes,
while from a short distance away I heard the clang of pitched horseshoes.

At dusk came a steady drumbeat from a wooded grove a few hundred   6
yards away. Though no one had told us ahead of time, we all seemed to
understand this was a signal to head toward the trees with the drums we'd
each been asked to bring. A drum not being the sort of thing one has lying
around the house, before flying down from New York I'd hastily visited a
48th Street music store, where I was persuaded to buy a dusty silver instrument lying forgotten in a corner. It was a type of drum used by old
mambo bands, and for the next two days, whenever I thumped it, I could
not remove the image from my mind of Ricky Ricardo leading his band at
the Tropicana nightclub.

Inside a grove of Spanish oaks, we assembled. Hay bales were arranged   7
in a large circle, and a fire burned at the center. Soon we would learn to
call this the Sacred Grove. Tribal masks hung in trees to inspire us with
their fierce, primitive maleness. The mask closest to me was a scowling
African face with slit eyes, cow horns and a fringe of snakeskin.

The drumming ended with a burst of whistles and cheers. At the center   8
of the circle, Marvin Allen asked us to introduce ourselves to our immediate
neighbors, and to "tell them if you were afraid to come tonight." The man
to my left, Jim, who was from Houston, confided at length and with much
feeling that he'd been fearful of showing up.

Allen turned over the proceedings to his co-leader for the weekend,   9
John Lee, the author of one of the best-selling books of the new masculinity, "The Flying Boy." In the book Lee relates how he once "overvalued the
feminine" side of himself, cultivating a sensitive nature and wearing his
hair long like a girl. He became a Peter Pan—like figure unable to make
commitments to women or begin a career. To get on in life, he had to
embrace the "deep masculine" side of his personality.

Striding around the grove in calf-high mud boots, Lee indeed cut a   10
rugged profile. He wore jeans and a denim shirt. He had a salt-and-pepper

beard and he now wore his hair in a Marine cut. He spoke confidently in a rich Southern accent.

Lee told us his father, a machinist, was a "tough s.o.b." who would   11
think what we were doing this weekend was "a crock." Lee said his dad had been an angry alcoholic who was always emotionally and physically absent. He never taught his son how to have close male friends, and he never showed him that it was all right to express his feelings. "And," Lee said, drawing out the words for effect, "he never taught me how to cry."

"Ho," said many men, uttering the American Indian word we'd been told   12
to use to signal our assent or understanding.

Lee told us to close our eyes and imagine our fathers standing 100   13
yards behind us outside the circle. "They're mad at us," Lee said. "They're scared we're leaving them out." He said he was going to try something. He told us to take slow, deep breaths. Then, as if intoning a mantra, he said, "Dad." He repeated it "Dad." Then he said, "Father." He paused, "Father. Daddy."

Remarkably, men began to break down. At first, with eyes closed, I   14
didn't recognize the sound. How often had I heard men weep? Almost never. It began like a strangled cry, as if the men were gargling. Then their anguish burst forth in heaving sobs that rolled through the grove. Beside me, Jim cried freely. A couple of places to my right, a man gasped, "Hug me!" and he was embraced by the man next to him.

I was surprised and somewhat confused. What depths of sorrow did   15
these men feel, what scars could they be carrying associated with their fathers? Furthermore, who were they who could, at the incantatory mention of a parent, spill over in such showy, if nonetheless sincere, emotions? I felt distant from the public expression of grief. Dry-eyed, I returned to my tent. That night I slept restlessly and had vivid, disquieting dreams.

The concept of the wildman was introduced by Robert Bly, a National   16
Book Award—winning poet, about 10 years ago. Bly looked around in the early 80's and decided the nation was populated by many wimpified men, whom he labeled "soft males." These soft men, influenced by the cultural upheaval of the women's movement, could read poetry and talk to their wives and girlfriends. But they lacked energy, assertiveness, and the ability to make commitments. Bly did not believe that men should look to John Wayne or Arnold Schwarzenegger as role models. He spurned these caricatures of masculinity. Rather, he noted that almost every pre-industrial culture, from ancient Greece to the Middle Ages, projected in its myths and poetry an image of an ideal man as a forceful, spontaneous, primal being. "What I'm proposing," Bly once said, "is that every modern male has, lying at the bottom of his psyche, a large, primitive man covered with hair down to his feet. Making contact with this wildman is the step the 70's man has not yet taken: this is the process that still hasn't taken place in contemporary culture."

The men's movement says it's not a reactionary response to feminism.   17

Rather, it sees itself as a parallel development. While feminism has often dealt with politics and the outward conditions of women's lives, the men's movement is about internal issues, about men's psyches. At the Wildman Gathering I figured I'd hear a lot of grousing about wives and mothers, but in two full days women were hardly mentioned. Men were too busy talking about themselves.

Bly, 63 years old, is a white-haired paterfamilias whom many in the men's movement regard as a guru. They buy his audio tapes and his volumes of poetry, and invariably, whether they've met him or not, refer to him as "Robert." At one point in our weekend someone mentioned that Bly was lecturing in Portland, Oregon, at that very moment, whereupon John Lee encouraged everyone to shout over the tops of the trees, "Hello, Robert!" 18

A stirring storyteller and poetry reader, Bly has spread his message in week-long workshops and weekend lectures that draw huge crowds (and earn him up to $20,000 a pop). One event in San Francisco in May attracted 700 men, plus a waiting list of 700. Bly bars TV cameras from these gatherings and has been known to tell members of the audience not to take photographs or make recordings. The reason, a participant says, is that these are intrusions into the "ritual space" of the gatherings. 19

A major theme of Bly's is that men feel a great sense of grief and loss, often unacknowledged. On the subject of what, specifically, men have to grieve over, Bly can be vague. "It's as if grief is impersonal with men," he told Bill Moyers. "It's always present. You don't know if it's about the absence from their father, or it may be about all of the animals that we were in touch with all the millions of years we were hunters, and all the animals that died. . . . Men have lived for centuries out there, and they feel that terrific grief of nature and the out-of-doors and pine trees." 20

John Lee and Marvin Allen, who are both trained psychotherapists, are much more specific: the grief men feel is for the wounds inflicted on them by their fathers. Men feel a sense of loss that their fathers were never the kind of fathers they wished them to be, or needed. 21

Saturday morning in the Sacred Grove, Allen said: "Probably every way a man could be wounded by his father is represented here. Fathers have shamed us and criticized us. Some of our fathers have whipped us." 22

Quietly, several men answered, "Ho." 23

Allen told of his own father, a fighter pilot, and the image that came to mind was of the swaggering Robert Duvall in *The Great Santini*. Allen's father sounded distant and disapproving, and he passed onto his son the image of a man as someone who never felt pain or fear. 24

Allen is slight, with blue eyes and a neatly trimmed, professorial beard. He has a gentle, unthreatening manner. If one were to picture him as a high school athlete, the last sports that would come to mind are football and boxing. Yet to win his father's approval, Allen said, those are the sports he took up. "I got into Golden Gloves boxing, and I never lost because I had a burning desire to win," he told us. "But never once did he come to watch or tell me he was proud." 25

"Ho," responded many men. 26

"So I got into high-school football, and I was the skinniest guy on the 27 team, 125 pounds. Every time I got tackled I got hurt." Once, he said, he tried extra hard because his father was attending a game. He made a couple of big plays and heard his name announced on the loudspeaker. "I knew he was up there hearing my name, which was his name too: Allen." The son came home thinking that now, certainly, his father would give him the love and praise he thirsted for. But the father only grunted as the son entered the house. "Out of all the times he beat me and criticized me, that was the worst," Allen said in a voice thickening with emotion. "I realized seven or eight years ago that I spent most of my life trying to get him to appreciate me and validate me. Later he was able to. But it didn't mean that much by then. The little boy had already grown up."

Around the grove, several men were sniffling sympathetically. Others 28 had put their arms around one another as they listened. If there was concern the wildman would turn out to be just another male brute, unable to express his feelings or to nurture, it was not in evidence here.

It seemed that many men listening to Allen had heard their own stories 29 told. Indeed, over the weekend, I heard a surprising number of accounts of men who'd had outstanding athletic careers, primarily, they said, to win the love of distant fathers. It may have been that because we were in Texas, home of overvalued college and high school sports, that father-son dynamics had worked themselves out this way. One burly man, who said he'd been a state champion wrestler, said: "My father instilled a competitive fierceness in me. Somehow it wasn't good enough to be second. I loved him and he loved me, but that's not all there is to it."

Another man, whose dad, like Allen's was a fighter pilot, recalled: "My 30 father always told me of all the things I could do in this world, if I didn't fly a fighter, I'd failed. But I never flew a fighter and I don't want to."

The men were largely in their 30's and 40's, healthy and presentable- 31 looking guys. With only a few exceptions, they didn't strike me as life's losers. Most had weathered the traditional rites of passage for American males — college or the military, marriage, a successful career — but these passages left them somehow uncertain of their masculine identity. A Vietnam veteran, a survivor of the hoariest tradition of all for forging men, said, "I went to Vietnam a boy, and I came back an emotional baby."

There was a minister present, two judges, psychologists and entrepre- 32 neurs with their own businesses. The gathering included many lawyers. One confessed a desire to switch careers because, after 20 years of adversarial dickering, he realized he'd only been "re-enacting the kind of abusive relationship I've always had with my father."

What men were saying was that the traditional images of masculinity 33 had failed them, especially as represented by a hard-boiled figure who might be a football coach, a litigator, or a fighter pilot. Many men spoke of having had distant fathers like Allen's, prone to wound themselves and their families with alcohol or workaholism. A surprising number of men indicated they had received frequent beatings.

Allen said he wanted everyone to go off by himself for a while. "Go and 34 draw a circle, get inside it, and invite your father in," he said. "Tell him what you've always wanted to, the fear, the anger."

We left the grove and headed to the far corners of the ranch. I walked 35 a few hundred yards and sat down in front of a half circle of pine trees, with a view of a marshy frog pond. Behind me, I heard a man's tormented voice shouting at an imaginary father, "I hate your violence!" Another man, below me near the pond, whacked the trunk of a tree over and over with a branch.

I tried to zap some hostility onto an image of my dad. Although there'd 36 been plenty of times I'd been angry in his presence, I found that in such a warm, sunny spot, with crickets and frogs making a chirpy racket, it was impossible to feel bitter about much of anything. My father had not hit or neglected me, and if he was sometimes insensitive and unable to express his feelings, I could be equally insensitive and mute around him. I did not think he'd wounded me to the degree that other men described in moving terms.

I was uncertain what to grieve over. I tried to sense the more general 37 "grief of pine trees" that Bly referred to. The problem was, I've always felt upbeat around pine trees. I have always liked the outdoors. I'd sometimes wished for a more outdoorsy father, one who might have taught me to identify trees and animal tracks and to survive in the wilderness. As it happened, his back-country lore was pretty much limited to barbecuing in our suburban yard. One of the few nature skills he did teach me was how to blow on a blade of grass to make a whistle. Thinking of my father, I yanked a blade from the ground, stretched it between my thumbs, and blew into them to make the blade vibrate in a low, mournful whistle.

People in the men's movement believe there was once a golden age of 38 masculinity, when strong men hugged, expressed their feelings, honored their elders and served as mentors to younger men. This era is sometimes said to have existed during Arthurian times, when kings, warriors and wise magicians served as role models. These ancient societies offered men clear road maps of how they ought to behave through myths, legends and poetry. There were ceremonies to show respect, and rites to initiate adolescents into adulthood.

In modern times, rites and myths no longer exist to set men right, and 39 thus many are deeply confused. A major focus at men's retreats is to enact latter-day rituals to replace the old ones. Saturday afternoon and evening was to be our time to recover the rituals our post-industrial age denied us. I came to think of it as our time of Dungeons and Dragons.

After a lunch of rabbit stew, we returned to the Sacred Grove, where 40 Allen and Lee had spread an inner circle of dry hay around the fire. "I'd like to take this time to bring up and honor the elders," Lee said. He invited all the men over 50, about fifteen in all, to step forward and be seated on the dry hay. "These men know secrets, mysteries, truths," Lee said solemnly. "I bet if you ask them over the weekend they'll share some things we in our

30's and 40's don't know." He paused. "We're going to drum for these men. And drum for the lost fathers."

We pounded our drums. After many minutes the drumming had a lulling 41 effect that lent a kind of gravity to what struck me as a frivolous ritual. When we stopped, it was determined the oldest man present was 73. He was helped to his feet by the others. "We honor the eldest of the eldest," Lee said. We drummed furiously.

Our co-leaders spoke often of the wildman inside us, but they regularly 42 insisted that the wildman is not hostile, insensitive, or full of rage. That creature, Lee and Allen said, is known as the savageman. The savageman represents the macho, aggressive side of masculinity, which is what women and others may fear is what the men's movement has in mind when it speaks of getting in touch with "deep masculinity." This fear is erroneous, say the men. In order to feel the difference between the savageman and the wildman, we were to act them out in a pair of improvisational dances.

We paraded from the Sacred Grove to a large pasture doing the "king 43 walk," striding with chests puffed out, expressing pride without arrogance. Once in the pasture, we were encouraged to do a savageman dance. At first most men stood looking embarrassed, a perfectly normal reaction to being told to express oneself spontaneously. When Allen suggested "you might want to growl to express the savagery within" more than 100 men suddenly began running through the field snarling like rabid dogs. Most were enthusiastic savages. My own snarling left me hoarse the rest of the day.

Then it was time to dance like wildmen, and here many seemed at a 44 loss. One man skipped. Another jumped from side to side across a tractor rut. I picked up heavy rocks and threw them into the next pasture, thinking the gist of the wildman might lie in the primitive expression of strength and control. When Allen suggested we might wish to raise our arms in praise of the rosy sunset, many men took his suggestion. Whatever this wildman was, I thought, he still seemed to be an abstraction. We'd been far more convincing as savages.

All day, two mysterious structures had been taking shape beyond the 45 ranch corral. They were built of wood boughs bent in the skeletons of Indian lodges, which were heavily covered with blankets. The structures were sweat lodges, natural saunas that in some American Indian tribes are used for rituals of renewal and rebirth.

As night fell, we stripped off our clothes and lined up to enter the 46 lodges. A smoldering fire heated rocks for our natural saunas. A man named Lance conducted the ceremony in the lodge I entered. He compared the cave-dark enclosure to the womb of Mother Earth. Inside, we were squeezed together shoulder to shoulder and hip to hip, the great sweaty brotherhood of naked men that stretched back ritualistically, if not to a golden age, at least to the locker rooms of junior high.

Lance ordered the glowing rocks to be shoveled in. He sprinkled them 47 with water and cedar chips,and lung-scalding steam boiled up. Soon it was hot and claustrophobic. Earlier Lance had warned us that the sweat lodge could be an ordeal. "Pain is a powerful teacher," he said. "In a way, in the lodge we suffer a little bit. It takes that to open us up."

Lance, who is part Sac and Fox Indian, sang Indian prayers in a fine, soft voice. I scooped up cool mud from the ground to smear across my face, as a cricket crawled over my bare leg. After 40 minutes or so, the ceremony was over. I stumbled out beneath a brilliant starry sky and immediately found a cattle trough to use as a cold plunge. When I emerged, I indeed felt very good. But was I spiritually cleansed? Was I now a born-again wildman? I wasn't sure. My body hummed all over, but I've felt a similar uplift after a day's skiing and a hot tub. 48

It seemed to me there is a problem with the search for latter-day rituals by the men's movement. In themselves, rituals performed outside a cultural context don't mean very much. The power of a rite, be it a Christmas Mass or an Indian sweat lodge, comes from what the participants bring to it, which is a result of a long history of beliefs and expectations. It may be that American culture fails to respect the earned wisdom of its elderly, but 10 minutes of drumming isn't going to redress the hurt feelings of the oldsters. Enacted without a pre-existing system of beliefs, the drumming, dancing and vision-questing of the new masculinity feel pretty silly — at least they do to this camper. 49

The rituals were only part of our weekend, however. They provided a rough structure, but in between times, in what seemed to me ultimately a subtle subversion of the wildman's agenda, men would stand up spontaneously in the grove and tell chapters from their life stories. That's what these men apparently wanted to do most, just talk. The format derived from self-help groups where participants identify themselves by first names only and share their experiences. Many of the men were veterans of A.A. or groups for adult children of alcoholics or child-abuse victims, so they knew the program. The others got with it pretty quickly. 50

What emerged in the testimonies of men was a deep confusion at having to live up to conventional expectations of masculinity. Men said they'd tried to be fearless, invulnerable, all-knowing. Their fathers and their culture had taught them this was the way to act manly. But no one had prepared them for real life, for the breakup of a marriage and the sadness they would be unable to express. No one had prepared them for the emptiness of growing old without having gained maturity and wisdom. No one had showed them how to face death. 51

On Sunday morning, with a sense that time was running out, various men stood up to address the group. One took a step into the circle, an athletic-looking man in his mid-30's who was bare-chested in the sun. "I'm Randy," he said in a deep southern accent. His voice was shaky but he held himself rigidly erect, as if hoping to control powerful emotions through his posture. "I buried my father about a week ago," he said, choking out the words. "Before he died, I saw a scared old man. And I don't want to die that way." 52

"Ho," a few men said very softly.   53

"And like a lot of y'all," he went on, "I have the fear that I don't know   54
what's. . . . I don't know how. . . . I don't know what to do with it. He didn't
know a damn thing about feelings. See, I don't know if I grieved enough.
It was all so fast. He died Wednesday. We bought the coffin Thursday. And
we buried him Friday. Come Saturday I shut the hell down. Sunday I wished
I was here. The rest of the week I was scared I wasn't going to come.

Randy paused to take several breaths. All around the circle, men had   55
inhaled sharply when he began to speak of burying his father only the week
before. Now there was silence.

He struggled to continue. Tears were running freely down his cheeks.   56
"Now I don't want what he gave me. I still remember him walking like a
child among men. *I don't want to walk like a child among men.* I want to
stand up and walk. . . . I don't remember feeling this feeling before. . . .
Yeah, I think I was alone all of my damn life."

"Ho." Many others had been moved to tears.   57

"Thank you," Randy said in conclusion.   58

Lee commanded him, "Walk around the fire." Randy did so, his posture   59
as rod-straight as when he had begun to speak.

The Wildman Gathering was at an end, and for me it was ending on a   60
note of pitched emotion and some confusion. On the one hand, there
seemed a patent foolishness in the rituals we enacted—the drumming and
dancing. But on the other hand, who could not be moved by stories like
Randy's? The men around the fire had seemed at times ridiculous, but they
were ridiculous and real. Many were struggling to overcome the image of
a man, passed down by their fathers, as someone who is miserly with his
feelings and in whom any sign of vulnerability is a sign of weakness. They
had bought into this code of masculinity, and in all cases, they said, it had
stunted them.

I didn't know how the concept of a fierce, elemental wildman fit into   61
this realization. Nor, I suspect, did many others. The wildman weekend
hadn't made men fierce so much as it had tenderized them. The men's
movement hardly needs its sweat lodges and sacred groves. What most
men seem to want are more forums in which they can talk directly to one
another, a kind of recovery program for victims of errant notions of masculinity, a sort of Men's Anonymous.

Around the fire, there was applause and drumming in support of Randy,   62
and then Lee said: "Look at this man. God. When he was standing there,
you just saw it, a man feeling his feelings. As strong as the goddamn Rock
of Gibraltar with tears running down his face."

He embraced Randy, and then, one after another, other men got up to   63
join in, until almost the entire group was standing in a kind of huddle around
the man, swaying slowly like a rugby scrum, or a many-legged amoeba,
while wood smoke rose through the sunlight in the grove.

Questions to Start You Thinking

1. What is Gabriel's reaction to his experience of the Wildman Gathering? What is his attitude toward the goals of the men's movement?

2. How does Gabriel use reported conversations to convey his impression of the gathering?

3. Find examples of the vocabulary of sight and sound in this essay. How does such language make Gabriel's experience real to his readers?

4. Contrast the images of men discussed in this essay with those described by Scott Russell Sanders in "The Men We Carry in Our Minds" (p. 461).

Suggestions for Writing

1. What are the "conventional expectations of masculinity" (paragraph 51) in our society? Write a brief essay explaining why you do or do not feel that men are limited by such expectations. Use your own experience and observations, as well as Gabriel's essay, to help you develop and support your argument.

2. Using recall as a resource, describe a meeting or other gathering you have attended. How did the meeting or gathering make you feel? What was the mood of the group? Characterize the group through observation and reported conversation.

SUSAN FALUDI was born in New York City in 1959 and is best known as the author of *Backlash: The Undeclared War on American Women* (1991). After graduating from Harvard in 1981, Faludi worked at the *Miami Herald* and the *San Jose News.* Now a reporter for the *Wall Street Journal,* she revised the introduction of *Backlash* into the following essay, which appeared in *Mother Jones* in 1991. In it she cites numerous polls and statistics to support her argument that contemporary American women are the victims of a backlash against the women's movement.

BLAME IT ON FEMINISM
Susan Faludi

To be a woman in America at the close of the twentieth century—what 1
good fortune. That's what we keep hearing, anyway. The barricades have
fallen, politicians assure us. Women have "made it," Madison Avenue
cheers. Women's fight for equality has "largely been won," *Time* magazine
announces. Enroll at any university, join any law firm, apply for credit at
any bank. Women have so many opportunities now, corporate leaders say,
that they don't really need opportunity policies. Women are so equal now,
lawmakers say, that they no longer need an Equal Rights Amendment.

Women have "so much," former president Ronald Reagan says, that the White House no longer needs to appoint them to high office. Even American Express ads are saluting a woman's right to charge it. At last, women have received their full citizenship papers.

And yet . . . 2

Behind this celebration of the American woman's victory, behind the 3 news, cheerfully and endlessly repeated, that the struggle for women's rights is won, another message flashes: You may be free and equal now, but you have never been more miserable.

This bulletin of despair is posted everywhere—at the newsstand, on 4 the TV set, at the movies, in advertisements and doctors' offices and academic journals. Professional women are suffering "burnout" and succumbing to an "infertility epidemic." Single women are grieving from a "man shortage." The *New York Times* reports: Childless women are "depressed and confused" and their ranks are swelling. *Newsweek* says: Unwed women are "hysterical" and crumbling under a "profound crisis of confidence." The health-advice manuals inform: High-powered career women are stricken with unprecedented outbreaks of "stress-induced disorders," hair loss, bad nerves, alcoholism, and even heart attacks. The psychology books advise: Independent women's loneliness represents "a major mental-health problem today." Even founding feminist Betty Friedan has been spreading the word: She warns that women now suffer from "new problems that have no name."

How can American women be in so much trouble at the same time that 5 they are supposed to be so blessed? If women got what they asked for, what could possibly be the matter now?

The prevailing wisdom of the past decade has supported one, and only 6 one, answer to this riddle: It must be all that equality that's causing all that pain. Women are unhappy precisely because they are free. Women are enslaved by their own liberation. They have grabbed at the gold ring of independence, only to miss the one ring that really matters. They have gained control of their fertility, only to destroy it. They have pursued their own professional dreams—and lost out on romance, the greatest female adventure. "Our generation was the human sacrifice" to the women's movement, writer Elizabeth Mehren contends in a *Time* cover story. Baby-boom women, like her, she says, have been duped by feminism: "We believed the rhetoric." In *Newsweek*, writer Kay Ebeling dubs feminism the "Great Experiment That Failed" and asserts, "Women in my generation, its perpetrators, are the casualties."

In the eighties, publications from the *New York Times* to *Vanity Fair* to 7 *The Nation* have issued a steady stream of indictments against the women's movement, with such headlines as "When Feminism Failed" or "The Awful Truth About Women's Lib." They hold the campaign for women's equality responsible for nearly every woe besetting women, from depression to meager savings accounts, from teenage suicides to eating disorders to bad complexions. The *Today* show says women's liberation is to blame for bag ladies. A guest columnist in the *Baltimore Sun* even proposes that feminists produced the rise in slasher movies. By making the "violence" of abortion more acceptable, the author reasons, women's-rights activists made it all right to show graphic murders on screen.

At the same time, other outlets of popular culture have been forging 8 the same connection: In Hollywood films, of which *Fatal Attraction* is only the most famous, emancipated women with condominiums of their own slink wild-eyed between bare walls, paying for their liberty with an empty bed, a barren womb. "My biological clock is ticking so loud it keeps me awake at night," Sally Field cries in the film *Surrender*, as, in an all-too-common transformation in the cinema of the eighties, an actress who once played scrappy working heroines is now showcased groveling for a groom. In prime-time television shows, from *thirtysomething* to *Family Man*, single, professional, and feminist women are humiliated, turned into harpies, or hit by nervous breakdowns; the wise ones recant their independent ways by the closing sequence. In popular novels, from Gail Parent's *A Sign of the Eighties* to Stephen King's *Misery*, unwed women shrink to sniveling spinsters or inflate to fire-breathing she-devils; renouncing all aspirations but marriage, they beg for wedding bands from strangers or swing axes at reluctant bachelors. Even Erica Jong's high-flying independent heroine literally crashes by the end of the decade, as the author supplants *Fear of Flying*'s saucy Isadora Wing, an exuberant symbol of female sexual emancipation in the seventies, with an embittered careerist-turned-recovering-"codependent" in *Any Woman's Blues* — a book that is intended, as the narrator bluntly states, "to demonstrate what a dead end the so-called sexual revolution had become and how desperate so-called free women were in the last few years of our decadent epoch."

Popular psychology manuals peddle the same diagnosis for contem- 9 porary female distress. "Feminism, having promised her a stronger sense of her own identity, has given her little more than an identity *crisis*," the best-selling advice manual *Being a Woman* asserts. The authors of the era's self-help classic, *Smart Women/Foolish Choices*, proclaim that women's distress was "an unfortunate consequence of feminism" because "it created a myth among women that the apex of self-realization could be achieved only through autonomy, independence, and career."

In the Reagan and Bush years, government officials have needed no 10 prompting to endorse this thesis. Reagan spokeswoman Faith Ryan Whittlesey declared feminism a "straitjacket" for women, in one of the White House's only policy speeches on the status of the American female population — entitled "Radical Feminism in Retreat." The U.S. attorney general's Commission on Pornography even proposed that women's professional advancement might be responsible for rising rape rates: With more women in college and at work now, the commission members reasoned in their report, women just have more opportunities to be raped.

Legal scholars have railed against the "equality trap." Sociologists 11 have claimed that "feminist-inspired" legislative reforms have stripped women of special "protections." Economists have argued that well-paid working women have created a "less stable American family." And demographers, with greatest fanfare, have legitimated the prevailing wisdom with so-called neutral data on sex ratios and fertility trends; they say they actually have the numbers to prove that equality doesn't mix with marriage and motherhood.

Finally, some "liberated" women themselves have joined the lamentations. In *The Cost of Loving: Women and the New Fear of Intimacy*, Megan Marshall, a Harvard-pedigreed writer, asserts that the feminist "Myth of Independence" has turned her generation into unloved and unhappy fast-trackers, "dehumanized" by careers and "uncertain of their gender identity." Other diaries of mad Superwomen charge that "the hard-core feminist viewpoint," as one of them puts it, has relegated educated executive achievers to solitary nights of frozen dinners and closet drinking. The triumph of equality, they report, has merely given women hives, stomach cramps, eye "twitching" disorders, even comas.

But what "equality" are all these authorities talking about?

If American women are so equal, why do they represent two-thirds of all poor adults? Why are more than 70 percent of full-time working women making less than twenty-five thousand dollars a year, nearly double the number of men at that level? Why are they still far more likely than men to live in poor housing, and twice as likely to draw no pension? If women "have it all," then why don't they have the most basic requirements to achieve equality in the work force: unlike that of virtually all other industrialized nations, the U.S. government still has no family-leave and child-care programs.

If women are so "free," why are their reproductive freedoms in greater jeopardy today than a decade earlier? Why, in their own homes, do they still shoulder 70 percent of the household duties—while the only major change in the last fifteen years is that now men *think* they do more around the house? In thirty states, it is still generally legal for husbands to rape their wives; and only ten states have laws mandating arrest for domestic violence—even though battering is the leading cause of injury to women (greater than rapes, muggings, and auto accidents combined).

The word may be that women have been "liberated," but women themselves seem to feel otherwise. Repeatedly in national surveys, majorities of women say they are still far from equality. In poll after poll in the decade, overwhelming majorities of women said they need equal pay and equal job opportunities, they need an Equal Rights Amendment, they need the right to an abortion without government interference, they need a federal law guaranteeing maternity leave, they need decent child-care services. They have none of these. So how exactly have women "won" the war for women's rights?

Seen against this background, the much ballyhooed claim that feminism is responsible for making women miserable becomes absurd—and irrelevant. The afflictions ascribed to feminism, from "the man shortage" to "the infertility epidemic" to "female burnout" to "toxic day care," have had their origins not in the actual conditions of women's lives but rather in a closed system that starts and ends in the media, popular culture, and advertising—an endless feedback loop that perpetuates and exaggerates its own false images of womanhood. And women don't see feminism as their enemy, either. In fact, in national surveys, 75 to 95 percent of women credit the feminist campaign with *improving* their lives, and a similar proportion say that the women's movement should keep pushing for change.

18   If the many ponderers of the Woman Question really wanted to know what is troubling the American female population, they might have asked their subjects. In public-opinion surveys, women consistently rank their own *inequality*, at work and at home, among their most urgent concerns. Over and over, women complain to pollsters of a lack of economic, not marital, opportunities; they protest that working men, not working women, fail to spend time in the nursery and the kitchen. It is justice for their gender, not wedding rings and bassinets, that women believe to be in desperately short supply.

19   As the last decade ran its course, the monitors that serve to track slippage in women's status have been working overtime. Government and private surveys are showing that women's already vast representation in the lowliest occupations is rising, their tiny presence in higher-paying trade and craft jobs stalled or backsliding, their minuscule representation in upper management posts stagnant or falling, and their pay dropping in the very occupations where they have made the most "progress."

20   In national politics, the already small numbers of women in both elective posts and political appointments fell during the eighties. In private life, the average amount that a divorced man paid in child support fell by about 25 percent from the late seventies to the mid-eighties (to a mere $140 a month). And government records chronicled a spectacular rise in sexual violence against women. Reported rapes more than doubled from the early seventies—at nearly twice the rate of all other violent crimes and four times the overall crime rate in the United States.

21   The truth is that the last decade has seen a powerful counterassault on women's rights, a backlash, an attempt to retract the handful of small and hard-won victories that the feminist movement did manage to win for women. This counterassault is largely insidious: in a kind of pop-culture version of the big lie, it stands the truth boldly on its head and proclaims that the very steps that have elevated women's position have actually led to their downfall.

22   The backlash is at once sophisticated and banal, deceptively "progressive" and proudly backward. It deploys both the "new" findings of "scientific research" and the dime-store moralism of yesteryear; it turns into media sound bites both the glib pronouncements of pop-psych trend-watchers and the frenzied rhetoric of New Right preachers. The backlash has succeeded in framing virtually the whole issue of women's rights in its own language. Just as Reaganism shifted political discourse far to the right and demonized

liberalism, so the backlash convinced the public that women's "liberation" was the true contemporary American scourge—the source of an endless laundry list of personal, social, and economic problems.

But what has made women unhappy in the last decade is not their "equality"—which they don't yet have—but the rising pressure to halt, and even reverse, women's quest for that equality. The "man shortage" and the "infertility epidemic" are not the price of liberation; in fact, they do not even exist. But these chimeras are part of a relentless whittling-down process—much of it amounting to outright propaganda—that has served to stir women's private anxieties and break their political wills. Identifying feminism as women's enemy only furthers the ends of a backlash against women's equality by simultaneously deflecting attention from the backlash's central role and recruiting women to attack their own cause.   23

Questions to Start You Thinking

1. How does Faludi define the "backlash" against feminism? Whom does she see as responsible for it?

2. How does Faludi challenge those cause and effect arguments that she considers mistaken?

3. Define *opportunity policies* (paragraph 1), *stress-induced disorders* (paragraph 4), *prevailing wisdom* (paragraph 6), *codependent* (paragraph 8), *ballyhooed* (paragraph 17), and *chimeras* (paragraph 23).

4. Does the comedy of Roseanne Arnold, as Barbara Ehrenreich presents it in "The Wretched of the Hearth" (p. 543), help counter the backlash against feminism? If so, how?

Suggestions for Writing

1. In a short personal essay, discuss what "feminism" means to you. Would you call yourself a "feminist"? Why or why not?

2. "In prime-time television shows . . . single, professional, and feminist women are humiliated, turned into harpies, or hit by nervous breakdowns," writes Faludi (paragraph 8). Do you agree or disagree? Write a short essay evaluating images of women in television. How do these images seem accurate? How do they seem inaccurate?

CHAPTER 23

American Diversity

RICHARD RODRIGUEZ, born in 1944 in San Francisco, could speak only fifty words of English when his parents enrolled him in a Catholic grammar school in Sacramento, California. But he proceeded to earn a B.A. at Stanford University and an M.A. in philosophy at Columbia University as well as a Ph.D. in English Renaissance literature. His best-known work, *Hunger of Memory: The Education of Richard Rodriguez* (1982), supports from his own experience his opposition to bilingual education. Although all academic doors were open to him, Rodriguez left academia because, as he told an interviewer, he felt he had "benefited on the backs ... of truly disadvantaged Mexican-Americans." He now works as a freelance writer and lecturer, often debating the merits of bilingual education. The following essay appeared in *Harper's* magazine in March 1984.

DOES AMERICA STILL EXIST?
Richard Rodriguez

For the children of immigrant parents the knowledge comes easier. 1 America exists everywhere in the city—on billboards, frankly in the smell of French fries and popcorn. It exists in the pace: traffic lights, the assertions of neon, the mysterious bong-bong-bong through the atriums of department stores. America exists as the voice of the crowd, a menacing sound—the high nasal accent of American English.

When I was a boy in Sacramento (California, the fifties), people would 2
ask me, "Where you from?" I was born in this country, but I knew the
question meant to decipher my darkness, my looks.

My mother once instructed me to say, "I am an American of Mexican 3
descent." By the time I was nine or ten, I wanted to say, but dared not
reply, "I am an American."

Immigrants come to America and, against hostility or mere loneliness, 4
they recreate a homeland in the parlor, tacking up postcards or calendars
of some impossible blue — lake or sea or sky. Children of immigrant parents
are supposed to perch on a hyphen between two countries. Relatives assume the achievement as much as anyone. Relatives are, in any case,
surprised when the child begins losing old ways. One day at the family
picnic the boy wanders away from their spiced food and faceless stories to
watch other boys play baseball in the distance.

There is sorrow in the American memory, guilty sorrow for having left 5
something behind — Portugal, China, Norway. The American story is the
story of immigrant children and of their children — children no longer able
to speak to grandparents. The memory of exile becomes inarticulate as it
passes from generation to generation, along with wedding rings and pocket
watches — like some mute stone in a wad of old lace. Europe. Asia. Eden.

But, it needs to be said, if this is a country where one stops being 6
Vietnamese or Italian, this is a country where one begins to be an American.
America exists as a culture and a grin, a faith and a shrug. It is clasped in
a handshake, called by a first name.

As much as the country is joined in a common culture, however, Amer- 7
icans are reluctant to celebrate the process of assimilation. We pledge
allegiance to diversity. America was born Protestant and bred Puritan, and
the notion of community we share is derived from a seventeenth-century
faith. Presidents and the pages of ninth-grade civics readers yet proclaim
the orthodoxy: We are gathered together — but as individuals, with separate
pasts, distinct destinies. Our society is as paradoxical as a Puritan congregation: We stand together, alone.

Americans have traditionally defined themselves by what they refused 8
to include. As often, however, Americans have struggled, turned in good
conscience at last to assert the great Protestant virtue of tolerance. Despite
outbreaks of nativist frenzy, America has remained an immigrant country,
open and true to itself.

Against pious emblems of rural America — soda fountain, Elks hall, Prot- 9
estant church, and now shopping mall — stands the cold-hearted city,
crowded with races and ambitions, curious laughter, much that is odd.
Nevertheless, it is the city that has most truly represented America. In the
city, however, the millions of singular lives have had no richer notion of
wholeness to describe them than the idea of pluralism.

"Where you from?" the American asks the immigrant child. "Mexico," 10
the boy learns to say.

Mexico, the country of my blood ancestors, offers formal contrast to 11 the American achievement. If the United States was formed by Protestant individualism, Mexico was shaped by a medieval Catholic dream of one world. The Spanish journeyed to Mexico to plunder, and they may have gone, in God's name, with an arrogance peculiar to those who intend to convert. But through the conversion, the Indian converted the Spaniard. A new race was born, the *mestizo*, wedding European to Indian. José Vasconcelos, the Mexican philosopher, has celebrated this New World creation, proclaiming it the "cosmic race."

Centuries later, in a San Francisco restaurant, a Mexican-American law-   12
yer of my acquaintance says, in English, over *salade niçoise*, that he does not intend to assimilate into gringo society. His claim is echoed by a chorus of others (Italian-Americans, Greeks, Asians) in this era of ethnic pride. The melting pot has been retired, clanking, into the museum of quaint disgrace, alongside Aunt Jemima and the Katzenjammer Kids. But resistance to assimilation is characteristically American. It only makes clear how inevitable the process of assimilation actually is.

For generations, this has been the pattern. Immigrant parents have   13
sent their children to school (simply, they thought) to acquire the "skills" to survive in the city. The child returned home with a voice his parents barely recognized or understood, couldn't trust, and didn't like.

In eastern cities—Philadelphia, New York, Boston, Baltimore—class   14
after class gathered immigrant children to women (usually women) who stood in front of rooms full of children, changing children. So also for me in the 1950s. Irish-Catholic nuns. California. The old story. The hyphen tipped to the right, away from Mexico and toward a confusing but true American identity.

I speak now in the chromium American accent of my grammar school   15
classmates—Billy Reckers, Mike Bradley, Carol Schmidt, Kathy O'Grady.
. . . I believe I became like my classmates, became German, Polish, and (like my teachers) Irish. And because assimilation is always reciprocal, my classmates got something of me. (I mean sad eyes; belief in the Indian Virgin; a taste for sugar skulls on the Feast of the Dead.) In the blending, we became what our parents could never have been, and we carried America one revolution further.

"Does America still exist?" Americans have been asking the question   16
for so long that to ask it again only proves our continuous link. But perhaps the question deserves to be asked with urgency now. Since the black civil rights movement of the 1960s, our tenuous notion of a shared public life has deteriorated notably.

The struggle of black men and women did not eradicate racism, but it   17
became the great moment in the life of America's conscience. Water hoses, bulldogs, blood—the images, rendered black, white, rectangular, passed into living rooms.

It is hard to look at a photograph of a crowd taken, say, in 1890 or in   18
1930 and not notice the absence of blacks. (It becomes an impertinence to wonder if America *still* exists.)

In the sixties, other groups of Americans learned to champion their rights by analogy to the black civil rights movement. But the heroic vision faded. Dr. Martin Luther King, Jr., had spoken with Pauline eloquence° of a nation that would unite Christian and Jew, old and young, rich and poor. Within a decade, the struggles of the 1960s were reduced to a bureaucratic competition for little more than pieces of a representational pie. The quest for a portion of power became an end in itself. The metaphor for the American city of the 1970s was a committee: one black, one woman, one person under thirty . . . 19

If the small town had sinned against America by too neatly defining who could be an American, the city's sin was a romantic secession. One noticed the romanticism in the antiwar movement — certain demonstrators who demonstrated a lack of tact or desire to persuade and seemed content to play secular protestants. One noticed the romanticism in the competition among members of "minority groups" to claim the status of Primary Victim. To Americans unconfident of their common identity, minority standing became a way of asserting individuality. Middle-class Americans — men and women clearly not the primary victims of social oppression — brandished their suffering with exuberance. 20

The dream of a single society probably died with *The Ed Sullivan Show*. The reality of America persists. Teenagers pass through big-city high schools banded in racial groups, their collars turned up to a uniform shrug. But then they graduate to jobs at the phone company or in banks, where they end up working alongside people unlike themselves. Typists and tellers walk out together at lunchtime. 21

It is easier for us as Americans to believe the obvious fact of our separateness — easier to imagine the black and white Americas prophesied by the Kerner report° (broken glass, street fires) — than to recognize the reality of a city street at lunchtime. Americans are wedded by proximity to a common culture. The panhandler at one corner is related to the pamphleteer at the next who is related to the banker who is kin to the Chinese old man wearing an MIT sweatshirt. In any true national history, Thomas Jefferson begets Martin Luther King, Jr., who begets the Gray Panthers. It is because we lack a vision of ourselves entire — the city street is crowded and we are each preoccupied with finding our own way home — that we lack an appropriate hymn. 22

Under my window now passes a little white girl softly rehearsing to herself a Motown obbligato. 23

Questions to Start You Thinking

1. Is Rodriguez's answer to the title question yes or no? Briefly explain why. What does he mean by *America*?

Pauline eloquence. Refers to Saint Paul's oratorical powers.

Kerner report. A 1968 report on racial unrest in America by the President's National Advisory Commission on Civil Disorders.

2. How does Rodriguez use specific examples to support his analysis of American culture? Why does he use so many different examples of national origins, heritages, and names?

3. Define *nativist* (paragraph 8), *pluralism* (paragraph 9), *assimilation* (paragraph 12), and *secession* (paragraph 20).

4. How would Rodriguez evaluate the experience of Ti-Hua Chang in "Downtown Cousin" (p. 492)? Do Chang's feelings of alienation from Chinese immigrants support Rodriguez's view that assimilation is inevitable?

Suggestions for Writing

1. Write a brief personal essay explaining how your family's heritage has shaped your experiences of America. Are you proud of your ancestry? Does American society encourage pride in one's heritage?

2. Using Rodriguez's ideas as a springboard, write a response to the question "Does America still exist?" How do you define *America*? What, in your opinion, are the most important factors in American culture today? How important are people's national or cultural origins to their participation in American culture?

TI-HUA CHANG was born in New York City in 1950. After attending the University of Pennsylvania, he earned an M.A. at Columbia University's School of Journalism. He began his broadcasting career in Biloxi, Mississippi, reported for WKYW in Philadelphia and KBTV in Denver, and won three Emmy Awards for his reporting at WJBK in Detroit. After a brief stint as an investigative reporter for ABC's *Prime Time Live,* he joined CBS in the fall of 1991. The following short narrative appeared in the *New York Times Magazine* March 17, 1991. In it Chang presents several different "types" of Chinese Americans and explores the complex feelings that can arise as an ethnic American confronts his background and struggles with stereotypes.

DOWNTOWN COUSIN
Ti-Hua Chang

I had just finished a spending spree for suits, a binge delayed for years, 1 when I hailed a taxi. I wanted to head uptown to buy a sing-along tape machine at a discount electronics store. The cabdriver, like me, was Chinese, and somewhere in our conversation about my good English and his tough life as an immigrant, he learned that I was heading for a midtown store. "Why you do that? You should go Chinatown! Much better than uptown, cousin. You know Chinatown cheaper. Much cheaper."

"You sure it will save me money?"   2

"Ah, ya! You save . . . one hundred dollar." In his enthusiasm he   3
seemed to levitate briefly.

A small smile breached my lips. I liked him, this friendly, hustling   4
cabby, his breed rare among the muttering, angry men who cursed gasoline
prices and scarce riders. I enjoyed his boisterous loudness; he appeared
untamed by a nation that prided itself on being composed of immigrants,
yet still regarded Asians as alien. He was not like me—a quiet Asian-
American who avoids loud talk in public places, fearing attention from that
one bigot who seemingly lurks in every crowd.

"Look, I got Chinese newspaper. We call before go. I no waste your   5
money."

"O.K. We can do that," I said, assuming he wanted to help a fellow   6
Asian. He pulled over to the curb a block from Radio City Music Hall and
theatrically paged through a blue-and-red bannered Chinese newsweekly.

"I can't find store ad. Ah, ya. Very good store," he said and told me its   7
name.

"You're sure they have sing-along machines? With a microphone, and   8
your voice is mixed with the background music?"

"Yeah, sure. I know they got!"   9

"Forget about calling, then. Just go. I trust you." I wanted to trust him,   10
to connect with this newfound buddy. But my fear of being conned lingered.

Flooring the accelerator, he cut the cab across Madison Avenue and   11
began a tortured route past the throngs at Union Square's outdoor clothing
stands, the alcoholics on the Bowery and then the Chinese in Chinatown.
I wondered why only here we looked like a serried mass of black-haired
sheep, and instantly flushed with shame. Even I have been affected by
movies about Fu Manchu, Charlie Chan, and attacking hordes of yellow
"gooks." How could I view myself this way—I, a television-news producer
who once led student demonstrations against racism?

"This best store. You see." The cabby glanced down, adding as an   12
aside, "13 dollar." This seemed excessive, but ethnic obligation and
pleasure at the prospect of saving more money produced a rare $3 tip from
me.

The door to the electronics store was wedged open with an egg carton.   13
The salesmen were eating lunch with chopsticks out of Chinese takeout
containers. No one spoke. The only sounds were the hum of a plastic fan
and the slurping of lo mein.

One salesman, standing by the toaster ovens, was not eating. He ended   14
his telephone conversation and smiled. He looked like the stereotype my
father demanded I not be: skinny, with glasses and squinting eyes.

I noted with pride that I measured several inches taller and weighed   15
30 pounds more than he. I stood up straight, chest out. My father posed
for every picture this way. Chest out, head up. "Chinese," he lectured my
brother and me for years, "too stooped."

In one sepia photograph, frayed at the edges, my father stood straight   16
with his head cocked back, chest out, a Thompson submachine gun cradled

in his arms. This was during World War II, in Burma, where my father, a Chinese journalist, reported on the campaign against Japan. I, too, cocked my head.

"Do you sell sing-along machines?"   17

"What?" the salesman asked.   18

"Sing-along machines."   19

"What that?"   20

"The Japanese sing-along, kareoke machine."   21

"Oh, you mean ka-RA-oke."   22

"That's what I said."   23

"No, you say wrong, it ka-RA-oke."   24

"Look, do you have them or not?"   25

"We got plenty. Over here." When he reached the one and only karaoke   26
machine, he paused and turned as if setting up for a classroom lecture. With a heavy Chinese accent, he began a long discourse on the machine. He gesticulated expansively. Laser disk not tape, video not sound alone. All of which I knew meant expensive not cheap. I imagined carnival music and a barker in a red-striped jacket and straw hat sermonizing with a bamboo cane: "And here my friends you have your quadrasound, superturbo, nuclear-injected, atomic-powered machine."

With repressed sarcasm, I asked, "Can I change the pitch?"   27

Through a tight smile, the salesman said: "You must let me finish. You   28
start from end, I start from beginning."

Anger rising, I wanted to leave the store. I did not. Our shared ethnicity   29
prevented me, knowing that he undoubtedly struggled as my parents had in a new country.

I noticed he rarely looked me in the eyes. Other salesmen were listen-   30
ing, and he seemed to be putting on a show for them. I wondered if he would try to cheat me because I was an American-born Chinese who dressed, acted and spoke like a *beiren*, a white man. I wondered if he hated me for my American upbringing, for my expensive new suits slung over my shoulder. Was he angry at his stained plaid tie and red shirt? Did he resent my luck at having been born here, at having had more chances to succeed? Could he understand the poverty and racial slurs of *my* childhood, growing up in Spanish Harlem, attending private school on scholarship with rich kids?

He droned on, disingenuous grin never fading. Finally I asked again,   31
"Can I change the pitch?"

"You don't need pitch. Here, look this, this laser, don't need change   32
nothing, hah!" He smiled more broadly, turning to another salesman.

"That's all I need to know," I said as I turned and walked out, incensed   33
that he had wasted my time. He could have immediately answered my question about the stupid machine. Fuming, I thought to myself that from his accent he was from Hong Kong, having arrived in the States probably five or six years ago, possibly within the last few years. Hong Kong Chinese

would cheat anyone, I thought. Chinese from that quintessential free market cheated everyone. It was a malicious, intentional stereotyping. Angry at the salesman, I found myself debasing the people of his region.

I decided not to ride the subway but to spend the extra money and take 34 a taxi home. I hoped the driver would not be Chinese, preferring an unintelligible immigrant from some obscure country, one of those angry, silent men from a place so foreign to me that I would not care. I threw my arm up, stopped a cab and, wordlessly, pointed uptown.

Questions to Start You Thinking

1. How does Chang present the Chinese American community in this selection? Is his view of Chinatown's culture positive or negative?

2. Look carefully at how Chang contrasts his family's and his own attitudes with those of the cabdriver and the salesman. How does he use recall to create this contrast? What other resources does he use?

3. How is Chang's speech different from that of the salesman and the cabdriver? How does this difference underscore his theme? Define *levitate* (paragraph 3), *boisterous* (paragraph 4), *serried* (paragraph 11), and *disingenuous* (paragraph 31).

4. To what stereotypes of Asian American men is Chang reacting? How do they differ from the stereotypes of African American men Brent Staples discusses in "Black Men and Public Space" (p. 507)?

Suggestions for Writing

1. "He looked like the stereotype my father demanded I not be," says Chang of the salesman (paragraph 14). Have your parents encouraged you to challenge stereotypes? To conform to them? Write a brief personal essay discussing how your parents have expected you to relate to cultural stereotypes.

2. In a short essay, analyze the presentation of Asian Americans or another ethnic group in American popular culture. You may want to use examples from film, television, fiction, or journalism; you may also recall your own experience.

TONI MORRISON, born Chloe Anthony Wofford in 1931 in Lorain, Ohio, received a B.A. from Howard University and an M.A. from Cornell University. Since 1964 she has lived in New York City, working as an editor on the autobiographies of Angela Davis and Muhammad Ali, among other projects. Morrison's novels include *Song of Solomon* (1977); *Tar Baby* (1981); *Beloved* (1986), for which she won the Pulitzer Prize; and *Jazz* (1992). The following article was published in the *New York Times Magazine* on the United States' bicentennial, July 4, 1976, apt timing because of Morrison's sense of this country's unique diversity and the struggles it has occasioned. The selection demonstrates Morrison's ability to interweave personal and social history into a vivid and compelling narrative.

A SLOW WALK OF TREES
Toni Morrison

His name was John Solomon Willis, and when at age 5 he heard from the old folks that "the Emancipation Proclamation was coming," he crawled under the bed. It was his earliest recollection of what was to be his habitual response to the promise of white people: horror and an instinctive yearning for safety. He was my grandfather, a musician who managed to hold on to his violin but not his land. He lost all 88 acres of his Indian mother's inheritance to legal predators who built their fortunes on the likes of him. He was an unreconstructed black pessimist who, in spite of or because of emancipation, was convinced for 85 years that there was no hope whatever for black people in this country. His rancor was legitimate, for he, John Solomon, was not only an artist but a first-rate carpenter and farmer, reduced to sending home to his family money he had made playing the violin because he was not able to find work. And this during the years when almost half the black male population were skilled craftsmen who lost their jobs to white ex-convicts and immigrant farmers. 1

His wife, however, was of a quite different frame of mind and believed that all things could be improved by faith in Jesus and an effort of the will. So it was she, Ardelia Willis, who sneaked her seven children out of the back window into the darkness, rather than permit the patron of their sharecropper's existence to become their executioner as well, and headed north in 1912, when 99.2 percent of all black people in the U.S. were native-born and only 60 percent of white Americans were. And it was Ardelia who told her husband that they could not stay in the Kentucky town they ended up in because the teacher didn't know long division. 2

They have been dead now for 30 years and more and I still don't know which of them came closer to the truth about the possibilities of life for black people in this country. One of their grandchildren is a tenured professor at Princeton. Another, who suffered from what the Peruvian poet called "anger that breaks a man into children," was picked up just as he entered his teens and emotionally lobotomized by the reformatories and mental institutions specifically designed to serve him. Neither John Solomon nor Ardelia lived long enough to despair over one or swell with pride over the other. But if they were alive today each would have selected and collected enough evidence to support the accuracy of the other's original point of view. And it would be difficult to convince either one that the other was right. 3

Some of the monstrous events that took place in John Solomon's America have been duplicated in alarming detail in my own America. There was 4 the public murder of a president in a theater in 1865 and the public murder of another president on television in 1963. The Civil War of 1861 had its encore as the civil rights movement of 1960. The torture and mutilation of a black West Point Cadet (Cadet Johnson Whittaker) in 1880 had its rerun with the 1970s murders of students at Jackson State College, Texas Southern, and Southern University in Baton Rouge. And in 1976 we watch for what must be the thousandth time a pitched battle between the children of slaves and the children of immigrants—only this time, it is not the New York draft riots of 1863, but the busing turmoil in Paul Revere's home town, Boston.

Hopeless, he'd said. Hopeless. For he was certain that white people of 5 every political, religious, geographical, and economic background would band together against black people everywhere when they felt the threat of our progress. And a hundred years after he sought safety from the white man's "promise," somebody put a bullet in Martin Luther King's brain. And not long before that some excellent samples of the master race demonstrated their courage and virility by dynamiting some little black girls to death. If he were here now, my grandfather, he would shake his head, close his eyes and pull out his violin—too polite to say, "I told you so." And his wife would pay attention to the music but not to the sadness in her husband's eyes, for she would see what she expected to see—not the occasional historical repetition, but, *like the slow walk of certain species of trees from the flatlands up into the mountains*, she would see the signs of irrevocable and permanent change. She, who pulled her girls out of an inadequate school in the Cumberland Mountains, knew all along that the gentlemen from Alabama who had killed the little girls would be rounded up. And it wouldn't surprise her in the least to know that the number of black college graduates jumped 12 percent in the last three years: 47 percent in 20 years. That there are 140 black mayors in this country; 14 black judges in the District Circuit, 4 in the Courts of Appeals and one on the Supreme Court. That there are 17 blacks in Congress, one in the Senate; 276 in state legislatures—223 in state houses, 53 in state senates. That there are 112 elected black police chiefs and sheriffs, 1 Pulitzer Prize winner; 1 winner of the Prix de Rome; a dozen or so winners of the Guggenheim; 4 deans of predominantly white colleges. . . . Oh, her list would go on and on. But so would John Solomon's sweet sad music.

While my grandparents held opposite views on whether the fortunes of 6 black people were improving, my own parents struck similarly opposed postures, but from another slant. They differed about whether the moral fiber of white people would ever improve. Quite a different argument. The old folks argued about how and if black people could improve themselves, who could be counted on to help us, who would hinder us and so on. My parents took issue over the question of whether it was possible for white people to improve. They assumed that black people were the humans of the globe, but had serious doubts about the quality and existence of white humanity. Thus my father, distrusting every word and every gesture of every white man on earth, assumed that the white man who crept up the stairs one afternoon had come to molest his daughters and threw him down the stairs and then our tricycle after him. (I think my father was wrong, but considering what I have seen since, it may have been very healthy for me to have witnessed that as my first black-white encounter.) My mother, however, *believed* in them—their possibilities. So when the meal we got on relief was bug-ridden, she wrote a long letter to Franklin Delano Roosevelt. And when white bill collectors came to our door, it was she who received them civilly and explained in a sweet voice that we were people of honor and that the debt would be taken care of. Her message to Roosevelt got through—our meal improved. Her message to the bill collectors did not always get through and there was occasional violence when my father (self-exiled to the bed-room for fear he could not hold his temper) would hear that her reasona-bleness had failed. My mother was always wounded by these scenes, for she thought the bill collector knew that she loved good credit more than life and that being in arrears on a payment horrified her probably more than it did him. So she thought he was rude because he was white. For years she walked to utility companies and department stores to pay bills in person and even now she does not seem convinced that checks are legal tender. My father loved excellence, worked hard (he held three jobs at once for 17 years) and was so outraged by the suggestion of personal slackness that he could explain it to himself only in terms of racism. He was a fastidious worker who was frightened of one thing: unemployment. I can remember now the dooms day-cum-graveyard sound of "laid off" and how the minute school was out he asked us, "Where you workin'?" Both my parents believed that all succor and aid came from themselves and their neighborhood, since "they"—white people in charge and those not in charge but in obstructionist positions—were in some way fundamentally, genetically corrupt.

So I grew up in a basically racist household with more than a child's   7
share of contempt for white people. And for each white friend I acquired who made a small crack in that contempt, there was another who repaired it. For each one who related to me as a person, there was one who in my presence at least, became actively "white." And like most black people of my generation, I suffer from racial vertigo that can be cured only by taking what one needs from one's ancestors. John Solomon's cynicism and his deployment of his art as both weapon and solace, Ardelia's faith in the magic that can be wrought by sheer effort of the will; my mother's open-mindedness in each new encounter and her habit of trying reasonableness first; my father's temper, his impatience and his efforts to keep "them" (throw them) out of his life. And it is out of these learned and selected attitudes that I look at the quality of life for my people in this country now. These widely disparate and sometimes conflicting views, I suspect, were held not only by me, but by most black people. Some I know are clearer in their positions, have not sullied their anger with optimism or dirtied their hope with despair. But most of us are plagued by a sense of being worn shell-thin by constant repression and hostility as well as the impression of

being buoyed by visible testimony of tremendous strides. There *is* repetition of the grotesque in our history. And there *is* the miraculous walk of trees. The question is whether our walk is progress or merely movement. O. J. Simpson leaning on a Hertz car *is* better than the Gold Dust Twins on the back of a soap box. But is "Good Times" better than Stepin Fetchit? Has the first order of business been taken care of? Does the law of the land work for us?

Questions to Start You Thinking

1. Are Morrison's feelings about race relations more in line with her father and grandfather's pessimism or with her mother and grandmother's optimism? Explain why.

2. Discuss Morrison's use of comparison and contrast. How does she compare her grandparents with her parents? Her grandparents with each other? Her parents with each other? How does her own experience contrast with theirs?

3. How does Morrison use words ironically? (For a definition of *irony* see p. 238.) Consider *patron* (paragraph 2), *excellent samples of the master race* (paragraph 5), and *fundamentally, genetically corrupt* (paragraph 6).

4. Does Morrison suggest that black women's experiences of and reactions to racism are different from black men's experiences and reactions? How does her experience compare with Paula Gunn Allen's in "Where I Come from Is like This" (p. 500)?

Suggestions for Writing

1. Morrison says here that she "grew up in a basically racist household" (paragraph 7). In a brief essay, take a stand on whether African Americans and other non-European Americans can indeed be "racist" as we usually define the term. Support your stand with examples from Morrison's essay and your own experience.

2. Write a short personal essay discussing a racial or ethnic stereotype you encountered in your childhood, and discuss how your family's views challenged or reinforced this stereotype.

PAULA GUNN ALLEN, born in 1939, is a Laguna Pueblo Sioux who has dedicated her life to studying and writing about her heritage. She is a professor of English and American Indian literature at the University of California, Los Angeles, and has written several celebrated volumes of poetry; a novel, *The Woman Who Owned the Shadows* (1983); and *The Sacred Hoop: Recovering the Feminine in American Indian Traditions* (1986), the source from which the following selection has been excerpted. In her writing, Allen informs readers about basic differences between American Indian and European-based religions and culture, especially as they relate to women. She also uses her own experience to address the unique difficulties faced by American Indians, whose environment and values have been submerged by American culture.

WHERE I COME FROM IS LIKE THIS
Paula Gunn Allen

I

Modern American Indian women, like their non-Indian sisters, are deeply 1
engaged in the struggle to redefine themselves. In their struggle they must reconcile traditional tribal definitions of women with industrial and post-industrial non-Indian definitions. Yet while these definitions seem to be more or less mutually exclusive, Indian women must somehow harmonize and integrate both in their own lives.

An American Indian woman is primarily defined by her tribal identity. In 2
her eyes, her destiny is necessarily that of her people, and her sense of herself as a woman is first and foremost prescribed by her tribe. The defi-nitions of woman's roles are as diverse as tribal cultures in the Americas. In some she is devalued, in others she wields considerable power. In some she is a familial/clan adjunct, in some she is as close to autonomous as her economic circumstances and psychological traits permit. But in no tribal definitions is she perceived in the same way as are women in western industrial and postindustrial cultures.

In the west, few images of women form part of the cultural mythos, 3
and these are largely sexually charged. Among Christians, the madonna is the female prototype, and she is portrayed as essentially passive: her con-tribution is simply that of birthing. Little else is attributed to her and she certainly possesses few of the characteristics that are attributed to mythic figures among Indian tribes. This image is countered (rather than balanced) by the witch-goddess/whore characteristics designed to reinforce cultural beliefs about women, as well as western adversarial and dualistic percep-tions of reality.

The tribes see women variously, but they do not question the power of 4
femininity. Sometimes they see women as fearful, sometimes peaceful, sometimes omnipotent and omniscient, but they never portray women as mindless, helpless, simple, or oppressed. And while the women in a given tribe, clan, or band may be all these things, the individual woman is pro-vided with a variety of images of women from the interconnected super-natural, natural, and social worlds she lives in.

As a half-breed American Indian woman, I cast about in my mind for 5
negative images of Indian women, and I find none that are directed to Indian women alone. The negative images I do have are of Indians in general and in fact are more often of males than of females. All these images come to

me from non-Indian sources, and they are always balanced by a positive image. My ideas of womanhood, passed on largely by my mother and grand-mothers, Laguna Pueblo women, are about practicality, strength, reason-ableness, intelligence, wit, and competence. I also remember vividly the women who came to my father's store, the women who held me and sang to me, the women at Feast Day, at Grab Days,° the women in the kitchen of my Cubero home, the women I grew up with; none of them appeared weak or helpless, none of them presented herself tentatively. I remember a certain reserve on those lovely brown faces; I remember the direct gaze of eyes framed by bright-colored shawls draped over their heads and cas-cading down their backs. I remember the clean cotton dresses and carefully pressed hand-embroidered aprons they always wore; I remember laughter and good food, especially the sweet bread and the oven bread they gave us. Nowhere in my mind is there a foolish woman, a dumb woman, a vain woman, or a plastic woman, though the Indian women I have known have shown a wide range of personal style and demeanor.

My memory includes the Navajo woman who was badly beaten by her 6 Sioux husband; but I also remember that my grandmother abandoned her Sioux husband long ago. I recall the stories about the Laguna woman beaten regularly by her husband in the presence of her children so that the children would not believe in the strength and power of femininity. And I remember the women who drank, who got into fights with other women and with the men, and who often won those battles. I have memories of tired women, partying women, stubborn women, sullen women, amicable women, selfish women, shy women, and aggressive women. Most of all I remember the women who laugh and scold and sit uncomplaining in the long sun on feast days and who cook wonderful food on wood stoves, in beehive mud ovens, and over open fires outdoors.

Among the images of women that come to me from various tribes as 7 well as my own are White Buffalo Woman, who came to the Lakota long ago and brought them the religion of the Sacred Pipe which they still prac-tice; Tinotzin the goddess who came to Juan Diego to remind him that she still walked the hills of her people and sent him with her message, her demand and her proof to the Catholic bishop in the city nearby. And from Laguna I take the images of Yellow Woman, Coyote Woman, Grandmother Spider (Spider Old Woman), who brought the light, who gave us weaving and medicine, who gave us life. Among the Keres she is known as Thought Woman who created us all and who keeps us in creation even now. I re-member Iyatiku, Earth Woman, Corn Woman, who guides and counsels the people to peace and who welcomes us home when we cast off this coil of flesh as huskers cast off the leaves that wrap the corn. I remember Iyatiku's sister, Sun Woman, who held metals and cattle, pigs and sheep, highways and engines and so many things in her bundle, who went away to the east saying that one day she would return.

Grab Days. Laguna ritual in which women throw food and small items to those who attend.

II

Since the coming of the Anglo-Europeans beginning in the fifteenth century,   8
the fragile web of identity that long held tribal people secure has gradually
been weakened and torn. But the oral tradition has prevented the complete
destruction of the web, the ultimate disruption of tribal ways. The oral
tradition is vital; it heals itself and the tribal web by adapting to the flow
of the present while never relinquishing its connection to the past. Its
adaptability has always been required, as many generations have experienced. Certainly the modern American Indian woman bears slight resemblance to her forebears — at least on superficial examination — but she is
still a tribal woman in her deepest being. Her tribal sense of relationship
to all that is continues to flourish. And though she is at times beset by her
knowledge of the enormous gap between the life she lives and the life she
was raised to live, and while she adapts her mind and being to the circumstances of her present life, she does so in tribal ways, mending the tears
in the web of being from which she takes her existence as she goes.

My mother told me stories all the time, though I often did not recognize   9
them as that. My mother told me stories about cooking and childbearing;
she told me stories about menstruation and pregnancy; she told me stories
about gods and heroes, about fairies and elves, about goddesses and spirits; she told me stories about the land and the sky, about cats and dogs,
about snakes and spiders; she told me stories about climbing trees and
exploring the mesas; she told me stories about going to dances and getting
married; she told me stories about dressing and undressing, about sleeping
and waking; she told me stories about herself, about her mother, about
her grandmother. She told me stories about grieving and laughing, about
thinking and doing; she told me stories about school and about people;
about darning and mending; she told me stories about turquoise and about
gold; she told me European stories and Laguna stories; she told me Catholic stories and Presbyterian stories; she told me city stories and country
stories; she told me political stories and religious stories. She told me
stories about living and stories about dying. And in all of those stories she
told me who I was, who I was supposed to be, whom I came from, and who
would follow me. In this way she taught me the meaning of the words she
said, that all life is a circle and everything has a place within it. That's what
she said and what she showed me in the things she did and the way she
lives.

Of course, through my formal, white, Christian education, I discovered   10
that other people had stories of their own — about women, about Indians,
about fact, about reality — and I was amazed by a number of startling sup-
positions that others made about tribal customs and beliefs. According to
the un-Indian, non-Indian view, for instance, Indians barred menstruating
women from ceremonies and indeed segregated them from the rest of the
people, consigning them to some space specially designed for them. This
showed that Indians considered menstruating women unclean and not fit
to enjoy the company of decent (nonmenstruating) people, that is, men. I

was surprised and confused to hear this because my mother had taught me that white people had strange attitudes toward menstruation: they thought something was bad about it, that it meant you were sick, cursed, sinful, and weak and that you had to be very careful during that time. She taught me that menstruation was a normal occurrence, that I could go swimming or hiking or whatever else I wanted to do during my period. She actively scorned women who took to their beds, who were incapacitated by cramps, who "got the blues."

As I struggled to reconcile these very contradictory interpretations of   11
American Indians' traditional beliefs concerning menstruation, I realized that the menstrual taboos were about power, not about sin or filth. My conclusion was later borne out by some tribes' own explanations, which, as you may well imagine, came as quite a relief to me.

The truth of the matter as many Indians see it is that women who are   12
at the peak of their fecundity are believed to possess power that throws male power totally out of kilter. They emit such force that, in their presence, any male-owned or -dominated ritual or sacred object cannot do its usual task. For instance, the Lakota say that a menstruating woman anywhere near a yuwipi man, who is a special sort of psychic, spirit-empowered healer, for a day or so before he is to do his ceremony will effectively disempower him. Conversely, among many if not most tribes, important ceremonies cannot be held without the presence of women. Sometimes the ritual woman who empowers the ceremony must be unmarried and virginal so that the power she channels is unalloyed, unweakened by sexual arousal and penetration by a male. Other ceremonies require tumescent women, others the presence of mature women who have borne children, and still others depend for empowerment on post-menopausal women. Women may be segregated from the company of the whole band or village on certain occasions, but on certain occasions men are also segregated. In short, each ritual depends on a certain balance of power, and the positions of women within the phases of womanhood are used by tribal people to empower certain rites. This does not derive from a male-dominant view; it is not a ritual observance imposed on women by men. It derives from a tribal view of reality that distinguishes tribal people from feudal and industrial people.

Among the tribes, the occult power of women, inextricably bound to our   13
hormonal life, is thought to be very great; many hold that we possess innately the blood-given power to kill—with a glance, with a step, or with a judicious mixing of menstrual blood into somebody's soup. Medicine women among the Pomo of California cannot practice until they are sufficiently mature; when they are immature, their power is diffuse and is likely to interfere with their practice until time and experience have it under control. So women of the tribes are not especially inclined to see themselves as poor helpless victims of male domination. Even in those tribes where something akin to male domination was present, women are perceived as powerful, socially, physically, and metaphysically. In times past, as in times

present, women carried enormous burdens with aplomb. We were far indeed from the "weaker sex," the designation that white aristocratic sisters unhappily earned for us all.

I remember my mother moving furniture all over the house when she 14 wanted it changed. She didn't wait for my father to come home and help— she just went ahead and moved the piano, a huge upright from the old days, the couch, the refrigerator. Nobody had told her she was too weak to do such things. In imitation of her, I would delight in loading trucks at my father's store with cases of pop or fifty-pound sacks of flour. Even when I was quite small I could do it, and it gave me a belief in my own physical strength that advancing middle age can't quite erase. My mother used to tell me about the Acoma Pueblo women she had seen as a child carrying huge ollas (water pots) on their heads as they wound their way up the tortuous stairwell carved into the face of the "Sky City" mesa, a feat I tried to imitate with books and tin buckets. ("Sky City" is the term used by the Chamber of Commerce for the mother village of Acoma, which is situated atop a high sandstone table mountain.) I was never very successful, but even the attempt reminded me that I was supposed to be strong and balanced to be a proper girl.

Of course, my mother's Laguna people are Keres Indian, reputed to be 15 the last extreme mother-right people on earth. So it is no wonder that I got notably nonwhite notions about the natural strength and prowess of women. Indeed, it is only when I am trying to get non-Indian approval, recognition, or acknowledgment that my "weak sister" emotional and intellectual ploys get the better of my tribal woman's good sense. At such times I forget that I just moved the piano or just wrote a competent paper or just completed a financial transaction satisfactorily or have supported myself and my children for most of my adult life.

Nor is my contradictory behavior atypical. Most Indian women I know 16 are in the same bicultural bind: we vacillate between being dependent and strong, self-reliant and powerless, strongly motivated and hopelessly insecure. We resolve the dilemma in various ways: some of us party all the time; some of us drink to excess; some of us travel and move around a lot; some of us land good jobs and then quit them; some of us engage in violent exchanges; some of us blow our brains out. We act in these destructive ways because we suffer from the societal conflicts caused by having to identify with two hopelessly opposed cultural definitions of women. Through this destructive dissonance we are unhappy prey to the self-disparagement common to, indeed demanded of, Indians living in the United States today. Our situation is caused by the exigencies of a history of invasion, conquest, and colonization whose searing marks are probably ineradicable. A popular bumper sticker on many Indian cars proclaims: "If You're Indian You're In," to which I always find myself adding under my breath, "Trouble."

III

No Indian can grow to any age without being informed that her people were 17 "savages" who interfered with the march of progress pursued by respectable, loving, civilized white people. We are the villains of the scenario when we are mentioned at all. We are absent from much of white history except when we are calmly, rationally, succinctly, and systematically dehumanized. On the few occasions we are noticed in any way other than as howling, bloodthirsty beings, we are acclaimed for our noble quaintness. In this definition, we are exotic curios. Our ancient arts and customs are used to draw tourist money to state coffers, into the pocketbooks and bank accounts of scholars, and into support of the American-in-Disneyland promoters' dream.

As a Roman Catholic child I was treated to bloody tales of how the 18 savage Indians martyred the hapless priests and missionaries who went among them in an attempt to lead them to the one true path. By the time I was through high school I had the idea that Indians were people who had benefited mightily from the advanced knowledge and superior morality of the Anglo-Europeans. At least I had, perforce, that idea to lay beside the other one that derived from my daily experience of Indian life, an idea less dehumanizing and more accurate because it came from my mother and the other Indian people who raised me. That idea was that Indians are a people who don't tell lies, who care for their children and their old people. You never see an Indian orphan, they said. You always know when you're old that someone will take care of you—one of your children will. Then they'd list the old folks who were being taken care of by this child or that. No child is ever considered illegitimate among the Indians, they said. If a girl gets pregnant, the baby is still part of the family, and the mother is too. That's what they said, and they showed me real people who lived according to those principles.

Of course the ravages of colonization have taken their toll; there are 19 orphans in Indian country now, and abandoned, brutalized old folks; there are even illegitimate children, though the very concept still strikes me as absurd. There are battered children and neglected children, and there are battered wives and women who have been raped by Indian men. Proximity to the "civilizing" effects of white Christians has not improved the moral quality of life in Indian country, though each group, Indian and white, explains the situation differently. Nor is there much yet in the oral tradition that can enable us to adapt to these inhuman changes. But a force is growing in that direction, and it is helping Indian women reclaim their lives. Their power, their sense of direction and of self will soon be visible. It is the force of the women who speak and work and write, and it is formidable.

Through all the centuries of war and death and cultural and psychic 20 destruction have endured the women who raise the children and tend the fires, who pass along the tales and the traditions, who weep and bury the dead, who are the dead, and who never forget. There are always the women, who make pots and weave baskets, who fashion clothes and cheer their children on at powwow, who make fry bread and piki bread, and corn soup and chili stew, who dance and sing and remember and hold within their hearts the dream of their ancient peoples—that one day the woman who thinks will speak to us again, and everywhere there will be peace. Meanwhile we tell the stories and write the books and trade tales of anger and woe and stories of fun and scandal and laugh over all manner of things that happen every day. We watch and we wait.

My great-grandmother told my mother: Never forget you are Indian. And   21
my mother told me the same thing. This, then, is how I have gone about remembering, so that my children will remember too.

Questions to Start You Thinking

1. How does Paula Gunn Allen feel that American Indian views of women differ from those of mainstream American society?

2. Discuss how Allen uses recall as a resource to construct her comparison and contrast of American Indian and European American cultures.

3. Define *postindustrial* (paragraph 1), *familial/clan adjunct, autonomous* (paragraph 2), *adversarial, dualistic* (paragraph 3), *fecundity, feudal* (paragraph 12), and *metaphysically* (paragraph 13). From what academic discipline do most of these words come?

4. How is Allen's integration of her American Indian childhood into her adult experience similar to the process of assimilation Richard Rodriguez describes in "Does America Still Exist?" (p. 488)? How is it different?

Suggestions for Writing

1. How are men's and women's roles traditionally defined in the specific culture or cultures that make up your ethnic heritage? Write a brief essay both describing these traditional views and explaining how they have or have not shaped your vision of yourself as a woman or man.

2. How did experiences and observations from your childhood help shape your ideas of what constitutes "masculine" and "feminine" behavior? In a short essay, analyze how your childhood experiences taught you to perceive gender. Use specific examples to support your position.

BRENT STAPLES, born in 1951 in Chester, Pennsylvania, earned a Ph.D. in psychology from the University of Chicago and worked for the *Chicago Sun-Times* and *Down Beat* magazine before joining the *New York Times* in 1985. A member of the *Times* editorial board, he has contributed to many publications and is the author of *Parallel Time: A Memoir* (1991). In the following piece, published in a slightly different version in *Ms.* magazine in September 1986, Staples reflects on the anxiety his presence arouses in nighttime pedestrians.

BLACK MEN AND PUBLIC SPACE
Brent Staples

My first victim was a woman—white, well dressed, probably in her 1
late twenties. I came upon her late one evening on a deserted street in
Hyde Park, a relatively affluent neighborhood in an otherwise mean, impoverished section of Chicago. As I swung onto the avenue behind her,
there seemed to be a discreet, uninflammatory distance between us.
Not so. She cast back a worried glance. To her, the youngish black man—
a broad six feet two inches with a beard and billowing hair, both hands
shoved into the pockets of a bulky military jacket—seemed menacingly
close. After a few more quick glimpses, she picked up her pace and was
soon running in earnest. Within seconds, she disappeared into a cross
street.

That was more than a decade ago. I was twenty-two years old, a grad- 2
uate student newly arrived at the University of Chicago. It was in the echo
of that terrified woman's footfalls that I first began to know the unwieldy
inheritance I'd come into—the ability to alter public space in ugly ways. It
was clear that she thought herself the quarry of a mugger, a rapist, or
worse. Suffering a bout of insomnia, however, I was stalking sleep, not
defenseless wayfarers. As a softy who is scarcely able to take a knife to a
raw chicken—let alone hold one to a person's throat—I was surprised,
embarrassed, and dismayed all at once. Her flight made me feel like an
accomplice in tyranny. It also made it clear that I was indistinguishable
from the muggers who occasionally seeped into the area from the surrounding ghetto. That first encounter, and those that followed, signified that a
vast, unnerving gulf lay between nighttime pedestrians—particularly
women—and me. And I soon gathered that being perceived as dangerous
is a hazard in itself. I only needed to turn a corner into a dicey situation,
or crowd some frightened, armed person in a foyer somewhere, or make
an errant move after being pulled over by a policeman. Where fear and
weapons meet—and they often do in urban America—there is always the
possibility of death.

In that first year, my first away from my hometown, I was to become 3
thoroughly familiar with the language of fear. At dark, shadowy intersec-
tions, I could cross in front of a car stopped at a traffic light and elicit the
thunk, thunk, thunk, thunk of the driver—black, white, male, or female—
hammering down the door locks. On less traveled streets after dark, I grew
accustomed to but never comfortable with people crossing to the other side
of the street rather than pass me. Then there were the standard unpleas-
antries with policemen, doormen, bouncers, cabdrivers, and others whose
business it is to screen out troublesome individuals *before* there is any
nastiness.

I moved to New York nearly two years ago and I have remained an avid 4
night walker. In central Manhattan, the near-constant crowd cover mini-
mizes tense one-on-one street encounters. Elsewhere—in SoHo, for ex-

ample, where sidewalks are narrow and tightly spaced buildings shut out the sky—things can get very taut indeed.

After dark, on the warrenlike streets of Brooklyn where I live, I often 5 see women who fear the worst from me. They seem to have set their faces on neutral, and with their purse straps strung across their chests bandolier-style, they forge ahead as though bracing themselves against being tackled. I understand, of course, that the danger they perceive is not a hallucination. Women are particularly vulnerable to street violence, and young black males are drastically overrepresented among the perpetrators of that violence. Yet these truths are no solace against the kind of alienation that comes of being ever the suspect, a fearsome entity with whom pedestrians avoid making eye contact.

It is not altogether clear to me how I reached the ripe old age of twenty- 6 two without being conscious of the lethality nighttime pedestrians attributed to me. Perhaps it was because in Chester, Pennsylvania, the small, angry industrial town where I came of age in the 1960s, I was scarcely noticeable against a backdrop of gang warfare, street knifings, and murders. I grew up one of the good boys, had perhaps a half-dozen fistfights. In retrospect, my shyness of combat has clear sources.

As a boy, I saw countless tough guys locked away; I have since buried 7 several, too. They were babies, really—a teenage cousin, a brother of twenty-two, a childhood friend in his mid-twenties—all gone down in episodes of bravado played out in the streets. I came to doubt the virtues of intimidation early on. I chose, perhaps unconsciously, to remain a shadow—timid, but a survivor.

The fearsomeness mistakenly attributed to me in public places often 8 has a perilous flavor. The most frightening of these confusions occurred in the late 1970s and early 1980s, when I worked as a journalist in Chicago. One day, rushing into the office of a magazine I was writing for with a deadline story in hand, I was mistaken for a burglar. The office manager called security and, with an ad hoc posse, pursued me through the labyrinthine halls, nearly to my editor's door. I had no way of proving who I was. I could only move briskly toward the company of someone who knew me.

Another time I was on assignment for a local paper and killing time 9 before an interview. I entered a jewelry store on the city's affluent Near North Side. The proprietor excused herself and returned with an enormous red Doberman pinscher straining at the end of a leash. She stood, the dog extended toward me, silent to my questions, her eyes bulging nearly out of her head. I took a cursory look around, nodded, and bade her good night.

Relatively speaking, however, I never fared as badly as another black 10 male journalist. He went to nearby Waukegan, Illinois, a couple of summers ago to work on a story about a murderer who was born there. Mistaking the reporter for the killer, police officers hauled him from his car at gunpoint and but for his press credentials would probably have tried to book him. Such episodes are not uncommon. Black men trade tales like this all the time.

Over the years, I learned to smother the rage I felt at so often being 11
taken for a criminal. Not to do so would surely have led to madness. I now
take precautions to make myself less threatening. I move about with care,
particularly late in the evening. I give a wide berth to nervous people on
subway platforms during the wee hours, particularly when I have exchanged
business clothes for jeans. If I happen to be entering a building behind
some people who appear skittish, I may walk by, letting them clear the
lobby before I return, so as not to seem to be following them. I have been
calm and extremely congenial on those rare occasions when I've been
pulled over by the police.

And on late-evening constitutionals I employ what has proved to be an 12
excellent tension-reducing measure: I whistle melodies from Beethoven
and Vivaldi and the more popular classical composers. Even steely New
Yorkers hunching toward nighttime destinations seem to relax, and occasionally they even join in the tune. Virtually everybody seems to sense that
a mugger wouldn't be warbling bright, sunny selections from Vivaldi's *Four
Seasons*. It is my equivalent of the cowbell that hikers wear when they know
they are in bear country.

Questions to Start You Thinking

1. How does Staples react to others' misconceptions of him? What does he feel
   causes such misconceptions?

2. How does Staples use recall? What other resources does he use? How does he
   use analysis? What other critical thinking skills does he use?

3. Define *affluent, uninflammatory* (paragraph 1), *unwieldy, quarry, errant* (paragraph 2), *bandolier, solace* (paragraph 5), *lethality* (paragraph 6), and *bravado*
   (paragraph 7). Why does Staples use such formal language in this essay?

4. Staples attempts to counter stereotypes of African American men by whistling
   "melodies from . . . the more popular classical composers" (paragraph 12). How
   does this response to stereotyping differ from that described by Henry Louis
   Gates, Jr., in "2 Live Crew, Decoded" (p. 558)?

Suggestions for Writing

1. How are African American men stereotyped in our society? How accurate are
   these stereotypes? Write a brief essay evaluating the typical view of the African
   American man in the United States. Use examples from Staples's essay and your
   own experience as the basis for your evaluation.

2. Staples writes about his feelings as the object of prejudiced fear. Have you ever
   been the object of such a fear or of other misconceptions based on prejudice or
   stereotypes? Write a short personal essay discussing the causes and effects of
   such an experience. Of what preconceptions were you the victim? How did you
   respond?

WILLIAM RASPBERRY was born in 1935 in Okolona, Mississippi. He graduated from Indiana Central College in 1960 and began working for the *Washington Post.* Raspberry received several awards for his coverage of the Watts riots during the civil rights unrest of the 1960s, and since 1966 his nationally syndicated column has originated weekly in the *Washington Post.* Raspberry was once described in *Time* as "the Lone Ranger of columnists," and the following article, condensed from a speech he gave in 1990 at Hillsdale College, Michigan, demonstrates his readiness to argue forcefully on a controversial topic.

THE MYTH THAT IS CRIPPLING BLACK AMERICA
William Raspberry

A myth has crippled black America: the myth that racism is the dominant influence in our lives. 1

Two things flow from this racism-is-all myth. It puts the solution to our difficulties outside our control. And it encourages the fallacy that attacking racism as the source of our problems is the same as attacking our problems. As a result, we expend precious time, energy and imagination searching (always successfully) for evidence of racism—while our problems grow worse. 2

Consider poor whites. They can vote, live where their money permits them, eat where their appetites dictate, work at jobs for which their skills qualify them. They have their civil rights. And yet they are in desperate straits. It doesn't seem to occur to us that the full grant of our civil rights would leave black Americans in about the same situation that poor whites are now in. 3

There is another minority whose situation may be more instructive. I refer to Asian-Americans. Neither the newly arrived Southeast Asians nor the earlier-arriving Japanese-Americans, Chinese-Americans and Korean-Americans are loved by white people. But these groups have spent little time and energy proving that white people don't love them. 4

While our myth is that racism accounts for our shortcomings, their belief is that their own efforts can make the difference, no matter what white people think. They have looked at America like children with their noses pressed to the candystore window: if only I could get in there, boy, could I have a good time. And when they get in, they work and study and save and create businesses and jobs for their people. 5

But we, born inside the candy store, focus only on the maldistribution of the candy. Our myth leads us to become consumers when victories accrue to the producers. 6

This is a fairly recent phenomenon. Following the Civil War, free blacks and former slaves, though denied many of the rights we take for granted today, were entrepreneurs—artisans and inventors, shopkeepers and in- 7 dustrialists, bankers and financiers. The first female millionaire in America was a black woman, Madame C. J. Walker. Fifty years after emancipation, in 1913, as Robert L. Woodson observed in his book *On the Road to Economic Freedom*, black America "could take pride in owning 550,000 homes, 40,000 businesses and 937,000 farms."

What has happened since? Hundreds of thriving restaurants, hotels, service outlets and entertainment centers have gone out of business because we preferred integration to supporting our own painstakingly established institutions. Indeed, aside from black churches and black colleges, little remains to show for that entrepreneurial spurt early this century. 8

We overlearned the lessons of the civil rights era. That courageous movement enabled black Americans, for the first time, to enjoy the full panoply of civil rights. Unfortunately, the movement also taught us to see in terms of civil rights things that might more properly be achieved by enterprise and exertion. 9

Even when we speak of business now, our focus is on set-asides and affirmative action. We insist on a fair distribution of jobs in businesses created and run by others. But the emphasis ought to be on getting more of us into our own businesses, creating jobs ourselves and encouraging an entrepreneurial approach to our social problems. 10

I am not suggesting that government has no role. But we need government-backed programs that, instead of merely making our problems more bearable, help solve them. We are forever talking about the lack of day care as an impediment to work for welfare families. Why aren't we lobbying for legislation to permit some of the money now spent on public welfare to be used to establish child-care centers? Why aren't we looking for ways to create small jitney services to transport job seekers to distant jobs? 11

I leave to others the specifics. I will tell you only that increasing the economic success of black America can be done—and is being done by an encouraging number of us. When people believe that their problems can be solved, they tend to get busy solving them. 12

On the other hand, when people believe that their problems are beyond solution, they tend to position themselves so as to avoid blame. Take the woeful inadequacy of education in the predominantly black central cities. Does the black leadership see the ascendancy of black teachers, school administrators and politicians as an asset to be used in improving those dreadful schools? Rarely. You are more likely to hear charges of white abandonment, white resistance to integration, white conspiracies to isolate black children, even when the schools are officially desegregated. In short, white people are accused of being responsible for the problem. But if the youngsters manage to survive those awful school systems and achieve success, leaders want to claim credit. They don't hesitate to attribute that success to the glorious civil rights movement. 13

Many of us, of course, aren't succeeding. Teen-age pregnancy, dope trafficking, lawlessness, and lack of ambition make many doubt that we ever will succeed. But when we see failure among our people and have 14 reason to believe the failure is permanent, our leaders say racism is the culprit. Mistakenly, we credit black pride for our successes and blame prejudice for our shortfalls. My simple suggestion is that we stop using the plight of the black underclass as a scourge for beating up on white racists.

I used to play a little game in which I'd tell black leaders: "Let's say 15 you're exactly right, that racism is the overriding reason for our situation and that an all-out attack on racism is our most pressing priority.

"Now let us suppose that we eventually win the fight against racism 16 and put ourselves in the position currently occupied by poor whites—that is, in full possession of civil rights, but economically disadvantaged. What would you urge we do next?

"Pool our resources? Establish and support black businesses? Insist 17 that our children take advantage of the opportunities that a society free of racism would offer?

"Well, just for the hell of it, why don't we pretend the racist dragon has 18 been slain already—and take that next step right now?"

Questions to Start You Thinking

1. How does Raspberry feel that the situation of African Americans differs from the situation of other minority groups in the United States?

2. Discuss how Raspberry uses cause and effect to make a strong argument for his proposed solution.

3. Define *fallacy* (paragraph 2), *straits* (paragraph 3), *maldistribution* (paragraph 6), *panoply* (paragraph 9), and *scourge* (paragraph 14).

4. With which of Toni Morrison's ancestors, as depicted in "A Slow Walk of Trees" (p. 567), would Raspberry be most likely to sympathize? Why?

Suggestions for Writing

1. In this piece, Raspberry proposes "increasing the economic success of black America" (paragraph 12) as one solution to the problem of African American social inequality in the United States. In a brief essay, propose a solution of your own to the same problem, or to another problem of inequality.

2. Raspberry refers to the belief that "racism is the dominant influence" (paragraph 1) in African American lives as a "myth." What does he mean by this? Write a short essay supporting or challenging his claim.

CHAPTER 24

The World of Work

JESSICA MITFORD was born in 1917 in rural Gloucestershire, England. Her first husband, a nephew of Winston Churchill, was killed early in World War II. Two years later, Mitford remarried, moved to the United States, and began her career as a muckraking journalist, mercilessly exposing the absurdities of such subjects as the American funeral industry. Her *Poison Penmanship: The Gentle Art of Muckraking* (1979) was described as "a virtual textbook on investigative reporting." In the following essay, excerpted from her book *The American Way of Death* (1963), Mitford provides a graphic account of the work performed by the embalmer.

BEHIND THE FORMALDEHYDE CURTAIN
Jessica Mitford

The drama begins to unfold with the arrival of the corpse at the mortuary.   1

Alas, poor Yorick!° How surprised he would be to see how his counter-   2
part of today is whisked off to a funeral parlor and is in short order sprayed,
sliced, pierced, pickled, trussed, trimmed, creamed, waxed, painted,
rouged, and neatly dressed — transformed from a common corpse into a

---

Alas, poor Yorick! Mitford echoes Shakespeare: Hamlet's line as he examines the skull of his old friend, the court jester, who was buried without a coffin in a common grave (*Hamlet* V.i.184).

Beautiful Memory Picture. This process is known in the trade as embalming and restorative art, and is so universally employed in the United States and Canada that the funeral director does it routinely, without consulting corpse or kin. He regards as eccentric those few who are hardy enough to suggest that it might be dispensed with. Yet no law requires embalming, no religious doctrine commends it, nor is it dictated by considerations of health, sanitation, or even of personal daintiness. In no part of the world but in Northern America is it widely used. The purpose of embalming is to make the corpse presentable for viewing in a suitably costly container; and here too the funeral director routinely, without first consulting the family, prepares the body for public display.

Is all this legal? The processes to which a dead body may be subjected   3
are after all to some extent circumscribed by law. In most states, for instance, the signature of next of kin must be obtained before an autopsy may be performed, before the deceased may be cremated, before the body may be turned over to a medical school for research purposes; or such provision must be made in the decedent's will. In the case of embalming, no such permission is required nor is it ever sought. A textbook, *The Principles and Practices of Embalming*, comments on this: "There is some question regarding the legality of much that is done within the preparation room." The author points out that it would be most unusual for a responsible member of a bereaved family to instruct the mortician, in so many words, to *"embalm"* the body of a deceased relative. The very term "embalming" is so seldom used that the mortician must rely upon custom in the matter. The author concludes that unless the family specifies otherwise, the act of entrusting the body to the care of a funeral establishment carries with it an implied permission to go ahead and embalm.

Embalming is indeed a most extraordinary procedure, and one must   4
wonder at the docility of Americans who each year pay hundreds of millions of dollars for its perpetuation, blissfully ignorant of what it is all about, what is done, how it is done. Not one in ten thousand has any idea of what actually takes place. Books on the subject are extremely hard to come by. They are not to be found in most libraries or bookshops.

In an era when huge television audiences watch surgical operations in   5
the comfort of their living rooms, when, thanks to the animated cartoon, the geography of the digestive system has become familiar territory even to the nursery school set, in a land where the satisfaction of curiosity about almost all matters is a national pastime, the secrecy surrounding embalming can, surely, hardly be attributed to the inherent gruesomeness of the subject. Custom in this regard has within this century suffered a complete reversal. In the early days of American embalming, when it was performed in the home of the deceased, it was almost mandatory for some relative to stay by the embalmer's side and witness the procedure. Today, family members who might wish to be in attendance would certainly be dissuaded by the funeral director. All others, except apprentices, are excluded by law from the preparation room.

A close look at what does actually take place may explain in large 6
measure the undertaker's intractable reticence concerning a procedure that
has become his major *raison d'être*. Is it possible he fears that public
information about embalming might lead patrons to wonder if they really
want this service? If the funeral men are loath to discuss the subject outside the trade, the reader may, understandably, be equally loath to go on
reading at this point. For those who have the stomach for it, let us part the
formaldehyde curtain. . . .

The body is first laid out in the undertaker's morgue — or rather, Mr. 7
Jones is reposing in the preparation room — to be readied to bid the world
farewell.

The preparation room in any of the better funeral establishments has 8
the tiled and sterile look of a surgery, and indeed the embalmer-restorative
artist who does his chores there is beginning to adopt the term "derma-
surgeon" (appropriately corrupted by some mortician-writers as "demi-
surgeon") to describe his calling. His equipment, consisting of scalpels,
scissors, augers, forceps, clamps, needles, pumps, tubes, bowls, and ba-
sins, is crudely imitative of the surgeon's, as is his technique, acquired in
a nine- or twelve-month post-high school course in an embalming school.
He is supplied by an advanced chemical industry with a bewildering array
of fluids, sprays, pastes, oils, powders, creams, to fix or soften tissue,
shrink or distend it as needed, dry it here, restore the moisture there. There
are cosmetics, waxes, and paints to fill and cover features, even plaster of
Paris to replace entire limbs. There are ingenious aids to prop and stabilize
the cadaver: a Vari-Pose Head Rest, the Edwards Arm and Hand Positioner,
the Repose Block (to support the shoulders during the embalming), and the
Throop Foot Positioner, which resembles an old-fashioned stocks.

Mr. John H. Eckels, president of the Eckels College of Mortuary Science, 9
thus describes the first part of the embalming procedure: "In the hands of
a skilled practitioner, this work may be done in a comparatively short time
and without mutilating the body other than by slight incision — so slight that
it scarcely would cause serious inconvenience if made upon a living person.
It is necessary to remove the blood, and doing this not only helps in the
disinfecting, but removes the principal cause of disfigurements due to
discoloration."

Another textbook discusses the all-important time element: "The earlier 10
this is done, the better, for every hour that elapses between death and
embalming will add to the problems and complications encountered. . . ."
Just how soon should one get going on the embalming? The author tells
us, "On the basis of such scanty information made available to this profession through its rudimentary and haphazard system of technical research,
we must conclude that the best results are to be obtained if the subject is
embalmed before life is completely extinct — that is, before cellular death
has occurred. In the average case, this would mean within an hour after
somatic death." For those who feel that there is something a little rudimentary, not to say haphazard, about this advice, a comforting thought is

offered by another writer. Speaking of fears entertained in early days of premature burial, he points out, "One of the effects of embalming by chemical injection, however, has been to dispel fears of live burial." How true; once the blood is removed, chances of live burial are indeed remote.

To return to Mr. Jones, the blood is drained out through the veins and replaced by embalming fluid pumped in through the arteries. As noted in *The Principles and Practices of Embalming*, "every operator has a favorite injection and drainage point—a fact which becomes a handicap only if he fails or refuses to forsake his favorites when conditions demand it." Typical favorites are the carotid artery, femoral artery, jugular vein, subclavian vein. There are various choices of embalming fluid. If Flextone is used, it will produce a "mild, flexible rigidity. The skin retains a velvety softness, the tissues are rubbery and pliable. Ideal for women and children." It may be blended with B. and G. Products Company's Lyf-Lyk tint, which is guaranteed to reproduce "nature's own skin texture . . . the velvety appearance of living tissue." Suntone comes in three separate tints: Suntan; Special Cosmetic Tint, a pink shade "especially indicated for female subjects"; and Regular Cosmetic Tint, moderately pink.

About three to six gallons of a dyed and perfumed solution of formaldehyde, glycerin, borax, phenol, alcohol, and water is soon circulating through Mr. Jones, whose mouth has been sewn together with a "needle directed upward between the upper lip and gum and brought out through the left nostril," with the corners raised slightly "for a more pleasant expression." If he should be bucktoothed, his teeth are cleaned with Bon Ami and coated with colorless nail polish. His eyes, meanwhile, are closed with flesh-tinted eye caps and eye cement.

The next step is to have at Mr. Jones with a thing called a trocar. This is a long, hollow needle attached to a tube. It is jabbed into the abdomen, poked around the entrails and chest cavity, the contents of which are pumped out and replaced with "cavity fluid." This done, and the hole in the abdomen sewn up, Mr. Jones's face is heavily creamed (to protect the skin from burns which may be caused by leakage of the chemicals), and he is covered with a sheet and left unmolested for a while. But not for long— there is more, much more, in store for him. He has been embalmed, but not yet restored, and the best time to start the restorative work is eight to ten hours after embalming, when the tissues have become firm and dry.

The object of all this attention to the corpse, it must be remembered, is to make it presentable for viewing in an attitude of healthy repose. "Our customs require the presentation of our dead in the semblance of normality . . . unmarred by the ravages of illness, disease, or mutilation," says Mr. J. Sheridan Mayer in his *Restorative Art*. This is rather a large order since few people die in the full bloom of health, unravaged by illness and unmarked by some disfigurement. The funeral industry is equal to the challenge: "In some cases the gruesome appearance of a mutilated or disease-ridden subject may be quite discouraging. The task of restoration may seem impossible and shake the confidence of the embalmer. This is the time for intestinal fortitude and determination. Once the formative work is begun and affected tissues are cleaned or removed, all doubts of success vanish. It is surprising and gratifying to discover the results which may be obtained."

The embalmer, having allowed an appropriate interval to elapse, returns to the attack, but now he brings into play the skill and equipment of sculptor and cosmetician. Is a hand missing? Casting one in plaster of Paris is a simple matter. "For replacement purposes, only a cast of the back of the hand is necessary; this is within the ability of the average operator and is quite adequate." If a lip or two, a nose or an ear should be missing, the embalmer has at hand a variety of restorative waxes with which to model replacements. Pores and skin texture are simulated by stippling with a little brush, and over this cosmetics are laid on. Head off? Decapitation cases are rather routinely handled. Ragged edges are trimmed, and head joined to torso with a series of splints, wires, and sutures. It is a good idea to have a little something at the neck—a scarf or a high collar—when time for viewing comes. Swollen mouth? Cut out tissue as needed from inside the lips. If too much is removed, the surface contour can easily be restored by padding with cotton. Swollen necks and cheeks are reduced by removing tissue through vertical incisions made down each side of the neck. "When the deceased is casketed, the pillow will hide the suture incisions . . . as an extra precaution against leakage, the suture may be painted with liquid sealer."

The opposite condition is more likely to present itself—that of emaciation. His hypodermic syringe now loaded with massage cream, the embalmer seeks out and fills the hollowed and sunken areas by injection. In this procedure the backs of the hands and fingers and the under-chin area should not be neglected.

Positioning the lips is a problem that recurrently challenges the ingenuity of the embalmer. Closed too tightly, they tend to give a stern, even disapproving expression. Ideally, embalmers feel, the lips should give the impression of being ever so slightly parted, the upper lip protruding slightly for a more youthful appearance. This takes some engineering, however, as the lips tend to drift apart. Lip drift can sometimes be remedied by pushing one or two straight pins through the inner margin of the lower lip and then inserting them between the two front upper teeth. If Mr. Jones happens to have no teeth, the pins can just as easily be anchored in his Armstrong Face Former and Denture Replacer. Another method to maintain lip closure is to dislocate the lower jaw, which is then held in its new position by a wire run through holes which have been drilled through the upper and lower jaws at the midline. As the French are fond of saying, *il faut souffrir pour être belle.*°

If Mr. Jones has died of jaundice, the embalming fluid will very likely turn him green. Does this deter the embalmer? Not if he has intestinal

15

16

17

18

---

il faut . . . belle. You have to suffer to be beautiful.

fortitude. Masking pastes and cosmetics are heavily laid on, burial garments and casket interiors are color-correlated with particular care, and Jones is displayed beneath rose-colored lights. Friends will say "How *well* he looks." Death by carbon monoxide, on the other hand, can be rather a good thing from the embalmer's viewpoint: "One advantage is the fact that this type of discoloration is an exaggerated form of a natural pink coloration." This is nice because the healthy glow is already present and needs but little attention.

The patching and filling completed, Mr. Jones is now shaved, washed, 19 and dressed. Cream-based cosmetic, available in pink, flesh, suntan, brunette, and blond, is applied to his hands and face, his hair is shampooed and combed (and, in the case of Mrs. Jones, set), his hands manicured. For the horny-handed son of toil special care must be taken; cream should be applied to remove ingrained grime, and the nails cleaned. "If he were not in the habit of having them manicured in life, trimming and shaping is advised for better appearance—never questioned by kin."

Jones is now ready for casketing (this is the present participle of the 20 verb "to casket"). In this operation his right shoulder should be depressed slightly "to turn the body a bit to the right and soften the appearance of lying flat on the back." Positioning the hands is a matter of importance, and special rubber positioning blocks may be used. The hands should be cupped slightly for a more lifelike, relaxed appearance. Proper placement of the body requires a delicate sense of balance. It should lie as high as possible in the casket, yet not so high that the lid, when lowered, will hit the nose. On the other hand, we are cautioned, placing the body too low "creates the impression that the body is in a box."

Jones is next wheeled into the appointed slumber room where a few 21 last touches may be added—his favorite pipe placed in his hand or, if he was a great reader, a book propped into position. (In the case of little Master Jones a Teddy bear may be clutched.) Here he will hold open house for a few days, visiting hours 10 A.M. to 9 P.M.

All now being in readiness, the funeral director calls a staff conference 22 to make sure that each assistant knows his precise duties. Mr. Wilber Kriege writes: "This makes your staff feel that they are a part of the team, with a definite assignment that must be properly carried out if the whole plan is to succeed. You never heard of a football coach who failed to talk to his entire team before they go on the field. They have drilled on the plays they are to execute for hours and days, and yet the successful coach knows the importance of making even the bench-warming third-string substitute feel that he is important if the game is to be won." The winning of *this* game is predicated upon glass-smooth handling of the logistics. The funeral director has notified the pallbearers whose names were furnished by the family, has arranged for the presence of clergyman, organist, and soloist, has provided transportation for everybody, has organized and listed the flowers sent by friends. In *Psychology of Funeral Service* Mr. Edward A. Martin points out: "He may not always do as much as the family thinks he is doing, but it is his helpful guidance that they appreciate in knowing they are proceeding as they should. . . . The important thing is how well his services can be used to make the family believe they are giving unlimited expression to their own sentiment."

The religious service may be held in a church or in the chapel of the 23
funeral home; the funeral director vastly prefers the latter arrangement, for not only is it more convenient for him but it affords him the opportunity to show off his beautiful facilities to the gathered mourners. After the clergyman has had his say, the mourners queue up to file past the casket for a last look at the deceased. The family is *never* asked whether they want an open-casket ceremony; in the absence of their instruction to the contrary, this is taken for granted. Consequently well over 90 percent of all American funerals feature the open casket—a custom unknown in other parts of the world. Foreigners are astonished by it. An English woman living in San Francisco described her reaction in a letter to the writer:

> I myself have attended only one funeral here—that of an elderly fellow 24
> worker of mine. After the service I could not understand why everyone was walking towards the coffin (sorry, I mean casket), but thought I had better follow the crowd. It shook me rigid to get there and find the casket open and poor old Oscar lying there in his brown tweed suit, wearing a suntan makeup and just the wrong shade of lipstick. If I had not been extremely fond of the old boy, I have a horrible feeling that I might have giggled. Then and there I decided that I could never face another American funeral—even dead.

The casket (which has been resting throughout the service on a Classic 25
Beauty Ultra Metal Casket Bier) is now transferred by a hydraulically operated device called Porto-Lift to a balloon-tired, Glide Easy casket carriage which will wheel it to yet another conveyance, the Cadillac Funeral Coach. This may be lavender, cream, light green—anything but black. Interiors, of course, are color-correlated, "for the man who cannot stop short of perfection."

At graveside, the casket is lowered into the earth. This office, once the 26
prerogative of friends of the deceased, is now performed by a patented mechanical lowering device. A "Lifetime Green" artificial grass mat is at the ready to conceal the sere earth, and overhead, to conceal the sky, is a portable Steril Chapel Tent ("resists the intense heat and humidity of summer and the terrific storms of winter . . . available in Silver Grey, Rose or Evergreen"). Now is the time for the ritual scattering of earth over the coffin, as the solemn words "earth to earth, ashes to ashes, dust to dust" are pronounced by the officiating cleric. This can today be accomplished "with a mere flick of the wrist with the Gordon Leak-Proof Earth Dispenser. No grasping of a handful of dirt, no soiled fingers. Simple, dignified, beautiful, reverent! The modern way!" The Gordon Earth Dispenser (at $5) is of nickel-plated brass construction. It is not only "attractive to the eye and long wearing"; it is also "one of the 'tools' for building better public relations" if presented as "an appropriate non-commercial gift" to the clergyman. It is shaped something like a saltshaker.

Untouched by human hand, the coffin and the earth are now united.   27

It is in the function of directing the participants through this maze of   28
gadgetry that the funeral director has assigned to himself his relatively new
role of "grief therapist." He has relieved the family of every detail, he has
revamped the corpse to look like a living doll, he has arranged for it to nap
for a few days in a slumber room, he has put on a well-oiled performance
in which the concept of *death* has played no part whatsoever—unless it
was inconsiderately mentioned by the clergyman who conducted the religious service. He has done everything in his power to make the funeral a
real pleasure for everybody concerned. He and his team have given their
all to score an upset victory over death.

Questions to Start You Thinking

1. Is Mitford's view of the funeral industry positive or negative? Point to examples in the text that support your opinion.

2. Where does Mitford interrupt her analysis of the process of embalming to analyze and evaluate the funeral industry and its attitudes?

3. In this essay, Mitford juxtaposes blunt, descriptive language with the jargon of the funeral industry. Identify examples of both types of language. What effect does the juxtaposition have? Define *decedent* (paragraph 3), *formaldehyde* (paragraph 6), *reposing* (paragraph 7), *cadaver* (paragraph 8), *somatic* (paragraph 10), and *stippling* (paragraph 15).

4. How is the view of death Mitford depicts here different from that presented by Annie Dillard in "Fecundity" (p. 586)?

Suggestions for Writing

1. Using Mitford's essay as a model, write a short process analysis explaining each step that was involved in a job you once held. Your goal should be to describe these steps so clearly that readers of your essay would actually be able to perform your job.

2. Write an essay explaining the rituals of death. Describe these rituals as you have experienced them. What is their function? How have they made you feel?

STEVE OLSON was born in 1946 in Rice Lake, Wisconsin, and currently lives in northern Wisconsin with his wife and two sons. Unadorned by the usual list of degrees, awards, and publications, Olson identified himself simply as "a construction worker" when asked for biographical information recently. Claiming that he writes "mostly for [him]self," he seems to be speaking for the average American. In the following piece, which appeared as a "My Turn" essay in *Newsweek* on November 6, 1989, Olson strives to honor the dialect and ethic of a group of Americans who are often stereotyped but rarely heard from.

YEAR OF THE BLUE-COLLAR GUY
Steve Olson

While the learned are attaching appropriate labels to the 1980s and speculating on what the 1990s will bring, I would like to steal 1989 for my own much maligned group and declare it "the year of the blue-collar guy (BCG)." BCGs have been portrayed as beer-drinking, big-bellied, bigoted rednecks who dress badly. Wearing a suit to a cement-finishing job wouldn't be too bright. Watching my tie go around a motor shaft followed by my neck is not the last thing I want to see in this world. But, more to the point, our necks are too big and our arms and shoulders are too awesome to fit suits well without expensive tailoring. Suits are made for white-collar guys.

But we need big bellies as ballast to stay on the bar stool while we're drinking beer. And our necks are red from the sun and we are somewhat bigoted. But aren't we all? At least our bigotry is open and honest and worn out front like a tattoo. White-collar people are bigoted, too. But it's disguised as the pat on the back that holds you back: "You're not good enough so you need affirmative action." BCGs aren't smart enough to be that cynical. I never met a BCG who didn't respect an honest day's work and a job well done — no matter who did it.

True enough, BCGs aren't perfect. But, I believe this: we are America's last true romantic heroes. When some twenty-first-century Louis L'Amour writes about this era he won't eulogize the greedy Wall Street insider. He won't commend the narrow-shouldered, wide-hipped lawyers with six-digit unearned incomes doing the same work women can do. His wide-shouldered heroes will be plucked from the ranks of the blue-collar guy. They are the last vestige of the manly world where strength, skill and hard work are still valued.

To some extent our negative ratings are our own fault. While we were building the world we live in, white-collar types were sitting on their ever-widening butts redefining the values we live by. One symbol of America's opulent wealth is the number of people who can sit and ponder and comment and write without producing a usable product or skill. Hey, get a real job — make something — then talk. These talkers are the guys we drove from the playgrounds into the libraries when we were young and now for 20 years or more we have endured the revenge of the nerds.

BCGs fidgeted our way out of the classroom and into jobs where, it seemed, the only limit to our income was the limit of our physical strength and energy. A co-worker described a BCG as "a guy who is always doing things that end in the letter 'n' — you know — huntin', fishin', workin' . . ." My wise friend is talking energy! I have seen men on the job hand-nail 20 square of shingles (that's 6,480 nails) or more a day, day after day, for weeks. At the same time, they were remodeling their houses, raising children, and coaching Little League. I've seen crews frame entire houses in a day — day after day. I've seen guys finish concrete until 11 P.M., go out on a date, then get up at 6 A.M. and do it all over again the next day.

These are amazing feats of strength. There should be stadiums full 6
of screaming fans for these guys. I saw a 40-year-old man neatly fold a
350-pound piece of rubber roofing, put it on his shoulder and, alone, carry
it up a ladder and deposit it on a roof. Nobody acknowledged it because
the event was too common. One day at noon this same fellow wrestled a
22-year-old college summer worker. In the prime of his life, the college kid
was a 6-foot-3, 190-pound body-builder and he was out of his league. He
was on his back to stay in 90 seconds flat.

GREAT SKILLED WORK FORCE

Mondays are tough on any job. But in our world this pain is eased by stories 7
of weekend adventure. While white-collar types are debating the value of
reading over watching TV, BCGs are doing stuff. I have honest to God heard
these things on Monday mornings about BCG weekends: "I tore out a wall
and added a room," "I built a garage," "I went walleye fishing Saturday and
pheasant hunting Sunday," "I played touch football both days" (in January),
"I went skydiving," "I went to the sports show and wrestled the bear." Pack
a good novel into these weekends.

My purpose is not so much to put down white-collar people as to stress 8
the importance of blue-collar people to this country. Lawyers, politicians,
and bureaucrats are necessary parts of the process, but this great skilled
work force is so taken for granted it is rarely seen as the luxury it truly is.
Our plumbing works, our phones work, and repairs are made as quickly as
humanly possible. I don't think this is true in all parts of the world. But this
blue-collar resource is becoming endangered. Being a tradesman is viewed
with such disdain these days that most young people I know treat the trades
like a temporary summer job. I've seen young guys take minimum-wage
jobs just so they can wear suits. It is as if any job without a dress code is
a dead-end job. This is partly our own fault. We even tell our own sons,
"Don't be like me, get a job people respect." Blue-collar guys ought to brag
more, even swagger a little. We should drive our families past the latest
job site and say, "That house was a piece of junk, and now it's the best
one on the block. I did that." Nobody will respect us if we don't respect
ourselves.

Our work is hard, hot, wet, cold, and always dirty. It is also often very 9
satisfying. Entailing the use of both brain and body there is a product — a
physical result of which to be proud. We have fallen from your roofs, died
under heavy equipment, and been entombed in your dams. We have done
honest, dangerous work. Our skills and energy and strength have transformed lines on paper into physical reality. We are this century's Renaissance men. America could do worse than to honor us. We still do things
the old-fashioned way, and we have earned the honor.

Questions to Start You Thinking

1. Why does Olson feel there should be a "Year of the Blue-Collar Guy"? What would
be the purpose of such a year?

2. How does Olson compare and contrast the "blue-collar guy" with the "white-collar types" to support his stand?

3. Is Olson's choice of vocabulary sometimes surprising for a self-named "blue-collar guy"? Define *ballast* (paragraph 2), *eulogize* (paragraph 3), *opulent* (paragraph 4), *disdain* (paragraph 8), and *Renaissance men* (paragraph 9).

4. Compare this essay with Mary Kay Blakely's "Psychic Income" (page 537). Both writers use humor to make a serious point. How is their use of humor similar? How does it differ?

Suggestions for Writing

1. Suggest a group you feel should have a year of its own (for example, college students, teachers, secretaries, mothers) and write a short essay taking a stand on why this group deserves such an honor.

2. In a brief essay, discuss images of blue-collar workers that you have encountered in television, film, music, and literature. How accurate do these images seem to you?

WILLIAM OUCHI, born in 1943 in Honolulu, has drawn in his adult work on the dual heritage of his state of birth. Educated at Williams College, Stanford University, and the University of Chicago, Ouchi consults and writes on management strategies. His books include *The M-Form Society: How American Business Can Recapture the Competitive Edge* (1984) and *Theory Z: How American Business Can Meet the Japanese Challenge* (1981). In the following essay, excerpted from *Theory Z*, Ouchi compares and contrasts the Japanese and the American work ethic and argues that the Japanese are better able to cope with modern industrialism because of their emphasis on cooperation.

JAPANESE AND AMERICAN WORKERS: TWO CASTS OF MIND
William Ouchi

Perhaps the most difficult aspect of the Japanese for Westerners to   1
comprehend is the strong orientation to collective values, particularly a collective sense of responsibility. Let me illustrate with an anecdote about a visit to a new factory in Japan owned and operated by an American electronics company. The American company, a particularly creative firm, frequently attracts attention within the business community for its novel approaches to planning, organizational design, and management systems. As a consequence of this corporate style, the parent company determined to make a thorough study of Japanese workers and to design a plant that would combine the best of East and West. In their study they discovered

that Japanese firms almost never make use of individual work incentives, such as piecework or even individual performance appraisal tied to salary increases. They concluded that rewarding individual achievement and individual ability is always a good thing.

In the final assembly area of their new plant long lines of young Japa-   2
nese women wired together electronic products on a piece-rate system: the more you wired, the more you got paid. About two months after opening, the head foreladies approached the plant manager. "Honorable plant manager," they said humbly as they bowed, "we are embarrassed to be so forward, but we must speak to you because all of the girls have threatened to quit work this Friday." (To have this happen, of course, would be a great disaster for all concerned.) "Why," they wanted to know, "can't our plant have the same compensation system as other Japanese companies? When you hire a new girl, her starting wage should be fixed by her age. An eighteen-year-old should be paid more than a sixteen-year-old. Every year on her birthday, she should receive an automatic increase in pay. The idea that any one of us can be more productive than another must be wrong, because none of us in final assembly could make a thing unless all of the other people in the plant had done their jobs right first. To single one person out as being more productive is wrong and is also personally humiliating to us." The company changed its compensation system to the Japanese model.

Another American company in Japan had installed a suggestion system   3
much as we have in the United States. Individual workers were encouraged to place suggestions to improve productivity into special boxes. For an accepted idea the individual received a bonus amounting to some fraction of the productivity savings realized from his or her suggestion. After a period of six months, not a single suggestion had been submitted. The American managers were puzzled. They had heard many stories of the inventiveness, the commitment, and the loyalty of Japanese workers, yet not one suggestion to improve productivity had appeared.

The managers approached some of the workers and asked why the   4
suggestion system had not been used. The answer: "No one can come up with a work improvement idea alone. We work together, and any ideas that one of us may have are actually developed by watching others and talking to others. If one of us was singled out for being responsible for such an idea, it would embarrass all of us." The company changed to a group suggestion system, in which workers collectively submitted suggestions. Bonuses were paid to groups which would save bonus money until the end of the year for a party at a restaurant or, if there was enough money, for family vacations together. The suggestions and productivity improvements rained down on the plant.

One can interpret these examples in two quite different ways. Perhaps   5
the Japanese commitment to collective values is an anachronism that does not fit with modern industrialism but brings economic success despite that collectivism. Collectivism seems to be inimical to the kind of maverick

creativity exemplified in Benjamin Franklin, Thomas Edison, and John D. Rockefeller. Collectivism does not seem to provide the individual incentive to excel which has made a great success of American enterprise. Entirely apart from its economic effects, collectivism implies a loss of individuality, a loss of the freedom to be different, to hold fundamentally different values from others.

The second interpretation of the examples is that the Japanese collec- 6 tivism is economically efficient. It causes people to work well together and to encourage one another to better efforts. Industrial life requires inter-dependence of one person on another. But a less obvious but far-reaching implication of the Japanese collectivism for economic performance has to do with accountability.

In the Japanese mind, collectivism is neither a corporate or individual 7 goal to strive for nor a slogan to pursue. Rather, the nature of things op-erates so that nothing of consequence occurs as a result of individual effort. Everything important in life happens as a result of teamwork or collective effort. Therefore, to attempt to assign individual credit or blame to results is unfounded. A Japanese professor of accounting, a brilliant scholar trained at Carnegie-Mellon University who teaches now in Tokyo, remarked that the status of accounting systems in Japanese industry is primitive compared to those in the United States. Profit centers, transfer prices, and computerized information systems are barely known even in the largest Japanese companies, whereas they are a commonplace in even small United States organizations. Though not at all surprised at the dif-ference in accounting systems, I was not at all sure that the Japanese were primitive. In fact, I thought their system a good deal more efficient than ours.

Most American companies have basically two accounting systems. One 8 system summarizes the overall financial state to inform stockholders, bank-ers, and other outsiders. That system is not of interest here. The other system, called the managerial or cost accounting system, exists for an entirely different reason. It measures in detail all of the particulars of trans-actions between departments, divisions, and key individuals in the organi-zation, for the purpose of untangling the interdependencies between people. When, for example, two departments share one truck for deliveries, the cost accounting system charges each department for part of the cost of maintaining the truck and driver, so that at the end of the year, the performance of each department can be individually assessed, and the better department's manager can receive a larger raise. Of course, all of this information processing costs money, and furthermore may lead to ar-guments between the departments over whether the costs charged to each are fair.

In a Japanese company a short-run assessment of individual per- 9 formance is not wanted, so the company can save the considerable expense of collecting and processing all of that information. Companies still keep track of which department uses a truck how often and for what purposes, but like-minded people can interpret some simple numbers for themselves and adjust their behavior accordingly. Those insisting upon clear and precise measurement for the purpose of advancing individual interests must have an elaborate information system. Industrial life, however, is essentially integrated and interdependent. No one builds an automobile alone, no one carries through a banking transaction alone. In a sense the Japanese value of collectivism fits naturally into an industrial setting, whereas the Western individualism provides constant conflicts. The image that comes to mind is of Chaplin's silent film "Modern Times" in which the apparently insignificant hero played by Chaplin successfully fights against the unfeeling machinery of industry. Modern industrial life can be aggravating, even hostile, or natural: all depends on the fit between our culture and our technology.

The *shinkansen* or "bullet train" speeds across the rural areas of Japan 10
giving a quick view of cluster after cluster of farmhouses surrounded by rice paddies. This particular pattern did not develop purely by chance, but as a consequence of the technology peculiar to the growing of rice, the staple of the Japanese diet. The growing of rice requires construction and maintenance of an irrigation system, something that takes many hands to build. More importantly, the planting and the harvesting of rice can only be done efficiently with the cooperation of twenty or more people. The "bottom line" is that a single family working alone cannot produce enough rice to survive, but a dozen families working together can produce a surplus. Thus the Japanese have had to develop the capacity to work together in harmony, no matter what the forces of disagreement or social disintegration, in order to survive.

Japan is a nation built entirely on the tips of giant, suboceanic volcan- 11
oes. Little of the land is flat and suitable for agriculture. Terraced hillsides make use of every available square foot of arable land. Small homes built very close together further conserve the land. Japan also suffers from natural disasters such as earthquakes and hurricanes. Traditionally homes are made of light construction materials, so a house falling down during a disaster will not crush its occupants and also could be quickly and inexpensively rebuilt. During the feudal period until the Meiji restoration of 1868, each feudal lord sought to restrain his subjects from moving from one village to the next for fear that a neighboring lord might amass enough peasants with which to produce a large agricultural surplus, hire an army and pose a threat. Apparently bridges were not commonly built across rivers and streams until the late nineteenth century, since bridges increased mobility between villages.

Taken all together, this characteristic style of living paints the picture 12
of a nation of people who are homogeneous with respect to race, history, language, religion, and culture. For centuries and generations these people have lived in the same village next door to the same neighbors. Living in close proximity and in dwellings which gave very little privacy, the Japanese survived through their capacity to work together in harmony. In this situa-

tion, it was inevitable that the one most central social value which emerged, the one value without which the society could not continue, was that an individual does not matter.

To the Western soul this is a chilling picture of society. Subordinating 13 individual tastes to the harmony of the group and knowing that individual needs can never take precedence over the interests of all is repellent to the Western citizen. But a frequent theme of Western philosophers and sociologists is that individual freedom exists only when people willingly subordinate their self-interests to the social interest. A society composed entirely of self-interested individuals is a society in which each person is at war with the other, a society which has no freedom. This issue, constantly at the heart of understanding society, comes up in every century, and in every society, whether the writer be Plato, Hobbes, or B. F. Skinner. The question of understanding which contemporary institutions lie at the heart of the conflict between automatism and totalitarianism remains. In some ages, the kinship group, the central social institution, mediated between these opposing forces to preserve the balance in which freedom was realized; in other times the church or the government was most critical. Perhaps our present age puts the work organization as the central institution.

In order to complete the comparison of Japanese and American living 14 situations, consider a flight over the United States. Looking out of the window high over the state of Kansas, we see a pattern of a single farmhouse surrounded by fields, followed by another single homestead surrounded by fields. In the early 1800s in the state of Kansas there were no automobiles. Your nearest neighbor was perhaps two miles distant; the winters were long, and the snow was deep. Inevitably, the central social values were self-reliance and independence. Those were the realities of that place and age that children had to learn to value.

The key to the industrial revolution was discovering that nonhuman 15 forms of energy substituted for human forms could increase the wealth of a nation beyond anyone's wildest dreams. But there was a catch. To realize this great wealth, nonhuman energy needed huge complexes called factories with hundreds, even thousands of workers collected into one factory. Moreover, several factories in one central place made the generation of energy more efficient. Almost overnight, the Western world was transformed from a rural and agricultural country to an urban and industrial state. Our technological advance seems to no longer fit our social structure: in a sense, the Japanese can better cope with modern industrialism. While Americans still busily protect our rather extreme form of individualism, the Japanese hold their individualism in check and emphasize cooperation.

Questions to Start You Thinking

1. According to Ouchi, how are Japanese and American workers similar and how are they different? What does he see as the single biggest difference between them? What are some of the causes of the differences he discusses?

2. How does Ouchi evaluate the American and the Japanese work ethic in order to compare and contrast them?

3. Define *incentives, appraisal* (paragraph 1), *anachronism* (paragraph 5), *feudal* (paragraph 11), *homogeneous* (paragraph 12).

4. How does Ouchi's depiction of the Japanese workplace differ from Gary Katzenstein's in "The Salaryman" (p. 528)?

Suggestions for Writing

1. Write a short essay evaluating how your goals have conflicted or still conflict with your family's or society's goals. How did you or do you resolve the conflict?

2. Using both the observations in this essay and your own knowledge and experience as evidence, write an essay proposing a solution to the problems of American industry.

GARY KATZENSTEIN was born in 1956 in New York City. After earning a B.A. at Brown University and two degrees in computer science at UCLA, he traveled widely in the Far East and received a fellowship from Sony in the early 1980s to work at its corporate headquarters in Tokyo. While in Japan he had the opportunity to observe some of the darker, rarely reported aspects of Japan's economic "miracle." His book, *Funny Business: An Outsider's View of Japan* (1989), from which the following essay is excerpted, concerns some of the negative aspects of Japan's success.

THE SALARYMAN
Gary Katzenstein

Returning to Tokyo, I sought out Takagi-san and spoke to him about 1 my situation in the office. He had been introduced to me as my liaison in the division, my English-speaking go-between. I understood now that he was my *senpai*, my immediate superior in the hierarchy—my senior. It was to Takagi-san that I communicated my frustrations about the role I had been assigned. He, in turn, would advise me, his junior, instruct me by example, and report the situation to the assistant manager, if necessary. Only the assistant manager was allowed to speak to the manager, and only the manager spoke to the general manager, Murata-bucho.

It was a system and a structure that had not appeared on the organi- 2 zation charts I had been shown, which enumerated relatively few levels. But it was the daily reality within the company, and I was observing its unwritten strictures in speaking to Takagi-san.

I was, I explained, terribly frustrated. I had yet to do a stitch of 3 computer-related work, or real work of any sort, since I had arrived. Certainly, I had had no opportunity for hands-on experience in Japanese management. I was still far from the fluency needed to understand technical manuals or follow the exchanges I would overhear in the Computer Division. I did not explain that I now knew that American employees in the company had come in technically well trained and fluent, or else knew no Japanese and performed menial work.

There was no way I was going to learn Japanese in the time permitted. Would it not be advisable to place me elsewhere in the firm where language was not a problem? 4

Takagi-san listened to my grievance in perfect silence. I thanked him for his time and left. 5

Every day that I came to work, I checked with Takagi-san and did whatever he asked me to. Despite his terse style and reserved character, we had developed a rapport. As the weeks passed, however, I sensed something was wrong. Takagi-san, the star of our team who always did his work well, began to come in late, appearing at the gate after 8:30. I cringed at first, expecting that he would be fetched by the boss and escorted to his desk, the shaming procedure I had been told by personnel was the norm, but it thankfully never happened (neither was anyone ever chastised over the public-address system for forgetting to set location cards). 6

Takagi-san's behavior evinced discontent, even defeat. I was amazed and worried. He was a top graduate of Tokyo University, the Harvard of Japan, with a reputation as a brilliant abstract mathematician. He went to work at Sony right out of college, first as a trainee, of course, then as a programmer in the Computer Division. He had been a programmer for six years and had mastered the job years earlier. He wanted to move on, to assume tasks better suited to his intellectual abilities, but he couldn't. Promotions were accorded by seniority, so his might not come for five years, or seven, or even another ten. 7

He was a *sarariman*, a "salaryman," and could not seek a better position elsewhere. It simply wasn't done, nor was it probably attainable, as another company was unlikely to hire him anyway. No firm would take on someone who had left another's employ because of dissatisfaction — or, really, any other reason — and one was self-evidently dissatisfied if one wished to leave a position. Few *sararimen* even attempted to change jobs for this reason, and those who did, merely by making the attempt, were labeled as peculiar. The conventional thinking was that if an employee was prepared to leave one firm, he might well be disposed to leave another, making him untrustworthy. 8

Nor could one hide previous employment. Your *rirekisho*, or "work history," was dutifully maintained by your employer, and (although denied) managements would certainly avail other firms of the contents of such files. 9

The only alternatives available to an unhappy employee were to seek out a small company or business, or to go into business for himself. Neither avenue provided prestige or security, nor the same level of monetary reward as a large firm. 10

The system allegedly offered stability and certitude, and eliminated the 11
stress of competition. It also eliminated the need for regular review and
formal evaluation, thereby avoiding potential conflict and maintaining *wa,*
"social harmony." However, Takagi-san did not seem at all so confident of
his future or content with his career. Although single, he dreaded the over-
seas tour Sony would require of him within the next few years. He just did
not want to leave Japan and his family, yet it would probably be asked of
him, and he would have to accept if he was to keep hoping for a job upgrade
or advancement.

It began to dawn on me that the man I had complained to about my 12
inherently temporary dilemma was facing a built-in, permanent one with a
lifetime guarantee, and I began to see variations of Takagi-san's mute
unhappiness in the situations of other workers around me.

A good *sarariman* worked long hours, constantly. Overtime was a way 13
of life and one of the first words I had learned at Sony: *zangyo.* Much of it
was counterproductive, if not downright silly. Wives actually worried if their
husbands came home too early. Rather than embarrass her with the neighbors, spouses followed the work-overtime-play ritual by putting in the obligatory overtime and spending the rest of the evening eating and cavorting
with their colleagues. Starting around ten each evening the *sararimen* began staggering homeward.

Nohara-san admitted to me privately that he would be coming to work 14
the next Saturday not because he had anything to finish but simply to "show
his face," thereby demonstrating his commitment and support to those who
were legitimately there. I questioned the efficacy of so much extra work
done over so many hours. Why was it a constant?

One reason seemed to be the standards set for them. Often they were 15
impossibly high. Since failure would mean a terrible loss of face, failure
was unacceptable. Seeing the world in Zen black and white, they considered anything less than 100 percent as completely inadequate. It was like
being in a nation of perfectionists, and the overall goals were set by managers who had grown up in merciless postwar poverty and remained obsessed with the need to survive through arduous work, even though the
reality had obviously changed. Excessive work and absurd hours were not
just virtuous, they were a mindlessly worshiped fetish.

Procedures and policies were rigid, arbitrary, and usually doubled the 16
time necessary to complete assigned tasks. The physical work conditions
were wearing. The place was noisy, crowded, and messy, and made everything hard. The work itself was usually boring, which made it tedious. Even
the group meetings, held every Friday after lunch, were in reality boring,
compulsory, and mostly useless exercises. No one really listened. Yet not
to attend would have been a grievous transgression, so everyone showed
up, bowed formally to the boss, and sat there, bored. I saw no evidence of
the enthusiasm Western reporters and writers extolled as a major factor
underlying Japan's economic success.

There weren't nearly enough secretaries and assistants, and there was 17 insufficient rest. The buzzer would sound at 5:30, officially ending the paid workday, yet usually no one would react. They would just keep on working, right through their dinnertime. Most stayed until 7:00 P.M., "finishing what needed to be done." They went home late and exhausted, night after night.

Often, it seemed to me, they would have been better off stopping and 18 taking up their tasks again the next day, fresh instead of fatigued. But they couldn't. Management pressure had created a peer pressure that had become self-perpetuating. Respect was accorded by co-workers and supervisors to those who worked long hours. The more hours, the more praise.

Similarly, normal vacations of two and three weeks, to which my col- 19 leagues were entitled, were almost never taken. The implication was that one's contribution was important to the group. He or she could not responsibly take more than two or three days at a time. Such self-indulgence would increase the burden of the other team members. Likewise, sick days were theoretically available but were taken only when someone was gravely ill. Usually, workers came in with bad colds, fevers, flu, whatever. Not surprisingly, this resulted in near-epidemic illness in our claustrophobic, humid office during several weeks of the winter season. And a whole office of sick people was not productive, which meant—more overtime! Even the rare national holiday did not constitute totally free time. Invariably, everyone had to come in the following weekend to make up for the lost time. Takagi-san actually said it one day: "Overtime itself breeds more overtime."

The one way in which Sony favorably differed from other companies was 20 that Sony employees worked Saturdays only occasionally. In most firms, employees put in the extra day as a matter of course. Recently, the government had actually recognized the physical and psychological toll of this national workaholism and was encouraging businesses to cut back hours. The necessity of the six-day, sixty-hour week, it argued, was over; the postwar economy had been rebuilt.

The bureau set up to promote this concept was called the Office of Not 21 Working on Saturday. According to the papers, the bureau was not having much success despite a valiant effort. The staff was working day and night, six days a week.

Questions to Start You Thinking

1. Does Katzenstein present his friend Takagi-san as typical of Japanese workers? Explain why or why not.

2. Point out some specific observations Katzenstein uses as evidence in his analysis. What other writer's resources does he use?

3. Define *hierarchy* (paragraph 1), *strictures* (paragraph 2), *grievance* (paragraph 5), *fetish* (paragraph 15), *arbitrary*, and *compulsory* (paragraph 16).

4. Compare the structure of this essay with that of Jessica Mitford's "Behind the Formaldehyde Curtain" (p. 513). How is Katzenstein's subject analysis different from Mitford's process analysis?

Suggestions for Writing

1. Using Katzenstein's essay and your own experience as evidence, write a brief essay comparing and contrasting the expectations placed on Japanese workers with the expectations U.S. industry has of American workers.

2. Write a short personal essay about a time when you were expected to do too much in the workplace, at home, or at school. How did the pressure make you feel? What did you do to lessen the burden of expectations?

MANNING MARABLE, born in 1950 in Dayton, Ohio, earned degrees from Earlham College, the University of Wisconsin, and the University of Maryland and has taught at Tuskegee Institute, Cornell University, Fisk University, and Williams College. He is currently Professor of Political Science and History at the University of Colorado's Center for Studies of Ethnicity and Race in America. Winner of two prizes for his poetry, he focuses on his scholarly writing and in his teaching on the African American experience. His books include *How Capitalism Underdeveloped Black America* (1982), *W. E. B. Du Bois* (1986), and *Race, Reform, and Rebellion: The Second Reconstruction* (second revised edition, 1991). Like many scholars of the post–World War II generation, he has progressed from the ivory tower to open engagement with pressing social issues. In the following essay from his recent work, *The Crisis of Color and Democracy* (1991), he argues that corporate America has a responsibility to address the needs of African Americans.

RACISM AND CORPORATE AMERICA
Manning Marable

For years, Reagan economist Milton Friedman asserted that the 1
free enterprise system is virtually "free" of racism. More recently, black
Reaganites such as Thomas Sowell and Walter Williams have championed
the corporations as being interested in the uplifting and development of
African Americans. But the actual record of the relationship between blacks
and corporate America, particularly in terms of black employment in managerial positions, has been similar to *apartheid* in South Africa.

Before 1965, the white corporate establishment didn't realize that Af- 2
rican Americans even existed. College-trained blacks and middle-class businesspeople were attached to the separate economy of the ghetto. African
Americans who applied for jobs at white-owned companies found that their
resumes weren't accepted. Blacks who were hired were placed in low-paying
clerical or maintenance positions.

With the impact of the civil rights movement, the public demonstrations 3
and boycotts against corporations which Jim Crowed blacks, businesses

were forced to change their hiring policies. However, most blacks were placed in minority neighborhoods, having little contact with whites in supervisory roles. In the 1960s and 1970s, the careers of most black executives were "racialized." They were given responsibilities which focused exclusively on racial matters, rather than the broad issues which affected the profit and loss of the corporation as a whole. They were assigned to mediate black employees' grievances, or to direct affirmative action policies, rather than being placed in charge of a major division of the company. Their managerial experiences were limited, and therefore their prospects for upward mobility into senior executive positions were nonexistent.

In 1977, only 3.6 percent of all managers in the United States were 4 people of color. The *Fortune* magazine survey of the 1,000 largest U.S. companies that year indicated that, out of 1,708 senior executives, there were only three African Americans, two Asians, two hispanics, and eight women.

In the 1980s and 1990s, progress for African Americans inside cor- 5 porations slowed, and in some cases has been reversed. African Americans now represent about 13 percent of the total U.S. population, but less than 5 percent of all managers, and less than 1 percent of all mid-to-upper level executives. Why this pattern of corporate apartheid?

One reason is the racial segregation of U.S. business schools. African 6 Americans represent only 3 to 4 percent of all students in MBA programs. Blacks are less than 2 percent in graduate level programs in the sciences and computer programming. With the Bush administration's threat to eliminate minority scholarships at universities, and a decline in federal enforcement of affirmative action, universities aren't as aggressive in recruiting students of color.

Many heads of major corporations have racial attitudes which are dis- 7 criminatory. But even more pervasive is what I would term the "passive racism" inside the corporate suites. White executives recognize that racism exists within their corporations, but they are unwilling to do anything about it. They refuse to compensate victims of past or current discrimination, or to take positive steps to subsidize development programs within minority communities, such as internships or scholarships.

Black and Hispanic executives usually lack the informal connections 8 most whites take for granted. They usually don't belong to the same social clubs, churches, fraternities or political parties. They aren't mentored for possible openings for career advancement by senior white executives. From their perspective, a "glass ceiling" exists which blocks their mobility.

Unless policies of greater corporate accountability and social respon- 9 sibility are pursued, blacks, Latinos and women will continue to be marginalized inside corporations. Part of this strategy for reform must transcend the request for jobs within the corporate structure. The private sector must be forced to address the basic needs of the black community. This will not occur until the system of corporate capitalism is transformed, and economic decisions are based first upon human needs rather than private profits.

Questions to Start You Thinking

1. What evidence does Marable cite to support his claim that racism exists within American corporations? What does he feel should be done to address the inequalities he discusses?

2. How does Marable use cause and effect to support the stand he takes?

3. Define *free enterprise, apartheid* (paragraph 1), *Jim Crowed* (paragraph 3), and *mentored* (paragraph 8). How would you describe Marable's tone in this selection?

4. Compare this selection with William Raspberry's "The Myth that Is Crippling Black America" (p. 510). What solutions to the problems of economic inequality does each author propose? How do their solutions differ?

Suggestions for Writing

1. Marable suggests that women and minorities are held back in American society by a "glass ceiling" — an invisible barrier that keeps them from advancing. Do you think this is true? Write a brief essay taking a stand on this topic. Use examples from your own experience and knowledge to support your opinion.

2. Identify a social problem that interests or concerns you and write a short essay outlining the problem's causes and effects, taking a stand, and proposing a solution to the problem. Use Marable's essay as a model; be as concise as possible.

ELLEN GOODMAN, born in 1941 in Newton, Massachusetts, is a nationally syndicated columnist writing on current social and political issues, especially as they affect women. Before becoming a columnist at the *Boston Globe,* Goodman worked as a researcher, reporter, and feature writer for *Newsweek,* the *Detroit Free Press,* and the *Globe.* She won a Pulitzer Prize for Commentary in 1980 and was named Columnist of the Year by the New England Women's Press Association in 1975. Her books, collections of her newspaper columns, include *Close to Home* (1979), *Keeping in Touch* (1985), and *Making Sense* (1989). The following article, first published in 1987, reflects Goodman's strong support for affirmative action.

WAS THE WOMAN REALLY LESS QUALIFIED?
Ellen Goodman

By now I am not surprised at any reaction to affirmative action. The issue has been hanging around so long that attitudes have hardened into reflexes.   1

Indeed, last week when the Supreme Court made a definitive — at last, at last — decision upholding a voluntary plan in Santa Clara County, California, that takes gender into account in hiring and promoting, the comments sounded as if they were all pre-scripted.   2

The winner, Diane Joyce, cried out: "A giant victory for womanhood."   3

The loser, Paul Johnson, growled: "Putting it mildly, I think it stinks."

From the left, Judith Lichtman of the Women's Legal Defense Fund 4 volleyed: "Ecstatic."

From the Reagan right, Clarence Thomas of the Equal Employment 5 Opportunity Commission thundered: "Social engineering."

So it wasn't the predictable public noises that struck me this past week. 6 It was, rather, the undertone. I heard the low and lingering rumble of those who believe that affirmative action is a pole used by inferior candidates to jump over their superiors.

In the wake of this decision, almost all of those opposed to affirmative 7 action, and even some who support it, talk as if the court had simply chosen gender over merit. As if they were allowing employers to favor random women or minorities over qualified men and whites.

These are the same perverse or reverse rumblings heard in a thousand 8 offices when someone "new" gets a post from which "their kind" was excluded. At least one disgruntled coworker is sure to suggest that "if Diane Joyce had been Don Joyce, she wouldn't have her promotion today." With this widespread sort of sentiment, it is possible to win the advantages of affirmative action in the courts and lose them in the public consciousness.

But if this case can clear up the fuzzy legal status of plans such as the 9 Santa Clara County one, it can also be used to clarify the whole peculiar matter of "qualifications."

Consider the protagonists, Diane Joyce and Paul Johnson. When the 10 job of road dispatcher came open in 1979, Diane, a 42-year-old widow and Paul, a 54-year-old, were among twelve applicants. Nine of the twelve were considered "qualified." They went before a board and got ranked. Paul tied for second with a 75 and Diane came in right behind with a 73. This is how Paul got the public title of "more qualified."

These very objective, even scientific-sounding numbers were assigned 11 by a very subjective oral interviewing process. In the real world, there is little pure and perfect ranking of qualifications.

Paul and Diane were then given a second interview by three agency 12 supervisors. Who were these arbiters of merit? The same men who had been selecting and promoting the candidates for skilled work at this agency throughout its recent history. Not a one of their 238 skilled workers was female.

Diane, who was also the first woman to be a road maintenance worker, 13 had reportedly had some run-ins with two of the three men. Indeed one is said to have called her "a rabble-rousing, skirt-wearing person," whatever that might mean.

As you might have predicted from this history, the board unanimously 14 chose Paul. So it is not shocking that the county, instead, gave Diane the job. Their affirmative-action plan was made for the Diane Joyces, excellent candidates for jobs in a carefully kept male preserve.

The scales of tradition were balanced against her; the affirmative- 15 action plan did just what it was intended to do, added weight to her side, to open up the door for women.

As the Brennan opinion makes clear, the plan didn't discharge a white   16
male, it didn't set up quotas, and most of all it didn't give preference to
women whose only credential was in their chromosomes. It said, in essence, that a subjective two-point difference between Diane and Paul
wasn't as important as a 238-job difference between men and women.

I think this distinction is important, because there is something insidi-   17
ous about the "qualification" issue. For most of history, the men in power
determined that women were intrinsically disqualified for "men's jobs."
Eventually we labeled that attitude discrimination. But when we implement
plans to open up the work world, many carry along the closed mind.

Women, such as Diane Joyce, who were once barred on account of their   18
sex are now told they were only chosen on account of their sex. Permit me
a groan.

After this decision, Charles Murray, a conservative political scientist,   19
commented that "affirmative action is just leaking a poison into the system." But the poison was already there. It's wearing the same old label:
prejudice.

Questions to Start You Thinking

1. According to Goodman, what is the major misconception shared by almost everyone who opposes affirmative action for women?
2. How does Goodman use the example of the Joyce-Johnson case to support her
   stand? What other methods of development does she use?
3. What are the meanings of *affirmative action* (paragraph 1), *protagonists* (paragraph 10), *arbiters* (paragraph 12), and *intrinsically* (paragraph 17)?
4. In "Year of the Blue-Collar Guy" (p. 521), Steve Olson describes affirmative action
   as "the pat on the back that holds you back" (paragraph 2). How might he and
   Goodman disagree on this issue? Why?

Suggestions for Writing

1. In a short essay, take a stand on affirmative action. Do you think it is necessary?
   Why or why not? In what cases is it helpful, and in what cases is it hurtful? Draw
   on your own experience and knowledge to support your stand.
2. Write a brief personal essay analyzing a situation in which you were the victim
   of a subjective judgment. What happened? Who judged you unfairly, and why?
   What prejudices or preconceptions did the person or persons hold that motivated
   the unfair judgment? What action did you take in response?

MARY KAY BLAKELY was born in Chicago in 1948. She has taught at Purdue
University and the New School for Social Research in New York City. A prolific
freelance writer, she contributes columns to *Vogue, Lear's,* and the *Ladies'*

Home Journal. Blakely is the editor of *Pulling Our Own Strings: A Collection of Feminist Humor* (1980), whose title suggests her gift for using humor to make serious points, as she does in the following piece, first published in the *New York Times* in 1981.

PSYCHIC INCOME
Mary Kay Blakely

I used to be an unbeliever. I questioned the integrity of an economic system that valued women's work only half as much as men's. I was—and this seems almost preposterous to admit now—dissatisfied with the lot of women.

Before I reached enlightenment, I suffered from a common form of math anxiety caused by statistics from the Department of Labor. I was easily susceptible to depression whenever the words "supply and demand" came up in conversation. I kept getting lost in the void of the earnings gap. Years of investigation about women revealed many things to me, but didn't make sense of those numbers: Women earn 59 percent of what men earn. Until last week, I was like a haunted woman—devils of injustice chasing me, demons of inequity plaguing me.

My conversion happened unexpectedly, during a business meeting with a highly placed administrator. I had noticed—because skeptics habitually pay attention to damning facts—that the women employed by his prestigious institution were being paid much less money than the men. Like most unbelievers I was there to complain about the inequity. That's the major problem with those who don't have the gift of faith in our economic system. They have their visions trained on the temporal facts of their lives.

The discussion began predictably enough. With benign paternal tolerance, he reviewed the intricate principles of economics, the baffling nuances of budgets, the confounding factors behind the salary schedules. With the monosyllabic vocabulary educators use to address slow learners, he explained the familiar platitudes.

He invoked the dogma of salary surveys—the objective instruments used to determine what "the market will bear." They prove, beyond a shadow of doubt, that women workers are "a dime a dozen." That's reality, he reported almost regretfully, that's how life is outside of Eden. Practitioners of sound business—the members of the faith, so to speak—can in good conscience pay them no more. If he didn't adhere to the precepts of salary surveys, it would cause economic chaos. Other women, in other institutions, would begin to think they were worth more, too. The brethren in other administrations would expel him from the faith.

"You have to think about what the job is worth, not the person in it," he cautioned me. It always gets you into trouble, thinking about what a person is worth. He warned me against engaging in the fallacy of "comparing apples and oranges," a comparison odious to the members of the faith. It is only the unbelievers, the kumquats, who try to argue for the fruits of their labors. Mixing the categories would produce uncontrollable hybrids on the salary scale. Men are men and women are women and their paychecks are just further evidence of their vast biological differences, the powerful influence of the X and Y chromosomes.

I confess, I had heard these tenets of the faith many times before. It 7 was the kind of conversation that might inspire the vision of a lawsuit. So it wasn't with an open heart that I asked the question one more time. How could he accept women's invaluable contributions to the success of his institution, witness their obvious dedication, and withhold their just rewards?

He paused, regarding me carefully, deliberating, apparently, on 8 whether I was prepared to hear the truth, to embrace the amazing mystery of women's wages. Then slowly, respectfully, he revealed the fantastic reason.

Women came seeking positions with an intense longing for work, but 9 with a paucity of credentials and experience. They were filled with gratitude when they were offered a job. They worked in a pleasant environment, doing meaningful work, and had the privilege of writing the name of the prestigious institution on their résumés. They received such an extraordinary sense of well-being, it would be almost a violation of female sensibilities to compensate them with cold, hard cash. Instead, they received something much more valuable; they earned a "psychic income."

I heard my voice becoming hysterical. Hysteria is not at all uncommon 10 during conversions. I was loud—perhaps I was even shouting—when I asked him how much of his income was "psychic." Like many doubters, I didn't immediately see the light. I thought one of us was mad.

But not an hour later, enlightenment came. I was in a car dealership, 11 chatting with the amiable mechanic who had repaired my transmission. He seemed to enjoy his job, especially when he handed me the bill. I gasped, knowing that the balance in my checkbook wouldn't cover the charge. Then I remembered my "psychic income" and that people who love their work, who are dedicated to it, are better paid with congratulations and a pat on the back. I told him what a wonderful job he did, how much I appreciated it. And then I wrote a "psychic check."

Suddenly, I was filled with the spirit. A happiness, a release flooded 12 over me. I realized that every act of spending my "psychic income" was an act of faith. I had so much catching up to do. I worked steadily to increase my state of grace. Immediately, I applied for a loan at the employee credit union at the prestigious institution, authorizing payments through "psychic payroll deductions." I used my "psychic credit cards" to charge two pairs of spiritual Adidas for my kids, whose real toes were poking through their real tennis shoes.

I was filled with a fervor to spread the Word. At a rally of working women, 13

I brought them the message of "psychic incomes," and many converts came into the fold.

Nurses, who had an extraordinary love for their work, felt "psychic bonuses" coming to them. Their sense of self-esteem expanded miraculously, and they no longer bowed down to the false gods in the hospitals.   14

Clerical workers grasped the theory of "psychic work for psychic pay" and began typing only intangible letters, filing transcendental folders, and making celestial phone calls.   15

Prior to their conversions, working mothers thought they had to do all the housework, because their earnings were only half of their husbands' salaries. But when they learned how to bank on their "psychic incomes," they never cooked dinner again. They served their families supernatural pot roasts.   16

Of course, everyone will not accept the gift of the Word. There are those who will try to persecute us for practicing our faith. We must learn to smile serenely at the unfortunate creditors who lack the vision. We must have a charitable attitude toward the bill collectors whose interests are rooted in temporal assets. Beware of the pharisees who pay spiritual salaries but still demand physical work.   17

And judge not the angry women who file the interminable lawsuits, who still rail against the status quo. Their daily struggle to exist prevents them from accepting the good news. Remember that there, but for the gift of "psychic economics," go we.   18

Questions to Start You Thinking

1. What does Blakely mean by the term "psychic income"? Does Blakely feel that earning a psychic income is enough for women? Why or why not?

2. How does Blakely use imagination as a resource in this essay? What stand does she take and how does her use of imagination help her to support it?

3. Define *preposterous* (paragraph 1), *inequity* (paragraph 2), *temporal* (paragraph 3), *platitudes* (paragraph 4), *dogma* (paragraph 5), *tenets* (paragraph 7), *paucity* (paragraph 9), and *hysteria* (paragraph 10).

4. How is Blakely's view of women's role in corporate America similar to Manning Marable's view of the role of minorities, especially African Americans, in "Racism and Corporate America" (p. 532)? How do the two writers differ in the presentation of their positions?

Suggestions for Writing

1. Mary Kay Blakely shows how "expert opinion" can be used to silence complaints. Write a brief essay describing an occasion when you felt unfairly silenced by an "expert." How did you respond? How might you respond today?

2. Write a satiric essay on an issue that you feel strongly about. Like Blakely, express your opinion by pretending to take the position with which you disagree. Try to support the position you oppose in such an exaggerated, ridiculous way that you make the opposition look foolish.

CHAPTER 25

Popular Culture

URSULA KROEBER LE GUIN was born in 1929 in Berkeley, California, into an astonishingly creative family of writers, scholars, and teachers. She earned degrees at Radcliffe College and Columbia University and has taught and been writer-in-residence at schools including UCLA, Kenyon College, and Tulane University. She has won many awards for her science fiction, notably *The Left Hand of Darkness* (1969), *The Lathe of Heaven* (1975), and the *EarthSea* trilogy (completed in 1990). In the following essay, which first appeared in *The Language of the Night: Essays of Fantasy and Fiction* (1975), Le Guin examines the portrayal of the "Other" or alien in science fiction writing in light of broader social issues.

AMERICAN SF AND THE OTHER
Ursula K. Le Guin

One of the great early socialists said that the status of women in a society is a pretty reliable index of the degree of civilization of that society. If this is true, then the very low status of women in SF should make us ponder about whether SF is civilized at all. 1

The women's movement has made most of us conscious of the fact that SF has either totally ignored women, or presented them as squeaking 2 dolls subject to instant rape by monsters — or old-maid scientists desexed by hypertrophy of the intellectual organs — or, at best, loyal little wives or mistresses of accomplished heroes. Male elitism has run rampant in SF. But is it only male elitism? Isn't the "subjection of women" in SF merely a symptom of a whole which is authoritarian, power-worshiping, and intensely parochial?

The question involved here is the question of The Other — the being who 3
is different from yourself. This being can be different from you in its sex; or in its annual income; or in its way of speaking and dressing and doing things; or in the color of its skin, or the number of its legs and heads. In other words, there is the sexual Alien, and the social Alien, and the cultural Alien, and finally the racial Alien.

Well, how about the social Alien in SF? How about, in Marxist terms, 4
"the proletariat"? Where are they in SF? Where are the poor, the people who work hard and go to bed hungry? Are they ever *persons*, in SF? No. They appear as vast anonymous masses fleeing from giant slime-globules from the Chicago sewers, or dying off by the billion from pollution or radiation, or as faceless armies being led to battle by generals and statesmen. In sword and sorcery they behave like the walk-on parts in a high school performance of *The Chocolate Prince*. Now and then there's a busty lass amongst them who is honored by the attentions of the Captain of the Supreme Terran Command, or in a spaceship crew there's a quaint old cook, with a Scots or Swedish accent, representing the Wisdom of the Common Folk.

The people, in SF, are not people. They are masses, existing for one 5
purpose: to be led by their superiors.

From a social point of view most SF has been incredibly regressive and 6
unimaginative. All those Galactic Empires, taken straight from the British Empire of 1880. All those planets — with 80 trillion miles between them! — conceived of as warring nation-states, or as colonies to be exploited, or to be nudged by the benevolent Imperium of Earth toward self-development — the White Man's Burden all over again. The Rotary Club on Alpha Centauri, that's the size of it.

What about the cultural and the racial Other? This is the Alien everybody 7
recognizes as alien, supposed to be the special concern of SF. Well, in the old pulp SF, it's very simple. The only good alien is a dead alien — whether he is an Aldebaranian Mantis-Man, or a German dentist. And this tradition still flourishes: witness Larry Niven's story "Inconstant Moon" (in *All the Myriad Ways*, 1971) which has a happy ending — consisting of the fact that America, including Los Angeles, was not hurt by a solar flare. Of course a few million Europeans and Asians were fried, but that doesn't matter, it just makes the world a little safer for democracy, in fact. (It is interesting that the female character in the same story is quite brainless; her only function is to say Oh? and Ooooh! to the clever and resourceful hero.)

Then there's the other side of the same coin. If you hold a thing to be 8
totally different from yourself, your fear of it may come out as hatred, or

as awe—reverence. So we get all those wise and kindly beings who deign to rescue Earth from her sins and perils. The Alien ends up on a pedestal in a white nightgown and a virtuous smirk—exactly as the "good woman" did in the Victorian Age.

In America, it seems to have been Stanley Weinbaum who invented the 9 sympathetic alien, in *A Martian Odyssey*. From then on, via people like Cyril Kornbluth, Ted Sturgeon, and Cordwainer Smith, SF began to inch its way out of simple racism. Robots—the alien intelligence—begin to behave nicely. With Smith, interestingly enough, the racial alien is combined with the social alien, in the "Underpeople," and they are allowed to have a revolution. As the aliens got more sympathetic, so did the heroes. They began to have emotions, as well as rayguns. Indeed they began to become almost human.

If you deny any affinity with another person or kind of person, if you 10 declare it to be wholly different from yourself—as men have done to women, and class has done to class, and nation has done to nation—you may hate it, or deify it; but in either case you have denied its spiritual equality, and its human reality. You have made it into a thing, to which the only possible relationship is a power relationship. And thus you have fatally impoverished your own reality. You have, in fact, alienated yourself.

This tendency has been remarkably strong in American SF. The only 11 social change presented by most SF has been toward authoritarianism, the domination of ignorant masses by a powerful elite—sometimes presented as a warning, but often quite complacently. Socialism is never considered as an alternative, and democracy is quite forgotten. Military virtues are taken as ethical ones. Wealth is assumed to be a righteous goal and a personal virtue. Competitive free enterprise capitalism is the economic destiny of the entire Galaxy. In general, American SF has assumed a permanent hierarchy of superiors and inferiors with rich, ambitious, aggressive males at the top, then a great gap, and then at the bottom the poor, the uneducated, the faceless masses, and all the women. The whole picture is, if I may say so, curiously "un-American." It is a perfect baboon patriarchy, with the Alpha Male on top, being respectfully groomed, from time to time, by his inferiors.

Is this speculation? Is this imagination? Is this extrapolation? I call it 12 brainless regressivism.

I think it's time SF writers—and their readers!—stopped daydreaming 13 about a return to the age of Queen Victoria, and started thinking about the future. I would like to see the Baboon Ideal replaced by a little human idealism, and some serious consideration of such deeply radical, futuristic concepts as Liberty, Equality, and Fraternity. And remember that about 53 percent of the Brotherhood of Man is the Sisterhood of Woman.

Questions to Start You Thinking

1. What is Le Guin's chief complaint with American science fiction? How does she define "The Other" in this essay?

2. How does Le Guin use the resource of evaluation? Also identify the stand she takes and explain how she supports her argument.

3. Define *hypertrophy, elitism, parochial* (paragraph 2), *regressive, Imperium, White Man's Burden* (paragraph 6), and *affinity* (paragraph 10). How do such words help reveal Le Guin's tone?

4. Would Le Guin agree with Barbara Ehrenreich in "The Wretched of the Hearth" (p. 543) that working-class culture is "the neglected underside of the eighties" (paragraph 3)? How do their presentations of the problems of the working class differ?

Suggestions for Writing

1. Using Le Guin's ideas as a springboard, write an essay analyzing the presentation of the "Other" in movies or television today. You may choose to discuss any of the types of "Other" Le Guin outlines: "the sexual Alien, and the social Alien, and the cultural Alien, and finally the racial Alien" (paragraph 3). How does our media depict the "Other"?

2. Briefly retell a fairy tale or other well-known story from the point of view of the "Other." You might want to retell "Little Red Riding Hood" from the wolf's viewpoint; "Cinderella" from the stepsisters' side; "Batman" from the Joker's perspective; or any story that strikes you as being one-sided. How might the "Other" feel that he or she has been portrayed unfairly?

BARBARA EHRENREICH was born in Butte, Montana, in 1941, and studied at Reed College and Rockefeller University. Cochair of Democratic Socialists of America, Ehrenreich is a columnist for *Ms.* and *Mother Jones* magazines, and her books include *The American Health Empire: Power, Profits, and Politics* (1970), and *The Worst Years of Our Lives: Irreverent Notes from a Decade of Greed* (1990). The following article, from the *New Republic* of April 1990, views the condition of women from the dual perspectives of gender and class, exemplified in the nineties feminist and pop icon Roseanne Arnold.

THE WRETCHED OF THE HEARTH
Barbara Ehrenreich

In the second half of the eighties, when American conservatism had 1 reached its masochistic zenith with the reelection of Ronald Reagan, when women's liberation had been replaced by the more delicate sensibility known as post-feminism, when everyone was a yuppie and the heartiest word of endorsement in our vocabulary was "appropriate," there was yet this one paradox: our favorite TV personages were a liberal black man and a left-wing feminist. Cosby could be explained as a representative of America's officially profamily mood, but Roseanne is a trickier case. Her idea of humor is to look down on her sleeping family in the eponymous sitcom and muse, "Mmmm, I wonder where we could find an all-night taxidermist."

If zeitgeist were destiny, Roseanne would never have happened. Only a few years ago, we learn from her autobiography, Roseanne Barr° was just your run-of-the-mill radical feminist mother-of-three, writing poems involving the Great Goddess, denouncing all known feminist leaders as sellout trash, and praying for the sixties to be born again in a female body. Since the entertainment media do not normally cast about for fat, loudmouthed feminists to promote to superstardom, we must assume that Roseanne has something to say that many millions of people have been waiting to hear. Like this, upon being told of a woman who stabbed her husband thirty-seven times: "I admire her restraint."

Roseanne is the neglected underside of the eighties, bringing together its great themes of poverty, obesity, and defiance. The overside is handled well enough by Candice Bergen (*Murphy Brown*) and Madonna, who exist to remind us that talented women who work out are bound to become fabulously successful. Roseanne works a whole different beat, both in her sitcom and in the movie *She-Devil*, portraying the hopeless underclass of the female sex: polyester-clad, overweight occupants of the slow track; fast-food waitresses, factory workers, housewives, members of the invisible pink-collar army; the despised, the jilted, the underpaid.

But Barr — and this may be her most appealing feature — is never a victim. In the sitcom, she is an overworked mother who is tormented by her bosses at such locales as Wellman Plastics (where she works the assembly line) and Chicken Divine (a fast-food spot). But Roseanne Connor, her sitcom character, has, as we say in the blue-collar suburbs, a mouth on her. When the cute but obnoxious boss at Wellman calls the workers together and announces, "I have something to tell you," Roseanne yells out, "What? That you feel you're a woman trapped in a man's body?" In *She-Devil*, where Barr is unfortunately shorn of her trademark deadpan snarl, revenge must take more concrete forms: she organizes an army of the wretched of the earth — nursing home patients and clerical workers — to destroy her errant husband and drive the slender, beautiful, rich-and-famous Other Woman dotty.

At some point the women's studies profession is bound to look up from its deconstructions and "rethinkings" and notice Roseanne. They will then observe, in article and lecture form, that Barr's radicalism is distributed over the two axes of gender and class. This is probably as good an approach as any. Barr's identity is first of all female — her autobiography is titled *My Life as a Woman* — but her female struggles are located in the least telegenic and most frequently overlooked of social strata — the white, blue-collar working class. In anticipation of Roseannology, let us begin with Barr's contribution to the sociology of social class, and then take up her impressive achievements in the area of what could be called feminist theory.

Roseanne Barr. Now Roseanne Arnold.

Roseanne the sitcom, which was inspired by Barr the stand-up comic, is a radical departure simply for featuring blue-collar Americans — and for depicting them as something other than half-witted greasers and low-life louts. The working class does not usually get much of a role in the American entertainment spectacle. In the seventies mumbling, muscular blue-collar males (*Rocky, The Deer Hunter, Saturday Night Fever*) enjoyed a brief mod-ishness on the screen, while Archie Bunker, the consummate blue-collar bigot, raved away on the tube. But even these grossly stereotyped images vanished in the eighties, as the spectacle narrowed in on the brie-and-chardonnay class. Other than *Roseanne,* I can find only one sitcom that deals consistently with the sub-yuppie condition: *Married . . . with Children*, a relentlessly nasty portrayal of a shoe salesman and his cognitively disabled family members. There may even be others, but sociological zeal has not sufficed to get me past the opening sequences of *Major Dad, Full House,* or *Doogie Howser.*

Not that *Roseanne* is free of class stereotyping. The Connors must bear part of the psychic burden imposed on all working-class people by their economic and occupational betters: they inhabit a zone of glad-handed gemeinschaft,° evocative, now and then, of the stock wedding scene (*The Godfather, The Deer Hunter, Working Girl*) that routinely signifies lost old-world values. They indulge in a manic physicality that would be unthinkable among the more controlled and genteel Huxtables. They maintain a tradi-tional, low-fiber diet of white bread and macaroni. They are not above a fart joke.

Still, in *Roseanne* I am willing to forgive the stereotypes as markers designed to remind us of where we are: in the home of a construction worker and his minimum-wage wife. Without the reminders, we might not be aware of how thoroughly the deeper prejudices of the professional class are being challenged. Roseanne's fictional husband, Dan (played by the irresistibly cuddly John Goodman), drinks domestic beer and dedicates Sundays to football; but far from being a Bunkeresque boor, he looks to this feminist like the fabled "sensitive man" we have all been pining for. He treats his rotund wife like a sex goddess. He picks up on small cues signaling emo-tional distress. He helps with homework. And when Roseanne works over-time, he cooks, cleans, and rides herd on the kids without any of the piteous whining we have come to expect from upscale males in their rare, and lavishly documented, encounters with soiled Pampers.

Roseanne Connor has her own way of defying the stereotypes. Variously employed as a fast-food operative, a factory worker, a bartender, and a telephone salesperson, her real dream is to be a writer. When her twelve-year-old daughter Darlene (brilliantly played by Sara Gilbert) balks at a poetry-writing assignment, Roseanne gives her a little talking-to involving Sylvia Plath: "She inspired quite a few women, including *moi.*" In another episode, a middle-aged friend thanks Roseanne for inspiring her to dump her chauvinist husband and go to college. We have come a long way from the dithering, cowering Edith Bunker.

gemeinschaft. German for "community."

Most of the time the Connors do the usual sitcom things. They have   10
the little domestic misunderstandings that can be patched up in twenty-
four minutes with wisecracks and a round of hugs. But *Roseanne* carries
working-class verisimilitude into a new and previously taboo dimension—
the workplace. In the world of employment, Roseanne knows exactly where
she stands: "All the good power jobs are taken. Vanna turns the letters.
Leona's got hotels. Margaret's running England . . . 'Course she's not doing
a very good job. . . ."

And in the workplace as well as the kitchen, Roseanne knows how to   11
dish it out. A friend of mine, herself a denizen of the low-wage end of the
work force, claims to have seen an episode in which Roseanne led an
occupational health and safety battle at Wellman Plastics. I missed that
one, but I have seen her, on more than one occasion, reduce the boss's
ego to rubble. At Chicken Divine, for example, she is ordered to work weekends—an impossibility for a working mother—by an officious teenage boss
who confides that he doesn't like working weekends either. In a sequence
that could have been crafted by Michael Moore, Roseanne responds: "Well,
that's real good 'cause you never do. You sit in your office like a little
Napoleon, making up schedules and screwing up people's lives." To which
he says, "That's what they pay me for. And you are paid to follow my orders."
Blah blah blah. To which she says, staring at him for a long time and then
observing with an evil smile: "You know, you got a little prize hanging out
of your nose there."

The class conflict continues on other fronts. In one episode, Roseanne   12
arrives late for an appointment with Darlene's history teacher, because she
has been forced to work overtime at Wellman. The teacher, who is leaning
against her desk stretching her quadriceps when Roseanne arrives, wants
to postpone the appointment because she has a date to play squash. When
Roseanne insists, the teacher tells her that Darlene has been barking in
class, "like a dog." This she follows with some psychobabble—on emotional problems and dysfunctional families—that would leave most mothers, whatever their social class, clutched with guilt. Not Roseanne, who
calmly informs the yuppie snit that, in the Connor household, everybody
barks like dogs.

Now this is the kind of class-militant populism that the Democrats,   13
most of them anyway, never seem to get right: up with the little gal; down
with the snotty, the pretentious, and the overly paid. At least part of the
appeal of *Roseanne* is that it ratifies the resentments of the underdog
majority. But this being a sitcom, and Barr being a pacifist, the class-anger
never gets too nasty. Even the most loathsome bosses turn out to be human, and in some cases pathetically needy. Rather than hating the bad
guys, we end up feeling better about ourselves, which is the function of all
good and humanistic humor anyway.

According to high conservative theory, the leftist cast to a show like   14
Roseanne must reflect the media manipulations of the alleged "liberal
elite." But the politics of *Roseanne*—including its feminist side, which we

will get to in a minute—reflects nothing so much as the decidedly unelite politics of Barr herself. On the Larry King show a few weeks ago, Barr said that she prefers the term "working class" to "blue collar" because (and I paraphrase) it reminds us of the existence of class, a reality that Americans are all too disposed to forget. In her autobiography, right up front in the preface, she tells us that it is a "book about the women's movement . . . a book about the left."

Roseanne: My Life As a Woman traces her journey from alienation to 15 political commitment. It must stand as another one of Barr's commanding oddities. Where you would expect a standard rags-to-riches story, you find a sort of rags-to-revolution tale: more an intellectual and spiritual memoir than the usual chronicle of fearsome obstacles and lucky breaks. She was born the paradigmatic outsider, a Jew in Mormon Utah, and a low-income Jew at that. Within the Mormon culture, she was the "Other" (her own term), the "designated Heathen" in school Christmas pageants, always being reminded that "had we been in a Communist country, I would never have been allowed to express my religion, because 'dissent' is not tolerated there." At home she was loved and encouraged, but the emotional density of the Holocaust-haunted Barr family eventually proved too much for her. After a breakdown and several months of hospitalization, she ran away, at nineteen, to find the sixties, or what was left of them in 1971.

Her hippie phase left Barr with some proto-politics of the peace-and- 16 love variety, three children, and an erratic wage-earner for a husband. It was in this condition that she wandered into the Woman to Woman bookstore on Colfax Avenue in Denver, where she discovered the Movement. Barr seems to have required very little in the way of consciousness-raising. With one gigantic "click," she jumped right in, joined the collective, and was soon occupied giving "seminars on racism, classism, anti-Semitism, pornography, and taking power." If this seems like a rather sudden leap to political leadership, I can attest from my own experience with venues like Woman to Woman that it happens every day.

But even within the ecumenical embrace of feminism, Barr remained 17 the Outsider. "We did not agree anymore," she tells us of her collective, "with Betty Friedan, Gloria Steinem, or party politics within the women's movement," which she believes has turned into "a professional, careerist women's thing." When she found her "voice," it spoke in a new tone of working-class existentialism: "I began to speak as a working-class woman who is a mother, a woman who no longer believed in change, progress, growth, or hope." It was this special brand of proletarian feminism that inspired her stand-up comic routine. "I am talking about organizing working-class women and mothers," she tells us, and her comic persona was her way of going about it.

Middle-class feminism has long admitted the possibility of a working- 18 class variant, but the general expectation has been that it would be a diluted version of the "real," or middle-class, thing. According to the conventional wisdom, working-class women would have no truck with the more antimale aspects of feminism, and would be repelled by the least insult to the nuclear family. They would be comfortable only with the bread-and-butter issues of pay equity, child care, and parental leave. They would be culturally conservative, sensible, dull.

But we had not met Barr. Her stand-up routine was at first almost too vulgar and castrating for Denver's Comedy Works. In her autobiography, Barr offers an example. Heckled by a drunk for not being "feminine," she turned around, stared at her assailant, and said, "Suck my dick." I wish *Roseanne: My Life As a Woman* gave more examples of her early, Denver-era, stand-up style, but the recently released videotape *Roseanne* (made later in a Los Angeles club) may be a fair representation. On it she promotes a product called "Fem-Rage," designed to overcome female conditioning during that "one day of the month when you're free to be yourself," and leaves her female fans with the memorable question: "Ever put those maxi-pads on adhesive side up?" 19

In *Roseanne*, the sitcom, however, Barr has been considerably tamed. No longer standing bravely, and one must admit massively, alone with the microphone, she comes to us now embedded in the family: overwhelmed by domestic detail, surrounded by children too young for R-rated language, padding back and forth between stove, refrigerator, and kitchen table. Some of the edge is off here. There are no four-letter words, no menstruation jokes; and Roseanne's male-baiting barbs just bounce off her lovable Dan. Still, what better place for the feminist comic than in a family sitcom? Feminist theory, after all, cut its teeth on the critique of the family. Barr continues the process — leaving huge gaping holes where there was sweetness and piety. 20

All family sitcoms, of course, teach us that wisecracks and swift put-downs are the preferred modes of affectionate discourse. But Roseanne takes the genre a step further — over the edge, some may say. In the era of big weddings and sudden man shortages, she describes marriage as "a life sentence, without parole." And in the era of the biological time clock and the petted yuppie midlife baby, she can tell Darlene to get a fork out of the drawer and "stick it through your tongue." Or she can say, when Dan asks, "Are we missing an offspring?" at breakfast, "Yeah. Where do you think I got the bacon?" 21

It is Barr's narrow-eyed cynicism about the family, even more than her class consciousness, that gives *Roseanne* its special frisson. Archie Bunker got our attention by telling us that we (blacks, Jews, "ethnics," WASPS, etc.) don't really like each other. Barr's message is that even within the family we don't much like each other. We love each other (who else do we have?); but The Family, with its impacted emotions, its lopsided division of labor, and its ancient system of age-graded humiliations, just doesn't work. Or rather, it doesn't work unless the contradictions are smoothed out with irony and the hostilities are periodically blown off as humor. Coming from Mom, 22 rather than from a jaded teenager or a bystander dad, this is scary news indeed.

So Barr's theoretical outlook is, in the best left-feminist tradition, dialectical. On the one hand, she presents the family as a zone of intimacy and support, well worth defending against the forces of capitalism, which drive both mothers and fathers out of the home, scratching around for paychecks. On the other hand, the family is hardly a haven, especially for its grown-up females. It is marred from within by—among other things—the patriarchal division of leisure, which makes Dad and the kids the "consumers" of Mom's cooking, cleaning, nurturing, and (increasingly) her earnings. Mom's job is to keep the whole thing together—to see that the mortgage payments are made, to fend off the viperish teenagers, to find the missing green sock—but Mom is no longer interested in being a human sacrifice on the altar of "profamily values." She's been down to the feminist bookstore; she's been reading Sylvia Plath. 23

This is a bleak and radical vision. Not given to didacticism, Barr offers no programmatic ways out. Surely, we are led to conclude, pay equity would help, along with child care, and so on. But Barr leaves us hankering for a quality of change that goes beyond mere reform: for a world in which even the lowliest among us—the hash-slinger, the sock-finder, the factory hand—will be recognized as the poet she truly is. 24

Maybe this is just too radical. The tabloids have taken to stalking Barr as if she were an unsightly blot on the electronic landscape of our collective dreams. The *New York Times* just devoted a quarter of a page to some upscale writer's prissy musings on Roseanne. "Was I just being squeamish" for disliking Barr, she asks herself: "a goody-two-shoes suburban feminist who was used to her icons being chic and sugar-coated instead of this gum-chewing, male-bashing . . . working-class mama with a big mouth?" No, apparently she is not squeamish. Barr is just too, well, unfeminine. 25

We know what Barr would say to that, and exactly how she would say it. Yeah, she's crude, but so are the realities of pain and exploitation she seeks to remind us of. If middle-class feminism can't claim Roseanne, maybe it's gotten a little too dainty for its own good. We have a long tradition of tough-talking females behind us, after all, including that other great working-class spokesperson, Mary "Mother" Jones, who once advised the troops, "Whatever you do, *don't* be ladylike." 26

Questions to Start You Thinking

1. According to Ehrenreich, what is the political message of Roseanne Arnold's comedy?

2. How does Ehrenreich support her evaluation of Arnold's politics with examples from Arnold's work?

3. Is Ehrenreich's vocabulary different from Arnold's? Why might that be? Define *masochistic, zenith, eponymous* (paragraph 1), *zeitgeist* (paragraph 2), *telegenic*

(paragraph 5), *populism* (paragraph 13), *paradigmatic* (paragraph 15), *proletarian* (paragraph 17), and *dialectical* (paragraph 23).

4. How is Arnold's comic exaggeration of working-class and female stereotypes like the exaggeration of African American stereotypes that Henry Louis Gates, Jr., analyzes in "2 Live Crew, Decoded" (p. 558)?

Suggestions for Writing

1. Ehrenreich says that "Candice Bergen . . . and Madonna . . . exist to remind us that talented women who work out are bound to become fabulously successful" (paragraph 3). How accurate is this assessment? Write a brief essay analyzing some media images of successful women. What qualities do these images share? How does the media define women's success? How realistic are these images?

2. Throughout this selection, Ehrenreich talks about stereotypes of "the white, blue-collar working class" (paragraph 5). In a short essay, describe these stereotypes as you have seen them in the media and in society at large. Are these stereotypes destructive?

JACK SHAHEEN was born in Pittsburgh in 1935, the son of Lebanese immigrants. He earned degrees from Carnegie Tech, Penn State, and the University of Missouri. Since 1969 he has taught mass communications at Southern Illinois University and has worked as a freelance reporter and critic. His writing often draws together his concerns as an Arab American and his professional training, as do his books *The TV Arab* (1984) and *The Hollywood Arab* (1990), which trace negative stereotyping in the media. That also is Shaheen's focus in the following selection, published in *Newsweek* on February 29, 1988.

THE MEDIA'S IMAGE OF ARABS
Jack G. Shaheen

America's bogyman is the Arab. Until the nightly news brought us TV   1
pictures of Palestinian boys being punched and beaten, almost all portraits of Arabs seen in America were dangerously threatening. Arabs were either billionaires or bombers—rarely victims. They were hardly ever seen as ordinary people practicing law, driving taxis, singing lullabies or healing the sick. Though TV news may portray them more sympathetically now, the absence of positive media images nurtures suspicion and stereotype. As an Arab-American, I have found that ugly caricatures have had an enduring impact on my family.

I was sheltered from prejudicial portraits at first. My parents came from   2
Lebanon in the 1920s; they met and married in America. Our home in the steel city of Clairton, Pa., was a center for ethnic sharing—black, white,

Jew and gentile. There was only one major source of media images then, at the State movie theater where I was lucky enough to get a part-time job as an usher. But in the late 1940s, Westerns and war movies were popular, not Middle Eastern dramas. Memories of World War II were fresh, and the screen heavies were the Japanese and the Germans. True to the cliché of the times, the only good Indian was a dead Indian. But when I mimicked or mocked the bad guys, my mother cautioned me. She explained that stereotypes blur our vision and corrupt the imagination. "Have compassion for all people, Jackie," she said. "This way, you'll learn to experience the joy of accepting people as they are, and not as they appear in films. Stereotypes hurt."

Mother was right. I can remember the Saturday afternoon when my son, 3
Michael, who was seven, and my daughter, Michele, six, suddenly called out: "Daddy, Daddy, they've got some bad Arabs on TV." They were watching that great American morality play, TV wrestling. Akbar the Great, who liked to hear the cracking of bones, and Abdullah the Butcher, a dirty fighter who liked to inflict pain, were pinning their foes with "camel locks." From that day on, I knew I had to try to neutralize the media caricatures.

It hasn't been easy. With my children, I have watched animated heroes 4
Heckle and Jeckle pull the rug from under "Ali Boo-Boo, the Desert Rat," and Laverne and Shirley stop "Sheik Ha-Mean-Ie" from conquering "the U.S. and the world." I have read comic books like the "Fantastic Four" and "G.I. Combat" whose characters have sketched Arabs as "lowlifes" and "human hyenas." Negative stereotypes were everywhere. A dictionary informed my youngsters that an Arab is a "vagabond, drifter, hobo and vagrant." Whatever happened, my wife wondered, to Aladdin's good genie?

To a child, the world is simple: good versus evil. But my children and 5
others with Arab roots grew up without ever having seen a humane Arab on the silver screen, someone to pattern their lives after. Is it easier for a camel to go through the eye of a needle than for a screen Arab to appear as a genuine human being?

Hollywood producers must have an instant Ali Baba kit that contains 6
scimitars, veils, sunglasses and such Arab clothing as *chadors* and *kufiyahs.* In the mythical "Ay-rabland," oil wells, tents, mosques, goats and shepherds prevail. Between the sand dunes, the camera focuses on a mock-up of a palace from "Arabian Nights"—or a military air base. Recent movies suggest that Americans are at war with Arabs, forgetting the fact that out of twenty-one Arab nations, America is friendly with nineteen of them. And in "Wanted Dead or Alive," a movie that starred Gene Simmons, the leader of the rock group Kiss, the war comes home when an Arab terrorist comes to the United States dressed as a rabbi and, among other things, conspires with Arab-Americans to poison the people of Los Angeles. The movie was released last year.

The Arab remains American culture's favorite whipping boy. In his mem- 7
oirs, Terrel Bell, Ronald Reagan's first secretary of education, writes about an "apparent bias among mid-level, right-wing staffers at the White House"

who dismissed Arabs as "sand niggers." Sadly, the racial slurs continue. At a recent teacher's conference, I met a woman from Sioux Falls, S.D., who told me about the persistence of discrimination. She was in the process of adopting a baby when an agency staffer warned her that the infant had a problem. When she asked whether the child was mentally ill, or physically handicapped, there was silence. Finally, the worker said: "The baby is Jordanian."

To me, the Arab demon of today is much like the Jewish demon of yesterday. We deplore the false portrait of Jews as a swarthy menace. Yet a similar portrait has been accepted and transferred to another group of Semites — the Arabs. Print and broadcast journalists have started to challenge this stereotype. They are now revealing more humane images of Palestinian Arabs, a people who traditionally suffered from the myth that Palestinian equals terrorist. Others could follow that lead and retire the stereotypical Arab to a media Valhalla. 8

It would be a step in the right direction if movie and TV producers developed characters modeled after real-life Arab-Americans. We could then see a White House correspondent like Helen Thomas, whose father came from Lebanon, in "The Golden Girls," a heart surgeon patterned after Dr. Michael DeBakey on "St. Elsewhere," or a Syrian-American playing tournament chess like Yasser Seirawan, the Seattle grandmaster. 9

Politicians, too should speak out against the cardboard caricatures. They should refer to Arabs as friends, not just as moderates. And religious leaders could state that Islam like Christianity and Judaism maintains that all mankind is one family in the care of God. When all imagemakers rightfully begin to treat Arabs and all other minorities with respect and dignity, we may begin to unlearn our prejudices. 10

Questions to Start You Thinking

1. How does Shaheen describe the American media's portrayal of Arabs? How accurate does he think this portrayal is?

2. How does Shaheen use recall and evaluation to support the stand he takes in this essay?

3. Define *bogyman, caricatures* (paragraph 1), *scimitars, chadors, kufiyahs* (paragraph 6), *whipping boy* (paragraph 7), and *Valhalla* (paragraph 8). Look up the definition of *Semites* (paragraph 8). What do we usually mean by the word "anti-Semitism?" How might the prejudice against Arabs that Shaheen describes be thought of as a new kind of "anti-Semitism"?

4. Does Shaheen's essay concern the same kind of stereotyping that Ursula K. Le Guin describes in "American SF and The Other" (p. 540)? Why or why not?

Suggestions for Writing

1. In a brief essay, discuss your own encounters with media stereotypes of Arabs and Arab Americans or of other ethnic groups.

2. Shaheen proposes that the media present positive "characters modeled after real-

life Arab-Americans" (paragraph 9). Select another group that might benefit from better media role models, and write a brief essay creating some positive characters from that group who might be included in television shows or films. (For example, an African American general, like General Colin Powell, could appear on *Major Dad*, or an Asian American designer could be a character on *Designing Women*.)

ROBERT PALMER, born in 1945 in Little Rock, Arkansas, is a professional jazz and rock musician and an award-winning author of five books on popular music, including *Deep Blues* (1981). A former music critic for the *New York Times*, he is a frequent contributor to *Rolling Stone* and other publications. Among Palmer's main interests has been tracing the changes in African music as it developed in the United States, influencing every form of music from symphonies to rock-'n'-roll. The following essay appeared in a slightly different form in the *New York Times* of February 24, 1985, and in it Palmer examines evidence that rock lyrics are a primary barometer of larger changes in society.

WHAT POP LYRICS SAY TO US TODAY
Robert Palmer

Bruce Springsteen became the first rock lyricist to be courted by both 1
of the major candidates in a presidential election last fall.° First Ronald Reagan singled him out as an artist whose songs instill pride in America. Walter Mondale retaliated, asserting that *he* had won the rock star's endorsement. "Bruce may have been born to run," Mr. Mondale quipped, quoting the title of a Springsteen hit, "but he wasn't born yesterday."

Rock is part of adult culture now, to an extent that would have been 2
unthinkable as recently as a decade ago. It is no longer the exclusive reserve of young people sending messages to each other. But pop music has always reflected and responded to the currents of its own time, and today's pop music is no exception. What does it seem to be telling us about our own time? Part of the message is in the music itself—in the insistence of the beat, the shriek of heavily amplified guitars. But lyrics remain the most accurate barometer of what makes *these* times different from, for example, the 1960s and 70s.

Today's pop music is sending several dominant messages. Material 3
values are on the ascendant, but idealism is by no means a spent force. Most pop songs are love songs, as always, but today's versions try to look

presidential . . . fall. The 1984 presidential election.

at relationships without rose-colored glasses. Romantic notions are viewed with some suspicion; so are drugs. And important rock artists and rappers, while no longer anticipating radical change, are addressing issues, and challenging their listeners to actively confront the world around them. There have probably been more angry protest lyrics written and recorded in the last three or four years than in any comparable period of the 60s.

In the 60s, it would have been unthinkable for a politician to seek   4
endorsements from rock musicians; rock was rebel music. Stars like Bob Dylan and the Rolling Stones wrote and recorded outspoken lyrics that urged sweeping social change and an end to war and flirted with the rhetoric of revolution. They sang openly about sex and drugs. The music was the voice of a new generation and a constant reminder of the generation gap. The battle lines were drawn.

The rock lyricists of the 60s were fond of talking about "love." To the   5
Beatles, "love" was transcendent, an irresistible force for good that could accomplish practically anything. [As they put it in one song, "All You Need Is Love."]°

Love is still something one hears a great deal about in pop lyrics, but   6
the contemporary version is more hard-headed and down-to-earth than the cosmic, effulgent Love of the 60s. Many of today's songwriters argue that romance isn't as important as material values or sex. "What's love got to do with it?" Tina Turner asked in her recent heavy-breathing hit of the same title. And Madonna, whose come-hither pout and undulating style have made her pop's hottest video star, serves notice in her hit "Material Girl" (written by Peter Brown and Robert Rans) that she won't worry much about love as long as there's money in the bank.

Madonna's carefully calculated image has struck a chord among many   7
of today's more affluent young listeners, though she is perhaps too one-dimensional to be Queen of the Yuppies. And she will never be the darling of the feminists.

Nevertheless, during the past decade, the hue and cry against rock   8
lyrics that demeaned women seemed to have a broad and salutary effect. One didn't hear many songs of the sort the Rolling Stones and other 60s bands used to perform, songs like the Stones' "Under My Thumb," [in which Mick Jagger brags that his woman has learned to say what he wants when she's spoken to.]

The title tune from Mick Jagger's new solo album, "She's the Boss," is   9
sung like a taunt or a tease, but that doesn't disguise its message; Mr. Jagger seems to have experienced a shift in values since he wrote "Under My Thumb."

> She's the boss! She's the boss!
> She's the boss in bed, she's the boss in my head
> She's got the pants on, now she's the boss.

The use of brackets indicates material that has been slightly revised by the author since this piece first appeared in the *New York Times*.

Still, many of today's pop lyrics continue to celebrate male dominance. 10
[Aggressively macho hard rock tends to treat women as either temptresses
or chattel, although a number of hard rock and heavy metal bands demonstrate a clear awareness of issues of sexual and social equality.]

Amid these changes in attitude, the old-fashioned romantic love song, 11
always the staple of pop lyrics, continues to flourish. Prince, another of
today's biggest-selling artists, has progressed from early songs that dealt
explicitly with various sexual situations and permutations to love lyrics of
a more conventional sort. [In] "Take Me With U" (sic), a song from his
phenomenally successful album "Purple Rain," [he tells a "pretty baby" that
she can go anywhere or do anything, if only she takes him with her. Such
sentiments] could have been written decades ago or yesterday.

Pop songs can do more than chart changing attitudes toward love and 12
romance; they can address topical issues and appeal to our social conscience. In the 60s, Bob Dylan and other songwriters composed anthems
that were sung by civil rights workers as they headed south, and by
hundreds of thousands demonstrating for peace and equal rights. "How
many deaths will it take till we know that too many people have died," Dylan
asked. "The answer, my friend, is blowin' in the wind." And, he added, in
a line in another song that provided a name for the radical faction within
Students for a Democratic Society, "You don't need a weatherman to tell
which way the wind blows."

By the late 60s, the peace and civil rights movements were beginning 13
to splinter. The assassinations of the Kennedys and Martin Luther King had
robbed a generation of its heroes, the Vietnam war was escalating despite
the protests, and at home, violence was on the rise. Young people turned
to rock, expecting it to ask the right questions and come up with answers,
hoping that the music's most visionary artists could somehow make sense
of things. But rock's most influential artists—Bob Dylan, the Beatles, the
Rolling Stones—were finding that serving as the conscience of a generation
exacted a heavy toll. Mr. Dylan, for one, felt the pressures becoming un-
bearable, and wrote about his predicament in songs like "All Along the
Watchtower."

> There must be some way out of here, said the joker to the thief.
> There's too much confusion, I can't get no relief.
> Businessmen they drink my wine, plowmen dig my earth.
> None of them along the line knows what any of it is worth.

Many rock artists of the 60s turned to drugs before the decade ended. 14
For a while, songs that were thought to be about drugs, whatever their
original intentions (Bob Dylan's "Mr. Tambourine Man," the Byrds' "Eight
Miles High," the Rolling Stones' "Get Off My Cloud"), were widely heard.
Bob Dylan sang that "everybody must get stoned," and many young people
seemed to agree. But the fad for drug lyrics was short-lived. They were
never again as prevalent as during that brief Indian summer of the counterculture. One hears few drug references in today's pop lyrics, and when
drugs *are* mentioned, listeners are usually advised to stay away from them;

"Don't do it," Grandmaster Flash and the Furious Five cautioned listeners about to experiment with drugs in their rap hit "White Lines."

The mainstream rock of the 1970s produced little in the way of socially 15 relevant lyrics. But toward the end of that decade a change began to be felt. The rise of punk rock in Britain brought to the country's pop charts angry songs about unemployment and nuclear Armageddon. In America, the issue of nuclear energy and the threat of nuclear war enlisted the sympathies of many prominent rock musicians. But attempts by Graham Nash, John Hall, and other anti-nuclear activists to turn their concerns into anthems were too self-conscious; the songs were quickly forgotten.

Rap, the new pop idiom that exploded out of New York's black and Latin 16 neighborhoods in the late 70s, seemed to concern itself mostly with hedonism and verbal strutting—at first. Then, in the early 80s, came "The Message," the dance-single by Grandmaster Flash and the Furious Five that provided listeners with an angry, eyewitness account of inner-city neighborhoods and people abandoned to rot, prey to crime, poverty, and disease. [In his vocal the group's champion rapper, Melle Mel, wonders how he's managed to survive in the junglelike streets.]

The rap records of the last several years have confronted similar issues 17 head-on, and they have been danceable enough to attract a sizable audience. Run-D.M.C.'s recent hit single "It's Like That" ticked off a list of some of the daily horrors many black Americans have to contend with. But you can't give up, Run-D.M.C. insisted to their young, predominately black and urban audience. You have to make something of yourself, to rise above "the way it is."

Bruce Springsteen's recent songs have also been topical and deeply 18 felt. They have also been the most popular music of his career. He is writing for and about the America of his dreams and the America he sees around him, and his lyrics are followed closely by a huge audience, as last year's presidential campaign references made abundantly clear.

The narrator of Mr. Springsteen's recent hit "Born in the U.S.A." is a 19 Vietnam veteran who returns home to confront harsh realities.

> Went down to see my V.A. man
> He said "Son don't you understand now"
> Had a brother at Khe Sahn fighting off the Viet Cong
> They're still there he's all gone

Other songs on Mr. Springsteen's most recent album suggest that there 20 is a pervasive gloom hanging over the country's decaying inner cities and factory towns. But their message is a positive one. "Hold on," the songs seem to say, "you've got to have something to believe in." The laborer in "Working on the Highway" is certainly hanging on to *his* dream:

> I work for the county out on 95
> All day I hold a red flag and watch the traffic pass me by
> In my head I keep a picture of a pretty little miss
> Someday mister I'm gonna lead a better life than this.

Mr. Springsteen's songs look at America and find both despair and   21
hope. And like Chuck Berry and so many other rock and roll lyricists, past
and present, he finds a source of strength and inspiration in rock itself.
Singing of his schooldays, he captures rock and roll's heart:

> We learned more from a three-minute record than we ever learned in school
> Tonight I hear the neighborhood drummer sound
> I can feel my heart begin to pound
> We made a promise we swore we'd always remember
> No retreat, no surrender.

Questions to Start You Thinking

1. Does Palmer think that pop lyrics of the 1980s are primarily about personal or about political issues? What examples does he use to support his opinion?
2. How does Palmer use comparison and contrast in his evaluation of 1980s pop lyrics?
3. How does the language of this essay differ from the language of the lyrics it describes? Define *transcendent* (paragraph 5), *undulating* (paragraph 6), *salutary* (paragraph 8), and *counterculture* (paragraph 14).
4. Would Ursula K. Le Guin in "American SF and The Other" (p. 540) find that pop lyrics, as Palmer describes them, adequately portray the "Other"? Which of her critiques of science fiction would also apply to pop music today? Which might not?

Suggestions for Writing

1. Select two popular songs of the same type (both love songs, for example, or both songs about teenage rebellion), one from the 1960s or 1970s and one from the 1980s or 1990s. Compare and contrast their lyrics. How are their messages similar? How do they differ?
2. Write a short personal essay about a song that has meant a great deal to you. What is its message? What role has the song played in your life?

HENRY LOUIS GATES, JR., was born in Keyser, West Virginia, in 1950. He has taught at Yale and Cornell universities and is currently W.E.B. Du Bois Professor of the Humanities and chairman of the Afro-American Studies Department at Harvard University. A frequent contributor to scholarly journals and popular magazines, in 1982 Gates created a TV series for PBS called *The Image of the Black in the Western Imagination.* His many books include *Figures in Black: Words, Signs, and the Racial Self* (1987). As this title suggests, in recent years Gates has been increasingly concerned with decoding the slang that enriches popular music and speech but whose meanings are often obscure to those outside a particular ethnic or racial group. In the following piece, originally published in the *New York Times* on June 19, 1990, Bates considers the controversial lyrics of the rap group 2 Live Crew.

2 LIVE CREW, DECODED
Henry Louis Gates, Jr.

The rap group 2 Live Crew and their controversial hit recording "As Nasty 1
as They Wanna Be" may well earn a signal place in the history of First
Amendment rights. But just as important is how these lyrics will be interpreted and by whom.

For centuries, African-Americans have been forced to develop coded 2
ways of communicating to protect them from danger. Allegories and double
meanings, words redefined to mean their opposites ("bad" meaning
"good," for instance), even neologisms ("bodacious") have enabled blacks
to share messages only the initiated understood.

Many blacks were amused by the transcripts of Marion Barry's sting 3
operation, which reveals that he used the traditional black expression about
one's "nose being opened." This referred to a love affair and not, as Mr.
Barry's prosecutors have suggested, to the inhalation of drugs. Understanding this phrase could very well spell the difference (for the Mayor) between
prison and freedom.

2 Live Crew is engaged in heavy-handed parody, turning the stereotypes 4
of black and white American culture on their heads. These young artists
are acting out, to lively dance music, a parodic exaggeration of the age-
old stereotypes of the oversexed black female and male. Their exuberant
use of hyperbole (phantasmagoric sexual organs, for example) under-
mines—for anyone fluent in black cultural codes—a too literal-minded
hearing of the lyrics.

This is the street tradition called "signifying" or "playing the dozens," 5
which has generally been risqué, and where the best signifier or "rapper"
is the one who invents the most extravagant images, the biggest "lies," as
the culture says. (H. "Rap" Brown earned his nickname in just this way.) In
the face of racist stereotypes about black sexuality, you can do one of two
things: You can disavow them or explode them with exaggeration.

2 Live Crew, like many "hip-hop" groups, is engaged in sexual carni- 6
valesque. Parody reigns supreme, from a take-off of standard blues to a
spoof of the black power movement; their off-color nursery rhymes are part
of a venerable Western tradition. The group even satirizes the culture of
commerce when it appropriates popular advertising slogans ("Tastes
great!" "Less filling!") and puts them in a bawdy context.

2 Live Crew must be interpreted within the context of black culture 7
generally and of signifying specifically. Their novelty, and that of other
adventuresome rap groups, is that their defiant rejection of euphemism
now voices for the mainstream what before existed largely in the "race
record" market—where the records of Redd Foxx and Rudy Ray Moore once
were forced to reside.

Rock songs have always been about sex but have used elaborate sub- 8
terfuges to convey that fact. 2 Live Crew uses Anglo-Saxon words and is
self-conscious about it: a parody of a white voice in one song refers to

"private personal parts," as a coy counterpart to the group's bluntness.

Much more troubling than its so-called obscenity is the group's overt 9 sexism. Their sexism is so flagrant, however, that it almost cancels itself out in a hyperbolic war between the sexes. In this, it recalls the inter-sexual jousting in Zora Neale Hurston's novels. Still, many of us look toward the emergence of more female rappers to redress sexual stereotypes. And we must not allow ourselves to sentimentalize street culture: the appreciation of verbal virtuosity does not lessen one's obligation to critique bigotry in all of its pernicious forms.

Is 2 Live Crew more "obscene" than, say, the comic Andrew Dice Clay? 10 Clearly, this rap group is seen as more threatening than others that are just as sexually explicit. Can this be completely unrelated to the specter of the young black male as a figure of sexual and social disruption, the very stereotypes 2 Live Crew seems determined to undermine?

This question—and the very large question of obscenity and the First 11 Amendment—cannot even be addressed until those who would answer them become literate in the vernacular traditions of African-Americans. To do less is to censor through the equivalent of intellectual prior restraint— and censorship is to art what lynching is to justice.

Questions to Start You Thinking

1. What criticisms of 2 Live Crew does Gates's article address? How valid does he believe these criticisms are?

2. How does Gates use cause and effect to support the stand he takes?

3. How does Gates use word choice to establish his own authority as a professor and cultural critic? Define *allegories, neologisms* (paragraph 2), *parody, hyperbole, phantasmagoric* (paragraph 4), *euphemism* (paragraph 7), and *vernacular* (paragraph 11).

4. "Rock songs have always been about sex but have used elaborate subterfuges to convey that fact," writes Gates (paragraph 8). Would Robert Palmer in "What Pop Lyrics Say to Us Today" (p. 553) agree?

Suggestions for Writing

1. Choose a controversial musical group, performer, television show, film, book, or play that has been criticized for its sexual, violent, or political content. In a brief essay, describe the group or work that has been criticized, evaluate the criticism, and take a stand for or against it. How is the criticism fair? How is it unfair?

2. Write a short personal essay giving your impressions of rap music. How do rap performers challenge stereotypes? How do they conform to them?

EMILY PRAGER, born in 1952, writes fiction featuring a surreal and coldly humorous blend of pop culture slogans and classical allusions. Her novel *Clea and Zeus Divorce* (1987) has been called "a music video in the form of a novel." A former contributing editor to the *National Lampoon,* Prager suggests in the following piece, published in *Interview* in December 1991, that absurd features of post–World War II consumerism influence us more than we know.

OUR BARBIES, OURSELVES
Emily Prager

MAJOR BARBIE

I read an astounding obituary in the *New York Times* not too long ago. It 1
concerned the death of one Jack Ryan. A former husband of Zsa Zsa Gabor, it said, Mr. Ryan had been an inventor and designer during his lifetime. A man of eclectic creativity, he designed Sparrow and Hawk missiles when he worked for the Raytheon Company, and, the notice said, when he consulted for Mattel he designed Barbie.

If Barbie was designed by a man, suddenly a lot of things made sense 2
to me, things I'd wondered about for years. I used to look at Barbie and wonder, What's wrong with this picture? What kind of woman designed this doll? Let's be honest: Barbie looks like someone who got her start at the Playboy Mansion. She could be a regular guest on *The Howard Stern Show.* It is a fact of Barbie's design that her breasts are so out of proportion to the rest of her body that if she were a human woman, she'd fall flat on her face.

If it's true that a woman didn't design Barbie, you don't know how much 3
saner that makes me feel. Of course, that doesn't ameliorate the damage. There are millions of women who are subliminally sure that a thirty-nine-inch bust and a twenty-three-inch waist are the epitome of lovability. Could this account for the popularity of breast implant surgery?

I don't mean to step on anyone's toes here. I loved my Barbie. Secretly, 4
I still believe that neon pink and turquoise blue are the only colors in which to decorate a duplex condo. And like many others of my generation, I've never married, simply because I cannot find a man who looks as good in clam diggers as Ken.

The question that comes to mind is, of course, Did Mr. Ryan design 5
Barbie as a weapon? Because it *is* odd that Barbie appeared about the same time in my consciousness as the feminist movement—a time when women sought equality and small breasts were king. Or is Barbie the dream date of weapons designers? Or perhaps it's simpler than that: perhaps Barbie is Zsa Zsa if she were eleven inches tall. No matter what, my discovery of Jack Ryan confirms what I have always felt: there is something indescribably masculine about Barbie—dare I say it, phallic. For all her

giant breasts and high-heeled feet, she lacks a certain softness. If you asked a little girl what kind of doll she wanted for Christmas, I just don't think she'd reply, "Please, Santa, I want a hard-body."

On the other hand, you could say that Barbie, in feminist terms, is 6 definitely her own person. With her condos and fashion plazas and pools and beauty salons, she is definitely a liberated woman, a gal on the move. And she has always been sexual, even totemic. Before Barbie, American dolls were flat-footed and breastless, and ineffably dignified. They were created in the image of little girls or babies. Madame Alexander was the queen of doll makers in the 50s, and her dollies looked like Elizabeth Taylor in *National Velvet.* They represented the kind of girls who looked perfect in jodhpurs, whose hair was never out of place, who grew up to be Jackie Kennedy—before she married Onassis. Her dolls' boyfriends were figments of the imagination, figments with large portfolios and three-piece suits and presidential aspirations, figments who could keep dolly in the style to which little girls of the 50s were programmed to become accustomed, a style that spasm-ed with the 60s and the appearance of Barbie. And perhaps what accounts for Barbie's vast popularity is that she was also a 60s woman: into free love and fun colors, anticlass, and possessed of a real, molded boyfriend, Ken, with whom she could chant a mantra.

But there were problems with Ken. I always felt weird about him. He 7 had no genitals, and, even at age ten, I found that ominous. I mean, here was Barbie with these humongous breasts, and that was O.K. with the toy company. And then, there was Ken with that truncated, unidentifiable lump at his groin. I sensed injustice at work. Why, I wondered, was Barbie designed with such obvious sexual equipment and Ken not? Why was his treated as if it were more mysterious than hers? Did the fact that it was treated as such indicate that somehow his equipment, his essential maleness, was considered more powerful than hers, more worthy of the dignity of concealment? And if the issue in the mind of the toy company was obscenity and its possible damage to children, I still object. How do they think I felt, knowing that no matter how many water beds they slept in, or hot tubs they romped in, or swimming pools they lounged by under the stars, Barbie and Ken could never make love? No matter how much sexuality Barbie possessed, she would never turn Ken on. He would be forever withholding, forever detached. There was a loneliness about Barbie's situation that was always disturbing. And twenty-five years later, movies and videos are still filled with topless women and covered men. As if we're all trapped in Barbie's world and can never escape.

God, it certainly has cheered me up to think that Barbie was designed 8 by Jack Ryan. There's only one thing that could make me happier, and that's if Gorbachev would come over here and run for president on the Democratic ticket. If they don't want him in Russia, fine. We've got the capitalist system in place, ready to go; all we need is someone to run it.

Gorbachev for president and Barbie designed by a man. A blissful end 9 to 1991.

Questions to Start You Thinking

1. What is Prager's main point in this piece? What does she mean when she says that "if Barbie was designed by a man, suddenly a lot of things made sense to me" (paragraph 2)?

2. How does Prager use the resource of imagination in this essay? How does she use humor in her evaluation of Barbie's design and Barbie's impact on young girls?

3. Prager's tone seems to be a parody of formal academic speech. Is this tone appropriate to her article? Explain why or why not. Define *eclectic* (paragraph 1), *ameliorate, subliminally, epitome* (paragraph 3), *phallic* (paragraph 5), and *truncated* (paragraph 7).

4. Are the attitudes toward women described by Prager similar to or different from those that Ursula K. Le Guin discusses in "American SF and The Other" (p. 540)?

Suggestions for Writing

1. In a brief personal essay, describe a childhood toy that had a strong influence on you. How did the toy encourage you to see the world? How did it encourage you to see yourself?

2. Write a short essay evaluating the stereotypes of women's appearance that are presented in our culture. What standards of appearance are held up as the norm? What effects do these stereotypes have?

JOYCE CAROL OATES has published more than twenty novels, fifteen volumes of short stories, and nine books of poetry and has won a dozen national awards for her fiction and essays. Born in 1938 in Lockport, New York, and raised on her grandparents' farm, Oates attended a one-room schoolhouse and submitted her first novel for publication at age fifteen. She has taught writing at several universities and since 1978 has been writer-in-residence at Princeton University. Her fictional milieus range from the migrant poor (in *A Garden of Earthly Delights* (1967) to the suburban rich in *Expensive People* (1968) to the urban working class in *them* (1969). Throughout her writing run themes of violence and sexuality. In the following article, published in *Newsweek* on February 24, 1992, Oates brings these themes together in a meditation on boxing and the trial of a heavyweight champ.

RAPE AND THE BOXING RING
Joyce Carol Oates

Mike Tyson's conviction on rape charges in Indianapolis is a minor   1
tragedy for the beleaguered sport of boxing, but a considerable triumph for women's rights. For once, though bookmakers were giving 5–1 odds that

Tyson would be acquitted, and the mood of the country seems distinctly conservative, a jury resisted the outrageous defense that a rape victim is to be blamed for her own predicament. For once, a celebrity with enormous financial resources did not escape trial and a criminal conviction by settling with his accuser out of court.

That boxing and "women's rights" should be perceived as opposed is   2 symbolically appropriate, since of all sports, boxing is the most aggressively masculine, the very soul of war in microcosm. Elemental and dramatically concise, it raises to an art the passions underlying direct human aggression; its fundamentally murderous intent is not obscured by the pursuit of balls or pucks, not can the participants expect help from teammates. In a civilized, humanitarian society, one would expect such a blood sport to have died out, yet boxing, sponsored by gambling casinos in Las Vegas and Atlantic City, and broadcast by cable television, flourishes: had the current heavyweight champion, Evander Holyfield, fought Mike Tyson in a title defense, Holyfield would have earned no less than $30 million. If Tyson were still champion, and still fighting, he would be earning more.

The paradox of boxing is that it so excessively rewards men for inflicting   3 injury upon one another that, outside the ring, with less "art," would be punishable as aggravated assault, or manslaughter. Boxing belongs to that species of mysterious masculine activity for which anthropologists use such terms as "deep play": activity that is wholly without utilitarian value, in fact contrary to utilitarian value, so dangerous that no amount of money can justify it. Sports car racing, stunt flying, mountain climbing, bullfighting, dueling—these activities, through history, have provided ways in which the individual can dramatically, if sometimes fatally, distinguish himself from the crowd, usually with the adulation and envy of the crowd, and traditionally, the love of women. Women—in essence, Woman—is the prize, usually self-proffered. To look upon organized sports as a continuum of Darwinian theory—in which the sports-star hero flaunts the superiority of his genes— is to see how displays of masculine aggression have their sexual component, as ingrained in human beings as any instinct for self-preservation and reproduction. In a capitalist society, the secret is to capitalize upon instinct.

Yet even within the very special world of sports, boxing is distinct. Is   4 there any athlete, however celebrated in his own sport, who would not rather reign as the heavyweight champion of the world? If, in fantasy at least, he could be another Muhammad Ali, or Joe Louis, or indeed, Mike Tyson in his prime? Boxing celebrates the individual man in his maleness, not merely in his skill as an athlete—though boxing demands enormous skill, and its training is far more arduous than most men could endure for more than a day or two. All athletes can become addicted to their own adrenaline, but none more obviously than the boxer, who, like Sugar Ray Leonard, already a multimillionaire with numerous occupations outside the ring, will risk serious injury by coming back out of retirement; as Mike Tyson has said, "Outside of boxing, everything is so boring." What makes boxing repulsive to many observers is precisely what makes boxing so fascinating to participants.

BLOOD SACRIFICE:
This is because it is a highly organized ritual that violates taboo. It flouts 5 such moral prescriptions as "Thou shalt not kill." It celebrates, not meekness, but flamboyant aggression. No one who has not seen live boxing matches (in contrast to the sanitized matches broadcast over television) can quite grasp its eerie fascination—the spectator's sense that he or she is a witness to madness, yet a madness sanctioned by tradition and custom, as finely honed by certain celebrated practitioners as an artist's performance at the highest level of genius, and, yet more disturbing, immensely gratifying to the audience. Boxing mimics our early ancestors' rite of bloody sacrifice and redemption; it excites desires most civilized men and women find abhorrent. For some observers, it is frankly obscene, like pornography; yet, unlike pornography, it is not fantasy but real, thus far more subversive.

The paradox for the boxer is that, in the ring, he experiences himself 6 as a living conduit for the inchoate, demonic will of the crowd: the expression of their collective desire, which is to pound another human being into absolute submission. The more vicious the boxer, the greater the acclaim. And the financial reward—Tyson is reported to have earned $100 million. (He who at the age of 13 was plucked from a boys' school for juvenile delinquents in upstate New York.) Like the champion gladiators of Roman decadence, he will be both honored and despised, for, no matter his celebrity, and the gift of his talent, his energies spring from the violation of taboo and he himself is tainted by it.

Mike Tyson has said that he does not think of boxing as a sport. He 7 sees himself as a fantasy gladiator who, by "destructing" opponents, enacts others' fantasies in his own being. That the majority of these others are well-to-do whites who would themselves crumple at a first blow, and would surely claim a pious humanitarianism, would not go unnoted by so wary and watchful a man. Cynicism is not an inevitable consequence of success, but it is difficult to retain one's boyish naiveté in the company of the sort of people, among them the notorious Don King, who have surrounded Tyson since 1988, when his comanager, Jim Jacobs, died. As Floyd Patterson, an ex-heavyweight champion who has led an exemplary life, has said, "When you have millions of dollars, you have millions of friends."

It should not be charged against boxing that Mike Tyson *is* boxing in 8 any way. Boxers tend to be fiercely individualistic, and Tyson is, at the least, an enigma. He began his career, under the tutelage of the legendary trainer Cus D'Amato, as a strategist, in the mode of such brilliant technicians as Henry Armstrong and Sugar Ray Robinson. He was always aware of a lineage with Jack Dempsey, arguably the most electrifying of all heavyweight champions, whose nonstop aggression revolutionized the sport and whose shaved haircut and malevolent scowl, and, indeed, penchant for dirty fighting, made a tremendous impression upon the young Tyson.

In recent years, however, Tyson seems to have styled himself at least   9
partly on the model of Charles (Sonny) Liston, the "baddest of the bad"
black heavyweights. Liston had numerous arrests to his credit and served
time in prison (for assaulting a policeman); he had the air, not entirely
contrived, of a sociopath; he was always friendly with racketeers, and died
of a drug overdose that may in fact have been murder. (It is not coincidental
that Don King, whom Tyson has much admired, and whom Tyson has empowered to ruin his career, was convicted of manslaughter and served time
in an Ohio prison.) Like Liston, Tyson has grown to take a cynical pleasure
in publicly condoned sadism (his "revenge" bout with Tyrell Biggs, whom
he carried for seven long rounds in order to inflict maximum damage) and
in playing the outlaw; his contempt for women, escalating in recent years,
is a part of that guise. The witty obscenity of a prefight taunt of Tyson's—
"I'll make you into my girlfriend"—is the boast of the rapist.

Perhaps rape itself is a gesture, a violent repudiation of the female, in   10
the assertion of maleness that would seem to require nothing beyond physical gratification of the crudest kind. The supreme macho gesture—like
knocking out an opponent and standing over his fallen body, gloves raised
in triumph.

In boxing circles it is said—this with an affectionate sort of humor—   11
that the heavyweight champion is the 300-pound gorilla who sits anywhere
in the room he wants; and, presumably, takes any female he wants. Such
a grandiose sense of entitlement, fueled by the insecurities and emotions
of adolescence, can have disastrous consequences. Where once it was
believed that Mike Tyson might mature into the greatest heavyweight of all
time, breaking Rocky Marciano's record of 49 victories and no defeats, it
was generally acknowledged that, since his defeat of Michael Spinks in
1988, he had allowed his boxing skills to deteriorate. Not simply his ig-
nominious loss of his title to the mediocre James (Buster) Douglas in 1990,
but subsequent lackluster victories against mediocre opponents made it
clear that Tyson was no longer a serious, nor even very interesting, boxer.

The dazzling reflexes were dulled, the shrewd defensive skills drilled   12
into him by D'Amato were largely abandoned: Tyson emerged suddenly as
a conventional heavyweight like Gerry Cooney, who advances upon his opponent with the hope of knocking him out with a single punch—and does
not always succeed. By 25, Tyson seemed already middle aged, burnt out.
He would have no great fights after all. So, strangely, he seemed to invite
his fate outside the ring, with sadomasochistic persistence, testing the
limits of his celebrity's license to offend by ever-escalating acts of aggression and sexual effrontery.

The familiar sports adage is surely true, one's ultimate opponent is   13
oneself.

It may be objected that these remarks center upon the rapist, and not   14
his victim; that sympathy, pity, even in some quarters moral outrage flow
to the criminal and not the person he has violated. In this case, ironically,
the victim, Desiree Washington, though she will surely bear psychic scars
through her life, has emerged as a victor, a heroine: a young woman whose

traumatic experience has been, as so few traumas can be, the vehicle for a courageous and selfless stand against the sexual abuse of women and children in America. She seems to know that herself, telling *People* magazine, "It was the right thing to do." She was fortunate in drawing a jury who rejected classic defense ploys by blaming the victim and/or arguing consent. Our criminal justice system being what it is, she was lucky. Tyson, who might have been acquitted elsewhere in the country, was unlucky.

"POOR GUY":
Whom to blame for this most recent of sports disgraces in America? The 15 culture that flings young athletes like Tyson up out of obscurity, makes millionaires of them and watches them self-destruct? Promoters like Don King and Bob Arum? Celebrity hunters like Robin Givens, Tyson's ex-wife, who seemed to have exploited him for his money and as a means of promoting her own acting career? The indulgence generally granted star athletes when they behave recklessly? When they abuse drugs and alcohol, and mistreat women?

I suggest that no one is to blame, finally, except the perpetrator him- 16 self. In Montieth Illingworth's cogently argued biography of Tyson, "Mike Tyson: Money, Myth and Betrayal," Tyson is quoted, after one or another public debacle: "People say 'Poor guy.' That insults me. I despise sympathy. So I screwed up. I made some mistakes. 'Poor guy,' like I'm some victim. There's nothing poor about me."

Questions to Start You Thinking

1. Does Oates sympathize primarily with Mike Tyson or with Desiree Washington? How can you tell?
2. How does Oates use cause and effect to support the stand she takes?
3. Oates discusses the issues of sports, violence, and rape in language that might be referred to as "professorial." Why do you think she chose such an approach? Define *beleaguered* (paragraph 1), *microcosm, elemental* (paragraph 2), *utilitarian, Darwinian* (paragraph 3), *inchoate, gladiators, decadence* (paragraph 6), *enigma, tutelage* (paragraph 8), *condoned* and *sadism* (paragraph 9).
4. Does Mike Tyson embody the stereotypes Brent Staples argues against in "Black Men and Public Space" (p. 507)?

Suggestions for Writing

1. Write a short essay taking a stand on whether professional sports such as boxing, football, and ice hockey reinforce violence in our society.
2. In a brief essay, discuss how images of violence and images of sexuality are linked in today's culture. Use examples from the media to support your claim. What effect could this linking have?

CHAPTER 26

Nature and the Environment

ALICE WALKER was born in 1944 in Eatonton, Georgia, and graduated from Sarah Lawrence College in 1965. Since 1968 she has been a writer-in-residence and teacher at schools including Wellesley College and Brandeis University. She has won numerous awards for her poetry and fiction, including the Pulitzer Prize for her novel *The Color Purple* (1983), and in 1984 she cofounded Wild Trees Press. Her most recent publication is the novel *Possessing the Secret of Joy* (1992). Walker writes on cultural and political issues, from a feminist and third world perspective. She has also blended these concerns with her interest in the environment, evident in the following article, published in *Ms.* magazine in January 1984.

WHEN A TREE FALLS
Alice Walker

> *There are people who think that only people have emotions like pride, fear, and joy, but those who know will tell you all things are alive, perhaps not in the same way we are alive, but each in its own way, as should be, for we are not all the same. And though different from us in shape and life span, different in Time and Knowing, yet are trees alive. And rocks. And water. And all know emotion.* —Anne Cameron,
> *Daughters of Copper Woman*
> (Press Gang of Canada)

Some years ago a friend and I decided to go into the countryside to   1
listen to what the Earth was saying. Because countryside is almost always
privately owned, we went to a national forest many miles from the city. By
the time we had walked a hundred yards, I felt I need go no further, and
laid myself down where I was, across the path in a grove of trees. For
several hours I lay there, and other people entering the forest had to walk
around me. I hardly noticed them, so intense was my dialogue with the
trees.

As I was lying there, really, across their feet, I felt or "heard" with my   2
feelings, the distinct request from them that I remove myself. But these
are not feet, I thought, peering at them, but roots. Roots do not tell you to
go away. It was then that I looked up and around me into the "faces." These
"faces" were all middle-aged to old conifers, and they were all suffering
from some kind of disease, the most obvious sign of which was a light
green fungus, resembling moss and lichen, that nearly covered them, giving
them — in spite of the bright spring sunlight — an eerie, fantastical aspect.
Beneath this greenish envelopment, the limbs of the trees, the "arms,"
were bent in a profusion of deformity. Indeed, the trees reminded me of
nothing so much as badly rheumatoid elderly people, as I began to realize
how difficult it would be for their limbs to move freely in the breeze. Clearly
these were sick people, or trees; irritable, angry, and growing old in pain.
And they did not want me lying on their gnarled and no doubt aching feet.

Looking again at their feet, or roots — which stuck up all over the ground   3
and directly under my own cheek — I saw that the ground from which they
emerged was gray and dead-looking, as if it had been poisoned. Aha, I
thought, this is obviously a place where chemicals were dumped. The soil
has been poisoned, the trees afflicted, slowly dying, and they do not like
it. I hastily communicated this to the trees and asked that they understand
it was not *I* who had poisoned them. I just moved to this part of the country,
I said. They were not appeased. Get up. Go away, they replied. But I refused
to move. Nor could I. I needed to make them agree to my innocence.

The summer before this encounter I lived in the northern hills of Cali-   4
fornia where much logging is done. Each day on the highway as I went to
buy groceries or to the river to swim, I saw the loggers' trucks, like enormous hearses, carrying the battered bodies of the old sisters and brothers,
as I thought of them, down to the lumberyards in the valley. In fact, this
sight, in an otherwise peaceful setting, distressed me — as if I lived in a
beautiful neighborhood that lost hundreds of its finest members daily, while
I sat mournful but impotent beside the avenue that carried them away.

It was of this endless funeral procession that I thought, as I lay across   5
the feet of these sick old relatives whose "safe" existence in a public park
(away from the logging trucks) had not kept them safe at all.

I *love* trees, I said.   6

Human, *please*, they replied.   7

But I do not cut you down in the prime of life. I do not haul your muti-   8
lated and stripped bodies shamelessly down the highway. It is the lumber
companies, I said.

Just go away, said the trees.   9

All my life you have meant a lot to me, I said. I love your grace, your   10
dignity, your serenity, your generosity. . . .

Well, said the trees, before I finished this list, we find you without grace,   11
without dignity, without serenity, and there is no generosity in you either—
just ask any tree. You butcher us, you burn us, you grow us only to destroy
us. Even when we grow ourselves you kill us, or cut off our limbs. That we
are alive and have feelings means nothing to you.

But *I* as an individual, am innocent, I said. Though it did occur to me   12
that I live in a wood house, I eat at a wood table, I sleep on a wood bed.

My uses of wood are modest, I said, and always tailored to my needs.   13
I do not slash through whole forests, destroying hundreds of trees in the
process of "harvesting" a few.

But finally, after much discourse, I understood what the trees were   14
telling me: being an individual didn't matter. Just as to human beings all
trees are perceived as one (Didn't an American official say recently that
"when you've seen one tree, you've seen 'em all"?), all human beings, to
the trees, are one. The earth holds us responsible for our crimes against
it, not as individuals, but as a species, was the message of the trees: I
found this to be a terrifying thought. For I had assumed that the earth, the
spirit of the earth, noticed exceptions. Those who wantonly damage it and
those who do not. But the earth is wise. It has given itself into the keeping
of all, and all are therefore accountable.

And how hard it will be to change our worst behavior!   15

Last spring I moved even deeper into the country and went eagerly up   16
the hill from my cabin to start a new garden. As I was patting the soil
around the root of a new tomato plant, I awakened a small garden snake
who lived in the tomato bed. Though panicked and not knowing at the time
what kind of snake it was, I tried calmly to direct it out of the garden—now
that I, a human being, had arrived to take possession of it. It went. The
next day, however, because the tomato bed *was* its home, the snake came
back. Once more I directed it away. The third time it came back, I called a
friend—who thought I was badly frightened, from my nervous behavior—
and he killed it. It looked very small and harmless, hanging from the end
of his hoe.

Everything I was ever taught about snakes—that they are dangerous,   17
frightful, repulsive, sinister—went into the murder of this snake person,
who was only, after all, trying to remain in his or her home, perhaps the
only home he or she had ever known. Even my ladylike "nervousness" in
its presence, was learned behavior. I knew at once that killing the snake
was not the first act that should have occurred in my new garden, and I
grieved that I had apparently learned nothing—as a human being—since
the days of Adam and Eve.

Even on a practical level, killing this small, no doubt bewildered and   18
disoriented, creature made poor sense, because throughout the summer,
snakes just like it regularly visited the garden (and deer ate all the toma-

toes), so that it appeared to me that the little snake I killed was always with me. Occasionally a very large mama or papa snake wandered into the cabin yard, as if to let me know its child had been murdered, and it knew who was responsible for it.

These garden snakes, said my neighbors, are harmless: they eat mice   19 and other pests that invade the garden. In this respect, they are even helpful to humans. And yet, I am still afraid of them, because that is how I was taught to be. Deep in the psyche of most of us there is this fear — and long ago, I do not doubt, in the psyche of ancient peoples, there was a similar fear of trees. And of course, a fear of other human beings, for that is where all fear of natural things leads us. To fear of ourselves, fear of each other, and fear even of the spirit of the universe, because out of fear we often greet its outrageousness with murder.

> *That fall, they say, the last of the bison herds was slaughtered by the*   20
> *Wasichus.° I can remember when the bison were so many that they could not*
> *be counted, but more and more Wasichus came to kill them until there were*
> *only heaps of bones scattered where they used to be. The Wasichus did not*
> *kill them to eat; they killed them for the metal that makes them crazy, and they*
> *took only the hides to sell. Sometimes they did not even take the hides, only*
> *the tongues; and I have heard that fire-boats came down the Missouri River*
> *loaded with dried bison tongues. You can see that the men who did this were*
> *crazy. Sometimes they did not even take the tongues; they just killed and killed*
> *because they liked to do that. When we hunted bison, we killed only what we*
> *needed. And when there was nothing left but heaps of bones, the Wasichus*
> *came and gathered up even the bones and sold them.*   —*Black Elk Speaks,*
>   by John G. Niehardt
>   (Washington Square Press)

In this way, the Wasichus starved the Indians into submission, and   21 forced them to live on impoverished "reservations" in their own land. Like the little snake in my garden, many of the Indians returned again and again to their ancient homes and hunting grounds, only to be driven off with greater brutality until they were broken or killed.

The Wasichus in Washington who ordered the slaughter of bison and   22 Indian, and those on the prairies who did the deed, are frequently thought of, by some of us, as "fathers of our country," along with the Indian-killers and slaveowners Washington and Jefferson and the like.

Yet what "father" would needlessly exterminate any of his children.   23

Are not the "fathers" rather those Native Americans, those "wild Indi-   24 ans" like Black Elk, who said, "It is the story of all life that is holy and is good to tell, and of us two-leggeds sharing in it with the four-leggeds and the wings of the air and all green things; for these are children of one mother and their father is one Spirit"?

Indeed, America, the country, acts so badly, so much like a spoiled   25 adolescent boy, because it has never acknowledged the "fathers" that ex-

---

Wasichu. A term used by the Ogalala Sioux to designate the white man, but having no reference to the color of his skin. It means: He who takes the fat. (author's note)

isted before the "fathers" of its own creation. It has been led instead — in every period of its brief and troubled history — by someone who might be called Younger Brother (after the character in E. L. Doctorow's novel, *Ragtime*, set in turn-of-the-century America) who occasionally blunders into good and useful deeds, but on the whole never escapes from the white Victorian house of racist and sexist repression, puritanism, and greed.

The Wasichu speaks, in all his American history books, of "opening up virgin lands." Yet there were people living here, on Turtle Island (which is an ancient Indian name for America), for thousands of years; but living so gently on the land that to Wasichu eyes it looked untouched. Yes, it was "still," as they wrote over and over again, with lust, "virginal." If it were a bride, the Wasichu would have permitted it to wear a white dress.　26

It is ironic to think that if the Indians who were here then "discovered" America as it is now they would find little reason to want to stay. This is a fabulous *land* not because it is a country, but because it is soaked in so many years of love. And though the Native Americans fought as much as any other people among themselves (much to their loss!) never did they fight against the earth, which they correctly perceived as their mother, or against their father, the sky; now thought of mainly as "outer space" where primarily bigger and "better" wars have a projected future.　27

The Wasichu may be Father of the country, but the Native Americans, the Indians, are the parents ("guardians" as they've always said they are°) of the land. And, in my opinion, as Earthling above all, we must get to know these parents "from our mother's side" before it is too late. It has been proved that the land can exist without the country — and be better for it — it has not been proved (though some space enthusiasts appear to think so) that the country can exist without the land. And the land is being killed.　28

Sometimes, when I teach, I try to help my students understand what it must feel like to be a slave. Not many of them can go to South Africa and ask the black people enslaved by the Wasichu there, or visit the migrant laborer camps kept hidden from their neighborhoods, so we talk about slavery as it existed in America, a little over a hundred years ago. One day I asked if any of them felt they had ever been "treated like dirt." No, many of them felt they had been treated badly at some time in their lives (they were largely middle class and white), but no one felt she or he had been treated like dirt. Yet what pollution you breathe, I pointed out, which the atmosphere also breathes; what a vast number of poisons you eat with your food, which the earth has eaten just before you. How unexpectedly many of you will fall ill and die from cancer because the very ground on which you build your homes will be carcinogenic.　29

Some of us have become used to thinking that woman is the nigger of　30

° Though much of what we know of our Indian ancestors concerns the male, it is good to remember who produced him; that women in some tribes were shamans, could vote, and, among the Onondaga still elect the men who lead the tribe. And, inasmuch as "women's work" has always involved cleaning up after, as well as teaching the young principles by which to live, we have our Indian female parent to thank for her care of Turtle Island, as well as the better documented male who took her instructions so utterly to heart. (author's note)

the world, that a person of color is the nigger of the world, that a poor person is the nigger of the world. But, in truth, earth itself has become the nigger of the world. Perceived, ironically, as "other"—alien, evil, and threatening—by those who are finding they cannot draw a healthful breath without its cooperation. While the earth is poisoned, everything it supports is poisoned. While the earth is enslaved, none of us is free. While the earth is "a nigger," it has no choice but to think of us all as Wasichu. While it is "treated like dirt," so are we.

In this time, when human life—because of greed, avarice, ignorance, 31 and fear—hangs by a thread, it is of disarmament that every thoughtful person thinks; for regardless of whether we all agree that we deserve to live as a species, most of us have the desire. Abandoning of weapons is of what we think; but disarmament must also occur in the heart and in the spirit. We must absolutely reject the way of the Wasichu that we are so disastrously traveling. The way that most respects (above nature, obviously, above life itself, above even the spirit of the universe) the "metal that makes men crazy."

Our primary connection is to the earth, our mother and father; regard- 32 less of who "owns" pieces and parts, we, as sister and brother beings to the "four-leggeds (and the fishes) and the wings of the air," share the whole. No one should be permitted to buy a part of our earth to dump poisons in, just as we would not sell one of our legs to be used as a trash can.

Many of us are afraid to abandon the way of the Wasichu because we 33 have become so addicted to his way of death. The Wasichu has promised us so many good things, and has actually delivered several. But "progress," once claimed by the present chief of the Wasichu to be their "most impor- tant product," had meant hunger, misery, enslavement, unemployment, and worse to millions of people on the globe. The many time-saving devices we've become addicted to because of our "progress" have freed us to watch endless reruns of commercials, sit-coms, and murders.

Our thoughts must now be on how to restore to the earth its dignity as 34 a living being; to stop raping and plundering it as a matter of course. We must begin to develop the consciousness that everything has equal rights because existence itself is equal. In other words, we are all here: trees, people, snakes, alike. We must realize that even tiny insects in the South American jungle know how to make plastic, for instance; they have simply chosen not to cover the earth with it. The Wasichu's uniqueness is not his ability to "think" and "invent"—from the evidence almost everything does this in some fashion or other—it is his profound unnaturalness. His lack of harmony with other peoples and places, and with the very environment to which he owes his life.

In James Mooney's *Myths of the Cherokee* and *Sacred Formulas of the* 35 *Cherokees*, collected between 1887 and 1890, he relates many interesting practices among the original inhabitants of this land, among them the custom of asking pardon of slain or offended animals. And in writing about the needless murder of the snake who inhabited our garden—the snake's and mine—I ask its pardon, and in the telling of its death, hope to save the lives of many of its kin.

"The missionary Washburn," says Mooney, "tells how, among the Cher- 36 okees of Arkansas, he was once riding along, accompanied by an Indian on foot, when they discovered a poisonous snake coiled beside the path. 'I observed Blanket° turned aside to avoid the serpent, but made no sign of attack, and I requested the interpreter to get down and kill it. He did so, and I then inquired of Blanket why he did not kill the serpent. He answered, "I never kill snakes and so snakes never kill me." '

"The trader Henry," Mooney observes elsewhere, "tells of similar be- 37 havior among the Objibwa of Lake Superior in 1764. While gathering wood he was startled by a sudden rattle . . . 'I no sooner saw the snake, than I hastened to the canoe, in order to procure my gun; but, the Indians observing what I was doing, inquired the occasion, and being informed, begged me to desist. At the same, they followed me to the spot, with their pipes and tobacco pouches in their hands. On returning, I found the snake still coiled.

" 'The Indians, on their part, surrounded it, all addressing it by turns, 38 and calling it their *grandfather*; but yet keeping at some distance. During this part of the ceremony, they filled their pipes; and now each blew the smoke toward the snake, who, as it appeared to me, really received it with pleasure. In a word, after remaining coiled, and receiving incense, for the space of half an hour, it stretched itself along the ground, in visible good humor. Its length was between four and five feet. Having remained outstretched for some time, at last it moved slowly away, the Indians following it, and still addressing it by the title of grandfather, beseeching it to take care of their families during their absence, and to be pleased to open the heart of Sir William Johnson (the British Indian Agent, whom they were about to visit) so that he might *show them charity*, and fill their canoe with rum. One of the chiefs added a petition, that the snake would take no notice of the insult which had been offered by the Englishman, who would even have put him to death, but for the interference of the Indians to whom it was hoped he would impute no part of the offense. They further requested that he would remain, and inhabit their country, and not return among the English. . . .' "

What makes this remarkable tale more so is that the "bite" of the 39 Englishman's rum was to afflict the Indians far more severely than the bite of any tremendous number of poisonous snakes.

That the Indians were often sexist, prone to war, humanly flawed, I do 40 not dispute. It is their light step upon the earth that I admire and would have us emulate. The new way to exist on the earth may well be the ancient

---

Blanket. A derogatory appellation, short for "blanket Indian." The Indians were eventually reduced to wearing blankets because the Wasichu had destroyed their homes, clothing, and everything else. It is recorded that the blankets often sold or given to the Indians by the Wasichu were infected with diseases such as smallpox. (author's note)

way of the steadfast lovers of this particular land. Whereas to the Wasichu only the white man attains full human status, everything to the Indian was a relative. Everything was a human being.

Perhaps a rule for permissible murder should be that beyond feeding and clothing and sheltering ourselves, even abundantly, we should be allowed to destroy only what we ourselves can create. We cannot recreate this world. We cannot recreate "wilderness." We cannot even, truly, recreate ourselves. Only our behavior can we recreate, or create anew. 41

> *Hear me, four quarters of the world—a relative I am! Give me the strength* 42
> *to walk the soft earth, a relative to all that is! Give me the eyes to see and the*
> *strength to understand, that I may be like you. . . .*
> *Great Spirit, Great Spirit, my Grandfather, all over the earth the faces of*
> *living things are all alike. With tenderness have these come up out of the*
> *ground. Look upon these faces of children without number and with children*
> *in their arms, that they may face the winds and walk the good road to the day*
> *of quiet.* —Black Elk

Questions to Start You Thinking

1. What does Walker see as the central message of American Indian cultures concerning the relationship between humans and the natural world?

2. How does Walker use quotation to support her stand? How does she use the resource of imagination?

3. Would you describe Walker's language as formal or informal? Define *conifers, rheumatoid* (paragraph 2), *psyche* (paragraph 19), *carcinogenic* (paragraph 29), *avarice* (paragraph 31).

4. How do Walker's perceptions of American Indian culture differ from Paula Gunn Allen's in "Where I Come from Is like This" (p. 500)?

Suggestions for Writing

1. Using imagination as a resource, write a brief essay in which you, too, talk to and listen to the trees or some other element of nature. What does nature say to you? How do you respond to its challenges or accusations?

2. "While the earth is enslaved, none of us is free. . . . While it is 'treated like dirt,' so are we," writes Walker (paragraph 30). What does she mean? Do you agree? Write an essay taking a stand on this question. Use examples from your own experience to support your stand.

PETER P. SWIRE, born in 1958 in Albany, New York, is a professor of law at the University of Virginia. As a senior at Princeton University, he combined his personal and professional interests, writing his thesis on environmental law.

After graduating from Yale Law School in 1985, Swire practiced in Washington, D.C., and, shortly before turning to teaching, wrote the following piece, which appeared in the *New Republic* on January 30, 1989. Swire addresses the problems of rain forest degradation and global warming and proposes a remedy that recognizes both the differences and the shared interests of developed and developing nations.

TROPICAL CHIC
Peter P. Swire

In case anyone is wondering where Peter Max has been since the early 1970s, the answer is "in creative retreat," according to a spokesman. But now Max is back, and he's determined to use his art "to show his concern for planetary issues," especially the preservation of tropical forests. For instance, Max has produced a "quality line of sportswear" that features shirts saying "Save the Rainforest" and "Hug a Tree." The proceeds will be donated to Peter Max's bank account. But don't get the wrong idea; Max says he plans to hold a $1 million auction of his work, and *that* money will go to the Rainforest Action Network, a San Francisco–based organization devoted to linking rain forest activists.

That's a lot of linking. Max is but one of many cultural heroes who have lined up for the hottest political cause since world hunger. The British rock star Sting has done a rain forest benefit concert at the Kennedy Center. And the Grateful Dead, though long known for consciousness raising, had never raised it for any specific political cause until last September's benefit concert for tropical forests at Madison Square Garden. The audience received an extensive information kit, including ready-to-send postcards to officials at the World Bank, at the United Nations Environment Program, in Congress, and in Brazil. Also: quotes from band members, including drummer Mickey Hart's meditation on "a profound understanding of man's biochemical relationship with nature." Suzanne Vega and Roger Hornsby sang at the concert, and Kermit the Frog was featured in a "Save the Rainforests" film.

Tropical chic is particularly evident in Washington, D.C. The Smithsonian is featuring a major exhibition on rain forests, the National Zoo is raising money to start its own tropical forest, and environmental groups are staffing up on lobbyists and grass-roots activists in the area. Among politicians, tropical forest preservation has moved up the charts to rate mention not only by members of Congress, but by former presidents Ford and Carter and President-elect Bush.

There is one problem with all of this. Backers of the rain forest movement are mostly in the United States or other modern industrialized countries. The rain forests are not. They're mostly in developing countries, which face other, more pressing issues, such as feeding their growing populations. So two questions must be answered. First, why is it our business to tell Brazil, Indonesia, and other forested countries what to do with their forests? And, assuming there's an answer to that question, how can we in developed countries convince the forested countries they should listen to us?

The standard answer to the first question is that the whole world is   5
affected by tropical deforestation, so everyone should have a say in what happens to the forests. The best-known spillover effect is global warming, caused by emission of carbon dioxide and other gases. Deforestation (often to create farmland or ranch land, or just for the lumber) contributes to the greenhouse effect in two ways: burning the trees releases carbon dioxide into the environment, and cutting them reduces the number of trees on hand to convert carbon dioxide back into oxygen. The effect of deforestation on warming is substantial, perhaps one-third of the effect of all burning of fossil fuels. Estimates of the rate of tropical deforestation vary from 27,000 square miles per year (a bit larger than West Virginia) to 77,000 square miles (Nebraska). At the latter rate, the tropical forests, now covering about seven percent of the world's land surface, will disappear by 2050. Recent satellite photos that show thousands of fires in Brazil, ruining 31,000 square miles of virgin forest per year, suggest the higher number may be more accurate.

Unfortunately, the problem of global warming can seem abstract and   6
distant to political leaders struggling with crises of debt, hunger, population growth, and urbanization. More to the point, even if, say, Brazil does recognize the gravity of the greenhouse effect, why should it sacrifice for the entire world? After all, northern countries don't have a long history of such sacrifice. They got rich by cutting their forests and exploiting their minerals. In fact, even since the environmental toll of economic development became evident, northern nations haven't posted a strong record. The United States, for example, has been blocked by political bickering from taking strong action on acid rain. So third world leaders can justifiably tell us to clean up our own back yard before telling them to clean up theirs. In particular, they can demand that we cut our own, sky-high consumption of fossil fuels, which contributes substantially to global warming.

In short, demanding unilateral action from the Southern Hemisphere in   7
the name of the greenhouse effect is unlikely to do any good. And it may backfire, since U.S. pressure is easily seen as Yankee imperialism.

To be sure, in trying to drive home the urgency of saving the rain forests,   8
we can always note, correctly, that the greenhouse effect is not the only problem. Consider the loss of "biodiversity." Tropical forests hold over half of all terrestrial species, and perhaps over 90 percent. Deforestation, at current rates, will lead to a greater extinction of species than accompanied the demise of the dinosaurs. It is hard to reduce this issue to costs and

benefits. Ecologists warn about the large and unpredictable effects that would follow such a mass extinction. Scientists worry about losing the world's most complex ecosystems before most species there are even catalogued, much less studied. Genetic engineers will feel cheated by the loss of their chief feedstock, new genes, just when biotechnology is opening the tropics' genetic diversity to myriad new uses. And many people find human-caused extinctions wrong for moral and aesthetic reasons (which, of all the concerns about biodiversity, turn out to carry the greatest political clout).

Still, with biodiversity as with the greenhouse effect, the question 9 arises: Why should southern nations especially care? Clearing the forests brings them short-term economic gains—at least to their cattle ranchers and governing elites—even if it impedes sustainable economic development. But the long-term, more abstract benefits of saving the forests accrue mostly to the north. That's where the bioengineering and pharmaceutical companies are, and that's where most of the biologists and taxonomists and National Geographic photographers are.

Given that moral suasion is largely unconvincing and ineffective, how 10 are we to get tropical nations to do what we want? Some have proposed boycotting imports of beef raised on burned-out forest plantations, or wood logged in nonsustainable ways. This approach may sometimes work, but it also risks trade retaliation, and it suggests a moral high ground that we may not, in fact, have. Suppose the tropical countries, or other countries, started boycotting U.S. products whose manufacture entailed the burning of fossil fuels (i.e., most U.S. products). How would we feel about that?

The fact is that if the world wants southern nations to stop burning their 11 tropical forests, the world is going to have to pay them to do it. It can either pay them in the same currency, by forging some international environmental agreement under which all nations cut their various contributions to the greenhouse effect, or it can pay them with money. For now, the latter is simpler. And the mechanism for it already exists. The World Bank and the other multilateral development banks (MDBs), such as the Inter-American Development Bank, make more than $24 billion in loans and credits available each year to developing countries. These agencies have been criticized for funding projects that cause great environmental harm. Because the United States and other developed nations provide the funding, they can require the MDBs to pick projects that preserve the forests. There are signs that this is starting already.

The idea of subsidizing the preservation of rain forests has been picked 12 up by some environmental groups in the form of "debt-for-nature swaps" that have offered an attractive deal to debtor nations including Costa Rica, Bolivia, and Ecuador. In these swaps, environmental groups buy up debt in hard-to-get dollars. In return, the debtor government agrees to make conservation investments in the local currency. The symbolism is apt: rather than "borrowing" short-term from their natural resources, the nations reduce debt by preserving those resources. The swaps expand parklands, sponsor environmental education and research, and provide funding for maintaining parklands that otherwise often exist only in theory.

But debt-for-nature swaps remain tiny compared with the economics of the overall debt problem. A far greater help to the rain forests would be an aggressive debt reduction plan that would directly ease the pressure on developing countries to exploit their resources so rapidly. Tropical forest preservation can become a major issue in LDC debt negotiations, joining traditional concerns about promoting democracy and maintaining economic stability. Environmental groups are pushing for such a solution, and Latin American governments are starting to see how effective the greenhouse effect could be in getting them more debt relief than they receive under the Baker Plan's renewed loans. 13

As the debt-for-nature swaps illustrate, environmental groups have done a fair amount of hard-nosed thinking about saving the rain forests. And the statements attributed to their celebrity patrons, for the most part, have been strikingly well informed. But it's important to remember that conscience alone won't save a single tree, and the forested countries are unlikely to respond favorably to stirring moral pleas or self-righteous demands. 14

Resisting faddish rain forest proposals is a particular challenge for Congress. A bill introduced by Representative Claudine Schneider of Rhode Island would require a forest conservation plan from every tropical country (a significant bureaucratic burden for some countries), and *all* activities supported by direct U.S. foreign assistance would then have to be consistent with the plan. Saving the rain forests is important, but not important enough to trump all other goals of foreign aid. 15

Among the better congressional proposals: part of the Agency for International Development (AID) appropriation has been earmarked for rain forest projects, with good results. The next step is to increase the overall level of aid and use it as leverage in the rain forest issues. 16

And what will professed environmentalist George Bush do? He has promised to convene a global conference on the environment in 1989, and to place tropical forest preservation high on the agenda. Sounds fine. But remember: presidents go to Moscow to duck tough domestic issues. Similarly, perhaps Bush will want to go to the international conference rather than tackling the tough, expensive, and controversial environmental issues that await him at home. 17

Be that as it may, the Bush administration can help save tropical forests through AID and the MDBs, by its support on debt-for-nature issues, and by starting to see forest preservation as integrally tied to the debt crisis. Bush can also use his bully pulpit to educate Americans about environmental issues. Perhaps a joint appearance with the Grateful Dead at the Kennedy Center? 18

Questions to Start You Thinking

1. What does Swire see as the chief cause of the rain forest crisis? What solution(s) to this crisis does he propose?

2. How does Swire's evaluation of celebrity involvement in rain forest action help him develop his overall argument?

3. Define *chic* (paragraph 3), *industrialized countries, developing countries* (paragraph 4), *unilateral* (paragraph 7), *biodiversity, ecosystems, biotechnology* (paragraph 8), *taxonomists* (paragraph 9), *suasion* (paragraph 10), and *bully pulpit* (paragraph 18).

4. Would Swire agree with any of the points that Kirkpatrick Sale makes in "The Environmental Crisis Is Not Our Fault" (p. 579)? Which points and why? On what points would the two authors disagree? Why?

Suggestions for Writing

1. Write a short essay discussing your own exposure to a particular environmental issue. Analyze the problem's causes and effects and propose a solution. You should focus on a specific issue that affects you, such as a controversy over the use of incinerators in your hometown or the dumping of hazardous waste.

2. Swire seems skeptical of the effectiveness of celebrity involvement in political and social issues. Write an essay discussing the following questions: On what kinds of issues should celebrities make their opinions known? How seriously should the public take them? What dangers are there in celebrity politics?

KIRKPATRICK SALE was born in 1937 in Ithaca, New York, and received his B.A. from Cornell University in 1958. He has been an editor and correspondent for the *New Leader*, the *San Francisco Chronicle*, and the *New York Times Magazine*. A frequent contributor to a range of journals, Sale deals in his work with the relatedness of environmental and political issues. His books include *The CIA and World Peace* (1976) and *Human Scale* (1980). In the following article, which appeared in *The Nation* on April 30, 1990, Sale argues that while individual efforts celebrated at events like Earth Day are valuable, they are inadequate solutions to the ecological crisis.

THE ENVIRONMENTAL CRISIS IS NOT OUR FAULT
Kirkpatrick Sale

I am as resonsible as most eco-citizens: I bike everywhere; I don't own   1
a car; I recycle newspapers, bottles, cans and plastics; I have a vegetable
garden in the summer; I buy organic products; and I put all vegetable waste

into my backyard compost bin, probably the only one in all of Greenwich Village. But I don't at the same time believe that I am saving the planet, or in fact doing anything of much consequence about the various eco-crises around us. What's more, I don't even believe that if "all of us" as individuals started doing the same it would make any but the slightest difference, and then only of degree and not—where it counts—of kind.

Leave aside ozone depletion and rain forest destruction—those are patently corporate crimes that no individual actions will remedy to any degree. Take, instead, energy consumption in this country. In 1987 (the most recent figures) residential consumption was 7.2 percent of the total, commercial 5.5 percent and industrial 23.3 percent; of the remainder, 27.8 percent was transportation (about one-third of it by private car) and 36.3 percent was electric generation (about one-third for residential use). Individual energy use, in sum, was something like 28 percent of total consumption. Therefore, although you and I cutting down on energy consumption would have some small effect (and should be done), it is surely the energy consumption of industry and other large institutions such as government and agribusiness that needs to be addressed first. And it is industry and government that must be forced to explain what their consumption is for, what is produced by it, how necessary it is and how it can be drastically reduced. They need an Earth Day more than we do.

The point is that the ecological crisis *is* essentially beyond "our" control, as citizens or householders or consumers or even voters. It is not something that can be halted by recycling or double-pane insulation. It is the inevitable by-product of our modern industrial civilization, dominated by capitalist production and consumption and serviced and protected by various institutions of government, federal to local. It cannot possibly be altered or reversed by simple individual actions, even by the actions of the millions who will take part in Earth Day—and even if they all went home and fixed their refrigerators and from then on walked to work. Nothing less than a drastic overhaul of this civilization and an abandonment of its ingrained gods—progress, growth, exploitation, technology, materialism, humanism and power—will do anything substantial to halt our path to environmental destruction, and it's hard to see how the lifestyle solutions offered by Earth Day will have an effect on that.

What I find truly pernicious about such solutions is that they get people thinking they are actually making a difference and doing their part to halt the destruction of the earth: "There, I've taken all the bottles to the recycling center and used my string bag at the grocery store; I guess that'll take care of global warming." It is the kind of thing that diverts people from the hard truths and hard choices and hard actions, from the recognition that they have to take on the larger forces of society—corporate and governmental—where true power, and true destructiveness, lie.

And to the argument that, well, you have to start somewhere to raise people's consciousness, I would reply that this individualistic approach does not in fact raise consciousness. It does not move people beyond their old familiar liberal perceptions of the world, it does nothing to challenge the belief in technofix or write-your-Congressperson solutions and it does not begin to provide them with the new vocabulary and modes of thought necessary for a true change of consciousness. We need, for example, to think of recycling centers not as the answer to our waste problems, as Earth Day suggests, but as a confession that the system of packaging and production in this society is out of control. Recycling centers are like hospitals; they are the institutions at the end of the cycle that take care of problems that would never exist if ecological criteria had operated at the beginning of the cycle. Until we have those kinds of understandings, we will not do anything with consciousness except reinforce it with the same misguided ideas that created the crisis. . . .

Questions to Start You Thinking

1. What does Sale mean when he says that the environmental crisis is not our fault? Is he arguing that we should not attempt to be ecologically responsible? Explain.
2. How does Sale use facts and figures to support his stand?
3. Define *patently, agribusiness* (paragraph 2), *capitalist* (paragraph 3), and *pernicious* (paragraph 4).
4. Would Sale agree with the views Alice Walker expresses in "When a Tree Falls" (p. 567)? How might the two writers disagree?

Suggestions for Writing

1. Taking on the role of an investigative reporter, write a brief essay examining how you and others in your home, school, or workplace are attempting to be environmentally responsible. How will your efforts help improve the environment?
2. Evaluate Sale's argument in this essay. What kinds of solutions does he propose to the ecological crisis? How reasonable are these solutions? In a short essay, take a stand for or against Sale's position.

DAVID QUAMMEN was born in Cincinnati in 1948. He earned degrees at Yale University and, as a Rhodes Scholar, at Oxford University, after which he returned to the United States to live and write in Bozeman, Montana. He has written three novels and two books on the environment, *Natural Acts* (1985) and *The Flight of the Iguana* (1988). He is a frequent contributor to the magazine *Outside,* in which the following piece appeared in May 1983. Although he is not a scientist by training, Quammen is a writer of great curiosity, insight, and wit, always ready to take an unusual approach to a subject.

A REPUBLIC OF COCKROACHES:
WHEN THE ULTIMATE EXTERMINATOR
MEETS THE ULTIMATE PEST
David Quammen

In the fifth chapter of Matthew's gospel, Christ is quoted as saying that 1
the meek shall inherit the earth, but other opinion lately suggests that, no,
more likely it will go to the cockroaches.

A decidedly ugly and disheartening prospect: our entire dear planet— 2
after the final close of all human business—ravaged and overrun by great
multitudes of cockroaches, whole plagues of them, whole scuttering herds
shoulder to shoulder like the old herds of bison, vast cockroach legions
sweeping as inexorably as driver ants over the empty prairies. Unfortunately
this vision is not just the worst Kafkaesque fantasy of some fevered pessimist. There is also a touch of hard science involved.

The cockroach, as it happens, is a popular test subject for laboratory 3
research. It adapts well to captivity, lives relatively long, reproduces
quickly, and will subsist in full vigor on Purina Dog Chow. The largest American species, up to two inches in length and known as *Periplaneta americana*, is even big enough for easy dissection. One eminent physiologist
has written fondly: "The laboratory investigator who keeps up a battle to
rid his rat colony of cockroaches may well consider giving up the rats and
working with the cockroaches instead. From many points of view the roach
is practically made to order as a laboratory subject. Here is an animal of
frugal habits, tenacious of life, eager to live in the laboratory and very
modest in its space requirements." Tenacious of life indeed. Not only in
kitchen cupboards, not only among the dark corners of basements, is the
average cockroach a hard beast to kill. Also in the laboratory. And so also
it would be, evidently, in the ashes of civilization. Among the various biological studies for which cockroaches have served as the guinea pigs—on
hormone activity, parasitism, development of resistance against insecti-
cides, and numerous other topics—have been some rather suggestive experiments concerning cockroach survival and atomic radiation.

Survival. Over the centuries, over the millennia, over the geologic 4
epochs and periods and eras, that is precisely what this animal has proved
itself to be good at. The cockroach is roughly 250 million years old, which
makes it the oldest of living insects, possibly even the oldest known air-
breathing animal. Admittedly "250 million years" is just one of those stupe-
fying and inexpressive paleontological numbers, so think of it this way:
long before the first primitive mammal appeared on earth, before the first
bird, before the first pine tree, before even the reptiles began to assert
themselves, cockroaches were running wild. They were thriving in the great
humid tropical forests that covered much of the Earth then, during what
geologists now call the Carboniferous period (because so much of that thick
swampy vegetation was eventually turned into coal). Cockroaches were by
far the dominant insect of the Carboniferous, outnumbering all other spe-

cies together, and among the most dominant of animals. In fact, sometimes this period is loosely referred to as the Age of Cockroaches. But unlike the earlier trilobites, unlike the later dinosaurs, cockroaches lingered on quite successfully (though less obtrusively) long after their heyday—because, unlike the trilobites and the dinosaurs, cockroaches were versatile.

They were generalists. Those primitive early cockroaches possessed a 5 simple and very practical anatomical design that remains almost unchanged in the cockroaches of today. Throughout their evolutionary history they have avoided wild morphological experiments like those of their near relatives, the mantids and walking sticks, and so many other bizarrely evolved insects. For cockroaches the byword has been: keep it simple. Consequently today, as always, they can live almost anywhere and eat almost anything.

Unlike most insects, they have mouthparts that enable them to take 6 hard foods, soft foods, and liquids. They will feed on virtually any organic substance. One study, written a century ago and still considered authoritative, lists their food preferences as "Bark, leaves, the pith of living cycads [fern palms], paper, woollen clothes, sugar, cheese, bread, blacking, oil, lemons, ink, flesh, fish, leather, the dead bodies of other Cockroaches, their own cast skins and empty egg-capsules," adding that "Cucumber, too, they will eat, though it disagrees with them horribly." So much for cucumber.

They are flattened enough to squeeze into the narrowest hiding place, 7 either in human habitations or in the wild. They are quick on their feet, and can fly when they need to. But the real reason for their long-continued success and their excellent prospects for the future is that, beyond these few simple tools for living, they have never specialized.

It happens to be the very same thing that, until recently, could be said 8 of *Homo sapiens.*

Now one further quote from the experts, in summary, and because it 9 has for our purposes here a particular odd resonance. "Cockroaches," say two researchers who worked under sponsorship of the United States Army, "are tough, resilient insects with amazing endurance and the ability to recover rapidly from almost complete extermination."

It was Jonathan Schell's best-selling jeremiad *The Fate of the Earth,* 10 published in 1982, that started me thinking about cockroach survival. *The Fate of the Earth* is a very strange sort of book, deeply unappealing, not very well written, windy and repetitious, yet powerful and valuable beyond measure. In fact, it may be the dreariest piece of writing that I ever wished everyone in America would read. Its subject is, of course, the abiding danger of nuclear Armageddon. Specifically, it describes in relentless scientific detail the likelihood of total human extinction following a full-scale nuclear war. In a section that Schell titles "A Republic of Insects and Grass," there is a discussion of the relative prospects for different animal species surviving to propagate again after mankind's final war. Schell takes his facts from a 1970 symposium held at Brookhaven National Laboratory, and in summarizing that government-sponsored research he says:

> For example, the lethal doses of gamma radiation for animals in pasture, where 11
> fallout would be descending on them directly and they would be eating fallout
> that had fallen on the grass, and would thus suffer from doses of beta radiation
> as well, would be one hundred and eighty rads [a standard unit of absorbed
> radiation] for cattle; two hundred and forty rads for sheep; five hundred and
> fifty rads for swine; three hundred and fifty rads for horses; and eight hundred
> rads for poultry. In a ten-thousand-megaton attack, which would create levels
> of radiation around the country averaging more than ten thousand rads, most
> of the mammals of the United States would be killed off. The lethal doses for
> birds are in roughly the same range as those for mammals, and birds, too,
> would be killed off. Fish are killed at doses of between one thousand one
> hundred rads and about five thousand six hundred rads, but their fate is less
> predictable. On the one hand, water is a shield from radiation, and would afford
> some protection; on the other hand, fallout might concentrate in bodies of
> water as it ran off from the land. (Because radiation causes no pain, animals,
> wandering at will through the environment, would not avoid it.) The one class
> of animals containing a number of species quite likely to survive, at least in
> the short run, is the insect class, for which in most known cases the lethal
> doses lie between about two thousand rads and about a hundred thousand
> rads. Insects, therefore, would be destroyed selectively. Unfortunately for the
> rest of the environment, many of the phytophagous species [the plant-eaters]
> . . . have very high tolerances, and so could be expected to survive dispropor-
> tionately, and then to multiply greatly in the aftermath of an attack.

Among the most ravaging of those phytophagous species referred to 12
by Schell is an order of insects called the Orthoptera. The order Orthoptera
includes locusts, like those Moses brought down on Egypt in plagues. It
also includes crickets, mantids, walking sticks, and cockroaches.

Ten thousand rads, according to Schell's premises, is roughly the aver- 13
age dosage that might be received by most living things during the week
immediately following Armageddon. By coincidence, 10,000 rads is also
the dosage administered to certain test animals in a study conducted, some
twenty-four years ago, by two researchers named Wharton and Wharton.
The write-up can be found in a 1959 volume of the journal *Radiation Research*. The experiment was performed under the auspices, again, of the
U.S. Army. The radiation was administered from a two-million-electron-volt
Van de Graaff accelerator. The test animals were *Periplaneta americana*,
those big American cockroaches.

Remember now, a dose of 180 rads is enough to kill a Hereford. A 14
horse will die after taking 350 rads. The average lethal dose for humans
isn't precisely known (because no one is performing quite such systematic
experiments on humans, though again the Army has come closest, with
those hapless GIs forced to ogle detonations at the Nevada Test Site), but
somewhere around 600 rads seems to be a near guess.

By contrast, cockroaches in the laboratory dosed with 830 rads rou- 15 tinely survive to die of old age. Their *average* lethal dose seems to be up around 3200 rads. And of those that Wharton and Wharton blasted with 10,000 rads, *half* of the group were still alive two weeks later.

The Whartons in their *Radiation Research* paper don't say *how much* 16 longer those hardiest cockroaches lasted. But it was long enough, evidently, for egg capsules to be delivered, and hatch, and for the cycle of cockroach survival and multiplication—unbroken throughout the past 250 million years—to continue on. Long enough to suggest that, if the worst happened, cockroaches in great and growing number would be around to dance on the grave of the human species.

With luck maybe it won't happen—that ultimately ugly event foreseen 17 so vividly by Jonathan Schell. With luck, and with also a gale of informed and persistent outrage by citizenries more sensible than their leaders. But with less luck, less persistence, what I can't help but envision for our poor raw festering planet, in those days and years after the After, is, like once before, an Age of Cockroaches.

PARTIAL SOURCES

Cornwell, P. B. *The Cockroach.* London: Hutchinson, 1968.

Guthrie, D. M., and A. R. Tindall. *The Biology of the Cockroach.* New York: St. Martin's Press, 1968.

Miall, L. C., and Alfred Denny. *The Structure and Life-History of the Cockroach* (Periplaneta orientalis). London: L. Reeve, 1886.

Rau, Phil. "The Life History of the American Cockroach, *Periplaneta americana* Linn. (Orthop.: Blattidae)." *Entomological News* 51 (1940).

Schell, Jonathan. *The Fate of the Earth.* New York: Knopf, 1982.

Wharton, D. R. A., and Martha L. Wharton. "The Effect of Radiation on the Longevity of the Cockroach, *Periplaneta americana,* as Affected by Dose, Age, Sex, and Food Intake." *Radiation Research* 11 (1959).

Questions to Start You Thinking

1. Why does Quammen introduce the subject of nuclear war into an essay on cockroaches? How does he connect these two topics? What overall point is he trying to make in this piece?

2. How does Quammen use Jonathan Schell's *The Fate of the Earth* as a springboard for his own ideas in this essay? How does he work quotations from his reading into his argument?

3. Is Quammen's language very technical? Who is his intended audience? Define *Kafkaesque* (paragraph 2), *tenacious* (paragraph 3), *paleontological* (paragraph 4), *morphological* (paragraph 5), *jeremiad* and *Armageddon* (paragraph 10).

4. Compare this essay with Annie Dillard's "Fecundity" (p. 586). Both are about death and the persistence of species, but are the two selections similar in other ways? How do they differ?

Suggestions for Writing

1. In this selection, Quammen implies that the human race has much to learn from the cockroach's adaptability. Select an animal from which you think humanity could learn a lesson, and write a short essay analyzing the animal's strengths and explaining why we would do well to imitate it.

2. Write an essay taking a stand on the issue of nuclear education. In your opinion, is nuclear war still an important concern? What should people know about nuclear armament?

ANNIE DILLARD, born in 1945 in Pittsburgh, writes essays, poetry, and fiction that offer a philosophic and quietly passionate response to the natural world. Educated at Hollins College, Virginia, Dillard won a wide following and a Pulitzer Prize with her first book of essays, *Pilgrim at Tinker Creek* (1974). Her later writings include *Teaching a Stone to Talk* (1982), *An American Childhood* (1987), *The Writing Life* (1989), and *The Living* (1992). In the following excerpt from *Tinker Creek*, Dillard contemplates her mixed responses to the realization that nature is indifferent to human suffering.

FECUNDITY
Annie Dillard

I have to look at the landscape of the blue-green world again. Just think: in all the clean beautiful reaches of the solar system, our planet alone is a blot; our planet alone has death. I have to acknowledge that the sea is a cup of death and the land is a stained altar stone. We the living are survivors huddled on flotsam, living on jetsam. We are escapees. We wake in terror, eat in hunger, sleep with a mouthful of blood. 1

Death: W. C. Fields called death "the Fellow in the Bright Nightgown." He shuffles around the house in all the corners I've forgotten, all the halls I dare not call to mind or visit for fear I'll glimpse the hem of his shabby, dazzling gown disappearing around a turn. This is the monster evolution loves. How could it be? 2

The faster death goes, the faster evolution goes. If an aphid lays a million eggs, several might survive. Now, my right hand, in all its human cunning, could not make one aphid in a thousand years. But these aphid eggs — which run less than a dime a dozen, which run absolutely free — can make aphids as effortlessly as the sea makes waves. Wonderful things, wasted. It's a wretched system. Arthur Stanley Eddington, the British physicist and astronomer who died in 1944, suggested that all of "Nature" could conceivably run on the same deranged scheme. "If indeed she has 3 no greater aim than to provide a home for her greatest experiment, Man, it would be just like her methods to scatter a million stars whereof one might haply achieve her purpose." I doubt very much that this is the aim, but it seems clear on all fronts that this is the method.

Say you are the manager of the Southern Railroad. You figure that you   4
need three engines for a stretch of track between Lynchburg and Danville. It's a mighty steep grade. So at fantastic effort and expense you have your shops make nine thousand engines. Each engine must be fashioned just so, every rivet and bolt secure, every wire twisted and wrapped, every needle on every indicator sensitive and accurate.

You send all nine thousand of them out on the runs. Although there are   5
engineers at the throttles, no one is manning the switches. The engines crash, collide, derail, jump, jam, burn. . . . At the end of the massacre you have three engines, which is what the run could support in the first place. There are few enough of them that they can stay out of each others' paths.

You go to your board of directors and show them what you've done. And   6
what are they going to say? You know what they're going to say. They're going to say: It's a hell of a way to run a railroad.

Is it a better way to run a universe?   7

Evolution loves death more than it loves you or me. This is easy to   8
write, easy to read, and hard to believe. The words are simple, the concept clear—but you don't believe it, do you? Nor do I. How could I, when we're both so lovable? Are my values then so diametrically opposed to those that nature preserves? This is the key point.

Must I then part ways with the only world I know? I had thought to live   9
by the side of the creek in order to shape my life to its free flow. But I seem to have reached a point where I must draw the line. It looks as though the creek is not buoying me up but dragging me down. Look: Cock Robin may die the most gruesome of slow deaths, and nature is no less pleased; the sun comes up, the creek rolls on, the survivors still sing. I cannot feel that way about your death, nor you about mine, nor either of us about the robin's—nor even the barnacles'. We value the individual supremely, and nature values him not a whit. It looks for the moment as though I might have to reject this creek life unless I want to be utterly brutalized. Is human culture with its values my only real home after all? Can it possibly be that I should move my anchor-hold to the side of a library? This direction of thought brings me abruptly to a fork in the road where I stand paralyzed, unwilling to go on, for both ways lead to madness.

Either this world, my mother, is a monster, or I myself am a freak.   10

Consider the former: the world is a monster. Any three-year-old can see   11
how unsatisfactory and clumsy is this whole business of reproducing and dying by the billions. We have not yet encountered any god who is as merciful as a man who flicks a beetle over on its feet. There is not a people in the world who behaves as badly as praying mantises. But wait, you say, there is no right and wrong in nature; right and wrong is a human concept. Precisely: we are moral creatures, then, in an amoral world. The universe

that suckled us is a monster that does not care if we live or die — does not care if it itself grinds to a halt. It is fixed and blind, a robot programmed to kill. We are free and seeing; we can only try to outwit it at every turn to save our skins.

This view requires that a monstrous world running on chance and death, 12 careening blindly from nowhere to nowhere, somehow produced wonderful us. I came from the world, I crawled out of a sea of amino acids, and now I must whirl around and shake my fist at that sea and cry Shame! If I value anything at all, then I must blindfold my eyes when I near the Swiss Alps. We must as a culture dissemble our telescopes and settle down to back-slapping. We little blobs of soft tissue crawling around on this one planet's skin are right, and the whole universe is wrong.

Or consider the alternative. 13

Julian of Norwich, the great English anchorite and theologian, cited, in 14 the manner of the prophets, these words from God: "See, I am God: see, I am in all things: see, I never lift my hands off my works, nor ever shall, without end. . . . How should anything be amiss?" But now not even the simplest and best of us sees things the way Julian did. It seems to us that plenty is amiss. So much is amiss that I must consider the second fork in the road, that creation itself is blamelessly, benevolently askew by its very free nature, and that it is only human feeling that is freakishly amiss. The frog that the giant water bug sucked had, presumably, a rush of pure feeling for about a second, before its brain turned to broth. I, however, have been sapped by various strong feelings about the incident almost daily for several years.

Do the barnacle larvae care? Does the lacewing who eats her eggs 15 care? If they do not care, then why am I making all this fuss? If I am a freak, then why don't I hush?

Our excessive emotions are so patently painful and harmful to us as a 16 species that I can hardly believe that they evolved. Other creatures manage to have effective matings and even stable societies without great emotions, and they have a bonus in that they need not ever mourn. (But some higher animals have emotions that we think are similar to ours: dogs, elephants, otters, and the sea mammals mourn their dead. Why do that to an otter? What creator could be so cruel, not to kill otters, but to let them care?) It would seem that emotions are the curse, not death — emotions that appear to have devolved upon a few freaks as a special curse from Malevolence.

All right then. It is our emotions that are amiss. We are freaks, the 17 world is fine, and let us all go have lobotomies to restore us to a natural state. We can leave the library then, go back to the creek lobotomized, and live on its banks as untroubled as any muskrat or reed. You first.

Of the two ridiculous alternatives, I rather favor the second. Although 18 it is true that we are moral creatures in an amoral world, the world's amorality does not make it a monster. Rather, I am the freak. Perhaps I don't need a lobotomy, but I could use some calming down, and the creek is just the place for it. I must go down to the creek again. It is where I belong, although as I become closer to it, my fellows appear more and more freakish, and my home in the library more and more limited. Imperceptibly at first, and now consciously, I shy away from the arts, from the human emotional stew. I read what the men with telescopes and microscopes have to say about the landscape. I read about the polar ice, and I drive myself deeper and deeper into exile from my own kind. But, since I cannot avoid the library altogether—the human culture that taught me to speak in its tongue—I bring human values to the creek, and so save myself from being brutalized.

What I have been after all along is not an explanation but a picture.   19
This is the way the world is, altar and cup, lit by the fire from a star that has only begun to die. My rage and shock at the pain and death of individuals of my kind is the old, old mystery, as old as man, but forever fresh, and completely unanswerable. My reservations about the fecundity and waste of life among other creatures is, however, mere squeamishness. After all, I'm the one having the nightmares. It is true that many of the creatures live and die abominably, but I am not called upon to pass judgment. Nor am I called upon to live in that same way, and those creatures who are are mercifully unconscious.

I don't want to cut this too short. Let me pull the camera back and look   20
at that fork in the road from a distance, in the larger context of the speckled and twining world. I could be that the fork will disappear, or that I will see it to be but one of many interstices in a network, so that it is impossible to say which line is the main part and which is the fork.

The picture of fecundity and its excesses and of the pressures of growth   21
and its accidents is of course no different from the picture I painted before of the world as an intricate texture of a bizarre variety of forms. Only now the shadows are deeper. Extravagance takes on a sinister, wastrel air, and exuberance blithers. When I added the dimension of time to the landscape of the world, I saw how freedom grew the beauties and horrors from the same live branch. This landscape is the same as that one, with a few more details added, and a different emphasis. I see squashes expanding with pressure and a hunk of wood rapt on the desert floor. The rye plant and the Bronx ailanthus are literally killing themselves to make seeds, and the animals to lay eggs. Instead of one goldfish swimming in its intricate bowl, I see tons and tons of goldfish laying and eating billions and billions of eggs. The point of all the eggs is of course to make goldfish one by one— nature loves the *idea* of the individual, if not the individual himself—and the point of a goldfish is pizzazz. This is familiar ground. I merely failed to mention that it is death that is spinning the globe.

It is harder to take, but surely it's been thought about. I cannot really   22
get very exercised over the hideous appearance and habits of some deep-sea jellies and fishes, and I exercise easy. But about the topic of my own death I am decidedly touchy. Nevertheless, the two phenomena are two branches of the same creek, the creek that waters the world. Its source is

freedom, and its network of branches is infinite. The graceful mockingbird that falls drinks there and sips in the same drop a beauty that waters its eyes and a death that fledges and flies. The petals of tulips are flaps of the same doomed water that swells and hatches in the ichneumon's gut.

That something is everywhere and always amiss is part of the very stuff 23 of creation. It is as though each clay form had baked into it, fired into it, a blue streak of nonbeing, a shaded emptiness like a bubble that not only shapes its very structure but that also causes it to list and ultimately explode. We could have planned things more mercifully, perhaps, but our plan would never get off the drawing board until we agreed to the very compromising terms that are the only ones that being offers.

The world has signed a pact with the devil; it had to. It is a covenant 24 to which every thing, even every hydrogen atom, is bound. The terms are clear: if you want to live, you have to die; you cannot have mountains and creeks without space, and space is a beauty married to a blind man. The blind man is Freedom, or Time, and he does not go anywhere without his great dog Death. The world came into being with the signing of the contract. A scientist calls it the Second Law of Thermodynamics. A poet says, "The force that through the green fuse drives the flower/Drives my green age." This is what we know. The rest is gravy.

Questions to Start You Thinking

1. Why does Dillard find it frightening to contemplate evolution? What does she mean when she says that "evolution loves death more than it loves you or me" (paragraph 8)?

2. Select one of Dillard's uses of cause and effect and examine it closely. How does it help in her analysis? How does it support her main idea?

3. How does Dillard use language to convey sensory images? Define *jetsam* (paragraph 1), *anchorite* (paragraph 14), *patently* (paragraph 16), *fecundity* (paragraph 21), and *exercised* (paragraph 22).

4. Compare Dillard's essay with E. B. White's "Once More to the Lake" (p. 425). How are the writers' experiences of nature similar? How do they differ?

Suggestions for Writing

1. Write a short personal essay about an observation of nature that affected you deeply. Describe the event using images of sight, sound, touch, and smell. Try to make the reader feel the experience as you felt it. What thoughts did it inspire? What emotions?

2. "There is no right and wrong in nature; right and wrong is a human concept. . . . we are moral creatures, then, in an amoral world," writes Dillard (paragraph 11). In a brief essay, compare and contrast animal behavior with human behavior. Is the animal world "crueler" than our own? What are human ideals of right and wrong; do humans behave according to these ideals? Include examples from your experience and observations.

STEPHEN JAY GOULD, born in 1941 in New York City, may be the most creative and widely read biologist of our times. He earned his B.A. at Antioch College and his Ph.D. at Columbia University and since 1967 has taught at Harvard University and written widely for a general audience. His books include *Ever Since Darwin* (1977), *The Mismeasure of Man* (1981), and *Time's Arrow, Time's Cycle* (1987). Like Margaret Mead, Gould has a gift for making science entertaining and accessible to all readers, and he is not shy about discussing social issues such as the value of IQ tests. In the following essay, published in the *New York Times Magazine* on April 30, 1987, Gould takes a concerned but unsentimental look at the biological context of AIDS and draws inferences on how best to resist the virus, not only with science but with new attitudes.

THE TERRIFYING NORMALCY OF AIDS
Stephen Jay Gould

Disney's Epcot Center in Orlando, Fla., is a technological tour de force 1 and a conceptual desert. In this permanent World's Fair, American industrial giants have built their versions of an unblemished future. These masterful entertainments convey but one message, brilliantly packaged and relentlessly expressed: progress through technology is the solution to all human problems. G.E. proclaims from Horizons: "If we can dream it, we can do it." A.T.&T. speaks from on high within its giant golf ball: We are now "unbounded by space and time." United Technologies bubbles from the depths of Living Seas: "With the help of modern technology, we feel there's really no limit to what can be accomplished."

Yet several of these exhibits at the Experimental Prototype Community 2 of Tomorrow, all predating last year's space disaster, belie their stated message from within by using the launch of the shuttle as a visual metaphor for technological triumph. The Challenger disaster may represent a general malaise, but it remains an incident. The AIDS pandemic, an issue that may rank with nuclear weaponry as the greatest danger of our era, provides a more striking proof that mind and technology are not omnipotent and that we have not canceled our bond to nature.

In 1984, John Platt, a biophysicist who taught at the University of Chi- 3 cago for many years, wrote a short paper for private circulation. At a time when most of us were either ignoring AIDS, or viewing it as a contained and peculiar affliction of homosexual men, Platt recognized that the limited data on the origin of AIDS and its spread in America suggested a more frightening prospect: we are all susceptible to AIDS, and the disease has been spreading in a simple exponential manner.

Exponential growth is a geometric increase. Remember the old kiddy 4 problem: if you place a penny on square one of a checkerboard and double the number of coins on each subsequent square — 2, 4, 8, 16, 32 . . . — how big is the stack by the 64th square? The answer: about as high as the universe is wide. Nothing in the external environment inhibits this increase, thus giving to exponential processes their relentless character. In the real, noninfinite world, of course, some limit will eventually arise, and the process slows down, reaches a steady state, or destroys the entire system: the stack of pennies falls over, the bacterial cells exhaust their supply of nutrients.

Platt noticed that data for the initial spread of AIDS fell right on an 5 exponential curve. He then followed the simplest possible procedure of extrapolating the curve unabated into the 1990s. Most of us were incredulous, accusing Platt of the mathematical gamesmanship that scientists call "curve fitting." After all, aren't exponential models unrealistic? Surely we are not all susceptible to AIDS. Is it not spread only by odd practices to odd people? Will it not, therefore, quickly run its short course within a confined group?

Well, hello 1987 — worldwide data still match Platt's extrapolated 6 curve. This will not, of course, go on forever. AIDS has probably already saturated the African areas where it probably originated, and where the sex ratio of afflicted people is 1-to-1, male-female. But AIDS still has far to spread, and may be moving exponentially, through the rest of the world. We have learned enough about the cause of AIDS to slow its spread, if we can make rapid and fundamental changes in our handling of that most powerful part of human biology — our own sexuality. But medicine, as yet, has nothing to offer as a cure and precious little even for palliation.

This exponential spread of AIDS not only illuminates its, and our, biol- 7 ogy, but also underscores the tragedy of our moralistic misperception. Exponential processes have a definite time and place of origin, an initial point of "inoculation" — in this case, Africa. We didn't notice the spread at first. In a population of billions, we pay little attention when 1 increases to 2, or 8 to 16, but when 1 million becomes 2 million, we panic, even though the *rate* of doubling has not increased.

The infection has to start somewhere, and its initial locus may be little 8 more than an accident of circumstance. For a while, it remains confined to those in close contact with the primary source, but only by accident of proximity, not by intrinsic susceptibility. Eventually, given the power and lability of human sexuality, it spreads outside the initial group and into the general population. And now AIDS has begun its march through our own heterosexual community.

What a tragedy that our moral stupidity caused us to lose precious 9 time, the greatest enemy in fighting an exponential spread, by downplaying the danger because we thought that AIDS was a disease of three irregular groups of minorities: minorities of lifestyle (needle users), of sexual preference (homosexuals) and of color (Haitians). If AIDS had first been imported from Africa into a Park Avenue apartment, we would not have dithered as the exponential march began.

The message of Orlando — the inevitability of technological solutions — 10
is wrong, and we need to understand why.

Our species has not won its independence from nature, and we cannot 11
do all that we can dream. Or at least we cannot do it at the rate required
to avoid tragedy, for we are not unbounded from time. Viral diseases are
preventable in principle, and I suspect that an AIDS vaccine will one day
be produced. But how will this discovery avail us if it takes until the millennium, and by then AIDS has fully run its exponential course and saturated our population, killing a substantial percentage of the human race?
A fight against an exponential enemy is primarily a race against time.

We must also grasp the perspective of ecology and evolutionary biology 12
and recognize, once we reinsert ourselves properly into nature, that AIDS
represents the ordinary workings of biology, not an irrational or diabolical
plague with a moral meaning. Disease, including epidemic spread, is a
natural phenomenon, part of human history from the begining. An entire
subdiscipline of my profession, paleopathology, studies the evidence of
ancient diseases preserved in the fossil remains of organisms. Human
history has been marked by episodic plagues. More native peoples died of
imported disease than ever fell before the gun during the era of colonial
expansion. Our memories are short, and we have had a respite, really, only
since the influenza pandemic at the end of World War I, but AIDS must be
viewed as a virulent expression of an ordinary natural phenomenon.

I do not say this to foster either comfort or complacency. The evolu- 13
tionary perspective is correct, but utterly inappropriate for our human scale.
Yes, AIDS is a natural phenomenon, one of a recurring class of pandemic
diseases. Yes, AIDS may run through the entire population, and may carry
off a quarter or more of us. Yes, it may make no *biological* difference to
Homo sapiens in the long run: there will still be plenty of us left and we
can start again. Evolution cares as little for its agents — organisms struggling for reproductive success — as physics cares for individual atoms of
hydrogen in the sun. But *we* care. These atoms are our neighbors, our
lovers, our children, and ourselves. AIDS is both a natural phenomenon
and, potentially, the greatest natural tragedy in human history.

The cardboard message of Epcot fosters the wrong attitudes; we must 14
both reinsert ourselves into nature and view AIDS as a natural phenomenon
in order to fight properly. If we stand above nature and if technology is all-
powerful, then AIDS is a horrifying anomaly that must be trying to tell us
something. If so, we can adopt one of two attitudes, each potentially fatal.
We can either become complacent, because we believe the message of
Epcot and assume that medicine will soon generate a cure, or we can panic
in confusion and seek a scapegoat for something so irregular that it must
have been visited upon us to teach us a moral lesson.

But AIDS is not irregular. It is part of nature. So are we. This should 15
galvanize us and give us hope, not prompt the worst of all responses: a

kind of "new-age" negativism that equates natural with what we must accept and cannot, or even should not, change. When we view AIDS as natural, and when we recognize both the exponential property of its spread and the accidental character of its point of entry into America, we can break through our destructive tendencies to blame others and to free ourselves of concern.

If AIDS is natural, then there is no *message* in its spread. But by all   16
that science has learned and all that rationality proclaims, AIDS works by a *mechanism* — and we can discover it. Victory is not ordained by any principle of progress, or any slogan of technology, so we shall have to fight like hell, and be watchful. There is no message, but there is a mechanism.

Questions to Start You Thinking

1. According to Gould, what is the "message" of the Epcot Center? How does Gould connect his discussion of this "message" with the problem of AIDS?

2. What evidence does Gould cite to support his stand that technology cannot solve all our problems? Does Gould propose a solution to the AIDS crisis? If so, what is it?

3. How does Gould's choice of language help establish his authority? Define *tour de force* (paragraph 1), *malaise, omnipotent* (paragraph 2), *affliction* (paragraph 3), *exponential* (paragraph 4), *palliation* (paragraph 6), *locus, proximity, intrinsic* (paragraph 8), *millennium* (paragraph 11), *epidemic, pandemic* (paragraph 12), and *anomaly* (paragraph 14).

4. How does Gould's view of nature differ from Annie Dillard's in "Fecundity" (p. 586). Why might this be?

Suggestions for Writing

1. What should society do about the AIDS crisis? What should governments do to solve the AIDS problem? What actions should individuals take? Write a short essay proposing a solution and taking a stand on this issue.

2. Gould writes that "the message of Orlando — the inevitability of technological solutions — is wrong" (paragraph 10). What does he mean? In a brief essay, discuss another problem of modern life to which Gould's statement might apply. How does society have blind faith that science will solve this problem? What other actions may need to be taken?

A
WRITER'S
RESEARCH
MANUAL

To do research is, in a sense, to venture into the unknown: to explore, to experiment, to discover, to revise thinking. When its object is to probe the mysterious recesses of the human brain or the far galaxies, research can be thrilling. That may be why some people devote their lives to such investigation—in libraries, in the field, in laboratories.

In one college research paper due in a month, you may not make any earth-shaking discoveries. You won't be expected to unfold the secrets of the brain or the Spiral Nebula. Even so, you just might find a little excitement as you become increasingly aware that in doing research you don't merely paste together information and opinions taken from other people; you use that material to think for yourself. You arrive at your own fresh view.

To help you find your own view and express it convincingly, our assignment for a library research paper in Chapter 27 is fairly simple. If you take our advice, you will conduct a short investigation, not an extremely deep one. But you *will* learn how to do research in a library, how to use various useful sources to fulfill a purpose, and how to bring together your findings in a readable, trustworthy paper.

The second chapter in this section, Chapter 28, "Knowing Your College Library," provides valuable information. It explains the many sources available in a library.

Chapter 29 will take you into field research, in which you observe and converse with people to find out something brand-new. This chapter includes a paper by a college student who broke new ground: he revealed new knowledge about a little-known, much-maligned, sometimes glamorized business—bail bonding.

Chapter 30, "Documenting Sources," explains and illustrates the patterns to use to indicate where you got your information. It is there to be consulted when you type up your paper in finished form.

CHAPTER 27

Writing from Library Research

All around us, information keeps exploding. From day to day, television, books, newspapers, and magazines shower us with facts and figures, statements and reports, views and opinions — some of them half-baked, some revealing and trustworthy. College gives you experience in sorting through this massive burst of words. It asks you to distinguish between fact and opinion, off-the-wall claims and expert interpretations. Writing a library research paper helps you gain such skills, and expand the frontiers of what you know already.

In Chapter 3, "Writing from Reading," if you did the main assignment, you read works by other writers and wrote a paper that one of your readings inspired. You may want to review that chapter now. When you wrote, you gave credit to those other writers in an informal way. That experience will prove good preparation for writing a research paper. This new task, though, will be different in the following ways.

All your reading will point in one direction.

You'll draw from more sources.

You'll do more interpreting, more evaluating, more piecing together, more throwing away of the unnecessary.

You'll learn to cite and list your sources in the exact form that many scholars and other professionals follow in writing research reports and articles.

To be able to write a library research paper is a useful skill. This kind of writing is essential not only in an academic community but in business and the professions. Lawyers preparing legal briefs and arguments research previous cases that have a bearing on their own. Engineers rely on research studies when they write feasibility reports. Doctors synthesize discoveries from research to help them decide on treatment for patients. Business owners depend on market research to sell their products.

LEARNING FROM ANOTHER WRITER: ONE STUDENT'S EXPERIENCE

To give you a sense of what one student encountered in fulfilling a typical research paper assignment, we will tell you a true story. It's about a freshman who began her investigation with enthusiasm, found herself stopped in her tracks, and had to start over in a fresh direction. Her story will give you an idea of how a typical research paper is written.

At first, Lisa Chickos wasn't daunted to find herself taking English 102 that spring, even though it was a course many students dreaded. Its notorious requirement — a research paper — made some people register for it unhappily. But in high school back in Apollo, Pennsylvania, Chickos had coped with more than one writing assignment that had taken her into the library. Research, in her experience, hadn't been a cause for despair.

Even so, the English 102 assignment presented challenges. As often happens in college, the nature of the course itself suggested a direction for its students' research papers. That spring, Ms. Miller's section was centered on a theme: the changing roles of men and women in contemporary society. To start their thinking along that broad and promising line, the students had been reading *On the Contrary,* a collection of essays on male and female roles. Within the large area of that topic, the research paper assignment left the way wide open: "Write a paper of at least 2000 words on a subject from our discussions."

A month would be an awfully short time to go from a tentative topic to a finished research paper. But along the way, the instructor would confer with each student at least twice in her office to follow the student's progress and offer counsel.

Right at the start, Chickos's investigation ran head-on into its tallest obstacle. Chickos had decided on a general direction: to find out more about women who make movies, their roles as producers, directors, and workers behind the scenes. That subject keenly appealed to her, but it led to immediate discouragement. She made a preliminary search of her college library's catalog and of the database NewsBank but turned up very little recent material. It may have been that she wasn't looking in the right places or that the best sources weren't available in her library. Had she consulted a specialized index, such as *Film Literature Index,* she might have found more leads. She did find articles on women filmmakers and skimmed through them, but they struck her as too slight — lacking in facts and figures, in clearly stated views. From them, she couldn't get a clear sense of the extent of women's influence on filmmaking. Besides, what could her conclusion be? Probably something obvious: "Hooray for women filmmakers—more power to them!" Disappointed, Chickos realized that in the time she had, she probably couldn't write a strong paper on that subject.

All wasn't lost. In the reference room, she dug into indexes. In the *Readers' Guide to Periodical Literature* she found a promising article listed: "A Bright Woman Is Caught in a Double Bind." She looked up the article in *Psychology Today* and found it thought-provoking. Some women, said psychologist Matina Horner, won't aspire to administrative positions because they fear success: if they succeed, they might find themselves cast out from society. This point confirmed an idea Chickos had met in her introductory psychology course. The textbook contained a discussion about some women's feelings that to deviate from traditional sex roles is more frightening than to fail. Ideas were coming together. Chickos began to take notes.

Although she was moving in a clearer direction, she didn't have a definite topic yet. Administration—that seemed a discouragingly broad subject to investigate. What particular field of endeavor for bright women might she concentrate on? She looked over the anthology of essays her English class had discussed, and she did some random thinking. In elementary and secondary schools, most teachers are women. But what about their administrators—the principals, the superintendents? She reasoned, We tend to think that a school administrator has to be a man, but is that necessarily the case?

She decided to find out. With the aid of the library catalog, she tracked down two books that promised to light the way: collections of essays by various writers entitled *Women and Educational Leadership* and *Academic Women on the Move.* When she looked into them, she found helpful comments by the fistful. Her research began to soar in its new direction.

In the second book, she came across a passage that annoyed her and made her want to keep investigating. Patricia Albjerg Graham, a teacher of history and education at Columbia University, made a revealing comment:

> Administrators are expected to be independent and assertive, behaviors understood as "tough and bitchy" when displayed by women, but "clear-headed and attentive to detail" when found in a man.

Graham's remark indicated sex discrimination in the hiring of school administrators, and Chickos felt her resentment continue to rise. Just how prevalent was this attitude? She read further. By happenstance, a kind of luck that sometimes favors research paper writers, she soon met (in *Women and Educational Leadership*) another quotation that fruitfully irritated her. A male administrator frankly admitted, "It's easier to work without women. Principals and superintendents are a management team. . . . I wonder if we could hang together so well if some of us were women."

Chickos was beginning to feel involved personally. This paper would be well worth writing! Could she find out more about this outrageous situation? Could she find some recent articles and books, some up-to-date statistics?

Could she find enough evidence to make some suggestions for changing the situation? If so, maybe the toil of shuffling note cards, outlining, and citing sources would all be justified. She set to work with confidence. A couple of times Ms. Miller met with Chickos to monitor her progress and offer advice. "But she didn't try to tell me what avenues to follow," Chickos recalls. "The direction of my research had to be original."

As Chickos looked over the interesting information she had found, she realized her sources were not up to date — 1969, 1973, 1980 — and she wondered if what was true then was still true. With little trouble she located several more recent books and articles and scanned them to find that the authors made the same claims as the earlier writers. She couldn't find any recent statistics, although she looked in the usually reliable references — the library catalog, *Readers' Guide,* and NewsBank. She realized that if she wanted to show that sex discrimination existed in school administration, she would need recent figures. She decided to check ERIC (Educational Resources Information Center), an information service available on microfiche. She typed the descriptors "women" and "school administration" into the computer, but the search of the database turned up nothing useful. She tried "women" and "leadership," then "women" and "sex discrimination," but still nothing. Finally, with the help of a friendly librarian, she used the combination "employment" and "statistics" and "public school" — success! These descriptors turned up the report of a survey on staffing in schools conducted in 1987–88 by the National Center for Education Statistics, U.S. Department of Education, and published by the Government Printing Office in 1990. Here were the statistics she needed, and they showed that nothing had changed much in the last two decades.

When Chickos did some early freewriting on her topic, she set down her points as they occurred to her. As she reviewed her thoughts, one idea stood out from the rest. Educator Jacqueline Clement had posed a problem: "Administrators usually start out as teachers and move up through the ranks. Why, then, if women make up the pool of potential educational leaders, are so few of them at the top?" On her notes, Chickos penned a red star next to this thought. She had found her basic research question, and in her paper she would try to answer it.

In this chapter, we'll show you some of the research materials Lisa Chickos consulted, some notes she took, and some of her experiences along the way. Finally, we'll give you her completed paper, "Educational Leadership: A Man's World."

LEARNING BY WRITING

Lisa Chickos's experience of getting momentarily stopped at the start could have happened to anyone at any college. As a rule, in any composition course a research paper is your most complicated job.

Some of our advice in this chapter may be old news to you. You may have learned in high school how to take research notes or how to make a working bibliography. At times, as we guide you through writing your paper, we'll pause to explain those special skills. Mastering them, if you haven't mastered them already, will speed you toward that triumphant day when you bang a final staple through your paper. But if at any moment you find us telling you more than you need to know, just skim that part and go on. Later, should you want to review that information, you can return to it.

The Assignment: Writing from Library Research

Find a topic that intrigues you. To learn as much about it as you can, research that topic in the library. Then, based on your research, write a paper that calls on you to use one or all of the critical thinking skills you honed in Part Two of this book: analyzing, taking a stand, evaluating, identifying causes and effects, perhaps proposing a solution to a problem. Your purpose will be to come to some conclusions about your chosen topic. Assume that your audience is your instructor and your classmates. Here's how you proceed, in more or less this order.

1. Choose a general subject you care to investigate.
2. Do a little reading around in it, to see exactly what aspects of the subject most keenly interest you.

(If you know, from early on, exactly what interests you, you can skip these first two steps.)

3. State, in the form of a question, exactly what you care to find out.
4. By means of library research, find an answer to your question. This answer may be tentative — just a healthy hunch — but if it is your best hunch, go ahead and stick up for it.
5. Then, in a paper of at least 2000 words, set forth the conclusions you have drawn from your study. Give evidence from your research to support them.
6. If your topic seems to call for it, propose some action that should be taken. Suggest to your readers what they might do, if it is an action in which they can effectively take part.

This paper, as you can see, will be more than a stack of facts. Reading and digesting the ideas of ten or twelve other writers is just the first step. In the process of writing your paper, you'll be called on as well to bring your own intelligence to bear on what you have read.

Among student research papers we have seen recently, the following were the most informative.

A woman researched and then praised the British system of supplying drug addicts with drugs, thus making business for drug dealers less profitable.

A man analyzed the process through which an unpublished song by an unknown composer might be recorded and go on to hit the top of the charts. He concluded that if you are an unknown composer, your chances of such success are remote, but the odds aren't hopeless.

A man, after considering several possible solutions to the problem of America's national debt, came to the conclusion that the best solution would be a national lottery. He supported his proposal with evidence from his research into national lotteries held in other countries.

A woman researching the health problems of Vietnam veterans concluded that the ill effects of their exposure to Agent Orange would haunt them and their families well into the twenty-first century.

A Chinese-American student examined what he called "the myth of the model minority"—the perception in the United States that Asian immigrants generally succeed in spite of all obstacles—and found it to be little more than a justification for racism.

To define the poet's role in the society of his times, a man analyzed and evaluated the political poetry of Seamus Heaney.

A woman, seeking causes for what she perceived as the decline of our national parks, concluded that underfunding and understaffing were paramount.

A note on schedules   Along with the assignment to write a research paper, some instructors will suggest a schedule. Lisa Chickos's instructor blocked out the students' obligations like this:

February 26: Topic due (the question to be answered)

March 5: Working bibliography due (citations—on cards—of the sources you think will be useful) [one week]

March 19: Note cards due [two weeks]

March 26: Thesis statement (a one-sentence statement of what the paper will demonstrate) and preliminary outline due [one week]

April 9: Draft—with proper documentation—due [two weeks]

April 16: Completed revised paper due [one week]

But if your instructor doesn't give you a series of deadlines, you'll be wise to set some for yourself. You can depend on this: a research paper will require more time than you expect. You'll find this huge job much more manageable if you break it into a series of small tasks. Writing the final draft, you'll need hours to cite all your sources accurately. You'll need time, then, to look it all over and proofread it, not be forced to toss everything together in a desperate all-night siege. A clear-cut schedule will help.

Generating Ideas

How can we most effectively help long-term prisoners, on their release, to return to society?

Did Walt Disney make any admirable and original contributions to American art, or was he a mere imitator, a purveyor of slick schlock, as some of his critics have charged?

What should be done about acid rain?

Should the U.S. State Department act to prevent American soldiers of fortune — hired mercenaries — from fighting in the Middle East?

What can be done to help the homeless in America?

If you already have a narrowly defined research question in mind, such as the preceding examples — congratulations. You can just skip to the discovery checklist on page 606. But if you don't have a question yet, read on.

Choosing your territory   To explore, you need a territory — a subject that interests you. Perhaps, as Lisa Chickos found, your work in this very course or in another course will suggest an appropriate territory. Chickos wrote a paper suggested by a theme that ran through all the readings and discussions in her writing course. A psychology course might encourage you to investigate mental disorders; a sociology course, labor relations; a geography course, tropical forests.

You'll have an easier time from the start if you can make your territory smaller than "mental disorders" or "labor relations." "Schizophrenia" or "steel-workers' strikes" or "effects of rain forests on global weather" would be smaller, more readily explorable territories. But if you don't feel that you can make your topic so narrow and definite yet, go ahead and start with a broad subject.

For finding your general subject, the following questions may help you. They'll send you back once more to every writer's five basic resources.

DISCOVERY CHECKLIST: CHOOSING YOUR TERRITORY

- Can you *recall* from your work or leisure experience, from travel or study, something you'd care to read more about?
- What have you *observed* recently that you could more thoroughly investigate with the aid of books and magazines? (Suggestion: try watching the evening news, taking notes as you watch.)
- What have you recently *read* that has left you still wondering?
- In recent *conversation* with friends, in class discussions, what topics have arisen that you'd care to explore?
- What can you imagine that might be confirmed or denied by your reading? If, for instance, you can *imagine* life as a peasant on a feudal manor or as a slave on a plantation, you might go to some history books to have your mental picture corrected and enlarged. If you can imagine yourself living on a space station in orbit, you might learn from recent science writers what such a space station will probably be like.

Your next move is to take an overall look at your subject, to see what's in it for you.

Taking an overview   Before launching an expedition into a little-known territory, a smart explorer first makes a reconnaissance flight and takes an overview. Having seen the terrain, the explorer then chooses the very spot to set up camp: the point on the map that looks most promising. Research writers do something like that, too. Before committing themselves to a topic, they first look over a broader territory to see what parts of it look most attractive and then zero in on one small area that seems interesting.

How do you take an overview? You might begin by looking up your subject in an encyclopedia and reading the general articles about it — *unions* or *labor relations, schizophrenia* or *mental illness* or (still more general) *psychiatry.* By now, you are a veteran reader of encyclopedias, but if you care for any tips on using both general encyclopedias and specialized ones, see Chapter 28 (pp. 662–663). When you write your paper later, you'll probably find the information in the encyclopedia too general to use.

In your library's reference room, you might check the *Readers' Guide to Periodical Literature,* that index of recent articles in popular magazines. It will direct you to the latest information and opinion, classified by many subjects. You can also look in NewsBank, a computerized file now available in many libraries. Browsing in an introductory textbook, if any seems likely to help, is also a useful early step. For the general subjects we've been considering, labor relations, mental illness, and tropical forests, you might go to a textbook in political science or psychology or geography.

When Lisa Chickos began investigating women in school administration, she had only a large, vague subject in mind. But as she kept reading and thinking, she saw a smaller idea she wanted to concentrate on: "discrimination against women school administrators." That seemed plenty to consider in a 2000-word research paper. As you read, keep a lookout for any ideas that intrigue you and that you might like to explore.

How much time should you devote to your overview? Many students find that they can make such a reconnaissance flight in an evening or a few hours. At this point, your investigation need go only far enough to suggest a question you'd care to answer — one like Chickos's "In educational administration, why are so few women at the top?" Let's see what goes into a workable, researchable question.

Stating your question   Once you have zeroed in on part of a territory to explore, you can ask a definite question. Ask what you want to find out, and your task will leap into focus. Having begun with a broad, general interest in (let's say) social problems in large cities, a writer might then ask, "What happens to teenage runaways on the streets of Manhattan?" Or, if a writer has started with a general yen to know more about contemporary architecture, a definite question might be "Who in America today is good at designing sports arenas?"

Brainstorm. You might start with a brainstorming session. For fifteen or twenty minutes, let your thoughts revolve, and jot down whatever questions come to mind—even useless ones. Then, looking over your list, you may find one that appears promising.

Size up your question. A workable question has to be narrow enough to allow a fruitful investigation in the library. However, a question can be too immense and the research it would call for too overwhelming to complete in two months—"How is the climate of the earth changing?" "Who are the world's best living storytellers?" "Why are there poor among us?" "What's going on in outer space?"

On the other hand, a question can be too narrow or too insignificant. If a mere source or two could answer it, the resulting paper may be a thin summary, not a true research paper. "How does the First Lady do her hair?" would be a shallow question. It would turn up facts but few opinions. All you would need to answer it would be one popular magazine interview with a White House hairdresser. But even if you were to find such an interview, you would lack sufficient material. The subject has provoked a lot of gossip, but little serious thought. Probably you could either search out an answer to that question in fifteen minutes or waste days and find nothing worth taking a note about. So instead, ask a question that will lead you to a lot of meaty books and articles. "How does the First Lady influence the politics of this administration?" That might be worth several weeks of research work.

A caution: if you pick a topic currently in the news, you may have trouble finding useful material—deep analysis, critical thought, ample historical background, intelligent controversy. For many current topics, the only printed sources may be recent newspapers and news magazines. The topic may be too new for anyone yet to have done a thought-provoking book or a really thorough magazine analysis about it.

Hone your question. Try to keep the wording of your question as simple as you can: set yourself one thing to find out, not several. A question that reads "How do current art and music reflect the cultural revolution of the 1960s?" is too big. You could split such a question into two parts and then pick one of them: "How does art reflect the cultural revolution of the 1960s?" or "How does music . . . ?" By qualifying the word *music*, you might cut the question still further down to size: "How does last year's rock music . . . ?" Focus on whatever you most keenly wish to learn.

A well-wrought research question suggests ways to answer it. Say the question is "What has caused a shortage of low-income housing in northeastern cities?" The wording suggests subject headings that may be found in the library catalog or the *Readers' Guide* or NewsBank: *housing, housing shortage, low-income housing, urban housing.*

Until you start working in the library, of course, you can't know for certain how fruitful your question will be. If it doesn't lead you to any definite facts, if it doesn't start you thinking critically, you'll need to reword it or throw it out and ask a new question. But at the very least, the question you first ask can give you a definite direction in which to start looking.

When you have tentatively stated your question, you can test it by asking other questions about it.

- Is the scope of the question appropriate — not too immense and not too narrow?
- Is this question answerable — at least partly answerable — in the time you have? Does it need to be reduced or expanded?
- Can you find books and articles on this question?
- Does the question refer to a matter that has been written about only lately? Or, like a more promising question for library research, will it send you to books and magazines of at least a year earlier?
- Have you worded your question as plainly and simply as you can? Do you understand exactly what you'll be looking for?
- Does the question ask for just one answer, not several?
- Does your question interest you? Do you honestly crave the answer to it? If so, your research is likely to cruise along at a great rate, and you will find yourself enjoying a sense of discovery. Interest yourself and you are also likely to interest your reader.

Making a preliminary search You can quickly see whether your question is likely to lead to an ample research paper by conducting a short, fast search that shouldn't take you more than an hour. Just check the library catalog to see what books appear under your subject heading. If possible go into the stacks and look over the shelves. Take a quick check of magazine articles: consult the last annual *Readers' Guide* and a recent electronic database, looking under the subject headings closest to your special concern. Don't look up the articles yet; just see how many there are and whether their titles sound promising. If your subject is "Women: School Administrators," an article called "Iona Dawes Honored with Birthday Cake for Fourteen Years as Principal" is probably going to be too specific to help.

This preliminary search has a simple purpose: to ascertain that you'll have enough material to do the job. If the material looks so skimpy that you won't have anything to choose from, and you'll need to force every crumb of it into your paper to get 2000 words, you might better ask another question. If your first trip into the stacks reveals ten yards of books, alarm bells should start ringing. Did someone other than Shakespeare write Shakespeare's plays? A thousand books have dealt with that question. What caused the Civil War? Every United States history book offers a few explanations. You might want to ask a different question. Instead of a question that only two books might answer, or a question that a hundred articles might answer, pick a question that a dozen or twenty sources might.

Making a working bibliography Before going on with your investigation, you need a working bibliography: a detailed list of books and articles you plan to consult. Later, after examining the sources on this list, you may discover that some are useful, but others are not.

Your overview and preliminary search may have given you a good rough notion of where your most promising material lies. Now you need titles and information. Some writers keep track of everything in a notebook small enough to fit in a pocket. Most find that a convenient and efficient way to compile such a working bibliography is on 4-by-6-inch note cards, one source to a card. Cards are handy to work with: you can arrange and shuffle them. The more care you take in recording your tentative sources, the more time you'll save later, when at the end of your paper you compile a list of works actually used and cited. At that point, you'll be grateful to find all the necessary information at your fingertips. Otherwise, you'll have to make a frantic trip back to the library.

What should each source card contain? Everything necessary to find the source later as well as to write the final list of sources to be placed at the end of your paper. Include the following for books (see Figure 27.1).

1. The library catalog call number, in the upper left corner of the card.
2. The last name of the book's author in the upper right corner, in uppercase letters, so that you can identify the source at a glance.
3. The author's full name, last name first.
4. The book's title, including its subtitle if it has one, underlined.
5. The publication information: place, publisher, and year of publication.

For each source card, you may also include a brief note to yourself on your impression of the usefulness of the work—"GREAT INFO!" or "Really packed" or "Maybe a few gems here" or "Probably not much use."

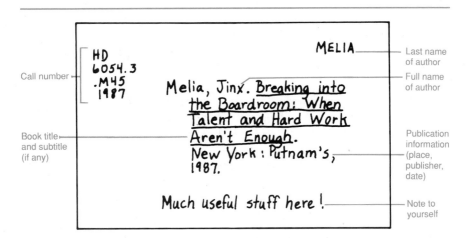

FIGURE 27.1 A bibliography card for a book with one author, in MLA style

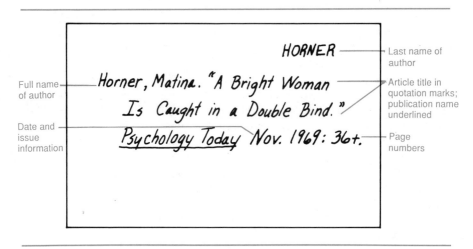

FIGURE 27.2   A bibliography card for an article in a monthly magazine, in MLA style

For a magazine article, your source card need contain no library catalog call number, but if your library classifies periodicals, the call number will be useful. You'll definitely need the following data (see Figure 27.2 and 27.3).

1.   The last name of the person who wrote the article in the upper right corner, in uppercase letters.
2.   The author's full name.
3.   The title of the article, in quotation marks, followed by the name of the publication, underlined.
4.   For a scholarly journal, the volume number, sometimes followed by the issue number.
5.   The date of the issue. (Form varies with the type of magazine. See Chapter 30 for correct form.)

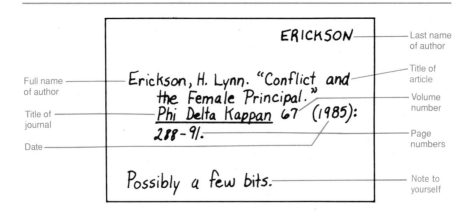

FIGURE 27.3   A bibliography card for an article in a scholarly journal with a volume number, in MLA style

6. The page numbers of the article (A "+" indicates that the article covers more than one page, but not consecutive pages.)

This may seem like a lot of record keeping. But it will take you less time to jot down all this information in full now than to make future trips to the library to dig out something you have not recorded. You'll need every last bit of this information in citing your sources and in making your list of works cited. On the night before your draft is due, you'll thank your stars you got all this stuff early and accurately.

To locate promising sources to look for, what do you consult? The following five references are essential. You probably know them already, but if you don't, you will quickly get some hands-on experience. (They are also discussed in detail in Chapter 28.)

1. **The library catalog,** for the titles, publication information, and locations of books. Early on, you'll no doubt consult this master listing of every book and bound periodical in the library. Are you acquainted with the *Library of Congress Subject Headings*? This useful directory can help you find a particular subject in the catalog even if you don't know exactly what to call it. For more about this helpful aid, see page 658. For a basic description of the library catalog, how it works, and how it can serve you, see pages 657–660.

2. **An index to periodicals,** for the titles of magazine articles. In high school, you probably used at least the *Readers' Guide to Periodical Literature,* which covers popular magazines, but if your subject falls into the category of art, music, theater, film, architecture, law, business, or education, other indexes can be helpful. Some cover specialized magazines and scholarly journals. If you'd like a short description of these indexes — there may be one just right for your project — see pages 665–667.

3. **The *New York Times Index,*** for a list of all the articles published each day in this comprehensive newspaper. You remember that Mount St. Helens erupted sometime in the 1980s, but you need the exact date. Check it here, and also find out how many people were killed and other details.

4. **NewsBank,** for an up-to-date, computerized, comprehensive list of articles in periodicals. This electronic reference also contains a database of the articles themselves. Now you can look through ten years' issues of fifty magazines without leaving the computer screen. Think how much time you'll save!

5. **A ready-made bibliography,** for a list of books and articles on a certain subject, often with a brief descriptive opinion of each item. Imagine what a good start you'll have if someone has already drawn up a bibliography for your subject. For more about such bibliographies, see page 665.

For your present short-range investigation, those five basic sources will probably lead to more books and articles than you can weave into 1500 or 2000 words. But what if they don't, and you need still more material? In that case, you can find thumbnail descriptions of other likely sources in Chapter 28. Whenever a college course calls on you to do a longer and deeper research paper, such as a term paper at the end of a course or an honors thesis, you will surely need more sources than the basic ones suggested here. Your present task, though limited, is still large: to think with the aid of printed sources and, with their help, to speak your mind.

Evaluating your sources   With any luck, in making your working bibliography you will have turned up some books and articles by writers of deep knowledge and high integrity. You may also have turned up a few hasty hunks of verbiage written by hacks or some material written with biases—which may be perfectly good as long as you recognize the biases. How do you know what sources are trustworthy? Here are some questions to ask yourself:

Is the source timely? A good indication of a source's reliability is a recent date of publication. If you are using a book that has been revised, use the latest edition. Use material published in recent years so that the facts and opinions will be up to date. In a fast-changing information age, additional information and discoveries in most fields come out every year. If you cite five-year-old procedures for treating AIDS, for example, you may be all wrong.

Is the writer a recognized, reliable authority? See whether any credentials are given in a *blurb,* or biographical note, at the beginning or end of a book or article. If still in doubt, you might check whether the writer is listed in the library catalog as the author of other books on the subject and in *Who's Who, Contemporary Authors,* or reference works covering specialized fields, such as *American Men and Women of Science.* Inclusion in such works isn't a guarantee that the writer is absolutely trustworthy, but you may be able to get an idea of the author's background. Ask your reference librarian whether the writer's name is familiar. But ultimately, the best test of a writer's authority is whether his or her work meets the critical demands of other authorities. You might find some authorities on campus to talk with. Your instructor is an authority on some things. And you might do some more reading in the field and start becoming an authority yourself.

Is the source primary or secondary? In most research papers you'll need both primary and secondary sources. A *primary source* is an observer: someone, let's say, who witnessed a fire and writes an account of it. A primary source may also be the person who originally makes a statement: the fire chief who gives his report on the blaze. A *secondary source* is a writer or speaker who refers to primary sources—such as a newspaper reporter who writes of the fire after talking with eyewitnesses or a historian who has read the reporter's account in an old newspaper. If you quote a book written by child psychologist Jean Piaget, you quote a primary source; a secondary source might be a book by another writer discussing Piaget's theories.

Secondary sources aren't necessarily less trustworthy just because they are not firsthand reports. Eyewitnesses can be prejudiced, self-serving, or simply unable to know as much as a later writer who has talked with *many* eyewitnesses. In writing a history paper on the attitudes of American social workers toward World War I, you might quote a primary source: Jane Addams, founder of Chicago's Hull House, who was a pacifist. If you relied only on Addams's words, though, you might get the idea that social workers were unanimously opposed to the war effort. To put Addams's views into perspective you'd also need secondary sources, which would show that most of her peers didn't want to identify with her unpopular pacifism and publicly disagreed with her.

If your source is a weekly news magazine like *Time, Newsweek,* or *U.S. News & World Report,* the writer of an article is likely to be a reporter, not always a famous name, perhaps not a world-renowned authority. Such magazines do, however, feature some articles by experts; and all such magazines have a good reputation for checking their facts carefully. They try to present a range of opinions but sometimes *select* facts to mirror the opinions of their editors. In a serious, reputable periodical of general interest, other than a news weekly—a magazine such as *New York Review of Books,* the *Atlantic, Harper's,* or the *American Scholar*—articles are often written by well-known authorities.

Who are its readers? In testing another writer's statements, it helps to notice the audience for which they were written. Does the periodical have a predictable point of view? Is it written toward any special audience? *The Nation,* a magazine of commentary from a left-leaning political point of view, is likely to give you a different picture of the world from that found in the *National Review,* edited by conservative William F. Buckley, Jr. How can you find out, if you don't already know, the general outlook of the periodical you're examining?

Read the advertisements, if any. Ads are usually the surest guide to a magazine's audience. To whom are its editors trying to appeal? *Time, Newsweek,* and *U.S. News & World Report,* for instance, address mostly college-educated professionals. A large part of this audience consists of businesspeople—as shown by the many ads for office copiers, delivery services, hotels for business travelers, and corporations.

Read more than one issue of the magazine. Browse, at least, through several issues—as many as necessary to understand the magazine's assumptions and its audience.

Read the editorials, in which the editors, making no pretense of being impartial, set forth their views. In most magazines, these will be in a front section and may not even be signed, since the name of the editor is on the masthead, near the contents. If you can find an editorial commenting on a familiar issue, you may soon know the magazine's bias.

Read any featured columnists who appear regularly. Usually their jobs depend on their voicing opinions congenial to the magazine's editors and publishers. But this test isn't foolproof. Sometimes a dissenting columnist is hired to lend variety.

Read with an analytic eye the lead features or news stories (those most prominently placed in the front of the issue), paying special attention to the last paragraph, in which the writer often declares what it all means. Sometimes this will betray assumptions that reveal where the magazine stands: "Despite the stern criticisms leveled at Centro Oil by environmentalists, the company has weathered this small storm and no doubt will outlast many to come." The voice is clearly that of a friend of the oil company.

Read the letters to the editor. Some magazines, like *Time,* strive to offer space to a diversity of opinion. (When *Time* prints two letters on a subject, one is generally pro and one is con.) You can often get a line on the level of schooling and intelligence shown by who writes the letters and thereby understand something about the magazine's readers.

A helpful work of reference that evaluates magazines is *Magazines for Libraries.* It mentions biases, tells what sort of material specific magazines customarily print, and gives circulation figures.

For still more advice on evaluating evidence, turn back to "Testing Evidence," on pages 154–156.

DISCOVERY CHECKLIST: DEVELOPING A WORKING BIBLIOGRAPHY

- ✔ Have you made a bibliography card for every book, part of a book, magazine article, and newspaper article that you think will be useful for your topic?
- ✔ Do you have sufficient sources to write a good research paper? What if you discover that some are useless or repetitious? If you have to discard some, will you still have enough?
- ✔ Are the sources up to date?
- ✔ Do you have a variety of types of sources? A range of opinions?
- ✔ Are the authors recognized experts in the field? Are the publications reliable (not sensational)?
- ✔ Is each entry relevant to your restricted topic?
- ✔ Have you included all the necessary information for each entry?
- ✔ Is each entry in the proper form?
- ✔ Have you made annotations to yourself about the probable usefulness of each source so that you can read the best ones first?
- ✔ Are the bibliography cards in alphabetical order by authors' names?

Setting out: note taking   Once you have a working bibliography and have evaluated your sources and winnowed out any you don't trust, you need to begin reading and accumulating material. What will you look for? Facts, ideas, and opinions as well as examples and illustrations of the ideas you're pursuing along with evidence to support them—and to refute them.

Skim each source to decide whether to take notes and, if so, how extensively. You can't always guess the usefulness of a source in advance. Sometimes a likely article turns out to yield nothing much, and a book that had promised to be a juicy plum shrivels to a prune in your hands. Read the entire article or section of a book before beginning to take notes in order to help you to avoid distorting the meaning.

Take thorough notes. When you take notes from your reading, take ample ones. Many a writer has come to grief by setting down sketchy jottings and trusting memory to fill in the blanks. You'll probably find that using note cards will work better than taking notes on pieces of paper because, when the time comes to organize the material you've gathered, you can shuffle your cards into an order that makes most sense to you. Roomy 4-by-6-inch or 5-by-8-inch cards will hold more than 3-by-5-inch cards. Even a meaty idea ought to fit on one card. *Use one card per idea.* Putting two or more ideas on the same card complicates your task when you reach the planning and drafting stages.

Some research writers insist that the invention of photocopying has done away with the need to take notes. Indeed, judicious photocopying can save you time as you gather materials for your paper, but the key word here is *judicious.* Simply photocopying everything you read with the vague notion that some of it contains material valuable for your essay is likely in the end to waste money and to cost you more time rather than less. Much of it won't be worth saving. Most important, you won't have digested and evaluated what was on the page; you will merely have copied it. Selecting what is essential, transcribing it by hand, perhaps nutshelling or paraphrasing it (see p. 615), helps make it yours. When later you start drafting, unless your paper is to be very short, it will take you longer to digest great bundles of photocopied material than to work from carefully thought-out note cards.

If, however, you're using a source that doesn't circulate, such as a reference book always kept in the reference room, you may want to photocopy the relevant pages so that you can use them whenever and wherever is convenient for you. Just make sure that the name of the source and the page number appear on your copy so that you can make a source card for it. If not, pencil it on the photocopy. When you start organizing your notes, you may find it convenient to scissor out of a photocopied page what you're going to use and stick it onto a note card.

A good rule is to make your notes and citations full enough so that, once they're written, you're totally independent of the source from which they came. That way you'll avoid having to rush back to the library in a panic trying to find again, in a book or periodical you returned weeks ago, some nugget of material you want to include in your paper. Good, thoughtful notes can sometimes be copied verbatim from note card to first draft. But usually they will take rewriting to fit them in so they don't stand out like boulders in the stream of your prose.

A useful note card includes three elements:

An identifier, usually the last name of the author whose work you're citing, followed by the *page number or numbers* on which the information can be found.

A subject heading, some keyword or phrase you make up yourself to help you decide where in your paper the information will best fit.

The fact, idea, or quotation you plan to use in your paper.

You'll need all these elements so that later, when it's time to incorporate your notes into your paper or develop your ideas from multiple sources, you'll

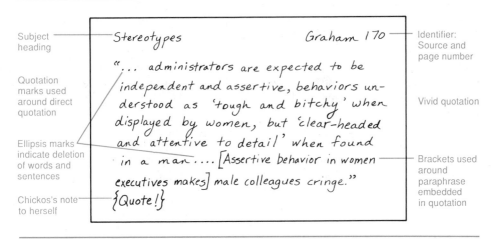

Subject heading

Quotation marks used around direct quotation

Ellipsis marks indicate deletion of words and sentences

Chickos's note to herself

Identifier: Source and page number

Vivid quotation

Brackets used around paraphrase embedded in quotation

> *Stereotypes*   *Graham 170*
>
> " ... *administrators are expected to be independent and assertive, behaviors understood as 'tough and bitchy' when displayed by women, but 'clear-headed and attentive to detail' when found in a man.* .... [*Assertive behavior in women executives makes*] *male colleagues cringe.*"
> {Quote!}

FIGURE 27.4   A sample note card giving a direct quotation from a source

have an accurate record of what you found in each source. You'll also know exactly where you found it, and you will be able to cite every source without difficulty. (For sample note cards, see Figures 27.4, 27.5, and 27.6.)

While you're taking notes, you should keep evaluating. Decide whether the stuff is going to be greatly valuable, fairly valuable, or only a little bit valuable. Some note takers put a star at the top of any note they assign great value to, a question mark on a note that might or might not be useful. Later, when they're organizing their material, they can see what especially stands out and will need emphasis. Others write a notation to themselves at the bottom of the card.

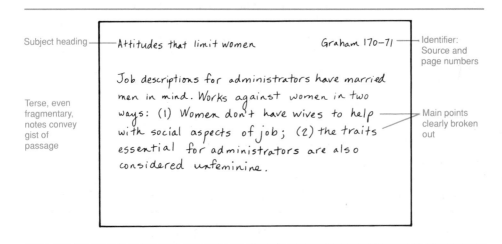

Subject heading

Terse, even fragmentary, notes convey gist of passage

Identifier: Source and page numbers

Main points clearly broken out

> *Attitudes that limit women*   *Graham 170-71*
>
> *Job descriptions for administrators have married men in mind. Works against women in two ways: (1) Women don't have wives to help with social aspects of job; (2) the traits essential for administrators are also considered unfeminine.*

FIGURE 27.5   Nutshelling, or summarizing, a paragraph

<table>
<tr><td>

Paraphrase is about half the length of original passage.

No interpretation or evaluation of original passage is included.

</td><td>

Roadblocks   Graham 170-71

Women aspiring to administrative positions in
education are limited by the assumption that
administrators are married men whose wives
can provide social support. Because job
descriptions are written with such men in mind,
they also call for skills considered natural for
men but unfeminine for women. On the job men
are given latitude in how they carry out their
duties, but there is pressure on women to
walk a fine line between competence and femininity.

</td><td>

Although emphasis of original is maintained, word choice and order have been reworked to avoid the danger of plagiarism.

</td></tr>
</table>

FIGURE 27.6   Paraphrasing the quotation from Graham's article

Bristle while you work. In reading the material you are collecting, looking at it a little sourly and suspiciously might be to your advantage. Mary-Claire van Leunen, author of *A Handbook for Scholars* (New York: Knopf, 1978), has advised researchers who must read much scholarly writing: "Do not smile sweetly as you read through pages of graceless, stilted, maundering bombast. Fume, fuss, be angry. Your anger will keep you up to the mark when you turn to writing yourself."

Take sufficient notes. How many notes are enough? When you find that the sources you consult are mostly repeating what you've learned from previous sources, you have probably done enough reading and note taking. But before you reach that point, we'd like to remind you of three ways of setting down notes that will help you write a good, meaty paper. (You have met them before in Chapter 3, "Writing from Reading.")

Writing from sources: quoting, nutshelling, paraphrasing You have an obligation to repay the researchers, scholars, and writers who came before you. That is why, in doing research, you cite your source materials so carefully, mentioning the names of all other writers you get information from. You do this not only for quotations you take but also for ideas, even though you have nutshelled or paraphrased them in your own words. If a writer fails to acknowledge all sources or uses the original writer's words without quotation marks, he or she has plagiarized, a very serious offense in the academic, business, and industrial communities. The writer is suspected of a rip-off, when he or she merely failed to make a debt clear. Chapter 30 offers information about how to cite and list sources so that, like any good scholar, you will know exactly how to pay your debts in full.

While preparing to write her paper on women in educational administration, Lisa Chickos found a thought-provoking paragraph in Patricia Albjerg

Graham's "Status Transitions of Women Students, Faculty, and Administrators," a chapter in *Academic Women on the Move*:

> Violation of cultural stereotypes may be another factor working against women faculty members moving into upper-level administrative positions. It generally is assumed that women can make their best contributions in positions subordinate to men. Hence the university administrator's job description is almost invariably drawn with a man in mind, particularly a married man whose wife can provide auxiliary social support. Moreover, administrators are expected to be independent and assertive, behaviors understood as "tough and bitchy" when displayed by women, but "clear-headed and attentive to detail" when found in a man. Tolerance for men's behavior is a good deal broader than it is for that of women. Men are permitted their idiosyncracies of whatever sort, but women are expected to maintain a much more precarious balance between conspicuous competence and tactful femininity. Manifestations of independence and autonomy are expected in a male executive; their presence in women makes some male colleagues cringe.

Quoting. To quote selectively — to choose the words with life and pith in them — is one convincing way to demonstrate and refute ideas and to marshal evidence. To do so, you'll need to copy a brief quotation carefully onto a card, making sure to reproduce exactly the words, the spelling, the order, and the punctuation, even if they're unusual. Go back over what you've written to make sure that you've copied it correctly. *Put quotation marks around the material* so that when you come to include it in your paper, you'll remember that it's a direct quotation. You might also want to remind yourself in a bracketed note that you intend to use the author's words in a quotation. Lisa Chickos extracted a lively quotation for the note card shown in Figure 27.4.

Quoting needs to be done sparingly, and for good reason — to add support and authority to your assertions. Otherwise, it raises needless complications. Some writers of college research papers do much pointless quoting. This notion is understandable, but dubious. Mary-Claire van Leunen in *A Handbook for Scholars* gives cogent advice:

> Quote only the quotable. Quote for color; quote for evidence. Otherwise, don't quote. When you are writing well, your sentences should join each other like rows of knitting, each sentence pulling up what went before it, each sentence supporting what comes after. Quotation introduces an alien pattern — someone else's diction, someone else's voice, someone else's links before and afterward. Even necessary quotations are difficult to knit smoothly into your structure. Over-quotation will result in something more like a bird's nest than like fine handiwork.

That quotation, by the way, seems to us worth quoting. Its words are memorable, worth taking to heart.

Sometimes it doesn't pay to transcribe a quotation word for word. Parts may fail to serve your purpose, such as transitions ("as the reader will recall from Chapter 14"), parenthetical remarks ("which data slightly modifies the earlier view of Pflug"), and other information useless to you. Lisa Chickos, quoting a sentence on her note card shown in Figure 27.4, doesn't bother to take down the transition word "Moreover" with which the sentence begins. But she faithfully indicates the omission by using an ellipsis mark (. . .).

Nutshelling. Nutshelling, or summarizing, takes less room than quoting extensively and will be more useful when you write the paper. To give your reader just the sense of a passage from another writer, you can condense it *in your own words.* If Lisa Chickos had put into nutshell form the essential ideas she wished to take from the paragraph in Graham's article, her note card might have looked like Figure 27.5.

Paraphrasing. A third strategy useful in taking research notes, paraphrasing also transforms an author's ideas *into your own words.* Unlike nutshelling, though, paraphrasing doesn't necessarily make your notes any briefer. Why paraphrase? It is especially helpful when the language of another writer isn't particularly vivid and memorable (unlike the phrase from Graham that Lisa Chickos quotes: "tough and bitchy"). When the writer's ideas look valuable but the words seem not worth preserving in the original, paraphrase them. Don't, however, hover so close to the writer's words that your paraphrase is merely an echo. If your source writes, "In staging an ancient Greek tragedy today, most directors do not mask the actors," and you write, merely changing the word order, "Most directors, in staging an ancient Greek tragedy today, do not mask the actors," you have stuck too closely to the original. Write instead: "Few contemporary directors of Greek tragedy insist that their actors wear masks." When you paraphrase, also avoid the temptation to merely substitute a synonym here and there. Paraphrasing too close to the source is a form of plagiarism. The style in paraphrasing, as in nutshelling, has to be yours. When you paraphrase, by the way, you aren't judging or interpreting another writer's ideas — you are simply trying to express them fairly and accurately in different words. If Lisa Chickos had chosen to paraphrase Graham, her note card might have looked like Figure 27.6.

How do you abstract the main idea from another writer's thoughts? Before you nutshell or paraphrase, we suggest that you do the following.

1. Read the original passage a couple of times.
2. Without looking at it, try to state its gist, the point it makes, the main sense you remember.
3. Go back and reread the original passage one more time, making sure you got its point faithfully. Revise as necessary.

If you have dealt carefully with the material, you won't have to put quotation marks around anything in your paraphrase. However, if you quote a single significant word or phrase, you must use quotation marks.

Unless an assignment strictly confines you to library sources, which it might, no law forbids your using any promising nonlibrary materials in your research paper. To make a point, you can recall your own experience, observations, conversations, past reading. And why park your imagination outside the library? You might want to bring together sources not usually related. One fine research paper we have read, by a prelaw student, compared gambling laws in ancient Rome with gambling laws in present-day Atlantic City. Placing Rome and Atlantic City cheek to cheek took imagination.

DISCOVERY CHECKLIST: TAKING NOTES

- ↙ Do you identify the source (by last name of author or an important word from the title) and the exact page for each note card?
- ↙ Do you take notes most of the time in your own words—summarizing or paraphrasing?
- ↙ Do you retain the meaning of the original so that you are true to the source?
- ↙ Do you quote sparingly—only pithy, striking short passages?
- ↙ When you quote, do you quote exactly? Do you use quotation marks and ellipsis marks as needed? Do you use quotation marks around significant words or phrases from the original sources?
- ↙ Do you avoid lengthy notes?
- ↙ Does each card contain only one idea?
- ↙ Do you avoid paraphrasing too close to the source?
- ↙ Have you made a bibliography card for each new source you discovered during your reading?

Planning, Drafting, and Developing

You began gathering material with a question in mind. It asked what you wanted to find out. By now, if your research has been thorough and fruitful, you know the answer. The moment has come to weave together the material you have gathered. We can vouch for two time-proven methods.

The thesis method. Decide what your research has led you to believe. What does it all mean? Sum up that view in a sentence. It is your thesis, the one main idea your paper will demonstrate. Lisa Chickos's preliminary thesis sentence might be "The scarcity of women school administrators can be alleviated." (For more advice on composing such a sentence, see p. 322.) You can then start outlining or drafting, including only material that supports your thesis, concentrating from beginning to end on making that thesis clear.

The answer method. Some writers have an easier time of writing if they plunge in and start writing without first trying to state any thesis at all. If you care to try this method, recall your original question and start writing with the purpose of answering it, lining up evidence as you go. You may discover what you want to say as you write. This method usually requires much revising.

Evaluating your material   About now, you will probably wish to sift through all the evidence you have collected. If you've been taking notes on cards, the labor of sorting the cards into piles according to subject will be made easier. But thinking will be the hardest part of sorting: you'll need to reflect on each item, imagining it as a piece of your finished paper. At this point it will be useful to write a subject heading in the top left corner of each note card to make the sorting easier. Another useful method is to categorize your notes into three categories: essential material, good but less important material, and material not worth the powder to blow it up.

How to decide what is essential? *A useful note will plainly help answer your original question.* If that question was "How far advanced is Soviet computer technology?" then a comment by a Norwegian engineer who was permitted to use a large computer at the Soviet Academy of Sciences and who evaluated its performance would obviously be very valuable. Of lesser import might be an American tourist's recollection of seeing a large computer in Moscow being unloaded from a truck. Yet if for any reason the latter note seemed memorable, you should hang on to it, at least until writing a draft.

You aren't trying to impose your will on your material so that it proves only what you want to prove. Still, the rough rule we can offer for evaluating your material is this: *Does this note help you say what you now want to say?*

Organizing your ideas   If your material seems not to want to shape up, you may find it helpful to plan the order of the ideas by writing an outline. You might arrange all your note cards in an order that makes sense. Then the stack of cards becomes your plan, and, as you write, turning over card after card, you follow it. Or you can make an informal outline on paper (see p. 332). For such a complex writing task, you will probably find writing out the plan helpful. That's what Lisa Chickos did at first. She made a rough preliminary listing of the points she planned to cover, moving from problem to causes of the problem to solution.

As you can see, Chickos included the heading "Fear of success," and at that point she found the outline prompting her ideas. Next to "Fear of success" she wrote, "Say something about deviating from prescribed roles." Obviously

Introduction

Leadership in American education

Barriers to women who might go into administration
   Perceptions of women's ability
   Socialization
   "Fear of success"
   Departure from traditional roles
   Family and geographic ties
   Female stereotypes

Solutions
   Mutual support
   Support from male colleagues
   Encouragement of children
   Support from family
   Openness of employers
   Support from organizations and legislation

young women in educational administration might be afraid of being branded as "tough and bitchy" (to quote Graham again). "I may need another category," Chickos realized, noting to herself that "women who have reached positions. Maybe a separate category for barriers that inhibit both women from rising in administration and employers from hiring them." This early outline was tentative, and Chickos changed her plan as she drafted her ideas, but just looking over her rough outline proved stimulating: it made thoughts start to flow.

From notes to outline to draft Note cards are only the raw material for a research paper. If they are to end up in a readable, unified whole, they need shaping and polishing. Much verbiage in your notes probably won't need to go into your paper. When you draft, you'll find yourself summarizing your notes or selecting just the useful parts of them.

You may need a formal outline to guide your drafting. But remember that an outline is a skeleton to which you will add flesh (details). Use the outline as a suggested organization and change the subdivisions or the order of the parts if you discover a better way.

When you look over your outline, compare each section with the notes you have on hand for it. If for a certain section you have no notes, or only a single note, your research has a gap, so go back to the library.

When you are satisfied that your notes fall into some kind of order and you have material for every part of your outline, you can start to write. If things don't fall into perfect order, start writing anyway. Get something down on paper so that you will have something to revise.

As you write, document all the ideas, facts, summaries, and paraphrases

---

WRITING WITH A COMPUTER: SHAPING A RESEARCH PAPER DRAFT
In writing a research paper, you'll find word processing a great boon. Any material you collect can be sorted and grouped on screen — laid in the very place it should go. Material can be shifted about, a wonderful power to have in organizing long blocks of copy. And especially in a research paper where everything has to be documented and chances to make mistakes abound, you'll appreciate the ease of making corrections. Then, too, word processing lets you easily add any stray material that may turn up late in the process of writing. (For suggestions for rewriting with a computer, see p. 633.)

from your reading. All the while, keep citing: referring your reader to the exact sources of your material. In the body of your paper, right after every fact, idea, or quotation you have borrowed, you tell your reader where you found it. In Chapter 30, we show you in detail how to cite. It's probably easiest to cite your sources carefully *while you're drafting your paper.* Although to do so takes a little extra time as you write, it saves fuss when you're putting your paper into final form. And it prevents unintentional plagiarism.

Note in your draft, right after each borrowed item, the name of the author and the page of the book or article you took it from. If you're using two or more works by the same author, you need one more detail to tell them apart. Shorten the titles — the first word or phrase will do — and include the shortened title with the author's name.

```
An assassin outrages us not only by his deed but also by

offering an unacceptable reason for violence.  Nearly as

offensive as his act of wounding President Reagan was

Hinckley's explanation that he fired in order to impress

screen star Jody Foster.  (Szasz, "Intentionality," 5)
```

The title in parenthesis is short for an article by Thomas Szasz, "Intentionality and Insanity," to distinguish it from another work by Szasz that the writer also cites: *The Myth of Mental Illness.*

When in writing a draft you include a direct quotation, you might as well save copying time. Just paste or tape in the whole note card bearing the quotation. Your draft may look sloppy, but who cares? Drafts usually are. You're going to recopy the quotation anyway when you type your final version.

When you lay the quotation into place, add a few words to introduce it. A brief transition might go something like "A more negative view of standardized intelligence tests is that of Harry S. Baum, director of the Sooner Research Center." Then comes Baum's opinion, that IQ tests aren't very reliable. The transition announces why Baum will be quoted. Evidently, you have previously written about somebody else's praise of IQ tests; now Baum will cast cold water on them. And the transition, brief as it is, tells us a little about Baum: his professional title. Indicating that he is a recognized authority, this bit of information makes us more willing to accept his expert view. (For more suggestions on introducing ideas, see "Transitions," p. 354.)

But if no transition occurs at the moment, don't sit around waiting for it. Slap that card into place and keep writing while the spirit is moving you along. Later, when you rewrite, you can always add connective tissue. Just remember to add it, though — a series of slapped-in summaries and quotations would make rough reading.

Using sources (not letting sources use you)   Sometimes you can get drawn into discussing something that really doesn't have anything much to do with your investigation, perhaps because the material is interesting and you happen to have a heap of it. It's a great temptation, when a note has cost you time and toil, to want to include it at all costs. Resist. Include only material that answers your research question. Your paper will be far stronger as a result. A note dragged in by force always sticks out like a pig in the belly of a boa constrictor.

Using long passages Nutshell and paraphrase are fine ways to avoid quoting excessively. We first talked about these useful methods on page 615, and earlier in this chapter we saw how Lisa Chickos used them. Both methods translate another writer's ideas into your own words.

If, to save time in the library, you made photocopies of long passages, you now have to face the task of selecting from them, boiling them down, and weaving them into your paper. To illustrate once again how nutshelling and paraphrasing can serve you, let's first look at a passage from historian Barbara W. Tuchman. In *The Distant Mirror: The Calamitous 14th Century* (New York: Knopf, 1978), Tuchman sets forth the effects of that famous plague the Black Death. In her foreword to her study, she admits that any historian dealing with the Middle Ages faces difficulties. For one, large gaps exist in the supply of recorded information:

ORIGINAL

A greater hazard, built into the very nature of recorded history, is overload of the negative: the disproportionate survival of the bad side — of evil, misery, contention, and harm. In history this is exactly the same as in the daily newspaper. The normal does not make news. History is made by the documents that survive, and these lean heavily on crisis and calamity, crime and misbehavior, because such things are the subject matter of the documentary process — of lawsuits, treaties, moralists' denunciations, literary satire, papal Bulls. No Pope ever issued a Bull to approve of something. Negative overload can be seen at work in the religious reformer Nicolas de Clamanges, who, in denouncing unfit and worldly prelates in 1401, said that in his anxiety for reform he would not discuss the good clerics because "they do not count beside the perverse men."

Disaster is rarely as pervasive as it seems from recorded accounts. The fact of being on the record makes it appear continuous and ubiquitous whereas it is more likely to have been sporadic both in time and place. Besides, persistence of the normal is usually greater than the effect of disturbance, as we know from our own times. After absorbing the news of today, one expects to face a world consisting entirely of strikes, crimes, power failures, broken water mains, stalled trains, school shutdowns, muggers, drug addicts, neo-Nazis, and rapists. The fact is that one can come home in the evening — on a lucky day — without having encountered more than one or two of these phenomena.

This passage in a nutshell, or summary, might become as follows:

NUTSHELL

Tuchman reminds us that history lays stress on misery and misdeeds because these negative events attracted notice in their time and so were reported in writing;

```
just as in a newspaper today, bad news predominates.  But
we should remember that suffering and social upheaval
didn't prevail everywhere all the time.
```

As you can see, this nutshell merely abstracts from the original. Not everything in the original has been preserved: not Tuchman's thought about papal bulls, not the specific examples such as Nicolas de Clamanges and the modern neo-Nazis and rapists. But the gist—the summary of the main idea— echoes Tuchman faithfully.

Before you write a nutshell, or summary, an effective way to sense the gist of a passage is carefully to pare away examples, details, modifiers, offhand remarks, and nonessential points. Here is the original quotation from Tuchman as one student marked it up on a photocopy, crossing out elements she decided to omit from her paraphrase:

> ~~A greater hazard,~~ built into the ~~very~~ nature of recorded history, is ~~overload of the negative.~~ the disproportionate survival of the bad side ~~of evil, misery, contention, and harm. In history~~ this is exactly the same as in the daily newspaper. ~~The normal does not make news.~~ ~~History is made by the~~ documents that survive, ~~and these~~ lean heavily on crisis and calamity, crime and misbehavior, because such things are the subject matter of the documentary process ~~of lawsuits, treaties, moralists' denunciations, literary satire, papal Bulls. No Pope ever issued a Bull to approve of something. Negative overload can be seen at work in the religious reformer Nicolas de Clamanges, who, in denouncing unfit and worldly prelates in 1401, said that in his anxiety for reform he would not discuss the good clerics because "they do not count beside the perverse men."~~
>
> Disaster is rarely as pervasive as it seems from recorded accounts. ~~The fact of being on the record makes it appear~~ continuous and ~~ubiquitous whereas~~ it is more likely to have been sporadic both in time and place. Besides, persistence of the normal is usually greater than the effect of disturbance, as we know from our own times. ~~After absorbing the news of today, one expects to face a world consisting entirely of strikes, crimes, power failures, broken water mains, stalled trains, school shutdowns, muggers, drug addicts, neo-Nazis, and rapists. The fact is that one can come home in the evening—on a lucky day—without having encountered more than one or two of these phenomena.~~

Rewording what was left, she wrote the following nutshell version:

NUTSHELL

```
    History, like a daily newspaper, reports more bad
than good.  Why?  Because the documents that have come
down to us tend to deal with upheavals and disturbances,
which are seldom as extensive and long-lasting as history
books might lead us to believe.
```

In filling her nutshell, you'll notice, the student couldn't simply omit the words she had deleted. The result would have been less readable and still long. She knew she couldn't use Tuchman's very words: that would be plagiarism. To make a good, honest, compact nutshell that would fit smoothly into her research paper, she had to condense most of the original words into her own.

Now here is Tuchman's passage in paraphrase. The writer has put Tuchman's ideas into other words but retained her major points. Note that the writer gives Tuchman credit for the ideas.

PARAPHRASE

> Tuchman points out that historians find some distortion of the truth hard to avoid, for more documentation exists for crimes, suffering, and calamities than for the events of ordinary life. As a result, history may overplay the negative. The author reminds us that we are familiar with this process from our contemporary newspapers, in which bad news is played up as being of greater interest than good news. If we believed that newspapers told all the truth, we would think ourselves threatened at all times by technical failures, strikes, crime, and violence—but we are threatened only some of the time, and normal life goes on. The good, dull, ordinary parts of our lives do not make the front page, and praiseworthy things tend to be ignored. "No Pope," says Tuchman, "ever issued a Bull to approve of something." But in truth, social upheaval did not prevail as widely as we might think from the surviving documents of medieval life. Nor, the author observes, can we agree with a critic of the church, Nicolas de Clamanges, in whose view evildoers in the clergy mattered more than men of goodwill.

In that reasonably complete and accurate paraphrase, about three-quarters the length of the original, most of Tuchman's points have been preserved and spelled out fully, even though they have been rearranged. Paraphrasing enables the writer to emphasize the ideas important to his or her research and makes the reader more aware of them as support for the writer's thesis than if the whole passage had been quoted directly. But notice that Tuchman's great remark about papal bulls has been kept a direct quotation because the statement is short and memorable, and it would be hard to improve on her words. The writer, you'll observe, doesn't interpret or evaluate Tuchman's ideas — she only passes them on.

When you use the information from a source in your paper, make sure that, like the writer of the nutshell and the paraphrase just given, you indicate your original source. You can pay due credit in a terse phrase — "Barbara W. Tuchman believes that . . ." or "According to Barbara W. Tuchman. . ." — and then give the page number in parentheses.

Often you paraphrase to emphasize one essential point. Here is an original passage from Evelyn Underhill's classic study *Mysticism*:

ORIGINAL

In the evidence given during the process for St. Teresa's beatification, Maria de San Francisco of Medina, one of her early nuns, stated that on entering the saint's cell whilst she was writing this same "Interior Castle" she found her [St. Teresa] so absorbed in contemplation as to be unaware of the external world. "If we made a noise close to her," said another, Maria del Nacimiento, "she neither ceased to write nor complained of being disturbed." Both these nuns, and also Ana de la Encarnacion, prioress of Granada, affirmed that she wrote with immense speed, never stopping to erase or to correct, being anxious, as she said, to write what the Lord had given her before she forgot it.

Suppose that the names of the witnesses do not matter, but the researcher wishes to emphasize, in fewer words, the celebrated mystic's writing habits. To bring out that point, the passage might be paraphrased (and quoted in part) like this:

PARAPHRASE

Evelyn Underhill has recalled the testimony of those
who saw St. Teresa at work on The Interior Castle.
Oblivious to noise, the celebrated mystic appeared to
write in a state of complete absorption, driving her pen
"with immense speed, never stopping to erase or to correct, being anxious, as she said, to write what the Lord
had given her before she forgot it."

Avoiding plagiarism   Here is a point we can't stress too strongly. When you paraphrase, never lift another writer's words or ideas without giving that writer due credit or without transforming them into words of your own. If you do, you are plagiarizing. You have seen in this chapter examples of honest nutshelling and paraphrasing. Introducing them into a paper, a writer would clearly indicate that they belong to Barbara Tuchman (or some other originator). Now here are a few horrible examples: paraphrases of Barbara Tuchman's original passage (on p. 622) that lift, without thanks, her ideas and even her very words. Finding such gross borrowings in a paper, an instructor might hear the ringing of a burglar alarm. First is an egregious example that lifts both thoughts and words.

PLAGIARIZED

Sometimes it's difficult for historians to learn the truth about the everyday lives of people from past societies because of the disproportionate survival of the bad side of things. Historical documents, like today's newspapers, tend to lean rather heavily on crisis, crime, and misbehavior. Reading the newspaper could lead one to expect a world consisting entirely of strikes, crimes, power failures, muggers, drug addicts, and rapists. In fact, though, disaster is rarely so pervasive as recorded accounts can make it seem.

What are the problems here? The phrase "the disproportionate survival of the bad side" is quoted directly from Tuchman's passage (line 2). The series "crisis, crime, and misbehavior" is too close to Tuchman's series "crisis and calamity, crime and misbehavior" (line 5); only the words "and calamity" have been omitted. The words "lead one to expect a world consisting entirely" is almost the same as the original "one expects to face a world consisting entirely" (lines 16–17). The phrase "strikes, crimes, power failures, muggers, drug addicts, and rapists" simply records — and in the same order — six of the ten examples Tuchman provides (lines 17–18). The last sentence in the plagiarized passage ("In fact, though, disaster is rarely so pervasive as recorded accounts can make it seem") is almost the same — and thus too close to the source — as the first sentence of Tuchman's second paragraph ("Disaster is rarely as pervasive as it seems from recorded accounts"). The student who wrote this attempted paraphrase failed to comprehend Tuchman's passage sufficiently to be able to put her ideas in his or her own words.

A more subtle theft, lifting thoughts but not words:

PLAGIARIZED

It's not always easy to determine the truth about the everyday lives of people from past societies because bad news gets recorded a lot more frequently than good news does. Historical documents, like today's newspapers, tend to pick up on malice and disaster and ignore flat normality. If I were to base my opinion of the world on what I see on the seven o'clock news, I would expect to see death and destruction around me all the time. Actually, though, I rarely come up against true disaster.

By using the first person pronoun *I*, this student suggests that Tuchman's ideas are his or her own. That is just as dishonest as quoting without using quotation marks, as reprehensible as not citing the source of ideas.

Here is an example that fails to make clear which ideas belong to the writer and which belong to Tuchman (although none of them belong to the writer):

```
        Barbara Tuchman explains that it can be difficult
    for historians to learn about the everyday lives of
    people who lived a long time ago because historical
    documents tend to record only the bad news.  Today's
    newspapers are like that, too: disaster, malice, and con-
    fusion take up a lot more room on the front page than
    happiness and serenity.  Just as the ins and outs of our
    everyday lives go unreported, we can suspect that upheav-
    als do not really play so important a part in the making
    of history as they seem to do.
```

After rightfully attributing the ideas in the first sentence to Tuchman, the student researcher makes a comparison to today's world in sentence 2. Then in sentence 3 he or she goes back to Tuchman's ideas without giving Tuchman credit. The placement of the last sentence suggests that this last idea is the student's whereas it is really Tuchman's.

To avoid falling into such habits, observe the cautions in the following checklist.

DISCOVERY CHECKLIST: AVOIDING PLAGIARISM

- Remember that taking notes is as much a process of understanding what you read as it is of writing.
- Carefully check each paraphrase or summary against the original. Be sure you have not misinterpreted or distorted the meaning of the original.
- When you quote from the original, be sure to quote exactly and use quotation marks. Quote no significant words from the original without placing them in quotation marks.
- Use ellipsis marks (. . .) to indicate where you have omitted something from the original, and use square brackets ([ ]) to indicate changes or additions you have made in a quotation.
- Take pains to identify the author of any quotation, paraphrase, or summary. Credit by name the originator of any fact, idea, or quotation you use.
- Make sure you indicate where another writer's ideas stop and where yours begin. (You might end your paraphrase with some clear phrase or phrases of transition: "—or so Tuchman affirms. In my own view. . . .")

📝 If, all the way through, your paraphrase slavishly parallels the author's sentence structure (the author asks three questions, so you ask three questions), rewrite it and vary it.

📝 If, at any place, your paraphrase looks close to the exact words of the original, carefully rewrite it in your own words.

Exercise: Paraphrasing

Study one of the following passages until you understand it thoroughly. Then using your own words, write a paraphrase of the passage. Compare and contrast your version with that of your classmates in your peer group. Finally, evaluate your own version: What are its strengths and weaknesses? Where should it be revised? When you take notes from library research, be sure to avoid the problems that you identify in this group activity.

PASSAGE 1

Within the next decades education will change more than it has changed since the modern school was created by the printed book over three hundred years ago. An economy in which knowledge is becoming the true capital and the premier wealth-producing resource makes new and stringent demands on the schools for educational performance and educational responsibility. A society dominated by knowledge workers makes even newer — and even more stringent — demands for social performance and social responsibility. Once again we will have to think through what an educated person is. At the same time, how we learn and how we teach are changing drastically and fast — the result, in part, of new theoretical understanding of the learning process, in part of new technology. Finally, many of the traditional disciplines of the schools are becoming sterile, if not obsolescent. We thus also face changes in *what* we learn and teach and, indeed, in what we mean by knowledge.

— Peter F. Drucker, *The New Realities*

PASSAGE 2

The New Obsolescence. For most of human history, the norm had been continuity. Change was news. Daily lives were governed by tradition. The most valued works were the oldest. The great works of architecture were monuments that survived from the past. Furnishings became increasingly valuable by becoming antique. Great literature never went out of date. "Literature," Ezra Pound observed, "is news that *stays* news." The new enriched the old and was enriched by the old. Shakespeare enriched Chaucer. Shaw enriched Shakespeare. It was a world of the enduring and the durable.

The laws of our Republic of Technology are quite different. The importance of a scientific work, as the German mathematician David Hilbert once observed, can be measured by the number of previous publications it makes superfluous to read. Scientists and technologists dare not wait for their current journals. They must study "preprints" of articles, use the telephone, and refer to the latest information "on line" to be sure that their work has not been made obsolete by what somebody else did this morning.

The Republic of Technology is a world of obsolescence. Our characteristic printed matter is not a deathless literary work but today's newspaper that makes yesterday's newspaper worthless. Old objects simply become secondhand, to be ripe for the next season's recycling. An H. H. Richardson or a Louis Sullivan building is torn down to make way for a parking garage. Progress seems to have become quick, sudden, and wholesale.

Most novel of all is our changed attitude toward change. Now nations seem to be distinguished not by their heritage or their stock of monuments, by what was once called their civilization, but by their pace of change. Rapidly "developing" nations are those that are most speedily obsolescing their inheritance. While it once took centuries or even millennia to build a civilization, now the transformation of an "underdeveloped" nation can be accomplished in mere decades. —Daniel J. Boorstin, *Hidden History*

PASSAGE 3

When I look to the future of humanity beyond the twenty-first century, I see on my list of things to come the extension of our inquisitiveness from the objective domain of science to the subjective domain of feeling and memory. Homo sapiens, the exploring animal, will not be content with merely physical exploration. Our curiosity will drive us to explore the dimensions of mind as vigorously as we explore the dimensions of space and time. For every pioneer who explores a new asteroid or a new planet, there will be another pioneer who explores from the inside the minds of our fellow passengers on planet Earth. It is our nature to strive to explore everything, alive and dead, present and past and future. When once the technology exists to read and write memories from one mind into another, the age of mental exploration will begin in earnest. Instead of admiring the beauties of nature from the outside, we will look at nature directly through the eyes of the elephant, the eagle, and the whale. We will be able, through the magic of science, to feel in our own minds the pride of the peacock and the wrath of the lion. That magic is no greater than the magic that enables me to see the rocking horse through the eyes of the child who rode it sixty years ago. —Freeman Dyson, *Infinite in All Directions*

Beginning and ending Perhaps, as we have suggested, only after you have written the body of your paper will a good beginning and a concluding paragraph or paragraphs occur to you. The head and tail of your paper might then make clear your opinion of whatever you have found out. But that is not the only way to begin and end a research paper. Lisa Chickos began her draft with a short summary of what her investigation revealed:

> Whoever first said "It's lonely at the top" must have had the field of education in mind--more specifically, women in education. Although women predominate at the lower levels in education, the "top" of the educational field is overwhelmingly composed of men.

Chickos then used facts and figures to support her view. That's a strong, concise beginning, and it makes the situation clear. A different opening paragraph might have answered the question she had investigated ("In educational administration, why are so few women at the top?").

> For a woman to become a school administrator, she must battle stereotyped attitudes. This obstacle defeats many teachers who try to rise in their profession and discourages many others from trying.

That opening may not be as lively as the one Chickos actually wrote, but it would do. Still another way to begin a research paper is to sum up the findings of other scholars. One research biologist, Edgar F. Warner, has reduced this kind of opening to a formula:

> First, in one or two paragraphs, you review everything that has been said about your topic, naming the most prominent earlier commentators. Next you declare why all of them are wrong. Then you set forth your own claim, and you spend the rest of your paper supporting it.

That pattern may seem cut and dried, but it is clear and useful. If you browse in specialized journals in many fields — literary criticism, social studies, the sciences — you may be surprised how many articles begin and go on in that very way. Of course, you don't need to damn every earlier commentator. One or two other writers may be enough to argue with. Erika Wahr, a student writing on the American poet Charles Olson, starts her research paper by disputing two views of him:

> To Cid Corman, Charles Olson of Gloucester, Massachusetts, is "the one dynamic and original epic poet twentieth-century America has produced" (116). To Allen Tate, Olson is "a loquacious charlatan" (McFinnery 92). In my opinion, the truth lies between these two extremes, nearer to Corman's view.

Whether or not you have stated your view in your beginning, you will certainly need to make it clear in your closing paragraph or paragraphs. A suggestion: before writing the last lines of your paper, read back over what you have written earlier. Then, without looking at your paper, try to put your view into writing. (For more suggestions on starting and finishing, see pp. 347 and 350.)

Revising and Editing

Because in writing a library research paper it is easy to lose sight of what you're saying, why not ask a classmate to read over your draft and give you reactions? Ask your peer editor to answer the questions in the peer editing checklist.

PEER EDITING CHECKLIST: WRITING FROM LIBRARY RESEARCH

- What is your overall reaction to this paper?
- What do you understand the research question to be? Did the writer answer that question?
- What promises has the writer made that should be met in the paper? Did he or she meet them?
- How interested were you in continuing to read the paper? If you didn't have to, would you have kept on reading? Why or why not?
- What changes might you make to the introduction that would wake up a sleepy instructor drinking coffee at 3:00 A.M. and enlist his or her careful attention?
- Does the conclusion merely restate the introduction? If so, suggest some specific changes to improve it.
- Is the conclusion too abrupt or too hurried? If so, suggest three specific revisions that would make the reader feel that the essay has ended exactly as it should.
- Are there any places where the essay becomes hard to follow? Star these.
- Do you know which information is from the student writer and which from the research sources? Star any facts, opinions, or questions that you think should be documented.

When you set about the task of revising, you can start by backtracking at the trouble spots your peer editor has starred. If you need to improve connections between parts, try summarizing the previous section of your paper. By so doing, you remind your reader of what you have already said. This strategy can come in handy, especially in a long paper when, after a few pages, the reader's memory may need refreshing and a summary of the argument so far will be welcome. Such a brief summary might go like this: "As we can infer from the previous examples, most veteran career counselors are reluctant to encourage women undergraduates to apply for jobs as principals in elementary schools."

When you look over your draft, here are a few other points to inspect critically (and, if need be, try to improve).

REVISION CHECKLIST: LOOKING OVER EVERYTHING

- Do you honestly feel you have said something, not just heaped facts and statements by other writers that don't add up to anything? If your answer is no, a mere heap of meaningless stuff is all you've got, then you face a painful decision. Take a long walk and try to define what your research has shown you. Don't despair: talk to other students, talk to your instructor. It may be that you need a whole new question whose answer you care about. Or it may be that you need to do some harder thinking.

▸ Does your paper make clear the research question it began with? Does it reveal, early on, what you wanted to find out and why this might be important to the reader?

▸ Does it sum up your findings? Does it clearly present your findings as it goes along?

▸ Have you included only library materials that told you something and left out any that seem useless (even though you worked hard to look them up and take notes on them)?

▸ Have you digressed in any places from answering the question you set out to answer? If so, does the digression help your reader understand the nature of the problem, or does it add extraneous material that might simply be omitted? (Although it is a shock to discover you have written, say, six pages that don't advance your research, be brave—use those scissors, feed that wastebasket.)

▸ Does each new idea or piece of information seem to follow from the one before it? Can you see any stronger order in which to arrange things? Have you connected the parts?

▸ Is the source of every quotation, every fact, every idea you have borrowed made unmistakably clear? If your readers cared to look up your sources, could they readily find them in a library?

Documenting sources A research paper calls on you to follow special rules in documenting your sources—in citing them as you write and in listing them at the end of your paper. At first, these rules may seem fiendishly fussy, but for good reason professional writers of research papers swear by them and follow them to a *T*. The rules will make sense if you imagine a world in which scholarly and professional writers could prepare their research papers in any old way they pleased. The result would be a new tower of Babel. Research papers go by the rules in order to be easily readable, easily set into type. The rules also ensure that all necessary information is there to enable any reader interested in the same subject to look up the original sources.

Quotation style. One special manuscript convention for research papers is that for direct quotations. When you use a direct quotation from one of your sources, ordinarily you simply put into quotation marks, in the body of your paper, the words you're using, along with the name of the person who said them and the page number from the source of the quotation.

```
It was Patrick Henry who said, "Give me liberty or give
me death."

Johnson puts heavy emphasis on the importance of "giving
the child what she needs at the precise moment in her
life when it will do the most good" (23).
```

When you include a quotation longer than four typed lines, you set it off in your text by indenting the whole quotation ten spaces from the left margin if you're following MLA style, five for APA style. You double-space the quotation, just as you do the rest of your paper. Don't place quotation marks around an indented quotation and, if the quotation is a paragraph or less, don't indent its first line. Following is an example, a critic's comment on Emily Dickinson's use of language:

> Cynthia Griffin Wolff in her biography <u>Emily Dickin-</u>
> <u>son</u> comments on this nineteenth-century poet's incisive
> use of language:
>
>> Language, of course, was a far subtler weapon
>> than a hammer. Dickinson's verbal maneuvers
>> would increasingly reveal immense skill in
>> avoiding a frontal attack; she preferred the
>> silent knife of irony to the strident battering
>> of loud complaint. She had never suffered
>> fools gladly. The little girl who had written
>> of a dull classmate, "He is the silliest crea-
>> ture that ever lived I think," grew into a
>> woman who could deliver wrath and contempt with
>> excruciating economy and cunning. Scarcely sub-
>> missive, she had acquired the cool calculation
>> of an assassin. (170-71)

(For detailed instructions about quoting sources, see Chapter 30.)

WRITING WITH A COMPUTER: LIBRARY RESEARCH

REWRITING

If you plan to use traditional bottom-of-the-page footnotes, see if your word processing program will format them for you. A program that does so even figures out for you how much space to allow for the footnote at the bottom of each page.

Research papers, being rich in names and numbers, invite misspellings and other typographical errors. A great way to proofread your finished research paper, before you print it out, is to go to the bottom of the document you have been writing, scroll backward, and reread what you have written line by line. This technique prevents you from getting so interested in what you've written that you forget to notice mistakes. Instead, it keeps you looking at spelling, punctuation, and such mechanical matters, concentrating on one line at a time. Another proofreading help is the spellchecker. It will identify not only misspelled words but also proper names not in its dictionary, and you can check each in isolation.

(For suggestions on shaping a draft with a computer, see p. 620.)

Style guides. In humanities courses and the social sciences, most writers of research papers follow the style of the Modern Language Association (MLA) or the American Psychological Association (APA). Your instructor will probably suggest which style to observe; if you are not told, use MLA. The first time you prepare a research paper according to MLA or APA rules, you'll need extra time to look up just what to do in each situation. Chapter 30 gives examples of most of the usual situations.

Works cited. At the very end of a library research paper, you supply a list of all the sources you have cited: books, periodicals, and any other materials. Usually this list is the last thing you write. It will be easy to make if, when you compiled your working bibliography, you included on each note card all the necessary information (as shown in Figures 27.1 and 27.2). If you did, you can now simply arrange the works you used in alphabetical order, and then type the information about each source, following the MLA or APA guidelines (given in Chapter 30, pp. 707 and 721). The MLA specifies that you title your list "Works Cited"; the APA, "References." Any leftover parts — cards for sources you haven't used after all — may now be sailed into the wastebasket. Resist the temptation to transcribe them, too, and impressively lengthen your list.

Manuscript form. A note following Chapter 18 tells you how to style a finished (typewritten or word-processed) manuscript. Its advice on proper formatting applies not only to library research papers but to any other college papers you may write.

Last pass. Before you hand in your final revision, go over it one last time for typographical and mechanical errors. If you have written your paper on a word processor, it's an easy matter to correct all errors right on the screen before you print it. If you find any mistakes in a paper you have typewritten, don't despair. Your instructor knows how difficult and frustrating it would be to retype a whole page to fix one flyspeck error. Correct it neatly in ink. (How to be neat? See p. 398 and the proofreading symbols at the back of the book.)

A COMPLETED LIBRARY RESEARCH PAPER

Lisa Chickos's irritation at men who would call a hard-working woman school administrator "tough and bitchy" led her to write a paper she strongly cared about. The completed paper is more than a compilation of facts, more than a string of quotations. Chickos sets forth a problem that irritates her, and she proposes action.

She prefaced her paper with a formal outline. Written in complete statements, it is a *sentence outline*. (If your instructor asks for such an outline, see the advice on formal outlines on p. 334.)

In her later college life, Chickos found, the training she acquired as a freshman researcher proved valuable. "Now that I'm a history major," she said, "I'm *always* doing research papers."

Title page contains, on separate lines, centered and double-spaced, the title of the paper, the writer's name, the instructor's name, the course number, and the date.

Educational Leadership: A Man's World

Lisa Chickos

Professor Laura Miller

English 102

May 12, 199-

Chickos ii

Outline

Thesis: To achieve fair representation in educational administration, women must change the current system.

I. Women are not adequately represented in educational administration.

    A. More men than women are in top positions.

    B. The situation is not improving.

II. There are various barriers to women who might go into educational administration.

    A. Biased social attitudes keep women out of supervisory positions.

        1. Females are stereotyped as emotional and non-task-oriented.

        2. Women are not perceived as capable of running a school system.

        3. The belief that women are not as capable as men is erroneous.

    B. Women may not aspire to positions of leadership because of the way they are socialized.

        1. They are not socialized to be leaders.

        2. Some have less financial need than men.

        3. They have a fear of success.

        4. They have a fear of disapproval.

    C. Young girls have few role models.

    D. Family ties may interfere with career advancement.

Type "Outline" centered, one inch from the top. Double-space to the first line of text.

The thesis states the main idea of the paper.

This outline is in sentence form rather than in the shorter topic form. It is a skeleton of the research paper.

Chickos iii

1. Family responsibilities are time-consuming.
2. Conflicting roles cause stress.
3. A wife and mother may be perceived as not being able to relocate easily.

III. Women must work to change the current system.

    A. Attitudes must change.

        1. Leadership should be redefined.

        2. Attitudes toward gender roles must change.

        3. Early education should change.

        4. Women must overcome their internal barriers.

        5. Women need the understanding of their families.

    B. Practices within the educational system must change.

        1. Hiring practices must change.

        2. Women must encourage other women.

        3. Women should enlist the support of male colleagues.

All pages after the title page are numbered in the upper right corner, half an inch from the top. The writer's name appears before the page number. Outline pages are numbered with small roman numerals (the title page is counted but is not numbered).

Chickos 1

Educational Leadership: A Man's World

Whoever first said "It's lonely at the top" must have had the field of education in mind-- more specifically, women in education. Although the number of women in administrative positions is increasing in many professional fields, the number of women moving up the career ladder in education is not increasing significantly (Whitaker and Lane 12). If women are to be more fairly represented in educational administration, they must overcome the restrictions imposed by the current system, a system built on erroneous perceptions about women's work and women's abilities.

Women definitely are not adequately represented in educational administration. In 1972, 62 percent of the professional staff of public schools were female, yet 99 percent of the superintendents, 98 percent of high school principals, and 80 percent of elementary school principals were male (Schmuck 244). In 1982, two thirds of public school teachers were women, but the great majority of administrative positions were still held by men (Truett 1). More recently, in 1988, 70 percent of public school teachers were women (Hammer and Gerald, Teachers), but men occupied 75 percent of administrative positions (Hammer and Gerald, Administrators). Unfortunately the figures haven't improved much over the last two decades.

There are various barriers to women entering educational administration. Biased social

Title is repeated, ce
tered, on the first
page of the text, an
the writer's name an
page number are
omitted. Double-spa
from the title to the
first line of text.

Citation of work by
two or three authors
gives the names of a
authors.

Thesis is stated here

First section of body
establishes the current situation.

Paraphrase and summary rather than direct quotation to
discuss the results of
most studies.

Citations within text
are placed in parentheses before sentence period.

Second section of essay identifies and pro
vides evidence of the
causes of the current
situation.

Chickos 2

attitudes are the basis of the inequity in women's representation at the top. The female stereotype that categorizes women as being emotional and non-task-oriented (Whitaker and Lane 15) can cause problems. It holds that women can be part of the system, obeying its rules and taking orders, but that they are not capable of running the system--making the rules and giving the orders (Biklen 10). This societal attitude convinces some women that they don't have what it takes to be a leader. As Sari Knopp Biklen states, "People's perceptions about their ability influence achievement more than their actual ability or level of aspiration" (8).

This stereotype may also prevent women from being hired for administrative positions. There is a particular stereotype of the ambitious woman, especially prevalent among men:

> a self-righteous female, smug and intolerant, obstructive and naive, focused on process without discernible result, given to judgmental bitchiness, unwilling to take her licks like the rest of the guys, and demanding protection even as she screams for independence. (Melia 49)

Because the educational leaders are primarily men, they may not even consider hiring women for administrative positions (Schmuck 248). An interview with a male administrator reflected their feelings:

> It's easier to work without women.

Text pages are numbered with arabic numerals in the upper right corner, preceded by writer's last name. Leave one-inch margins at the top, bottom, and sides of the paper. Place page number half an inch from the top.

Direct quotation rather than paraphrasing for the source's strong, effective language.

Source's names mentioned at the beginning of the quotation, so the citation gives only the page number.

Quotation of more than four typed lines is indented ten spaces from the left margin and is double-spaced with no quotation marks. Citation of source is in parentheses following the end punctuation of the quotation.

Direct quotation for the exact words of the respondent in this study.

Chickos 3

> Principals and superintendents are a
> management team. It fosters interde-
> pendence and mutual support. We need
> each other for survival. It's no
> evil liaison--it's just pure politics.
> I wonder if we could hang together
> so well if some of us were women.
> (Biklen 12)

This brings up another difficulty that
women must confront. Because there are so few
women in educational administration, a woman who
reaches such a position may see herself (and may
be seen by others) as a token or representative
of all women. Performing naturally becomes
very difficult (Biklen 16). Because she is in
the spotlight and because she may feel like an
outsider in a male-dominated profession, a woman
may adopt "female behavior" (passive, agreeable,
compromising), which in turn contributes to the
negative image of her role as an administrator
(Clement 136).

Quotation marks around two important words from source.

Could it be that men actually have more
ability than women to be effective leaders?
This hardly seems the case. Kathryn S. Whitaker
and Kenneth Lane, experts in educational leadership, assert,

> Although attitudinal barriers exist,
> several research studies point out
> that female administrators are just as
> capable as their male counterparts.
> (12)

One study that supports this conclusion was

Chickos 4

conducted by Andrew Fishel and Janice Pottker, researchers who asked teachers to evaluate women principals. Their findings showed no significant differences in the behavior of women principals compared with that of men principals, and the women were definitely viewed as competent leaders (qtd. in Biklen 10). Another study that surveyed attitudes toward women school district administrators found that the terms used to describe the most effective women were "conscientious, sensitive to the needs of others, reliable, adaptable, and tactful" (Temmen 9).

Other studies suggest that women, in fact, may be more effective educational leaders than men. One study, for example, indicated that when placed in competitive situations, men become very aggressive and tend to act in ways that are most advantageous for themselves whereas women usually try to consider the interests of all involved, not just themselves (Conoley 39). Furthermore, the study showed that in educational settings, groups accomplish more when they have a leader who works with them rather than ruling over them--someone who listens to the opinions of all the group members and tries to do what is best for all involved, as women do (Conoley 40). In another study Alan Hein found that women were actually rated as better than men in several important categories: flexibility, constructive criticism, communication, assuming responsibility, and ex-

Biklen is a secondary source for the study by Fishel and Pottker, so citation reads "qtd. in."

Writer uses transitional words and phrases to link paragraphs discussing various studies.

Chickos 5

ercising leadership (qtd. in Whitaker and Lane 14). Neal Gross and Anne Trask identified additional strengths of female administrators: they provide better instructional supervision than men, use more effective managerial techniques, and place more emphasis on teaching skills for evaluation (qtd. in Whitaker and Lane 14).

    Clearly, women do have the ability to be effective educational leaders. Therefore, the reasons that more men reach higher positions must lie elsewhere.

    One possibility may be that women simply do not aspire to positions of leadership. Overall, women are socialized to nurture others whereas men are taught to persevere toward success (Whitaker and Lane 12). From early childhood, boys are encouraged to be competitive. Organized sports and other games send young boys a clear message--be the best. For young girls, however, emphasis is placed mainly on looks and personality. They are not encouraged to reach high goals (Clement 134), and few are told they have leadership potential (Melia 2). Because of this socialization, women usually do not attach the same importance to administrative positions as men do. Thus, fewer women complete training programs and fewer apply for high-level positions (Whitaker and Lane 13).

    Although more women are working outside the home today, few in the educational system are the sole or main breadwinner for the family.

Transition paragraph: to summarize and to point forward.

Writer indicates that she will list other reasons and uses transitional words such as *one* and *also* to highlight each new reason.

In a survey of public school administrators, the working husbands of the female administrators made more money than their wives, while the working wives of male administrators made less money than their husbands (Truett 9). It can be speculated that most men still see their jobs as the main source of family income and there- fore go after the highest-paying positions, while some women in education continue to view their jobs as a second income and have less financial need for a better position.

Women also may not aspire to administrative positions because of a "fear of success." So- ciety's concept of femininity tells young girls that achievement is a masculine quality. It doesn't mix with a pretty face and pleasant personality. Many girls, therefore, fear that they will be socially rejected if they succeed in reaching a position of authority (Horner 36).

Some experts have suggested that women may not actually have a fear of success; instead, they may fear disapproval. According to Jinx Melia, women have "a strong, overriding need for approval" (41). Women who were tested for fear of success showed a fear of losing love or of being socially rejected. The small number of men who showed some fear of success questioned the value of the success rather than showing any fears about possible rejection (Johnson 176). For this reason it has been speculated that women have a fear of what might happen if they deviate from traditional sex roles, not a fear

Chickos 7

of succeeding (Wortman, Loftus, and Marshall 368).

Fear of the consequences of "unfeminine" behavior is certainly legitimate. Society's attitudes are unfavorable toward women in traditionally male professions. As Dr. Patricia Albjerg Graham, a member of the history and education faculty at Barnard College and Teachers College, Columbia University, states,

> administrators are expected to be independent and assertive, behaviors understood as "tough and bitchy" when displayed by women, but "clear-headed and attentive to detail" when found in a man. (170)

Obviously, no woman (or man, for that matter) would want to be described as "tough and bitchy." Young girls need to see that they can fill administrative positions and still gain approval. What better place for this to start than in the educational system?

Unfortunately, because there are so few women already in high positions in education, young girls have few role models to follow. They need to see that other women have succeeded and that they too can succeed and thus strive to seek better jobs (Antonucci 188). There are plenty of men for girls to pattern themselves after, but it is easier for children to model themselves after someone they can identify with and in most cases a young girl can most easily identify with a woman (Antonucci 186).

Title and credentials establish the source as an authority.

One of the major reasons women don't reach for administrative jobs may be family ties and responsibilities. If a woman is a wife and mother, she may not be able to put as much time as she would like into a demanding job (Graham 170) and may experience a lot of stress because she tries to be "superwoman" (Erickson 291). She is assertive and makes important decisions all day, yet when she goes home, more than likely her husband will expect her to assume the role of the "little woman," the helpmate, without complaint. One woman expressed this conflict by saying, "I feel resentful and a little ridiculous when I have to ask my husband for $10 for groceries and he questions the expenditure, after I have just spent the day managing a budget of thousands of dollars" (Erickson 290).

Perception of a woman's geographic mobility may also influence her lack of advancement. There is nothing strange about a family's relocating because of the husband's job transfer, but it is less commonplace for a family to move to a new location for the wife's job. The possibility of relocating may keep some women from pursuing certain jobs and may also keep women who do pursue such jobs from being hired. School boards, assuming that a man would be able to relocate easily and a woman might not, probably do not give equal consideration to women for certain positions. Interestingly, however, the survey of public school administrators revealed that the person who had moved the most

Chickos 9

(three times in the past five years) was a woman
(Truett 13). This same survey showed no real
difference between men and women in willingness
to relocate: 16.7 percent of the men anticipated
a future move to obtain a better job, as did 14
percent of the women (15). Actually, neither
men nor women seem very eager to relocate for a
higher position, but women are certainly no less
willing to relocate than men (Truett 22).

Chickos gives her interpretation of some data in sentence form and then presents the statistics themselves.

Women must work to change the current system if they are ever to become an equal part of
educational administration. First, attitudes
must change. Leadership must be redefined
(Sadler 617), and social attitudes toward gender
roles must change (Whitaker and Lane 15). During the school years, boys and girls can be
taught that there is nothing wrong with pursuing
nontraditional careers and can be encouraged to
reach for their own goals--not the goals society
has set for them (Johnson 180).

Third and final section of essay proposes solutions to the problem.

As Jinx Melia points out, women must overcome their "internal barriers" (33), such as
reluctance to take risks (39), overwhelming desire for approval (41), and expectation of reward for good behavior (44). In addition, they
need the support of their family. If a career
woman is also a wife and mother, she is actually
carrying two jobs. Cooperation from her husband and the independent behavior of her children may give a woman a chance to pursue a
position she thought was not within her reach
(Biklen 14).

Chickos 10

Practices within the system also must change. First, hiring practices must be changed. Since administrative staffs are essentially male, and they tend to hire men over women (Weitzman 485), affirmative action laws require women to be involved in the selection processes. Nevertheless, although those who review applications and make hiring decisions cannot legally consider marital status and family, because of personal biases they probably sometimes consider a family to be a burden for a woman's career but not for a man's. Furthermore, more programs to encourage women to go into leadership positions should be established, and additional research should be conducted into the equities of access to school administration (Whitaker and Lane 15).

The women already in leadership positions must encourage women who are on the way up, and they all need to support one another. One female administrator pointed out:

> It used to be when I walked into a room full of men and only one woman I would tend to ignore her. Now when I walk into a similar situation the woman and I at least have eye-contact. There's too damn few of us women; we found out we need to support each other. If there were more of us we would be free to act just as folks, but because there are so few of us, there is the common bond of being women. (Schmuck 254)

Chickos 11

But women cannot just join forces and try to overthrow the system. They must consciously try to project a positive image to their male colleagues (Schmuck 249). Women need to have male support because men are in the power positions and have the ability to make changes. Also, if women banded together and excluded men from their efforts, that in itself would be discrimination, which is exactly what must be overcome (Schmuck 251).

A number of organizations and some legislation, such as Sex Equity in Educational Leadership (SEEL), the National Council of Administrative Women in Education (NCAWE), the Leadership and Learning Cooperative (LLC), and the Women's Educational Equity Act (WEEA), have been designed to facilitate the changes that are necessary to ensure equity in educational leadership. With the help of such groups and legislation, along with an enlightened public, perhaps equality in educational administration will soon be realized. Then "powerful women may create a massive upheaval in education as it is now practiced in the United States" (Melia 160).

Organizations are considered common knowledge, and no source citation is needed.

Conclusion suggests what can happen if system is changed.

Chickos 12

Works Cited

Antonucci, Toni. "The Need for Female Role
Models in Education." Biklen and Brannigan 185-95.

Biklen, Sari Knopp. "Introduction: Barriers to
Equity--Women, Educational Leadership, and
Social Change." Biklen and Brannigan
1-23.

Biklen, Sari Knopp, and Marilyn B. Brannigan,
eds. Women and Educational Leadership.
Lexington: Lexington, 1980.

Clement, Jacqueline. "Sex Bias in School
Administration." Biklen and Brannigan
131-37.

Conoley, Jane Close. "The Psychology of Leadership: Implications for Women." Biklen
and Brannigan 35-46.

Erickson, H. Lynn. "Conflict and the Female
Principal." Phi Delta Kappan 67(1985):
288-91.

Graham, Patricia Albjerg. "Status Transitions
of Women Students, Faculty, and Administrators." Academic Women on the Move.
Ed. Alice S. Rossi and Ann Calderwood.
New York: Sage, 1973. 163-72.

Hammer, Charles, and Elizabeth Gerald. "Table
1: Number and Percentage of Teachers by
Selected Characteristics." Selected Characteristics of Public and Private School
Teachers: 1987-88. United States. Department of Education. National Center
for Education Statistics. NCES-90-087.
Washington: GPO, 1990. ERIC ED 323 195.

Works cited parenthet-
ically in text of paper
are listed here alpha-
betically by authors'
last names. Type
"Works Cited" cen-
tered, one inch from
top. Double-space to
first entry and double-
space within and be-
tween entries. Indent
second and following
lines of each entry
five spaces.

Book itself is not cited
parenthetically in text
of paper, but more
than two entries in the
list of works cited are
taken from it. Publica-
tion information is
given here, and short
cross-references to it
are used in the other
entries.

Article in a monthly
magazine.

Chapter in an edited
book with publication
information given in
this entry.

Statistical table from
ERIC system.

Chickos 13

---. "Table 1: Number and Percentage of Admin-
istrators by Selected Characteristics."
Selected Characteristics of Public and
Private School Administrators: 1987-1988.
United States. Department of Education.
National Center for Education Statistics.
NCES-90-085. Washington: GPO, 1990. ERIC
ED 318 128.

Horner, Matina. "A Bright Woman Is Caught in a
Double Bind." Psychology Today Nov. 1969:
36+.

Johnson, Marilyn. "How Real Is Fear of Success?" Biklen and Brannigan 175-82.

Melia, Jinx. Breaking into the Boardroom: When
Talent and Hard Work Aren't Enough. New
York: Putnam's, 1987.

Sadler, Lynn Veach. "Continuing to Grow in Administration (or What Next?)." June 3-4,
1991. Vital Speeches of the Day 1 Aug.
1991: 614-20.

Schmuck, Patricia A. "Changing Women's Representation in School Management: A Systems
Perspective." Biklen and Brannigan
239-59.

Temmen, Karen. "A Research Study of Selected
Successful Women Administrators in the
Educational Field." St. Louis: CEMREL,
1982.

Truett, Carol. "Professional and Geographic
Mobility of a Selected Sample of Nebraska
Public School Administrators: Differences

Source by same au-
thors as in preceding
entry.

Book title with
subtitle.

Study sponsored by
corporation.

Unpublished paper
presented at a confe
ence.

Chickos 14

between Men and Women." Paper. Annual
Meeting of the National Conference of Pro-
fessors of Educational Administration.
San Marcos, TX, 1982.

Weitzman, Lenore J. "Affirmative Action Plans
for Eliminating Sex Discrimination in Aca-
deme." Academic Women on the Move. Ed.
Alice S. Rossi and Ann Calderwood. New
York: Sage, 1973. 463-504.

Whitaker, Kathryn S., and Kenneth Lane. "What
Is 'A Woman's Place' in Educational Administration?" Education Digest Nov. 1990:
12-15.

Wortman, Camille B., Elizabeth F. Loftus, and
Mary Marshall. Psychology. New York:
Knopf, 1981.

Chapter from book with two editors.

Book with three authors.

Questions to Start You Thinking

1. Which of the reasons given in this paper for women's failure to advance in the field of education seems to you the strongest? What makes that reason hard to refute?

2. Do any of the points that Chickos includes for support seem to you less convincing? What are they? If you were her peer editor, what suggestions would you make that might strengthen her main point?

3. What other professions can you name in which men hold most positions of leadership? Why do you think this is so?

Other Assignments

Using your library sources, write a short research paper, under 3000 words (Chickos's paper is 2400 words), in which you give a rough survey of the state of current knowledge on one of the following topics or on another that you and your instructor agree offers promising opportunities for research. Proceed as if you had chosen to work on the main assignment that is described on p. 628.

1. The health of the economy or the stability of the government in a third world country

2. Career opportunities in a certain line of work that interests you

3. Another planet in the solar system, or comets, novas, black holes, perhaps even a neighboring star

4. Progress in the cure and prevention of a disease or syndrome

5. Treatment of drug abuse or the rehabilitation of users

6. The "greenhouse effect" (a phenomenon causing a change in worldwide climate)

7. Recent changes in a European, Asian, or African country

8. A comparison of the relative effectiveness of present methods of disposing of nuclear wastes

9. Effects of banning smoking in public places

10. The growth of telecommuting: the tendency of people to work in their own homes, keeping in touch by phone and computer modem with the main office

APPLYING WHAT YOU LEARN: SOME USES OF LIBRARY RESEARCH

In many courses beyond your English course you will be asked to write papers from library research. The more deeply you move into core requirements and specialized courses for your major, the more independent research and thinking you will do. At some colleges, a long research paper is required of all seniors to graduate. Beyond college, the demand for writing based on library research is evident. Scholars explore issues that absorb and trouble them and the community of scholars to which they belong. In the business world, large companies often maintain their own specialized libraries since information and opinions are worth money and decisions have to be based on them. If you should take an entry-level job in the headquarters of a large corporation, don't be surprised to be told, "We're opening a branch office in Sri Lanka, and Graham (the executive vice-president) doesn't know a thing about the place. Can you write a report on it? Customs, geography, climate, government, state of the economy, political stability, religion, lifestyle, and all that?" In a large city newspaper, reporters and feature writers continually do library research (as well as field research), and the newspaper's library of clippings on subjects covered in the past (the "morgue") is in constant use. Many popular magazine articles were obviously researched in a library: "The Strangest Career in Movies" (for which the writer looked up all the biographies and biographical facts about Greta Garbo), "New Findings about Sunburn" (for which the writer went through the past year's crop of medical journals).

As one of the ways they become prominent in their disciplines, academics and professionals in many fields — law, medicine, English, geography, social studies, art and music history, the history of science — write and publish papers and whole books based on library research in specialized and scholarly journals. In an exciting study of urban architecture, *Spaces: Dimensions of the Human Landscape* (New Haven: Yale UP, 1981), Barrie B. Greenbie draws connections between our notion of "self" — a personal universe bounded by the skin — and our sense of the kind of dwelling we feel at home in. In exploring

FOR GROUP LEARNING

To write a collaborative essay from library research is a complex job, and we recommend that you attempt it only if your writing group has already had some success in writing a collaborative paper. If you do embark on such an endeavor, you will find that working as a research team can make your project advance with alacrity. After consulting with your instructor and getting a go-ahead, your group might develop a research paper following one of the assignments in this chapter. (An instructor who agrees to accept a collaborative research paper will give the same grade to all participants.)

You will need to fix a series of deadlines, parcel out the work, and meet faithfully according to a schedule. Here is a sample schedule that one group followed for an eight-week research project:

Week 1: Members individually seek a topic for the group project.

Week 2: The group meets and members agree on a topic: a research question. They choose a coordinator to keep the project moving, someone willing to make phone calls to keep in touch with people when necessary. The group clears the topic with the instructor.

Weeks 3–4: Assisted by two people, the coordinator makes a preliminary search and compiles a tentative bibliography. The group meets to divide up responsibilities: who will collect what material. Then, without further meetings, all begin work.

Week 5: Each member continues his or her assigned portion of the research, reading and taking relevant notes.

Week 6: The group meets to evaluate the material and to see where any further information may be needed. Members collaborate on a rough plan or outline.

Week 7: Three writers divide up the outline and each writes part of a draft (if possible, with the aid of a word processor). The other group members read over the writing for at least one hour during this week and help solve any problems in it.

Week 8: All group members meet for one long evening session and carefully review the draft. All write comments and corrections on it. Then two fresh writers divide the criticized draft and type it up smoothly. Whoever has done the least work to date is designated the proofreader. The coordinator gives the whole paper another, final proofreading.

Obviously such a plan can succeed only if your group can work in a close, friendly, and responsible fashion. No one should enter into such an arrangement without first making sure of enough unobstructed time to meet all assigned responsibilities — or else the whole project can bog down in an awful mess. But if it succeeds, as it probably will, your research will generate excitement. You'll know the pleasure of playing your part on a dynamic, functioning team.

this relationship (and the need to build dwellings that correspond to our psychic needs), Greenbie brings together sources in psychology, architecture, economics, and literature (the poetry of Emily Dickinson). This passage from the beginning of his book may give you a sense of his way of weaving together disparate materials:

> The psychoanalyst Carl Jung placed great emphasis on the house as a symbol of self, and many others have elaborated this idea.[1] Of course Jung considered "self" both in a social as well as individual sense, and in fact the concept of *self* has no meaning except in the context of *others.* Most of us share our houses with some sort of family group during most of our lives, and while parts of an adequately sized house may belong primarily to one or another individual, the boundaries of the home are usually those of a cluster of selves which form a domestic unit. Even people who by choice or circumstance live alone express in their homes the images and traditions formed at one time in a family group.
>
> The architects Kent C. Bloomer and Charles W. Moore view buildings as the projection into space of our awareness of our own bodies. Fundamental and obvious as this relationship might seem, it has been to a great extent ignored in contemporary architecture. Bloomer and Moore sum up the personal situation very well in their book, *Body, Memory, and Architecture:*
>
>> One tell-tale sign remains, in modern America, of a world based not on a Cartesian abstraction, but on our sense of ourselves extended beyond the boundaries of our bodies to the world around: that is the single-family house, free-standing like ourselves, with a face and a back, a hearth (like a heart) and a chimney, an attic full of recollections of *up,* and a basement harboring implications of *down.*[2]
>
> Many North American tract houses fit this characterization less adequately than they might. But whatever the deficiencies of domestic and other kinds of contemporary architecture may be, they are as nothing compared to the shortcomings of most urban design. . . . This book will focus on the hierarchical structures that extend from the "skin" of the family home to the street and beyond.

Notice that Greenbie uses endnote form (see p. 718) because the amount of information he has to put in his notes might have interrupted the flow of his prose. Endnote 1, for instance, reads:

> [1]Carl G. Jung, *Memories, Dreams, and Reflections* (London: Fontana Library Series, 1969). For an exceptionally good summary and elaboration, see Clare Cooper, "The House as Symbol of the Self," in *Designing for Human Behavior,* ed. J. Lang et al. (Stroudsburg, Pa.: Dowden, Hutchinson, and Ross, 1974).

Earlier, we pointed out that unless your assignment confines you to library materials, your research paper may draw on any other sources you have: recall of your personal experience, observation, conversation, previous reading, even imagination. Here is a memorable example of two professional writers on biology, Anne and Paul Ehrlich, combining library materials with their own experience.

> The direct benefits supplied to humanity by other species are often little appreciated, but nonetheless they can be very dramatic. In 1955 Paul's father died

after a grim thirteen-year battle with Hodgkin's disease, a leukemia-like disorder of the lymphatic system. Just after his death, some Canadian scientists discovered that an extract of the leaves of a periwinkle plant from Madagascar caused a decrease in the white blood cell count of rats. Chemists at Eli Lilly and Company analyzed the chemistry of periwinkle leaves, and the analysis turned up a large number of alkaloids, poisonous chemicals that plants apparently have evolved to protect themselves from animals that eat them and parasites that infest them.[1] Two of these alkaloids, vincristine and vinblastine, have proven to be effective in treating Hodgkin's disease. Indeed, treatment with vincristine in combination with other chemical agents now gives a very high remission rate and long periods where no further treatment is required in patients even in the advanced stage of the disease.

Thus a chemical found in a plant species might have helped greatly to prolong Bill Ehrlich's life — and is now available to help the five to six thousand people in the United States alone who contract Hodgkin's disease annually. As some measure of its economic value, total sales of vincristine worldwide in 1979 were $35 million.[2] Vincristine also is used along with other compounds to fight a wide variety of cancers and cancerlike diseases, including one form of leukemia, breast cancer, and cancers that afflict children. Had the periwinkle plant been wiped out before 1950, humanity would have suffered a loss — even though no one would have realized it. (*Extinction: The Causes and Consequences of the Disappearance of Species* [New York: Random, 1981], 53–54)

---

[1] P. R. Ehrlich and P. H. Raven, "Butterflies and Plants: A Study of Coevolution," *Evolution* 18 (1964): 586–608.

[2] Information on origins of vincristine is from G. E. Trease and W. C. Evans, *Pharmacognosy,* 10th ed. (Baltimore: Williams and Wilkins, 1972). The figure on the value of sales is from Norman Myers, "What Is a Species Worth?" manuscript for *Science Digest,* 1980.

As you can see from that remarkable illustration, these writers care very much about a topic for library research. In a personal way, they combine what they discover with what they already know.

CHAPTER 28

Knowing Your College Library:

A Directory of Sources

In the previous chapter, we didn't want to bore you with anything you know already. Neither did we want to ply you with additional information, lest you lose sight of what library research is all about. But there is a good deal that most of us ordinary citizens not trained in library school don't know about a large library. Now that you have seen the process of thoughtful writing that goes into a library research paper, perhaps you would like to see in greater depth what your library has to offer.

Certainly, public service announcements on television have made us aware that our libraries contain more than books. It is true: libraries today also lend recordings, software, videotapes, musical scores, and works of art. Through computer terminals, libraries may have access to one or more data banks, bringing a world of information to your fingertips.

Yet for all these changes, in a college library, books are still indispensable properties. Technology may have altered our methods of storing, retrieving, and transmitting ideas, but the book still remains a compact and relatively inexpensive source.

Most libraries have reference librarians who can find anything from a two-letter word for "ancient Egyptian sun god" (for a distraught crossword puzzle addict) to an 1898 news story stored on microfilm. Know your reference librarians. You might be surprised at the resources they can reveal for you.

By the way, when you set out to do college research, don't forget your *local* library. In large towns and cities, it may be less busy than your college library. Some of its facilities—reference room, current newspapers, and popular magazines—may be just as extensive as your college's, if not more so.

Whatever library you use, you'll save time if you first know your way around. You'll need to locate the centers of action: circulation desk where you charge out books; reference section; library catalog (drawers of cards or a computer terminal); microform readers; special collections of materials on specific subjects; periodicals (newspapers, magazines, and journals); photocopiers. Here are five small questions worth knowing the answers to. If any stumps you, ask a librarian.

DISCOVERY CHECKLIST: FIVE PRACTICAL MATTERS

- ✓ If another borrower has a book out, how can you get it held for you on its return?
- ✓ If this library doesn't have a certain book you need, can you order it on interlibrary loan?
- ✓ If you haven't previously taken a guided tour of your college library, is one available?
- ✓ Is there a pamphlet mapping the library's rooms and explaining its services?
- ✓ Are there any available study carrels—usually small cubicles with desks in the stacks—that you can use while working on your research paper?

CONSULTING THE LIBRARY CATALOG

Like the ignition key that starts the car, a library catalog starts your book search moving. You consult it for detailed information on every book in the library.

If your library's catalog is a traditional sort, it is housed in file drawers, on 3-by-5-inch cards. In many libraries, although a catalog may still have cards, you view them or lists of books on a screen. They are filed on microfilm or microfiche or on a computer, and you scroll through them.

The library catalog lets you look up a book in any of three ways: (1) by author, (2) by title, or (3) by subject. In some libraries, author cards are contained in one file, title cards in a second, subject cards in a third. In other libraries, all cards are filed together alphabetically. On the author card, the main card for each book, you find the following information—which often will give you some ideas about the book before you look for it. (Figure 28.1 shows a typical author card.)

1. The call number. The combination of letters and numbers tells you exactly where to find the book.
2. The author's full name, last name first, with birth and death dates (if known).
3. The title as it appears on the book's title page; the fact that the book has been revised in a second (or later) edition if that is the case.

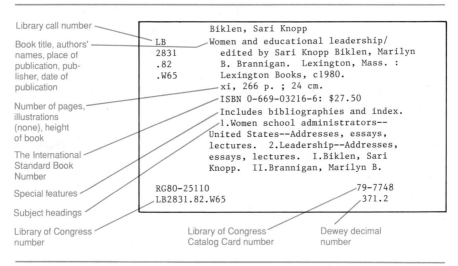

Library call number

Book title, authors' names, place of publication, publisher, date of publication

Number of pages, illustrations (none), height of book

The International Standard Book Number

Special features

Subject headings

Library of Congress number

```
                    Biklen, Sari Knopp
    LB          Women and educational leadership/
    2831            edited by Sari Knopp Biklen, Marilyn
    .82             B. Brannigan. Lexington, Mass. :
    .W65            Lexington Books, c1980.
                    xi, 266 p. ; 24 cm.
                    ISBN 0-669-03216-6: $27.50
                    Includes bibliographies and index.
                    1.Women school administrators--
                United States--Addresses, essays,
                lectures. 2.Leadership--Addresses,
                essays, lectures. I.Biklen, Sari
                Knopp. II.Brannigan, Marilyn B.

    RG80-25110                              79-7748
    LB2831.82.W65                            371.2
```

Library of Congress   Library of Congress   Dewey decimal
number   Catalog Card number   number

FIGURE 28.1 A Library of Congress author card

4. Publication information: city, name of publisher, and date of publication.

5. The number of pages, the height of the book, and mention of any maps, charts, or illustrations the book may contain.

6. A list of whatever special features the book may have—bibliographies, appendices, indexes, illustrations.

7. All subject headings under which the book is filed in the library.

8. The International Standard Book Number (ISBN) used by librarians to order books. (You need pay no attention to it.)

The title card looks like the author card except that it lists the book's title at the top, above the name of the author (see Figure 28.2).

FIGURE 28.2 A Library of Congress title card

```
    LB          Women and educational leadership/
    2831            edited by Sari Knopp Biklen, Marilyn
    .82             B. Brannigan. Lexington, Mass. :
    .W65            Lexington Books, c1980.
                    xi, 266 p. ; 24 cm.
                    Includes bibliographies and index.
                    ISBN 0-669-03216-6: $27.50
                    1.Women school administrators--
                United States--Addresses, essays,
                lectures. 2.Leadership--Addresses,
                essays, lectures. I.Biklen, Sari
                Knopp. II.Brannigan, Marilyn B.

    RG80-25110                              79-7748
    LB2831.82.W65                            371.2
```

```
                    LEADERSHIP--ADDRESSES, ESSAYS,
                      LECTURES.
        LB          Women and educational leadership/
        2831          edited by Sari Knopp Biklen, Marilyn
        .82           B. Brannigan. Lexington, Mass. :
        .W65          Lexington Books, c1980.
```

```
                    WOMEN SCHOOL ADMINISTRATORS--UNITED
                      STATES--ADDRESSES, ESSAYS, LECTURES.
        LB          Women and educational leadership/
        2831          edited by Sari Knopp Biklen, Marilyn
        .82           B. Brannigan. Lexington, Mass. :
        .W65          Lexington Books, c1980.
                      xi, 266 p. ; 24 cm.
                      Includes bibliographies and index.
                      ISBN 0-669-03216-6: $27.50
                      1. Women school administrators--
                    United States--Addresses, essays,
                    lectures.  2.Leadership--Addresses,
                    essays, lectures.  I.Biklen, Sari
                    Knopp.  II.Brannigan, Marilyn B.

        RG80-25110                         79-7748
        LB2831.82.W65                        371.2
```

FIGURE 28.3   Library of Congress subject cards with subject subdivisions

When you start your research, you may find subject cards more useful than author cards. They will often lead you to useful titles. Also, the subject you look under may direct you to related subjects and thus to still more titles. The subject card looks just like the author card except the author's name appears under a subject heading (see Figure 28.3).

Library of Congress Subject Headings

Whether you use the subject cards or the subject option in the computer catalog, your first attempt with a subject may come up empty. Never fear: an excellent reference is at hand to help you put your search in the words the library uses to categorize its material. The source is the *Library of Congress Subject Headings (LCSH)*, a set of books on hand near the library catalog. Suppose, for example, you look up "Women School Administrators" in the catalog and there isn't any such subject. In fact, the library may own several books on the subject, listed in the catalog under "School administrators" and "Women in education" — but how are you to know that? Simply look up "Women school administrators" in a copy of *Library of Congress Subject Headings*. Figure 28.4 shows how entries look in the *LCSH*. Please note: If your library files books under the Dewey Decimal System instead of the Library of Congress System, you can consult the *Dewey Decimal Classification and Relative Index*. (Both of these systems are described in the next section.)

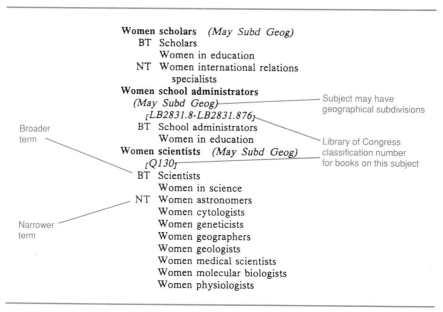

FIGURE 28.4   Entries from the *Library of Congress Subject Headings*

UNDERSTANDING SYSTEMS OF CLASSIFICATION

Assuming that the book you want is in the library, you can expect its call number to help you find it. The first letter or letters of the call number point you to its neighborhood. A book, for instance, whose call number starts with an *S* is about agriculture or forestry. To help you find books easily, every library organizes its shelves by a system of classification. We will look at the two most widely used. Some people claim that it pays to memorize these systems; then when you have to trek from one section of the library to another looking for books, your head will save your feet. At least, you may care to recognize the call numbers of books in the category of your investigation.

Library of Congress System

Most college libraries use the same system of book classification used by the Library of Congress in Washington, D.C. If your library does, you'll find that call letters and numbers direct you to books grouped in subject areas.

A	General Works	E–F	America
B	Philosophy, Psychology, Religion	G	Geography, Anthropology, Sports and Games
C–D	Foreign History and Topography	H	Social Sciences
		J	Political Science

K	Law	S	Agriculture and Forestry
L	Education	T	Engineering, Technology
M	Music	U	Military Science
N	Fine Arts	V	Naval Science
P	Language and Literature	Z	Bibliography and Library Science
Q	Science		
R	Medicine		

Dewey Decimal System

Small libraries often still use the older Dewey decimal system of classifying books. Other libraries, in transition, have some books filed according to the Dewey decimal system and some according to the Library of Congress method. The Dewey decimal system files books into large categories by numbers.

000–099	General Works
100–199	Philosophy
200–299	Religion
300–399	Social Sciences, Government, Customs
400–499	Language
500–599	Natural Sciences
600–699	Applied Sciences
700–799	Fine and Decorative Arts
800–899	Literature
900–999	History, Travel, Biography

Incidentally, neither Admiral George Dewey, who took Manila, nor educator John Dewey started the Dewey decimal system. The credit goes to Melvil Dewey (1851–1931), founder of the American Library Association.

Count yourself lucky if you can follow your own call number into the stacks. Shelved near the book you've come for may be others by the same author or on the same subject. Browse around in the neighborhood. Lisa Chickos, who discovered *Women and Educational Leadership* in the library catalog, might have found on the same shelf another title full of promise for her research: *Academic Women on the Move*. The golden rule for research in the stacks is this: *to do right unto others, don't put a book back in place hastily*. Replace it wrong and no one else will be able to locate it.

USING PERIODICALS

The periodicals area houses current and recent issues of magazines and newspapers. Many of the items on your working bibliography that you found listed in the latest *Readers' Guide to Periodical Literature* will be there. Older issues, bound into volumes for previous years, may be shelved by call numbers. Some are kept on microfiche or microfilm (see p. 670). A list or file of periodicals' names and their call numbers is usually posted conspicuously in the periodicals area; if you can't find it, look up the name of the periodical in your library catalog.

In the periodicals area, too, current newspapers are available. Even in most small libraries, you'll find at least the *New York Times* and your nearest big city's daily, possibly also the *Washington Post* and the *Christian Science Monitor,* two newspapers noted for their coverage of national and international affairs. Most libraries have back issues of the *New York Times* on microfilm and the *New York Times Index* (see "News Indexes," p. 667). The *Wall Street Journal,* an extremely well written and edited daily newspaper, not only covers business news but reviews films and books and often features articles of interest to the general public.

SURVEYING THE REFERENCE SECTION

Make your own tour of that treasure trove for researchers: the reference section. See what is available. Interesting reference books exist on subjects you may never have dreamed had been covered. You may find whole shelves devoted to general areas in which you plan to do research. A helpful listing is provided by the *American Library Association Guide to Reference Books,* edited by Eugene P. Sheehy.

Here is a short tour of a few groups of reference books.

Encyclopedias

Back in high school when you had to do a research paper, you shot like a comet straight to an encyclopedia. (Sometimes you read *two* encyclopedias, and that was all the research required.) An encyclopedia can still help you get an overview of your subject and may be especially valuable when you are first casting around for a topic. But when you start investigating more deeply, you will need to go to other sources as well.

General encyclopedias are written for the reader who isn't a specialist, who wants a decent smattering of information, or who wants some fact he or she is missing. In all but the cheapest encyclopedias, notable experts write the longer and more important articles. The *New Encyclopaedia Britannica,* now published in Chicago, is the largest general (that is, unspecialized) encyclopedia on the shelves. More sprightly in style, and sometimes beating the *Britannica* to the shelves with recent information, are other popular encyclopedias: *Encyclopedia Americana, Collier's, New Columbia, World Book,* and several more.

All encyclopedias struggle with a problem: how to give a reader not only specific facts but a broader, more inclusive view. If you look something up, how do you find out that your subject relates to larger matters that also might interest you? If, for instance, you look up Marie Curie, how do you learn that she and her work are discussed under "Chemistry," "Curie, Pierre," "Physics," "Polonium," "Radiation," "Radioactivity," and "Uranium" as well? To help you find all the places where a topic is discussed, some encyclopedias offer an index in a separate volume referring to other articles. *World Book* gives cross-references after an article ("See also . . ."). The *Britannica* now comes in two parts. The shorter part, the *Micropaedia* (which you consult first, like any other encyclopedia), offers a concise, pointed article and may also refer you to other places in the larger *Macropaedia,* which contains longer articles, wider in scope.

Specialized Encyclopedias

Specialized encyclopedias are written for the searcher interested in a single area: art, movies, music, religion, science, rock and roll. How do you know that someone has prepared one in the very field you are investigating? Look up your subject in the library catalog. If a specialized encyclopedia about your subject exists, you will find it indicated on a subject card. The *Encyclopedia of World Art,* for instance, is usually listed under "Art—Dictionaries." (Specialized encyclopedias are often classified as dictionaries, even though they contain much more than short definitions.) Better yet, dwell a while in the area of the reference section that involves your subject and glance at the books shelved there. If your subject is from science, see the *McGraw-Hill Encyclopedia of Science and Technology* or *Van Nostrand's Scientific Encyclopedia.* If you are writing about some aspect of life in a less industrialized, developing nation, the *Encyclopedia of the Third World* might be valuable. If existentialism is your subject, likely places to look might be the *Dictionary of the History of Ideas,* the *Encyclopedia of Philosophy,* and the *Harper Dictionary of Modern Thought.* The *Encyclopedia Judaica* and the *New Catholic Encyclopedia* concentrate on matters of faith, tradition, ritual, history, philosophy, and theology. Just to give you a notion of the variety of other specialized encyclopedias, here is a sampling of titles:

Black's Law Dictionary
Encyclopedia of Banking and Finance
Encyclopedia of Biochemistry
Encyclopedia of Pop, Rock, and Soul
Harper's Bible Dictionary
International Encyclopedia of the Social Sciences
New Grove Dictionary of Music and Musicians
Oxford Companion to American Literature
Oxford Dictionary of the Christian Church

Dictionaries

Besides desk dictionaries, of the kind on every college student's desk, your library's reference section stocks large and specialized dictionaries. You'll find

sla·pstick. orig. *U.S.* Also **slap-stick.** [f. SLAP *v.*[1] + STICK *sb.*[1]] **1.** Two flat pieces of wood joined together at one end, used to produce a loud slapping noise; *spec.* such a device used in pantomime and low comedy to make a great noise with the pretence of dealing a heavy blow (see also quot. 1950).

1896 *N.Y. Dramatic News* 4 July 9/3 What a relief, truly, from the slap-sticks, rough-and-tumble comedy couples abounding in the variety ranks. **1907** *Weekly Budget* 19 Oct. 1/2 The special officer in the gallery, armed with a 'slap-stick', the customary weapon in American theatre galleries, made himself very officious amongst the small boys. **1925** M. W. DISHER *Clowns & Pantomimes* 13 What has caused the playgoers' sudden callousness? The slapstick. Towards the end of the seventeenth century Arlequin had introduced into England the double-lath of castigation, which made the maximum amount of noise with the minimum of injury. **1937** M. COVARRUBIAS *Island of Bali* iv. 77 Life-size scarecrows are erected, but soon the birds become familiar with them... Then watchmen circulate among the fields beating bamboo drums and cracking loud bamboo slap-sticks. **1950** *Sun* (Baltimore) 10 Apr. 3/1 The 50-year-old clown..said that when he bent over another funnyman accidentally hit him with the wrong side of a slap-stick. He explained that a slap-stick contains a blank ·38-caliber cartridge on one side to make a bang.

2. a. *attrib.* passing into *adj.* Of or pertaining to a slapstick; of or reminiscent of knock-about comedy.

1906 *N.Y. Even. Post* 25 Oct. 10 It required all the untiring efforts of an industrious 'slap-stick' coterie..to keep the enthusiasm up to a respectable degree. **1914** *Photoplay* Sept. 91 (*heading*) Making slap-stick comedy.

1923 *Weekly Dispatch* 4 Mar. 9 He likes good comedies.. but thinks the slapstick ones ridiculous. **1928** *Daily Sketch* 7 Aug. 4/3 The jokes..are rapier-like in their keenness, not the usual rolling-pin or slapstick form of humour. **1936** W. HOLTBY *South Riding* IV. v. 258 She took a one-and-threepenny ticket, sat in comfort, and watched a Mickey Mouse film, a slapstick comedy, and the tragedy of Greta Garbo acting Mata Hari. **1944** [see *POCHO]. **1962** A. NISBETT *Technique Sound Studio* x. 173 Decidedly unobvious effects, such as the cork-and-resin 'creak' or the hinged slapstick 'whip'. **1977** R. L. WOLFF *Gains & Losses* II. iv. 296 The prevailing tone of the book is highly satirical, with strong overtones of slapstick farce.

b. *absol.* Knockabout comedy or humour, farce, horseplay.

1926 *Amer. Speech* I. 437/2 *Slap-stick*, low comedy in its simplest form. Named from the double paddles formerly used by circus clowns to beat each other. **1930** *Publishers' Weekly* 25 Jan. 420/2 The slapstick of 1929 was often exciting. The Joan Lowell episode was regarded as exposing the gullibility of the critics... The popularity of 'The Specialist' made the whole book business look cockeyed. **1955** *Times* 6 June 9/1 A comic parson (Mr. Noel Howlett) is added for good measure, mainly to play on the piano while other people crawl under it. Even on the level of slapstick the farce seemed to keep in motion with some difficulty and raised but moderate laughter. **1967** M. KENYON *Whole Hog* xxv. 253 A contest which had promised..to be short and cruel, had become slapstick. **1976** *Oxf. Compan. Film* 640/1 As it developed in the decade 1910–20..slapstick depended on frenzied, often disorganized, motion that increased in tempo as visual gags proliferated.

FIGURE 28.5   Entry from the *Oxford English Dictionary*, 2nd ed.

dictionaries of foreign languages; dictionaries of slang; dictionaries of regionalisms; dictionaries of medical, scientific, and other specialized terms. If you don't know what NATO or RSVP stands for, a specialized dictionary such as the *Acronyms, Initialisms, and Abbreviations Dictionary* might help. An unabridged dictionary, such as *Webster's Third New International*—the kind so hefty it sits on a stand of its own, tied down with a chain—tries to include every word and phrase in current use in the language. The *New Century Cyclopedia of Names,* a dictionary of names of people and peoples, places, works of art, and other proper names of every kind, is useful for tracking down allusions—mentions of things that a writer believes are common knowledge but that you may not happen to know.

The massive and monumental *Oxford English Dictionary (OED)* is a historical dictionary: that is, it lists words with dated examples of their occurrences in the language, from the twelfth century to the twentieth, arranged in chronological order. Any shade of meaning an English word ever had is there, making it a beloved treasure for any word freak (who probably owns the two-volume edition in reduced print, which comes with a magnifying glass). It is invaluable if you are tracing the history of an idea through the centuries: you can see how the meaning of a word may have changed. Along with those changes, sometimes, go major changes in society and its people. One student, writing a paper on pollution in the environment, looked up the word *pollution* in the *OED* and as a result was able to reinvigorate the contemporary meaning of the word with earlier meanings of shame and sin. If, in defining terms used in your paper, you need a definition of *freedom,* consult the *OED* and an immense storehouse will swing open to you. You'll find quotations using this luminous word in a whole spectrum of ways, starting with its earliest recorded appearance in the language.

Because the original edition of this great dictionary was completed in 1933, it does not cover words that have recently entered the language. However, the second edition of the *Oxford English Dictionary,* published in 1989, includes (in handy *A*-to-*Z* sequence) material previously published in four supplementary volumes. It adds about five thousand new words or new meanings to the original *OED,* among them *slapstick* (see Figure 28.5) and *yuppie.* Look to see whether your library has this latest edition. If you like words, you'll enjoy browsing in it.

Bibliographies

It takes work to make a working bibliography. Wouldn't it be great if a bibliography came ready-made for you? Perhaps it does.

Each field of knowledge has its own bibliography, often more than one, which may appear in an issue of a learned journal or as a separate publication, like the *International Bibliography of Sociology.* Is there a bibliography in your area of interest? Consult the latest *Bibliographic Index: A Cumulative Bibliography of Bibliographies.* A quarterly, it is gathered into one volume each year. Turn to it for listings, by subject, of specialized bibliographies and also of books and articles that contain specialized bibliographies. Some bibliographies you track down will be *annotated*; that is, they will give a short summary of what a book or article contains. Sometimes the bibliographer will venture a judgment about a book's worth.

Some encyclopedias, after the end of an article, will also give you a short list of relevant works worth reading. Often such a list will include the best-known and most popular books on a subject. Such lists are usually directed to a reader who knows nothing much about the subject rather than to a specialist, and they may be long out of date. We recommend that you look first into the *Bibliographic Index.* It's a wonderful instrument for the serious specialist.

Indexes to Periodicals

Magazines, because they can be published faster than books, often print the latest information and opinions months before they appear in book form. Look to them for the most up-to-date material.

To find recent articles on any subject you're investigating, start with the *Readers' Guide to Periodical Literature,* issued monthly, collected into thicker issues quarterly, and bound into a heavyweight volume in each new year. The *Readers' Guide* classifies, by author and subject, recent articles from popular magazines aimed toward general readers — *Time, The New Yorker, Psychology*

Today — but not scholarly or professional magazines such as *American Zoologist, Harvard Business Review, Physics Today,* or *Journal of Music Theory,* which address specialized audiences. It gives cross-references so that with a little digging you can usually find headings that will lead you to useful articles. Under each heading, entries give you the title and author of an article and the name of the periodical, its volume number and date, and the pages on which the article can be found.

When you're making a working bibliography with the aid of the *Readers' Guide* and you want the most up-to-date material, begin with the most recent issue, then work backward through previous issues or annual volumes. If, like Lisa Chickos, you had decided to investigate the role of women in college administration, you would have found in the 1991 volume of the *Readers' Guide* the headings "Women college officials" and "Women school administrators." Under the first you would have found indexed an article from the August 1, 1991, issue of a periodical called *Vital Speeches of the Day* that seemed promising enough to follow up (see Figure 28.6). After combing through earlier issues of the *Readers' Guide* for more leads, you would have amassed a list of perhaps seven or eight articles that seemed to promise valuable information on your topic. At that point, you'd be ready to check out your library's collection of periodicals to see how many of the listed articles you could find and read.

Naturally, the *Readers' Guide* falls short of including every periodical your investigation might call for. One supplement, *Access: The Supplementary Index to Periodicals,* has since 1975 been listing the contents of many magazines, some regional, not found in the *Readers' Guide,* like *Alaska, Sporting News,* and *TV Guide.*

If you find too few leads in the *Readers' Guide* or *Access* or not enough solid information in popular magazine articles, you may want to consult a selected subject index for more scholarly or professional materials. Here is a short list of some indexes widely available.

Art Index	*Environment Index*
Biological Abstracts RRM	*Film Literature Index*
Business Periodicals Index	*General Science Index*
Criminology Index	*Humanities Index*
Education Index	*Social Sciences Index*

Art Index is broader in scope than its name implies: it lists not only articles on graphic arts but also many on archeology, architecture, city planning, crafts, films, industrial design, interior design, and photography. For a research paper on women as school and college administrators, the relevant section of *Education Index* for July 1990–June 1991 is illustrated in Figure 28.7.

Many of the periodical indexes already mentioned are now available on computer, as well as in book format. Some computerized indexes will even display the full text of the articles indexed. (Computer databases are discussed on p. 670.) Other indexes, like *Magazine Index* and *InfoTrac,* which index

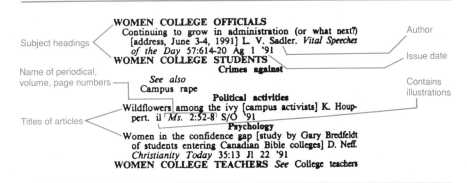

FIGURE 28.6   Entries from the *Readers' Guide to Periodical Literature*

more periodicals than *Readers' Guide,* are available only in microform or as a database.

News Indexes

To locate a newspaper account of virtually any recent event or development, a popular printed aid is the *New York Times Index.* Most libraries subscribe to the *Times,* and many keep back years of it on microfilm. Its semimonthly *Index,* bound into a volume each year, directs you to stories in daily and Sunday issues all the way back to the newspaper's founding in 1851.

Say you're pursuing the question of why relatively few women hold top jobs as administrators in schools and colleges. "Women" might seem your largest, most central idea, so in the 1987 volume you look up "Women" and under it find the subheading "Education." This is a mere cross-reference that

FIGURE 28.7   Entry from *Education Index*

Women as coaches *See* Coaches and coaching (Athletics)
Women as college presidents *See* Women as educators
Women as doctors *See* Women as physicians
Women as economists
   Confessions of a feminist economist: why I haven't yet
    taught an economics course on women's issues. L.
    J. Bassi. *Women's Stud Q* 18:42-5 Fall/Wint '90
Women as educators
    See also
    American Association of University Professors. Com-
     mittee W on the Status of Women in the Academic
     Profession
   165 female college presidents 'honor progress, connect
    with each other,' and commiserate. D. E. Blum. il
    Chron Higher Educ 37:A13+ D 19 '90
   Administrative promotion: the power of gender. L. K.
    Johnsrud. bibl *J Higher Educ* 62:119-49 Mr/Ap '91
   Are women changing the nature of the academic profes-
    sion? A. M. T. Lomperis. bibl *J Higher Educ* 61:643-77
    N/D '90
   Behind the bastion [why do so many women spurn
    academic life?] J. Johnson. il *Times Higher Educ Suppl*
    911:14 Ap 20 '90

lists the dates of five stories about women in education; it doesn't have room to tell you what the stories are about. It directs you to a larger category, "Education and Schools," where you find listed and briefly summarized all the stories about education, in chronological order. You skim down the listing and check the five dates that interest you. For April 5, three stories about education are listed (see Figure 28.8). Clearly, the first one will be the most promising story for this topic. And the story will be easy to find. The legend "Ap 5, I, 23:1" indicates that it appeared on April 5 in section I of the newspaper, page 23, column 1. The length of the story is also indicated: "L" for a long story (more than three columns), "M" for a story of medium length (between one and three columns), "S" for a short item (less than a column long). This system points you to substantial stories especially worth looking up and (if your time is scarce) saves you from bothering with short items that might not prove worthwhile.

Other newspapers that publish indexes include the *Wall Street Journal,* the *Washington Post,* and the *Times* of London. *Facts on File* (discussed on p. 669) publishes an index twice a month to help readers locate its summaries of recent news. Also, some libraries now receive computerized indexes, such as *National Newspaper Index,* which lists the contents not only of the *New York Times* but also the *Christian Science Monitor,* the *Wall Street Journal,* the *Washington Post,* and the *Los Angeles Times.*

Another kind of newspaper index is NewsBank, which draws on more than 450 local U.S. newspapers. Updated monthly, it is available both in paper format or on compact disk for computer searching. NewsBank provides the indexed articles on sheets of microfiche, and libraries who subscribe to this index usually have both readers and photocopiers (microfiche is explained on p. 670).

Biographical Sources

If you want to know about someone's life and work, you have a rich array of sources. To find quickly the names and dates of famous people now dead, *Webster's New Biographical Dictionary* can be handy. For more extensive

FIGURE 28.8   Entry from the *New York Times Index*

Report by National Organization for Women claims most American women are vulnerable to sex discrimination in schools and universities, as members of student body and faculty; report says only seven states and territory of Guam have adequate protection against sex discrimination in education; states are Alaska, California, Florida, Maine, Nebraska, Oregon and Rhode Island (M), Ap 5,I,23:1
    Glenwood D Brogan, 18-year-old student at Hammond High School in Columbia, Md, is sentenced to six months in jail for spiking coffee of Janet Thurman, teacher of home economics, with derivative of cayenne pepper; Thurman has undergone minor surgery several times since she drank coffee (S), Ap 5,I,44:6
    April 7 elections in 550 of New Jersey's 606 school districts will determine makeup of local school boards and also fate of budgets; remaining 56 districts have appointed school boards; education officials are hoping for greater voter turnout but most do not count on it (M), Ap 5,XI,8:4

treatment of outstanding Americans (dead ones only), see the *Dictionary of American Biography (DAB)* in 20 volumes (1928–36 and later supplements). The British equivalent is the *Dictionary of National Biography*. Lately, a multivolume set has filled many gaps in the *DAB: Notable American Women, 1607–1950*. *Who Was Who* (for Britain) and *Who Was Who in America* preserve facts on those no longer alive.

For the lives of living celebrities of all nations, see *Current Biography* (published monthly and gathered in one volume each year), a highly readable and entertaining compilation. Bare facts on the lives and works of celebrities and people prominent in their fields are listed in *Who's Who* (for Britain), *Who's Who in America,* and *Who's Who in the World.* Regional American editions (*Who's Who in the West* as well as volumes for the Midwest, South and Southwest, and East) and *Who's Who of American Women* encapsulate people not included in the nationwide volume. See if your library has the latest edition of *Who's Who Among Black Americans.* Marquis, publisher of *Who's Who in America,* also offers specialized *Who's Who*'s: *Who's Who in American Law* and similar volumes for finance and industry, frontier science and technology, religion, and science.

The lives of writers are usually well documented. For early writers' biographies, see *American Authors, 1600–1900, British Authors before 1800, British Authors of the Nineteenth Century, Twentieth Century Authors* and its supplement, and *World Authors,* which covers writers since 1950. Writers from all countries, including hundreds not found in encyclopedias, are usually to be found in *Contemporary Authors* and its revisions, a vast series that covers not just poets and fiction writers but popular writers in every field. *Contemporary Novelists, Contemporary Poets,* and *Contemporary Dramatists* contain not only biographies and bibliographies, but critical estimates as well.

Yearbooks and Almanacs

Encyclopedia publishers, realizing that time gallops on and that their product rapidly becomes obsolete, bring out an annual yearbook of recent events and discoveries in an attempt to look up to date. We consider these to be rather cumbersomely organized sources, designed to extract more money from owners of encyclopedias. If you want a short account of a recent event or development, try *Facts on File.* Calling itself a "Weekly World News Digest, with Cumulative Index," it is a concise list of news events. Important events rate more space. Twice a month it publishes an index on blue paper, and then quarterly yellow indexes supersede the blue ones. The weekly issues are gathered into a binder every year and placed on the library's shelves.

Many miscellaneous facts—news events, winners of prizes, athletic records—are compiled in a yearly almanac such as the *World Almanac and Book of Facts,* a popular, variously useful work that many people like to have as a desk-top reference. In it you can find out everything from the population of Bloomington, Indiana, to information about job openings and current earnings, from the locations of hazardous waste sites to the time the moon rises on any given date—and much more. Your library may also offer specialized almanacs: *American Jewish Year Book, Catholic Almanac, Canadian Almanac and Directory.*

Gazetteers and Atlases

Gazetteers list places and give basic facts about them. Two popular gazetteers are the *Columbia Lippincott Gazetteer of the World* and *Webster's New Geographical Dictionary.*

For maps, see atlases such as *The Times Atlas of the World, National Atlas of the United States of America,* and (for maps that show political boundaries in the past—fascinating!) the *Historical Atlas.*

EXPLORING OTHER SOURCES

Besides reference books, your library may have other sources that will supply you with ideas and information not available elsewhere.

Microforms

Most libraries take advantage of microforms (microfilm and microfiche) to store newspapers, magazines, and other materials that would otherwise take up acres of valuable shelf space. If you aren't acquainted with it, you should be, for marvelous research opportunities are available to you if you are. If, for instance, you are writing a paper on World War II, wouldn't it be great to see the front page of a newspaper for December 8, 1941, the day the U.S. Congress declared war? Or to quote from a magazine article written just after that fateful day? Microforms make such a search possible, and usually you can get a printed copy of any page.

Microfilm is small photographic film that contains the images of printed pages in reduced form. A whole week's file of daily newspapers or several years' issues of a magazine can be preserved on a strip of microfilm two inches wide and seven or eight feet long. Wound into a roll and stashed in a small, labeled box, the microfilm can be stored in a few square inches of space. To view a roll of microfilm, you place it in a viewing projector (usually called a reader). You advance the film through the machine from one reel to another until you come to the page you are looking for.

A *microfiche* is a sheet of microfilm bearing images of sixty to one hundred printed pages. A reader shows each frame of the microfiche on a viewing screen.

Databases

As a modern researcher, you have access to more information than ever before. Increasingly, libraries are supplementing printed resources with those available on computer. The *Readers' Guide,* for example, may now be searched as a computer database—a computerized listing of thousands of articles from periodicals and newspapers, all of which can be explored in just minutes by subject, author, or numerous other identifiers. Databases can be real timesavers for you; for example, by entering your subject into the computer just once, you can search *Readers' Guide* from 1983 to the present.

Databases that index periodicals are most useful when you are searching for information published after 1980. Some popular general database indexes are *Readers' Guide, InfoTrac* (a system of several databases of periodicals and newspapers), and NewsBank (an index of newspapers). Specialized databases are available in just about any field that you may study in college. A few well-known examples include MLA BIBLIOGRAPHY (for languages and literature), ABI/Inform (business and finance), PsycINFO (psychology), SCISEARCH (biological and applied sciences), and ERIC (for education topics).

Different databases will give you different information. Some, like the *Readers' Guide,* index only publishing information. Others give an abstract of each article, still others a more detailed summary, and a few even contain entire articles. See what your library has to offer. You will quickly learn what to expect from each database you use.

If you're not a computer genius, don't worry. A librarian can instruct or assist you. With an ever-increasing number of databases available on compact disc (known as CD-ROM: Compact Disc—Read Only Memory), as well as a growing number of cooperative networks that allow libraries to lower costs for online use, computer searches are no longer the costly ventures they once were for student researchers.

Government Documents

"A glance at the organization of our government documents," says Mary-Claire van Leunen, author of *A Handbook for Scholars,* "may suggest that the United States is neither a democracy nor a republic, but an anarchy. Writing a good reference to a federal document would be simple if only one of those brainy forefathers of ours had thought to write at the bottom of the Declaration of Independence, 'Serial #1,' but it's too late now." It is true that because government documents differ widely in format, depending on which branch of the government published them, they are sometimes hard to find, but often they contain valuable material worth searching for.

Among major American publishers is the United States Congress. Its primary publications include the *Congressional Record,* a daily transcript of what is said in both the House and the Senate, together with anything else members of Congress wish inserted; bills, acts, laws, and statutes (after a bill is enacted into law it is bound into *Statutes at Large*); and the minutes of congressional committee hearings. Most college libraries carry at least the *Congressional Record.*

The judicial branch of the government doesn't publish anything except cases. But other executive departments and state governments publish prolifically, as do various agencies of the United Nations. John L. Andriot's *Guide to U.S. Government Publications* lists and explains the printed products of most federal agencies. The U.S. Government Printing Office in Washington, D.C., publishes and distributes some popular works, including *Your Child from 1 to 6* and the *Government Manual,* an explanation of how the government is organized.

There is, by the way, a *Monthly Catalog of United States Government Publications,* compiled into one volume annually. Matthew Lesko's guidebook *Lesko's Info-Power* (Kensington: Information USA, 1990) is valuable for library and field research. It lists both federal libraries (some offering free telephone reference service) and federal databases (some available for low-cost or free searches).

Brochures, Handouts, and Annual Reports

For other kinds of printed material, your library may have a vertical file for pamphlets, documents, or corporate reports. Otherwise you may need to round it up on your own. Often, on a visit to a museum or historic site, you are given (along with your ticket of admission) a pamphlet to carry with you, containing a terse history of the place and perhaps a map of its exhibits. This kind of material can prove valuable to researchers. Usually it is the work of curators and other dedicated experts who know their locales, and sometimes the information it contains is hard to find anywhere else. If, say, you are making a field trip to a computer museum before writing about the history of early computers, you might carefully save any handout. You might also peruse the gift shop or the pamphlet rack at the information desk, even if the offerings cost money. If you can't visit the museum or historic site, a phone call might tell you how to order its publications by mail.

Many concerned organizations, such as the American Cancer Society, the American Heart Association, Physicians for Social Responsibility, and others, sometimes publish surveys and reports that they will send you on request. Some of their valuable handouts are made known through public service announcements on radio and television. For names, addresses, and telephone numbers of a variety of organizations and agencies, see the *Encyclopedia of Associations.* This useful guide includes a brief overview of each organization and lists its available publications and reports.

The U.S. Government's Consumer Information Center in Pueblo, Colorado, sends free pamphlets (*Occupations in Demand, Being Your Own Boss*) and sells larger brochures at low prices (*The Job Outlook in Brief, Exercise and Weight Control*). A list of publications with an order form is available on request; the zip code is 81002.

Most large corporations produce hefty annual reports, copies of which are yours for the asking. Few people except investors write to a corporation for an annual report, but the corporations are willing to give a copy to practically anyone seriously interested in their activities. You are likely to receive a vast, handsomely printed document favorably portraying the past year's operations and future expectations of the company so that present stockholders will be reassured and future investors will be attracted; the report usually contains graphs, charts, photographs, and other documents. Writing a research paper on recent developments in artificial intelligence, a student we know requested the annual reports of several computer and software firms. For the cost of a few postage stamps, he received hundreds of pages of up-to-date information and professional opinion that would have been difficult to find elsewhere.

CHAPTER 29

Writing from Research in the Field

Finding material in a library is only one way to do research. You can also generate your own ideas and information—in other words, tap your own primary sources.

Most often in college, field research is required in upper-level courses. For a term paper in the social sciences, education, or business studies, you may be expected to interview people, conduct a survey, or gather statistics. Usually, course assignments in field research are directed toward specific ends. A psychology assignment to test a hypothesis, for example, might ask you to observe people in a situation of stress and to report their behavior.

If you enjoy meeting and talking with people and don't mind what news reporters call "legwork," you will relish the fun and satisfaction of obtaining ideas and information at first hand. Perhaps you will even investigate matters that few researchers have investigated before. Many rich, unprinted sources of ideas and information lie beyond library walls. This chapter will reveal a few of them. It will show you how to write a research paper not only by reading but also by observing, conversing with people, recalling, and imagining, or by combining several of these sources. In the future, researchers may be able to cite *you*.

Like library research, field research should be more than a squirreling-up of facts—or else you may end up with a great heap of rotting acorns and no nourishment. Field research (and kindly underline this sentence) has to be the sensitive, intelligent, and critical selection of *meaningful* ideas and information. As the chapter proceeds, we'll give you more specific suggestions for picking out what is meaningful from what isn't. Right now, it is sufficient to note that you can expect to change your initial hunches while at work out in the field. You'll be exercising your critical thinking skills: sifting evidence, evaluating, drawing conclusions, revising and correcting your early thoughts, forming clearer ideas. When you begin a project on identical twins, say, you might seek evidence to back up your hunch that identical twins are likely to enter the same line of work in later life. Perhaps, though, the evidence, based on interviews with several sets of twins, will refuse to march in the path you want it to follow. You might end up disproving your hunch and coming to a fresh realization: that some twins, perhaps, develop in independent directions.

LEARNING FROM ANOTHER WRITER: ONE STUDENT'S EXPERIENCE

To show you a student thinking and solving problems in the field, changing his mind while collecting material and coming to fresh realizations, let us tell the story of Jamie Merisotis. A political science major with an assignment to write an honors thesis, Merisotis became interested in studying the lives and work of people engaged in an unusual profession: bail bonding. He grew increasingly curious about this business of supplying bail money for suspected criminals who have been arrested.

Whatever your field research topic, you will probably have an easier time gathering ideas and information than Jamie Merisotis had. First, because he found little recent published research on his topic, he decided to try to interview every bondsman practicing in an East Coast state he knew well, where the bail bond system still thrives. His labors were complicated by the fact that while attending college in Maine, he pursued his research in another state. It took him most of a year to obtain his evidence, for he had only weekends and vacations for interviewing.

"The hardest part," Merisotis recalls, "was getting the bondsmen to talk to me." Busy people who shun publicity, many bondsmen flatly turned down the student's request for interviews. At first, Merisotis had trouble even getting in touch with the bondsmen, since many publish only their phone numbers, not their addresses. The phone numbers connect to an answering service that relays only calls from people in need of bail money. Luckily, a friendly bail commissioner took an interest in Merisotis's study and encouraged the bondsmen to talk to him. Even with this help, one bondsman had to be called ten times before he consented to an interview. "I think he finally broke down just to get rid of me," Merisotis says. In the end, he succeeded in interviewing eighteen bail bondsmen — about half of all those practicing in the state, perhaps the largest number ever interviewed by any researcher, student or professional.

Although the bail bondsman is a familiar figure in detective movies and fiction, surprisingly little about his life has been documented. A few facts may help you glimpse the nature of Merisotis's project. In effect, a bail bond is a promissory note stating that if the defendant does not appear in court to stand trial, he or she will forfeit a sum of money. When a person arrested and charged with a crime has to post bail, needs money to do so, and cannot raise it alone, he or she calls a bail bondsman. In some commentaries Merisotis read, the bondsmen are "mindless thugs," "moronic leeches," "cigar-chomping social parasites living off the misfortunes of others." Reports have circulated that bondsmen use guns and brass knuckles to whip their errant clients into submission. On television they are romanticized: in the series *The Fall Guy* (now in reruns), glamorous bondswoman Big Jack sometimes sends muscle man Lee Majors to track down missing clients for her.

Curious to learn the truth behind the stereotypes, Merisotis formulated his question for research: "What is the life and work of a typical bail bondsman really like?" As he interviewed practicing bondsmen, he found his preliminary ideas changing. In some cases, he learned, bondsmen do indeed threaten violence against clients they suspect will fail to appear ("I'll break your legs," "I'll get a gorilla over to take you in") or they threaten financial disaster ("Your mother will pay if you don't show"). Empowered to arrest clients who run out on them, they sometimes (but seldom) risk their necks tracking down a fugitive. Compared to their stereotypes on television, however, their lives are quiet. If some of their tactics are unpleasant, bondsmen do provide a useful service. Slow to risk their money, suspicious of some prospects, they nevertheless assist many low-income people who otherwise would languish in jail. They help make the legal system work. Because they assume responsibility for their clients' appearing in court, they often pester a client, browbeat him, and see that he shows up for trial.

In our legal system, then, bondsmen are valuable people. Yet to his surprise Merisotis found little recent literature on the topic in his college library. We'll continue to trace his story in this chapter and finally show you a chapter from his completed paper.

LEARNING BY WRITING

The Assignment: Researching a Subculture

Here is a typical *general* writing assignment for a field research paper, one that leaves up to you the task of finding a specific topic. Try to find a topic that, because you care about it, will elicit your desire to write. Of course, for a college composition paper, you are not expected to do as extensive a job of research as Merisotis did.

Consider some group of people in our society about whose lives and activities you would like deeper knowledge. The group you choose should be one whose members you would be able to engage in conversation—the homeless, amateur rock musicians, members of the Society of Friends, aspiring painters, women construction workers, model railroad buffs, hospital patients, people who live in a certain locality, or any other group of people that for any reason keenly interests you. Find out as much as you can about the group by observing, by conversing with people, by questioning them, by seeking any other evidence that you do not find in print but discover for yourself.

From what you have learned, draw some conclusion or make some generalization. Present it in a paper, supporting it with evidence you have collected. You will not need all the data you have gathered: focus and be selective. Write for an audience of your classmates, but to keep your paper fair and accurate write it so that it might also be read by members of the group you have observed.

Among successful papers we have seen written from this assignment are the following.

> Using her own observations, a questionnaire she had devised, and a series of interviews, a woman set out to test the validity of an idea she had read: that the tradition of the family dinner was fast disappearing from middle-class life. She wrote this paper for a freshman English course centering on the theme "The Way We Live Now."
>
> A man studying child development, after observing two- and three-year-olds at a day-care center and keeping a log of his observations for three weeks, wrote about the many ways the two groups of children differed from each other.
>
> In a sociology course, in an effort to find out what forces had driven homeless people to the streets and what was being done for them, a man sought out and interviewed people in the helping professions who worked with street people in his city and also talked with some of the homeless people themselves.
>
> A man conducted a survey among his fellow students to learn their reasons for choosing the college they attended. He sorted out their answers, emerging with a varied list and increased respect for his college's reputation.
>
> A woman who had recently moved from Baltimore to Portland, Oregon, relied on recall, observation, and conversation to record and interpret cultural differences between easterners and westerners. After writing the paper for an English class, she sold part of it to a newspaper as a feature article.

Generating Ideas

Before you set out on your field research, you first have to decide on a subject you want to investigate — the later lives of identical twins, say, or the methods of designing hang gliders. Start by casually looking into something that appeals to you, and decide whether to persist in further investigation. Those trusty resources for writers discussed in Part One may prove their usefulness. You might observe your subject in action (twins, hang gliders, or whatever) and recall what you already know about it. You might talk with anyone familiar with it, do some reading about it in a library, and imagine yourself doing field research into it (interviewing twins or builders of hang gliders). The more you look into a subject, the more it is likely to interest you.

DISCOVERY CHECKLIST: FINDING A TOPIC

- Is there a career you are considering but don't know much about? Talk to some people working in this field.
- Is there a local group you have become curious about through recent news reports?
- Is there a group of students (a club, an ethnic group, some athletes) on campus you'd like to know more about?
- Is there a nursing home or senior citizens' center near your college or home? A day-care center?
- Have you ever wondered why some people are so intense about an activity (fishing, motocross, poetry, exercise)?
- Have you checked the local newspaper for hobby club meetings?

Once you feel sure of your direction, state a research question — exactly what are you trying to find out? How to word such a question is discussed in Chapter 27 on page 604. The research question is the central question to ask yourself and to keep living with: Do identical twins go into the same line of work as adults? Or, does an identical twin resent or relish having someone so much like himself or herself? The following questions are other, smaller ones.

DISCOVERY CHECKLIST: WEIGHING POSSIBILITIES

- Where will you find more ideas and information about this subject? Whom might you consult for suggestions?
- What places should you visit?
- Whom should you talk with?
- How much time and effort is this investigation likely to take? Is your project reasonable?

You may not be able to answer this last question accurately until you start investigating, but make a rough guess. Set yourself a schedule, with deadlines for completing your research, for drafting, for revising. For any project in which you interview people, an excellent rule of thumb is to allow 50 percent more time than you might reasonably think necessary. People may be out when you call or you may find that one interview didn't supply all you need and that you'll have to do a follow-up. For a college paper, a field research project has to be humanly possible. Four to six weeks is usually a reasonable amount of time. If you begin with the intention of interviewing all the identical twins in your county, you might take a look at your deadline (and your course load) and then decide to limit your research to a sampling of, say, twenty individuals. Robert A. Day, author of *How to Write and Publish a Scientific Paper* (Philadelphia: ISI P, 1983), offers this sound advice: "Don't start vast projects with half-vast ideas." Don't start half-vast projects, either.

Reading for background   Jamie Merisotis didn't plunge blindly into field research. Even though it was slim, his reading gave him leads to follow up. Books such as Roy B. Flemming's *Punishment before Trial: An Organizational Perspective of Felony Bail Processes* (New York: Longman, 1982) helped fill him in on how the bail bond business operates. He also found a few helpful articles on bail bonding in professional law journals, such as *Criminal Law Bulletin, Justice System Journal,* and *Law and Society Review.*

A useful question for you before you start to do field research is What helpful background material on your topic can you find first of all in your library? Read what is available and take notes, citing the sources carefully (see Chapter 27, pp. 632–633).

Directing an interview   People in all walks of life are often willing, sometimes even eager, to talk to a college student writing a research paper. Many, you may find, will seem flattered by your attention. Interviews — conversations with a purpose — may prove to be your main source of material. In Chapter 4 (p. 84), we gave advice that once again may come in handy:

1. Make sure your prospect is willing to be quoted in writing.
2. Plan an appointment for a day when this person will have enough time — if possible, an hour — to have a thorough talk with you.
3. Appear promptly, with carefully thought-out questions to ask.
4. Really listen. Let the person open up.
5. Be flexible and allow the interview to go in unanticipated directions if some come up.
6. If a question draws no response, don't persist and make a nuisance of yourself; just go on to the next question.
7. Make additional notes right after the interview to preserve anything you didn't have time to record during the interview. This strategy is the main one Truman Capote used to gather information for *In Cold Blood.*

Despite bondsmen's initial reluctance to talk to him, in the end Jamie Merisotis came up with a trove of exciting material. His interviews were never shorter than forty-five minutes. Some bondsmen, apparently gratified by his taking their work seriously, opened up and talked candidly for as long as two hours. As is usual in studies of criminal justice, Merisotis's research paper gave the bondsmen anonymity. Because some bondsmen's activities (such as coercing clients to appear) hover on the borderline of the law, Merisotis had to assure them that he would not cite their names. He wouldn't even identify the state they practiced in. Some bondsmen, in fact, would agree to be interviewed only on the condition that their voices not be tape-recorded. If you want to use a tape recorder, remember to ask permission of the interviewee.

For his own guidance, Merisotis first made himself a list of questions he wanted to ask. To persuade the bondsmen to trust him, he began with questions that voiced his genuine interest in them as people:

> Tell me about yourself—where you live, where you grew up, your personal background.
>
> How long have you been working as a bondsman? Do you plan to stay in the business?
>
> Let's suppose you're having an average day. Could you tell me what this average day as a bondsman is like? In other words, what happens that you consider "regular"?

Then he probed more deeply, pursuing his main interest in his paper: how the bondsman operates. He asked questions to zero in on the bondsman's activities and reveal certain parts of them in detail:

> What do you consider when deciding to post bond for a defendant?
> Do you consider his or her ties to the community?
> His past record?
> His financial situation?
> The offense he is charged with?
> Are there any other things you take into account?

To round out his view of the bondsmen's activities, Merisotis sought interviews with legal professionals. To his disappointment, although he asked them many times, no judges would consent to be interviewed. But Merisotis persisted. He talked with others in the legal system: police, prosecutors, public defenders, private attorneys, sheriffs, and bail commissioners. They confirmed, and sometimes supplemented, what the bondsmen had told him in confidence.

As Merisotis collected more and more evidence, not only his ideas changed but also the language he couched them in. From reading about bail bondsmen in legal journals, he had picked up the term *deposit bail,* which he used in his first interviews. But he soon found that the phrase belonged to classrooms and law offices, not to bondsmen in the field. He had to change it to *ten percent bail* so that the bondsmen would understand him.

Inquiring by telephone   If you can't talk to an expert in person, your next best resource may be a telephone interview. A busy person whom you call during a working day may not be able to give you a half hour of conversation on the spur of a moment, and it is polite to ask for a time when you may call again. You will waste the person's time (and yours) if you try to wing your interview; have written questions in hand before you dial. Take notes.

Federal regulations, by the way, forbid recording an interview over the phone without notifying the person who is talking that you are recording his or her remarks and without using a recorder connector with a warning device that emits a beep signal every fifteen seconds. For a charge, some telephone companies will now make a beep-punctuated recording of your conversation and mail you a tape cassette; ask your operator whether this service is available.

The telephone, of course, has other uses besides interviewing. Early in his project Jamie Merisotis placed scores of phone calls to set up his face-to-face interviews. Later he checked some facts by making further calls.

Preparing a questionnaire From each of the eighteen bail bondsmen who consented to talk with him, Jamie Merisotis sought even more evidence than his interview alone would bring. When the conversation came to an end, he would hand each person a questionnaire to fill out and return.

Questionnaires, as you know, are part of contemporary life. You probably filled out one the last time you applied for a job or for college. Many people, in our experience, enjoy having their knowledge tapped or their opinion solicited. Indeed, filling out a questionnaire has a gamelike appeal, as you can tell from the frequency with which self-quiz features appear in popular magazines: "How Rigid Are You?" followed by a thirty-question quiz to score yourself.

As a rule, when researching a particular question, professional pollsters, opinion testers, and survey takers survey thousands of individuals, chosen to represent a certain segment of society or perhaps a broad range of the populace (widely diversified in geography, income, ethnic background, and education). Their purpose may be to inform manufacturers who are test-marketing new products or trying to identify a new market. It may be to help a politician in planning a campaign. Questionnaires are widely used because they deliver large stores of useful information quickly and efficiently.

To make it easy for his interviewees to return his questionnaire, Merisotis provided each with a stamped, self-addressed envelope. Apparently, the bondsmen, after they opened up and talked, felt involved in his research and became willing also to reply to written questions.

Merisotis's questionnaire is reprinted in Figure 29.1. The questions call for short answers, easy to supply. He had used his most complicated questions in his interviews. This questionnaire asks for information revealing the bondsman's personal history, his family circumstances and background, his income, his education, his religious and political views. In keeping with his promise to the bondsmen to maintain their anonymity, Merisotis identified each questionnaire by a number and did not use the respondent's name.

WRITING WITH A COMPUTER: FIELD RESEARCH

GENERATING IDEAS
Database software can sort all the numbers from your questionnaire and do the statistical calculations for you. It might save you hours of tallying with pencil and paper. Databases will probably be available in the campus computer lab or business department.

Questionnaire

Interview number_____

Age:

Marital status:

Number of dependents:

Father's occupation:

Mother's occupation:

How old were you when you became a bondsman?

How did you learn to become a bondsman?

_____ family member was a bondsman   _____ taught myself
_____ friend was a bondsman   _____ other (Please explain)

How long, in months and years, would you estimate it took you to learn about bail bonding?

How many days a week do you work as a bondsman?

Do you hold another job?

Estimate your earnings as a bondsman last year:

_____ less than $10,000   _____ $20,000 to $30,000
_____ $10,000 to $15,000   _____ more than $30,000
_____ $15,000 to $20,000

How many employees do you have (excluding other bondsmen)?

In what state were you born?

In what state have you lived the most number of years?

How long have you been a resident of this state?

Do you speak any foreign languages?

If so, which?

Estimate the percentage of your clients who do not speak English:

_____ less than 10 percent
_____ 10 percent to 50 percent
_____ more than 50 percent

Which best describes the education you have received?

_____ some high school   _____ some four-year college
_____ graduated high school   _____ graduated four-year college
_____ some two-year college   _____ post-college or graduate study

List the schools and colleges you have attended, starting with high school:

What newspapers and magazines do you read regularly?

FIGURE 29.1 Jamie Merisotis's questionnaire to bail bondsmen

Know your purpose. If you think you want to use a survey to gather information for your paper, ask yourself: What am I trying to discover with this questionnaire? Merisotis's questionnaire delivered good results because it addressed the questions its author wanted answered, and it was directed to the people able to answer it. Since bail bondsmen often are asked to aid

```
Questionnaire / page 2

Which of the following best describes your partisan political preference?

_____ sometimes vote Democrat        _____ always vote Republican
_____ usually vote Democrat          _____ independent
_____ always vote Democrat           _____ don't vote
_____ sometimes vote Republican      _____ usually vote for another
_____ usually vote Republican                party  (Please name)

Which word best describes your political beliefs?

_____ left-liberal                   _____ moderate conservative
_____ liberal                        _____ conservative
_____ middle-of-the-road

Are you a veteran of any U.S. wars?  If so, which ones?


How many of the following kinds of organizations do you belong to?

_____ veterans' organizations (VFW, American Legion, etc.)
_____ religious organizations (Knights of Columbus, etc.)
_____ fraternal and service organizations (Masons, Elks, etc.)
_____ service organizations (Kiwanis, Boy Scout leader, etc.)
_____ business organizations (Chamber of Commerce, etc.)
_____ advocate or lobbyist organizations (National Rifle Association,
       Greenpeace, Common Cause, etc.)

Please indicate any you contribute to or otherwise actively support.


What is your religious affiliation?

_____ Protestant                     _____ Muslim
_____ Roman Catholic                 _____ Other  (Please name)
_____ Eastern Orthodox               _____ None
_____ Jewish

How often do you attend religious services?

_____ very regularly                 _____ infrequently
_____ fairly regularly               _____ never

Please list any hobbies or special interests:
```

FIGURE 29.1   (Continued)

disadvantaged minorities, people who don't have personal lawyers or large bank accounts, Merisotis correctly guessed that the bondsmen's views, allegiances, education, and personal circumstances might well throw some light on their policies in deciding whether or not to take a risk on a client and write a bond.

By using this questionnaire, Merisotis soon found a clear picture of typical bondsmen emerging—one quite different from the image in the popular mind. Most bondsmen, the responses indicated, are not lone wolves, glamorously racing around cornering fugitives, but are cautious middle-class citizens: most of them married, with children, people of more education than he had expected, churchgoers and templegoers involved in community activities. From the responses to his questionnaire, he concluded that most bondsmen are not pistol-packing vigilantes but "day-to-day businessmen determined to make a living within the limits of the law."

You too will want to define the purpose of your questionnaire and then thoughtfully invent questions to fulfill it. If, for instance, you want to know how effective a day-care center is in the eyes of working mothers who entrust their children to it, you might ask questions like these: Do your children report that they are happy there? Have you ever had reason to complain? If so, about what?

Keep it simple. Any questionnaire you design has to be one that people are willing to answer. The main point to remember in writing a questionnaire is to make it easy and inviting to fill out. If you make it too complex and time-consuming, the recipient will throw it away. Ask questions that call for a check mark, a simple yes or no, for one word or a few words. Ask yourself as you write each question what information you want to acquire with the question. Then read it over to be sure that it will work the way it is written. It's a good idea to ask for just one piece of information per question. Like Merisotis, keep it simple: list alternative answers with blanks for your respondent to check.

Avoid slanted questions. Write unbiased questions that will solicit factual responses. Merisotis did not ask, "How religious are you?" Instead he asked, "What is your religious affiliation?" and "How often do you attend religious services?" From the facts he gathered in response to these two questions, he could report these facts and draw logical inferences about the respondents.

Be flexible in approaching respondents. If possible, give the questionnaire to your interviewees at the end of your discussion as Merisotis did. If not, assemble a group of people (at, say, an evening coffee for parents or children in a day-care center) and have them fill out your questionnaire on the spot. Facing the group, you can explain the purpose of your research, and, to enlist their confidence, you can invite questions and answer them. If you must send your questionnaire to people, include a concise letter or note explaining what you are trying to do and what use you will make of the replies. You might say, "This questionnaire should take no more than ten minutes of your time to complete" or give some such estimate that will make the task look reasonable to the respondents. Some professional questioners offer a morsel of bait: a small check or a coupon good for a free jar of pickles. You might promise a copy of your finished paper or article, a brief report of the results, or a listing of each respondent's name in an acknowledgment.

Even with such little enticements, professional poll takers and opinion testers find that a 40 percent response to a mailed questionnaire is unusually high. That is why they often conduct surveys by telephone, with the phone caller making a phone appointment and then filling in the questionnaire for the respondent. Better results will come if you distribute your questionnaire in person, laying a copy in your prospects' hands.

If you can't interview a person, you might find it worthwhile to add to your questionnaire some "open questions," questions that call for short written responses. Although responses to these questions will be difficult to tally and you are likely to get a smaller number responding, the answers might supply you with something worth quoting or might suggest facts for you to consider when you mull over the findings. Urge your recipients to flip over the questionnaire and use the back side if they need more room.

Tally your responses. When you get back all your questionnaires, sit down and tally the results. That is easy enough to do if you are just counting short answers ("Republican," "Democrat"), but longer answers to open questions ("What is your goal in life?") will need to be summed up in paraphrase and then sorted into rough categories ("To grow rich," "To serve humanity," "To travel," "To save own soul"). By this means, you can count similar replies and accurately measure the extent of a pattern of responses.

Making a field trip A visit to observe at first hand may well be essential in field research, as it certainly was in Jamie Merisotis's study. Merisotis visited four criminal courts, where he observed the bondsmen in action. In his paper, his observations supplied the evidence for his contention that the work of a bondsman has some socially redeeming use:

> In the crowded, often disorganized environment of a lower criminal court, bondsmen are a stabilizing influence. Their presence is unmistakable. They can be seen conferring with family and friends of defendants in courthouse corridors, speaking with prosecutors during a court recess, and keeping track of defendants still to be presented in court. Bondsmen help keep order in the courtroom, and they locate people. One bondsman was observed frequently assisting in translating for Spanish-speaking defendants when the official courtroom interpreter was unavailable.

Merisotis also observed the bondsmen on their daily rounds. He accompanied several as they made calls, observing them talking with clients and writing bonds. This firsthand experience supplied authentic details from which his writing profited.

In making an observational visit of your own, you may care to recall the suggestions we give in Chapter 4. You will need to make an appointment. Right away when you arrive, identify yourself and your business. Some receptionists will insist on identification. You might ask your instructor for a statement on college letterhead, declaring that you are a bona fide student doing field research. Follow-up field trips may be necessary if, while you are writing, you find gaps in your research or if new ideas occur that you'll need to test by further observation.

Interviews, telephone inquiries, questionnaires, and observations are the sources of evidence you are likely to find most useful in field research. (To see how Jamie Merisotis drew from all these sources, see the chapter from his honors thesis beginning on p. 694.) But other sources of ideas and information will serve you, too, for other kinds of field research. Briefly, we'll run through them.

Letter writing   Do you know a person whose knowledge or opinions you need but who lives too far away to interview? Write him or her a letter. Make it short and polite, enclose your questionnaire, or ask a few pointed questions, and enclose a stamped, self-addressed envelope for a reply.

Large corporations, huge organizations such as the Red Cross and the National Wildlife Federation, branches of the military and the federal government, and elected officials are accustomed to getting such mail. In fact, many of them employ public relations officers whose duty is to answer you. Sometimes they will unexpectedly supply you with a bonus: free brochures, press releases, or other material that they think might interest you. Many such nuggets of material valuable for research are available for nothing, from people trying hard to give it away.

Using television and radio programs, films, and recordings   Intriguing possibilities for writing lie in the media. If you ever care to do a research paper about television, radio, movies, or contemporary theater or music, you may find yourself doing field research as original as if you went out and interviewed eighteen bail bondsmen. Because your material lies close at hand (in the case of television, it may be yours at the click of a remote control), our only advice to you is to get plenty of it. Watch (or listen to) a large amount of it and draw conclusions.

Successful papers based on such research are legion. One student we know wrote an excellent research paper on public service commercials, free time devoted to good causes (like accident prevention and saving whales), which all television channels are required by law to make available. She classified the different causes being promoted and their different pitches or appeals, and she found unanticipated correlations between the causes given air time and the presumed interests of a station's advertisers. For example, one station that aired many beer commercials rarely aired a public service message about the dangers of alcohol. Another student fruitfully compared the news coverage of an election by three major networks and the Public Broadcasting System by first recording a dozen televised newscasts with the aid of a VCR. Her main finding was that the networks seemed determined to cast the election into a more dramatic form — similar to a prizefight or a football game — than Public Broadcasting did, even though the outcome became clear very early.

Program guides (*TV Guide,* a station's own guide, or a daily newspaper) can save you time by directing you to the most relevant programs. For easy reference, the script of a broadcast or telecast may be available on request (or for a small charge) from a station or network; if the end credits do not proclaim that it is available, you can write to inquire.

In writing about movies or plays, don't forget to check out reviews in magazines and newspapers. In writing about a recording, inspect any information supplied on an insert or on the album jacket. Record labels, too, sometimes provide dates, names of members of a group, and song composers.

Using a camera or a videocamera   Even if you are only an amateur photographer, taking pictures in the field may greatly advance your research. Some photographs may serve as illustrations to include in your paper; others may help you remember details while you write. One student of architecture, making a survey of the best-designed buildings in her city, carried a 35-mm camera and photographed each building she proposed to describe. A student of sociology, looking into methods used to manage large crowds, found it effective to carry a videocamera to a football game. Later, watching a few crowd scenes in slow motion, he felt better able to write lively and accurate accounts of how police and stadium guards performed their jobs.

Attending lectures and conferences   Professionals in virtually every walk of life — and also special-interest groups — sometimes convene for a regional or national conference. Such conferences bring together doctors, lawyers, engineers, scientists, librarians, teachers, and assorted people bound together by some mutual concern (a conference to protest acid rain, a convention of science fiction fans). These meetings can be fertile sources of fresh ideas.

Fortunately, college campuses sometimes welcome such conferences, and if there are any of possible use to you, go take them in. An idea for a field research paper might result. At some conferences, lectures and panel discussions are open to the public. At others, to gain admission you might have to register for the conference and pay a fee. This drawback might discourage a casual researcher, but if your honors thesis depends on material to be discussed at the conference, or if you are thinking of a possible career in that profession, you might find it worthwhile to pay the fee. To attend a professional conference, to meet and talk with speakers and fellow attendees, can be an excellent way to learn the language of a discipline. If you plan to be an ornithologist, start thinking and talking and writing like an ornithologist. Learn the vocabulary, the habits of mind. To steep yourself in the language of a specialized conference is one way to begin. You can take notes on the lectures, which are given by speakers who usually are distinguished in their specialties, and thus get some firsthand live opinions. You may even be able to ask questions from the audience or corner the speakers later for informal talk.

Proceedings of important conferences may be published later (unfortunately, often months or years later) and eventually can be tracked down in a library. A paper presented at one such conference of professors of educational administration is cited in the research paper by Lisa Chickos on page 650.

Check the weekly schedules of events listed on your college bulletin boards and in your campus newspaper. These may alert you to other lectures (besides those delivered at conferences) that may hold ideas and information useful to you.

Planning, Drafting, and Developing

All the while you have been gathering material, you have been evaluating it, deciding what to trust, which evidence looks most likely to answer your basic research question. Presumably, you have been doing some heavy sifting and discarding along the way. If you have, you will have saved yourself much toil at the present moment, when you are ready to shape your material into a paper.

At this point, as you glance over what you have collected, you can again be critical of it. Do you have *enough* material to answer your research question? If not, you may need to go out and get more. How much is enough? To answer that, we can't lay down any hard-and-fast rule. But the larger the generalization you make from your investigation, the more evidence it calls for in support. Clearly, you cannot decide that all day-care centers in the state of Washington are safe, well-managed facilities from having visited only five of them in Seattle; and in a research project bounded by the limited time of a college course, you may need to trim down your generalization: "The day-care centers *I visited in Seattle* impressed me by their safety and professional management" [emphasis ours].

Most college writers find, at the moment they begin to shape a first draft, that they have collected a bewildering array of material. If you've done much legwork, the amount and variety of your evidence may dismay you. Do you feel frozen as you contemplate your difficulties? Don't know how you will ever pull this jumble into shape? Stop trying to plan; start writing. Don't worry about which part of your paper to write first—start with anything at all. If you just get something down on paper, then later you can decide where to place it. Absorb yourself in your task. Maybe your material will start falling into shape as you write.

Organizing your ideas   With any luck, your material may fall readily into shape, but if it is various and extensive, you may find you need to outline beforehand. In Chapter 15, we offer detailed advice on outlining (p. 331).

In organizing your field research, remember that, as is true of most other kinds of writing, some intuitive art is called for. It is not enough to relate the steps you took in answering your research question: you aren't writing a memoir; you're reporting the significance of what you found out. Try putting your material together in various combinations until you find out what seems most engaging and clear. In a guidebook titled *How to Write and Publish*

Engineering Papers and Reports (Philadelphia: ISI P, 1982), Herbert B. Michaelson remarks:

> Because there is no one best way to organize all engineering manuscripts, the role of the imagination cannot be overemphasized. Writing progress seldom follows the same sequence as progress on an engineering project. Designing a device or developing a process may get off to a false start, or may be sidetracked into a wrong approach, or may undergo modifications before the work is completed. A manuscript describing all these stages of the design or process would be difficult to read. After the problems have been solved in the laboratory, it is time for a new exercise of the imagination: the design of the manuscript.

If you began with a clear, carefully worded question for research (first discussed on p. 604), you will generally have an easier time in selecting and organizing your evidence to answer it. Of course, research questions often may change and re-form while you're at work in the field. Don't be afraid, when the time comes to organize, to junk an original question that no longer works and to try to reorganize your material around a newly formed question. In the long run, you'll save both time and toil.

With pencil in hand, reread any notes you have taken. Think critically about the evidence that you have gathered. Try to answer your research question. One way to structure your essay is to pose your research question in the introduction, report and interpret your evidence in the body, and answer the research question in the conclusion. As you plan and draft the body, group related ideas and have a reason for the order of the sections of evidence.

Interpreting your evidence   To be sure, organizing the facts you collect is an important part of your task. You might easily mistake that part for the most important part of field research. But still more important is *interpreting* those facts. What do they indicate? In themselves, facts and statistics may not always make much sense. Much more likely to communicate meaning to your reader is what you make of your figures—your summaries of what statistics mean. Instead of reporting that 34.1 percent of your respondents favor capital punishment (with no further comment on the statistic), it might make more sense to write, "More than a third of the people I questioned said that they believe capital punishment is sometimes justified, although many of these people qualified their answers. They said they believed in it only to punish violent crimes such as murder and rape."

Evaluate your sources. You can probably trust anyone you interviewed who has a good reputation among other experts in the same field. Did some person you interviewed seem indifferent, half asleep? Did he appear not to know what he was talking about? Discard his testimony or give it only a passing mention. Did any others impress you with their competence? Rely on them more heavily.

If you used a questionnaire and tabulated the replies, show them to fellow students whose opinions you respect. What conclusions do they draw? Test their interpretations against your own.

Here are some evidence-testing questions.

DISCOVERY CHECKLIST: EVALUATING EVIDENCE

- Is any of your evidence hearsay ("I understand she was a pretty reckless driver in her younger days")? If so, can you support or discount a speaker's view by comparing it with any other evidence?

- Was anyone who described an important event actually on the scene? Is it likely that the passage of time has distorted his or her memory?

- Does the testimony agree with published accounts—in books, magazines, and newspapers?

- Have you compared different people's opinions or accounts of the same thing? In general, the more people, the better.

- Do you base any large generalization on a single example, one fact, one individual opinion? If so, reconsider your claim.

- If you have tried to question a random sampling of people, do you feel they are truly representative?

- Did an interviewee exhibit prejudice or bias? Some remarks may need to be discounted.

- How detailed is your evidence? How extensive?

For more suggestions on evaluating facts and testimony, glance back over the section "Testing Evidence" in Chapter 7 (pp. 154–156).

Using sources (not letting sources use you) While you write, it is easy to get distracted from your central inquiry—from your attempt to answer the research question you started out with. No doubt you will have collected experiences, comments from people, and miscellaneous delightful facts that you think you just have to include in your paper. Maybe they belong in an informal paper — a memoir, say, of your life as a field researcher — but be willing to omit them in writing up your field research. Some material that you may have taken great pains to collect may not prove useful when you draft. If it doesn't serve your inquiry, leave it out — don't yank it in by the heels.

A common danger, besides letting sources dominate a draft and receive undeserved prominence, is for a writer to swagger in triumph over what he or she discovered. Cultivate a certain detachment. Make no exorbitant claims for what you have discovered ("Thus I have shown that day-care centers universally deserve the trust of any parent in the state of Washington"). You have probably not answered your research question for all time; you need not claim to be irrefutable. Norman Tallent, in his guidebook *Psychological Report Writing* (Englewood Cliffs: Prentice, 1976), quotes a professional reader of reports in the field of psychology: "I have seen some reports which affected me adversely because of a tendency to sound pompous with the implication 'This is the final word!' rather than 'This is an opinion intended to be helpful in understanding the whole.' "

As you write, introduce pieces of evidence with transitions, such as "*Two other bail bondsmen disagreed* that first-time offenders make the best risks" or "*Elsewhere, in the southwest end, a more ethnically various part of the city,* few respondents felt that the problem of unemployment was serious." On the art of smoothly weaving quotations and other material into your paper, Chapter 27 makes a few suggestions (pp. 620–627).

Revising and Editing

As in writing a library research paper, you will probably find it easier to write the beginning and ending of your paper after you have done your research and written it up. You'll now better understand what you have demonstrated.

Looking over your evidence and your draft, you may quite possibly find your conclusion changing. Don't be afraid to make a whole new interpretation.

Not every spoken remark you've collected will be worth quoting, and if you faithfully introduce every one, word for word, the result may sound like drivel. In that case, summarize and paraphrase in your own words. To test whether a quotation is worth quoting, ask yourself:

> Are these words memorable? Would you recall them if you hadn't written them down? If not, away with them!

> Does the speaker's remark support any point you're trying to make? Or does it seem mere maundering chin music? If so, out with it!

When you sit down to rewrite, there are other, possibly useful questions to ask yourself (see the revision checklist on p. 692).

Once you have done all you can do by yourself to make your paper informative, tightly reasoned, and interesting to read, you might wish to take one last step: show it to one of your friends and ask for his or her criticisms.

REVISION CHECKLIST: LOOKING OVER YOUR RESULTS

- Have you put in only evidence that makes a point?
- Have you ever yielded to the temptation to put in some fact or quotation just because it cost effort to obtain?
- Are your sources of information trustworthy? Do you have lingering doubts about anything anyone told you? (If so, whom might you consult to verify it?)
- Did you take advantage of any library material that supplied background information or helped you test the validity of your evidence?
- Is your conclusion (or generalization) made clear?
- Do you spend much space announcing what you are going to do or repeating what you demonstrated? (If you do, consider whether such passages might be whittled down or done without.)
- If you include observations made on a field trip or visit, do you now need to make any follow-up visit?
- Do you need more evidence to back up any point? If so, where might you obtain it?

Answering your peer editor's comments will probably take extra time; but if you take this step seriously, the final result will almost surely be a better paper than the one you might otherwise have handed in. Ask your peer reader to answer the questions in the following peer editing checklist.

PEER EDITING CHECKLIST: WRITING FROM RESEARCH IN THE FIELD

- Describe your overall reaction to the paper.
- What do you think about the conclusions the writer has drawn from his or her research? Do they seem fair and logical? Describe any problems you have with the conclusions.
- Is the organization logical and easy to follow?
- Does the writer need all the quotations he or she has used? Point out any that puzzled you or that you thought were not well incorporated.
- Do you have any questions about the writer's evidence? Point out any areas where the writer has not fully backed up his or her conclusions.
- Has the writer described the results of a survey or questionnaire clearly? Do you need any additional information or explanation?
- Look carefully at the conclusion. Does it clearly enough answer the writer's research question? Did you learn anything in the paper that you think should be somehow included in the conclusion?
- Did the writer commit any logical fallacies (see Chapter 18)?
- Look carefully at transitions and put an asterisk anywhere you think the writer needs to work harder.

Preparing your manuscript   The form of your field research paper isn't much different from that of a library research paper. (For further instructions, see also "A Note on Manuscript Style," p. 396.) One difference may occur when, if you are following APA style, you come to prepare a list of your sources ("References") at the end of your paper. You do not list personal communications that you have cited in your paper (such as letters, interviews, and phone conversations). You need list only sources that a reader can verify: published works and public records. (If you are using the MLA style, you will list all sources, including interviews.) For specific advice on citing and listing your sources, see Chapter 30.

Proofreading a field research paper calls for checking information carefully — not against neatly printed sources, which are easier to check, but against your original notes and jottings. Allow yourself ample time to give your paper a final going-over.

A COMPLETED FIELD RESEARCH PAPER

When Jamie Merisotis completed his honors thesis, it caused a local stir. Friends and roommates who read it were greatly intrigued and impressed by it. As his academic department required, large parts of his thesis were devoted to explaining recent and pending legislation as it affected the bail bond business and to giving an account of his methods of research (which account we have already summarized). But let us show you one short, self-contained chapter of the paper, which illustrates how Merisotis put his field research to use. The paper is written in APA style, so both direct quotations and indirect quotations, taken from interviews, are cited with dates. Unlike most field research papers, this one contains no names, for in order to persuade the bondsmen to talk freely, Merisotis had to agree to keep them all anonymous. In preserving anonymity, he followed the practice of *Law and Society Review,* a professional journal that sometimes publishes articles quoting criminals who want to conceal their identities. He dated all facts and quotations he obtained from interviews, but lest anyone see a pattern in the responses and try to identify the speakers, he did not distinguish one speaker from another.

Unlike a library research paper, this field research paper has no listing of its sources titled "References." Merisotis's information came entirely from personal communications, mostly from interviews and responses to his questionnaire, which he distributed privately. But if, using the APA style, you were writing a field research paper that referred to public sources, such as a lecture to an audience or records in courthouses, which are open for anyone's inspection, then at the end of your paper you would add a list of "References." And if you were to submit your paper for publication in a journal, you would need to include a title page with the title, your name and affiliation, and an abbreviation of the title at the bottom of the title page for the journal to use as running head copy. Your name would then be omitted from the first page of the paper, now page 2.

How a Bondsman 1

How a Bondsman Decides to Post Bail

Jamie Merisotis

The bail bondsman's decision whether or not
to post bond for a defendant is probably the
single greatest power he wields in the legal
system. People who seek the services of a
bondsman normally do not have the means to raise
the full bond amount themselves. Thus the
bondsman is often the deciding factor in determining a defendant's pretrial status. Defendants unable to secure the services of a bondsman
often remain in the custody of the state until
the trial, which may be several months later.

When a bondsman is asked to write a bond,
he considers several factors. This decision-
making process is complex, and most bondsmen
stress that each client is considered on his own
terms. Nevertheless, from this research several clear patterns have emerged. (All evidence cited in this study is from personal
communications.)

By far the most important factor, at least
initially, is the amount of the bond. After
all, it is the bond amount that ultimately
yields the bondsman's fee. Of course, the
bondsman is also aware that the greater fee
carries the greater risk. One telltale sign of
the importance of the bond amount may be seen
from the bondsman's method of screening prospective clients. A defendant, or someone

To persuade those
interviewed to talk
freely, the writer had
to guarantee anonym-
ity, and thus cites no
names. To prevent
readers from noticing
a pattern in the re-
sponses and trying to
identify the speakers
the writer did not dis-
tinguish one speaker
from another.

How a Bondsman 2

close to him, can call the bondsman by looking
under "Bonds--Bail" in the telephone book or
requesting the list of bondsmen from the police
station. But a phone call does not bring direct access to the bondsman. In most cases, a
professional answering service fields calls for
the bondsman, then notifies him through an
electronic beeper. The bondsman then calls the
answering service and takes the message. What
is interesting is that the answering service
asks callers only three questions: (1) name,
(2) where they are at the moment, and (3) the
bond amount. Clearly this amount is of tanta-
mount importance to the bondsman, and he makes
note of it immediately when taking the message.
Bondsmen concur that the bond amount is very
important in their decision-making process, as
these comments reveal:

> Let's say I get a call at three
> o'clock a.m. I've just gotten into bed
> and the service beeps me with a call.
> It's late but I take the call and find out
> it's for a five hundred dollar bond out in
> [a town about 20 miles from the bondsman's
> house]. My answer to that is simple. No.
> There's no way I drag myself out of bed for
> a 50 dollar fee. As a matter of fact, I
> might even call the service back and tell
> them not to bother me with nickel fees.
> (November 29, 1985)

Double space between all lines of the manuscript.

Because all facts and quotations cited were obtained from *private* interviews and personal communication (mostly interviews and questionnaires) sources are not identified. A paper that cites public sources (e.g., lectures, courthouse records) would include a list of "References" at the end.

How a Bondsman 3

Running head is abbreviated title.

I don't write bonds for under five hundred. Whether I'm taking a call or sitting in court during arraignments, I can't--won't--even sneeze at a guy who wants my services on a two-fifty bond. It's not worth my time. (December 27, 1985)

Do you know how much paperwork there is on a bond? Do you? I'm not saying I won't write a bond because of the paper-work, but any bondsman will tell you that paperwork is the worst part of this job. If I write only a few bonds a week, you better believe they're good risks for good money. (November 9, 1985)

In APA style, both direct quotations and indirect quotations taken from interviews are cited with dates of interviews in parentheses. When citing from other sources (e.g., books, articles, videos), APA style prescribes parenthetical in-text citation of author and date; when quoting directly, cite page(s) as well. More details on APA in-text citation appear in Chapter 30, pages 721–727.

Bondsmen who have a large bond volume, but deal in very low bonds, rarely survive in the modern bail bond business.

Bondsmen consider another important factor: the alleged offense. It tells them something about the defendant, which in turn gives them an idea of the likelihood that he will appear. Probably the single offense that causes greatest apprehension to bondsmen is a failure to appear, also referred to as FTA. Obviously, a defend-ant who did not face the court in a previous case is not a good risk. Failing to appear is a sin that many bondsmen will not forgive, and thus recidivist criminals may often find that they have no benefactors in the community of

How a Bondsman 4

bondsmen. In other cases, bondsmen have personal preferences for not wanting to bond out
certain defendants. Sample responses demonstrate this eclecticism:

> I don't bond sex offenders. Perverts
> don't deserve to be free. (November 29,
> 1985)

> I try to stay away from people who are
> charged with violent crimes, especially if
> it involves a gun. Will he turn around
> and use it on me? I don't want to find
> out. (January 11, 1986)

> No prostitutes, and no one that deals
> in heroin. You never know where those
> kind of people will be in the morning.
> (October 5, 1985)

Another factor that bondsmen take into account is the defendant's community ties. Most
bondsmen ask the defendant where he lives, what
kind of job he has, and how long he has lived in
the area. This information is important to a
bondsman because it gives him an idea of the
likelihood of a defendant's returning for trial;
it also gives him some information about how
difficult the client would be to trace if he
failed to appear in court. Bondsmen are wary
of out-of-state defendants because the costs of
retrieving a client from a long distance are
naturally higher. But information on community
ties can also be used to measure the client's

How a Bondsman 5

credibility. As one bondsman stated, "A guy
who's got a good job, wife, kids, whatever, is a
lot better risk than some chump with no address"
(October 5, 1985).

Some bondsmen express no apprehensions
about career criminals if they "know the guy or
his family" (November 16, 1985; January 4,
1986). Others, however, are unwilling to assume the risk for repeat offenders. "If I'm in
another business," one bondsman said, "steady
clients are great. In this business, steady
clients are bad news" (December 30, 1985).

Several bondsmen said they take the defendant's age into consideration because they
believe that young clients have high rates of
failure to appear. That the defendant is living with his parents, however, bondsmen take as
a sign of stability. One bondsman noted that
if a parent has "gone down" (engaged a bondsman
before), "you know the kid will have someone
around making sure he gets to court" (November
6, 1985).

It should be noted that a majority of
bondsmen denied that race is a factor in their
decisions. Others, quite vocal about their
racial preferences, said they do not bond out
black defendants. The reasons offered were
mostly stereotypes:

I'll bond out a black person if he
comes from a good neighborhood. But I

In APA style, short
quotations are incor-
porated into the text
and enclosed by quo-
tation marks. Paren-
thetical citation
precedes period at
end of sentence.

How a Bondsman   6

definitely check the address. A lot of
the time, I read [the name of a predominantly black area] and say to myself, "If
this guy skips, are you gonna go in there
and drag him out?" Unless I'm in a daring
mood, there's no way. (January 11, 1986)

Women defendants are also approached cautiously
by some bondsmen. One remarked that women are
sometimes difficult to trace because "once the
case comes up, months or even a year later, she
could be married and change her name. That
makes tracing difficult" (November 6, 1985).

In many cases the bondsman requires an indemnitor on the bond. This person is often a
relative or friend, usually the person who
called the bondsman. The indemnitor agrees to
compensate the bondsman for his losses in the
event of forfeiture or to deposit collateral
with the bondsman. The bondsman's decision to
post bond is often contingent on who the indemnitor is and what he has to offer as security
or collateral. Only in extenuating circum-
stances--if he knows the defendant well or is
feeling extraordinarily compassionate--will the
bondsman not require an indemnitor. Indeed,
the indemnitor in some ways plays a more important role in the bondsman's business than does
the defendant, as the following comments show:

I deal strictly with the indemnitor.
I want to know who this person is, how much

In APA style, long quo-
tations are displayed
in double-spaced
block, indented
5 spaces, with no
quotation marks.
Parenthetical citation
follows after sen-
tence; no additional
period needed after
citation.

How a Bondsman 7

money he's got, and what he can offer me
for collateral. Otherwise, no deal.
(November 8, 1985)

Really, my financial leverage--you
know, how I'm gonna get my money back if
the client skips--is with the indemnitor.
As co-signer, they're putting their butt on
the line for this guy. . . . Most times,
I don't even see the defendant until it's
time to sign the papers. (December 30,
1985)

Bondsmen accept an array of things as security or collateral: for example, stocks, savings account passbooks, real estate, and car
titles. A bondsman wants to know how much leverage he will have with a defendant in the event
of forfeiture. Clearly, a majority of this
leverage is with the indemnitor, the person who
has the most to lose (at least financially) if
the client absconds.

Whether any of these factors that bondsmen
consider really affects the defendant's likelihood of appearance for trial--a most important
question in every bondsman's mind--goes beyond
the scope of the present study. Nevertheless,
each bondsman perceives these factors and weighs
them differently. His analysis ultimately
yields the decision whether or not to assume the
risk for a defendant.

Most APA-style paper
end with a list of "Re
erences" that gives
credit to the sources
cited in the paper. Fo
information about pre
paring a "References
list and sample refer-
ences, see Chapter
30, pages 724—727.

Questions to Start You Thinking

1. How is a bail bondsman similar to other businesspeople you know? In what ways is the job of bondsman strikingly different?

2. How does Merisotis demonstrate his opening contention that the bondsman wields great power within the legal system?

3. In his concluding paragraph, how does he separate his own view from the views of the bondsmen? With what opinions that the bondsmen have expressed (and which he has quoted) do you suppose he might disagree?

4. What other interesting, unusual, or unfamiliar occupations come to mind about which you might enjoy doing field research?

Other Assignments

1. As Jamie Merisotis did, investigate a job or profession. Interview people in this line of work, explain what they do, and try to characterize them. Your topic need not be as colorful and hard to research as bail bonding; just pick a profession you care to know more about, perhaps one that you consider a career possibility, such as data processing, nursing, or accounting.

2. Write a portrait of life in your town or neighborhood as it was in the past based on interviews with senior citizens. Any photographs or other visual evidence you can gather might be valuable to include. Try to verify any testimony you receive by comparing it with a file of old newspapers (probably available at a local newspaper office) or by talking with a local historian.

3. Write a short history of your immediate family from interviews, photographs, scrapbooks, old letters, written but unpublished records, and any other sources.

4. Study the reasons students today give for going to college. Gather your information from actual interviews with and possibly a questionnaire of students at your college. Try to contact a variety of types of students for your research.

5. Investigate a current trend you have noticed on television (collecting evidence by observing news programs, other programs, or commercials).

6. Write a survey of recent films of a certain kind (detective movies, horror movies, science fiction movies, comedies, love stories), making generalizations that you support with evidence from your own film watching.

FOR GROUP LEARNING

While writing your field research paper, hold meetings with your writing group. At the outset, you can draw on the knowledge of others: perhaps they can suggest sources unknown to you. Later in the process, meet to talk over any problems you encounter and exchange drafts for reactions and criticism. Because this is likely to be a large project, you might want to team up with another student and write your field research paper in collaboration. If you think working with a partner is a good idea for your project, get your instructor's approval before you proceed.

7. Study the lyrics of contemporary popular songs and draw a conclusion about them, citing a dozen or more examples.

8. Prepare a questionnaire to find out about the reading or television habits of college students today — what, when, why, and other aspects of interest to you.

APPLYING WHAT YOU LEARN: SOME USES OF FIELD RESEARCH

Opportunities may arise to do field research in almost any college course, at any level, in which you are called on to collect evidence and to observe. If you happen to be a student of journalism, you may be sent out to cover news stories: one of the most practical applications of field research. In education and social studies courses, field trips and observational visits are commonplace. (Columbia College offers a well-known undergraduate course in the sociology of New York City that includes trips to police lockups, morgues, and charity hospitals.) In a course in psychology, medical care, or political science, you may have to observe people's behavior and interpret it.

In the world beyond the campus, to carry out useful field research is an enormous and bustling concern. Sociologists seek to explain the components of the population. Bankers and stockbrokers and businesspeople seek to predict trends in the economy. Businesspeople seek new products that will sell, or they try to learn why an established product isn't selling better. Often they seek to understand a potential market and how to appeal to it. Professionals who conduct research often set forth their findings in reports and articles — sharing these discoveries is the reason specialized technical and professional journals abound. Anthropologists and sociologists study how people live, archeologists dig up evidence of how people lived in the past, biologists and students of the environment collect evidence about the behavior of species of wildlife.

Here, for instance, is the anthropologist E. Richard Sorenson reporting his observations of children of the Fore, a tribal people in New Guinea who live by agriculture. He published his findings in "Cooperation and Freedom among the Fore in New Guinea" (in *Learning Non-Aggression: The Experience of Non-Literate Societies,* ed. Ashley Montague [New York: Oxford UP, 1978]). Taking movies with a concealed camera that went unnoticed and taking still pictures without alerting the tribesmen in advance, Sorenson photographed growing children and their families in their daily activities. From the pictures and his notes, he formed several interesting generalizations about the Fore people's practices in childrearing.

> The core discovery was that young infants remained in almost continual bodily contact with their mother, her housemates, or her gardening associates. At first, mothers' laps were the center of activity, and infants occupied themselves there by nursing, sleeping, and playing with their own bodies or those of their caretakers. They were not put aside for the sake of other activities, as when food

was being prepared or heavy loads were being carried. Remaining in close, un-interrupted physical contact with those around them, their basic needs, such as rest, nourishment, stimulation, and security, were continuously satisfied without obstacle. . . .

A second crucial thread running from infancy through childhood was the unrestricted manner in which exploratory activity and pursuit of interest were left to the initiative of the child. As the infant's awareness increased, his interests broadened to the things his mother and other caretakers did and to the objects and materials they used. Then these youngsters began crawling out to explore things nearby that attracted their attention. By the time they were toddling their interests continually took them on short sorties to nearby objects and persons. As soon as they could walk well, the excursions extended to the entire hamlet and its gardens, and then beyond with other children. Developing without inter-ference or supervision, this personal exploratory quest freely touched on what-ever was around, even axes, knives, machetes, and fire [Figure 29.2].

FIGURE 29.2   A generally practiced deference to the desires of the young in the choice of play objects permitted them to investigate and handle knives and other potentially harmful objects frequently. They were expected to make use of the tools and materials which belonged to their adult associates and were indulged in this expectation. As a result, use of knives was common, particularly for exploratory play.

Initially astonished by the ability of young children to manage so independently without being hurt, I eventually began to see how this capability also emerged from the infants' milieu of close human physical proximity and tactile interaction. Touch and bodily contact lent themselves naturally to satisfying the basic needs of the babies and provided the basis for an early kind of communicative experience based on touch. In continual physical touch with people engaged in daily pursuits, infants and toddlers began to learn the forms of behavior and response characteristic of Fore life. Muscle tone, movement, and mood were components of this learning process; formal instruction was not. . . . Competence with the tools of life developed quickly, and by the time they were able to walk, Fore youngsters could safely handle axes, knives, fire, and so on.

The early pattern of exploratory activity included frequent return to one of the "mothers." Serving as a home base, the bastion of security, a woman might occasionally give the youngster a nod of encouragement, if he glanced in her direction with uncertainty. Yet rarely did anyone attempt to control or direct, nor did they participate in a child's quests or jaunts.

At first I found it quite remarkable that toddlers did not recklessly thrust themselves into unappreciated dangers, the way our own children tend to do. Eventually I came to see that they had no reason to do so. From their earliest days, they enjoyed a benevolent sanctuary from which the world could be confidently viewed, tested, and appreciated. These human bases were neither demanding nor restrictive, so there was no need to escape or evade them in the manner so frequently seen in Western culture. Confidently, not furtively, the youngsters were able to extend their inquiry, widening their understanding as they chose. There was no need to play tricks or deceive in order to pursue life. Nor did they have to act out impulsively to break through subliminal fears induced by punishment or parental anxiety. Such children could safely move out on their own, unsupervised and unrestricted.

Most of us may never go on a field research expedition to New Guinea, but the techniques that Sorenson demonstrates — patiently collecting evidence, laying aside his own unwarranted assumptions, and finally making generalizations about the behavior patterns he observed — may serve for any investigation of the unfamiliar. You might try emulating Sorenson's accuracy, patience, and open-mindedness the next time you write a paper about people or a lifestyle different from your own.

In the sciences, social sciences, and fields of business (such as marketing or advertising), writers of articles frequently report on still another kind of study: their observations of tests and practical inquiries they have made. People in the helping professions, after testing and observing their patients, interviewing their families, and studying information from other professionals who have known them, often write case studies, which they keep on file and sometimes share with their colleagues. Only rarely are case studies meant for publication. Here, from a mental health center, is an example of one such case study.

Debbie is a twelve and a half-year-old girl from a broken home (father deserted six years ago and continues to upset the family by calling to complain to Debbie's mother about his present wife). Debbie is thought to be underachieving in school. Her teachers see her as an angry, troubled child. Debbie herself complains that schoolwork overwhelms her, tires her out. The following report seeks to achieve an understanding of Debbie as a basis for taking further action.

Debbie's intellectual status is above average. Her observations are accurate and there is originality of thought. She is an insecure child who has many fears. She fears the loss of her integrity, attack from others, and her own impulses. Debbie has a great need for acceptance and affection, but is inhibited by an overpowering fear of being rejected and hurt. There seems to be hostility directed to the mother. The relationship has not been mutually satisfying, often leaving Debbie frustrated. It is my impression that the mother's inconsistencies in handling the child may be a source of anger. Now she wants her own way and is conflicted about her dependency. Her attitudes to men are also unwholesome. They are seen as weak and mutilated. And she is confused about herself. She feels inadequate, and having a specific learning disability she requires more guidance and love than most children her age. However, not being able successfully to reach out to others has only left her more frustrated. Since Debbie finds it difficult to relate to people and because her own feelings are threatening to her, she withdraws to an immature fantasy world that provides little refuge. Even her fantasy is fearful, involving aggression and fear of being injured emotionally. Debbie is a very unhappy child.

In one memorable college paper, a business student reported the results of his attempt to give out free samples of a new margarine to supermarket customers. When he spread globs of the stuff on soft white bread, he had very little luck trying to give away samples. But when he dabbed the stuff daintily on tempting-looking crackers studded with sesame seeds, it moved well. He then tried dainty dabs of margarine on bread (with a little more success, but not much) and sometimes fat globs on the crackers (which moved fairly well). His conclusion: the crackers were the catalyst that made the margarine move. But in margarine samples, he decided, smaller offerings had proved more appealing than generous ones. These findings may not seem earthshaking to you, but to a merchant of margarine they might prove worth their weight in butter.

Anybody, in practically any field, can conduct an experiment. You might even ask yourself, What experiment might I conduct that might produce interesting results? In fact, what experiments might you conduct in order to write an interesting paper *for this very course?* Once again, you'll need your imagination.

CHAPTER 30

Documenting Sources: Using a Style Book

In newspaper language, a *style book* is a list of usages that every writer for the paper observes. A style book might instruct reporters, for instance, to refer to women as *Ms.,* to use a lowercase letter and not a capital on names of the seasons (*spring,* not *Spring*), to put quotation marks around the title of a book, a film, or a song. Every newspaper makes up its own style book and every staff writer has a copy. The style book helps determine the personality of a newspaper. For years, the *Chicago Tribune* insisted on spelling *philosophy* "filosofy," while the New York *Daily News* referred to no woman as a *lady* unless she was a convicted prostitute. More important, a style book saves each writer from having to deliberate about every fussy little thing: to capitalize or not to capitalize? It keeps all the articles in a newspaper consistent and so makes the paper more readable.

A similar logic operates in scholarly writing. Writers of college research papers most often follow the rules for documenting sources from either of two handbooks, one compiled by the Modern Language Association (MLA), the other by the American Psychological Association (APA). The style of the MLA is generally observed in papers for English composition, literature, and foreign language courses. APA style usually prevails in papers for the social sciences and business. If your research takes you into any scholarly or professional journals in those special areas, you will probably find all the articles following a recognizable style.

In other disciplines, other handbooks prescribe style: the *CBE Style Manual* of the Council of Biology Editors (1983), for instance, is used in the biological sciences and medicine. You will need to familiarize yourself with it, or with other manuals, if you ever do much research writing in those or other disciplines.

The purpose of citing and listing your sources is to enable any interested reader to look them up and verify what you say. The mechanics of documentation may seem fussy, but the obligation to cite and list sources keeps research writers truthful and responsible.

This chapter is here for handy reference. We try to tell you no more than you will need to know to write a freshman research paper. To know MLA style or APA style will be useful at these moments:

> *In citing while you write* — at any time when you want to document, often on a note card or in your paper, exactly where you obtained a fact, idea, opinion, or quotation.

> *In listing all your sources* — that is, in adding a final bibliography, a list entitled "Works Cited" or "References."

CITING SOURCES: MLA STYLE

As you write, you need to indicate in the text of your paper or in a parenthetical reference what you borrowed and where you found it. For complete information about your source, the reader can then turn to the end of your paper and refer to your list titled "Works Cited" (see p. 712). The *MLA Handbook for Writers of Research Papers,* 3rd ed. (New York: MLA, 1988) has extensive and exact recommendations. If you want more detailed advice than that given here, you can purchase a copy of the *MLA Handbook* or see a copy in the reference room of your college library.

Citing Printed Sources: Nonfiction Books

To cite a book in the text of a paper, you usually place in parentheses the author's last name and the number of the page containing the information cited. You do this as close as possible to your mention of the information you have borrowed, as in the following examples.

SINGLE AUTHOR

```
At least one critic maintains that Dean Rusk's exposure
to Nazi power in Europe in the 1930s permanently influ-
enced his attitude toward appeasement:

            In contrast to Acheson, who had attended Gro-
            ton, Yale, and Harvard despite his family's
            genteel poverty, Rusk was sheer Horatio Alger
            stuff.  He had grown up barefoot, the son of a
            tenant farmer in Georgia's Cherokee county, and
```

```
had worked his way through Davidson. . . .
Then came the moment that transformed his life
and his thinking.  He won a Rhodes scholarship
to Oxford.  More important, his exposure to
Europe in the early 1930s, as the Nazis con-
solidated their power in Germany, scarred his
mind, leading him to share Acheson's hostility
to appeasement in any form anywhere.  (Karnow
194)
```

```
One reason we admire Simone de Beauvoir is that "she
lived the life she believed" (Morgan 58).
```

Notice that a direct quotation longer than four lines is indented ten spaces and needs no quotation marks to set it off from the text of your paper.

For the sake of readability and transition, you'll sometimes want to mention an author or authors in your text, putting only the page number in parentheses.

TWO OR MORE AUTHORS

```
Taylor and Wheeler present yet another view (25).
```

MULTIPLE WORKS BY THE SAME AUTHOR

If you have used two or more works by the same author (or authors), you need to indicate with an abbreviated title which one you are citing in the text. In a paper that uses as sources two books by Iona and Peter Opie, *The Lore and Language of Schoolchildren* and *The Oxford Nursery Rhyme Book*, you would cite the first book as follows:

```
The Opies found that the children they interviewed were
more straightforward when asked about their "magic prac-
tices" or their "ways of obtaining luck or averting ill-
luck" than when asked about their "superstitions" (Lore
210).
```

A MULTIVOLUME WORK

For a work with multiple volumes, provide the author's name and the volume number followed by a colon and the page number.

```
In ancient times, astrological predictions were sometimes
used as a kind of black magic (Sarton 2: 319).
```

ENTIRE WORK

If you refer to an entire work and include the title and the name of the author, a specific page reference is unnecessary.

In The Story of My Boyhood and Youth, John Muir details
his boyhood in Scotland, his immigration to America, and
the hardships of farm life.

SECONDARY SOURCE

Whenever possible, cite the original source. If that source is unavailable
to you (as often happens with published accounts of spoken remarks), use
the abbreviation "qtd. in" (for "quoted in") before the secondary source you
cite in your parenthetical citation.

Zill says that, psychologically, children in stepfamilies
most resemble children in single-parent families, even if
they live in a two-parent household (qtd. in Derber 119).

Citing Printed Sources: Literature

NOVEL OR SHORT STORY

In A Tale of Two Cities, Dickens describes the aptly
named Stryver, who "had a pushing way of shouldering himself (morally and physically) into companies and conversations, that argued well for his shouldering his way up
in life" (110; bk. 2, ch. 4).

MORE THAN ONE NOVEL OR SHORT STORY

When referring to more than one novel or short story in your paper,
distinguish citations by using authors' names.

The character Naomi spends money like water, buying a new
kimono every month (Tanizaki 74; ch. 9). Dina's desires,
however, are limited by her income. Early in White
Horses she complains that her family cannot afford a new
car (Hoffman 12; ch. 1).

PLAY

For classic plays, leave out page numbers and include the act, scene, and
line numbers, separating them with periods.

Love, Iago says, "is merely a lust of the blood and a
permission of the will" (Othello 1.3.326).

In Equus, Dora says, "What the eye does not see, the
heart does not grieve over, does it?" (1.7).

POETRY

When you cite poetry, use the word "line" or "lines" in the first reference
and cite only numbers in subsequent references, as in the following examples

from William Wordsworth's "The World Is Too Much with Us." The first reference:

> "The world is too much with us; late and soon / Getting
>
> and spending, we lay waste our powers" (lines 1-2).

The subsequent reference:

> "Or hear old Triton blow his wreathed horn" (14).

Citing Printed Sources: Reference Books and Periodicals

ARTICLE IN A REFERENCE BOOK

In citing a one-page article from a work with entries arranged alphabetically, include the author's name in the text or in a parenthetical reference and omit the page number.

> Some intellectuals have offered unusual definitions of
>
> love, with one calling it the force that enables individ-
>
> uals to "understand the separateness of other people"
>
> (Havell).

If a reference article is long, give the page number.

> Gordon discusses Carver's "implosive" technique of ending
>
> stories just before epiphany (176).

If the article is unsigned, include a brief title in the text or in a parenthetical citation.

> She alienated many feminists with her portraits of women
>
> "who seemed to accept victimization" ("Didion").

JOURNAL ARTICLE

If the author is named in the text, cite just the page number(s) in the parenthetical reference.

> Mueller notes that Arthur's quest "aims at a goal that
>
> is, suggestively, beyond the immediate context of the
>
> narrative" (751).

If the author is not named in the text, provide the name in the reference.

> Arthur's quest "aims at a goal that is, suggestively, be-
>
> yond the immediate context of the narrative" (Mueller
>
> 751).

MAGAZINE OR NEWSPAPER ARTICLE

In citing a one-page magazine or newspaper article, include the author's name in the text or in a parenthetical reference. Do not include the page number, which will be noted in the list of works cited at the end of the paper.

```
Vacuum-tube audio equipment is making a comeback, with
aficionados praising the warmth and glow from the tubes,
as well as the sound (Patton).
```

When citing articles longer than one page, provide the specific page number(s) in a parenthetical reference.

```
Some less-than-perfect means have been used to measure
television viewership, including a sensor that scans
rooms for "hot bodies" (Larson 69).
```

When citing an anonymous magazine article, put the title of the article in parentheses, beginning with the word by which it is alphabetized in the list of works cited.

```
At least one former gang member has gone on to write
about his experiences ("Other Side of Cool").
```

Omit the page number when citing a one-page article.

```
Conservatives have attacked public television lately,
with one calling Sesame Street "just another kids' show"
(Carter).
```

THE BIBLE

```
The Bible speaks of the sacrifice God made to save the
world (John 3.16).
```

No bibliographic entry is necessary.

Citing Nonprint Sources

In both library and field research, it is likely that some of your material will be drawn from nonprint sources: interviews, questionnaires, phone calls, tapes and recordings, personal letters, films, filmstrips, slide programs, videotapes, computer programs. Finding material in the field (as in an interview) means that *you* are the source. You should document all your material as faithfully as you credit books, newspapers, and periodicals. Probably the easiest way to do that is to weave your mention of each source into the body of your paper.

```
Hearing Yeats read "The Song of the Old Mother" on tape
sheds new light on several lines in the poem.

On the H. L. Mencken recording, journalist Donald Howe
```

Kirkley, Sr., was able to persuade the veteran writer to
talk about his defeats as well as his triumphs.

In your list of works cited you give complete information about each source.
Transitions—phrases to introduce quotations, statistical tables, and other
blocks of material—can also serve you well. (For weaving material in gracefully, see the suggestions in Chapter 27, p. 617.)

LISTING SOURCES: MLA STYLE

At the end of your paper, you will provide a list of the sources from which
you have gleaned ideas or information. If you have indicated the work and
page number on each of your note cards, you will have little trouble compiling
this list. For most English courses you will follow the guidelines set forth by
the Modern Language Association (MLA).

The list of sources is called "Works Cited," includes only those sources
actually used in your paper, and is placed at the end of your paper. Center
the title at the top of a page. Double-space the list and alphabetize the entries
by authors' last names, or, for works with no author, by title. When an entry
exceeds one line, indent the second and subsequent lines five spaces.

Listing Printed Sources: Books

Notice that the information about each source is divided into three sections,
each followed by a period: author or agency's name (if there is one), title,
and publishing information. Give the author's name, last name first, and the
title in full as they appear on the title page. If the publisher lists more than
one city, include just the first. Use just the first name of a publisher with
multiple names: not Holt, Rinehart and Winston, but simply Holt. Omit initials
too. For J. B. Lippincott Co., simply write Lippincott.

SINGLE AUTHOR

Karnow, Stanley. <u>Vietnam: A History</u>. Rev. ed. New
York: Viking, 1991.

TWO OR MORE AUTHORS

Taylor, Edwin F., and John A. Wheeler. <u>Spacetime
Physics</u>. San Francisco: Freeman, 1966.

MULTIPLE WORKS BY THE SAME AUTHOR

Opie, Iona, and Peter Opie. <u>The Lore and Language of
Schoolchildren</u>. Oxford: Clarendon-Oxford UP, 1960.

---, eds. <u>The Oxford Nursery Rhyme Book</u>. Oxford:
Clarendon-Oxford UP, 1955.

CORPORATE AUTHOR

American Red Cross. Lifesaving: Rescue and Water Safety.
     New York: Doubleday, 1974.

GOVERNMENT DOCUMENT

United States. Dept. of Health and Human Services.
     Mosquito Control Measures in Gulf Coast States.
     Washington: GPO, 1986.

TWO OR MORE GOVERNMENT DOCUMENTS
BY THE SAME GOVERNMENT AGENCY

Hammer, Charles, and Elizabeth Gerald. "Table 1: Number
     and Percentage of Teachers by Selected Characteris-
     tics." United States Department of Education. Na-
     tional Center for Education Statistics. NCES-90-
     087. Selected Characteristics of Public and Private
     School Teachers: 1987-1988. Washington: GPO, 1990.

---. "Table 1: Number and Percentage of Administrators
     by Selected Characteristics." United States Depart-
     ment of Education. National Center for Education
     Statistics. NCES-90-085. Selected Characteristics
     of Public and Private School Administrators: 1987-
     1988. Washington: GPO, 1990.

UNKNOWN AUTHOR

Alcoholism and You. Pearl Island: Okra, 1986.

EDITED BOOK

If your paper focuses on the work or its author, cite the author first.

Hardy, Thomas. Tess of the D'Urbervilles. Ed. Scott
     Elledge. 3rd ed. New York: Norton, 1991.

If your paper focuses on the editor or the edition used, cite the editor first.

Elledge, Scott, ed. Tess of the D'Urbervilles. By
     Thomas Hardy. 3rd ed. New York: Norton, 1991.

EDITED COLLECTION OF ONE AUTHOR'S WORK

Irving, Washington. "Legend of the Moor's Legacy." The
     Complete Tales of Washington Irving. Ed. Charles
     Neider. Garden City: Doubleday, 1975. 536-56.

TRANSLATED WORK

Chekhov, Anton. <u>Love and Other Stories</u>. Trans. Constance Garnett. New York: Ecco, 1987.

If your paper focuses on the translation used, cite the translator first.

Garnett, Constance, trans. <u>Love and Other Stories</u>. By Anton Chekhov. New York: Ecco, 1987.

MULTIVOLUME WORK

Risjord, Norman K., ed. <u>America: A History of the United States</u>. 2 vols. Englewood Cliffs: Prentice, 1985.

McKenzie, D. F. "Printing in England from Caxton to Milton." <u>The Age of Shakespeare</u>. Ed. Boris Ford. New York: Penguin, 1982. 207-44. Vol. 2 of <u>The New Pelican Guide to English Literature</u>. 8 vols. 1982-84.

REVISED EDITION

Eble, Kenneth E. <u>The Craft of Teaching</u>. 2nd ed. San Francisco: Jossey, 1988.

Cuddon, J. A., ed. <u>A Dictionary of Literary Terms</u>. Rev. ed. Garden City: Doubleday, 1976.

BOOK IN A SERIES

U.S. Civil Service Commission. <u>Personnel Policies and Practices</u>. Personnel Bibliography Ser. 102. Washington: GPO, 1978.

Listing Printed Sources: Parts of Books

CHAPTER OR SECTION IN A BOOK

Galbraith, John Kenneth. "The Military Power." <u>The Nuclear Crisis Reader</u>. Ed. Gwyn Prins. New York: Vintage, 1984. 197-209.

ESSAY IN AN EDITED COLLECTION

Berthoff, Werner. "The Example of <u>Billy Budd</u>." <u>Twentieth Century Interpretations of</u> Billy Budd: A Collection of Critical Essays. Ed. Howard P. Vincent. Englewood Cliffs: Prentice, 1971. 58-60.

SHORT STORY, POEM, OR PLAY
IN AN EDITED COLLECTION

Le Guin, Ursula K. "Nine Lives." The World Treasury of
    Science Fiction. Ed. Clifton Fadiman. Boston:
    Little, 1989. 572-94.

TWO OR MORE WORKS FROM THE SAME EDITED COLLECTION

The following example shows citations for articles in the collection
Women and Educational Leadership as well as the citation for the collection
itself.

Antonucci, Toni. "The Need for Female Role Models in Ed-
    ucation." Biklen and Brannigan 185-95.

Biklen, Sari Knopp, and Marilyn B. Brannigan, eds. Women
    and Educational Leadership. Lexington: Lexington,
    1980.

Clement, Jacqueline. "Sex Bias in School Administra-
    tion." Biklen and Brannigan 131-37.

Listing Printed Sources: Reference Books

It is unnecessary to supply the editor, publisher, or place of publication for
well-known references such as *Websters, The Random House Dictionary,
World Book Encyclopedia,* and *Encyclopaedia Britannica.* Omit volume and
page numbers when citing a reference that is arranged alphabetically.

SIGNED DICTIONARY ENTRY

Turner, V. W. "Divination." A Dictionary of the Social
    Sciences. Ed. Julius Gould and William L. Kolb.
    New York: Free, 1964.

UNSIGNED DICTIONARY ENTRY

"Organize." Webster's Third New International Diction-
    ary. 1981 ed.

SIGNED ENCYCLOPEDIA ARTICLE

Binder, Raymond C., et al. "Mathematical Aspects of
    Physical Theories." Encyclopaedia Britannica:
    Macropaedia. 1981 ed.

UNSIGNED ENCYCLOPEDIA ARTICLE

"Jellyfish." Encyclopaedia Britannica: Micropaedia.
    1981 ed.

Listing Printed Sources: Periodicals

JOURNAL ARTICLE WITH SEPARATE PAGINATION

To list an article from a journal that paginates each issue of a volume separately, provide the volume number and issue number, separated by a period. If no volume number is available, put the month or season in parentheses before the year.

> Fitzgerald, Kathryn R. "Rhetorical Implications of
>   School Discourse for Writing Placement." Journal of
>   Basic Writing 7.1 (1988): 61-72.

> Fitzgerald, Kathryn R. "Rhetorical Implications of
>   School Discourse for Writing Placement." Journal of
>   Basic Writing 7 (Jan. 1988): 61-72.

JOURNAL ARTICLE WITH CONTINUOUS PAGINATION

In journals with continuous pagination, page numbers run continuously through all issues of a volume. To cite these journals, give the volume number, year, and page numbers.

> Walker, Cheryl. "Feminist Literary Criticism and the Au-
>   thor." Critical Inquiry 16 (1990): 551-71.

SIGNED MAGAZINE ARTICLE

> Alvarez, A. "Sleep." New Yorker 10 Feb. 1992: 85-94.

If the article's page numbers are not numbered consecutively, list the starting page number followed by +.

> Yudkin, Marcia. "Inspiration Made Easy." New Age Aug.
>   1991: 41+.

UNSIGNED MAGAZINE ARTICLE

> "Other Side of Cool." Mother Jones May-June 1992: 19.

SIGNED NEWSPAPER ARTICLE

> Putka, Gary. "Cat and Mouse: SAT Coaching Schools Inten-
>   sify Their Battle with College Board." Wall Street
>   Journal 14 Apr. 1992, eastern ed.: A1+.

> Brindle, David. "Psychiatric Care Crisis Hits Prisons."
>   Manchester Guardian Weekly 15 Dec. 1991: 3.

UNSIGNED NEWSPAPER ARTICLE

> "Israelis Honor Holocaust's Dead." Boston Globe 1 May
>   1992: 4.

SIGNED EDITORIAL

Ferguson, Tim W.   "Tales of the Cat and GM, Joined by a
    Union."   Editorial.   Wall Street Journal 14 Apr.
    1992, eastern ed.: A19.

UNSIGNED EDITORIAL

"Grounding Racism."   Editorial.   Nation 25 Feb. 1991: 1.

PUBLISHED INTERVIEW

Truffaut, François.   Interview.   "Truffaut at Mid-
    Career."   Saturday Review Jan. 1982: 42-45.

Listing Other Printed Sources

PAMPHLET

Association of American Publishers.   An Author's Primer
    to Word Processing.   New York: Assn. of American
    Publishers, 1983.

LETTER

Meyer, Kraig R.   Letter.   Esquire Sept. 1990: 32.

Jones, Sam.   Letter to the author.   3 May 1992.

MATERIAL FOUND WITH A COMPUTER DATABASE

Rocco, Pier L.   "Lithium and Suicidal Behavior in Bipolar
    Patients."   Medical Science Research 19 (1991): 910-
    16.   PsycLIT Disc 2, item 78-34111.

MATERIAL FOUND WITH AN INFORMATION SERVICE
OR COMPUTER DATABASE

Rocco, Pier L.   "Lithium and Suicidal Behavior in Bipolar
    Patients."   Medical Science Research 19 (1991): 910-
    16.   PsycLIT 78-34111.

Listing Nonprint Sources

AUDIOTAPE OR RECORDING

Begin with the name of the speaker, the writer, or the production director,
depending on what you want to emphasize.

Mencken, H. L.   H. L. Mencken Speaking.   Caedmon, TC
    1082, 1960.

```
Yeats, William Butler.  "The Song of the Old Mother."
      The Poems of William Butler Yeats.  Audiotape.  Read
      by William Butler Yeats, Siobhan McKenna, and
      Michael MacLiammoir.  Spoken Arts, SAC 8044, 1974.
```

TELEVISION OR RADIO PROGRAM

```
The Infinite Voyage.  PBS.  WNET, New York.  6 May 1992.
```

```
"A Dangerous Man: Lawrence after Arabia."  With Ralph
      Fiennes and Siddig el Fadil.  Great Performances.
      PBS.  WNET, New York.  6 May 1992.
```

FILM

```
Knights of the Round Table.  Dir. Richard Thorpe.  MGM,
      1953.
```

If you cite a person connected with the film, start with his or her name.

```
Thorpe, Richard, dir.  Knights of the Round Table.  MGM,
      1953.
```

FILMSTRIP, SLIDE PROGRAM, VIDEOTAPE

```
Wildlife Conservation.  Sound filmstrip.  Prod. Wildlife
      Research Group, 1986.  87 fr., 11 min.
```

SPEECH OR LECTURE

```
Hurley, James.  Address.  Opening General Sess. American
      Bar Assn. Convention.  Chicago, 17 Jan. 1987.
```

BROADCAST INTERVIEW

```
Edelman, Marian Wright.  Interview.  WBUR, Boston.  7 May
      1992.
```

PERSONAL INTERVIEW

```
Boyd, Dierdre.  Personal interview.  5 Feb. 1990.

Ladner, John.  Telephone interview.  20 Oct. 1987.
```

CITING SOURCES: ENDNOTES

Some people continue to prefer notes rather than simple parenthetical citations for documentation, especially when the citations need to be long.

   If you use endnotes, you number your citations consecutively in the body
of your text, like this:[1]. You roll your typewriter platen up a notch or learn
the command in your word processing program for superscripts. Then, at the

end of the text, on a new page, you center the title "Notes," double-space, and cite each source, in sequence, with a corresponding number. Double-space the entire list, and indent the first line of each entry five spaces. Unless your instructor prefers otherwise, this method can eliminate the need for a "Works Cited" list since it contains the same publishing information, merely adding the specific page number for each citation. Only the form is slightly different.

A comma separates the authors' names from the title. The publishing information is in parentheses, and the number of the page containing the borrowed information is not set off with a comma or any other punctuation. The note for the first sentence of this paragraph would look like this (this example also shows how to cite a second or later edition of a book):

FIRST REFERENCE TO A WORK

    [1] Joseph Gibaldi and Walter S. Achtert, MLA Handbook for Writers of Research Papers, 3rd ed. (New York: MLA, 1988) 183.

SUBSEQUENT REFERENCES

Should you cite the same work a second time, you use just the authors' last names and a page number.

    [2] Gibaldi and Achtert 181.

Printed Sources: Books

REFERENCES TO MULTIPLE WORKS BY THE SAME AUTHOR

If you have consulted more than one work by the same author (or authors), give full documentation for each one the first time it is mentioned. In subsequent references, include an abbreviated title after the author's name. For instance, if you have previously referred to two books by Iona and Peter Opie, *The Lore and Language of Schoolchildren* and *The Oxford Nursery Rhyme Book,* a later citation might look like this:

    [3] Opie and Opie, Lore 192.

MULTIVOLUME WORK

When you cite a multivolume work, indicate which volume contains the pages from which you have borrowed.

    [4] Francis James Child, ed., The English and Scottish Popular Ballads, vol. 2 (New York: Cooper Square, 1962) 373-76.

WORK IN AN EDITED COLLECTION

    [5] Warner Berthoff, "The Example of Billy Budd," Twentieth-Century Interpretations of Billy Budd: A

Collection of Critical Essays, ed. Howard P. Vincent (Englewood Cliffs: Prentice, 1971) 58-60.

Printed Sources: Periodicals

JOURNAL ARTICLE

6 Carol Cook, "'The Sign and Semblance of Her Honor': Reading Gender Difference in Much Ado about Nothing," PMLA 101 (1986): 200.

NEWSPAPER OR MAGAZINE ARTICLE

7 Richard D. Lamm, "English Comes First," New York Times 1 July 1986, natl. ed.: A23.

8 Robin Morgan, "The World without de Beauvoir," Ms. July 1986: 58.

Other Printed Sources

WORK WITH A CORPORATE AUTHOR

9 American Red Cross, Lifesaving: Rescue and Water Safety (New York: Doubleday, 1974) 181.

GOVERNMENT DOCUMENT

10 United States, Dept. of Health and Human Services, Mosquito Control Measures in Gulf Coast States (Washington: GPO, 1986) 25.

UNKNOWN AUTHOR

11 Alcoholism and You (Pearl Island: Okra, 1986) 3.

Nonprint Sources

AUDIOTAPE OR RECORDING

12 H. L. Mencken, H. L. Mencken Speaking, Caedmon, TC 1082, 1960.

13 William Butler Yeats, "The Song of the Old Mother," The Poems of William Butler Yeats, audiotape, read by William Butler Yeats, Siobhan McKenna, and Michael MacLiammoir, Spoken Arts, SAC 8044, 1974.

FILMSTRIP, SLIDE PROGRAM, VIDEOTAPE

[14] <u>Wildlife Conservation</u>, sound filmstrip, prod. Wildlife Research Group, 1986 (87 fr., 11 min.).

LECTURE

[15] Lois DeBakey, "The Intolerable Wrestle with Words and Meaning," International Technical Communication Conference, Washington, 2 May 1971.

PERSONAL COMMUNICATION

[16] Helen Nearing, personal interview, 12 Nov. 1985.

[17] John Bowlby, telephone interview, 3 June 1983.

[18] Charles G. Sherwood, letter to the author, 29 Sept. 1986.

For more detailed information about using endnotes to cite sources, see the *MLA Handbook for Writers of Research Papers.*

CITING SOURCES: APA STYLE

The American Psychological Association (APA) supplies a guide to the style most commonly used in the social sciences. This style is set forth in its *Publication Manual,* 3rd ed. (Washington, DC: APA, 1983). As in MLA style, APA citations are placed in parentheses in the body of the text.

Citing Printed Sources

To cite a study in the APA style, you usually place in parentheses the author's last name and the year the source was published. Do this as close as possible to your mention of the information you have borrowed.

SINGLE AUTHOR

A number of experts now believe that cognitive development begins much earlier than Piaget had thought (Gelman, 1978).

Notice that, because it is often necessary to refer to a whole study, only the author's name and the publication year are generally included in the citation. If the author's name appears in the body of the text, only the date is given in parentheses.

As Gelman (1978) points out, a number of experts now believe that cognitive development begins much earlier than
Piaget had thought.

If you do refer to a specific page, use "p." and set it off with a comma.

Dean Rusk's exposure to Nazi power in Europe in the 1930s
seems to have permanently influenced his attitude toward
appeasement (Karnow, 1991, p. 194).

When the author's name appears in the text, the page number still belongs
in parentheses after the cited material.

Karnow (1991) maintains that Dean Rusk's exposure to Nazi
power in Europe in the 1930s "scarred his mind" (p. 194).

If you set off a long quotation in a block, the author's name and the
publication year can follow the quotation with no additional period.

At least one critic maintains that Dean Rusk's exposure
to Nazi power in Europe in the 1930s permanently influenced his attitude toward appeasement:

> Then came the moment that transformed his life and
> his thinking. He won a Rhodes scholarship to Ox-
> ford. More important, his exposure to Europe in the
> early 1930s, as the Nazis consolidated their power
> in Germany, scarred his mind, leading him to share
> Acheson's hostility to appeasement in any form any-
> where. (Karnow, 1983, p. 194)

TWO AUTHORS

Refer to coauthors by their last names, in the order in which they appear
in the book or article you cite. Join the names by "and" if you mention them
in the body of your text, by an ampersand ("&") if your citation is in parentheses.

Ex-mental patients released from institutions but given
no follow-up care will almost surely fail to cope with
the stresses of living on their own (Bassuk & Gerson,
1978).

Bassuk and Gerson (1978) hold out little hope for ex-
mental patients who are released from institutions but
are given no follow-up care.

THREE OR MORE AUTHORS

When a book or article you cite has three or more authors (but fewer than six), include all the last names in your first reference only. In referring to the same source again, use the first author's name only, followed by "et al.," which means "and others." For *more* than six authors, use "et al." even in the first reference.

> In one study, the IQs of adopted children were found to correlate more closely with the IQs of their biological mothers than with those of their adoptive mothers (Horn, Loehlin, & Wellerman, 1975).

> Later studies have challenged the genetic view advanced by Wesson et al. (1978) by citing, among other things, selective placement on the part of adoption agencies.

CORPORATE AUTHOR

> There are three signs of oxygen deprivation (American Red Cross, 1974).

GOVERNMENT DOCUMENT

In the first citation in your text, identify the document by originating agency, followed by its abbreviation (if any) and year of publication (and page number, if appropriate).

> Clearly, it is of paramount importance to stop the spread of mosquito-borne diseases (Department of Health and Human Services [DHHS], 1986, p. 25).

Later citations would use just the abbreviation for the agency and the date (DHHS, 1986).

UNKNOWN AUTHOR

When you cite an anonymous work, identify it with a short title and a date.

> There are questions people can ask themselves if they suspect their drinking has gotten out of hand (Alcoholism, 1986).

MULTIPLE WORKS BY THE SAME AUTHOR

Identifying sources with dates is especially useful when you need to cite more than one work by the same author.

> One nuclear energy proponent for years has insisted on the importance of tight controls for the industry (Wein-

```
berg, 1972). . . . He goes so far as to call on utility
companies to insure each reactor with their own funds
(Weinberg, 1977).
```

When citing two or more sources written by the same author during the same year, arrange the titles alphabetically in the reference list (see p. 725) and identify each with a lowercase letter placed after the date (1976a, 1976b, 1976c, and so on). Identify them the same way in your text.

```
Those who advocate the "genesis strategy" would have the
world store up food in preparation for future climatic
changes (Schneider, 1976b).
```

Citing Nonprint Sources

PERSONAL INTERVIEW

Personal communications are not given in the reference list according to APA style. But in the text of your paper, you should include the initials and surname of your communicator, with the date remembered as exactly as possible.

```
C. G. Sherwood (personal communication, September 29,
1986) has specific suggestions about the market in
Belgium.
```

```
It is important to keep in mind the cultural differences
between countries, especially in this case the differ-
ences between the United States and Belgium (C. G. Sher-
wood, personal communication, September 29, 1986).
```

LISTING SOURCES: APA STYLE

If you're using APA guidelines (which you might do in listing both field and library materials), each entry should contain most of the same information given in an MLA citation, but the format is slightly different. In the APA style, the list of works cited is called "References" and appears at the end of the text. For entries that run past the first line, indent subsequent lines three spaces.

Organize your list alphabetically by author. The year appears immediately following the author's name, in parentheses. In the title only the first word, proper names, and the word following a colon are capitalized. For the author's first and middle names, only initials are used. Note that APA style uses a more complete name for a publisher (including "Press") than does MLA style.

Listing Printed Sources: Books

SINGLE AUTHOR

Karnow, S. (1983). <u>Vietnam: A history</u>. New York: Viking
    Press.

TWO OR MORE AUTHORS

Miller, G. A., Galanter, E., & Pribram, K. H. (1960).
    <u>Plans and the structure of behavior</u>. New York: Holt,
    Rinehart and Winston.

CORPORATE AUTHOR

American Red Cross. (1974). <u>Lifesaving: Rescue and</u>
    <u>water safety</u>. New York: Doubleday.

UNKNOWN AUTHOR

<u>Alcoholism and you</u>. (1986). Pearl Island: Okra Press.

MULTIPLE WORKS BY THE SAME AUTHOR,
PUBLISHED DURING THE SAME YEAR

Arrange the titles alphabetically and identify their order with lowercase
letters beginning with "a."

Schneider, S. H. (1976a). <u>Climate change and the world</u>
    <u>predicament: A case study for interdisciplinary</u>
    <u>research</u>. Boulder, CO: National Center for Atmos-
    pheric Research.

Schneider, S. H. (1976b). <u>The genesis strategy: Climate</u>
    <u>and global survival</u>. New York: Plenum Press.

CHAPTER OR SECTION OF A BOOK

Galbraith, J. K. (1984). The military power. In Gwyn
    Prins (Ed.), <u>The nuclear crisis reader</u> (pp. 197-209).
    New York: Vintage.

WORK IN AN EDITED COLLECTION

Lewontin, R. C. (1976). Race and intelligence. In
    N. J. Block & G. Dworkin (Eds.), <u>The IQ controversy</u>
    (pp. 78-92). New York: Pantheon.

Listing Printed Sources: Periodicals

ARTICLE FROM A JOURNAL WITH SEPARATE PAGINATION

Bassuk, E. L., & Gerson, S. (1978, February). Deinsti-

tutionalization and mental health services. Scientific American, pp. 46-53.

ARTICLE FROM A JOURNAL WITH CONTINUOUS PAGINATION

Gelman, R. (1978). Cognitive development. Annual Review of Psychology, 29, 297-332.

MAGAZINE ARTICLE

Laycock, G. (1991, September-October). Good times are
killing the Keys. Audubon, pp. 38-49.

SIGNED NEWSPAPER ARTICLE

Auerbach, J. D. (1986, June 22). Nuclear freeze at a
crossroads. Boston Globe, p. A19.

UNSIGNED NEWSPAPER ARTICLE

Human rights and public health. (1991, May 5). Manches-
ter Guardian, p. 16.

Listing Other Printed Sources

GOVERNMENT DOCUMENT

Start with the name of the department and then give the date of publication, the title (and author, if any), identifying number, and publisher.

Department of Health and Human Services. (1986). Mosquito control measures in Gulf Coast states (DHHW Publication No. F 82-06000). Washington, DC: U.S.
Government Printing Office.

MATERIAL FOUND WITH AN INFORMATION SERVICE
OR COMPUTER DATABASE

Rocco, P. L. (1991). Lithium and suicidal behavior in
bipolar patients. Medical Science Research, 19,
910-916. (PsycLIT Accession No. 78-34111).

Listing Nonprint Sources

RECORDING

Mencken, H. L. (Interviewee), with Donald Howe Kirkley,
Sr. (Interviewer). (1960). H. L. Mencken speaking
(Record No. TC 1082). New York: Caedmon.

Burns, K. (Producer). (1992). <u>Empire of the air</u>
    [Videotape].

The location of the distributor, if it is known, appears at the end of the citation.

FILM OR FILMSTRIP

Wildlife Research Group (Producer). (1986). <u>Wildlife
    conservation</u>. [Sound filmstrip].

PERSONAL INTERVIEW

The newest APA guidelines suggest omitting personal interviews from the reference list because they do not provide recoverable data. You would of course mention such sources in the body of your paper — even if you do so simply, as Jamie Merisotis does in reporting his conversations with bail bondsmen ("One bondsman stated . . .").

A NOTE ON THE NUMBER SYSTEM OF DOCUMENTATION

The MLA style is an example of the *author/page* approach to in-text citation; the APA style is an example of the *author/date* approach. A third common approach to in-text citation that you may encounter in your reading, and which you may be required to use in your writing, is the *number system.* This approach, which is often employed in the sciences and technologies, assigns a number to each source in a reference list. As each source is referred to in the text, the number is cited:

Females dominate males in spotted hyena clans (1).

Depending on the writer's preference or the guidelines prescribed, the number may appear in parentheses, (1); brackets, [2]; as superscript, ^{3}; or underlined in parentheses, (4).

In the sciences and technologies, where articles and books frequently have multiple authors, the number system is less cumbersome than author/page or author/date systems. It allows a writer to cite multiple sources with minimal disruption to a sentence:

Monogamous behavior among spectral tarsiers (2, 3) and
tree shrews (6, 7, 12) has been well documented.

As you can see, the number system is also less immediately informative than author/page or author/date systems. The writer generally cites whole works, not pages within works, and rarely quotes directly. Still, number system citations can be more specific and informative, if necessary:

Sagan writes that "when Velikovsky is original he is very
likely wrong" (8, p. 95).

This citation incorporates an author's name, a page reference, and a quotation.

In the number system, in-text citations are keyed to a numbered list of references that is included at the end of the paper. The list is organized either alphabetically according to author, or according to the order in which the works were cited in the text of the paper. In either case, if a source is referred to more than once in the text, the same reference number is cited each time. The list of references is given a title such as "References Cited" or "Literature Cited."

Here are a few sample Reference Cited entries that use the number system.

BOOK

1. Kruuk, H. The spotted hyena. Chicago: Univ. of Chicago Press; 1972.

PART OF A BOOK

2. Niemitz, C. Outline of the behavior of <u>Tarsius bancanus</u>. In: Doyle, G.; Martin, R. D., eds. The study of prosimian behavior. New York: Academic Press; 1979:p. 631–660.

JOURNAL ARTICLE

3. Tilson, R. L.; Tenaza, R. R. Monogamy and duetting in an old world monkey. Nat. 263:320–321; 1976.

These samples follow the recommendations of the *CBE Style Manual* of the Council of Biology Editors. Note that the title of the journal *Nature* has been abbreviated in the third reference. Because many scientific journals have lengthy titles, some style guides in the sciences require that the journal titles in the References Cited list be abbreviated according to the recommendations of the *American National Standard for Abbreviations of Titles and Periodicals.*

Although there are style manuals for every branch of science and technology, and variations in style among different publications within every branch, the basic features of the number system — in-text numbers and a numbered reference list — stay the same. If you are assigned a paper using the number system, be sure to ask the instructor to specify the style sheet or manual guidelines you are expected to follow.

A
WRITER'S
HANDBOOK

HANDBOOK

LADY: Little boy, it's cold out! Where's your coat?

BOY: I ain't got none.

LADY: "Ain't got none?" My stars, where's your grammar?

BOY: She's home settin' by the TV watchin' *Murphy Brown*.

In this dialogue, the lady speaks of *grammar* as a set of rules for using language, like chalk-drawn lines that writers and speakers of English must toe. She seems more shocked by the boy's uttering the forbidden word *ain't* than by his running around coatless in the cold. We can describe her approach as *prescriptive*: there are right ways and wrong ways to use the English language.

An alternative is a *descriptive* approach: **grammar** is that study of language concerned with the regular, systematic, and predictable ways in which words work together. How do speakers of English create sentences? How do they understand each other's sentences? In the last fifty years, grammarians haven't been laying down strict rules so much as they have been listening, observing, and trying to define those implicit rules by which the language operates.

From this point of view, the boy in the street speaks according to regular patterns, just as the lady does. His grammar may be different from hers, or perhaps less efficient as a means of communication, but it too consists of regular patterns of usage. Indeed, every speaker of English, even a child, commands a grammatical system of tremendous complexity.

Take the sentence "A bear is occupying a telephone booth while a tourist impatiently waits in line." In theory, there are nineteen billion different ways to state the idea in that sentence.[1] (Another is "A tourist fumes while he waits for a bear to finish yakking on a pay phone.") How do we understand a unique sentence like that one? For we do understand it, even though we have never heard it before — not in those very same words, not in the very same order.

To begin with, we recognize familiar words and we know their meanings. Just as significantly, we recognize grammatical structures. As we read or hear the sentence, we know that it contains a familiar pattern of **syntax**, or word order. This meaningful order helps the sentence make sense to us.

Ordinarily, we aren't even conscious of such an order, for we don't need to think about it; but it is there. To notice it, all we need do is rearrange the words of our sentence:

Telephone a impatiently line in waits tourist bear a occupying is a booth while.

The result is nonsense: it defies English grammar. The would-be sentence doesn't follow familiar rules or meet our expectations of order.

[1]Richard Ohmann, "Grammar and Meaning," *The American Heritage Dictionary* (Boston: Houghton Mifflin, 1979), pp. xxxi–xxxii.

Hundreds of times a day, with wonderful efficiency, we perform tasks of understanding and of sentence construction more complex than any computer can even try. (Were artificial intelligence equally far advanced, a computer could not only scan books but make sense of them for you, and it could put together words sensitively enough to write your papers.) Indeed, linguist Noam Chomsky has suggested that the human brain probably contains some kind of language-grasping structure. Built into us before birth, it enables us to understand what we hear (whether that is English, Chinese, or Swahili) and equips us to put together our own sentences. Certainly some kind of language-grasping ability is part of our makeup. For we can understand and create sentences even as toddlers, before we know anything about "grammar."

Why, then, think about grammar in college? Isn't it entirely possible to write well without contemplating grammar at all? Yes. If your innate sense of grammar is reliable, you can write clearly and logically and forcefully without knowing a predicate nominative from a handsaw. Many of the writers featured in current magazines and newspapers would be hard pressed to name all the parts of speech they use. Most successful writers, though, have been practicing for so many years that grammar has become second nature to them. Few students we know have a built-in sense so infallible. When you doubt a word or a construction, a glance in a handbook can clear up your confusion and restore your confidence — just as referring to a dictionary can help your spelling.

Besides helping us solve problems and bolstering our self-confidence, the study of grammar can be unexpectedly satisfying. Some students enjoy knowing, for instance, exactly why it makes more sense to say "Our soccer team is better than any other" than to say "Our soccer team is better than any." (For a grammatical reason, see p. H–95.) After all, to write without knowledge of grammar is a little like driving a car without caring what goes on under the hood. Most of the time, you can drive around without knowing a thing except how to steer and brake and tromp on the gas; but at times you may thank your stars you know how a carburetor works and, when it won't work, what to do about it.

More complex than a car, the English language provides subtler challenges. For one thing, merely following accepted practices doesn't guarantee good writing. The so-called grammatical conventions you'll find in this handbook are not mechanical specifications, but accepted ways in which skilled writers and speakers put words together to convey meaning efficiently and clearly. They come from observations of what educated, accomplished users of English actually do — how they utilize the language to communicate their ideas successfully. The amateur writer can learn by following their example, just as an amateur athlete, artist, or even auto mechanic can learn by watching the professionals. Knowing how the English language works, and how its parts get along together, is of enormous value to you as a writer. Once you understand what goes on under the hood, so to speak, you will have a keener sense of words and of why at times they won't go — so that when you write, you drive smoothly to your destination.

CHAPTER 31

Basic Grammar

1 PARTS OF SPEECH

Grammar deals with the elements that make up sentences. These elements may be single words or whole phrases and clauses. Let's look first at the simplest building blocks of sentences: words.

We sort words into eight classes: the **parts of speech**. We tell them apart by their functions (the jobs they do in sentences), by their forms, and by their meanings. Like most classifications, the parts of speech are a convenience: it is easier to refer to *an adjective modifying a noun* than "that word there that tells something about that thing." Here is a quick review of the celebrated eight.

1a *Nouns*

A **noun** names. A **common noun** names a general class of person (*clergyman, believer*), place (*town, dormitory*), thing (*car, dog*), or concept (*freedom, industrialization*). A **proper noun** names a specific person, place, thing, or concept: *Billy Graham, Milwaukee, Cadillac, New Deal*.

1b *Pronouns*

A **pronoun** stands in place of a noun. Without pronouns, most writing would be top-heavy with repeated nouns. Imagine writing an essay on Martin Luther King, Jr., in which you had to say "Martin Luther King, Jr." or "the clergyman and civil rights leader" every time you mentioned your subject. Instead, you can handily use *personal pronouns* (*he* and *him*) and the *possessive pronoun* (*his*).

There are nine types of pronouns.

1. **Personal pronouns** (*I, you, it*) stand for nouns that name persons or things. "Mark awoke slowly, but suddenly *he* bolted from the bed."

2. **Possessive pronouns** (*his, our/ours*) are a form of personal pronoun showing ownership. They are used in place of nouns or as adjectives modifying nouns. "*His* trophy is on the left; *hers* is on the right."

3. **Intensive pronouns** (*yourself, themselves*) emphasize a noun or another pronoun. "Michael Jackson *himself* opened the door."

4. **Relative pronouns** (*who, that, which*) start a subordinate clause (see p. H–21) that functions as an adjective modifying a noun or pronoun in another clause. "The gift *that* you give them ought to be handsome."

5. **Reflexive pronouns** have the same form as intensive pronouns but are used as objects referring back to subjects. "She helped *herself*."

6. **Interrogative pronouns** (*who, what*) ask or introduce questions. "*What* did you give them?"

7. **Indefinite pronouns** (*any, no one*) stand for persons or things not specified. "*No one* ran because of the rain."

8. **Demonstrative pronouns** (*this, those*) point to nouns. "*That's* the man, officer!"

9. **Reciprocal pronouns** (*each other, one another*) express relationship between two or more nouns or other pronouns. "Joe and Donna looked at *each other* with complete understanding."

PRONOUNS

	SINGULAR	PLURAL
PERSONAL PRONOUNS		
First person	I, me	we, us
Second person	you	you
Third person	he, she, it, him, her	they, them
POSSESSIVE PRONOUNS		
First person	my, mine	our, ours
Second person	your, yours	your, yours
Third person	his, her, hers, its	their, theirs

INTENSIVE AND REFLEXIVE PRONOUNS

First person	myself	ourselves
Second person	yourself	yourselves
Third person	himself, herself, itself	themselves

RELATIVE PRONOUNS

that, what, whatever, which, who, whoever, whom, whomever, whose

INTERROGATIVE PRONOUNS

what, which, who, whom, whose

INDEFINITE PRONOUNS

all, another, any, anybody, anyone, anything, both, each, either, everybody, everyone, everything, few, many, neither, nobody, none, no one, nothing, one, several, some, somebody, someone, something

DEMONSTRATIVE PRONOUNS

such, that, these, this, those

RECIPROCAL PRONOUNS

each other, one another

Exercise 1–1: Identifying Nouns and Pronouns

Underline the nouns and pronouns in the following sentences. Identify each noun as common or proper. Identify the type of each pronoun (personal, possessive, relative, and so on). Answers for the lettered sentences appear in the back of the book. Example:

> Little Boy Blue, come blow your horn.
>
> Little Boy Blue [proper noun], come blow your [possessive pronoun] horn [common noun].

a. If Lois sells two paintings, her husband will be delighted.

b. The price seems high, but Lois herself makes only a small profit.

c. The bulk of the money that she earns pays for her supplies.

d. Lewis wants to sell his Corvette to someone who appreciates it.

e. I can't help myself; I love you and no one else.

1. Which do you yourself prefer?

2. Is that the woman to whom Mr. Snopes spoke on the phone?

3. I heard that Linda plans to buy herself the first pair of jeans that fits her.

4. Why don't you give her the old Calvin Kleins that don't fit you anymore?

5. The members of the task force congratulated one another for meeting the deadline.

1c *Verbs*

A **verb** shows action ("The cow *jumped* over the moon") or a state of being ("The cow *is* brown," "The cow *felt* frisky").

Verbs like *is* or *felt* often show a state of being by linking the sentence's subject with another word that renames or describes it, as in the last two examples. Such verbs are called **linking verbs**. (See also 5a.)

A verb that shows action is called **transitive** when it has a direct object.

> VT   DO
> Jim *hit* the *ball* hard.

> VT   DO
> *Does* she *resemble* her *mother?*

A transitive verb must have an object to complete its meaning. You can't write just *Jim hit* or *Does she resemble?* But if a verb is complete in itself and needs no object, we call it **intransitive**.

> The surgeon *paused.*

> Sally *lives* on Boilermaker Street.

Look up a verb in your dictionary and you will find it classified *vt* (for "verb, transitive") or *vi* (for "verb, intransitive"). Many verbs can work either way.

> The bus *stopped.*

> The driver *stopped* the bus.

Not all verbs consist of just one word. The **main verb** in a sentence identifies the central action (*hit, stopped*). We can show variations on this action by adding **helping verbs**, such as *do, can, have,* or *will.* The main verb with its helping verbs is the *complete verb* or *verb phrase.*

> HV   MV
> Alan *did* not *hit* the ball.

> ┌─HV─┐ MV
> The bus *will have stopped* six times before we reach Main Street.

HELPING VERBS

There are twenty-three helping verbs in English. Fourteen of them can also function as main verbs:

be, is, am, are, was, were, being, been
do, does, did
have, has, had

The other nine can function only as helping verbs, never as main verbs:

can, could, should, would, may, might, must, shall, will

Exercise 1–2: Identifying Verbs

Underline the verbs in the following sentences. Identify each one as transitive (VT), intransitive (VI), linking (LV), or helping (HV). Answers for the lettered sentences appear in the back of the book. Example:

Marie released the ball too early and it rolled into the gutter.

        VT   VI
Marie released the ball too early and it rolled into the gutter.

a. When Jorge goes to Providence, Jim will accompany him.
b. Our coach dislikes players who are arrogant.
c. Never give yellow roses to a French friend: they symbolize infidelity.
d. The president should have spent more time on our proposal.
e. Harry dreams of becoming a famous novelist, but he rarely reads fiction.

1. If your letter comes in today's mail, I will mail you an answer tomorrow.
2. Louise introduced herself to Leon while he was walking his dog.
3. Leon is the musician whose band she likes so much.
4. Woodpeckers must have a padded lining inside their skulls.
5. If the sky were not so cloudy, would the ocean look blue?

1d Adjectives

An **adjective** describes, or modifies, a noun or a pronoun. In doing so it often answers the question Which? or What kind? Usually an adjective is a single word.

War is a *primitive* activity.
Young men kill other *young* men.
The *small brown* cow let out a *lackluster* moo.

ARTICLES

In the preceding examples, some grammarians would classify *the* and *a* as adjectives. Others would call them by a special name: *articles. The* is called the **definite article** because it indicates one particular item.

I need to borrow *the* car.

A and *an* are the **indefinite articles** because they indicate any old whatever-it-is.

I need to borrow *a* car.

1e Adverbs

An **adverb** modifies a verb, an adjective, or another adverb.

The cow bawled *loudly*. [The adverb *loudly* modifies the verb *bawled*.]

The cow bawled *very loudly indeed.* [Three adverbs in a row: *loudly* modifies the verb *bawled,* while *very* and *indeed* modify the adverb *loudly.*]

Adverbs often flesh out thoughts by showing how, when, or where an action happens.

The cow *quickly* [how] galloped *outside* [where] and *immediately* [when] kicked the farmer.

Exercise 1–3: Identifying Adjectives and Adverbs

Underline and identify the adjectives, definite articles, indefinite articles, and adverbs in the following sentences. For each adverb, draw an arrow to the word it modifies and mark that word as a verb, adjective, or adverb. Answers for the lettered exercises appear in the back of the book. Example:

The opera was too long, but Judith sang beautifully.

ADV ADJ   V   ADV

The opera was <u>too</u> long, but Judith <u>sang</u> beautifully.

a. After such a mild winter, the environmental experts greatly fear a drought.
b. James's elderly grandparents are incredibly mobile for their years.
c. The wildly beautiful Natasha often made wise men act foolishly.
d. She had a very short life, but she lived it fully.
e. We were absolutely delighted to get tickets to such a lovely play.

1. The character of Mercutio is not bad; the actor just played him badly.
2. The part of Juliet, in contrast, was remarkably well acted.
3. With someone so young in the role of Juliet, Romeo probably should have been younger.
4. My favorite parts are the romantic scenes.
5. Angela prefers the many comical scenes.

1f Prepositions

A **preposition** is a transitional word, usually short, that leads into a phrase. The preposition and its object (a noun or pronoun), plus any modifiers, form a **prepositional phrase**: *in the bar, under a rickety table, with you.*

A prepositional phrase can function as an adjective or an adverb. When it modifies a noun or pronoun, a prepositional phrase is called an **adjective phrase**.

I want a room *with a view.* [The adjective phrase *with a view* modifies the noun *room.*]

Everybody *in Hillsdale* knows Big Jake. [The adjective phrase *in Hillsdale* modifies the pronoun *Everybody.*]

When it modifies a verb, an adjective, or an adverb, a prepositional phrase is called an **adverb phrase**.

> Jarvis, the play reviewer, always leaves *after the first act.* [The adverb phrase *after the first act* modifies the verb *leaves.*]
>
> Alice is miserable *without you.* [The adverb phrase *without you* modifies the adjective *miserable.*]
>
> Ken works far *from home.* [The adverb phrase *from home* modifies the adverb *far.*]

There are dozens of prepositions in English. The chart includes the most common ones. Notice that some prepositions consist of more than one word. Also, some prepositions occasionally play other roles: *since,* for example, can be a preposition (*I've known him since childhood*), or an adverb (*He has since left town*), or a subordinating conjunction (*Let's go, since there's nothing to do here*).

COMMON PREPOSITIONS

about	below	except for	on	to
above	beneath	for	onto	toward
according to	beside	from	opposite	under
across	besides	in	out	underneath
after	between	in addition to	outside	unlike
against	beyond	inside	over	until
along	but (except)	in spite of	past	up
among	by	instead of	plus	upon
around	concerning	into	regarding	with
as	considering	like	since	within
at	despite	near	than	without
because of	down	next to	through	
before	during	of	throughout	
behind	except	off	till	

Exercise 1–4: Identifying Prepositional Phrases

Underline each prepositional phrase in the following sentences, and identify it as an adjective or adverb phrase. Circle the preposition. Answers for the lettered sentences appear in the back of the book. Example:

> (In) the beginning was the Word.
>
> In the beginning was the Word. [Adverb phrase.]

a. Rarely has anyone ever behaved so rudely to me.

b. The muffin on the table was supposed to be Jeffrey's.

c. Ann warned us before the meeting that her proposal might cause trouble.

   d. She presented it strictly according to the rules, but some committee members tried to block the discussion.

   e. My belief is that all but a few troublemakers will be reasonable once they understand her position.

  1. The politicians at City Hall would welcome a chance to intervene.

  2. Let's stop beating around the bush and make some decisions.

  3. Luis wants to go to the game this afternoon.

  4. From his seat beyond the foul pole he can hardly see the batter.

  5. I hope he can find an apartment in this neighborhood so we can see him more often.

1g *Conjunctions*

A **conjunction** links words or groups of words and connects them in sense.

A **coordinating conjunction** is a one-syllable word that joins elements with equal or near-equal importance: "Jack *and* Jill," "Sink *or* swim."

> COORDINATING CONJUNCTIONS
>
> and, but, for, nor, or, so, yet

A word used to make one clause dependent on, or subordinate to, another is called a **subordinating conjunction**.

Before we left the party, six people had fainted.

They passed out *because* Roger had spiked the punch.

I heard *that* they went looking for him the next day.

> COMMON SUBORDINATING CONJUNCTIONS
>
> | | | | |
> |---|---|---|---|
> | after | even if | since | when |
> | although | even though | so | whenever |
> | as | how | so that | where |
> | as if | if | than | wherever |
> | as soon as | in order that | that | whether |
> | as though | once | though | while |
> | because | provided that | unless | why |
> | before | rather than | until | |

Some conjunctions consist of paired words, such as *either . . . or*, that appear separately but work together to join elements of a sentence. Such a pair is called a **correlative conjunction**.

Not only for her money *but also* for her cooking, Augustus courted Serena.

Neither his friends *nor* hers thought the marriage would last.

When you use a correlative conjunction, remember to complete the pair.

INCOMPLETE   *Not only* was Robert saving money for his college tuition, he was saving for a new car.

REVISED   *Not only* was Robert saving money for his college tuition, *but* he was *also* saving for a new car.

CORRELATIVE CONJUNCTIONS

as . . . as	just as . . . so	not only . . . but also
both . . . and	neither . . . nor	whether . . . or
either . . . or	not . . . but	

Certain adverbs also can function as conjunctions. Called **conjunctive adverbs**, these linking words show a relationship between two ideas, such as addition (*also, besides*), comparison (*likewise, similarly*), contrast (*instead, however*), emphasis (*namely, certainly*), cause and effect (*thus, therefore*), or time (*finally, subsequently*).

Armando is a serious student; *therefore,* he studies every day.

COMMON CONJUNCTIVE ADVERBS

accordingly	furthermore	moreover	then
also	hence	nevertheless	thereafter
anyway	however	next	therefore
as	incidentally	nonetheless	thus
besides	indeed	now	undoubtedly
certainly	instead	otherwise	
consequently	likewise	similarly	
finally	meanwhile	still	

1h Interjections

An **interjection** inserts an outburst of feeling at the beginning, middle, or end of a sentence.

I'd go, but, *oh,* I don't want to.

Ow! What torture it was to read that essay!

There are pigeons on the grass, *alas.*

An entire phrase can work as an interjection.

Who *the dickens* are you?

What *in the world* is my term paper doing in the waste basket?

Exercise 1–5: Identifying Conjunctions and Interjections

Underline and identify the conjunctions and interjections in the following sentences. Mark each conjunction as coordinating, subordinating, or correlative. Answers for the lettered sentences appear in the back of the book. Example:

> Do we have to eat liver and onions again, for heaven's sake?

>   COORD CONJ   INTERJ
> Do we have to eat liver <u>and</u> onions again, <u>for heaven's sake</u>?

a. Oh, well, the team will do better when Smoots gets back in the game.

b. According to Polonius and many others, neither borrowing nor lending is wise.

c. Geraldine and her sister took both piano and ballet lessons.

d. Holy mackerel, what a big fish!

e. Although time and tide wait for no man, Juan is taking hours to launch his boat.

1. I'll dive in if you will, but, oh, that water's cold!

2. Neither Larry's father nor Kevin's is tall, yet both boys grew up to be over six feet tall.

3. How in the world are you and Elwood going to patch up your differences if neither of you will talk to the other?

4. While I can't eat either potato chips or pretzels, I love peanuts.

5. Susan and Lee enjoy their Spanish class more than they expected.

Exercise 1–6: Identifying Parts of Speech

Identify the part of speech of each underlined word in the following passages. Answers for the lettered words appear in the back of the book. Example:

> <u>We</u> <u>live</u> by <u>our</u> imaginations, by our admirations, by our <u>sentiments</u>.
>   —Ralph Waldo Emerson, "Illusions," in *The Conduct of Life*
> <u>We</u>: pronoun; <u>live</u>: verb; <u>our</u>: pronoun; <u>sentiments</u>: noun.

A. It is a mellow day, <u>very</u> <u>gentle</u>. The ash has lost its leaves and <u>when</u> I went
                    a.   **b.**   **c.**

out to get the mail <u>and</u> stopped to look <u>up</u> at <u>it</u>, I <u>rejoiced</u> to think that soon
                    d.   **e.** **1.**   **2.**

<u>everything</u> here will be honed down to structure. It is all a rich <u>farewell</u> now to
  3.   **4.**

leaves, to color. I think <u>of</u> the trees and how <u>simply</u> they let go, let fall the riches of
                    5.   **6.**

a season, how <u>without</u> grief (it seems) they <u>can</u> let go and go <u>deep</u> into <u>their</u> roots
         7.   **8.**   **9.**   **10.**

for renewal and sleep.

            —May Sarton, *Journal of a Solitude,* October 6, 1977

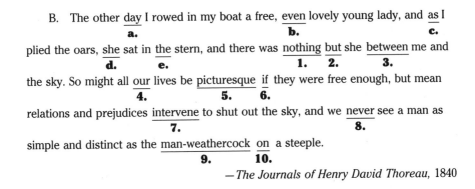

B. The other <u>day</u> I rowed in my boat a free, <u>even</u> lovely young lady, and <u>as</u> I
a.   b.   c.

plied the oars, <u>she</u> sat in <u>the</u> stern, and there was <u>nothing</u> <u>but</u> she <u>between</u> me and
d.   e.   1.   2.   3.

the sky. So might all <u>our</u> lives be <u>picturesque</u> <u>if</u> they were free enough, but mean
4.   5.   6.

relations and prejudices <u>intervene</u> to shut out the sky, and we <u>never</u> see a man as
7.   8.

simple and distinct as the <u>man-weathercock</u> <u>on</u> a steeple.
9.   10.

—The Journals of Henry David Thoreau, 1840

2   SENTENCE STRUCTURE

PARTS OF SENTENCES

Every sentence has two basic parts: a subject and a predicate. The *subject* names something—a person, an object, an idea, a situation. The *predicate* makes an assertion about the subject. Any word group that is missing either of these elements is not a complete sentence.

SENTENCE PARTS AT A GLANCE

The **subject** of a sentence identifies some person, place, thing, activity, or idea.

The **predicate** of a sentence makes an assertion about the subject.

An **object** is the target or recipient of the action described by a verb.

A **complement** renames or describes a subject or object.

For basic sentence patterns, see page H–19.

Both subject and predicate may consist of either one word or a group of words. A one-word subject is always a noun or pronoun; a one-word predicate is always a verb.

SUBJ PRED
Birds fly.

Many subjects and most predicates contain other elements as well, such as modifiers, objects, and complements. A modifier (such as an adjective or adverb) provides more information about the subject or some part of the predicate. A *direct* or *indirect object*, which always appears in the predicate, is the target or recipient of the action indicated by the verb. A *complement*, which also appears in the predicate, renames or describes the sentence's subject or object.

Let's look more closely at subjects, predicates, objects, and complements. Then we can explore the various ways of combining these elements in sentences.

2a *Subject*

The **subject** of a sentence identifies some person, place, thing, activity, or idea. Often the subject is the agent of the action identified by the predicate ("*Jill* hit the ball"). Sometimes the subject is the receiver of the action of the predicate ("The *ball* was hit by Jill"; "*Baseball* came up for discussion"). Because the subject names something, it almost always is (or includes) a noun or pronoun. That noun or pronoun is the **simple subject**.

> *Queen Elizabeth* waved to the crowd.
>
> *I* waved back.

Often a subject includes additional nouns or pronouns, modifiers, or both. A subject that consists of two or more nouns or pronouns linked by a conjunction is called a **compound subject**.

> *The Queen and I* exchanged waves.
>
> *My mother, my father, and my sister* just stood and stared.

The **complete subject** consists of the simple or compound subject plus any words that modify it.

> *The imposing, world-famous Queen* smiled at me.
>
> *Prince Charles on her left and Princess Anne on her right* didn't notice me.

Occasionally a subject is a phrase or clause that contains no nouns at all.

> *Whether or not to smile back* was the question.

In a command, the subject is understood to be *you*, even though the word does not appear in the sentence.

> Don't [*you*] stand so close to me.

2b *Predicate*

The **predicate** of a sentence makes an assertion about the subject. This assertion can involve an action ("Birds *fly*"), a relationship ("Birds *have* feathers"), or a state of being ("Birds *are* cold-blooded"). The **simple predicate** consists of the main verb plus any helping verbs that accompany it (*will fly, should have flown*). (For a full list of helping verbs, see 1c.) The **complete predicate** consists of the verb plus any other words that help it make its assertion, such as modifiers, objects, and complements.

Geese normally *can fly* more gracefully than chickens. [Simple predicate.]

Geese *normally can fly more gracefully than chickens.* [Complete predicate.]

Hiram *showed* me a goose that bites. [Simple predicate.]

Hiram *showed me a goose that bites.* [Complete predicate.]

In many sentences, the subject appears between two parts of the predicate.

When I visited his farm, Hiram *showed* me a goose that bites. [Simple predicate.]

When I visited his farm, Hiram *showed me a goose that bites.* [Complete predicate.]

You can tell that the opening clause *When I visited his farm* is part of the predicate because it modifies the verb (*showed*), not the subject (*Hiram*).

Just as a sentence may have a compound subject, a sentence may also have a compound predicate.

The child *screamed, cried, and kicked* until he got his way. [Simple compound predicate.]

The child *screamed, cried, and kicked until he got his way.* [Complete compound predicate.]

The receiver *intercepted* the pass *and ran* for a touchdown. [Simple compound predicate.]

The receiver *intercepted the pass and ran for a touchdown.* [Complete compound predicate.]

Exercise 2–1: Identifying Subjects and Predicates

Identify each simple subject (SS), complete subject (CS), simple predicate (SP), and complete predicate (CP) in the following sentences. Answers for the lettered sentences appear in the back of the book. Example:

Does your brother George really dye his hair?

Does your brother George really dye his hair?

a. Most wild animals do not make good pets.

b. War, that curse of the human race, has plagued civilizations throughout history.

c. Even after he became deaf, the composer Beethoven continued to write music.

d. One cup of coffee in the morning keeps me awake all day.

e. John Updike's mother, who had been a writer herself, always encouraged her son's literary aspirations.

1. Until the 1850s, the city now known as San Francisco was a tiny outpost with few human inhabitants.

2. The Golden Gate Bridge was named after the harbor entrance, long known as the Golden Gate.

3. The introduction of the telegraph enabled San Franciscans to find out when a ship was approaching the city.

4. San Francisco, like many California cities, was given its name by Spanish missionaries.

5. It was the Gold Rush that brought a flood of easterners and other outsiders to northern California.

6. Today people still flock to California, but few expect to get rich by finding gold.

7. During the 1989 World Series, an earthquake hit the San Francisco area and caused millions of dollars of damage.

8. Buildings burned, roads buckled, and bridges collapsed.

9. Frightened people called for help, ran into the streets, and cried when they saw the devastation.

10. Immediately after the earthquake the number of visitors to San Francisco decreased; however, the slump in tourism did not last long.

2c *Objects*

An **object** is the target or recipient of the action of a verb. Whereas the subject of a sentence does something, the object has something done to it or for it. Objects, like subjects, usually are (or include) nouns or pronouns.

> Some geese bite *people.*

A sentence can have two types of objects: direct and indirect. A **direct object** completes the action performed by the subject or asserted about the subject; it is the verb's target. (Not all verbs take direct objects. Those that do are called *transitive verbs*; see 1c.)

> She sells *seashells* by the seashore.
> Birds have *feathers.*
> Give me *your tired, your poor.* . . .

An **indirect object** names a person or other entity that is affected by the subject's action. Usually an indirect object is the recipient of the direct object, via the action indicated by the verb. Only certain transitive verbs take indirect objects. Among them are *ask, bring, buy, get, lend, offer, pay, promise, sell, show, tell,* and *write.*

> She sells *the tourists* seashells.
> Give *me* your tired, your poor. . . .

As you can see, the word *to* is implied before an indirect object. Often you can identify an indirect object by rearranging the sentence and inserting *to.*

> She sells seashells *to the tourists.*
> Give your tired and your poor *to me.*

2d *Complements*

A **complement** renames or describes a subject or object. It consists of a word or group of words in the predicate that completes the assertion in a sentence.

A complement that renames or describes the subject of a sentence is called a **subject complement**. It always follows a linking verb such as *be, am, were, seem, feel* (see 1c, 5a). A subject complement can be a noun, an adjective, or a group of words that functions as a noun or adjective.

    S   SC
That *dog* looks *friendly*. [Describes.]

    S   SC
Manute Bol must be *the tallest basketball player in the NBA*. [Renames.]

A complement that renames or describes a direct or indirect object is called an **object complement**. Like a subject complement, an object complement can be a noun, an adjective, or a group of words that functions as a noun or adjective.

          DO   OC
Leroy calls *Julie the hostess with the mostest*. [Renames.]

               DO   OC
This new computer will keep *Professor Mutt happy*. [Describes.]

SENTENCE PATTERNS

With a subject, a verb, an object or two, a complement or two, and some modifiers, you can build virtually any English sentence. As complex as our language is, most sentences that we recognize as grammatical follow one of five patterns. Sometimes the order of the ingredients changes, and sometimes the pattern is obscured by modifying words and phrases. Here are the five basic sentence patterns, with examples. (Only simple subjects, verbs, objects, and complements are marked.)

1. **subject/verb**

    S   V
The *king lives*.

       S   V
The former *king* now *lives* in a cottage on the palace grounds.

    V   S
Long *live* the *king*!

2. **subject/verb/subject complement**

    S   V   SC
This *plum tastes ripe*.

```
                               S         V        V    V    SC
```
When this plum was picked, *it* probably *would* not *have tasted ripe.*

```
        SC   V      S     V
```
How *ripe does* this *plum taste* to you?

3. subject/verb/direct object

```
S      V            DO
```
I photographed the *sheriff.*

```
S V                       V         DO
```
I did not, however, *photograph* the *deputy.*

```
V      S V          V           DO
```
Would I have photographed Sheriff Brown if he were a kinder man?

4. subject/verb/indirect object/direct object

```
    S      V    IO    DO
```
Charlene asked you a *question.*

```
 V   IO         DO
```
Ask me no more *questions* than you wish to hear answered. [The subject of the
verb *Ask* is *you,* understood.]

```
 V        S    V   IO     DO
```
*Did*n't *Charlene ask you* a *question?*

5. subject/verb/direct object/object complement

```
      S    V    DO              OC
```
The *judges rated Hugo* the best *skater.*

```
                S     V   V    DO           OC
```
Last year's *judges had rated Hugo* second *best* of all the skaters.

```
 V         S     V  DO  OC
```
Will the *judges rate Hugo first* again next year?

Exercise 2–2: Identifying Objects and Complements

Underline and identify the subject complements (SC), indirect objects (IO),
direct objects (DO), and object complements (OC) wherever they appear in
the following sentences. Mark the whole complement or object, not just its
key noun or pronoun. Answers for the lettered sentences appear in the back
of the book. Example:

Venus, the goddess of love, considered Adonis her equal.

```
                                       DO       OC
```
Venus, the goddess of love, considered <u>Adonis</u> <u>her equal</u>.

a. You are an educated person; how can you believe such a story?

b. By meowing, Timothy tells Judith his needs.

c. Elizabeth, a cynical observer, believes that the president is an evasive man.

d. Holography is an interesting art, but it requires expensive equipment.

e. Many people call Chicago the windy city.

1. Greyhounds are the dogs most often used for racing, which involves chasing a mechanical rabbit around a track.

2. The scorers named Michael Jordan most valuable player in last week's game.

3. The outfielder's agent negotiated him a new contract.

4. Within a month, Juanita had become the toast of San Clemente.

5. My friend Alicia calls her yellow Volkswagen Buttercup.

3 PHRASES AND CLAUSES

Grammar deals not only with single words but also with groups of words known as phrases and clauses. A **phrase** consists of two or more related words that work together: *my uncle Zeke, in the attic, will have been*. Words that do not work together do not make up a phrase: *Zeke uncle my, in attic the, been have will*.

Notice that a phrase doesn't make complete sense the way a sentence does. Useful as it may be, it is lacking. It may lack a subject (*will have been*), a verb (*my uncle Zeke*), or both (*in the attic*).

A **clause** too is a group of related words that work together. However, it has more going for it than a phrase: it contains both a subject and a verb. Clauses come in two forms: main and subordinate. A **main clause** needs only end punctuation to make it a complete sentence.

> S   V
> *Uncle Zeke likes* solitude.

A **subordinate clause** contains a subject and a verb, but it cannot stand alone; it depends on a main clause to help it make sense.

> S   V
> *who plays* the oboe

Only in combination with a main clause does a subordinate clause work in a sentence.

> Uncle Zeke, *who plays the oboe*, likes solitude.

TYPES OF PHRASES

Phrases, being incomplete by themselves, are versatile. They can function as nouns, verbs, adjectives, or adverbs. Every compound subject or object is a phrase by definition: *Zeke and Jake, my father and I*. So is every verb that consists of more than one word: *will have played, sang and danced.* Other types of phrases can play varied roles in sentences.

> *Playing the oboe* is Uncle Zeke's favorite pastime. [Noun phrase — subject.]
>
> He really enjoys *making music.* [Noun phrase — object.]
>
> Uncle Zeke plays an oboe *custom-made for him.* [Adjective phrase modifying *oboe.*]
>
> My music teacher says he plays *like a professional.* [Adverb phrase modifying *plays.*]

To determine whether a phrase functions as a noun, adjective, or adverb in a sentence, you can ask yourself what question the phrase answers. If it answers the question Who? or What?, it is a noun phrase. If it answers the question What kind?, it is an adjective phrase. If it answers the question When? or Where? or How?, it is usually an adverb phrase.

We can name phrases by the roles they play in a sentence: noun phrase, adjective phrase, adverb phrase. We can also name them by their form: prepositional phrase, verbal phrase, absolute phrase, appositive phrase. Because the form of a phrase determines the roles it can play, our discussion of phrases will classify them by form.

3a *Prepositional Phrases*

What do the following sentences have in common?

> Doesn't Lew have other friends besides Pat?
>
> Over the next sand dune lies the ocean.
>
> To understand his comments you must read between the lines.

Each sentence contains a **prepositional phrase**, so named because it starts with a preposition: *besides Pat, Over the next sand dune, between the lines.* (See the prepositions chart in 1f.)

Prepositional phrases are a common and very useful sentence ingredient. Most often, they function as adjectives or adverbs. When a prepositional phrase does the work of an adjective — that is, when it modifies a noun — it is an **adjective phrase**.

> Joyce wanted to live in a city *without smokestacks.* [Adjective phrase modifying *city.*]
>
> Tyrone is a man *of honor.* [Adjective phrase modifying *man.*]

When a prepositional phrase does the work of an adverb — that is, when it modifies a verb, an adjective, or another adverb — it is an **adverb phrase**.

> She writes *with vigor.* [Adverb phrase modifying the verb *writes.*]
>
> Jake feels indebted *to his coach.* [Adverb phrase modifying the adjective *indebted.*]
>
> Mr. Francis phoned early *in the morning.* [Adverb phrase modifying the adverb *early.*]

Some prepositional phrases function as nouns; they are **noun phrases.**

Over the river and through the woods is the long way to Grandmother's house.

3b *Verbal Phrases*

A **verbal** is a form of a verb that cannot function as a simple predicate in a sentence. Verbals include infinitives (*to live, to dream*), present participles (*falling, dancing*), and past participles (*lived, fallen*).

A verbal and its modifiers, if any, constitute a **verbal phrase.** The three types of verbal phrases are infinitive phrases (*to live alone, to dream vividly*); participial phrases (*falling behind, written in stone*); and gerund phrases (*smoking in the boys' room, slow dancing*). Verbal phrases (and verbals) can operate as nouns, adjectives, and adverbs.

INFINITIVE PHRASES

An **infinitive phrase** consists of the infinitive form of a verb preceded by *to* (*to quit*) plus any modifiers or objects (*to quit suddenly; to quit the job*). Infinitive phrases function as nouns, adjectives, and adverbs.

To err is human. [Noun phrase used as subject.]

Their goal is *to stop the pipeline project.* [Noun phrase used as subject complement.]

Jennifer is the candidate *to watch.* [Adjective phrase modifying *candidate.*]

Melvin lives *to eat.* [Adverb phrase modifying *lives.*]

He is too fat *to play tennis.* [Adverb phrase modifying *fat.*]

PHRASES AT A GLANCE

A **prepositional phrase** contains a preposition and its object(s) and any modifiers: "*In the old mansion* we found a stack *of books* hidden *behind the fireplace.*" (3a)

A **verbal phrase** consists of a verbal and its modifiers: "All she wanted was *to attend college someday*" [**infinitive phrase**]; "*Swimming in cold water,* we hardly noticed that the air temperature was 101 degrees" [**participial phrase**]; "*Combing the dog's hair* took at least thirty minutes every other day" [**gerund phrase**]. (3b)

An **absolute phrase** does not modify any one word in a sentence but modifies the entire sentence: It usually consists of a noun followed by a participial phrase: "*The 12:30 bus having already passed,* Arturo waited in the hot sun for the next one." (3c)

An **appositive phrase** is a group of words that adds information about a subject or object by identifying it in a different way: "Magali, *a student from France,* learned colloquial English by living with an American family." (3d)

An infinitive phrase is easy to distinguish from a prepositional phrase starting with *to*: in an infinitive phrase, *to* is followed first by a verb (*to row*) and only then by an object, if any (*to row a boat*). In a prepositional phrase, *to* is followed directly by its object, a noun or pronoun (*to me, to the lighthouse, to the boat*).

PARTICIPIAL PHRASES

A **participial phrase** is an adjective phrase that opens with the present or past participle of a verb. Here are examples of the infinitive and participial forms of a few common verbs:

INFINITIVE	PRESENT PARTICIPLE	PAST PARTICIPLE
(to) find	finding	found
(to) fly	flying	flown
(to) go	going	gone
(to) see	seeing	seen
(to) walk	walking	walked

All participial phrases share two characteristics: they start with participles, and they function as adjectives.

> *Leading the pack,* Michael sprinted into the final straightaway. [Modifies *Michael.*]
>
> He made the most of the few seconds *remaining in his race.* [Modifies *seconds.*]
>
> *Worn out by the intensity of his effort,* Michael fell. [Modifies *Michael.*]

GERUND PHRASES

A **gerund phrase** is a noun phrase that begins with the present participle of a verb. It can serve as the subject of a sentence, a direct object, a subject complement, or the object of a preposition.

> *Giving blood* is a valuable public service. [Subject.]
>
> Audrey loves *performing in plays.* [Direct object.]
>
> Phil's job is *making doughnuts.* [Subject complement.]
>
> My mother is nervous about *traveling by herself.* [Object of a preposition.]

3c *Absolute Phrases*

An **absolute phrase** usually consists of a noun followed by a participle. It does not modify any one word; rather, it modifies an entire clause or sentence. It can appear anywhere in the sentence.

> The stallion pawed the ground, *nostrils flaring, chestnut mane and tail swirling in the wind.*
>
> *Nostrils flaring, chestnut mane and tail swirling in the wind,* the stallion pawed the ground.

3d *Appositive Phrases*

An appositive is a word that adds to what we know about a subject or object simply by identifying it in a different way ("my dog *Rover*," "Harvey's brother *Fred*"). An **appositive phrase** is a group of words that provides the same kind of amplification.

> Bess, *the landlord's daughter,* had long black hair.
>
> I walked across the field, *a golden sea of wheat flecked with daisies,* to the stone wall.

Exercise 3–1: Identifying Phrases

Underline and identify the prepositional, verbal (infinitive, participial, and gerund), absolute, and appositive phrases in the following sentences. For each prepositional and verbal phrase, also identify its role in the sentence (noun, adjective, adverb). Answers for the lettered sentences appear in the back of the book. Example:

> The hero of the movie *Robocop* is half human, half machine.
>
> The hero <u>of the movie</u> *Robocop* is half human, half machine. [Prepositional; adjective.]

  a. Identifying parts of speech has never been my strong point.
  b. The fellow in the beret is a fourth-generation Californian.
  c. The Rolls-Royce, its silver hood ornament gleaming in the morning sun, stood waiting.
  d. I heard their astonishing news through the grapevine.
  e. The Confederacy, gone with the wind, remains a cherished southern memory.

  1. The North, Civil War victor, is less nostalgic.
  2. Looking out on the morning rain, Carole used to feel uninspired.
  3. Raymond's Las Vegas escapade gave playing blackjack a bad name.
  4. Elsa didn't want to get on the plane, but Rick insisted.
  5. Geoff's only accomplishment has been rebuilding that boat.
  6. The money stolen from Gene's wallet would have paid his rent.
  7. Cordelia, her father's favorite, loved King Lear the most.
  8. Your loud music having interrupted my concentration, I can't finish my essay right now.
  9. Blinded by the light, Bruce waved to his invisible audience.
  10. Steve's dream is to ride his motorcycle across the country.

TYPES OF CLAUSES

The main difference between a clause and a phrase is that a clause has both a subject and a verb. Some clauses, indeed, can stand alone as complete sentences. They are called **main clauses** (or **independent clauses**).

My *sister has* a friend.

The *flowers were* beautiful.

Clauses that cannot stand alone are called **subordinate clauses** (or **dependent clauses**).

who comes from Lebanon

that *Dan gave* Nicola

A subordinate clause must be linked with a main clause for its meaning to be entirely clear.

My sister has a friend who comes from Lebanon.

The flowers that Dan gave Nicola were beautiful.

Subordinate clauses, like phrases, are versatile: they can function as nouns, adjectives, and adverbs. You can generally tell noun, adjective, and adverb clauses apart by asking, What question does this clause answer? A clause that answers the question What? or Who? is a noun clause. One that answers the question What kind? or Which one? is an adjective clause. One that answers the question When? or How? or Where? is usually an adverb clause.

3e *Noun Clauses*

A subordinate clause that serves as a sentence subject, object, or complement is called a **noun clause**. Usually a noun clause begins with *how, what, when, where, whether, who* (or *whom*), *whoever* (or *whomever*), or *that*.

What I believe is none of their business. [Noun clause as subject.]

James doesn't know *whom he should blame.* [Noun clause as direct object.]

In both of these examples, the relative pronoun that opens the subordinate clause (*What, whom*) is followed by the subject and verb of the clause.

S   V

what *I believe*

$\overset{S}{\text{whom}} \overset{V}{\textit{he should blame}}$

Sometimes, however, the relative pronoun that opens the subordinate clause also serves as the subject of the clause.

James doesn't know *who did it*. [Noun clause as direct object.]

Sarah tells *whoever will listen* her complaints about Mrs. Quigley. [Noun clause as indirect object.]

In these two sentences, no additional noun or pronoun comes between *who* or *whoever* and the verb of the clause. The relative pronoun links the subordinate clause to the main clause, and it also functions as the subject of the subordinate clause.

3f *Adjective Clauses*

Subordinate clauses can serve as adjectives by modifying nouns or pronouns. Usually an adjective clause is introduced by one of the relative pronouns: *who, which,* or *that.* Sometimes the relative pronoun is implied: "I got the letter [*that*] you sent me." You can tell an adjective clause from a noun clause by its role in a sentence.

I like people *who are optimistic.* [Adjective clause modifying *people.*]

I plan to major in psychology, *which I have always found fascinating.* [Adjective clause modifying *psychology.*]

Science is a tide *that can only rise.* —Jonathan Schell [Adjective clause modifying *tide.*]

3g *Adverb Clauses*

An adverb clause plays the role of an adverb in a sentence, modifying a verb, an adjective, or another adverb.

Larry left *before I could explain my mistake.* [Adverb clause modifying the verb *left.*]

He was sure *that I had insulted him.* [Adverb clause modifying the adjective *sure.*]

He loses his temper faster *than most people do.* [Adverb clause modifying the adverb *faster.*]

Generally, subordinate clauses acting as adverbs are introduced by one of the common subordinating conjunctions, such as the following:

after	before	than	until	wherever
although	if	that	when	while
as	since	though	whenever	why
because	so that	unless	where	

(For a complete list of subordinating conjunctions, see 1g.) As with adjective clauses, the subordinating conjunction in an adverb clause sometimes is implied rather than stated: "You paint so well [*that*] you could be a professional."

Exercise 3–2: Identifying Clauses

Underline the subordinate clauses in the following sentences, and identify each one as a noun, adjective, or adverb clause. Answers for the lettered sentences appear in the back of the book. Example:

> The man whose toe Susan had stepped on yelped in pain.
>
> The man <u>whose toe Susan had stepped on</u> yelped in pain. [Adjective clause.]

a. My grandfather was a rolling stone; wherever he lived at the moment was his home.

b. While we were still arguing about its value, the statue was removed from the gallery.

c. The shirt that I took to the cleaner's came back with a ripped sleeve.

d. Ann did so badly on the exam that she may fail the course.

e. Lee can't decide whether he should invite James.

1. Before you leave for the summer, we should discuss plans for the fall semester.

2. The man who we all thought was so charming has been arrested for fraud.

3. Sailing, which is Charlie's favorite summer pastime, has been banned in Rock Harbor.

4. Lewis sent us more postcards than we had time to read.

5. Blame John's death on the cocaine he refused to give up.

4 TYPES OF SENTENCES

What is a **sentence**? There is more than one answer. In conversation, the single word *Where?* can be a sentence. But in striving to write clear, readable prose, you will find it useful to think of a sentence as the expression of a complete thought containing at least one *main clause* — that is, a subject and a verb (see p. H–25). So defined, sentences come in four varieties according to their structure.

4a Simple Sentences

Any sentence that contains only one clause is a **simple sentence**, even if it includes modifiers, objects, complements, and any number of phrases in addition to its subject and verb.

> Even amateur stargazers can easily locate the Big Dipper in the night sky.
>
> George Washington exhibited courage and leadership during a crucial period in our country's history.

Fred and Sandy have already applied for summer jobs.

The spectators laughed and cried at the same time.

Notice in the last two examples that a simple sentence may have a compound subject (*Fred and Sandy*) or a compound verb (*laughed and cried*). Still, it remains a simple sentence, for it contains only one main clause. Sometimes the subject of a simple sentence is not stated but is clearly understood. In the command "Run!," the subject is *you*.

4b Compound Sentences

A **compound sentence** consists of two or more main clauses joined by a coordinating conjunction such as *and*, *but*, or *for* or by a semicolon. Sometimes the semicolon is followed by a *conjunctive adverb* such as *however*, *nevertheless*, or *therefore*. (For complete lists of coordinating conjunctions and conjunctive adverbs, see 1g.)

```
                                         MAIN
┌──────── MAIN CLAUSE ────────┐   ┌CLAUSE┐
```
I would like to accompany you, but I can't.

```
┌ MAIN CLAUSE ┐  ┌ MAIN CLAUSE ┐
```
Two's company; three's a crowd.

```
┌──────── MAIN CLAUSE ────────┐        ┌──────────────── MAIN
```
Henry Kissinger was born in Europe; therefore, he cannot be a candidate for the

```
CLAUSE ──────────────┐
```
presidency of the United States.

4c Complex Sentences

A **complex sentence** consists of one main clause and one or more subordinate clauses.

```
                        SUBORDINATE
┌── MAIN CLAUSE──┐ ┌── CLAUSE ──┐
```
I will be at the airport when you arrive.

```
┌── SUBORDINATE CLAUSE ──┐  ┌──── MAIN CLAUSE ────┐
```
Since Amy bought a computer, she has been out of circulation.

```
┌──────── SUBORDINATE CLAUSE ────────┐ ┌MAIN CLAUSE┐ ┌──── SUBORDINATE
```
Because George has to travel widely, he is grateful whenever his far-flung

```
CLAUSE ──────────────────────┐
```
acquaintances invite him to a home-cooked meal.

In some sentences, the relative pronoun linking the subordinate clause to the main clause is implied rather than stated.

```
  MAIN        SUBORDINATE
┌ CLAUSE┐┌──── CLAUSE────┐
```
I know [that] you saw us.

Sometimes the relative pronoun linking the main and subordinate clauses serves as the subject of the subordinate clause.

SUBORDINATE
┌─MAIN CLAUSE─┐ ┌─ CLAUSE ──┐
Paulette likes men *who* flatter her.

SUBORDINATE
┌─MAIN CLAUSE ─┐ ┌── CLAUSE ──┐
Don't bite the hand *that* feeds you.

4d *Compound-Complex Sentences*

As its name implies, **a compound-complex sentence** shares the attributes of both a compound sentence (it contains two or more main clauses) and a complex sentence (it contains at least one subordinate clause).

┌──SUBORDINATE CLAUSE──┐ ┌────── MAIN CLAUSE ──────┐   ┌─────────MAIN
Where politics is concerned, Michael seems indifferent and Joanne seems ill
CLAUSE─┐
informed.

SUBORDINATE   MAIN
┌──────MAIN CLAUSE──────┐ ┌─CLAUSE─┐┌─CLAUSE──┐
I'd gladly wait until you're ready; but if I do, I'll miss the boat.

Exercise 4–1: Identifying Sentence Types

Identify each of the following sentences as simple, compound, complex, or compound-complex. Don't just pin labels on them: briefly explain what elements each sentence contains that make you classify it as you do. Answers for the lettered sentences appear in the back of the book. Example:

> If a bullfrog had wings, he wouldn't bump his tail so much, but he'd have a hard time swimming.
>
> ┌SUBORDINATE CLAUSE┐ ┌──────MAIN CLAUSE──────┐   ┌─────────MAIN
> If a bullfrog had wings, he wouldn't bump his tail so much, but he'd have a hard
> CLAUSE──────┐
> time swimming. [Compound-complex.]

a. Not only women but also men and children benefit from society's increasing resistance to sex-role stereotypes.

b. Even in a life-or-death emergency, I know you can count on Marlene.

c. Biology is interesting, but I prefer botany as it is taught by Professor Haines.

d. Do you prefer bacon and eggs or cereal and toast for breakfast this morning?

e. Most people believe that poverty begets poverty; however, recent studies have shown that, more often than not, when children from welfare families reach adulthood, they achieve economic independence.

1. Geraldine believes that the sexual revolution, without compensating women for their losses, has robbed them of all the advantages automatically bestowed by old-fashioned marriage.

2. In my favorite television series, the detective invariably sends his assistant on some mysterious errand.

3. Do you want to dance, or would you rather take time out for pizza?

4. Since Jennifer moved to the city, her attendance at concerts, plays, and museum shows has increased markedly; and she dines out at least once a week.

5. As a boy, Mike couldn't wait to qualify for the Little League baseball team; a few weeks after joining, he wanted only to quit.

6. Executives who promote incompetent workers can drive a corporation to the brink of disaster.

7. In the Virgin Islands the sun shines every day, the temperature drops to a comfortable level every night, and the breeze rustles through the palm trees at all hours.

8. No one can say exactly how long ago it was that dinosaurs ceased to walk the earth.

9. At some point in the long and surprisingly complex history of popular music, rock-'n'-roll acquired its present identity as the music of youth and rebellion.

10. If a man makes a better mousetrap, the world will beat a path to his door.
                                                                —Ralph Waldo Emerson

CHAPTER 32

Grammatical Sentences

5 VERBS

Most verbs show action (*swim*, *fight*, *eat*, *hide*, *pay*, *sleep*, *win*). Some verbs indicate a state of being by linking the subject of a sentence with a word that renames or describes it; they are called *linking verbs*. A few verbs work with a main verb to give more information about its action; they are called *helping verbs* or *auxiliary verbs*.

VERB FORMS

5a *Use a linking verb to connect the subject of a sentence with a subject complement.*

A **linking verb** indicates what the subject of a sentence *is* or *is like*. Some common linking verbs are *be*, *appear*, *feel*, and *grow*. A linking verb creates a sort of equation, either positive or negative, between the subject and its complement (see p. H–19). The subject complement can be a noun, a pronoun, or an adjective.

> LV   SC
> Julia will *make* a good *doctor*. [Noun.]

> LV   SC
> George *is* not the *one*. [Pronoun.]

> LV   SC
> London weather *seems foggy*. [Adjective.]

A verb may be a linking verb in some sentences and not in others.

> I often *grow* sleepy after lunch. [Linking verb with subject complement *sleepy*.]
>
> I often *grow* tomatoes in my garden. [Transitive verb with direct object *tomatoes*.]

If you pay attention to what the verb means, you can usually tell whether it is functioning as a linking verb.

COMMON LINKING VERBS
Some linking verbs tell what a noun is, was, or will be.

> *be, become, remain*
> *grow*: The sky *is growing* dark.
> *make*: One plus two *makes* three.
> *prove*: His warning *proved* accurate.
> *turn*: The weather *turned* cold.

Some linking verbs tell what a noun might be.

> *appear, seem, look*

Most verbs of the senses can operate as linking verbs.

> *feel, smell, sound, taste*

5b *Use helping verbs to add information about the main verb.*

A **helping** or **auxiliary verb** can add essential information about a main verb's action or state of being. Adding a helping verb to a simple verb (*go, shoot, be*) allows you to express a wide variety of tenses and moods (*am going, did shoot, would have been*). (See 5g–5l and 5n–5p.)

All the forms of *be*, *do*, and *have* can function as helping verbs. The other helping verbs are *can*, *could*, *may*, *might*, *must*, *shall*, *should*, *will*, and *would*. These last nine can function only as helping verbs, never as main verbs.

A main verb plus one or more helping verbs is called a **verb phrase**. The parts of a verb phrase need not appear together but may be separated by other words.

I probably *am going* to France this summer.

You *should* not *have shot* that pigeon.

This change *may* well *have been* seriously *contemplated* by the governor even before the election.

5c Use the correct principal parts of the verb.

The principal parts are the forms the verb can take—alone or with helping verbs—to indicate the full range of times when an action or state of being does, did, or will occur. Verbs have three principal parts: the infinitive, the past tense, and the past participle.

The **infinitive** is the simple or dictionary form of the verb (*go*, *sing*, *laugh*) or the simple form preceded by *to* (*to go*, *to sing*, *to laugh*). (See p. H–23.)

The **past tense** signals that the verb's action is completed (*went*, *sang*, *laughed*).

The **past participle** is combined with helping verbs to indicate action occurring at various times in the past or future (*have gone*, *had sung*, *will have laughed*). It is also used with forms of *be* to make the passive voice. (See pp. H–47 and H–48.)

In addition to the three principal parts, all verbs have a present participle, which consists of the *-ing* form of the verb. The present participle is used to make the progressive tenses. (See 5k and 5l.) It also can modify nouns and pronouns ("the *leaking* bottle"); and, as a gerund, it can function as a noun ("*sleeping all day* pleases me"). (See p. H–24.)

5d Use -d or -ed to form the past tense and past participle of a regular verb.

Most verbs in English are *regular verbs*: they form the past tense and past participle in a standard, predictable way. Regular verbs that end in *-e* add *-d* to the infinitive; those that do not end in *-e* add *-ed*.

INFINITIVE	PAST TENSE	PAST PARTICIPLES
(to) smile	smiled	smiled
(to) act	acted	acted
(to) please	pleased	pleased
(to) trick	tricked	tricked

5e *Use the correct forms for the past tense and past participle of irregular verbs.*

The English language has at least two hundred *irregular verbs*, which form their past tense and past participle in some other way than by adding *-d* or *-ed*. Most irregular verbs are familiar to native English speakers and pose no problem, although they can be a torment to people trying to learn the language. The principal parts chart lists just the most troublesome irregular verbs.

PRINCIPAL PARTS OF COMMON IRREGULAR VERBS

INFINITIVE	PAST TENSE	PAST PARTICIPLE
be	was	been
become	became	become
begin	began	begun
blow	blew	blown
break	broke	broken
bring	brought	brought
burst	burst	burst
catch	caught	caught
choose	chose	chosen
come	came	come
do	did	done
draw	drew	drawn
drink	drank	drunk
drive	drove	driven
eat	ate	eaten
fall	fell	fallen
fight	fought	fought
freeze	froze	frozen
get	got	got, gotten
give	gave	given
go	went	gone
grow	grew	grown
have	had	had
hear	heard	heard
hide	hid	hidden
know	knew	known
lay	laid	laid
lead	led	led
let	let	let
lie	lay	lain
make	made	made
raise	raised	raised
ride	rode	ridden

(continued)

INFINITIVE	PAST TENSE	PAST PARTICIPLE
ring	rang	rung
rise	rose	risen
run	ran	run
say	said	said
see	saw	seen
set	set	set
sit	sat	sat
sing	sang	sung
slay	slew	slain
slide	slid	slid
speak	spoke	spoken
spin	spun	spun
stand	stood	stood
steal	stole	stolen
swim	swam	swum
swing	swung	swung
teach	taught	taught
tear	tore	torn
think	thought	thought
throw	threw	thrown
wake	woke, waked	woken, waked
write	wrote	written

For the appropriate form of any irregular verb not on this list, consult your dictionary. (Some dictionaries list principal parts for all verbs, some just for irregular verbs.)

5f *Use the correct forms of the principal parts of* lie *and* lay *and* sit *and* set.

Among the most troublesome verbs in English are *lie* and *lay*. If you have difficulty choosing between them, you can forever eliminate confusion by taking two easy steps. The first is to memorize the principal parts and present participles of both verbs (see the chart).

The second step in deciding whether to use *lie* or *lay* is to fix in memory that *lie*, in all its forms, is intransitive. *Lie* never takes a direct object: "The island *lies* due east," "Jed *has lain* on the floor all day." *Lay*, on the other hand, is a transitive verb. It always requires an object: "*Lay* that pistol down."

The same distinction exists between *sit* and *set*. Usually, *sit* is intransitive: "He *sits* on the stairs." *Set*, on the other hand, almost always takes an object: "He *sets* the bottle on the counter." There are, however, a few easily memorized exceptions. The sun *sets*. A hen *sets*. Gelatin *sets*. You *sit* a horse. You can *sit* yourself down at a table that *sits* twelve.

lie: recline

PRESENT TENSE	I lie	we lie
	you lie	you lie
	he/she/it lies	they lie
PAST TENSE	I lay	we lay
	you lay	you lay
	he/she/it lay	they lay

PAST PARTICIPLE lain (We have *lain* in the sun long enough.)

PRESENT PARTICIPLE lying (At ten o'clock he was still *lying* in bed.)

lay: put in place, deposit

PRESENT TENSE	I lay	we lay
	you lay	you lay
	he/she/it lays	they lay
PAST TENSE	I laid	we laid
	you laid	you laid
	he/she/it laid	they laid

PAST PARTICIPLE laid (Having *laid* his clothes on the bed, Mark jumped into the shower.)

PRESENT PARTICIPLE laying (*Laying* her cards on the table, Lola cried, "Gin!")

sit: be seated

PRESENT TENSE	I sit	we sit
	you sit	you sit
	he/she/it sits	they sit
PAST TENSE	I sat	we sat
	you sat	you sat
	he/she/it sat	they sat

PAST PARTICIPLE sat (I have *sat* here long enough.)

PRESENT PARTICIPLE sitting (Why are you *sitting* on that rickety bench?)

set: place

PRESENT TENSE	I set	we set
	you set	you set
	he/she/it sets	they set
PAST TENSE	I set	we set
	you set	you set
	he/she/it set	they set

PAST PARTICIPLE	set	(Paul has *set* the table for eight.)
PRESENT PARTICIPLE	setting	(Jerry has been *setting* pins at the Bowl-a-drome.)

Exercise 5–1: Using Irregular Verb Forms

Underline each incorrectly used irregular verb in the following sentences and substitute the verb's appropriate form. Some sentences may be correct. Answers for the lettered sentences appear in the back of the book. Example:

Lie your books on the windowsill near the spot where the flowers are setting.

Lay your books on the windowsill near the spot where the flowers are sitting.

a. When Joe's mother catched him laying around the house during school hours, she throwed him out.

b. We woke soon after the sun rose, and then we swam to the raft.

c. He lay his cards triumphantly on the table but soon found that he was not setting in a lucky chair after all.

d. Wendy knew how much Roger had drank, but she gone with him anyway.

e. I have laid awake, tossing and turning, every night since exams begun.

1. Why don't you lay down for a while after you have lain a fire in the fireplace?

2. How could Ricardo have knew that Cindy drunk his coffee?

3. I have laid in an ample supply of groceries for tonight's birthday dinner, which we should have eaten yesterday.

4. Frank throwed a rock through the window and then teared down the curtains climbing inside.

5. I have set here for so long my legs won't move.

TENSES

The **tense** of a verb is the *time* when its action did, does, or will occur. With the *simple tenses* we can indicate whether the verb's action took place in the past, takes place in the present, or will take place in the future. The *perfect tenses* enable us to narrow the timing even further, specifying that the action was or will be completed by the time of some other action. The *progressive tenses* let readers know that the verb's action did, does, or will continue.

5g *Use the simple present tense for an action that takes place once, recurrently, or continuously in the present.*

The simple present tense is the infinitive form of a regular verb plus *-s* or *-es* for the third person singular.

I like, I go	we like, we go
you like, you go	you like, you go
he/she/it likes, he/she/it goes	they like, they go

Notice that some irregular verbs, such as *go,* form their simple present tense following the same rules as regular verbs. Other irregular verbs, such as *be* and *have,* are special cases for which you should learn the correct forms.

I am, I have	we are, we have
you are, you have	you are, you have
he/she/it is, he/she/it has	he/she/it is, he/she/it has

You can use the simple present tense for an action that is happening right now ("I *welcome* this news"), an action that happens repeatedly in the present ("Judy *goes* to church every Sunday"), or an ongoing present action ("Wesley *likes* ice cream"). In some cases, usually to ask a question or intensify the action, the helping verb *do* or *does* appears before the infinitive form of the main verb.

I *do think* you should take the job.

Does Andy *want* it?

Besides present action, you can use the simple present for future action: "Football season *starts* Wednesday."

Use the simple present for a general truth, even if the rest of the sentence is in a different tense:

Columbus proved in 1492 that the world *is* round.

Mr. Hammond will argue that people *are* basically good.

5h *Use the simple past tense for actions already completed.*

VERB TENSES AT A GLANCE
Note: the examples show first person only.

SIMPLE TENSES	REGULAR	IRREGULAR
Present	I cook	I see
Past	I cooked	I saw
Future	I will cook	I will see
PERFECT TENSES		
Present perfect	I have cooked	I have seen
Past perfect	I had cooked	I had seen
Future perfect	I will have cooked	I will have seen
PROGRESSIVE TENSES	**REGULAR**	**IRREGULAR**
Present progressive	I am cooking	I am seeing
Past progressive	I was cooking	I was seeing
Future progressive	I will be cooking	I will be seeing

PROGRESSIVE TENSES	REGULAR	IRREGULAR
Present perfect		
progressive	I have been cooking	I have been seeing
Past perfect		
progressive	I had been cooking	I had been seeing
Future perfect	I will have been	I will have been seeing
progressive	cooking	

Indicate the simple past tense with the verb's past tense form. Regular verbs form the past tense by adding *-d* or *-ed* to the infinitive; the past tense of irregular verbs must be memorized. (See p. H–35.)

Jack *enjoyed* the party. [Regular verb.]

Suzie *went* home early. [Irregular verb.]

If you add the helping verb *do,* use the past tense (*did*) with the infinitive form of the main verb.

I went, I did go	we went, we did go
you went, you did go	you went, you did go
he/she/it went, he/she/it did go	they went, they did go

NOTE: In some cases, spoken language may interfere with written language, causing problems with forming the past tense. Although speakers may not always pronounce the *-d* or *-ed* ending clearly, standard written English requires that you add the *-d* or *-ed* on all regular past tense verbs.

NONSTANDARD   I *use* to wear weird clothes when I was a child.

STANDARD   I *used* to wear weird clothes when I was a child.

5i *Use the simple future tense for actions that are expected to happen but have not happened yet.*

George *will arrive* in time for dinner.

Will you please *show* him where to park?

To form the simple future tense, add *will* to the infinitive form of the verb.

I will go	we will go
you will go	you will go
he/she/it will go	they will go

You can also use *shall* for first person or (for any person) to inject a tone of determination: "We *shall overcome!*"

Although the present tense can indicate future action ("We *go* on vacation next Monday"), most actions that have not yet taken place are expressed in the simple future tense ("Surely it *will snow* tomorrow").

ESL GUIDELINES: THE SIMPLE TENSES

Present Tense: base form of the verb (+ *-s* or *-es* for third person singular: *he, she, it*)

- Use the simple present tense to express general statements of fact or habitual activities or customs. Although it is called "present," this tense is really *general* or "timeless."

    The earth *spins* on its axis.

    You *make* wonderful coffee.

    Henry *goes* to the movies every Sunday afternoon.

    To form negatives and questions, use *do* or *does* + base form.

    Henry *does not* (*doesn't*) *go* to the movies during the week.

    Do you still *make* wonderful coffee?

Past Tense: base form + *-d* or *-ed* for regular verbs (memorize for irregular verbs [see p. H–35])

- Use the simple past tense to express an action that occurred at a specific time in the past. The specific time may be stated or implied by the context.

    The package *arrived* yesterday.

    Jack *impressed* us with his speaking ability.

    They *went* to San Juan for spring break.

    To form negatives and questions, use *did* + base form.

    They *did not* (*didn't*) *go* to Fort Lauderdale.

    Did the package *arrive* yesterday?

Future Tense: *will* or *be going to* + base form

- Use the simple future tense to express an action that will take place in the future. *Will* is also used to imply promises, predictions, and other meanings besides simply the future.

    The students *will study* hard for their exam.

    The students *are going to study* hard for their exam.

    We *will help* you move. [Promise.]

    Computers *will* soon *replace* most typewriters. [Prediction.]

    To form a question, use *will* + base form.

    Will computers *replace* typewriters?

    To form the negative, use *will* + *not* or *won't* + base form.

    Jose *will not graduate* this year.

    Jose *won't graduate* this year.

NOTE: Use the simple present, not the future, to express future meaning in time clauses (usually beginning with *before, after,* or *when*).

INCORRECT   When my mother *will get* home from work, we will make dinner.

CORRECT   When my mother *gets* home from work, we will make dinner.

5j *Use the perfect tense for an action completed at the time of another action.*

The present perfect, past perfect, and future perfect tenses consist of the past participle plus a form of the helping verb *have*. The tense of *have* determines the tense of the whole verb phrase.

The action of a *present perfect* verb was completed before the sentence is uttered. Its helping verb is in the present tense: *have* or *has*.

> I *have* never *been* to Spain, but I *have been* to Oklahoma.
>
> Mr. Grimaldi *has gone* home for the day.
>
> *Have* you *seen* John Sayles's new film?

You can use the present perfect tense either for an action completed before some other action ("I *have washed* my hands of the whole affair but I am watching from a safe distance") or for an action begun in the past and still going on ("Max *has worked* in this office for twelve years").

The action of a *past perfect* verb was completed before some other action in the past. Its helping verb is in the past tense: *had.*

> The concert *had ended* by the time we found a parking space.
>
> Until I met her, I *had pictured* Jenna as a redhead.
>
> *Hadn't* you *wanted* to clean the house before Mother arrived?

The action of a *future perfect* verb will be completed by some point (specified or implied) in the future. Its helping verb is in the future tense: *will have.*

> The builders *will have finished* the house by June.
>
> When I get the Dutch Blue, I *will have collected* every stamp I need.
>
> *Won't* the store *have closed* by the time we get there?

ESL GUIDELINES: THE PERFECT TENSES

Present Perfect Tense: *has* or *have* + past participle

- Use the present perfect tense when an action took place at some unspecified time in the past. The action may have occurred repeatedly.

> I *have traveled* to many countries.
>
> The dog *has bitten* my aunt twice.

Use the present perfect tense with *for* and *since* to indicate that an action began in the past, is occurring now, and will probably continue.

> I *have gone* to school with Jim and Susan since fifth grade.
>
> Jenny *has lived* next door to the Kramers for twelve years.

Past Perfect Tense: *had* + past participle

- Use the past perfect tense when an action was completed in the past before some other past action.

> Josef *had worn* jeans for many years before he began wearing suits.
>
> We got rid of the dog because he *had bitten* my aunt twice.

Future Perfect Tense: ***will* + *have*** + past participle

- Use the future perfect tense when an action will take place before some time in the future.

> The package *will have* already *arrived* by the time we get home from work.
>
> By June, the students *will have studied* ten chapters.

5k *Use the simple progressive tenses for an action in progress.*

The present progressive, past progressive, and future progressive tenses consist of the present participle plus a form of the helping verb *be*. (You can form the present participle of any verb, regular or irregular, by adding *-ing* to the infinitive.) The tense of *be* determines the tense of the whole verb phrase.

The *present progressive* expresses an action that is taking place now. Its helping verb is in the present tense: *am, is,* or *are.*

> I *am thinking* of a word that starts with *R.*
>
> *Is* Joe *babysitting* while Marie *is* off *visiting* her sister?

You can also express future action with the present progressive of *go* plus an infinitive phrase:

> I *am going to read* Tolstoy's *War and Peace* some day.
>
> *Are* you *going to sign up* for Professor Blaine's course on the sixties?

The *past progressive* expresses an action that took place continuously at some time in the past, whether or not that action is still going on. Its helping verb is in the past tense: *was* or *were.*

> The old men *were sitting* on the porch when we passed.
>
> Lucy *was planning* to take the weekend off.

The *future progressive* expresses an action that will take place continuously at some time in the future. Its helping verb is in the future tense: *will be.*

> They *will be answering* the phones while she is gone.
>
> *Will* we *be dining* out every night on our vacation?

ESL GUIDELINES: THE SIMPLE PROGRESSIVE TENSES

Present Progressive Tense: present tense of *be* + present participle (*-ing* form)

- Use the present progressive tense when an action began in the past, is happening now, and will end at some time in the future.

  Aimée *is learning* to drive a stick shift.

  The students *are studying* for their exam.

  My sister *is living* with us until she graduates from college.

You can also use the present progressive tense to show a future action.

  Maria *is flying* to Pittsburgh on July 8.

NOTE: Linking verbs such as *be, seem, look*), verbs that express an emotional or mental state (such as *trust, like, guess, realize*), and verbs without action (such as *belong, have, need*) are not generally used in the present progressive tense. For these verbs, use the present tense to express a continuous state.

  INCORRECT   I think I *am liking* you very much.

  CORRECT   I think I *like* you very much.

Past Progressive Tense: *was* or *were* + present participle (*-ing* form)

- Use the past progressive tense when an action began and continued at a specific time in the past.

  The dog *was chewing* a bone when I arrived.

  The students *were studying* for their exam all day.

Future Progressive Tense: *will be* + present participle (*-ing* form); or present tense of *be* + *going to be* + present participle (*-ing* form)

- Use the future progressive tense when an action will begin and will continue in the future.

  Josef *will be wearing* blue jeans to the party.

  The students *are going to be studying* until one o'clock in the morning.

---

51 *Use the perfect progressive tenses for a continuing action that began in the past.*

Use the present perfect progressive, the past perfect progressive, or the future perfect progressive tense for an action that started in the past and did, does, or will continue.

The *present perfect progressive* indicates an action that started in the past and is continuing in the present. Form it by adding the present perfect of *be* (*has been* or *have been*) to the present participle of the main verb.

All morning Fred *has been singing* the blues about his neighbor's wild parties.

Have you *been reading* Janine's postcards from England?

The *past perfect progressive* expresses a continuing action that was completed before another past action. Form it by adding the past perfect of *be* (*had been*) to the present participle of the main verb.

> By the time Dave finally arrived, I *had been waiting* for twenty minutes.

The *future perfect progressive* expresses an action that is expected to continue into the future beyond some other future action. Form it by adding the future perfect of *be* (*will have been*) to the present participle of the main verb.

> By 1995 Joanne *will have been attending* school longer than anyone else I know.

The main thing to remember about verb tenses is to avoid changing from one to another without reason. (See 11a.) Studying tenses can improve your writing by making you aware of the variety of verb forms at your disposal and by giving you practice at using them effectively.

ESL GUIDELINES: THE PERFECT PROGRESSIVE TENSES

Present Progressive Tense: **have/has been** + present participle (*-ing* form)

- Use the present perfect progressive tense when an action began at some time in the past and has continued to the present. Although the words **for** and **since** are not necessary, they are usually used with this tense.

  > She *has been answering* questions all day.

  > The students *have been studying* for a long time.

  > The dog *has been biting* people since he was a puppy.

Past Perfect Progressive Tense: **had been** + present participle (*-ing* form)

- Use the past perfect progressive tense when an action began and continued in the past and then was completed before some other past action.

  > The students *had been studying* for three hours before they finally decided to take a break.

  > The letter carrier *had been ringing* the bell for five minutes when we pulled in the driveway.

Future Perfect Progressive Tense: **will have been** + present participle (*-ing* form

- Use the future perfect progressive tense when an action will continue in the future for a specific amount of time and then end before another future action.

  > The students *will have been studying* for twenty-four hours by the time they take the exam tomorrow.

  > The seafarer *will have been sailing* for ten days when she arrives in Jamaica.

Exercise 5–2: Identifying Verb Tenses

Underline and identify the tense of each verb or verb phrase in the following sentences. Answers for the lettered sentences appear in the back of the book. Example:

> John is living in Hinsdale, but he prefers Joliet.
>
> John is living [present progressive] in Hinsdale, but he prefers [simple present] Joliet.

a. Yesterday Joan broke her leg because she was skiing too fast.

b. Bill sleeps for nine hours every night; even so, he is always yawning.

c. Until last weekend, Josh had never seen a whale, except on those nature specials the public television station runs.

d. The upcoming tour represents the first time the band will have performed together since they split up.

e. After I finish college, I probably will attend graduate school.

1. When they had eaten breakfast, Kate and Matthew strapped on their snowshoes.

2. As of December 1, Ira and Sandy will have been going together for three years.

3. I was thinking about all the fun we've had since we met in third grade.

4. Dan will have embarked on his career by the time his brother starts college.

5. Have you been hoping that Carlos will come to your party?

6. If so, you should know that he will not yet have returned from Chicago.

7. His parents had been expecting him home any day until they heard that he was still waiting for the bus.

8. Probably he is sitting in the depot right now, unless he has switched to the train.

9. I will be keeping my ears open for further news, since I know how much you had counted on Carlos.

10. Still, by the time the party has ended, you will have had so much fun that you won't be holding his absence against him.

VOICE

> Intelligent students read challenging books.
>
> Challenging books are read by intelligent students.

These two statements convey similar information, but their emphasis is different. In the first sentence, the subject (*students*) performs the verb's action (*read*); in the second sentence, the subject (*books*) receives the verb's action (*are read*). One sentence states its idea directly, the other indirectly. We say that the first sentence is in the *active voice* and the second is in the *passive voice*.

5m *Use the active voice rather than the passive voice.*

Verbs in the **active voice** consist of principal parts and helping verbs. Verbs in the **passive voice** consist of the past participle preceded by a form of *be* ("you *are given*," "I *was given*," "she *will be given*"). Most writers prefer the active to the passive voice because it is clearer and simpler, requires fewer words, and identifies the actor and the action more explicitly.

> ACTIVE VOICE   *Sergeants give* orders. *Privates obey* them.

Some writers use a verb in the passive voice when the active voice would be more effective. Normally the subject of a sentence is the focus of the readers' attention. If that subject does not perform the verb's action but instead receives the action, readers may wonder: What did the writer mean to emphasize? Just what is the point?

> PASSIVE VOICE   *Orders are given* by sergeants. *They are obeyed* by privates.

Other writers misuse the passive voice to try to lend pomp to a humble truth (or would-be truth). The nervous student, trying to impress the professor, says, "Your help is greatly appreciated by me." When the airplane needs repairs, the flight attendant tells the passengers, "Slight technical difficulties are being experienced."

Some writers use the passive voice deliberately to obscure the truth—a contradiction of the very purpose of writing. One of the witnesses in the congressional Iran-Contra hearings tried to dodge a key question by replying, "Whether full knowledge had been attained by us at that time is uncertain." If he had answered in the active voice—"I don't know whether we knew everything then or not"—his listeners easily would have recognized an evasion.

You do not need to eliminate the passive voice entirely from your writing. In some contexts the performer of the verb's action in a sentence is unknown or irrelevant. With a passive voice verb, you can simply omit the performer, as in "Many fortunes were lost in the stock market crash of 1929" or "The passive voice is often misused." It's a good idea, though, as you comb through a rough draft, to substitute the active voice for the passive unless you have a good reason for using the passive.

ESL GUIDELINES: THE PASSIVE VOICE

Passive Voice: *be* + past participle (*-ed/-en*); (memorize irregular forms [see p. H–35])

- In a passive voice sentence, the subject *receives* the action of the verb instead of performing it.

> ACTIVE   The university *awarded* Hamid a scholarship. [The university is doing the action.]
>
> PASSIVE   Hamid *was awarded* a scholarship by the university. [Hamid is receiving the action.]

If the identity of the action's performer is not important or is understood, the *by* phrase may be omitted.

PASSIVE   Automobiles are built in Detroit. [It is understood that they are built *by people*.]

Be careful to maintain the tense of the original active sentence when forming the passive by using the appropriate tense of *be*.

ACTIVE   Bongo the clown *entertains* most children. [Present tense, active voice.]

PASSIVE   Most children *are entertained* by Bongo the clown. [Present tense, passive voice.]

ACTIVE   Bongo the clown *entertained* the children. [Past tense, active voice.]

PASSIVE   The children *were entertained* by Bongo the clown. [Past tense, passive voice.]

NOTE: Intransitive verbs are not used in the passive voice (see p. H–8).

INCORRECT   The plane *was arrived*.

CORRECT   The plane *arrived*.

INCORRECT   The boy *was fallen*.

CORRECT   The boy *fell*.

NOTE: The future progressive and future perfect progressive tenses are not generally used in the passive voice.

Exercise 5–3: Using Active and Passive Voice Verbs

Change the following sentences to the active voice unless you can justify keeping the passive. (You may change more than the verb if doing so improves the sentence.) Example:

Only lip service is paid to moral values by too many of us.

Too many of us pay only lip service to moral values.

a. The *World Book Encyclopedia*'s article about opossums was recently read by me.
b. A resemblance can be noted between the rat and the opossum.
c. Food is caught at night by the opossum.
d. Like all marsupials, the young are carried in a stomach pouch by their mothers.
e. From fifteen to eighteen newborn opossums can be placed in a teaspoon.

1. They are carried by their mothers for two months after birth.
2. Almost any kind of animal or vegetable food is eaten by the opossum.
3. Because opossums have long toes, their tracks are easily recognized.
4. Both North America and South America are lived in by these interesting animals.
5. "Playing possum" (pretending to be dead) was invented by these ingenious animals to fool their predators.

MOOD

Still another characteristic of verbs is mood. Every verb is in one of three **moods**: the **indicative**, the **imperative**, or the **subjunctive**. The indicative mood is the most common. The imperative mood and subjunctive mood add valuable versatility to the English language.

5n *Use the indicative mood to state a fact, to ask a question, or to express an opinion.*

The vast majority of verbs in English are in the indicative mood.

    FACT   Pat *left* home two months ago.

    QUESTION   *Will* she *find* happiness as a belly dancer?

    OPINION   I *think* not.

5o *Use the imperative mood to make a request or to give a command or direction.*

The understood but usually unstated subject of a verb in the imperative mood is *you*. The verb's form is the infinitive.

    REQUEST   Please *be* there before noon. [*You* please be there . . .]

    COMMAND   *Hurry!* [*You* hurry!]

    DIRECTION   To reach my house, *drive* east on State Street. [*you* drive east . . .]

5p *Use the subjunctive mood to express a wish, a requirement, a suggestion, or a condition contrary to fact.*

The subjunctive mood is used in a subordinate clause to suggest uncertainty: the action expressed by the verb may or may not actually take place as specified. In any clause opening with *that* and expressing a requirement, the verb is in the subjunctive mood and its form is the infinitive.

    Professor Avery requires that every student *deliver* his or her work promptly.

    She asked that we *be* on time for all meetings.

When you use the subjunctive mood to describe a condition that is contrary to fact, use *were* if the verb is *be;* for other verbs, use the simple past tense. Wishes, whether present or past, follow the same rules.

    If I *were* rich, I would be happy.

    If I *had* a million dollars, I would be happy.

    Elissa wishes that Ted *were* more goal-oriented.

    Elissa wished that Ted *knew* what he wanted to do.

For a condition that was contrary to fact at some point in the past, use the past perfect tense.

ESL GUIDELINES: CONDITIONALS

Conditional sentences usually contain an *if* clause, which states the condition, and a result clause.

- When the condition is true or possibly true in the present or future, use the present tense in the *if* clause and the present or future tense in the result clause.

    If Jane *prepares* her composition early, she usually *writes* very well.

    If Claudia *saves* any money this month, she *will buy* a new album.

    NOTE: The future tense is not used in the *if* clause.

- When the condition is not true in the present, use the past tense in the *if* clause and use **would**, **could**, or **might** + infinitive form in the result clause.

    If Claudia *saved* enough money, she *could buy* a new pair of jeans. [Condition is not true: Claudia hasn't saved enough money.]

- When the condition was not true in the past, use the past perfect tense in the *if* clause, and use **would have** + past participle (**-ed/-en**) in the result clause.

    If Claudia *had saved* enough money last month, she *would have bought* a new pair of jeans. [Condition is not true: Claudia didn't save enough money.]

If I *had been* awake, I would have seen the meteor showers.

If Jessie *had known* you were coming, she would have cleaned her room.

Although use of the subjunctive mood has grown scarcer over the years, it still sounds crude to write "If I *was* you...." If you ever feel that the subjunctive mood makes a sentence sound stilted, you can rewrite it, substituting an infinitive phrase.

Professor Avery requires every student *to deliver* his or her work promptly.

Exercise 5–4: Using the Correct Mood of Verbs

Correct any errors in mood of verbs in the following sentences. Identify the mood of the incorrect verb as well as of its correct replacement. Some sentences may be correct. Answers for the lettered sentences appear in the back of the book. Example:

If a wish was a horse, then a beggar could ride.

If a wish *were* a horse, then a beggar could ride. [*Was* indicative; *were* subjunctive.]

a. When Janet cooks, she insists that Tom washes the dishes.
b. If Pete want me to help him, he can call and ask me himself.
c. If I was a licensed plumber, I could install the washing machine myself.
d. The IRS recommends that tax forms are filled out as soon as they become available.

e. If that man do not go away, call the police.

1. My sister's teacher insists that every girl wear a skirt to class.
2. You are at my house at six or we'll leave you behind.
3. I would feel more comfortable about leaving if someone was watching my things.
4. Courtesy demands that Jill returns your call.
5. I will pay him only if he give me the book by Friday.

6 SUBJECT-VERB AGREEMENT

What does it mean for a subject and a verb to agree? Practically speaking, it means that their forms are in accord: plural subjects take plural verbs, third-person subjects take third-person verbs, and so forth. Creating agreement in a sentence is like making sure that all the instruments in a song are playing in the same key. When your subjects and verbs agree, you prevent a discord that could distract readers from your message.

6a *A verb agrees with its subject in person and number.*

Subject and verb agree in person (first, second, or third):

> *I write* my research papers on a typewriter. [Subject and verb in first person.]
>
> *Jim writes* his research papers on a word processor. [Subject and verb in third person.]

Subject and verb agree in number (singular or plural):

> *Susan has enjoyed* college. [Subject and verb singular.]
>
> *She and Jim have enjoyed* their vacation. [Subject and verb plural.]

The present tense of most verbs is the infinitive form, with no added ending except in the third-person singular. (See 5g–5l.)

I enjoy	we enjoy
you enjoy	you enjoy
he/she/it enjoys	they enjoy

Forms of the verb *be* vary from this rule.

I am	we are
you are	you are
he/she/it is	they are

6b *A verb agrees with its subject, not with any words that intervene.*

> My *favorite* of O. Henry's short stories *is* "The Gift of the Magi."
>
> *Dollars,* once the dominant currency in international trade, *have fallen* behind the yen.

A singular subject linked to another noun or pronoun by a prepositional phrase such as *as well as, along with,* or *in addition to* remains a singular subject and takes a singular verb.

My cousin *James* as well as his wife and son *plans* to vote for the Democratic candidate.

6c Subjects joined by and *usually take a plural verb.*

Two or more nouns or pronouns linked by *and* constitute a *compound subject.* (See 2a.) In most cases, a compound subject counts as plural and takes a plural verb.

"Howl" and "Gerontion" are Barry's favorite poems.

Sugar, salt, and fat adversely *affect* people's health.

However, for phrases like *each man and woman* or *every dog and cat,* where the subjects are considered individually, use a singular verb.

Each man and woman in the room *has* a different story to tell.

Use a singular verb for two singular subjects that refer to the same thing.

Lime juice and soda quenches your thirst.

6d With subjects joined by or *or* nor, *the verb agrees with the part of the subject nearest to it.*

Either they or *Max is* guilty.

Neither Sally nor *I am* willing to face the truth.

Subjects containing *not . . . but* follow this rule also.

Not we but *George knows* the whole story.

You can remedy the awkwardness of such constructions by rephrasing the offending sentences.

Either they are guilty or Max is.

Sally and I are unwilling to face the truth.

We do not know the whole story, but George does.

6e Most collective nouns take singular verbs.

What do you do when the number of a subject is not obvious? Collective nouns, such as *committee, congregation, family, group, jury,* and *trio,* represent more than one person. When a collective noun refers to a group of people acting in unison, it takes a singular verb.

The *jury finds* the defendant guilty.

My *family upholds* traditional values.

ESL GUIDELINES: COUNT NOUNS

- Nouns that refer to items that can be counted are called count (or count-able) nouns. Count nouns can be made plural.

  table, chair, egg

  two *tables*, several *chairs*, a dozen *eggs*

- Singular count nouns must be preceded by an article or other determiner. The class of words called *determiners* includes possessives (***John's***, ***your***, ***his***, ***my***, and so on), demonstratives (***this***, ***that***, ***these***, ***those***), numbers (***three***, ***the third***, and so on), and indefinite quantity words (***no***, ***some***, ***many***, and so on).

  a dog, *the* football, *one* reason, *the first* page, *no* chance

- When plural count nouns are used in a general way, they are not preceded by an article, but when they are used in a definite or specific way, either because they have already been mentioned or because the context makes them specific, they must be preceded by ***the*** or another determiner.

  Horses don't eat meat, and neither do *cows*.

  Hal is feeding *the horses* in the barn.

  He has already fed *his cows*.

When the members act individually, use a plural verb.

The *jury do* not yet *agree* on a verdict.

Alice's *family* rarely *eat* together.

If you feel that using a plural verb with a collective subject results in an awkward sentence, reword the subject so that it refers to members of the group individually. (Also see 9e.)

The *jurors do* not yet *agree* on a verdict.

The *members* of Alice's family rarely *eat* together.

ESL GUIDELINES: NONCOUNT NOUNS

Nouns that cannot be counted are called ***noncount*** or uncountable nouns. Noncount nouns cannot be made plural.

- Common categories of noncount nouns include types of food (***cheese***, ***meat***, ***bread***, ***broccoli***, and so on), solids (***dirt***, ***salt***, ***chalk***), liquids (***milk***, ***juice***, ***gasoline***), gases (***methane***, ***hydrogen***, ***air***), and abstract ideas, in-cluding emotions (***love***, ***jealousy***, ***democracy***, ***gravity***).

  Water is essential to life.

  Hatred is the opposite of *love*.

  Democracy means "rule by the people."

- Another category of noncount nouns is **mass** nouns, which usually represent a large group of countable nouns, such as **furniture, equipment, luggage, mail,** and **clothing**.

    Our collection of antique *furniture* includes chairs, tables, and sofas.

    We received a letter, two postcards, and other *mail*.

    Lee brought a great deal of *luggage* on his trip.

- The only way to count noncount nouns is to use a countable noun with them; these countable nouns usually indicate a quantity or a container.

    a *piece* of furniture

    two *quarts* of water

    an *example* of jealousy

- Noncount nouns are never preceded by the indefinite article; they are often preceded by **some**.

    | INCORRECT | She gave us *a* good advice. |
    | CORRECT | She gave us good advice. |
    | CORRECT | She gave us *some* good advice. |
    | INCORRECT | I need to learn more *vocabularies*. |
    | CORRECT | I need to learn more *vocabulary*. |

- When noncount nouns are **general** in meaning, no article is required, but when the context makes them specific (usually in a phrase or a clause **after** the noun), the definite article is used.

    | GENERAL | Deliver us from *evil*. |
    | SPECIFIC | The *evil* that humans do lives after them. |

6f *Most indefinite pronouns take a third-person singular verb.*

With the indefinite pronouns *each, either, neither, anyone, anybody, anything, everyone, everybody, everything, one, no one, nobody, nothing, someone, somebody,* and *something* are considered singular and take a third-person singular verb.

Someone is bothering me.

Even when one of these subjects is followed by a phrase containing a noun or pronoun of a different person or number, use a singular verb.

Each of you *is* here to stay.

One of the pandas *seems* dangerously ill.

6g *The indefinite pronouns* all, any, *and* some *use a singular or plural verb depending on their meaning.*

I have no explanation. *Is any* needed?

Any of the changes that really needed to be made *have* been made already.

All is lost.

All of the bananas *are gone*.

Some of the blame *is* mine.

Some of us *are* Democrats.

None — like *all*, *any*, and *some* — takes a singular or a plural verb, depending on the sense in which the pronoun is used. (See also 9d, 9f.)

None of you *is* exempt.

None of his wives *were* blond.

6h In a subordinate clause with a relative pronoun as the subject, the verb agrees with the antecedent.

When you are writing a subordinate clause that modifies a noun, the subject may be a relative pronoun: *who*, *which*, or *that*. To determine the person and number of the verb in the clause, look back at the pronoun's antecedent, the word to which the pronoun refers. (See 9a–9f.) The antecedent is usually (but not always) the noun closest to the relative pronoun.

I have a friend *who studies* day and night. [The antecedent of *who* is the third-person singular noun *friend*. Therefore the verb in the subordinate clause is third-person singular, *studies*.]

Unfortunately, I bought one of the two hundred recently manufactured cars *that have* defective upholstery. [The antecedent of *that* is *cars*, so the verb is third-person plural, *have*.]

This is the only one of the mayor's new ideas *that has* any worth. [Here *one*, not *ideas*, is the antecedent of *that*. Thus the verb in the subordinate clause is third-person singular, *has*, not *have*.]

6i A verb agrees with its subject even when the subject follows the verb.

A writer need not necessarily place the subject of a sentence before the verb. In some sentences, an introductory phrase or a word such as *there* or *here* changes the ordinary subject-verb order. If a sentence opens with such a phrase or word, look for the subject after the verb. Remember that verbs agree with subjects, and that *here* and *there* are never subjects.

Here *is* a *riddle* for you.

There *are* forty *people* in my law class.

Under the bridge *were* a broken-down *boat and* a worn *tire*.

6j A linking verb agrees with its subject, not its subject complement.

In some sentences, a form of the verb *be* is used to link two or more nouns ("Matthew *is* the composer"). The linking verb's subject is the noun that precedes it. Nouns that follow the linking verb are subject complements. (See 2d.) Take care to make a linking verb agree with the subject of the sentence, not with the subject complement.

> *Jim is* a gentleman and a scholar.
>
> Amy's *parents are* her most enthusiastic audience.

6k *When the subject is a title, use a singular verb.*

> When I was younger, *James and the Giant Peach* by Roald Dahl *was* my favorite book.
>
> "Memories" sung by Barbra Streisand *is* my favorite song.

6l *Singular nouns that end in -s take singular verbs.*

Some nouns look plural even though they refer to a singular subject: *news, measles, logistics, mathematics, physics, electronics, economics.* Such nouns take singular verbs.

> The *news is* that *economics has become* one of the most popular majors.

Exercise 6–1: Making Subjects and Verbs Agree

Find and correct any errors of subject-verb agreement in the following sentences. Some sentences may be correct. Answers for the lettered sentences appear in the back of the book. Example:

> Addressing the audience tonight is the nominees for club president.
>
> Addressing the audience tonight *are* the nominees for club president.

a. Our foreign policy in Cuba, Nicaragua, El Salvador, and Panama have not been as successful as most Americans had hoped.

b. The large amount of metal and chlorine in our water makes it taste funny.

c. I read about a couple who is offering to trade their baby for a brand-new Chevrolet.

d. A shave, a haircut, and a new suit has turned Bill into a different person.

e. Neither the fruit nor the vegetables is fresh.

1. Each of us, including Alice, want this to be a successful party.

2. The police force, after the recent rash of burglaries, have added more patrols in this neighborhood.

3. More disturbing than John's speech was the gestures that accompanied it.

4. Samantha is one of those women who never wear shoes indoors.

5. Nearly everybody who traveled by air during the last six weeks were aware of increased security precautions.

6. The bad news about interest rates have been widely publicized.

7. Most of the class believed that both the private sector and the government was taking appropriate action on homelessness.

8. Lee's sister, as well as his brothers, have always been involved in the family business.

9. Ron Wood is not the only member of the Rolling Stones who have played in the band Faces.

10. Here among the geraniums lie the other rosebush you and Lois planted last spring.

7 PRONOUN CASE

As you know, pronouns come in distinctive forms. The first-person pronoun can be *I*, or it can be *me, my, mine, we, us, our,* or *ours*. Which form do you pick? It depends on what job you want the pronoun to do. Filling these jobs may sound easy, but now and again every writer has a hard time hiring the pronoun that is properly qualified.

To choose correctly, it may help you to know the three *cases* used to classify pronouns. Depending on a pronoun's function in a sentence, we say that it is in the **subjective case**, the **objective case**, or the **possessive case**.

Some pronouns change form when they change case and some do not. The personal pronouns *I, he, she, we,* and *they* and the relative pronoun *who* have different forms in the subjective, objective, and possessive cases. Other pronouns, such as *you, it, that,* and *which,* have only two forms: the plain case (which serves as both subjective and objective) and the possessive case.

PRONOUN CASES

SUBJECTIVE	OBJECTIVE	POSSESSIVE
I	me	my, mine
you	you	your, yours
he, she, it	him, her, it	his, her, hers, its
we	us	our, ours
you	you	your, yours
they	them	their, theirs
who	whom	whose

We can pin the labels *subjective, objective,* and *possessive* on nouns as well as on pronouns. Nouns, after all, do the same jobs as pronouns. However, like the pronouns *you, it, that,* and *which,* nouns shift out of their plain form only in the possessive case (*teacher's* pet, the *Joneses'* poodle).

Beware, when you are not sure which case to choose, of the temptation to fall back on a reflexive pronoun (*myself, himself*). Reflexive pronouns have limited, specific uses in writing (see 1b). They do not take the place of subjective or objective pronouns. If you catch yourself writing, "You can return the form to John or *myself*" or "John and *myself* are in charge," replace the reflexive pronoun with one that is grammatically correct: "You can return the form to John or *me*"; "John and *I* are in charge."

7a *Use the subjective case for the subject of a sentence or clause.*

I ate the granola.

Who cares?

Mark recalled that *she* played jai alai.

Election officials are the people *who* count.

Sometimes a compound subject will lead a writer astray: "Jed and *me* ate the granola." *Me*, an objective pronoun, is the wrong one for this job. Use the subjective form, *I*, instead.

A pronoun serving as subject for a verb is subjective even when the verb isn't written but is only implied:

Jed is hungrier than *I* [am].

Don't be fooled by a pronoun that appears immediately after a verb, as if it were a direct object, but that functions as the subject of a clause. The pronoun's case is determined by its role in the sentence, not its position.

The judge didn't believe *I* hadn't been the driver.

We were happy to interview *whoever* was running [Subject of *was running*.]

7b *Use the subjective case for a subject complement.*

A pronoun can function as a subject complement after a linking verb such as *is, seems,* or *appears.* (See 2d for more on subject complements, 5a for more on linking verbs.) Because it plays essentially the same role as the subject, the pronoun's case is subjective.

The phantom graffiti artist couldn't have been *he*. It was *I*.

7c *Use the subjective case for an appositive to a subject or a subject complement.*

A pronoun placed in apposition to a subject or subject complement is like an identical twin to the noun it stands beside. It has the same meaning and the same case. (See also 3d.)

The class *officers*—Jed and *she*—announced a granola breakfast.

7d *Use the objective case for a direct object, an indirect object, or the object of a preposition.*

> The custard pies hit *him* and *me*. [Direct object.]
>
> *Whom* do you love? [Direct object.]
>
> Mona threw *us* towels. [Indirect object.]
>
> Tell *her* your feelings. [Indirect object.]
>
> Mona threw towels to *him* and *us*. [Object of a preposition.]
>
> Binks is the professor of *whom* I hear glowing reports. [Object of a preposition.]

7e *Use the objective case for an appositive to a direct or indirect object or the object of a preposition.*

> Mona helped *us* all—Mrs. Van Dumont, *him*, and *me*. [*Him* and *me* are in apposition to the direct object *us*.]
>
> Binks gave his favorite *students*, Tom and *her*, an approving nod. [*Her* is in apposition to the indirect object *students*.]
>
> Yelling, the persistent pie flingers ran after *us*—Mrs. Van Dumont, Mona, *him*, and *me*. [*Him* and *me* are in apposition to *us*, the object of the preposition *after*.]

> POSSESSIVE PRONOUNS
> my, mine, our, ours, his, her, hers, its, your, yours, their, theirs

7f *Use the possessive case to show ownership.*

Possessive pronouns can function as adjectives or as nouns. The pronouns *my, your, his, her, its, our,* and *their* function as adjectives by modifying nouns or pronouns.

> *Their* apartment is bigger than *our* house.
>
> *My* new bike is having *its* first road test today.

Notice that the possessive pronoun *its* does not contain an apostrophe. *It's* with an apostrophe is not a possessive pronoun, but a contraction for *it is*, as in "*It's* a beautiful day." If you want to write about the day and *its* beauty, be sure to omit the apostrophe.

The possessive pronouns *mine, yours, his, hers, ours,* and *theirs* can discharge the whole range of noun duties. These pronouns can serve as subjects, subject complements, direct objects, indirect objects, or objects of prepositions.

> *Yours* is the last vote we need. [Subject.]
>
> This day is *ours*. [Subject complement.]
>
> Don't take your car; take *mine*. [Direct object.]

If we're honoring requests in chronological order, give *hers* top priority. [Indirect object.]

Give her request priority over *theirs*. [Object of a preposition.]

7g *Use the possessive case to modify a gerund.*

A possessive pronoun (or a possessive noun) is the appropriate escort for a gerund, a form of verb that functions as a noun: *griping, being, drinking*. (See 3b.) As a noun, a gerund requires an adjective, not another noun, for a modifier.

> Mary is tired of *his griping*. [The possessive pronoun *his* modifies the gerund *griping*.]
>
> I can stand *their being* late every morning, but not *his drinking* on the job. [The possessive pronoun *their* modifies the gerund *being*; the possessive pronoun *his* modifies the gerund *drinking*.]

Gerunds can cause confusion when you edit your writing because they look exactly like participles. (See 5c.) Whereas a gerund functions as a noun, a participle often functions as an adjective modifying a noun or pronoun.

> Mary heard *him griping* about work. [The participle *griping* modifies the direct object *him*.]

If you are not sure whether to use a possessive or an objective pronoun with a word ending in *-ing*, look closely at your sentence. Which word—the pronoun or the *-ing* word—is the object of your main verb? That word functions as a noun; the other word modifies it.

> Mr. Phipps remembered *them* smoking in the boys' room.
>
> Mr. Phipps remembered *their* smoking in the boys' room.

In the first sentence, Mr. Phipps's memory is of *them*, those naughty students. *Them* is the object of the verb, so *smoking* is a participle modifying *them*. In the second sentence, Mr. Phipps remembers *smoking*, that nasty habit. The gerund *smoking* is the object of the verb, so the possessive pronoun *their* is the right choice to modify it.

In everyday speech, the rules about pronoun case apply less rigidly. Someone who correctly asks in conversation, "To whom are you referring?" is likely to sound pretentious. You are within your rights to reply, as did the comic-strip character Pogo Possum, "Youm, that's whom!" Say, if you like, "It's *me*," but write "It is *I*." Say, if you wish, "*Who* did he ask to the party?" but write "*Whom* did he ask?"

Exercise 7–1: Using Pronouns Correctly

Replace any pronouns that are used incorrectly in the following sentences. (Consider all these examples as written—not spoken—English, and so apply the rules strictly.) Explain why each pronoun was incorrect. Some sentences may be correct. Answers for the lettered sentences appear in the back of the book. Example:

> In the photograph, that's him at the age of seven.
>
> In the photograph, that's *he* at the age of seven. [*He* is a subject complement.]

a. She can run faster than me.

b. Mrs. Van Dumont awarded the prize to Mona and I.

c. Jud laughed at both of us—she and I.

d. Were you referring to we?

e. Jerry, myself, and the pizza chef regard you and she as the very women who we wish to get acquainted with.

1. I like to watch them swimming in the hotel pool.

2. Whoever you wish to invite along is acceptable to Jeff and I.

3. The waiters and us busboys are highly trustworthy.

4. I won't tolerate you whistling in the courtroom.

5. Strictly platonic affairs suit us—Biff, the Flipper, and me.

6. Dean Fitts and them, who I suspect of being the pie throwers, flung crusty missiles at Mona, Mrs. Van Dumont, he, and myself.

7. Have I reached the party who I spoke to yesterday?

8. I didn't appreciate you laughing at her and I.

9. They—Jerry and her—are the troublemakers.

10. It was him asking about the clock that started me suspecting him.

11. Juliana isn't as old-fashioned in her views as them.

12. She gave Jed and I some bad advice.

13. There is a lack of communication among you and he and Dean.

14. The counterattack was launched by Dusty and myself.

15. Whomever this anonymous letter writer is, I resent him lying about Jules and me and the cabbages.

8 PRONOUN REFERENCE

Look hard at just about any piece of writing—this discussion, if you like—and you'll find that practically every pronoun in it points to some noun. This is the main use of pronouns: to refer in a brief, convenient form to some **antecedent** that has already been named. A pronoun usually has a noun or another pronoun as its antecedent. Often the antecedent is the subject or object of the same clause in which the pronoun appears.

> Josie hit the *ball* after *its* first bounce.
>
> Smashing into *Greg*, the ball knocked off *his* glasses.

The antecedent also can appear in a different clause or even a different sentence from the pronoun.

Josie hit the *ball* when *it* bounced back to *her*.

The *ball* smashed into *Greg*. *It* knocked off *his* glasses.

A pronoun as well as a noun can be an antecedent.

My *dog* hid in the closet when *she* had *her* puppies. [*Dog* is the antecedent of *she*; *she* is the antecedent of *her*.]

EDITING CHECKLIST: MAKING PRONOUN REFERENCE CLEAR

- ✓ Do all pronouns have named, not just implied, antecedents? (8a)
- ✓ Is the meaning of the pronoun *it*, *this*, *that*, or *which* always clear? (8b)
- ✓ Where there is more than one noun preceding a pronoun, is the identity of the antecedent clear? (8c)
- ✓ Is every pronoun close enough to its antecedent to make the relationship clear? (8d)

8a *Name the pronoun's antecedent—don't just imply it.*

In editing, in combing over what you write, be sure you have identified clearly the antecedent of each pronoun. A writer who leaves a key idea unsaid is likely to confuse readers.

> **VAGUE** Ted wanted a Norwegian canoe because he'd heard that *they* produce the lightest canoes afloat.

What does *they* refer to? Not to *Norwegian*, which is an adjective; the antecedent of a pronoun has to be a noun or pronoun. We may guess that this writer has in mind Norwegian canoe builders, but no such noun has been mentioned. To make the sentence work, the writer must supply an antecedent for *they*.

> **CLEAR** Ted wanted a Norwegian canoe because he'd heard that Norway produces [*or* Norwegians produce] the lightest canoes afloat.

Watch out for possessive nouns. They won't work as antecedents.

> **VAGUE** On William's canoe *he* painted a skull and bones. (For all we know, *he* might be some joker named Fred.)
>
> **CLEAR** On his canoe William painted a skull and bones.

8b *Give the pronoun it, this, that, or which a clear antecedent.*

Vagueness arises, thick as fog, whenever *it, this, that,* or *which* points to something a writer assumes he or she has said but indeed hasn't. Is the reference of a pronoun fuzzy? Might a reader get lost in the fog? Often the best way out of the fog is to substitute a specific noun or phrase for the pronoun.

VAGUE   I was an only child, and *it* was hard.

CLEAR   I was an only child, and *my solitary life* was hard. ·

VAGUE   Ruth majored in economics and applied for a job in a broker's office, *which* caused her father to exult. Still, *it* was not what she desired.

CLEAR   Ruth majored in economics and applied for a job in a broker's office, *decisions* that pleased her father. Still, *a career in finance* was not what she desired.

8c *Make the pronoun's antecedent clear.*

Confusion strikes again if the antecedent of a pronoun is ambiguous — that is, if the pronoun seems to point in two or more directions. In such a puzzling situation, there's no lack of antecedent; the trouble is that more than one antecedent looks possible. Baffled, the reader wonders which the writer means.

CONFUSING   Rob shouted to Jim to take off his burning sweater.

Whose sweater does *his* mean — Jim's or Rob's? Simply changing a pronoun won't clear up the confusion. The writer needs to revise the sentence drastically enough to move the two antecedents out of each other's way.

CLEAR   "Help, Rob!" Jim shouted. "My sweater's on fire! Take it off!"

CLEAR   "Jim!" shouted Rob. "Your sweater's on fire! Take it off!"

CLEAR   Flames were shooting from Jim's sweater. Rob shouted to Jim to take it off.

As you can tell from that first fogbound sentence, pronouns referring to nouns of the same gender are particular offenders. How would you straighten out this grammatical tangle?

CONFUSING   Linda welcomed Lee-Ann's move into the apartment next door. Little did she dream that soon she would be secretly dating her husband.

Let meaning show the way. If you had written these sentences, you would know which person is the sneak. One way to clarify the antecedents of *she* and *her* is to add more information.

CLEAR   In welcoming Lee-Ann to the apartment next door, Linda didn't dream that soon her own husband would be secretly dating her former sorority sister.

Instead of *her own husband*, you can identify that philanderer by name if you have previously identified him as Linda's husband: "Ned would be secretly dating. . . ." (Grammatical tangles are easier than human tangles to straighten out.)

8d *Place the pronoun close to its antecedent to keep the relationship clear.*

Watch out for distractions that slip in between noun and pronoun. If, before your readers come to a pronoun in your sentence, they meet other nouns—interesting nouns—that might look like antecedents, they may become bewildered.

CONFUSING   Harper steered his dinghy alongside the polished mahogany cabin cruiser that the drug smugglers had left anchored under an overhanging willow in the tiny harbor and eased it to a stop.

What did Harper ease to a stop? By the time readers reach the end of the sentence, they are likely to have forgotten. To avoid confusion, keep the pronoun and its antecedent reasonably close together.

CLEAR   Harper steered his dinghy into the tiny harbor and eased it to a stop alongside the polished mahogany cabin cruiser that the drug smugglers had left anchored under an overhanging willow.

Never force your readers to stop and think, "What does that pronoun stand for?" You, the writer, have to do this thinking for them.

Exercise 8–1: Making Pronoun Reference Clear

Rewrite each sentence or group of sentences so that any pronoun needing an antecedent clearly points to one. Possible revisions for the lettered sentences appear in the back of the book. Example:

If your dog tries to bite your guest, tie him up in the yard.

If your dog tries to bite your guest, tie the dog up in the yard.

a. When computers cost the same as television sets, every American will own one.

b. After Sarah's meeting with her newspaper's editor, she reported that she wasn't sure if she agreed with her position on freedom of speech.

c. I cannot speak of epileptic seizures with firsthand knowledge because I have never had any.

d. Marsha didn't know Russian and had allergies, but this didn't stop her from summering on a Ukrainian wheat farm.

e. Swaying gently in his parachute, floating lazily to earth, Edgar felt pure joy. It had been the finest thing he'd ever tried, and he was all for it.

1. Glancing down, Edgar saw the cactus loom and heard the rattlesnake hiss, which promised an uncertain landing.

2. The delicacy of the statue's carving, which obviously dates from a period when sculptors were highly respected, is what makes it valuable.

3. American auto workers and their Japanese counterparts differ in that they place less emphasis on quality. Detroit car manufacturers, however, are taking steps to solve this.

4. Casper told Damon he was an embezzler and he had been doing it for several

years. It was, he added, none of his business; and he would thank him to keep quiet about it.

5. Beachcombing, picking up shells, bottles, and driftwood, I found one containing a yellowed message dated 1792. "Why," he pleaded, "has no one answered the message I launched in 1789?"

9   PRONOUN-ANTECEDENT AGREEMENT

A pronoun's job is to fill in for a noun, much as an actor's double fills in for the actor. Pronouns are a short, convenient way for writers to avoid repeating the same noun over and over. The noun that a pronoun stands for is called its **antecedent**.

> The sheriff drew a six-shooter; he fired twice.

This action-packed sentence unfolds in a familiar order. First comes a noun (*sheriff*), and then a pronoun (*he*) that refers back to it. *Sheriff* is the antecedent of *he*.

Just as verbs need to agree with their subjects, pronouns need to agree with the nouns they stand for. A successful writer takes care not to shift number, person, or gender in mid-sentence ("The *sheriff* and the *outlaw* drew *their* six-shooters; *he* fired twice"). Rather, the writer starts each sentence with nouns clearly in mind and picks appropriate pronouns to refer to them.

9a   *Pronouns agree with their antecedents in person and number.*

A pronoun matches its antecedent in person (first, second, or third) and in number (singular or plural), even when a string of intervening words separates the pronoun and its antecedent. (See the pronoun chart in 1b.)

> **FAULTY**   All *campers* should bring *your* knapsacks.

Here, noun and pronoun disagree in person: *campers* is third person, but *your* is second person.

> **FAULTY**   Every *camper* should bring *their* knapsack.

EDITING CHECKLIST: MAKING PRONOUNS AGREE WITH THEIR ANTECEDENTS

- Do pronouns agree with their antecedents in number (singular or plural)? (9a)
- Do pronouns agree with their antecedents in person (first, second, or third)? (9a)
- Do pronouns agree with their antecedents in gender (masculine, feminine, or neuter)? (9f)

Here, noun and pronoun disagree in number: *camper* is singular, but *their* is plural.

> **REVISED**   All *campers* should bring *their* knapsacks.
>
> **REVISED**   Every *camper* should bring *his or her* knapsack.

(See also 9f.)

9b *Most antecedents joined by* and *require a plural pronoun.*

What if the subject of your sentence is two nouns (or a noun and a pronoun) connected by *and?* Such a compound subject is plural; use a plural pronoun to refer to it.

> *George,* who has been here before, *and Susan,* who hasn't, should bring *their* knapsacks.

However, if the nouns in a compound subject refer to the same person or thing, they make up a singular antecedent. In that case, the pronoun too is singular.

> The *owner and founder* of this camp carries *his* own knapsack everywhere.

9c *A pronoun agrees with the closest part of an antecedent joined by* or *or* nor.

If your subject is two or more nouns (or a combination of nouns and pro-nouns) connected by *or* or *nor,* look closely at the subject's parts. Are they all singular? If so, your pronoun should be singular.

> Neither *Joy nor Jean* remembered *her* knapsack last year.
>
> If *Sam, Arthur, or Max* shows up, tell *him* I'm looking for *him.*

If the part of the subject closest to the pronoun is plural, the pronoun should be plural.

> Neither *Joy nor her sisters* remembered *their* knapsacks last year.
>
> If you see *Sam, Arthur, or their friends,* tell *them* I'm looking for *them.*

9d *An antecedent that is an indefinite pronoun takes a singular pronoun.*

An indefinite pronoun is one that does not refer to any specific person, place, or thing: *anybody, each, either.* (For a complete list, see the pronoun chart in 1b.) Indefinite pronouns are usually singular in meaning, so a pronoun referring to one of them is also singular.

> *Either* of the boys can do it, as long as *he's* on time.
>
> Warn *anybody* who's still in *her* swimsuit that a uniform is required for dinner.

Sometimes the meaning of an indefinite pronoun is plural. To avoid awkwardness, avoid using such a pronoun as an antecedent.

Tell *everyone* in Cabin B that I'm looking for *him*.

This sentence works better if it is phrased differently.

Tell *all the campers* in Cabin B that I'm looking for *them*.

(See also 6f, 9f.)

9e Most collective nouns used as antecedents require singular pronouns.

A collective noun is a singular word for a group of people or items: *army, band, committee, jury*. When the members of such a group act as a unit, use a singular pronoun to refer to them.

The *cast* for the camp play will be posted as soon as our theater counselor chooses *it*.

When the group members act individually, use a plural pronoun.

The *cast* will go *their* separate ways when summer ends.

(See also 6e.)

9f A pronoun agrees with its antecedent in gender.

If *one of your parents* brings you to camp, invite *him* to stay for lunch.

While technically correct (the singular pronoun *he* is used to refer to the singular antecedent *one*), this sentence overlooks the fact that some parents are male, some female. To make sure the pronoun refers to both, a writer has two choices. (See 22a, 22c, 22d.)

If *one of your parents* brings you to camp, invite *him or her* to stay for lunch.

If your *parents* bring you to camp, invite *them* to stay for lunch.

Exercise 9–1: Making Pronouns and Antecedents Agree

If any nouns and pronouns disagree in number, person, or gender in the following sentences, substitute pronouns that will get along better. If you prefer, strengthen any sentence by rewriting it. Some sentences may be correct. Possible revisions for the lettered sentences appear in the back of the book. Example:

A cat expects people to feed them often.

A *cat* expects people to feed *it* often.

Cats expect people to feed *them* often.

a. All students are urged to complete your registration on time.

b. When a baby doesn't know their own mother, they may have been born with some kind of vision deficiency.

c. Each member of the sorority has to make his own bed.

d. If you don't like the songs the choir sings, don't join them.

e. Selfish people always look out for oneself.

1. Everyone is expected to keep their own clothes clean.

2. Bill refuses to kill spiders because he says it eats other bugs.

3. Neither Melissa nor James has received their application form yet.

4. He is the kind of man who gets their fun out of just sipping one's beer and watching his Saturday games on TV.

5. Many an architect finds work their greatest pleasure.

6. Although a business executive may work long hours, he should try to spend time with his family.

7. When our players heard the other team's jeers, they jumped to their feet.

8. Both they and Joyce have said she regrets the argument.

9. When one enjoys one's work, it's easy to spend all your spare time thinking about it.

10. If you love someone, set them free.

10 ADJECTIVES AND ADVERBS

An adjective is a word that modifies a noun or pronoun. (See 1d.) A phrase also can function as an adjective. (See 3a, 3b, 3f.) An adjective's job is to provide information about the person, place, object, or idea named by the noun or pronoun. The adjective typically answers the question Which? or What kind?

> Karen bought a *small red* car.
>
> The radios *on sale* are an *excellent* value.

An adverb is a word (or a phrase) that modifies a verb, an adjective, or another adverb. (See 1e, 3a, 3b, 3g.) An adverb typically answers the question How? or When? or Where? Sometimes it answers the question Why?

> Karen bought her car *quickly*.
>
> The radios arrived *yesterday*; Max put them *in the electronics department*.
>
> Karen needed her new car *to commute to school.*

The most common problems that writers have with adjectives and adverbs involve mixing them up: sending an adjective to do an adverb's job or vice versa.

ESL GUIDELINES: THE DEFINITE ARTICLE (the)

- Use the definite article, *the*, with a specific count or noncount noun (p. H–53) when both the writer and the reader know the identity of what is referred to or when the noun has been mentioned before.

  Did you feed *the* baby? [Both the reader and the writer know which baby is referred to.]

  The coffee tastes strong today. [Both the reader and the writer know which coffee is referred to.]

  She got a huge box in the mail. *The* box contained oranges from Florida. [*The* is used the second time the noun is mentioned.]

- Use the definite article, *the*, before specific count or noncount nouns when the reader is given enough information to identify what is being referred to.

  The furniture in my apartment is old and faded. [Specific furniture.]

  The young woman wearing blue is my sister. [Specific young woman.]

- Use the definite article, *the*, before a singular count noun to make a generality.

  The dog has been humans' favorite pet for centuries. [*The dog* here refers to all dogs.]

- Use the definite article before some geographical names.

  Collectives: the United States, the United Kingdom

  Groups of Islands: the Bahamas, the Canary Islands

  Large Bodies of Water (except lakes): the Atlantic Ocean, the Dead Sea, the Monongahela River, the Gulf of Mexico

  Mountain Ranges: the Rockies, the Himalaya Mountains

ESL GUIDELINES: THE INDEFINITE ARTICLE (a, an)

- Use the indefinite article, *a* or *an*, with a nonspecific, singular count noun when it is not known to the reader or to either the reader or the writer.

  My brother has *an* antique car. [The car's identity is unknown to the reader.]

  I saw *a* dog in my backyard this morning. [The dog's identity is unknown to both the reader and writer.]

- Use the indefinite article when the noun is mentioned for the first time. Use the definite article when the noun is mentioned again.

  I saw *a* car that I would love to buy. *The* car was red and had a leather interior.

> • Use **some** or no article instead of *a* or *an* with noncount nouns or plural nouns used in a general sense.
>
> INCORRECT   I am going to buy *a* furniture for my apartment.
>
> CORRECT   I am going to buy *some* furniture for my apartment.
>
> CORRECT   I am going to buy furniture for my apartment.

10a *Use an adverb, not an adjective, to modify a verb, adjective, or adverb.*

FAULTY   Karen bought her car *quick*.

FAULTY   It's *awful* hot today.

Although an informal speaker might be able to get away with these sentences, a writer cannot. *Quick* and *awful* are adjectives, so they can modify only nouns or pronouns. To modify the verb *bought* we need the adverb *quickly*; to modify the adjective *hot* we need the adverb *awfully*.

REVISED   Karen bought her car *quickly*.

REVISED   It's *awfully* hot today.

ADJECTIVES AND ADVERBS AT A GLANCE

ADJECTIVES
1. Typically answer the question Which? or What kind?
2. Modify nouns or pronouns

ADVERBS
3. Answer the question How? When? Where? or sometimes Why?
4. Modify verbs, adjectives, and other adverbs

10b *Use an adjective, not an adverb, as a subject complement or object complement.*

If we write, "Her old car looked awful," *awful* is a subject complement: it follows a linking verb and modifies the subject, *car*. (See 2d, 5a.)

FAULTY   Her old car looked *awfully*.

REVISED   Her old car looked *awful*.

An object complement is a word that renames a direct object or completes the sentence's description of it. (See 2d.) Object complements can be adjectives or nouns, but never adverbs.

Early to bed and early to rise makes a man *healthy, wealthy,* and *wise*. [Adjectives modifying the direct object *man*.]

When you are not sure whether you're dealing with an object complement or an adverb, look closely at the word's role in the sentence. If it modifies a noun, it is an object complement and therefore should be an adjective.

> The coach called the referee *stupid* and *blind*. [*Stupid* and *blind* are adjectives modifying the direct object *referee*.]

If it modifies a verb, you want an adverb instead.

> In fact, though, the ref had called the play *correctly*. [*Correctly* is an adverb modifying the verb *called*.]

10c Use good *as an adjective and* well *as an adverb.*

A common adjective-adverb mix-up occurs when writers confuse *good* and *well* as subject complements. *Good* is almost always an adjective; *well* is almost always an adverb.

> This sandwich tastes *good*. [The adjective *good* is a subject complement following the linking verb *tastes* and modifying the noun *sandwich*.]
>
> Heloise's skin healed *well* after surgery. [The adverb *well* modifies the verb *healed*.]

Only if the verb is a linking verb (see list in 5a) can you safely follow it with *good*. Other kinds of verbs do not take subject complements. Instead, they need adverbs to modify them.

> **FAULTY**   That painting came out *good*.
>
> **REVISED**   That painting came out *well*.

Complications arise when we write or speak about health. It is perfectly correct to say *I feel good*, using the adjective *good* as a subject complement after the linking verb *feel*. However, generations of confusion have nudged the adverb *well* into the adjective category, too. A nurse may speak of "a well baby"; and greeting cards urge patients to "get well"—meaning, "become healthy." Just as *healthy* is an adjective here, so is *well*.

What, then, is the best answer when someone asks, "How do you feel?" If you want to duck the issue, reply, "Fine!" Otherwise, in speech either *good* or *well* is acceptable; in writing, use *good*.

10d Form comparatives and superlatives of most adjectives with -er *and* -est *and of most adverbs with* more *and* most.

Comparatives and superlatives are special adjective and adverb forms that allow us to describe one thing in relation to another. You can put most adjectives into their comparative form by adding *-er* and into their superlative form by adding *-est*.

> The budget deficit is *larger* than the trade deficit.
>
> This year's trade deficit is the *largest* ever.

ESL GUIDELINES: CUMULATIVE ADJECTIVES

- Cumulative adjectives usually have a specific order of placement before a noun (25d). Use the following chart as a guideline for writing sentences with adjectives, but keep in mind that the order can be flexible.

  1. *Articles or determiners*
     a, an, the, some, this, these, his, my, several
  2. *Evaluative adjectives*
     beautiful, wonderful, hardworking, distasteful
  3. *Size or dimension*
     big, small, huge, obese, petite, six-foot
  4. *Length or shape*
     Long, short, round, square, oblong, oval
  5. *age*
     old, young, new, fresh, ancient
  6. *Color*
     red, pink, aquamarine, orange
  7. *Nation or place of origin*
     American, Japanese, European, Bostonian, Floridian
  8. *Religion*
     Protestant, Muslim, Hindu, Buddhist, Catholic
  9. *Matter or substance*
     wood, gold, cotton, plastic, pine, metal
  10. *Noun used as an adjective*
      telephone (as in *telephone operator*), computer (as in *computer software*)
  11. *The noun being modified*
      woman, house, book, flower, desk, wedding

- Cumulative adjectives do not require commas when used in a series.

  She is an *attractive older French* woman.

  His *expressive large brown* eyes moved me.

We usually form the comparative and superlative of long adjectives with *more* and *most* rather than with *-er* and *-est*, to keep them from becoming cumbersome.

Our national debt is *enormous.*

It may become *more enormous* over the next few years.

For short adverbs that do not end in *-ly*, usually add *-er* and *-est* in the comparative and superlative forms. With all other adverbs, use *more* and *most.*

Spending *faster* than one earns will plunge a person into debt *sooner* than any other way I know.

The *more indiscriminately* we import foreign goods, the *more rapidly* the trade deficit grows.

It grows *fastest* and *most uncontrollably* when exports are down.

For negative comparisons, use *less* and *least* for both adjectives and adverbs.

> Michael's speech was *less interesting* than Louie's.
>
> Paulette spoke *less interestingly* than Michael.
>
> Bud's speech was the *least interesting* of all.

The comparative and superlative forms of irregular adjectives and adverbs (such as *bad* and *badly*) are also irregular and should be used with special care.

> Tom's golf is *bad*, but no *worse* than George's.
>
> Tom plays golf *badly*, but no *worse* than George does.

COMPARISON OF IRREGULAR ADJECTIVES AND ADVERBS

POSITIVE	COMPARATIVE	SUPERLATIVE
ADJECTIVES		
good	better	best
bad	worse	worst
little	less, littler	least, littlest
many, some, much	more	most
ADVERBS		
well	better	best
badly	worse	worst
little	less	least

10e *Omit* more *and* most *with an adjective or adverb that is already comparative or superlative.*

Some words become comparative or superlative when we tack on *-er* or *-est*. Others, such as *top*, *favorite*, and *unique*, mark whatever they modify as one of a kind by definition. Neither category requires further assistance to make its point. To say "a *more worse* fate" or "my *most favorite* movie" is redundant—"a *worse* fate" or "my *favorite* movie" does the job.

> FAULTY   Lisa is *more uniquely* qualified for the job than any other candidate.
>
> REVISED   Lisa is *better* qualified for the job than any other candidate.
>
> REVISED   Lisa is *uniquely* qualified for the job.

10f *Use the comparative form of an adjective or adverb to compare two people or things, the superlative form to compare more than two.*

No matter how fantastic, wonderful, and terrific something is, we can call it the *best* only when we compare it with more than one other thing. Any comparison between two things uses the comparative form, not the superlative.

FAULTY	Their chocolate and vanilla are both good, but I like the chocolate *best*.
REVISED	Their chocolate and vanilla are both good, but I like the chocolate *better*.
FAULTY	Of his two dogs, he treats Bonzo *most affectionately*.
REVISED	Of his two dogs, he treats Bonzo *more affectionately*.

ESL GUIDELINES: NEGATIVES

- You can make a sentence negative by using either **not** or another negative adverb (such as **never, hardly,** or **seldom**).

With **not**: subject + helping verb + **not** + main verb

Regina has *not* driven across the country before.

Jerry did *not* go to the concert.

They will *not* call again.

For questions: helping verb + subject + **not** + main verb

Has Regina *not* driven across the country before?

Did Jerry *not* go to the concert?

Will they *not* call again?

With contraction **n't** (for **not**): helping verb + **n't** + subject + main verb

Hasn't Regina driven across the country before?

Didn't Jerry go to the concert?

Won't [for *Will not*] they call again?

- With a negative adverb: subject + negative adverb + main verb; **or** subject + helping verb + negative adverb + main verb

Negative adverbs include **seldom, rarely, never, hardly, hardly ever,** and **almost never**.

My son *seldom* watches TV.

John may *never* see them again.

Maxine is *rarely* in a bad mood.

When a negative adverb is placed at the beginning of a clause: negative adverb + helping verb + subject + verb

Not only does Emma play tennis well, but she also excels in golf.

Never before have I been so happy.

Exercise 10–1: Using Adjectives and Adverbs Correctly

Find and correct any improperly used adjectives and adverbs in the following sentences. Some sentences may be correct. Answers for the lettered sentences appear in the back of the book. Example:

Nobody on our team pitches as good as Jesse.

Nobody on our team pitches as *well* as Jesse.

a. Which of your two brothers is the oldest?

b. Since Mrs. Fox developed arthritis, she can't move as quick as she used to.

c. Using adjectives correct is tricky, but using adverbs correct is trickiest.

d. Among spring's greatest joys are the birds that sing so sweet every morning.

e. Judy talks a lot about Scott, but she spends all her time with Todd, so she must like Todd the most.

1. Hank's science project didn't work out as bad as he had feared.

2. Implanting the electrodes proved to be less harder than regulating the dosage.

3. That song sounds great when the drummer plays real loud.

4. After Luke's dog bit a skunk, the house didn't smell very good.

5. Would Snow White and her prince have lived happier ever after with the Seven Dwarfs out of the picture?

6. Even more worse than marrying a woman with seven jealous male friends would be having a witch for a mother-in-law.

7. Which dwarf in the Disney film is funnier: Sleepy, Dopey, or Doc?

8. Lucy's most favorite Disney film is *Dumbo*.

9. Her father, Tim, says that the excitingest filmmaker today is not George Lucas but Martin Scorsese.

10. Tim considered *Duck Soup* better than *A Day at the Races*, and he liked the middle film in the *Star Wars* trilogy the least.

11 SHIFTS

When you look at a scene, you view it from a particular position in time and space. If you go to your favorite spot at the beach at dawn, at noon, at twilight, and at midnight, the scene will appear different each time. If you look at the scene standing on a sand dune, lying flat on the sand, or swimming in the surf, it will appear different from each location. Your perspective or point of view determines the details of the scene.

Similarly, when you perceive a subject, you may consider it from various positions. If the time or the actor changes, your writing should reflect the change. However, writers sometimes shift point of view unconsciously or unnecessarily, causing ambiguity and confusion for readers. Such shifts are evident in grammatical inconsistencies.

11a *Maintain consistency in verb tense.*

When you write a paragraph or an essay, keep the verbs in the same tense unless the time changes.

INCONSISTENT	Football *is* a favorite spectator sport in my hometown. When the quarterback *threw* for a touchdown, everyone in the bleachers *stood* up and *cheered*.
CONSISTENT	Football *is* a favorite spectator sport in my hometown. When the quarterback *throws* for a touchdown, everyone in the bleachers *stands* up and *cheers*.
INCONSISTENT	The driver *yelled* at us to get off the bus, so I *ask* him why and he *tells* me it *is* none of my business.
CONSISTENT	The driver *yells* at us to get off the bus, so I *ask* him why and he *tells* me it *is* none of my business. [All verbs are present tense.]
CONSISTENT	The driver *yelled* at us to get off the bus, so I *asked* him why and he *told* me it *was* none of my business. [All verbs are past tense.]

11b *If the time changes, change the verb tense.*

Tense indicates time. Shifts in tense should indicate an actual change in time. If you are writing about something that occurred in the past, use past tense verbs. If you are writing about something that occurs in the present, use present tense verbs. If the time shifts, change the verb tense.

> I *do* not *like* the new television programs this year. The situation comedies *are* too realistic to be amusing, the adventure shows *don't have* much action, and the courtroom dramas *drag* on and on. Last year the television programs *were* different. The sitcoms *were* hilarious, the adventure shows *were* action-packed, and the courtroom dramas *were* fast-paced. I *prefer* reruns of last year's programs to new episodes of this year's choices.

The time and the verb tense change appropriately from present (*do like, are, do have, drag*) to past (*were, were, were, were*) back to present (*prefer*), indicating contrast between this year's *present* programming and last year's *past* programming and ending with *present* opinion.

> **NOTE:**   When writing papers about literature, the accepted practice is to use present tense verbs to summarize what happens in a story, poem, or play. When discussing other aspects of a work, use present tense for present time, past tense for past, and future tense for future.
>
> John Steinbeck *wrote* "The Chrysanthemums" in 1937. [Past tense for past time.]
>
> In "The Chrysanthemums" John Steinbeck *describes* the Salinas Valley as "a closed pot" cut off from the world by fog.

11c *Maintain consistency in the voice of verbs.*

In most writing, active voice is preferable to passive voice (see 5m). Shifting unnecessarily from active to passive voice causes confusion for readers.

INCONSISTENT	My roommates and I *sit* up late many nights talking about our problems. Grades, teachers, jobs, money, and dates *are discussed* at length.

CONSISTENT   My roommates and I *sit* up late many nights talking about our problems. We *discuss* grades, teachers, jobs, money, and dates at length.

11d Maintain consistency in person.

Person indicates the perspective from which an essay is written. First person (*I, we*) establishes a personal, informal relationship with readers. Second person (*you*) is also informal and personal, bringing the readers into the writing. Third person (*he, she, it, they*) is more formal and objective than the other two persons. (See 7.) In a formal scientific report, first person and second person are seldom appropriate. In a personal essay, using *he, she,* or *one* to refer to yourself sounds stilted. Choose the person appropriate for your purpose and stick to it.

INCONSISTENT   In *my* composition class there is a divorced woman returning to school after fifteen years of raising her children. Watching her, *you* can tell she is uncertain about her decision to enter college.

CONSISTENT   In *my* composition class there is a divorced woman returning to school after fifteen years of raising her children. Watching her, *I* can tell she is uncertain about her decision to enter college.

INCONSISTENT   Today college *students* need transportation, but *you* need a job to pay for the insurance and the gasoline.

CONSISTENT   Today college *students* need transportation, but *they* need jobs to pay for the insurance and the gasoline.

INCONSISTENT   *Anyone* can go skydiving if *you* have the guts.

CONSISTENT   *Anyone* can go skydiving if *he or she* has the guts.

11e Maintain consistency in the mood of verbs.

Closely related to shift in person is shift in the mood of the verb, usually from the indicative to the imperative. (See 5n–5p.)

INCONSISTENT   Counselors *advised* the students to register early to choose the best professors. Also *pay* tuition on time to avoid being dropped from classes. [Shift from indicative to imperative.]

CONSISTENT   Counselors *advised* the students to register early to choose the best professors. They also *advised* them to pay their tuition on time to avoid being dropped from classes. [Both verbs in indicative.]

11f Maintain consistency in level of language.

Attempting to impress readers, writers sometimes inappropriately use inflated language or slip into slang or a too informal tone. The level of language should be appropriate to your purpose and your audience throughout an essay.

If you are writing a personal essay, use informal language.

INCONSISTENT   I felt like a typical tourist. I carried an expensive camera with lots of gadgets I didn't quite know how to operate, and I had brought as much film as I could carry. But I was in a quandary because there was such a plethora of picturesque tableaus to record for posterity.

The sudden shift to formal language is inappropriate. The writer could end the passage simply: *But there was so much beautiful scenery all around that I just couldn't decide where to start.*

If you are writing an academic essay, use formal language.

INCONSISTENT   Puccini's final work *Turandot* is set in a China of legends, riddles, and fantasy. Brimming with beautiful melodies masterfully orchestrated—including the famed tenor aria "Nessum dorma"—this opera is music drama at its most spectacular. Man, I dig this gig!

The shift from formal language to slang is unnecessary. The last sentence can be cut without weakening the rest of the paragraph.

Exercise 11–1: Maintaining Grammatical Consistency

Revise the following sentences to eliminate shifts in verb tense, voice, and mood, person, and level of language. Possible revisions for the lettered sentences appear in the back of the book. Example:

> I needed the job at the restaurant, so I tried to tolerate the insults of my boss, but there is only so much a person can take.

> I needed the job at the restaurant, so I tried to tolerate the insults of my boss, but I could take only so much.

a. Sometimes late at night, I hear stereos booming from passing cars. The vibrations are so great you can feel your house shake.

b. Dr. Jamison is an erudite professor who cracks jokes in class.

c. The audience listened intently to the lecture, but the message was not understood.

d. The fire fighters tried repeatedly to put out the fire, but after five hours it was still not put out.

e. Most of the people in my psychology class are very interesting, and you can get into some exciting discussions with them.

1. Scientists can no longer evade the social, political, and ethical consequences of what they did in the laboratory.

2. To have good government, citizens must become informed on the issues. Also, be sure to vote.

3. Good writing is essential to success in many professions, especially in business, where ideas must be communicated in down-to-earth lingo.

4. Our legal system made it extremely difficult to prove a bribe. If the charges are not proven to the satisfaction of a jury or a judge, then we jump to the conclusion that the absence of a conviction demonstrates the innocence of the subject.

5. Before Morris K. Udall, Democrat from Arizona, resigns his seat in the U.S. House of Representatives, he helped preserve hundreds of acres of wilderness.

12 FRAGMENTS

A **complete sentence** is one that has both a subject and a predicate and can stand alone. (See 2a, 2b.) A **fragment** lacks a subject or a predicate or both or for some other reason fails to express a complete thought. We all use fragments in everyday speech, where their context and the way they are said make them understandable and therefore acceptable.

> That bicycle over there.
> Good job.
> Not if I can help it.

In writing, fragments like these fail to communicate complete, coherent ideas. Notice how much more effective they are when we turn them into complete sentences.

> I'd like to buy that bicycle over there.
> Hal did a good job sanding the floor.
> Nobody will steal your seat if I can help it.

Some writers purposefully use fragments. For example, advertisers are fond of them because short, emphatic fragments command attention, like a series of quick jabs to the head.

> Seafood special. Every Tuesday night. All you can eat. Specially priced at $6.95. For seafood lovers.

Professional writers use fragments, too, especially in journals, descriptions, and fiction—often to good effect, as in this passage from the beginning of Vladimir Nabokov's novel *Lolita*:

> Lolita, light of my life, fire of my loins. My sin, my soul. Lo-lee-ta: the tip of the tongue taking a trip of three steps down the palate to tap, at three, on the teeth. Lo. Lee. Ta.

In your college writing, though, it is good practice to express your ideas in complete sentences. Writing a paper or a report is a more formal, less experimental activity than writing fiction. Besides, complete sentences usually convey more information than fragments—a big advantage in expository writing. Sprinkling fragments through your work, unless you do so with great skill and style, tends to make readers wonder if you can tell a piece of thought from a whole thought completely thought through.

If you sometimes write fragments without recognizing them, learn to edit your work. Luckily, fragments are fairly easy to correct. Often you can attach a fragment to a neighboring sentence with a comma, a dash, or a colon.

Sometimes you can combine two thoughts without adding any punctuation at all.

12a *If a fragment is a phrase, link it to an adjoining sentence or make it a complete sentence.*

A freestanding phrase is a fragment because it lacks a subject or a verb or both. You have two choices for revising a fragment if it is a phrase: (1) link it to an adjoining sentence using punctuation such as a comma or a colon or (2) add a subject or a verb to the phrase to make it a complete sentence.

FRAGMENT	Malcolm has two goals in life. *Wealth and power.*
FRAGMENT	Schmidt ended his stories as he mixed his martinis. *With a twist.*
FRAGMENT	*To stamp out the union.* That was the bosses' plan.
FRAGMENT	The students taking the final exam in the auditorium.

Wealth and power is a phrase rather than a sentence because it has no verb. *With a twist* has neither a subject nor a verb. *To stamp out the union* has a verbal, which cannot be used as the main verb of a sentence, and it has no subject. *Taking* is not a complete verb: it is a participle and requires a helping verb to make it complete. You can make each of these phrases express a complete thought by linking it with a neighboring sentence or by adding the missing element. In each case there are several ways to complete the thought. Here is one set of possibilities:

REVISED	Malcolm has two goals in life: wealth and power. [A colon links *wealth and power* to *goals.*]
REVISED	Schmidt ended his stories as he mixed his martinis, with a twist. [The prepositional phrase *with a twist* is connected to the main clause with a comma.]
REVISED	To stamp out the union was the bosses' plan. [The infinitive phrase *To stamp out the union* becomes the subject of the sentence.]
REVISED	The students taking the final exam in the auditorium were interrupted by the fire alarm. [The predicate *were interrupted by the fire alarm* completes the sentence.]
REVISED	The students were taking the final exam in the auditorium. [The helping verb *were* completes the verb and thus makes a sentence.]

✓ Is the fragment a phrase? If so, link it to an adjoining sentence. (12a)

✓ Is the fragment a clause? If so, link it to an adjoining sentence or eliminate its subordinating conjunction. (12b)

✓ Does the fragment use *being* or another participle as its verb? If so, either change the participle to a main verb or link the fragment to an adjoining sentence. (12c)

✓ Is the fragment part of a compound predicate? If so, link it to the other part of the predicate. (12d)

12b *If a fragment is a subordinate clause, link it to an adjoining sentence or eliminate the subordinating conjunction.*

Some fragments are missing neither subject nor verb. Instead, they are subordinate clauses, unable to express complete thoughts unless linked with main clauses. (See 3e–3g, 4c.) As you examine your writing for sentence fragments, be on the lookout for *subordinating conjunctions*. (Some of the most common subordinating conjunctions are *although, because, if, since, unless, until,* and *while*; for a complete list, see 1g.) When you find a subordinating conjunction at the start or in the middle of a word group that looks like a sentence, that word group may be a subordinate clause and not a sentence at all.

FRAGMENT   The new law will stem the tide of inflation. *If it passes.*

FRAGMENT   Wealth doesn't guarantee happiness. *Whereas poverty does guarantee unhappiness.*

FRAGMENT   George loves winter in the mountains. *Because he is an avid skier.*

If you find that you have treated a subordinate clause as if it were a complete sentence, you can correct the problem in one of two ways: (1) you can combine the fragment with a main clause nearby or (2) you can make the subordinate clause into a complete sentence by dropping the subordinating conjunction.

REVISED   The new law will stem the tide of inflation, if it passes.

REVISED   Wealth doesn't guarantee happiness, whereas poverty does guarantee unhappiness.

REVISED   George loves winter in the mountains. He is an avid skier.

A sentence is not necessarily a fragment just because it opens with a subordinating conjunction. Some perfectly legitimate complex or compound-complex sentences have their conjunctions up front instead of in the middle. (See 4c, 4d.)

If you leave early, say good-bye.

Because of rain, the game was canceled.

12c If a fragment has a participle but no other verb, change the participle to a main verb or link the fragment to an adjoining sentence.

A participle (the *-ing* form of the verb, such as *being, writing, looking*) can serve as the main verb in a sentence only when it is accompanied by a form of *be* ("Jeffrey *is working* harder than usual"). When a writer mistakenly uses a participle alone as a main verb, the result is a fragment.

> FRAGMENT   *Sally being the first athlete on the team to compete in a national contest.* She received many congratulatory telegrams.

> FRAGMENT   Jon was used to the pressure of deadlines. *Having worked the night shift at the daily newspaper.*

One solution is to combine the fragment with an adjoining sentence.

> REVISED   Being the first athlete on the team to compete in a national contest, Sally received many congratulatory telegrams.

> REVISED   Jon was used to the pressure of deadlines, having worked the night shift at the daily newspaper.

Another solution is to turn the fragment into a complete sentence by choosing a form of the verb other than the participle.

> REVISED   Sally *was* the first athlete on the team to compete in a national contest. She received many congratulatory telegrams.

> REVISED   Jon was used to the pressure of deadlines. He *had worked* the night shift at the daily newspaper.

12d If a fragment is part of a compound predicate, link it with the complete sentence containing the rest of the predicate.

> FRAGMENT   In spite of a pulled muscle, Jeremy ran the race. *And won.*

A fragment such as *And won* sounds satisfyingly punchy. Still, it cannot stand on its own. "Ran . . . and won" is a compound predicate — two verbs with the same subject. You can create a complete sentence by linking the verbs.

> REVISED   In spite of a pulled muscle, Jeremy *ran* the race *and won.*

If you want to keep more emphasis on the second verb, you can turn the fragment into a full clause by adding punctuation and another subject.

> REVISED   In spite of a pulled muscle, Jeremy ran the race — and *he* won.

(See a review of the rules about punctuating linked phrases and clauses, 18a.)

Exercise 12–1: Eliminating Fragments

Eliminate fragments where they appear in the following examples. Some examples may be correct. Possible revisions for the lettered exercises appear in the back of the book. Example:

Bryan hates parsnips. And loathes squash.

Bryan hates parsnips and loathes squash.

a. Polly and Jim plan to see the new Woody Allen movie. Which was reviewed in last Sunday's *New York Times*.

b. For democracy to function at all, two elements are crucial. An educated populace and a firm collective belief in people's ability to chart their own course.

c. Scholastic achievement is important to Alex. Being the first person in his family ever to attend college.

d. Does our society rob children of their childhood? By making them aware too soon of adult ills?

e. It was one of those days. Complete chaos. Friends coming over in an hour. A term paper to write.

1. If the German people had known Hitler's real plans. Would they have made him führer?

2. Lisa advocated sleeping no more than four hours a night. Until she started nodding through her classes.

3. Have you ever noticed that most children's books seem to be written for girls? With some notable exceptions, of course.

4. Jack seemed well qualified for a career in the air force. Except for his tendency to get airsick.

5. Illness often accompanies stress. After the death of a loved one, for example, catching a cold is common.

6. None of the board members objected to Butch's proposal at the time. Only afterward, when they realized its implications.

7. Michael volunteered to build the wall. Having nothing better to do over the weekend.

8. Richard III supposedly had the young princes murdered. No one has ever found out what really happened to them.

9. They met. They talked. They fought. They reached agreement.

10. I can't think about modern philosophy. Especially in hot weather.

Exercise 12–2: Eliminating Fragments

Rewrite the following paragraph, eliminating all fragments. Explain why you made each change.

When I was about eleven years old. I played on a Little League baseball team. Played, that is, when I wasn't sitting on the bench. Which was most of the time. I got into the lineup only because the rules said every kid had to get a chance at bat. A rule my coach didn't like. Because he wanted our team to win every game. I rarely got to play in the field. Only when a shortage of players made my presence there necessary. Then always right field. Unless there were a lot of lefties coming up to bat on the opposing team. Believe me when I say that, for me, Little League baseball was no fun.

13 COMMA SPLICES AND FUSED SENTENCES

Splice two ropes, or two strips of movie film, and you join them into one. Splice two main clauses by putting only a comma between them, however, and you get an ungainly construction called a **comma splice**. Here, for instance, are two perfectly good main clauses, each separate, each able to stand on its own as a sentence:

> The detective wriggled on his belly toward the campfire. The drunken smugglers didn't notice him.

Now let's splice those sentences with a comma.

> COMMA SPLICE   The detective wriggled on his belly toward the campfire, the drunken smugglers didn't notice him.

The resulting comma splice makes for difficult reading.

Even more confusing than a comma splice is a **fused** (or **run-on**) **sentence**: two main clauses joined without any punctuation.

> FUSED SENTENCE   The detective wriggled on his belly toward the campfire the drunken smugglers didn't notice him.

Lacking clues from the writer, a reader cannot tell where to pause. To understand the sentence, he or she must halt and reread.

Even writers who know better can fall at times into fusing and comma splicing. Temptation may overwhelm them when, having written one sentence, they want to add some further thought. Either they simply jam the two thoughts together or they push in a comma, like a thumbtack, to stick on the second thought.

Here are five simple ways to eliminate both comma splices and fused sentences. Your choice depends on the length and complexity of your main clauses and the effect you want to achieve.

REVISING COMMA SPLICES AND FUSED SENTENCES
Try any of these five strategies:

1. Make each main clause a separate sentence. (13a)
2. Link the two main clauses with a comma and a coordinating conjunction. (1g); (13b)
3. Link the two main clauses with a semicolon or, if appropriate, a colon. (13c)
4. Subordinate one clause to the other. (13d)
5. Link the two main clauses with a semicolon, a conjunctive adverb, and a comma. (13e)

13a Write separate complete sentences to correct a comma splice or fused sentence.

COMMA SPLICE   Sigmund Freud has been called an enemy of sexual repression, the truth is that he is not a friend of free love.

FUSED SENTENCE Sigmund Freud has been called an enemy of sexual repression the truth is that he is not a friend of free love.

Neither sentence yields its meaning without a struggle. To point readers in the right direction, separate the clauses.

REVISED   Sigmund Freud has been called an enemy of sexual repression. The truth is that he is not a friend of free love.

13b Use a comma and a coordinating conjunction to correct a comma splice or a fused sentence.

Is it always incorrect to join two main clauses with a comma? No. If both clauses are of roughly equal weight, you can use a comma to link them—as long as you add a coordinating conjunction (*and, but, for, nor, or, so, yet*) after the comma.

COMMA SPLICE   Hurricane winds hit ninety miles an hour, they tore the roof from every house on Paradise Drive.

REVISED   Hurricane winds hit ninety miles an hour, *and* they tore the roof from every house on Paradise Drive.

13c Use a semicolon or a colon to correct a comma splice or a fused sentence.

Joining two clauses with a comma and a coordinating conjunction usually yields a smooth, grammatically correct sentence. Smoothness, however, is not always the writer's goal. If two clauses are unequal in weight, or if the writer wants to emphasize both, a different option may work better.

A semicolon can keep two thoughts connected while giving full emphasis to each one.

COMMA SPLICE   Hurricane winds hit ninety miles an hour, they tore the roof from every house on Paradise Drive.

REVISED   Hurricane winds hit ninety miles an hour; they tore the roof from every house on Paradise Drive.

If the second thought clearly illustrates or explains the first, add it on with a colon.

The hurricane caused extensive damage: it tore the roof from every house on Paradise Drive.

Remember that the only punctuation powerful enough to link two main clauses single-handed is a semicolon, a colon, or a period. A lone comma won't do the job.

13d Use subordination to correct a comma splice or a fused sentence.

If one main clause is more important than the other, or if you want to give it more importance, you can subordinate the less important clause to it. Using subordination helps your reader more than simply dividing a fused sentence or comma splice into two sentences. When you make one clause subordinate, you throw weight on the main clause. In effect, you show your reader how one idea relates to another—you decide which matters more.

> **FUSED SENTENCE**   Hurricane winds hit ninety miles an hour they tore the roof from every house on Paradise Drive.
>
> **REVISED**   *When hurricane winds hit ninety miles an hour*, they tore the roof from every house on Paradise Drive.
>
> **REVISED**   Hurricane winds *hit ninety miles an hour, tearing the roof from every house on Paradise Drive.*

For a rundown of different ways to use subordination, see 3e–3g and 18d–18f.

13e Use a conjunctive adverb with a semicolon and a comma to correct a comma splice or a fused sentence.

A writer who is sharp enough to beware of fused sentences and comma splices but who still wants to cram more than one clause into a sentence may join two clauses with a *conjunctive adverb*. Some common conjunctive adverbs are *also, besides, consequently, even so, finally, furthermore, however, indeed, moreover, nevertheless,* and *therefore.* (See 1g.) These transitional words and phrases can be a useful way of linking clauses—but only if used with the right punctuation.

> **COMMA SPLICE**   Sigmund Freud has been called an enemy of sexual repression, however the truth is that he is not a friend of free love.

The writer might consider a comma plus the conjunctive adverb *however* glue enough to combine the two main clauses; but that cheap fish glue won't hold. Stronger binding is called for.

> **REVISED**   Sigmund Freud has been called an enemy of sexual repression; however, the truth is that he is not a friend of free love.

A writer who fuses and comma splices sentences is like a man trying to join two boards. If he comma splices, he tries to put them together with only one nail; if he fuses, he puts them together with no nail at all. But most thoughts, to hang together, need plenty of hammering.

EXCEPTION   Certain very short, similar main clauses can be joined with a comma.

Only if you now feel sure that you can tell a comma splice or a fused sentence when you see one, read on: here comes a fine point. We hate to admit it, lest it complicate life, but once in a great while you'll see a competent writer joining main clauses with nothing but a comma between them.

> Jill runs by day, Tom walks by night.
>
> I came, I saw, I conquered.

Commas are not obligatory with short, similar clauses. If you find this issue confusing, you can stick with semicolons to join all main clauses, short or long.

> Jill runs by day; Tom walks by night.
>
> I came; I saw; I conquered.

Exercise 13–1: Revising Comma Splices and Fused Sentences

In the following examples, revise each comma splice or fused sentence in two ways and decide which way you believe works best. Be creative — don't revise every sentence in the same way. Some sentences may be correct as written. Possible revisions for the lettered sentences appear in the back of the book. Example:

> The castle looked eerie from a distance, it filled us with nameless fear as we approached.
>
> 1. The castle looked eerie from a distance. It filled us with nameless fear as we approached.
>
> 2. The castle looked eerie from a distance; it filled us with nameless fear as we approached.
>
> 3. The castle, which looked eerie from a distance, filled us with nameless fear as we approached.

a. Everyone had heard alarming rumors in the village about strange goings-on, we hesitated to believe them.

b. Bats flew about our ears as the carriage pulled up under a stone archway an assistant stood waiting to lead us to our host.

c. We followed the scientist down a flight of wet stone steps at last he stopped before a huge oak door.

d. From a jangling keyring Dr. Frankenstein selected a heavy key, he twisted it in the lock.

e. The huge door gave a groan it swung open on a dimly lighted laboratory.

1. Our guide turned, with a lopsided smile, silently he motioned us into the room.

2. Before us on a dissecting table lay a form with closed eyes to behold it sent a quick chill down my spine.

3. With glittering eyes the scientist strode to the table, he lifted a white-gloved hand.

4. The form lying before us seemed an obscenely large baby in disbelief I had to rub my eyes.

5. It resembled no human child instead it seemed constructed of rubber or clay.

6. With a hoarse cry Frankenstein flung a power switch, blue streamers of static electricity crackled about the table, the creature gave a grunt and opened smoldering eyes.

7. "I've won!" exclaimed the scientist in triumph he circled the room doing a demented Irish reel.

8. The creature's right hand strained, the heavy steel manacle imprisoning his wrist groaned in torment.

9. Like a staple wrenched from a document, the manacle yielded.

10. The creature sat upright and tugged at the shackles binding his ankles, Frankenstein uttered a piercing scream.

Exercise 13–2: Revising Comma Splices and Fused Sentences

Identify each of the following errors as either a fused sentence or a comma splice. Revise each, using either subordination or a conjunctive adverb. Some sentences may be correct. Possible revisions for the lettered sentences appear in the back of the book. Example:

> The scientist's shriek echoed through the cavernous cellar, it roused a flapping cloud of frightened bats.
>
> [Comma splice.] The scientist's shriek echoed through the cavernous cellar, rousing a flapping cloud of frightened bats.

a. The creature lumbered toward its terrified creator, Frankenstein shrank back against a wall.

b. To defend himself the scientist grabbed a wooden mallet it had been sitting on a cabinet nearby.

c. Frankenstein wore a smile of contemptuous superiority, his triumph proved brief in duration.

d. With one sweep of an arm the creature dashed aside the mallet its wooden head splintered on the stone floor.

e. What followed is engraved upon my dreams, I hesitate to disclose it lest it trouble your own.

1. Many psychologists believe that fantasy stories can be valuable they are a means of exploring our secret fears.

2. We identify with the characters and situations, this helps us to face threatening experiences without going through them.

3. The hero is good, the villain is evil, and virtue triumphs.

4. We all carry around our own monsters some of them we created ourselves.

5. We fear an inner Frankenstein, otherwise why would we shiver whenever we enter a dark cellar?

Exercise 13–3: Revising Comma Splices and Fused Sentences

Write six fused sentences and comma splices. Then trade papers with a class-mate and revise each other's deliberate errors in whatever ways yield the best results.

CHAPTER 33

Effective Sentences

14   MISPLACED AND DANGLING MODIFIERS

The purpose of a modifier is to give readers additional information. To do so, the modifier must be linked clearly to whatever it is meant to modify. If you wrote, "We saw a stone wall around a house on a grassy hill, beautiful and distant," your readers would be hard put to figure out whether *beautiful* and *distant* modify *wall, house,* or *hill.* When you finish writing, double-check your modifiers—especially prepositional phrases and subordinate clauses—to make sure each one is in the right place.

14a   *Keep modifiers close to what they modify.*

Misplaced modifiers—phrases and clauses that wander away from what they modify—produce results that are more likely to amuse your readers than inform them. To avoid confusion, place your modifiers as close as possible to whatever they modify.

> MISPLACED   She offered handcrafted toys to all the orphans in colorful packages. [Does the phrase *in colorful packages* modify *toys* or *orphans*?]
>
> CLEAR   She offered handcrafted toys in colorful packages to all the orphans.
>
> MISPLACED   Today's assignment is to remove the dishes from the crates that got chipped. [Does the clause *that got chipped* modify *dishes* or *crates*?]
>
> CLEAR   Today's assignment is to remove from the crates the dishes that got chipped.

Sometimes, when you move a misplaced modifier to a better place, an additional change or two will help you to clarify the sentence.

> MISPLACED   Jim offered cream and sugar to his guests in their coffee.
>
> CLEAR   Jim offered his guests cream and sugar in their coffee. [When *guests* is made an indirect object, *to* is cut.]

14b *Place each modifier so that it clearly modifies only one thing.*

A **squinting modifier** is one that looks two ways, leaving the reader uncertain whether it modifies the word before it or the word after it. Don't let your modifiers squint. Make sure each modifies only one element in a sentence. A good tactic is to place your modifier close to the word or phrase it modifies and away from any others that might cause confusion.

> SQUINTING   The best-seller that appealed to Mary *tremendously* bored Max.
>
> CLEAR   The best-seller that *tremendously* appealed to Mary bored Max.
>
> CLEAR   The best-seller that appealed to Mary bored Max *tremendously.*

Exercise 14–1: Placing Modifiers

Improve the following sentences, which contain modifiers that are misplaced or squinting. Possible revisions for the lettered sentences appear in the back of the book. Example:

> Miranda placed the book on the table that was overdue at the library.
>
> Miranda placed on the table the book that was overdue at the library.

a. The team that lost miserably remained silent on the trip home.

b. Complete the writing assignment in the textbook that follows Chapter 2.

c. Those who make mistakes frequently learn valuable lessons.

d. Margaret was mortified at not having learned her lines for the duration of the rehearsal.

e. A person who snacks often gets fat.

1. Leo hid the stolen diamonds as soon as he heard the police siren under the driver's seat.

2. How can Jeannie keep that house looking so elegant at such an advanced age?

3. The city council voted to open a clinic for people with AIDS, which they can ill afford.

4. Don't ask one of the boys to carry the groceries out to the car when there are so few.

5. Horace squinted at the frog with myopic eyes.

14c *Have something in the sentence for each modifier to modify.*

Generally we assume that a modifying phrase that appears at the start of a sentence will modify the subject of the main clause to follow. If we encounter a modifying phrase midway through a sentence, we assume that it modifies something just before or (less often) after it.

> *Feeling sick to his stomach, Jason* went to bed.
>
> *An early bird by nature, Felix* began at eight o'clock.
>
> *Alice, while sympathetic,* was not inclined to help.

Occasionally a writer will slip up by allowing a modifying phrase to dangle. A **dangling modifier** is one that, on close inspection, is found to be shirking its job: it doesn't modify anything in its sentence.

> **DANGLING** *Noticing a slight pain behind his eyes*, an aspirin seemed like a good idea. [The introductory phrase cannot be said to modify *aspirin*. In fact, it doesn't modify anything.]
>
> **DANGLING** *To do a good job*, the right tools were needed.

To correct a dangling modifier, recast the sentence. First, figure out what noun, pronoun, or noun phrase the modifier is meant to modify and then make that word or phrase the subject of the main clause.

> **CLEAR** *Noticing a slight pain behind his eyes, he* decided to take an aspirin.
>
> **CLEAR** *To do a good job, the plumber* needed the right tools.

CORRECTING DANGLING MODIFIERS

Try either of these two strategies:

1. Figure out what noun, pronoun, or noun phrase the dangling modifier is meant to modify. Then make that word or phrase the subject of the main clause.
2. Turn the dangling modifier into a clause that includes the missing noun or pronoun.

Another way to correct a dangling modifier is to turn the dangler into a clause that includes the missing noun or pronoun.

DANGLING	Her progress, *although talented*, has been slowed by poor work habits.
CLEAR	*Although she is talented*, her progress has been slowed by poor work habits.

Sometimes a bit of rewriting will clarify what the modifier modifies and improve the sentence as well.

CLEAR	*Although talented*, *she* has been handicapped by poor work habits.

Exercise 14–2: Revising Dangling Modifiers

Revise any sentences that contain dangling modifiers. Some sentences may be correct. Possible revisions for the lettered sentences appear in the back of the book. Example:

Angry at her poor showing, geology would never be Joan's favorite class.

Angry at her poor showing, Joan knew that geology would never be her favorite class.

a. After working for six hours, the job was done.

b. Unable to fall asleep, a warm bath relaxes you.

c. To join the college choir, a singer's voice has to be loud.

d. It's common, feeling lonely, to want to talk to someone.

e. Having worried all morning, relief flooded over him when his missing son returned.

1. Once gripped by the urge to sail, it never leaves you.

2. Further information can be obtained by calling the following number.

3. Passing the service station, the bank will appear on your right.

4. Having created strict ethical standards, there should be some willingness on Congress's part to live up to them.

5. Recalling Ben Franklin's advice, "hanging together" became the club members' new policy.

15 INCOMPLETE SENTENCES

A fragment fails to qualify as a sentence because it lacks a subject or a predicate or both (see 12). However, a sentence can contain these two essentials and still miss the mark. If it lacks some other key element—a crucial word or phrase—the sentence is *incomplete*. Often the problem is carelessness: the writer sets down too few words to cover a whole idea. The resulting incomplete sentence is likely to lose the reader. Like a bridge open to the public, it invites us to cross; but it has unexpected gaps that we topple through.

Incomplete sentences catch writers most often in two writing situations: comparisons and the abbreviated type of parallel structure called elliptical constructions.

COMPARISONS

15a *Make your comparisons clear by stating fully what you are comparing with what.*

> **INCOMPLETE**   Roscoe loves spending time with a computer more than Diane.

What is the writer of this sentence trying to tell us? Does Roscoe prefer the company of a keyboard to the company of his friend? Or, of these two people, is Roscoe (and not Diane) the computer addict? We can't be sure, because the writer has not completed the comparison. Adding a word would solve the problem.

> **REVISED**   Roscoe loves spending time with a computer more than Diane *does*.
>
> **REVISED**   Roscoe loves spending time with a computer more than *with* Diane.

In editing what you write, double-check your comparisons to be sure they are complete.

> **INCOMPLETE**   Miami has more newcomers from Havana than New York.
>
> **REVISED**   Miami has more newcomers from Havana than New York *has*.
>
> **REVISED**   Miami has more newcomers from Havana than *from* New York.

15b *When you start to draw a comparison, finish it.*

The unfinished comparison is a favorite trick of advertisers—"Our product is better!"—because it dodges the question "Better than what?" A sharp writer (or shopper) knows that any item being compared must be compared *with* something else.

> **INCOMPLETE**   Scottish tweeds are warmer.
>
> **REVISED**   Scottish tweeds are warmer *than any other fabric you can buy*.

15c *Be sure the things you compare are of the same kind.*

The saying "You can't compare apples and oranges" makes a useful grammatical point. A sentence that draws a comparison should assure its readers that the items involved are similar enough for comparison to be appropriate. When you compare two things, be sure the terms of the comparison are clear and logical.

> **INCOMPLETE**   The engine of a Ford truck is heavier than a Piper Cub airplane.

What is being compared? Truck and airplane? Or engine and engine? If we consider, we can guess: since a truck engine is unlikely to outweigh an airplane, the writer must mean to compare engines. Readers, however, should not have to make the effort to complete a writer's incomplete thought.

REVISED   The engine of a Ford truck is heavier than *that of* a Piper Cub airplane.

REVISED   A Ford truck's engine is heavier than a *Piper Cub's*.

In this last example, parallel structure (*Ford truck's* and *Piper Cub's*) helps to make the comparison concise as well as clear. (See 17a, 17c for more on parallel structure.)

15d *To compare an item with others of its kind, use* any other.

A comparison using *any* shows how something relates to a group without belonging to the group.

Alaska is larger than *any* country in Central America.

Bluefish has as much protein as *any* meat.

A comparison using *any other* shows how one member of a group relates to other members of the same group.

Death Valley is drier than *any other* place in the United States.

Bluefish has as distinctive a flavor as *any other* fish.

Exercise 15–1: Completing Comparisons

Add needed words to any of the following comparisons that strike you as incomplete. (Depending on how you interpret the sentence, there may be more than one way to complete a comparison.) Some sentences may be correct. Possible revisions for the lettered sentences appear in the back of the book. Example:

I hate hot weather more than you.

I hate hot weather more than you *do*.

I hate hot weather more than *I hate* you.

a. She plays the *Moonlight Sonata* more brilliantly than any pianist her age.

b. Driving a sports car means more to Jake than his professors.

c. People who go to college aren't necessarily smarter, but they will always have an advantage at job interviews.

d. I don't have as much trouble getting along with Michelle as Karin.

e. One-eyed Bill was faster on the draw than any gunslinger in West Texas.

1. The brain of an ape is larger than a hippopotamus.

2. A more sensible system of running the schools would be to appoint a school board.

3. A hen lays fewer eggs than any turtle.

4. The town meeting form of government doesn't function as efficiently as a mayor.

5. Sex is closer to prayer than a meal of Chicken McNuggets.

ELLIPTICAL CONSTRUCTIONS

A well-known poem by Robert Frost begins:

> Some say the world will end in fire, some say in ice.

When Frost wrote that sentence, he avoided needless repetition by implying certain words rather than stating them. The result is more concise and more effective than a complete version of the same sentence would be:

> Some say the world will end in fire, some say the world will end in ice.

This common writer's tactic — leaving out (for the sake of concision) an unnecessary word — produces an **elliptical construction**. Readers can easily fill in the words that, although not written, are clearly understood. Elliptical constructions can create confusion, however, if the writer gives readers too little information to fill in those missing words accurately.

15e *When you eliminate repetition, keep all words that are essential for clarity.*

An elliptical construction saves repeating what a reader already knows. But whenever you use this strategy, make sure to omit only words that are stated elsewhere in the sentence. Otherwise, your reader may fill the gap incorrectly.

> INCOMPLETE   How can I date her, seeing that she is a senior, I a mere freshman?

This elliptical construction won't work. A reader supplying the missing verb in the last part of the sentence would get "I *is* a mere freshman." Although the writer means *am, is* is the verb already stated.

> REVISED   How can I date her, seeing that she is a senior and I *am* a mere freshman?

Leaving out a necessary preposition also can produce a faulty elliptical construction.

> INCOMPLETE   The train neither goes nor returns from Middletown.

Without a *to* after *goes*, readers are likely to fill in an extra *from* to complete the verb's action. Write instead:

> REVISED   The train neither goes *to* nor returns from Middletown.

15f *In a compound predicate, leave out only verb forms that have already been stated.*

Compound predicates are especially prone to incomplete elliptical constructions. Writing in haste, we accidentally omit part of a verb that is needed for the sentence to make sense. When you write a sentence with a compound predicate, check your verbs most carefully if they are in different tenses. Be sure that no necessary part is missing.

INCOMPLETE   The committee never has and never will vote to raise taxes.

REVISED   The committee never has *voted* and never will vote to raise taxes.

15g If you mix comparisons using as *and* than, include both words.

To contrast two things that are different, we normally use the comparative form of an adjective followed by *than: better than, more than, fewer than.* To show a similarity between two things that are alike, we normally use the simple form of an adjective sandwiched between *as* and *as: as good as, as many as, as few as.* Often we can combine two *than* comparisons or two *as* comparisons into an elliptical construction.

The White House is smaller [than] and newer than Buckingham Palace.

Some corporate executives live in homes as large [as] and as grand as the White House.

If you want to combine a *than* comparison with an *as* comparison, however, an elliptical construction won't work.

INCOMPLETE   The White House is smaller but just as beautiful as Buckingham Palace.

REVISED   The White House is smaller *than* but just *as* beautiful *as* Buckingham Palace.

INCOMPLETE   Some corporate executives live in homes as large, and no less grand, than the White House.

REVISED   Some corporate executives live in homes *as* large *as,* and no less grand *than,* the White House.

Exercise 15–2: Completing Sentences

Add needed words to each of the following sentences that strikes you as incomplete. (Depending on how you interpret the sentence, there may be more than one way to fill in a gap.) Some sentences may be correct. Possible revisions for the lettered sentences appear in the back of the book. Example:

President Kennedy should have but didn't see the perils of invading Cuba.

President Kennedy should have *seen* but didn't see the perils of invading Cuba.

a. The sand pit is just as wide but deeper than the quarry.

b. Pembroke was never contacted, much less involved with, the election committee.

c. I haven't yet but soon will finish my term paper.

d. Ron likes his popcorn with butter, Linda with parmesan cheese.

e. George Washington always has been and will be regarded as the father of his country.

1. You have traveled to exotic Tahiti; Maureen, to Asbury Park, N.J.
2. The mayor refuses to negotiate or even talk to the civic association.
3. Building a new sewage treatment plant would be no more costly and just as effective as modifying the existing one.
4. We favor this proposal, Louise that one.
5. The board has not and will not accept such an unfair proposal.

16 MIXED CONSTRUCTIONS AND FAULTY PREDICATION

Sometimes a sentence contains all the necessary parts and still doesn't work. Reading it, we feel uneasy, although we may not know why. The problem is a discord between two or more parts of the sentence: the writer has combined phrases or clauses that don't fit together (a *mixed construction*) or mismatched a verb and its subject, object, or modifier (*faulty predication*). The resulting tangle looks like a sentence at first glance, but it fails to make sense.

16a *Link phrases and clauses logically.*

A **mixed construction** results when a writer connects phrases or clauses (or both) that don't work together as a sentence.

> MIXED   In her efforts to solve the tax problem only caused the mayor additional difficulties.

The prepositional phrase *In her efforts to solve the tax problem* is a modifier; it cannot function as the subject of a sentence. The writer, however, has used this phrase as a noun—the subject of the verb *caused.* To untangle the mixed construction, the writer has two choices: (1) rewrite the phrase so that it works as a noun or (2) use the phrase as a modifier rather than as the sentence's subject.

> REVISED   Her efforts to solve the tax problem only caused the mayor additional difficulties. [With *in* gone, *efforts* becomes the subject of the sentence.]

> REVISED   In her efforts to solve the tax problem, the mayor created additional difficulties. [The prepositional phrase now modifies the verb *created.*]

To avoid mixed constructions, check the links that join your phrases and clauses—especially prepositions and conjunctions. A sentence, like a chain, is only as strong as its weakest link.

> MIXED   Jack, although he was picked up by the police, but was not charged with anything.

Using both *although* and *but* gives this sentence one link too many. We can unmix the construction in two ways.

> REVISED   Jack was picked up by the police but was not charged with anything.

> REVISED   Although he was picked up by the police, Jack was not charged with anything.

16b   *Relate the parts of a sentence logically.*

Faulty predication refers to a skewed relationship between a verb and some other part of a sentence.

> FAULTY   *The temperature of water freezes* at 32 degrees Fahrenheit.

At first glance, that sentence looks all right. It contains both subject and predicate. It expresses a complete thought. What is wrong with it? The writer has slipped into faulty predication by mismatching the subject and verb. The sentence tells us that *temperature freezes,* when science and common sense tell us it is *water* that freezes. To correct this error, the writer must find a subject and verb that fit each other.

> REVISED   *Water freezes* at 32 degrees Fahrenheit.

Faulty predication also can result from a mismatch between a verb and its direct object.

> FAULTY   Rising costs *diminish college* for many students.

Costs don't *diminish college.* To correct this predication error, the writer must change the sentence so its direct object follows logically from its verb.

> REVISED   Rising costs *diminish the number of students who can attend college.*

Subtler predication errors result when a writer uses a linking verb to forge a false connection between the subject and a subject complement.

> FAULTY   *Industrial waste* has become *an important modern priority*.

Is it really *waste* that has become a *priority*? Or, rather, is it *working to solve the problems caused by careless disposal of industrial waste*? A writer who says all that, though, risks wordiness. Why not just replace *priority* with a closer match for *waste*?

> REVISED   *Industrial waste* has become *a modern menace.*

Predication errors tend to plague writers who are too fond of the passive voice. Mismatches between a verb and its subject, object, or another part of the sentence are easier to avoid (and to spot during editing) when the verb is active than when it is passive. To improve your sentences, cast them in the active voice whenever possible. (See 5m.)

> FAULTY   The idea of giving thanks for a good harvest *was not done* first by the Pilgrims.
>
> REVISED   The idea of giving thanks for a good harvest *did not originate* with the Pilgrims.

16c   *Avoid starting a definition with* when *or* where.

Many inexperienced writers slip into predication errors when they define terms. A definition, like any other phrase or clause, needs to fit grammatically with the rest of the sentence.

FAULTY	Dyslexia is when you have a reading disorder.
REVISED	Dyslexia is a reading disorder.
FAULTY	A lay-up is where a player drives in close to the basket and then makes a usually one-handed, banked shot.
REVISED	To shoot a lay-up, a player drives in close to the basket and then makes a usually one-handed, banked shot.

16d *Avoid using* the reason is because . . .

Anytime you start an explanation with *the reason is,* what follows *is* should be a subject complement: an adjective, a noun, or a noun clause. (See 2d.) *Because* is a conjunction; it cannot function as a noun or adjective.

FAULTY	*The reason* Gerard hesitates *is because* no one supported him two years ago.
REVISED	*The reason* Gerard hesitates *is simple*: no one supported him two years ago.
REVISED	*The reason* Gerard hesitates *is that no one supported him two years ago.*
REVISED	*The reason* Gerard hesitates *is his lack of support two years ago.*

Exercise 16–1: Correcting Mixed Constructions and Faulty Predication

Correct any mixed constructions and faulty predication you find in the following sentences. Possible revisions for the lettered sentences appear in the back of the book. Example:

"Coming about" is when a sailboat makes a turn into the wind.

"Coming about" is a sailboat's turn into the wind.

A sailboat "comes about" when it makes a turn into the wind.

a. The characteristics of a balanced budget call for careful planning.

b. Among the candidates for school committee head are unimpressive this year.

c. Financial aid searches for able students and decides to pay their college costs.

d. One good reason for financial aid is because it enables capable lower-income students to attend college.

e. In one sizzling blast, the destruction of the enemy space fleet was instantly wiped out.

1. Inflation is where money keeps decreasing in value.

2. From all the debates over rising energy costs failed to accomplish any positive action.

3. The damp weather swelled Joe's arthritis.

4. Getting a job can improve a person's status symbols in the community.

5. The air force's explanation for the crash is because heavy snow forced an emergency landing.

6. Life's saddest moments are experienced by the loss of a loved one.

7. One solution to urban decay is when old neighborhoods are revitalized rather than torn down.

8. Addiction to crack cocaine has become a national crusade.

9. Market research demonstrates to a manufacturer the consumers using its products.

10. American cars try to look flashier than foreign cars.

17   PARALLEL STRUCTURE

An important tool for any writer is **parallel structure,** or parallelism. You use this tool when you create a series of words, phrases, clauses, or sentences with the same grammatical form. The pattern created by the series—its parallel structure—emphasizes the similarities or differences among the items, which may be things, qualities, actions, or ideas.

> My favorite foods are roast beef, deep-dish apple pie, and linguine with clam sauce.
>
> Louise is charming, witty, intelligent, and talented.
>
> Jeff likes to swim, ride, and run.
>
> Dave likes movies that scare him and books that make him laugh.

Each series is a perfect parallel construction, composed of equivalent words: nouns in the first example, adjectives in the second, verbs in the third, and adjective clauses in the fourth.

17a *In a series linked by a coordinating conjunction, keep all elements in the same grammatical form.*

Whenever you connect items with a coordinating conjunction (*and, but, for, or, nor, so,* and *yet*), you cue your readers to expect a parallel structure. Whether your series consists of single words, phrases, or clauses, its parts should balance one another.

> **AWKWARD**   The puppies are *tiny, clumsily bumping* into each other, *and cute.*

Two elements in this series are parallel one-word adjectives, but the third is a verb phrase. The writer can improve this awkward sentence by making the series consistent.

> **PARALLEL**   The puppies are *tiny, clumsy, and cute.*

Don't mix verb forms in a series. Avoid, for instance, pairing a gerund and an infinitive.

AWKWARD	Switzerland is a good place for a winter vacation if you like *skiing and to skate.*
PARALLEL	Switzerland is a good place for a winter vacation if you like *skiing and skating.*
PARALLEL	Switzerland is a good place for a winter vacation if you like *to ski and to skate.*

In a series of phrases or clauses, be sure that all elements in the series are similar in form, even if they are not similar in length.

AWKWARD	The fight in the bar happens after the two lovers have their scene together but before the car chase. [The clause starting with *after* is not parallel to the phrase starting with *before.*]
PARALLEL	The fight in the bar happens after the love scene but before the car chase.
AWKWARD	You can take the key, or don't forget to leave it under the mat. [The declarative clause starting with *You can* is not parallel to the imperative clause starting with *don't forget.*]
PARALLEL	You can take the key, or you can leave it under the mat.

EDITING CHECKLIST: KEEPING PARALLEL STRUCTURE

- Are all the elements in a series in the same grammatical form? (17a–17c)
- Are the elements in a comparison parallel in form? (17c)
- Are articles, conjunctions, or prepositions between elements in a series repeated rather than mixed? (17d)
- In a series of clauses, are lead-in words repeated? (17e)

17b *In a series linked by correlative conjunctions, keep all elements in the same grammatical form.*

When you use a correlative conjunction (*either ... or, neither ... nor, not only ... but also*), follow each part of the conjunction with a similarly structured word, phrase, or clause.

AWKWARD	I'm looking forward *to either attending* Saturday's wrestling match *or to seeing* it on closed-circuit TV. [Parallel structure is violated because *to* precedes the first part of the correlative conjunction (*to either*) but follows the second part (*or to*).]
PARALLEL	I'm looking forward *either to attending* Saturday's wrestling match *or to seeing* it on closed-circuit television.
AWKWARD	Take my advice: try *neither to be first nor last* in the lunch line. [Parallel structure is violated because *to be* follows the first part of the correlative conjunction but not the second part.]
PARALLEL	Take my advice: try to be *neither first nor last* in the lunch line.

17c *Make the elements in a comparison parallel in form.*

A comparative word such as *than* or *as* cues the reader to expect a parallel structure. This makes logical sense: to be compared, two things must resemble each other, and parallel structure emphasizes this resemblance. (See also 15g.)

AWKWARD	Philip likes *fishing* better than *to sail.*
PARALLEL	Philip likes *fishing* better than *sailing.*
PARALLEL	Philip likes *to fish* better than *to sail.*
AWKWARD	*Maintaining* railway lines is as important to our public transportation system as *to buy* new trains.
PARALLEL	*Maintaining* railway lines is as important to our public transportation system as *buying* new trains.

17d *Reinforce parallel structure by repeating rather than mixing articles, conjunctions, or prepositions.*

When you write a series involving articles, conjunctions, or prepositions, be consistent. Try to repeat rather than to vary the word that begins each phrase or clause.

> "The time has come," the Walrus said,
> "To talk of many things:
> Of shoes — and ships — and sealing-wax —
> Of cabbages — and — kings — "

In this famous rhyme from *Through the Looking-Glass,* Lewis Carroll builds a beautiful parallel structure on three *of*'s and three *and*'s, each followed by a noun. The repetition of preposition and conjunction makes clear the equivalence of the nouns.

Sometimes the same lead-in word won't work for all elements in a series. In such cases you may be able to preserve a parallel structure by changing the order of the elements to minimize variation.

AWKWARD	The new school building is large but not very comfortable, and expensive but unattractive.
PARALLEL	The new school building is large and expensive, but uncomfortable and unattractive.

17e *In a series of clauses, repeat lead-in words to emphasize parallel structure.*

Parallel structures are especially useful in complex sentences expressing equivalent ideas. Whenever you write a sentence containing a series of long, potentially confusing clauses, try to precede each clause with *that, who, when, where,* or some other connective, repeating the same connective every time. To do so not only helps you to keep your thoughts in order as you write but helps readers to follow them with ease.

> No one in this country needs a government that aids big business at the expense of farmers and laborers; that ravages the environment in the name of progress; that slashes budgets of health and education; that turns its back on the unemployed, the illiterate, the mentally ill, the destitute; that constantly swaggers and rattles its sabers; that spends billions piling up missiles it would be insane to use.
>
> —Student essay

Repeating an opening phrase can accomplish the same goal in a series of parallel sentences, as the following graceful example shows.

> The Russian dramatist is one who, walking through a cemetery, does not see the flowers on the graves. The American dramatist is one who, walking through a cemetery, does not see the graves under the flowers.   —George Jean Nathan

Exercise 17–1: Making Sentences Parallel

First figure out what the writer is trying to say in each of the following sentences. Then revise, substituting parallel structures for awkward ones. Possible revisions for the lettered sentences appear in the back of the book. Example:

> Not only are you wasting your time but mine.
>
> You are wasting not only your time but mine.

a. I like movies about the Old West, documentaries, and I like foreign films.

b. Better than starting from scratch would be to build on what already has been done.

c. Her apartment needed fresh paint, a new rug was a necessity, and Mary Lou wished she had a neater roommate and that she had chosen quieter friends.

d. All my brothers are blond and athletes.

e. For breakfast the waiter brought scrambled eggs, which I like, and kippers, although I don't like them.

1. The United States must start either focusing more attention on education or we must accept a future as a second-rate power.

2. Not only are you a gentleman but a scholar.

3. The best teachers are kind, firm, are smart, and have a sense of humor.

4. Like Polonius in *Hamlet,* I believe neither in being a borrower nor a lender.

5. Jules contends that our science facilities are inadequate, we need a new student center, a gym, and that an arts center would add much to the quality of life on campus.

6. Melrose would rather carry his battle to the Supreme Court than he would be willing to give up without a fight.

7. My landlady is tidy, generous, easygoing, and a talker.

8. Are problem novels for the young really good for children or merely exploit them by making life appear more burdensome, chaotic, more wretched and evil than it really is?

9. When you first start out, running halfway around the track is as big a challenge as to complete several circuits.

10. Her excuses were the difficulty of the task, the instructions were awkwardly worded, and having only four hours to complete the assignment.

11. In my drama class so far we've read a Shakespearean tragedy, another by Marlowe, and one of Webster's.

12. When you are broke and unemployed and your friends have deserted you, while you have nowhere to sleep but under a bridge, then and only then should you call this number.

13. Learn both winning with grace and to lose with dignity.

14. Not only should we accept Marinda's kind offer, but thank her for making it.

15. How often Reuben has done this kind of work is less important than the quality of his output.

18 COORDINATION AND SUBORDINATION

A good piece of writing is greater than the sum of its parts. Links between sentences help the reader to see how one thought relates to another and to share the writer's overview of the topic.

When you write, you can use coordination and subordination to bring out the relationships between your ideas. Coordination clarifies the connection between thoughts of equal importance; subordination shows how one thought affects another. These two techniques will help you produce sentences, paragraphs, and essays that function as a coherent whole.

18a Coordinate clauses or sentences that are related in theme and equal in importance.

> The car skidded for a hundred yards. It crashed into a brick wall.

These two clauses make equally significant statements about the same subject, a car accident. Because the writer has indicated no link between the sentences, we can only guess that the crash followed from the skid; we cannot be sure.

Suppose we join the two with a conjunction.

> The car skidded for a hundred yards, and it crashed into a brick wall.

Now the sequence is clear: first the car skidded, then it crashed. That's coordination.

Another way to coordinate the two clauses is to combine them into a single sentence with a compound verb. The second main clause, losing its subject, becomes a phrase.

> The car skidded for a hundred yards and crashed into a brick wall.

Now the connection is so clear we can almost hear screeching brakes and crunching metal.

Once you decide to coordinate two clauses, there are three ways you can do it: with a conjunction, with a conjunctive adverb, or with punctuation.

1. Join two main clauses with a coordinating conjunction (*and*, *but*, *for*, *or*, *nor*, *so*, or *yet*).

UNCOORDINATED	George does not want to be placed on your mailing list. He does not want a salesperson to call him.
COORDINATED	George does not want to be placed on your mailing list, nor does he want a salesperson to call him.
COORDINATED	George does not want to be placed on your mailing list or called by a salesperson.

EDITING CHECKLIST: COORDINATING AND SUBORDINATING

- Are all coordinated clauses related in theme and equal in importance? (18a)
- Are all coordinated clauses clearly and logically related? (18b)
- Do all coordinated clauses work together to make a coherent point? (18c)
- Is subordination used to link a less important idea to a more important idea? (18d)
- Is the main idea always expressed in the main clause? (18e)

---

2. Join two main clauses with a semicolon and a conjunctive adverb such as *furthermore*, *however*, *moreover*, or *therefore*.

UNCOORDINATED	The guerrillas did not observe the truce. They never intended to.
COORDINATED	The guerrillas did not observe the truce; furthermore, they never intended to.

3. Join two main clauses with a semicolon or a colon. (For details on when to use which punctuation mark, see 26 and 27.)

UNCOORDINATED	The government favors negotiations. The guerrillas prefer to fight.
COORDINATED	The government favors negotiations; the guerrillas prefer to fight.
UNCOORDINATED	The guerrillas have two advantages. They know the terrain, and the people support them.
COORDINATED	The guerrillas have two advantages: they know the terrain, and the people support them.

18b Coordinate clauses only if they are clearly and logically related.

Whenever you hitch together two sentences, make sure they get along. Will the relationship between them be evident to your readers? Have you chosen a coordinating conjunction, conjunctive adverb, or punctuation mark that accurately reflects this relationship?

FAULTY   The sportscasters were surprised by Easy Goer's failure to win the Kentucky Derby, but it rained on Derby day.

The writer has not included enough information for the reader to see why these two clauses are connected.

COORDINATED   The sportscasters were surprised by Easy Goer's failure to win the Kentucky Derby; *however, he runs poorly on a muddy track*, and it rained on Derby day.

Another route to faulty coordination is a poorly chosen link between clauses.

FAULTY   The sportscasters all expected Easy Goer to win the Kentucky Derby, and Sunday Silence beat him.

The conjunction *and* implies that both clauses reflect the same assumptions. This is not the case, so the writer should choose a conjunction that expresses difference.

COORDINATED   The sportscasters all expected Easy Goer to win the Kentucky Derby, *but* Sunday Silence beat him.

18c Coordinate clauses only if they work together to make a coherent point.

When a writer strings together several clauses in a row, often the result is excessive coordination. Trying to pack too much information into a single sentence can make readers dizzy, unable to pick out which points really matter.

EXCESSIVE   Easy Goer was the Kentucky Derby favorite, and all the sportscasters expected him to win, but he runs poorly on a muddy track, and it rained on Derby day, so Sunday Silence beat him.

What are the main points in this passage? Each key idea deserves its own sentence so that readers will recognize it as important.

REVISED   Easy Goer was the Kentucky Derby favorite, and all the sportscasters expected him to win. However, he runs poorly on a muddy track, and it rained on Derby day; so Sunday Silence beat him.

Excessive coordination also tends to result when a writer uses the same conjunction repeatedly.

| EXCESSIVE | Phil was out of the house all day, so he didn't know about the rain, so he went ahead and bet on Easy Goer, so he lost twenty bucks, so now he wants to borrow money from me. |
| REVISED | Phil was out of the house all day, so he didn't know about the rain. He went ahead and bet on Easy Goer, and he lost twenty bucks. Now he wants to borrow money from me. |

One solution to excessive coordination is subordination: making one clause dependent on another instead of giving both clauses equal weight. (See 18d.)

Exercise 18–1: Writing Using Coordination and Subordination

Rewrite the following sentences to add coordination where it is needed and to remove faulty or excessive coordination wherever you find it. Possible revisions for the lettered sentences appear in the back of the book. Example:

> The wind was rising, and leaves tossed on the trees, and the air seemed to crackle with electricity, and we knew that a thunderstorm was on the way.

> The wind was rising, leaves tossed on the trees, and the air seemed to crackle with electricity. We knew that a thunderstorm was on the way.

a. Congress is expected to pass the biotechnology bill. The president already has said he will veto it.

b. Mortgage rates have dropped. Home buying is likely to increase in the near future.

c. Find Mrs. Fellowes a seat. She looks tired.

d. I left the house in a hurry and ran to the bank so I could cash a check to buy lunch, but it was the bank's anniversary, and the staff was busy serving coffee and cake, so by the time I left, after chatting and eating for twenty minutes, I wasn't hungry anymore.

e. The U.S. Postal Service handles millions of pieces of mail every day. It is the largest postal service in the world.

1. Jackson may go through with his lawsuit. He may settle out of court.

2. If you want to take Spanish this semester, you have only one choice. You must sign up for the 8 a.m. course.

3. Peterson's Market has raised its prices. Last week tuna fish cost $.89 a can. Now it's up to $1.09.

4. Joe starts the morning with a cup of coffee, which wakes him up, and then at lunch he eats a chocolate bar, so that the sugar and caffeine will bring up his energy level.

5. I like Chinese food. I often eat it. Some Szechuan dishes are too hot for me.

18d Subordinate less important ideas to more important ideas.

Subordination is one of the most useful of all writing strategies. By subordinating a less important clause to a more important one, you show your readers that one fact or idea follows from another or affects another. You stress what counts, thereby encouraging your readers to share your viewpoint—an important goal, whatever you are writing.

When you have two sentences that contain ideas in need of connecting, you can subordinate one to the other in any of the following three ways.

1. Turn the less important idea into a subordinate clause by introducing it with a subordinating conjunction such as *although, because, if,* or *when.* (See 1g for a list of subordinating conjunctions.)

> Jason has a keen sense of humor. He has an obnoxious, braying laugh.

From that pair of sentences, a reader doesn't know what to feel about Jason. Is he likable or repellent? The writer needs to decide which trait matters more and to emphasize it.

> *Although Jason has a keen sense of humor,* he has an obnoxious, braying laugh.

The revision makes Jason's sense of humor less important than his annoying hee-haw. The less important idea is stated as a subordinate clause opening with *although,* the more important idea as the main clause.

The writer could reverse the meaning by combining the two ideas the other way around:

> *Although Jason has an obnoxious, braying laugh,* he has a keen sense of humor.

That version makes Jason sound fun to be with, despite his mannerism.

Which of Jason's traits to emphasize is up to the writer. What matters is that, in both combined versions of the original two separate sentences, the writer takes a clear stand by making one sentence a main clause and the other a subordinate clause.

2. Turn the less important idea into a subordinate clause by introducing it with a relative pronoun such as *who, which,* or *that.* (See 1b for a list of relative pronouns.)

> Jason, *who has an obnoxious, braying laugh,* has a keen sense of humor.
> Jason, *whose sense of humor is keen,* has an obnoxious, braying laugh.

3. Turn the less important idea into a phrase.

> Jason, *a keen humorist,* has an obnoxious, braying laugh.
> *Despite his obnoxious, braying laugh,* Jason has a keen sense of humor.

18e *Express the most important idea in the main clause.*

Sometimes a writer accidentally subordinates a more important idea to a less important idea and turns the sentence's meaning upside down.

> **FAULTY SUBORDINATION** Although the Algonquin Round Table lives on in spirit, the writers who created it are nearly all dead now.

This sentence is factually accurate. Does the writer, however, really want to stress death over life? This is the effect of putting *are nearly all dead* in the main clause and *lives on* in the subordinate clause. Recognizing a case of faulty subordination, the writer can reverse the two clauses.

REVISED   Although the writers who created it are nearly all dead now, the Algonquin Round Table lives on in spirit.

18f *Limit the number of subordinate clauses in a sentence.*

The cause of excessive subordination is usually that a writer has tried to cram too much information into one sentence. The result is a string of ideas in which readers may not be able to pick out what matters.

EXCESSIVE   Debate over the Strategic Defense Initiative (SDI), which was
SUBORDINATION   originally proposed as a space-based defensive shield that would protect America from enemy attack, but which critics have suggested amounts to creating a first-strike capability in space, has to some extent focused on the wrong question because it concentrates on the plan's technological flaws and thus fails to consider adequately whether SDI would in fact lower or increase the odds of nuclear war.

In revising this sentence, the writer needs to decide which are the main points and turn each one into a main clause. Lesser points can remain as subordinate clauses, arranged so that each of them gets an appropriate amount of emphasis.

REVISED   Debate over the Strategic Defense Initiative (SDI) has to some extent focused on the wrong question. The plan was originally proposed as a space-based defensive shield that would protect America from enemy attack; but critics have suggested that it amounts to creating a first-strike capability in space. However, most arguments about SDI have concentrated on its technological flaws and thus have failed to consider adequately whether SDI would in fact lower or increase the odds of nuclear war.

Exercise 18–2: Using Subordination

Rewrite the following sentences to subordinate where it is appropriate and to remove faulty or excessive subordination wherever you find it. Possible revisions for the lettered sentences appear in the back of the book. Example:

Some playwrights like to work with performing theater companies. It is helpful to hear a script read aloud by actors.

Some playwrights like to work with performing theater companies because it is helpful to hear a script read aloud by actors.

a. Although we occasionally hear horror stories about fruits and vegetables being unsafe to eat because they were sprayed with toxic chemicals or were grown in contaminated soil, the fact remains that, given their high nutritional value, these fresh foods are generally much better for us than processed foods.

b. Renata claims that cats make the best pets. They are adorable, affectionate, and easy to care for.

c. At the end of Verdi's opera *La Traviata,* Alfredo has to see his beloved Violetta again. He knows she is dying and all he can say is good-bye.

d. Violetta gives away her money. She bids adieu to her faithful servant. After that she dies in her lover's arms.

e. Some television cartoon shows have become cult classics. This has happened years after they went off the air. Examples include *Rocky and Bullwinkle* and *George of the Jungle.*

1. Cape Cod is a peninsula in Massachusetts. It juts into the Atlantic Ocean south of Boston. The Cape marks the northern turning point of the Gulf Stream.

2. Renata likes cats. However, her husband bought a German shepherd. He said it would protect their house against intruders.

3. Tim spent his last twenty dollars to buy his mother a big bouquet of flowers. He adores her.

4. Although bank customers have not yet begun to shift their money out of savings accounts, the interest rate on NOW accounts has gone up.

5. I usually have more fun at a concert with Rico than with Morey. Rico loves music. Morey merely tolerates it.

19 SENTENCE VARIETY

Just as the special-effects experts in movies use the unexpected to shock or to please, writers may combine sentence elements in unexpected ways to achieve special effects. Writers use some patterns more than others to express ideas directly and efficiently, but sometimes they vary the normal expectations in sentences to emphasize ideas and surprise readers.

19a *Normal Sentences*

In a **normal sentence** a writer puts the subject before the verb at the beginning of the main clause. This pattern is the most common in English because it expresses ideas in the most straightforward manner.

> Most college *students* today *are* not *interested* in reading.
>
> *Franklin sighed* because he was frustrated over his inability to solve the quadratic equation.

19b *Inverted Sentences*

In an **inverted sentence** a writer inverts or reverses the subject-verb order to emphasize an idea in the predicate.

> NORMAL   My peers are uninterested in reading.
>
> INVERTED   How uninterested in reading are my peers!

19c *Balanced Sentences*

In a **balanced sentence** a writer purposefully repeats key words and uses parallel sentence patterns to emphasize ideas.

> In studying the heavens, we are debarred from all senses except sight. *We cannot* touch the sun, *or* travel to it: *we cannot* walk around the moon, *or* apply a foot-rule to the Pleiades. —Bertrand Russell

19d *Cumulative Sentences*

In a **cumulative sentence** a writer piles details at the end of a sentence to help readers visualize a scene or understand an idea.

> They came walking out in heavily brocaded yellow and black costumes, the familiar "toreador" suit, heavy with gold embroidery, cape, jacket, shirt and collar, knee breeches, pink stockings, and low pumps.
> —Ernest Hemingway, "Bull Fighting a Tragedy"

19e *Periodic Sentences*

The positions of emphasis in a sentence are the beginning and the end. In a **periodic sentence** a writer suspends the main clause for a climactic ending, emphasizing an idea by withholding it until the end.

> Leaning back in his chair, shaking his head slowly back and forth, frustrated over his inability to solve the quadratic equation, Franklin scowled.

Exercise 19–1: Identifying Sentence Variety

Identify each sentence as normal, inverted, cumulative, balanced, periodic, or a combination of these types. Answers for the lettered sentences appear in the back of the book. Example:

> Watching Katrina walk down the long aisle of the arena to receive her diploma, and remembering the many hours of work and sacrifice that brought her to this moment, I felt great pride. [Cumulative.]

a. Surprising himself, bobbing and weaving rapidly and expertly down the field through the hulking defensive linemen, the third string quarterback ran.

b. In Mexico City I was always being told that there were places I should and should not go, things I should and should not do, and meals I should and should not eat.

c. He was waiting at the ramp, smiling and cordial, arms outstretched, eyes twinkling, a bit portly in a green sweatsuit.

d. Education is increasingly and necessarily specialized and conducted by specialists.

e. At the end of the dirt road, under an ancient oak covered with Spanish moss, was the decaying mansion.

1. He was an undersized little man, with a head too big for his body—a sickly little man.
   —Deems Taylor, "The Monster"

2. If education is the transmission of civilization, we are unquestionably progressing.
   —Will and Ariel Durant, *The Lessons of History*

3. I wanted not an obvious rhetorical exchange about why America had no national heroes anymore; I wanted to get at how one kept one's world from collapsing once its mythic underpinnings had given way.   —Joe McGinnis, *Heroes*

4. The classification "conservative" is so frayed at the edges that it is becoming an impediment to clear thinking and prudent government.
   —George F. Will, *Statecraft as Soulcraft*

5. The only purpose for which power can rightfully be exercised over any member of a civilized community against the will is to prevent harm to others.
   —John Stuart Mill, *Utilitarianism, Liberty, and Republican Government*

Exercise 19–2: Generating Sentence Variety

Try your hand—either alone or with your peer group—at composing each of these types of sentences: a normal sentence, an inverted sentence, a balanced sentence, a cumulative sentence, and a periodic sentence.

CHAPTER 34

Word Choice

20   APPROPRIATENESS

When you talk to people face to face, you can gauge how they are reacting to what you say. Often their responses guide your tone of voice and your choice of words: if your listener chuckles at your humor, you go on being humorous. If your listener frowns, you cut the comedy and speak more seriously.

Like a speaker's voice, a writer's voice may come across as warm and friendly or cool and aloof, furious or merely annoyed, playful or grimly serious. Its quality depends on how the writer feels toward his or her material and toward the reader. The devices the writer uses to show these feelings create the *tone* of the piece of writing.

The tone of your writing, like the tone of your speaking voice, strongly influences your audience's response to the points you are making. Judging a reader's reaction, however, is harder than judging a listener's. To know whether your presentation is successful, usually you must imagine yourself in the reader's place.

Although you may consider your readers from time to time as you gather material and as you write, you probably focus most closely on their response when you reread your writing. What attitude do you want readers to take toward your topic? What tone is likely to convey this attitude most effectively? Do your choices of sentence length, vocabulary, and other elements of style work together to create an appropriate tone?

20a Choose an approach and a level of formality appropriate for your topic and audience.

Tone may include choice of formal or informal language, colorful or bland words, coolly objective words or words loaded with emotional connotations ("You pig!" "You angel!"). A tone that seems right (to a reader) comes when the writer has written with an accurate sense of how the reader will react. If the writer is unaware of or is wrong about the reader's responses, then the writer's tone is inappropriate. For instance, taking a humorous approach to a disease such as cancer or AIDS probably would yield an inappropriate tone. The reader, not finding the topic funny, is likely to read without sympathy.

Being aware of your audience helps you choose words that are neither too formal nor too informal. By *formal* language we mean the impersonal language of educated persons, usually written. In general, formal language is marked by relatively long and complex sentences and by a large vocabulary. It doesn't use contractions (such as *doesn't*), and its attitude toward the topic is serious.

Informal (or colloquial) language more closely resembles ordinary conversation. Its sentences tend to be relatively short and simple. Informal language may include contractions, slang, and references to everyday objects and activities (cheeseburgers, T-shirts, car repair). It may address the reader as "you."

The right language for most essays, especially those you write for class assignments, lies somewhere between formal and informal. If your topic and your tone are serious (say, for an expository paper on the United Nations), then your language is likely to lean toward formality. If your topic is not weighty and your tone is light or humorous (say, for a narrative paper about giving your dog a bath), then your language can be more informal.

20b Choose common words instead of jargon.

Whatever your tone and your level of formality, certain types of language are best avoided when you write an essay. **Jargon** is the name given to the specialized vocabulary used by people in a particular field. Nearly every academic, professional, and even recreational field—music, carpentry, the law, computer programming, sports—has its own jargon. In baseball, pitcher Dennis Eckersley says that when he faces a dangerous batter, he thinks: "If I throw him *the heater,* maybe he *juices it out* on me" (emphasis added). Translation: "If I throw him a fastball, he might hit a home run."[1]

To a specialist addressing other specialists, jargon is convenient and necessary. Without technical terms, after all, two surgeons could hardly discuss a patient's anatomy. To an outsider, though, such terms may be incomprehensible. If your writing is meant (as it should be) to communicate information to your readers and not to make them feel excluded or confused, you should avoid unnecessary jargon.

Commonly, we apply the name *jargon* to any private, pretentious, or needlessly specialized language. Jargon can include not only words but ways of using words. Some politicians and bureaucrats like to make nouns into verbs by tacking on suffixes like *-ize.*

JARGON	Let us *prioritize* our objectives.
CLEAR	Let us *assign priorities to* our objectives.
CLEAR	Let us *rank* our objectives *in order of urgency.*
JARGON	The government intends to *privatize* federal land holdings.
CLEAR	The government intends to *sell* federal land holdings *to private buyers.*

Although *privatize* implies merely "convert to private ownership," usually its real meaning is "sell off" — as might occur, say, were a national park to be auctioned to developers. *Privatize* thus also can be called a *euphemism,* which is any pleasant term that masks an unpleasant meaning (see 20c).

Besides confusing readers, jargon is likely to mislead them. Recently, high technology has made verbs of the familiar nouns *access, boot,* and *format.* Other terms that have entered the popular vocabulary include *interface, x amount of, database,* and *parameters.* Such terms are useful to explain technical processes; but when thoughtlessly applied to nontechnical ideas, they can obscure meaning.

JARGON	A democracy needs the electorate's *input.*
CLEAR	A democracy needs the electorate *to vote and to express its views to elected officials.*

Here's how to shun needless jargon.

1. Beware of choosing any trendy new word when a perfectly good old word will do.

2. Before using a word ending in *-ize, -wise,* or *-ism,* count to ten. This will give you time either to think of a clearer alternative or to be sure that none exists.

3. Avoid the jargon of a special discipline — say, psychology or fly-fishing — unless you are writing of psychological or fly-fishing matters and you know for sure that your reader, too, is familiar with them. If you're writing for an audience of general readers about some field in which you are an expert — if, for instance, you're explaining the fundamentals of hang gliding —

[1] Quoted by Mike Whiteford, *How to Talk Baseball* (New York: Dembner, 1983), 51.

define any specialized terms. Even if you're addressing fellow hang-gliding experts, use plain words and you'll rarely go wrong.

Exercise 20–1: Using Appropriate Language

The following sentences bog down in jargon. Turn them into standard English. If you see a need to change them extensively, go ahead. If you can't tell what a sentence means, decide what it might mean and rewrite it so that its meaning is clear. Possible revisions for the lettered sentences appear in the back of the book. Example:

> The proximity of Mr. Fitton's knife to Mr. Schering's arm produced a violation of the integrity of the skin.
>
> Mr. Fitton's knife cut Mr. Schering's arm.

a. Diagnosiswise, Mrs. Pitt, your husband's heart looks considerably failure-prone at this particular point in time.

b. In the heart area, Mr. Pitt is a prime candidate-elect for intervention of a multiple bypass nature.

c. Within the parameters of your insurance company's financial authorization, he can either be regimed dietwise or be bypass prognosticated.

d. We of the State Department have carefully contexted the riots in Lebanon intelligencewise, and after full and thorough database utilization, find them abnormalling rapidly.

e. Certain antinuclearistic and pacifistic/prejudicial factions have been picketing the missile conference in hopes of immobilizing these vital peacekeeping deliberations.

1. Regarding the issue as to whether foreknowledge of the operation was obtained by the secretary in this instance, it has been ascertained that no definite affirmative conclusion is warranted.

2. Engaging in a conversational situation with the Deity permits an individual to maximally interface with the Lord.

3. The deer hunters number-balanced the ecological infrastructure by quietizing x amount of the deer populace.

4. "I am very grateful that we have education up where it is, high on the educational agenda of this country."
   —Secretary of Education T. H. Bell, in a speech, June 1983

5. All student personnel are directed to prioritize their efforts to the nth degree toward minimization of excessive dormitory litter generation.

20c Use euphemisms sparingly.

Euphemisms are plain truths dressed in attractive words, sometimes hard facts stated gently and pleasantly. To say that someone *passed away* instead of *died* is a common euphemism — useful and humane, perhaps, in breaking terrible news to an anxious family. In such shock-absorbing language, an army that retreats *makes a strategic withdrawal;* a poor old man becomes a *disadvantaged senior citizen.* But euphemisms aren't always oversized words. If you call someone *slim* whom you think *underweight* or *skinny,* you use a euphemism, though it has only one syllable.

Because they can bathe glum truths in a kindly glow, euphemisms are beloved by advertisers — like the *mortician (undertaker)* who offered *pre-need arrangements.* Euphemisms also can make ordinary things sound more impressive. Some acne medications treat not *pimples* but *blemishes.* In Madison, Wisconsin, a theater renamed its candy counter the *patron assistance center.*

Euphemisms may serve grimmer purposes. During World War II, Jewish prisoners sent to Nazi extermination camps carried papers stamped *Rückkehr Unerwünscht* (Return Unwanted). In 1984, the Doublespeak Award of the National Council of Teachers of English went to the U.S. State Department for its announcement that it would no longer use the word *killing* in its official reports but would substitute *unlawful or arbitrary deprivation of life.*

Even if you aren't prone to using euphemisms in your own writing, be aware of them when you read, especially when collecting evidence from biased sources and official spokespersons.

Exercise 20–2: Avoiding Euphemisms

Rewrite the following statements, turning euphemisms into plainer words. Possible revisions for the lettered sentences appear in the back of the book. Example:

> I am temporarily between jobs, so I am currently experiencing a negative cash flow.
>
> I'm out of work and in debt.

a. This entry-level position offers a challenging career opportunity with a relatively modest initial salary.

b. The ship sank because of loss of hull integrity.

c. The new K27 missile will effectively depopulate the cities of any aggressor nation.

d. In our town, sanitation engineers when making their rounds must wear professional apparel.

e. Freddie the Rocker has boarded a first-class flight for the great all-night discotheque in the sky.

1. Our security forces have judiciously thinned an excessive number of political dissidents.

2. The champion's uppercut landed, and on the challenger's lip a tea-rose bloomed.

3. To bridge the projected shortfall between collections and expenditures in next year's budget, the governor advocates some form of revenue enhancement.

4. Saturday's weather forecast calls for extended periods of shower activity.

5. Uncle Eb, a gentleman of extremely mature years, was a faithful worshiper at the Follies Bar, a shrine of progressive corporeal revelation.

20d Avoid slang in formal writing.

Poet Carl Sandburg once said, "Slang is language that takes off its coat, spits on its hands, and gets to work." Clearly, Sandburg approved. Probably even the purists among us will concede that slang, especially when new, can be colorful ("She's not playing with a full deck"), playful ("He's wicked cute!"), and apt (*ice* for diamonds, a *stiff* for a corpse).

The trouble with most slang, however, is that it quickly comes to seem quaint, even incomprehensible. We don't hear anyone say *groovy* anymore except on reruns of *The Brady Bunch. Bad vibes*, ubiquitous in the 1960s, today wear spiderwebs. Even the lately minted *bummer* and *grody to the max* already seem as old and wrinkled as the Jazz Age's favorite exclamation of glee, *twenty-three skidoo!*

In the classroom and out of it, your writing communicates your thoughts. To be understood, your best bet is to stick to standard English. Most slang is less than clever. The newest of it, apt though it may seem, like any fad is in danger of being quickly tossed aside in favor of something newer still. Seek words that are usual but exact, not the latest thing, and your writing will stay young longer.

Exercise 20–3: Avoiding Slang

Revise the following sentences to replace slang with standard English. Possible revisions for the lettered sentences appear in the back of the book. Example:

> I can see that something is bugging you, so you may as well lay it on me.
>
> I can see that something is bothering you, so you may as well tell me about it.

a. Judy doesn't dig the way Paul's been coming on to her.

b. If large animals do not clear out of the combat zone, the army's policy is to waste them.

c. Judge Lehman's reversal of the *Smith v. Jones* verdict shows that his lights are on but nobody's home.

d. Once that eyewitness spilled his guts, Jones's goose was cooked.

e. If he can make bail, he'll probably split.

1. Otherwise he could draw five to ten in the slammer.

2. Blue-collar criminals get nailed; white-collar criminals walk.

3. The insider trading thing on Wall Street has turned out to be a major scam.

4. One honcho actually offed himself.

5. If the Iranians had the hardware, they'd probably nuke us.

21 EXACT WORDS

What would you think if you read in a newspaper that a certain leading citizen is a *pillow of the community?* How would you react to a foreign dignitary's statement that he has no children because his wife is *inconceivable?* Good writing — that is, effective written communication — depends on more than good grammar. Just as important are knowing what words and phrases mean and using them precisely.

21a Choose words for their connotations as well as their denotations.

The **denotation** of a word is its basic meaning — its dictionary definition. *Stone,* for instance, has the same denotation as *rock. Excited, agitated,* and *exhilarated* all denote a similar state of physical and emotional arousal. When you look up a word in a dictionary or thesaurus, the synonyms you find have been selected for their shared denotation.

The **connotations** of a word are the shades of meaning that set it apart from its synonyms. We say *Phil's house is a stone's throw from mine,* not *a rock's throw.* You might be *agitated* by the prospect of exams next week, but *exhilarated* by your plans for a vacation afterward. When you choose one out of several synonyms listed in a dictionary or thesaurus, you base your choice on connotation.

Paying attention to connotation helps a writer to say exactly what he or she intends, instead of almost but not quite.

IMPRECISE	Advertisers have given light beer a macho image by showing football players *sipping* the product with *enthusiasm.*
REVISED	Advertisers have given light beer a macho image by showing football players *guzzling* the product with *gusto.*
IMPRECISE	The cat's eyes *shone* as she *pursued* the mouse.
REVISED	The cat's eyes *glittered* as she *stalked* the mouse.

21b Avoid clichés.

A **cliché** is a trite expression, worn out from too much use. It may have glinted once, like a coin fresh from the mint, but now it is dull and flat from years of passing from hand to hand. If a story begins, "It was a dark and stormy night," and introduces a *tall, dark, and handsome* man and a woman who is *a vision of loveliness,* then its author is obviously using worn coins.

A cliché isn't just any old dull expression: it is one whose writer mistakenly assumes is bright. "Let's run this up the flagpole and see if anyone salutes," proposes the executive, while his or her colleagues yawn at the effort to sound clever. Stale, too, is the suggestion to put an idea *on the back burner.* Clichés abound when writers and speakers try hard to sound vigorous and colorful but don't trouble to invent anything vigorous, colorful, and new.

George Orwell once complained about prose made up of phrases "tacked together like the sections of a prefabricated henhouse." If you read newspapers, you are familiar with such ready-made constructions. A strike is usually settled after *a marathon bargaining session* that *narrowly averts a walkout,* often *at the eleventh hour.* Fires customarily *race* and *gut.* Some writers use clichés to exaggerate, giving a statement more force than they feel. The writer to whom everything is *fantastic* or *terrific* arouses a reader's suspicion that it isn't.

No writer can entirely avoid clichés or avoid echoing colorful expressions first used by someone else. You need not ban from your writing all proverbs ("It takes a thief to catch a thief"), well-worked quotations from Shakespeare ("Neither a borrower nor a lender be"), and other faintly dusty wares from the storehouse of our language. "Looking for a needle in a haystack" may be a time-worn phrase, yet who can put that idea any more memorably?

Nor should you fear that every familiar expression is a cliché. *Just in time, more or less, sooner or later*—these are old, familiar expressions, to be sure; but they are not clichés, for they don't try to be vivid or figurative. Inevitably, we all rely on them.

When editing your writing, you will usually recognize any really annoying cliché you'll want to eradicate. If you feel a sudden guilty desire to surround an expression with quotation marks, as if to apologize for it—

In his campaign speeches for his fourteenth term, Senator Pratt shows that he cannot "cut the mustard" any longer.

—then strike it out. Think again: what do you want to say? Recast your idea more clearly, more exactly.

At age seventy-seven, Senator Pratt no longer can hold a crowd with an impassioned, hour-long speech, as he could when he first ran for Congress.

By what other means can you spot a cliché? One way is to show your papers to friends, asking them to look for anything trite. As you go on in college, your awareness of clichés will grow with reading. The more you read, the easier it is to recognize a cliché on sight, for you will have met it often before.

Meanwhile, here is a list of a few clichés still in occasional circulation. If any is a favorite of yours, try replacing it with something more vivid and original.

Achilles' heel	in my wildest dreams
acid test	last but not least
add insult to injury	little did I dream
apple of one's eye	make a long story short
as American as apple pie	natural inclination
an astronomical sum	neat as a pin
beyond a shadow of a doubt	nutty as a fruitcake
born with a silver spoon in one's mouth	old as the hills
	on the ball
bosom companions, bosom buddies	on the brink of disaster
burn the midnight oil	over and above the call of duty
burn one's bridges	pay through the nose
busy as a beaver (or a bee)	piece of cake
But that's another story.	point with pride
come hell or high water	proud as a peacock
cool as a cucumber	pull the wool over someone's eyes

cream of the crop	salad days
cut like a knife	sell like hotcakes
dead as a doornail	a sheepish grin
do your own thing	since the dawn of time
dressed fit to kill	skating on thin ice
eager beaver	a skeleton in the closet
easy as taking candy from a baby	slow as molasses
easy as falling off a log	smell a rat
a face that would stop a clock	a sneaking suspicion
feeling on top of the world	stab me in the back
few and far between	stack the deck
fine and dandy	stagger the imagination
fly in the ointment	stick out like a sore thumb
from (or since) time immemorial	sweet as honey
golden years	That's the way the ball bounces.
greased lightning	tip of the iceberg
hands-on learning experience	through thick and thin
hard as a rock	time-honored
high as a kite	too little and too late
holler bloody murder	tried but true
honest as the day is long	You could have knocked me over with
In conclusion, I would like to say . . .	a feather.

21c *Use idioms in their correct form.*

Every language contains **idioms,** or *idiomatic expressions:* phrases that, through long use, have become standard even though their construction may defy logic or grammar. Idioms can be difficult for a native speaker of English to explain to someone just learning the language. They sound natural, however, to those who have heard them since childhood.

Many idiomatic expressions require us to choose the right preposition. We say we live *in* the city, but vacation *at* the seashore, even though we might be hard pressed to explain why we use *in* in one phrase and *at* in the other. To pause *for* a minute is not the same as to pause *in* a minute. We work *up* a sweat while working *out* in the gym. We argue *with* someone, but *about* something. We can also argue *for* or *against* it.

For some idioms we must know which article to use before a noun—or whether to use any article at all. We can be *in motion,* but we have to be *in the swim.* We're occasionally in *a tight spot* but never in *a trouble.* Certain idioms vary from country to country: in Britain, a patient has an operation *in hospital*; in America, *in the hospital.* Idioms can involve choosing the right verb with the right noun: we *seize* an opportunity, but we *catch* a plane. We *break* a law but *explode* a theory.

Sometimes even the best writers draw a blank when they confront a common idiomatic expression. Is *compared with* or *compared to* the right phrase? Should you say *agree to, agree on,* or *agree with? Disgusted at* or *disgusted with? Smile about, smile at, smile on,* or *smile over?*

Depending on what you mean, sometimes one alternative is correct, sometimes another. When you're at work on a paper, the dictionary can help you choose. Look up *agree* in *The American Heritage Dictionary*, for instance, and you will find *agree to, agree with, agree about, agree on,* and *agree that* illustrated with sentence examples that make clear just where and when each combination is appropriate. You can then pick the idiom that belongs in the sentence you are working on. In the long run, though, you learn to use idioms accurately in your writing by reading the work of careful writers, by absorbing what they do, and by doing likewise.

Exercise 21–1: Selecting Words

Revise the following sentences to replace inappropriate connotations, clichés, and faulty idioms. Possible revisions for the lettered sentences appear in the back of the book. Example:

> The premier's tantamount objective is to defeat the guerrillas by giving them some of their own medicine.

> The premier's paramount objective is to defeat the guerrillas using their own tactics.

a. Since time immemorial, the Sahara has had a legendary reputation as one of the most overheated and arid regions on earth.

b. The intrepid explorers knew they were taking their lives in their hands as they sallied forth to cross the featureless sands.

c. After six days of travel, every member of the party was red as a beet and faint because of thirst.

d. Even the camels were on the verge to falling over in their tracks when the scouts laid their eyes on an oasis.

e. With furrowed brow, the caravan leader peered into the blinding sun.

1. As the distant speck loomed larger on the horizon, everyone could see it was no optical illusion, but a long-waited-for refuge.

2. "At last! Water!" screamed the very pleased caravan leader.

3. Cleaning his damp, dusty brow, he led the party into the welcome darkness under the palm trees.

4. Their throats felt as dry as bones, but before wetting their whistles, they watered the camels.

5. As the dead-on-their-feet explorers scurried under their mosquito netting for forty winks, their leader muttered that crossing the Sahara was a pleasure compared to searching for the North Pole.

22 BIAS-FREE LANGUAGE

The words we use reveal out attitudes — our likes and dislikes, our preferences and prejudices. Favorable or unfavorable connotations help us to express how we feel. A *brat* is quite different from a *little angel*, a *childish prank* from an *act of vandalism*, a *jalopy* from a *limousine*.

Language with unfavorable connotations has the power to insult or hurt someone. Thoughtful writers attempt to avoid harmful bias in language. They respect their readers, and they don't want to insult them or make them angry. They realize that discriminatory language can impede communication. According to Rosalie Maggio, "Ordinary people have chosen to replace linguistic pejoration and disrespect with words that grant full humanity and equality to all of us."[1] You may not be able to eliminate discrimination from society, but you can eliminate discriminatory language in your writing. Be on the lookout for words that insult or stereotype individuals or groups by gender, age, race, ethnic origin, or religion.

22a *To eliminate sexist language, use alternatives that make no reference to gender.*

Among the prime targets of American feminists in the 1960s and 1970s was the male bias built into the English language. Why, they asked, do we talk about *prehistoric man, manpower,* and *the brotherhood of man,* when by *man* we mean the entire human race? Why do we focus attention on the gender of an accomplished woman by calling her a *poetess* or a *lady doctor*? Why does a letter to a corporation have to begin "Gentlemen:"?

Early efforts to provide alternatives to sexist language often led to awkward, even ungrammatical solutions. To substitute "Everyone prefers their own customs" for "Everyone prefers *his* own customs" is to replace sexism with bad grammar. "Everyone prefers his or her [*or* his/her] own customs" is correct, but sometimes clumsy. Even clumsier is "Was it George or Jane who submitted his or her [his/her] resignation?" *Chairperson, policeperson, businessperson, spokesperson,* and *congressperson* do not flow easily from tongue or pen; and some people object to *chairwoman, policewoman,* and similar words because they call attention to gender where gender ought not to matter. *Male nurse* or *female supervisor* elicits the same objection.

Some writers try to eliminate sexual bias by alternating between the masculine and feminine genders every few sentences. Dr. Benjamin Spock, when referring to babies in recent revisions of his well-known *Baby and Child Care,* uses *he* and *she* in roughly equal numbers. Some readers find this approach refreshing. Why should we, after all, think of every baby as a boy, every parent as a woman? Other readers find such gender switches confusing.

Well-meaning attempts to invent or borrow neutral third-person pronouns (*thon asks* instead of *he asks* or *she asks,* for instance) have not gained general acceptance. How then can we as sensitive writers minimize the sexist constraints that the English language places in our path? Although there are no hard-and-fast rules, no perfect solutions, we can be aware of the potholes and try to steer around them as smoothly as possible.

[1] *The Dictionary of Bias-Free Usage: A Guide to Nondiscriminatory Language* (Oryx, 1991), vii.

22b *Avoid terms that include or imply* man.

We all know from experience that the most obvious way to neuter *man* or a word starting with *man* is to substitute *human.* The result, however, is often clumsy.

SEXIST   Mankind has always been obsessed with man's inhumanity to man.

NONSEXIST   Humankind has always been obsessed with humans' inhumanity to other humans.

Adding *hu-* to *man* alleviates sexism but weighs down the sentence. When you run into this problem, think for a moment. Usually you can find a more graceful solution.

REVISED   Human beings have always been obsessed with people's cruelty to one another.

Similarly, when you face a word that ends with *-man,* you need not simply replace that ending with *-person.* Take a different approach: think about what the word means and find a synonym that is truly neutral.

SEXIST   Did you leave a note for the mailman?

REVISED   Did you leave a note for the mail carrier?

The same tactic works for designations with a male and a female ending, such as *waiter* and *waitress.*

SEXIST   Ask your waiter [or waitress] for today's specials.

NONSEXIST   Ask your waitperson for today's specials.

REVISED   Ask your server for today's specials.

22c *Use plural instead of singular.*

SEXIST   Today's student values his education.

REVISED   Today's students value their education.

Sexism is not the only problem in the first sentence. Anytime you let a singular noun stand for a group of people, you run the risk of creating a stereotype. Using plurals thus can sometimes help you to avoid ethnic and racial, as well as sexual, bias.

STEREOTYPED The Chinaman eats his rice with chopsticks.

REVISED   Chinese people eat their rice with chopsticks.

STEREOTYPED The American Indian lost his land to the white man.

REVISED   American Indians lost their land to whites.

22d *Where possible, omit words that denote gender.*

SEXIST   For optimal results, there must be rapport between a stockbroker and his client, a teacher and her student, a doctor and his patient.

REVISED	For optimal results, there must be rapport between stockbroker and client, teacher and student, doctor and patient.
SEXIST	The girls in the secretarial pool bought President Schmutz a birthday cake.
REVISED	The secretarial pool [or the secretaries] bought President Schmutz a birthday cake.

22e Avoid condescending words.

A responsible writer does not call women *blondes, coeds, gals, working girls, woman drivers,* or any other names that imply that they are not to be taken seriously. Nor should an employee ever be referred to as a *girl* or *boy.* Avoid any terms that put down individuals or groups because of age (*old goat, the grannies*); race or ethnic background (*Indian giver, Chinaman's chance*); disability (*amputee, handicapped*).

CONDESCENDING	I'll have my girl call your girl and make a date for lunch.
REVISED	I'll have my secretary call your secretary and make a date for lunch.
CONDESCENDING	Mario said he'd send one of the boys to drive Linda to the airport.
REVISED	Mario said he'd send a driver to take Linda to the airport.
CONDESCENDING	My neighbor is just an old fogy.
REVISED	My neighbor has old-fashioned ideas.
CONDESCENDING	Few decisions in life are black and white.
REVISED	Few decisions in life are simple either/or choices.

22f Avoid implied stereotypes.

Sometimes a negative stereotype is linked to a title or designation indirectly. Aside from a few obvious exceptions such as *mothers* and *fathers,* never assume that all the members of a group are the same.

STEREOTYPE	A bunch of yuppies in our condo plays golf every Sunday afternoon.
REVISED	A group of residents in our condo plays golf every Sunday afternoon.
STEREOTYPE	Astronauts have little time to spend with their wives and children.
REVISED	Astronauts have little time to spend with their families.
STEREOTYPE	Rock musicians meet plenty of eager women, but few who are worth getting to know.
REVISED	Rock musicians meet plenty of eager fans, but few who are worth getting to know.

22g Use Ms. for a woman with no other known title.

Ms. is a wonderfully useful form of address. Comparable to *Mr.* for a man, it is easier to use than either *Miss* or *Mrs.* for someone whose marital status you don't know. Now that many married women are keeping their original last names, either professionally or in all areas of their lives, *Ms.* is often the best choice even for someone whose marital status you do know. However, if the woman to whom you are writing holds a doctorate, a professional office, or some other position that comes with a title, use that title rather than *Ms.*

Ms. Jane Doe, Editor. Dear Ms. Doe:

Professor Jane Doe, Department of English. Dear Professor Doe:

Senator Jane Doe, Washington, D.C. Dear Senator Doe:

Accept your inability to change the English language overnight, single-handed. As more people come to regard themselves as equals, the language will increasingly reflect the reality. Meanwhile, in your writing, try to be fair to all individuals without succumbing either to clumsiness or to grammatical error.

22h *Avoid labeling with biased titles or names.*

Sometimes we debase individuals or groups by assigning a negative or gender-specific descriptor to them. Be alert for these widespread biases.

BIASED	She's just a gypsy at heart.
REVISED	She's a free spirit who enjoys traveling.
BIASED	My uncle is a male nurse and my aunt is a woman doctor.
REVISED	My uncle is a nurse and my aunt is a doctor.
BIASED	The townies voted for the bond issue to build a new school.
REVISED	The townspeople voted for the bond issue to build a new school.

Exercise 22–1: Avoiding Bias

Revise the following sentences to eliminate biased words. Possible revisions for the lettered sentences appear in the back of the book. Example:

When the bartender brought the check to Linda and John, Linda suggested that they go dutch.

When the bartender brought the check to Linda and John, Linda suggested that they each pay half.

a. My cousin volunteered as a candy-striper at the old folks' home.

b. Michelle and Roberto welshed on the real estate deal.

c. My high school history teacher was an old battle-ax.

d. The television crew conducted a series of man-on-the street interviews on the proposal for an increase in the gasoline tax.

e. The American politician must watch his words carefully.

1. Only WASP's belong to that country club.

2. Mother Nature has been good to us, but we have returned her bounteous blessings by exploiting her goodness.

3. Joanie began to swear like a trooper while she was in college.
4. The senator was highly regarded by voters in her district even though she was a spinster.
5. The bar was filled with rednecks guzzling cheap beer.

23 WORDINESS

Writers who try to impress their audience by offering few ideas in many words rarely fool anyone but themselves. Concision takes more effort than wordiness, but it pays off in clarity. (For more on how to unpad your prose, see "Cutting and Whittling," p. 386.)

The following list contains common words and phrases that take up more room than they deserve. Each has a shorter substitute. If this list contains some of your favorite expressions, don't worry. Not even the best professional writer is perfectly terse. Still, being aware of verbal short cuts may help you avoid rambling. The checklist can be useful for self-editing, particularly if you ever face a strict word limit. When you write an article for a college newspaper where space is tight, or a laboratory report that you must squeeze into a standard worksheet, or an assignment limited to 600 words, use this list to pare your prose to the bone.

CHECKLIST OF WINDY WORDS AND PHRASES

WORDY VERSION	CONCISE VERSION
adequate enough	adequate
a period of a week	a week
approximately	about
area of, field of	[Omit.]
arrive at an agreement, conclude an agreement	agree
as a result of	because
as far as . . . is concerned	about
as to whether	whether
as you are already well aware	as you know
at an earlier point in time	before, earlier
at a later moment	after, later
join together	join
kind of, sort of, type of	[Omit.]
large in size, large-sized	large
a large number of	many
lend assistance to	assist, aid, help
main essentials	essentials
make contact with	call, talk with
members of the opposition	opponents

merge together	merge
numerous	many
numerous and sundry	many different
on the occasion of	on
on a daily basis	daily
other alternatives	alternatives
past experience, past history	experience, history
persons of the female gender	women
persons of the homosexual persuasion	homosexuals, gays, lesbians
persons of the Methodist faith	Methodists
pertaining to	about, on
plan ahead for the future	plan
prior to	before
put an end to, terminate	end
rarely ever, seldom ever	rarely, seldom
strongly urge	urge
sufficient amount of	enough
the reason why	the reason
refer to by the name of	call, name
refer back to	refer to
remarks of a humorous nature, remarks on the humorous side	humorous remarks
render completely inoperative	break, smash, destroy
repeat again	repeat
resemble in appearance	look like
respective, respectively	[Omit.]
returning back	returning
similar to	like
subsequent to	after
subsequently	later, then
sufficient number (or amount) of	enough
true facts	facts, truth
until such time as	until
utilize, make use of	use
very	[Omit unless you very much need it.]
wastage	waste
way in which	way
whether or not	whether

Exercise 23–1: Eliminating Wordiness.

Rewrite the following sentences to eliminate wordiness. Possible revisions for the lettered sentences appear in the back of the book. Example:

Professor Scott assures us that as of the present moment she does not feel any necessity for an increase in bookshelf space.

Professor Scott says she does not need more bookshelves right now.

a. It is my personal suspicion that the manner in which this inquiry is being handled has a strong likelihood of obscuring the true facts.

b. In order to begin utilization of our new computer system, all individuals are requested to make their selection of a password at their earliest possible convenience.

c. As you are already aware, there is a very low probability at this point in time of your remittance being expeditiously returned back to you.

d. If a sufficient number of people press the elevator call button within a short duration of time, the elevator will be rendered inoperative.

e. It was impossible for the secretary to ascertain whether or not Mr. Jones and Ms. Cunningham had presented to the board by telephone their respective decisions to resign.

1. Dr. Glidden wishes to urge strongly that the entertainment committee refrain from hiring any comedian who is prone to making remarks of a so-called humorous nature about persons of Italian, Irish, Polish, or other ancestry.

2. It was Ms. Howe's impression prior to accepting this job that she was assured of regular salary increases on a semiannual schedule.

3. Implementation of our organization's plan for the future will not take place on schedule due to the fact that a substantial number of the details remain to be finalized.

4. With regard to the proposal for the recycling of paper, it is management's position that restraint by all personnel in their amount of paper utilization will adequately decrease wastage.

5. Consumption of apples on a daily basis has been shown to significantly decrease the necessity for medical attention.

CHAPTER 35

Punctuation

24   END PUNCTUATION

Three marks can signal the end of a sentence: the period, the exclamation point, and the question mark.

24a   *Use a period to end a declarative sentence, a directive, or an indirect question.*

The great majority of English sentences are *declarative*, meaning simply that they make a statement. No matter what its topic, a declarative sentence properly ends with a period.

> Most people on earth are malnourished.

> The Cadillac rounded the corner on two wheels and careened into a newsstand.

A period is also used after a *directive*, a statement telling someone to do something.

Please send a check or money order with your application.

Put down your weapons and come out with your hands up.

Some readers are surprised to find a period, not a question mark, at the end of an *indirect question*. But an indirect question is really a kind of declarative sentence: it states that a question was asked or is being asked. Therefore, a period is the right way to end it.

The counselor asked Marcia why she rarely gets to class on time.

I wonder why George didn't show up.

If those sentences were written as *direct questions*, they would require a question mark.

The counselor asked, "Marcia, why do you rarely get to class on time?"

Why, I wonder, didn't George show up?

24b Use a period after most abbreviations.

A period within a sentence shows that what precedes it has been shortened.

Dr. Hooke's plane arrived in Washington, D.C., at 8:00 p.m.

The names of most organizations (YMCA, PTA), countries (USA, UK), and people (JFK, FDR) are abbreviated without periods. Other abbreviations, such as those for academic degrees and designations of time, use periods. (See 32e.)

When an abbreviation that uses periods falls at the end of a sentence, follow it with just one period, not two.

Jim hopes to do graduate work at UCLA after receiving his B.A.

24c Use a question mark to end a direct question.

How many angels can dance on the point of a pin?

The question mark comes at the end of the question even if the question is part of a longer declarative sentence. (See 29a for advice about punctuating indirect quotations/questions.)

"What'll I do now?" Marjorie wailed.

Only if the question is rewritten into indirect form does it end in a period.

Marjorie, wailing, wanted to know what she should do now.

You can use a question mark, also, to indicate doubt about the accuracy of a number or date.

Aristophanes, born in 450 (?) B.C., became the master comic playwright of Greece's Golden Age.

Usually, however, the same purpose can be accomplished more gracefully in words:

> Aristophanes, born around 450 B.C., became the master comic playwright of Greece's Golden Age.

In formal writing, avoid using a question mark to express irony or sarcasm: *her generous (?) gift.* If your doubts are worth including, state them directly: *her meager but highly publicized gift.*

24d *Use an exclamation point to end an interjection or an urgent command.*

An exclamation point signals strong, even violent, emotion. It can end any sentence that requires unusually strong emphasis.

> We've struck an iceberg! We're sinking! I can't believe it! This is horrible!

It may mark the short, emphatic structure known as an *interjection*. (See 1h.)

> Oh, no! Fire!

Or it may indicate an urgent directive.

> Hurry up! Help me!

Because most essays appeal to readers' reason more than to their passions, you will rarely need this punctuation mark in expository writing. In newspaper parlance, exclamation points are *astonishers*. Although they can grab a reader's attention, they cannot hold it. Tossing in an exclamation point, as if it were a firecracker, is no substitute for carefully selected emphatic words and syntax.

Exercise 24–1: Using End Punctuation

Where appropriate, correct the end punctuation and internal periods in the following sentences. Give reasons for any changes you make. Some sentences may be correct. Answers for the lettered sentences appear in the back of the book. Example:

> Mary asked if George could manage to get to the church on time?
>
> Mary asked if George could manage to get to the church on time.

a. Unlike Gerald Ford and L.B.J., who came to the vice-presidency from Congress, George Bush won that office after heading the C.I.A..

b. The population of California is much greater than that of Nevada!

c. Do you think I'm going to clean up this mess.

d. "When will the world end," my four-year-old nephew asked in a quavering voice?

e. Yes! The Republicans are worried about the gender gap! They fear that women in increasing numbers will vote for the Democrats! How can the Republicans fight back!

1. If you're too cold, why don't you just switch off the air conditioner.
2. "Help, help. It's a murder. Call the police," cried Jim.
3. Jim asked the officer how else the woman would have been strangled by her own scarf?
4. "Does it make sense to you?" he asked, "that she did that herself?"
5. In the history of the Cape Cod Community Players (C.C.C.P.), only one managing director has had an MA in theater.
6. Where do we go from here!
7. I didn't ask Sylvia, "Will you go to the meeting?" I told her, "You *will* go to the meeting!"
8. How do you expect me to learn the Latin names of fifty plants in an hour.
9. "Why is the sky blue" is a question that any physicist can answer.
10. Don't you think that teachers' salaries ought to be higher than they are!

25   THE COMMA

Speech without pauses would be hard to listen to. Likewise, writing without commas would make hard reading. Like a split-second pause in conversation, a **comma** helps your readers to catch the train of your thought. It keeps them, time and again, from stumbling over a solid block of words. A comma can direct readers' attention, pointing them to what you want them to notice. And a well-placed comma can prevent misreading: it keeps your audience from drawing an inaccurate conclusion about what you are trying to tell them.

Consider the following sentence:

Lyman paints fences and bowls.

From this statement, we can deduce that Lyman is a painter who works with both a large and a small brush. But add commas before and after *fences* and the portrait changes:

Lyman paints, fences, and bowls.

Now our man wields a paintbrush, a sword, and a bowling ball. What the reader learns about Lyman's activities depends on how the writer punctuates the sentence. Carefully placed commas prevent misreading and ensure that readers meet the real Lyman.

25a Use a comma with a coordinating conjunction to join two main clauses.

The joint between main clauses has two parts: a coordinating conjunction (*and, but, for, or, nor, so,* or *yet*) and a comma. The comma comes after the first clause, right before the conjunction.

The chocolate pie whooshed through the air, and it landed in Lyman's face.

The pie whooshed with deadly aim, but the agile Lyman ducked.

If your clauses are short and parallel in structure, you may omit the comma.

Spring passed and summer came.

They urged but I refused.

Or you may keep the comma. It can lend your words a speechlike ring, throwing a bit of emphasis on your second clause.

Spring passed, and summer came.

They urged, but I refused.

CAUTION: Don't use a comma with a coordinating conjunction that links two phrases or that links a phrase and a clause.

FAULTY   The mustangs galloped, and cavorted across the plain.

REVISED   The mustangs galloped and cavorted across the plain.

EDITING CHECKLIST: USING THE COMMA WHERE REQUIRED

- Are two main clauses joined with a coordinating conjunction and a comma? (25a)
- Is there a comma after each introductory clause, phrase, or word? (25b)
- Are items in a series separated by commas? (25c)
- Is there a comma or commas between adjectives that are separate and equal modifiers of the same noun (coordinate adjectives)? (25d)
- Is there a comma before and after each nonrestrictive phrase or clause? (25e)

See 25f–25m for other uses of the comma.

25b   *Use a comma after an introductory clause, phrase, or word.*

Weeping, Lydia stumbled down the stairs.

Before that, Arthur saw her reading an old love letter.

If he knew who the writer was, he didn't tell.

Placed after any such opening word, phrase, or subordinate clause, a comma tells your reader: "Enough preliminaries—now the main clause starts." (See 3 for a quick refresher on phrases and clauses.)

EXCEPTION: You need not use a comma after a single introductory word or a short phrase or clause if there is no danger of misreading.

Sooner or later Lydia will tell us the whole story.

Exercise 25–1: Using Commas

Add any necessary commas to the following sentences and remove any commas that do not belong. Some sentences may be correct. Answers for the lettered sentences appear in the back of the book. Example:

> Your dog may have sharp teeth but my lawyer can bite harder.
>
> Your dog may have sharp teeth, but my lawyer can bite harder.

a. When Enrique gets to Paris I hope he'll drop me a line.

b. Beethoven's deafness kept him from hearing his own music yet he continued to compose.

c. Debbie plans to apply for a grant, and if her application is accepted, she intends to spend a year in Venezuela.

d. The cherries are overripe for picking has been delayed.

e. The robin yanked at the worm, but was unable to pull it from the ground.

1. During the summer of the great soybean failure Larry took little interest in national affairs.

2. Unaware of the world he slept, and grew within his mother's womb.

3. While across the nation farmers were begging for mortgages he swam without a care.

4. Neither the mounting agricultural crisis, nor any other current events, disturbed his tranquillity.

5. In fact you might have called him irresponsible.

25c *Use a comma between items in a series.*

When you list three or more items, whether they are nouns, verbs, adjectives, adverbs, or entire phrases or clauses, separate them with commas.

> Country ham, sweet corn, tacos, bratwurst, and Indian pudding weighted Aunt Gertrude's table.
>
> Joel prefers music that shakes, rattles, and rolls.
>
> In one afternoon, we rode a Mississippi riverboat, climbed the Matterhorn, voyaged beneath the sea, and flew on a rocket through space.

Notice that no comma *follows* the final item in the series.

NOTE: Some writers (especially Britons and journalists) omit the comma *before* the final item in the series. This custom has no noticeable advantage. It has the disadvantages of throwing off the rhythm of a sentence and, in some cases, obscuring the writer's meaning. Using the comma in such a case is never wrong; omitting it can create confusion.

> I was met at the station by my cousins, brother and sister.

Who are these people? Are they a brother-and-sister pair who are the writer's cousins or a group consisting of the writer's cousins, her brother, and her sister? If they are in fact more than two people, a comma would clear up the confusion.

> I was met at the station by my cousins, brother, and sister.

25d Use a comma between coordinate adjectives, but not between cumulative adjectives.

Adjectives that function independently of each other, even though they modify the same noun, are called **coordinate adjectives**. Set them off with commas.

> Ruth was a clear, vibrant, persuasive speaker.
>
> Life is nasty, brutish, and short.

To check whether adjectives are coordinate, apply two tests. Can you rearrange the adjectives without distorting the meaning of the sentence? (*Ruth was a persuasive, vibrant, clear speaker.*) Can you insert *and* between them? (*Life is nasty and brutish and short.*)

If the answer to both questions is yes, the adjectives are coordinate. Removing any one of them would not greatly affect the others' impact. Use commas between them to show that they are separate and equal.

> NOTE: If you choose to link coordinate adjectives with *and* or another conjunction, omit the commas.

> New York City is huge and dirty and beautiful.

Cumulative adjectives work together to create a single unified picture of the noun they modify. Remove any one of them and you change the picture. No commas separate cumulative adjectives.

> Ruth has two small white poodles.
>
> Who's afraid of the big bad wolf?

If you rearrange cumulative adjectives or insert *and* between them, the effect of the sentence is distorted (*two white small poodles; the big and bad wolf*).

Exercise 25–2: Using Commas

Add any necessary commas to the following sentences; remove any commas that do not belong; and change any punctuation that strikes you as incorrect. Some sentences may be correct. Revisions for the lettered sentences appear in the back of the book. Example:

> Mel has been a faithful hard-working consistent pain in the neck.
>
> Mel has been a faithful, hard-working, consistent pain in the neck.

a. Mrs. Carver looks like a sweet, little, old lady, but she plays a wicked electric guitar.

b. Her bass player, her drummer and her keyboard player all live at the same rest home.

c. They practice individually in the afternoon, rehearse together at night and play at the home's Saturday night dances.

d. The Rest Home Rebels have to rehearse quietly, and cautiously, to keep from disturbing the other residents.

e. Mrs. Carver has two Fender guitars, a Stratocaster and a Telecaster, and she also has an acoustic twelve-string Gibson.

1. When she breaks a string, she doesn't want her elderly crew to have to grab the guitar change the string and hand it back to her, before the song ends.

2. The Rest Home Rebels' favorite bands are U-2, the Talking Heads and Lester Lanin and his orchestra.

3. They watch a lot of MTV because it is fast-paced colorful exciting and informative and it has more variety than soap operas.

4. Just once, Mrs. Carver wants to play in a really, huge, sold-out, arena.

5. She hopes to borrow the rest home's big, white, van to take herself her band and their equipment to a major, professional, downtown, recording studio.

25e *Use commas to set off a nonrestrictive phrase or clause.*

A **nonrestrictive modifier** adds a fact that, while perhaps interesting and valuable, isn't essential. You could leave it out of the sentence and still make good sense. When a word in your sentence is modified by a nonrestrictive phrase or clause, set off the modifier with commas before and after it.

> Potts Alley, *which runs north from Chestnut Street*, is too narrow and crowded for cars to get through.

> At the end of the alley, *where the street fair book sale was held last summer*, a getaway car waited.

A **restrictive modifier** is essential. Omit it and you significantly change the meaning of both the modified word and the sentence. Such a modifier is called *restrictive* because it limits what it modifies: we are talking about this specific place, person, action, or whatever, and no other. Because a restrictive modifier is part of the identity of whatever it modifies, no commas set it off from the rest of the sentence.

> They picked the alley *that runs north from Chestnut Street* because it is close to the highway.

> Anyone *who robs my house* will regret it.

Leave out the modifier in that last sentence — write instead *Anyone will regret it* — and you change the meaning of your subject from potential robbers to all humankind.

Here are two more examples to help you tell a nonrestrictive modifier, which you set off with commas, from a restrictive modifier, which you don't.

Germans, who smoke, live to be 120.

Germans who smoke live to be 120.

See what a difference a couple of commas make? The first sentence declares that all Germans smoke, but they nevertheless live to old age. The second sentence singles out smokers from the rest of the population and declares that they reach age 120.

NOTE: Use *that* to introduce (or to recognize) a restrictive phrase or clause. Use *which* to introduce (or to recognize) a nonrestrictive phrase or clause.

The food *that I love best* is chocolate.

Chocolate, *which I love*, is not on my diet.

25f Use commas to set off nonrestrictive appositives.

An **appositive** is a noun or noun phrase that renames or amplifies the noun it follows. (See 3d.) Like the modifiers discussed in 25e, an appositive can be either restrictive or nonrestrictive. If it is nonrestrictive—if the sentence still makes sense when the appositive is omitted or changed—then set it off with commas before and after.

My third ex-husband, *Hugo,* will be glad to meet you.

We are bringing dessert, *a blueberry pie,* to follow your wonderful dinner.

Hugo created the recipe for his latest cookbook, *Pies! Surprise!*

If the appositive is restrictive—if you can't take it out or change it without changing your meaning—then include it without commas.

Of all the men I've been married to, my ex-husband *Hugo* is the best cook.

His cookbook *Pies! Surprise!* is selling better than his beef, wine, and fruit cookbooks.

Exercise 25–3: Using Commas

Add any necessary commas to the following sentences and remove any commas that do not belong. You may have to draw your own conclusions about what the writer meant to say. Some sentences may be correct. Revisions for the lettered sentences appear in the back of the book. Example:

Jay and his wife the former Nancy Montez were high school sweethearts.

Jay and his wife, the former Nancy Montez, were high school sweethearts.

a. The rain which wasn't due until tomorrow is falling right now.

b. The party, a dismal occasion ended earlier than we had expected.

c. Secretary Stern warned that the concessions, that the West was prepared to make, would be withdrawn if not matched by the East.

d. Although both of Don's children are blond, his daughter Sharon has darker hair than his son Jake.

e. Herbal tea which has no caffeine makes a better after-dinner drink than coffee.

1. The emerald, that Richard gave Elizabeth, is more valuable than the famous family diamonds, which went to his brother's wife.

2. If the base commanders had checked their gun room where powder is stored, they would have found several hundred pounds missing.

3. Brazil's tropical rain forests which help produce the air we breathe all over the world, are being cut down at an alarming rate.

4. Senator Edward Kennedy's late brothers, Joe and Jack, were older than his third brother, Bobby.

5. Mr. O'Neil told me that by next Monday, which is the day we agreed to meet, the issue already will have been decided.

25g   *Use commas to set off conjunctive adverbs.*

A key function of the comma, as you probably have noticed, is to insert material into a sentence. To perform this service, commas work in pairs. When you drop a conjunctive adverb such as *furthermore, however,* or *nevertheless* into the midst of a clause, set it off with commas before and after it. (See 1g for a full list of conjunctive adverbs.)

> Using lead paint in homes has been illegal, *however,* since 1973.
>
> Builders, *indeed,* gave it up some twenty years earlier.

25h   *Use commas to set off parenthetical expressions.*

Use a pair of commas around any parenthetical expression — that is, a transitional expression (*for example, as a result, in contrast*) or any kind of aside from you to your reader.

> Professional home inspectors, *for this reason,* are often asked to test for lead paint.
>
> The idea, *of course,* is to protect small children who might eat flaking paint.
>
> The Cosmic Construction Company never used lead paint, *or so their spokesperson says,* even when it was legal.

25i   *Use commas to set off a phrase or clause expressing contrast.*

> It was Rudolph, *not Dasher,* who had a red nose.

EXCEPTION: Short contrasting phrases beginning with *but* need not be set off by commas.

> It was not Dasher but Rudolph who had a red nose.

25j *Use commas to set off an absolute phrase.*

An **absolute phrase** modifies an entire clause rather than a single word. (See 3c.) The link between an absolute phrase and the rest of the sentence is a comma, or two commas if the phrase falls in mid-sentence.

> *Our worst fears drawing us together*, we huddled over the telegram.

> Luke, *his knife being the sharpest*, slit the envelope.

Exercise 25–4: Using Commas

Add any necessary commas to the following sentences, remove any commas that do not belong, and change any inappropriate punctuation. Revisions for the lettered sentences appear in the back of the book. Example:

> The screenwriter unlike the director, believes the film should be shown unedited.

> The screenwriter, unlike the director, believes the film should be shown unedited.

a. Before we begin however I want to thank everyone who made this evening possible.

b. Our speaker, listed in your program as a professor, tells us that on the contrary she is a teaching assistant.

c. The discussion that followed was not so much a debate, as a free-for-all.

d. Alex insisted that predestination not free will shapes human destiny.

e. Shirley on the other hand, who looks so calm, passionately defended the role of choice.

1. Philosophy not being one of my strong points I was unable to contribute much to the argument.

2. The car rolled down the hill, a problem Bill should have anticipated when he left it in gear and crashed into a telephone pole.

3. This attic apartment its windows notwithstanding, is very hot in summer.

4. The orchard smelled fruity and felt squishy underfoot; hundreds of apples having fallen from the trees.

5. Not Jerome in the judge's opinion but Lewis was responsible for the accident.

25k *Use commas to set off a direct quotation from your own words, and vice versa.*

When you briefly quote someone, distinguish the source's words from yours with commas (and, of course, quotation marks). When you insert an explanation into a quotation (such as *he said*), set that off with commas.

> It was Shakespeare who wrote, "Some are born great, some achieve greatness, and some have greatness thrust upon them."

> "The best thing that can come with success," commented the actress Liv Ullmann, "is the knowledge that it is nothing to long for."

Notice that the comma always comes *before* the quotation marks. (For more on how to use other punctuation with quotation marks, see 29h and 29i.)

EXCEPTION: Do not use a comma with a very short quotation or one introduced by *that*.

Don't tell me "yes" if you mean "maybe."

Jules said that "Nothing ventured, nothing gained" is his motto.

Don't use a comma with any quotation that is run into your own sentence and that reads as part of your sentence. Often such quotations are introduced by linking verbs.

Her favorite statement at age three was "I can do it myself."

It was Shakespeare who originated the expression "my salad days, when I was green in judgment."

25l *Use commas around* yes *and* no*, mild interjections, tag questions, and the name or title of someone directly addressed.*

YES AND NO	*Yes*, I would like to own a Rolls-Royce, but, *no*, I didn't place an order for one.
INTERJECTIONS	*Well*, don't blame it on me.
TAG QUESTIONS	It would be fun to drive down Main Street in a Silver Cloud, *wouldn't it?*
DIRECT ADDRESS	Drive us home, *James*.

25m *Use commas to set off dates, states, countries, and addresses.*

On June 6, 1969, Ned Shaw was born.

East Rutherford, New Jersey, seemed like Paris, France, to him.

Shortly after his tenth birthday his family moved to 11 Maple Street, Middletown, Ohio.

NOTE: Do not use a comma between a state and a zip code: *Bedford, MA 01730*.

Exercise 25–5: Using Commas

Add any necessary commas to the following sentences, remove any commas that do not belong, and change any inappropriate punctuation. Some sentences may be correct. Revisions for the lettered sentences appear in the back of the book. Example:

When Alexander Graham Bell said "Mr. Watson come here, I want you" the telephone entered history.

When Alexander Graham Bell said, "Mr. Watson, come here, I want you," the telephone entered history.

a. On October 2 1969 the future discoverer of antigravity tablets was born.
b. Corwin P. Grant entered the world while his parents were driving to a hospital in Costa Mesa California.
c. The car radio was playing that old song "Be My Baby."
d. Today ladies and gentlemen Corwin enjoys worldwide renown.
e. Schoolchildren from Augusta Maine to Azuza California can recite his famous comment "It was my natural levity that led me to overcome gravity."

1. I don't mean to prod you Belinda, but yes that was your cue.
2. Move downstage Gary, for Pete's sake or you'll run into Mrs. Clackett.
3. Vicki my precious, when you say, "great" or "terrific," look as though you mean it.
4. As your director darling I am not responsible for your props.
5. Well Dotty, it only makes sense that when you say, "Sardines!," you should go off to get the sardines.

25n Do not use a comma to separate a subject from its verb or a verb from its object.

FAULTY   The slim athlete driving the purple Jaguar, was the Reverend Mr. Fuld. [Subject separated from verb.]

REVISED   The slim athlete driving the purple Jaguar was the Reverend Mr. Fuld.

FAULTY   The new president should not have given his campaign manager, such a prestigious appointment. [Verb separated from direct object.]

REVISED   The new president should not have given his campaign manager such a prestigious appointment.

25o Do not use a comma between words or phrases joined by correlative or coordinating conjunctions.

Be careful not to divide a compound subject or predicate unnecessarily with a comma.

FAULTY   Neither Peter Pan, nor the fairy Tinkerbell, saw the pirates sneaking toward their hideout. [Compound subject.]

REVISED   Neither Peter Pan nor the fairy Tinkerbell saw the pirates sneaking toward their hideout.

FAULTY   The chickens clucked, and pecked, and flapped their wings. [Compound predicate.]

REVISED   The chickens clucked and pecked and flapped their wings.

25p *Do not use a comma before the first or after the last item in a series.*

> FAULTY We had to see, my mother's doctor, my father's lawyer, and my dog's veterinarian, in one afternoon.
>
> REVISED We had to see my mother's doctor, my father's lawyer, and my dog's veterinarian in one afternoon.

25q *Do not use a comma to set off a restrictive word, phrase, or clause.*

A restrictive modifier is essential to the definition or identification of whatever it modifies; a nonrestrictive modifier is not. If you are not sure whether an element in your sentence is restrictive, review 25e.

> FAULTY The fireworks, that I saw on Sunday, were the best ones I've ever seen.
>
> REVISED The fireworks that I saw on Sunday were the best ones I've ever seen.

25r *Do not use commas to set off indirect quotations.*

When *that* introduces a quotation, the quotation is an indirect one and requires neither a comma nor quotation marks.

> FAULTY He told us that, we shouldn't have done it.
>
> FAULTY He told us that, "You shouldn't have done it."
>
> REVISED He told us that we shouldn't have done it.

This sentence also would be correct if it were recast as a direct quotation, with a comma and quotation marks.

> REVISED He told us, "You shouldn't have done that."

EDITING CHECKLIST: RECOGNIZING MISUSED COMMAS

- Have you used a comma between adjectives that depend on each other (cumulative adjectives)? (25d)
- Have you used a comma to separate a subject from its verb or a verb from its object? (25n)
- Have you used a comma between words or phrases joined by a coordinating conjunction? (25o)
- Have you divided a compound subject or predicate unnecessarily with a comma? (25o)
- Have you used a comma before the first or after the last item in a series? (25p)
- Have you used a comma to set off a restrictive word, phrase, or clause? (25q)

↳ Have you used a comma to set off an indirect quotation? (25r)

If the answer to any of these questions is yes, the comma is used incorrectly.

26 THE SEMICOLON

A semicolon is a sort of compromise between a comma and a period: it creates a stop without ending a sentence.

26a *Use a semicolon to join two main clauses not joined by a coordinating conjunction.*

Suppose, having written one statement, you want to add another. You could start a new sentence, but let's say that both statements are closely related in sense. You decide to keep them both in a single sentence.

> Shooting clay pigeons was my mother's favorite sport; she would smash them for hours at a time.

A semicolon is a good substitute for a period when you don't want to bring your readers to a complete stop.

> By the yard life is hard; by the inch it's a cinch.

> I never travel without my diary; one should always have something sensational to read in the train. — Oscar Wilde

Remember that usually, when you join two statements with a coordinating conjunction (*and, but, for, or, nor, so, yet*), no semicolon is called for — just use a comma. (For exceptions to this general rule, see 26d.)

EDITING CHECKLIST: USING THE SEMICOLON

↳ Does a semicolon join two main clauses not joined with a coordinating conjunction? (26a)

↳ Does a semicolon join two main clauses that are linked by a conjunctive adverb? (26b)

↳ Do semicolons separate items in a series that contain internal punctuation or that are long and complex? (26c)

↳ Do semicolons separate main clauses that contain internal punctuation or that are long and complex? (26d)

↳ Does a comma, not a semicolon, separate a phrase or subordinate clause from the rest of the sentence? (26d)

26b Use a semicolon to join two main clauses that are linked by a conjunctive adverb.

When the second of two statements begins with (or includes) a conjunctive adverb, you can join it to the first statement with a semicolon. Common conjunctive adverbs include *also, consequently, however, indeed, nevertheless, still, therefore,* and *thus.* (For a complete list, see 1g.)

> Bert is a stand-out player; *indeed,* he's the one hope of our team.
>
> We yearned to attend the concert; tickets, *however,* were hard to come by.

Note in the second sentence that the conjunctive adverb falls within the second main clause. No matter where the conjunctive adverb appears, the semicolon is placed between the two clauses.

26c Use a semicolon to separate items in a series that contain internal punctuation or that are long and complex.

The semicolon is especially useful for setting off one group of items from another. More powerful than a comma, it divides a series of series.

> The auctioneer sold clocks, watches, and cameras; freezers of steaks and tons of bean sprouts; motorcycles, cars, speedboats, canoes, and cabin cruisers; and rare coins, curious stamps, and precious stones.

If the writer had used commas in place of semicolons in that sentence, the divisions would have been harder to notice.

Commas are not the only internal punctuation that warrants the extra force of semicolons between items.

> The auctioneer sold clocks and watches (with or without hands); freezers of steaks and tons of bean sprouts; trucks and motorcycles (some of which had working engines); and dozens of smaller items.

26d Use a semicolon to separate main clauses that are long and complex or that contain internal punctuation.

The semicolon also separates the clauses in a long sentence of two or more clauses, at least one of which contains internal punctuation.

> Though we had grown up together, laughing and playing like brother and sister, I had never regarded Spike as a possible lover; and his abrupt proposal took me by surprise.

In that sentence, an important break between clauses needs a mark stronger than a comma to give it impact. A semicolon is appropriate, even though it stands before a coordinating conjunction—where, ordinarily, a comma would suffice.

You can see the difference between a compound sentence joined with a comma and one joined with a semicolon in these examples:

Captain Bob planned the hog-riding contest for Thursday, but it rained.

Captain Bob, that old cynic, planned the hog-riding contest for Thursday despite a ban by the city council; but it rained.

You would not be wrong if you kept the original comma between clauses. The sentence is easier to read, however, with a semicolon at its main intersection.

A semicolon can do the same job for clauses that contain internal punctuation other than commas.

Captain Bob—that cynical crowd assembler—planned the hog-riding contest for Thursday (although the city council had banned such events); but it rained.

You also can use a semicolon with a coordinating conjunction to link clauses that have no internal punctuation but that are long and complex.

The powers behind Her Majesty's secret service occasionally deem it advisable to terminate the infiltrations of an enemy agent by ending his life; and in such cases they generally call on James Bond.

26e *Use a comma, not a semicolon, to separate a phrase or subordinate clause from the rest of a sentence.*

Remember that a semicolon has the force of a period; its job is to create a strong pause in a sentence, especially between main clauses. When your purpose is simply to add a phrase to a clause, use a comma, not a semicolon.

FAULTY   The road is long; winding through many towns.

REVISED   The road is long, winding through many towns.

Similarly, use a comma, not a semicolon, to join a subordinate clause to a main clause.

FAULTY   Columbus sailed unknowingly toward the New World; while Ferdinand and Isabella waited for news from China.

REVISED   Columbus sailed unknowingly toward the New World, while Ferdinand and Isabella waited for news from China.

Exercise 26–1: Using Semicolons

Repunctuate the following sentences as necessary, adding semicolons when they are needed and changing any that are incorrectly used. Some sentences may be correct. Revisions for the lettered sentences appear in the back of the book. Example:

If you knew all the facts; you would see that I am right.

If you knew all the facts, you would see that I am right.

a. Gasoline prices almost always rise at the start of tourist season, this year will be no exception.

b. I disagree with your point, however I appreciate your reasons for stating it.

   c. The garden is a spectacular display of fountains and gargoyles, beds of lilies, zinnias, and hollyhocks, bushes shaped like animals, climbing roses, wisteria, and ivy, and lawns as wide as golf greens.

   d. Luther missed the conference in Montreal; but he plans to attend the one in Memphis.

   e. Dr. Elliott's intervention in the dispute was well intentioned, nevertheless it was unfortunate.

1. The banquet menu included soup; fish; roast beef; ham; a variety of vegetables; a cheese board; and salad.

2. If that shyster deceives you once, shame on him, if he deceives you twice, shame on you.

3. A Newfoundland dog is huge and furry; much like a Saint Bernard.

4. Senator Blank favors increasing state aid to small businesses, he believes however that such a bill cannot pass this year.

5. A robin's red breast is the color of rust, a grosbeak's is the rosier hue of maraschino cherries.

6. The town council voted to approve the affordable housing project, a decision that may, over time, lead to a tax increase.

7. If the residents and tourists of Athens were willing to leave their automobiles outside the city, air pollution would not threaten the caryatids on the Acropolis, but the impracticality of banning cars has forced authorities to move those stone maidens to a museum.

8. The resolution must pass by a two-thirds majority, otherwise it fails and its supporters must reintroduce it next year.

9. The Democrats on the Ways and Means Committee are hoping the bill will pass; for they are its primary supporters.

10. Don't listen to Dr. Bromberg, she doesn't understand the situation.

27   THE COLON

A colon introduces a further thought, one added to throw light on a first. In using it, a writer declares: "What follows will clarify what I've just said."

> Her Majesty's navy has three traditions: rum, sodomy, and the lash.
> —Winston Churchill

Some writers use a capital letter to start any complete sentence that follows a colon; others prefer a lowercase letter. Both habits are acceptable; but whichever you choose, be consistent. A *phrase* that follows a colon always begins with a lowercase letter.

27a *Use a colon between two main clauses if the second exemplifies, explains, or summarizes the first.*

Like a semicolon, a colon can join two sentences into one. The chief difference is this: a semicolon says merely that two main clauses are related; a colon says that the second clause gives an example or explanation of the point made in the first clause. You can think of a colon as an abbreviation for *that is* or *for example*.

> Mayor Curley was famed as a silver-tongued orator: it is said that, with a few well-chosen words, he could extract campaign contributions from a mob intent on seeing him hanged.

> She tried everything: she scoured the library, made dozens of phone calls, wrote letters, even consulted a lawyer.

27b *Use a colon to introduce a list or a series.*

A colon can introduce a word, a phrase, or a series as well as a second main clause. Sometimes the introduction is made stronger by *as follows* or *the following*.

> The dance steps are as follows: forward, back, turn, and glide.

> Engrave the following truth upon your memory: a colon is always constructed of two dots.

When a colon introduces a series of words or phrases, it often means *such as* or *for instance*. A list of examples after a colon need not include *and* before the last item unless all possible examples have been stated.

> On a Saturday night many different kinds of people crowd our downtown area: gamblers, drifters, bored senior citizens, college students out for a good time.

27c *Use a colon to introduce an appositive.*

An *appositive* is a noun or noun phrase that renames another noun. A colon can introduce an appositive when the colon is preceded by an independent clause.

> I have discovered the key to the future: plastics.

27d *Use a colon to introduce a long or comma-filled quotation.*

Sometimes you can't conveniently introduce a quoted passage with a comma. Perhaps the quotation is too long or heavily punctuated; perhaps your prefatory remarks demand a longer pause than a comma provides. In either case, use a colon.

> God told Adam and Eve: "Be fruitful, and multiply, and replenish the earth, and subdue it."

27e *Use a colon when convention calls for it.*

AFTER A SALUTATION	Dear Professor James: Dear Sir or Madam:
BIBLICAL CITATIONS	Genesis 4:7 [The book of Genesis, chapter four, seventh verse.]

BOOK TITLES AND SUBTITLES	*In the Beginning: Creation Stories from around the World* *Convergences: Essays on Art and Literature*
SOURCE REFERENCES	Welty, Eudora. *The Eye of the Story: Selected Essays and Reviews.* New York: Random, 1978.
TIME OF DAY	2:02 p.m.

27f *Use a colon only at the end of a main clause.*

In a sentence, a colon always follows a clause, never a phrase. Avoid using a colon between a verb and its object, between a preposition and its object, and before a list introduced by *such as*. Any time you are in doubt about whether to use a colon, first make sure that the preceding statement is a complete sentence. Then you will not litter your writing with unnecessary colons.

FAULTY   My mother and father are: Jill and Jim.

REVISED   My mother and father are Jill and Jim.

FAULTY   Many great inventors have changed our lives, such as: Edison, Marconi, and Hymie Glutz.

REVISED   Many great inventors have changed our lives, such as Edison, Marconi, and Hymie Glutz. *Or* Many great inventors have changed our lives: Edison, Marconi, Hymie Glutz.

Use either *such as* or a colon. You don't need both.

Exercise 27–1: Using Colons

Add, cut, or substitute colons wherever appropriate in the following sentences. If necessary, rewrite to support your changes in punctuation. Some sentences may be correct. Revisions for the lettered sentences appear in the back of the book. Example:

> Yum-Yum Burger has franchises in the following cities; New York, Chicago, Miami, San Francisco, and Seattle.
>
> Yum-Yum Burger has franchises in the following cities: New York, Chicago, Miami, San Francisco, and Seattle.

a. The personnel director explained that the job requirements include: typing, filing, and answering telephones.

b. The interview ended with a test of skills, taking dictation, operating the switchboard, proofreading documents, and typing a sample letter.

c. The sample letter began, "Dear Mr. Jones, Please accept our apologies for the late shipment."

d. Candace quoted Proverbs 8, 18: "Riches and honor are with me."

e. A book that profoundly impressed me was Kurt Vonnegut's *Cat's Cradle* (New York, Dell, 1963).

1. The following line is my favorite, "It is not possible to make a mistake."
2. You should have no trouble starting the car if you remember three important steps: depress the clutch, turn the key, and press briefly on the accelerator.
3. These are my dreams, to ride in a horse-drawn sleigh, to fly in a small plane, to gallop down a beach on horseback, and to cross the ocean in a sailboat.
4. The reason for the delay is: The train left Philadelphia twenty minutes late.
5. Paris at night presents an array of characters; sidewalk artists, jugglers, and break-dancers; rap musicians and one-man bands; hippies, bohemians, and amazed tourists.
6. He ended his speech with a quotation from Homer's *Iliad,* "Whoever obeys the gods, to him they particularly listen."
7. To get onto Route 6: take Bay Lane to Old Stage Road, turn right, and go straight to the end.
8. Professor Bligh's book is called *Management, A Networking Approach.*
9. George handed Cynthia a note, "Meet me after class under the big clock on Main Street."
10. She expected to arrive at 4.10, but she didn't get there until 4.20.

28 THE APOSTROPHE

Use apostrophes for three purposes: to show possession, to indicate an omission, and to add an ending to a number, letter, or abbreviation.

28a To make a singular noun possessive, add -'s.

The *plumber's* wrench left grease stains on *Harry's* shirt.

Even when your singular noun ends with the sound of *s*, form its possessive case by adding -*'s*.

Felix's roommate enjoys reading *Henry James's* novels.

Some writers find it awkward to add -*'s* to nouns that already end in an -*s*, especially those of two syllables or more. You may, if you wish, form such a possessive by adding only an apostrophe.

The Egyptian king *Cheops'* death occurred more than two thousand years before *Socrates'.*

28b To make a plural noun ending in -s possessive, add an apostrophe.

A *stockbrokers'* meeting combines *foxes'* cunning with the noisy chaos of a *boys'* locker room.

28c *To make a plural noun not ending in -s possessive, add -'s.*

Nouns such as *men, mice, geese,* and *alumni* form the possessive case the same way as singular nouns: with -*'s.*

What effect has the *women's* liberation movement had on *children's* literature?

28d *To show joint possession by two people or groups, add an apostrophe or -'s to the second noun of the pair.*

I left my *mother and father's* house with our *friends and neighbors'* good wishes.

If the two members of a noun pair possess a set of things individually, add an apostrophe or -*'s* to each noun.

Men's and *women's* marathon records are improving steadily.

28e *To make a compound noun possessive, add an apostrophe or -'s to the last word in the compound.*

A compound noun consists of more than one word (*commander in chief, sons-in-law*); it may be either singular or plural. (See 37a–5 for plurals of compound words.)

The *commander in chief's* duties will end on July 1.

Esther does not approve of her *sons-in-law's* professions, but she is glad to see her daughters happily married.

28f *To make an indefinite pronoun possessive, add -'s.*

Indefinite pronouns such as *anyone, nobody,* and *another* are usually singular in meaning, so they form the possessive case the same way as singular nouns: with -*'s.* (See 28a.)

What caused the accident is *anybody's* guess; but it appears to be *no one's* fault.

28g *To indicate the possessive of a personal pronoun, use its possessive case.*

The personal pronouns—*I, me, he, she, it, him, her, we, us, they, them,* and *who*—are irregular; each has its own possessive form. No possessive personal pronoun contains an apostrophe. If you are ever tempted to make a personal pronoun possessive by adding an apostrophe or -*'s,* resist the temptation.

NOTE: If you learn nothing else this year, learn when to write *its* (no apostrophe) and when to write *it's* (with an apostrophe). *Its* is always a possessive pronoun.

I retreated when the Murphys' German shepherd bared *its* fangs.

POSSESSIVE CASE OF PERSONAL PRONOUNS

PERSONAL PRONOUN	POSSESSIVE CASE
I	my, mine
you	your, yours (*not* your's)
he	his
she	her, hers (*not* her's)
it	its (*not* it's)
we	our, ours (*not* our's)
they	their, theirs (*not* their's)
who	whose (*not* who's)

It's is always a contraction.

> *It's* [It is] not our fault.
>
> *It's* [It has] been a memorable evening.

28h Use an apostrophe to indicate an omission in a contraction.

> *They're* [They are] too sophisticated for me.
>
> *I've* [I have] learned my lesson.
>
> Pat *didn't* [did not] finish her assignment.
>
> *Bill's* [Bill has] been in jail for a week.
>
> Americans grow up admiring the Spirit of *'76* [1776].
>
> It's nearly eight *o'clock* [of the clock].
>
> When you are presented to the Queen, say "Your Majesty"; after that, say "*Ma'am*" [Madam].

28i Use an apostrophe to form the plural of an abbreviation and of a letter, word, or number mentioned as a word.

ABBREVIATION	Do we need I.D.'s at YMCA's outside our hometown?
LETTER	How many *n*'s are there in *Cincinnati*?
WORD	Try replacing all the *should*'s in that sentence with *could*'s.
NUMBER	Cut out two *3*'s to sew on Larry's shirt.

NOTE: A letter, word, or number named as a word is usually italicized (underlined).

EXCEPTION: To refer to the years in a decade, simply add *-s* without an apostrophe.

> The 1980s differed greatly from the 1970s.

APOSTROPHES AND PLURAL NOUNS

Using apostrophes with plural nouns may cause confusion for writers because both plural nouns and possessive nouns often end with the letter -*s*. To avoid confusion in your writing, remember that *plural* means more than one (two *dogs*, six *friends*), but *possessive* means ownership (the *dogs'* biscuits, my *friends'* cars). If you can substitute the word *of* instead of the -*s* and apostrophe (the biscuits *of* the dog, the cars *of* my friends) you need the plural possessive with an apostrophe after the -*s*. If you cannot substitute *of*, you need the simple plural with no apostrophe (the *dogs* are well fed, my *friends* have no *money for gas*).

Exercise 28–1: Using the Apostrophe

Correct any errors in the use of the apostrophe and other related usage in the following sentences. Some sentences may be correct. Revisions for the lettered sentences appear in the back of the book. Example:

> Youd better put on you're new shoes.
>
> You'd better put on your new shoes.

a. Its not easy to be old in our society.
b. I dont understand the Jameses's objections to our plans for a block party.
c. As the saying goes, "Every dog has it's day."
d. Is this collection of 50's records your's or your roommates?
e. Alas, Brian got two Ds on his report card.

1. Joe and Chucks' fathers were both in the class of 53.
2. They're going to finish their term papers as soon as the party ends.
3. Jane deplored her mother's-in-law habit of visiting unannounced.
4. Be sure your 7s don't look like ls.
5. Ted and Virginia's son is marrying the editor's in chief's daughter.
6. I think I know who's barn this is; that big house in the village is their's, too.
7. Its hard to join a womens' basketball team because so few of them exist.
8. I had'nt expected to hear Janice' voice again.
9. Don't give the Murphy's dog it's biscuit until it's sitting up.
10. Isnt' it the mother and fathers' job to teach kid's to mind their *p*s and *q*s?

29 QUOTATION MARKS

Quotation marks always come in pairs: one at the start and one at the finish of a quoted passage. In the United States, the double quotation mark (") is preferred over the single one (') for most uses. Use quotation marks to set off a quoted or highlighted word or words from the rest of your text.

"Injustice anywhere is a threat to justice everywhere," wrote Martin Luther King, Jr.

29a Use quotation marks around direct quotations from another writer or speaker.

You can enrich the content, language, and authority of your writing by occasionally quoting a source whose ideas support your own. When you do this, you owe credit to the quoted person. If you use his or her exact words, enclose them in quotation marks.

> The Arab concept of community is reflected in Egyptian leader Anwar el-Sadat's comment "A man's village is his peace of mind."

> Minnesota-born songwriter Bob Dylan told an interviewer, "When I was growing up in Hibbing, home was a place to run away from."

(See 33j for correct capitalization with quotation marks.)

In an indirect quotation, you report someone else's idea without using his or her exact words. Do not enclose an indirect quotation in quotation marks. Do, however, name your source; and stay as close as you can to what the source actually said.

> Anwar el-Sadat asserted that a person's community provides a sense of well being.

(For punctuation of direct and indirect questions, see 24a, 24c, and 25r.)

29b Use single quotation marks around a quotation inside another quotation.

Sometimes a source you are quoting quotes someone else or puts a word or words in quotation marks. When that happens, use single quotation marks around the internal quotation (even if your source used double ones), and put double quotation marks around the larger passage that you are quoting.

> "My favorite advice from Socrates, 'Know thyself and fear all women,' " said Dr. Blatz, "has been getting me into trouble lately."

29c Indent a quotation of more than four lines, instead of using quotation marks.

Suppose you are writing an essay about Soviet dissidents living in the United States. You might include a paragraph like this:

> In a June 1978 commencement address at Harvard University, the writer Alexander Solzhenitsyn commented:
>
> > I have spent all my life under a Communist regime, and I will tell you that a society without any objective legal scale is a terrible one indeed. But a society with no other scale but

```
the legal one is not quite worthy of man
either.
```

Merely by indenting this passage, you have shown that it is a direct quotation. You need not frame it with quotation marks. Simply double-space above and below the quoted passage, indent it ten spaces from your left margin, and double-space the quoted lines.

Follow the same practice if your quoted material is a poem.

```
Phillis Wheatley, the outstanding black poet of co-
lonial America, expresses a sense that she is condemned
to write in obscurity and be forgotten:
                 No costly marble shall be reared,
                     No Mausoleum's pride--
                 Nor chiselled stone be raised to tell
                     That I have lived and died.
```

Notice that not only the source's words but her punctuation, capitalization, indentation, and line breaks are quoted exactly. (See also 33j.)

29d *In dialogue, use quotation marks around a speaker's words, and mark each change of speaker with a new paragraph.*

> Randolph gazed at Ellen and uttered a heartfelt sigh. "What extraordinary beauty."
> "They are lovely," she replied, staring at the roses, "aren't they?"

29e *Use quotation marks around the title of a speech, an article in a newspaper or magazine, a short story, a poem shorter than book length, a chapter in a book, a song, and an episode of a television or radio program.*

> The article "An Updike Retrospective" praises "Solitaire" as the best story in John Updike's collection *Museums and Women*.
>
> In Chapter 5, "Expatriates," Schwartz discusses Eliot's famous poem "The Waste Land."
>
> My favorite *Miami Vice* episode was "Smuggler's Blues," based on Glen Frey's song "Smuggler's Blues."

(Most other types of titles are underlined. See 35a.)

29f *Avoid using quotation marks to indicate slang or to be witty.*

Quotation marks should not be used around slang or would-be witticisms. By "quoting" them, you make them stand out like the nose of a W. C. Fields; and your discomfort in using them becomes painfully obvious.

| INADVISABLE | Liza looked like a born "loser," but Jerry was "hard up" for companionship. |
| REVISED | Liza looked like a born loser, but Jerry was hard up for companionship. |

Stick your neck out. If you really want to use those words, just go ahead.

Some writers assume that, by placing a word in quotation marks, they wax witty and ironic:

| INADVISABLE | By the time I finished all my chores, my long-awaited "day off" was over. |
| REVISED | By the time I finished all my chores, my long-awaited day off was over. |

No quotation marks are needed after *so-called* and other words with similar meaning.

| FAULTY | Call me "a dreamer," but I believe we can win. |
| REVISED | Call me a dreamer, but I believe we can win. |

29g *Put commas and periods inside quotation marks.*

A comma or a period always comes before quotation marks, even if it is not part of the quotation.

We pleaded and pleaded, "Keep off the grass," in hope of preserving the lawn.

(Also see 25k.)

29h *Put semicolons and colons outside quotation marks.*

We said, "Keep off the grass"; they still tromped onward.

29i *Put other punctuation inside or outside quotation marks depending on its function in the sentence.*

Parentheses that are part of the quotation go inside the quotation marks. Parentheses that are your own, not part of the quotation, go outside the quotation marks.

We said, "Keep off the grass (unless it's artificial turf)."

They tromped onward (although we had said, "Keep off the grass") all the way to the road.

If a question mark, exclamation point, or dash is part of the quotation, place it inside the quotation marks.

She hollered, "Fire!"

"Marjorie?" he called. "I thought you—"

If any of these marks is not part of the quoted passage, place it after the closing quotation marks.

> Who hollered "Fire"?
>
> "Marjorie"—he paused for breath—"we'd better go."

As these examples show, don't close a sentence with two end punctuation marks, one inside and one outside the quotation marks. If the quoted passage ends with a dash, exclamation point, question mark, or period, you need not add any further end punctuation. If the quoted passage falls within a question asked by you, however, it should finish with a question mark, even if that means cutting other end punctuation (*Who hollered "Fire"?*).

Exercise 29–1: Using Quotation Marks

Add quotation marks wherever they are needed in the following sentences, and correct any other errors. Revisions for the lettered sentences appear in the back of the book. Example:

> How do you say This is a holdup in Spanish? Etta asked the Sundance Kid.
>
> "How do you say 'This is a holdup' in Spanish?" Etta asked the Sundance Kid.

a. Don't think about it, advised Jason; it will only make you unhappy.

b. Should I go, Marcia asked, or should I stay here?

c. In her story The Wide Net, Eudora Welty wrote, The excursion is the same when you go looking for your sorrow as when you go looking for your joy.

d. Who's supposed to say the line Tennis, anyone? asked the director.

e. Robert Burns's poem To a Mouse opens, Wee, sleekit, cow'rin, tim'rous beastie, / O, what a panic's in thy breastie!

1. How now! a rat? exclaimed Hamlet when Polonius stirred behind the curtain.

2. That so-called "sculpture" is what I call "junk."

3. Irving Berlin wrote God Bless America, which some people think should replace The Star-Spangled Banner as our national anthem.

4. When Ann remarked that people who live in glass houses shouldn't throw stones, Bill replied, That's the pot calling the kettle black!

5. Dame Edith Sitwell wrote, Rhythm was described by Schopenhauer as melody deprived of its pitch.

30 THE DASH

A **dash** is a horizontal line used to separate parts of a sentence—a more dramatic substitute for a comma, semicolon, or colon. To type a dash, hit your hyphen key twice. When using a pen, make your dashes good and long, so that readers can tell them from hyphens.

30a *Use a dash to indicate a sudden break in thought or shift in tone.*

The dash signals that a surprise is in store: a shift in viewpoint, perhaps, or an unfinished statement.

> Ivan doesn't care which team wins — he bet on both.
>
> I didn't even pay much attention to my parents' accented and ungrammatical speech — at least not at home.   — Richard Rodriguez
>
> Stunned, Jake stood there muttering, "What in the — ?"

30b *Use a dash to introduce an explanation, an illustration, or a series.*

When you want the kind of preparatory pause that a colon provides, but without the formality of a colon, try a dash.

> My advice to you is simple — stop complaining.

You can use a dash to introduce an appositive (a noun or noun phrase that renames the noun it follows) if the appositive needs drama or contains commas.

> Elliott still cherishes the pastimes of the '60s — drugs, sex, and rock-'n'-roll.
>
> Longfellow wrote about three young sisters — grave Alice, laughing Allegra, and Edith with golden hair — in "The Children's Hour."

30c *Use dashes to set off an emphatic aside or parenthetical element from the rest of a sentence.*

> It was as hot — and I mean *hot* — as a seven-dollar pistol on Fourth of July in Death Valley.
>
> If I went through anguish in botany and economics — for different reasons — gymnasium work was even worse.   — James Thurber

Dashes set off a phrase or clause with more punch than commas or parentheses can provide. (Compare commas, 25, and parentheses, 31a–31b.)

30d *Avoid overusing dashes.*

Like a physical gesture of emphasis — a jab of a pointing finger — the dash becomes meaningless if used too often. Use it only when a comma, a colon, or parentheses don't seem strong enough.

> EXCESSIVE Algy's grandmother — a sweet old lady — asked him to pick up some things at the store — milk, eggs, apples, and cheese.
>
> REVISED Algy's grandmother, a sweet old lady, asked him to pick up some things at the store: milk, eggs, apples, and cheese.

Exercise 30–1: Using the Dash

Add, replace, or cut dashes wherever appropriate in the following sentences. Some sentences may be correct. Revisions for the lettered sentences appear in the back of the book. Example:

> Stanton had all the identifying marks, boating shoes, yellow slicker, khaki pants, and tennis racquet, of a preppie.

> Stanton had all the identifying marks — boating shoes, yellow slicker, khaki pants, and tennis racquet — of a preppie.

a. I enjoy going fishing with my friend John — whom I've known for fifteen years.

b. His new boat is spectacular: a regular seagoing Ferrari.

c. Bella and Scott spent their vacation doing exactly what they wanted to do surfing.

d. We were just rounding the point when — WHAM!

e. "A rock!" I cried. "John, I'm afraid we're"

1. The sport of fishing — or at least some people call it a sport — is boring, dirty — and tiring.

2. Everything in John's tackle box, however, flies, spinners, hooks, lines, and sinkers, went flying into the water.

3. Three states in the Sunbelt, Florida, California, and Arizona, are the fastest growing in the nation.

4. Three-year-old Jody wrote a song, if that's the right word, consisting of two lines.

5. LuLu was ecstatic when she saw her grades, all A's!

31 PARENTHESES, BRACKETS, AND THE ELLIPSIS MARK

Like quotation marks, parentheses (singular, *parenthesis*) work in pairs. So do brackets. Both sets of marks usually surround bits of information added to make a statement perfectly clear. An ellipsis mark is a trio of periods inserted to show that some bit of information has been cut.

PARENTHESES

31a *Use parentheses to set off interruptions that are useful but not essential.*

> FDR (as people called Franklin D. Roosevelt) won four presidential elections.

> In fact, he occupied the White House for so many years (1933 to mid-1945) that babies became teenagers without having known any other president.

The material within the parentheses may be helpful, but it isn't essential. Were the writer to omit it altogether, the sentence would still make good sense. Use parentheses when adding in mid-sentence a qualifying word or phrase, a helpful date, or a brief explanation — words that, in conversation, you might introduce in a changed tone of voice.

31b *Use parentheses around letters or numbers indicating items in a series.*

> Archimedes asserted that, given (1) a lever long enough, (2) a fulcrum, and (3) a place to stand, he could move the earth.

You need not put parentheses around numbers or letters in a list that you set off from the text by indentation.

Exercise 31–1: Using Parentheses

Correct any improper use of parentheses in the following sentences. Some sentences may be correct. Revisions for the lettered sentences appear in the back of the book. Example:

> The Islamic fundamentalist Ayatollah Khomeini — 1903–1989 — was described as having led Iran forward into the fifteenth century.
>
> The Islamic fundamentalist Ayatollah Khomeini (1903–1989) was described as having led Iran forward into the fifteenth century.

a. In *The Last Crusade,* archeologist Indiana Jones, who took his name from the family dog, joins his father in a quest for the Holy Grail.

b. Our cafeteria serves the four basic food groups: white — milk, bread, and mashed potatoes — brown — mystery meat and gravy — green — overcooked vegetables and underwashed lettuce — and orange — squash, carrots, and tomato sauce.

c. The ambassador says that if, 1, the United States will provide more aid and, 2, the guerrillas will agree to a cease-fire, his government will hold free elections.

d. When Phil said he works with whales (as well as other marine mammals) for the Whale Stranding Network, Lisa thought he meant that his group lures whales onto beaches.

e. Actually, the Whale Stranding Network, WSN, rescues whales that have stranded themselves.

1. The new pear-shaped bottles will hold 200 milliliters, 6.8 fluid ounces, of lotion.

2. The letter from Agatha — not her real name — told a heart-wrenching story of abandonment and abuse.

3. Al's policeman costume was a fantastic success (even his mother was fooled).

4. Communicorp had enough applicants, 39, and enough jobs, 27, to qualify for the program, but the personnel manager failed to submit the proper paperwork.

5. Although he enjoys her company, Maxwell says he hopes to marry a better-established — meaning wealthier — woman than Lydia.

BRACKETS

Brackets, those open-ended typographical boxes, work in pairs like parentheses. They serve a special purpose: they mark changes in quoted material.

If your typewriter lacks brackets, you can draw them in by hand or you can construct passable brackets out of slashes and underlines.

[Franklin D. *]* Roosevelt

31c   *Use brackets to add information or to make changes within a direct quotation.*

A quotation must be quoted exactly. If you need to add or alter a word or a phrase in a quotation from another writer, place brackets around your changes. When is it appropriate to make such a change? Most often the need arises when you weave into your own prose a piece of someone else's, and you want to get rid of dangling threads.

Suppose you are writing about James McGuire's being named chairman of the board of directors of General Motors. In your source, the actual words are these: "A radio bulletin first brought the humble professor of philosophy the astounding news." But in your paper, you want readers to know the professor's identity. So you add that information, in brackets.

"A radio bulletin first brought the humble professor of philosophy [James McGuire] the astounding news."

Be careful never to alter a quoted statement any more than you have to. Every time you consider an alteration, ask yourself: do I really need this word-for-word quotation, or should I paraphrase?

31d   *Use brackets around* sic *to indicate an error in a direct quotation.*

When you faithfully quote a statement that contains an error and you don't want your reader to blame you for it, follow the error with a bracketed *sic* (Latin for "so" or "so the writer says").

"President Ronald Reagan foresaw a yearly growth of 29,000,000,000 [*sic*] in the American populace."

Of course, any statement as incorrect as that one is not worth quoting. Usually you're better off paraphrasing an error-riddled passage than pointing out its weaknesses. The writer who uses *sic* is like someone who goes around with a mean dog, siccing it on fellow writers. Never unleash your dog unless your target truly deserves a bite.

THE ELLIPSIS MARK

31e   *Use the ellipsis mark to signal that you have omitted part of a quotation.*

Occasionally, in quoting a passage of prose, you will want to cite just those parts that relate to your topic. It's all right to make judicious cuts in a quotation, as long as you acknowledge them. To do this, use the *ellipsis mark*: three periods with a space before and after each one (. . .).

Let's say you are writing an essay, "Today's Children: Counselors on Marital Affairs." One of your sources is Marie Winn's book *Children without Childhood,* in which you find this passage:

> Consider the demise of sexual innocence among children. We know that the casual integration of children into adult society in the Middle Ages included few sexual prohibitions. Today's nine- and ten-year-olds watch pornographic movies on cable TV, casually discourse about oral sex and sadomasochism, and not infrequently find themselves involved in their own parents' complicated sex lives, if not as actual observers or participants, at least as advisers, friendly commentators, and intermediaries.

You want to quote Winn's last sentence, but it has too much detail for your purposes. You might shorten it by omitting two of its parts.

> Today's nine- and ten-year-olds . . . not infrequently find themselves involved in their own parents' complicated sex lives, . . . at least as advisers, friendly commentators, and intermediaries.

If you want to include parts of two or more sentences, use a period plus the ellipsis mark—four periods altogether. The period that ends the first sentence appears in its usual place, followed by the three spaced periods that signal the omission.

> Consider the demise of sexual innocence among children. . . . Today's nine- and ten-year-olds [and the rest].

31f Avoid using the ellipsis mark at the beginning or end of a quotation.

Even though the book *Children without Childhood* keeps on going after the quoted passage, you don't need an ellipsis mark at the end of your quotation. Nor do you ever need to begin a quotation with three dots. Save the ellipsis mark for words or sentences you omit *inside* whatever you quote.

Anytime you decide to alter a quotation, with an ellipsis or with brackets, pause to ask yourself whether the quoted material is still necessary and still effective as changed. A passage full of ellipsis marks starts to look like Swiss cheese. If you plan to cut more than one or two sections from a quotation, think about paraphrasing instead.

Exercise 31–2: Using Brackets and the Ellipsis Mark

The following are two hypothetical passages from original essays. Each one is followed by a set of quotations. Adapt or paraphrase each quotation, using brackets and ellipsis marks, and splice it into the essay passage.

1. ESSAY PASSAGE

Has evil lost its capacity to frighten us? Today's teenagers use words like *wicked, bad,* and *evil* not to condemn another person's behavior or style but to show that they approve of it. Perhaps the declining power of organized religion has allowed us to stop worrying about evil. Perhaps the media's coverage of war, genocide, and murder has made us feel impotent against it. Perhaps the worldwide spread of nuclear weapons has made evil too huge and uncontrollable for our imaginations to grapple with.

QUOTATIONS

a. It was as though in those last minutes he was summing up the lessons that this long course in human wickedness had taught us — the lesson of the fearsome, word-and-thought-defying *banality of evil.*
   —Philosopher Hannah Arendt, writing about the Nazi leader Adolf Eichmann

b. I am not a pessimist; to perceive evil where it exists is, in my opinion, a form of optimism.   —Filmmaker Roberto Rossellini

c. The world has achieved brilliance without conscience. Ours is a world of nuclear giants and ethical infants.   —General Omar Bradley

2. ESSAY PASSAGE

Every human life is touched by the natural world. Before the modern industrial era, most people recognized the earth as the giver and supporter of existence. Nowadays, with the power of technology, we can (if we choose) destroy many of the complex balances of nature. With such power comes responsibility. We are no longer merely nature's children, but nature's parents as well.

QUOTATIONS

a. A land ethic for tomorrow should be as honest as Thoreau's *Walden,* and as comprehensive as the sensitive science of ecology. It should stress the oneness of our resources and the live-and-help-live logic of the great chain of life. If, in our haste to "progress," the economics of ecology are disregarded by citizens and policy makers alike, the result will be an ugly America.
   —Former Secretary of the Interior Stewart Lee Udall

b. The overwhelming importance of the atmosphere means that there are no longer any frontiers to defend against pollution, attack, or propaganda. It means, further, that only by a deep patriotic devotion to one's country can there be a hope of the kind of protection of the whole planet, which is necessary for the survival of the people of other countries.   —Anthropologist Margaret Mead

c. The survival of our wildlife is a matter of grave concern to all of us in Africa. These wild creatures amid the wild places they inhabit are not only important as a source of wonder and inspiration but are an integral part of our natural resources and of our future livelihood and well-being.
   —Former President of Tanzania Julius Nyerere

d. [Religion] is a force in itself and it calls for the integration of lands and peoples in harmonious unity. The lands wait for those who can discern their rhythms. The peculiar genius of each continent, each river valley, the rugged mountains, the placid lakes, all call for relief from the constant burden of exploitation.
   —American Indian leader Vine Deloria, Jr., a Standing Rock Sioux

Exercise 31–3: Punctuation Review

Punctuate each of the following sentences correctly, changing capitalization if necessary.

1. Being a dedicated beachcomber Truman my aunts former accountant found life in Okracoke North Carolina to be just his cup of punch

2. He would jump through waves by the hour he would shriek back at the gulls

3. Some mornings feeling lazy hed sit in the sun and talk with shipwrecked sailors or were they dope runners whose planes had been shot down

4. What Truman wondered was the meaning of success

5. Lieutenant Binks officer in charge of Cape Hatteras lighthouse a Coast Guard station lent him a willing no a compassionate ear

6. One night without warning crash a colossal yacht struck the beach not far from Trumans tiny rain-drenched tent

7. Good grief he cried leaping to his feet whats happened

8. As he ran along the beach into his wondering gaze came a vision of naked loveliness

9. She seemed a moon-washed phantom her lightly stepping feet moving like a dancers through the surf

10. Such delicacy such grace Truman always a sucker for beauty instantly resolved to befriend this charming castaway

11. Shaking her sea-drenched coat she gave him a head-to-foot saltwater bath

12. Her tongue was blue which coupled with her auburn hue told Truman an expert in such matters that she must be a chow chow

13. Scoffers their eyes fixed on high-paying jobs may well laugh but Truman P Kelp CPA fugitive from society recognized love

14. With his devoted friend partner and organic bed warmer he lived to pick a trite expression happily ever after although dog food was always in scant supply

15. Heres an interesting bit of advice for young writers from Tennessee Williams All you have to do is close your eyes and wait for the symbols.

CHAPTER 36

Mechanics

32 ABBREVIATIONS

Abbreviations are a form of shorthand that enables a writer to include certain necessary information in capsule form. In your writing, limit abbreviations to those that are common enough for readers to recognize and understand without pausing. When a reader has to stop and ask, "What does this mean?" your writing loses impact.

If ever you're unsure about whether to abbreviate a word, remember: when in doubt, spell it out.

32a *Use abbreviations for some titles with proper names.*

Abbreviate the following titles:

Mr. and Mrs. Hubert Collins   Dr. Martin Luther King, Jr.
Ms. Martha Reading   St. Matthew

Write out other titles in full:

General Douglas MacArthur   Senator Nancy L. Kassebaum
President George Bush   Professor Shirley Fixler

Titles that are unfamiliar to readers of English, such as *M.* (for the French *Monsieur*) or *Sr.* (for the Spanish *Señor*), should be spelled out.
Spell out most titles that appear without proper names:

FAULTY   Fred is studying to be a dr.

REVISED   Fred is studying to be a doctor.

When an abbreviated title (such as an academic degree) follows a proper name, set it off from the name and from the rest of the sentence with commas.

Alice Martin, C.P.A., is the accountant for Charlotte Cordera, Ph.D., and John Hoechst, Jr., Esq.

Lucy Chen, M.D., and James Filbert, D.D.S., have moved their offices to the Millard Building.

An academic degree that appears without a proper name can be abbreviated, but it is not set off with commas.

My brother has a B.A. in economics.

Avoid repeating different forms of the same title before and after a proper name. You can properly refer to a doctor of dental surgery as either *Dr. Jane Doe* or *Jane Doe, D.D.S.*, but not as *Dr. Jane Doe, D.D.S.*

32b Use a.m., p.m., B.C., A.D., and $ with numbers.

9:05 a.m.   3:45 p.m.
2000 B.C.   A.D. 1066

The words we use to pinpoint years and times are so commonly abbreviated that many English speakers have forgotten what the letters stand for. In case you are curious: *a.m.* means *ante meridiem*, Latin for "before noon"; *p.m.* means *post meridiem*, "after noon." A.D. is *anno domini*, Latin for "in the year of the Lord"—that is, since the official year of Jesus' birth. B.C. stands for "before Christ." You may also run into alternative designations such as B.P., "before present," and B.C.E., "before the common era." If you think your readers may not know what an abbreviation stands for, spell it out or add an explanation.

The ruins date from 1200 B.P. (before present).

For prices, use a dollar sign with numbers (*$17.95, $10*).
Avoid using an abbreviation together with a word or words that mean the same thing: write *$1 million* or *one million dollars*, not *$1 million dollars*. Write *9:05 a.m.* or *9:05 in the morning*, not *9:05 a.m. in the morning*.

32c *Avoid abbreviating names of months, days of the week, units of measurement, or parts of literary works.*

Many references that can be abbreviated in footnotes or citations should be spelled out when they appear in the body of an essay.

NAMES OF MONTHS AND DAYS OF THE WEEK

FAULTY   After their meeting on 9/3, they did not see each other again until Fri., Dec. 12.

REVISED   After their meeting on September 3 [*or* the third of September], they did not see each other again until Friday, December 12.

UNITS OF MEASUREMENT

FAULTY   It would take 10,000 lb. of concrete to build a causeway 25 ft × 58 in. [*or* 25′ × 58″].

REVISED   It would take 10,000 pounds of concrete to build a causeway 25 feet by 58 inches.

PARTS OF LITERARY WORKS

FAULTY   Von Bargen's reply appears in vol. II, ch. 12, p. 187.

REVISED   Von Bargen's reply appears in volume II, chapter 12, page 187.

FAULTY   Leona first speaks in Act I, sc. 2.

REVISED   Leona first speaks in Act I, scene 2 [*or* the second scene of Act I].

32d *Use the full English version of most Latin abbreviations.*

Unless you are writing for an audience of ancient Romans, translate Latin abbreviations into English and spell them out whenever possible.

COMMON LATIN ABBREVIATIONS

ABBREVIATION	LATIN	ENGLISH
et al.	*et alia*	and others, and other people, and the others (people)
etc.	*et cetera*	and so forth, and others, and the rest (things)
i.e.	*id est*	that is
e.g.	*exempli gratia*	for example, such as

Latin abbreviations are acceptable, however, for source citations and for comments in parentheses and brackets. (See also 31d.)

32e *Use abbreviations for familiar organizations, corporations, and people.*

Most sets of initials that are read as letters do not require periods between the letters (CIA, JFK, UCLA). You will not be wrong if you insert periods (C.I.A., J.F.K., U.C.L.A.), as long as you are consistent.

A set of initials that is pronounced as a word is called an **acronym** (NATO, AIDS, UNICEF) and never has periods between letters.

To avoid misunderstanding, write out an organization's full name the first time you mention it, followed by its initials in parentheses. Then, in later references, you can rely on initials alone. (With very familiar initials, such as FBI, CBS, and YMCA, you need not give the full name.)

32f Avoid abbreviations for countries.

When you mention the United States or another country, give its full name, unless the name is repeated so often that it would weigh down your paragraph.

The president will return to the United States [not *U.S.*] on Tuesday from a trip to the United Kingdom [not *U.K.*].

EXCEPTION: Although it is not advisable to use *U.S.* as a noun, you can use it as an adjective: *U.S. Senate, U.S. foreign policy*. For other countries, find an alternative: *British ambassador*.

Exercise 32–1: Using Abbreviations

Substitute abbreviations for words and vice versa wherever appropriate in the following sentences. Correct any incorrectly used abbreviations. Answers for the lettered sentences appear in the back of the book. Example:

My history teacher, Doctor Lembas, got her doctor of philosophy degree at the University of Southwest Florida.

My history teacher, Dr. Lembas, got her Ph.D. at the University of Southwest Florida.

a. Built for the Paris Exposition of 1889, the Eiffel Tower contains 15 million lb. of pig iron, protected by 37 T of paint.

b. Fri., 7/14, 1989, was the Eiffel Tower's 100th anniversary.

c. M. Eiffel would be pleased that Pres. Mitterrand et al. now accept his controversial "iron giraffe" as a national landmark.

d. In some Parisian tourist traps, a cup of coffee costs as much as 5 dollars.

e. France is a member of NATO, but the French historically have mistrusted some of their fellow NATO members, e.g., the U.K.

1. Amb. and Mrs. Collins stand several in. shorter than Gen. Garcia and his wife.

2. When the Senate considered whether the U.S. should aid the famine victims, Sens. Kerry, Kennedy, and Biden requested an authorization of $1.2 million dollars.

3. When John Fitzgerald Kennedy picked Lyndon Baines Johnson for VP, Democrats never guessed that three yrs later JFK would be dead and LBJ would be in the White House.

4. At 8:20 p.m. this evening we heard that Dr. Reginald Styx M.D. had stumbled upon relics dating to 1400 B.C.

5. The children in Middletown who collected pennies for U.N.I.C.E.F. at Halloween brought in more than 70 dollars.

33 CAPITAL LETTERS

The main thing to remember about capital letters is to use them only with good reason. If you think a word will work in lowercase letters, you're probably right.

33a Capitalize proper names and adjectives made from proper names.

Proper names designate individuals, places, organizations and institutions, brand names, and certain other distinctive things.

Miles Standish	University of Iowa
Belgium	a Volkswagen
United Nations	a Xerox machine

Any proper name can have an adjective as well as a noun form. The adjective form too is capitalized.

Australian beer	a Renaissance man
Shakespearean comedy	Machiavellian tactics

33b Capitalize a title or rank before a proper name.

Now in her second term, Senator Wilimczyk serves on two important committees.

In his lecture Professor Jones went on and on about fossil evidence.

In formal writing, titles that do not come before proper names are not capitalized.

Ten senators voted against the missile research appropriation.

Jones is the department's only full professor.

EXCEPTION: The abbreviation for the full name of an academic or professional degree is capitalized, whether or not it accompanies a proper name. The informal name of a degree is not capitalized.

Dora E. McLean, M.D., also holds a B.A. in music.

Dora holds a bachelor's degree in music.

33c Capitalize a family relationship only when it is part of a proper name or when it substitutes for a proper name.

Do you know the song about Mother Machree?

I've invited Mother to visit next weekend.

I'd like you to meet my aunt, Emily Smith.

CAPITALIZATION AT A GLANCE
Capitalize the following.

PROPER NAMES AND ADJECTIVES MADE FROM THEM
Marie Curie   Cranberry Island   Smithsonian Institution
a Freudian reading

RANK OR TITLE BEFORE A PROPER NAME
Ms. Olson   Professor Harvey

FAMILY RELATIONSHIP ONLY WHEN IT SUBSTITUTES FOR OR IS PART OF A PROPER NAME
Grandma Jones   Father Time

RELIGIONS, THEIR FOLLOWERS, AND DEITIES
Islam   Orthodox Jew   Buddha

PLACES, REGIONS, AND GEOGRAPHIC FEATURES
Palo Alto   the Berkshire Mountains

DAYS OF THE WEEK, MONTHS, AND HOLIDAYS
Wednesday   July   Labor Day

HISTORICAL EVENTS, PERIODS, DOCUMENTS, AND MOVEMENTS
the Boston Tea Party   the Middle Ages   the Constitution
the Abolitionist movement

SCHOOLS, COLLEGES, UNIVERSITIES, AND SPECIFIC COURSES
Temple University   Introduction to Clinical Psychology

FIRST, LAST, AND MAIN WORDS IN TITLES OF PAPERS, BOOKS, ARTICLES, AND WORKS OF ART
The Decline and Fall of the Roman Empire

THE FIRST LETTER OF A QUOTED SENTENCE
She called out, "Come in! The water's not cold."

33d *Capitalize the names of religions, their deities, and their followers.*

Christianity   Islam
Muslims   Methodists
Jehovah   Allah
Krishna   the Holy Spirit

33e *Capitalize proper names of places, regions, and geographic features.*

Los Angeles   Death Valley
the Black Hills   Big Sur
the Atlantic Ocean   the Philippines

Do not capitalize compass points unless they are parts of proper names (*West Virginia, South Orange*) or refer to formal geographic locations.

Drive south to Chicago and then east to Cleveland.

Jim, who has always lived in the South, likes to read about the mysterious East.

A common noun such as *street, avenue, boulevard, park, lake,* or *hill* is capitalized when part of a proper name.

Meinecke Avenue	Hamilton Park
Sunset Boulevard	Lake Michigan

33f *Capitalize days of the week, names of months, and holidays, but not seasons or academic terms.*

By the Monday after Passover I have to choose between the January study plan and junior year abroad.

At Easter we'll be halfway through the spring term.

33g *Capitalize historical events, periods, documents, and movements.*

Black Monday	Magna Charta
the Civil War	Declaration of Independence
the Holocaust	Atomic Energy Act
the Bronze Age	the Pre-Raphaelite Brotherhood
the Roaring Twenties	the Wobblies

33h *Capitalize the names of schools and colleges, department names, and course titles.*

West End School, Central High School [*but* elementary school, high school]
Reed College, Arizona State University [*but* the college, a university]
Department of Geography [*but* geography department, departmental meeting]
Feminist Perspectives in Nineteenth-Century Literature [*but* literature course]

33i *Capitalize the first, last, and main words in titles.*

When you write the title of a media product, whether it is a comic book, a television show, or a ballet, capitalize the first and last words and all main words in between. Do not capitalize articles, conjunctions, or prepositions unless they come first or last in the title or follow a colon.

ESSAY	"Once More to the Lake"
NOVEL	*Of Mice and Men*
VOLUME OF POETRY	*Poems after Martial*
POEM	"A Valediction: Of Weeping"

(For advice about using quotation marks and italics for titles, see 29e, 35a.)

33j *Capitalize the first letter of a quoted sentence.*

> Oscar Wilde wrote, "The only way to get rid of a temptation is to yield to it."

Only the first word of a quoted sentence is capitalized, even when you break the sentence with words of your own.

> "The only way to get rid of a temptation," wrote Oscar Wilde, "is to yield to it."

If you quote more than one sentence, start each one with a capital letter.

> "Art should never try to be popular," said Wilde. "The public should try to make itself artistic."

(For advice about punctuating quotations, see 29g–29i.)

If the beginning of the quoted passage blends in with your sentence, use lowercase for the first word of the quotation.

> Oscar Wilde wrote that "the only way to get rid of a temptation is to yield to it."

Exercise 33–1: Using Capitalization

Correct any capitalization errors you find in the following sentences. Some sentences may be correct. Answers for the lettered sentences appear in the back of the book. Example:

> "The quality of mercy," says Portia in Shakespeare's *The Merchant Of Venice*, "Is not strained."
>
> "The quality of mercy," says Portia in Shakespeare's *The Merchant of Venice,* "is not strained."

a. At our Family Reunion, I met my Cousin Sam for the first time, and also my father's brother George.

b. I already knew from dad that his brother had moved to Australia years ago to explore the great barrier reef.

c. At the reunion, uncle George told me that he had always wanted to be a Marine Biologist.

d. He had spent the Summer after his Sophomore year of college in Woods Hole, Massachusetts, on cape cod.

e. At the Woods Hole oceanographic institution he studied Horseshoe Crabs.

1. "These crabs look like armored tanks," he told me. "They have populated the Northeast for millions of years."

2. "I'm writing a book," he said, "Entitled *Horseshoe Crabs are Good Luck.*"

3. I had heard that uncle George was estranged from his Mother, a Roman catholic, after he married an Atheist.

4. She told George that God created many religions so that people would not become Atheists.

5. When my Uncle announced that he was moving to a Continent thousands of miles Southwest of the United States, his Mother gave him a bible to take along.

6. My Aunt, Linda McCallum, received her Doctorate from one of the State Universities in California.

7. After graduation she worked there as Registrar and lived in the San Bernardino valley.

8. She has pursued her interest in Hispanic Studies by traveling to South America from her home in Northeastern Australia.

9. She uses her maiden name — Linda McCallum, Ph.D. — for her nonprofit business, Hands across the Sea.

10. After dinner we all toasted grandmother's Ninetieth Birthday and sang "For She's A Jolly Good Fellow."

34 NUMBERS

When do you write out a number (*twenty-seven*) and when do you use figures for it (*27*)? Unless your essay relies on statistics, you'll want in most cases to use words. Figures are most appropriate in contexts where readers are used to seeing them, such as times and dates (*11:05 P.M. on March 15*).

FIGURES AT A GLANCE	
ADDRESSES	4 East 74th Street; also, One Copley Place; 5 Fifth Avenue
DATES	May 20, 1992; 450 B.C.; also, Fourth of July
DECIMALS	98.6° Fahrenheit; .57 acre
FRACTIONS	$3\frac{1}{2}$ years ago; $1\frac{3}{4}$ miles; also, half a loaf; three-fourths of voters surveyed
PARTS OF LITERARY WORKS	volume 2, chapter 5, page 37; Act 1, Scene 2 (*or* Act I, Scene ii)
PERCENTAGES	25 percent; 99.9 percent
PRICES	$1.99; $200,000; also, $5 million; ten cents; a dollar
SCORES	a 114–111 victory; a final score of 5 to 3
STATISTICS	men in the 25–30 age group; odds of 5 to 1 (*or* 5–1 odds); height 5′7″; also, three out of four doctors
TIMES	2:29 P.M.; 10:15 tomorrow morning; also, three o'clock, half past four

34a *In general, write out a number that consists of one or two words and use figures for longer numbers.*

Short names of numbers are easily read (*ten, six hundred*); longer ones take more thought (*two thousand four hundred eighty-seven*). So for numbers of more than a word or two, use figures.

More than two hundred suckers paid twenty-five dollars apiece for that cheap plastic novelty item.

A frog's tongue has 970,580 taste buds, one-sixth as many as a human being's.

EXCEPTION: For multiples of a million or more, you can use a figure plus a word.

The earth is 93 million miles from the sun.

The Pentagon has requested a $3.4 billion increase.

34b *Use figures for most addresses, dates, decimals, fractions, parts of literary works, percentages, prices, scores, statistics, and times.*

Using figures is mainly a matter of convenience. If you think words will be easier for your readers to follow, you can always write out a number.

NOTE: Any number that precedes *o'clock* should be in words, not figures. (For pointers on writing the plurals of figures [*6's, 1960s*], see 28i.)

34c *Use words or figures consistently throughout a passage.*

Switching back and forth between words and figures for numbers can be distracting to readers. Choose whichever form suits most of the numbers in your passage and use that form for all of them, unless to do so would create excessive awkwardness.

Ten years ago, only a quarter of the land in town was developed; now, all but fifteen percent is occupied by buildings.

Of the 276 representatives who voted, 97 supported a 25 percent raise, while 179 supported an amendment that would implement a 30 percent raise over 5 years.

34d *Write out a number that begins a sentence.*

Readers recognize a new sentence by its initial capital; however, you can't capitalize a figure. When a number starts a sentence, either write it out or move it deeper into the sentence. If a number starting a sentence is followed by other numbers in the same category, write them out, too, unless to do so would make the sentence excessively awkward.

Five percent of the frogs in our aquarium ate sixty-two percent of the flies.

Ten thousand people packed an arena built for 8,550.

Exercise 34–1: Using Numbers

Correct any inappropriate uses of numbers in the following sentences. Some sentences may be correct. Answers for the lettered sentences appear in the back of the book. Example:

As Smith notes on page 197, a delay of 3 minutes cost the researchers 5 years' worth of work.

As Smith notes on page 197, a delay of three minutes cost the researchers five years' worth of work.

a. Wasn't it the 3 Musketeers whose motto was "One for all and all for one"?

b. In the 1970s, there were about ninety-two million ducks in America, but in the last 4 years their number has dropped to barely sixty-nine million.

c. Cruising around the world on a one-hundred-twenty-five-foot yacht with eight other people sounded glamorous until I saw our wooden berths, thirty-two inches wide by sixty-eight inches long.

d. Forty days and 40 nights would seem like 40 years if you were sailing on an ark with two of every kind of animal.

e. I doubt that I'll ever bowl a perfect 300, but I hope to break 250 if it takes me till I'm eighty.

1. The meeting has been rescheduled from three-thirty p.m. Tuesday to four o'clock this afternoon because $\frac{1}{2}$ the members couldn't make it.

2. A program to help save the sea otter transferred more than eighty animals to a new colony over the course of 2 years; however, all but 34 otters swam back home again.

3. 1 percent or less of the estimated fifteen to twenty billion pounds of plastic discarded annually in the United States is recycled.

4. The 1983 Little League World Series saw the Roosters beat the Dusters ninety-four to four before a throng of seven thousand five hundred and fifty.

5. In Act Two, Scene Nine of Shakespeare's *The Merchant of Venice,* Portia's 2nd suitor fails to guess which of 3 caskets contains her portrait.

6. *Fourscore* means 4 times 20; a *fortnight* means 2 weeks; and a *brace* is two of anything.

7. 50 years ago, traveling from New York City to San Francisco took approximately 15 hours by plane, 50 hours by train, and almost 100 hours by car.

8. A candy bar that cost $.05 in the nineteen-fifties costs $.35 to $.50 today.

9. If the backers cannot raise a hundred and fifty thousand dollars by noon tomorrow, they lose their ten-thousand-dollar deposit.

10. Justine finished volume one of Proust's *Remembrance of Things Past,* but by the time she got to page forty of volume two, she had forgotten the beginning and had to start over.

35 ITALICS

Italic type—as in this line—slants to the right. Slightly harder to read than perpendicular type, it is usually saved for emphasis or for special use of a word or phrase. In writing or typewriting, indicate italics by underlining.

35a *Underline the titles of magazines, newspapers, and long literary works (books, pamphlets, plays); the titles of films; the titles of paintings and other works of art; the titles of long* *musical works (operas, symphonies); the titles of record albums; and the names of television and radio programs.*

> We read the story "Araby" in James Joyce's book *Dubliners.*
>
> The Broadway musical *My Fair Lady* was based on Shaw's play *Pygmalion.*
>
> Pete read reviews in the *Washington Post* and *Newsweek* magazine of the Cleveland Philharmonic's recording of Beethoven's *Pastoral* symphony.
>
> I saw a *Miami Vice* episode that featured cuts from two Doors albums: *The Doors* and *Strange Days.*

The names of the Bible (King James Version, Revised Standard Version), the books of the Bible (Genesis, Matthew), and other sacred books (the Koran, the Rig-Veda) are not italicized.

(For titles that are put in quotation marks, see 29e.)

35b Underline the names of ships, boats, trains, airplanes, and spacecraft.

> The launching of the Venus probe *Magellan* was a heartening success after the *Challenger* disaster.
>
> The *Concorde* combines the elegance of an ocean liner like the *Queen Mary* with the convenience of high-speed air travel.

35c Underline a word or phrase from a foreign language if it is not in everyday use.

> Gandhi taught the principles of *satya* and *ahimsa:* truth and nonviolence.
>
> Although there is no one-word English equivalent for the French *chez,* we can translate *chez Bob* simply as "at Bob's."

Foreign words that are familiar to most American readers need not be underlined. (Check your dictionary to see which words are considered familiar.)

> After being declared passé several years ago, détente is making a reappearance in East-West politics.
>
> I prefer provolone to mozzarella.

35d Underline a word when you define it.

> The rhythmic, wavelike motion of the walls of the alimentary canal is called *peristalsis.*

When you give a synonym or a translation — a definition that is just one or two words long — italicize the word being defined and put the definition in quotation marks.

> The word *orthodoxy* means "conformity."
>
> *Trois, drei,* and *tres* are all words for "three."

ITALICS AT A GLANCE
Underline the following when typing or writing by hand.

TITLES

MAGAZINES AND NEWSPAPERS
Ms.   the *London Times*

LONG LITERARY WORKS
Heart of Darkness (a novel)   *The Less Deceived* (a collection of poems)

FILMS
Notorious   *Black Orpheus*

PAINTINGS AND OTHER WORKS OF ART
Four Dancers (a painting)   *The Thinker* (a sculpture)

LONG MUSICAL WORKS
Aïda   Handel's *Messiah*

RECORD ALBUMS
Sticky Fingers

TELEVISION AND RADIO PROGRAMS
I Love Lucy   *All Things Considered*

OTHER WORDS AND PHRASES

NAMES OF SPECIFIC VEHICLES AND SPACECRAFT
the *Orient Express*   the *Challenger*

A WORD OR PHRASE FROM A FOREIGN LANGUAGE IF IT IS NOT IN EVERYDAY USE
The Finnish sauna ritual uses a *vihta*, a brush made of fresh birch branches tied together.

A LETTER, NUMBER, WORD, OR PHRASE WHEN YOU DEFINE IT OR REFER TO IT AS A WORD
My lucky number is *12*.   What do you think *fiery* is referring to in the second line?

Note: See 29e for titles that need to be placed in quotation marks.

35e *Underline a letter, number, word, or phrase used as a word.*

George Bernard Shaw pointed out that *fish* could be spelled *ghoti*: *gh* as in *tough*, *o* as in *women*, and *ti* as in *fiction*.

Watching the big red *8* on a basketball player's jersey, I recalled the scarlet letter *A* worn by Hester Prynne.

Psychologists now prefer the term *unconscious* to *subconscious*.

35f Use underlining sparingly for emphasis.

When you absolutely *must* stress a point, underline it; but watch out. Frequent italics can make your writing look hysterical. In most cases, the structure of your sentence, not a typographical gimmick, should give emphasis where emphasis is due.

> He suggested putting the package *under* the mailbox, not *into* the mailbox.

> People committed to saving whales, sea otters, and baby seals may not be aware that *forty thousand children per day* die of starvation or malnutrition.

Exercise 35–1: Using Italics

Add or remove italics as needed in the following sentences. Some sentences may be correct. Revisions for the lettered sentences appear in the back of the book. Example:

> Hiram could not *believe* that his parents had seen *the Beatles'* legendary performance at Shea Stadium.

> Hiram could not believe that his parents had seen the Beatles' legendary performance at Shea Stadium.

a. Hiram's favorite Beatles album is "Sergeant Pepper's Lonely Hearts Club Band," but his father prefers "Magical Mystery Tour."

b. Hiram named his rowboat the "Yellow Submarine."

c. He was disappointed when I told him that the play *Long Day's Journey into Night* is *definitely not* a staged version of the movie "A Hard Day's Night."

d. I had to show him the article "Eugene O'Neill's Journey into Night" in "People" magazine to convince him.

e. Many different ethnic groups eat tomatoes and cheese in or on some form of cooked dough, whether they call this dish a *pizza*, an *enchilada*, a sandwich, or something else.

1. Is "avocado" Spanish for "lawyer"?

2. Our chorus and orchestra will perform Handel's Messiah at Christmas and Beethoven's Eroica in the spring.

3. You can pick out some of the best basketball players in the *NBA* by the 33 on their jerseys.

4. The nine musicians on the *Titanic* went down with the ship, playing "Nearer My God to Thee."

5. In one episode of "Rocky and Bullwinkle," the intrepid moose and squirrel landed on the *Isle of Lucy*.

6. "Eye" in France is "oeil," while "eyes" is "yeux."

7. "Deux yeux bleus" means "two blue eyes" in French.

8. Jan can never remember whether Cincinnati has three n's and one t or two n's and two t's.

9. My favorite comic bit in "The Pirates of Penzance" is Major General Stanley's confusion between "orphan" and "often."

10. In Tom Stoppard's play "The Real Thing," the character Henry accuses Bach of copying a *cantata* from a popular song by *Procol Harum*.

36 THE HYPHEN

The hyphen, that Scotch-tape mark of punctuation, is used to join words and to connect parts of words. You will find it indispensable for the following purposes.

36a *Use hyphens in compound words that require them.*

Compound words in the English language take three forms:

1. Two or more words combined into one (*crossroads, salesperson*)
2. Two or more words that remain separate but function as one (*gas station, high school*)
3. Two or more words linked by hyphens (*sister-in-law, window-shop*)

Compound nouns and verbs fall into these categories more by custom than by rule. When you're not sure which way to write a compound, refer to your dictionary. If the compound is not listed in your dictionary, write it as two words.

Use a hyphen in a compound word containing one or more elements beginning with a capital letter.

> Bill says that, as a *neo-Marxist* living in an *A-frame* house, it would be politically incorrect for him to wear a Mickey Mouse *T-shirt*.

> Bubba doesn't mind being labeled a *pre-Neanderthal*, but he'll break anyone's neck who calls him *anti-American*.

There are exceptions to this rule: *unchristian*, for one. If you think a compound word looks odd with a hyphen, check your dictionary.

36b *Use a hyphen in a compound adjective preceding a noun but not following a noun.*

> Jerome, a devotee of *twentieth-century* music, has no interest in the classic symphonies of the *eighteenth century*.

> I'd like living in an *out-of-the-way* place better if it weren't so far *out of the way*.

In a series of hyphenated adjectives with the same second word, you can omit that word (but not the hyphen) in all but the last adjective of the series.

> Julia is a lover of eighteenth-, nineteenth-, and twentieth-century music.

The adverb *well*, when coupled with an adjective, follows the same hyphenation rules as if it were an adjective.

It is *well known* that Tony has a *well-equipped* kitchen, although his is not as *well equipped* as the hotel's.

Do *not* use a hyphen to link an adverb ending in *-ly* with an adjective.

FAULTY   The sun hung like a newly-minted penny in a freshly-washed sky.

REVISED   The sun hung like a newly minted penny in a freshly washed sky.

36c Use a hyphen after the prefixes all-, ex-, and self- and before the suffix -elect.

Lucille's *ex-husband* is studying *self-hypnosis*.

This *all-important* debate pits Senator Browning against the *president-elect*.

Note that these prefixes and suffixes also can function as parts of words that are not hyphenated (*exit, selfish*). Whenever you are unsure whether to use a hyphen, check a dictionary.

36d Use a hyphen if an added prefix or suffix creates a double vowel, triple consonant, or ambiguous pronunciation.

The contractor told us that his *pre-estimate* did not cover any *pre-existing* flaws in the building.

The recreation department favors the *re-creation* of a summer activities program.

36e Use a hyphen in spelled-out fractions and compound whole numbers from twenty-one to ninety-nine.

When her sister gave Leslie's age as six and *three-quarters*, Leslie corrected her: "I'm six and *five-sixths!*"

If Fred makes *ninety-nine* mistakes, he has a hundred and one excuses.

36f Use a hyphen to indicate a series between two numbers.

The section covering the years 1975-1980 is found on pages 20-27.

36g Use a hyphen to break a word between syllables at the end of a line.

Words are divided as they are pronounced, by syllables. Break a hyphenated compound at its hyphen and a nonhyphenated compound between the words that make it up. For a noncompound word, saying it out loud usually will give you a good idea where to break it; if you still are not sure, check your dictionary.

FAULTY   Bubba hates to be called an-
          ti-American.

REVISED   Bubba hates to be called anti-
          American.

| FAULTY | Mr. Brown will not be in until lun-chtime. |
| REVISED | Mr. Brown will not be in until lunch-time. |

Don't split a one-syllable word, even if keeping it intact makes your line come out a bit too short or too long.

FAULTY	I'm completely drench-ed.
REVISED	I'm completely drenched.
FAULTY	Arnold is a tower of stren-gth.
REVISED	Arnold is a tower of strength.

Don't split a word after a one-letter syllable or before a one- or two-letter syllable.

FAULTY	What's that up the road a-head?
REVISED	What's that up the road ahead?
FAULTY	When did Thomas and Mari-a get married?
REVISED	When did Thomas and Ma-ria get married?

Don't split a word after a segment that looks like a whole word, even if a dictionary puts a syllable break there.

CONFUSING	The lusty sailor aimed his sex-tant at the stars.
CLEAR	The lusty sailor aimed his sextant at the stars.
CONFUSING	He is addicted to her-oin.
CLEAR	He is addicted to heroin.

Exercise 36–1: Using Hyphens

Add necessary hyphens or remove incorrectly used hyphens in the following sentences. Some sentences may be correct. Answers for the lettered sentences appear in the back of the book. Example:

Carlos presented Isabel with a beautifully-wrought silver necklace.

Carlos presented Isabel with a beautifully wrought silver necklace.

a. Do nonAmericans share our view of ourselves as a freedom loving people?

b. The dealer told George the two vases are within nine-tenths of an inch of being a perfect match.

c. Patrick Henry's words reecho down through the ages: "Give me liberty or give
me death!"

d. Those well-spoken words are well-remembered today.

e. The weather forecast calls for showers followed by sunshine.

1. How are you going to fit that heavy sweater into a fully-packed suitcase?

2. Henry's exact height is six feet, four and a half inches.

3. As Joyce walked away, a voice behind her called, "You-
're under arrest!"

4. Dubowski's last film was greatly improved by reediting.

5. Critics applauded the fast moving plot and fully realized characters.

6. As part of her recovery from hand surgery, Susan has learned to crossstitch.

7. Batman fended off the Joker's surprise attack with a powerful right hook to the jaw.

8. According to Dr. Shelby, selfactualization is the highest human need.

9. The guerrillas insist that being anticapitalist doesn't mean they are proSoviet.

10. The downpour that sent everyone running for shelter ended as quickly as it had started.

37 SPELLING

English spelling so often defies the rules that many speakers of the language wonder if, indeed, there *are* rules. You probably learned to spell—as most of us did—mainly by memorizing. By now you remember that there's a *b* in *doubt* but not in *spout,* a *k* in *knife* but not in *nine.* You know that the same sound can have several spellings, as in *here, ear, pier, sneer,* and *weird.* You are resigned to the fact that *ou* is pronounced differently in *four, round, ought,* and *double.* Still, like most people, you may have trouble with the spelling of certain words.

How many times have you heard someone say "ath-uh-lete" for *athlete,* "gov-er-ment" for *government,* or "nuc-yu-lar" for *nuclear*? Get the pronunciation right and you realize that the spelling has to be *arctic* (not *artic*), *mischievous* (not *mischievious*), *perform* (not *preform*), *surprise* (not *suprise*), *replenish* (not *replentish*), *similar* (not *similiar*).

The trouble is that careful pronunciation is only sometimes a reliable guide to English spelling. Knowing how to pronounce *psychology, whistle, light, gauge,* and *rhythm* doesn't help you spell them. How, then, are you to cope?

37a *Follow spelling rules.*

Fortunately, there are a few rules for spelling English words that work most of the time. Learning them, and some of their exceptions, will give you a sturdy foundation on which to build.

EI OR IE?

The best way to remember which words are spelled *ei* and which ones *ie* is to recall this familiar jingle:

> *I* before *e* except after *c,*
> Or when sounded like *a,* as in *neighbor* and *weigh.*

Niece, believe, field, receive, receipt, ceiling, beige, and *freight* are just a few of the words you'll be able to spell easily once you learn that rule. Then memorize a few of the exceptions:

counterfeit	foreign	kaleidoscope	protein	seize
either	forfeit	leisure	science	weird
financier	height	neither	seismograph	

Also among the rule breakers are words in which *cien* is pronounced "shen"; *ancient, efficient, conscience, prescience.*

HOMONYMS

Words that sound the same, or almost the same, but are spelled differently are called **homonyms.** Here are some of the most commonly confused homonyms, briefly identified, with examples of how to use them. (Also see the Glossary of Troublemakers at the end of the *Handbook.*)

COMMONLY CONFUSED HOMONYMS

accept (v., take); **except** (prep., other than)

Mimi could *accept* all of Lefty's gifts *except* his ring.

affect (v., influence); **effect** (n., result)

If the new rules *affect* us, what will be their *effect*?

allusion (n., reference); **illusion** (n., fantasy)

Any *allusion* to Norman's mother may revive his *illusion* that she is upstairs, alive, in her rocking chair.

capital (adj., uppercase; n., seat of government); **capitol** (n., government building)

The *Capitol* building in Washington, D.C. (our nation's *capital*), is spelled with a *capital* C.

COMMONLY CONFUSED HOMONYMS *(continued)*

cite (v., refer to); **sight** (n., vision or tourist attraction); **site** (n., place)

Did you *cite* Mother as your authority on which *sites* feature the most interesting *sights*?

complement (v., complete; n., counterpart); **compliment** (v. or n., praise)

For Lee to say that Sheila's beauty *complements* her intelligence may or may not be a *compliment*.

desert (v., abandon); **desert** (n., barren region); **dessert** (n., end-of-meal sweet)

Don't *desert* us by leaving before *dessert*.

elicit (v., bring out); **illicit** (adj., illegal)

By going undercover, Sonny should *elicit* some offers of *illicit* drugs.

formally (adv., officially); **formerly** (adv., in the past)

Jane and John Doe-Smith, *formerly* Jane Doe and John Smith, sent cards *formally* announcing their marriage.

led (v., past tense of *lead*); **lead** (n., metal)

Gil's heart was heavy as *lead* when he *led* the mourners to the grave.

principal (n. or adj., chief); **principle** (n., rule)

The *principal* problem is convincing the media that our school *principal* is a person of high *principles*.

stationary (adj., motionless); **stationery** (n., writing paper)

Hubert's *stationery* shop stood *stationary* for twenty years until a flood swept it down the river.

their (pron., belonging to them); **there** (adv., in that place); **they're** (contraction of *they are*)

Sue said *they're* going over *there* to visit *their* aunt.

to (prep., toward); **too** (adv., also or excessively); **two** (n. or adj., numeral: one more than one)

Let's not take *two* cars *to* town—that's *too* many unless Lucille and Harry are coming *too*.

who's (contraction of *who is*); **whose** (pron., belonging to whom)

Who's going to tell me *whose* dog this is?

your (pron., belonging to you); **you're** (contraction of *you are*)

You're not getting *your* own way this time!

PLURALS

1. To form the plural of most common nouns, add -s. If a noun ends in -ch, -sh, -s, or -x, form its plural by adding -es.

attack, attacks	umbrella, umbrellas
ridge, ridges	zone, zones
boss, bosses	trellis, trellises
sandwich, sandwiches	crash, crashes
tax, taxes	Betamax, Betamaxes

2. To form the plural of a common noun ending in -o, add -s if the -o follows a vowel and -es if it follows a consonant.

radio, radios	video, videos
hero, heroes	potato, potatoes

3. To form the plural of a common noun ending in -y, change the y to i and add -es if the y follows a consonant. Add only -s if the y follows a vowel.

baby, babies	sissy, sissies
fly, flies	wallaby, wallabies
toy, toys	monkey, monkeys
guy, guys	day, days

4. To form the plural of a proper noun, add -s or -es without changing the noun's ending.

Proper nouns follow the same rules as common nouns, with one exception: a proper noun never changes its spelling in the plural form.

Mary Jane, Mary Janes	Dr. Maddox, the Maddoxes
Mr. Curry, the Currys	Saturday, Saturdays
Professor Jones, the Joneses	

5. To form the plural of a compound noun, add -s or -es to the chief word, or to the last word if all the words are equal in weight.

brother-in-law, brothers-in-law	actor-manager, actor-managers
aide-de-camp, aides-de-camp	tractor-trailer, tractor-trailers

6. Memorize the plural forms of nouns that diverge from these rules. Certain nouns have special plurals. Here are a few:

alumna, alumnae	man, men
alumnus, alumni	medium, media
child, children	mouse, mice
half, halves	self, selves
goose, geese	tooth, teeth
leaf, leaves	woman, women

SUFFIXES

The -s added to a word to make it plural is one type of **suffix,** or tail section. Suffixes allow the same root word to do a variety of jobs, by giving it different forms for different functions. Keeping a few basic rules in mind will help you to use suffixes successfully.

1. Drop a silent *e* before a suffix that begins with a vowel.

move, mover, moved, moving
argue, arguer, argued, arguing
accrue, accruing, accrual

EXCEPTION: If the *e* has an essential function, keep it before *-ing.* In *singe,* for instance, the *e* changes the word's pronunciation from "sing" to "sinj." If you dropped the *e* in *singeing,* it would become *singing.*

singe, singed, singeing
tiptoe, tiptoed, tiptoeing

2. Keep a silent *e* before a suffix that begins with a consonant.

move, movement   hope, hopeless

EXCEPTION: In a word ending in a silent *e* preceded by a vowel, sometimes (but not always) drop the *e.*

argue, argument   true, truly

3. Change a final *y* to *i* before a suffix if the *y* follows a consonant but not if the *y* follows a vowel.

cry, crier, cried   joy, joyous, joyful
happy, happiest, happily   pray, prayed, prayer
hurry, hurried

EXCEPTION: Keep the *y* whenever the suffix is *-ing.*

hurry, hurrying   pray, praying

Drop a final *y* before the suffix *-ize.*

deputy, deputize   memory, memorize

4. Double the final consonant of a one-syllable word before a suffix if (1) the suffix starts with a vowel *and* (2) the final consonant follows a single vowel.

sit, sitter, sitting
flop, flopped, floppy
rob, robbed, robbery

Don't double the final consonant if it follows two vowels or another consonant.

fail, failed, failure
stack, stacking, stackable

Don't double the final consonant if the suffix starts with a consonant.

top, topless   cap, capful

5. Double the final consonant of a word with two or more syllables if (1) the suffix starts with a vowel *and* (2) the final consonant follows a single vowel *and* (3) the last syllable of the stem is accented once the suffix is added.

commit, committed, committing
rebut, rebuttal
regret, regretted, regrettable

Don't double the final consonant if it follows more than one vowel,

avail, available   repeat, repeating

or it follows another consonant,

accent, accented   depend, dependence

or the suffix starts with a consonant,

commit, commitment   jewel, jewelry

or, when the suffix is added, the final syllable of the stem is unaccented.

confer, conference (*but* conferred)
travel, traveler

PREFIXES

The main point to remember when writing a word with a *prefix* (or nose section) is that the prefix usually does not alter the spelling of the root word it precedes.

dis + appear = disappear
dis + satisfied = dissatisfied
mis + step = misstep
mis + understand = misunderstand
with + hold = withhold
un + necessary = unnecessary

For guidelines on when to use a hyphen to attach a prefix, see 36c and 36d.

37b *Develop spelling skills.*

Besides becoming familiar with the rules in this chapter, you can use several other tactics to teach yourself to be a better speller.

1. ***Use mnemonic devices.*** To make unusual spellings stick in your memory, invent associations. *Weird* behaves *weirdly*. Would you rather study *ancient science* or be an *efficient financier*? Using such *mnemonic devices* (tricks to aid memory) may help you not only with *ie* and *ei* but with whatever troublesome spelling you are determined to remember. Rise ag*ain*, Brit*ain*! One *d* in *dish*, one in *radish*. Why isn't *mathe*matics like *athle*tics? You write a lett*er* on station*ery*. Any silly phrase or sentence will do, as long as it brings tricky spellings to mind.

2. ***Keep a record of words you misspell.*** Buy yourself a little notebook in which to enter words that invariably trip you up. Each time you proofread a paper you have written and each time you receive one back from your instructor, write down any words you have misspelled. Then practice pronouncing, writing, and spelling them out loud until you have mastered them.

3. ***Check any questionable spelling by referring to your dictionary.*** Keep a dictionary at your elbow as you write. In matters of spelling, that good-as-gold book is your best friend. Use it to check words as you come up with them and to double-check them as you proofread and edit your work.

4. ***Learn commonly misspelled words.*** To save you the trouble of looking up every spelling bugbear, here is a list of words frequently misspelled. This list will serve to review our whole discussion of spelling, for it contains the trickiest words we've mentioned. Check-mark those that give you trouble—but don't stop there. Spend a few minutes each day going over them. Pronounce each one carefully or have a friend read the list to you. Spell every troublesome word out loud; write it ten times. Your spelling will improve rapidly.

Everybody has at least ten or twenty bugbears. Shoot down yours.

COMMONLY MISSPELLED WORDS

absence	aggressive	apology	audible
abundance	aging	apparatus	audience
academic	allege	apparent	average
acceptable	alleviate	appetite	awkward
accessible	all right	appearance	
accidentally	all together (all in	appreciate	balloon
accommodate	one group)	appropriate	barbarous
accustom	a lot	arctic	bearing
achievement	already	arrest	beginning
acknowledgment	although	argument	believe
acquaintance	altogether	ascend	beneficial
acquire	(entirely)	assassinate	benefited
acquitted	amateur	assistance	borne (carried)
across	analogous	association	boundary
address	analysis	athlete	breath (noun)
advertisement	analyze	athletics	breathe (verb)
advice	annual	attach	Britain
advise	antecedent	attendance	buoyant
aggravate	anxiety	attractive	*(continued)*

COMMONLY MISSPELLED WORDS (*continued*)

bureaucracy
business
cafeteria
calendar
candidate
capital
capitol
    (a building)
careful
casualties
category
causal
ceiling
cemetery
certain
changeable
changing
characteristic
chief
choose
    (present tense)
chose
    (past tense)
climbed
column
coming
commitment
committed
committee
comparative
competent
competition
complement
compliment
conceive
condemn
congratulate
connoisseur
conscience
conscientious
consistent
controlled
controversy
corollary
coroner
corps (a group)
corpse (a body)
costume
criticism

criticize
cruise
curiosity
curious
deceive
decision
defendant
deficient
definite
deity
dependent
descendant
describe
description
desirable
despair
desperate
detach
develop
develops
development
device (noun)
devise (verb)
diaphragm
diary
dietitian
difference
dilemma
dining
disappear
disappoint
disastrous
discipline
discussion
disease
disparate
dissatisfied
dissipate
divide
divine
doesn't
dominant
don't
drawer
drunkenness
ecstasy
efficiency
eighth
either

eligible
embarrass
emphasize
entirety
environment
equipped
equivalent
especially
exaggerate
exceed
excel
excellence
exercise
exhaust
existence
experience
explanation
extremely

fallacious
familiar
fascinate
February
fiery
finally
financial
foreign
foremost
foresee
foreword
    (a preface)
forfeit
forward
forty
fourth
    (number four)
forth
frantically
fraternities
friend
fulfill
fulfillment

gaiety
gauge
genealogy
generally
genuine
government
grammar

grief
grievous
guarantee
guard
guidance

harass
height
heroes
hoping
humorous
hurriedly
hurrying
hygiene
hypocrisy

illiterate
illogical
imaginary
imitation
immediately
incidentally
incredible
indefinite
independence
independent
indispensable
infinite
influential
inoculate
intelligence
intelligent
intentionally
interest
interpret
interrupt
irrelevant
irresistible
irritable
island
its (possessive)
it's (it is, it has)

jealousy
judgment

khaki
knowledge

laboratory
led (past tense
    of *lead*)
library

COMMONLY MISSPELLED WORDS (continued)

license
lightning
literature
loneliness
loose (adjective)
lose (verb)
losing
lying

magazine
maintenance
marriage
mathematics
medicine
miniature
mischievous
misspell
misstep
muscle
mysterious

necessary
neither
nickel
niece
ninety
ninth
noticeable
notorious
nuclear
nucleus
numerous

obstacle
occasion
occasionally
occur
occurred
occurrence
occurring
official
omission
omit
omitted
opinion
opportunity
originally
outrageous
overrun

paid
pamphlet

panicky
parallel
particularly
pastime
peaceable
perceive
perform
performance
perhaps
permanent
permissible
persistence
personnel
persuade
physical
picnic
playwright
possession
possibly
practically
precede
predominant
preferred
prejudice
preparation
prevalent
primitive
principal (adj.,
    main; n., head
    of a school)
principle (a rule
    or standard)
privilege
probably
procedure
proceed
professor
prominent
pronounce
pronunciation
propeller
psychology
psychological
pursue

quantity
quarantine
questionnaire
quiet
quizzes

realize
rebelled
recede
receipt
receive
received
receiving
recommend
recipe
reference
referring
regrettable
relevance
relief
relieve
religious
remembrance
reminisce
reminiscence
renown
repetition
replenish
representative
resistance
restaurant
review
rhythm
rhythmic
ridiculous
roommate

sacrifice
sacrilegious
safety
scarcely
scarcity
schedule
secretary
seize
separate
sergeant
shining
siege
similar
sincerely
sophomore
source
specifically
specimen
sponsor

stationary (in one
    place)
stationery (writing
    material)
strategy
strength
strenuous
stretch
studying
succeed
successful
suddenness
superintendent
supersede
suppress
surprise
suspicious
synonymous

technical
technique
temperature
tendency
therefore
thorough
thoroughbred
though
thought
throughout
tragedy
traveler
traveling
transferred
truly
twelfth
tyranny

unanimous
undoubtedly
unnecessary
unnoticed
until
useful
usually

vacancy
vacuum
valuable
vengeance
vicious
view

(continued)

COMMONLY MISSPELLED WORDS (*continued*)

villain	weird	whose (possessive	women
warrant	whether	of *who*)	writing
weather	wholly	withhold	yacht
Wednesday	who's (who is)	woman	

A Glossary
of Troublemakers

Usage refers to the way in which writers customarily use certain words and phrases. It includes matters of accepted practice or convention. To incorporate appropriate usage in your writing, you can observe (as dictionary makers carefully do) the practices followed by a majority of admirable writers.

This glossary lists words and phrases whose usage troubles student writers. Not every possible problem is listed — only some that frequently puzzle students. This brief list is meant to help you pinpoint a few sources of difficulty and wipe them out. Look it over; refer to it when you don't remember the preferred usage. It may clear up a few problems for you.

For advice on getting rid of long-winded expressions (*in the field of, in regards to*), see page 378. For advice on spelling, see 37.

a, an   Use *an* only before a word beginning with a vowel sound. "*An* asp can eat *an* egg *an* hour." (Note that some words, such as *hour* and *honest*, open with a vowel sound even though spelled with an *h*.)

above   Using *above* or *below* to refer back or forward in an essay is awkward and may not be accurate. Less awkward alternatives: "the *preceding* argument," "in the *following* discussion," "on the *next* page."

accept, except   *Accept* is a verb meaning "to receive willingly"; *except* is usually a preposition meaning "not including." "This motel *accepts* all children *except* infants under two." Sometimes *except* is a verb, meaning "to exempt." "The rate of $20 per person *excepts* children under twelve."

adverse, averse   *Adverse* means "unfavorable or antagonistic" and is used to modify things, not people. *Averse* means "reluctant or strongly opposed" and is followed by *to*. "Because of the *adverse* winds, the captain is *averse* to setting sail."

advice, advise   *Advice* is a noun, *advise* a verb. When someone *advises* you, you receive *advice*.

affect, effect Most of the time, the verb *affect* means "to act on" or "to influence." "Too much beer can *affect* your speech." *Affect* can also mean "to put on airs." "He *affected* an Oxford accent." *Effect,* a noun, means "a result": "Too much beer has a numbing *effect.*" But *effect* is also a verb, meaning "to bring about." "Beer *effected* his downfall."

aggravate Although in speech people often use *aggravate* to mean "to annoy," in formal writing use *aggravate* to mean "to make worse." "The noise of the jackhammers *aggravated* her headache."

agree to, agree with, agree on *Agree to* means "to consent to"; *agree with*, "to be in accord." "I *agreed to* attend the New Age lecture, but I didn't *agree with* the speaker's views." *Agree on* means "to come to or have an understanding about." "Chuck and I finally *agreed on* a compromise: the children would go to camp, but not overnight."

ain't Don't use *ain't* in writing; it is nonstandard English for *am not, is not (isn't)*, and *are not (aren't)*.

allusion, illusion An *allusion* is a reference to history, literature, music, science, or some other area of knowledge. In the statement "Two by two we hurried aboard Flight 937 as though the waters of the flood lapped at our heels," the writer makes an allusion to the biblical story of Noah's ark. An *illusion* is a misleading appearance ("an optical illusion") or a mistaken assumption. "He labors under the *illusion* that he's Romeo" (to give an example with an allusion in it).

a lot Many people mistakenly write the colloquial expression *a lot* as one word: *alot.* Use *a lot* if you must; but in writing, *much* or *a large amount* is preferable. See also *lots, lots of, a lot of.*

already, all ready *Already* means "by now"; *all ready* means "set to go." "At last our picnic was *all ready*, but *already* it was night."

altogether, all together *Altogether* means "entirely." "He is *altogether* mistaken." *All together* means "in unison" or "assembled." "Now *all together*—heave!" "Inspector Trent gathered the suspects *all together* in the drawing room."

among, between *Between* refers to two persons or things; *among*, to more than two. "Some disagreement *between* the two superpowers was inevitable. Still, there was general harmony *among* the five nations represented at the conference."

amoral, immoral *Amoral* means "neither moral nor immoral" or "not involved with moral distinctions or judgments." "Nature is *amoral*." "Some people think children are *amoral* and should not be held accountable for their actions." *Immoral* means "violating moral principles, morally wrong." "Stealing from the poor is *immoral.*"

amount, number Use *amount* to refer to quantities that cannot be counted or to bulk; use *number* to refer to countable, separate items. "The *number* of people you want to serve determines the *amount* of ice cream you'll need."

an, a See *a, an.*

and/or Usually use either *and* or *or* alone. "Tim *and* Elaine will come to the party." "Tim *or* Elaine will come to the party." If you mean three distinct options, write, "Tim *or* Elaine, *or both*, will come to the party, depending on whether they can find a babysitter."

ante-, anti- The prefix *ante* means "preceding." An *antechamber* is a small room that leads to a larger one; *antebellum* means "before the Civil War." *Anti* most often means "opposing": *antidepressant*. It needs a hyphen in front of *i* (*anti-inflationary*) or in front of a capital letter (*anti-Marxist*).

anxious, eager   Although the meanings of these two words overlap to some extent, in writing reserve *anxious* for situations involving anxiety or worry. *Eager* denotes joyous anticipation. "We are *eager* to see him, but we're *anxious* about his failing health."

anybody, any body   When *anybody* is used as an indefinite pronoun, write it as one word: "*Anybody* in his or her right mind abhors murder." (*Anybody* is singular; therefore it is wrong to say "Anybody in *their* right mind." See 22 for acceptable alternatives.)

   Any body, written as two words, is the adjective *any* modifying the noun *body*. "Name *any body* of water in Australia." "The coroner told his assistant to begin work on *any body* brought in from the crash site."

anyone, any one   *Anyone* is an indefinite pronoun written as one word. "Does *anyone* want dessert?" The phrase *any one* consists of the pronoun *one* modified by the adjective *any* and is used to single out something in a group: "Pick *any one* of the pies—they're all good."

anyplace   *Anyplace* is colloquial for *anywhere* and should not be used in formal writing.

anyways, anywheres   These are nonstandard forms of *anyway* and *anywhere* and should not be used in writing.

apt   Usually, *apt* means "likely." "That film is *apt* to bore you." "Jack's big feet make him *apt* to trip." *Apt* can also mean "fitting" and "quick to learn": "an apt nickname," "an apt student of French." See also *liable, likely*.

as   Sometimes using the subordinating conjunction *as* can make a sentence ambiguous. "*As* we were climbing the mountain, we put on heavy sweaters." Does *as* here mean "because" or "while"? Whenever using *as* would be confusing, use a more specific term instead, such as *because* or *while*.

as, like   Use *as, as if,* or *as though* rather than *like* to introduce clauses of comparison. "Dan's compositions are tuneful, *as* [not *like*] music ought to be." "Jeffrey behaves *as if* [not *like*] he were ill."

   Like, because it is a preposition, can introduce a phrase but not a clause. "My brother looks *like* me." "Henrietta runs *like* a duck."

as to   Usually this expression sounds stilted. Use *about* instead. "He complained *about* [not *as to*] the cockroaches."

at   See *where . . . at, where . . . to*.

averse   See *adverse*.

bad, badly   *Bad* is an adjective; *badly* is an adverb. They are commonly misused after linking verbs (*be, appear, become, grow, seem, prove*) and verbs of the senses (*feel, look, smell, sound, taste*). Following a linking verb, use the adjective form. "I feel *bad* that we missed the plane." "The egg smells *bad*." (See 10a, 10b.) The adverb form is used to modify a verb or an adjective. "They played so *badly* they lost to the last-place team." "It was a *badly* needed victory that saved the cellar-dwellers from elimination."

being as, being that   "*Being as* I was ignorant of the facts, I kept still" is a clumsy way to say "*Because* I was ignorant" or "*Not knowing* the facts."

beside, besides　*Beside* is a preposition meaning "by the side of." "Sheldon enjoyed sitting *beside* the guest of honor." *Besides* is an adverb meaning "in addition." "*Besides*, he has a sense of humor." *Besides* is also a preposition meaning "other than." "Something *besides* shyness caused his embarrassment."

between, among　See *among, between.*

between you and I　The preposition *between* always takes the objective case. "Between *you* and *me* [not *I*], that story about the dog's eating Joe's money sounds suspicious." "Between *us* [not *we*], what's going on between Chris and *her* [not *she*] is unfathomable."

bi-, semi-　These prefixes are often confused. *Bi-* means "two." *Semi-* means "half of." Thus, *semiautomatic* means "partly automatic," and *semiannual* means "happening every half year." *Biaxial* means "having two axes." Although sometimes people also use *bi-* to mean "happening twice in," avoid that use because it can be confusing (for example, it's difficult to know whether the person using *biweekly* means "twice a week" or "every two weeks").

but that, but what　"I don't know *but what* [or *but that*] you're right" is a wordy, imprecise way of saying "Maybe you're right" or "I believe you're right."

can, may　Use *can* to indicate ability. "Jake *can* bench press 650 pounds." *May* involves permission. "*May* I bench press today?" "You *may*, if you *can*."

capital, capitol　A *capital* is a city that is the center of government for a state or country. *Capital* can also mean "wealth." A *capitol* is a building in which legislators meet. "Who knows what the *capital* of Finland is?" "The renovated *capitol* is a popular tourist attraction."

censor, censure　*Censor* as a verb means "to evaluate and remove objectionable material." As a noun, it means "someone who censors." "All mail was *censored* before it left the country." *Censure* as a verb means "to find fault with, criticize." As a noun, it means "disapproval." "The governor's extreme actions were met with public *censure.*"

center around　Say "Class discussion *centered on* [or *revolved around*] her paper." In this sense, the verb *center* means "to have one main concern"—the way a circle has a central point. (Thus, to say a discussion centers *around* anything is a murky metaphor.)

cite, sight, site　*Cite*, a verb, means "to quote from or refer to." *Sight* as a verb means "to see or glimpse"; as a noun it means "a view, a spectacle." "When the police officer *sighted* my terrier running across the playground, she *cited* the leash laws and told me I'd be fined." *Site*, a noun, means "location." "Standing at the *site* of his childhood home, he wept tears of nostalgia. He was a pitiful *sight.*"

climatic, climactic　*Climatic*, from *climate*, refers to meteorological conditions. Saying "climatic conditions," however, is wordy—you can usually substitute "the climate": "*Climatic* conditions are [or "The *climate* is"] changing because of the ozone hole." *Climactic*, from *climax*, refers to the culmination of a progression of events. "In the *climactic* scene the hero drives his car off the pier."

compare, contrast　*Compare* has two main meanings. The first, "to liken or represent as similar" is followed by *to.* "She *compared* her room *to* a jail cell." "He *compared* me *to* a summer's day." In its second meaning, *compare* means "to analyze for similarities and differences" and is generally followed by *with.* "The speaker *compared* the American educational system *with* the Japanese system."

Contrast also has two main meanings. As a transitive verb, taking an object, it means "to compare or analyze to emphasize differences" and is generally followed by *with*. "The speaker *contrasted* the social emphasis of the Japanese primary grades *with* the academic emphasis of ours." As an intransitive verb, *contrast* means "to exhibit differences when compared." "The matted tangle of Sidney's fur *contrasted* sharply *with* its usual healthy sleekness."

complement, compliment   *Compliment* is a verb meaning "to praise" or a noun meaning "praise." "The professor *complimented* Sarah on her perceptiveness." *Complement* is a verb meaning "to complete or reinforce." "Jennifer's experiences as a practice teacher *complemented* what she learned in her education class."

continual, continuous   *Continual* means "often repeated." "Mike was in *continual* conflict with his neighbors." *Continuous* means "uninterrupted." "Lisa's *continuous* chatter made it impossible for Debbie to concentrate on her reading."

could care less   This is nonstandard English for *couldn't care less* and should not be used in writing. "The cat *couldn't* [not *could*] *care less* about which brand of cat food you buy."

could of   *Could of* is colloquial for *could have* and should not be used in writing.

couple of   Write "a *couple of* drinks" when you mean two. For more than two, say "a *few* [or *several*] drinks."

criteria, criterion   *Criteria* is the plural of *criterion*, which means "a standard or requirement on which a judgment or decision is based." "The main *criteria* for this job are attention to detail and good typing skills."

data   *Data* is a plural noun. Write "The data *are*" and "*these* data." The singular form of *data* is *datum* — rarely used because it sounds musty. Instead, use *fact*, *figure*, or *statistic*.

different from, different than   *Different from* is usually the correct form to use. "How is good poetry *different from* prose?" Use *different than* when a whole clause follows. "Violin lessons with Mr. James were *different than* I had imagined."

disinterested, uninterested   *Disinterested* means "impartial, fair, objective." "The defendant hoped for a *disinterested* judge." *Uninterested* means "indifferent." Suzanne was *uninterested* in world news.

don't, doesn't   *Don't* is the contraction for *do not*, and *doesn't* is the contraction for *does not*. "They *don't* want to get dressed up for the ceremony." "*Don't* feed the grizzly bears!" "The cat *doesn't* [not *don't*] like to be combed."

due to   *Due* is an adjective and must modify a noun or pronoun; it can't modify a verb. Begin a sentence with *due to* and you invite trouble: "*Due to rain*, the game was postponed." Write instead, "*Because of* rain." *Due to* works after the verb *be*. "His fall was *due to* a banana peel." There, *due* modifies the noun *fall*.

due to the fact that   A windy expression for *because*.

eager, anxious   See *anxious, eager*.

effect, affect   See *affect, effect*.

either   Use *either* when referring to one of two things. "Both internships sound great; I'd be happy with *either*." When referring to one of three or more things, use *any one* or *any*. "*Any one* of our four trained counselors will be able to help you."

elicit, illicit   *Elicit*, a verb, means "to bring or draw out." *Illicit*, an adjective, means "unlawful" or "not permissible." "Try as he might, Gus could not *elicit* details from Bob about his *illicit* nighttime activities."

emigrant, immigrant   An *emigrant* has left a country or region; an *immigrant* has moved into a country or region. The verb forms reflect the same distinction: *emigrate from*, *immigrate to*. "Even in the United States, *immigrants* often hold the lowest-paying positions." "Anders *emigrated* from Norway."

eminent, imminent   *Eminent* means "distinguished or outstanding"; *imminent* means "about to happen." "The *eminent* novelists shyly announced their *imminent* marriage."

enormity, enormousness, enormous   *Enormity* means "monstrous evil"; *enormousness* means "vastness or immensity"; and *enormous* means "vast or huge." "The *enormity* of the convicted woman's crimes baffled her acquaintances." "The *enormousness* of the lake impressed them."

enthuse   Good writers shun this verb. Instead of "The salesman *enthused* about the product," write, "The salesman *was enthusiastic* about the product."

et cetera, etc.   Replace *et cetera* (or its abbreviation, *etc.*) with exact words, and you will sharpen your writing. Even translating the Latin expression into English is an improvement: *and other things.* Rather than announcing an athletic meet to feature "high-jumping, shot-putting, *etc.*," you could say, "high-jumping, shot-putting, and other field events."

everybody, every body   When used as an indefinite pronoun, *everybody* is one word. "Why is *everybody* on the boys' team waving his arms?" Keep in mind that *everybody* is singular. It is a mistake to write, "Why is *everybody* waving *their* arms?" (See 7b and 9d for acceptable alternatives.) *Every body* written as two words refers to separate, individual bodies. "After the massacre, they buried *every body* in *its* [not *their*] own grave." "From the air, Kate could see *every body* of water in the country."

everyone, every one   Used as an indefinite pronoun, *everyone* is one word. "*Everyone* has *his or her* own ideas." Remember that *everyone* is singular. Therefore it is wrong to write, "*Everyone* has *their* own ideas." (See 7b and 9d for acceptable alternatives.) *Every one* written as two words refers to individual, distinct items. "I studied *every one* of the assigned exercises."

except, accept   See *accept, except.*

expect   In writing, avoid the informal use of *expect* to mean "suppose, assume, or think." "I *suppose* [not *expect*] you've heard that half the class flunked."

fact that   This is an expression that, nearly always, you can do without. "*The fact that* he was puny went unnoticed" is wordy; write, "That [not *The fact that*] he was puny went unnoticed." "Because [not *Because of the fact that*] it snowed, the game was canceled."

famous, infamous   Do something that attracts wide notice and you become celebrated, or *famous*: "Marcia dreamed of growing up to be a *famous* inventor." But if your deeds are detestable, you may instead become notorious, or *infamous,* like Bluebeard, the *infamous* wife killer.

farther, further   In your writing, use *farther* to refer to literal distance. "Chicago is *farther* from Nome than from New York." When you wish to denote additional degree, time, or quantity, use *further*: "Sally's idea requires *further* discussion."

fewer, less   *Less* refers to general quantity or bulk; *fewer*, to separate, countable items. "Eat *less* pizza." "Salad has *fewer* calories."

field   In a statement such as "He took courses *in the field of* economics," leave out *the field of* and save words.

firstly   The recommended usage is *first* (and *second*, not *secondly*; *third* not *thirdly*; and so on).

flaunt, flout   To *flaunt* is to show off. "She *flaunted* her wealth by buying much more than she needed." To *flout* is to defy. "George *flouted* the law by refusing to register for the draft."

former, latter   *Former* means "first of two"; *latter*, "second of two." They are an acceptable but heavy-handed pair, best done without. Too often, they oblige your reader to backtrack. Nine times out of ten, your writing will be clearer if you simply name again the persons or things you mean. Instead of writing, "The *former* great artist is the master of the flowing line, while the *latter* is the master of color," write, "Picasso is the master of the flowing line, while Matisse is the master of color."

further, farther   See *farther, further*.

get, got   *Get* has many meanings, especially in slang and colloquial use. Some, such as the following, are not appropriate in formal writing:
    "To start, begin": "Let's start [not *get*] painting."
    "To stir the emotions": "His frequent interruptions finally started annoying [not *getting to*] me." "The puppies' pathetic whimpers really upset [not *got to*] her."
    "To harm, punish, or take revenge on": "She's going to take revenge on [not *get*] him." Or better, be even more specific about what you mean. "She's going to spread rumors about him to ruin his reputation."

good, well   To modify a verb, use the adverb *well*, not the adjective *good*. "Jan dives *well* [not *good*]." Linking verbs (*be, appear, become, grow, seem, prove*) and verbs of the senses (such as *feel, look, smell, sound, taste*) call for the adjective *good*. "The paint job looks *good*." *Well* is an adjective used only to refer to health. "She looks *well*" means that she seems to be in good health. "She looks *good*" means that her appearance is attractive. (See 10b, 10c.)

great deal of   This informal expression means "much" and refers to things that come in bulk and can't be counted. "She had a *great deal of* training in psychology." Don't use it to mean "a large number." "*Many* people [or *a crowd*; not *a great deal of people*] jammed the stadium.

hanged, hung   Both words are the past tense of the verb *hang*. *Hanged* refers to an execution. "The murderer was *hanged* at dawn." For all other situations, use *hung*. "Jane *hung* her wash on the clothesline to dry."

have got to   In formal writing, avoid using the phrase *have got to* to mean "have to" or "must." "I *must* [not *have got to*] phone them right away."

he, she, he or she   Using *he* as a matter of course to refer to a person is considered sexist; so is using *she* with reference to traditionally female occupations or pastimes. However, peppering your writing with the phrase *he or she* can seem wordy and awkward. For alternatives, see 22.

herself   See *-self, -selves*.

himself   See *-self, selves*.

hopefully   *Hopefully* means "with hope." "The children turned *hopefully* toward the door, expecting Santa Claus." In writing, avoid *hopefully* when you mean "it is to be hoped" or "let us hope." "*I hope* [not *Hopefully*] the posse will arrive soon."

if, whether   Use *if* for conditional phrases. "*If* wishes were horses, beggars would ride." "*If* Dwayne calls while I'm out, please take a message." Use *whether* in indirect questions and to introduce alternatives. "Father asked me *whether* I was planning to sleep all morning." "I'm so confused I don't know *whether* it's day or night."

illicit   See *elicit, illicit*.

illusion, allusion   See *allusion, illusion*.

imminent   See *eminent, imminent*.

immoral   See *amoral, immoral*.

imply, infer   *Imply* means "to suggest"; *infer* means "to draw a conclusion." "Maria *implied* that she was too busy to see Tom. As their conversation proceeded, Tom *inferred* that Maria had lost interest in him."

in, into   *In* refers to a location or condition; *into* refers to the direction of movement or change. "The hero burst *into* the room and found the heroine *in* another man's arms." "Hiroko decided to go *into* banking."

individual   Don't use *individual* for *person*. "What kind of *person* [not *individual*] would do that?" Save the word to mean "one" as opposed to "many": "an *individual* thinker in a conforming crowd."

infer, imply   See *imply, infer*.

ingenious, ingenuous   *Ingenious* means "clever." "The *ingenious* inventor caught the mouse unharmed." *Ingenuous* has two related meanings: "naive, unsophisticated" and "frank, candid." "Little Lord Fauntleroy's *ingenuous* remarks touched even his ill-tempered grandfather."

in regards to   Write *in regard to, regarding,* or *about*.

inside of, outside of   As prepositions, *inside* and *outside* do not require *of*. "The students were more interested in what was going on *outside* [not *outside of*] the building than in what was happening *inside* [not *inside of*] the classroom." Do not use *inside of* to refer colloquially to time or *outside of* to mean "except." "I'll finish the assignment *within* [not *inside of*] two hours." "He told no one *except* [not *outside of*] a few friends."

irregardless   *Irregardless* is a double negative. Use *regardless*.

is because   See *reason is because*.

is when, is where   Using these expressions results in errors in predication. "Obesity *is when* a person is greatly overweight." "Biology *is where* students dissect frogs." *When* refers to a point in time, but *obesity* is not a point in time; *where* refers to a place, but *biology* is not a place. Write instead, "Obesity is the condition of extreme overweight." "Biology is a laboratory course in which students dissect frogs." (See faulty predication, 16.)

its, it's   *Its* is a possessive pronoun, never in need of an apostrophe. *It's* is a contraction for *it is*. "Every new experience has *its* bad moments. Still, *it's* exciting to explore the unknown."

it's me, it is I   Although *it's me* is widely used in speech, don't use it in formal writing. Write "It is *I*," which is grammatically correct. The same applies to other personal pronouns. "It was *he* [not *him*] who started the mutiny." (See pronoun case, 7.)

kind of, sort of, type of   When you use *kind, sort,* or *type* — singular words — make sure that the sentence construction is singular. "That *type* of show *offends* me." "Those *types* of shows *offend* me." In speech, *kind of* and *sort of* are used as qualifiers. "He is *sort of* fat." Avoid them in writing. "He is *rather* [or *somewhat* or *slightly*; not *sort of*] fat."

latter, former See *former, latter.*

lay, lie The verb *lay*, meaning "to put or place," takes an object. *Lie*, meaning "to rest or recline," does not. Their principal parts are *lay, laid, laid,* and *lie, lay, lain.* "*Lay* that pistol down." "*Lie* on the bed until your headache goes away." (See 5f.)

leave, let *Leave* means "to go away." *Let* means "to permit." "I'll *leave* on a jet plane." "*Let* the child run—she needs the exercise."

lend, loan Although *lend* and *loan* are used interchangeably in speech, avoid using *loan* as a verb. "Can you *lend* (not *loan*) me some money?"

less, fewer See *fewer, less.*

let, leave See *leave, let.*

liable, likely Use *likely* to mean "plausible" or "having the potential." "Jake is *likely* [not *liable*] to win." Save *liable* for "legally obligated" or "susceptible." "A stunt man is *liable* to injury."

lie, lay See *lay, lie.*

like, as See *as, like.*

likely, liable See *liable, likely.*

literally Don't sling *literally* around for emphasis. It means "strictly according to the meaning of a word (or words)"; if you are speaking figuratively, it will wreck your credibility. "Professor Gray *literally* flew down the hall to the chairman's office" means that Gray traveled on wings. "Rick was *literally* stoned out of his mind" means that someone drove Rick insane by pelting him with mineral specimens. Save *literally* to mean that, by everything holy, you're reporting a fact. "Chemical wastes travel on the winds, and it *literally* rains poison."

loan, lend See *lend, loan.*

loath, loathe *Loath* is an adjective meaning "reluctant." *Loathe* is a verb meaning "to detest." "We were *loath* to say good-bye." "We *loathed* our impending separation."

loose, lose *Loose,* an adjective, most commonly means "not fastened" or "poorly fastened." *Lose,* a verb, means "misplace" or "not win." "I have to be careful not to *lose* this button—it's so *loose.*"

lots, lots of, a lot of Use these expressions only in informal speech. In formal writing, say *many* or *much.* See also *a lot.*

mankind This term is considered sexist by many people. Use *humanity, humankind, the human race,* or *people* instead.

may, can See *can, may.*

media, medium *Media* is the plural of *medium* and most commonly refers to the various forms of public communication. "Some argue that of all the *media,* television is the worst for children because it leaves so little to the imagination."

might of *Might of* is colloquial for *might have* and should not be used in writing.

most Do not use *most* when you mean "almost" or "nearly." "*Almost* [not *Most*] all of the students felt that Professor Chartrand should have received tenure."

must of   *Must of* is colloquial for *must have* and should not be used in writing.

myself   See *-self, -selves.*

not all that   *Not all that* is colloquial for *not very*; do not use it in formal writing. "The movie was *not very* [not *not all that*] exciting."

number, amount   See *amount, number.*

of   See *could of, might of, must of, should of.*

off of   *Of* is unnecessary with *off.* Use *off* alone, or use *from*: "Cartoon heroes are forever falling *off* [or *from*] cliffs."

O.K., o.k., okay   In formal writing, do not use any of these expressions. *All right* and *I agree* are possible substitutes.

one   Like a balloon, *one,* meaning "a person," tends to inflate. One *one* can lead to another. "When *one* is in college, *one* learns to make up *one's* mind for *oneself.*" Realizing that the sentence sounds pompous, the writer might be tempted to switch to the more familiar-sounding *you*: "When *one* is in college, *you* learn . . . ," but the result is inconsistency. Substituting *a person* often leads to sexist constructions (*he, himself*) or awkward alternatives (*he or she, himself or herself*). Whenever possible, substitute *people* or a more specific plural noun. "When *students* are in college, *they* learn to make up their minds for *themselves.*" Also see *you.*

ourselves   See *-self, -selves.*

outside of, inside of   See *inside of, outside of.*

percent, per cent, percentage   When you specify a number, write *percent* (also written *per cent*). "Eight *percent* of the listeners responded to the offer." The only time to use *percentage,* meaning "part," is with an adjective, when you mention no number: "A high *percentage* [or *a large percentage*] of listeners responded." *A large number* or *a large proportion* sounds better yet, and we urge you to strike *percentage* from your vocabulary.

per se   Translate this Latin expression into English and you'll sound less stiff. Write "Getting a good education is important *in itself* [or *by itself*; not *per se*]."

phenomenon, phenomena   *Phenomena* is plural for *phenomenon,* which means "an observable fact or occurrence." "I've read about many mysterious supernatural *phenomena.*" "Clairvoyance is the strangest *phenomenon* of all."

pore over, pour over   *Pore over* a book and you study it intently; *pour over* a book and you get it wet.

precede, proceed   *Precede* means "to go before or ahead of"; *proceed* means "to go forward." "The fire drill *proceeded* smoothly; the children *preceded* the teachers into the safety of the yard."

principal, principle   *Principal* means "chief," whether used as an adjective or as a noun. "Marijuana is the *principal* cash crop of Colombia." "Our high school *principal* frowns on pot." Referring to money, *principal* means "capital." "Investors in marijuana earn as much as 850 percent interest on their *principal.*" *Principle,* a noun, means *rule* or *standard.* "Let's apply the *principle* of equality in hiring." "No marijuana for her: she's a woman of strict *principles.*"

proved, proven   Although both forms can be used as past participles, *proved* is recommended. Use *proven* as an adjective. "They had *proved* their skill in match after match." "Try this *proven* cough remedy: lemon, honey, whiskey, and hot water blended into a toddy."

quote, quotation   *Quote* is a verb meaning "to cite, to use the words of." *Quotation* is a noun meaning "something that is quoted." "The *quotation* [not *quote*] next to her yearbook picture fits her perfectly."

raise, rise   *Raise,* meaning "to cause to move upward," is a transitive verb and takes an object. *Rise,* meaning "to move up (on its own)" is intransitive and does not take an object: "I *rose* from my seat and *raised* my arm, but the instructor still didn't see me."

rarely ever   *Rarely* by itself is strong enough. "George *rarely* [not *rarely ever*] eats dinner with his family."

real, really   *Real* is an adjective, *really* an adverb. Do not use *real* to modify a verb or another adjective, and avoid overusing either word. "*The Ambassadors* is a *really* [not *real*] fine novel." Even better: "*The Ambassadors* is a fine novel."

reason is because, reason . . . is   *Reason . . . is* requires a clause beginning with *that.* Using *because* is nonstandard. "The *reason* I can't come *is that* [not *is because*] I have the flu." But *reason . . . is* is a wordy construction that can usually be rephrased more succinctly. It is simpler and more direct to write, "I can't come because I have the flu."

respectfully, respectively   *Respectfully* means "with respect, showing respect." *Respectively* means "each in turn" or "in the order given." "They stopped talking and stood *respectfully* as the prime minister walked by." "Joan, Michael, and Alfonso majored in history, sociology, and economics, *respectively.*"

rise   See *raise, rise.*

seldom ever   Let *seldom* stand by itself. "Martha *seldom* [not *seldom ever*] attends church."

-self, -selves   Don't use a pronoun ending in *-self* or *-selves* in place of *her, him, me, them, us,* or *you.* "Nobody volunteered but Jim and *me* [not *myself*]." Use the *-self* pronouns to refer back to a noun or another pronoun and to lend emphasis. "*We* did it *ourselves.*" "Sarah *herself* is a noted musician." (See 7b.)

semi-   See *bi-, semi-.*

sensual, sensuous   Both words have to do with stimulation of the senses, but *sensual* has more blatantly carnal overtones. "Gluttony and lust were the *sensual* millionaire's favorite sins." *Sensuous* pleasures are more aesthetic. "The *sensuous* beauty of the music stirred his soul."

set, sit   *Set,* meaning "to put or place," is a transitive verb and takes an object. *Sit,* meaning "to be seated," is intransitive and does not take an object. "At the security point we were asked to *set* our jewelry and metal objects on the counter and *sit* down." (See also 5f.)

shall, will; should, would   The helping verb *shall* formerly was used with first-person pronouns. It is still used to express determination ("We *shall* overcome"; "They *shall* not give in") or to ask consent ("*Shall* I let the cat out?"). Otherwise *will* is commonly used with all three persons. "I *will* enter medical school in the fall." "They *will* accept the bid if the terms are clear." *Should* is a helping verb that expresses obligation; *would,* a helping verb that expresses a hypothetical condition. "I *should* wash the dishes before I watch TV." "He *would* learn to speak English if you *would* give him a chance."

should of   *Should of* is colloquial for *should have* and should not be used in writing.

sight   See *cite, sight, site.*

since   Sometimes using *since* can make a sentence ambiguous. "*Since* the babysitter left, the children have been watching television." Does *since* here mean "because" or "from the time that"? If using *since* might be confusing to your readers, use an unambiguous term (*because, ever since*).

sit   See *set, sit.*

site   See *cite, sight, site.*

sort of   See *kind of, sort of, type of.*

stationary, stationery   *Stationary,* an adjective, means "fixed, unmoving." "The fireplace remained *stationary* though the wind blew down the house." *Stationery* is paper for letter writing. To spell it right, remember that *letter* also contains *-er.*

suppose to   Write *supposed to.* "He was *supposed to* appear for dinner at eight o'clock."

sure   *Sure* is an adjective, *surely* an adverb. Do not use *sure* to modify a verb or another adjective. If by *sure* you mean "certainly," write *certainly* or *surely* instead. "He *surely* [not *sure*] is crazy about cars."

than, then   *Than* is a conjunction used in comparisons; *then* is an adverb indicating time. "Marlene is brainier *than* her sister." "First crack six eggs; *then* beat them."

that, which   Which pronoun should open a clause—*that* or *which*? If the clause adds to its sentence an idea that, however interesting, could be left out, then the clause is nonrestrictive and should begin with *which* and be separated from the rest of the sentence with commas. "The vampire, *which* had been hovering nearby, leaped for Sarah's throat."

If the clause is essential to your meaning, it is restrictive and should begin with *that* and should not have commas around it. "The vampire *that* Mel brought from Transylvania leaped for Sarah's throat." The clause indicates not just any old vampire but one in particular.

Don't use *which* to refer vaguely to an entire clause. Instead of "Jack was an expert drummer in high school, *which* won him a college scholarship," write: "Jack's skill as a drummer won him. . . ." (See 25e.)

themselves   See *-self, -selves.*

then, than   See *than, then.*

there, their, they're   *There* is an adverb indicating place. *Their* is a possessive pronoun. *They're* is a contraction of *they are.* "After playing tennis *there* for three hours, Lamont and Laura went to change *their* clothes because *they're* going out to dinner."

to, too, two   *To* is a preposition. *Too* is an adverb meaning "also" or "in excess." *Two* is a number. "Janet wanted to go *too,* but she feared she was still *too* sick to travel in the car for *two* days. Instead, she went *to* bed."

toward, towards   *Toward* is preferred in the United States, *towards* in Britain.

try and   Use *try to.* "I'll *try to* [not *try and*] attend the opening performance of your play."

type of   See *kind of, sort of, type of.*

uninterested, disinterested   See *disinterested, uninterested.*

unique   Nothing can be *more unique, less unique, really unique, very unique,* or *somewhat unique. Unique* means "one of a kind."

use to   Write *used to.* "Jeffrey *used to* have a beard, but now he is clean-shaven."

wait for, wait on   Write *wait for* when you mean "await." *Wait on* means "to serve." "While *waiting for* his friends, George decided to *wait on* one more customer."

well, good   See *good, well.*

where at, where to   The colloquial use of *at* or *to* after *where* is redundant. Write "*Where* were you?" not "Where were you *at*?" "I know *where* she was rushing [not *rushing to*]."

where, that   Although speakers sometimes use *where* instead of *that,* you should not do so in writing. "I heard on the news *that* [not *where*] it got hot enough to fry eggs on car hoods."

whether   See *if, whether.*

which, that   See *that, which.*

who, which, that, whose   *Who* refers to people, *which* to things and ideas. "Was it Pogo *who* said, 'We have met the enemy and he is us'?" "The blouse, *which* was lime green embroidered with silver, accented her dark skin and eyes."

     That refers to things but can also be used for a class of people. "The team *that* puts in the most overtime will get a bonus."

     Using *of which* can be cumbersome; use *whose* even to refer to things. "The mountain, *whose* snowy peaks were famous world over, was covered in a dismal fog." See also *that, which.*

who, whom   *Who* is used as a subject, *whom* as an object. In "*Whom* do I see?" *Whom* is the object of *see.* In "*Who* goes there?" *Who* is the subject of "goes." (See also 7b.)

who's, whose   *Who's* is a contraction for *who is* or *who has.* "*Who's* going with Phil?" *Whose* is a possessive pronoun. "Bill is a conservative politician *whose* ideas are unlikely to change."

will, shall   See *shall, will.*

would, should   See *should, would.*

would of   *Would of* is colloquial for *would have* and should not be used in writing.

you   *You,* meaning "a person," occurs often in conversation. "When you go to college you have to work hard." In writing, use *one* or a specific noun. "When *students* go to college *they* have to work hard." But see also *one.*

your, you're   *Your* is a possessive pronoun; *you're* is the contraction for *you are.* "*You're* lying! It was *your* handwriting on the envelope."

yourself, yourselves   See *-self, -selves.*

Answers for Lettered Exercises

EXERCISE 1–1, page H–7
a. Proper noun: Lois; common nouns: paintings, husband; possessive pronoun: her; **b.** Proper noun: Lois; common nouns: price, profit; intensive pronoun: herself; **c.** Common nouns: bulk, money, supplies; relative pronoun: that; personal pronoun: she; possessive pronoun: her; **d.** Proper nouns: Lewis, Corvette; possessive pronoun: his; indefinite pronoun: someone; relative pronoun: who; personal pronoun: it; **e.** Personal pronouns: I, I, you; reflexive pronoun: myself; indefinite pronoun: no one

EXERCISE 1–2, page H–9
a. Transitive: accompany; intransitive: goes; helping: will; **b.** Transitive: dislikes; linking: are; **c.** Transitive: give, symbolize; **d.** Transitive: spent; helping: should have; **e.** Transitive: reads; intransitive: dreams

EXERCISE 1–3, page H–10
a. Adjectives: mild, environmental; indefinite articles: a, a; definite article: the; adverb: greatly, modifying verb fear; **b.** Adjectives: elderly, mobile; adverb: incredibly, modifying adjective mobile; **c.** Adjectives: beautiful, wise; definite article: The; adverbs: wildly, modifying adjective beautiful; often, modifying verb made; foolishly, modifying verb act; **d.** Adjective: short; indefinite article: a; adverbs: very, modifying adjective short; fully, modifying verb lived; **e.** Adjectives: delighted, lovely; indefinite article: a; adverb: absolutely, modifying adjective delighted

EXERCISE 1–4, page H–11
a. To me, preposition to; adverb phrase; **b.** On the table, preposition on; adjective phrase; **c.** Before the meeting, preposition before; adverb phrase; **d.** According to the rules, preposition according to; adverb phrase; **e.** But a few troublemakers, preposition but; adjective phrase

EXERCISE 1–5, page H–14
a. Conjunction: when (subordinating); interjection: Oh, well; **b.** Conjunctions: and (coordinating), neither . . . nor (correlative); **c.** Conjunctions: and (coordinating), both . . . and (correlative); **d.** Interjection: Holy mackerel; **e.** Conjunctions: Although (subordinating), and (coordinating)

EXERCISE 1–6, page H–14
A. a. adverb; **b.** adjective; **c.** subordinating conjunction; **d.** coordinating conjunction; **e.** adverb **B. a.** noun; **b.** adverb; **c.** subordinating conjunction; **d.** pronoun; **e.** adjective (article)

EXERCISE 2–1, page H–17
a. Simple subject: animals; complete subject: Most wild animals; simple predicate: do make; complete predicate: do not make good pets; **b.** Simple subject: War; complete subject: War, that curse of the human race; simple predicate: has plagued; complete predicate: has plagued civilizations throughout history; **c.** Simple subject: composer; complete subject: the composer Beethoven; simple predicate: continued;

complete predicate: Even after he became deaf . . . continued to write music; **d.** Simple subject: cup; complete subject: One cup of coffee in the morning; simple predicate: keeps; complete predicate: keeps me awake all day; **e.** Simple subject: mother; complete subject: John Updike's mother, who had been a writer herself; simple predicate: encouraged; complete predicate: always encouraged her son's literary aspirations

EXERCISE 2–2, page H–20

a. Subject complement: an educated person; direct object: such a story; **b.** Direct object: his needs; indirect object: Judith; **c.** Subject complement: an evasive man; **d.** Subject complement: an interesting art; direct object: expensive equipment; **e.** Direct object: Chicago; object complement: the windy city

EXERCISE 3–1, page H–25

a. Identifying parts of speech: gerund phrase, noun; **b.** in the beret: prepositional phrase, adjective; **c.** its silver hood ornament gleaming in the morning sun: absolute phrase; in the morning sun: prepositional phrase, adverb; **d.** through the grapevine: prepositional phrase, adverb; **e.** gone with the wind: participial phrase, adjective

EXERCISE 3–2, page H–28

a. wherever he lived at the moment: noun clause; **b.** While we were still arguing about its value: adverb clause; **c.** that I took to the cleaner's: adjective clause; **d.** that she may fail the course: adverb clause; **e.** whether he should invite James: noun clause

EXERCISE 4–1, page H–30

a. Simple sentence. Compound subject: Not only women but also men and children; verb: benefit; **b.** Complex sentence. Prepositional phrase: Even in a life-or-death emergency; main clause: I know; subordinate clause: [that] you can count on Marlene; **c.** Compound-complex sentence. Main clauses: Biology is interesting; I prefer botany; subordinate clause: as it is taught by Professor Haines; **d.** Simple sentence. Subject: you; verb: prefer; direct object: bacon and eggs or cereal and toast; **e.** Compound-complex sentence. Main clauses: Most people believe; recent studies have shown; subordinate clauses: that poverty begets poverty; that they achieve economic independence; when children from welfare families reach adulthood

EXERCISE 5–1, page H–38

a. When Joe's mother *caught* him *lying* around the house during school hours, she *threw* him out.

b. Correct
c. He *laid* his cards triumphantly on the table but soon found that he was not *sitting* in a lucky chair after all.
d. Wendy knew how much Roger had *drunk,* but she *went* with him anyway.
e. I have *lain* awake, tossing and turning, every night since exams *began.*

EXERCISE 5–2, page H–46

a. broke: simple past; was skiing: past progressive; **b.** sleeps: simple present; is yawning: present progressive; **c.** had seen: past perfect; run: simple present; **d.** represents: simple present; will have performed: future perfect; split: simple past; **e.** finish: simple present; will attend: simple future

EXERCISE 5–3, page H–48

Suggested revisions:

a. I recently read the *World Book Encyclopedia*'s article about opossums.
b. The rat and the opossum resemble each other.
c. The opossum catches food at night.
d. Like all marsupials, opossum mothers carry their young in a stomach pouch.
e. Passive is acceptable.

EXERCISE 5–4, page H–50

a. When Janet cooks, she insists that Tom *wash* the dishes. (Incorrect washes, indicative; correct wash, subjunctive)
b. If Pete *wants* me to help him, he can call and ask me himself. (Incorrect *want*, subjunctive; correct *wants*, indicative)
c. If I *were* a licensed plumber, I could install the washing machine myself. (Incorrect *was*, indicative; correct *were*, subjunctive)
d. The IRS recommends that tax forms *be* filled out as soon as they become available. (Incorrect *are*, indicative; correct *be*, subjunctive)
e. If that man *does* not go away, call the police. (Incorrect *do*, subjunctive; correct *does*, indicative)

EXERCISE 6–1, page H–56

a. Our foreign policy in Cuba, Nicaragua, El Salvador, and Panama *has* not been as successful as most Americans had hoped.
b. Correct
c. I read about a couple who *are* offering to trade their baby for a brand-new Chevrolet.
d. A shave, a haircut, and a new suit *have* turned Bill into a different person.
e. Neither the fruit nor the vegetables *are* fresh.

EXERCISE 7–1, page H–60

a. She can run faster than *I*. (*I* is the subject of the implied verb *can run*.)
b. Mrs. Van Dumont awarded the prize to Mona and *me*. (*Me* is an object of the preposition *to*.)
c. Jud laughed at both of us—*her* and *me*. (*Her* and *me* are appositives to *us*, the object of the preposition.)
d. Were you referring to *us*? (*Us* is the object of the preposition *to*.)
e. Jerry, the pizza chef, and *I* regard you and *her* as the very women *whom* we wish to get acquainted with. (*I* is a subject of the verb *regard*; *her* is a direct object of the verb *regard*; *whom* is the object of the preposition *with*.)

EXERCISE 8–1, page H–64

Suggested revisions:

a. Every American will own a computer when it costs the same as a television set.
b. After meeting with her newspaper's editor, Sarah reported that she wasn't sure if the editor agreed with her position on freedom of speech.
c. Never having had any epileptic seizures, I cannot speak of them with firsthand knowledge.
d. Marsha didn't know Russian and had allergies, but these problems didn't stop her from summering on a Ukrainian wheat farm.
e. Swaying gently in his parachute, floating lazily to earth, Edgar felt pure joy. The jump had been the finest thing he'd ever tried, and he was all for this new sport.

EXERCISE 9–1, page H–67

Suggested revisions:

a. All students are urged to complete *their* registration on time.
b. *Babies* who don't know *their* own mothers may have been born with some kind of vision deficiency.
c. Each member of the sorority has to make *her* own bed.
d. If you don't like the songs the choir sings, don't join *it*.
e. Selfish people always look out for *themselves*.

EXERCISE 10–1, page H–74

a. Change *oldest* to *older;* b. Change *quick* to *quickly;* c. Change *correct* to *correctly* (in both places); change *trickiest* to *trickier;* d. Change *sweet* to *sweetly;* e. Change *the most* to *more*

EXERCISE 11–1, page H–78

Suggested revisions:

a. Sometimes late at night, I hear stereos booming from passing cars. The vibrations are so great *I* can feel *my* house shake.
b. Dr. Jamison is an erudite professor who *tells amusing anecdotes in class.* [Formal.] Or Dr. Jamison is a *comical* teacher who cracks jokes in class. [Informal.]
c. The audience listened intently to the lecture but *did not understand* the message.
d. The fire fighters tried repeatedly to put out the fire, but after five hours *they still had not put it out.*
e. Most of the people in my psychology class are very interesting, and *I* can get into some exciting discussions with them.

EXERCISE 12–1, page H–82

Suggested revisions:

a. Polly and Jim plan to see the new Woody Allen movie, which was reviewed in last Sunday's *New York Times.*
b. For democracy to function at all, two elements are crucial: an educated populace and a firm collective belief in people's ability to chart their own course.
c. Scholastic achievement is important to Alex, the first person in his family ever to attend college.
d. Does our society rob children of their childhood by making them aware too soon of adult ills?
e. It was one of those days: complete chaos, friends coming over in an hour, and a term paper to write.

EXERCISE 13–1, page H–87

Suggested revisions:

a. Everyone had heard alarming rumors in the village about strange goings-on. We hesitated to believe them.
   Although everyone had heard alarming rumors in the village about strange goings-on, we hesitated to believe them.
b. Bats flew about our ears as the carriage pulled up under a stone archway. An assistant stood waiting to lead us to our host.
   Bats flew about our ears as the carriage pulled up under a stone archway, where an assistant stood waiting to lead us to our host.
c. We followed the scientist down a flight of wet stone steps. At last he stopped before a huge oak door.
   We followed the scientist down a flight of wet stone steps, until at last he stopped before a huge oak door.

d. From a jangling keyring Dr. Frankenstein selected a heavy key; he twisted it in the lock.
From a jangling keyring Dr. Frankenstein selected a heavy key, which he twisted in the lock.

e. The huge door gave a groan and swung open on a dimly lighted laboratory.
The huge door gave a groan; it swung open on a dimly lighted laboratory.

EXERCISE 13–2, page H–88

Suggested revisions:

a. Comma splice. As the creature lumbered toward its terrified creator, Frankenstein shrank back against a wall.

b. Fused sentence. To defend himself the scientist grabbed a wooden mallet that had been sitting on a cabinet nearby.

c. Comma splice. Frankenstein wore a smile of contemptuous superiority; however, his triumph proved brief in duration.

d. Fused sentence. With one sweep of an arm the creature dashed aside the mallet, splintering its wooden head on the stone floor.

e. Comma splice. What followed is engraved upon my dreams; therefore, I hesitate to disclose it lest it trouble your own.

EXERCISE 14–1, page H–91

Suggested revisions:

a. After they lost miserably, the team remained silent on the trip home. *Or* After they lost, the team remained miserably silent on the trip home.

b. Complete the writing assignment that follows Chapter 2 in the textbook.

c. Those who frequently make mistakes learn valuable lessons. *Or* Frequently those who make mistakes learn valuable lessons.

d. For the duration of the rehearsal, Margaret was mortified at not having learned her lines.

e. A person who often snacks gets fat. *Or* Often a person who snacks gets fat.

EXERCISE 14–2, page H–93

Suggested revisions:

a. After working for six hours, they finished the job. *Or* After they worked for six hours, the job was done.

b. When you are unable to fall asleep, a warm bath relaxes you.

c. To join the college choir, a singer has to have a loud voice.

d. It's common for a person feeling lonely to want to talk to someone.

e. Having worried all morning, he felt relief flood over him when his missing son returned.

EXERCISE 15–1, page H–95

Suggested revisions:

a. She plays the *Moonlight Sonata* more brilliantly than any *other* pianist her age.

b. Driving a sports car means more to Jake than *it does to* his professors. *Or* Driving a sports car means more to Jake than his professors *do.*

c. People who go to college aren't necessarily smarter *than those who don't,* but they will always have an advantage at job interviews.

d. I don't have as much trouble getting along with Michelle as *I do with* Karin. *Or* I don't have as much trouble getting along with Michelle as Karin *does.*

e. One-eyed Bill was faster on the draw than any *other* gunslinger in West Texas.

EXERCISE 15–2, page H–97

a. The sand pit is just as wide *as* but deeper than the quarry.

b. Pembroke was never contacted *by,* much less involved with, the election committee.

c. I haven't yet *finished* but soon will finish my term paper.

d. Ron likes his popcorn with butter; Linda *likes hers* with parmesan cheese.

e. Correct

EXERCISE 16–1, page H–100

Suggested revisions:

a. A balanced budget calls for careful planning.

b. The candidates for school committee head are unimpressive this year.

c. A college's financial aid staff searches for able students and decides to pay their costs.

d. One good reason for financial aid is that it enables capable lower-income students to attend college.

e. In one sizzling blast, the enemy space fleet was instantly wiped out.

EXERCISE 17–1, page H–104

Suggested revisions:

a. I like westerns, documentaries, and foreign films.

b. Better than starting from scratch would be building on what already has been done.

c. Her apartment needed fresh paint and a new rug, and Mary Lou wished she had a neater roommate and quieter friends.

d. All my brothers are blond and athletic.

e. For breakfast the waiter brought scrambled eggs, which I like, and kippers, which I don't like.

EXERCISE 18–1, page H–108

Suggested revisions:

a. Congress is expected to pass the biotechnology bill, but the president already has said he will veto it.
b. Mortgage rates have dropped, so home buying is likely to increase in the near future.
c. Find Mrs. Fellowes a seat; she looks tired.
d. I left the house in a hurry and ran to the bank so I could cash a check to buy lunch. However, it was the bank's anniversary, and the staff was busy serving coffee and cake. By the time I left, after chatting and eating for twenty minutes, I wasn't hungry anymore.
e. The U.S. Postal Service handles millions of pieces of mail every day; it is the largest postal service in the world.

EXERCISE 18–2, page H–110

Suggested revisions:

a. We occasionally hear horror stories about fruits and vegetables being unsafe to eat because they were sprayed with toxic chemicals or were grown in contaminated soil. The fact remains that, given their high nutritional value, these fresh foods are generally much better for us than processed foods.
b. Renata claims that cats make the best pets because they are adorable, affectionate, and easy to care for.
c. At the end of Verdi's opera *La Traviata,* Alfredo has to see his beloved Violetta again, even though he knows she is dying and all he can say is good-bye.
d. After giving away her money and bidding adieu to her faithful servant, Violetta dies in her lover's arms.
e. Some television cartoon shows, such as *Rocky and Bullwinkle* and *George of the Jungle,* have become cult classics years after they went off the air.

EXERCISE 19–1, page H–112

a. Periodic;   b. Balanced;   c. Cumulative;
d. Normal;   e. Inverted

EXERCISE 20–1, page H–117

Suggested revisions:

a. My diagnosis, Mrs. Pitt, is that your husband's heart may fail at any time.
b. I recommend multiple bypass heart surgery for Mr. Pitt.

c. If your insurance company will pay for it, he can be scheduled for bypass surgery; if not, he should go on a strict diet.
d. We the State Department staff have investigated the riots in Lebanon, and all our data indicate they are rapidly becoming worse.
e. Antinuclear protesters have been picketing the missile conference in hopes of stalling the negotiations.

EXERCISE 20–2, page H–118

Suggested revisions:

a. This starting job involves hard work for low pay at first, but it could lead to promotion.
b. The ship sank because of a hole in the hull.
c. The new K27 missile will kill everyone in the cities of any nation that attacks us.
d. In our town, trash collectors must wear uniforms at work.
e. Freddie the Rocker is dead.

EXERCISE 20–3, page H–119

Suggested revisions:

a. Judy doesn't like Paul's sexual advances.
b. If large animals don't leave the combat zone, the army's policy is to kill them.
c. Judge Lehman's reversal of the *Smith v. Jones* verdict shows that he cannot think clearly.
d. Once that eyewitness told everything he knew, Jones's case was lost.
e. If he can get the money to pay his bail, he'll probably flee.

EXERCISE 21–1, page H–123

Suggested revisions:

a. The Sahara has always been known as one of the hottest, most arid regions on earth.
b. The explorers knew they risked death as they set out to cross the desert.
c. After six days of travel, every member of the party was sunburned and faint from thirst.
d. Even the camels were about to collapse when the scouts noticed an oasis.
e. The caravan leader squinted into the sun.

EXERCISE 22–1, page H–127

Suggested revisions:

a. My cousin volunteered as an aide at the retirement home.
b. Michelle and Roberto backed out on the real estate deal.
c. My high school history teacher was an unpleasant woman.

d. The television crew conducted a series of on-the-street interviews on the proposal for an increase in the gasoline tax.

e. American politicians must watch their words carefully.

EXERCISE 23–1, page H–129

Suggested revisions:

a. I suspect that this inquiry is likely to obscure the facts.

b. Please choose a password as soon as possible so that we can start using our new computer system.

c. As you know, your payment probably won't be returned to you soon.

d. If enough people press the elevator call button in a short time, the elevator will break down.

e. The secretary could not find out whether Mr. Jones and Ms. Cunningham had telephoned their resignations to the board.

EXERCISE 24–1, H–133

a. Unlike Gerald Ford and LBJ, who came to the vice-presidency from Congress, President Bush won that office after heading the CIA.

b. The population of California is much greater than that of Nevada.

c. Do you think I'm going to clean up this mess?

d. "When will the world end?" my four-year-old nephew asked in a quavering voice.

e. Yes, the Republicans are worried about the gender gap. They fear that women in increasing numbers will vote for the Democrats. How can the Republicans fight back?

EXERCISE 25–1, page H–136

a. When Enrique gets to Paris, I hope he'll drop me a line.

b. Beethoven's deafness kept him from hearing his own music, yet he continued to compose.

c. Correct

d. The cherries are overripe, for picking has been delayed.

e. The robin yanked at the worm but was unable to pull it from the ground.

EXERCISE 25–2, page H–137

a. Mrs. Carver looks like a sweet little old lady, but she plays a wicked electric guitar.

b. Her bass player, her drummer, and her keyboard player all live at the same rest home.

c. They practice individually in the afternoon, rehearse together at night, and play at the home's Saturday night dances.

d. The Rest Home Rebels have to rehearse quietly and cautiously to keep from disturbing the other residents.

e. Correct

EXERCISE 25–3, page H–139

Suggested revisions:

a. The rain, which wasn't due until tomorrow, is falling right now.

b. The party, a dismal occasion, ended earlier than we had expected.

c. Secretary Stern warned that the concessions that the West was prepared to make would be withdrawn if not matched by the East.

d. Although both of Don's children are blond, his daughter, Sharon, has darker hair than his son, Jake.

e. Herbal tea, which has no caffeine, makes a better after-dinner drink than coffee.

EXERCISE 25–4, page H–141

a. Before we begin, however, I want to thank everyone who made this evening possible.

b. Our speaker, listed in your program as a professor, tells us that, on the contrary, she is a teaching assistant.

c. The discussion that followed was not so much a debate as a free-for-all.

d. Alex insisted that predestination, not free will, shapes human destiny.

e. Shirley, on the other hand, who looks so calm, passionately defended the role of choice.

EXERCISE 25–5, page H–142

a. On October 2, 1969, the future discoverer of antigravity tablets was born.

b. Corwin P. Grant entered the world while his parents were driving to a hospital in Costa Mesa, California.

c. Correct

d. Today, ladies and gentlemen, Corwin enjoys worldwide renown.

e. Schoolchildren from Augusta, Maine, to Azuza, California, can recite his famous comment "It was my natural levity that led me to overcome gravity."

EXERCISE 26–1, page H–147

a. Gasoline prices almost always rise at the start of tourist season; this year will be no exception.

b. I disagree with your point; however, I appreciate your reasons for stating it.

c. The garden is a spectacular display of fountains and gargoyles; beds of lilies, zinnias, and hollyhocks; bushes shaped like animals; climbing roses, wisteria, and ivy; and lawns as wide as golf greens.

d. Luther missed the conference in Montreal,

but he plans to attend the one in Memphis.

e. Dr. Elliott's intervention in the dispute was well intentioned; nevertheless, it was unfortunate.

EXERCISE 27–1, page H–150

Suggested revisions:

a. The personnel director explained that the job requirements include typing, filing, and answering telephones.

b. The interview ended with a test of skills: taking dictation, operating the switchboard, proofreading documents, and typing a sample letter.

c. The sample letter began, "Dear Mr. Jones: Please accept our apologies for the late shipment."

d. Candace quoted Proverbs 8:18: "Riches and honor are with me."

e. A book that profoundly impressed me was Kurt Vonnegut's *Cat's Cradle* (New York: Dell, 1963).

EXERCISE 28–1, page H–154

a. It's not easy to be old in our society.

b. I don't understand the Jameses' objections to our plans for a block party.

c. As the saying goes, "Every dog has its day."

d. Is this collection of '50s records yours or your roommate's?

e. Alas, Brian got two D's on his report card.

EXERCISE 29–1, page H–158

a. "Don't think about it," advised Jason; "it will only make you unhappy."

b. "Should I go," Marcia asked, "or should I stay here?"

c. In her story "The Wide Net," Eudora Welty wrote, "The excursion is the same when you go looking for your sorrow as when you go looking for your joy."

d. "Who's supposed to say the line 'Tennis, anyone?'" asked the director.

e. Robert Burns's poem "To a Mouse" opens, "Wee, sleekit, cow'rin, tim'rous beastie, / O, what a panic's in thy breastie!"

EXERCISE 30–1, page H–160

Suggested revisions:

a. I enjoy going fishing with my friend John, whom I've known for fifteen years.

b. His new boat is spectacular—a regular seagoing Ferrari.

c. Bella and Scott spent their vacation doing exactly what they wanted to do—surfing.

d. Correct

e. "A rock!" I cried. "John, I'm afraid we're—"

EXERCISE 31–1, page H–161

Suggested revisions:

a. In *The Last Crusade,* archeologist Indiana Jones (who took his name from the family dog) joins his father in a quest for the Holy Grail.

b. Our cafeteria serves the four basic food groups: white (milk, bread, and mashed potatoes), brown (mystery meat and gravy), green (overcooked vegetables and underwashed lettuce), and orange (squash, carrots, and tomato sauce).

c. The ambassador says that if (1) the United States will provide more aid and (2) the guerrillas will agree to a cease-fire, his government will hold free elections.

d. Correct

e. Actually, the Whale Stranding Network (WSN) rescues whales that have stranded themselves.

EXERCISE 32–1, page H–169

a. Built for the Paris Exposition of 1889, the Eiffel Tower contains 15 million pounds of pig iron, protected by 37 tons of paint.

b. Friday, July 14, 1989, was the Eiffel Tower's hundredth anniversary.

c. Monsieur Eiffel would be pleased that President Mitterrand and others now accept his controversial "iron giraffe" as a national landmark.

d. In some Parisian tourist traps, a cup of coffee costs as much as $5.

e. France is a member of the North Atlantic Treaty Organization (NATO), but the French historically have mistrusted some of their fellow NATO members, such as the United Kingdom.

EXERCISE 33–1, page H–173

a. At our family reunion, I met my cousin Sam for the first time, and also my father's brother George.

b. I already knew from Dad that his brother had moved to Australia years ago to explore the Great Barrier Reef.

c. At the reunion, Uncle George told me that he had always wanted to be a marine biologist.

d. He had spent the summer after his sophomore year of college in Woods Hole, Massachusetts, on Cape Cod.

e. At the Woods Hole Oceanographic Institution he studied horseshoe crabs.

EXERCISE 34–1, page H–175

a. Wasn't it the Three Musketeers whose motto was "One for all and all for one"?

b. In the 1970s, there were about 92 million

ducks in America, but in the last four years their number has dropped to barely 69 million.

c. Cruising around the world on a 125-foot yacht with eight other people sounded glamorous until I saw our wooden berths, 32 inches wide by 68 inches long.

d. Forty days and forty nights would seem like forty years if you were sailing on an ark with two of every kind of animal.

e. Correct

EXERCISE 35–1, page H–179

a. Hiram's favorite Beatles album is *Sergeant Pepper's Lonely Hearts Club Band,* but his father prefers *Magical Mystery Tour.*

b. Hiram named his rowboat the *Yellow Submarine.*

c. He was disappointed when I told him that the play *Long Day's Journey into Night* is definitely not a staged version of the movie *A Hard Day's Night.*

d. I had to show him the article "Eugene O'Neill's Journey into Night" in *People* magazine to convince him.

e. Many different ethnic groups eat tomatoes and cheese in or on some form of cooked dough, whether they call this dish a pizza, an enchilada, a sandwich, or something else.

EXERCISE 36–1, page H–182

a. Do non-Americans share our view of ourselves as a freedom-loving people?

b. The dealer told George the two vases are within nine-tenths of an inch of being a perfect match.

c. Patrick Henry's words re-echo down through the ages: "Give me liberty or give me death!"

d. Those well-spoken words are well remembered today.

e. The weather forecast calls for showers followed by sun-shine.

Acknowledgments (continued from p. ii)

Joan Jacobs Brumberg. "The Origins of Anorexia Nervosa." Reprinted by permission of the publishers from *Fasting Girls: The Emergence of Anorexia Nervosa as a Modern Disease* by Joan Jacobs Brumberg. Cambridge, Mass.: Harvard University Press. Copyright © 1988 by the President and Fellows of Harvard College.

Ti-Hua Chang. "Downtown Cousin." Copyright © 1991 by The New York Times Company. Reprinted by permission.

Consumer Reports. From "Is There a DAT in Your Future?" Copyright © 1989 by Consumers Union of the United States, Inc., Yonkers, NY 10703. Excerpted by permission from *Consumer Reports*, January 1989.

Norman Cousins. Originally appeared in *Saturday Review* (1978). Reprinted by permission of Eleanor Cousins.

Harry Crews. Excerpt from "The Car." From *Florida Frenzy*. Copyright © 1982 by Harry Crews. Reprinted by permission of John Hawkins & Associates, Inc.

Frank J. Cunningham. From "Writing Philosophy: Sequential Essays and Objective Tests," *College Composition and Communication*, May 1985. Copyright 1985 by the National Council of Teachers of English. Reprinted with permission.

Emily Dickinson. "A narrow Fellow in the Grass." Reprinted by permission of the publishers and the Trustees of Amherst College from *The Poems of Emily Dickinson*, Thomas H. Johnson, ed. Cambridge, Mass.: The Belknap Press of Harvard University Press. Copyright © 1951, 1955, 1979, 1983 by the President and Fellows of Harvard College.

Annie Dillard. "Fecundity." From *Pilgrim at Tinker Creek* by Annie Dillard. Copyright © 1974 by Annie Dillard. Reprinted by permission of HarperCollins Publishers.

Michael Dorris. "The Train Cake." From *The Broken Chord* by Michael Dorris. Copyright © 1989 by Michael Dorris. Reprinted by permission of HarperCollins Publishers.

Peter Drucker. From *The New Realities*. Copyright 1989 by HarperCollins Publishers.

Bob Dylan. Copyright © 1968 by Dwarf Music. All rights reserved. International copyright secured. Used by permission.

Freeman Dyson. From *Infinite in All Directions*. Copyright © 1988 by HarperCollins Publishers.

Barbara Ehrenreich. "The Wretched of the Hearth." From *The New Republic*, April 2, 1990. Reprinted by permission of the author.

Paul R. Ehrlich and Anne H. Ehrlich. Excerpt from *Extinction: The Causes and Consequences of the Disappearance of Species*. Copyright © 1981 by Random House, Inc. Reprinted by permission of the publisher.

Susan Faludi. "Blame It on Feminism." From *Backlash* by Susan Faludi. Copyright © 1991 by Susan Faludi. Reprinted by permission of Crown Publishers, Inc.

Kurt W. Fischer and Arlyne Lazerson. From *Human Development* by Kurt W. Fischer and Arlyne Lazerson. Copyright © 1984 by W. H. Freeman and Company. Reprinted by permission.

Robert Frost. "Putting in the Seed" and "The Road Not Taken." From *The Poetry of Robert Frost* edited by Edward Connery Lathem. Copyright 1916, © 1969 by Holt, Rinehart and Winston. Copyright 1944 by Robert Frost. Henry Holt and Company, Inc., Publisher.

Trip Gabriel. "Call of the Wildmen." Copyright © 1990 by The New York Times Company. Reprinted by permission.

Henry Louis Gates, Jr. "2 Live Crew, Decoded." Copyright © 1990 by The New York Times Company. Reprinted by permission.

Marcia Ann Gillespie. "A Different Take on the Ol' Bump and Grind." From *Ms.*, October 1987. Reprinted by permission of the author.

Ellen Goodman. From "Misunderstood Michelle" in *At Large* by Ellen Goodman. © 1981, The Boston Globe Newspaper Company/Washington Post Writers Group. Reprinted with permission.

Ellen Goodman. "Was the Woman Really Less Qualified?" From *Making Sense* by Ellen Goodman. Copyright © 1989 by the Washington Post Company. Used by permission of Atlantic Monthly Press.

Vivian Gornick. Excerpt retitled "Mama Went to Work." From *Fierce Attachments* by Vivian Gornick. Copyright © 1987 by Vivian Gornick. Reprinted by permission of Farrar, Straus & Giroux, Inc.

Stephen Jay Gould. Reprinted from *The Flamingo's Smile: Reflections in Natural History* by Stephen Jay Gould, by permission of W. W. Norton & Company, Inc. Copyright © 1985 by Stephen Jay Gould.

Stephen Jay Gould. "The Terrifying Normalcy of AIDS." Copyright © 1987 by The New York Times Company. Reprinted by permission.

Barrie B. Greenbie. From *Spaces: Dimensions of the Human Landscape* by Barrie B. Greenbie. Copyright © 1981 by Barrie B. Greenbie. Reprinted by permission of the publisher, Yale University Press.

Charlie Haas. "Tinsel Teens." From *Esquire*, June 1985. Reprinted by permission of the author.

Garrett Hardin. Reprinted with permission from *Naked Emperors: Essays of a Taboo Stalker* by Garrett Hardin. Copyright © 1982 by William Kaufmann, Inc., Los Altos, CA 94022. All rights reserved.

Shirley Jackson. "The Lottery." From *The Lottery and Other Stories* by Shirley Jackson. Copyright © 1948, 1949 by Shirley Jackson. Renewal copyright © 1976, 1977 by Laurence Hyman, Barry Hyman, Mrs. Sarah Webster, and Mrs. Joanne Schnurer. Reprinted by permission of Farrar, Straus & Giroux, Inc.

Mary Harris, "Mother" Jones. From *The Autobiography of Mother Jones* (Charles H. Kerr Co., Chicago, 1980).

Gary Katzenstein, "The Salaryman." From *Funny Business* by Gary Katzenstein, © 1989 by Symbiosis, Inc. Reprinted by permission of Simon & Schuster.

Jonathan Kozol, "Are the Homeless Crazy?" From *Rachel and Her Children: Homeless Families in America* by Jonathan Kozol. Reprinted by permission of Crown Publishers, Inc.

Jack G. Shaheen. "The Media's Image of Arabs." From *Newsweek*, February 29, 1988. Reprinted by permission of the author.

Richard Sorenson. Text excerpt and figure from *Learning Non-Aggression: The Experience of Non-Literate Societies* by Ashley Montagu. Copyright © 1978 by Ashley Montagu. Reprinted by permission of Oxford University Press, Inc.

Brent Staples. "Black Men and Public Space." From *Harper's*, December 1987. Reprinted by permission of the author.

Ann Swidler. From *Habits of the Heart: Individualism and Commitment in American Life* by Robert N. Bellah, Richard Madsen, William M. Sullivan, Ann Swidler, and Steven M. Tipton. Copyright © 1985 by the Regents of the University of California. Reprinted by permission of the University of California Press.

Peter P. Swire. "Tropical Chic." Reprinted by permission of *The New Republic*, © 1989, The New Republic, Inc.

Lewis Thomas. "The Art of Teaching Science." Originally "Humanities and Science," copyright © 1983 by Lewis Thomas, from *Late Night Thoughts on Listening to Mahler's Ninth* by Lewis Thomas. Used by permission of Viking Penguin, a division of Penguin Books USA, Inc.

Barbara W. Tuchman. From *A Distant Mirror: The Calamitous Fourteenth Century* by Barbara W. Tuchman. Copyright © 1978 by Barbara W. Tuchman. Reprinted by permission of Alfred A. Knopf, Inc.

John Updike. From "Venezuela for Visitors" in *Hugging the Shore: Essays and Criticism* by John Updike. Copyright © 1983 by John Updike. Reprinted by permission of Alfred A. Knopf, Inc. Originally appeared in *The New Yorker*.

Lindsy Van Gelder. "The Great Person-Hole Cover Debate." From *Ms.*, April 1980. Reprinted by permission of the author.

Charles Van Riper. Excerpt from *A Career in Speech Pathology*, © 1979, p. 29. Prentice Hall, Englewood Cliffs, New Jersey.

Alice Walker. "When a Tree Falls." Originally titled "Everything Is a Human Being" from *Living By the Word: Selected Writings 1973–1987*, copyright © 1984 by Alice Walker, reprinted by permission of Harcourt Brace Jovanovich, Inc.

Gerald Weissmann. Excerpt from "Foucault and the Bag Lady." Reprinted by permission of Dodd, Mead & Company, Inc., from *The Woods Hole Cantata: Essays on Science and Society* by Gerald Weissmann. Copyright © 1985 by Gerald Weissmann, M.D.

E. B. White. "Once More to the Lake." From *Essays of E. B. White*. Copyright 1944 by E. B. White. Reprinted by permission of HarperCollins Publishers.

Cynthia Griffin Wolff. Excerpt from *Emily Dickinson*. © 1988 by Cynthia Griffin Wolff. Reprinted with permission of Addison-Wesley Publishing Company.

Philip Zaleski. From "The Superstars of Heart Research." *Boston* Magazine, December 1982. Copyright © 1982 by Philip Zaleski. Reprinted by permission of the author.

Art and Photograph Credits

pages 44–45: Print of woodcut by The Master I.B. with the Bird (original version and forgery) from William M. Ivins, Jr., *How Prints Look*, published by Beacon Press, Boston.

page 50 (top): Peter Vandermark/Stock Boston. (bottom): James Holland/Stock Boston.

page 51: Eva Demjen/Stock Boston.

page 77: Photo of Barbara Pierre. Copyright © 1982 by William Least Heat Moon. Reprinted from *Blue Highways: A Journey Into America* by William Least Heat Moon by permission of the author.

pages 217–218: Drawings by Glen Baxter from *Atlas*, © 1979. Reprinted by permission of Uitgeverij De Harmonie, Amsterdam.

Figure 28.5: Entry from *The Oxford English Dictionary*, 2nd ed. © Oxford University Press 1989. Reprinted by permission.

Figure 28.6: Reader's Guide to Periodical Literature, 1991. Copyright © 1991 by the H. W. Wilson Company. Material reproduced with permission of the publisher.

Figure 28.7: Education Index, (July 1990–June 1991). Copyright © 1991 by the H. W. Wilson Company. Material reproduced with permission of the publisher.

Figure 28.8: Entries from *The New York Times Index*. Copyright © 1987 by The New York Times Company. Reprinted by permission.

Index

INDEX TO DOCUMENTATION MODELS

Use these standard proofreading marks when making minor corrections in your final draft. If extensive revision is necessary, type or print out a clean copy.

∿	Transpose
≡	Capitalize
/	Lowercase
#	Add space
⌒	Close up space
ℯ	Delete
⸺	Stet (undo deletion)
∧	Insert
⊙	Insert period
⋏	Insert comma
;/	Insert semicolon
:/	Insert colon
∨	Insert apostrophe
∨ ∨	Insert quotation marks
|=|	Insert hyphen
¶	New paragraph
no ¶	No new paragraph

CORRECTION SYMBOLS

Many instructors use these abbreviations and symbols to mark errors in student papers. Refer to this chart to find out what they mean.

Boldface numbers refer to sections of the handbook.

abbr	faulty abbreviation **32**		**om**	omitted word **15**
ad	misuse of adverb or adjective **10**		**p**	error in punctuation
agr	faulty agreement **6, 9**		⌃	comma **25**
appr	inappropriate language **20, 22**		**no ,**	no comma **25n–r**
awk	awkward		**;**	semicolon **26**
cap	capital letter **33**		**:**	colon **27**
case	error in case **7**		**⌄**	apostrophe **28**
coord	faulty coordination **18**		**" "**	quotation marks **29**
cs	comma splice **13**		**. ? !**	period, question mark, exclamation point **24**
dm	dangling modifier **14**		**– ( )** **[ ] . . .**	dash, parentheses, brackets, ellipsis **30–31**
exact	inexact language **21**		**par, ¶**	new paragraph
frag	sentence fragment **12**		**pass**	ineffective passive **5m**
fs	fused sentence **13**		**ref**	error in pronoun reference **8**
gl	see glossary of trouble-makers		**rev**	revise
gr	grammar **1–4**		**sp**	misspelled word **37**
hyph	error in use of hyphen **36**		**sub**	faulty subordination **18**
inc	incomplete construction **15**		**t**	error in verb tense **5c, g–l**
irreg	error in irregular verb **5e**		**v**	voice **5m**
ital	italics (underlining) **35**		**vb**	error in verb form **5**
lc	use lowercase letter **33**		**w**	wordy **23**
mixed	mixed construction **16**		**//**	faulty parallelism **17**
mm	misplaced modifier **14a–b**		**∧**	insert
mood	error in mood **5n–p**		**x**	obvious error
ms	manuscript form pp. 396–398		**#**	insert space
nonst	nonstandard usage **20, 21**		⌒	close up space
num	error in use of numbers **34**			

A GUIDE TO THE HANDBOOK